ADMINISTRATIVE LAW

SIXTH EDITION

By

PAUL CRAIG, MA (Oxon), BCL, QC (Hon), FBA

Professor of English Law
St John's College, Oxford

LONDON
SWEET & MAXWELL
2008

First edition	1983
Second edition	1989
Third edition	1994
Fourth edition	1999
Fifth edition	2003

Published in 2008 by
Sweet & Maxwell Limited of 100 Avenue Road,
http://www.sweetandmaxwell.co.uk
Typeset by YHT Ltd, London
Printed in England by Ashford Colour Press, Gosport, Hants

No natural forests were destroyed to make this product;
only farmed timber was used and re-planted.

British Library Cataloguing in Publication Data

A CIP catalogue record for this book
is available from the British Library

ISBN 978 1 847 032836

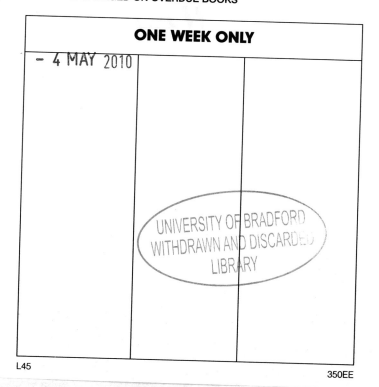

AUSTRALIA
Law Book Co
Sydney

CANADA AND USA
Carswell
Toronto

HONG KONG
Sweet & Maxwell Asia

NEW ZEALAND
Brookers
Wellington

SINGAPORE and MALAYSIA
Sweet & Maxwell Asia
Singapore and Kuala Lumpur

To my mother and the memory
of my father

PREFACE

There have been considerable developments in administrative law over the last five years. There has been important legislation on matters as diverse as tribunals, inquiries and local government. The courts have continued to be active and there have been many important new judicial decisions. There has been much interesting secondary literature. The Human Rights Act 1998 has, not surprisingly, generated a large amount of case law, as the courts have grappled with many of the key issues under this statute.

I have sought to incorporate all these changes, and to give a balanced account of the subject, which will be of equal use to those who are interested in the administrative system and those whose primary interest lies in judicial review. All chapters of the book have been revised to take account of the new developments, and several chapters have been substantially rewritten. The 6th edition contains two new chapters concerning review of fact and judicial review on grounds of equality. The discussion of the Human Rights Act and judicial review is now contained in a separate chapter, and the implications of the Act are also considered in other chapters of the book where appropriate.

I would like to thank all those at Sweet & Maxwell who have provided support in the production process with the book. I would also like to thank Anita and Ciaran for their help and understanding when work on the book impinged on family time.

The law is as stated on May 1, 2008.

Paul Craig
St John's College
Oxford

CONTENTS

	Page
Preface	vii
Table of Cases	xxvii
Table of Legislation	ci
European Union Treaties and Conventions	cxv

PART 1: THE ADMINISTRATIVE SYSTEM

1	**THE NATURE AND PURPOSE OF ADMINISTRATIVE LAW**	**3**
1	Introduction	3
2	Dicey, Unitary Democracy and the Ultra Vires Principle	4
	A. *The Basis of the Model*	4
	B. *The Implications of the Ultra Vires Model*	7
	C. *The Deficiencies of the Ultra Vires Model*	11
	D. *The Debate about the Ultra Vires Principle*	16
3	Rights, Legality and Abuse of Power	18
	A. *The Nature of the Model*	18
	B. *The Meaning of a Rights-Based Approach*	19
	C. *The Justifications for a Rights-Based Approach*	21
	D. *A Critique*	25
	E. *Response*	25
4	Particular Implications of the Model—I: Traditional Pluralism	31
	A. *Intellectual Foundations*	32
	B. *Implications for Administrative Law*	34
5	Particular Implications of the Model—II: Market-Orientated Pluralism	38
	A. *Intellectual Foundations*	38
	B. *Implications for Administrative Law*	39
6	Particular Implications of the Model—III: The Third Way	42
	A. *Intellectual Foundations*	42
	B. *Implications for Administrative Law*	44
7	Conclusion	44

2   THE ADMINISTRATIVE SYSTEM: AN HISTORICAL
    PERSPECTIVE   47
    1   Introduction   47
    2   The Nineteenth Century   47
        A. *Industrialisation and the Growth of Central Regulation*   47
        B. *The Machinery of Administration*   52
        C. *The Rationale for Administrative Growth*   56
        D. *Local Government*   59
        E. *The Evolution of Statutory Inquiries*   63
    3   The Twentieth Century   64
        A. *The Birth of the Welfare State and the Development of the
            Tribunal System*   64
        B. *Donoughmore, Franks, the 1980 Report and the 1988 Justice
            Report*   68

3   PARLIAMENT AND THE EXECUTIVE   71
    1   The Changing Pattern of Government   71
    2   The Foundations of Executive Power   72
        A. *The Expansion of the Franchise and the Increase in the
            Area of Governmental Responsibility*   73
        B. *The Centralisation of Legislative Initiative*   75
        C. *The Development of the Party System*   77
    3   The Role of the Legislature   78
        A. *The Commons and Scrutiny*   79
        B. *The Commons and Legislation*   84
    4   Reform of the House of Lords   89
    5   Conclusion   90

4   AGENCIES AND NON-DEPARTMENTAL PUBLIC BODIES   93
    1   Evolution of Executive Agencies and Non-Departmental
        Public Bodies   93
        A. *Fulton, Hiving Off and Agencies*   93
        B. *Rayner, Ibbs and Next Steps Agencies*   95
        C. *Non-Departmental Public Bodies*   97
        D. *Terminology*   98
        E. *Conclusion*   99
    2   Legal Status and Organisational Framework   99
        A. *NDPBs*   99
        B. *Executive Agencies*   101
    3   NDPBs: Appointments, Accountability and Efficiency   102
        A. *Appointments*   102
        B. *Control and Accountability*   103
        C. *Efficiency and Effectiveness*   106
    4   Executive Agencies: Staffing, Accountability and Efficiency   107
        A. *Staffing*   107
        B. *Control and Accountability*   108
        C. *Effectiveness*   111

5 Agencies: Institutional Design and Legal Principle 113
 A. *The Civil Aviation Authority* 113
 B. *Nationalisation and the Public Corporation* 116
 C. *Privatisation and Regulatory Control* 118
6 A Constitutional and Legal Framework for Agencies 122

5 CONTRACT, SERVICE PROVISION AND GOVERNANCE 125
 1 Introduction 125
 2 Towards "Better Procurement": The Framing of Government
  Procurement Policy 126
  A. *Institutional Responsibility* 126
  B. *Guidelines on Procurement* 128
  C. *The Range of Procurement Options* 129
  D. *Contract and Government Contracts* 130
 3 Towards "Better Government": Contract and Service Provision
  by Central Government 131
  A. *Contracting-Out: The Initial Conservative Policy* 131
  B. *Contracting-Out: The Labour Strategy* 132
  C. *Contracting-Out: Problems and Concerns* 134
  D. *Contracting-Out: Contract Formation and Legal Principle* 136
 4 Public Private Partnerships and the Private Finance Initiative:
  Contract and Service Provision by Central Government 138
 5 Towards "Best Value": Contract and Service Provision by Local
  Government 141
  A. *The Provision of Local Services: The Market and the
   Conservative Government's Approach* 141
  B. *The Provision of Local Services: "Best Value" and the Labour
   Government's Approach* 144
 6 The Private Finance Initiative: Contract and Service
  Provision by Local Government 147
 7 Public Procurement and the EC: Contract and Service
  Provision by Government 149
  A. *The Object of the EC Rules* 149
  B. *The Application of the Treaty* 150
  C. *The Directives on Public Procurement* 150
 8 Contract, Service Provision and Governance 154
  A. *Contract as an Instument of Policy* 154
  B. *The Source and Nature of Executive Power* 155
  C. *The Blurring of the Public/Private Divide and the
   Responsibility for Policy Formation* 156
 9 Making the Contract: General Principles 156
  A. *Capacity to Contract* 156
  B. *The Authority of an Agent* 159
  C. *Parliamentary Appropriation* 161
  D. *Proceedings Against the Crown* 162
  E. *Crown Service* 162
  F. *The Effect of an Unlawful Contract* 166

6 LOCAL GOVERNMENT, LOCAL GOVERNANCE AND
   DEMOCRACY   169
   1 The Changing Pattern of Local Government   169
   2 Local Authorities: Structure, Organisation, Powers and Finance 170
      A. *Structure*   170
      B. *Internal Organisation*   172
      C. *Functions and Powers*   174
      D. *Finances*   176
   3 Local Governance: Agencies and Service Delivery   180
   4 Central–Local Relations and Democracy   182

7 DEVOLUTION, WALES AND SCOTLAND   187
   1 Scotland   187
      A. *The Background*   187
      B. *The Composition of the Scottish Parliament*   188
      C. *The Formal Operation of the Scottish Parliament*   189
      D. *The Powers of the Scottish Parliament: Legislative Powers* 190
      E. *The Powers of the Scottish Parliament: The Powers of the*
          Executive   195
      F. *The Powers of the Scottish Parliament: Subordinate*
          Legislation   196
      G. *The Powers of the Scottish Parliament: Money*   199
      H. *Political Challenge to the Competence of the Scottish*
          Parliament   200
      I. *Judicial Challenge to the Competence of the Scottish*
          Parliament   201
      J. *Scottish Devolution: Some Reflections*   205
   2 Wales   208
      A. *The Background*   208
      B. *The Assembly*   209
      C. *The Executive*   210
      D. *Powers*   212
      E. *Judicial Challenge*   215
      F. *Welsh Devolution: Some Reflections*   219

8 INFORMATION, STANDARDS AND COMPLAINTS   223
   1 Freedom of Information: Rationale and Background   224
      A. *The Rationale for Freedom of Information*   224
      B. *The Move Towards Freedom of Information Legislation in the*
          UK   224
   2 The Freedom of Information Act 2000   226
   3 Standards of Conduct in Public Life   228
      A. *Cash, Sleaze and Concerns: The Development of the*
          Administrative Machinery   228
      B. *The Committee on Standards*   229
      C. *The Parliamentary Commissioner for Standards and the Select*
          Committee on Standards and Privileges   231

D. *Local Authorities and Standards of Conduct* 233
4 The Parliamentary Commissioner for Administration 233
   A. *General* 233
   B. *Who can be Investigated?* 235
   C. *What can be Investigated?* 235
   D. *Matters excluded from the PCA's Jurisdiction* 239
   E. *The Complainant and the Procedure* 241
   F. *Remedies* 243
   G. *Workload* 245
   H. *The Select Committee on the PCA* 246
   I. *Judicial Review and the PCA* 246
   J. *The Role of the PCA* 247
5 The Health Service Commissioners 250
6 Local Commissioners 252
   A. *Scope of Authority* 252
   B. *The Commissioners, Internal Complaints Procedures and*
      General Advice to Local Authorities 254
7 Ombudsman: Looking to the Future 256

9 TRIBUNALS AND INQUIRIES 257
1 Tribunals: Rationale and Nature 257
   A. *Introduction* 257
   B. *Reasons for their Creation* 257
   C. *The Nature of Tribunals* 258
2 Tribunal Reform: Franks and Leggatt 259
   A. *The Franks Report* 259
   B. *The Leggatt Report* 261
3 Tribunals: The Tribunals, Courts and Enforcement Act 2007 263
   A. *Senior President of Tribunals* 263
   B. *First-Tier Tribunal and Upper Tribunal* 264
   C. *Transfer of Functions to First-Tier Tribunal and*
      Upper Tribunal 265
   D. *First-Tier Tribunal and Upper Tribunal: Self-Review,*
      Appeal and Judicial Review 266
   E. *Tribunal Procedure Rules* 274
   F. *Mediation and Alternative Dispute Resolution* 278
   G. *The Tribunals Service, Administrative Support and*
      Staffing 279
   H. *Oversight: The Administrative Justice and Tribunals*
      Council 279
4 Statutory Inquiries 283
   A. *The Background* 283
   B. *The Franks Committee* 284
   C. *Inquiries: Practice and Procedure* 286
   D. *The Inquiries Act 2005* 294
   E. *Supervision* 296
   F. *Planning Inquiries, the Government and the Public* 297

10 THE EUROPEAN UNION   303
    1   The Institutions   303
        A. *The Council*   304
        B. *The Commission*   304
        C. *The European Parliament*   306
        D. *The European Council*   306
        E. *The European Court of Justice*   307
    2   The Legislative Process   307
    3   The Legal Order: Supremacy and Direct Effect   308
        A. *Supremacy*   308
        B. *Direct Effect*   313
        C. *Direct Effect: Rights and Remedies*   326
    4   The Impact of Community Law   328

11 A CASE STUDY: COMPETITION AND REGULATION   329
    1   Competition: Whether to Regulate   329
    2   Competition: Who Should Regulate?   330
    3   Competition: How to Regulate   332
        A. *Effectiveness and the Choice of the Legislative Criterion*   332
        B. *Procedure and Procedural Rights*   334
        C. *Defining the Public Interest: Rule Making and Discretion*   335
        D. *Defining the Public Interest: Politics, Policy and
            Justiciability*   336
        E. *Enforcement*   337
        F. *Accountability and Control*   338
        G. *The Importance of Competition Policy*   339
    4   Utilities and Market Power: Whether to Regulate   339
        A. *The Public Interest Rationale for Regulation*   339
        B. *The Private Interest Rationale for Regulation*   341
        C. *Natural Monopoly: Regulation or Structural Adjustment* 343
        D. *Whether to Regulate: The Government's Approach to
            Regulation*   345
        E. *Utilities Regulation: Political, Economic and Social
            Considerations*   346
        F. *Utilities Regulation: The Broader Context*   347
    5   Utilities and Market Power: Who Should Regulate?   348
        A. *The Common Law and the Courts*   348
        B. *Departmental Regulation*   350
        C. *Regulation by Tribunal or Board*   351
        D. *Public Ownership*   352
        E. *Privatisation and Agencies*   354
    6   Utilities and Market Power: How to Regulate   354
        A. *Selling State Assets: Constitutional Implications*   354
        B. *The Regulatory Regime: Legal Powers and Legal
            Constraints, the Initial Regime for Gas*   357
        C. *The Regulatory Regime: Legal Powers and Legal
            Constraints, the Modified Regime for Gas*   360

D. *The Regulatory Regime: Institutional Design*   362
E. *The Regulatory Regime: The Limits of Public Law*   365
F. *The Regulatory Regime: The Citizen's Charter and Subsequent Legislation*   366
7   Conclusion   367

PART 2: JUDICIAL REVIEW

12 NATURAL JUSTICE: HEARINGS   371
  1   Introduction   371
    A. *Historical Development*   371
    B. *The Rationale for Procedural Rights*   372
  2   Limitation of the Principle   373
    A. *Administrative v Judicial*   373
    B. *Rights and Remedies*   374
    C. *Rights v Privileges*   374
    D. *Statutory Hearings and Inquiries*   374
  3   The Principle Revived   375
    A. *Ridge v Baldwin*   375
    B. *Natural Justice and Fairness*   376
  4   Applicability of Procedural Protection   379
    A. *Categorisation: Administrative v Judicial v Legislative*   379
    B. *Rights, Interests and Legitimate Expectations*   380
  5   The Content of Procedural Protection: Balancing   388
    A. *Balancing: The Factors taken into Account*   388
    B. *Balancing: Preliminary Hearings—An Example*   390
    C. *Balancing: The Issue of Causation*   390
    D. *Balancing: The Nature of the Balancing Process*   392
  6   Content of Procedural Protection: Specific Procedural Norms   395
    A. *Notice*   395
    B. *Consultation*   396
    C. *The Hearing*   397
    D. *Representation*   400
    E. *Reasons*   401
    F. *Appeals and Rehearing*   409
    G. *Deciding Without Hearing*   409
    H. *The ECHR and the Content of Procedural Rights*   410
  7   Fairness: Non-Adjudicative Procedures   411
  8   Conclusion   415

13 NATURAL JUSTICE: BIAS AND INDEPENDENCE   417
  1   Introduction   417
  2   Bias: Personal Interest   417
    A. *Pecuniary Interest*   417
    B. *Other Personal Interests*   418
  3   Bias: Institutional   419
    A. *Prosecutor and Judge*   419

    B.   *Institutional Opinion*   420
4 Bias: The Test for Bias   422
    A.   *Past Confusion*   422
    B.   *From Gough to Porter*   422
5 Bias: Exceptions   424
    A.   *Necessity*   424
    B.   *Statute*   425
    C.   *Waiver*   425
6 The HRA and ECHR   426
    A.   *Article 6(1): The ECHR Legal Requirements*   426
    B.   *Article 6(1) in Domestic Courts: Fairness and Waiver*   427
    C.   *Article 6(1) in Domestic Courts: Planning and the*
        Distinction between Policy and Fact Finding   428
    D.   *Article 6(1) in Domestic Courts: Housing and the*
        Re-evaluation of the Policy/Fact-Finding Distinction   432
    E.   *Article 6(1) in Domestic Courts: Developments Since*
        Begum   434
7 A Common Law Requirement of "An Independent and
    Impartial Tribunal"   435

14 JURISDICTION AND ERROR OF LAW   437
1 Introduction   437
2 Theories of Jurisdiction   438
    A.   *Collateral Fact Doctrine*   439
    B.   *Limited Review*   441
    C.   *Extensive Review: The Academic Argument*   444
    D.   *Extensive Review: The Judicial Argument*   447
    E.   *Conclusion*   451
3 Case Law History   452
    A.   *Limited Intervention*   452
    B.   *Collateral or Preliminary Fact Cases*   453
    C.   *Attempts at Reconciliation*   454
4 The Current Case Law   454
    A.   *The Impact of Anisminic*   454
    B.   *From Anisminic to Racal*   457
    C.   *The Uncertainty of Racal*   458
    D.   *The Impact of Page*   459
    E.   *The Impact of South Yorkshire Transport*   460
    F.   *Summary*   461
    G.   *Error of Law within Jurisdiction*   462
    H.   *Statutory Review*   463
5 The Test for Review: Policy Considerations   464
    A.   *Clearing the Deck: The Demise of the Collateral Fact*
        Doctrine and Limited Review   468
    B.   *Judicial Control and Agency Automomy: Remembering the*
        Past when Constructing the Future   465
    C.   *The Modern Law: Review for Errors of Law*   466

D. *A Middle Way: Rightness and Rational Basis*   467
E. *A Middle Way: The Pragmatic and Functional Approach*   470
F. *The Middle Way: Concerns*   470
G. *Conclusion*   472

15 REVIEW OF FACT AND EVIDENCE   475
   1 Introduction   475
   2 The Meaning of Mistake of Fact   476
   3 *E v Secretary of State for the Home Department*   479
     A. *The Facts*   479
     B. *Judicial Review, Appeal and Fact*   480
   4 The Test for Mistake of Fact: Foundations   483
     A. *The Overview was Necessary*   484
     B. *The Conceptual Foundation for Judicial Intervention*   484
     C. *Difficulties with the Pre-Existing Narrow View*   486
   5 The Test for Mistake of Fact: The Criteria in the *E* Case   487
     A. *Mistake as to Existing Fact including Mistake as to Availability of Evidence*   487
     B. *The Fact or Evidence must be Uncontentious and Objectively Verifiable*   487
     C. *Responsibility for the Mistake*   491
     D. *The Mistake should have Played a Material Part in the Tribunal's Reasoning*   491
     E. *The Admissibility of Fresh Evidence*   491
   6 The Role of the Reviewing Court in the Determination of Factual Error   492
     A. *The Standard of Proof Required in Relation to Facts*   493
     B. *The Reviewing Court Should Not in General Engage in De Novo Review of Facts*   494
     C. *The Reviewing Court's Options when Engaged in Factual Scrutiny: Sufficiency of Evidence or Rationality*   495
     D. *The Reviewing Court's Role in Relation to Factual Error only Apparent in the Light of Fresh Evidence*   498
   7 Conclusion   499

16 FAILURE TO EXERCISE DISCRETION   501
   1 Introduction   501
     A. *Discretion: Types of Constraint*   501
     B. *Discretion: The Rationale for Intervention*   502
   2 Delegation   502
     A. *General Principles*   502
     B. *Agency and Delegation*   503
     C. *Government Departments*   506
     D. *Statutory Power*   510
   3 Fettering of Discretion: Rules, Policies and Discretion   510
     A. *An Existing Rule or Policy: The Present Law*   511
     B. *No Existing Rule or "Insufficient" Rules*   517

4 Fettering of Discretion: Contracts and the Exercise of
Discretion 521
   A. *The Problem* 521
   B. *The Incompatability Test* 522
   C. *Compensation* 526
   D. *The Position of the Crown* 530

17 ABUSE OF DISCRETION 531
  1 Illegality and Irrationality 531
  2 Reasonableness: The Two Meanings 532
  3 The Types of Power that can be Controlled 533
   A. *Statutory Power* 533
   B. *Prerogative Power* 534
   C. *Common Law Discretionary Power* 535
   D. *Non-statutory Bodies* 536
  4 Intensity of Review 536
  5 Illegality: Common Law Constraints 537
   A. *Improper Purposes* 538
   B. *Relevancy* 542
   C. *Bad Faith* 544
  6 Human Rights: The Common Law Background 545
   A. *The Common Law Jurisprudence* 545
   B. *The Secondary Literature* 548

18 THE HUMAN RIGHTS ACT AND JUDICIAL REVIEW 551
  1 Introduction 551
  2 The Genesis of the Human Rights Act 1998 552
   A. *The Status of the European Convention of Human Rights
prior to the HRA* 552
   B. *The HRA: "Bringing Rights Home"* 552
  3 Legislation: The Interpretative Obligation and the
Declaration of Incompatibility 554
   A. *The Statutory Provisions* 554
   B. *Legislative History* 556
   C. *Judicial Interpretation of Section 3: Early Case Law* 557
   D. *Judicial Interpretation of Section 3: Ghaidan v
Godin-Mendoza* 559
   E. *Judicial Interpretation of Section 3: The Post-Ghaidan
Case Law* 561
   F. *Reflections on the Courts' Jurisprudence* 563
  4 Acts of Public Authorities: A New Head of Illegality 565
   A. *Section 6(1) HRA* 565
   B. *Section 6(2) HRA* 566
   C. *Acts of Public Authorities: The Scope of Section 6* 569
   D. *Acts of Public Authorities: The Horizontal Effect of
the Human Rights Act* 579
   E. *Proceedings and Standing under Section 6* 582

F. *The Remedies for Breach of Section 6* 583
5 The Standard of Review 585
  A. *ECHR Precepts* 585
  B. *The Domestic Concept of Deference/Discretionary Area
    of Judgment/Respect* 586
  C. *Proportionality under the HRA: Daly* 591
  D. *Proportionality under the HRA: The Role of the Court
    and the Initial Decision-Maker* 593
  E. *The Standard of Review: The Academic Debate* 599
6 Rights: The EC Dimension 606
  A. *Legislative Competence and Human Rights* 607
  B. *Rights and Direct Effect* 607
  C. *Fundamental Rights* 608
  D. *The EU Charter of Rights* 609
  E. *The ECHR, HRA and EU* 610

19 RATIONALITY AND PROPORTIONALITY 613
1 The Limits of Judicial Intervention 613
2 *Wednesbury* Unreasonableness: Its Past, Present and Future 615
  A. *Wednesbury Unreasonableness: "The Touchstone of
    Legitimate Judicial Intervention"* 615
  B. *Wednesbury Unreasonableness: The Present Law* 616
  C. *Wednesbury Unreasonableness: The Future of the Test* 621
3 Proportionality in UK Law: Status, Meaning and Application 622
  A. *Legal Status of Proportionality* 623
  B. *Proportionality: Place and Meaning* 627
  C. *Proportionality: Application* 628
  D. *Proportionality: The Role of the Court and the Standard of
    Review* 630
4 Proportionality: The EC Dimension 631
  A. *Proportionality and Rights* 632
  B. *Proportionality and Penalties* 633
  C. *Proportionality and Discretion* 633
5 Reasonableness, Proportionality and Review 635
  A. *The Retention of Traditional Wednesbury alongside
    Proportionality* 635
  B. *The Retention of Modified Wednesbury alongside
    Proportionality* 636
  C. *Proportionality as the General Criterion of Review* 637
6 Substantive Control, Separation of Powers and the Limits of
  Judicial Review 640
  A. *The Traditional Approach* 640
  B. *An Alternative Approach* 642
7 The Interrelationship between Procedural and Substantive
  Principles of Review 643

20 LEGITIMATE EXPECTATIONS 647
  1 The Nature of the Problem 648
    A. *Actual and Apparent Retroactivity* 648
    B. *Legal Certainty, Legitimate Expectations and Legality* 649
  2 Intra Vires Representations: Types of Case 649
  3 Intra Vires Representations and Substantive Legitimate
    Expectations: The Contending Arguments 650
    A. *The Arguments in Favour* 650
    B. *The Arguments Against* 652
  4 Intra Vires Representations and Legitimate Expectations:
    Coughlan 654
    A. *The Law prior to Coughlan* 654
    B. *Coughlan* 654
  5 Intra Vires Representations: The Determination of whether the
    Expectation is Reasonable and Legitimate 659
  6 Intra Vires Representations: The Standard of Review Applied
    when the Administration seeks to Defeat a Legitimate
    Expectation 661
    A. *Coughlan* 661
    B. *Nadarajah* 663
    C. *Bibi* 666
  7 Intra Vires Representations and Legitimate Expectations:
    Types of Case 667
    A. *Changes of Policy* 667
    B. *Departure from an Existing Policy* 668
    C. *Individualised Representations* 670
    D. *Decisions, Final Determinations and Estoppel by Record* 672
  8 Ultra Vires Representations and Legitimate Expectations:
    The Current Law 675
    A. *The Jurisdictional Principle: The Relationship of Ultra Vires,*
      Agency and Delegation 675
    B. *The Jurisdictional Principle: Application* 677
    C. *The Jurisdictional Principle: The Conceptual Language,*
      Estoppel or Legitimate Expectations 679
    D. *The Jurisdictional Principle: Qualifications* 680
  9 Ultra Vires Representations: Re-Assessing the Jurisdictional
    Principle 682
    A. *The Policy behind the Jurisdictional Principle: The First*
      Rationale 682
    B. *The Policy behind the Jurisdictional Principle: The Second*
      and Third Rationales 683
 10 Ultra Vires Representations: Three Possible Strategies 684
    A. *Limited Qualifications to the Jurisdictional Principle* 685
    B. *Balancing the Public and Individual Interest* 685
    C. *Compensation* 691

21 EQUALITY 693
  1 Introduction 693
  2 Common Law 693
    A. *The Principle of Treating Like Groups Alike: The Basic*
       Precept 693
    B. *The Principle of Treating Like Groups Alike: The Case Law* 694
  3 Statutory Intervention and Statutory Interpretation 696
  4 The HRA 697
    A. *Article 14 and Protocol 12 ECHR* 697
    B. *The Determination of Discrimination* 698
    C. *Strict Scrutiny and Rationality Review* 701
    D. *Gender and Positive Discrimination* 706
  5 EU Law 708
    A. *Discrimination and Nationality* 708
    B. *Discrimination and Gender* 709
    C. *Discrimination and Article 13 EC* 710
    D. *Discrimination and Common Policies* 711
    E. *Discrimination and the Charter of Rights* 712

22 RULE-MAKING 715
  1 Introduction 715
  2 Delegated Legislation: History, Rationale and Form 716
    A. *History* 716
    B. *Rationale and Constitutional Concerns* 718
    C. *Form* 719
  3 Delegated Legislation: Passage and Publication 719
    A. *The Statutory Instruments Act 1946* 719
    B. *Publication and Making* 720
  4 Delegated Legislation: Control by Parliament 723
    A. *Scrutiny by the House* 723
    B. *Scrutiny by Committee: Delegated Legislation Committees* 725
    C. *Scrutiny in Committee: The Joint Committee on Statutory*
       Instruments 725
    D. *Scrutiny in Committee: The House of Lords' Merits of*
       Statutory Instruments Committee 727
    E. *Scrutiny of Regulatory Reform: A Special Regime* 728
    F. *Scrutiny of European Legislation* 730
  5 Delegated Legislation: Consultation 732
    A. *Consultation Rights and Statute* 732
    B. *Consultation Rights and the Common Law* 733
    C. *Consultation Rights and Future Prospects* 735
    D. *Consultation and the Code of Practice* 738
    E. *Conclusion* 739
  6 Delegated Legislation: Judicial Review 740
    A. *Procedural Ultra Vires and Formal Invalidity* 740
    B. *Substantive Ultra Vires* 741
    C. *Delegation* 744

    D. *Remedies*   744
  7 Delegated Legislation: Possible Reforms   745
    A. *Rippon Commission*   746
    B. *The Select Committee on Procedure*   749
    C. *The House of Lords' Merits of Statutory Instruments*
        Committee   750
  8 Rules Made by the Administration   751
    A. *Type and Rationale*   751
    B. *Legal Status*   752
    C. *Rules Made by the Administration: Problems*   753
    D. *Rules Made by the Administration: Possible Solutions*   754
  9 The Impact of Community Law   757

23 INVALIDITY   759
  1 Direct and Collateral Attack   759
    A. *Classification*   759
    B. *The Relationship between Direct and Collateral Attack: The*
        General Principle   760
    C. *The Relationship Between Direct and Collateral Attack:*
        Qualifications to the General Principle   762
  2 Void and Voidable: Correct and Incorrect Uses   764
    A. *Void: A Relative not Absolute Concept*   765
    B. *The Decision as to whether an Error Renders the*
        Administrative Act Void   767
    C. *The Consequences of Holding that an Act is Void*   768
    D. *Voidable: Different Uses*   769
  3 Void and Voidable: Theory, Reality and Judicial Discretion   771
    A. *The Reasons for Judicial Departure from the Traditional*
        Meanings of Void and Voidable: Administrative Convenience,
        Justice and Rigidity   771
    B. *Resolving the Problem*   773
  4 Void and Voidable: Natural Justice   777
    A. *Hearings*   777
    B. *Bias*   778
    C. *Waiver*   779
  5 Problems of Proof   780
    A. *The Burden of Proof*   780
    B. *Validity Pending Determination*   782
    C. *Partial Invalidity*   785

PART 3: REMEDIES

24 REMEDIES: STANDING   789
  1 Introduction   789
  2 The Position before 1978   790
    A. *Certiorari*   790
    B. *Prohibition*   790

Contents

C. *Mandamus*

D. *Injunction and Declaration*

3 The Attorney-General, Public Authorities and Statutory
   Appeals   79

   A. *Attorney-General*   794

   B. *Public Authorities*   795

   C. *Statutory Appeals*   796

4 Standing in Judicial Review Actions   798

   A. *Introduction*   798

   B. *The IRC Case*   798

   C. *Interpretation of the Test*   802

   D. *Locus Standi under the Human Rights Act 1998*   808

   E. *Locus Standi Outside Section 31*   810

5 Intervention in Judicial Review Actions   811

6 The Function of Standing   812

   A. *Vindication of Private Rights*   812

   B. *Fusion of Standing and Merits*   814

   C. *Citizen Action*   815

   D. *Injury in Fact*   821

7 Standing and Intervention: Looking to the Future   822

   A. *Standing*   822

   B. *Standing: Individuals and Groups*   823

   C. *Intervention*   824

25 JUDICIAL REMEDIES   827

1 Certiorari/Quashing Order and Prohibition/Prohibiting Order   828

   A. *Introduction*   828

   B. *The Scope of Certiorari/Quashing Orders and Prohibition/*
      Prohibiting Orders   829

   C. *Grounds for the Award of Certiorari and Prohibition*   835

   D. *Limitations on the Grant of the Remedies*   835

   E. *The Effect of an Award of Certiorari/Quashing Order*   837

2 Mandamus/Mandatory Order   837

   A. *Introduction*   837

   B. *The Ambit of Mandamus/Mandatory Order*   838

   C. *Limits on the Availability of Mandamus/Mandatory Order*   840

3 Declaration   841

   A. *Introduction*   841

   B. *The Scope of Declaration*   843

   C. *Limits on the Availability of Declaration*   845

   D. *The Impact of the Declaration*   850

   E. *Practice and Procedure*   851

4 Injunction   852

   A. *Introduction*   852

   B. *The Types of Injunction*   853

   C. *The Scope of Injunctive Relief*   853

   D. *Limits to Injunctive Relief*   856

    E. *Practice and Procedure*   856
  5 Other Remedies   857
    A. *Habeas Corpus*   857
    B. *Private Law Remedies*   858
    C. *Default Powers*   859

26 REMEDIES AND REFORM   861
  1 The Reforms   861
    A. *The Need for Reform*   861
    B. *The Ordinary Courts: The Legal Foundations of the
        Existing Procedure*   862
    C. *The Upper Tribunal: Legal Foundations for New Judicial
        Review Power*   863
    D. *The Application/Claim for Judicial Review*   863
    E. *O'Reilly v Mackman*   864
  2 The Exceptions: "Getting Out" of the Judicial Review
    Procedure   865
    A. *The Reasons for Seeking to Proceed outside Section 31*   865
    B. *Collateral Attack and Private Rights: The Initial Approach* 866
    C. *Collateral Attack and Private Rights: Broadening the
        Exception*   868
    D. *Collateral Attack: Beyond Private Rights*   871
    E. *The Impact of the Human Rights Act 1998*   872
    F. *The Impact of the CPR*   873
    G. *Summary*   874
    H. *Assessment*   875
  3 Public Law Cases: "Getting Into" the Judicial Review
    Procedure   877
    A. *The Reasons for Wishing to Use the Section 31 Procedure*   877
    B. *Public Law: Possible Tests*   878
    C. *The Boundaries of Public Law*   880
  4 Evaluation of the Present Law   894
    A. *The Unavoidable Issue: Which Bodies are Amenable to
        Review?*   894
    B. *The Central Issue: Do Public Bodies Require Special
        Protection?*   895
    C. *Protecting Public Bodies: Permission*   896
    D. *Protecting Public Bodies: Time Limits*   903
    E. *The Exclusivity Principle*   908
    F. *Disclosure and Inspection*   909
    G. *Conclusion*   912
  5 Procedure   912
    A. *Permission*   912
    B. *The Substantive Hearing*   913
    C. *Discretion to Refuse Relief*   915
  6 The Effect of Alternative Remedies   916
    A. *Choice of Remedies under CPR Pt 54*   916

   B. *Alternative Statutory Remedies* 916
   C. *Conclusion* 918
  7 Conclusion 919

27 REMEDIES: EXCLUSION OF REVIEW 921
  1 Complete Exclusion 921
   A. *Finality Clauses* 921
   B. *"No Certiorari" Clauses* 922
   C. *"Shall not be Questioned" Clauses* 923
   D. *"As if Enacted" and "Conclusive Evidence"* 923
   E. *Statutory Intervention* 925
  2 Time Limits 926
  3 The Effect of the Human Rights Act 1998 927
  4 Conclusion 928
   A. *Complete Ouster Clauses* 928
   B. *Time Limits* 929

28 PUBLIC INTEREST IMMUNITY AND CROWN LIABILITY 931
  1 Public Interest Immunity 931
   A. *"Crown Privilege"* 931
   B. *From Crown Privilege to Public Interest Immunity* 932
   C. *Public Interest Immunity: The Type of Body which can claim*
      Immunity 934
   D. *Public Interest Immunity and Confidentiality* 935
   E. *Public Interest Immunity: Duty or Discretion* 936
   F. *Public Interest Immunity: Duty, Discretion and the ECHR* 937
   G. *Public Interest Immunity: The Change in Governmental*
      Approach 938
   H. *Public Interest Immunity: The Balancing Process* 940
   I. *Public Interest Immunity: Inspection* 943
  2 Statutes and the Crown 945
   A. *Statutes Binding the Crown* 945
   B. *Statutes Benefiting the Crown* 947
  3 Procedure, Remedies and the Crown 947
   A. *General* 947
   B. *Injunctions and Interim Relief* 949
   C. *Contempt* 954

29 TORT AND RESTITUTION 957
  1 Introduction 957
   A. *Foundations of the Present Law* 957
   B. *The Available Options* 958
  2 Negligence, Statutory Duties and Statutory Powers 959
   A. *The "Liberal Approach"* 960
   B. *The "Cautious" or "Restrictive Approach"* 962
   C. *The "Middle Way"* 967
  3 Breach of Statutory Duty 975

		A.	*Criteria for Liability*	975
		B.	*Application of the Criteria*	977
		C.	*Comment*	977
	4	The Human Rights Act		978
		A.	*Criteria for Liability*	979
		B.	*Development and Application of the Criteria*	980
		C.	*Comment*	983
	5	Misfeasance in Public Office		983
		A.	*Criteria for Liability*	983
		B.	*Development and Application of the Criteria for Liability: Three Rivers*	986
		C.	*Comment*	989
	6	Nuisance		989
		A.	*Criteria for Liability*	989
		B.	*Application of the Criteria*	989
		C.	*Comment*	991
	7	Rylands v Fletcher		994
		A.	*Criteria for Liability*	994
		B.	*Application of the Criteria*	995
		C.	*Comment*	995
	8	The Crown		996
		A.	*The Law Prior to 1947*	996
		B.	*Crown Proceedings Act 1947*	997
	9	Judicial Immunity		998
	10	Restitution		999
		A.	*Duress*	999
		B.	*Mistake*	1000
		C.	*Recovery for Ultra Vires Demands*	1002
		D.	*Discretionary Payments*	1005
		E.	*Restitution from the Individual*	1005
	11	EU Law: Damages Liability and Recovery of Money		1006
		A.	*Criteria for Liability*	1006
		B.	*Development and Application of the Criteria*	1007
		C.	*The Implications for Domestic Law*	1011
		D.	*Recovery of Money*	1012
	12	Reform		1013
		A.	*Options for Reform*	1013
		B.	*Compensation via a Risk Theory*	1013
		C.	*Compensation for Invalidity*	1014
		D.	*Compensation on an Ex Gratia Basis*	1017
		E.	*The Impact of Community Law and Convention Jurisprudence*	1017
		F.	*Conclusion*	1018
Index				1019

TABLE OF CASES

A v Essex CC [2003] EWCA Civ 1848; [2004] 1 W.L.R. 1881; [2004] 1 F.L.R. 749; [2004] 1 F.C.R. 660; [2004] B.L.G.R. 587; (2004) 7 C.C.L. Rep. 98; [2004] Fam. Law 238; (2004) 148 S.J.L.B. 27, CA (Civ Div) 29–016

A v Scottish Ministers. *See* Anderson v Scottish Ministers

A v Secretary of State for the Home Department; sub nom. X v Secretary of State for the Home Department [2004] UKHL 56; [2005] 2 A.C. 68; [2005] 2 W.L.R. 87; [2005] 3 All E.R. 169; [2005] H.R.L.R. 1; [2005] U.K.H.R.R. 175; 17 B.H.R.C. 496; [2005] Imm. A.R. 103; (2005) 155 N.L.J. 23; (2005) 149 S.J.L.B. 28, HL 18–010, 18–036, 21–003

A v Secretary of State for the Home Department [2003] EWCA Civ 175; [2003] I.N.L.R. 249; (2003) 147 S.J.L.B. 114, CA (Civ Div) 15–003

A Local Authority (Inquiry: Restraint on Publication), Re; sub nom. Local Authority v Health Authority (Disclosure: Restriction on Publication) [2003] EWHC 2746 (Fam); [2004] Fam. 96; [2004] 2 W.L.R. 926; [2004] 1 All E.R. 480; [2004] 1 F.L.R. 541; [2004] 1 F.C.R. 113; [2004] B.L.G.R. 117; (2004) 7 C.C.L. Rep. 426; (2004) 76 B.M.L.R. 210; [2004] Fam. Law 179; (2004) 101(3) L.S.G. 33, Fam Div 18–028

ACT Construction Co Ltd v Customs and Excise Commissioners [1981] 1 W.L.R. 1542; [1982] 1 All E.R. 84; [1982] S.T.C. 25; (1981) 125 S.J. 864, HL 9–019, 9–021, 14–022, 14–031

Abbott v Sullivan [1952] 1 K.B. 189; [1952] 1 All E.R. 226; [1951] 2 Lloyd's Rep. 573; [1952] 1 T.L.R. 133; (1952) 96 S.J. 119, CA 12–001, 23–025

Abdulaziz v United Kingdom (A/94); Cabales v United Kingdom (9473/81); Balkandali v United Kingdom (9474/81) (1985) 7 E.H.R.R. 471, ECHR 21–005, 24–025

Ackerley v Parkinson (1815) 3 M. & S. 411 14–026

Adami v Ethical Standards Officer of the Standards Board for England; sub nom. R. (on the application of Adami) v Ethical Standards Officer of the Standards Board for England [2005] EWCA Civ 1754; [2006] B.L.G.R. 397, CA (Civ Div) 12–034

Adams v Adams [1971] P. 188 23–008

Adams v Lord Advocate. *See* Adams v Scottish Ministers

Adams v Naylor [1946] A.C. 543, HL 29–044

Adams v Scottish Ministers; sub nom. Adams v Advocate General for Scotland; Adams, Petitioner; Adams v Lord Advocate 2004 S.C. 665; 2004 G.W.D. 18–384, IH (2 Div) 7–007, 24–025

Adams v War Office [1955] 1 W.L.R. 1116; [1955] 3 All E.R. 245; (1955) 99 S.J. 746, QBD 29–046

Adams Fruit Company, Inc v Ramsford Barrett 494 U.S. 638 (1990) 14–041

Adan (Hassan Hussein) v Secretary of State for the Home Department; sub nom. Secretary of State for the Home Department v Adan (Hassan Hussein); R. v Secretary of State for the Home Department Ex p. Adan (Hassan Hussein) [1999] 1 A.C. 293; [1998] 2 W.L.R. 702; [1998] 2 All E.R. 453; [1998] Imm. A.R. 338; [1998]

I.N.L.R. 325; (1998) 95(18) L.S.G. 33; (1998) 148 N.L.J. 552; (1998) 142 S.J.L.B. 139, HL 15–002
Agricultural, Horticultural and Forestry Industry Training Board v Aylesbury Mushrooms [1972] 1 W.L.R. 190; [1972] 1 All E.R. 280, QBD 22–017
AL (Serbia) v Secretary of State for the Home Department [2006] EWCA Civ 1619; [2007] H.R.L.R. 7; [2007] U.K.H.R.R. 564; [2007] Imm. A.R. 369; [2007] I.N.L.R. 136; (2006) 150 S.J.L.B. 1606, CA (Civ Div) 21–007, 21–012
Air Canada v Secretary of State for Trade (No.2) [1983] 2 A.C. 394; [1983] 2 W.L.R. 494; [1983] 1 All E.R. 910, HL 26–006, 28–012, 28–013, 28–014
Alaska Department of Environmental Conservation v Environmental Protection Agency 540 U.S. 461 (2004) 14–042
Aldridge, Re (1893) 15 N.Z.L.R. 361 23–007
Alexander Machinery (Dudley) v Crabtree [1974] I.C.R. 120; [1974] I.R.L.R. 56; [1974] I.T.R. 182, NIRC 12–036
Alexandrou v Oxford [1993] 4 All E.R. 328; (1991) 3 Admin. L.R. 675; (1991) 155 L.G. Rev. 566, CA (Civ Div) 29–009
Alfred Crompton Amusement Machines Ltd v Customs and Excise Commissioners (No.2) [1974] A.C. 405; [1973] 3 W.L.R. 268; [1972] 1 W.L.R. 833; [1973] 2 All E.R. 1169; (1973) 117 S.J. 602, HL 28–006
Allen v Gulf Oil Refining Ltd [1981] A.C. 1001; [1981] 2 W.L.R. 188; [1981] 1 All E.R. 353; [1981] J.P.L. 353; (1981) 125 S.J. 101, HL 29–038
Allen v Sharp (1848) 2 Ex. 352 14–026
Allen and Matthews Arbitration, Re [1971] 2 Q.B. 518 14–031
Allentown Mack Sales and Service v National Labor Relations Board 522 U.S. 359 (1998) 15–026
Alliance des Professeurs Catholiques de Montreal v Labour Relations Board of Quebec [1953] 2 S.C.R. 140 12–008
Allingham v Minister of Agriculture and Fisheries [1948] 1 All E.R. 780; 64 T.L.R. 290; (1948) 112 J.P. 237; 46 L.G.R. 224, DC 16–003
Allinson v General Council of Medical Education and Registration [1894] 1 Q.B. 750; [1891–94] All E.R. Rep. 768, CA 13–003, 23–026
Allnutt v Inglis 104 E.R. 206; (1810) 12 East 527, KB 11–019
American Cyanamid Co (No.1) v Ethicon Ltd [1975] A.C. 396; [1975] 2 W.L.R. 316; [1975] 1 All E.R. 504; [1975] F.S.R. 101; [1975] R.P.C. 513; (1975) 119 S.J. 136, HL 25–032
Amherst (Lord) v Somers (Lord) (1788) 2 T.R. 372 .... 14–027, 15–002
Amministrazione delle Finanze dello Stato v Denkavit Italiana Srl (61/79) [1980] E.C.R. 1205; [1981] 3 C.M.L.R. 694, ECJ 29–060
Amministrazione delle Finanze dello Stato v San Giorgio SpA (199/82) [1983] E.C.R. 3595; [1985] 2 C.M.L.R. 658, ECJ 10–031, 29–060
Amministrazione delle Finanze dello Stato v Simmenthal SpA (106/77); sub nom. Italian Tax and Revenue Administration v SA Simmenthal, Monza (Italy) [1978] E.C.R. 629; [1978] 3 C.M.L.R. 263, ECJ 10–011
Amphitrite. *See* Rederiaktiebolaget Amphitrite v King, The
Amsterdam Bulb BV v Produktschap voor Siergewassen (C-50/76) [1977] E.C.R. 137; [1977] 2 C.M.L.R. 218, ECJ 10–022
Anderson v Scottish Ministers; sub nom. A v Scottish Ministers [2001] UKPC D 5; [2003] 2 A.C. 602; [2002] 3 W.L.R. 1460; 2002 S.C. (P.C.) 63; 2001 S.L.T. 1331; [2002] H.R.L.R. 6; [2002] U.K.H.R.R. 1; [2001] M.H.L.R. 192; 2001 G.W.D. 33–1312, PC (Sc) 7–006, 7–007
Andrews v Reading BC (No.1) [2004] EWHC 970 (Admin); [2005] Env. L.R. 2; [2004] U.K.H.R.R. 599; [2004] R.V.R. 272; [2005] A.C.D. 11, QBD (Admin) 29–041
Andrews v Reading BC (No.2) [2005] EWHC 256 (QB); [2006] R.V.R. 56, QBD 29–041
Anisminic Ltd v Foreign Compensation Commission [1969] 2 A.C. 147; [1969] 2 W.L.R. 163; [1969] 1 All E.R. 208; (1968) 113 S.J. 55, HL 14–004, 14–029, 23–026, 24–006, 27–004
Annamunthodo v Oilfields Workers Trade Union [1961] A.C. 945; [1961] 3 W.L.R. 650; [1961] 3 All E.R. 621; (1961) 105 S.J. 706, PC (WI) 12–024, 12–041
Anns v Merton LBC; sub nom. Anns v Walcroft Property Co Ltd [1978] A.C. 728; [1977] 2 W.L.R. 1024; [1977] 2 All E.R. 492; 75 L.G.R. 555; (1977) 243 E.G. 523; (1988) 4 Const. L.J. 100; [1977] J.P.L. 514; (1987) 84 L.S.G. 319; (1987) 137 N.L.J. 794; (1977) 121 S.J. 377, HL 29–005

Anufrijeva v Southwark LBC; sub nom. R. (on the application of Anufrijeva) v
 Southwark LBC [2003] EWCA Civ 1406; [2004] Q.B. 1124; [2004] 2 W.L.R. 603;
 [2004] 1 All E.R. 833; [2004] 1 F.L.R. 8; [2003] 3 F.C.R. 673; [2004] H.R.L.R. 1;
 [2004] U.K.H.R.R. 1; 15 B.H.R.C. 526; [2004] H.L.R. 22; [2004] B.L.G.R. 184;
 (2003) 6 C.C.L. Rep. 415; [2004] Fam. Law 12; (2003) 100(44) L.S.G. 30, CA (Civ
 Div) 29–027, 29–029
Apex Asphalt & Paving Co Ltd v Office of Fair Trading [2005] CAT 4; [2005] Comp.
 A.R. 507, CAT 23–011
Application des Gaz SA v Falks Veritas Ltd [1974] Ch. 381; [1974] 3 W.L.R. 235; [1974]
 3 All E.R. 51; [1974] 2 Lloyd's Rep. 493; [1974] 2 C.M.L.R. 75; [1974] F.S.R. 355;
 [1975] R.P.C. 421; (1974) 118 S.J. 363, CA (Civ Div) 29–059
Armah v Ghana (No.1); sub nom. R. v Governor of Brixton Prison Ex p. Armah
 (No.1); Kwesi Armah, Re [1968] A.C. 192; [1966] 3 W.L.R. 828; [1966] 3 All E.R.
 177; (1967) 131 J.P. 43; (1966) 110 S.J. 890, HL 25–038
Armstrong v Kane [1964] N.Z.L.R. 369 25–015
Armstrong World Industries, Inc v Commissioner of Internal Revenue 974 F. 2d 422
 (1992) 14–041
Arsenal Football Club Ltd v Ende [1979] A.C. 1 24–011
Arthur JS Hall & Co v Simons; sub nom. Harris v Scholfield Roberts & Hall; Barratt v
 Ansell (t/a Woolf Seddon) [2002] 1 A.C. 615; [2000] 3 W.L.R. 543; [2000] 3 All
 E.R. 673; [2000] B.L.R. 407; [2000] E.C.C. 487; [2000] 2 F.L.R. 545; [2000] 2
 F.C.R. 673; [2001] P.N.L.R. 6; [2000] Fam. Law 806; [2000] E.G. 99 (C.S.); (2000)
 97(32) L.S.G. 38; (2000) 150 N.L.J. 1147; (2000) 144 S.J.L.B. 238; [2000] N.P.C.
 87, HL 21–003
Ashbridge Investments Ltd v Minister of Housing and Local Government [1965] 1
 W.L.R. 1320; [1965] 3 All E.R. 371; (1965) 129 J.P. 580; 63 L.G.R. 400; (1965) 109
 S.J. 595, CA 14–037, 15–011
Ashbury Railway Carriage & Iron Co Ltd v Riche; sub nom. Riche v Ashbury Railway
 Carriage & Iron Co Ltd (1874–75) L.R. 7 H.L. 653, HL 5–048
Ashby v Ebdon [1985] Ch. 394; [1985] 2 W.L.R. 279; [1984] 3 All E.R. 869; (1985) 17
 H.L.R. 1; (1984) 81 L.S.G. 2935; (1984) 128 S.J. 686, Ch D 24–026
Ashby v White (1703) 2 Lld. Raym. 938 29–021
Asher v Secretary of State for the Environment [1974] Ch. 208; [1974] 2 W.L.R. 466;
 [1974] 2 All E.R. 156; 72 L.G.R. 333; (1974) 118 S.J. 258, CA (Civ Div) 25–040
Ashmole v Wainwright (1842) 2 Q.B. 837 11–020
Associated Industries v US Dept of Labor 487 F. 2d 342 (2d Cir.1973) 15–025
Associated Provincial Picture Houses Ltd v Wednesbury Corp [1948] 1 K.B. 223; [1947]
 2 All E.R. 680; (1947) 63 T.L.R. 623; (1948) 112 J.P. 55; 45 L.G.R. 635; [1948]
 L.J.R. 190; (1947) 177 L.T. 641; (1948) 92 S.J. 26, CA 17–002, 19–001, 20–018
Association of Data Processing Service Organizations, Inc v Board of Governors of the
 Federal Reserve System 745 F. 2d 677 (1984) 15–025
Aston Cantlow and Wilmcote with Billesley Parochial Church Council v Wallbank; sub
 nom. Wallbank v Aston Cantlow and Wilmcote with Billesley Parochial Church
 Council [2003] UKHL 37; [2004] 1 A.C. 546; [2003] 3 W.L.R. 283; [2003] 3 All E.R.
 1213; [2003] H.R.L.R. 28; [2003] U.K.H.R.R. 919; [2003] 27 E.G. 137 (C.S.);
 (2003) 100(33) L.S.G. 28; (2003) 153 N.L.J. 1030; (2003) 147 S.J.L.B. 812; [2003]
 N.P.C. 80, HL 18–018, 18–019, 18–020, 18–021, 18–024
Atkinson v Newcastle Waterworks Co (1877) 2 Ex D. 441 29–021
Atlan v United Kingdom (36533/97) (2002) 34 E.H.R.R. 33; [2001] Crim. L.R. 819,
 ECHR 28–008
Atlanta Amsterdam BV v Produktschap voor Vee en Vlees (240/78) [1979] E.C.R.
 2137 19–021
Attorney General v Able [1984] Q.B. 795; [1983] 3 W.L.R. 845; [1984] 1 All E.R. 277;
 (1984) 78 Cr. App. R. 197; [1984] Crim. L.R. 35; (1983) 127 S.J. 731, QBD 24–009
Attorney General v Bastow [1957] 1 Q.B. 514; [1957] 2 W.L.R. 340; [1957] 1 All E.R.
 497; (1957) 121 J.P. 171; 55 L.G.R. 122; (1957) 8 P. & C.R. 168; (1957) 101 S.J.
 192, QBD 24–009
Attorney General v Chaudry [1971] 1 W.L.R. 1614; [1971] 3 All E.R. 938; 70 L.G.R. 22;
 (1971) 115 S.J. 792, CA (Civ Div) 24–007, 25–033
Attorney General v Colchester Corp; sub nom. Attorney General Ex rel Allen v Colchester BC [1955] 2 Q.B. 207; [1955] 2 W.L.R. 913; [1955] 2 All E.R. 124; 53
 L.G.R. 415; (1955) 99 S.J. 291, QBD 25–026, 25–036

Attorney General v De Keyser's Royal Hotel Ltd [1920] A.C. 508 .   17–005, 22–004, 28–015
Attorney General v Horner (1912) 107 L.T. 547 11–020
Attorney General v Fulham Corp [1921] 1 Ch. 440, Ch D 24–009, 25–033
Attorney General v Guardian Newspapers Ltd (No.2) [1990] 1 A.C. 109 .... 8–003, 17–018,
18–002
Attorney General v Harris (No.1); sub nom. Harris v Attorney General [1961] 1 Q.B.
74; [1960] 3 W.L.R. 532; [1960] 3 All E.R. 207; 58 L.G.R. 242; (1960) 104 S.J. 704,
CA 24–009
Attorney General v Jonathan Cape Ltd [1976] Q.B. 752; [1975] 3 W.L.R. 606; [1975] 3
All E.R. 484; (1975) 119 S.J. 696, QBD 28–003
Attorney General v Lindegren (1819) 6 Price 287 16–022
Attorney General v London and Home Counties Joint Electricity Authority [1929] 1
Ch. 513, Ch D 25–034
Attorney General v Manchester Corp [1906] 1 Ch. 643, Ch D 24–009, 25–033
Attorney General v PYA Quarries Ltd (No.1) [1957] 2 Q.B. 169; [1957] 2 W.L.R. 770;
[1957] 1 All E.R. 894; (1957) 121 J.P. 323; 55 L.G.R. 208; (1957) 101 S.J. 338, CA   24–009
Attorney General v Pontypridd Waterworks Co [1908] 1 Ch. 388, Ch D 24–010
Attorney General v Premier Line Ltd [1932] 1 Ch. 303, Ch D 24–009
Attorney General v Ryan [1980] A.C. 718; [1980] 2 W.L.R. 143; (1979) 123 S.J. 621, PC
(Bah) 12–027, 12–030
Attorney General v St Ives Rural DC [1961] 1 Q.B. 366; [1961] 2 W.L.R. 111; [1961] 1
All E.R. 265; (1961) 125 J.P. 119; 59 L.G.R. 105; (1961) 105 S.J. 87, CA 25–021
Attorney General v Smith [1958] 2 Q.B. 173 .... 24–007, 25–033
Attorney General v Wilts United Dairies Ltd (1922) 38 T.L.R. 781, HL 22–027
Attorney General for Canada v Hallett & Carey Ltd [1952] A.C. 427 22–028
Attorney General of Ceylon v Silva (AD) [1953] A.C. 461; [1953] 2 W.L.R. 1185; [1953]
1 Lloyd's Rep. 563; (1953) 97 S.J. 384, PC (Cey) 20–032
Attorney General of the Gambia v N'Jie [1961] A.C. 617; [1961] 2 W.L.R. 845; [1961] 2
All E.R. 504; (1961) 105 S.J. 421, PC (West Africa) 24–011
Attorney General of Hong Kong v Ng Yuen Shiu [1983] 2 A.C. 629; [1983] 2 W.L.R.
735; [1983] 2 All E.R. 346; (1983) 127 S.J. 188, PC (HK) 12–016, 12–028,
16–015, 20–015, 22–018, 25–007
Attorney General ex rel Tilley v Wandsworth LBC [1981] 1 W.L.R. 854; [1981] 1 All
E.R. 1162; (1981) 11 Fam. Law 119; (1981) 125 S.J. 148, CA (Civ Div) 16–012
Attorney General's Reference (No.2 of 2004), Re; sub nom. R. v Neville (Daniel John)
[2004] EWCA Crim 1280; [2005] 1 Cr. App. R. (S.) 14, CA (Crim Div) 12–043
Auckland Harbour Board v King, The [1924] A.C. 318, PC (NZ) 29–055
Austria v Council of the European Union (C-445/00) [2003] E.C.R. I-8549, ECJ 23–021
Autologic Holdings Plc v Inland Revenue Commissioners; sub nom. Test Claimants in
Loss Relief Group Litigation v Inland Revenue Commissioners; Loss Relief
Group Litigation Order Claimants v Inland Revenue Commissioners [2005]
UKHL 54; [2006] 1 A.C. 118; [2005] 3 W.L.R. 339; [2005] 4 All E.R. 1141; [2005]
S.T.C. 1357; [2005] 3 C.M.L.R. 2; [2006] Eu. L.R. 131; 77 T.C. 504; [2005] B.T.C.
402; [2005] S.T.I. 1336; (2005) 155 N.L.J. 1277, HL 25–023
Avon CC v Buscott; sub nom. Buscott v Avon CC [1988] Q.B. 656; [1988] 2 W.L.R.
788; [1988] 1 All E.R. 841; (1988) 20 H.L.R. 385; 86 L.G.R. 569; [1988] E.G. 26
(C.S.); (1988) 85(14) L.S.G. 49; (1988) 132 S.J. 567, CA (Civ Div) 26–014
Ayr Harbour Trustees v Oswald (1882–83) L.R. 8 App. Cas. 623, HL 16–024
B v Attorney General of New Zealand [2003] UKPC 61 29–016
B v Secretary of State for the Home Department (Deportation: Proportionality) [2000]
2 C.M.L.R. 1086; [2000] Eu. L.R. 687; [2000] H.R.L.R. 439; [2000] U.K.H.R.R.
498; [2000] Imm. A.R. 478; [2000] I.N.L.R. 361, CA (Civ Div) 19–010
B, Petitioner [2007] CSOH 73; 2007 S.L.T. 566; 2007 G.W.D. 15–288, OH 7–010
BBC v Johns [1965] Ch. 32; [1964] 2 W.L.R. 1071; [1964] 1 All E.R. 923; [1964] R.V.R.
579; [1964] R.V.R. 579; 10 R.R.C. 239; 41 T.C. 471; (1964) 43 A.T.C. 38; [1964]
T.R. 45; (1964) 108 S.J. 217, CA 28–015
BL Cars Ltd (Formerly Leyland Cars) v Vyas. *See* Science Research Council v Nasse
Bagg's Case (1615) 11 Co. Rep. 93b 12–001, 12–015
Baines, Re (1840) Cr.& Ph.31 14–026
Baldock v Webster [2004] EWCA Civ 1869; [2006] Q.B. 315; [2006] 2 W.L.R. 1; [2005] 3
All E.R. 655; (2005) 102(7) L.S.G. 27, CA (Civ Div) 23–008
Baldwin & Francis Ltd v Patents Appeal Tribunal; sub nom. R. v Patents Appeal

Tribunal Ex p. Baldwin & Francis; Baldwin & Francis' Application, Re [1959]
A.C. 663; [1959] 2 W.L.R. 826; [1959] 2 All E.R. 433; [1959] R.P.C. 221; (1959) 103
S.J. 451, HL 14–036
Balkan Import Export GmbH v Hauptzollamt Berlin Packhof (5/73) [1973] E.C.R.
1091, ECJ 19–022
Bank of Scotland v Investment Management Regulatory Organisation Ltd, 1989 S.C.
107; 1989 S.L.T. 432; 1989 S.C.L.R. 386, IH (Ex Div) 26–027
Bankers Case (1700) 90 ER 270 5–035
Barber v Manchester Regional Hospital Board [1958] 1 W.L.R. 181; [1958] 1 All E.R.
322; (1958) 122 J.P. 124; (1958) 102 S.J. 140, QBD 12–015
Barnard v National Dock Labour Board [1953] 2 Q.B. 18; [1953] 2 W.L.R. 995; [1953] 1
All E.R. 1113; [1953] 1 Lloyd's Rep. 371; (1953) 97 S.J. 331, CA 12–042, 16–003,
26–001
Barnato, Re; sub nom. Joel v Sanges [1949] Ch. 258; [1949] 1 All E.R. 515; [1949] T.R.
97; [1949] L.J.R. 1109, CA 25–026
Barnham v Secretary of State for the Environment and Hertfordshire CC (1986) 52 P.
& C.R. 10; [1985] J.P.L. 861, QBD 9–041
Baron Reitzes de Marienwert v Administrator of Austrian Property [1924] 2 Ch. 282,
CA 25–023
Barraclough v Brown [1897] A.C. 615 .... 25–020, 25–023
Barrett v Enfield LBC [2001] 2 A.C. 550; [1998] 1 W.L.R. 277; [1999] 3 W.L.R. 79;
[1999] 3 All E.R. 193; [1999] 2 F.L.R. 426; [1999] 2 F.C.R. 434; (1999) 1 L.G.L.R.
829; [1999] B.L.G.R. 473; (1999) 11 Admin. L.R. 839; [1999] Ed. C.R. 833; (1999) 2
C.C.L. Rep. 203; [1999] P.I.Q.R. P272; (1999) 49 B.M.L.R. 1; [1999] Fam. Law
622; (1999) 96(28) L.S.G. 27; (1999) 143 S.J.L.B. 183, HL 29–006, 29–012,
29–013, 29–014, 29–015
Barrs v Bethell [1982] Ch. 294; [1981] 3 W.L.R. 874; [1982] 1 All E.R. 106; 81 L.G.R.
269; (1981) 125 S.J. 808, Ch D 24–007, 25–031
Barry v Arnaud (1839) 10 Ad. & E. 646 29–021
Bates v Lord Hailsham of St Marylebone [1972] 1 W.L.R. 1373; [1972] 3 All E.R. 1019;
(1972) 116 S.J. 584, Ch D 12–012, 12–028, 22–018
Battelley v Finsbury BC (1958) 122 J.P. 169; 56 L.G.R. 165 16–006
Beaudesert Shire Council v Smith (1966) 120 C.L.R. 145 29–032
Becker v Finanzamt Munster-Innenstadt (8/81) [1982] E.C.R. 53; [1982] 1 C.M.L.R.
499, ECJ 10–025
Beggs v Scottish Ministers (Contempt of Court) 2005 1 S.C. 342; 2005 S.L.T. 305; 2005
S.C.L.R. 640; 2005 G.W.D. 10–145, IH (1 Div) 28–023
Begum v Tower Hamlets LBC; sub nom. Tower Hamlets LBC v Begum (Runa) [2003]
UKHL 5; [2003] 2 A.C. 430; [2003] 2 W.L.R. 388; [2003] 1 All E.R. 731; [2003]
H.R.L.R. 16; [2003] U.K.H.R.R. 419; 14 B.H.R.C. 400; [2003] H.L.R. 32; [2003]
B.L.G.R. 205; 2003 Hous. L.R. 20; [2003] A.C.D. 41; (2003) 100(13) L.S.G. 28;
(2003) 147 S.J.L.B. 232; [2003] N.P.C. 21, HL 12–018, 12–019, 13–017,
13–018, 18–003
Bela-Muhle Josef Bergmann KG v Grows Farm GmbH & Co KG (114/76) [1977]
E.C.R. 1247; [1977] E.C.R. 1269; [1977] E.C.R. 1211; [1979] 2 C.M.L.R. 83, ECJ 19–021
Belfast City Council v Miss Behavin' Ltd (Northern Ireland); sub nom. Belfast City
Council v Miss Behavin' Ltd [2007] UKHL 19; [2007] 1 W.L.R. 1420; [2007] 3 All
E.R. 1007; [2007] N.I. 89; [2007] H.R.L.R. 26; [2008] B.L.G.R. 127; (2007) 104(19)
L.S.G. 27; (2007) 151 S.J.L.B. 575, HL 18–040, 18–043, 18–044, 18–051, 19–018
Bell v Ontario Human Rights Commission (1971) 9 Osgoode Hall L.J. 203 14–007
Bellinger v Bellinger [2003] UKHL 21; [2003] 2 A.C. 467; [2003] 2 W.L.R. 1174; [2003] 2
All E.R. 593; [2003] 1 F.L.R. 1043; [2003] 2 F.C.R. 1; [2003] H.R.L.R. 22; [2003]
U.K.H.R.R. 679; 14 B.H.R.C. 127; (2003) 72 B.M.L.R. 147; [2003] A.C.D. 74;
[2003] Fam. Law 485; (2003) 153 N.L.J. 594; (2003) 147 S.J.L.B. 472, HL 18–009
Benjamin v Storr (1873–74) L.R. 9 C.P. 400, CCP 24–006
Benthem v Netherlands (8848/80) (1986) 8 E.H.R.R. 1, ECHR 12–018, 13–012
Berezovsky v Forbes Inc (No.2) [2001] EWCA Civ 1251; [2001] E.M.L.R. 45, CA (Civ
Div) 18–028
Bhamjee v Forsdick [2003] EWCA Civ 1113; [2004] 1 W.L.R. 88; [2003] C.P. Rep. 67;
[2003] B.P.I.R. 1252; (2003) 100(36) L.S.G. 41, CA (Civ Div) 26–053
Bilbie v Lumley (1802) 2 East 469 29–050
Bilston Corp v Wolverhampton Corp [1942] Ch. 391, Ch D 25–034

Birkdale District Electric Supply Co Ltd v Southport Corp; sub nom. Southport Corp v
    Birkdale District Electric Supply Co Ltd [1926] A.C. 355, HL 16–024, 16–031
Bivens v Six Unknown Named Agents of the Federal Bureau of Narcotics 403 U.S. 388
    (1971) 29–025
Blackpool Corp v Locker [1948] 1 K.B. 349; [1948] 1 All E.R. 85; (1948) 112 J.P. 130; 46
    L.G.R. 58; [1948] L.J.R. 847, CA 16–006, 22–007
Blaizot v University of Liege (C-24/86) [1988] E.C.R. 379; [1989] 1 C.M.L.R. 57, ECJ   23–021
Blake (Valuation Officer) v Hendon Corp (No.1) [1962] 1 Q.B. 283; [1961] 3 W.L.R.
    951; [1961] 3 All E.R. 601; (1961) 125 J.P. 620; 59 L.G.R. 515; [1961] R.V.R. 552;
    (1961) 105 S.J. 666, CA 16–028
Blanchard v Control Data Canada Ltee [1984] 2 S.C.R. 476; 14 D.L.R. (4th) 289 ... 14–006
Board of Education v Rice; sub nom. R. v Board of Education [1911] A.C. 179,
    HL 12–001, 12–010, 25–004, 25–016
Board of Trade v Temperley Steam Shipping Co Ltd (1927) 27 Ll. L. Rep. 230, CA   16–025
Bocchi Food Trade International GmbH v Commission of the European Communities
    (T-30/99) [2001] E.C.R. II-943, CFI (5th Chamber) 19–022
Boddington v British Transport Police [1999] 2 A.C. 143; [1998] 2 W.L.R. 639; [1998] 2
    All E.R. 203; (1998) 162 J.P. 455; (1998) 10 Admin. L.R. 321; (1998) 148 N.L.J.
    515, HL 22–030, 23–002, 26–010
Bolam v Friern Hospital Management Committee [1957] 1 W.L.R. 582; [1957] 2 All
    E.R. 118; [1955–95] P.N.L.R. 7; (1957) 101 S.J. 357, QBD 29–015
Bolt v Stennett (1800) 8 TR 606 11–019
Bolton v Law Society [1994] 1 W.L.R. 512; [1994] 2 All E.R. 486; [1994] C.O.D. 295,
    CA (Civ Div) 19–010
Bombay Province v Bombay Municipal Corp [1947] A.C. 58; 62 T.L.R. 643; [1947]
    L.J.R. 380, PC (Ind) 28–015
Bonaker v Evans 117 E.R. 840; (1850) 16 Q.B. 162, Ex Chamber 12–001, 23–025
Bone v Mental Health Review Tribunal [1985] 3 All E.R. 330, QBD 12–034
Booth & Co (International) Ltd v National Enterprise Board [1978] 3 All E.R. 624,
    QBD 24–006, 24–030, 29–021
Boren v State Personnel Board 234 P.2d 981 (1951) 20–042
Bourgoin SA v Ministry of Agriculture, Fisheries and Food [1986] Q.B. 716; [1985] 3
    W.L.R. 1027; [1985] 3 All E.R. 585; [1986] 1 C.M.L.R. 267; (1985) 82 L.S.G. 3435,
    CA (Civ Div) 29–032
Bowen v Georgetown University Hospital 488 U.S. 204 (1988) 14–041, 20–003
Bowyer, Philpott & Payne Ltd v Mather [1919] 1 K.B. 419 16–005
Boyce v Paddington BC [1906] A.C. 1, HL 24–006, 25–031
Boyle v Wilson [1907] A.C. 45 .... 16–012, 16–013
Bradbury v Enfield LBC [1967] 1 W.L.R. 1311; [1967] 3 All E.R. 434; (1968) 132 J.P. 15;
    65 L.G.R. 115; (1967) 111 S.J. 701, CA (Civ Div) 24–007, 25–040
Bradford-Smart v West Sussex CC [2002] EWCA Civ 7; [2002] 1 F.C.R. 425; [2002]
    B.L.G.R. 489; [2002] E.L.R. 139; (2002) 99(10) L.S.G. 32; (2002) 152 N.L.J. 142;
    (2002) 146 S.J.L.B. 46, CA (Civ Div) 29–015
Bradlaugh Ex p. (1878) 3 Q.B.D. 509 .... 14–027, 27–003
Bradlaugh v Gossett (1883–84) L.R. 12 Q.B.D. 271, QBD 25–034
Bradley v Jockey Club [2005] EWCA Civ 1056, CA (Civ Div) 26–028
Brasserie du Pecheur SA v Germany (C-46/93); R. v Secretary of State for Transport
    Ex p. Factortame Ltd (C-48/93) [1996] Q.B. 404; [1996] 2 W.L.R. 506; [1996] All
    E.R. (EC) 301; [1996] E.C.R. I-1029; [1996] 1 C.M.L.R. 889; [1996] C.E.C. 295;
    [1996] I.R.L.R. 267, ECJ 10–032, 29–057, 29–067
Brayhead (Ascot) Ltd v Berkshire CC [1964] 2 Q.B. 303; [1964] 2 W.L.R. 507; [1964] 1
    All E.R. 149; (1964) 128 J.P. 167; 62 L.G.R. 162; (1964) 15 P. & C.R. 423; (1964)
    108 S.J. 178, QBD 12–034
Brayser v Maclean (1875) L.R. 6 P.C. 398 29–033
Breen v Amalgamated Engineering Union [1971] 2 Q.B. 175; [1971] 2 W.L.R. 742;
    [1971] 1 All E.R. 1148; 10 K.I.R. 120; (1971) 115 S.J. 203, CA (Civ Div) 12–027,
                                                                                    12–030
Bride v City of Slater 263 S.W. 2d 22 (1953) 20–042
Brinkmann Tabakfabriken GmbH v Skatteministeiet (C-319/96) [1998] E.C.R. I-5255;
    [1998] 3 C.M.L.R. 673, ECJ 29–058
Bristol DC v Clark [1975] 1 W.L.R. 1443; [1975] 3 All E.R. 976; 74 L.G.R. 3; (1975) 30
    P. & C.R. 441; (1975) 119 S.J. 659, CA (Civ Div) 17–013, 23–029

Bristol and North Somerset Railway Co, Re (1877) 3 Q.B.D. 10 .... 23–021, 25–018
British Airways Board v Laker Airways Ltd; sub nom. Laker Airways Ltd v Secretary
of State for Trade and Industry [1985] A.C. 58; [1984] 3 W.L.R. 413; [1984] 3 All
E.R. 39; [1985] E.C.C. 49; (1984) 81 L.S.G. 2849; (1984) 134 N.L.J. 746; (1984) 128
S.J. 531, HL 19–029
British Launderers Research Association v Hendon Rating Authority; sub nom. British
Launderers Research Association v Central Middlesex Assessment Committee
[1949] 1 K.B. 462; [1949] 1 All E.R. 21; 65 T.L.R. 103; (1949) 113 J.P. 72; 47
L.G.R. 113; 41 R. & I.T. 564; [1949] L.J.R. 416; (1949) 93 S.J. 58, CA 9–019
British Oxygen Co Ltd v South of Scotland Electricity Board (No.2); sub nom. British
Oxygen Gases Ltd v South of Scotland Electricity Board (No.2) [1959] 1 W.L.R.
587; [1959] 2 All E.R. 225; 1959 S.C. (H.L.) 17; 1959 S.L.T. 181; (1959) 103 S.J.
370, HL 29–049
British Oxygen Co Ltd v Board of Trade [1971] A.C. 610; [1969] 2 W.L.R. 892; [1970] 3
W.L.R. 488; [1970] 3 All E.R. 165, HL 16–013, 16–014
British Railways Board v Customs and Excise Commissioners [1977] 1 W.L.R. 588;
[1977] 2 All E.R. 873; [1977] S.T.C. 221; (1977) 121 S.J. 356, CA (Civ Div) 9–021
British Steel Corp v Granada Television Ltd [1981] A.C. 1096; [1980] 3 W.L.R. 774;
[1981] 1 All E.R. 417; (1980) 124 S.J. 812, HL 28–005
British Steel Plc v Customs and Excise Commissioners (No.1) [1997] 2 All E.R. 366, CA
(Civ Div) 26–009, 29–052
British Transport Commission v Westmoreland County Council [1958] A.C. 126 16–024
Brittain v Kinnaird (1819) 1 B. & B. 432 14–026
Broadbent v Rotherham Corp [1917] 2 Ch. 31, Ch D 25–033
Bromley LBC v Greater London Council [1983] 1 A.C. 768; [1982] 2 W.L.R. 92; [1982]
1 All E.R. 153; (1982) 126 S.J. 16, HL 17–011, 19–017
Brookes v Earl Rivers (1668) Hardr. 503 23–026
Brooks v Commissioner of Police of the Metropolis [2005] UKHL 24; [2005] 1 W.L.R.
1495; [2005] 2 All E.R. 489; [2005] Po. L.R. 157; (2005) 155 N.L.J. 653, HL ... 29–016
Brooks & Burton Ltd v Secretary of State for the Environment [1977] 1 W.L.R. 1294;
[1978] 1 All E.R. 733; 76 L.G.R. 53; (1978) 35 P. & C.R. 27; 244 E.G. 715; [1977]
J.P.L. 720; (1977) 121 S.J. 617, CA (Civ Div) 20–035
Broome v Broome [1955] P. 190; [1955] 2 W.L.R. 401; [1955] 1 All E.R. 201; (1955) 99
S.J. 114, PDAD 28–002
Brown v Executors of the Estate of HM Queen Elizabeth the Queen Mother [2008]
EWCA Civ 56, CA (Civ Div) 24–017
Brown v Gardner 513 U.S. 115 (1994) 14–042
Brown v Stott; sub nom. Stott (Procurator Fiscal) v Brown [2003] 1 A.C. 681; [2001] 2
W.L.R. 817; [2001] 2 All E.R. 97; 2001 S.C. (P.C.) 43; 2001 S.L.T. 59; 2001
S.C.C.R. 62; [2001] R.T.R. 11; [2001] H.R.L.R. 9; [2001] U.K.H.R.R. 333; 11
B.H.R.C. 179; (2001) 3 L.G.L.R. 24; (2001) 145 S.J.L.B. 100; 2000 G.W.D. 40–
1513, PC (Sc) 7–007, 18–035
Brownsea Haven Properties v Poole Corp [1958] Ch. 574; [1958] 2 W.L.R. 137; [1958] 1
All E.R. 205; (1958) 122 J.P. 97; 56 L.G.R. 91; (1958) 102 S.J. 84, CA .. 24–007, 25–021
Bryan v United Kingdom (A/335–A); sub nom. Bryan v United Kingdom (19178/91)
(1996) 21 E.H.R.R. 342; [1996] 1 P.L.R. 47; [1996] 2 E.G.L.R. 123; [1996] 28 E.G.
137, ECHR 13–012
Buckley v Law Society (No.2) [1984] 1 W.L.R. 1101; [1984] 3 All E.R. 313; (1984) 81
L.S.G. 3017; (1984) 128 S.J. 505, Ch D 28–005, 28–006
Bucknell (Frank) & Son v Croydon LBC; sub nom. Frank Bucknell & Son, Ltd v
Croydon LBC [1973] 1 W.L.R. 534; [1973] 2 All E.R. 165; 71 L.G.R. 175; [1973]
Crim. L.R. 182; (1973) 117 S.J. 244, QBD 25–021
Buckoke v Greater London Council [1971] Ch. 655; [1971] 2 W.L.R. 760; [1971] 2 All E.R.
254; [1971] R.T.R. 131; 69 L.G.R. 210; (1971) 115 S.J. 174, CA (Civ Div) 12–008
Bugdaycay v Secretary of State for the Home Department; sub nom. R. v Secretary of
State for the Home Department Ex p. Bugdaycay [1987] A.C. 514; [1987] 2 W.L.R.
606; [1987] 1 All E.R. 940; [1987] Imm. A.R. 250; (1987) 84 L.S.G. 902; (1987) 137
N.L.J. 199; (1987) 131 S.J. 297, HL 19–010
Bugg v DPP [1993] Q.B. 473; [1993] 2 W.L.R. 628; [1993] 2 All E.R. 815; (1993) 157 J.P.
673; (1993) 5 Admin. L.R. 633; [1993] Crim. L.R. 374; [1993] C.O.D. 8; (1993) 157
J.P.N. 329; (1993) 157 L.G. Rev. 621, DC 22–028, 23–002

Buitoni SA v Fonds d'Orientation et de Regularisation des Marches Agricoles (122/78)
[1979] E.C.R. 677; [1979] 2 C.M.L.R. 665, ECJ 19–021
Bunbury v Fuller (1853) 9 Ex. 111 14–027
Bunney v Burns Anderson Plc [2007] EWHC 1240 (Ch); [2008] Bus. L.R. 22; [2007] 4
All E.R. 246; [2008] 1 B.C.L.C. 17; [2008] Lloyd's Rep. I.R. 198; (2007) 104(25)
L.S.G. 36, Ch D 26–009
Burmah Oil Co Ltd v Bank of England [1980] A.C. 1090; [1979] 3 W.L.R. 722; [1979] 3
All E.R. 700; (1979) 123 S.J. 786, HL 28–012, 28–013
Burmah Oil Co (Burma Trading) Ltd v Lord Advocate [1965] A.C. 75; [1964] 2 W.L.R.
1231; [1964] 2 All E.R. 348; 1964 S.C. (H.L.) 117; 1964 S.L.T. 218; (1964) 108 S.J.
401, HL 17–005, 23–023, 29–039
Bushell v Secretary of State for the Environment [1981] A.C. 75; [1980] 3 W.L.R. 22;
[1980] 2 All E.R. 608; 78 L.G.R. 269; (1980) 40 P. & C.R. 51; [1980] J.P.L. 458;
(1981) 125 S.J. 168, HL 9–038, 12–031, 12–046
Butler v Thompson [2005] EWCA Civ 864, CA (Civ Div) 12–033
Buxton v Minister of Housing and Local Government [1961] 1 Q.B. 278; [1960] 3
W.L.R. 866; [1960] 3 All E.R. 408; (1960) 124 J.P. 489; 59 L.G.R. 45; (1961) 12 P.
& C.R. 77; (1960) 104 S.J. 935, QBD 9–040, 24–011
Buy Irish Campaign, Re (C-249/81); sub nom. Commission of the European Com-
munities v Ireland [1983] E.C.R. 4005; [1982] E.C.R. 4005; [1983] 2 C.M.L.R. 104,
ECJ 5–032
CGU International Insurance Plc v AstraZeneca Insurance Co Ltd (Permission to
Appeal); sub nom. AstraZeneca Insurance Co Ltd v CGU International Insurance
Plc (Permission to Appeal) [2006] EWCA Civ 1340; [2007] Bus. L.R. 162; [2007] 1
All E.R. (Comm) 501; [2007] 1 Lloyd's Rep. 142; [2007] C.P. Rep. 4; [2006] 2
C.L.C. 441; [2006] H.R.L.R. 43, CA (Civ Div) 18–027
CIA Security International SA v Signalson SA (C-194/94) [1996] All E.R. (EC) 557;
[1996] E.C.R. I-2201; [1996] 2 C.M.L.R. 781, ECJ 10–030
Cabo Verde v Secretary of State for the Home Department [2004] EWCA Civ 1726   15–018
Cadbury Schweppes and Lyons & Co's Agreement, Re; sub nom. Cadbury Schweppes
Agreement, Re [1975] 1 W.L.R. 1018; [1975] 2 All E.R. 307; [1975] I.C.R. 240;
(1975) 119 S.J. 458, Ch D (RPC) 11–004
Caffoor (Trustees of the Abdul Gaffoor Trust) v Income Tax Commissioner
(Colombo); sub nom. Gaffoor (Abdul) Trustees v Ceylon Commissioner of
Income Tax; Trustees of Abdul Gaffoor Trust v Income Tax Commissioner,
Colombo [1961] A.C. 584; [1961] 2 W.L.R. 794; [1961] 2 All E.R. 436; (1961) 40
A.T.C. 93; [1961] T.R. 97; (1961) 105 S.J. 383, PC (Cey) 20–030
California Pacific Bank v Small Business Administration 557 F. 2d 218 (1977) 20–048
Calveley v Merseyside Police. See R. v Chief Constable of Merseyside Ex p. Calveley
Calvin v Carr [1980] A.C. 574; [1979] 2 W.L.R. 755; [1979] 2 All E.R. 440; (1979) 123
S.J. 112, PC (Aus) 12–041, 23–009
Cambridge Water Co Ltd v Eastern Counties Leather Plc [1994] 2 A.C. 264; [1994] 2
W.L.R. 53; [1994] 1 All E.R. 53; [1994] 1 Lloyd's Rep. 261; [1994] Env. L.R. 105;
[1993] E.G. 211 (C.S.); (1994) 144 N.L.J. 15; (1994) 138 S.J.L.B. 24, HL 29–042
Cameron v Network Rail Infrastructure Ltd (formerly Railtrack Plc) [2006] EWHC
1133 (QB); [2007] 1 W.L.R. 163; [2007] 3 All E.R. 241; [2006] H.R.L.R. 31; [2007]
U.K.H.R.R. 245; [2006] P.I.Q.R. P28; (2006) 156 N.L.J. 881; (2006) 150 S.J.L.B.
739, QBD 18–029
Campbell v Tameside MBC [1982] Q.B. 1065; [1982] 3 W.L.R. 74; [1982] 2 All E.R. 791;
80 L.G.R. 700; (1982) 126 S.J. 361, CA (Civ Div) 28–013
Campbell v United Kingdom (7511/76); Cosans v United Kingdom (7743/76) (1981) 3
E.H.R.R. 531, Eur Comm HR 24–025
Canada (Attorney general) v Mossop [1993] 1 S.C.R. 554 14–043
Canal Satelite Digital SL v Administracion General del Estado (C-390/99) [2002]
E.C.R. I-607; [2003] 1 C.M.L.R. 27; [2002] E.C.D.R. 22; [2003] E.M.L.R. 12,
ECJ 19–020
Cannock Chase DC v Kelly [1978] 1 W.L.R. 1; [1978] 1 All E.R. 152; 76 L.G.R. 67;
(1978) 36 P. & C.R. 219; (1977) 244 E.G. 211; [1977] J.P.L. 655; (1977) 121 S.J.
593, CA (Civ Div) 17–013, 26–025
Caparo Industries Plc v Dickman [1990] 2 A.C. 605; [1990] 2 W.L.R. 358; [1990] 1 All
E.R. 568; [1990] B.C.C. 164; [1990] B.C.L.C. 273; [1990] E.C.C. 313; [1955–95]

P.N.L.R. 523; (1990) 87(12) L.S.G. 42; (1990) 140 N.L.J. 248; (1990) 134 S.J. 494,
HL 29–008
Capel v Child (1832) 2 Cr. & J. 588 .... 12–001, 23–025
Capital and Counties Plc v Hampshire CC [1997] Q.B. 1004; [1997] 3 W.L.R. 331;
    [1997] 2 All E.R. 865; [1997] 2 Lloyd's Rep. 161; (1997) 147 N.L.J. 599; (1997) 141
    S.J.L.B. 92, CA (Civ Div) 29–009
Carltona Ltd v Commissioners of Works [1943] 2 All E.R. 560, CA 5–012, 16–007,
                                                                                                                        16–010
Carnavon harbour Acts [1937] Ch.72 25–026
Carty v Croydon LBC [2005] EWCA Civ 19; [2005] 1 W.L.R. 2312; [2005] 2 All E.R.
    517; [2005] 1 F.C.R. 554; [2005] B.L.G.R. 319; [2005] E.L.R. 104; (2005) 102(10)
    L.S.G. 30, CA (Civ Div) 29–016
Case of Monopolies (1602) 11 Co. Rep. 84b 17–005
Cave v Mountain (1840) 1 M. & G. 257 14–026
Cayzer Irvine & Co Ltd v Board of Trade; Cayzer, Irvine & Co Ltd v Board of Trade
    [1927] A.C. 610; (1927) 28 Ll. L. Rep. 113, HL 28–016
Central Electricity Generating Board v Clwyd CC [1976] 1 W.L.R. 151; [1976] 1 All
    E.R. 251; (1976) 31 P. & C.R. 238; (1976) 120 S.J. 81, Ch D 9–021
Chagos Islanders v Attorney General [2004] EWCA Civ 997, CA (Civ Div) 29–036
Chamberlaine v Chester and Birkenhead Ry Co (1848) 1 Ex. 870 24–007
Chandler (Terence Norman) v DPP; sub nom. R. v Chandler (Terence Norman) (No.1)
    [1964] A.C. 763; [1962] 3 W.L.R. 694; [1962] 3 All E.R. 142; (1962) 46 Cr. App. R.
    347; (1962) 106 S.J. 588, HL 17–005
Charing Cross Electricity Supply Co v Hydraulic Power Co; sub nom. Charing Cross
    West End and City Electricity Supply Co v London Hydraulic Power Co [1914] 3
    K.B. 772, CA 29–043
Chaudhury v General Medical Council [2002] UKPC 41; [2004] Lloyd's Rep. Med. 251,
    PC (UK) 19–010, 19–011
Cheall v Association of Professional, Executive, Clerical and Computer Staff (APEX)
    [1983] 2 A.C. 180; [1983] 2 W.L.R. 679; [1983] 1 All E.R. 1130; [1983] I.C.R. 398;
    [1983] I.R.L.R. 215; (1983) 133 N.L.J. 538, HL 25–004
Chertsey Urban DC v Mixnam's Properties Ltd [1965] A.C. 735; [1964] 2 W.L.R. 1210;
    [1964] 2 All E.R. 627; (1964) 128 J.P. 405; 62 L.G.R. 528; (1964) 15 P. & C.R. 331;
    [1964] R.V.R. 632; (1964) 108 S.J. 402, HL 17–010
Chester v Bateson [1920] 1 K.B. 829, KBD 22–027
Chevron USA Inc v NRDC 467 U.S. 837 (1984) 14–041
Chew v Holroyd (1852) 8 Ex. 249 14–027
Chief Adjudication Officer v Foster [1993] A.C. 754; [1993] 2 W.L.R. 292; [1993] 1 All
    E.R. 705; [1993] C.O.D. 259; (1993) 137 S.J.L.B. 36, HL 23–002, 26–010
Chief Constable of Greater Manchester v McNally; sub nom. McNally v Chief Con-
    stable of Greater Manchester [2002] EWCA Civ 14; [2002] 2 Cr. App. R. 37; [2002]
    Po. L.R. 9; [2002] Crim. L.R. 832, CA (Civ Div) 28–013
Chief Constable of North Wales v Evans [1982] 1 W.L.R. 1155; [1982] 3 All E.R. 141;
    (1983) 147 J.P. 6; (1982) 79 L.S.G. 1257; (1982) 126 S.J. 549, HL 12–024, 12–042,
                                                                                                                        23–019, 25–018
Chilton v Saga Holidays [1986] 1 All E.R. 841, CA (Civ Div) 12–031
Ching v Surrey County Council [1910] 1 K.B. 736 29–021
Church v Inclosure Commissioners (1862) 11 C.B. (N.S.) 664 .... 25–005, 25–007
Cinnamond v British Airports Authority [1980] 1 W.L.R. 582; [1980] 2 All E.R. 368;
    [1980] R.T.R. 220; 78 L.G.R. 371; (1980) 124 S.J. 221, CA (Civ Div) 12–024
Citizens to Preserve Overton Park v Volpe 401 U.S. 402 (1971) 15–024
City of Long Beach v Mansell 476 P.2d 423 (1970) 20–048
Clairborne Sales Co v Collector of Revenue 99 So. 2d 345 (1957) 20–042, 20–043
Clark v Devon CC; sub nom. Devon CC v Clarke [2005] EWCA Civ 266; [2005] C.P.
    Rep. 42; [2005] 2 F.L.R. 747; [2005] 1 F.C.R. 752; [2005] E.L.R. 375, CA (Civ
    Div) 29–016
Clark v Epsom Rural DC [1929] 1 Ch. 287, Ch D 26–057
Clark v University of Lincolnshire and Humberside [2000] 1 W.L.R. 1988; [2000] 3 All
    E.R. 752; [2000] Ed. C.R. 553; [2000] E.L.R. 345; [2000] C.O.D. 293; (2000) 150
    N.L.J. 616; (2000) 144 S.J.L.B. 220, CA (Civ Div) 26–013
Clarke v Chadburn [1985] 1 W.L.R. 78; [1985] 1 All E.R. 211; [1984] I.R.L.R. 350;
    (1984) 81 L.S.G. 3094; (1984) 128 S.J. 767, Ch D 25–030

Clay, Re [1919] 1 Ch. 66 25–025
Clough v Bussan [1990] 1 All E.R. 431; [1990] R.T.R. 178, QBD 29–008
Clough v Ratcliffe (1847) 1 De G. and S. 164 25–020
Clunis v Camden and Islington HA [1998] Q.B. 978; [1998] 2 W.L.R. 902; [1998] 3 All
    E.R. 180; (1997–98) 1 C.C.L. Rep. 215; (1998) 40 B.M.L.R. 181; [1998] P.N.L.R.
    262; (1998) 95(2) L.S.G. 23; (1998) 142 S.J.L.B. 38, CA (Civ Div) 29–022
Cocks v Thanet DC [1983] 2 A.C. 286; [1982] 3 W.L.R. 1121; [1982] 3 All E.R. 1135;
    (1983) 6 H.L.R. 15; 81 L.G.R. 81; [1984] R.V.R. 31; (1982) 126 S.J. 820, HL . 26–007,
                                                                                   26–056
Coenen v Sociaal-Economische Raad (39/75); sub nom. Coenen v Social and Economic
    Council of the Netherlands [1976] E.C.R. 1547; [1975] E.C.R. 1547; [1976] 1
    C.M.L.R. 30; [1976] I.C.R. 104, ECJ 19–020
Coghurst Wood Leisure Park Ltd v Secretary of State for Transport, Local Govern-
    ment and the Regions [2002] EWHC 1091; [2003] J.P.L. 206; [2002] 24 E.G. 145
    (C.S.); [2002] N.P.C. 80, QBD (Admin) .... 20–036 , 20–049
Coleen Properties Ltd v Minister of Housing and Local Government [1971] 1 W.L.R.
    433; [1971] 1 All E.R. 1049; 69 L.G.R. 175; (1971) 22 P. & C.R. 417; (1971) 115 S.J.
    112, CA (Civ Div) 14–037, 15–011
Collins v Imtrat Handelsgesellschaft mbH (C-92/92); Patricia Im- und Export Ver-
    waltungsgesellschaft mbH v EMI Electrola GmbH (C-326/92) [1993] E.C.R. I-
    5145; [1993] 3 C.M.L.R. 773; [1994] E.M.L.R. 108; [1994] F.S.R. 166, ECJ 21–016
Colonial Bank of Australasia v Willan (1874) L.R. 5 P.C. 417 14–028
Commins v Massam (1643) March N.C. 196 .... 25–002, 25–006
Commission of the European Communities v Belgium (C-217/99) [2000] E.C.R. I-
    10251 19–020
Commission of the European Communities v Council (Generalized Tariff Preferences)
    (51/87) [1988] E.C.R. 5459 23–021
Commission of the European Communities v European Central Bank (C-11/00) [2003]
    E.C.R. I-7147, ECJ 19–022
Commission of the European Communities v Germany (C178/84); sub nom. Purity
    Requirements for Beer, Re [1987] E.C.R. 1227; [1988] 1 C.M.L.R. 780, ECJ .. 19–020,
                                                                                   29–057
Commission of the European Communities v Ireland (45/87); sub nom. Dundalk Water
    Supply Scheme, Re (No.3) (45/87) [1988] E.C.R. 4929; 44 B.L.R. 1; [1989] 1
    C.M.L.R. 225, ECJ 5–026
Commission of the European Communities v Ireland (C-249/81). See Buy Irish Cam-
    paign, Re (C-249/81)
Commission of the European Communities v Italy (3/88) [1989] E.C.R. 4035 5–026
Commission of the European Communities v United Kingdom (40/82) [1984] E.C.R.
    283, ECJ 19–020
Commissioners of Crown Lands v Page [1960] 2 Q.B. 274; [1960] 3 W.L.R. 446; [1960] 2
    All E.R. 726; (1960) 104 S.J. 642, CA 16–022, 16–025, 16–030
Company A. Re [1980] Ch.138 14–032
Company of Mercers and Ironmongers of Chester v Bowker (1726) 1 Stra. 639 23–026
Coney v Choyce [1975] 1 W.L.R. 422; [1975] 1 All E.R. 979; (1974) 119 S.J. 202,
    Ch D 25–026, 25–036, 26–057
Congreve v Home Office [1976] Q.B. 629; [1976] 2 W.L.R. 291; [1976] 1 All E.R. 697;
    (1975) 119 S.J. 847, CA (Civ Div) 17–010
Consolidated Edison Co v NLRB 305 U.S. 197 (1938) 15–025
Conway v Rimmer [1968] A.C. 910; [1968] 2 W.L.R. 998; [1968] 1 All E.R. 874; (1968)
    112 S.J. 191, HL 28–002, 28–003, 28–004, 28–013
Cook v Southend BC [1990] 2 Q.B. 1; [1990] 2 W.L.R. 61; [1990] 1 All E.R. 243; (1990)
    154 J.P. 145; 88 L.G.R. 408; (1990) 2 Admin. L.R. 115; [1989] R.V.R. 215; [1990]
    C.O.D. 120; (1990) 154 J.P.N. 73; (1989) 133 S.J. 1133, ... CA (Civ Div)
                                                                                   24–011
Cookson & Clegg Ltd v Ministry of Defence [2005] EWCA Civ 811; [2006] Eu. L.R.
    1092; (2005) 149 S.J.L.B. 771, CA (Civ Div) 5–031
Cooper v Wandsworth Board of Works 143 E.R. 414; (1863) 14 C.B. N.S. 180,
    CCP 12–001, 23–025, 26–015
Cooper v Wilson [1937] 2 K.B. 309 .... 12–015, 13–004, 23–026
Coppard v Customs and Excise Commissioners [2003] EWCA Civ 511; [2003] Q.B.

1428; [2003] 2 W.L.R. 1618; [2003] 3 All E.R. 351; (2003) 100(24) L.S.G. 36; (2003) 147 S.J.L.B. 475, CA (Civ Div) 23–008
Corsten, Re (C-58/98) [2000] E.C.R. I-7919, ECJ 19–020
Costa v Ente Nazionale per l'Energia Elettrica (ENEL) (6/64) [1964] E.C.R. 585; [1964] C.M.L.R. 425, ECJ 10–011
Cotter v Minister for Social Welfare (C-377/89) [1991] E.C.R. I-1155; [1991] 3 C.M.L.R. 507; [1991] I.R.L.R. 380, ECJ 10–032
Couch v Steel (1854) 3 E. & B. 402 29–021
Council v Hautala (C-353/99) [2001] E.C.R. I-9565 19–020
Council of Civil Service Unions v Minister for the Civil Service [1985] A.C. 374; [1984] 1 W.L.R. 1174; [1984] 3 All E.R. 935; [1985] I.C.R. 14; [1985] I.R.L.R. 28; (1985) 82 L.S.G. 437; (1984) 128 S.J. 837, HL 12–022, 12–028, 14–033, 16–015, 17–002, 19–002, 20–016, 20–018, 22–018, 25–004
County and Nimbus Estates v Ealing LBC 76 L.G.R. 624; (1978) 249 E.G. 339, DC   27–005
Cowan v Chief Constable of Avon and Somerset [2002] H.L.R. 44; [2001] Po. L.R. 425, CA (Civ Div) 29–009
Cowl v Plymouth City Council. *See* R. (on the application of Cowl) v Plymouth City Council
Crake v Supplementary Benefits Commission [1982] 1 All E.R. 498; (1981) 2 F.L.R. 264, QBD 9–024, 12–034
Cream Holdings Ltd v Banerjee [2004] UKHL 44; [2005] 1 A.C. 253; [2004] 3 W.L.R. 918; [2004] 4 All E.R. 617; [2005] E.M.L.R. 1; [2004] H.R.L.R. 39; [2004] U.K.H.R.R. 1071; 17 B.H.R.C. 464; (2005) 28(2) I.P.D. 28001; (2004) 101(42) L.S.G. 29; (2004) 154 N.L.J. 1589; (2004) 148 S.J.L.B. 1215, HL 25–032
Credit Suisse v Allerdale BC [1997] Q.B. 306; [1996] 3 W.L.R. 894; [1996] 4 All E.R. 129; [1996] 2 Lloyd's Rep. 241; [1996] 5 Bank. L.R. 249; (1997) 161 J.P. Rep. 88, CA (Civ Div) 5–048, 5–049
Credit Suisse v Waltham Forest LBC [1997] Q.B. 362; [1996] 3 W.L.R. 943; [1996] 4 All E.R. 176; (1997) 29 H.L.R. 115; 94 L.G.R. 686; (1997) 9 Admin. L.R. 517, CA (Civ Div) 5–048
Crew v Vernon (1627) Cro. Car. 97 23–007
Criminal Proceedings against Bernaldez (C-129/94) [1996] All E.R. (EC) 741; [1996] E.C.R. I-1829; [1996] 2 C.M.L.R. 889, ECJ (5th Chamber) 10–030
Criminal Proceedings against Burmanjer (C-20/03); sub nom. Openbaar Ministerie v Burmanjer [2005] E.C.R. I-4133; [2006] 1 C.M.L.R. 24; [2006] C.E.C. 173, ECJ (1st Chamber) 19–020
Crofton Investment Trust v Greater London Rent Assessment Committee [1967] 2 Q.B. 955; [1967] 3 W.L.R. 256; [1967] 2 All E.R. 1103; [1967] R.V.R. 284; (1967) 111 S.J. 334, DC 9–024, 12–031
Crooke's Case (1691) 1 Show K.B. 208 28–016
Crown Prosecution Service v T; sub nom. DPP v T [2006] EWHC 728 (Admin); [2007] 1 W.L.R. 209; [2006] 3 All E.R. 471; (2006) 170 J.P. 470; [2006] 3 F.C.R. 184; [2007] A.C.D. 71; (2006) 170 J.P.N. 835, DC 23–004
Cullen v Chief Constable of the Royal Ulster Constabulary [2003] UKHL 39; [2003] 1 W.L.R. 1763; [2004] 2 All E.R. 237; [2003] N.I. 375; [2003] Po. L.R. 337; (2003) 100(35) L.S.G. 38; (2003) 147 S.J.L.B. 873, HL (NI) 29–022
Cullen v Morris (1821) 2 Stark 577 29–033
Cummings v Birkenhead Corp [1972] Ch. 12; [1971] 2 W.L.R. 1458; [1971] 2 All E.R. 881; 69 L.G.R. 444; (1971) 115 S.J. 365, CA (Civ Div) 16–013, 16–014, 29–021
Cunliffe v Fielden; sub nom. Fielden v Cunliffe [2005] EWCA Civ 1508; [2006] Ch. 361; [2006] 2 W.L.R. 481; [2006] 2 All E.R. 115; [2006] 1 F.L.R. 745; [2005] 3 F.C.R. 593; [2006] W.T.L.R. 29; (2005–06) 8 I.T.E.L.R. 855; [2006] Fam. Law 263; (2006) 103(3) L.S.G. 26, CA (Civ Div) 12–033
Curran v Northern Ireland Coownership Housing Association Ltd [1987] A.C. 718; [1987] 2 W.L.R. 1043; [1987] 2 All E.R. 13; 38 B.L.R. 1; (1987) 19 H.L.R. 318; (1987) 84 L.S.G. 1574; (1987) 131 S.J. 506, HL (NI) 29–008
Customs and Excise Commissioners v Peninsular and Oriental Steam Navigation Co Ltd [1994] S.T.C. 259; (1994) 138 S.J.L.B. 52, CA (Civ Div) 19–016
Cutler v Wandsworth Stadium Ltd [1949] A.C. 398; [1949] 1 All E.R. 544; 65 T.L.R. 170; [1949] L.J.R. 824; (1949) 93 S.J. 163, HL 29–021
D v National Society for the Prevention of Cruelty to Children (NSPCC) [1978] A.C.

171; [1977] 2 W.L.R. 201; [1977] 1 All E.R. 589; 76 L.G.R. 5; (1977) 121 S.J. 119,
   HL 28–005, 28–006
D v Secretary of State for the Home Department. *See* R. (on the application of D) v
   Secretary of State for the Home Department
D (Infants), Re [1970] 1 W.L.R. 599; [1970] 1 All E.R. 1088; 68 L.G.R. 183; (1970) 114
   S.J. 188, CA (Civ Div) 28–006
D (Minors) (Adoption Reports: Confidentiality), Re [1996] A.C. 593; [1995] 3 W.L.R.
   483; [1995] 4 All E.R. 385; [1995] 2 F.L.R. 687; [1996] 1 F.C.R. 205; [1996] Fam.
   Law 8; (1995) 145 N.L.J. 1612, HL 12–030
DPP v Haw [2007] EWHC 1931 (Admin); [2007] H.R.L.R. 43; [2007] U.K.H.R.R. 1194;
   (2007) 104(33) L.S.G. 26; (2007) 157 N.L.J. 1198; [2008] 1 W.L.R. 379, DC 16–007
DPP v Head; sub nom. R. v Head (John Shortrig) [1959] A.C. 83; [1958] 2 W.L.R. 617;
   [1958] 1 All E.R. 679; (1958) 42 Cr. App. R. 98; (1958) 122 J.P. 259; (1958) 102 S.J.
   249, HL 23–001, 23–004
DPP v Hutchinson; sub nom. R. v Secretary of State for Defence Ex p. Parker; R. v
   Secretary of State for Defence Ex p. Hayman [1990] 2 A.C. 783; [1990] 3 W.L.R.
   196; (1991) 155 J.P. 71; 89 L.G.R. 1; (1990) 2 Admin. L.R. 741; [1991] C.O.D. 4;
   (1990) 154 J.P.N. 674; (1990) 154 L.G. Rev. 872; (1990) 140 N.L.J. 1035; (1990)
   134 S.J. 1041, HL 22–024, 23–033
DPP v Memery [2002] EWHC 1720 (Admin); (2003) 167 J.P. 238; [2003] R.T.R. 18;
   (2003) 167 J.P.N. 431, QBD (Admin) 23–004
DPP v T. *See* Crown Prosecution Service v T
DS v HM Advocate; sub nom. HM Advocate v DS [2007] UKPC D1; 2007 S.L.T. 1026;
   2007 S.C.C.R. 222; [2007] H.R.L.R. 28; 2007 S.C. (P.C.) 1, PC (Sc) 7–007
Dale v Pollard (1847) 10 Q.B. 505 14–027
Darker Enterprises v Dacorum BC [1992] C.O.D. 465 .... 13–005, 13–008
Darlassis v Minister of Education (1954) 118 J.P. 452; 52 L.G.R. 304; (1953–54) 4 P. &
   C.R. 281, QBD 9–040
David v Abdul Cader [1963] 1 W.L.R. 834; [1963] 3 All E.R. 579; (1963) 107 S.J. 615,
   PC (Cey) 29–033
Davidson v Scottish Ministers (No.1); sub nom. Davidson, Petitioner (No.1); Scott,
   Petitioner; Scott v Scottish Ministers [2005] UKHL 74; 2006 S.C. (H.L.) 41; 2006
   S.L.T. 110; 2006 S.C.L.R. 249; 2006 G.W.D. 4–72, HL 28–020
Davidson v Scottish Ministers (No.2); sub nom. Davidson, Petitioner (No.2) [2004]
   UKHL 34; 2005 1 S.C. (H.L.) 7; 2004 S.L.T. 895; 2004 S.C.L.R. 991; [2004]
   H.R.L.R. 34; [2004] U.K.H.R.R. 1079; [2005] A.C.D. 19; 2004 G.W.D. 27–572,
   HL 13–007
Davis v Radcliffe [1990] 1 W.L.R. 821; [1990] 2 All E.R. 536; [1990] B.C.C. 472; [1990]
   B.C.L.C. 647; (1990) 87(19) L.S.G. 43; (1990) 134 S.J. 1078, PC (IoM) 29–008
Davy v Spelthorne BC [1984] A.C. 262; [1983] 3 W.L.R. 742; [1983] 3 All E.R. 278; 82
   L.G.R. 193; (1984) 47 P. & C.R. 310; [1984] J.P.L. 269; (1983) 133 N.L.J. 1015;
   (1983) 127 S.J. 733, HL 26–007
Dawkins v Antrobus (1881) L.R. 17 Ch. D. 615, Ch D 12–001
Dawson v Bingley Urban District Council [1911] 2 K.B. 149 29–021
Daymond v South West Water Authority; sub nom. Daymond v Plymouth City
   Council [1976] A.C. 609; [1975] 3 W.L.R. 865; [1976] 1 All E.R. 39; 74 L.G.R. 128;
   (1975) 119 S.J. 846, HL 23–001
De Falco v Crawley BC [1980] Q.B. 460; [1980] 2 W.L.R. 664; [1980] 1 All E.R. 913;
   [1980] 1 C.M.L.R. 437; 78 L.G.R. 180; [1980] J.P.L. 392; (1980) 124 S.J. 82, CA
   (Civ Div) 29–021
De Freitas v Permanent Secretary of Ministry of Agriculture, Fisheries, Lands and
   Housing [1999] 1 A.C. 69; [1998] 3 W.L.R. 675; 4 B.H.R.C. 563; (1998) 142
   S.J.L.B. 219, PC (Ant) 18–039
De Haber v Queen of Portugal (1851) 17 Q.B. 171 .... 24–004, 25–009
De Verteuil v Knaggs [1918] A.C. 557, PC (Trin) 12–041
Defrenne v SA Belge de Navigation Aerienne (SABENA) (43/75); sub nom. Defrenne v
   SABENA [1981] 1 All E.R. 122; [1976] E.C.R. 455; [1976] 2 C.M.L.R. 98; [1976]
   I.C.R. 547, ECJ 10–021, 10–025, 18–054, 21–017, 23–021
Defrenne v SA Belge de Navigation Aerienne (SABENA) (149/77); sub nom. Defrenne
   v SA Belge d'Exploitation de la Navigation Aerienne (SABENA) [1978] E.C.R.
   1365; [1978] 3 C.M.L.R. 312, ECJ 21–017
Delta Properties Pty Ltd v Brisbane City Council (1956) 95 C.L.R. 11 12–008

Denkavit International BV v Bundesamt fur Finanzen (C-283/94) [1996] S.T.C. 1445; [1996] E.C.R. I-5063, ECJ (5th Chamber) 29–058

Dennis v Ministry of Defence [2003] EWHC 793 (QB); [2003] Env. L.R. 34; [2003] E.H.L.R. 17; [2003] 2 E.G.L.R. 121; [2006] R.V.R. 45; [2003] J.P.L. 1577; [2003] 19 E.G. 118 (C.S.); (2003) 153 N.L.J. 634; [2003] N.P.C. 55, QBD 29–041

Denton v Auckland City [1969] N.Z.L.R. 256 12–027

Department of the Treasury 494 U.S. 922 (1990) 14–041

Department of Transport v North West Water Authority [1984] A.C. 336; [1983] 3 W.L.R. 707; [1983] 3 All E.R. 273; 82 L.G.R. 207; (1983) 133 N.L.J. 1016; (1983) 127 S.J. 713, HL 29–038, 29–043, 29–044

Derbyshire CC v Times Newspapers Ltd [1993] A.C. 534; [1993] 2 W.L.R. 449; [1993] 1 All E.R. 1011; 91 L.G.R. 179; (1993) 143 N.L.J. 283; (1993) 137 S.J.L.B. 52, HL 17–018, 18–002

Deumeland v Germany (A/120); sub nom. Deumeland v Germany (9384/81) (1986) 8 E.H.R.R. 448, ECHR 12–018, 12–019

Deutsche Morgan Grenfell Group Plc v Inland Revenue Commissioners; sub nom. Inland Revenue Commissioners v Deutsche Morgan Grenfell Group Plc; Deutsche Morgan Grenfell Group Plc v Revenue and Customs Commissioners [2006] UKHL 49; [2007] 1 A.C. 558; [2006] 3 W.L.R. 781; [2007] 1 All E.R. 449; [2007] S.T.C. 1; [2007] 1 C.M.L.R. 14; [2007] Eu. L.R. 226; 78 T.C. 120; [2006] B.T.C. 781; 9 I.T.L. Rep. 201; [2006] S.T.I. 2386; (2006) 103(43) L.S.G. 29; (2006) 150 S.J.L.B. 1430, HL 29–050, 29–052

Deutsche Telekom AG v Schroder (C-50/96); Deutsche Post AG v Sievers (C-270/97); Deutsche Telekom AG v Vick (C-234/96) [2000] E.C.R. I-743; [2002] 2 C.M.L.R. 25; [2000] I.R.L.R. 353, ECJ (6th Chamber) 21–017

Devon CC v Clarke. *See* Clark v Devon CC

Devonport Corporation v Tozer [1903] 1 Ch. 759 24–010

Dickson, Re; sub nom. Local Government Act 1933, Re; Dickson v Hurle Hobbs [1948] 2 K.B. 95; [1948] 1 All E.R. 713; 64 T.L.R. 233; (1948) 112 J.P. 232; 46 L.G.R. 175; [1948] L.J.R. 1119; (1948) 92 S.J. 244, CA 20–042

Dickson v Hurle Hobbs. *See* Dickson, Re

Dilieto v Ealing LBC [2000] Q.B. 381; [1998] 3 W.L.R. 1403; [1998] 2 All E.R. 885; [1998] 2 P.L.R. 98; [1998] P.L.C.R. 212, DC 23–004

Dillenkofer v Germany (C-178/94); Erdmann v Germany (C-179/94); Schulte v Germany (C-188/94); Heuer v Germany (C189/94); Knor v Germany (C-190/94) [1997] Q.B. 259; [1997] 2 W.L.R. 253; [1996] All E.R. (EC) 917; [1996] E.C.R. I-4845; [1996] 3 C.M.L.R. 469; [1997] I.R.L.R. 60, ECJ 29–058

Dimes v Grand Junction Canal Proprietors 10 E.R. 301; (1852) 3 H.L. Cas. 759, HL 13–002, 23–026

Director General of Fair Trading v Proprietary Association of Great Britain (Costs); sub nom. Medicaments and Related Classes of Goods (No.4), Re [2001] EWCA Civ 1217; [2002] 1 W.L.R. 269; [2002] 1 All E.R. 853; (2001) 98(34) L.S.G. 37; (2001) 151 N.L.J. 1372; (2001) 145 S.J.L.B. 209, CA (Civ Div) 24–025

Director General of Fair Trading v Tobyward Ltd [1989] 1 W.L.R. 517; [1989] 2 All E.R. 266; (1990) 9 Tr. L.R. 41; (1989) 133 S.J. 184, Ch D 23–032

Disher v Disher [1965] P. 31; [1964] 2 W.L.R. 21; [1963] 3 All E.R. 933; (1964) 108 S.J. 37, DC 23–025

Dobson v Thames Water Utilities Ltd [2007] EWHC 2021 (TCC); [2008] 2 All E.R. 362; [2007] B.L.R. 465; [2007] T.C.L.R. 7; [2007] H.R.L.R. 45; [2007] C.I.L.L. 2518; [2007] N.P.C. 102, QBD (TCC) 29–041

Dr Q v College of Physicians and Surgeons of British Columbia [2003] 1 S.C.R. 226 . 14–043

Doe d. Bishop of Rochester v Bridges (1831) 1 B. & Ad. 847 25–040

Dole v United Steelworkers of America 494 U.S. 26 (1990) 14–041

Dombo Beheer BV v Netherlands (A/274–A) (1994) 18 E.H.R.R. 213, ECHR 12–043

Dorset Yacht Co Ltd v Home Office [1970] A.C. 1004; [1970] 2 W.L.R. 1140; [1970] 2 All E.R. 294; [1970] 1 Lloyd's Rep. 453; (1970) 114 S.J. 375, HL 29–005

Doswell v Impey (1823) 1 B. & C. 163 23–001

Douglas v Hello! Ltd (No.1) [2001] Q.B. 967; [2001] 2 W.L.R. 992; [2001] 2 All E.R. 289; [2001] E.M.L.R. 9; [2001] 1 F.L.R. 982; [2002] 1 F.C.R. 289; [2001] H.R.L.R. 26; [2001] U.K.H.R.R. 223; 9 B.H.R.C. 543; [2001] F.S.R. 40, CA (Civ Div) .. 18–028, 25–032

Dowty Boulton Paul Ltd v Wolverhampton Corp (No.1) [1971] 1 W.L.R. 204; [1971] 2
  All E.R. 277; 69 L.G.R. 192; (1970) 115 S.J. 76, Ch D 16–027, 16–033
Dowty Boulton Paul Ltd v Wolverhampton Corp (No.2) [1976] Ch. 13; [1973] 2 W.L.R.
  618; [1973] 2 All E.R. 491; 71 L.G.R. 323; (1973) 25 P. & C.R. 282; (1973) 117 S.J.
  304, CA (Civ Div) 16–027
Doyle v Northumbria Probation Committee [1991] 1 W.L.R. 1340; [1992] I.C.R. 121;
  (1992) 89(7) L.S.G. 28; (1991) 141 N.L.J. 855, QBD 26–015
Draper v British Optical Association [1938] 1 All E.R. 115 25–026
Drewe v Coulton (1787) 1 East 563n 29–033
Du Plessis v Du Klerk 1996 3 S.A.850 18–028
Duke v GEC Reliance Ltd; sub nom. Duke v Reliance Systems Ltd [1988] A.C. 618;
  [1988] 2 W.L.R. 359; [1988] 1 All E.R. 626; [1988] 1 C.M.L.R. 719; [1988] I.C.R.
  339; [1988] I.R.L.R. 118; [1988] 1 F.T.L.R. 398; (1988) 85(11) L.S.G. 42; (1988) 132
  S.J. 226, HL 10–029
Duke of Newcastle v Worksop Urban DC [1902] 2 Ch. 145, Ch D 11–020
Duncan v Cammell Laird & Co Ltd (Discovery) [1942] A.C. 624; [1942] 1 All E.R. 587;
  (1942) 73 Ll. L. Rep. 109; (1942) 86 S.J. 287, HL 28–002, 28–003
Duncan v Findlater (1839) Macl. & R. 911 29–005
Dunkley v Evans [1981] 1 W.L.R. 1522; [1981] 3 All E.R. 285; (1981) 125 S.J. 843,
  QBD 23–033
Dunlop v Woollahra Municipal Council [1982] A.C. 158; [1981] 2 W.L.R. 693; [1981] 1
  All E.R. 1202; (1981) 125 S.J. 199, PC (Aus) 29–015
Dunn v Macdonald [1897] 1 Q.B. 555, CA 5–041, 5–045
Dunn v Queen, The [1896] 1 Q.B. 116, CA 5–045
Dunne v North Western Gas Board [1964] 2 Q.B. 806; [1964] 2 W.L.R. 164; [1963] 3 All
  E.R. 916; 62 L.G.R. 197; (1963) 107 S.J. 890, CA 29–043
Durayappah v Fernando [1967] 2 A.C. 337; [1967] 3 W.L.R. 289; [1967] 2 All E.R. 152;
  (1967) 111 S.J. 397, PC (Cey) 23–009, 23–014, 23–019
Dyson v Attorney General (No.1) [1911] 1 K.B. 410, CA 25–020
E v Secretary of State for the Home Department [2004] EWCA Civ 49; [2004] Q.B.
  1044; [2004] 2 W.L.R. 1351; [2004] I.N.L.R. 268; [2004] B.L.G.R. 463; (2004)
  101(7) L.S.G. 35; (2004) 148 S.J.L.B. 180, CA (Civ Div) 15–001
Eagil Trust Co v Pigott-Brown [1985] 3 All E.R. 119, CA (Civ Div) 12–033
Ealing Corp v Jones; sub nom. Jones v Ealing BC [1959] 1 Q.B. 384; [1959] 2 W.L.R.
  194; [1959] 1 All E.R. 286; (1959) 123 J.P. 148; 57 L.G.R. 86; (1959) 10 P. & C.R.
  100, QBD 24–011
Ealing LBC v Race Relations Board [1972] A.C. 342; [1972] 2 W.L.R. 71; [1972] 1 All
  E.R. 105; 70 L.G.R. 219; (1971) 116 S.J. 60, HL 25–023
East Fremantle Corporations v Annois [1902] A.C. 213 29–005
East Suffolk Rivers Catchment Board v Kent [1941] A.C. 74, HL 29–005
Eastaway v Secretary of State for Trade and Industry [2007] EWCA Civ 425 12–043
Eastham v Newcastle United Football Club [1964] Ch. 413; [1963] 3 W.L.R. 574; [1963]
  3 All E.R. 139; (1963) 107 S.J. 574, Ch D 24–007, 25–021, 25–026
Editions Periscope v France (A/234–B) (1992) 14 E.H.R.R. 597, ECHR 12–018
Edwards (Inspector of Taxes) v Bairstow [1956] A.C. 14; [1955] 3 W.L.R. 410; [1955] 3
  All E.R. 48; 48 R. & I.T. 534; 36 T.C. 207; (1955) 34 A.T.C. 198; [1955] T.R. 209;
  (1955) 99 S.J. 558, HL 14–023
Edwards v Environment Agency. *See* R. (on the application of Edwards) v Environ-
  ment Agency (No.2)
Edwards v National Coal Board [1949] 1 K.B. 704; [1949] 1 All E.R. 743; 65 T.L.R.
  430; (1949) 93 S.J. 337, CA 29–023
Edwards v SOGAT [1971] Ch. 354 21–003
Edwards v United Kingdom (A/247B) (1993) 15 E.H.R.R. 417, ECHR 28–008
Edwards v United Kingdom (39647/98); Lewis v United Kingdom (40461/98) (2005) 40
  E.H.R.R. 24, ECHR (Grand Chambe) 28–008
Ejaz v Secretary of State for the Home Department [1995] C.O.D. 72 20–041
EI Du Pont de Nemours Italiana SpA v Unita Sanitaria Locale No.2 di Carrara (C-21/
  88) [1990] E.C.R. I-889; [1991] 3 C.M.L.R. 25, ECJ 5–026
El Farargy v El Farargy [2007] EWCA Civ 1149; [2007] 3 F.C.R. 711; (2007) 104(46)
  L.S.G. 26; (2007) 151 S.J.L.B. 1500, CA (Civ Div) 13–007
Eleko v Officer Administering Nigeria (No.2) [1931] A.C. 662, PC (Nig) 15–024
Elliniki Radiophonia Tileorassi AE (ERT) v Dimotiki Etairia Pliroforissis (DEP) (C-

260/89); Elliniki Radiophonia Tileorassi AE (ERT) v Sotirios Kouvelas [1991]
  E.C.R. I-2925; [1994] 4 C.M.L.R. 540, ECJ 18–055
Elliotson v Knowles (1842) 11 L.J. Ch. 399 25–020
Ellis v Dubowski [1921] 3 K.B. 621, KBD 16–003
Ellis v Home Office [1953] 2 Q.B. 135; [1953] 3 W.L.R. 105; [1953] 2 All E.R. 149; (1953)
  97 S.J. 436, CA 28–002
Elston v Rose (1868) L.R. 4 Q.B. 4 14–027
Enderby Town Football Club v Football Association [1971] Ch. 591; [1970] 3 W.L.R.
  1021; [1971] 1 All E.R. 215; (1970) 114 S.J. 827, CA (Civ Div) 12–032
English v Emery Reimbold & Strick Ltd [2002] EWCA Civ 605; [2002] 1 W.L.R. 2409;
  [2002] 3 All E.R. 385; [2002] C.P.L.R. 520; [2003] I.R.L.R. 710; [2002] U.K.H.R.R.
  957; (2002) 99(22) L.S.G. 34; (2002) 152 N.L.J. 758; (2002) 146 S.J.L.B. 123, CA
  (Civ Div) 12–033
Environmental Defense Fund Inc v Ruckelshaus 439 F. 2d 584 (1971) 19–032
Errington v Minister of Health [1935] 1 K.B. 249, CA 12–004
Esfandiari v Secretary of State for Work and Pensions [2006] EWCA Civ 282; [2006]
  H.R.L.R. 26, CA (Civ Div) 21–007, 21–011
Eshugbayi Eleko v Officer Administering Nigeria (No.2) [1931] A.C. 662, PC (Nig) . 23–029,
                                                                               25–038
Essex Incorporated Congregational Church Union v Essex County Council [1963] A.C.
  808 .... 23–027, 25–009
Esso Petroleum Co Ltd v Harper's Garage (Stourport) Ltd [1968] A.C. 269; [1967] 2
  W.L.R. 871; [1967] 1 All E.R. 699; (1967) 111 S.J. 174, HL 11–004
Estate & Trust Agencies (1927) Ltd v Singapore Improvement Trust [1937] A.C. 898,
  PC (Sing) 25–005
Etsi Pipeline Project v Missouri 484 U.S. 495 (1988) 14–041
European Parliament v Council of Ministers of the European Communities (C-295/90);
  sub nom. Students Rights, Re [1992] E.C.R. I-4193; [1992] 3 C.M.L.R. 281, ECJ 23–021
European Parliament v Council of the European Union (C-21/94); sub nom. Road
  Taxes, Re [1995] E.C.R. I-1827; [1996] 1 C.M.L.R. 94, ECJ 23–021
European Parliament v Council of the European Union (C-360/93) [1996] E.C.R. I-
  1195, ECJ 23–021
European Parliament v Council of the European Union (C-392/95) [1997] E.C.R. I-
  3213; [1997] 3 C.M.L.R. 896, ECJ 23–021
European Parliament v Council of the European Union (C-22/96) [1998] E.C.R. I-3231;
  [1999] 1 C.M.L.R. 160, ECJ 23–021
European Parliament v Council of the European Union (C-93/00) [2001] E.C.R. I-
  10119, ECJ 23–021
Evangelical United Brethren Church of Adna v State 407 P. 2d 440 (1965) 29–005
Everett v Griffiths [1921] 1 A.C. 631 29–047
Everett v Ryder (1926) 135 L.T. 302 25–026
Ezeh v United Kingdom (39665/98); Connors v United Kingdom (40086/98) (2002) 35
  E.H.R.R. 28; 12 B.H.R.C. 589; [2002] Prison L.R. 354; [2002] Crim. L.R. 918,
  ECHR 12–032
FEC v Democratic Senatorial Campaign Committee 454 U.S. 27 (1981) 14–042
FM (A Child) v Singer [2004] EWHC 793, QBD 29–047
Faccini Dori v Recreb Srl (C-91/92) [1995] All E.R. (E.C.) 1; [1994] E.C.R. I-3325;
  [1995] 1 C.M.L.R. 665, ECJ 10–025
Fairmount Investments Ltd v Secretary of State for the Environment; sub nom.
  Fairmount Investments Ltd v Southwark LBC [1976] 1 W.L.R. 1255; [1976] 2 All
  E.R. 865; 75 L.G.R. 33; (1976) 120 S.J. 801, HL 12–027
Farmer (Surveyor of Taxes) v Cotton's Trustees; sub nom. Cotton's Trustees v Farmer
  (Surveyor of Taxes); Cotton's Trustees v Inland Revenue Commissioners [1915]
  A.C. 922; 1915 S.C. (H.L.) 109; 1915 2 S.L.T. 2, HL 9–019, 9–021
Farquharson v Morgan [1894] 1 Q.B. 552 .... 23–027, 24–004, 25–009, 25–010
Farrington v Thomson [1959] V.R. 286 29–033
Fawcett v Fowlis (1827) 7 B. & C. 396 14–026
Fawcett Properties Ltd v Buckingham CC [1961] A.C. 636; [1960] 3 W.L.R. 831; [1960]
  3 All E.R. 503; (1961) 125 J.P. 8; 59 L.G.R. 69; (1961) 12 P. & C.R. 1; (1960) 104
  S.J. 912, HL 17–010, 22–028, 23–028
Fawdry & Co v Murfitt [2002] EWCA Civ 643; [2003] Q.B. 104; [2002] 3 W.L.R. 1354;
  [2003] 4 All E.R. 60; [2002] C.P. Rep. 62; [2002] C.P.L.R. 593, CA (Civ Div) .. 23–008

Federal Crop Insurance Corporation v Merrill 332 U.S. 380 (1947) 20–042
Feldbrugge v Netherlands (A/99); sub nom. A v Netherlands (8562/79) (1986) 8
  E.H.R.R. 425, ECHR 12–018, 12–019
Ferguson v Kinnoull (1842) 9 Cl. & F. 251 .... 29–021, 29–033
Fernley v Worthington (1840) 1 Man. & G. 491 .... 14–027, 15–002
Ferrazzini v Italy (44759/98) [2001] S.T.C. 1314; (2002) 34 E.H.R.R. 45; [2003] B.T.C.
  157; 3 I.T.L. Rep. 918; [2001] S.T.I. 1224, ECHR 12–019
56 Denton Road, Twickenham, Re; sub nom. War Damage Act 1943, Re [1953] Ch. 51;
  [1952] 2 All E.R. 799; [1952] 2 T.L.R. 676; [1952] W.N. 472, Ch D 20–029
Findlay, Re; sub nom. Findlay v Secretary of State for the Home Department [1985]
  A.C. 318; [1984] 3 W.L.R. 1159; [1984] 3 All E.R. 801; [1985] Crim. L.R. 154;
  (1985) 82 L.S.G. 38; (1984) 128 S.J. 816, HL 16–013, 20–013
Firma A Racke v Hauptzollamt Mainz (C-98/78) [1979] E.C.R. 69, ECJ 19–022
Firma A Racke v Hauptzollamt Mainz (283/83) [1984] E.C.R. 3791, ECJ 21–019
Firman v Ellis [1978] Q.B. 886; [1978] 3 W.L.R. 1; [1978] 2 All E.R. 851; (1978) 122 S.J.
  147, CA (Civ Div) 23–025
Firth v Staines [1897] 2 Q.B. 70, QBD 16–005
Fisher v Jackson (1891) 2 Ch. 824 .... 12–001, 12–015
Fisher v Ruislip Northwood Urban DC [1945] K.B. 584, CA 29–005
Fisher (Louis Walter) v Keane (1879) L.R. 11 Ch. D. 353, Ch D 12–001, 23–025
Fitzpatrick v Sterling Housing Association Ltd [2001] 1 A.C. 27; [1999] 3 W.L.R. 1113;
  [1999] 4 All E.R. 705; [2000] 1 F.L.R. 271; [1999] 2 F.L.R. 1027; [2000] 1 F.C.R. 21;
  [2000] U.K.H.R.R. 25; 7 B.H.R.C. 200; (2000) 32 H.L.R. 178; [2000] L. & T.R. 44;
  [2000] Fam. Law 14; [1999] E.G. 125 (C.S.); (1999) 96(43) L.S.G. 3; [1999] N.P.C.
  127; (2000) 79 P. & C.R. D4, HL 21–004
Flannery v Halifax Estate Agencies Ltd (t/a Colleys Professional Services) [2000] 1
  W.L.R. 377; [2000] 1 All E.R. 373; [2000] C.P. Rep. 18; [1999] B.L.R. 107; (1999)
  11 Admin. L.R. 465; (1999) 15 Const. L.J. 313; (1999) 96(13) L.S.G. 32; (1999) 149
  N.L.J. 284; [1999] N.P.C. 22, CA (Civ Div) 12–033
Fletcher's Application, Re [1970] 2 All E.R. 527 (Note), CA (Civ Div) 8–026, 17–014
Flynn (Patrick Anthony) v HM Advocate (No.1) [2004] UKPC D 1; 2004 S.C. (P.C.) 1;
  2004 S.L.T. 863; 2004 S.C.C.R. 281; [2004] H.R.L.R. 17; [2005] 1 Prison L.R. 154;
  2004 G.W.D. 16–360, PC (Sc) 7–007
Food and Drug Administration v Brown & Williamson Tobacco Corporation 529 U.S.
  120 (2000) 14–042
Ford Motor Co v NLRB 441 U.S. 488 (1979) 14–042
Ford Motor Credit Co v Milhollin 444 U.S. 555 (1980) 14–042
Forster v Forster and Berridge (1863) 4 B. & S. 187 24–004
Francovich v Italy (C-6/90); Bonifacti v Italy (C-9/90) [1991] E.C.R. I-5357; [1993] 2
  C.M.L.R. 66; [1995] I.C.R. 722; [1992] I.R.L.R. 84, ECJ 10–032, 29–056
Franklin v Attorney General [1974] Q.B. 185; [1973] 2 W.L.R. 225; [1973] 1 All E.R.
  879; (1972) 117 S.J. 143, QBD 5–043
Franklin v Minister of Town and Country Planning [1948] A.C. 87; [1947] 2 All E.R.
  289; (1947) 63 T.L.R. 446; (1947) 111 J.P. 497; 45 L.G.R. 581; [1947] L.J.R. 1440,
  HL 12–046, 13–005
Frankson v Secretary of State for the Home Department; sub nom. Rowe v Fryers
  [2003] EWCA Civ 655; [2003] 1 W.L.R. 1952; [2003] C.P. Rep. 52; [2003] Prison
  L.R. 395; [2003] Po. L.R. 197, CA (Civ Div) 28–005
Fraser v Mudge [1975] 1 W.L.R. 1132; [1975] 3 All E.R. 78; (1975) 119 S.J. 508, CA
  (Civ Div) 12–032
Freeman & Lockyer v Buckhurst Park Properties (Mangal) Ltd [1964] 2 Q.B. 480;
  [1964] 2 W.L.R. 618; [1964] 1 All E.R. 630; (1964) 108 S.J. 96, CA 16–005, 20–032
French Kier Developments Ltd v Secretary of State for the Environment [1977] 1 All
  E.R. 296; (1977) 244 E.G. 967; [1977] J.P.L. 30, QBD 9–041, 12–034
Friend v Lord Advocate; sub nom. Whaley v Lord Advocate [2007] UKHL 53; 2007
  S.L.T. 1209; 2008 S.C.L.R. 128; [2008] H.R.L.R. 11; [2008] U.K.H.R.R. 157;
  (2007) 151 S.J.L.B. 1565; 2007 G.W.D. 39–680, HL 7–007
Frome United Breweries Co Ltd v Bath Justices; sub nom. R. v Bath Compensation
  Authority [1926] A.C. 586, HL 13–004, 13–010
Frost v Minister of Health [1935] 1 K.B. 286, KBD 12–004
Fry, Ex p. [1954] 1 W.L.R. 730; [1954] 2 All E.R. 118; (1954) 118 J.P. 313; 52 L.G.R.
  320; (1954) 98 S.J. 318, CA 12–008

Fullbrook v Berkshire Magistrates Courts Committee (1970) 69 L.G.R. 75 25–024
Fuller v Fotch (1695) Carth. 346 23–001
Fulton v City of Lockwood 269 S.W. 2d 1 (1954) 20–042
G (A Child) v Bromley LBC (2000) 2 L.G.L.R. 237; [2000] Ed. C.R. 49; [1999] E.L.R.
    356, CA (Civ Div) 29–016
Gahan v Maingay (1793) Ridge. L. & S. 20 23–002
Galloway v London Corporation (1866) L.R. 1 H.L. 34 17–010
Gard v Callard (1817) 6 M & S 69 11–020
Garden Cottage Foods Ltd v Milk Marketing Board [1984] A.C. 130; [1983] 3 W.L.R.
    143; [1983] 2 All E.R. 770; [1983] Com. L.R. 198; [1983] 3 C.M.L.R. 43; [1984]
    F.S.R. 23; (1983) 127 S.J. 460, HL 29–059
Garland v British Rail Engineering Ltd [1983] 2 A.C. 751; [1982] 2 W.L.R. 918; [1982] 2
    C.M.L.R. 174; [1982] I.C.R. 420; [1982] I.R.L.R. 257; (1982) 126 S.J. 309, HL . 18–002
Garrett v Attorney General [1997] 2 N.Z.L.R. 332 29–033
Gaskin v Liverpool City Council [1980] 1 W.L.R. 1549; (1980) 124 S.J. 498, CA (Civ
    Div) 28–006, 28–014
Geddis v Bann Reservoir Proprietors (1877–78) L.R. 3 App. Cas. 430, HL (UK-Irl) 29–005
General Electric Co v Price Commission [1975] I.C.R. 1; (1974) 119 S.J. 166, CA (Civ
    Div) 15–011
General Medical Council v Spackman; sub nom. R. v General Medical Council Ex p.
    Spackman [1943] A.C. 627; [1943] 2 All E.R. 337; (1943) 59 T.L.R. 412; (1943) 169
    L.T. 226; (1943) 87 S.J. 298, HL 12–024, 25–005
Germany v Commission of the European Economic Community (24/62); sub nom.
    Tariff Quota on Wine, Re (24/62) [1963] E.C.R. 63; [1963] C.M.L.R. 347, ECJ 12–040
Germany v Commission of the European Economic Community (34/62); sub nom.
    Import Duties on Sweet Oranges, Re [1963] E.C.R. 131; [1963] C.M.L.R. 369,
    ECJ 21–019
Ghaidan v Godin-Mendoza; sub nom. Mendoza v Ghaidan; Ghaidan v Mendoza;
    Godin-Mendoza v Ghaidan [2004] UKHL 30; [2004] 2 A.C. 557; [2004] 3 W.L.R.
    113; [2004] 3 All E.R. 411; [2004] 2 F.L.R. 600; [2004] 2 F.C.R. 481; [2004]
    H.R.L.R. 31; [2004] U.K.H.R.R. 827; 16 B.H.R.C. 671; [2004] H.L.R. 46; [2005] 1
    P. & C.R. 18; [2005] L. & T.R. 3; [2004] 2 E.G.L.R. 132; [2004] Fam. Law 641;
    [2004] 27 E.G. 128 (C.S.); (2004) 101(27) L.S.G. 30; (2004) 154 N.L.J. 1013; (2004)
    148 S.J.L.B. 792; [2004] N.P.C. 100; [2004] 2 P. & C.R. DG17, HL ... 18–008, 18–011,
                                                              21–004, 21–007, 21–009
Gibson v United States of America [2007] UKPC 52; [2007] 1 W.L.R. 2367, PC (Bah) 25–038
Gillick v West Norfolk and Wisbech AHA [1986] A.C. 112; [1985] 3 W.L.R. 830; [1985]
    3 All E.R. 402; [1986] Crim. L.R. 113; (1985) 82 L.S.G. 3531; (1985) 135 N.L.J.
    1055; (1985) 129 S.J. 738, HL 19–029, 22–046
Gillies v Secretary of State for Work and Pensions; sub nom. Secretary of State for
    Work and Pensions v Gillies [2006] UKHL 2; [2006] 1 W.L.R. 781; [2006] 1 All
    E.R. 731; 2006 S.C. (H.L.) 71; 2006 S.L.T. 77; 2006 S.C.L.R. 276; [2006] I.C.R.
    267; (2006) 9 C.C.L. Rep. 404; (2006) 103(9) L.S.G. 33; (2006) 150 S.J.L.B. 127;
    2006 G.W.D. 3–66, HL 13–007
Gillingham BC v Medway (Chatham Docks) Co Ltd [1993] Q.B. 343; [1992] 3 W.L.R.
    449; [1992] 3 All E.R. 923; [1993] Env. L.R. 98; 91 L.G.R. 160; (1992) 63 P. & C.R.
    205; [1992] 1 P.L.R. 113; [1992] J.P.L. 458; [1991] E.G. 101 (C.S.); [1991] N.P.C.
    97, QBD 20–029, 29–038
Gillingham Corp v Kent CC [1953] Ch. 37; [1952] 2 All E.R. 1107; [1952] 2 T.L.R. 1009;
    (1953) 117 J.P. 39; 51 L.G.R. 52; (1952) 96 S.J. 803, Ch D 25–023
Givaudan v Minister of Housing and Local Government [1967] 1 W.L.R. 250 9–024,
                                                                       9–041, 12–034
Glasgow Corp v Central Land Board 1956 S.C. (H.L.) 1; 1956 S.L.T. 41; [1956] J.P.L.
    442, HL 28–002
Global Plant Ltd v Secretary of State for Health and Social Security; sub nom. Global
    Plant Ltd v Secretary of State for Social Services [1972] 1 Q.B. 139; [1971] 3
    W.L.R. 269; [1971] 3 All E.R. 385; (1971) 11 K.I.R. 284; (1971) 115 S.J. 506,
    QBD 9–019, 9–021
Glynn v Keele University; sub nom. Glynn v University of Keele [1971] 1 W.L.R. 487;
    [1971] 2 All E.R. 89; (1970) 115 S.J. 173, Ch D 12–014
Goldberg v Kelly (1970) 397 U.S. 254 12–047

Golden Chemical Products, Re [1976] Ch. 300; [1976] 3 W.L.R. 1; [1976] 2 All E.R. 543; (1976) 120 S.J. 401, Ch D 16–007
Golder v United Kingdom (A/18) (1979–80) 1 E.H.R.R. 524, ECHR 12–018, 12–043
Goldman v Hargrave; sub nom. Hargrave v Goldman [1967] 1 A.C. 645; [1966] 3 W.L.R. 513; [1966] 2 All E.R. 989; [1966] 2 Lloyd's Rep. 65; (1966) 110 S.J. 527, PC (Aus) 29–037
Goodridge v Chief Constable of Hampshire [1999] 1 W.L.R. 1558; [1999] 1 All E.R. 896, QBD 28–014
Gordon Dadds & Co v Morris [1945] 2 ALL e.r. 616 16–006
Gordondale Investments Ltd v Secretary of State for the Environment 70 L.G.R. 158; (1972) 23 P. & C.R. 334, CA (Civ Div) 14–037
Gorringe v Calderdale MBC; sub nom. Calderdale MBC v Gorringe [2004] UKHL 15; [2004] 1 W.L.R. 1057; [2004] 2 All E.R. 326; [2004] R.T.R. 27; [2004] P.I.Q.R. P32; (2004) 101(18) L.S.G. 35; (2004) 148 S.J.L.B. 419, HL 29–018
Gorris v Scott (1875) L.R. 9 Ex. 125 29–021
Gorton Local Board v Prison Commissioners [1904] 2 K.B. 165 (Note), KBD 28–015
Gough v Chief Constable of Derbyshire; sub nom. Miller v Leeds Magistrates Court [2002] EWCA Civ 351; [2002] Q.B. 1213; [2002] 3 W.L.R. 289; [2002] 2 All E.R. 985; [2002] 2 C.M.L.R. 11; [2002] Eu. L.R. 359; [2002] H.R.L.R. 29; [2002] Po. L.R. 68; [2002] A.C.D. 75; (2002) 99(18) L.S.G. 36; (2002) 152 N.L.J. 552; (2002) 146 S.J.L.B. 94, CA (Civ Div) 19–012
Gould v Stuart [1896] A.C. 575, PC (Aus) 5–045
Gould v Yukon Order of Pioneers [1996] 1 S.C.R. 571 14–043
Gouriet v Union of Post Office Workers; sub nom. Attorney General v Gouriet [1978] A.C. 435; [1977] 3 W.L.R. 300; [1977] 3 All E.R. 70; (1977) 121 S.J. 543, HL . 23–032, 24–007, 24–009, 24–026, 24–034, 25–020, 25–021, 25–033, 26–001
Governors of Bristol Poor v Wait (1834) 1 A. & E. 264 .... 14–027, 14–028, 15–002
Governors of the Peabody Donation Fund v Sir Lindsay Parkinson & Co Ltd [1985] A.C. 210; [1984] 3 W.L.R. 953; [1984] 3 All E.R. 529; 28 B.L.R. 1; 83 L.G.R. 1; [1984] C.I.L.L. 128; (1984) 81 L.S.G. 3179; (1984) 128 S.J. 753, HL 29–008
Graddage v Haringey LBC [1975] 1 W.L.R. 241; [1975] 1 All E.R. 224; (1975) 29 P. & C.R. 441; [1974] J.P.L. 723; (1974) 118 S.J. 775, Ch D 27–005
Graham v Public Works Commissioners; sub nom. Graham v HM's Commissioners of Public Works and Buildings [1901] 2 K.B. 781, KBD 5–036
Gray v Powell 314 U.S. 402 (1941) 14–042
Great Central Ry Co v Hewlett [1916] 2 A.C. 511 29–005
Great Western Railway Co v Sutton (1869–70) L.R. 4 H.L. 226, HL 11–020, 29–049
Greater Boston Television Corp v Federal Communications Comm. 444 F. 2d 841 (1970) 19–032
Greene v Associated Newspapers Ltd; sub nom. Green v Associated Newspapers Ltd [2004] EWCA Civ 1462; [2005] Q.B. 972; [2005] 3 W.L.R. 281; [2005] 1 All E.R. 30; [2005] E.M.L.R. 10; (2004) 101(45) L.S.G. 31; (2004) 148 S.J.L.B. 1318, CA (Civ Div) 25–032
Greene v Secretary of State for Home Affairs [1942] A.C. 284, HL 23–029
Gregory v Camden LBC [1966] 1 W.L.R. 899; [1966] 2 All E.R. 196; (1966) 130 J.P. 244; 64 L.G.R. 215; (1967) 18 P. & C.R. 69; 197 E.G. 19; (1966) 110 S.J. 213, QBD 24–006
Groenvelt v Burwell (1700) 3 Salk 354 .... 23–002, 25–002, 26–019
Groppera Radio AG v Switzerland (A/173); sub nom. Groppera Radio Ag v Switzerland (10890/84) (1990) 12 E.H.R.R. 321, ECHR 18–032
Grosvenor Hotel, London (No.2), Re [1965] Ch. 1210; [1964] 3 W.L.R. 992; [1964] 3 All E.R. 354; (1964) 108 S.J. 674, CA 28–002
Groves v Lord Wimborne [1898] 2 Q.B. 402 29–021
Grzelczyk v Centre Public d'Aide Sociale d'Ottignies Louvain la Neuve (C-184/99) [2003] All E.R. (EC) 385; [2001] E.C.R. I-6193; [2002] 1 C.M.L.R. 19; [2002] I.C.R. 566, ECJ 21–016
Guaranty Trust Co of New York v Hannay & Co [1915] 2 K.B. 536; 12 A.L.R. 1, CA   25–020
Guildford BC v Hein [2005] EWCA Civ 979; [2005] B.L.G.R. 797, CA (Civ Div) ... 24–010
H v Belgium (A/127); sub nom. H v Belgium (8950/80) (1988) 10 E.H.R.R. 339, ECHR 12–018
H Lavender & Son Ltd v Minister of Housing and Local Government [1970] 1 W.L.R. 1231; [1970] 3 All E.R. 871; 68 L.G.R. 408; (1970) 114 S.J. 636, QBD . 16–003, 16–013

HK (An Infant), Re; sub nom. K (H) (An Infant), Re [1967] 2 Q.B. 617; [1967] 2
W.L.R. 962; [1967] 1 All E.R. 226; (1967) 111 S.J. 296, QBD 12–009
HM Advocate v McIntosh (Robert) (No.1); sub nom. McIntosh (Robert) v HM
Advocate; McIntosh, Petitioner [2001] UKPC D 1; [2003] 1 A.C. 1078; [2001] 3
W.L.R. 107; [2001] 2 All E.R. 638; 2001 S.C. (P.C.) 89; 2001 S.L.T. 304; 2001
S.C.C.R. 191; [2001] 2 Cr. App. R. 27; [2001] H.R.L.R. 20; [2001] U.K.H.R.R.
463; (2001) 98(11) L.S.G. 43; (2001) 145 S.J.L.B. 83; 2001 G.W.D. 6–206, PC (Sc)   7–007
HM Advocate v R; sub nom. R v HM Advocate [2002] UKPC D 3; [2004] 1 A.C. 462;
[2003] 2 W.L.R. 317; 2003 S.C. (P.C.) 21; 2003 S.L.T. 4; 2003 S.C.C.R. 19; [2003]
U.K.H.R.R. 1; 2002 G.W.D. 39–1280, PC (Sc)   7–007
HTV v Price Commission [1976] I.C.R. 170; (1976) 120 S.J. 298, CA (Civ Div)   15–007,
                                                                                   20–004, 22–046
Hadmor Productions v Hamilton [1983] 1 A.C. 191; [1982] 2 W.L.R. 322; [1982] 1 All
E.R. 1042; [1982] I.C.R. 114; [1982] I.R.L.R. 102; (1982) 126 S.J. 134, HL   12–027
Hall & Co Ltd v Shoreham by Sea Urban DC [1964] 1 W.L.R. 240; [1964] 1 All E.R. 1;
(1964) 128 J.P. 120; 62 L.G.R. 206; (1964) 15 P. & C.R. 119; (1963) 107 S.J. 1001,
CA 19–004, 25–021
Hamilton, Re [1981] A.C. 1038   12–027
Hammersmith & City Railway Co v Brand; sub nom. Brand and Wife v Hammersmith
& City Railway Co; Brand v Hammersmith & City Railway Co (1869–70) L.R. 4
H.L. 171, HL   29–038
Hammerton v Hammerton [2007] EWCA Civ 248; [2007] 2 F.L.R. 1133; [2007] 3
F.C.R. 107; [2007] Fam. Law 798, CA (Civ Div)   18–027
Hammond v St Pancras Vestry (1873–74) L.R. 9 C.P. 316, CCP   29–043
Handyside v United Kingdom (A/24) (1979–80) 1 E.H.R.R. 737, ECHR   18–032
Hanks v Ministry of Housing and Local Government [1963] 1 Q.B. 999; [1962] 3
W.L.R. 1482; [1963] 1 All E.R. 47; (1963) 127 J.P. 78; 61 L.G.R. 76; (1964) 15 P. &
C.R. 246; [1962] R.V.R. 762; (1962) 106 S.J. 1032, QBD   17–012
Hannam v Bradford Corp; sub nom. Hannam v Bradford City Council [1970] 1 W.L.R.
937; [1970] 2 All E.R. 690; 68 L.G.R. 498; (1970) 114 S.J. 414, CA (Civ Div) ..   13–006
Hans-Otto Wagner GmbH Agrarhandel KG v Bundesanstalt fur Landwirtschaftliche
Marktordnung (C-8/82) [1983] E.C.R. 371, ECJ   21–019
Hanson v Church Commissioners for England; sub nom. Hanson v London Rent
Assessment Committee [1978] Q.B. 823; [1977] 2 W.L.R. 848; [1977] 3 All E.R.
404; (1977) 34 P. & C.R. 158; (1976) 241 E.G. 683; [1977] J.P.L. 245; (1976) 120
S.J. 837, CA (Civ Div)   12–030
Hardy v Pembrokeshire CC (Permission to Appeal) [2006] EWCA Civ 240; [2006] Env.
L.R. 28; [2007] J.P.L. 284; [2006] N.P.C. 34, CA (Civ Div)   26–046
Harman v Tappenden (1802) 1 East 555   29–033
Harper v Secretary of State for the Home Department; sub nom. Merricks v. Heathcoat
Amory [1955] Ch. 238; [1955] 2 W.L.R. 316; [1955] 1 All E.R. 331; (1955) 119 J.P.
148; 53 L.G.R. 244; (1955) 99 S.J. 95, CA   25–034
Harpin v St Albans City Council; sub nom. Harpin v St Albans Corp 67 L.G.R. 479;
(1969) 113 S.J. 426, DC   23–029
Harrington, Re; sub nom. Harrington v Roots; R. v Dorking Justices Ex p. Harrington
[1984] A.C. 743; [1984] 3 W.L.R. 142; [1984] 2 All E.R. 474; (1984) 79 Cr. App. R.
305; (1985) 149 J.P. 211; [1984] Crim. L.R. 622; (1984) 81 L.S.G. 2142; (1984) 134
N.L.J. 567; (1984) S.J. 434, HL   23–025
Harris v Packwood (1810) 3 Taunt 263   11–020
Harrison v Croydon LBC; sub nom. Croydon Development Plans 1954 and 1959, Re
[1968] Ch. 479; [1967] 3 W.L.R. 100; [1967] 2 All E.R. 589; 65 L.G.R. 338; (1967)
18 P. & C.R. 486; [1967] R.A. 270; (1967) 111 S.J. 255, Ch D   25–026
Hart v Relentless Records Ltd [2002] EWHC 1984 (Ch); [2003] F.S.R. 36; (2002) 152
N.L.J. 1562, Ch D   13–007
Hartnell v Minister of Housing and Local Government; sub nom. Minister of Housing
and Local Government v Hartnell [1965] A.C. 1134; [1965] 2 W.L.R. 474; [1965] 1
All E.R. 490; (1965) 129 J.P. 234; 63 L.G.R. 103; (1966) 17 P. & C.R. 60; (1965)
109 S.J. 156, HL   17–010
Hatton v United Kingdom (36022/97) [2002] 1 F.C.R. 732; (2002) 34 E.H.R.R. 1; 11
B.H.R.C. 634, ECHR   29–040
Hatton v United Kingdom (36022/97) (2003) 37 E.H.R.R. 28; 15 B.H.R.C. 259, ECHR
(Grand Chamber)   29–040

Hauer v Land Rheinland-Pfalz (44/79) [1979] E.C.R. 3727; [1980] 3 C.M.L.R. 42;
(1981) 3 E.H.R.R. 140, ECJ 19–020
Hawke's Bay Raw Milk Producers Cooperative Co v New Zealand Milk Board [1961]
N.Z.L.R. 218, CA (NZ) 22–029
Hawley v Steele (1877) 6 Ch.D. 521 29–039
Haydon v Kent CC [1978] Q.B. 343; [1978] 2 W.L.R. 485; [1978] 2 All E.R. 97; 76
L.G.R. 270; [1978] J.P.L. 174; (1977) 121 S.J. 894, CA (Civ Div) 29–023
Hazell v Hammersmith and Fulham LBC [1992] 2 A.C. 1; [1991] 2 W.L.R. 372; [1991] 1
All E.R. 545; 89 L.G.R. 271; (1991) 3 Admin. L.R. 549; [1991] R.V.R. 28; (1991)
155 J.P.N. 527; (1991) 155 L.G. Rev. 527; (1991) 88(8) L.S.G. 36; (1991) 141 N.L.J.
127, HL 5–038, 5–049, 6–010, 17–010, 29–050
Healey v Minister of Health [1955] 1 Q.B. 221; [1954] 3 W.L.R. 815; [1954] 3 All E.R.
449; (1955) 119 J.P. 242; (1954) 98 S.J. 819, CA 25–023
Helle v Finland (20772/92) (1998) 26 E.H.R.R. 159; [1998] H.R.C.D. 186, ECHR . 12–035,
12–043
Henry Boot Homes Ltd v Bassetlaw DC [2002] EWCA Civ 983; [2003] 1 P. & C.R. 23;
[2002] 4 P.L.R. 108; [2003] J.P.L. 1030; [2002] 50 E.G. 112 (C.S.); (2002) 99(49)
L.S.G. 20; (2002) 146 S.J.L.B. 277; [2002] N.P.C. 156, CA (Civ Div) ... 20–017, 20–049
Hermann Schrader HS Kraftfutter GmbH & Co KG v Hauptzollamt Gronau (265/87)
[1989] E.C.R. 2237, ECJ 19–022
Herring v Templeman [1973] 3 All E.R. 569; 72 L.G.R. 162; (1973) 117 S.J. 793, CA
(Civ Div) 25–004
Hetley v Boyer (1614) Cr. Jac. 336 17–009
Hilditch v Westminster City Council; sub nom. R. v Westminster City Council Ex p.
Hilditch [1990] C.O.D. 434, CA (Civ Div) 26–046, 26–057
Hill v Chief Constable of West Yorkshire [1989] A.C. 53; [1988] 2 W.L.R. 1049; [1988] 2
All E.R. 238; (1988) 152 L.G. Rev. 709; (1988) 85(20) L.S.G. 34; (1988) 138 N.L.J.
Rep. 126; (1988) 132 S.J. 700, HL 29–008
Hinds, Ex p. (No. 2); sub nom. Hinds, Re, *The Times*, February 15, 1961, HL 25–038
Hoffmann La Roche (F) & Co AG v Secretary of State for Trade and Industry [1975]
A.C. 295; [1974] 3 W.L.R. 104; [1974] 2 All E.R. 1128; [1975] 3 All E.R. 945; (1973)
117 S.J. 713; (1974) 118 S.J. 500, HL 11–005, 23–009, 23–010, 23–022,
23–030, 23–031, 23–032, 25–034, 28–021
Hoggard v Worsbrough Urban DC [1962] 2 Q.B. 93; [1962] 2 W.L.R. 676; [1962] 1 All
E.R. 468; (1962) 126 J.P. 104; 60 L.G.R. 198; [1962] R.V.R. 347; (1962) 106 S.J.
244, Assizes (Sheffield) 12–008
Holbeck Hall Hotel Ltd v Scarborough BC [2000] Q.B. 836; [2000] 2 W.L.R. 1396;
[2000] 2 All E.R. 705; [2000] B.L.R. 109; (2000) 2 T.C.L.R. 865; 69 Con. L.R. 1;
[2000] B.L.G.R. 412; [2000] E.G. 29 (C.S.); (2000) 97(9) L.S.G. 44; (2000) 97(11)
L.S.G. 36; (2000) 150 N.L.J. 307; (2000) 144 S.J.L.B. 109; [2000] N.P.C. 17, CA
(Civ Div) 29–037
Holder v Law Society [2003] EWCA Civ 39; [2003] 1 W.L.R. 1059; [2003] 3 All E.R. 62;
(2003) 100(11) L.S.G. 34; (2003) 147 S.J.L.B. 117, CA (Civ Div) 18–035
Hollis v Secretary of State for the Environment (1984) 47 P. & C.R. 351; (1983) 265
E.G. 476; [1983] J.P.L. 164, QBD 15–007
Hooper v Secretary of State for Work and Pensions. *See* R. (on the application of
Hooper) v Secretary of State for Work and Pensions
Hopkins v Smethwick Local Board of Health (1890) L.R. 24 Q.B.D. 712, CA 12–001,
12–004, 23–025
Hounslow LBC v Twickenham Garden Developments Ltd [1971] Ch. 233; [1970] 3
W.L.R. 538; [1970] 3 All E.R. 326; 7 B.L.R. 81; 69 L.G.R. 109; (1970) 114 S.J. 603,
Ch D 23–014, 23–025
Howard v Pickford Tool Co [1951] 1 K.B. 417; (1951) 95 S.J. 44; (1951) 95 S.J. 553,
CA 25–026
Howell v Falmouth Boat Construction Co Ltd [1951] A.C. 837; [1951] 2 All E.R. 278;
[1951] 2 Lloyd's Rep. 45; [1951] 2 T.L.R. 151; (1951) 95 S.J. 413, HL 16–034
Huang v Secretary of State for the Home Department [2007] UKHL 11; [2007] 2 A.C.
167; [2007] 2 W.L.R. 581; [2007] 4 All E.R. 15; [2007] 1 F.L.R. 2021; [2007]
H.R.L.R. 22; [2007] U.K.H.R.R. 759; [2007] Imm. A.R. 571; [2007] I.N.L.R. 314;
[2007] Fam. Law 587; (2007) 151 S.J.L.B. 435, HL 19–018
Hughes v Department of Health and Social Security [1985] A.C. 776; [1985] 2 W.L.R.

866; [1985] I.C.R. 419; [1985] I.R.L.R. 263; (1985) 82 L.S.G. 2009; (1985) 129 S.J.
315, HL 20–011
Human Fertilisation & Embryology Authority v Amicus Healthcare Ltd [2005] EWHC
1092, QBD 25–021
Huth v Clarke (1890) L.R. 25 Q.B.D. 391, QBD 16–006
IBA Health Ltd v Office of Fair Trading; sub nom. Office of Fair Trading v IBA
Healthcare Ltd [2004] EWCA Civ 142; [2004] 4 All E.R. 1103; [2005] 1 All E.R.
(Comm) 147; [2004] U.K.C.L.R. 683; [2005] E.C.C. 1; [2004] I.C.R. 1364; (2004)
101(11) L.S.G. 33; (2004) 154 N.L.J. 352, CA (Civ Div) 17–008
ISKON v UK (1994) 76A D.R. 90 13–012
Ibeneweka v Egbuna [1964] 1 W.L.R. 219; (1964) 108 S.J. 114, PC (Nig) 25–021
Immigration and Naturalization Service v Cardozo-Fonseca 480 U.S. 421 (1986) ... 14–041
Imperial Metal Industries (Kynoch) Ltd v Amalgamated Union of Engineering
Workers (Technical Administrative and Supervisory Section) [1979] 1 All E.R.
847; [1979] I.C.R. 23; [1978] I.R.L.R. 407, CA (Civ Div) 25–015
Inland Revenue Commissioners v Brooks; sub nom. Brooks v Inland Revenue Com-
missioners [1915] A.C. 478, HL 20–043
Inland Revenue Commissioners v Hambrook [1956] 2 Q.B. 641; [1956] 3 W.L.R. 643;
[1956] 3 All E.R. 338; 57 A.L.R.2d 790; (1956) 100 S.J. 632, CA 5–046
Innes v Wylie 174 E.R. 800; (1844) 1 Car. & K. 257, QB 23–025
Institute of Patent Agents v Lockwood; sub nom. Chartered Institute of Patent-Agents
v Lockwood [1894] A.C. 347; (1894) 21 R. (H.L.) 61; (1894) 2 S.L.T. 106, HL . 27–005
Instrumatic Ltd v Supabrase Ltd [1969] 1 W.L.R. 519; [1969] 2 All E.R. 131; (1969) 113
S.J. 144, CA (Civ Div) 9–021
International General Electric Co of New York v Customs and Excise Commissioners
[1962] Ch. 784; [1962] 3 W.L.R. 20; [1962] 2 All E.R. 398; [1962] R.P.C. 235; (1962)
106 S.J. 327, CA 25–030, 28–021
International Harvester Co v Ruckelshaus 478 F. 2d 615 (1973) 22–020
International Railway Co v Niagara Parks Commission [1941] A.C. 328, PC (Can) .. 5–036
International Transport Roth GmbH v Secretary of State for the Home Department;
sub nom. R. (on the application of . International Transport Roth GmbH) v
Secretary of State for the Home Department; Secretary of State for the Home
Department v International Transport Roth GmbH [2002] EWCA Civ 158; [2003]
Q.B. 728; [2002] 3 W.L.R. 344; [2002] 1 C.M.L.R. 52; [2002] Eu. L.R. 74; [2002]
H.R.L.R. 31; [2002] U.K.H.R.R. 479; [2002] A.C.D. 57, CA (Civ Div) 18–007
Investors in Industry Commercial Properties Ltd v South Bedfordshire DC [1986] Q.B.
1034; [1986] 2 W.L.R. 937; [1986] 1 All E.R. 787; 32 B.L.R. 1; 5 Con. L.R. 1; [1986]
1 E.G.L.R. 252; (1986) 2 Const. L.J. 108; (1986) 83 L.S.G. 441; (1986) 136 N.L.J.
118; (1986) 130 S.J. 71, CA (Civ Div) 29–008
Irving v Wilson (1791) 4 T.R. 485 29–049
Isaacs v Robertson [1985] A.C. 97; [1984] 3 W.L.R. 705; [1984] 3 All E.R. 140; (1984) 81
L.S.G. 2769; (1984) 134 N.L.J. 745, PC (StV) 23–009, 23–020
Island Records Ltd v Corkindale; sub nom Island Records Ltd, Ex p. [1978] Ch. 122;
[1978] 3 W.L.R. 23; [1978] 3 All E.R. 824; [1978] F.S.R. 505; (1978) 122 S.J. 298,
CA (Civ Div) 24–007, 24–030
Island Records Ltd, Ex p. *See* Island Records Ltd v Corkindale
Iveagh v Minister of Housing and Local Government [1964] 1 Q.B. 395; [1963] 3
W.L.R. 974; [1963] 3 All E.R. 817; (1964) 128 J.P. 70; 62 L.G.R. 32; (1964) 15 P. &
C.R. 233; [1963] R.V.R. 791; (1963) 107 S.J. 790; (1963) 107 S.J. 851, CA 9–041
JA Pye (Oxford) Estates Ltd v West Oxfordshire DC (1984) 47 P. & C.R. 125; (1982)
264 E.G. 533; [1982] J.P.L. 577, QBD 22–046
JD v East Berkshire Community Health NHS Trust; sub nom. MAK v Dewsbury
Healthcare NHS Trust; D v East Berkshire Community NHS Trust [2005] UKHL
23; [2005] 2 A.C. 373; [2005] 2 W.L.R. 993; [2005] 2 All E.R. 443; [2005] 2 F.L.R.
284; [2005] 2 F.C.R. 81; (2005) 8 C.C.L. Rep. 185; [2005] Lloyd's Rep. Med. 263;
(2005) 83 B.M.L.R. 66; [2005] Fam. Law 615; (2005) 155 N.L.J. 654, HL 29–016
Jackson v Turnley (1853) 1 Dr. 617 25–020
Jackson Stansfield & Sons v Butterworth [1948] 2 All E.R. 558; 64 T.L.R. 481; (1948)
112 J.P. 377; 46 L.G.R. 410; [1948] W.N. 315; (1948) 92 S.J. 469, CA 16–003
Jagendorf v Secretary of State [1987] J.P.L. 771 15–007
Jarrett Ex p. (1946) 52 T.L.R. 230 26–057

Jasper v United Kingdom (27052/95) (2000) 30 E.H.R.R. 441; [2000] Po. L.R. 25; [2000]
    Crim. L.R. 586, ECHR 28–008
Jayawardane (Don Leonard) v VP Silva; sub nom. Jayawardane v Silva [1970] 1
    W.L.R. 1365; (1970) 114 S.J. 787, PC (Cey) 25–006
Jayne v National Coal Board [1963] 2 All E.R. 220, Assizes (Monmouthshire) 29–023
Jeary v Chailey Rural DC (1973) 26 P. & C.R. 280, CA (Civ Div) 27–008
Jeffs v New Zealand Dairy Production and Marketing Board [1967] 1 A.C. 551; [1967] 2
    W.L.R. 136; [1966] 3 All E.R. 863; (1966) 110 S.J. 809, PC (NZ) 12–042, 13–009
John v Rees [1970] Ch. 345; [1969] 2 W.L.R. 1294; [1969] 2 All E.R. 274; (1969) 113 S.J.
    487, Ch D 12–024, 26–040
Johnson v Secretary of State for Health [2001] Lloyd's Rep. Med. 385, CA (Civ Div)   23–011
Johnson v Sargent [1918] 1 K.B. 101 22–006
Johnston v Chief Constable of the Royal Ulster Constabulary (222/84) [1987] Q.B. 129;
    [1986] 3 W.L.R. 1038; [1986] 3 All E.R. 135; [1986] E.C.R. 1651; [1986] 3 C.M.L.R.
    240; [1987] I.C.R. 83; [1986] I.R.L.R. 263; (1987) 84 L.S.G. 188; (1986) 130 S.J.
    953, ECJ 18–055
Jones v DAS Legal Expenses Insurance Co Ltd [2003] EWCA Civ 1071; [2004] I.R.L.R.
    218; (2003) 147 S.J.L.B. 932, CA (Civ Div) 13–007
Jones v James (1850) 19 L.J. Q.B. 257 25–010
Jones v Owen (1845) 5 D. & L. 669 25–010
Jones v Robson [1901] 1 Q.B. 673 22–006
Jones v Swansea City Council [1990] 1 W.L.R. 1453; [1990] 3 All E.R. 737; 89 L.G.R.
    90; (1990) 134 S.J. 1437, HL 29–033
Jory v Secretary of State for Transport, Local Government and the Regions [2002]
    EWHC 2724; [2003] 1 P.L.R. 54; [2003] J.P.L. 549; (2002) 99(45) L.S.G. 36; (2003)
    100(3) L.S.G. 33, QBD (Admin) 9–038
K v Secretary of State for the Home Department [2006] EWCA Civ 1037, CA (Civ
    Div) 15–002
Kanda v Malaya [1962] A.C. 322; [1962] 2 W.L.R. 1153; (1962) 106 S.J. 305, PC
    (FMS) 12–027
Kane v New Forest DC (No.1) [2001] EWCA Civ 878; [2002] 1 W.L.R. 312; [2001] 3 All
    E.R. 914; [2002] 1 P.L.R. 7; [2002] J.P.L. 409; [2001] 27 E.G. 132 (C.S.); [2001]
    N.P.C. 100, CA (Civ Div) 29–016
Kaplan v United Kingdom (1994) 76A DR 90 13–012
Kavanagh v Chief Constable of Devon and Cornwall; sub nom. Bankrupt, Ex p. v
    Chief Constable of Devon and Cornwall; Kavanagh, Re [1974] Q.B. 624; [1974] 2
    W.L.R. 762; [1974] 2 All E.R. 697; (1974) 118 S.J. 347, CA (Civ Div) . 12–030, 12–031
Kay v Lambeth LBC; sub nom. Leeds City Council v Price; Lambeth LBC v Kay [2006]
    UKHL 10; [2006] 2 A.C. 465; [2006] 2 W.L.R. 570; [2006] 4 All E.R. 128; [2006] 2
    F.C.R. 20; [2006] H.R.L.R. 17; [2006] U.K.H.R.R. 640; 20 B.H.R.C. 33; [2006]
    H.L.R. 22; [2006] B.L.G.R. 323; [2006] 2 P. & C.R. 25; [2006] L. & T.R. 8; [2006]
    11 E.G. 194 (C.S.); (2006) 150 S.J.L.B. 365; [2006] N.P.C. 29, HL 18–003
Kaydanyuk v Secretary of State for the Home Department [2006] EWCA Civ 368, CA
    (Civ Div) 15–015
Kemikalieinspektionen v Toolex Alpha AB (C-473/98) [2000] E.C.R. I-5681, ECJ .. 19–020
Kent CC v Batchelor (No.2) [1979] 1 W.L.R. 213; [1978] 3 All E.R. 980; 76 L.G.R. 714;
    (1979) 38 P. & C.R. 185; [1978] J.P.L. 179; (1978) 122 S.J. 47, QBD 24–010
Kibiti v Secretary of State for the Home Department [2000] Imm. A.R. 594, CA (Civ
    Div) 15–002, 15–027
Kilby v Basildon DC; sub nom. R. (on the application of Kilby) v Basildon DC [2007]
    EWCA Civ 479; [2007] H.R.L.R. 39; [2007] 22 E.G. 161 (C.S.); (2007) 151 S.J.L.B.
    712; [2007] N.P.C. 65, CA (Civ Div) 16–025
Kilmarnock Magistrates v Secretary of State for Scotland 1961 S.C. 350; 1961 S.L.T.
    333, OH 16–013
King Emperor v Benoari Lal Sarma [1945] A.C. 14; [1945] 1 All E.R. 210, PC (Ind)   16–003
Kingsley v United Kingdom (35605/97) (2001) 33 E.H.R.R. 13, ECHR 13–012
Kingston upon Thames RLBC v Secretary of State for the Environment [1973] 1
    W.L.R. 1549; [1974] 1 All E.R. 193; 71 L.G.R. 206; (1973) 26 P. & C.R. 480; (1973)
    117 S.J. 794, DC 17–010
Kingsway Investments (Kent) Ltd Kent CC [1971] A.C. 72; [1970] 2 W.L.R. 397; [1970]
    1 All E.R. 70; 68 L.G.R. 301; (1970) 21 P. & C.R. 58; (1970) 114 S.J. 73, HL . 23–033

Kiriri Cotton Co Ltd v Dewani; sub nom. Kiriri Cotton Ct v Dewani [1960] A.C. 192; [1960] 2 W.L.R. 127; [1960] 1 All E.R. 177; (1960) 104 S.J. 49, PC (EA) 29–050

Kirkham v Chief Constable of Greater Manchester; sub nom. Kirkham v Anderton [1990] 2 Q.B. 283; [1990] 2 W.L.R. 987; [1990] 3 All E.R. 246; (1990) 140 N.L.J. 209; (1990) 134 S.J. 758, CA (Civ Div) 29–008

Kleinwort Benson Ltd v Lincoln City Council [1999] 2 A.C. 349; [1998] 3 W.L.R. 1095; [1998] 4 All E.R. 513; [1998] Lloyd's Rep. Bank. 387; [1999] C.L.C. 332; (1999) 1 L.G.L.R. 148; (1999) 11 Admin. L.R. 130; [1998] R.V.R. 315; (1998) 148 N.L.J. 1674; (1998) 142 S.J.L.B. 279; [1998] N.P.C. 145, HL 29–048, 29–050

Knowles v United States of America [2006] UKPC 38; [2007] 1 W.L.R. 47, PC (Bah) 25–038

Kodeeswaran (Chelliah) v Attorney General of Ceylon; sub nom. Kodeeswaran v Attorney General of Ceylon [1970] A.C. 1111; [1970] 2 W.L.R. 456; (1969) 114 S.J. 87, PC (Cey) 5–046

Kruse v Johnson; sub nom. Knise v Johnson [1898] 2 Q.B. 91, QBD 21–003, 22–028

Kruslin v France (A176–B); sub nom. Kruslin v France (11801/85) (1990) 12 E.H.R.R. 547, ECHR 18–032

Kuddus v Chief Constable of Leicestershire [2001] UKHL 29; [2002] 2 A.C. 122; [2001] 2 W.L.R. 1789; [2001] 3 All E.R. 193; (2001) 3 L.G.L.R. 45; [2001] Po. L.R. 181; (2001) 98(28) L.S.G. 43; (2001) 151 N.L.J. 936; (2001) 145 S.J.L.B. 166, HL ... 29–035

Kydd v Liverpool Watch Committee; sub nom. Kydd v Watch Committee of Liverpool [1908] A.C. 327, HL 27–002

Laboratoires Pharmaceutiques Bergaderm SA v Commission of the European Communities (C-352/98 P) [2000] E.C.R. I-5291, ECJ 29–058

Laker Airways Ltd v Department of Trade [1977] Q.B. 643; [1977] 2 W.L.R. 234; [1977] 2 All E.R. 182; (1976) 121 S.J. 52, CA (Civ Div) 4–025, 17–005, 20–014, 20–036

Lancashire CC v Taylor; sub nom. Taylor v Lancashire CC [2005] EWCA Civ 284; [2005] 1 W.L.R. 2668; [2005] H.R.L.R. 17; [2005] U.K.H.R.R. 766; [2005] L. & T.R. 26; [2005] 2 E.G.L.R. 17; [2005] 23 E.G. 142; [2005] N.P.C. 43, CA (Civ Div) 24–025

Lapointe v L'Association de Bienfaisance et de Retraite de la Police de Montreal [1906] A.C. 535, PC (Can) 12–001, 23–025

Larner v Solihull MBC [2001] R.T.R. 32; (2001) 3 L.G.L.R. 31; [2001] B.L.G.R. 255; [2001] P.I.Q.R. P17; (2001) 98(8) L.S.G. 45, CA (Civ Div) 29–016

Lau Liat Meng v Disciplinary Committee [1968] A.C. 391; [1967] 3 W.L.R. 877; (1967) 111 S.J. 619, PC (Sing) 12–027

Law v Chartered Institute of Patent Agents [1919] 2 Ch. 276, Ch D 13–004

Law v National Greyhound Racing Club; sub nom. Tozer v National Greyhound Racing Club [1983] 1 W.L.R. 1302; [1983] 3 All E.R. 300; (1983) 80 L.S.G. 2367; (1983) 127 S.J. 619, CA (Civ Div) 25–004, 26–028

Lawal v Northern Spirit Ltd [2003] UKHL 35; [2004] 1 All E.R. 187; [2003] I.C.R. 856; [2003] I.R.L.R. 538; [2003] H.R.L.R. 29; [2003] U.K.H.R.R. 1024; (2003) 100(28) L.S.G. 30; (2003) 153 N.L.J. 1005; (2003) 147 S.J.L.B. 783, HL 13–007

Lawlor v Union of Post Office Workers [1965] Ch. 712; [1965] 2 W.L.R. 579; [1965] 1 All E.R. 353; (1964) 108 S.J. 879, Ch D 12–001

Lawrence v Pembrokeshire CC; sub nom. L v Pembrokeshire CC; SL v Pembrokeshire CC [2007] EWCA Civ 446; [2007] 2 F.L.R. 705; [2007] 2 F.C.R. 329; [2007] H.R.L.R. 30; (2007) 10 C.C.L. Rep. 367; (2007) 96 B.M.L.R. 158; [2007] Fam. Law 804; (2007) 104(22) L.S.G. 24; [2007] 1 W.L.R. 2991, CA (Civ Div) 29–016

Lazarus Estates Ltd v Beasley [1956] 1 Q.B. 702; [1956] 2 W.L.R. 502; [1956] 1 All E.R. 341; (1956) 100 S.J. 131, CA 17–015

Le Compte v Belgium (A/43); Van Leuven v Belgium (A/43); De Meyere v Belgium (A/43) [1982] E.C.C. 240; (1982) 4 E.H.R.R. 1, ECHR 12–018, 13–012

Leader v Moxon (1773) 2 W.B. 1 924 17–009

Leary v National Union of Vehicle Builders [1971] Ch. 34; [1970] 3 W.L.R. 434; [1970] 2 All E.R. 713; 9 K.I.R. 137, Ch D 12–041

Lee v Showmen's Guild of Great Britain [1952] 2 Q.B. 329; [1952] 1 All E.R. 1175; [1952] 1 T.L.R. 1115; (1952) 96 S.J. 296, CA 15–017

Leech v Deputy Governor of Parkhurst Prison. *See* R. v Deputy Governor of Parkhurst Prison Ex p. Leech

Leeds City Council v Price; sub nom. Price v Leeds City Council [2005] EWCA Civ 289; [2005] 1 W.L.R. 1825; [2005] 3 All E.R. 573; [2005] U.K.H.R.R. 413; [2005] H.L.R. 31; [2005] B.L.G.R. 782; [2005] 2 P. & C.R. 26; [2005] J.P.L. 1241; [2005] 12 E.G.

218 (C.S.); (2005) 102(19) L.S.G. 33; (2005) 149 S.J.L.B. 359; [2005] N.P.C. 41, CA
(Civ Div) 18–003
Leeson v General Council of Medical Education and Registration (1890) L.R. 43 Ch.
D. 366, CA 13–002
Lentz v McMahon 231 Cal.Rptr 622 (1986) 20–048
Leonesio v Italian Ministry of Agriculture and Forestry (93/71); sub nom. Leonesio v
Ministero dell'Agricoltura e Foreste [1972] E.C.R. 287; [1973] C.M.L.R. 343,
ECJ 10–022
Lever Brothers & Unilever Ltd v Manchester Ship Canal Co (1945) 78 Ll. L. Rep. 507,
Ch D 25–026
Lever (Finance) Ltd v Westminster Corp; sub nom. Lever (Finance) Ltd v Westminster
LBC [1971] 1 Q.B. 222; [1970] 3 W.L.R. 732; [1970] 3 All E.R. 496; 68 L.G.R. 757;
(1970) 21 P. & C.R. 778; [1971] J.P.L. 115; (1970) 114 S.J. 651, CA (Civ Div) . 16–005,
                                                        20–034, 20–042, 20–046, 20–052
Lewisham BC v Roberts [1949] 2 K.B. 608; [1949] 1 All E.R. 815; 65 T.L.R. 423; (1949)
113 J.P. 260; 47 L.G.R. 479; [1949] L.J.R. 1318, CA 16–006, 16–007
Lithgow v United Kingdom (A/102); sub nom. Lithgow v United Kingdom (9006/80);
Vosper Plc v United Kingdom (9262/81); English Electric Co Ltd v United
Kingdom (9263/81); Banstonian Co v United Kingdom (9265/81); Yarrow Plc v
United Kingdom (9266/81); Vickers Plc v United Kingdom (9313/81); Dowsett
Securities Ltd v United Kingdom (9405/81) (1986) 8 E.H.R.R. 329, ECHR 21–005
Litster v Forth Dry Dock & Engineering Co Ltd; sub nom. Forth Estuary Engineering
Ltd v Litster [1990] 1 A.C. 546; [1989] 2 W.L.R. 634; [1989] 1 All E.R. 1134; 1989
S.C. (H.L.) 96; 1989 S.L.T. 540; [1989] 2 C.M.L.R. 194; [1989] I.C.R. 341; [1989]
I.R.L.R. 161; (1989) 86(23) L.S.G. 18; (1989) 139 N.L.J. 400; (1989) 133 S.J. 455,
HL 10–029
Liversidge v Anderson [1942] A.C. 206, HL 22–025
Livingstone v Westminster Corp [1904] 2 K.B. 109, KBD 20–029
Lloyd v United Kingdom (29798/96) [2006] R.A. 329, ECHR 29–047
Local Government Board v Arlidge. *See* R. v Local Government Board Ex p. Arlidge
London and Brighton Ry Co v Truman (1886) 11 App. Cas. 45 .... 29–038, 29–039
London & Clydeside Estates Ltd v Aberdeen DC [1980] 1 W.L.R. 182; [1979] 3 All E.R.
876; 1980 S.C. (H.L.) 1; 1980 S.L.T. 81; (1980) 39 P. & C.R. 549; (1979) 253 E.G.
1011; (1980) 124 S.J. 100, HL 23–011
London Association of Shipowners and Brokers v London and India Docks Joint
Committee [1892] 3 Ch. 242, CA 25–021
London City Council v South Metropolitan Gas Company [1904] 1 Ch.76, CA 24–010
London County Council v Attorney General [1902] A.C. 165 24–009
London Passenger Transport Board v Moscrop; sub nom. Moscrop v London Pas-
senger Transport Board [1942] A.C. 332, HL 24–006
Longshore v County of Ventura 151 Cal. Rptr 708 (1979) 20–048
Lonrho Ltd v Shell Petroleum Co Ltd (No.2) [1982] A.C. 173; [1981] 3 W.L.R. 33;
[1981] 2 All E.R. 456; (1981) 125 S.J. 429, HL 24–007, 28–006, 29–021, 29–032
Lonrho plc v Secretary of State for Trade and Industry. *See* R. v Secretary of State for
Trade and Industry Ex p. Lonrho Plc
Lonrho Plc v Tebbit [1992] 4 All E.R. 280; [1992] B.C.C. 779; [1993] B.C.L.C. 96, CA
(Civ Div) 26–006, 26–009
Lord Advocate v Dumbarton DC [1990] 2 A.C. 580; [1989] 3 W.L.R. 1346; [1990] 1 All
E.R. 1; 1990 S.C. (H.L.) 1; 1990 S.L.T. 158; (1990) 2 Admin. L.R. 429; (1990) 87(4)
L.S.G. 39; (1990) 134 S.J. 165, HL 28–015
Lord Luke of Pavenham v Minister of Housing and Local Government [1968] 1 Q.B.
172; [1967] 3 W.L.R. 801; [1967] 2 All E.R. 1066; (1967) 131 J.P. 425; 65 L.G.R.
393; (1967) 18 P. & C.R. 333; (1967) 111 S.J. 398, CA (Civ Div) 9–040
Lovell v Simpson (1800) 3 Esp. 153 29–049
Luby v Newcastle under Lyme Corp [1965] 1 Q.B. 214; [1964] 3 W.L.R. 500; [1964] 3
All E.R. 169; (1964) 128 J.P. 536; 62 L.G.R. 622; [1964] R.V.R. 708; (1964) 108 S.J.
541, CA 17–014
Lucas v Lucas [1943] P. 68, PDAD 5–046
Ludwigshafener Walzmuhle Erling KG v Council of the European Communities (197/
80) [1981] E.C.R. 3211, ECJ 19–022, 21–019
M v Home Office [1994] 1 A.C. 377; [1993] 3 W.L.R. 433; [1993] 3 All E.R. 537; (1995) 7

Admin. L.R. 113; (1993) 90(37) L.S.G. 50; (1993) 143 N.L.J. 1099; (1993) 137
S.J.L.B. 199, HL 28–017, 28–022, 28–023
MB v Managers of Warley Hospital, July 30, 1998 25–038
MCI Telecommunications Corp v American Telephone & Telegraph Co 512 U.S. 218
(1994) 14–042
McC (A Minor), Re; sub nom. McC (A Minor) v Mullan [1985] A.C. 528; [1984] 3
W.L.R. 1227; [1984] 3 All E.R. 908; [1984] N.I. 186; (1985) 81 Cr. App. R. 54;
(1985) 149 J.P. 225; [1985] Crim. L.R. 152; (1985) 82 L.S.G. 117; (1984) 128 S.J.
837, HL 29–047
McClaren v Home Office; sub nom. McLaren v Secretary of State for the Home
Department [1990] I.C.R. 824; [1990] I.R.L.R. 338; (1990) 2 Admin. L.R. 652;
[1990] C.O.D. 257; (1990) 87(17) L.S.G. 31; (1990) 134 S.J. 908, CA (Civ Div) . 5–044,
26–031, 26–032
McEldowney v Forde [1971] A.C. 632; [1969] 3 W.L.R. 179; [1969] 2 All E.R. 1039;
[1970] N.I. 11; (1969) 113 S.J. 566, HL 22–028
McInnes v Onslow Fane [1978] 1 W.L.R. 1520; [1978] 3 All E.R. 211; (1978) 122 S.J.
844, Ch D 12–009, 12–016, 12–022, 12–027
McKerr's Application for Judicial Review, Re; sub nom. McKerr, Re [2004] UKHL 12;
[2004] 1 W.L.R. 807; [2004] 2 All E.R. 409; [2004] N.I. 212; [2004] H.R.L.R. 26;
[2004] U.K.H.R.R. 385; 17 B.H.R.C. 68; [2004] Lloyd's Rep. Med. 263; [2004]
Inquest L.R. 35; (2004) 101(13) L.S.G. 33; (2004) 148 S.J.L.B. 355, HL (NI) ... 24–025
McLaren v Secretary of State for the Home Department. *See* McClaren v Home Office
McWhirter v Independent Broadcasting Authority; sub nom. McWhirter's Applica-
tion, Re [1973] Q.B. 629; [1973] 2 W.L.R. 344; [1973] 1 All E.R. 689; (1973) 117 S.J.
126; (1973) 117 S.J. 71, CA (Civ Div) 25–040, 29–021
Maatschap Toeters v Productschap Vee en Vlees (C-171/03) [2004] E.C.R. I-10945,
ECJ 19–022
Machado v Secretary of State for the Home Department [2005] EWCA Civ 597; [2005]
2 C.M.L.R. 43; [2005] Eu. L.R. 851; [2006] I.N.L.R. 69, CA (Civ Div) 18–040
Madan v General Medical Council (Interim Suspension Order) [2001] EWHC Admin
577; [2001] Lloyd's Rep. Med. 539; [2002] A.C.D. 3, DC 12–018, 19–011
Madras Electric Supply Corp Ltd v Boarland [1955] A.C. 667; [1955] 2 W.L.R. 632;
[1955] 1 All E.R. 753; 48 R. & I.T. 189; 35 T.C. 612; (1955) 34 A.T.C. 53; [1955]
T.R. 57; (1955) 99 S.J. 217; (1955) 99 S.J. 127, HL 28–015
Maerkle v British Continental Fur Co [1954] 1 W.L.R. 1242; [1954] 3 All E.R. 50;
(1954) 98 S.J. 588, CA 25–025, 25–026
Magdalen College Case (1615) 11 Co. Rep. 66b 28–015
Mahon v Air New Zealand [1984] A.C. 808; [1984] 3 W.L.R. 884; [1984] 3 All E.R. 201;
(1984) 81 L.S.G. 3336; (1984) 128 S.J. 752, PC (NZ) 12–027, 15–011
Makanjuola v Commissioner of Police of the Metropolis [1992] 3 All E.R. 617, CA (Civ
Div) 28–007
Malloch v Aberdeen Corp (No.1) [1971] 1 W.L.R. 1578; [1971] 2 All E.R. 1278; 1971
S.C. (H.L.) 85; 1971 S.L.T. 245; (1971) 115 S.J. 756, HL 12–024, 26–031
Manchester Corp v Farnworth; sub nom. Farnworth v Lord Mayor of Manchester
[1930] A.C. 171, HL 29–038, 29–039
Manchester (Ringway Airport) Compulsory Purchase Order, Re (1935) 153 L.T. 219 . 13–009
Mann Ex p. (1916) 32 T.L.R. 479 25–015
Maradana Mosque (Board of Trustees) v Badiuddin Mahmud [1967] 1 A.C. 13; [1966] 2
W.L.R. 921; [1966] 1 All E.R. 545; (1966) 110 S.J. 310, PC (Cey) 12–027
Marcic v Thames Water Utilities Ltd; sub nom. Thames Water Utilities Ltd v Marcic
[2003] UKHL 66; [2004] 2 A.C. 42; [2003] 3 W.L.R. 1603; [2004] 1 All E.R. 135;
[2004] B.L.R. 1; 91 Con. L.R. 1; [2004] Env. L.R. 25; [2004] H.R.L.R. 10; [2004]
U.K.H.R.R. 253; [2003] 50 E.G. 95 (C.S.); (2004) 101(4) L.S.G. 32; (2003) 153
N.L.J. 1869; (2003) 147 S.J.L.B. 1429; [2003] N.P.C. 150, HL .. 29–039, 29–040, 29–063
Margate Pier Company v Hannam (1819) 3 B. & Ald. 266 23–007
Maritime Electrical Company Ltd v General Dairies Ltd [1937] A.C. 620 20–043
Marleasing SA v La Comercial Internacional de Alimentacion SA (C-106/89) [1990]
E.C.R. I-4135; [1993] B.C.C. 421; [1992] 1 C.M.L.R. 305, ECJ (6th Chamber) . 10–028,
18–006
Marriage v East Norfolk River Catchment Board [1950] 1 K.B. 284; [1949] 2 All E.R.
1021; 66 T.L.R. (Pt. 1) 225; (1950) 114 J.P. 38; (1950) 94 S.J. 32, CA 29–039
Marriott v Oxford and District Cooperative Society (No.2) [1970] 1 Q.B. 186; [1969] 3

W.L.R. 984; [1969] 3 All E.R. 1126; (1969) 7 K.I.R. 219; (1969) 3 I.T.R. 377; (1969)
113 S.J. 655, CA (Civ Div) 9–021
Marshall v Southampton and South West Hampshire AHA (152/84) [1986] Q.B. 401;
[1986] 2 W.L.R. 780; [1986] 2 All E.R. 584; [1986] E.C.R. 723; [1986] 1 C.M.L.R.
688; [1986] I.C.R. 335; [1986] I.R.L.R. 140; (1986) 83 L.S.G. 1720; (1986) 130 S.J.
340, ECJ 10–025
Marshall v Southampton and South West Hampshire AHA (C-271/91) [1994] Q.B. 126;
[1993] 3 W.L.R. 1054; [1993] 4 All E.R. 586; [1993] E.C.R. I-4367; [1993] 3
C.M.L.R. 293; [1993] I.C.R. 893; [1993] I.R.L.R. 445, ECJ 10–032
Marten v Flight Refuelling Ltd (No.1) [1962] Ch. 115; [1961] 2 W.L.R. 1018; [1961] 2
All E.R. 696; (1962) 13 P. & C.R. 389; (1961) 105 S.J. 442, Ch D 16–025, 29–038
Martindale v Falkner (1846) 2 C.B. 706 29–050
Martinez Sala v Freistaat Bayern (C-85/96) [1998] E.C.R. I-2691, ECJ 21–016
Mason v State of New South Wales (1958–1959) 102 C.L.R. 108 29–049
Matadeen v Pointu [1999] 1 A.C. 98; [1998] 3 W.L.R. 18; (1998) 142 S.J.L.B. 100, PC
(Mau) 21–003
Matrix Securities Ltd v Inland Revenue Commissioners. *See* R. v Inland Revenue
Commissioners Ex p. Matrix Securities Ltd
Matthews v Eldridge 424 U.S. 319 (1976) 12–020, 12–026
Matthews v Ministry of Defence [2003] UKHL 4; [2003] 1 A.C. 1163; [2003] 2 W.L.R.
435; [2003] 1 All E.R. 689; [2003] I.C.R. 247; [2004] H.R.L.R. 2; [2003] U.K.H.R.R.
453; 14 B.H.R.C. 585; [2003] P.I.Q.R. P24; [2003] A.C.D. 42; (2003) 100(13) L.S.G.
26; (2003) 153 N.L.J. 261; (2003) 147 S.J.L.B. 235, HL 18–007, 29–046
Maurice v London CC [1964] 2 Q.B. 362; [1964] 2 W.L.R. 715; [1964] 1 All E.R. 779;
(1964) 128 J.P. 311; 62 L.G.R. 241; [1964] R.V.R. 341; (1964) 108 S.J. 175, CA . 24–011
Maxwell v Department of Trade and Industry [1974] Q.B. 523; [1974] 2 W.L.R. 338;
[1974] 2 All E.R. 122; (1974) 118 S.J. 203, CA (Civ Div) 12–021, 12–023, 12–027
May v Beattie [1927] 2 K.B. 353, KBD 22–017
Maynard v Osmond [1977] Q.B. 240; [1976] 3 W.L.R. 711; [1977] 1 All E.R. 64; [1976]
Crim. L.R. 633; (1976) 120 S.J. 604, CA (Civ Div) 12–032
Mayor and Alderman of City of London v Cox (1867) L.R. 2 H.L. 239 23–027,
24–004, 25–002, 25–009
Meade v Haringey LBC [1979] 1 W.L.R. 637; [1979] 2 All E.R. 1016; [1979] I.C.R. 494;
77 L.G.R. 577; (1979) 123 S.J. 216 ,CA (Civ Div) 25–040, 29–021
Medicaments and Related Classes of Goods (No.2), [2001] 1 W.L.R. 700; [2001]
U.K.C.L.R. 550; [2001] I.C.R. 564; [2001] H.R.L.R. 17; [2001] U.K.H.R.R. 429;
(2001) 3 L.G.L.R. 32; (2001) 98(7) L.S.G. 40; (2001) 151 N.L.J. 17; (2001) 145
S.J.L.B. 29, CA (Civ Div) 13–007
Meerabux v Attorney General of Belize [2005] UKPC 12; [2005] 2 A.C. 513; [2005] 2
W.L.R. 1307, PC (Bze) 13–004
Mennitto v Italy (33804/96) (2002) 34 E.H.R.R. 48, ECHR 12–018
Merchandise Transport Ltd v British Transport Commission (No.1) [1962] 2 Q.B. 173;
[1961] 3 W.L.R. 1358; [1961] 3 All E.R. 495; 32 Traff. Cas. 19; 60 L.G.R. 1; (1961)
105 S.J. 1104, CA 16–012
Mercury Communications Ltd v Director General of Telecommunications [1996] 1
W.L.R. 48; [1996] 1 All E.R. 575; [1995] C.L.C. 266; [1998] Masons C.L.R. Rep.
39, HL 26–010, 26–011
Meroni & Co Industrie Metallurgiche SpA v High Authority of the European Coal and
Steel Community (9/56) [1957–58] E.C.R. 133, ECJ 12–040
Merricks v Heathcoat-Amory and the Minister of Agriculture, Fisheries and Food
[1955] Ch. 567; [1955] 3 W.L.R. 56; [1955] 2 All E.R. 453; (1955) 99 S.J. 400, Ch
D 28–020
Merricks v Nott-Bower [1965] 1 Q.B. 57; [1964] 2 W.L.R. 702; [1964] 1 All E.R. 717;
(1964) 128 J.P. 267; (1964) 108 S.J. 116, CA 28–002
Mersey Docks and Harbour Board Trustees v Gibbs (1866) L.R. 1 H.L. 93, HL ... 29–005
Metropolitan Asylum District v Hill (1881) 6 App. Cas. 193 29–038
Metropolitan Properties Co (FGC) Ltd v Lannon; sub nom. R. v London Rent
Assessment Panel Committee Ex p. Metropolitan Properties Co (FGC) Ltd [1969]
1 Q.B. 577; [1968] 3 W.L.R. 694; [1968] 3 All E.R. 304; (1968) 19 P. & C.R. 856;
[1968] R.V.R. 490; (1968) 112 S.J. 585, CA (Civ Div) 9–024, 13–003, 13–006
Michaelek v Wandsworth LBC; Michalak v Wandsworth LBC [2002] EWCA Civ 271;

[2003] 1 W.L.R. 617; [2002] 4 All E.R. 1136; [2003] 1 F.C.R. 713; [2002] H.L.R. 39;
[2002] N.P.C. 34, CA (Civ Div) 21–006, 21–009
Midwood & Co v Manchester Corp; sub nom. Midwood & Co Ltd v Mayor, Alder-
men, and Citizens of Manchester [1905] 2 K.B. 597, CA 29–043
Milac GmbH Gross- und Aussenhandel v Hauptzollamt Freiburg (C-8/78) [1978]
E.C.R. 1721, ECJ 21–015
Millar (David Cameron) v Dickson [2001] UKPC D 4; [2002] 1 W.L.R. 1615; [2002] 3
All E.R. 1041; 2002 S.C. (P.C.) 30; 2001 S.L.T. 988; 2001 S.C.C.R. 741; [2001]
H.R.L.R. 59; [2001] U.K.H.R.R. 999; 2001 G.W.D. 26–1015, PC (Sc) 13–013
Miller v Weymouth and Melcombe Regis Corp (1974) 27 P. & C.R. 468; (1974) 118 S.J.
421, QBD 14–037
Mills v London CC [1925] 1 K.B. 213, KBD 16–003
Mills (Kenneth Anthony) v HM Advocate (No.2) [2002] UKPC D 2; [2004] 1 A.C. 441;
[2002] 3 W.L.R. 1597; 2003 S.C. (P.C.) 1; 2002 S.L.T. 939; 2002 S.C.C.R. 860;
[2002] H.R.L.R. 44; [2002] U.K.H.R.R. 1074; 13 B.H.R.C. 549; 2002 G.W.D. 26–
886, PC (Sc) 7–007
Milward v Caffin (1778) 2 Black. W. 1330 .... 14–027, 15–002
Minister of Agriculture and Fisheries v Hulkin Unreported 1950 20–042
Minister of Agriculture and Fisheries v Matthews [1950] 1 K.B. 148; [1949] 2 All E.R.
724; 65 T.L.R. 655, KBD 20–042
Minister of Housing and Local Government v Hartnell. *See* Hartnell v Minister of
Housing and Local Government
Minister of National Revenue v Wrights Canadian Ropes Ltd [1947] A.C. 109, PC
(Can) 12.036, 23–028
Mississippi Power v Moore 487 U.S. 354 (1988) 14–041, 14–042
Mogul Steamship Co Ltd v McGregor Gow & Co [1892] A.C. 25; [1891–4] All E.R.
Rep. 263, HL 11–002
Money Markets International Stockbrokers Ltd (In Liquidation) v London Stock
Exchange Ltd [2002] 1 W.L.R. 1150; [2001] 4 All E.R. 223; [2001] 2 All E.R.
(Comm) 344; [2001] 2 B.C.L.C. 347; [2001] B.P.I.R. 1044, Ch D 18–028
Monks v East Northamptonshire DC; sub nom. Monks v Northamptonshire DC [2002]
EWHC 473; (2002) 166 J.P. 592; (2002) 166 J.P.N. 728; [2002] E.H.L.R. Dig. 6,
QBD (Admin) 24–010
Monro v Watson (1887) 57 L.T. 366 22–028
Montes v Secretary of State for the Home Department [2004] EWCA Civ 404; [2004]
Imm. A.R. 250, CA (Civ Div) 15–020
Montilla v United States 457 F. 2d 978 (1972) 20–048
Montgomery v HM Advocate; sub nom. HM Advocate v Montgomery (David Shields)
[2003] 1 A.C. 641; [2001] 2 W.L.R. 779; 2001 S.C. (P.C.) 1; 2001 S.L.T. 37; 2000
S.C.C.R. 1044; [2001] U.K.H.R.R. 124; 9 B.H.R.C. 641; 2000 G.W.D. 40–1487,
PC (Sc) 7–007
Moore v Gamgee (1890) 25 Q.B.D. 244 25–010
Morgan v Palmer (1824) 2 B. & C. 729 29–049
Mortimer v Labour Party, *Independent*, February 28, 2000, Ch D 24–026
Moser v United Sattes 341 U.S. 41 (1951) 20–048
Motor Vehicle Manufacturers Assn v State Farm Mutual Automobile Insurance Co
463 U.S. 29 (1983) 19–032
Mould v Williams (1844) 5 Q.B. 469 14–026
Mountview Court Properties Ltd v Devlin (1970) 21 P. & C.R. 689; [1971] J.P.L. 113;
(1970) 114 S.J. 474, QBD 9–024, 12–034
Moyna v Secretary of State for Work and Pensions; sub nom. Moyna v Secretary of
State for Social Security [2003] UKHL 44; [2003] 1 W.L.R. 1929; [2003] 4 All E.R.
162; (2003) 73 B.M.L.R. 201, HL 14–022, 15–024
Mulliner v Midland Railway Co; sub nom. Mulliner v Midland Railway (1879) L.R. 11
Ch. D. 611, Ch D 16–024
Mullins v McFarlane [2006] EWHC 986, QBD 25–021
Mulvenna v Admiralty, The 1926 S.C. 842; 1926 S.L.T. 568, IH (1 Div) 5–046
Municipal Mutual Insurance Co Ltd v Pontefract Corporation (1917) 33 T.L.R. 234 16–022
Munn v Illinois 94 US 113 (1877) 11–021
Murphy v Brentwood DC [1991] 1 A.C. 398; [1990] 3 W.L.R. 414; [1990] 2 All E.R. 908;
[1990] 2 Lloyd's Rep. 467; 50 B.L.R. 1; 21 Con. L.R. 1; (1990) 22 H.L.R. 502; 89

L.G.R. 24; (1991) 3 Admin. L.R. 37; (1990) 6 Const. L.J. 304; (1990) 154 L.G. Rev.
1010; [1990] E.G. 105 (C.S.); (1990) 87(30) L.S.G. 15; (1990) 134 S.J. 1076, HL . 29–008
Murphy (J) & Sons v Secretary of State for the Environment; sub nom. Murphy v
Secretary of State for the Environment [1973] 1 W.L.R. 560; [1973] 2 All E.R. 26;
71 L.G.R. 273; (1973) 25 P. & C.R. 268; (1973) 117 S.J. 304, QBD 9–040
NLRB v United Food and Commercial Workers Union, Local 23, AFL-CIO 484 U.S.
112 (1987) 14–041
NV Algemene Transport- en Expeditie Onderneming van Gend en Loos v Nederlandse
Administratie der Belastingen (26/62) [1963] E.C.R. 1; [1963] C.M.L.R. 105, ECJ . 10–019
Nagle v Fielden; sub nom. Nagle v Feilden [1966] 2 Q.B. 633; [1966] 2 W.L.R. 1027;
[1966] 1 All E.R. 689; (1966) 110 S.J. 286, CA 25–021
Nairn v University of St Andrews; sub nom. Nairn v University Courts of the Uni-
versities of St Andrews and Edinburgh; Nairn v University Courts of St Andrews
and Edinburgh [1909] A.C. 147; 1909 S.C. (H.L.) 10; (1908) 16 S.L.T. 619, HL . 21–002
Nakkuda Ali v MF de S Jayaratne; sub nom. Ali v Jayaratne [1951] A.C. 66; 66 T.L.R.
(Pt. 2) 214; (1950) 10 C.R. 421; (1950) 94 S.J. 516, PC (Cey) 12–004, 12–005,
12–008, 25–006
Napier v Scottish Ministers 2005 1 S.C. 307; 2005 S.L.T. 379; [2005] U.K.H.R.R. 268;
2005 G.W.D. 9–136, IH (1 Div) 7–010
Napier Ex p. (1852) 18 Q.B. 692 25–015
Nasser v United Bank of Kuwait (Security for Costs) [2001] EWCA Civ 556; [2002] 1
W.L.R. 1868; [2002] 1 All E.R. 401; [2001] C.P. Rep. 105, CA (Civ Div) 21–007
National Corn Growers' Assn v Canada Import Tribunal [1990] 2 S.C.R. 1324 14–043
Neil Martin Ltd v Revenue and Customs Commissioners [2007] EWCA Civ 1041;
[2007] S.T.C. 1802; [2007] B.T.C. 662; [2007] S.T.I. 2459; (2007) 151 S.J.L.B. 1403,
CA (Civ Div) 29–022
Neilson v Laugharne [1981] Q.B. 736; [1981] 2 W.L.R. 537; [1981] 1 All E.R. 829; (1981)
125 S.J. 202, CA (Civ Div) 28–007
Nelms v Roe [1970] 1 W.L.R. 4; [1969] 3 All E.R. 1379; (1970) 54 Cr. App. R. 43; [1970]
R.T.R. 45; (1969) 113 S.J. 942, DC 16–007
Hydro Electric Commission of the Township of Nepean v Ontario Hydro (1982) 132
D.L.R. (3d) 193; [1982] 1 S.C.R. 347, CA (Can) 29–050
New Fashions (London) Ltd v Revenue and Customs Commissioners; sub nom. New
Fashion (London) Ltd v Revenue and Customs Commissioners [2005] EWHC
1628 (Ch); [2006] S.T.C. 175; [2007] B.T.C. 694; [2005] S.T.I. 1317, Ch D 9–021
New South Wales v Bardolph (1934) 52 C.L.R. 455 .... 5–035, 5–042
New Zealand Licensed Victuallers' Association of Employers v Price Tribunal [1957]
N.Z.L.R. 167 12–008
Newbury DC v Secretary of State for the Environment [1981] A.C. 578; [1980] 2
W.L.R. 379; [1980] 1 All E.R. 731; 78 L.G.R. 306; (1980) 40 P. & C.R. 148; [1980]
J.P.L. 325; (1980) 124 S.J. 186, HL 17–010
Niarchos (London) Ltd v Secretary of State for the Environment and Westminster City
Council (No.2) [1981] J.P.L. 118, CA (Civ Div) 19–004
Nicholls v Tavistock Urban DC [1923] 2 Ch. 18, Ch D 24–007, 25–021
Nichols v Walker (1632–1633) Cro.Car. 394 .... 14–027, 15–002
Nilabati Bahera v State of Orissa (1993) A.I.R. 1960 29–025
Nisbet Shipping Co v Queen, The [1955] 1 W.L.R. 1031; [1955] 3 All E.R. 161; [1955] 2
Lloyd's Rep. 173; (1955) 99 S.J. 579, PC (Can) 28–016
Norris v Ireland (A/142); sub nom. Norris v Ireland (10581/83) (1991) 13 E.H.R.R. 186,
ECHR 24–025
Northern Territory v Mengel (1995) 69 A.L.J.R. 527 29–033
Norton Tool Co Ltd v Tewson [1973] 1 W.L.R. 45; [1973] 1 All E.R. 183; [1972] I.C.R.
501; [1972] I.R.L.R. 86; (1972) 13 K.I.R. 328; [1973] I.T.R. 23; (1973) 117 S.J. 33,
NIRC 12–036
Norwich City Council v Stringer (2001) 33 H.L.R. 15; (2000) 2 L.G.L.R. 1102, CA (Civ
Div) 29–052
Norwich Pharmacal Co v Customs and Excise Commissioners; sub nom. Morton-
Norwich Products Inc v Customs and Excise Commissioners [1974] A.C. 133;
[1973] 3 W.L.R. 164; [1973] 2 All E.R. 943; [1973] F.S.R. 365; [1974] R.P.C. 101;
(1973) 117 S.J. 567, HL 28–006
Nottinghamshire CC v Secretary of State for the Environment. *See* R. v Secretary of
State for the Environment Ex p. Nottinghamshire CC

Nyali Ltd v Attorney General [1957] A.C. 253; [1956] 3 W.L.R. 341; [1956] 2 All E.R.
689; (1956) 100 S.J. 489, HL 11–020, 25–021
OLL Ltd v Secretary of State for the Home Department [1997] 3 All E.R. 897; (1997)
147 N.L.J. 1099, QBD 29–009
Oakes v Sidney Sussex College (Cambridge) [1988] 1 W.L.R. 431; [1988] 1 All E.R.
1004; (1988) 132 S.J. 416, Ch D 12–014
Offer v Minister of Health [1936] 1 K.B. 40, CA 12–004
Office of Personnel Management v Richmond 496 U.S. 414 (1990) 20–042
Official Solicitor v K; sub nom. K (Infants), Re [1965] A.C. 201; [1963] 3 W.L.R. 408;
[1963] 3 All E.R. 191; (1963) 107 S.J. 616, HL 12–030
O'Kelly v Trusthouse Forte Plc [1984] Q.B. 90; [1983] 3 W.L.R. 605; [1983] 3 All E.R.
456; [1983] I.C.R. 728; [1983] I.R.L.R. 369, CA (Civ Div) 9–021
O'Reilly v Mackman [1983] 2 A.C. 237; [1982] 3 W.L.R. 1096; [1982] 3 All E.R. 1124;
(1982) 126 S.J. 820, HL 12–009, 14–016, 14–033, 23–005, 23–025, 24–015, 25–004,
25–005, 26–005, 26–006, 26–007, 26–008, 26–009, 26–011, 26–019, 26–032,
26–047, 27–006
Olotu v Secretary of State for the Home Department; sub nom. Olotu v Home Office;
Olotu v Crown Prosecution Service [1997] 1 W.L.R. 328; [1997] 1 All E.R. 385;
(1997) 94(1) L.S.G. 24; (1997) 141 S.J.L.B. 14, CA (Civ Div) 29–022
Olsson v Sweden (A/130); sub nom. Olsson v Sweden (10465/83) (1989) 11 E.H.R.R.
259, ECHR 18–032
Open Door Counselling Ltd v Ireland (A/246); sub nom. Open Door Counselling Ltd v
Ireland (14234/88, 14253/88); Dublin Well Woman Centre v Ireland (A/246) (1993)
15 E.H.R.R. 244, ECHR 24–025
Orange v Chief Constable of West Yorkshire [2001] EWCA Civ 611; [2002] Q.B. 347;
[2001] 3 W.L.R. 736; [2001] Inquest L.R. 36; [2001] Prison L.R. 263; [2001] Po.
L.R. 126; (2001) 98(24) L.S.G. 44; (2001) 145 S.J.L.B. 125, CA (Civ Div) 29–016
O'Rourke v Camden LBC [1998] A.C. 188; [1997] 3 W.L.R. 86; [1997] 3 All E.R. 23;
(1997) 29 H.L.R. 793; (1997) 9 Admin. L.R. 649; (1997) 161 J.P.N. 1038; (1997)
94(26) L.S.G. 30; (1997) 141 S.J.L.B. 139; [1997] N.P.C. 93, HL 26–007, 29–022
Osgood v Nelson (1871–72) L.R. 5 H.L. 636, HL 12–001, 23–025
Osman v United Kingdom (23452/94) [1999] 1 F.L.R. 193; (2000) 29 E.H.R.R. 245; 5
B.H.R.C. 293; (1999) 1 L.G.L.R. 431; (1999) 11 Admin. L.R. 200; [2000] Inquest
L.R. 101; [1999] Crim. L.R. 82; [1998] H.R.C.D. 966; [1999] Fam. Law 86; (1999)
163 J.P.N. 297, ECHR 29–019, 29–020
P v Hackney LBC [2007] EWHC 1365 (Admin), QBD (Admin) 16–013
P v S and Cornwall CC (C-13/94); sub nom. P v S (Sex Discrimination) (C13/94) [1996]
All E.R. (EC) 397; [1996] E.C.R. I-2143; [1996] 2 C.M.L.R. 247; [1996] C.E.C. 574;
[1996] I.C.R. 795; [1996] I.R.L.R. 347; [1996] 2 F.L.R. 347; [1997] 2 F.C.R. 180;
[1996] Fam. Law 609, ECJ 21–017
Padfield v Minister of Agriculture, Fisheries and Food; sub nom. R. v Minister of
Agriculture and Fisheries Ex p. Padfield [1968] A.C. 997; [1968] 2 W.L.R. 924;
[1968] 1 All E.R. 694; (1968) 112 S.J. 171, HL 12–036, 25–016, 28–017
Page v Hull University Visitor. See R. v Lord President of the Privy Council Ex p. Page
Palacegate Properties Ltd v Camden LBC (2001) 3 L.G.L.R. 18; (2001) 82 P. & C.R.
17; [2000] 4 P.L.R. 59; [2001] J.P.L. 373 (Note); [2001] A.C.D. 137; [2001] A.C.D.
23, DC 23–004
Panagis Pafitis v Trapeza Kentrikis Ellados AE (C-441/93) [1996] E.C.R. I-1347 ... 10–030
Parke Davis & Co v Comptroller-General of Patents, Designs and Trade Marks; sub
nom. R. v Comptroller-General of Patents and Designs Ex p. Parke Davis & Co
[1954] A.C. 321; [1954] 2 W.L.R. 531; [1954] 1 All E.R. 671; (1954) 71 R.P.C. 169;
(1954) 98 S.J. 211, HL 23–027, 25–009, 25–010
Pasmore v Oswaldtwistle Urban DC (No.2); sub nom. Peebles v Oswaldtwistle Urban
DC (No.2) [1898] A.C. 387, HL 25–040, 26–057, 29–021
Patchett v Leathem 65 T.L.R. 69; 47 L.G.R. 240; [1948] W.N. 386 .... 22–007, 22–024
Peak Park Joint Planning Board v Secretary of State for the Environment (1980) 39 P.
& C.R. 361; [1980] J.P.L. 114, QBD 14–037
Pearce v Secretary of State for Defence [1988] A.C. 755; [1988] 2 W.L.R. 1027; [1988] 2
All E.R. 348; (1988) 132 S.J. 699, HL 29–046
Pearlberg v Varty (Inspector of Taxes) [1972] 1 W.L.R. 534; [1972] 2 All E.R. 6; 48 T.C.
14; [1972] T.R. 5; (1972) 116 S.J. 335, HL 12–009, 12–023
Pearlman v Keepers and Governors of Harrow School [1979] Q.B. 56; [1978] 3 W.L.R.

736; [1979] 1 All E.R. 365; (1979) 38 P. & C.R. 136; (1978) 247 E.G. 1173; [1978] J.P.L. 829, CA (Civ Div) 14–031, 27–002

Peek v North Staffordshire Railway (1862) 11 E.R. 1109; (1863) 10 H.L. Cas. 473, HL 11–020

Pension Benefit Guaranty Corporation v LTV Corporation 496 U.S. 633 (1990) 14–041

Pepper (Inspector of Taxes) v Hart [1993] A.C. 593; [1992] 3 W.L.R. 1032; [1993] 1 All E.R. 42; [1992] S.T.C. 898; [1993] I.C.R. 291; [1993] I.R.L.R. 33; [1993] R.V.R. 127; (1993) 143 N.L.J. 17; [1992] N.P.C. 154, HL 18–006

Percy v Hall [1997] Q.B. 924; [1997] 3 W.L.R. 573; [1996] 4 All E.R. 523; (1996) 160 J.P. Rep. 788; (1996) 93(23) L.S.G. 36; (1996) 140 S.J.L.B. 130; [1996] N.P.C. 74, CA (Civ Div) 22–028, 23–012

Pergamon Press, Re [1971] Ch. 388; [1970] 3 W.L.R. 792; [1970] 3 All E.R. 535; (1970) 114 S.J. 569, CA (Civ Div) 12–009, 12–021, 12–023

Phelps v Hillingdon LBC; sub nom. G (A Child), Re [2001] 2 A.C. 619; [2000] 3 W.L.R. 776; [2000] 4 All E.R. 504; [2000] 3 F.C.R. 102; (2001) 3 L.G.L.R. 5; [2000] B.L.G.R. 651; [2000] Ed. C.R. 700; [2000] E.L.R. 499; (2000) 3 C.C.L. Rep. 156; (2000) 56 B.M.L.R. 1; (2000) 150 N.L.J. 1198; (2000) 144 S.J.L.B. 241, HL ... 29–012, 29–013, 29–015

Phillips v Berkshire CC [1967] 2 Q.B. 991; [1967] 3 W.L.R. 565; [1967] 2 All E.R. 675; (1967) 131 J.P. 382; 65 L.G.R. 377; (1967) 111 S.J. 498, DC 24–011

Phillips v Britannia Hygienic Laundry Co Ltd [1923] 2 K.B. 832, CA 29–021

Phillips v Eyre (1870–71) L.R. 6 Q.B. 1, Ex Chamber 13–009, 23–026

Pickering v James (1873) L.R. 7 C.P. 489 29–021

Pickwell v Camden LBC [1983] Q.B. 962; [1983] 2 W.L.R. 583; [1983] 1 All E.R. 602; 80 L.G.R. 798; (1982) 126 S.J. 397, QBD 17–002

Piersack v Belgium (A/53) (1983) 5 E.H.R.R. 169, ECHR 13–007

Pillai v Singapore City Council; sub nom. Pillai (M Vasudevan) v City Council of Singapore [1968] 1 W.L.R. 1278; (1968) 112 S.J. 440, PC (Sing) 12–041

Pioneer Aggregates (UK) Ltd v Secretary of State for the Environment [1985] A.C. 132; [1984] 3 W.L.R. 32; [1984] 2 All E.R. 358; 82 L.G.R. 488; (1984) 48 P. & C.R. 95; (1984) 272 E.G. 425; [1984] J.P.L. 651; (1984) 81 L.S.G. 2148; (1984) 128 S.J. 416, HL 17–010

Piper v St Marylebone Licensing Justices [1928] 2 K.B. 221, KBD 27–002

Pittston Coal Group v Sebben 488 U.S. 105 (1988) 14–041

Point of Ayr Collieries Ltd v Lloyd-George [1943] 2 All E.R. 546, CA 23–028

Polat (Bulent) v Secretary of State for the Home Department [2003] EWCA Civ 1059, CA (Civ Div) 15–003

Poplar Housing & Regeneration Community Association Ltd v Donoghue; sub nom. Donoghue v Poplar Housing & Regeneration Community Association Ltd; Poplar Housing & Regeneration Community Association Ltd v Donoghue [2001] EWCA Civ 595; [2002] Q.B. 48; [2001] 3 W.L.R. 183; [2001] 4 All E.R. 604; [2001] 2 F.L.R. 284; [2001] 3 F.C.R. 74; [2001] U.K.H.R.R. 693; (2001) 33 H.L.R. 73; (2001) 3 L.G.L.R. 41; [2001] B.L.G.R. 489; [2001] A.C.D. 76; [2001] Fam. Law 588; [2001] 19 E.G. 141 (C.S.); (2001) 98(19) L.S.G. 38; (2001) 98(23) L.S.G. 38; (2001) 145 S.J.L.B. 122; [2001] N.P.C. 84, CA (Civ Div) 5–013, 18–007, 18–022

Port Louis Corp v Attorney General (Mauritius) [1965] A.C. 1111; [1965] 3 W.L.R. 67; (1965) 109 S.J. 413, PC (Mau) 22–017

Porter v Magill; sub nom. Magill v Porter; Magill v Weeks [2001] UKHL 67; [2002] 2 A.C. 357; [2002] 2 W.L.R. 37; [2002] 1 All E.R. 465; [2002] H.R.L.R. 16; [2002] H.L.R. 16; [2002] B.L.G.R. 51; (2001) 151 N.L.J. 1886; [2001] N.P.C. 184, HL . 13–007, 17–010

Portland Cement Assn v Ruckelshaus 486 F. 2d 375 (1973) 22–020

Portugal v Commission of the European Communities (C-159/96) [1998] E.C.R. I-7379; [2001] 1 C.M.L.R. 33, ECJ (6th Chamber) 23–021

Portugal v Commission of the European Communities (C-365/99) [2001] E.C.R. I-5645, ECJ (5th Chamber) 19–021

Post Office v Gallagher [1970] 3 All E.R. 712; 9 K.I.R. 78, Ch D 22–017

Potato Marketing Board v Merricks [1958] 2 Q.B. 316; [1958] 3 W.L.R. 135; [1958] 2 All E.R. 538; (1958) 102 S.J. 510, QBD 23–028, 23–033

Potter v Scottish Prison Service; sub nom. Potter v Scottish Ministers [2007] CSIH 67; 2007 S.L.T. 1019; 2008 S.C.L.R. 81; [2007] U.K.H.R.R. 1361; 2007 G.W.D. 28–500, IH (1 Div) 7–010

Powergen UK Plc v Leicester City Council; sub nom. R. v Leicester City Council Ex p.
Powergen UK Plc (2001) 81 P. & C.R. 5; [2000] J.P.L. 1037; [2000] E.G. 64 (C.S.);
[2000] N.P.C. 57, CA (Civ Div) 20–034, 20–036, 20–049
Powley v Advisory, Conciliation and Arbitration Service (ACAS) [1978] I.C.R. 123;
[1977] I.R.L.R. 190; (1977) 121 S.J. 476, Ch D 22–017
Poyser and Mills Arbitration, Re; sub nom. Poyser v Mills [1964] 2 Q.B. 467; [1963] 2
W.L.R. 1309; [1963] 1 All E.R. 612; (1963) 107 S.J. 115, QBD 9–024, 12–034
Practice Sattement (Administrative Court: Listing and Urgent Cases) [2002] 1 W.L.R.
810 26–048
Prescott v Birmingham Corp [1955] Ch. 210; [1954] 3 W.L.R. 990; [1954] 3 All E.R. 698;
(1955) 119 J.P. 48; 53 L.G.R. 68; (1954) 98 S.J. 886, CA 17–010, 24–007
Prestatyn Urban DC v Prestatyn Raceway Ltd [1970] 1 W.L.R. 33; [1969] 3 All E.R.
1573; 68 L.G.R. 609; (1969) 113 S.J. 899, Ch D 24–010
Pride of Derby and Derbyshire Angling Association Ltd v British Celanese Ltd [1953]
Ch. 149; [1953] 2 W.L.R. 58; [1953] 1 All E.R. 179; (1953) 117 J.P. 52; 51 L.G.R.
121; (1953) 97 S.J. 28 CA 25–033, 25–036, 29–038
Prohibitions del Roy (1607) 12 Co. Rep. 63 17–005
Pubblico Ministero v Ratti (148/78) [1979] E.C.R. 1629; [1980] 1 C.M.L.R. 96, ECJ . 10–024,
10–025
Public Disclosure Commission v Isaacs [1988] 1 W.L.R. 1043; [1989] 1 All E.R. 137;
(1988) 138 N.L.J. Rep. 185, PC (Bah) 12–031
Public Service Alliance of Canada v Attorney General of Canada [1991] 1 S.C.R. 614 14–043
Pudsey Coal Gas Co v Corporation of Bradford (1872) L.R. 15 Eq. 167 24–006
Puhlhofer v Hillingdon LBC. *See* R. v Hillingdon LBC Ex p. Puhlhofer
Pullar v United Kingdom 1996 S.C.C.R. 755; (1996) 22 E.H.R.R. 391, ECHR 13–007
Punton v Ministry of Pensions and National Insurance [1963] 1 W.L.R. 186; [1963] 1
All E.R. 275; (1962) 106 S.J. 1010, CA 25–022
Punton v Ministry of Pensions and National Insurance (No 2) [1964] 1 W.L.R. 226;
[1964] 1 All E.R. 448; (1964) 108 S.J. 34, CA 25–022
Pushpanathan v Canada (Minister of Citizenship and Immigration) [1998] 1 S.C.R.
982 14–043
Pyrenees Shire Council v Day (1998) 192 C.L.R. 330 29–011
Pyx Granite Co Ltd v Ministry of Housing and Local Government [1960] A.C. 260;
[1959] 3 W.L.R. 346; [1959] 3 All E.R. 1; (1959) 123 J.P. 429; 58 L.G.R. 1; (1959)
10 P. & C.R. 319; (1959) 103 S.J. 633, HL 17–010, 25–021, 25–023, 26–056, 26–057
Quaquah v Group 4 Securities Ltd (No.2); sub nom. Quaquah v Group Four (Total
Security) Ltd (No.2) [2001] Prison L.R. 318, QBD 5–013
Quinn v Ministry of Defence [1998] P.I.Q.R. P387, CA (Civ Div) 5–044
R. v A (Complainant's Sexual History); sub nom. R. v A (No.2); R. v Y (Sexual
Offence: Complainant's Sexual History) [2001] UKHL 25; [2002] 1 A.C. 45; [2001]
2 W.L.R. 1546; [2001] 3 All E.R. 1; [2001] 2 Cr. App. R. 21; (2001) 165 J.P. 609;
[2001] H.R.L.R. 48; [2001] U.K.H.R.R. 825; 11 B.H.R.C. 225; [2001] Crim. L.R.
908; (2001) 165 J.P.N. 750, HL 18–007
R. v Acting Returning Officer for the Devon and East Plymouth Constituency Ex p.
Sanders; sub nom. Sanders Ex p. [1994] C.O.D. 497, QBD 27–004
R. v Admiralty Board of the Defence Council Ex p. Coupland [1996] C.O.D. 147,
QBD 19–010
R. v Advertising Standards Authority Ex p. Insurance Services (1990) 2 Admin. L.R.
77; (1990) 9 Tr. L.R. 169; [1990] C.O.D. 42; (1989) 133 S.J. 1545, DC 26–027
R. v Agricultural Land Tribunal for the Wales and Monmouth Area Ex p. Davies
[1953] 1 W.L.R. 722; [1953] 1 All E.R. 1182; 51 L.G.R. 368; (1953) 97 S.J. 335,
DC 25–005
R. v Alnwick DC Ex p. Robson [1998] C.O.D. 241; [1997] E.G. 144 (C.S.), QBD .. 16–015,
22–018
R. v Altrincham Justices Ex p. Pennington (Norman) [1975] Q.B. 549; [1975] 2 W.L.R.
450; [1975] 2 All E.R. 78; 73 L.G.R. 109; (1974) 119 S.J. 64, DC 13–006
R. v Archbishop of Canterbury Ex p. Morant [1944] K.B. 282, CA 12–001
R. v Arts Council of England Ex p. Women's Playhouse Trust [1998] C.O.D. 175,
QBD 26–006
R. v Askew (1768) 4 Burr. 2186 17–009
R. v Association of British Travel Agents Ex p. Sunspell Ltd (t/a Superlative Travel).

See R. (on the application of Sunspell Ltd (t/a Superlative Travel)) v Association of British Travel Agents

R. v Aston University Senate Ex p. Roffey; sub nom. R. v Senate of the University of Aston Ex p. Roffey [1969] 2 Q.B. 538; [1969] 2 W.L.R. 1418; [1969] 2 All E.R. 964; (1969) 133 J.P. 463; (1969) 113 S.J. 308, DC 12–014, 25–004

R. v Avon CC Ex p. Terry Adams Ltd [1994] Env. L.R. 442; [1994] N.P.C. 2, CA (Civ Div) 26–046

R. v BBC Ex p. Kelly [1996] C.O.D. 58, DC 16–015, 22–018

R. v BBC Ex p. Referendum Party [1997] E.M.L.R. 605; (1997) 9 Admin. L.R. 553; [1997] C.O.D. 459, QBD 26–025, 26–027

R. v BHB Community Healthcare NHS Trust Ex p. B; sub nom. B, Re [1999] 1 F.L.R. 106; (1999) 2 C.C.L. Rep. 5; [1999] Lloyd's Rep. Med. 101; (1999) 47 B.M.L.R. 112, CA (Civ Div) 25–038

R. v Bacon's School Governors Ex p. Inner London Education Authority [1990] C.O.D. 414, DC 26–055

R. v Badger (1856) 6 El. & Bl. 138 14–027

R. v Barker (1762) 3 Burr 1265 25–014

R. v Barnsley Licensing Justices Ex p. Barnsley and District Licensed Victuallers Association [1960] 2 Q.B. 167; [1960] 3 W.L.R. 305; [1960] 2 All E.R. 703; (1960) 124 J.P. 359; 58 L.G.R. 285; (1960) 104 S.J. 583, CA 13–003

R. v Barnsley MBC Ex p. Hook [1976] 1 W.L.R. 1052; [1976] 3 All E.R. 452; 74 L.G.R. 493; (1976) 120 S.J. 182, CA (Civ Div) 13–004, 19–010, 25–004

R. v Barnet LBC Ex p. Shah (Nilish) [1983] 2 A.C. 309; [1983] 2 W.L.R. 16; [1983] 1 All E.R. 226; 81 L.G.R. 305; (1983) 133 N.L.J. 61; (1983) 127 S.J. 36, HL . 9–019, 14–022

R. v Barnet & Camden Rent Tribunal Ex p. Frey Investments Ltd; sub nom. Frey Investments v Camden LBC [1972] 2 Q.B. 342; [1972] 2 W.L.R. 619; [1972] 1 All E.R. 1185; 70 L.G.R. 241; (1972) 24 P. & C.R. 202; (1971) 115 S.J. 967, CA (Civ Div) 17–014

R. v Barnsley MBC Ex p. Hook [1976] 1 W.L.R. 1052; [1976] 3 All E.R. 452; 74 L.G.R. 493; (1976) 120 S.J. 182, CA (Civ Div) 25–006, 26–025

R. v Bath City Council Ex p. Crombie [1995] C.O.D. 283, QBD 26–046

R. v Bedford Level Corporation (1805) 6 East 356 23–008

R. v Bedwelty Justices Ex p. Williams [1997] A.C. 225 ..... 14–033, 15–011, 15–017, 25–004

R. v Benjafield (Karl Robert) (Confiscation Order) [2002] UKHL 2; [2003] 1 A.C. 1099; [2002] 2 W.L.R. 235; [2002] 1 All E.R. 815; [2002] 2 Cr. App. R. 3; [2002] 2 Cr. App. R. (S.) 71; [2002] H.R.L.R. 20; [2002] Crim. L.R. 337; (2002) 99(10) L.S.G. 29; (2002) 146 S.J.L.B. 37, HL 18–003

R. v Birmingham and Gloucester Ry (1841) 2 Q.B. 47 25–018

R. v Birmingham City Council Ex p. Dredger, 91 L.G.R. 532; (1994) 6 Admin. L.R. 553; [1993] C.O.D. 340; (1994) 158 L.G. Rev. 1007; [1993] E.G. 9 (C.S.); [1993] N.P.C. 13, QBD 11–034, 16–015, 22–018, 26–025

R. v Birmingham Justices Ex p. Lamb [1983] 1 W.L.R. 339; [1983] 3 All E.R. 23; (1983) 147 J.P. 75; [1983] Crim. L.R. 329; (1983) 127 S.J. 119, DC 12–030

R. v Birmingham Licensing Planning Committee Ex p. Kennedy; sub nom. Kennedy v Birmingham Licensing Planning Committee [1972] 2 Q.B. 140; [1972] 2 W.L.R. 939; [1972] 2 All E.R. 305, CA (Civ Div) 17–013, 25–016

R. v Bishop of Stafford Ex p. Owen [2001] A.C.D. 14, CA (Civ Div) 26–016

R. v Bloomsbury Income Tax Commissioners [1915] 3 K.B. 768 14–029

R. v Board of Control Ex p. Rutty; sub nom. Rutty, Re [1956] 2 Q.B. 109; [1956] 2 W.L.R. 822; [1956] 1 All E.R. 769; (1956) 120 J.P. 153; 54 L.G.R. 276; (1956) 100 S.J. 263, DC 25–038

R. v Board of Visitors of the Maze Prison Ex p. Hone; sub nom. Hone and McCartan's Application, Re [1988] A.C. 379; [1988] 2 W.L.R. 177; [1988] 1 All E.R. 321; (1988) 132 S.J. 158, HL 12–032

R. v Board of Visitors of Hull Prison Ex p. St Germain (No.1) [1979] Q.B. 425; [1979] 2 W.L.R. 42; [1979] 1 All E.R. 701; (1979) 68 Cr. App. R. 212; (1978) 122 S.J. 697, CA (Civ Div) 12–008, 25–005, 25–007, 26–057

R. v Board of Visitors of Hull Prison Ex p. St Germain (No.2) [1979] 1 W.L.R. 1401; [1979] 3 All E.R. 545; [1979] Crim. L.R. 726; (1979) 123 S.J. 768, QBD 12–014, 12–024, 12–031

R. v Bolsover DC Ex p. Pepper. *See* R. (on the application of Pepper) v Bolsover DC

R. v Bolton (1841) 1 Q.B. 66 .... 14–026, 14–028

R. v Bolton Magistrates Court Ex p. Scally [1991] 1 Q.B. 537; [1991] 2 W.L.R. 239; [1991] 2 All E.R. 619; (1991) 155 J.P. 501; [1991] R.T.R. 84; [1991] Crim. L.R. 550; [1991] C.O.D. 118; (1991) 155 J.P.N. 43; (1990) 134 S.J. 1403, QBD 12–027

R. v Botmeh (Jawad); R. v Alami (Samar) [2001] EWCA Crim 2226; [2002] 1 W.L.R. 531; [2002] 1 Cr. App. R. 28; [2002] H.R.L.R. 13; [2002] Crim. L.R. 209; (2001) 98(46) L.S.G. 35; (2001) 145 S.J.L.B. 255, CA (Crim Div) 28–008

R. v Bouchereau (Pierre Roger) (30/77) [1978] Q.B. 732; [1978] 2 W.L.R. 251; [1981] 2 All E.R. 924; [1977] E.C.R. 1999; (1978) 66 Cr. App. R. 202; [1977] 2 C.M.L.R. 800; (1978) 122 S.J. 79, ECJ 19–020

R. v Boundary Commission for England Ex p. Gateshead BC; R. v Boundary Commission for England Ex p. Foot [1983] Q.B. 600; [1983] 2 W.L.R. 458; [1983] 1 All E.R. 1099; (1983) 127 S.J. 155, CA (Civ Div) 19–004

R. v Bow Street Metropolitan Stipendiary Magistrate Ex p. Pinochet Ugarte (No.2); Sub Nom. Pinochet Ugarte (No.2), Re; R. v Evans Ex p. Pinochet Ugarte (No.2); R. v Bartle Ex p. Pinochet Ugarte (No.2) [2000] 1 A.C. 119; [1999] 2 W.L.R. 272; [1999] 1 All E.R. 577; 6 B.H.R.C. 1; (1999) 11 Admin. L.R. 57; (1999) 96(6) L.S.G. 33; (1999) 149 N.L.J. 88, HL 13–004, 13–007, 13–011

R. v Bowman [1898] 1 Q.B. 663 17–013

R. v Boycott Ex p. Keasley [1939] 2 K.B. 651, KBD 25–005

R. v Bradford on Avon Urban DC Ex p. Boulton; sub nom. R. v Bradford upon Avon Urban DC Ex p. Boulton [1964] 1 W.L.R. 1136; [1964] 2 All E.R. 492; (1964) 128 J.P. 339; 62 L.G.R. 475; (1964) 15 P. & C.R. 304; (1964) 108 S.J. 710, QBD ... 24–003

R. v Brent LBC, Ex p. Gunning (1985) 84 L.G.R. 168, QBD 12–028, 22–017

R. v Bridgnorth DC Ex p. Prime Time Promotions Ltd [1999] C.O.D. 265; [1999] E.H.L.R. Dig. 455, QBD 19–004

R. v Brighton Justices Ex p. Jarvis [1954] 1 W.L.R. 203; [1954] 1 All E.R. 197; (1954) 118 J.P. 117; 52 L.G.R. 148; (1954) 98 S.J. 64, DC 24–003

R. v Bristol City Council Ex p. Bailey (1995) 27 H.L.R. 307; [1995] C.O.D. 347; (1995) 159 L.G. Rev. 221; [1994] E.G. 172 (C.S.), QBD 12–037

R. v Bristol City Council Ex p. Penfold (1997–98) 1 C.C.L. Rep. 315; [1998] C.O.D. 210, QBD 17–014

R. v Bristol Corp Ex p. Hendy [1974] 1 W.L.R. 498; [1974] 1 All E.R. 1047; 72 L.G.R. 405; (1974) 27 P. & C.R. 180, CA (Civ Div) 23–021, 25–016, 25–018, 26–055

R. v Bristol Crown Court Ex p. Cooper [1990] 1 W.L.R. 1031; [1990] 2 All E.R. 193; [1990] C.O.D. 312, CA (Civ Div) 13–005

R. v British Standards Institution Ex p. Dorgard Ltd [2001] A.C.D. 15, QBD 26–029

R. v Brixton Prison Governor Ex p. Ahsan [1969] 2 Q.B. 222; [1969] 2 W.L.R. 618; [1968] 2 All E.R. 347; (1969) 133 J.P. 407; (1968) 112 S.J. 422, DC 23–029

R. v BBC Ex p. Lavelle [1983] 1 W.L.R. 23; [1983] 1 All E.R. 241; [1983] I.C.R. 99; [1982] I.R.L.R. 404; (1983) 133 N.L.J. 133; (1982) 126 S.J.L.B. 836, QBD 23–027, 25–004, 26–004, 26–031

R. v British Coal Corp Ex p. Price (No.3) [1994] I.R.L.R. 72; [1993] C.O.D. 482, DC 12–028, 22–017

R. v Brixton Prison Governor Ex p. Enahoro (No.2) [1963] 2 Q.B. 455; [1963] 2 W.L.R. 1260; [1963] 2 All E.R. 477; (1963) 107 S.J. 357, QBD 16–007

R. v Broadcasting Complaints Commission Ex p. Granada Television Ltd [1995] E.M.L.R. 163; [1995] C.O.D. 207; (1995) 92(7) L.S.G. 36; (1995) 139 S.J.L.B. 48, CA (Civ Div) 17–019

R. v Broadcasting Complaints Commission Ex p. Owen [1985] Q.B. 1153; [1985] 2 W.L.R. 1025; [1985] 2 All E.R. 522, DC 17–012

R. v Buckinghamshire JJ (1843) 3 Q.B. 800 14–026

R. v Burton Ex p. Young [1897] 2 Q.B. 468 13–002

R. v Butt Ex p. Brooke (1922) 38 T.L.R. 537 24–003

R. v Calgary Ex p. Sanderson (1966) 53 D.L.R. 477 12–022

R. v Camborne Justices Ex p. Pearce [1955] 1 Q.B. 41; [1954] 3 W.L.R. 415; [1954] 2 All E.R. 850; (1954) 118 J.P. 488; (1954) 98 S.J. 577, QBD 13–006

R. v Cambridge DHA Ex p. B (No.1) [1995] 1 W.L.R. 898; [1995] 2 All E.R. 129; [1995] 1 F.L.R. 1056; [1995] 2 F.C.R. 485; [1995] 6 Med. L.R. 250; [1995] C.O.D. 407; [1995] Fam. Law 480; (1995) 145 N.L.J. 415, CA (Civ Div) 1–031, 19–001

R. v Camden LBC Ex p. Woolf [1992] C.O.D. 456 27–008

R. v Central Criminal Court Ex p. Boulding [1984] Q.B. 813; [1984] 2 W.L.R. 321;

[1984] 1 All E.R. 766; (1984) 79 Cr. App. R. 100; (1983) 5 Cr. App. R. (S.) 433;
(1984) 148 J.P. 174, QBD 12–030
R. v Central London County Court Ex p. London [1999] Q.B. 1260; [1999] 3 W.L.R. 1;
[1999] 3 All E.R. 991; [2000] C.P. Rep. 75; [1999] 2 F.L.R. 161; (1999) 2 C.C.L.
Rep. 256; [1999] C.O.D. 196; [1999] Fam. Law 452; (1999) 96(15) L.S.G. 30, CA
(Civ Div) 23–012
R. v Ceredigion CC Ex p. McKeown [1998] 2 P.L.R. 1; [1998] P.L.C.R. 90; [1997]
C.O.D. 463, QBD 26–046
R. v Chancellor of the University of Cambridge (1723) 1 Str. 557 .. 12–001, 12–015, 25–014
R. v Chapman Ex p. Arlidge [1918] 2 K.B. 298, KBD 16–005
R. v Cheltenham Commissioners (1841) 1 Q.B. 467 .... 23–026, 27–003
R. v Chertsey JJ Ex p. Franks [1961] 2 Q.B. 152 14–036
R. v Cheshire JJ Ex p. Heaver (1913) 108 L.T. 374 25–016
R. v Chesterfield BC, Ex p. Darker Enterprises [1992] C.O.D. 466 .... 13–003, 13–008
R. v Chichester Justices Ex p. Collins [1982] 1 W.L.R. 334; [1982] 1 All E.R. 1000; (1982)
74 Cr. App. R. 285; (1981) 3 Cr. App. R. (S.) 366; (1982) 126 S.J. 100, DC 12–027
R. v Chief Adjudication Officer Ex p. Bland, *The Times*, February 6, 1985, DC 24–021
R. v Chief Constable of Kent Ex p. Absalom, May 5, 1993 19–009
R. v Chief Constable of Merseyside Ex p. Calveley; sub nom. Calveley v Merseyside
Police [1986] Q.B. 424; [1986] 2 W.L.R. 144; [1986] 1 All E.R. 257; [1986] I.R.L.R.
177, CA (Civ Div) 26–057, 29–008, 29–032
R. v Chief Constable of North Wales Ex p. AB; sub nom. R. v Chief Constable of
North Wales Ex p. Thorpe [1999] Q.B. 396; [1998] 3 W.L.R. 57; [1998] 3 All E.R.
310; [1998] 2 F.L.R. 571; [1998] 3 F.C.R. 371; [1998] Fam. Law 529; (1998) 95(17)
L.S.G. 29, CA (Civ Div) 16–013, 17–019
R. v Chief Constable of Sussex Ex p. International Trader's Ferry Ltd [1999] 2 A.C.
418; [1998] 3 W.L.R. 1260; [1999] 1 All E.R. 129; [1999] 1 C.M.L.R. 1320; (1999)
11 Admin. L.R. 97; (1998) 95(47) L.S.G. 29; (1998) 148 N.L.J. 1750; (1998) 142
S.J.L.B. 286, HL 19–004, 19–012, 20–021
R. v Chief Constable of Thames Valley Ex p. Cotton; sub nom. R. v Deputy Chief
Constable of Thames Valley Ex p. Cotton [1990] I.R.L.R. 344, CA (Civ Div) . 12–024,
26–055
R. v Chief Constable of the West Midlands Ex p. Wiley [1995] 1 A.C. 274; [1994] 3
W.L.R. 433; [1994] 3 All E.R. 420; [1995] 1 Cr. App. R. 342; [1994] C.O.D. 520;
(1994) 91(40) L.S.G. 35; (1994) 144 N.L.J. 1008; (1994) 138 S.J.L.B. 156, HL . 28–007,
28–013
R. v Chief Immigration Officer, Heathrow Airport Ex p. Bibi (Salamat) [1976] 1
W.L.R. 979; [1976] 3 All E.R. 843; (1976) 120 S.J. 405, CA (Civ Div) . 18–002, 22–041
R. v Chief Rabbi of the United Hebrew Congregations of Great Britain and the
Commonwealth Ex p. Wachmann; sub nom. R. v Jacobovits Ex p. Wachmann
[1992] 1 W.L.R. 1036; [1993] 2 All E.R. 249; (1991) 3 Admin. L.R. 721; [1991]
C.O.D. 309, QBD 26–034
R. v Chiswick Police Superintendent Ex p. Sacksteder [1918] 1 K.B. 578, CA 16–007
R. v Churchwardens of All Saints Wigan (1876) 1 App. Cas. 611 25–018
R. v City of London Corp Ex p. Matson [1997] 1 W.L.R. 765; 94 L.G.R. 443; (1996) 8
Admin. L.R. 49; [1996] C.O.D. 161, CA (Civ Div) 12–037
R. v Civil Service Appeal Board Ex p. Bruce [1989] 2 All E.R. 907; [1989] I.C.R. 171,
CA (Civ Div) 5–044, 12–033, 26–027, 26–032
R. v Civil Service Appeal Board Ex p. Cunningham [1991] 4 All E.R. 310; [1992] I.C.R.
817; [1992] I.C.R. 816; [1991] I.R.L.R. 297; [1991] C.O.D. 478; (1991) 141 N.L.J.
455, CA (Civ Div) 12–036, 12–037
R. v Code of Practice Committee of the British Pharmaceutical Industry Ex p. Pro-
fessional Counselling Aids (1991) 3 Admin. L.R. 697; [1991] C.O.D. 228, QBD   26–027
R. v Collins Ex p. MS. *See* S (Application for Judicial Review), Re
R. v Collins Ex p. S. *See* S (Application for Judicial Review), Re
R. v Commission for Racial Equality Ex p. Cottrell and Rothon [1980] 1 W.L.R. 1580;
[1980] 3 All E.R. 265; [1980] I.R.L.R. 279; (1980) 255 E.G. 783; (1980) 124 S.J. 882,
DC 12–031, 12–042
R. v Commissioner of Police of the Metropolis Ex p. Blackburn (No.1) [1968] 2 Q.B.
118; [1968] 2 W.L.R. 893; [1968] 1 All E.R. 763; (1968) 112 S.J. 112, CA (Civ
Div) 16–012, 17–013, 24–005, 25–016

R. v Commissioner of Police of the Metropolis Ex p. Blackburn (No.3); sub nom.
Blackburn Ex p. (No.3) [1967] Crim. L.R. 541, DC 16–012, 25–016
R. v Commissioner of Police of the Metropolis Ex p. Parker [1953] 1 W.L.R. 1150;
[1953] 2 All E.R. 717; (1953) 117 J.P. 440; (1953) 97 S.J. 590, QBD 12–004, 25–006
R. v Commissioners for Special Purposes of Income Tax (1888) 21 Q.B.D. 313 14–028,
24–005
R. v Comptroller-General of Patents and Designs Ex p. Parke Davis & Co. *See* Parke
Davis & Co v Comptroller-General of Patents, Designs and Trade Marks
R. v Cornwall CC Ex p. Huntington [1994] 1 All E.R. 694, CA (Civ Div) 27–008
R. v Coventry City Council Ex p. Phoenix Aviation; sub nom. R. v Coventry Airport
Ex p. Phoenix Aviation [1995] 3 All E.R. 37; [1995] C.L.C. 757; (1995) 7 Admin.
L.R. 597; [1995] C.O.D. 300; (1995) 145 N.L.J. 559, DC 24–027
R. v Criminal Injuries Compensation Board Ex p. A [1999] 2 A.C. 330; [1999] 2 W.L.R.
974; [1999] C.O.D. 244; (1999) 96(17) L.S.G. 25; (1999) 149 N.L.J. 522; (1999) 143
S.J.L.B. 120, HL 15–003, 15–017, 26–046
R. v Criminal Injuries Compensation Board Ex p. Clowes [1977] 1 W.L.R. 1353; [1977]
3 All E.R. 854; (1977) 65 Cr. App. R. 289; [1977] Crim. L.R. 419; (1977) 121 S.J.
391, DC 25–015
R. v Criminal Injuries Compensation Board Ex p. Cobb [1995] P.I.Q.R. P90; [1995]
C.O.D. 126, QBD 12–037
R. v Criminal Injuries Compensation Board Ex p. Ince [1973] 1 W.L.R. 1334; [1973] 3
All E.R. 808; [1973] Crim. L.R. 624; (1973) 117 S.J. 616, CA (Civ Div) 16–015
R. v Criminal Injuries Compensation Board Ex p. Keane and Marsden [1998] C.O.D.
128 20–043
R. v Criminal Injuries Compensation Board Ex p. Lain [1967] 2 Q.B. 864; [1967] 3
W.L.R. 348; [1967] 2 All E.R. 770; (1967) 111 S.J. 331, QBD ... 2–005, 25–004, 29–006
R. v Criminal Injuries Compensation Board Ex p. Milton [1997] P.I.Q.R. P74; [1996]
C.O.D. 264, QBD 9–026
R. v Criminal Injuries Compensation Board Ex p. Pearce [1994] C.O.D. 235, QBD .. 9–026
R. v Criminal Injuries Compensation Board Ex p. Schofield [1971] 1 W.L.R. 926; [1971]
2 All E.R. 1011; (1971) 115 S.J. 367, DC 22–046, 29–066
R. v Criminal Injuries Compensation Board Ex p. Thompstone [1984] 1 W.L.R. 1234;
[1984] 3 All E.R. 572; (1984) 81 L.S.G. 3012; (1984) 128 S.J. 768, CA (Civ Div) 22–046
R. v Customs and Excise Commissioners Ex p. Cook; sub nom. R. v Customs and
Excise Commissioners Ex p. Cooke and Stevenson [1970] 1 W.L.R. 450; [1970] 1
All E.R. 1068; (1969) 114 S.J. 34, DC 24–005, 28–017
R. v Customs and Excise Commissioners Ex p. Eurotunnel Plc [1995] C.L.C. 392; [1995]
C.O.D. 291, DC 26–046
R. v Customs and Excise Commissioners Ex p. Tsahl [1990] C.O.D. 230, QBD 12–036
R. v DPP Ex p. Camelot Group Plc (No.2) (1998) 10 Admin. L.R. 93; [1998] C.O.D. 54;
(1998) 162 J.P.N. 67, QBD 26–057
R. v DPP Ex p. Merton LBC (No.2) [1999] C.O.D. 358, QBD 25–025
R. v DPP Ex p. Kebilene; sub nom. R. v DPP Ex p. Kebelene [2000] 2 A.C. 326; [1999]
3 W.L.R. 972; [1999] 4 All E.R. 801; [2000] 1 Cr. App. R. 275; [2000] H.R.L.R. 93;
[2000] U.K.H.R.R. 176; (2000) 2 L.G.L.R. 697; (1999) 11 Admin. L.R. 1026;
[2000] Crim. L.R. 486; (1999) 96(43) L.S.G. 32, HL 18–035
R. v Dacorum BC Ex p. Walsh (1992) 24 H.L.R. 401; [1992] C.O.D. 125, QBD 20–029
R. v Dairy Produce Quota Tribunal for England and Wales Ex p. Caswell [1990] 2 A.C.
738; [1990] 2 W.L.R. 1320; [1990] 2 All E.R. 434; (1990) 2 Admin. L.R. 765; [1990]
C.O.D. 243; (1990) 140 N.L.J. 742, HL 26–046
R. v Dairy Produce Quota Tribunal for England and Wales Ex p. PA Cooper & Sons
[1993] 19 E.G. 138; [1993] C.O.D. 276; [1993] E.G. 10 (C.S.), QBD 12–037
R. v Darlington School Governors (1844) 6 Q.B. 682 12–015
R. v Darlington BC and Darlington Transport Company Ltd Ex p. Association of
Darlington Taxi Owners and the Darlington Owner Drivers Association [1994]
C.O.D. 424 24–023
R. v Davey [1899] 2 Q.B. 301 23–004
R. v Dayman (1857) 7 El. & Bl. 672 25–016
R. v Denton (Clive) [2001] 1 Cr. App. R. 16; [2001] Crim. L.R. 225, CA (Crim Div) 12–033
R. v Deputy Governor of Parkhurst Prison Ex p. Hague; sub nom. Hague v Deputy
Governor of Parkhurst Prison [1992] 1 A.C. 58; [1991] 3 W.L.R. 340; [1991] 3 All

E.R. 733; (1993) 5 Admin. L.R. 425; [1992] C.O.D. 69; (1991) 135 S.J.L.B. 102,
HL 29–021
R. v Deputy Governor of Parkhurst Prison Ex p. Leech; sub nom. Leech v Deputy
Governor of Parkhurst Prison [1988] A.C. 533; [1988] 2 W.L.R. 290; [1988] 1 All
E.R. 485; (1988) 85(11) L.S.G. 42; (1988) 138 N.L.J. Rep. 38; (1988) 132 S.J. 191,
HL 12–014, 26–057
R. v Deputy Industrial Injuries Commissioner Ex p. Jones [1962] 2 Q.B. 677; [1962] 2
W.L.R. 1215; [1962] 2 All E.R. 430; (1962) 106 S.J. 311, DC 12–027
R. v Deputy Industrial Injuries Commissioner Ex p. Moore [1965] 1 Q.B. 456; [1965] 2
W.L.R. 89; [1965] 1 All E.R. 81; (1964) 108 S.J. 1030, CA 9–024, 12–030, 15–011
R. v Derbyshire CC Ex p. Noble [1990] I.C.R. 808; [1990] I.R.L.R. 332, CA (Civ Div)   26–031
R. v Devon CC Ex p. Baker [1995] 1 All E.R. 73; 91 L.G.R. 479; (1994) 6 Admin. L.R.
113; [1993] C.O.D. 253, CA (Civ Div) 12–012, 12–017, 16–015, 20–018, 26–057
R. v Diggines Ex p. Rahmani; sub nom. R. v Immigration Appeal Adjudicator Ex p.
Rahmani; R. v Immigration Appeal Tribunal Ex p. Rahmani; Rahmani v Diggines
[1986] A.C. 475; [1986] 2 W.L.R. 530; [1986] 1 All E.R. 921; [1986] Imm. A.R. 195,
HL 12–027
R. v Director of the Serious Fraud Office Ex p. Johnson (Malcolm Keith) [1993] C.O.D.
58 24–020
R. v Disciplinary Committee of the Jockey Club Ex p. Aga Khan [1993] 1 W.L.R. 909;
[1993] 2 All E.R. 853; [1993] C.O.D. 234; (1993) 143 N.L.J. 163, CA (Civ Div) .   26–016,
                                                                        26–029, 26–037
R. v Disciplinary Committee of the Jockey Club Ex p. Massingberd-Mundy [1993] 2 All
E.R. 207; (1990) 2 Admin. L.R. 609; [1990] C.O.D. 260, DC 26–028
R. v Dorking Justices Ex p. Harrington. *See* Harrington, Re
R. v Doutre (1883–84) L.R. 9 App. Cas. 745, PC (Can) 5–045
R. v Dyfed CC Ex p. Manson [1995] Env. L.R. 83; [1994] C.O.D. 366; [1994] N.P.C. 27,
QBD 24–021
R. v East Berkshire HA Ex p. Walsh [1985] Q.B. 152; [1984] 3 W.L.R. 818; [1984] 3 All
E.R. 425; [1984] I.C.R. 743; [1984] I.R.L.R. 278, CA (Civ Div) 12–015,
                                                                        26–016, 26–019
R. v East Sussex CC Ex p. Reprotech (Pebsham) Ltd. *See* R. (on the application of
Reprotech (Pebsham) Ltd) v East Sussex CC
R. v East Sussex CC Ex p. Tandy; sub nom. T (A Minor), Re [1998] A.C. 714; [1998] 2
W.L.R. 884; [1998] 2 All E.R. 769; [1998] 2 F.C.R. 221; (1998) 10 Admin. L.R. 453;
[1998] Ed. C.R. 206; [1998] E.L.R. 251; (1997–98) 1 C.C.L. Rep. 352; (1998) 42
B.M.L.R. 173; (1998) 95(24) L.S.G. 33; (1998) 148 N.L.J. 781; (1998) 142 S.J.L.B.
179, HL 17–014
R. v Eastleigh BC Ex p. Betts; sub nom. Eastleigh BC v Betts; Betts, Re [1983] 2 A.C.
613; [1983] 3 W.L.R. 397; [1983] 2 All E.R. 1111; (1983) 10 H.L.R. 94; [1984] Fam.
Law 25; (1983) 133 N.L.J. 893; (1983) 127 S.J. 537, HL 16–013
R. v Electricity Commissioners Ex p. London Electricity Joint Committee Co (1920)
Ltd; sub nom. R. v Electricity Commissioners [1924] 1 K.B. 171, CA ..   12–005, 25–003
R. v Enfield LBC Ex p. TF Unwin (Roydon) 46 B.L.R. 1; (1989) 1 Admin. L.R. 51;
[1989] C.O.D. 466; (1989) 153 L.G. Rev. 890, DC 26–025
R. v Epping and Harlow General Commissioners Ex p. Goldstraw [1983] 3 All E.R.
257; [1983] S.T.C. 697; 57 T.C. 536, CA (Civ Div) 26–057
R. v Epping Forest DC Ex p. Green [1993] C.O.D. 81, CA (Civ Div) 26–057
R. v Essex Justices Ex p. Perkins [1927] 2 K.B. 475; (1927) 96 L.J. K.B. 530, KBD .   13–011
R. v Falmouth and Truro Port HA Ex p. South West Water Ltd; sub nom. Falmouth
and Truro Port HA v South West Water Ltd [2001] Q.B. 445; [2000] 3 W.L.R.
1464; [2000] 3 All E.R. 306; [2000] Env. L.R. 658; [2000] E.H.L.R. 306; (2000) 2
L.G.L.R. 1061; [2000] J.P.L. 1174 (Note); [2000] E.G. 50 (C.S.); (2000) 97(23)
L.S.G. 41; [2000] N.P.C. 36, CA (Civ Div) 12–016, 16–015, 22–018, 26–057
R. v Felixstowe Justices Ex p. Leigh [1987] Q.B. 582; [1987] 2 W.L.R. 380; [1987] 1 All
E.R. 551; (1987) 84 Cr. App. R. 327; (1987) 151 J.P. 65; [1987] Crim. L.R. 125;
(1987) 151 J.P.N. 31; (1987) 84 L.S.G. 901; (1986) 136 N.L.J. 988; (1986) 130 S.J.
767, QBD 24–019
R. v Financial Intermediaries Managers and Brokers Regulatory Association Ex p.
Cochrane [1991] B.C.L.C. 106; [1990] C.O.D. 33, DC 26–027
R. v Flintshire County Council Licensing (Stage Plays) Committee Ex p. Barrett [1957]
1 Q.B. 350 16–012

R. v Football Association Ex p. Football League; sub nom. Football Association v
  Football League [1993] 2 All E.R. 833; (1992) 4 Admin. L.R. 623; [1992] C.O.D.
  52, QBD 26–029
R. v Football Association of Wales Ex p. Flint Town United Football Club [1991]
  C.O.D. 44, DC 26–029
R. v Frankland Prison Board of Visitors Ex p. Lewis [1986] 1 W.L.R. 130; [1986] 1 All
  E.R. 272; [1986] Crim. L.R. 336; (1986) 83 L.S.G. 125; (1986) 130 S.J. 52, QBD . 13–004
R. v Fulham, Hammersmith and Kensington Rent Tribunal Ex p. Hierowski [1953] 2
  Q.B. 147; [1953] 2 W.L.R. 1028; [1953] 2 All E.R. 4; (1953) 117 J.P. 295; 51 L.G.R.
  363; (1953) 97 S.J. 335, DC 14–029
R. v Fulham, Hammersmith and Kensington Rent Tribunal Ex p. Zerek [1951] 2 K.B.
  1; [1951] 1 All E.R. 482; [1951] 1 T.L.R. 423; (1951) 115 J.P. 132; 49 L.G.R. 275;
  (1951) 95 S.J. 237, QBD 14–029
R. v Gaisford [1892] 1 Q.B. 381, QBD 13–002, 13–004
R. v Gaming Board for Great Britain Ex p. Benaim [1970] 2 Q.B. 417; [1970] 2 W.L.R.
  1009; [1970] 2 All E.R. 528; (1970) 114 S.J. 266, CA (Civ Div) 12–012, 25–005
R. v Gaming Board for Great Britain Ex p. Kingsley (No.2) [1996] C.O.D. 241,
  QBD 20–013, 20–017
R. v General Council of the Bar Ex p. Percival [1991] 1 Q.B. 212; [1990] 3 W.L.R. 323;
  [1990] 3 All E.R. 137; (1990) 2 Admin. L.R. 711; (1990) 87(24) L.S.G. 44, DC . 24–019
R. v Gloucestershire CC Ex p. Barry; sub nom. R. v Gloucestershire CC Ex p. Mah-
  food [1997] A.C. 584; [1997] 2 W.L.R. 459; [1997] 2 All E.R. 1; (1997) 9 Admin.
  L.R. 209; (1997–98) 1 C.C.L. Rep. 40; (1997) 36 B.M.L.R. 92; [1997] C.O.D. 304;
  (1997) 94(14) L.S.G. 25; (1997) 147 N.L.J. 453; (1997) 141 S.J.L.B. 91, HL 17–013
R. v Gough (Robert) [1993] A.C. 646; [1993] 2 W.L.R. 883; [1993] 2 All E.R. 724;
  (1993) 97 Cr. App. R. 188; (1993) 157 J.P. 612; [1993] Crim. L.R. 886; (1993) 157
  J.P.N. 394; (1993) 143 N.L.J. 775; (1993) 137 S.J.L.B. 168, HL 13–007
R. v Governor of Blundeston Prison Ex p. Gaffney; sub nom. R. v Home Office Ex p.
  Gaffney [1982] 1 W.L.R. 696; [1982] 2 All E.R. 492; (1982) 75 Cr. App. R. 42;
  [1982] Crim. L.R. 519; (1982) 126 S.J. 330, DC 25–004
R. v Governor of Brixton Prison Ex p. Armah (No.1). *See* Armah v Ghana (No.1)
R. v Governor of Brixton Prison Ex p. Soblen (No.2) [1963] 2 Q.B. 243, CA 17–010,
                                                                                      17–012
R. v Governor of Brockhill Prison Ex p. Evans (No.2); sub nom. Evans v Governor of
  Brockhill Prison [2001] 2 A.C. 19; [2000] 3 W.L.R. 843; [2000] 4 All E.R. 15; [2000]
  U.K.H.R.R. 836; [2000] Prison L.R. 160; [2000] Po. L.R. 290; (2000) 97(32) L.S.G.
  38; (2000) 144 S.J.L.B. 241, HL 23–012
R. v Governor of Pentonville Prison Ex p. Herbage; sub nom. R. v Secretary of State
  for the Home Department Ex p. Herbage (No.1) [1987] Q.B. 872; [1986] 3 W.L.R.
  504; [1986] 3 All E.R. 209; (1986) 83 L.S.G. 2750; (1986) 130 S.J. 697, QBD ... 28–019
R. v Governor of Pentonville Prison Ex p. Osman (No.1); sub nom .Osman (No.1), Re
  [1990] 1 W.L.R. 277; [1989] 3 All E.R. 701; (1990) 90 Cr. App. R. 281; [1988] Crim.
  L.R. 611; (1990) 87(7) L.S.G. 32; (1990) 134 S.J. 458, QBD 25–038
R. v Governor of Pentonville Prison Ex p. Osman (No.3) [1990] 1 W.L.R. 878; [1990] 1
  All E.R. 999; (1990) 91 Cr. App. R. 409; [1990] C.O.D. 92, DC 25–038
R. v Governor of Risley Remand Centre Ex p. Hassan; sub nom. Hassan (Wajid), Re
  [1976] 1 W.L.R. 971; [1976] 2 All E.R. 123; (1976) 120 S.J. 333, DC 23–029
R. v Governors of Haberdashers Aske's Hatcham College Trust Ex p. Tyrell; sub nom.
  R. v Governors of Haberdashers Aske's Hatcham College Trust Ex p. T [1995]
  C.O.D. 399, QBD 26–027
R. v Grays Justices Ex p. Graham [1982] Q.B. 1239; [1982] 3 W.L.R. 596; [1982] 3 All
  E.R. 653; (1982) 75 Cr. App. R. 229; [1982] Crim. L.R. 594; (1982) 79 L.S.G. 920;
  (1982) 126 S.J. 447, QBD 12–027
R. v Great Northern Ry, (1883) 11 Q.B.D. 30 25–037
R. v Greater London Council Ex p. Blackburn [1976] 1 W.L.R. 550; [1976] 3 All E.R.
  184; 74 L.G.R. 464; (1976) 120 S.J. 421, CA (Civ Div) 16–003, 24–007
R. v Greenwich LBC Ex p. Lovelace [1991] 1 W.L.R. 506; [1991] 3 All E.R. 511; 89
  L.G.R. 549; (1991) 3 Admin. L.R. 525; (1991) 155 L.G. Rev. 386; (1991) 135 S.J.
  184, CA (Civ Div) 17–012
R. v H [2003] 1 W.L.R. 3006 28–008
R. v H [2004] 2 A.C. 134 28–008

R. v HM Coroner for Greater Manchester Ex p. Tal [1985] Q.B. 67; [1984] 3 W.L.R. 643; [1984] 3 All E.R. 240; [1984] Crim. L.R. 557; (1984) 128 S.J. 500, QBD ... 14–033

R. v HM Coroner for Inner London West District Ex p. Dallaglio; R. v HM Coroner for Inner London West District Ex p. Lockwood-Croft [1994] 4 All E.R. 139; (1995) 159 J.P. 133; (1995) 7 Admin. L.R. 256; [1995] C.O.D. 20, CA (Civ Div) 13–007

R. v HM Inspectorate of Pollution Ex p. Chapman [1996] C.O.D. 154; [1996] Env. L.R. D31, QBD 25–026

R. v HM Treasury Ex p. British Telecommunications Plc [1994] 1 C.M.L.R. 621; [1995] C.O.D. 56, CA (Civ Div) 25–034

R. v HM Treasury Ex p. British Telecommunications Plc (C-392/93) [1996] Q.B. 615; [1996] 3 W.L.R. 203; [1996] All E.R. (EC) 411; [1996] E.C.R. I-1631; [1996] 2 C.M.L.R. 217; [1996] C.E.C. 381; [1996] I.R.L.R. 300; (1996) 93(32) L.S.G. 33, ECJ 29–058

R. v HM Treasury Ex p. Smedley; sub nom. R. v Economic Secretary to the Treasury Ex p. Smedley [1985] Q.B. 657; [1985] 2 W.L.R. 576; [1985] 1 All E.R. 589; [1985] 1 C.M.L.R. 665; [1985] F.L.R. 180; (1985) 82 L.S.G. 761; (1985) 129 S.J. 48, CA (Civ Div) 22–028, 24–019

R. v Halliday [1917] A.C. 260, HL 22–025

R. v Hammersmith and Fulham LBC Ex p. Beddowes [1987] Q.B. 1050; [1987] 2 W.L.R. 263; [1987] 1 All E.R. 369; (1986) 18 H.L.R. 458; 85 L.G.R. 270; [1987] R.V.R. 189; (1986) 83 L.S.G. 3001; (1986) 130 S.J. 696, CA (Civ Div) 16–028

R. v Hammersmith and Fulham LBC Ex p. Burkett. *See* R. (on the application of Burkett) v Hammersmith and Fulham LBC (No.1)

R. v Hammond (1863) 9 L.T. (N.S.) 423 13–002

R. v Hampstead Borough Council Ex p. Woodward (1917) 116 L.T. 213 ... 23–021, 25–018

R. v Hanley Revising Barrister [1912] 3 K.B. 518, KBD 25–017

R. v Haringey LBC Ex p. Secretary of State for the Environment [1990] R.V.R. 261; [1991] C.O.D. 135, DC 24–019

R. v Harrow Crown Court Ex p. Dave [1994] 1 W.L.R. 98; [1994] 1 All E.R. 315; (1994) 99 Cr. App. R. 114; (1994) 158 J.P. 250; [1994] Crim. L.R. 346; (1993) 143 N.L.J. 1676, DC 12–033

R. v Head Teacher of Fairfield Primary School Ex p. W [1998] C.O.D. 106, QBD .. 25–026

R. v Hendon Rural District Council Ex p. Chorley [1933] 2 K.B. 696 .... 13–003, 25–006

R. v Hendon Justices Ex p. DPP [1994] Q.B. 167; [1993] 2 W.L.R. 862; [1993] 1 All E.R. 411; (1993) 96 Cr. App. R. 227; (1993) 157 J.P. 181; [1993] Crim. L.R. 215; [1993] C.O.D. 61; (1992) 156 J.P.N. 746; (1992) 142 N.L.J. 1303, QBD 23–009

R. v Hereford Corp Ex p. Harrower [1970] 1 W.L.R. 1424; [1970] 3 All E.R. 460; 69 L.G.R. 28; (1970) 114 S.J. 705, DC 24–005

R. v Hereford Magistrates Court Ex p. Rowlands [1998] Q.B. 110; [1997] 2 W.L.R. 854; [1997] 2 Cr. App. R. 340; (1997) 161 J.P. 258; (1997) 9 Admin. L.R. 186; [1997] C.O.D. 236; (1997) 161 J.P. Rep. 308, QBD 26–057

R. v Herrod Ex p. Leeds City Council [1976] Q.B. 540 23–021

R. v Hertfordshire JJ (1845) 6 Q.B. 753 23–026

R. v Hide (1647) Style 60 .... 25–002, 25–006

R. v Highbury Corner Magistrates Court Ex p. Uchendu (Sentencing) [1994] R.A. 51; (1994) 158 L.G. Rev. 481, QBD 19–010

R. v Higher Education Funding Council Ex p. Institute of Dental Surgery [1994] 1 W.L.R. 242; [1994] 1 All E.R. 651; [1994] C.O.D. 147, DC 12–037, 12–038

R. v Hillingdon LBC Ex p. Puhlhofer; sub nom. Puhlhofer v Hillingdon LBC [1986] A.C. 484; [1986] 2 W.L.R. 259; [1986] 1 All E.R. 467; [1986] 1 F.L.R. 22; (1986) 18 H.L.R. 158; [1986] Fam. Law 218; (1986) 83 L.S.G. 785; (1986) 136 N.L.J. 140; (1986) 130 S.J. 143, HL 19–029

R. v Hillingdon LBC Ex p. Royco Homes Ltd [1974] Q.B. 720; [1974] 2 W.L.R. 805; [1974] 2 All E.R. 643; 72 L.G.R. 516; (1974) 28 P. & C.R. 251; (1974) 118 S.J. 389, QBD 19–004, 25–006, 26–057

R. v Horsham DC Ex p. Wenman [1995] 1 W.L.R. 680; [1994] 4 All E.R. 681; (1995) 7 Admin. L.R. 73; [1992] C.O.D. 427; (1995) 159 L.G. Rev. 365; (1993) 143 N.L.J. 1477; [1993] N.P.C. 129, QBD 25–017

R. v Hounslow LBC Ex p. Pizzey [1977] 1 W.L.R. 58; [1977] 1 All E.R. 305; 75 L.G.R. 168; [1977] J.P.L. 29; (1976) 120 S.J. 857, DC 26–057

R. v Housing Appeal Tribunal [1920] 3 K.B. 334 12–030

R. v Hull University Visitor Ex p. Page; R. v Visitor of the University of Hull Ex p.

Page [1993] A.C. 682; [1993] 3 W.L.R. 1112; [1993] 1 All E.R. 97; [1993] I.C.R. 114;
(1993) 143 N.L.J. 15; (1993) 137 S.J.L.B. 45, HL 14–020, 14–033
R. v Hunt (1856) 6 El. & Bl. 409 27–002
R. v Huntingdon Confirming Authority Ex p. George and Stanford Hotels Ltd [1929] 1
K.B. 698 23–025
R. v Hutchings [1881] 6 Q.B.D. 300 20–030
R. v Hyde [1912] 1 K.B. 645 17–013
R. v ITC Ex p. T.VNi Ltd and TVS Ltd, *The Times*, December 30, 1991 26–046
R. v Imam of Bury Park Mosque, Luton Ex p. Ali (Sulaiman); sub nom. Ali (Sulaiman)
v Imam of Bury Park Mosque, Luton [1994] C.O.D. 142, CA (Civ Div) 26–034
R. v Immigration Appeal Tribunal Ex p. Joyles [1972] 1 W.L.R. 1390; [1972] 3 All E.R.
213; (1972) 116 S.J. 823, DC 22–008
R. v Immigration Appeals Adjudicator Ex p. Khan [1972] 1 W.L.R. 1058; [1972] 3 All
E.R. 297; (1972) 116 S.J. 600, DC 17–012
R. v Immigration Appeal Tribunal Ex p. Khan (Mahmud) [1983] Q.B. 790; [1983] 2
W.L.R. 759; [1983] 2 All E.R. 420; [1982] Imm. A.R. 134, CA (Civ Div) 12–036
R. v Immigration Appeal Tribunal Ex p. Singh (Bakhtaur) [1986] 1 W.L.R. 910; [1986]
2 All E.R. 721; [1986] Imm. A.R. 352; (1986) 83 L.S.G. 2488; (1986) 130 S.J. 525,
HL 22–041
R. v Independent Television Commission Ex p. Flextech Plc [1999] E.M.L.R. 880;
[1999] C.O.D. 108, QBD 20–017
R. v Independent Television Commission Ex p. TSW Broadcasting Ltd [1996]
E.M.L.R. 291, HL 14–033
R. v Industrial Court Ex p. ASSET [1965] 1 Q.B. 377; [1964] 3 W.L.R. 680; [1964] 3 All
E.R. 130; (1964) 108 S.J. 691, QBD 24–005, 25–015
R. v Industrial Injuries Commissioner Ex p. Amalgamated Engineering Union (No.2)
[1966] 2 Q.B. 31; [1966] 2 W.L.R. 97; [1966] 1 All E.R. 97; (1965) 109 S.J. 934,
CA 14–031
R. v Inhabitants of Leake 110 E.R. 863; (1833) 5 B. & Ad. 469, KB 16–023
R. v Inland Revenue Commissioners Ex p. Bishopp; sub nom. Inland Revenue Com-
missioners v Pricewaterhouse Coopers; Inland Revenue Commissioners v Ernst &
Young [1999] S.T.C. 531; (1999) 11 Admin. L.R. 575; 72 T.C. 322; [1999] B.T.C.
158; [1999] C.O.D. 354; (1999) 149 N.L.J. 682; [1999] N.P.C. 50, QBD 25–025
R. v Inland Revenue Commissioners Ex p. MFK Underwriting Agents Ltd; sub nom.
R. v Inland Revenue Commissioners Ex p. MFK Underwriting Agencies [1990] 1
W.L.R. 1545; [1990] 1 All E.R. 91; [1990] S.T.C. 873; 62 T.C. 607; [1990] C.O.D.
143; (1989) 139 N.L.J. 1343, QBD 20–014, 20–017, 20–041, 20–043, 20–048
R. v Inland Revenue Commissioners Ex p. Matrix Securities Ltd; sub nom. Matrix
Securities Ltd v Inland Revenue Commissioners [1994] 1 W.L.R. 334; [1994] 1 All
E.R. 769; [1994] S.T.C. 272; 66 T.C. 629, HL 20–014, 20–017
R. v Inland Revenue Commissioners Ex p. National Federation of Self Employed and
Small Businesses Ltd; sub nom. Inland Revenue Commissioners v National Fed-
eration of Self Employed and Small Businesses Ltd [1982] A.C. 617; [1981] 2
W.L.R. 722; [1981] 2 All E.R. 93; [1981] S.T.C. 260; 55 T.C. 133; (1981) 125 S.J.
325, HL 24–011, 26–004
R. v Inland Revenue Commissioners Ex p. Preston; sub nom. Preston v Inland Revenue
Commissioners [1985] A.C. 835; [1985] 2 W.L.R. 836; [1985] 2 All E.R. 327; [1985]
S.T.C. 282; 59 T.C. 1, HL 15–007, 19–006, 20–014, 26–056, 26–057
R. v Inland Revenue Commissioners Ex p. Rossminster Ltd; sub nom. Inland Revenue
Commissioners v Rossminster Ltd; Rossminster and Tucker, Re [1980] A.C. 952;
[1980] 2 W.L.R. 1; [1980] 1 All E.R. 80; [1980] S.T.C. 42; (1980) 70 Cr. App. R.
157; [1979] T.R. 427, HL 23–028, 25–030, 26–006, 28–013, 28–021
R. v Inland Revenue Commissioners Ex p. Taylor (No.1) [1989] 1 All E.R. 906; [1988]
S.T.C. 832; 62 T.C. 562; [1988] B.T.C. 451, CA (Civ Div) 26–006
R. v Inland Revenue Commissioners Ex p. Unilever Plc [1996] S.T.C. 681; 68 T.C. 205;
[1996] C.O.D. 421, CA (Civ Div) 20–013
R. v Inland Revenue Commissioners Ex p. Woolwich Equitable Building Society [1990]
1 W.L.R. 1400; [1991] 4 All E.R. 92; [1990] S.T.C. 682; 63 T.C. 589; (1990) 134 S.J.
1404, HL 29–051
R. v Inner London Education Authority Ex p. Ali (1990) 2 Admin. L.R. 822; [1990]
C.O.D. 317; (1990) 154 L.G. Rev. 852, QBD 25–018
R. v Inner London Education Authority Ex p. Westminster City Council [1986] 1

W.L.R. 28; [1986] 1 All E.R. 19; 84 L.G.R. 120; (1986) 83 L.S.G. 359; (1986) 130
S.J. 51, QBD 17–012
R. v Inner South London Coroner Ex p. Douglas-Williams [1999] 1 All E.R. 344 .. 14–035
R. v Inspectorate of Pollution Ex p. Greenpeace Ltd (No.2) [1994] 4 All E.R. 329;
[1994] 2 C.M.L.R. 548; [1994] Env. L.R. 76; [1994] C.O.D. 116; [1993] N.P.C. 126,
QBD 24–022
R. v Insurance Ombudsman Bureau Ex p. Aegon Life Assurance Ltd [1995] L.R.L.R.
101; [1994] C.L.C. 88; [1994] C.O.D. 426, DC 26–029
R. v International Stock Exchange of the United Kingdom and the Republic of Ireland
Ltd Ex p. Else (1982) Ltd [1993] Q.B. 534; [1993] 2 W.L.R. 70; [1993] 1 All E.R.
420; [1993] B.C.C. 11; [1993] B.C.L.C. 834; [1993] 2 C.M.L.R. 677; (1994) 6
Admin. L.R. 67; [1993] C.O.D. 236, CA (Civ Div) 19–009, 24–019
R. v Intervention Board for Agricultural Produce Ex p. ED&F Man (Sugar) Ltd (181/
84) [1986] 2 All E.R. 115; [1985] E.C.R. 2889; [1985] 3 C.M.L.R. 759, ECJ (5th
Chamber) 19–021
R. v Jockey Club Ex p. RAM Racecourses Ltd [1993] 2 All E.R. 225; (1991) 5 Admin.
L.R. 265; [1990] C.O.D. 346, QBD 20–017, 26–028
R. v Judge Amphlett [1915] 2 K.B. 223, KBD 12–030
R. v Jukes (1800) 8 T.R. 542 27–002
R. v Justices of the Central Criminal Court (1886) 17 Q.B.D. 598 14–026
R. v Justices of Cheshire (1838) 8 Ad. & E. 398 14–026
R. v Kansal (Yash Pal) (Change of Law); sub nom. R. v Kansal (Yash Pal) (No.2) [2001]
UKHL 62; [2002] 2 A.C. 69; [2001] 3 W.L.R. 1562; [2002] 1 All E.R. 257; [2002] 1
Cr. App. R. 36; [2002] H.R.L.R. 9; [2002] U.K.H.R.R. 169; [2002] B.P.I.R. 370;
[2002] Crim. L.R. 498; (2002) 99(3) L.S.G. 25; (2001) 145 S.J.L.B. 275, HL 18–003,
18–015
R. v Kensington and Chelsea RLBC Ex p. Birdwood 74 L.G.R. 424; [1976] J.P.L. 232,
DC 25–016
R. v Kensington and Chelsea RLBC Ex p. Grillo (1996) 28 H.L.R. 94; [1995] N.P.C. 85,
CA (Civ Div) 12–037
R. v Kensington and Chelsea RLBC Ex p. Hammell; sub nom. Hammell v Kensington
and Chelsea RLBC [1989] Q.B. 518; (1988) 20 H.L.R. 666, CA (Civ Div) 25–033
R. v Kent Police Authority Ex p. Godden; sub nom. Godden, Re [1971] 2 Q.B. 662;
[1971] 3 W.L.R. 416; [1971] 3 All E.R. 20; 69 L.G.R. 533; (1971) 115 S.J. 640, CA
(Civ Div) 12–027, 13–004, 25–005
R. v Kerrier DC Ex p. Guppys (Bridport) Ltd 76 L.G.R. 129; (1976) 32 P. & C.R. 411;
(1976) 242 E.G. 955; [1976] J.P.L. 695; (1976) 120 S.J. 646, CA (Civ Div) 25–018
R. v Kirk (Kent) (C-63/83) [1985] 1 All E.R. 453; [1984] E.C.R. 2689; [1984] 3 C.M.L.R.
522, ECJ 18–055
R. v Knightsbridge Crown Court Ex p. International Sporting Club (London) [1982] Q.B.
304; [1981] 3 W.L.R. 640; [1981] 3 All E.R. 417; (1981) 125 S.J. 589, QBD 12–036,
14–036, 25–010
R. v Knightsbridge Crown Court Ex p. Marcrest Properties; sub nom. R. v Gaming
Board of Great Britain Ex p. Marcrest Properties [1983] 1 W.L.R. 300; [1983] 1 All
E.R. 1148; (1983) 127 S.J. 87, CA (Civ Div) 25–010
R. v Lambert (Steven) [2001] UKHL 37; [2002] 2 A.C. 545; [2001] 3 W.L.R. 206; [2001]
3 All E.R. 577; [2002] 1 All E.R. 2; [2001] 2 Cr. App. R. 28; [2001] H.R.L.R. 55;
[2001] U.K.H.R.R. 1074; [2001] Crim. L.R. 806; (2001) 98(33) L.S.G. 29; (2001)
145 S.J.L.B. 174, HL 18–003, 18–007
R. v Lambeth LBC Ex p. Ghous [1993] C.O.D. 302 16–014
R. v Lancashire CC Ex p. Guyer; sub nom. Guyer's Application, Re [1980] 1 W.L.R.
1024; [1980] 2 All E.R. 520; 78 L.G.R. 454; (1980) 40 P. & C.R. 376; [1980] J.P.L.
736; (1980) 124 S.J. 375, CA (Civ Div) 25–018
R. v LAUTRO Ex p. Tee; sub nom. R. v Life Assurance and Unit Trust Regulatory
Organisation Ltd Ex p. Tee (1995) 7 Admin. L.R. 28, CA (Civ Div) 24–020
R. v Lee Ex p. Shaw [1882] 9 Q.B.D. 394 13–004
R. v Leeds City Council Ex p. Cobleigh [1997] C.O.D. 69, QBD 26–025
R. v Leeds Crown Court Ex p. Hunt [1999] 1 W.L.R. 841 25–038
R. v Legal Aid Area No.8 (Northern) Appeal Committee Ex p. Angel [1990] COD
355 12–034
R. v Legal Aid Board Ex p. Bateman [1992] 1 W.L.R. 711; [1992] 3 All E.R. 490; (1992)

4 Admin. L.R. 692; [1992] C.O.D. 388; (1992) 142 N.L.J. 347; (1992) 136 S.J.L.B.
98, DC 24–020
R. v Legal Aid Board Ex p. Donn & Co [1996] 3 All E.R. 1, QBD 26–025
R. v Legal Aid Board Ex p. Hughes (1992) 24 H.L.R. 698; (1992) 142 N.L.J. 1304, CA
(Civ Div) 26–040
R. v Legislative Committee of the Church Assembly Ex p. Haynes-Smith [1928] 1 K.B.
411, KBD 12–005, 12–008, 25–006
R. v Leicester City Council Ex p. Powergen UK Plc. *See* Powergen UK Plc v Leicester
City Council
R. v Leicester Guardians; sub nom. R. v Leicester Union [1899] 2 Q.B. 632, QBD . 25–040,
26–057
R. v Leicestershire CC Ex p. Blackfordby and Boothorpe Action Group Ltd; sub nom.
R. v Leicester City Council Ex p. Blackfordby and Boothcorpe Action Group Ltd;
R. v Leicestershire CC Ex p. Blackfordby and Boothcorpe Action Group Ltd
[2001] Env. L.R. 2; [2000] E.H.L.R. 215; [2000] J.P.L. 1266, QBD 24–022
R. v Leman Street Police Station Inspector Ex p. Venicoff [1920] 3 K.B. 72, KBD . 12–004,
12–006
R. v Leonard Cheshire Foundation. *See* R. (on the application of Heather) v Leonard
Cheshire Foundation
R. v Lewis (Michael William) [2005] EWCA Crim 859; [2005] Crim. L.R. 796, CA
(Crim Div) 28–008
R. v Lewisham LBC Ex p. Shell UK [1988] 1 All E.R. 938; (1988) 152 L.G. Rev. 929,
DC 5–019, 26–025
R. v Lewisham Union [1897] 1 Q.B. 498 24–005
R. v Leyland Justices Ex p. Hawthorn; sub nom. R. v Leyland Magistrates Ex p.
Hawthorn [1979] Q.B. 283; [1979] 2 W.L.R. 28; [1979] 1 All E.R. 209; (1979) 68 Cr.
App. R. 269; [1979] R.T.R. 109; [1978] Crim. L.R. 627, DC 25–004
R. v Licensing Authority Ex p. Smith Kline & French Laboratories Ltd (No.2) [1990] 1
Q.B. 574; [1989] 2 W.L.R. 378; (1989) 133 S.J. 263, CA (Civ Div) 28–019
R. v Lichfield DC Ex p. Lichfield Securities Ltd [2001] EWCA Civ 304; (2001) 3
L.G.L.R. 35; [2001] 3 P.L.R. 33; [2001] P.L.C.R. 32; [2001] J.P.L. 1434 (Note);
[2001] 11 E.G. 171 (C.S.); (2001) 98(17) L.S.G. 37; (2001) 145 S.J.L.B. 78, CA (Civ
Div) 26–045, 26–046
R. v Life Assurance Unit Trust Regulatory Organisation Ex p. Ross; sub nom. R. v
LAUTRO Ex p. Ross [1993] Q.B. 17; [1992] 3 W.L.R. 549; [1993] 1 All E.R. 545;
[1993] B.C.L.C. 509; (1993) 5 Admin. L.R. 573; [1992] C.O.D. 455, CA (Civ Div) . 12–021
R. v Liverpool City Council Ex p. Muldoon; sub nom. R. v Rent Officer Service Ex p.
Muldoon [1996] 1 W.L.R. 1103; [1996] 3 All E.R. 498; (1997) 29 H.L.R. 163;
(1996) 8 Admin. L.R. 552; [1996] C.O.D. 495; (1996) 160 J.P. Rep. 875; (1996)
93(33) L.S.G. 25; (1996) 146 N.L.J. 1057; (1996) 140 S.J.L.B. 184, HL 24–027
R. v Liverpool Corp Ex p. Liverpool Taxi Fleet Operators Association; sub nom.
Liverpool Taxi Fleet Operators Association, Re; Liverpool Taxi Owners Asso-
ciation, Re [1972] 2 Q.B. 299; [1972] 2 W.L.R. 1262; [1972] 2 All E.R. 589; 71
L.G.R. 387; (1972) 116 S.J. 201, CA (Civ Div) 12–012, 12–017, 12–028,
16–015, 20–048, 22–018, 25–005
R. v Lloyd's of London Ex p. Briggs [1993] 1 Lloyd's Rep. 176; [1993] C.O.D. 66,
QBD 12–017, 26–029
R. v Local Government Board (1882) 10 Q.B.D. 309 25–002
R. v Local Government Board Ex p. Arlidge; sub nom. Local Government Board v
Arlidge [1915] A.C. 120, HL 9–038, 12–004, 12–007, 12–042
R. v London CC Ex p. Corrie [1918] 1 K.B. 68, KBD 16–012
R. v London CC Ex p. Empire Theatre (1894) 71 L.T. 638 13–005
R. v London CC Ex p. Entertainments Protection Association [1931] 2 K.B. 215, CA . 25–004
R. v London Metal Exchange Ltd Ex p. Albatros Warehousing BV, March 30, 2000,
QBD 26–027
R. v London Quarter Sessions Ex p. Westminster Corporation [1951] 2 K.B. 508 ... 24–011
R. v London Residuary Body Ex p. Inner London Education Authority, The Times,
July 24, 1987; Independent, July 6, 1987, DC 15–006, 15–017
R. v London Transport Executive Ex p. Greater London Council [1983] Q.B. 484;
[1983] 2 W.L.R. 702; [1983] 2 All E.R. 262; 81 L.G.R. 474; (1983) 127 S.J. 106,
DC 17–011
R. v Lord Chancellor Ex p. Lightfoot; sub nom. Lightfoot v Lord Chancellor [2000]

Q.B. 597; [2000] 2 W.L.R. 318; [1999] 4 All E.R. 583; [2000] B.C.C. 537; [2000] H.R.L.R. 33; [2000] B.P.I.R. 120; (1999) 96(31) L.S.G. 35; (1999) 149 N.L.J. 1285, CA (Civ Div) 17–020, 18–004

R. v Lord Chancellor Ex p. Witham [1998] Q.B. 575; [1998] 2 W.L.R. 849; [1997] 2 All E.R. 779; [1997] C.O.D. 291; (1997) 147 N.L.J. 378; (1997) 141 S.J.L.B. 82, QBD 17–020, 22–027, 24–027

R. v Lord Chancellor Ex p. Hibbit & Saunders [1993] C.O.D. 326, DC 26–025

R. v Lord Chancellor's Department Ex p. Nangle [1992] 1 All E.R. 897; [1991] I.C.R. 743; [1991] I.R.L.R. 343; [1991] C.O.D. 484, QBD 5–044

R. v Lord President of the Privy Council Ex p. Page; sub nom. Page v Hull University Visitor; R. v Hull University Visitor Ex p. Page; R. v Visitor of the University of Hull Ex p. Page [1993] A.C. 682; [1993] 3 W.L.R. 1112; [1993] 1 All E.R. 97; [1993] I.C.R. 114; (1993) 143 N.L.J. 15; (1993) 137 S.J.L.B. 45, HL 12–014

R. v Lord Saville of Newdigate Ex p. B (No.2); sub nom. R. v Lord Saville of New- digate Ex p. A [2000] 1 W.L.R. 1855; [1999] 4 All E.R. 860; [1999] C.O.D. 436; (1999) 149 N.L.J. 1201, CA (Civ Div) 19–004

R. v McKenzie [1892] 2 Q.B. 519 13–002

R. v Mahony [1910] 2 I.R. 695 14–029

R. v Manchester City Justices Ex p. Davies (Barry); sub nom. R. v Manchester City Magistrates Court Ex p. Davies; Davies v Manchester City Justices; R. v Man- chester City Justices Ex p. Davies (No.2) [1989] Q.B. 631; [1988] 3 W.L.R. 1357; [1989] 1 All E.R. 90; (1988) 152 J.P. 605; [1988] R.A. 261; (1988) 152 J.P.N. 722; (1988) 138 N.L.J. Rep. 260; (1988) 132 S.J. 1732, CA (Civ Div) 29–047

R. v Manchester Corporation [1911] 1 K.B. 560 .... 22–030, 24–005

R. v RA Manchester Legal Aid Committee Ex p. Brand & Co [1952] 2 Q.B. 413; [1952] 1 All E.R. 480; [1952] 1 T.L.R. 476; (1952) 96 S.J. 183, DC 25–006

R. v Manchester Metropolitan University Ex p. Nolan, *Independent*, July 15, 1993, DC 19–010

R. v Marie L, The Mayor and Burgesses of the London Borough of Barking & Dagenham [2001] 2 F.L.R. 763 20–017

R. v May (Raymond George) [2005] EWCA Crim 97; [2005] 1 W.L.R. 2902; [2005] 3 All E.R. 523; [2005] 2 Cr. App. R. (S.) 67; (2005) 149 S.J.L.B. 176, CA (Crim Div) 28–008

R. v Mayor of Peterborough (1875) 44 L.J. Q.B. 85 .... 23–021, 25–018

R. v Mayor of Tewkesbury (1868) L.R. 3 Q.B. 629 29–050

R. v Medical Appeal Tribunal Ex p. Gilmore; sub nom. Gilmore's Application, Re [1957] 1 Q.B. 574; [1957] 2 W.L.R. 498; [1957] 1 All E.R. 796; (1957) 101 S.J. 248, CA 14–036, 27–002, 27–003

R. v Mental Health Tribunal Ex p. Pickering [1986] 1 All E.R. 99, QBD 12–034

R. v Merton Sutton and Wandsworth HA Ex p. P (2000) 3 C.C.L. Rep. 378; [2001] Lloyd's Rep. Med. 73; [2001] A.C.D. 9, QBD 20–015

R. v Metropolitan Borough of Knowsley Ex p. Maguire [1992] C.O.D. 499 29–064

R. v Milk Marketing Board Ex p. North (1934) 50 T.L.R. 559 25–004

R. v Minister of Agriculture, Fisheries and Food Ex p. Bell Lines Ltd [1984] 2 C.M.L.R. 502, QBD 19–012

R. v Minister of Health [1939] 1 K.B. 232 14–029

R. v Minister of Health Ex p. Yaffe; sub nom. Minister of Health v King, The [1931] A.C. 494, HL 25–004, 25–007, 27–005

R. v Minister of Housing and Local Government Ex p. Chichester Rural DC [1960] 1 W.L.R. 587; [1960] 2 All E.R. 407; (1960) 124 J.P. 322; 58 L.G.R. 198; (1960) 11 P. & C.R. 295; (1960) 104 S.J. 449, DC 12–034

R. v Ministry of Agriculture, Fisheries and Food Ex p. Astonquest Ltd [2000] Eu. L.R. 371, CA (Civ Div) 19–012

R. v Ministry of Agriculture, Fisheries and Food Ex p. British Pig Industry Support Group [2000] Eu. L.R. 724; [2001] A.C.D. 3, QBD 24–023

R. v Ministry of Agriculture, Fisheries and Food Ex p. Cox [1993] 2 C.M.L.R. 917; (1994) 6 Admin. L.R. 421; [1993] 22 E.G. 111; [1993] E.G. 27 (C.S.), QBD 20–029

R. v Ministry of Agriculture, Fisheries and Food Ex p. Dairy Trade Federation Ltd [1998] Eu. L.R. 253; [1995] C.O.D. 237; [1995] C.O.D. 3, QBD 26–046

R. v Ministry of Agriculture, Fisheries and Food Ex p. Federation Europeene de la Sante Animale (FEDESA) (C-331/88) [1990] E.C.R. I-4023; [1991] 1 C.M.L.R. 507, ECJ (5th Chamber) 19–022

R. v Ministry of Agriculture, Fisheries and Food Ex p. First City Trading Ltd (1996)
[1997] 1 C.M.L.R. 250; [1997] Eu. L.R. 195, QBD 19–001, 19–012,
19–026, 19–027, 19–031
R. v Ministry of Agriculture, Fisheries and Food Ex p. Hamble (Offshore) Fisheries
Ltd [1995] 2 All E.R. 714; [1995] 1 C.M.L.R. 533; (1995) 7 Admin. L.R. 637; [1995]
C.O.D. 114, QBD 20–007
R. v Ministry of Agriculture, Fisheries and Food Ex p. Hedley Lomas (Ireland) Ltd (C-
5/94) [1997] Q.B. 139; [1996] 3 W.L.R. 787; [1996] All E.R. (EC) 493; [1996] E.C.R.
I-2553; [1996] 2 C.M.L.R. 391; [1996] C.E.C. 979; (1996) 15 Tr. L.R. 364, ECJ . 29–058
R. v Ministry of Agriculture Fisheries and Food Ex p. Lay [1998] C.O.D. 387, QBD . 29–058,
29–059
R. v Ministry of Agriculture, Fisheries and Food Ex p. Live Sheep Traders Ltd [1995]
C.O.D. 297, QBD 25–026
R. v Ministry of Agriculture, Fisheries and Food Ex p. Monsanto Plc (No.2) [1999]
Q.B. 1161; [1999] 2 W.L.R. 599; [1998] 4 All E.R. 321; [1999] F.S.R. 223, DC . 25–032
R. v Ministry of Agriculture, Fisheries and Food Ex p. Roberts; sub nom. R. v Ministry
of Agriculture, Fisheries and Food Ex p. Royal Society for the Prevention of
Cruelty to Animals [1991] 1 C.M.L.R. 555; [1991] C.O.D. 172, QBD 19–012
R. v Ministry of Defence Ex p. Murray [1998] C.O.D. 134, DC 12–038
R. v Ministry of Defence Ex p. Smith [1996] Q.B. 517; [1996] 2 W.L.R. 305; [1996] 1 All
E.R. 257; [1996] I.C.R. 740; [1996] I.R.L.R. 100; (1996) 8 Admin. L.R. 29; [1996]
C.O.D. 237; (1995) 145 N.L.J. 1689, CA (Civ Div) 17–019, 18–002, 18–038, 19–005
R. v Ministry of Defence Ex p. Walker [2000] 1 W.L.R. 806; [2000] 2 All E.R. 917;
[2000] C.O.D. 153; (2000) 97(19) L.S.G. 43; (2000) 144 S.J.L.B. 198, HL 20–016
R. v Monopolies and Mergers Commission Ex p. Argyll Group Plc; sub nom. R. v
Monopolies and Mergers Commission and Secretary of State for Trade and
Industry, Ex p. Argyll Group Plc [1986] 1 W.L.R. 763; [1986] 2 All E.R. 257;
(1986) 2 B.C.C. 99086, CA (Civ Div) 24–017, 25–029
R. v Monopolies and Mergers Commission Ex p. Elders IXL Ltd [1987] 1 W.L.R. 1221;
[1987] 1 All E.R. 451; (1986) 2 B.C.C. 99179; [1987] E.C.C. 259; (1987) 84 L.S.G.
2764; (1987) 131 S.J. 1120, QBD 11–009
R. v Monopolies and Mergers Commission Ex p. Matthew Brown Plc [1987] 1 W.L.R.
1235; [1987] 1 All E.R. 463; (1988) 4 B.C.C. 171; (1987) 84 L.S.G. 2606; (1987) 131
S.J. 1120, QBD 11–009
R. v Monopolies and Mergers Commission Ex p. Milk Marque Ltd [2000] C.O.D. 329,
DC 24–027
R. v Monopolies and Mergers Commission Ex p. South Yorkshire Transport Ltd; sub
nom. South Yorkshire Transport v Monopolies and Mergers Commission [1993] 1
W.L.R. 23; [1993] 1 All E.R. 289; [1993] B.C.C. 111; [1994] E.C.C. 231; (1993) 143
N.L.J. 128, HL 14–034, 14–040, 14–042
R. v Moreley (1760) 2 Burr. 1040 27–002
R. v Nailsworth Licensing Justices Ex p. Bird [1953] 1 W.L.R. 1046; [1953] 2 All E.R.
652; (1953) 117 J.P. 426; 51 L.G.R. 532; (1953) 97 S.J. 541, DC 13–005, 13–011
R. v Nat Bell Liquors Ltd [1922] 2 A.C. 128, PC (Can) 14–029, 14–036, 15–017, 27–002
R. v National Dock Labour Board Ex p. National Amalgamated Stevedores & Dockers
[1964] 2 Lloyd's Rep. 420, QBD 25–018
R. v National Joint Council for the Craft of Dental Technicians (Disputes Committee)
Ex p. Neate [1953] 1 Q.B. 704; [1953] 2 W.L.R. 342; [1953] 1 All E.R. 327; (1953)
97 S.J. 116, DC 25–004
R. v Newham LBC Ex p. Bibi; R. v Newham LBC Ex p. Al-Nashed. *See* R. (on the
application of Bibi) v Newham LBC (No.1)
R. v Norfolk CC Ex p. Thorpe [1998] C.O.D. 208; [1998] N.P.C. 11, QBD 17–014
R. v North Ex p. Oakey [1927] 1 K.B. 491, CA 12–001, 23–025, 26–057
R. v North and East Devon HA Ex p. Coughlan [2001] Q.B. 213; [2000] 2 W.L.R. 622;
[2000] 3 All E.R. 850; (2000) 2 L.G.L.R. 1; [1999] B.L.G.R. 703; (1999) 2 C.C.L.
Rep. 285; [1999] Lloyd's Rep. Med. 306; (2000) 51 B.M.L.R. 1; [1999] C.O.D. 340;
(1999) 96(31) L.S.G. 39; (1999) 143 S.J.L.B. 213, CA (Civ Div) 19–004, 20–012,
20–013, 20–015, 20–016, 20–018, 20–019, 26–023
R. v North Hertfordshire DC Ex p. Cobbold [1985] 3 All E.R. 486, QBD 23–033
R. v North West Leicestershire DC Ex p. Moses (No.1) [2000] J.P.L. 733; (1999) 96(37)
L.S.G. 33, QBD 24–020
R. v North Yorkshire CC Ex p. M (No.1) [1989] Q.B. 411; [1988] 3 W.L.R. 1344; [1989]

1 All E.R. 143; (1989) 153 J.P. 390; [1989] 1 F.L.R. 203; [1989] F.C.R. 128; [1989] C.O.D. 190; [1989] Fam. Law 102; (1989) 153 J.P.N. 288; (1989) 153 L.G. Rev. 652; (1989) 86(5) L.S.G. 42; (1988) 132 S.J. 1731, QBD 25–033
R. v Northamptonshire CC Ex p. D; sub nom. R. v Northamptonshire CC Ex p. W [1998] Ed. C.R. 14; [1998] E.L.R. 291; [1998] C.O.D. 110, QBD 12–039
R. v Northamptonshire CC Ex p. Marshall [1998] Ed. C.R. 262; [1998] C.O.D. 457, QBD 9–024, 12–034
R. v Northumberland Compensation Appeal Tribunal Ex p. Shaw [1952] 1 K.B. 338; [1952] 1 All E.R. 122; [1952] 1 T.L.R. 161; (1952) 116 J.P. 54; 50 L.G.R. 193; (1951–52) 2 P. & C.R. 361; (1952) 96 S.J. 29, CA 14–036, 25–002, 25–018
R. v Paddington and St Marylebone Furnished Houses Rent Tribunal Ex p. Kendal Hotels Ltd; sub nom. R. v Paddington and St Marylebone Rent Tribunal Ex p. Kendal Hotels Ltd [1947] 1 All E.R. 448; 63 T.L.R. 239; [1947] W.N. 103; 176 L.T. 330, KBD 23–026
R. v Paddington Valuation Officer Ex p. Peachey Property Corp (No.2) [1966] 1 Q.B. 380; [1965] 3 W.L.R. 426; [1965] 2 All E.R. 836; (1965) 129 J.P. 447; 63 L.G.R. 353; [1965] R.A. 177; [1965] R.V.R. 384; 11 R.R.C. 141; (1965) 109 S.J. 475, CA .. 23–010, 24–003, 24–005, 25–018, 26–057
R. v Paddington and St Marylebone Rent Tribunal Ex p. Perry [1956] 1 Q.B. 229; [1955] 3 W.L.R. 744; [1955] 3 All E.R. 391; (1955) 119 J.P. 565; 53 L.G.R. 670; (1955) 99 S.J. 816, DC 14–029, 14–030, 23–026
R. v Panel of the Federation of Communication Services Ltd Ex p. Kubis (1999) 11 Admin. L.R. 43; [1998] C.O.D. 5, QBD 26–029
R. v Panel on Takeovers and Mergers Ex p. Datafin Plc [1987] Q.B. 815; [1987] 2 W.L.R. 699; [1987] 1 All E.R. 564; (1987) 3 B.C.C. 10; [1987] B.C.L.C. 104; [1987] 1 F.T.L.R. 181; (1987) 131 S.J. 23, CA (Civ Div) 25–004, 25–029, 26–016, 26–018, 26–020, 26–027, 26–028
R. v Panel on Take-overs and Mergers Ex p. Guinness Plc [1990] 1 Q.B. 146; [1989] 2 W.L.R. 863; [1989] 1 All E.R. 509; (1988) 4 B.C.C. 714; [1989] B.C.L.C. 255; (1988) 138 N.L.J. Rep. 244; (1989) 133 S.J. 660, CA (Civ Div) 26–027, 26–057
R. v Parliamentary Commissioner for Administration Ex p. Balchin (No.1) [1998] 1 P.L.R. 1; [1997] J.P.L. 917; [1997] C.O.D. 146; [1996] E.G. 166 (C.S.); [1996] N.P.C. 147, QBD 8–015, 8–031, 19–004
R. v Parliamentary Commissioner for Administration Ex p. Balchin (No.2) (2000) 2 L.G.L.R. 87; (2000) 79 P. & C.R. 157; [2000] R.V.R. 303; [2000] J.P.L. 267; [1999] E.G. 78 (C.S.), QBD 8–031
R. v Parliamentary Commissioner for Administration Ex p. Dyer [1994] 1 W.L.R. 621; [1994] 1 All E.R. 375; [1994] C.O.D. 331; (1993) 137 S.J.L.B. 259, DC 8–031
R. v Parliamentary Commissioner for Standards Ex p. Al-Fayed [1998] 1 W.L.R. 669; [1998] 1 All E.R. 93; (1998) 10 Admin. L.R. 69; [1998] C.O.D. 139; (1997) 94(42) L.S.G. 31; (1997) 147 N.L.J. 1689, CA (Civ Div) 26–033
R v Parole Board Ex p. Wilson [1992] Q.B. 740; [1992] 2 W.L.R. 707; [1992] 2 All E.R. 576; (1992) 4 Admin. L.R. 525; [1992] C.O.D. 331; (1992) 89(17) L.S.G. 49; (1992) 136 S.J.L.B. 83, CA (Civ Div) 12–014
R. v Peak Park Joint Planning Board Ex p. Jackson (1976) 74 L.G.R. 376, DC 25–018
R. v Pease (1832) 4 B. & Ad. 30 29–038
R. v Pembrokeshire Justices 109 E.R. 1188; (1831) 2 B. & Ad. 391, KB 25–018
R. v Personal Investment Authority Ombudsman Ex p. Burns-Anderson Independent Network Plc (1998) 10 Admin. L.R. 57; [1997] C.O.D. 379, CA (Civ Div) 25–026
R. v Plowright (1686) 3 Mod. 94 .... 25–002, 27–002
R. v Police Complaints Board Ex p. Madden [1983] 1 W.L.R. 447; [1983] 2 All E.R. 353; [1983] Crim. L.R. 263; (1983) 127 S.J. 85, QBD 16–003
R. v Police Complaints Authority Ex p. Wells [1991] C.O.D. 95 26–057
R. v Poplar MBC Ex p. London CC (No.2) [1922] 1 K.B. 95, CA 26–057
R. v Port of London Authority Ex p. Kynoch Ltd [1919] 1 K.B. 176, CA 16–013, 16–015, 25–016
R. v Post Office Ex p. Byrne [1975] I.C.R. 221; (1975) 119 S.J. 341, DC 25–004
R. v Powell (1841) 1 Q.B. 352 28–017
R. v Preston Supplementary Benefits Appeal Tribunal Ex p. Moore [1975] 1 W.L.R. 624; [1975] 2 All E.R. 807; (1975) 119 S.J. 285, CA (Civ Div) 14–031
R. v Pwllheli Justices Ex p. Soane [1948] 2 All E.R. 815; 64 T.L.R. 574; (1948) 112 J.P. 441; 46 L.G.R. 557; [1948] W.N. 411; (1948) 92 S.J. 634, DC 13–004

R. v Quarter Sessions (Surrey) Ex p. Lilley [1951] 2 K.B. 749; [1951] 2 All E.R. 659; [1951]
  2 T.L.R. 546; (1951) 115 J.P. 507; 49 L.G.R. 802; (1951) 95 S.J. 697, DC 24–011
R. v R. [1992] 1 A.C. 599 21–004
R. R. [2000] 1 F.L.R. 451 28–021
R. v Race Relations Board Ex p. Selvarajan; sub nom. Selvarajan v Race Relations
  Board; Selvarajan, Re [1975] 1 W.L.R. 1686; [1976] 1 All E.R. 12; [1975] I.R.L.R.
  281; (1975) 119 S.J. 644, CA (Civ Div) 12–042, 16–003
R. v Rand (1865–66) L.R. 1 Q.B. 230, QB 13–002
R. v Reading Crown Court Ex p. Hutchinson [1988] Q.B. 384; [1987] 3 W.L.R. 1062;
  [1988] 1 All E.R. 333; (1988) 87 Cr. App. R. 36; (1988) 152 J.P. 47; 86 L.G.R. 71;
  [1987] Crim. L.R. 827; (1987) 151 J.P.N. 825; (1988) 152 L.G. Rev. 50; (1987) 131
  S.J. 1987, QBD 26–014
R. v Redbridge LBC Ex p. G [1991] C.O.D. 398, DC 26–046, 26–048
R. v Registrar of Companies Ex p. Central Bank of India. *See* R. v Registrar of
  Companies Ex p. Esal (Commodities) Ltd (In Liquidation)
R. v Registrar of Companies Ex p. Esal (Commodities) Ltd (In Liquidation); sub nom.
  R. v Registrar of Companies Ex p. Central Bank of India [1986] Q.B. 1114; [1986]
  2 W.L.R. 177; [1986] 1 All E.R. 105; (1985) 1 B.C.C. 99501; [1986] P.C.C. 235;
  (1985) 129 S.J. 755, CA (Civ Div) 14–033, 27–005, 27–006
R. v Rent Officer Service Ex p. Muldoon. *See* R. v Liverpool City Council Ex p.
  Muldoon
R. v Rochdale MBC, Ex p. Cromer Ring Mill Ltd [1982] 3 All E.R. 761, QBD 16–013
R. v Rochdale MBC Ex p. Schemet [1993] 1 F.C.R. 306; 91 L.G.R. 425; [1993] C.O.D.
  113, QBD 12–017
R. v Romsey Justices Ex p. Gale (1992) 156 J.P. 567; [1992] Crim. L.R. 451; [1992]
  C.O.D. 323; (1992) 156 J.P.N. 202, DC 13–004
R. v Russell Ex p. Beaverbrook Newspapers [1969] 1 Q.B. 342; [1968] 3 W.L.R. 999;
  [1968] 3 All E.R. 695; (1968) 133 J.P. 27; (1968) 112 S.J. 800, DC 24–003
R. v Ruyton (Inhabitants) 121 E.R. 813; (1861) 1 B. & S. 534, QB 27–003
R. v St Albans Crown Court Ex p. Cinnamond [1981] Q.B. 480; [1981] 2 W.L.R. 681;
  [1981] 1 All E.R. 802; (1980) 2 Cr. App. R. (S.) 235; [1981] R.T.R. 139; [1981]
  Crim. L.R. 243, QBD 19–004
R. v St Edmundsbury BC Ex p. Investors in Industry Commercial Properties [1985] 1
  W.L.R. 1168; [1985] 3 All E.R. 234; (1986) 51 P. & C.R. 251; [1986] J.P.L. 38;
  (1985) 82 L.S.G. 2741; (1985) 129 S.J. 623, DC 13–008, 17–010
R. v St Lawrence's Hospital Statutory Visitors Ex p. Pritchard [1953] 1 W.L.R. 1158 . 12–005,
                                                                                          25–005
R. v Salop JJ [1859] 2 El. & El. 386 23–027
R. v Searby (Alan Edward) [2003] EWCA Crim 1910; [2003] 3 C.M.L.R. 15; [2003] Eu.
  L.R. 819, CA (Crim Div) 23–002
R. v Secretary of Companies Ex p. Central Bank of India [1986] Q.B. 1114 24–019
R. v Secretary of State for Defence Ex p. Sancto (1993) 5 Admin. L.R. 673; [1993]
  C.O.D. 144, DC 24–020
R. v Secretary of State for Education and Employment Ex p. Begbie; sub nom. R. v
  Department of Education and Employment Ex p. B (A Minor); R. v Secretary of
  State for Education and Employment Ex p. B (A Minor) [2000] 1 W.L.R. 1115;
  [2000] Ed. C.R. 140; [2000] E.L.R. 445; (1999) 96(35) L.S.G. 39, CA (Civ Div) . 20–016,
                                                                                          20–021
R. v Secretary of State for Education and Science Ex p. J [1993] C.O.D. 146 26–006
R. v Secretary of State for Education and Science Ex p. Skitt [1995] C.O.D. 270, QBD   15–017
R. v Secretary of State for Education and Science Ex p. Southwark LBC [1994] C.O.D.
  298, QBD 16–015, 22–018
R. v Secretary of State for the Environment Ex p. Haringey LBC 92 L.G.R. 538; [1994]
  C.O.D. 518; (1995) 159 L.G. Rev. 21, CA (Civ Div) 5–020
R. v Secretary of State for Employment Ex p. Equal Opportunities Commission [1995]
  1 A.C. 1; [1994] 2 W.L.R. 409; [1994] 1 All E.R. 910; [1995] 1 C.M.L.R. 391; [1994]
  I.C.R. 317; [1994] I.R.L.R. 176; 92 L.G.R. 360; [1994] C.O.D. 301; (1994) 91(18)
  L.S.G. 43; (1994) 144 N.L.J. 358; (1994) 138 S.J.L.B. 84, HL 10–014, 24–022,
                                                                            24–024, 25–021, 26–004
R. v Secretary of State for the Environment Ex p. Alconbury [2003] 2 A.C. 295 15–007
R. v Secretary of State for the Environment Ex p. Brent LBC [1982] Q.B. 593; [1982] 2

W.L.R. 693; [1983] 3 All E.R. 321; 80 L.G.R. 357; (1982) 126 S.J. 118, DC ... 12–022, 12–024, 13–005, 16–013, 16–013

R. v Secretary of State for the Environment Ex p. Camden LBC (1996) 28 H.L.R. 321; [1995] C.O.D. 203, QBD 29–055

R. v Secretary of State for the Environment Ex p. Doncaster BC [1990] C.O.D. 441 26–006

R. v Secretary of State for the Environment Ex p. Hackney LBC [1984] 1 W.L.R. 592; [1984] 1 All E.R. 956; 84 L.G.R. 32; (1984) 81 L.S.G. 664; (1984) 128 S.J. 280, CA (Civ Div) 20–030

R. v Secretary of State for the Environment Ex p. Hammersmith and Fulham LBC [1991] 1 A.C. 521; [1990] 3 W.L.R. 898; [1990] 3 All E.R. 589; 89 L.G.R. 129; [1990] R.V.R. 188; (1991) 155 L.G. Rev. 48; (1990) 140 N.L.J. 1422; (1990) 134 S.J. 1226, HL 17–008, 22–028

R. v Secretary of State for the Environment Ex p. Hillingdon LBC [1986] 1 W.L.R. 807; [1986] 2 All E.R. 273; (1988) 55 P. & C.R. 241; [1987] R.V.R. 6; [1987] J.P.L. 717; (1986) 83 L.S.G. 2331; (1986) 130 S.J. 481, CA (Civ Div) 16–011

R. v Secretary of State for the Environment Ex p. Kent [1990] J.P.L. 124; [1990] C.O.D. 78; (1990) 154 L.G. Rev. 53; [1989] E.G. 72 (C.S.), CA (Civ Div) 27–008

R. v Secretary of State for the Environment Ex p. Kirkstall Valley Campaign Ltd; sub nom. R. v Secretary of State for the Environment Ex p. William Morrison Supermarket Plc [1996] 3 All E.R. 304; [1997] 1 P.L.R. 8; [1996] J.P.L. 1042; [1996] C.O.D. 337; (1996) 160 J.P. Rep. 699; [1996] E.G. 46 (C.S.); (1996) 146 N.L.J. 478; [1996] N.P.C. 41, QBD 13–008

R. v Secretary of State for the Environment and the Secretary of State for Wales Ex p. NALGO [1992] C.O.D. 282 .... 19–010, 20–017

R. v Secretary of State for the Environment Ex p. Norwich City Council; sub nom. Norwich City Council v Secretary of State for the Environment [1982] Q.B. 808; [1982] 2 W.L.R. 580; [1982] 1 All E.R. 737; (1981–82) 2 H.L.R. 1; 80 L.G.R. 498; (1982) 126 S.J. 119, CA (Civ Div) 12–027, 25–040

R. v Secretary of State for the Environment Ex p. Nottinghamshire CC; sub nom. Nottinghamshire CC v Secretary of State for the Environment [1986] A.C. 240; [1986] 2 W.L.R. 1; [1986] 1 All E.R. 199; 84 L.G.R. 305; (1986) 83 L.S.G. 359; (1985) 135 N.L.J. 1257; (1986) 130 S.J. 36, HL 22–028, 25–034

R. v Secretary of State for the Environment Ex p. Ostler; sub nom. R. v Secretary of State for the Home Department Ex p. Ostler [1977] Q.B. 122; [1976] 3 W.L.R. 288; [1976] 3 All E.R. 90; 75 L.G.R. 45; (1976) 32 P. & C.R. 166; (1976) 238 E.G. 971; [1976] J.P.L. 301; (1976) 120 S.J. 332, CA (Civ Div) .. 15–011, 17–015, 27–007, 27–011

R. v Secretary of State for the Environment Ex p. Rose Theatre Trust Co (No.2) [1990] 1 Q.B. 504; [1990] 2 W.L.R. 186; [1990] 1 All E.R. 754; (1990) 59 P. & C.R. 257; [1990] 1 P.L.R. 39; [1990] J.P.L. 360; [1990] C.O.D. 186; [1989] E.G. 107 (C.S.); (1990) 87(6) L.S.G. 41; (1990) 134 S.J. 425, QBD 24–022

R. v Secretary of State for the Environment Ex p. Upton Brickworks [1992] J.P.L. 1044; [1992] C.O.D. 301 27–008

R. v Secretary of State for the Environment Ex p. West Oxfordshire DC (1994) 26 H.L.R. 417; [1994] C.O.D. 134, QBD 20–026, 21–003

R. v Secretary of State for Foreign and Commonwealth Affairs Ex p. Everett [1989] Q.B. 811; [1989] 2 W.L.R. 224; [1989] 1 All E.R. 655; [1989] Imm. A.R. 155; [1989] C.O.D. 291; (1989) 86(8) L.S.G. 43; (1989) 133 S.J. 151, CA (Civ Div) 17–005

R. v Secretary of State for Foreign and Commonwealth Affairs Ex p. Lord Rees-Mogg [1994] Q.B. 552; [1994] 2 W.L.R. 115; [1994] 1 All E.R. 457; [1993] 3 C.M.L.R. 101; [1994] C.O.D. 119; (1993) 143 N.L.J. 1153; (1993) 137 S.J.L.B. 195, DC 24–022

R. v Secretary of State for Foreign and Commonwealth Affairs Ex p. World Development Movement Ltd [1995] 1 W.L.R. 386; [1995] 1 All E.R. 611; [1995] C.O.D. 211; (1995) 145 N.L.J. 51, DC 24–022

R. v Secretary of State for Health Ex p. British American Tobacco (Investments) Ltd (C-491/01). *See* R. (on the application of British American Tobacco (Investments) Ltd) v Secretary of State for Health (C-491/01)

R. v Secretary of State for Health Ex p. Hackney LBC [1994] C.O.D. 432, QBD ... 26–006

R. v Secretary of State for Health Ex p. Scotia Pharmaceuticals International Ltd (No.2) [1997] Eu. L.R. 650 25–032

R. v Secretary of State for Health Ex p. United States Tobacco International Inc [1992] Q.B. 353; [1991] 3 W.L.R. 529; [1992] 1 All E.R. 212; (1991) 3 Admin. L.R. 735; (1992) 11 Tr. L.R. 1; [1991] C.O.D. 268, DC 12–017, 20–013, 25–007

R. v Secretary of State for Health Ex p. Wagstaff; sub nom. R. (on the application of Wagstaff) v Secretary of State for Health; R. (on the application of Associated Newspapers Ltd) v Secretary of State for Health [2001] 1 W.L.R. 292; [2000] H.R.L.R. 646; [2000] U.K.H.R.R. 875; (2000) 56 B.M.L.R. 199; [2001] A.C.D. 24; (2000) 97(37) L.S.G. 39; (2000) 144 S.J.L.B. 249, DC 19–004

R. v Secretary of State for the Home Department Ex p. Abdi (Khalif Mohamed) [1996] 1 W.L.R. 298; [1996] 1 All E.R. 641; [1996] Imm. A.R. 288; (1996) 8 Admin. L.R. 248; (1996) 146 N.L.J. 245; (1996) 140 S.J.L.B. 63, HL 25–026

R. v Secretary of State for the Home Department Ex p. Adams (No.1) [1995] All E.R. (E.C.) 177, DC 19–012

R. v Secretary of State for the Home Department Ex p. Al-Fayed (No.1)[1998] 1 W.L.R. 763; [1997] 1 All E.R. 228; [1997] I.N.L.R. 137; [1997] C.O.D. 205, CA (Civ Div) 12–037

R. v Secretary of State for the Home Department Ex p. Al-Mehdawi; sub nom. Al-Mehdawi v Secretary of State for the Home Department [1990] 1 A.C. 876; [1989] 3 W.L.R. 1294; [1989] 3 All E.R. 843; [1990] Imm. A.R. 140; (1990) 2 Admin. L.R. 367; [1990] C.O.D. 188; (1990) 134 S.J. 50, HL 12–027, 12–030

R. v Secretary of State for the Home Department Ex p. Amnesty International, January 31, 2000 24–022

R. v Secretary of State for the Home Department Ex p. Anderson; sub nom. R. v Governor of Wormwood Scrubs Prison Ex p. Anderson [1984] Q.B. 778; [1984] 2 W.L.R. 725; [1984] 1 All E.R. 920; [1984] Crim. L.R. 295; (1984) 81 L.S.G. 658; (1984) 128 S.J. 62, QBD 12–032

R. v Secretary of State for the Home Department Ex p. BH [1990] C.O.D. 445 26–006

R. v Secretary of State for the Home Department Ex p. Begum (Angur) [1990] Imm. A.R. 1; [1990] C.O.D. 107, CA (Civ Div) 26–040

R. v Secretary of State for the Home Department Ex p. Bentley [1994] Q.B. 349; [1994] 2 W.L.R. 101; [1993] 4 All E.R. 442; [1994] C.O.D. 65; (1993) 143 N.L.J. 1025; (1993) 137 S.J.L.B. 194, DC 17–005

R. v Secretary of State for the Home Department Ex p. Benwell [1985] Q.B. 554; [1984] 3 W.L.R. 843; [1984] 3 All E.R. 854; [1984] I.C.R. 723; [1985] I.R.L.R. 6; (1984) 81 L.S.G. 2544; (1984) 128 S.J. 703, QBD 12–015, 26–016, 26–031

R. v Secretary of State for the Home Department Ex p. Brind [1991] 1 A.C. 696; [1991] 2 W.L.R. 588; [1991] 1 All E.R. 720; (1991) 3 Admin. L.R. 486; (1991) 141 N.L.J. 199; (1991) 135 S.J. 250, HL 17–008, 17–018, 18–002, 19–005, 19–009

R. v Secretary of State for the Home Department Ex p. Capti-Mehmet; sub nom. R. v Secretary of State for the Home Department Ex p. Capti (Mehmet) [1997] C.O.D. 61, QBD 26–057

R. v Secretary of State for the Home Department Ex p. Cheblak [1991] 1 W.L.R. 890; [1991] 2 All E.R. 319; (1992) 4 Admin. L.R. 353; [1991] C.O.D. 394; (1991) 141 N.L.J. 201, CA (Civ Div) 25–038

R. v Secretary of State for the Home Department Ex p. Chahal (No.2); sub nom. Chahal (Karamjit Singh) v Secretary of State for the Home Department [1995] 1 W.L.R. 526; [1995] 1 All E.R. 658; [1994] Imm. A.R. 107; (1994) 6 Admin. L.R. 789; (1993) 90(46) L.S.G. 38; (1993) 137 S.J.L.B. 255, CA (Civ Div) 18–002

R. v Secretary of State for the Home Department Ex p. Daly [2001] UKHL 26; [2001] 2 A.C. 532; [2001] 2 W.L.R. 1622; [2001] 3 All E.R. 433; [2001] H.R.L.R. 49; [2001] U.K.H.R.R. 887; [2001] Prison L.R. 322; [2001] A.C.D. 79; (2001) 98(26) L.S.G. 43; (2001) 145 S.J.L.B. 156, HL 19–004

R. v Secretary of State for Home Affairs Ex p. Dannenberg; sub nom. Dannenberg v Secretary of State for Home Affairs [1984] Q.B. 766; [1984] 2 W.L.R. 855; [1984] 2 All E.R. 481; (1984) 148 J.P. 321; [1984] 2 C.M.L.R. 456; [1984] Imm. A.R. 33; [1984] Crim. L.R. 362; (1984) 128 S.J. 349, CA (Civ Div) 12–034

R. v Secretary of State for the Home Department Ex p. Doody [1994] 1 A.C. 531; [1993] 3 W.L.R. 154; [1993] 3 All E.R. 92; (1995) 7 Admin. L.R. 1; (1993) 143 N.L.J. 991, HL 12–002

R. v Secretary of State for the Home Department Ex p. Doorga (Davendranath) [1990] Imm. A.R. 98; [1990] C.O.D. 109, CA (Civ Div) 26–039, 26–040

R. v Secretary of State for the Home Department Ex p. Ejaz (Naheed) [1994] Q.B. 496; [1994] 2 W.L.R. 534; [1995] C.O.D. 72, CA (Civ Div) 23–019

R. v Secretary of State for the Home Department Ex p. Follen [1996] C.O.D. 169, QBD 12–037

R. v Secretary of State for the Home Department Ex p. Gangadeen; sub nom.
Gangadeen v Secretary of State for the Home Department; Khan (Khalid) v
Secretary of State for the Home Department [1998] 1 F.L.R. 762; [1998] 2 F.C.R.
96; [1998] Imm. A.R. 106; [1998] I.N.L.R. 206; [1998] C.O.D. 216; [1998] Fam.
Law 248; (1998) 95(1) L.S.G. 24; (1998) 142 S.J.L.B. 27, CA (Civ Div) 16–015,
20–014, 20–026, 21–003, 22–018, 22–046
R. v Secretary of State for the Home Department Ex p. Hargreaves [1997] 1 W.L.R.
906; [1997] 1 All E.R. 397; [1997] C.O.D. 214; (1997) 94(5) L.S.G. 33; (1997) 141
S.J.L.B. 6, CA (Civ Div) 16–015, 19–009, 20–011, 20–013, 22–018, 24–027
R. v Secretary of State for the Home Department Ex p. Harrison [1988] 3 All E.R. 86;
(1988) 138 N.L.J. Rep. 187, QBD 12–033
R. v Secretary of State for the Home Department Ex p. Herbage (No.1). *See* R. v
Governor of Pentonville Prison Ex p. Herbage
R. v Secretary of State for the Home Department Ex p. Hickey (No.2) [1995] 1 W.L.R.
734; [1995] 1 All E.R. 490; (1995) 7 Admin. L.R. 549; (1994) 144 N.L.J. 1732, DC   12–037
R. v Secretary of State for the Home Department Ex p. Hosenball [1977] 1 W.L.R. 766;
[1977] 3 All E.R. 452; (1977) 121 S.J. 255, CA (Civ Div) 22–041
R. v Secretary of State for the Home Department Ex p. Jeyeanthan; sub nom. R. v
Immigration Appeal Tribunal Ex p. Jeyeanthan; Secretary of State for the Home
Department v Ravichandran [2000] 1 W.L.R. 354; [1999] 3 All E.R. 231; [2000]
Imm. A.R. 10; [1999] I.N.L.R. 241; (1999) 11 Admin. L.R. 824; [1999] C.O.D. 349,
CA (Civ Div) 23–011
R. v Secretary of State for the Home Department Ex p. Khan (Asif Mahmood); sub
nom. Khan (Asif Mahmood) v Immigration Appeal Tribunal [1984] 1 W.L.R.
1337; [1985] 1 All E.R. 40; [1984] Imm. A.R. 68; [1984] Fam. Law 278; (1984) 81
L.S.G. 1678; (1984) 128 S.J. 580, CA (Civ Div) 12–017, 12–028,
16–015, 20–004, 22–018, 25–007
R. v Secretary of State for the Home Department Ex p. Khawaja [1984] A.C. 74; [1983]
2 W.L.R. 321; [1983] 1 All E.R. 765; [1982] Imm. A.R. 139; (1983) 127 S.J. 137,
HL 15–023, 23–029, 26–006
R. v Secretary of State for the Home Department Ex p. Lancashire Police Authority
[1992] C.O.D. 161, QBD 22–046
R. v Secretary of State for the Home Department Ex p. Launder (No.2) [1997] 1
W.L.R. 839; [1997] 3 All E.R. 961; (1997) 94(24) L.S.G. 33; (1997) 147 N.L.J. 793;
(1997) 141 S.J.L.B. 123 HL 15–008
R. v Secretary of State for the Home Department Ex p. Leech (No.2) [1994] Q.B. 198;
[1993] 3 W.L.R. 1125; [1993] 4 All E.R. 539; (1993) 137 S.J.L.B. 173, CA (Civ
Div) 17–019, 19–010, 22–027
R. v Secretary of State for the Home Department Ex p. McAvoy [1998] 1 W.L.R. 790;
[1998] C.O.D. 148; (1998) 95(1) L.S.G. 23; (1998) 142 S.J.L.B. 39, CA (Civ Div)   12–037
R. v Secretary of State for the Home Department Ex p. McQuillan [1995] 4 All E.R.
400; [1995] C.O.D. 137, QBD 17–019, 19–010
R. v Secretary of State for the Home Department Ex p. Mehari [1994] Q.B. 474; [1994]
2 W.L.R. 349; [1994] 2 All E.R. 494; [1994] Imm. A.R. 151; [1994] C.O.D. 231,
DC 25–026
R. v Secretary of State for the Home Department Ex p. Mehta (Satyen) [1992] Imm.
A.R. 512; [1992] C.O.D. 484, DC 27–004
R. v Secretary of State for the Home Department Ex p. Moon [1997] I.N.L.R. 165;
(1996) 8 Admin. L.R. 477; [1996] C.O.D. 54, QBD 17–019
R. v Secretary of State for the Home Department Ex p. Mowla; sub nom. Secretary of
State for the Home Department v Mowla [1992] 1 W.L.R. 70; [1991] Imm. A.R.
210; [1991] C.O.D. 304, CA (Civ Div) 20–011
R. v Secretary of State for the Home Department Ex p. Muboyayi [1992] Q.B. 244;
[1991] 3 W.L.R. 442; [1991] 4 All E.R. 72; [1992] C.O.D. 37, CA (Civ Div) 25–038
R. v Secretary of State for the Home Department Ex p. Murphy [1997] C.O.D. 478,
QBD 12–037
R. v Secretary of State for the Home Department and the Parole Board Ex p. Norney
(1995) 7 Admin. L.R. 861; [1996] C.O.D. 81, QBD 17–019, 18–002
R. v Secretary of State for the Home Department Ex p. Oladehinde [1991] 1 A.C. 254;
[1990] 3 W.L.R. 797; [1990] 3 All E.R. 393; (1991) 3 Admin. L.R. 393; (1990) 140
N.L.J. 1498; (1990) 134 S.J. 1264, HL 16–007

R. v Secretary of State for the Home Department Ex p. Oloniluyi [1989] Imm. A.R.
135; [1989] C.O.D. 275, CA (Civ Div) 20–011
R. v Secretary of State for the Home Department Ex p. Pegg [1995] C.O.D. 84, DC 12–037
R. v Secretary of State for the Home Department Ex p. Ruddock [1987] 1 W.L.R. 1482;
[1987] 2 All E.R. 518; (1987) 131 S.J. 1550, QBD 12–028, 16–015,
17–005, 20–014, 20–026, 22–018, 26–046
R. v Secretary of State for the Home Department Ex p. Salem [1999] 1 A.C. 450; [1999]
2 W.L.R. 483; [1999] 2 All E.R. 42; (1999) 11 Admin. L.R. 194; [1999] C.O.D. 486;
(1999) 96(9) L.S.G. 32; (1999) 143 S.J.L.B. 59, HL 25–026
R. v Secretary of State for the Home Department Ex p. Saleem; sub nom. R. v
Immigration Appeal Tribunal Ex p. Saleem; Saleem v Secretary of State for the
Home Department [2001] 1 W.L.R. 443; [2000] 4 All E.R. 814; [2000] Imm. A.R.
529; [2000] I.N.L.R. 413, CA (Civ Div) 13–018
R. v Secretary of State for the Home Department Ex p. Santillo (No.2) [1981] Q.B. 778;
[1981] 2 W.L.R. 362; [1981] 2 All E.R. 897; (1981) 73 Cr. App. R. 71; [1981] 1
C.M.L.R. 569, CA (Civ Div) 12–027
R. v Secretary of State for the Home Department Ex p. Simms; sub nom. R. v Secretary
of State for the Home Department Ex p. Main [2000] 2 A.C. 115; [1999] 3 W.L.R.
328; [1999] 3 All E.R. 400; [1999] E.M.L.R. 689; 7 B.H.R.C. 411; (1999) 11 Admin.
L.R. 961; [1999] Prison L.R. 82; [1999] C.O.D. 520; (1999) 96(30) L.S.G. 28; (1999)
149 N.L.J. 1073; (1999) 143 S.J.L.B. 212, HL 15–008, 17–020
R. v Secretary of State for the Home Department Ex p. Sivakumaran [1988] A.C. 958;
[1988] 1 All E.R. 193; [1988] Imm. A.R. 147; (1988) 85(6) L.S.G. 37; (1988) 132 S.J.
22, HL 24–027
R. v Secretary of State for the Home Department Ex p. Swati; sub nom. Swati v
Secretary of State for the Home Department [1986] 1 W.L.R. 477; [1986] 1 All E.R.
717; [1986] Imm. A.R. 88; (1986) 83 L.S.G. 780; (1986) 136 N.L.J. 189; (1986) 130
S.J. 186, CA (Civ Div) 26–057
R. v Secretary of State for the Home Department Ex p. Tarrant (James); sub nom. R. v
Board of Visitors of Albany Prison Ex p. Tarrant (James) [1985] Q.B. 251; [1984] 2
W.L.R. 613; [1984] 1 All E.R. 799; (1984) 81 L.S.G. 1045; (1984) S.J. 223, DC . 12–031,
12–032
R. v Secretary of State for the Home Department Ex p. Tawfick; sub nom. R. (on the
application of Tawfick) v Secretary of State for the Home Department [2001]
A.C.D. 28; [2001] A.C.D. 171; (2001) 98(2) L.S.G. 40, DC 19–004
R. v Secretary of State for the Home Department Ex p. Turgut; sub nom. Turgut v
Secretary of State for the Home Department [2001] 1 All E.R. 719; [2000]
H.R.L.R. 337; [2000] U.K.H.R.R. 403; [2000] Imm. A.R. 306; [2000] I.N.L.R. 292;
[2001] A.C.D. 12; (2000) 97(7) L.S.G. 40; (2000) 150 N.L.J. 131, CA (Civ Div) 15–002
R. v Secretary of State for the Home Department Ex p. Urmaza [1996] C.O.D. 479,
QBD 16–015, 20–014, 20–026, 21–003, 22–018
R. v Secretary of State for the Home Department Ex p. Venables [1998] A.C. 407; [1997]
3 W.L.R. 23; [1997] 3 All E.R. 97; [1997] 2 F.L.R. 471; (1997) 9 Admin. L.R. 413;
[1997] Fam. Law 789; (1997) 94(34) L.S.G. 27; (1997) 147 N.L.J. 955, HL 16–014,
17–013, 24–027
R. v Secretary of State for the Home Department Ex p. Watts [1997] C.O.D. 152,
QBD 26–057
R. v Secretary of State for the Home Department Ex p. Westminster Press (1992) 4
Admin. L.R. 445; [1992] C.O.D. 303, DC 22–046
R. v Secretary of State for the Home Department Ex p. Zeqiri. See R. (on the appli-
cation of Zeqiri) v Secretary of State for the Home Department
R. v Secretary of State for Social Security Ex p. Association of Metropolitan Autho-
rities (1993) 25 H.L.R. 131; (1993) 5 Admin. L.R. 6; [1993] C.O.D. 54, QBD . 12–028,
22–017, 26–055
R. v Secretary of State for Social Security Ex p. Joint Council for the Welfare of
Immigrants [1997] 1 W.L.R. 275; [1996] 4 All E.R. 385; (1997) 29 H.L.R. 129;
(1997) 9 Admin. L.R. 1; (1996) 146 N.L.J. 985, CA (Civ Div) 17–019, 22–026
R. v Secretary of State for Social Security Ex p. Sherwin (1996) 32 B.M.L.R. 1, QBD . 4–010,
16–009
R. v Secretary of State for Social Security Ex p. Sutton (C-66/95) [1997] All E.R. (EC)
497; [1997] E.C.R. I-2163; [1997] 2 C.M.L.R. 382; [1997] C.E.C. 1110; [1997] I.C.R.
961; [1997] I.R.L.R. 524, ECJ 10–032

R. v Secretary of State for Social Services Ex p. Association of Metropolitan Authorities [1986] 1 W.L.R. 1; [1986] 1 All E.R. 164; (1985) 17 H.L.R. 487; 83 L.G.R. 796; (1986) 130 S.J. 35, QBD 25–007, 25–029, 26–055

R. v Secretary of State for Social Services Ex p. Child Poverty Action Group [1990] 2 Q.B. 540; [1989] 3 W.L.R. 1116; [1989] 1 All E.R. 1047; (1989) 86(41) L.S.G. 41; (1989) 133 S.J. 1373, CA (Civ Div) 24–019

R. v Secretary of State for Social Services Ex p. Wellcome Foundation Ltd; sub nom. SEPTRIN Trade Mark [1988] 1 W.L.R. 635; [1988] 2 All E.R. 684; [1988] 3 C.M.L.R. 95; [1988] 2 F.T.L.R. 206; (1988) 132 S.J. 821, HL 17–014

R. v Secretary of State for Trade Ex p. Anderson Strathclyde Plc [1983] 2 All E.R. 233; [1983] Com. L.R. 94; [1984] E.C.C. 249, QBD 11–007

R. v Secretary of State for Trade and Industry Ex p. Greenpeace Ltd (No.1) [1998] Eu. L.R. 48; [1998] Env. L.R. 415; [1998] C.O.D. 59, QBD 26–046

R. v Secretary of State for Trade and Industry Ex p. Greenpeace Ltd (No.2) [2000] 2 C.M.L.R. 94; [2000] Eu. L.R. 196; [2000] Env. L.R. 221; [2000] C.O.D. 141, QBD 26–046

R. v Secretary of State for Trade and Industry Ex p. Lonrho Plc [1989] 1 W.L.R. 525; [1989] 2 All E.R. 609; (1989) 5 B.C.C. 633; (1989) 139 N.L.J. 717; (1989) 133 S.J. 724, HL 11–009, 12–036

R. v Secretary of State for Transport Ex p. APH Road Safety (No.1)[1993] C.O.D. 150 26–006

R. v Secretary of State for Transport Ex p. Factortame Ltd (C-213/89) [1990] 2 Lloyd's Rep. 351; [1990] E.C.R. I-2433; [1990] 3 C.M.L.R. 1; (1990) 140 N.L.J. 927, ECJ 10–031, 28–019

R. v Secretary of State for Transport Ex p. Factortame Ltd (C-221/89) [1992] Q.B. 680; [1992] 3 W.L.R. 288; [1991] 3 All E.R. 769; [1991] 2 Lloyd's Rep. 648; [1991] E.C.R. I-3905; [1991] 3 C.M.L.R. 589; (1991) 141 N.L.J. 1107, ECJ 29–057

R. v Secretary of State for Transport Ex p. Factortame Ltd (No.1) [1990] 2 A.C. 85; [1989] 2 W.L.R. 997; [1989] 2 All E.R. 692; [1989] 3 C.M.L.R. 1; [1989] C.O.D. 531; (1989) 139 N.L.J. 715, HL 10–011, 10–013, 28–019

R. v Secretary of State for Transport Ex p. Factortame Ltd (No.2) [1991] 1 A.C. 603; [1990] 3 W.L.R. 818; [1991] 1 All E.R. 70; [1991] 1 Lloyd's Rep. 10; [1990] 3 C.M.L.R. 375; (1991) 3 Admin. L.R. 333; (1990) 140 N.L.J. 1457; (1990) 134 S.J. 1189, HL 10–031, 23–032, 25–032, 25–034, 28–020

R. v Secretary of State for Transport Ex p. Factortame Ltd (No.5) [2000] 1 A.C. 524; [1999] 3 W.L.R. 1062; [1999] 4 All E.R. 906; [1999] 3 C.M.L.R. 597; [2000] Eu. L.R. 40; (1999) 96(43) L.S.G. 32; [1999] N.P.C. 126, HL 29–059

R. v Secretary of State for Transport Ex p. GLC [1986] Q.B. 556 23–033

R. v Secretary of State for Transport Ex p. Factortame Ltd (No.6); sub nom. R. v Secretary of State for the Environment, Transport and the Regions Ex p. Factortame Ltd; Factortame Ltd v Secretary of State for Transport (No.6) [2001] 1 W.L.R. 942; [2001] 1 C.M.L.R. 47; [2001] Eu. L.R. 207; (2001) 98(12) L.S.G. 42; (2001) 145 S.J.L.B. 19, QBD (TCC) 29–059

R. v Secretary of State for Transport Ex p. Gwent CC [1988] Q.B. 429; [1987] 2 W.L.R. 961; [1987] 1 All E.R. 161; [1987] J.P.L. 645; (1987) 84 L.S.G. 1327; (1987) 131 S.J. 472, CA (Civ Div) 9–038, 12–046

R. v Secretary of State for Transport Ex p. Pegasus Holdings (London) [1988] 1 W.L.R. 990; [1989] 2 All E.R. 481; (1988) 132 S.J. 1182, QBD 12–030

R. v Secretary of State for Transport Ex p. Richmond upon Thames LBC (No.1) [1994] 1 W.L.R. 74; [1994] 1 All E.R. 577; [1994] Env. L.R. 134, QBD 20–013

R. v Secretary of State for War [1891] 2 Q.B. 326, CA 25–015

R. v Sefton MBC Ex p. Help the Aged [1997] 4 All E.R. 532; [1997] 3 F.C.R. 573; (1997–98) 1 C.C.L. Rep. 57; (1997) 38 B.M.L.R. 135; [1998] C.O.D. 69, CA (Civ Div) 17–014

R. v Servite Houses Ex p. Goldsmith (2001) 33 H.L.R. 35; (2000) 2 L.G.L.R. 997; [2001] B.L.G.R. 55; (2000) 3 C.C.L. Rep. 325; [2001] A.C.D. 4, QBD ... 5–013, 26–023

R. v Sevenoaks DC Ex p. Terry [1985] 3 All E.R. 226; [1984] J.P.L. 420, QBD 13–008

R. v Shayler (David Michael) [2002] UKHL 11; [2003] 1 A.C. 247; [2002] 2 W.L.R. 754; [2002] 2 All E.R. 477; [2002] H.R.L.R. 33; [2002] U.K.H.R.R. 603; [2002] A.C.D. 58; (2002) 99(17) L.S.G. 34; (2002) 146 S.J.L.B. 84, HL 18–038

R. v Shoreditch Assessment Committee Ex p. Morgan [1910] 2 K.B. 859, CA 14–009

R. v Skinner (Edward George) [1968] 2 Q.B. 700; [1968] 3 W.L.R. 408; [1968] 3 All E.R.
124; (1968) 52 Cr. App. R. 599; (1968) 112 S.J. 565, CA (Crim Div) 16–007
R. v Somerset CC Ex p. Dixon [1998] Env. L.R. 111; (1998) 75 P. & C.R. 175; [1997]
J.P.L. 1030; [1997] C.O.D. 323; [1997] N.P.C. 61, QBD 24–017
R. v Somersetshire JJ (1826) 5 B. & C. 816 27–003
R. v South Hams DC Ex p. Gibb; sub nom. Davies v Gloucestershire CC; Gibb v
Devon CC and South Hams DC; Rolls v Dorset CC [1995] Q.B. 158; [1994] 3
W.L.R. 1151; [1994] 4 All E.R. 1012; 93 L.G.R. 59; [1994] C.O.D. 448; [1995]
C.O.D. 9; (1994) 158 L.G. Rev. 861; (1994) 91(32) L.S.G. 41; (1994) 138 S.J.L.B.
132, CA (Civ Div) 15–024
R. v Southwark LBC Ex p. Bannerman (1990) 22 H.L.R. 459; (1990) 2 Admin. L.R.
381; [1990] R.V.R. 33; [1990] C.O.D. 115; (1990) 154 L.G. Rev. 376, QBD 20–035
R. v Special Educational Needs Tribunal Ex p. F; sub nom. R. v Special Educational
Needs Tribunal Ex p. Fairpo (No.1) [1996] E.L.R. 213; [1996] C.O.D. 180, QBD . 26–057
R. v Speyer [1916] 2 K.B. 858, CA 24–004, 25–035
R. v Stafford JJ Ex p. Stafford Corporation [1940] 2 K.B. 33 24–003
R. v Stimpson (1863) 4 B. & S. 301 14–027
R. v Stratford upon Avon DC Ex p. Jackson [1985] 1 W.L.R. 1319; [1985] 3 All E.R.
769; 84 L.G.R. 287; (1986) 51 P. & C.R. 76; (1985) 82 L.S.G. 3533; (1985) 129 S.J.
854, CA (Civ Div) 26–045
R. v Stoke on Trent City Council Ex p. Highgate Projects (1997) 29 H.L.R. 271, CA
(Civ Div) 24–021
R. v Stoke on Trent Justices Ex p. Cawley [1996] C.O.D. 292 25–038
R. v Sunderland JJ [1901] PI 122 13–006
R. v Surrey JJ (1870) L.R. 5 Q.B. 466 24–003
R. v Sussex Justices Ex p. McCarthy; sub nom. R. v Sussex JJ Ex p. McCarthy [1924] 1
K.B. 256, KBD 13–004, 13–006
R. v Swansea Income Tax Commissioners Ex p. English Crown Spelter Co Ltd [1925] 2
K.B. 250, KBD 14–029
R. v Sykes (David) (1875–76) L.R. 1 Q.B.D. 52, QBD 12–036
R. v Thames Magistrates Court Ex p. Greenbaum (1957) 55 L.G.R. 129, CCA 24–003
R. v Thames Magistrates Court Ex p. Polemis (The Corinthic); sub nom. R. v Thames
Justices Ex p. Polemis [1974] 1 W.L.R. 1371; [1974] 2 All E.R. 1219; [1974] 2
Lloyd's Rep. 16; (1974) 118 S.J. 734, QBD 12–024, 12–027
R. v Thomas [1892] 1 Q.B. 426 12–036
R. v Torquay Licensing Justices Ex p. Brockman [1951] 2 K.B. 784; [1951] 2 All E.R.
656; [1951] 2 T.L.R. 652; (1951) 115 J.P. 514; 49 L.G.R. 733, KBD 16–012, 16–015
R. v Tower Hamlets LBC Ex p. Abbas Ali (1993) 25 H.L.R. 158; [1993] C.O.D. 131,
CA (Civ Div) 21–003
R. v Tower Hamlets LBC Ex p. Begum (Ferdous) [1993] Q.B. 447; [1993] 2 W.L.R. 9;
[1993] 1 All E.R. 447; (1992) 24 H.L.R. 715, CA (Civ Div) 15–024
R. v Tower Hamlets LBC Ex p. Chetnik Developments Ltd [1988] A.C. 858; [1988] 2
W.L.R. 654; [1988] 1 All E.R. 961; 86 L.G.R. 321; [1988] R.A. 45; [1988] E.G. 36
(C.S.); (1988) 138 N.L.J. Rep. 89; (1988) 132 S.J. 4621 HL 25–016, 29–054
R. v Tower Hamlets LBC Ex p. Kayne-Levenson; sub nom. R. v Tower Hamlets LBC
[1975] Q.B. 431; [1975] 2 W.L.R. 164; [1975] 1 All E.R. 641; 73 L.G.R. 64; (1975)
119 S.J. 85, CA (Civ Div) 16–012, 16–013
R. v Traffic Commissioners for the North Western Ex p. Brake [1996] C.O.D. 248;
[1995] N.P.C. 167, QBD 24–023
R. v Twiss; sub nom. R. v Sir Travers Twiss (1868–69) L.R. 4 Q.B. 407, QB 24–004
R. v Visitors to the Inns of Court Ex p. Calder; sub nom. Calder v General Council of
the Bar [1994] Q.B. 1; [1993] 3 W.L.R. 287; [1993] 2 All E.R. 876; [1993] C.O.D.
242; (1993) 143 N.L.J. 164, CA (Civ Div) 26–027
R. v Wandsworth Licensing Justices Ex p. Whitbread & Co Ltd [1921] 3 K.B. 487,
KBD 17–013
R. v Warwick Crown Court Ex p. Smalley (No.2) [1987] 1 W.L.R. 237; (1987) 84 Cr.
App. R. 51; [1987] Crim. L.R. 112; (1987) 84 L.S.G. 654; (1987) 131 S.J. 257,
QBD 19–010
R. v Westminster City Council Ex p. Ermakov [1996] 2 All E.R. 302; [1996] 2 F.C.R.
208; (1996) 28 H.L.R. 819; (1996) 8 Admin. L.R. 389; [1996] C.O.D. 391; (1996)
160 J.P. Rep. 814; (1996) 140 S.J.L.B. 23, CA (Civ Div) 12–034, 12–039

R. v Westminster Assessment Committee Ex p. Grosvenor House (Park Lane) Ltd
[1941] 1 K.B. 53, CA 9–024, 12–031
R. v Whitfield (1885) 15 Q.B.D. 122 14–026
R. v Wicks (Peter Edward) [1998] A.C. 92; [1997] 2 W.L.R. 876; [1997] 2 All E.R. 801;
(1997) 161 J.P. 433; (1997) 9 Admin. L.R. 349; [1997] 2 P.L.R. 97; [1997] J.P.L.
1049; (1997) 161 J.P.N. 628; (1997) 94(35) L.S.G. 34; (1997) 147 N.L.J. 883; (1997)
141 S.J.L.B. 127; [1997] N.P.C. 85, HL 22–030, 26–010
R. v Williams Ex p. Phillips; sub nom. R. v Justices of Swansea Ex p. Phillips [1914] 1
K.B. 608, KBD 13–011, 23–027, 25–010
R. v Wilson (1844) 6 Q.B. 620 14–026
R. v Winchester Crown Court Ex p. Morris [1996] C.O.D. 104, Crown Ct 12–033
R. v Windsor Licensing Justices Ex p. Hodes; sub nom. Hodes v Windsor Licensing
Justices [1983] 1 W.L.R. 685; [1983] 2 All E.R. 551; (1983) 147 J.P. 353; (1983) 127
S.J. 378, CA (Civ Div) 16–013
R. v Wood (1855) 5 El. & Bl. 49 .... 14–026, 27–003, 27–005
R. v Woodhouse [1906] 2 K.B. 501 .... 25–005, 25–006
R. (on the application of A) v B Council [2007] EWHC 1529 (Admin); [2007] B.L.G.R.
813, QBD (Admin) 26–026
R. (on the application of AA (Afghanistan)) v Secretary of State for the Home
Department [2006] EWCA Civ 1550; [2007] A.C.D. 32; (2006) 103(47) L.S.G. 30;
(2006) 150 S.J.L.B. 1570, CA (Civ Div) 19–004
R. (on the application of Abbasi) v Secretary of State for Foreign and Commonwealth
Affairs; sub nom. R. (on the application of Abassi) v Secretary of State for Foreign
and Commonwealth Affairs [2002] EWCA Civ 1598; [2003] U.K.H.R.R. 76; (2002)
99(47) L.S.G. 29, CA (Civ Div) 17–005, 20–016, 23–029
R. (on the application of Afzal) v Election Court [2005] EWCA Civ 647; [2005]
B.L.G.R. 823, CA (Civ Div) 12–031
R. (on the application of Aggregate Industries UK Ltd) v English Nature; sub nom.
Aggregate Industries UK Ltd v English Nature [2002] EWHC 908 (Admin); [2003]
Env. L.R. 3; [2002] A.C.D. 67; [2002] N.P.C. 58, QBD (Admin) 13–016
R. (on the application of Al Rawi) v Secretary of State for Foreign and Commonwealth
Affairs [2006] EWCA Civ 1279; [2007] 2 W.L.R. 1219; [2006] H.R.L.R. 42; [2007]
U.K.H.R.R. 58; (2006) 103(41) L.S.G. 33, CA (Civ Div) 17–008, 17–013
R. (on the application of Al-Skeini) v Secretary of State for Defence [2007] UKHL 26;
[2007] 3 W.L.R. 33; [2007] 3 All E.R. 685; [2007] H.R.L.R. 31; [2007] U.K.H.R.R.
955; 22 B.H.R.C. 518; (2007) 104(26) L.S.G. 34; (2007) 157 N.L.J. 894; (2007) 151
S.J.L.B. 809; [2008] 1 A.C. 153, HL 18–012
R. (on the application of Alconbury Developments Ltd) v Secretary of State for the
Environment, Transport and the Regions [2001] 2 W.L.R. 1389 .... 12–046, 13–014,
13–015, 18–003, 18–015, 18–035, 19–007
R. (on the application of Amin (Imtiaz)) v Secretary of State for the Home Depart-
ment; sub nom. R. (on the application of Middleton) v HM Coroner for Western
Somerset [2003] UKHL 51; [2004] 1 A.C. 653; [2003] 3 W.L.R. 1169; [1998] 1
W.L.R. 972; [2003] 4 All E.R. 1264; [2004] H.R.L.R. 3; [2004] U.K.H.R.R. 75; 15
B.H.R.C. 362; (2004) 76 B.M.L.R. 143; [2003] Inquest L.R. 1; [2004] Prison L.R.
140; (2003) 100(44) L.S.G. 32; (2003) 153 N.L.J. 1600, HL 18–003
R. (on the application of Anderson) v Secretary of State for the Home Department; sub
nom. R. v Secretary of State for the Home Department Ex p. Anderson; R. v
Secretary of State for the Home Department Ex p. Taylor [2002] UKHL 46; [2003]
1 A.C. 837; [2002] 3 W.L.R. 1800; [2002] 4 All E.R. 1089; [2003] 1 Cr. App. R. 32;
[2003] H.R.L.R. 7; [2003] U.K.H.R.R. 112; 13 B.H.R.C. 450; [2003] Prison L.R.
36; (2003) 100(3) L.S.G. 31; (2002) 146 S.J.L.B. 272, HL 18–003, 18–008
R. (on the application of Animal Defenders International) v Secretary of State for
Culture, Media and Sport [2008] UKHL 15; (2008) 152(12) S.J.L.B. 30, HL 18–038
R. (on the application of Anufrijeva) v Secretary of State for the Home Department
[2003] UKHL 36; [2004] 1 A.C. 604; [2003] 3 W.L.R. 252; [2003] 3 All E.R. 827;
[2003] H.R.L.R. 31; [2003] Imm. A.R. 570; [2003] I.N.L.R. 521; (2003) 100(33)
L.S.G. 29, HL 12–027, 17–020, 25–026
R. (on the application of Asha Foundation) v Millennium Commission [2003] EWCA
Civ 88; [2003] A.C.D. 50; (2003) 100(11) L.S.G. 31, CA (Civ Div) 12–037
R. (on the application of Association of British Civilian Internees (Far East Region)) v
Secretary of State for Defence; sub nom. Association of British Civilian Internees

(Far East Region) v Secretary of State for Defence [2003] EWCA Civ 473; [2003] Q.B. 1397; [2003] 3 W.L.R. 80; [2003] A.C.D. 51; (2003) 100(23) L.S.G. 38, CA (Civ Div) 19–009, 20–017, 21–003

R. (on the application of Association of British Travel Agents Ltd (ABTA)) v Civil Aviation Authority; sub nom. Association of British Travel Agents Ltd v Civil Aviation Authority [2006] EWCA Civ 1356; [2007] 2 All E.R. (Comm) 898; [2007] 2 Lloyd's Rep. 249; (2006) 150 S.J.L.B. 1430, CA (Civ Div) 22–046

R. (on the application of Axon) v Secretary of State for Health [2006] EWHC 37 (Admin); [2006] Q.B. 539; [2006] 2 W.L.R. 1130; [2006] 2 F.L.R. 206; [2006] 1 F.C.R. 175; [2006] H.R.L.R. 12; (2006) 88 B.M.L.R. 96; [2006] A.C.D. 58; [2006] Fam. Law 272; (2006) 103(8) L.S.G. 25, QBD (Admin) 22–046

R. (on the application of B) v Camden LBC [2001] EWHC Admin 271; (2001) 4 C.C.L. Rep. 246; (2002) 63 B.M.L.R. 154, QBD (Admin) 20–015

R. (on the application of B) v Haddock (Responsible Medical Officer) [2006] EWCA Civ 961; [2006] H.R.L.R. 40; [2006] Lloyd's Rep. Med. 433; (2007) 93 B.M.L.R. 52; [2006] M.H.L.R. 306, CA (Civ Div) 12–031, 26–051

R. (on the application of BAPIO Action Ltd) v Secretary of State for the Home Department [2007] EWCA Civ 1139; [2008] A.C.D. 7, CA (Civ Div) ... 16–015, 22–018

R. (on the application of Baiai) v Secretary of State for the Home Department; R. (on the application of Trzcinska) v Secretary of State for the Home Department; R. (on the application of Tilki) v Secretary of State for the Home Department; R. (on the application of Bigoku) v Secretary of State for the Home Department [2007] EWCA Civ 478; [2007] 3 W.L.R. 573; [2007] 4 All E.R. 199; [2007] 2 F.L.R. 627; [2007] 2 F.C.R. 421; [2007] H.R.L.R. 29; [2007] U.K.H.R.R. 771; [2007] Imm. A.R. 730; [2007] Fam. Law 806; (2007) 104(23) L.S.G. 33; (2007) 151 S.J.L.B. 711, CA (Civ Div) 21–011

R. (on the application of Balchin) v Parliamentary Commissioner for Administration (No.3); sub nom. R. v Parliamentary Commissioner for Administration Ex p. Balchin (No.3) [2002] EWHC 1876, QBD (Admin) 8–031

R. (on the application of BAPIO Action Ltd) v Secretary of State for the Home Department [2007] EWCA Civ 1139; [2008] A.C.D. 7, CA (Civ Div) 12–028

R. (on the application of BBC) v Information Tribunal [2007] 1 W.L.R. 2583 14–034

R. (on the application of Bagdanavicius) v Secretary of State for the Home Department [2005] UKHL 38; [2005] 2 A.C. 668; [2005] 2 W.L.R. 1359; [2005] 4 All E.R. 263; [2005] H.R.L.R. 24; [2005] U.K.H.R.R. 907; [2005] Imm. A.R. 430; [2005] I.N.L.R. 422, HL 15–003

R. (on the application of Baiai) v Secretary of State for the Home Department [2006] EWHC 1035 (Admin), QBD (Admin) 29–028

R. (on the application of Bamber) v Revenue and Customs Commissioners [2005] EWHC 3221 (Admin); [2006] S.T.C. 1035; [2006] B.T.C. 146; [2006] S.T.I. 46, QBD (Admin) 20–020

R. (on the application of Bancoult) v Secretary of State for Foreign and Commonwealth Affairs [2007] EWCA Civ 498; (2007) 104(23) L.S.G. 31; (2007) 151 S.J.L.B. 707; [2007] 3 W.L.R. 768, CA (Civ Div) 17–005, 20–019, 20–025, 22–028

R. (on the application of Bancoult) v Secretary of State for the Foreign and Commonwealth Office; sub nom. R. (on the application of Bancoult) v Secretary of State for Foreign and Commonwealth Affairs; R. v Secretary of State for the Foreign and Commonwealth Office Ex p. Bancoult [2001] Q.B. 1067; [2001] 2 W.L.R. 1219; [2001] A.C.D. 18; (2000) 97(47) L.S.G. 39, QBD (Admin) 22–028

R. (on the application of Beer (t/a Hammer Trout Farm)) v Hampshire Farmers Markets Ltd; sub nom. Hampshire CC v Beer (t/a Hammer Trout Farm) [2003] EWCA Civ 1056; [2004] 1 W.L.R. 233; [2004] U.K.H.R.R. 727; [2003] 31 E.G. 67 (C.S.); (2003) 100(36) L.S.G. 40; (2003) 147 S.J.L.B. 1085; [2003] N.P.C. 93, CA (Civ Div) 26–027

R. (on the application of Beeson) v Dorset CC; sub nom. Secretary of State for Health v Beeson's Personal Representative [2002] EWCA Civ 1812; [2003] H.R.L.R. 11; [2003] U.K.H.R.R. 353; [2003] H.L.R. 39; [2004] B.L.G.R. 92; (2003) 6 C.C.L. Rep. 5; [2003] A.C.D. 40; (2003) 100(10) L.S.G. 30, CA (Civ Div) 13–017

R. (on the application of Begum) v Denbigh High School Governors; sub nom. R. (on the application of SB) v Denbigh High School Governors [2006] UKHL 15; [2007] 1 A.C. 100; [2006] 2 W.L.R. 719; [2006] 2 All E.R. 487; [2006] 1 F.C.R. 613; [2006]

H.R.L.R. 21; [2006] U.K.H.R.R. 708; 23 B.H.R.C. 276; [2006] E.L.R. 273; (2006) 103(14) L.S.G. 29; (2006) 156 N.L.J. 552, HL 18–040, 18–044, 18–045, 18–046, 18–051, 19–018

R. (on the application of Ben-Abdelaziz) v Haringey LBC [2001] EWCA Civ 803; [2001] 1 W.L.R. 1485; [2001] A.C.D. 88; (2001) 98(26) L.S.G. 44; (2001) 145 S.J.L.B. 150, CA (Civ Div) 25–002, 26–002

R. (on the application of Bernard) v Enfield LBC [2002] EWHC 2282 (Admin); [2003] H.R.L.R. 4; [2003] U.K.H.R.R. 148; [2003] H.L.R. 27; [2003] B.L.G.R. 423; (2002) 5 C.C.L. Rep. 577; [2003] A.C.D. 26; (2002) 99(48) L.S.G. 27, QBD (Admin) .. 29–028

R. (on the application of Bewry) v Norwich City Council [2001] EWHC Admin 657; [2002] H.R.L.R. 2, QBD (Admin) 13–018, 13–020

R. (on the application of Bibi) v Newham LBC (No.1); sub nom. R. v Newham LBC Ex p. Bibi; R. v Newham LBC Ex p. Al-Nashed [2001] EWCA Civ 607; [2002] 1 W.L.R. 237; (2001) 33 H.L.R. 84; (2001) 98(23) L.S.G. 38; [2001] N.P.C. 83, CA (Civ Div) 20–017, 20–022, 20–023, 20–025, 20–048

R. (on the application of Bidar) v Ealing LBC (C-209/03) [2005] Q.B. 812; [2005] 2 W.L.R. 1078; [2005] All E.R. (EC) 687; [2005] E.C.R. I-2119; [2005] 2 C.M.L.R. 3; [2005] C.E.C. 607; [2005] E.L.R. 404, ECJ 21–016

R. (on the application of Bloggs 61) v Secretary of State for the Home Department [2003] EWCA Civ 686; [2003] 1 W.L.R. 2724; [2007] Inquest L.R. 206; [2003] Prison L.R. 426; [2003] Po. L.R. 221; (2003) 100(33) L.S.G. 29; (2003) 147 S.J.L.B. 780, CA (Civ Div) 20–032

R. (on the application of Bono) v Harlow DC [2002] EWHC 423; [2002] 1 W.L.R. 2475; [2002] H.R.L.R. 38; [2002] A.C.D. 73; [2002] N.P.C. 46, QBD (Admin) 18–014

R. (on the application of Bradley) v Secretary of State for Work and Pensions [2008] EWCA Civ 36, CA (Civ Div) 8–022, 19–004

R. (on the application of British American Tobacco (Investments) Ltd) v Secretary of State for Health (C-491/01); sub nom. R. v Secretary of State for Health Ex p. British American Tobacco (Investments) Ltd [2003] All E.R. (EC) 604; [2002] E.C.R. I-11453; [2003] 1 C.M.L.R. 14; [2003] C.E.C. 53; [2003] E.T.M.R. CN10; [2003] E.T.M.R. CN5, ECJ 19–022

R. (on the application of Bulger) v Secretary of State for the Home Department; sub nom. R. v Secretary of State for the Home Department Ex p. Bulger; R. (on the application of Bulger) v Lord Chief Justice [2001] EWHC Admin 119; [2001] 3 All E.R. 449, DC 24–020

R. (on the application of Burkett) v Hammersmith and Fulham LBC (No.1); sub nom. Burkett, Re; R. v Hammersmith and Fulham LBC Ex p. Burkett [2002] UKHL 23; [2002] 1 W.L.R. 1593; [2002] 3 All E.R. 97; [2002] C.P. Rep. 66; [2003] Env. L.R. 6; [2003] 1 P. & C.R. 3; [2002] 2 P.L.R. 90; [2002] J.P.L. 1346; [2002] A.C.D. 81; [2002] 22 E.G. 136 (C.S.); (2002) 99(27) L.S.G. 34; (2002) 152 N.L.J. 847; (2002) 146 S.J.L.B. 137; [2002] N.P.C. 75, HL 26–046

R. (on the application of C) v Brent, Kensington and Chelsea, and Westminster Mental Health NHS Trust [2002] EWHC 181 (Admin); (2003) 6 C.C.L. Rep. 335; [2002] Lloyd's Rep. Med. 321; [2002] M.H.L.R. 265, QBD (Admin) 20–017

R. (on the application of Carroll) v Secretary of State for the Home Department; sub nom. R. v Secretary of State for the Home Department Ex p. Carroll [2005] UKHL 13; [2005] 1 W.L.R. 688; [2005] 1 All E.R. 927; [2005] H.R.L.R. 12; 19 B.H.R.C. 282; [2005] 2 Prison L.R. 120; (2005) 102(15) L.S.G. 35, HL 13–007

R. (on the application of Carson) v Secretary of State for Work and Pensions; sub nom. Carson v Secretary of State for Work and Pensions [2005] UKHL 37; [2006] 1 A.C. 173; [2005] 2 W.L.R. 1369; [2005] 4 All E.R. 545; [2005] H.R.L.R. 23; [2005] U.K.H.R.R. 1185; 18 B.H.R.C. 677, HL 17–008, 21–007

R. (on the application of Castille Ltd) v Secretary of State for Trade and Industry [2002] EWHC 16; [2002] Eu. L.R. 209; [2002] A.C.D. 52, QBD (Admin) 19–012

R. (on the application of Cavanagh) v Health Service Commissioner [2005] EWCA Civ 1578; [2006] 1 W.L.R. 1229; [2006] 3 All E.R. 543; [2006] 1 F.C.R. 7; (2006) 91 B.M.L.R. 40, CA (Civ Div) 8–035

R. (on the application of Chief Constable of the West Midlands) v Birmingham Magistrates Court; sub nom. R. (on the application of Chief Constable of the West Midlands) v Birmingham Justices [2002] EWHC 1087 (Admin); [2002] Po. L.R. 157; [2003] Crim. L.R. 37; [2003] A.C.D. 18; (2002) 99(28) L.S.G. 32; (2002) 146 S.J.L.B. 159, QBD (Admin) 16–008

R. (on the application of Clear Channel UK Ltd) v Southwark LBC [2007] EWCA Civ
1328; [2007] N.P.C. 133, CA (Civ Div) 20–036
R. (on the application of Clift) v Secretary of State for the Home Department; sub
nom. Hindawi v Secretary of State for the Home Department; Secretary of State
for the Home Department v Hindawi; Secretary of State for the Home Department
v Headley [2006] UKHL 54; [2007] 1 A.C. 484; [2007] 2 W.L.R. 24; [2007] 2 All
E.R. 1; [2007] H.R.L.R. 12; [2007] U.K.H.R.R. 348; 21 B.H.R.C. 704; [2007]
A.C.D. 27, HL 18–010, 21–005
R. (on the application of Coghlan) v Chief Constable of Greater Manchester [2004]
EWHC 2801; [2005] 2 All E.R. 890; [2005] A.C.D. 34, QBD (Admin) 20–026
R. (on the application of Condron) v National Assembly for Wales; sub nom. Condron
v National Assembly for Wales; National Assembly for Wales v Condron [2006]
EWCA Civ 1573; [2007] B.L.G.R. 87; [2007] 2 P. & C.R. 4; [2007] J.P.L. 938; [2006]
49 E.G. 94 (C.S.); [2006] N.P.C. 127; [2007] Env. L.R. D7, CA (Civ Div) 13–007
R. (on the application of Conville) v Richmond upon Thames LBC; sub nom. Conville
v Richmond upon Thames LBC [2006] EWCA Civ 718; [2006] 1 W.L.R. 2808;
[2006] 4 All E.R. 917; [2006] H.L.R. 45; (2006) 103(25) L.S.G. 30; (2006) 150
S.J.L.B. 811; [2006] N.P.C. 70, CA (Civ Div) 17–014
R. (on the application of Corner House Research) v Secretary of State for Trade and
Industry [2005] EWCA Civ 192; [2005] 1 W.L.R. 2600; [2005] 4 All E.R. 1; [2005]
C.P. Rep. 28; [2005] 3 Costs L.R. 455; [2005] A.C.D. 100; (2005) 102(17) L.S.G. 31;
(2005) 149 S.J.L.B. 297, CA (Civ Div) 26–054
R. (on the application of Countryside Alliance) v Attorney General [2007] UKHL 52;
[2007] 3 W.L.R. 922; [2008] 2 All E.R. 95; [2008] H.R.L.R. 10; [2008] U.K.H.R.R.
1; (2007) 104(48) L.S.G. 23; (2007) 157 N.L.J. 1730; (2007) 151 S.J.L.B. 1564;
[2007] N.P.C. 127, HL 18–035
R. (on the application of Cowl) v Plymouth City Council; sub nom. Cowl v Plymouth
City Council; Cowl (Practice Note), Re [2001] EWCA Civ 1935; [2002] 1 W.L.R.
803; [2002] C.P. Rep. 18; (2002) 5 C.C.L. Rep. 42; [2002] A.C.D. 11; [2002] Fam.
Law 265; (2002) 99(8) L.S.G. 35; (2002) 146 S.J.L.B. 27, CA (Civ Div) 26–048
R. (on the application of D) v Secretary of State for the Home Department; sub nom. D
v Secretary of State for the Home Department [2002] EWHC 2805 (Admin); [2003]
1 W.L.R. 1315; [2003] U.K.H.R.R. 221; [2003] M.H.L.R. 193; [2003] Prison L.R.
178; [2003] A.C.D. 84, QBD (Admin) 18–007
R. (on the application of Daly) v Secretary of State for the Home Department; sub
nom. R. v Secretary of State for the Home Department Ex p. Daly [2001] UKHL
26; [2001] 2 A.C. 532; [2001] 2 W.L.R. 1622; [2001] 3 All E.R. 433; [2001] H.R.L.R.
49; [2001] U.K.H.R.R. 887; [2001] Prison L.R. 322; [2001] A.C.D. 79; (2001) 98(26)
L.S.G. 43; (2001) 145 S.J.L.B. 156, HL 18–038, 21–006
R. (on the application of E) v Ashworth Hospital Authority [2001] EWHC Admin
1089; [2002] M.H.L.R. 150; [2002] A.C.D. 23, QBD (Admin) 18–038
R. (on the application of Ealing LBC) v Audit Commission; sub nom. Ealing LBC v
Audit Commission; Audit Commission for England and Wales v Ealing LBC
[2005] EWCA Civ 556; (2005) 8 C.C.L. Rep. 317, CA (Civ Div) 16–003
R. (on the application of East Hertfordshire DC) v First Secretary of State [2007]
EWHC 834 (Admin); [2007] J.P.L. 1304, QBD (Admin) 20–030
R. (on the application of Edwards) v Environment Agency (No.1) [2004] EWHC 736
(Admin); [2004] 3 All E.R. 21; [2004] Env. L.R. 43; [2004] 2 P. & C.R. 20; [2004]
J.P.L. 1691; [2004] A.C.D. 82; [2004] N.P.C. 56, QBD (Admin) 24–019
R. (on the application of Edwards) v Environment Agency (No.2); sub nom. Edwards v
Environment Agency [2006] EWCA Civ 877; [2007] Env. L.R. 9; [2007] J.P.L. 82;
(2006) 103(30) L.S.G. 32, CA (Civ Div) 9–038, 12–028
R. (on the application of Elias) v Secretary of State for Defence; sub nom. Secretary of
State for the Home Department v Elias; Elias v Secretary of State for Defence
[2006] EWCA Civ 1293; [2006] 1 W.L.R. 3213; [2006] I.R.L.R. 934, CA (Civ
Div) 16–012, 21–004
R. (on the application of European Roma Rights Centre) v Immigration Officer,
Prague Airport; sub nom. European Roma Rights Centre v Immigration Officer,
Prague Airport; R. (on the application of European Roma Rights Centre) v
Secretary of State for the Home Department [2004] UKHL 55; [2005] 2 A.C. 1;
[2005] 2 W.L.R. 1; [2005] 1 All E.R. 527; [2005] I.R.L.R. 115; [2005] H.R.L.R. 4;

[2005] U.K.H.R.R. 530; 18 B.H.R.C. 1; [2005] Imm. A.R. 100; [2005] I.N.L.R. 182; (2004) 154 N.L.J. 1893; (2005) 149 S.J.L.B. 26, HL 21–004
R. (on the application of Ewing) v Office of the Deputy Prime Minister; sub nom. Ewing v Office of the Deputy Prime Minister [2005] EWCA Civ 1583; [2006] 1 W.L.R. 1260; [2005] N.P.C. 146, CA (Civ Div) 26–039
R. (on the application of Farrakhan) v Secretary of State for the Home Department; sub nom. Farrakhan v Secretary of State for the Home Department; Secretary of State for the Home Department v Farrakhan [2002] EWCA Civ 606; [2002] Q.B. 1391; [2002] 3 W.L.R. 481; [2002] 4 All E.R. 289; [2002] U.K.H.R.R. 734; 12 B.H.R.C. 497; [2002] Imm. A.R. 447; [2002] I.N.L.R. 257; [2002] A.C.D. 76; (2002) 99(22) L.S.G. 33; (2002) 152 N.L.J. 708; (2002) 146 S.J.L.B. 124, CA (Civ Div) 19–004, 19–011
R. (on the application of Ferguson) v Visitor of the University of Leicester [2003] EWCA Civ 1082; [2003] E.L.R. 562, CA (Civ Div) 14–036
R. (on the application of Fingle Glen Junction Business and Community Action Group) v Highways Agency [2007] EWHC 2446 (Admin), QBD (Admin) 20–020
R. (on the application of Fivepounds.co.ukLtd) v Transport for London [2005] EWHC 3002 20–017
R. (on the application of Friends Provident Life Office) v Secretary of State for the Environment, Transport and the Regions; sub nom. Friends Provident Life Office v Secretary of State for the Environment, Transport and the Regions; R. (on the application of Friends Provident Life & Pensions Ltd) v Secretary of State for Transport, Local Government and the Regions; Friends Provident Life & Pensions Ltd v Secretary of State for Transport, Local Government and the Regions [2001] EWHC Admin 820; [2002] 1 W.L.R. 1450; [2002] J.P.L. 958; [2001] 44 E.G. 147 (C.S.); [2001] N.P.C. 152, QBD (Admin) 13–016
R. (on the application of G) v Barnet LBC [2003] UKHL 57; [2004] 2 A.C. 208; [2003] 3 W.L.R. 1194; [2004] 1 All E.R. 97; [2004] 1 F.L.R. 454; [2003] 3 F.C.R. 419; [2004] H.R.L.R. 4; [2004] H.L.R. 10; [2003] B.L.G.R. 569; (2003) 6 C.C.L. Rep. 500; [2004] Fam. Law 21; (2003) 100(45) L.S.G. 29; [2003] N.P.C. 123, HL 17–014
R. (on the application of G) v Immigration Appeal Tribunal; R. (on the application of M) v Immigration Appeal Tribunal [2004] EWCA Civ 1731; [2005] 1 W.L.R. 1445; [2005] 2 All E.R. 165; [2005] Imm. A.R. 106; [2005] I.N.L.R. 329; (2005) 102(6) L.S.G. 32; (2005) 149 S.J.L.B. 59, CA (Civ Div) 26–057
R. (on the application of Galligan) v University of Oxford [2001] EWHC Admin 965; [2002] E.L.R. 494; [2002] A.C.D. 33, QBD (Admin) 12–016
R. (on the application of Georgiou) v Enfield LBC [2004] EWHC 779 (Admin); [2004] B.L.G.R. 497; [2004] 2 P. & C.R. 21; [2005] J.P.L. 62; (2004) 101(17) L.S.G. 33, QBD (Admin) 13–008
R. (on the application of Gill) v Lord Chancellor's Department [2003] EWHC 156, QBD (Admin) 20–026
R. (on the application of Godfrey) v Conwy CBC [2001] EWHC Admin 640, QBD (Admin) 20–017
R. (on the application of Greenfield) v Secretary of State for the Home Department [2005] UKHL 14; [2005] 1 W.L.R. 673; [2005] 2 All E.R. 240; [2005] H.R.L.R. 13; [2005] U.K.H.R.R. 323; 18 B.H.R.C. 252; [2005] 2 Prison L.R. 129; (2005) 102(16) L.S.G. 30; (2005) 155 N.L.J. 298, HL 29–028, 29–029
R. (on the application of Greenpeace Ltd) v Secretary of State for Trade and Industry [2007] EWHC 311 (Admin); [2007] Env. L.R. 29; [2007] J.P.L. 1314; [2007] N.P.C. 21, QBD (Admin) 12–028, 16–015, 20–017, 22–018, 22–022
R. (on the application of Gurung) v Ministry of Defence [2002] EWHC 2463 (Admin); (2003) 100(6) L.S.G. 25, QBD (Admin) 21–003
R. (on the application of H) v Mental Health Review Tribunal for North and East London Region; sub nom. R. (on the application of H) v London North and East Region Mental Health Review Tribunal; R. (on the application of H) v North and East London Regional Mental Health Review Tribunal [2001] EWCA Civ 415; [2002] Q.B. 1; [2001] 3 W.L.R. 512; [2001] H.R.L.R. 36; [2001] U.K.H.R.R. 717; (2001) 4 C.C.L. Rep. 119; [2001] Lloyd's Rep. Med. 302; (2001) 61 B.M.L.R. 163; [2001] M.H.L.R. 48; [2001] A.C.D. 78; (2001) 98(21) L.S.G. 40; (2001) 145 S.J.L.B. 108, CA (Civ Div) 18–007
R. (on the application of H) v Secretary of State for Health; sub nom. H v Secretary of State for Health; R. (on the application of MH) v Secretary of State for Health

[2005] UKHL 60; [2006] 1 A.C. 441; [2005] 3 W.L.R. 867; [2005] 4 All E.R. 1311; [2006] H.R.L.R. 1; [2006] Lloyd's Rep. Med. 48; (2005) 86 B.M.L.R. 71; [2005] M.H.L.R. 60, HL 18–014

R. (on the application of H) v Wood Green Crown Court [2006] EWHC 2683 (Admin); [2007] 1 W.L.R. 1670; [2007] 2 All E.R. 259; [2007] H.R.L.R. 2; [2007] Crim. L.R. 727; (2006) 156 N.L.J. 1722, DC 29–028

R. (on the application of Haile) v Immigration Appeal Tribunal; sub nom. Haile v Immigration Appeal Tribunal [2001] EWCA Civ 663; [2002] Imm. A.R. 170; [2002] I.N.L.R. 283, CA (Civ Div) 15–003

R. (on the application of Hammond) v Secretary of State for the Home Department [2005] UKHL 69; [2006] 1 A.C. 603; [2005] 3 W.L.R. 1229; [2006] 1 All E.R. 219; [2006] H.R.L.R. 5; 20 B.H.R.C. 198; [2006] 1 Prison L.R. 1; [2006] A.C.D. 33; (2006) 103(3) L.S.G. 27; (2005) 155 N.L.J. 1886; (2006) 150 S.J.L.B. 29, HL ... 18–010

R. (on the application of Hamsher) v First Secretary of State [2004] EWHC 2299 (Admin); [2005] J.P.L. 491, QBD (Admin) 9–038

R. (on the application of Heather) v Leonard Cheshire Foundation [2002] EWCA Civ 366; [2002] 2 All E.R. 936; [2002] H.R.L.R. 30; [2002] U.K.H.R.R. 883; [2002] H.L.R. 49; (2002) 5 C.C.L. Rep. 317; (2003) 69 B.M.L.R. 22; [2002] A.C.D. 43, CA (Civ Div) 5–013, 18–022, 18–023

R. (on the application of Hereford Waste Watchers Ltd) v Herefordshire CC; sub nom. Hereford Waste Watchers Ltd v Hereford Council [2005] EWHC 191 (Admin); [2005] Env. L.R. 29; [2005] J.P.L. 1469; [2005] 9 E.G. 188 (C.S.), QBD (Admin) . 12–039

R. (on the application of Holding & Barnes Plc) v Secretary of State for the Environment, Transport and the Regions; sub nom. R. v Secretary of State for the Environment, Transport and the Regions Ex p. Holdings & Barnes Plc [2001] UKHL 23; [2003] 2 A.C. 295; [2001] 2 W.L.R. 1389; [2001] 2 All E.R. 929; [2002] Env. L.R. 12; [2001] H.R.L.R. 45; [2001] U.K.H.R.R. 728; (2001) 3 L.G.L.R. 38; (2001) 82 P. & C.R. 40; [2001] 2 P.L.R. 76; [2001] J.P.L. 920; [2001] 20 E.G. 228 (C.S.); (2001) 98(24) L.S.G. 45; (2001) 151 N.L.J. 727; (2001) 145 S.J.L.B. 140; [2001] N.P.C. 90, HL 13–014

R. (on the application of Hooper) v Secretary of State for Work and Pensions; sub nom. Hooper v Secretary of State for Work and Pensions [2005] UKHL 29; [2005] 1 W.L.R. 1681; [2006] 1 All E.R. 487; [2005] 2 F.C.R. 183; [2005] H.R.L.R. 21; [2005] U.K.H.R.R. 717; [2005] Pens. L.R. 337, HL 18–007, 18–015, 21–013

R. (on the application of Hoverspeed Ltd) v Customs and Excise Commissioners; sub nom. Hoverspeed Ltd v Customs and Excise Commissioners [2002] EWCA Civ 1804; [2003] Q.B. 1041; [2003] 2 W.L.R. 950; [2003] 2 All E.R. 553; [2003] S.T.C. 1273; [2003] 1 C.M.L.R. 24; [2002] Eu. L.R. 668; (2003) 100(8) L.S.G. 30, CA (Civ Div) 19–012

R. (on the application of Hirst) v Secretary of State for the Home Department (Contact with Media) [2002] EWHC 602 (Admin); [2002] 1 W.L.R. 2929; [2002] U.K.H.R.R. 758; [2002] Prison L.R. 260; [2002] A.C.D. 93; (2002) 99(19) L.S.G. 32; (2002) 146 S.J.L.B. 100, QBD (Admin) 18–038

R. (on the application of Howard) v Secretary of State for Health; sub nom. Howard v Secretary of State for Health [2002] EWHC 396; [2003] Q.B. 830; [2002] 3 W.L.R. 738; (2002) 99(18) L.S.G. 37; (2002) 146 S.J.L.B. 86, QBD (Admin) 19–004

R. (on the application of the Howard League for Penal Reform) v Secretary of State for the Home Department (No.1) [2002] EWHC 1750 (Admin), QBD (Admin) 24–027

R. (on the application of Hurst) v HM Coroner for Northern District London; sub nom. R. (on the application of Hurst) v London Northern District Coroner; R. (on the application of Hurst) v Northern District of London Coroner; Commissioner of Police of the Metropolis v Hurst [2007] UKHL 13; [2007] 2 A.C. 189; [2007] 2 W.L.R. 726; [2007] 2 All E.R. 1025; [2007] H.R.L.R. 23; [2007] U.K.H.R.R. 797; (2007) 157 N.L.J. 519; (2007) 151 S.J.L.B. 466, HL 18–003

R. (on the application of Husain) v Asylum Support Adjudicator [2001] EWHC Admin 852; [2002] A.C.D. 10, QBD (Admin) 12–019

R. (on the application of Imperial Tobacco Ltd) v Secretary of State for Health; sub nom. Imperial Tobacco Ltd v Secretary of State for Health; R. v Secretary of State for Health Ex p. Imperial Tobacco Ltd [2001] 1 W.L.R. 127; [2001] 1 All E.R. 850; [2001] 1 C.M.L.R. 34; [2001] Eu. L.R. 191; [2001] A.C.D. 32, HL 25–032

R. (on the application of International Transport Roth GmbH. *See* International Transport Roth GmbH v Secretary of State for the Home Department

R (Iran) v Secretary of State for the Home Department; sub nom. R. (on the application of R) v Secretary of State for the Home Department [2005] EWCA Civ 982; [2005] Imm. A.R. 535; [2005] I.N.L.R. 633, CA (Civ Div) 15–001

R. (on the application of Isiko) v Secretary of State for the Home Department; sub nom. Secretary of State for the Home Department v Isiko; R. v Secretary of State for the Home Department Ex p. Isiko [2001] 1 F.L.R. 930; [2001] 1 F.C.R. 633; [2001] H.R.L.R. 15; [2001] U.K.H.R.R. 385; [2001] Imm. A.R. 291; [2001] I.N.L.R. 175; [2001] A.C.D. 39; [2001] Fam. Law 419, CA (Civ Div) 18–038

R. (on the application of J) v Special Educational Needs and Disability Tribunal (SENDIST) [2005] EWHC 3315, QBD (Admin) 19–004

R. (on the application of Jackson) v Attorney General; sub nom. Jackson v Attorney General [2005] UKHL 56; [2006] 1 A.C. 262; [2005] 3 W.L.R. 733; [2005] 4 All E.R. 1253; (2005) 155 N.L.J. 1600; [2005] N.P.C. 116, HL 17–004

R. (on the application of Javed) v Secretary of State for the Home Department; sub nom. Secretary of State for the Home Department v Javed; R. v Secretary of State for the Home Department Ex p. Ali; R. v Secretary of State for the Home Department Ex p. Javed [2001] EWCA Civ 789; [2002] Q.B. 129; [2001] 3 W.L.R. 323; [2001] Imm. A.R. 529; [2001] I.N.L.R. 645; (2001) 98(26) L.S.G. 44; (2001) 145 S.J.L.B. 149, CA (Civ Div) 22–026

R. (on the application of K) v Camden and Islington HA; sub nom. R. v Camden and Islington HA Ex p. K [2001] EWCA Civ 240; [2002] Q.B. 198; [2001] 3 W.L.R. 553; [2001] U.K.H.R.R. 1378; (2001) 4 C.C.L. Rep. 170; [2001] Lloyd's Rep. Med. 152; (2001) 61 B.M.L.R. 173; [2001] M.H.L.R. 24; (2001) 98(16) L.S.G. 34; (2001) 145 S.J.L.B. 69, CA (Civ Div) 29–020

R. (on the application of KB) v Mental Health Review Tribunal (Damages); sub nom. R. (on the application of KB) v South London and South West Region Mental Health Review Tribunal (Damages) [2003] EWHC 193 (Admin); [2004] Q.B. 936; [2003] 3 W.L.R. 185; [2003] 2 All E.R. 209; [2003] U.K.H.R.R. 499; (2003) 6 C.C.L. Rep. 96; [2003] P.I.Q.R. Q3; [2003] M.H.L.R. 29; [2003] A.C.D. 43; (2003) 100(14) L.S.G. 27, QBD (Admin) 29–028

R. (on the application of Kathro) v Rhondda Cynon Taff CBC [2001] EWHC Admin 527; [2002] Env. L.R. 15; [2001] 4 P.L.R. 83; [2002] J.P.L. 304, QBD (Admin) . 13–016

R. (on the application of Kehoe) v Secretary of State for Work and Pensions; sub nom. Secretary of State for Work and Pensions v Kehoe; Kehoe v Secretary of State for Work and Pensions [2005] UKHL 48; [2006] 1 A.C. 42; [2005] 3 W.L.R. 252; [2005] 4 All E.R. 905; [2005] 2 F.L.R. 1249; [2005] 2 F.C.R. 683; [2005] H.R.L.R. 30; [2006] U.K.H.R.R. 360; [2005] Fam. Law 850; (2005) 155 N.L.J. 1123; (2005) 149 S.J.L.B. 921, HL 13–015

R. (on the application of Kides) v South Cambridgeshire DC [2002] EWCA Civ 1370; [2003] 1 P. & C.R. 19; [2002] 4 P.L.R. 66; [2003] J.P.L. 431; [2002] 42 E.G. 160 (C.S.); (2002) 99(43) L.S.G. 35; (2002) 146 S.J.L.B. 230; [2002] N.P.C. 121, CA (Civ Div) 24–020

R. (on the application of Kilby) v Basildon DC. *See* Kilby v Basildon DC

R. (on the application of L (A Child)) v Manchester City Council [2001] EWHC Admin 707; [2002] 1 F.L.R. 43; (2002) 5 C.C.L. Rep. 268; [2002] A.C.D. 45; [2002] Fam. Law 13, QBD (Admin) 18–038, 19–011, 19–031

R. (on the application of L) v Secretary of State for the Home Department; sub nom. R. (on the application of ZL) v Secretary of State for the Home Department [2003] EWCA Civ 25; [2003] 1 W.L.R. 1230; [2003] 1 All E.R. 1062; [2003] Imm. A.R. 330; [2003] I.N.L.R. 224; (2003) 100(11) L.S.G. 33, CA (Civ Div) 12–015

R. (on the application of L) v Wandsworth LBC [2006] EWHC 694 (QB); [2006] E.L.R. 376, QBD 15–015

R. (on the application of LH) v Lambeth LBC [2006] EWHC 1190 (Admin); [2006] 2 F.L.R. 1275; [2006] 2 F.C.R. 348; (2006) 9 C.C.L. Rep. 622; [2006] Fam. Law 931, QBD (Admin) 19–004

R. (on the application of Leung) v Imperial College of Science, Technology and Medicine [2002] EWHC 1358 (Admin); [2002] E.L.R. 653; [2002] A.C.D. 100, QBD (Admin) 12–039

R. (on the application of Lindley) v Tameside MBC [2006] EWHC 2296 (Admin); (2006) 103(39) L.S.G. 35; (2006) 150 S.J.L.B. 1252; [2006] N.P.C. 102, QBD (Admin) 20–017

R. (on the application of Livermore) v Nursing and Midwifery Council [2005] EWHC
2339, QBD (Admin) 19–010
R. (on the application of M (A Child)) v School Organisation Committee [2001] EWHC
Admin 245; [2001] A.C.D. 77, QBD (Admin) 26–046
R. (on the application of M) v Secretary of State for Constitutional Affairs [2004]
EWCA Civ 312; [2004] 1 W.L.R. 2298; [2004] 2 All E.R. 531; (2004) 168 J.P. 529;
[2004] B.L.G.R. 417; (2004) 168 J.P.N. 818; (2004) 101(15) L.S.G. 27; (2004) 148
S.J.L.B. 385, CA (Civ Div) 12–027
R. (on the application of McKay) v First Secretary of State [2005] EWCA Civ 774; [2006]
1 P. & C.R. 19; [2006] J.P.L. 52; [2005] 24 E.G. 178 (C.S.), CA (Civ Div) 23–011
R. (on the application of McLellan) v Bracknell Forest BC; sub nom. R. (on the
application of Johns) v Bracknell Forest DC; Forrest v Reigate and Banstead BC;
McLellan v Bracknell Forest BC [2001] EWCA Civ 1510; [2002] Q.B. 1129; [2002]
2 W.L.R. 1448; [2002] 1 All E.R. 899; [2002] H.R.L.R. 12; [2002] U.K.H.R.R. 45;
(2001) 33 H.L.R. 86; [2002] B.L.G.R. 191; [2002] A.C.D. 54; (2001) 98(46) L.S.G.
35; (2001) 145 S.J.L.B. 258; [2001] N.P.C. 149, CA (Civ Div) 13–018
R. (on the application of Machi) v Legal Services Commission [2001] EWCA Civ 2010;
[2002] 1 W.L.R. 983; (2002) 99(9) L.S.G. 29; (2002) 146 S.J.L.B. 22, CA (Civ
Div) 20–028
R. (on the application of Mahmood (Amjad)) v Secretary of State for the Home
Department ; sub nom. R. v Secretary of State for the Home Department Ex p.
Mahmood (Amjad); Mahmood (Amjad) v Secretary of State for the Home
Department [2001] 1 W.L.R. 840; [2001] 1 F.L.R. 756; [2001] 2 F.C.R. 63; [2001]
H.R.L.R. 14; [2001] U.K.H.R.R. 307; [2001] Imm. A.R. 229; [2001] I.N.L.R. 1;
(2001) 3 L.G.L.R. 23; [2001] A.C.D. 38; [2001] Fam. Law 257, CA (Civ Div) .. 18–038
R. (on the application of Marper) v Chief Constable of South Yorkshire [2002] EWCA
Civ 1275 18–035
R. (on the application of Menai Collect Ltd) v Department for Constitutional Affairs
[2006] EWHC 724 (Admin), QBD (Admin) 26–025
R. (on the application of Molinaro) v Kensington and Chelsea RLBC [2001] EWHC
Admin 896; [2002] B.L.G.R. 336, QBD (Admin) 26–026
R. (on the application of Montpeliers and Trevors Association) v Westminster City
Council [2005] EWHC 16 (Admin); [2006] B.L.G.R. 304; [2005] 3 E.G. 117 (C.S.),
QBD (Admin) 20–017
R. (on the application of Morgan Grenfell & Co Ltd) v Special Commissioners of
Income Tax; sub nom. R. v Inland Revenue Commissioners Ex p. Morgan
Grenfell & Co Ltd; R. v Special Commissioners of Income Tax Ex p. Morgan
Grenfell & Co Ltd [2002] UKHL 21; [2003] 1 A.C. 563; [2002] 2 W.L.R. 1299;
[2002] 3 All E.R. 1; [2002] S.T.C. 786; [2002] H.R.L.R. 42; 74 T.C. 511; [2002]
B.T.C. 223; 4 I.T.L. Rep. 809; [2002] S.T.I. 806; (2002) 99(25) L.S.G. 35; (2002) 146
S.J.L.B. 126; [2002] N.P.C. 70, HL 17–020
R. (on the application of Morris) v Westminster City Council (No.3); sub nom.
Westminster City Council v Morris [2005] EWCA Civ 1184; [2006] 1 W.L.R. 505;
[2005] H.R.L.R. 43; [2006] U.K.H.R.R. 165; [2006] H.L.R. 8; [2006] B.L.G.R. 81;
[2006] A.C.D. 29, CA (Civ Div) 18–016
R. (on the application of Mullins) v Jockey Club Appeal Board (No.1) [2005] EWHC
2197 (Admin); [2006] A.C.D. 2, QBD (Admin) 26–028
R. (on the application of Munjaz) v Mersey Care NHS Trust; sub nom. Munjaz v
Mersey Care NHS Trust; S v Airedale NHS Trust; R. (on the application of
Colonel M) v Ashworth Hospital Authority (now Mersey Care NHS Trust); R.
(on the application of Munjaz) v Ashworth Hospital Authority (now Mersey Care
NHS Trust) [2005] UKHL 58; [2006] 2 A.C. 148; [2005] 3 W.L.R. 793; [2006] 4 All
E.R. 736; [2005] H.R.L.R. 42; [2006] Lloyd's Rep. Med. 1; (2005) 86 B.M.L.R. 84;
[2005] M.H.L.R. 276, HL 20–026, 22–046
R. (on the application of N) v M [2002] EWCA Civ 1789; [2003] 1 W.L.R. 562; [2003] 1
F.L.R. 667; [2003] 1 F.C.R. 124; [2003] Lloyd's Rep. Med. 81; (2003) 72 B.M.L.R.
81; [2003] M.H.L.R. 157; [2003] Fam. Law 160; (2003) 100(8) L.S.G. 29, CA (Civ
Div) 12–031, 26–051
R. (on the application of Nadarajah) v Secretary of State for the Home Department;
sub nom. Abdi v Secretary of State for the Home Department; Nadarajah v
Secretary of State for the Home Department [2005] EWCA Civ 1363, CA (Civ
Div) 19–010, 20–017, 20–020

R. (on the application of Nahar) v Social Security Commissioners; sub nom. R. (on the application of Nahar) v Secretary of State for Work and Pensions [2002] EWCA Civ 859; [2002] A.C.D. 105, CA (Civ Div) 20–030

R. (on the application of Nash) v Chelsea College of Art and Design [2001] EWHC Admin 538, QBD (Admin) 12–039

R. (on the application of National Association of Guardians ad Litem and Reporting Officers) v Children and Family Court Advisory and Support Service [2001] EWHC Admin 693; [2002] 1 F.L.R. 255; [2002] A.C.D. 44; [2001] Fam. Law 877, QBD (Admin) 12–017, 24–021

R. (on the application of National Association of Health Stores) v Secretary of State for Health; sub nom. National Association of Health Stores v Department of Health [2005] EWCA Civ 154, CA (Civ Div) 23–033

R. (on the application of Nemeth) v West Berkshire DC, December 8, 2000, QBD (Admin) 20–017

R. (on the application of Niazi) v Secretary of State for the Home Department [2007] EWHC 1495 (Admin); [2007] A.C.D. 75, DC 12–028, 16–015, 20–017, 22–018

R. (on the application of Northern Ireland Human Rights Commission) v Greater Belfast Coroner; sub nom. Northern Ireland Human Rights Commission's Application for Judicial Review, Re; Northern Ireland Human Rights Commission, Re [2002] UKHL 25; [2002] N.I. 236; [2002] H.R.L.R. 35; [2002] A.C.D. 95, HL (NI) 24–027

R. (on the application of O) v Harrow Crown Court; sub nom. O (Writ of Habeas Corpus), Re; R. (on the application of O) v Crown Court at Harrow [2006] UKHL 42; [2007] 1 A.C. 249; [2006] 3 W.L.R. 195; [2006] 3 All E.R. 1157; [2007] 1 Cr. App. R. 9; [2006] H.R.L.R. 35; [2006] U.K.H.R.R. 1062; [2007] Crim. L.R. 63; (2006) 103(32) L.S.G. 22; (2006) 150 S.J.L.B. 1021, HL 18–010

R. (on the application of Omega Air Ltd) v Secretary of State for the Environment, Transport and the Regions (C-27/00) [2002] E.C.R. I-2569; [2002] 2 C.M.L.R. 9, ECJ 19–022

R. (on the application of Orange Personal Communications Ltd) v Secretary of State for Trade and Industry; sub nom. R. (on the application of Orange Personal Communications Services Ltd) v Secretary of State for the Environment, Transport and the Regions; R. v Secretary of State for Trade and Industry Ex p. Orange Personal Communications Services Ltd [2001] 3 C.M.L.R. 36; [2001] Eu. L.R. 165; (2000) 97(45) L.S.G. 42, QBD (Admin) 22–028

R. (on the application of Partingdale Lane Residents Association) v Barnet LBC [2003] EWHC 947, QBD (Admin) 12–028, 22–017

R. (on the application of Paul-Coker) v Southwark LBC [2006] EWHC 497 (Admin); [2006] H.L.R. 32, QBD (Admin) 19–004

R. (on the application of Pepper) v Bolsover DC; sub nom. R. v Bolsover DC Ex p. Pepper (2001) 3 L.G.L.R. 20; [2001] B.L.G.R. 43; [2001] J.P.L. 804; [2000] E.G. 107 (C.S.), QBD (Admin) 26–025

R. (on the application of Ponting) v Governor of Whitemoor Prison [2002] EWCA Civ 224; [2002] Po. L.R. 221, CA (Civ Div) 18–038

R. (on the application of ProLife Alliance) v BBC; sub nom. ProLife Alliance v BBC; R. (on the application of Quintavalle) v BBC [2003] UKHL 23; [2004] 1 A.C. 185; [2003] 2 W.L.R. 1403; [2003] 2 All E.R. 977; [2003] E.M.L.R. 23; [2003] H.R.L.R. 26; [2003] U.K.H.R.R. 758; [2003] A.C.D. 65; (2003) 100(26) L.S.G. 35; (2003) 153 N.L.J. 823; (2003) 147 S.J.L.B. 595, HL 18–003

R. (on the application of Quark Fishing Ltd) v Secretary of State for Foreign and Commonwealth Affairs (No.1); sub nom. Secretary of State for Foreign and Commonwealth Affairs v Quark Fishing Ltd [2002] EWCA Civ 1409, CA (Civ Div) 12–015, 12–022

R. (on the application of Quark Fishing Ltd) v Secretary of State for Foreign and Commonwealth Affairs (No.2) [2005] UKHL 57; [2006] 1 A.C. 529; [2005] 3 W.L.R. 837; [2006] 3 All E.R. 111; [2006] Eu. L.R. 424; [2005] H.R.L.R. 41; [2006] U.K.H.R.R. 535, HL 18–012, 29–064

R. (on the application of Rashid) v Secretary of State for the Home Department; sub nom. Rashid v Secretary of State for the Home Department [2005] EWCA Civ 744; [2005] Imm. A.R. 608; [2005] I.N.L.R. 550, CA (Civ Div) 20–017, 20–021, 20–026

R. (on the application of Reprotech (Pebsham) Ltd) v East Sussex CC; sub nom. Reprotech (Pebsham) Ltd v East Sussex CC; R. v East Sussex CC Ex p. Reprotech

(Pebsham) Ltd; East Sussex CC v Reprotech (Pebsham) Ltd [2002] UKHL 8; [2003] 1 W.L.R. 348; [2002] 4 All E.R. 58; [2003] 1 P. & C.R. 5; [2002] 2 P.L.R. 60; [2002] J.P.L. 821; [2002] 10 E.G. 158 (C.S.); [2002] N.P.C. 32, HL 20–036, 20–049
R. (on the application of Richards) v Pembrokeshire CC [2004] EWCA Civ 1000; [2005] B.L.G.R. 105, CA (Civ Div) 27–008, 27–009
R. (on the application of Roberts) v Parole Board; sub nom. Roberts v Parole Board [2005] UKHL 45; [2005] 2 A.C. 738; [2005] 3 W.L.R. 152; [2006] 1 All E.R. 39; [2005] H.R.L.R. 38; [2005] U.K.H.R.R. 939; (2005) 155 N.L.J. 1096, HL 12–030
R. (on the application of Robinson) v Torridge DC [2006] EWHC 877 (Admin); [2007] 1 W.L.R. 871; [2006] 3 All E.R. 1148; [2006] Env. L.R. 40; (2006) 156 N.L.J. 760, QBD (Admin) 25–026
R. (on the application of Rogers) v Swindon NHS Primary Care Trust; sub nom. Rogers v Swindon NHS Primary Care Trust [2006] EWCA Civ 392; [2006] 1 W.L.R. 2649; (2006) 9 C.C.L. Rep. 451; [2006] Lloyd's Rep. Med. 364; (2006) 89 B.M.L.R. 211; (2006) 103(17) L.S.G. 23; (2006) 156 N.L.J. 720; (2006) 150 S.J.L.B. 575, CA (Civ Div) 17–014, 19–001
R. (on the application of Rose) v Secretary of State for Health; sub nom. Rose v Secretary of State for Health [2002] EWHC 1593 (Admin); [2002] 2 F.L.R. 962; [2002] 3 F.C.R. 731; [2002] U.K.H.R.R. 1329; (2003) 69 B.M.L.R. 83; [2003] A.C.D. 6; [2003] Fam. Law 19; (2002) 99(39) L.S.G. 38, QBD (Admin) 18–012
R. (on the application of Rusbridger) v Attorney General; sub nom. Rusbridger v Attorney General [2003] UKHL 38; [2004] 1 A.C. 357; [2003] 3 W.L.R. 232; [2003] 3 All E.R. 784; [2003] H.R.L.R. 32; (2003) 153 N.L.J. 1029; (2003) 147 S.J.L.B. 812, HL 25–025
R. (on the application of S) v Secretary of State for the Home Department [2007] EWCA Civ 546; [2007] Imm. A.R. 781; [2007] I.N.L.R. 450; [2007] A.C.D. 94; (2007) 104(27) L.S.G. 30; (2007) 151 S.J.L.B. 858, CA (Civ Div) 19–006, 20–019
R. (on the application of S) v Chief Constable of South Yorkshire [2004] UKHL 39; [2004] 1 W.L.R. 2196; [2004] 4 All E.R. 193; [2004] H.R.L.R. 35; [2004] U.K.H.R.R. 967; 21 B.H.R.C. 408; [2004] Po. L.R. 283; [2005] Crim. L.R. 136; (2004) 101(34) L.S.G. 29; (2004) 154 N.L.J. 1183; (2004) 148 S.J.L.B. 914, HL . 16–013
R. (on the application of S (A Child)) v Brent LBC; sub nom. R. (on the application of P (A Child)) v Oxfordshire CC Exclusion Appeals Panel [2002] EWCA Civ 693; [2002] E.L.R. 556; [2002] A.C.D. 90; (2002) 99(26) L.S.G. 38; (2002) 146 S.J.L.B. 137, CA (Civ Div) 9–014
R. (on the application of Samaroo) v Secretary of State for the Home Department; sub nom:. R. v Secretary of State for the Home Department Ex p. Samaroo; Samaroo v Secretary of State for the Home Department [2001] EWCA Civ 1139; [2001] U.K.H.R.R. 1150; [2002] I.N.L.R. 55; (2001) 98(34) L.S.G. 40; (2001) 145 S.J.L.B. 208, CA (Civ Div) 19–011
R. (on the application of Sheikh) v Secretary of State for the Home Department; sub nom:. Sheikh v Secretary of State for the Home Department; R. v Secretary of State for the Home Department Ex p. Sheik; Sheik v Secretary of State for the Home Department; R. v Secretary of State for the Home Department Ex p. Sheikh [2001] Imm. A.R. 219; [2001] I.N.L.R. 98; [2001] A.C.D. 33; (2001) 98(6) L.S.G. 46, CA (Civ Div) 25–038
R. (on the application of Sinclair Gardens Investments (Kensington) Ltd) v Lands Tribunal; sub nom. Sinclair Gardens Investments (Kensington) Ltd v Lands Tribunal [2005] EWCA Civ 1305; [2006] 3 All E.R. 650; [2006] H.L.R. 11; [2006] 1 E.G.L.R. 7; [2006] 06 E.G. 172; [2006] R.V.R. 66; [2006] A.C.D. 16; (2005) 102(46) L.S.G. 27; [2005] N.P.C. 128, CA (Civ Div) 14–035, 26–057
R. (on the application of Sivasubramaniam) v Wandsworth County Court; sub nom. Sivasubramaniam v Wandsworth County Court; R. (on the application of Sivasubramaniam) v Guildford College of Further & Higher Education [2002] EWCA Civ 1738; [2003] 1 W.L.R. 475; [2003] 2 All E.R. 160; [2003] C.P. Rep. 27; (2003) 100(3) L.S.G. 34, CA (Civ Div) 14–035, 26–057, 27–002
R. (on the application of Smith) v East Kent Hospital NHS Trust [2002] EWHC 2640; (2003) 6 C.C.L. Rep. 251, QBD (Admin) 12–028
R. (on the application of Smith) v Parole Board; sub nom. Smith v Parole Board [2005] UKHL 1; [2005] 1 W.L.R. 350; [2005] 1 All E.R. 755; [2005] H.R.L.R. 8; 18 B.H.R.C. 267; [2005] 2 Prison L.R. 14; (2005) 102(12) L.S.G. 26; (2005) 149 S.J.L.B. 145, HL 12–030

R. (on the application of Spink) v Wandsworth LBC [2005] EWCA Civ 302; [2005] 1 W.L.R. 2884; [2005] 2 All E.R. 954; [2005] 1 F.C.R. 608; [2005] H.L.R. 41; [2005] B.L.G.R. 561; (2005) 8 C.C.L. Rep. 272; (2005) 84 B.M.L.R. 169; (2005) 102(19) L.S.G. 34; (2005) 149 S.J.L.B. 390, CA (Civ Div) 17–014

R. (on the application of Sunspell Ltd (t/a Superlative Travel)) v Association of British Travel Agents; sub nom. R. v Association of British Travel Agents Ex p. Sunspell Ltd (t/a Superlative Travel) [2001] A.C.D. 16, QBD (Admin) 26–029

R. (on the application of Swedish Match AB) v Secretary of State for Health (C-210/03); sub nom. Swedish Match AB v Secretary of State for Health [2004] E.C.R. I-11893; [2005] 1 C.M.L.R. 26, ECJ 19–022

R. (on the application of Theophilus) v Lewisham LBC [2002] EWHC 1371; [2002] 3 All E.R. 851; [2002] Eu. L.R. 563; [2003] B.L.G.R. 98; [2002] E.L.R. 719, QBD (Admin) 20–015

R. (on the application of Tucker) v Director General of the National Crime Squad [2003] EWCA Civ 2; [2003] I.C.R. 599; [2003] I.R.L.R. 439; [2003] Po. L.R. 9; [2003] A.C.D. 37; (2003) 100(10) L.S.G. 29, CA (Civ Div) 26–025

R. (on the application of Varma) v Duke of Kent; sub nom. R. (on the application of Varma) v Visitor to Cranfield University [2004] EWHC 1705; [2004] E.L.R. 616; [2004] A.C.D. 81, QBD (Admin) 14–036

R. (on the application of Vary) v Secretary of State for the Home Department [2004] EWHC 2251 (Admin), QBD (Admin) 20–017

R. (on the application of von Brandenburg) v East London and the City Mental Health NHS Trust; sub nom. R. v East London and the City Mental Health NHS Trust Ex p. von Brandenburg; R. v Tower Hamlets Healthcare NHS Trust Ex p. von Brandenburg [2003] UKHL 58; [2004] 2 A.C. 280; [2003] 3 W.L.R. 1265; [2004] 1 All E.R. 400; [2004] H.R.L.R. 6; (2004) 7 C.C.L. Rep. 121; [2004] Lloyd's Rep. Med. 228; (2004) 76 B.M.L.R. 168; [2004] M.H.L.R. 44; (2004) 101(5) L.S.G. 28; (2003) 147 S.J.L.B. 1366, HL 19–004

R. (on the application of Wainwright) v Richmond upon Thames LBC [2001] EWCA Civ 2062; (2002) 99(9) L.S.G. 29, CA (Civ Div) 12–028, 22–017

R. (on the application of Waite) v Hammersmith and Fulham LBC; sub nom. Waite v Hammersmith and Fulham LBC [2002] EWCA Civ 482; [2003] H.L.R. 3, CA (Civ Div) 21–006

R. (on the application of Walker) v Secretary of State for the Home Department; sub nom. Wells v Parole Board; Walker v Secretary of State for the Home Department; Secretary of State for Justice v Walker; R. (on the application of Wells) v Parole Board; Secretary of State for Justice v James [2008] EWCA Civ 30; (2008) 158 N.L.J. 263, CA (Civ Div) 1–031, 19–001

R. (on the application of Wandsworth LBC) v Secretary of State for Transport. *See* Wandsworth LBC v Secretary of State for Transport, Local Government and the Regions (Enforcement Notice)

R. (on the application of Wardle) v Leeds Crown Court; sub nom. R. v Leeds Crown Court Ex p. Stubley; R. v Leeds Crown Court Ex p. Wardle [2001] UKHL 12; [2002] 1 A.C. 754; [2001] 2 W.L.R. 865; [2001] 2 All E.R. 1; [2001] 2 Cr. App. R. 20; (2001) 165 J.P. 465; [2001] H.R.L.R. 29; [2001] Crim. L.R. 468; [2001] A.C.D. 82; (2001) 165 J.P.N. 327; (2001) 98(21) L.S.G. 39; (2001) 151 N.L.J. 386; (2001) 145 S.J.L.B. 117, HL 18–032

R. (on the application of Ware) v Neath Port Talbot CBC; sub nom. Neath Port Talbot CBC v Ware [2007] EWCA Civ 1359; [2008] 7 E.G. 144; [2007] N.P.C. 138, CA (Civ Div) 13–008

R. (on the application of Warren) v Mental Health Review Tribunal London & North East Region [2002] A.C.D. 84 14–033

R. (on the application of West) v Lloyd's of London [2004] EWCA Civ 506; [2004] 3 All E.R. 251; [2004] 2 All E.R. (Comm) 1; [2004] 2 C.L.C. 649; [2004] H.R.L.R. 27; [2004] Lloyd's Rep. I.R. 755; (2004) 148 S.J.L.B. 537, CA (Civ Div) 26–029

R. (on the application of Western Riverside Waste Authority) v Wandsworth LBC [2005] EWHC 536 (Admin); [2005] Env. L.R. 41; [2005] B.L.G.R. 846; [2006] J.P.L. 270, QBD (Admin) 17–014

R. (on the application of Wilkinson) v Broadmoor Hospital; sub nom. R. (on the application of Wilkinson) v Responsible Medical Officer Broadmoor Hospital; R. (on the application of Wilkinson) v Broadmoor Special Hospital Authority [2001] EWCA Civ 1545; [2002] 1 W.L.R. 419; [2002] U.K.H.R.R. 390; (2002) 5 C.C.L.

Rep. 121; [2002] Lloyd's Rep. Med. 41; (2002) 65 B.M.L.R. 15; [2001] M.H.L.R. 224; [2002] A.C.D. 47; (2001) 98(44) L.S.G. 36; (2001) 145 S.J.L.B. 247, CA (Civ Div) 26–051

R. (on the application of Wilkinson) v Inland Revenue Commissioners; sub nom. Wilkinson v Inland Revenue Commissioners [2005] UKHL 30; [2005] 1 W.L.R. 1718; [2006] 1 All E.R. 529; [2006] S.T.C. 270; [2005] U.K.H.R.R. 704; 77 T.C. 78; [2005] S.T.I. 904; (2005) 102(25) L.S.G. 33, HL 18–007, 18–010

R. (on the application of Wilson) v Wychavon DC; sub nom. Wilson v Wychavon DC [2007] EWCA Civ 52; [2007] 2 W.L.R. 798; [2007] H.R.L.R. 16; [2007] U.K.H.R.R. 835; [2007] B.L.G.R. 540; [2007] 2 P. & C.R. 13; [2007] J.P.L. 1158; [2007] 7 E.G. 142 (C.S.); [2007] N.P.C. 15; [2007] Q.B. 801, CA (Civ Div) 21–012

R. (on the application of Wirral HA) v Mental Health Review Tribunal [2001] EWCA Civ 1901; [2002] M.H.L.R. 34; (2002) 99(2) L.S.G. 27; (2001) 145 S.J.L.B. 270, CA (Civ Div) 23–020

R. (on the application of Wooder) v Feggetter [2002] EWCA Civ 554; [2003] Q.B. 219; [2002] 3 W.L.R. 591; [2002] M.H.L.R. 178; [2002] A.C.D. 94; (2002) 99(22) L.S.G. 33; (2002) 146 S.J.L.B. 125, CA (Civ Div) 12–037

R. (on the application of Wright) v Secretary of State for Health [2007] EWCA Civ 999; [2008] 1 All E.R. 886; [2008] H.R.L.R. 4; [2008] 2 W.L.R. 536, CA (Civ Div) . 12–019, 13–018, 18–010

R. (on the application of X) v Chief Constable of the West Midlands; sub nom. X v Chief Constable of the West Midlands [2004] EWCA Civ 1068; [2005] 1 W.L.R. 65; [2005] 1 All E.R. 610; [2005] Po. L.R. 24; (2004) 101(35) L.S.G. 34; (2004) 148 S.J.L.B. 1119, CA (Civ Div) 12–027

R. (on the application of X) v Headteachers and Governors of Y School [2007] EWHC 298 (Admin); [2008] 1 All E.R. 249; [2007] H.R.L.R. 20; [2007] B.L.G.R. 698; [2007] E.L.R. 278, QBD (Admin) 18–038

R. (on the application of Zeqiri) v Secretary of State for the Home Department; sub nom. R. v Secretary of State for the Home Department Ex p. Zeqiri; Secretary of State for the Home Department v Zeqiri [2002] UKHL 3; [2002] Imm. A.R. 296; [2002] I.N.L.R. 291; [2002] A.C.D. 60, HL 20–016

R, Re [2002] 1 F.L.R. 755 .... 28–012, 28–013

RCA Corp v Pollard [1983] Ch. 135; [1982] 3 W.L.R. 1007; [1982] 3 All E.R. 771; [1983] F.S.R. 9, CA (Civ Div) 24–007, 24–030

RJR-MacDonald Inc v Attorney General of Canada [1995] 3 S.C.R. 199, Sup Ct (Can) 18–049

Racal Communications Ltd, Re; sub nom. Company (No.00996 of 1979), Re [1981] A.C. 374; [1980] 3 W.L.R. 181; [1980] 2 All E.R. 634, HL 14–004, 14–016, 14–032, 25–004

Racal Communications v Pay Board [1974] 1 W.L.R. 1149; [1974] 3 All E.R. 263; [1974] I.C.R. 590; [1974] I.R.L.R. 209; (1974) 118 S.J. 564, Ch D 25–021

Racz v Home Office [1994] 2 A.C. 45; [1994] 2 W.L.R. 23; [1994] 1 All E.R. 97; (1994) 144 N.L.J. 89; (1994) 138 S.J.L.B. 12, HL 29–035

Rahman, Re [1996] C.O.D. 465 25–038

Raley v California tahoe Regional Planning Agency 137 Cal. Rptr 699 (1977) 20–051

Ransom (Inspector of Taxes) v Higgs; sub nom. Dickinson v Kilmorie (Aldridge) Downes [1974] 1 W.L.R. 1594; [1974] 3 All E.R. 949; [1974] S.T.C. 539; [1974] T.R. 281; (1974) 118 S.J. 849, HL 9–021

Ransom & Luck Ltd v Surbiton BC [1949] Ch. 180; [1949] 1 All E.R. 185; 65 T.L.R. 57; (1949) 113 J.P. 95; 47 L.G.R. 467; [1949] L.J.R. 809; (1949) 93 S.J. 41, CA 16–025

Rape Crisis Centre v Secretary of State for the Home Department; sub nom. Rape Crisis Centre, Petitioners 2000 S.C. 527; 2001 S.L.T. 389; 2000 S.C.L.R. 807; 2000 G.W.D. 25–946, OH 24–022

Ratnagopal (Rajah) v Attorney General; sub nom. Ratnagopal v Attorney General [1970] A.C. 974; [1969] 3 W.L.R. 1056; (1969) 113 S.J. 688, PC (Cey) 16–003

Rawlinson v Rice [1997] 2 N.Z.L.R. 651 29–033

Razzouk v Commission of the European Communities (75/82); Beydoun v Commission of the Eurpoean Communities (117/82) [1984] E.C.R. 1509; [1984] 3 C.M.L.R. 470, ECJ 21–017

Read v Croydon Corporation [1938] 4 All E.R. 631 29–021

Reading BC v Secretary of State for the Environment and Commercial Union Properties (Investments) Ltd (1986) 52 P. & C.R. 385; [1986] J.P.L. 115, QBD 9–041

R. v Secretary of State for Scotland [1999] 2 W.L.R. 28 15–011
Rechberger v Austria (C-140/97) [1999] E.C.R. I-3499; [2000] 2 C.M.L.R. 1, ECJ ... 29–058
Reddaway v Lancs County Council (1925) 41 T.L.R. 422 27–005
Rederiaktiebolaget Amphitrite v King, The [1921] 3 K.B. 500; (1921) 8 Ll. L. Rep. 443,
    KBD 16–024
Reeves v Commissioner of Police of the Metropolis [2000] 1 A.C. 360; [1999] 3 W.L.R.
    363; [1999] 3 All E.R. 897; (2000) 51 B.M.L.R. 155; [1999] Prison L.R. 99; (1999)
    96(31) L.S.G. 41; (1999) 143 S.J.L.B. 213, HL 29–016
Reffell v Surrey CC [1964] 1 W.L.R. 358; [1964] 1 All E.R. 743; (1964) 128 J.P. 261; 62
    L.G.R. 186; (1964) 108 S.J. 119, QBD 29–021
Reilly v King, The [1934] A.C. 176, PC (Can) 5–044, 5–046, 5–045
Repton School Governors v Repton Rural DC [1918] 2 K.B. 133, CA 22–028
Retarded Children's Aid Society v Barnet LBC [1969] 2 Q.B. 22; [1969] 2 W.L.R. 65;
    [1969] 1 All E.R. 300; (1969) 133 J.P. 140; 67 L.G.R. 294; (1968) 112 S.J. 906, DC 17–013
Revell v Blake (1872–73) L.R. 8 C.P. 533, Ex Chamber 14–026
Rewe-Handelsgesellschaft Nord mbH v Hauptzollamt Kiel (C-158/80) [1981] E.C.R.
    1805; [1982] 1 C.M.L.R. 449, ECJ 10–031
Rewe-Zentral AG v Bundesmonopolverwaltung fur Branntwein (120/78); sub nom.
    Cassis de Dijon, Re [1979] E.C.R. 649; [1979] 3 C.M.L.R. 494, ECJ 19–020
Reyners v Belgium (2/74) [1974] E.C.R. 631; [1974] 2 C.M.L.R. 305, ECJ 10–020
Richards (t/a Colin Richards & Co) v Hughes; sub nom. Hughes v Richards (t/a Colin
    Richards & Co) [2004] EWCA Civ 266; [2004] P.N.L.R. 35; (2004) 148 S.J.L.B.
    353, CA (Civ Div) 29–013
Richardson v West Lindsey DC [1990] 1 W.L.R. 522; [1990] 1 All E.R. 296; 48 B.L.R. 1;
    [1989] E.G. 127 (C.S.); (1989) 139 N.L.J. 1263, CA (Civ Div) 29–008
Rickards v Lothian [1913] A.C. 263, PC (Aus) 29–042
Ridge v Baldwin [1964] A.C. 40; [1963] 2 W.L.R. 935; [1963] 2 All E.R. 66; (1963) 127
    J.P. 295; (1963) 127 J.P. 251; 61 L.G.R. 369; 37 A.L.J. 140; 234 L.T. 423; 113 L.J.
    716; (1963) 107 S.J. 313, HL 12–005, 12–008, 12–009, 12–012, 12–015,
                12–024, 12–041, 12–048, 23–009, 25–007, 25–021, 26–031, 27–006
Ringeisen v Austria (No.1) (A/13) (1979–80) 1 E.H.R.R. 455, ECHR 12–018, 13–012
Ringer Ex p. (1909) 73 J.P. 436 27–005
Riordan v War Office [1961] 1 W.L.R. 210; [1960] 3 All E.R. 774, CA 5–045
Roberts v Hopwood; sub nom. R. v Roberts Ex p. Scurr; R. v Roberts Ex p. Scurr
    [1925] A.C. 578, HL 17–010
Roberts v Parole Board. *See* R. (on the application of Roberts) v Parole Board
Robertson v Department for the Environment, Food and Rural Affairs; sub nom.
    Department for the Environment, Food and Rural Affairs v Robertson [2005]
    EWCA Civ 138; [2005] I.C.R. 750; [2005] I.R.L.R. 363; (2005) 102(15) L.S.G. 33,
    CA (Civ Div) 4–018, 16–006
Robertson v Minister of Pensions [1949] 1 K.B. 227; [1948] 2 All E.R. 767; 64 T.L.R.
    526; [1949] L.J.R. 323; (1948) 92 S.J. 603, KBD 5–045, 16–034, 20–034, 20–043
Robinson v South Australia (No.2) [1931] A.C. 704 28–002
Rochdale BC v Anders [1988] 3 All E.R. 490; [1988] 3 C.M.L.R. 431; (1988) 138 N.L.J.
    Rep. 212, QBD 23–032
Roche v United Kingdom (32555/96) (2006) 42 E.H.R.R. 30; 20 B.H.R.C. 99, ECHR
    (Grand Chamber) 29–046
Rochester Tel Corp v United Sattes 307 U.S. 125 (1939) 14–042
Rodwell v Thomas [1944] K.B. 596, KBD 5–045
Roebuck v National Union of Mineworkers (Yorkshire Area) (No.2); sub nom.
    O'Brien v National Union of Mineworkers (Yorkshire Area) (No.2) [1978] I.C.R.
    676, Ch D 13–004
Rogers v Secretary of State for the Home Department [1973] A.C. 388; [1972] 3 W.L.R.
    279; [1972] 2 All E.R. 1057; (1972) 116 S.J. 696, HL 28–004
Rolled Steel Products (Holdings) Ltd v British Steel Corp [1986] Ch. 246; [1985] 2
    W.L.R. 908; [1985] 3 All E.R. 52; (1984) 1 B.C.C. 99158, CA (Civ Div) 5–048
Rollo v Minister of Town and Country Planning [1948] 1 All E.R. 13; 64 T.L.R. 25;
    (1948) 112 J.P. 104; 46 L.G.R. 114; [1948] L.J.R. 817; (1948) 92 S.J. 40, CA ... 22–017
Rolls v Dorset CC. *See* R. v South Hams DC Ex p. Gibb
Roncarelli v Duplessis [1952] 1 D.L.R. 680 .... 17–015, 29–033
Rootkin v Kent CC [1981] 1 W.L.R. 1186; [1981] 2 All E.R. 227; 80 L.G.R. 201; (1981)
    125 S.J. 496, CA (Civ Div) 20–029

Rose v Secretary of State for Health. *See* R. (on the application of Rose) v Secretary of
State for Health
Routh v Reading Corp (1970) 217 E.G. 1337, CA (Civ Div) 27–008
Rowe v United Kingdom (28901/95); Davis v United Kingdom (28901/95) (2000) 30
E.H.R.R. 1; 8 B.H.R.C. 325; [2000] Po. L.R. 41; [2000] Crim. L.R. 584, ECHR   28–008
Rowland v Environment Agency [2003] EWCA Civ 1885; [2005] Ch. 1; [2004] 3 W.L.R.
249; [2004] 2 Lloyd's Rep. 55; (2004) 101(8) L.S.G. 30; [2003] N.P.C. 165, CA (Civ
Div) 20–021, 20–052
Rowling v Takaro Properties Ltd [1988] A.C. 473; [1988] 2 W.L.R. 418; [1988] 1 All
E.R. 163, PC (NZ) 29–006, 29–008, 29–023, 29–065
Rowning v Goodchild (1772) 1 W Black 906 29–021
Roy v Kensington and Chelsea and Westminster Family Practitioner Committee [1992]
1 A.C. 624; [1992] 2 W.L.R. 239; [1992] 1 All E.R. 705; [1992] I.R.L.R. 233; (1992)
4 Admin. L.R. 649; [1992] 3 Med. L.R. 177; (1992) 142 N.L.J. 240; (1992) 136
S.J.L.B. 63, HL 26–008, 26–010
Royal College of Nursing of the United Kingdom v Department of Health and Social
Security [1981] A.C. 800; [1981] 2 W.L.R. 279; [1981] 1 All E.R. 545; [1981] Crim.
L.R. 322; (1981) 125 S.J. 149, HL 22–046, 24–021
Royal Scholten-Honig (Holdings) Ltd v Intervention Board for Agricultural Produce
(103/77); Tunnel Refineries Ltd v Intervention Board for Agricultural Produce
(145/77); Koninklijke Scholten-Honig NV v Hoofdproduktschap voor Akker-
bouwprodukten (125/77) [1978] E.C.R. 2037; [1979] 1 C.M.L.R. 675, ECJ   21–019
Ruckdeschel (Albert) & Co v Hauptzollamt Hamburg-St Annen (117/76); Diamalt AG
v Hauptzollamt Itzehoe (16/77) [1977] E.C.R. 1753; [1979] 2 C.M.L.R. 445,
ECJ 25–015, 21–019
Ruislip-Northwood Urban DC v Lee (1931) 145 L.T. 208 25–026
Ruiz-Mateos v Spain (A/262) (1993) 16 E.H.R.R. 505, ECHR 12–043
Russell v Duke of Norfolk [1949] 1 All E.R. 109; 65 T.L.R. 225; (1949) 93 S.J. 132,
CA 12–010
Russian Commercial and Industrial Bank v British Bank of Foreign Trade Ltd [1921] 2
A.C. 438 25–021
Rust v Sullivan 111 S. Ct. 1759 (1991) 14–041
Rutili v Ministre de l'Iinterieur (36/75) [1975] E.C.R. 1219; [1976] 1 C.M.L.R. 140,
ECJ 19–020
Rydqvist v Secretary of State for Work and Pensions [2002] EWCA Civ 947; [2002] 1
W.L.R. 3343; [2002] I.C.R. 1383; (2002) 146 S.J.L.B. 247, CA (Civ Div)   25–009
Rylands v Fletcher; sub nom. Fletcher v Rylands (1868) L.R. 3 H.L. 330, HL   29–042
S v France (1990) 65 D. & R. 250, Eur Comm HR 29–040
S v Gloucestershire CC; sub nom. RL v Gloucestershire CC; DS v Gloucestershire CC;
RL v Tower Hamlets LBC [2001] Fam. 313; [2001] 2 W.L.R. 909; [2000] 3 All E.R.
346; [2000] 1 F.L.R. 825; [2000] 2 F.C.R. 345; (2000) 2 L.G.L.R. 848; (2000) 3
C.C.L. Rep. 294; [2000] Fam. Law 474, CA (Civ Div) 29–016
S (A Barrister), Re [1981] Q.B. 683; [1981] 3 W.L.R. 129; [1981] 2 All E.R. 952, Visitors
(Inns of Ct) 13–004
S (A Minor) v Special Educational Needs Tribunal [1996] 1 W.L.R. 382; [1996] 2 All
E.R. 286; [1996] 1 F.L.R. 663; [1996] 2 F.C.R. 292; [1996] E.L.R. 228; [1996]
C.O.D. 430; [1996] Fam. Law 405, CA (Civ Div) 9–024, 12–034
S (Application for Judicial Review), Re; sub nom. R. v Collins Ex p. MS; R. v Collins
Ex p. S [1998] 1 F.L.R. 790; [1998] 1 F.C.R. 368; [1998] C.O.D. 52; [1997] Fam.
Law 790, CA (Civ Div) 26–046, 28–021
S (Children) (Care Order: Implementation of Care Plan), Re; sub nom. W and B
(Children) (Care Plan), Re; W (Children) (Care Plan), Re [2002] UKHL 10; [2002]
2 A.C. 291; [2002] 2 W.L.R. 720; [2002] 2 All E.R. 192; [2002] 1 F.L.R. 815; [2002]
1 F.C.R. 577; [2002] H.R.L.R. 26; [2002] U.K.H.R.R. 652; [2002] B.L.G.R. 251;
[2002] Fam. Law 413; (2002) 99(17) L.S.G. 34; (2002) 146 S.J.L.B. 85, HL ...   18–007,
                                                                                   18–009
S-C (Mental Patient: Habeas Corpus), Re [1996] Q.B. 599; [1996] 2 W.L.R. 146; [1996]
1 All E.R. 532; [1996] 1 F.L.R. 548; [1996] 2 F.C.R. 692; (1996) 29 B.M.L.R. 138;
[1996] Fam. Law 210, CA (Civ Div) 25–038
SEC v Chenery Corp 332 U.S. 194 (1947) 14–042
Sabey (H) & Co Ltd v Secretary of State for the Environment [1978] 1 All E.R. 586;
(1977) 245 E.G. 397; [1977] J.P.L. 661, QBD 12–027

Sadler v Sheffield Corp [1924] 1 Ch. 483, Ch D 17–013, 25–021
St Pancras BC v Frey [1963] 2 Q.B. 586; [1963] 2 W.L.R. 894; [1963] 2 All E.R. 124; 61
    L.G.R. 276; (1963) 107 S.J. 256, DC 23–029
Sagnata Investments Ltd v Norwich Corp; sub nom. Norwich Corp v Sagnata
    Investments Ltd [1971] 2 Q.B. 614; [1971] 3 W.L.R. 133; [1971] 2 All E.R. 1441; 69
    L.G.R. 471; (1971) 115 S.J. 406, CA (Civ Div) 16–013, 16–014
Salaried Persons Postal Loans Ltd v Revenue and Customs Commissioners; sub nom.
    Revenue and Customs Commissioners v Salaried Persons Postal Loans Ltd [2006]
    EWHC 763 (Ch); [2006] S.T.C. 1315; [2006] B.T.C. 423; [2006] S.T.I. 1269, Ch D . 9–021
Salesi v Italy (A/257–E) (1998) 26 E.H.R.R. 187, ECHR 12–018
Samaroo v Secretary of State for the Home Department. *See* R. (on the application of
    Samaroo) v Secretary of State for the Home Department
San Diego County v California Water and Telephone Co 186 P. 2d 124 (1947) 20–042
Save Britain's Heritage v Number 1 Poultry Ltd; sub nom. Save Britain's Heritage v
    Secretary of State for the Environment [1991] 1 W.L.R. 153; [1991] 2 All E.R. 10;
    89 L.G.R. 809; (1991) 3 Admin. L.R. 437; (1991) 62 P. & C.R. 105; [1991] 3 P.L.R.
    17; (1991) 155 L.G. Rev. 429; [1991] E.G. 24 (C.S.); (1991) 88(15) L.S.G. 31; (1991)
    135 S.J. 312, HL 12–034
Scadding v Lorant (1851) 3 H.L.C. 418 23–007
Schinotti v Bumsted (1796) 6 T.R. 646 29–021
Schmidt v Secretary of State for Home Affairs [1969] 2 Ch. 149; [1969] 2 W.L.R. 337;
    [1969] 1 All E.R. 904; (1969) 133 J.P. 274; (1969) 113 S.J. 16, CA (Civ Div) ... 12–013,
                                                                                    12–015
Schrader v Hauptzollamt Gronau. *See* Hermann Schrader HS Kraftfutter GmbH &
    Co KG v Hauptzollamt Gronau (265/87)
Schweiker v Hansen 450 U.S. 785 (1981) 20–042
Science Research Council v Nasse; sub nom. Nasse v Science Research Council; Vyas v
    Leyland Cars [1980] A.C. 1028; [1979] 3 W.L.R. 762; [1979] 3 All E.R. 673; [1979]
    I.C.R. 921; [1979] I.R.L.R. 465; (1979) 123 S.J. 768, HL 28–005, 28–013
Seal v Chief Constable of South Wales [2007] UKHL 31; [2007] 1 W.L.R. 1910; [2007] 4
    All E.R. 177; [2007] H.R.L.R. 37; 22 B.H.R.C. 769; [2007] B.P.I.R. 1396; (2007) 10
    C.C.L. Rep. 695; (2007) 97 B.M.L.R. 172; (2007) 104(29) L.S.G. 25; (2007) 151
    S.J.L.B. 927, HL 23–011
Secretary of State for Education and Science v Tameside MBC [1977] A.C. 1014; [1976]
    3 W.L.R. 641; [1976] 3 All E.R. 665; (1976) 120 S.J. 735, HL . 12–036, 15–003, 17–012
Secretary of State for the Home Department v E [2007] UKHL 47; [2007] 3 W.L.R. 720;
    [2008] 1 All E.R. 699; [2008] H.R.L.R. 7; [2008] U.K.H.R.R. 69; (2007) 157 N.L.J.
    1578; (2007) 151 S.J.L.B. 1433, HL 18–039
Secretary of State for the Home Department v JJ; sub nom. JJ, Re [2007] UKHL 45;
    [2007] 3 W.L.R. 642; [2008] 1 All E.R. 613; [2008] H.R.L.R. 5; [2008] U.K.H.R.R.
    80; (2007) 157 N.L.J. 1576; (2007) 151 S.J.L.B. 1432, HL 18–039
Secretary of State for the Home Department v MB; sub nom. MB, Re [2007] UKHL
    46; [2007] 3 W.L.R. 681; [2008] 1 All E.R. 657; [2008] H.R.L.R. 6; [2008]
    U.K.H.R.R. 119; (2007) 157 N.L.J. 1577; (2007) 151 S.J.L.B. 1437, HL 18–010
Secretary of State for the Home Department v Ravichandran. *See* R. v Secretary of
    State for the Home Department Ex p. Jeyeanthan
Secretary of State for the Home Department v Rehman; sub nom. Rehman v Secretary
    of State for the Home Department [2001] UKHL 47; [2003] 1 A.C. 153; [2001] 3
    W.L.R. 877; [2002] 1 All E.R. 122; 11 B.H.R.C. 413; [2002] Imm. A.R. 98; [2002]
    I.N.L.R. 92; [2002] A.C.D. 6; (2001) 98(42) L.S.G. 37; (2001) 145 S.J.L.B. 238,
    HL 15–023
Sedleigh-Denfield v O'Callagan (Trustees for St Joseph's Society for Foreign Missions)
    [1940] A.C. 880; [1940] 3 All E.R. 349, HL 29–037
Sempra Metals Ltd (formerly Metallgesellschaft Ltd) v Inland Revenue Commissioners
    [2007] UKHL 34; [2007] 3 W.L.R. 354; [2008] Bus. L.R. 49; [2007] 4 All E.R. 657;
    [2007] S.T.C. 1559; [2008] Eu. L.R. 1; [2007] B.T.C. 509; [2007] S.T.I. 1865; (2007)
    104(31) L.S.G. 25; (2007) 157 N.L.J. 1082; (2007) 151 S.J.L.B. 985, HL 29–050
Serjeant v Dale (1876–77) L.R. 2 Q.B.D. 558, QBD 23–026
Sevenoaks District Council v Emmett (1979) 79 L.G.R. 346 26–025
Shaheen v Secretary of State for the Home Department [2005] EWCA Civ 1294; [2006]
    Imm. A.R. 57; [2006] I.N.L.R. 245, CA (Civ Div) 15–018
Shamoon v Chief Constable of the Royal Ulster Constabulary [2003] UKHL 11; [2003]

2 All E.R. 26; [2003] N.I. 174; [2003] I.C.R. 337; [2003] I.R.L.R. 285; (2003) 147
    S.J.L.B. 268, HL (NI) 21–007
Sharp v Wakefield; sub nom. Sharpe v Wakefield [1891] A.C. 173, HL 17–013
Shaw (Inspector of Taxes) v Vicky Construction Ltd; sub nom. Vicky Construction Ltd
    v Shaw (Inspector of Taxes) [2002] EWHC 2659 (Ch); [2002] S.T.C. 1544; 75 T.C.
    26; [2003] B.T.C. 68; [2002] S.T.I. 1689, Ch D 9–021
Sheikh v Secretary of State for the Home Department. *See* R. (on the application of
    Sheikh) v Secretary of State for the Home Department
Sheldrake v DPP [2004] UKHL 43; [2005] 1 A.C. 264; [2004] 3 W.L.R. 976; [2005] 1 All
    E.R. 237; [2005] 1 Cr. App. R. 28; (2004) 168 J.P. 669; [2005] R.T.R. 2; [2004]
    H.R.L.R. 44; [2005] U.K.H.R.R. 1; 17 B.H.R.C. 339; [2005] Crim. L.R. 215;
    (2005) 169 J.P.N. 19; (2004) 101(43) L.S.G. 33; (2004) 148 S.J.L.B. 1216, HL .. 18–010
Shenton v Smith [1895] A.C. 229, PC (Aus) 5–045
Sheridan v Stanley Cole (Wainfleet) Ltd. *See* Stanley Cole (Wainfleet) Ltd v Sheridan
Short v Poole Corp [1926] Ch. 66, CA 17–013, 19–002
Sidebotham, Ex p. sub nom. Sidebotham, Re (1880) L.R. 14 Ch. D. 458, CA 24–011
Silver v United Kingdom (A/161) (1983) 5 E.H.R.R. 347, ECHR 18–032
Simeon (Assessment of Compensation), Re; Isle of Wight Rural DC, Re [1937] Ch. 525,
    Ch D 29–038
Simplex GE (Holdings) Ltd v Secretary of State for the Environment (1989) 57 P. &
    C.R. 306; [1988] 3 P.L.R. 25; [1988] J.P.L. 809; [1988] E.G. 65 (C.S.), CA (Civ
    Div) 15–007
Simpson v Attorney General [1994] 3 N.Z.L.R. 667 29–025
Sinfield v London Transport Executive [1970] Ch. 550; [1970] 2 W.L.R. 1062; [1970] 2
    All E.R. 264; 68 L.G.R. 512; (1970) 114 S.J. 285, CA (Civ Div) 22–017
Sirros v Moore [1975] Q.B. 118; [1974] 3 W.L.R. 459; [1974] 3 All E.R. 776; (1974) 118
    S.J. 661, CA (Civ Div) 29–047
Skarby v Sweden (A/180–B) (1991) 13 E.H.R.R. 90, ECHR 12–018
Skipper v Calderdale MBC [2006] EWCA Civ 238; [2006] E.L.R. 322; (2006) 103(13)
    L.S.G. 23; (2006) 150 S.J.L.B. 362, CA (Civ Div) 29–016
Slater v Mayor of Burnley (1888) 59 L.T. 636 29–050
Smeaton v Ilford Corp [1954] Ch. 450; [1954] 2 W.L.R. 668; [1954] 1 All E.R. 923;
    (1954) 118 J.P. 290; 52 L.G.R. 253; (1954) 98 S.J. 251, Ch D 29–038, 29–043
Smeeton v Attorney General [1920] 1 Ch. 85, Ch D 25–021, 26–057
Smith (Kathleen Rose) v East Elloe Rural DC [1956] A.C. 736; [1956] 2 W.L.R. 888;
    [1956] 1 All E.R. 855; (1956) 120 J.P. 263; 54 L.G.R. 233; (1956) 6 P. & C.R. 102;
    (1956) 100 S.J. 282, HL 14–037, 17–015, 23–010, 27–007, 29–033
Smith v Kvaerner Cementation Foundations Ltd [2006] EWCA Civ 242; [2007] 1
    W.L.R. 370; [2006] 3 All E.R. 593; [2006] C.P. Rep. 36; [2006] B.L.R. 244; [2006]
    A.C.D. 51; (2006) 103(14) L.S.G. 33; (2006) 156 N.L.J. 721; [2006] N.P.C. 35, CA
    (Civ Div) 13–011
Smith v United Kingdom (33985/96); Grady v United Kingdom (33986/96) [1999]
    I.R.L.R. 734; (2000) 29 E.H.R.R. 493; (1999) 11 Admin. L.R. 879, ECHR 18–038,
    19–010
Smyth v Ames 169 U.S. 466 (1898) 11–021
Societe Comateb v Directeur General des Douanes et Droits Indirects (C-192/95) [1997]
    S.T.C. 1006; [1997] E.C.R. I-165; [1997] 2 C.M.L.R. 649, ECJ 29–060
Society for the Protection of Unborn Children (Ireland) Ltd (SPUC) v Grogan (C-159/
    90) [1991] E.C.R. I-4685; [1991] 3 C.M.L.R. 849, ECJ 18–055
Society of Lloyd's v Henderson; sub nom. Society of Lloyd's v Lowe [2007] EWCA Civ
    930, CA (Civ Div) 29–031
Society of Medical Officers of Health v Hope (Valuation Officer) [1960] A.C. 551; [1960]
    2 W.L.R. 404; [1960] 1 All E.R. 317; (1960) 124 J.P. 128; 58 L.G.R. 165; 5 R.R.C.
    388; 53 R. & I.T. 102; (1960) 104 S.J. 147, HL 20–030
Solihull MBC v Maxfern Ltd [1977] 1 W.L.R. 127; [1977] 2 All E.R. 177; 75 L.G.R.
    327; [1977] J.P.L. 171, Ch D 24–010
Somerville v Scottish Ministers [2007] UKHL 44; [2007] 1 W.L.R. 2734; 2007 S.L.T.
    1113; 2007 S.C.L.R. 830; [2008] H.R.L.R. 3; (2007) 151 S.J.L.B. 1398; 2007
    G.W.D. 37–656, HL 7–007
South Buckinghamshire DC v Flanagan; sub nom. Flanagan v South Bucks DC [2002]
    EWCA Civ 690; [2002] 1 W.L.R. 2601; [2002] 3 P.L.R. 47; [2002] J.P.L. 1465;
    (2002) 99(25) L.S.G. 35; (2002) 146 S.J.L.B. 136; [2002] N.P.C. 71, CA (Civ Div) 20–035

South Buckinghamshire DC v Porter (No.1); sub nom. South Bucks DC v Porter [2003] UKHL 26; [2003] 2 A.C. 558; [2003] 2 W.L.R. 1547; [2003] 3 All E.R. 1; [2003] H.R.L.R. 27; [2003] U.K.H.R.R. 1344; [2003] B.L.G.R. 449; [2003] 2 P.L.R. 101; [2003] J.P.L. 1412; [2003] 23 E.G. 135 (C.S.); (2003) 100(22) L.S.G. 32; (2003) 147 S.J.L.B. 626; [2003] N.P.C. 70, HL 19–010, 25–033

South Buckinghamshire DC v Porter (No.2); sub nom. South Buckinghamshire DC v Secretary of State for Transport, Local Government and the Regions [2004] UKHL 33; [2004] 1 W.L.R. 1953; [2004] 4 All E.R. 775; [2005] 1 P. & C.R. 6; [2004] 4 P.L.R. 50; [2004] 28 E.G. 177 (C.S.); (2004) 101(31) L.S.G. 25; (2004) 148 S.J.L.B. 825; [2004] N.P.C. 108, HL 9–024

South East Asia Fire Bricks Sdn Bhd v Non Metallic Mineral Products Manufacturing Employees Union [1981] A.C. 363; [1980] 3 W.L.R. 318; [1980] 2 All E.R. 689; (1980) 124 S.J. 496, PC (Mal) 14–033, 27–003

South Eastern Railway Co v Cooper [1924] 1 Ch. 211, CA 16–024

South of Scotland Electricity Board v British Oxygen Co (No.1); sub nom. British Oxygen Co Ltd v South West Scotland Electricity Board (No.1) [1956] 1 W.L.R. 1069; [1956] 3 All E.R. 199; 1956 S.C. (H.L.) 112; 1956 S.L.T. 278; (1956) 100 S.J. 602, HL 17–013

South of Scotland Electricity Board v British Oxygen. *See* British Oxygen Co Ltd v South of Scotland Electricity Board (No.2)

South Wales Sea Fisheries Committee v National Assembly for Wales [2001] EWHC Admin 1162 7–042

South Yorkshire Transport v Monopolies and Mergers Commission. *See* R. v Monopolies and Mergers Commission Ex p. South Yorkshire Transport Ltd

Southampton Port HA v Seahawk Marine Foods Ltd; sub nom. R. (on the application of Seahawk Marine Foods Ltd) v Southampton Port HA; Seahawk Marine Foods Ltd v Southampton Port HA [2002] EWCA Civ 54; [2002] E.H.L.R. 15; [2002] A.C.D. 35, CA (Civ Div) 19–011, 19–013, 19–017

Southend on Sea Corp v Hodgson (Wickford) [1962] 1 Q.B. 416; [1961] 2 W.L.R. 806; [1961] 2 All E.R. 46; (1961) 125 J.P. 348; 59 L.G.R. 193; (1961) 12 P. & C.R. 165; (1961) 105 S.J. 181, DC 20–034

Southwark LBC v Dennett [2007] EWCA Civ 1091; [2008] B.L.G.R. 94; [2007] N.P.C. 115, CA (Civ Div) 29–035, 29–036

Southwark LBC v Williams Southwark LBC v Anderson [1971] Ch. 734; [1971] 2 W.L.R. 467; [1971] 2 All E.R. 175; 69 L.G.R. 145, CA (Civ Div) 25–040

Spackman v Plumstead Board of Works; sub nom. Plumstead Board of Works v Spackman (1884–85) L.R. 10 App. Cas. 229, HL 23–025

Sparks v Edward Ash Ltd [1943] K.B. 223; [1943] 1 All E.R. 1, CA 22–028

Special Effects Ltd v L'Oreal SA [2007] EWCA Civ 1; [2007] Bus. L.R. 759; [2007] R.P.C. 15; (2007) 151 S.J.L.B. 126; [2007] E.T.M.R. 51, CA (Civ Div) 20–030

Spiegelman v Hocker (1933) 50 T.L.R. 87 28–002

Sporrong & Lonnroth v Sweden (A/52) (1983) 5 E.H.R.R. 35, ECHR 12–018

Square Meals Frozen Foods v Dunstable Corp [1974] 1 W.L.R. 59; [1974] 1 All E.R. 441; 72 L.G.R. 180; (1973) 26 P. & C.R. 560; (1973) 117 S.J. 875, CA (Civ Div) 25–023

Stafford BC v Elkenford [1977] 1 W.L.R. 324; 75 L.G.R. 337; [1977] J.P.L. 170; (1977) 121 S.J. 34; (1978) 122 S.J. 34, CA (Civ Div) 24–010

Staffordshire Area Health Authority v South Staffordshire Waterworks Co [1978] 1 W.L.R. 1387 25–021

Stamford Corp v Pawlett 148 E.R. 1334; (1830) 1 Cr. & J. 57, KB 11–020

Stanley Cole (Wainfleet) Ltd v Sheridan; sub nom. Sheridan v Stanley Cole (Wainfleet) Ltd [2003] EWCA Civ 1046; [2003] 4 All E.R. 1181; [2003] I.C.R. 1449; [2003] I.R.L.R. 885; (2003) 100(38) L.S.G. 33, CA (Civ Div) 12–030

Starey v Graham [1899] 1 Q.B. 406 22–006

Starrs v Ruxton; sub nom. Ruxton v Starrs 2000 J.C. 208; 2000 S.L.T. 42; 1999 S.C.C.R. 1052; [2000] H.R.L.R. 191; [2000] U.K.H.R.R. 78; 8 B.H.R.C. 1; 1999 G.W.D. 37–1793, HCJ 7–007

Steaua Romana, The and Oltenia, The [1944] P. 43, PDAD 16–034

Steele v Minister of Housing and Local Government and West Ham County BC (1956) 6 P. & C.R. 386, CA 9–040

Steele v Williams (1853) 8 Ex. 625 29–049

Steenhorst-Neerings v Bestuur van de Bedrijfsvereniging voor Detailhandel,

Ambachten en Huisvrouwen (C-338/91) [1993] E.C.R. I-5475; [1995] 3 C.M.L.R.
  323; [1994] I.R.L.R. 244, ECJ 10–032
Steeples v Derbyshire DC [1985] 1 W.L.R. 256; [1984] 3 All E.R. 468; [1981] J.P.L. 582;
  (1985) 82 L.S.G. 358, QBD 24–026
Stefan v General Medical Council (No.1) [1999] 1 W.L.R. 1293; [2000] H.R.L.R. 1; 6
  B.H.R.C. 487; [1999] Lloyd's Rep. Med. 90; (1999) 49 B.M.L.R. 161; (1999) 143
  S.J.L.B. 112, PC (UK) 12–035, 13–012
Stepney Metropolitan Borough v John Walker & Sons Ltd [1934] A.C. 365, HL 26–057
Sterling v Turner (1672) 1 Ventris 206 29–021
Stevenson v United Road Transport Union [1977] 2 All E.R. 941; [1977] I.C.R. 893, CA
  (Civ Div) 12–015
Stockport District Waterworks Co v Manchester Corporation (1863) 9 Jur. 9N.S.)
  266 24–006
Stoke on Trent City Council v B&Q (Retail) Ltd [1984] A.C. 754; [1984] 2 W.L.R. 929;
  [1984] 2 All E.R. 332; 82 L.G.R. 473; (1984) 128 S.J. 364; (1985) 4 Tr. L. 9, HL . 24–009
Stoke on Trent City Council v B&Q Plc [1991] 1 A.C. 49 19–027
Stolting v Hauptzollamt Hamburg-Jonas (138/78) [1979] E.C.R. 713; [1979] 3 C.M.L.R.
  588, ECJ 19–022
Stourcliffe Estate Co Ltd v Bournemouth Corp [1910] 2 Ch. 12, CA 16–024
Stovin v Wise [1996] A.C. 923; [1996] 3 W.L.R. 388; [1996] 3 All E.R. 801; [1996]
  R.T.R. 354; (1996) 93(35) L.S.G. 33; (1996) 146 N.L.J. 1185; (1996) 140 S.J.L.B.
  201, HL 29–006, 29–007, 29–011
Stretch v United Kingdom (44277/98) (2004) 38 E.H.R.R. 12; [2004] B.L.G.R. 401;
  [2004] 1 E.G.L.R. 11; [2004] 03 E.G. 100; [2003] 29 E.G. 118 (C.S.); [2003] N.P.C.
  125, ECHR 5–049, 20–040
Stretch v West Dorset DC (No.1) (2000) 2 L.G.L.R. 140; (1998) 10 Admin. L.R. 129;
  (1999) 77 P. & C.R. 342; [1998] 3 E.G.L.R. 62; [1998] 48 E.G. 183; (1998) 162
  J.P.N. 202; (1997) 94(46) L.S.G. 30; (1998) 75 P. & C.R. D26, CA (Civ Div) 5–048
Stringer v Minister for Housing and Local Government [1970] 1 W.L.R. 1281; [1971] 1
  All E.R. 65; 68 L.G.R. 788; (1971) 22 P. & C.R. 255; [1971] J.P.L. 114; (1970) 114
  S.J. 753, QBD 16–013
Strong v County of Santa Cruz 543 P. 2d 264 (1975) 20–048
Sullivan v Everhart 494 U.S. 83 (1990) 14–041
Sunday Times v United Kingdom (A/30) (1979–80) 2 E.H.R.R. 245; (1979) 76 L.S.G.
  328, ECHR 18–032
Sutherland Shire Council v Heyman [1955–95] P.N.L.R. 238; 157 C.L.R. 424; (1985) 60
  A.L.R. 1; (1985) 59 A.L.J.R. 564; (1986) 2 Const. L.J. 161, HC (Aus) 29–011
Sutton v Attorney General (1923) 39 T.L.R. 294 5–045
Sutton v Clarke (1815) 6 Taunt 29 29–005
Swedish Engine Drivers Union v Sweden (A/20); sub nom. Svenska Lokmanna-
  forbundet v Sweden (A/20) [1978] E.C.C. 1; (1979–80) 1 E.H.R.R. 617, ECHR . 18–018
Swinney v Chief Constable of Northumbria (No.1) [1997] Q.B. 464; [1996] 3 W.L.R.
  968; [1996] 3 All E.R. 449; [1996] P.N.L.R. 473; (1996) 146 N.L.J. 878, CA (Civ
  Div) 29–009
Swinney v Chief Constable of Northumbria (No.2) (1999) 11 Admin. L.R. 811, QBD   29–009
TA Miller Ltd v Minister of Housing and Local Government [1968] 1 W.L.R. 992;
  [1968] 2 All E.R. 633; [1969] R.P.C. 91; 66 L.G.R. 39; (1968) 19 P. & C.R. 263;
  (1968) 112 S.J. 522, CA (Civ Div) 9–038
Tate & Lyle Industries Ltd v Greater London Council; sub nom. Tate & Lyle Food &
  Distribution Ltd v Greater London Council [1983] 2 A.C. 509; [1983] 2 W.L.R.
  649; [1983] 1 All E.R. 1159; [1983] 2 Lloyd's Rep. 117; 81 L.G.R. 4434; (1983) 46 P.
  & C.R. 243, HL 29–038
Taylor v Lawrence (Appeal: Jurisdiction to Reopen) [2002] EWCA Civ 90; [2003] Q.B.
  528; [2002] 3 W.L.R. 640; [2002] 2 All E.R. 353; [2002] C.P. Rep. 29; (2002) 99(12)
  L.S.G. 35; (2002) 152 N.L.J. 221; (2002) 146 S.J.L.B. 50, CA (Civ Div) 13–007
Taylor v Munrow (District Auditor) [1960] 1 W.L.R. 151; [1960] 1 All E.R. 455; (1960)
  124 J.P. 207; 58 L.G.R. 135; (1960) 104 S.J. 169, DC 17–010
Taylor v National Union of Seamen [1967] 1 W.L.R. 532; [1967] 1 All E.R. 767; [1966] 2
  Lloyd's Rep. 504; 1 K.I.R. 702; (1967) 111 S.J. 192, Ch D 12–014
Taylor v Williamsons (A Firm) [2002] EWCA Civ 1380; [2003] C.P. Rep. 20; (2002)
  99(36) L.S.G. 39, CA (Civ Div) 13–007

Tehrani v Rostron [1972] 1 Q.B. 182; [1971] 3 W.L.R. 612; [1971] 3 All E.R. 790; (1971)
　　115 S.J. 641, CA (Civ Div) 27–002
Terrell v Secretary of State for the Colonies [1953] 2 Q.B. 482; [1953] 3 W.L.R. 331;
　　[1953] 2 All E.R. 490; (1953) 97 S.J. 507, QBD 5–045
Terry v Huntington (1668) Hrd. 480 23–001
Tesco Stores Ltd v Secretary of State for the Environment [1995] 1 W.L.R. 759; [1995] 2
　　All E.R. 636; 93 L.G.R. 403; (1995) 70 P. & C.R. 184; [1995] 2 P.L.R. 72; [1995] 2
　　E.G.L.R. 147; [1995] 27 E.G. 154; [1995] E.G. 82 (C.S.); (1995) 92(24) L.S.G. 39;
　　(1995) 145 N.L.J. 724; (1995) 139 S.J.L.B. 145; [1995] N.P.C. 89A, HL 17–013
Texas & Pacific Ry. v Abilene Cotton Oil Co 204 U.S. 426 (1906) 11–021
Thames Water Authority v Elmbridge BC [1983] Q.B. 570; [1983] 2 W.L.R. 744; [1983]
　　1 All E.R. 836; 81 L.G.R. 678; [1983] J.P.L. 470; (1983) 127 S.J. 187, CA (Civ
　　Div) 23–033
Thanet DC v Ninedrive Ltd [1978] 1 All E.R. 703; 76 L.G.R. 320; [1977] J.P.L. 718;
　　(1977) 121 S.J. 706, Ch D 24–010
Thomas v University of Bradford; sub nom. Thomas v Bradford University [1987] A.C.
　　795; [1987] 2 W.L.R. 677; [1987] 1 All E.R. 834; [1987] I.C.R. 245; (1987) 84 L.S.G.
　　980; (1987) 137 N.L.J. 220; (1987) 131 S.J. 296, HL 12–014
Thompson v Ingham (1850) 14 Q.B. 710 .... 14–027, 14–028
Thompson v Lacy (1820) 3 B. & Ald. 283 11–020
Thorne Rural DC v Bunting (No.1) [1972] Ch. 470; [1972] 2 W.L.R. 517; [1972] 1 All
　　E.R. 439; 71 L.G.R. 51; (1972) 23 P. & C.R. 23; (1972) 116 S.J. 200, Ch D 24–007
Thrasyvoulou v Secretary of State for the Environment [1990] 2 A.C. 273; [1990] 2
　　W.L.R. 1; [1990] 1 All E.R. 65; 88 L.G.R. 217; (1990) 2 Admin. L.R. 289; (1990) 59
　　P. & C.R. 326; [1990] 1 P.L.R. 69; [1990] 13 E.G. 69; (1990) 154 L.G. Rev. 192;
　　[1989] E.G. 178 (C.S.), HL 20–030, 20–043
Three Rivers DC v Bank of England (Disclosure) (No.1); sub nom. Three Rivers DC v
　　HM Treasury; Three Rivers DC v Bank of England (No.5); Three Rivers DC v
　　Bank of England (No.4) [2002] EWCA Civ 1182; [2003] 1 W.L.R. 210; [2002] 4 All
　　E.R. 881; [2003] C.P. Rep. 9; [2003] C.P.L.R. 181; (2002) 99(39) L.S.G. 40, CA
　　(Civ Div) 26–050
Three Rivers DC v Bank of England (No.3) [2003] 2 A.C. 1; [2000] 2 W.L.R. 1220;
　　[2000] 3 All E.R. 1; [2000] Lloyd's Rep. Bank. 235; [2000] 3 C.M.L.R. 205; [2000]
　　Eu. L.R. 583; (2000) 2 L.G.L.R. 769; (2000) 97(23) L.S.G. 41, HL 29–031,
　　　　　　　　　　　　　　　　　　　　　　　　　　　29–034, 29–035
Tithe Redemption Committee v Wynne [1943] K.B. 756, CA 14–029
Tito v Waddell (No.2) [1977] Ch. 106; [1977] 3 W.L.R. 972; [1977] 2 W.L.R. 496; [1977]
　　3 All E.R. 129 (Note), Ch D 24–007
Town Investments Ltd v Department of the Environment; sub nom. London County
　　Freehold and Leasehold Properties v Department of the Environment; HEPC
　　(Mayfair Properties) v Department of the Environment [1978] A.C. 359; [1977] 2
　　W.L.R. 450; [1977] 1 All E.R. 813; (1977) 34 P. & C.R. 48; (1977) 121 S.J. 203,
　　HL 5–036, 5–037
Tozer v Child (1857) 7 E. & B. 377 29–033
Transco Plc v Stockport MBC; sub nom. British Gas Plc v Stockport MBC; Stockport
　　MBC v British Gas Plc [2003] UKHL 61; [2004] 2 A.C. 1; [2003] 3 W.L.R. 1467;
　　[2004] 1 All E.R. 589; 91 Con. L.R. 28; [2004] Env. L.R. 24; [2003] 48 E.G. 127
　　(C.S.); (2003) 153 N.L.J. 1791; (2003) 147 S.J.L.B. 1367; [2003] N.P.C. 143; [2004]
　　1 P. & C.R. DG12, HL 29–042
Trawnik v Gordon Lennox; sub nom. Trawnik v Ministry of Defence [1985] 1 W.L.R.
　　532; [1985] 2 All E.R. 368, CA (Civ Div) 29–046
Tre Traktorer AB v Sweden (A/159); sub nom. Tre Traktorer AB v Sweden (10873/84)
　　(1991) 13 E.H.R.R. 309, ECHR 13–012
Triggs v Staines Urban DC; sub nom. Staines Urban DC's Agreement, Re [1969] 1 Ch.
　　10; [1968] 2 W.L.R. 1433; [1968] 2 All E.R. 1; (1968) 132 J.P. 255; 66 L.G.R. 618;
　　(1968) 19 P. & C.R. 450; (1968) 112 S.J. 171, Ch D 16–025
Trojani v Centre Public d'Aide Sociale de Bruxelles (CPAS) (C-456/02) [2004] All E.R.
　　(EC) 1065; [2004] E.C.R. I-7573; [2004] 3 C.M.L.R. 38; [2005] C.E.C. 139, ECJ   21–016
Trustees of Dennis Rye Pension Fund v Sheffield City Council [1998] 1 W.L.R. 840;
　　[1997] 4 All E.R. 747; (1998) 30 H.L.R. 645; (1998) 10 Admin. L.R. 112; (1998) 162
　　J.P.N. 145, CA (Civ Div) 26–00, 26–014

Tsfayo v United Kingdom (60860/00) [2007] H.L.R. 19; [2007] B.L.G.R. 1, ECHR . 13–018, 13–019

Turner v Secretary of State for the Environment 72 L.G.R. 380; (1974) 28 P. & C.R. 123; (1973) 228 E.G. 335, QBD 9–052, 24–011

Tweed v Parades Commission for Northern Ireland [2006] UKHL 53; [2007] 1 A.C. 650; [2007] 2 W.L.R. 1; [2007] 2 All E.R. 273; [2007] N.I. 66; [2007] H.R.L.R. 11; [2007] U.K.H.R.R. 456; 22 B.H.R.C. 92; (2007) 151 S.J.L.B. 24, HL (NI) 26–006, 26–051

Twyford v Manchester Corp [1946] Ch. 236; [1946] 1 All E.R. 621; 62 T.L.R. 367; (1946) 110 J.P. 196; [1946] W.N. 70; [1947] L.J.R. 12; 175 L.T. 124; (1946) 90 S.J. 164, Ch D 29–049

US v Mead Corporation 533 U.S. 218 (2001) 14–042

Underhill v Ministry of Food [1950] 1 All E.R. 591; 66 T.L.R. (Pt. 1) 730; [1950] W.N. 133; (1950) 94 S.J. 194, Ch D 25–030, 28–021

Unectef v Heylens. *See* Union Nationale des Entraineurs et Cadres Techniques Professionnels du Football (UNECTEF) v Heylens (222/86)

Union des Employes de Srvice, Local 298 v Bibeault [1988] 2 S.C.R. 1048 14–043

Union Nationale des Entraineurs et Cadres Techniques Professionnels du Football (UNECTEF) v Heylens (222/86) [1987] E.C.R. 4097; [1989] 1 C.M.L.R. 901, ECJ 12–040

United Kingdom Association of Professional Engineers (UKAPE) v Advisory, Conciliation and Arbitration Service (ACAS); sub nom. Advisory, Conciliation and Arbitration Service v United Kingdom Association of Professional Engineers and Butchart; UKAPE v ACAS [1981] A.C. 424; [1980] 2 W.L.R. 254; [1980] 1 All E.R. 612; [1980] I.C.R. 201; [1980] I.R.L.R. 124; (1980) 124 S.J. 1547, HL .. 19–002, 19–004

United States v Certain Parcels of Land 131 F. Supp. 65 (1955) 20–048

United States v Florida East Coast Railway 410 U.S. 224 (1973) 22–020

United States v Lazy FC Ranch 481 F. 2d 98 (1973) 20–048

United States v Ruby Company 588 F. 2d 697 (1978) 20–048

Universal Camera Corp v NLRB 340 U.S. 474 (1951) 15–024

Usill v Hales; sub nom. Usil v Hales (1877–78) L.R. 3 C.P.D. 319, CPD 14–026

Utah Power and Light Company v United States 243 U.S. 389 (1917) 20–042

Van Binsbergen v Bestuur van de Bedrijfsvereniging voor de Metaalnijverheid (33/74) [1974] E.C.R. 1299; [1975] 1 C.M.L.R. 298, ECJ 19–020

Van de Hurk v Netherlands (A/288) (1994) 18 E.H.R.R. 481, ECHR 12–035, 13–012

Van der Mussele v Belgium (8919/80) (1984) 6 E.H.R.R. 163, ECHR 21–008

Van Duyn v Home Office (41/74) [1975] Ch. 358; [1975] 2 W.L.R. 760; [1975] 3 All E.R. 190; [1974] E.C.R. 1337; [1975] 1 C.M.L.R. 1; (1974) 119 S.J. 302, ECJ . 10–023, 10–024

Van Gend en Loos v Nederlandse Administratie der Belastingen (26/62). *See* NV Algemene Transport- en Expeditie Onderneming van Gend en Loos v Nederlandse Administratie der Belastingen (26/62)

Vaughan v Taff Vale Ry Co (1860) 5 H. & N. 679 29–038

Vaughan Ex p. (1866) L.R. 2 Q.B. 114 14–027

Vellino v Chief Constable of Greater Manchester [2001] EWCA Civ 1249; [2002] 1 W.L.R. 218; [2002] 3 All E.R. 78; [2002] P.I.Q.R. P10; [2001] Po. L.R. 295; (2001) 151 N.L.J. 1441, CA (Civ Div) 29–009

Vermont Yankee Nuclear Power Corp v Natural Resources Defence Council, Inc 435 U.S. 519 (1978) 22–020

Vernon v Vestry of St james Westminster (1880) 16 Ch.D 449 29–038

Vestal v Commissioner of Internal Revenue 152 F. 2d 132 (1945) 20–048

Victoria Square Property Co v Southwark LBC [1978] 1 W.L.R. 463; [1978] 2 All E.R. 281; 76 L.G.R. 349; (1977) 34 P. & C.R. 275; (1977) 247 E.G. 989; [1978] J.P.L. 243; (1977) 121 S.J. 816, CA (Civ Div) 17–013

Vidyodaya University of Ceylon v Silva [1965] 1 W.L.R. 77; [1964] 3 All E.R. 865; (1964) 108 S.J. 896, PC (Cey) 12–015, 25–004, 25–005

Vine v National Dock Labour Board [1957] A.C. 488; [1957] 2 W.L.R. 106; [1956] 3 All E.R. 939; [1956] 2 Lloyd's Rep. 567; (1957) 101 S.J. 86, HL 12–042, 16–003

Voice Construction Ltd v Construction & General Workers Union [2004] 1 S.C.R. 609 14–043

Von Colson v Land Nordrhein-Westfahlen (C-14/83); Harz v Deutsche Tradax GmbH (C-79/83) [1984] E.C.R. 1891; [1986] 2 C.M.L.R. 430, ECJ 5–028, 10–028, 18–006

W v Staffordshire CC [2006] EWCA Civ 1676; [2007] E.L.R. 208, CA (Civ Div) 15–016

W v United Kingdom (A/121); sub nom. W v United Kingdom (9749/82)(1988) 10
    E.H.R.R. 29, ECHR 13–012
W Beus GmbH & Co v Hauptzollamt Munchen Landsbergerstrasse (5/67) [1968]
    E.C.R. 83; [1968] C.M.L.R. 131, ECJ 12–040, 21–019
W. Whiteley Ltd v King (1909) 101 L.T. 741 29–050
Wachauf v Germany (C-5/88); sub nom. Wachauf v Bundesamt fur Ernahrung und
    Forstwirtschaft [1989] E.C.R. 2609; [1991] 1 C.M.L.R. 328, ECJ (3rd Chamber) . 12–040,
                                                                                      18–055
Wainwright v Home Office; sub nom. Secretary of State for the Home Department v
    Wainwright; Wainwright v Secretary of State for the Home Department [2003]
    UKHL 53; [2004] 2 A.C. 406; [2003] 3 W.L.R. 1137; [2003] 4 All E.R. 969; [2004]
    U.K.H.R.R. 154; 15 B.H.R.C. 387; [2004] Prison L.R. 130; (2003) 100(45) L.S.G.
    30; (2003) 147 S.J.L.B. 1208, HL 18–028
Waite v Hammersmith and Fulham LBC. *See* R. (on the application of Waite) v
    Hammersmith and Fulham LBC
Waite v United Kingdom (53236/99) (2003) 36 E.H.R.R. 54; [2003] Prison L.R. 160,
    ECHR 12–024
Wakefield Corp v Cooke [1904] A.C. 31, HL 20–030
Waldron, Re; sub nom. R. v Hallstrom Ex p. W (No.1)[1986] Q.B. 824; [1985] 3 W.L.R.
    1090; [1985] 3 All E.R. 775; (1986) 83 L.S.G. 199; (1985) 129 S.J. 892, CA (Civ
    Div) 27–003
Wallace v Quinn [2003] NICA 48; [2004] N.I. 164, CA (NI) 23–011
Wallasey Local Board v Gracey (1887) 36 Ch. D. 593 24–010
Waltham Forest LBC v Roberts [2004] EWCA Civ 940; [2005] H.L.R. 2; (2004) 148
    S.J.L.B. 910; [2004] N.P.C. 118, CA (Civ Div) 25–023
Wandsworth LBC v A [2000] 1 W.L.R. 1246; (2001) 3 L.G.L.R. 3; [2000] B.L.G.R. 81;
    [2000] Ed. C.R. 167; [2000] E.L.R. 257; (2000) 97(3) L.S.G. 35; (2000) 144 S.J.L.B.
    47, CA (Civ Div) 15–006
Wandsworth LBC v Secretary of State for Transport, Local Government and the
    Regions (Enforcement Notice); sub nom. R. (on the application of Wandsworth
    LBC) v Secretary of State for Transport, Local Government and the Regions
    [2003] EWHC 622 (Admin); [2004] 1 P. & C.R. 32; [2004] J.P.L. 291; [2003] N.P.C.
    11, QBD (Admin) 20–017
Wandsworth LBC v Winder (No.1) [1985] A.C. 461; [1984] 3 W.L.R. 1254; [1984] 3 All
    E.R. 976; (1985) 17 H.L.R. 196; 83 L.G.R. 143; (1985) 82 L.S.G. 201; (1985) 135
    N.L.J. 381; (1984) 128 S.J. 838, HL 26–007, 26–010, 26–015
Warwick Rural DC v Miller-Mead; sub nom. Miller-Mead v Warwick Rural DC [1962]
    Ch. 441; [1962] 2 W.L.R. 284; [1962] 1 All E.R. 212; (1962) 126 J.P. 143; 60 L.G.R.
    29; (1961) 105 S.J. 1124, CA 16–005
Warwickshire CC v British Railways Board [1969] 1 W.L.R. 1117; [1969] 3 All E.R.
    631; (1969) 113 S.J. 447, CA (Civ Div) 24–010
Waterloo Bridge Company v Cull (1858) 1 El. & El. 213 23–007
Watkins v Secretary of State for the Home Department; sub nom. Watkins v Home
    Office [2006] UKHL 17; [2006] 2 A.C. 395; [2006] 2 W.L.R. 807; [2006] 2 All E.R.
    353; [2006] 1 Prison L.R. 268, HL 29–035
Watson v British Boxing Board of Control Ltd [2001] Q.B. 1134; [2001] 2 W.L.R. 1256;
    [2001] P.I.Q.R. P16; (2001) 98(12) L.S.G. 44; (2001) 145 S.J.L.B. 31, CA (Civ
    Div) 29–016
Watt v Kesteven CC [1955] 1 Q.B. 408; [1955] 2 W.L.R. 499; [1955] 1 All E.R. 473;
    (1955) 119 J.P. 220; 53 L.G.R. 254; (1955) 99 S.J. 149, CA 29–021
Waverley BC v Hilden [1988] 1 W.L.R. 246; [1988] 1 All E.R. 807; 86 L.G.R. 271; [1988]
    J.P.L. 175; (1988) 152 L.G. Rev. 190; (1988) 132 S.J. 192, Ch D 26–014
Weaver v Price (1832) 3 B. & Ad. 409 .... 14–027, 15–002
Webb v EMO Air Cargo (UK) Ltd [1995] 1 W.L.R. 1454; [1995] 4 All E.R. 577; [1996] 2
    C.M.L.R. 990; [1995] I.C.R. 1021; [1995] I.R.L.R. 645, HL 10–029
Webb v Minister of Housing and Local Government [1965] 1 W.L.R. 755; [1965] 2 All
    E.R. 193; (1965) 129 J.P. 417; 63 L.G.R. 250; (1965) 16 P. & C.R. 259; (1965) 109
    S.J. 374, CA 14–037, 17–015, 27–007
Webb v R. (1994) 181 c.l.r. 41 13–007
Wednesbury Corp v Ministry of Housing and Local Government (No.2) [1966] 2 Q.B.
    275; [1965] 3 W.L.R. 956; [1965] 3 All E.R. 571; (1966) 130 J.P. 34; 63 L.G.R. 460;
    (1966) 17 P. & C.R. 190; (1965) 109 S.J. 630, CA 9–038

Welsh v Chief Constable of Merseyside [1993] 1 All E.R. 692, QBD 29–008
West v Sullivan 973 F. 2d 179 (1992) 14–041, 28–002
West Glamorgan CC v Rafferty [1987] 1 W.L.R. 457; [1987] 1 All E.R. 1005; (1986) 18
    H.L.R. 375; 85 L.G.R. 793; (1989) 57 P. & C.R. 261; [1988] J.P.L. 169; (1987) 84
    L.S.G. 1493; (1987) 131 S.J. 472, CA (Civ Div) 19–004, 26–014
Westdeutsche Landesbank Girozentrale v Islington LBC; sub nom. Islington LBC v
    Westdeutsche Landesbank Girozentrale [1996] A.C. 669; [1996] 2 W.L.R. 802;
    [1996] 2 All E.R. 961; [1996] 5 Bank. L.R. 341; [1996] C.L.C. 990; 95 L.G.R. 1;
    (1996) 160 J.P. Rep. 1130; (1996) 146 N.L.J. 877; (1996) 140 S.J.L.B. 136, HL . 29–050
Western Fish Products Ltd v Penwith DC [1981] 2 All E.R. 204; 77 L.G.R. 185; (1979)
    38 P. & C.R. 7; [1978] J.P.L. 627; (1978) 122 S.J. 471, CA (Civ Div) 16–005,
                                                                    20–035, 20–038, 20–039
Westminster City Council v Great Portland Estates Plc; sub nom. Great Portland
    Estates Plc v Westminster City Council [1985] A.C. 661; [1984] 3 W.L.R. 1035;
    [1984] 3 All E.R. 744; (1985) 50 P. & C.R. 20; [1985] J.P.L. 108; (1984) 81 L.S.G.
    3501; (1984) 128 S.J. 784, HL 9–024, 12–034
Westminster City Council v Mendoza; sub nom. R. v Horseferry Road Magistrates
    Court Ex p. Rezouali [2001] EWCA Civ 216; [2001] E.H.L.R. 16; [2001] N.P.C. 56,
    CA (Civ Div) 23–011
Westminster Corporation v L & NW Ry [1905] A.C. 426 17–010
Wetherall v Harrison [1976] Q.B. 773; [1976] 2 W.L.R. 168; [1976] 1 All E.R. 241; [1976]
    R.T.R. 125; [1976] Crim. L.R. 54; (1975) 119 S.J. 848, QBD 12–031
Whaley v Lord Watson of Invergowrie; sub nom. Whalley v Lord Watson of Inver-
    gowrie 2000 S.C. 340; 2000 S.L.T. 475; 2000 S.C.L.R. 279; 2000 G.W.D. 8–272, IH
    (1 Div) 7–026
Whippingham and East Cowes, St James (The Union of the Benefices of), Re; sub nom.
    Derham v Church Commissioners for England [1954] A.C. 245; [1954] 2 W.L.R.
    804; [1954] 2 All E.R. 22; (1954) 98 S.J. 268, PC (UK) 22–017
White v White [2001] 2 All E.R. 43 10–029
Whitelegg v Richards (1823) 2 B. & C. 45 29–033
Whyte Ridsdale & Co Ltd v Attorney General [1927] 1 Ch. 548, Ch D 25–026
Wildes v Russell (1866) L.R. 1 C.P. 722 23–026
Wilkinson v Barking Corp [1948] 1 K.B. 721; [1948] 1 All E.R. 564; 64 T.L.R. 230; (1948)
    112 J.P. 215; 46 L.G.R. 169; [1948] L.J.R. 1164; (1948) 92 S.J. 205, CA 13–009,
                                                                                    25–023
Wilkinson v Inland Revenue Commissioners. *See* R. (on the application of Wilkinson)
    v Inland Revenue Commissioners
William Cory & Son Ltd v London Corp [1951] 2 K.B. 476; [1951] 2 All E.R. 85; [1951]
    1 Lloyd's Rep. 475; [1951] 2 T.L.R. 174; (1951) 115 J.P. 371; (1951) 95 S.J. 465,
    CA 16–025, 16–030
Williams v Giddy [1911] A.C. 381, PC (Aus) 19–002
Williams v Home Office (No.1) [1981] 1 All E.R. 1151, QBD 28–013
Willion v Berkley (1561) 1 Plowden 223 28–015
Willis v Childe (1851) 13 Beav. 117 12–015
Wilover Nominees v Inland Revenue Commissioners [1974] 1 W.L.R. 1342; [1974] 3 All
    E.R. 496, CA (Civ Div) 23–028
Wilson v Weller (1819) 1 B. & B. 57 14–026
Wilson, Walton International (Offshire Services) v Tees and Hartlepools Port
    Authority [1969] 1 Lloyd's Rep. 120; (1969) 119 N.L.J. 390, Ch D 24–006
Wilson, Re [1985] A.C. 750 12–030
Winterbottom v Derby (1866–67) L.R. 2 Ex. 316, Ex Ct 24–006
Winterwerp v Netherlands (A/33) (1979–80) 2 E.H.R.R. 387, ECHR 18–032
Wiseman v Borneman [1971] A.C. 297; [1969] 3 W.L.R. 706; [1969] 3 All E.R. 275; 45
    T.C. 540; [1969] T.R. 279; (1969) 113 S.J. 838, HL 12–009, 12–012, 12–023
Wood v Ealing LBC [1967] Ch. 364; [1966] 3 W.L.R. 1209; [1966] 3 All E.R. 514; (1966)
    130 J.P. 22; 65 L.G.R. 282; (1966) 110 S.J. 944, Ch D 25–040, 29–021
Wood v Holden (Inspector of Taxes); sub nom. R v Holden (Inspector of Taxes) [2006]
    EWCA Civ 26; [2006] 1 W.L.R. 1393; [2006] S.T.C. 443; [2006] 2 B.C.L.C. 210; 78
    T.C. 1; [2006] B.T.C. 208; 8 I.T.L. Rep. 468; [2006] S.T.I. 236; (2006) 150 S.J.L.B.
    127, CA (Civ Div) 9–021
Wood v Woad (1874) L.R. 9 Ex. 190; (1873) 43 L.J. Ex. 153, Ex Ct 12–001, 23–025

Woodhouse v Peter Brotherhood Ltd [1972] 2 Q.B. 520; [1972] 3 W.L.R. 215; [1972] 3 All
    E.R. 91; [1972] I.C.R. 186; 13 K.I.R. 45; (1972) 116 S.J. 467, CA (Civ Div)   9–019,
                                                                                         9–021
Woollett v Minister of Agriculture and Fisheries [1955] 1 Q.B. 103; [1954] 3 W.L.R.
    776; [1954] 3 All E.R. 529; 53 L.G.R. 1; (1954–55) 5 P. & C.R. 18; (1954) 98 S.J.
    804, CA 16–007, 27–007
Woolwich Equitable Building Society v Inland Revenue Commissioners [1993] A.C. 70;
    [1992] 3 W.L.R. 366; [1992] 3 All E.R. 737; [1992] S.T.C. 657; (1993) 5 Admin.
    L.R. 265; 65 T.C. 265; (1992) 142 N.L.J. 1196; (1992) 136 S.J.L.B. 230, HL   29–048
Worthington v Jeffries (1875) L.R. 10 C.P. 379 ....   24–004, 25–009
Wright v Bruister (1832) 4 B. & Ald. 116   11–020
X v Scottish Ministers [2007] CSIH 45; 2007 S.L.T. 657; 2007 G.W.D. 20–348; 2007
    S.C. 631, IH (1 Div)   7–010
X NHS Trust v T (Adult Patient: Refusal of Medical Treatment) [2004] EWHC 1279
    (Fam); [2005] 1 All E.R. 387; [2004] 3 F.C.R. 297; (2005) 8 C.C.L. Rep. 38; [2004]
    Lloyd's Rep. Med. 433; (2004) 80 B.M.L.R. 184, Fam Div 25–030, 28–021
X (Minors) v Bedfordshire CC [1995] 2 A.C. 633; [1995] 3 W.L.R. 152; [1995] 3 All E.R.
    353; [1995] 2 F.L.R. 276; [1995] 3 F.C.R. 337; 94 L.G.R. 313; (1995) 7 Admin. L.R.
    705; [1995] Fam. Law 537; (1996) 160 L.G. Rev. 123; (1996) 160 L.G. Rev. 103;
    (1995) 145 N.L.J. 993, HL   29–021
YL v Birmingham City Council [2007] 3 W.L.R. 112 ....   5–013, 18–018
Yeoman's Row Management Ltd v London Rent Assessment Committee [2002]
    EWHC 835; [2002] N.P.C. 56, QBD (Admin)   9–024
York Corp v Henry Leetham & Sons Ltd [1924] 1 Ch. 557, Ch D   16–024
Yotvin v State of Israel (1979)   28–021
Yuen Kun Yeu v Attorney General of Hong Kong [1988] A.C. 175; [1987] 3 W.L.R.
    776; [1987] 2 All E.R. 705; [1987] F.L.R. 291; (1987) 84 L.S.G. 2049; (1987) 137
    N.L.J. 566; (1987) 131 S.J. 1185, PC (HK)   29–008
Zander v Sweden (A/279–B) (1994) 18 E.H.R.R. 175, ECHR   12–018
Zardi v Consorzio Agrario Provinciale di Ferrara (C-8/89) [1990] E.C.R. I-2515; [1991]
    3 C.M.L.R. 417, ECJ (5th Chamber)   19–022
Zurich Insurance Co v Revenue and Customs Commissioners; sub nom. Revenue and
    Customs Commissioners v Zurich Insurance Co [2007] EWCA Civ 218; [2007]
    S.T.C. 1756; [2007] 2 C.M.L.R. 53; [2007] B.T.C. 5314; [2007] B.V.C. 283, CA (Civ
    Div)   9–021

TABLE OF LEGISLATION

Statutes

1531	Statute of Sewers	22–002
1539	Statute of Proclamations	22–002
1601	Poor Relief Act (43 Eliz.1	
	c.2)	2–003
1679	Habeas Corpus Act (31 Car.2	
	c.2)	25–038
1742	Justices Jurisdiction Act (16	
	Geo.2 c.18)	13–010
1801	Inclosure Act	2–015
1832	Reform Act 2–012, 2–013	
1833	Judicial Committee Act (3 & 4	
	Will.4 c.41)	
	s.4	25–025
	Factory Act	2–003
1834	Poor Law (Amendment) Act	
	(4 & 5 Will.4 c.76)	2–004,
	2–007, 2–013, 22–002	
1835	Municipal Corporations Act	2–012,
	2–013, 2–014	
1840	Railways Regulation Act (3 &	
	4 Vict. c.97)	11–022
1845	General Inclosure Act (8 & 9	
	Vict. c.118)	2–015
1846	Commissioners of Railways	
	Act	11–022
1848	Public Health Act (11 & 12	
	Vict. c.63)	2–005
1852	Court of Chancery Procedure	
	Act (15 & 16 Vict. c.87)	25–020
1855	Metropolis Management Act	
	(18 & 19 Vict. c.120)	
	s.62	17–010
1860	Petitions of Right Act (23 &	
	24 Vict. c.34)	5–043
1872	Public Health Act	2–005
	s.258	13–010
1873	Regulation of Railways Act	
	(36 & 37 Vict. c.48)	11–022
	Supreme Court of Judicature	
	Act (36 & 37 Vict. c.66)	

	s.25(8)	25–037
1875	Public Health Act (38 & 39	
	Vict. c.55) 2–005, 2–015	
1883	Judicature Act	25–020
1888	Local Government Act (51 &	
	52 Vict. c.41)	2–014
1894	Merchant Shipping Act (57 &	
	58 Vict. c.60)	10–011
1897	Workmen's Compensation	
	Act (60 & 61 Vict. c.37)	2–017
1906	Workmen's Compensation	
	Act (6 Edw.7 c.58)	2–017
1908	Children's Act (8 Edw.7	
	c.67)	2–016
1909	Labour Exchanges Act (9	
	Edw.7 c.7)	2–017
1911	Parliament Act (1 & 2 Geo.5	
	c.13)	3–021
	National Insurance Act (1 & 2	
	Geo.5 c.55) 2–016, 3–005	
	Pt I 2–016, 2–017	
	Pt II	2–017
1914	Defence of the Realm Act ..	22–002
1918	Education Act (8 & 9 Geo.5	
	c.39)	2–018
1920	Unemployment Insurance	
	Act	2–018
	Emergency Powers Act (10 &	
	11 Geo.5 c.55)	22–002
	Government of Ireland Act	
	(10 & 11 Geo.5 c.67)	7–005
1921	Tribunals of Inquiry (Evi-	
	dence) Act (11 & 12	
	Geo.5 c.7)	9–047
1925	Rating and Valuation Act (15	
	& 16 Geo.5 c.90)	6–009
1933	Local Government Act (23 &	
	24 Geo.5 c.51)	16–028
	s.276	24–010
1934	Unemployment Act (24 & 25	
	Geo.5 c.29)	2–018

1937 Local Government Super-
     annuation (1 Edw.8 & 1
     Geo.6 c.68)
     s.35 25–024
1938 Administration of Justice
     (Miscellaneous Provi-
     sions) Act (1 & 2 Geo.6
     c.63)
     s.9 25–035
1939 Import, Export and Customs
     Powers (Defence) Act (2
     & 3 Geo.6 c.69) 22–003
     Trust Indenture Act, 15
     USCA (United States)
     s.77(c) 20–049
     Public Utility Holding Act, 15
     USCA (United States)
     s.79 I(d) 20–049
1940 Emergency Powers (Defence)
     Act (3 & 4 Geo.6 c.20)   22–002,
                                22–029
1944 Education Act (7 & 8 Geo.6
     c.31) 9–043
1945 Statutory Orders (Special
     Procedure) Act (9 & 10
     Geo.6 c.18) 22–004
1946 Statutory Instruments Act (9
     & 10 Geo.6 c.36) 18–005,
                        22–001, 22–005
     s.1(1) 22–005
        (b) 22–005
        (2) 22–005
     s.1(1A) 22–005
     s.2(1) 22–006
     s.3(2) 22–006
     s.4 .... 22–006, 22–008, 22–009
        (2) 22–006
     s.5 22–009
     s.6 22–009
     s.11(2) 22–005

     Coal Industry Nationalisation
     Act (9 & 10 Geo.6 c.59)   4–027
     National Insurance Act (9 &
     10 Geo.6 c.67) 2–018
     Civil Aviation Act (9 & 10
     Geo.6 c.70) 4–027
     Transport Act 4–027
     Administrative Procedure Act
     (USA) 12–020
     s.5(c) 13–004
     s.553(b) 22–043
     s.706(2)(a) 19–032
1947 Crown Proceedings Act (10 &
     11 Geo.6 c.44) .. 5–043, 29–046
     s.1 5–043
     s.2 28–015
        (1) 29–046
        (2) 29–046
        (3) 29–046
        (5) 29–046
        (6) 29–046

     s.4 28–017
     s.10 .... 18–007, 29–046
     s.17 28–017
     s.21 ...... 25–004, 28–019, 28–017
        (1) 28–019
        (2) 28–019
     s.23(2)(b) 28–019
     s.25(3) 28–017
        (4) 28–017
     s.27 5–046
     s.31(1) 28–016
     s.37 28–017
     s.38(2) 28–019, 29–046
     s.40(1) 5–043
        (2)(b) 5–043
        (c) 5–043
        (f) 28–015, 29–046
     Town and Country Planning
     Act (10 & 11 Geo.6 c.51)
     s.17(1) 25–023
     Portal-to-Portal Act, 29
     USCA (United States)
     ss.258–259 20–049
1948 Gas Act 4–027
     Local Government Act 6–009
     Monopolies and Restrictive
     Practices (Inquiry and
     Control) Act 11–003
     National Assistance Act
     s.21 18–023
        (1) 18–022, 18–025
        (4) 18–022, 18–025
        (5) 18–022
     s.26 26–023
1949 Iron and Steel Act (12, 13 &
     14 Geo.6 c.72) 4–027
     Parliament Act 3–021
1950 Foreign Compensation Act
     (14 Geo.6 c.12) 27–007
     s.4(4) 27–004
     Defence Production Act, 50
     USCA (United States)
     s.2157 20–049
1952 Prison Act (15 & 16 Geo.6 & 1
     Eliz.2 c.52)
     s.47(1) 18–038
1953 Post Office Act (1 & 2 Eliz.2
     c.36)
     s.58 24–007
     s.68 24–007
1956 Restrictive Trade Practices
     Act (4 & 5 Eliz.2 c.68) .. 11–003
1957 Housing Act (5 & 6 Eliz.2
     c.56)
     s.111 17–014
1958 Tribunals and Inquiries Act (6
     & 7 Eliz.2 c.66) 2–020,
              9–006, 12–034, 27–006
     s.1(2)(c) 9–036
     s.12 14–036
1960 Finance Act (8 & 9 Eliz.2 c.44)
     s.28 12–023

1961 Rating and Valuation Act (9
& 10 Eliz.2 c.45) 6–009
1964 Administrative Conference
Act (USA)
s.51 9–032
1965 Nuclear Installations Act
(c.57) 29–044
s.12 29–044
1966 Local Government Act
(c.42) 6–009
Tribunals and Inquiries Act . 9–043
1967 Parliamentary Commissioner
Act (c.13)
s.4(1) 8–013
(3A) 8–019
(3B) 8–019
(8) 8–013
s.5(1) 8–013, 8–015,
8–018, 8–025
s.5(1A)-(1C) 8–015
(2) 8–021
(3) 8–022
(5) 8–026, 8–031
(5A) 8–019
(5B) 8–019
s.6(3) 8–024
(4) 8–024
(5) 8–024
s.7(1) 8–026
(2) 8–026, 8–031
(3) 8–026
(4) 8–026, 8–027
s.8(1) 8–026
(2) 8–026
(3) 8–026
(4) 8–026
s.10(1) 8–026
(2) 8–026
(3) 8–026
(4) 8–026, 8–027
s.11(3) 8–026, 8–039
s.12(3) 8–018
Sch.3 8–022
Malaysian Industrial Relations Act
s.29(3)(a) 27–003
1969 Parliamentary Commissioner
(Northern Ireland) Act
(c.10) 8–012
Commissioner for Complaints
Act (Northern Ireland)
(c.25) 8–012
Transport (London) Act (c.35)
s.1 17–011
s.3 17–011
(1) 17–011
s.7(3)(b) 17–011
(6) 17–011
1970 Equal Pay Act (c.41) 5–047, 21–004
s.1(8) 5–044, 5–047
Chronically Sick and Disabled
Persons Act (c.44)

s.2(1) 17–013
1971 Misuse of Drugs Act (c.38)
s.28 18–007
Tribunals and Inquiries Act
(c.62) 27–006
Civil Aviation Act (c.75) 4–025,
4–026
s.3(1) 4–025
(2) 4–025
s.4 4–025
Town and Country Planning
Act (c.78)
s.29 20–035
1972 Gas Act (c.60) 11–023
European Communities Act
(c.68)
s.2(2) 22–028
Local Government Act (c.70)
s.2(2) 7–032
s.46 6–002
s.53 6–002
s.82 13–010
s.92 25–035
s.94 13–010
s.97 13–010
s.101 16–011
s.102 16–011
s.111 5–038
s.135 5–017
Sch.2 5–017
Deposit of Poisonous Waste
Act 29–044
s.2 29–044
1973 Land Compensation Act
(c.26) 29–044, 29–063
s.1 29–040
(2) 29–040
(6) 29–040
(8) 29–040
s.2 29–040
s.4 29–040
ss.5–6 29–040
Fair Trading Act (c.41)
s.50 11–003
s.51 11–003
s.56 11–008
s.73 11–008
s.76 11–003
s.81(2) 11–005
s.84 11–006
s.88 11–008
Independent Broadcasting Act
s.5 22–041
s.9 22–041
s.13 22–041
1974 Local Government Act (c.7) . 6–010
s.23 8–040
(12A) 8–041
s.25 8–038
s.26(5) 8–038
(6) 8–038
(7) 8–038

(8) 8–038
s.30 8–039
s.31 8–039
s.32(3) 8–039
s.34(1) 8–038
Sch.5 8–038
1975 Ministers of the Crown Act
(c.26) 9–014
s.8(1) 7–014
Local Government (Scotland)
Act (c.30)
Pt II 8–038
Sex Discrimination act (c.65) 5–047,
21–004
s.85 5–047
(2) 5–044
Administrative Appeals Tribunal Act (Australia) ...
s.48 9–032
1976 Restrictive Practices Court
Act (c.33) 11–003
Restrictive Trade Practices
Act (c.34) 11–003, 11–004
s.1(2)(c) 11–005
s.10 11–005
s.19 11–005
s.21 11–005
Resale Prices Act (c.53) 11–003
Race Relations Act (c.74) ... 21–004
s.75 5–044
s.76 5–044
1977 Restrictive Trade Practices
Act (c.19) 11–003
Housing (Homeless Persons)
Act 26–007
1978 Local Government (Scotland)
Act (c.4) 7–005
Employment   Protection
(Consolidation)   Act
(c.44)
Pt V 5–047
1979 Vaccine Damage Payments
Act (c.17) 29–063
1980 Competition Act (c.21)
ss.2–10 11–003
s.4 11–008
s.5 11–003
s.8 11–008
s.9 11–008
s.10 11–008
Limitation Act (c.58)
s.32(1)(c) 29–050
Civil Aviation Act (c.60)
s.12 4–026
s.13 4–026
Local Government, Planning
and Land Act (c.65) 6–013
Pt III 5–020
s.2 22–041
s.3 22–041
ss.54–62 6–010
ss.112–113 29–040

s.184 8–039
Highways Act (c.66) 9–043
1981 British   Telecommunications
Act (c.38) 4–030
s.8 4–030
s.9 4–030
Supreme Court Act (c.54) ... 26–002
s.28 25–004
s.29 ...... 25–001, 25–004, 26–004
(1A) 25–001
s.30 25–035
s.31 .... 23–010, 24–001,
24–006, 24–014, 24–026,
25–031, 25–037, 26–005,
26–006, 26–007, 26–008,
26–012, 26–014, 26–015,
26–016, 26–017, 26–019,
26–020, 26–021, 26–022,
26–027, 26–028, 26–031,
26–032, 26–047, 28–019
(1) 26–004
(2) 25–030, 25–037,
26–004, 26–004
(3) 24–012, 24–016, 26–053
(4) 26–004
(5) 25–013
(5)-(5A) 26–054
(5B) 26–054
(6) 20–050, 26–045, 26–046
s.31A 9–022, 26–003, 26–054
s.37 .... 25–034, 25–037
s.42 26–039
Broadcasting Act (c.68) 17–018,
19–009
Parliamentary   Commissioner
(Consular   Complaints)
Act 8–019
1982 Planning Inquiries (Attendance of Public) Act
(c.12) 9–039
Transport Act (c.49)
s.60 22–041
1983 National Audit Act (c.44) 3–012
1984 Telecommunications   Act
(c.12) 4–030, 4–031, 11–035
Pt III 4–030
s.1 4–030
s.2 4–030
s.3 4–030
s.5 4–030
s.7 4–030
s.12 4–030
s.13 4–030
s.16 4–030
s.18(6) 4–030
(8) 4–030
s.27 4–031
s.27A 4–031
s.27B 4–031
s.27C 4–031
s.27D 4–031
s.27E 4–031

s.50 4–030
Housing and Building Control
   Act (c.29) 6–007
Rates Act (c.33) 6–010
   s.2 6–010
Police and Criminal Evidence
   Act (c.60)
   Pt IX 28–013
1985 Local Government Act
   (c.51) 6–003
Housing Act (c.68)
   s.63 26–007
1986 Gas Act (c.44) 11–027,
                11–030, 11–035
   s.2 11–027
   s.3 11–027
   s.4 11–027
   s.4AA 11–030
   s.7 .... 11–027, 11–030
     (7) 11–029
     (9) 11–027
   s.9 11–030
     (2) 11–028
   s.10(5) 11–028
   s.14 11–028
   s.23 11–029
   s.24 11–029
   s.26 11–029
   s.28 11–029
   s.29 11–029
   s.30 11–029
   s.31 11–029
   s.33A 11–035
   s.33B 11–035
   ss.33C-D 11–035
   s.34 11–029
   s.35 11–029
   s.38 11–029
   ss.49–61 11–028
1987 Local Government Finance
   Act (c.6)
   s.6 6–010
   s.7 6–010
   s.8 6–010
Crown Proceedings (Armed
   Forces) Act (c.25)
   s.1 29–046
Local Government Act (c.44)
   ss.1–5 6–010
1988 Income and Corporation
   Taxes Act (c.1)
   s.262 18–014
Local Government Act (c.9) 5–020,
                    6–007
   s.2 5–020
   s.7 5–020
   s.17 5–018
     (5) 5–018, 5–019
     (e) 5–018
   s.18 5–018
   s.19(7) 5–018
     (8) 5–018

     (10) 5–018
   s.20 5–018
Merchant Shipping Act
   (c.12) . 10–011, 10–013, 29–059
   Pt II 29–057
Criminal Justice Act (c.33)
   Pt VII 29–066
Education Reform Act
   (c.40) 6–007
Local Government Finance
   Act (c.41) 6–009
1989 Electricity Act (c.29) 11–035
Children Act (c.41)
   s.38 18–009
Local Government and
   Housing Act (c.42)
   s.23 8–040
   s.26 8–039
   s.31 8–040
1990 Town and Country Planning
   Act (c.8)
   Pt III 9–052
   s.11 9–051
   s.12 9–051
   s.13 9–051
   s.20 .... 9–051, 9–052
   s.31 9–051
   s.33 9–052
   s.35 .... 9–051, 9–052
   s.36 9–051
   ss.39–42 9–051
   ss.39–45 9–052
   s.77 13–014
   s.78 13–014
   s.79 13–014
     (7) 9–044
   ss.82–87 9–052
   ss.88–90 9–052
   s.101 9–045
   s.179 9–052
   s.183 21–012
   Sch.6 9–044
   Sch.8 9–045
National Health Service and
   Community Care Act
   (c.19)
   s.47 26–023
Government Trading Act
   (c.30) 4–010
Courts and Legal Services Act
   (c.41) 8–012
Import and Export Control
   Act 22–003
1991 Water Industry Act (c.56) .. 11–035
1992 Social Security Contributions
   and Benefits Act (c.4) .. 22–026
Local Government Finance
   Act (c.14) 6–009
   Pt IVA 6–011
Local Government Act
   (c.19) 5–020, 6–003, 6–007
   s.8 6–007

(3) 22–017
(4) 22–017
Competition and Service
  (Utilities) Act (c.43) 4–031,
          4–033, 11–035
s.1 4–031
s.2 4–031
s.3 4–031
s.4 4–031
s.5 4–031
s.6 4–031
s.11 11–035
ss.12–13 11–035
s.37 11–027
ss.76–78 4–031
Tribunals and Inquiries Act
  (c.53) 9–003, 9–006, 27–006
s.1 9–005
  (1)(c) 9–035, 9–048
s.2 9–005
s.8 .... 9–006, 9–023
s.9 .... 9–037, 9–042
s.10 .... 9–006, 9–024, 9–025
  (1)(b) 9–041
  (2) 9–024
  (3) 9–024
  (4) 9–043
  (5)(b) 9–024
  (6) 9–024
  (7) 9–024
s.11 .... 9–006, 9–019
s.12 .... 9–006, 27–006, 27–010
  (1) 27–006
  (2) 27–006
  (3) 27–006
s.14 9–024
s.16(1)(b) 9–043
  (2) 9–043
s.93 9–043
s.302 9–043
Civil Service (Management
  Functions) Act (c.61) ... 4–018
1993 Asylum and Immigration
  Appeals Act (c.23) 22–026
Education Act (c.35)
s.298 17–014
Health Service Commissioners
  Act (c.46)
s.2 8–036
s.2A 8–036
s.2B 8–036
s.3 8–036
Administration of Justice
  (Miscellaneous Provi-
  sions) Act
s.5 26–039
1994 Deregulation and Contracting
  Out Act (c.40) .. 22–003, 22–013
Pt II 5–012, 16–010
s.69 .... 5–012, 16–010
  (5)(c) 5–012
s.70 16–010

s.71 5–012
  (1) 16–010
  (3) 16–010
s.72(2) 5–012, 16–010
  (3)(a) 5–012, 16–010
  (b) 5–012, 16–010
1995 Gas Act (c.45) 11–030
Disability Discrimination Act
  (c.50) 21–004
s.64 5–044
Criminal Injuries Compensa-
  tion Act (c.53) 29–066
1996 Health Service Commissioners
  (Amendment) Act (c.5)
s.6 8–037
Employment Rights Act
  (c.18) 5–047
s.94 5–047
Housing Act (c.52)
Pt VII 12–019
Statutory Instruments (Pro-
  duction and Sale) Act
  (c.54) 22–006
1997 Civil Procedure Act (c.12) ... 9–025
Local Government (Con-
  tracts) Act (c.65) 5–049
s.1(1) 5–049
  (2) 5–049
s.2 5–049
s.4 5–049
s.5 5–049
  (3) 5–049
s.6 5–049
s.7 5–049
1998 Employment Rights (Dispute
  Resolution) Act (c.8)
s.191 5–047
s.193 5–047
Audit Commission Act
  (c.18) 6–012
Public Interest Disclosure Act
  (c.23)
s.10 5–047
Government of Wales Act
  (c.38) 7–001, 7–028
s.22 .... 7–036, 7–045
s.28 7–037
  (1)(a)-(b) 7–037
  (c)-(d) 7–037
ss.53–56 7–031
Competition Act (c.41) 4–031
s.1 11–003
s.2(1) 11–004
s.3 11–009
s.6 11–009
ss.6–9 11–006
s.14 11–003
s.17 11–003
s.18 11–004
s.19 11–009
s.22 11–003
ss.25–31 11–005

ss.32–33 11–008
ss.35–36 11–008
ss.45–46 11–003
s.46 11–005
s.49 11–005
s.51 11–006
s.54 .... 4–030, 4–031
ss.66–67 11–005
Sch.8, para.9 11–005
Sch.9, para.2 11–006
Sch.10 .... 4–030, 4–031,
                        11–005, 11–035
Human Rights Act (c.42) ... 5–013,
            7–008, 12–001, 13–001,
            17–001, 17–016, 17–017,
            18–002, 22–003, 26–012,
            27–010, 29–024, 29–067
s.1 18–003
s.2 12–018
  (1) 18–003
s.3 .... 18–004, 18–006,
          18–007, 18–008, 18–009,
          18–010, 18–011, 18–012,
          18–013, 18–015, 18–016,
                    18–027, 18–050
  (1) 18–008
  (2) 18–004
    (a) 18–004
    (b) 18–004
    (c) 18–004
ss.3–4 11–025
s.4 .... 18–004, 18–010, 18–012,
          18–013, 18–016, 18–027,
          18–031, 18–050, 18–057
  (1) 18–004
  (2) 18–004
  (3) 18–004
  (4) 18–004
  (5) 18–004
  (6) 18–004
s.5 18–004
s.6 .... 18–001, 18–012, 18–017,
          18–022, 18–027, 18–030,
          18–031, 18–050, 24–025,
                            26–035
  (1) 18–012, 18–013, 18–015,
          18–016, 18–017, 18–027,
          18–028, 18–029, 18–030,
                    26–012, 29–027
  (2) 18–013, 18–014,
          18–015, 18–016, 18–050
    (a) 18–015, 18–016
    (b) 18–015, 18–016
  (3)(a) 18–017
    (b) . 18–017, 18–020, 18–021,
          18–022, 18–023, 18–024
  (5) 18–017
  (6) 18–030
s.7 .... 24–025, 26–012
  (1) 18–029, 24–025
    (a) 18–029, 18–030
    (b) 18–029

(2) 18–029
(3) 24–025, 26–012
(5) 18–029
(6) 18–029, 24–025
(7) 18–029
(9) 18–029
(11) 18–030
s.8 .... 29–025, 29–026,
                29–028, 29–030
  (1) 18–030, 29–025
  (2) 29–025
  (3) 18–030, 29–025
  (4) 29–025
  (6) 18–030
s.9(1) 18–029
  (2) 18–029
  (3) 29–027
s.10 ...... 18–005, 22–003, 22–012
  (2) 18–005
s.12(3) 25–032
s.19 18–004
  (1)(a) 18–004
    (b) 18–004
Sch.1 18–003
Sch.2, para.1(1)(b) 18–005
  (2) 18–005
    (a) 18–005
    (b) 18–005
  (4) 18–005
para.3 18–005
para.5 18–005
Regional Development Agencies Act (c.45) 6–013
s.4 6–013
s.5 6–013
s.6 6–013
Scotland Act (c.46) ... 7–001, 7–005
s.1 7–003
  (2) 7–003
  (3) 7–003
s.2(2) 7–003
s.6 7–003
s.11(1) 7–003
s.19 7–004
s.20 7–004
s.21(2) 7–004
  (3) 7–004
s.22(1) 7–004
s.28 7–006
  (7) 7–006
s.29(1) 7–006
  (2) 7–007
    (b) 7–008, 7–009, 7–026
    (c) 7–009
  (3) 7–007
  (4) 7–007
s.31(1) 7–007
  (2) 7–007
s.32(2) 7–019
  (3) 7–019
s.33(1) 7–019
  (2) 7–019

s.34 7–019
s.36(1) 7–006
s.39 7–004
s.44(1) 7–004
  (2) 7–004
s.45 .... 7–004, 7–014
s.46(1) 7–004
s.47 7–014
  (1)-(2) 7–004
s.48 7–004
s.51 7–004
s.52 7–013
  (1) 7–010
  (1)-(3) 7–010
  (6) 7–014
  (7) 7–010
s.53 7–013
  (1) 7–010, 7–014
  (2) 7–010
  (c) 7–010
  (3) 7–013
s.54 7–013
  (2)-(3) 7–010
ss.56–57 7–010
s.57(2) 7–010
s.58 7–017
  (1)-(2) 7–017
  (4) 7–017
s.59 7–004
s.60(1) 7–014
s.63 7–010
s.73 7–016
s.91 8–012
s.98 7–018
s.101(2) 7–018
  (3) 7–018
s.102(2) 7–024
  (3) 7–024
  (4) 7–024
s.103(1) 7–019
s.104 .... 7–013, 7–014
s.105 .... 7–013, 7–014
s.106 7–010
  (1) 7–014
s.107 .... 7–013, 7–014, 7–024
s.108 7–010
  (1) 7–014
s.112 7–014
  (1) 7–014
  (5) 7–014
s.117 7–014
s.118(2) 7–015
s.126 7–013
Sch.1, para.1 7–003
  para.2 7–003
Sch.2, para.4(1) 7–004
Sch.3 7–004
  para.3(1) 7–004
Sch.4 7–009
  para.1 7–008
  para.2(1) 7–009
  (2) 7–009

  para.3(1) 7–009
  para.7(1) 7–009
  paras 12–14 7–010
Sch.5 .... 7–008, 7–009
  Pt II 7–009
  Pt III 7–009
Sch.6 7–023
  para.1 7–018
  para.4 7–020
  (3) 7–021
  paras 5–6 7–019
  para.15 7–020
  (3) 7–021
  paras 16–17 7–019
  para.18 7–021
  para.19 7–021
  para.20 7–021
  para.21 7–021
  para.22 7–021
  para.23 7–021
  para.25 7–020
  (3) 7–021
  paras 26–27 7–019
  para.32 7–021
  para.33 7–019
  paras 34–35 7–019
Sch.7 7–015
Sch.7, para.1 7–015
  (2) 7–013, 7–024
  para.2 7–013
1999 European Parliamentary
    Elections Act (c.1) 10–006
  Disability Rights Commission
    Act (c.17) 21–004
  Access to Justice Act (c.22)
    s.55(1) 9–018
  Youth Justice and Criminal
    Evidence Act (c.23)
    s.41 18–007
    (3) 18–007
  Employment Relations Act
    (c.26)
    Sch.8 5–047
  Local Government Act
    (c.27) 5–021, 5–022,
                        6–007, 6–011
    Pt I 6–017
    s.1 5–021
    s.3(1) 5–021
    (2) 5–021
    s.3A 5–021
    s.4 5–021
    s.5(1) 5–021
    s.6(1) 5–021
    s.7 5–021
    s.19 5–018
    s.21 5–021
    Sch.1 .... 6–011, 6–017
  Greater London Authority
    Act (c.29) 6–003, 6–005
  Welfare Reform and Pensions
    Act (c.30) 21–013

Immigration and Asylum Act
  (c.33)
  Pt II 18–007
House of Lords Act (c.34) ... 3–020
  s.1 3–020
  s.2 3–020
  s.3 3–020
2000 Terrorism Act (c.11)
  s.11(1) 18–010
  (2) 18–010
Care Standards Act (c.14) .. 13–019
  s.82(4) 13–019
Local Government Act
  (c.22) 6–004, 6–005, 6–017
  Pt III 6–017, 8–011
  s.2 5–038
  s.11(2) 6–004
  (5)-(6) 6–004
  s.11(2A) 6–005
  (5)-(6) 6–005
  s.12 .... 6–004, 6–005
  s.14(2) 6–005
  (a) 6–004
  (b) 6–004
  (6) 6–004, 6–005
  s.21 6–005
  s.22 6–005
  ss.25–27 6–004
  ss.33A-33O 6–005
  s.37 6–005
  ss.49–67 8–040
  s.50 8–011
  s.51 8–011
  s.52 8–011
  ss.53–55 8–011
  s.57 8–011
  ss.59–67 8–011
  ss.75–76 8–011
Utilities Act (c.27) 11–030
  s.9 11–030
  s.76 11–030
  s.79 11–030
  ss.90–91 11–035
  ss.90–96 11–035
  s.94 11–035
Race Relations (Amendment)
  Act (c.34) 21–004
Freedom of Information Act
  (c.36) 4–015, 8–004
  Pt II 8–004, 8–005
  s.1 8–005
  (1) 8–004
  (3) 8–004
  s.2 8–004
  s.3 8–004
  s.9 8–004
  s.10 8–004
  s.12 8–004
  s.14 8–005
  s.18 8–005
  s.19 8–004
  s.20 8–004

ss.21–22 8–005
ss.23–24 8–005
ss.47–49 8–005
ss.50–51 8–005
s.52 8–005
s.53 8–005
s.54 8–005
ss.57–61 8–005
Sch.1 8–004
2001 Regulatory Reform Act (c.6) 11–015,
                22–003, 22–013
Anti-terrorism, Crime and
  Security Act (c.24)
  s.21 21–011
  s.23 .... 18–010, 21–011
2002 Nationality, Immigration and
  Asylum Act (c.41) 9–014
2003 Communications Act (c.21) . 4–031,
                    11–035
  ss.65–72 11–016
Local Government Act
  (c.26) 6–012, 6–017
  ss.31–33 6–011
Extradition Act (c.41) 8–022
2004 Planning and Compulsory
  Purchase Act (c.5) 9–051
Asylum and Immigration
  (Treatment of Claimants,
  etc.) Act (c.19) 9–014
Domestic Violence, Crime and
  Victims Act (c.28)
  s.32 8–015
  ss.35–44 8–015
Hunting Act (c.37) 18–035
2005 Constitutional Reform Act
  (c.4)
  s.19 9–014
  Sch.2 9–022
  Sch.7 9–014
  Sch.9, para.66(4) 18–017
  para.96 7–019
  Sch.11(1), para.1 24–012,
             25–001, 26–002
Public Services Ombudsman
  (Wales) Act (c.10) 8–012
Inquiries Act (c.12) 9–047
  s.1 9–047
  s.2 9–047
  s.5 9–047
  ss.8–9 9–047
  s.15 9–047
  s.17 9–047
  s.18 9–047
  s.19 9–047
  s.21 9–047
  s.24 9–047
  ss.25–26 9–047
2006 Government of Wales Act
  (c.32) 7–028, 8–012
  Pt 3 7–034
  s.1 7–029
  (2) 7–029

s.2(1) 7–029
  (2) 7–029
  (4) 7–029
s.3(1) 7–029
s.6 7–029
  (3) 7–029
  (4) 7–029
  (5) 7–029
s.25 7–030
s.26 7–030
s.27 7–030
ss.28–30 7–030
s.31 7–030
  (5) 7–030
s.35(1) 7–030
  (2) 7–030
s.36 7–030
s.45 7–031
s.46 7–031
s.47(1) 7–031
s.48 7–031
ss.49–50 7–031
s.51 7–031
s.57 7–032
s.58 7–032
s.59 7–032
s.60 7–032
s.61 7–032
ss.72–75 7–032
ss.76–79 7–032
s.80 7–032
s.81 7–032
s.82 7–032
s.93 7–034
  (5) 7–034
s.94(1) 7–034
  (2) 7–034
  (4) 7–034
  (5) 7–034
  (6) 7–034
s.95 7–034
ss.97–102 7–034
s.103 7–035
ss.107–108 7–035
s.150 7–044
s.151 7–044
s.153 7–044
  (2) 7–044
  (3) 7–044
  (4)-(6) 7–044
Sch.5, Pt 1 7–034
  Pt 2 7–034
  Pt 3 7–034
Sch.6 7–035
Sch.9 7–043
  para.1(1) 7–038
  (2) 7–041
  para.2 7–038
  para.4 7–040
  para.5(1) 7–039
  (2) 7–039
  para.6 7–041

  para.7(1) 7–041
  (2) 7–041
  para.8 7–041
  para.9 7–041
  para.10 7–041
  para.11 7–041
  para.29(1) 7–039
  para.30(1) 7–039
  (2) 7–039
  Sch.11, para.30 7–036
  Para.31 7–036
Legislative and Regulatory
  Reform Act (c.51) 11–015,
    22–013
s.12 22–013
s.13 22–013
s.14 .... 22–012, 22–013
s.15 22–013
  (6) 22–013
s.16 22–013
  (4)-(5) 22–013
s.17(3)-(4) 22–014
s.18 .... 22–012, 22–014
s.27 22–015
2007 Tribunals, Courts and Enforcement Act (c.15) 9–001,
    9–003, 9–011, 26–044
s.2 9–012
  (3) 9–012
s.3 9–013
ss.4–5 9–013
s.7 9–013
  (1) 9–012
  (9) 9–012
s.8 9–012
s.9 9–016
  (1) 9–016
s.10 9–016
s.11 9–017
  (5) 9–017
  (f) 9–017
  (6) 9–017
ss.11–14 26–044
s.12 9–017
  (2) 9–017
s.13 9–018
  (6) 9–018
  (7) 9–018, 9–023
  (8) 9–018
  (12) 9–018
s.14 9–018
  (2) 9–018
  (b)(i) 9–018
  (5) 9–018
s.15 .... 9–022, 9–023, 26–003
  (1) 9–022
ss.15–19 26–054
ss.15–21 26–044
s.16(6) 9–022
  (8) 9–022
s.17 9–022
s.18 9–022

(3) 9–022
(4) 9–022
(5) 9–022
(6) 9–022
(8) 9–022
(9) 9–022
s.19 .... 9–022, 26–003, 26–054
ss.20–21 9–022
s.22 9–025
(4) 9–025
s.23 .... 9–012, 9–025
s.24 9–027
(1) 9–027
s.26 9–013
s.27 9–013
s.28 9–013
s.29 9–013
s.30 9–014
(5)-(8) 9–014
s.31(1) 9–014
(2) 9–014
ss.32–34 9–014
s.35 9–014
(8)-(9) 9–014
s.36 9–014
s.39 9–028
s.40 9–028
s.42(5) 9–012
s.43 9–012
s.44 .... 9–029, 9–048
s.45 .... 9–029, 9–048
s.141 26–054
Sch.1 9–012
Sch.2, para.2(2) 9–012
para.6(2) 9–012
para.8 9–012
Schs 2–3 9–013
Sch.3, para.2(2) 9–012
para.6(2) 9–012
para.9 9–012
Sch.4 9–013
Sch.5 9–025
Sch.6 9–014
Sch.7 9–031
para.1(2) 9–031
para.4(2) 9–031
para.7(2) 9–031
para.13(1)-(2) 9–031
(4) 9–031, 9–032
para.14 9–031
(2) 9–032
para.15 .... 9–032, 9–048
para.16 .... 9–032, 9–048
para.17 ... 9–031, 9–032, 9–048
para.20 9–031
para.21 9–031
para.24(1) 9–032
(2) 9–032
para.25 .... 9–031, 9–032
Greater London Authority
Act (c.24) 6–003, 6–005

Further Education and
Training Act (c.25)
s.27 7–034
Local Government and Public
Involvement in Health
Act (c.28) 5–022, 6–003,
6–004, 6–007
ss.1–23 6–004
s.235 .... 7–034, 7–046
Sch.17 .... 7–034, 7–046
Legal Services Act (c.29)
ss.114–115 8–012
s.159 8–012

Statutory Instruments

1948 Statutory Instruments Regulations (SI 1948/1) 22–005
reg.4 22–006
(2) 22–006
reg.5 22–006
reg.6 22–006
reg.7 22–006
reg.8 22–006
reg.11(1) 22–006
1962 Foreign Compensation
(Egypt) (Determination
and Registration of
Claims) Order (SI 1962/
2187) 14–029
Art.4(1)(b)(ii) 14–029
1965 Rules of the Supreme Court
(SI 1965/1776)
Ord.15, r.16 ...... 26–005, 26–006
Ord.24, r.13 28–012
(1) 26–050
Ord.53 .... 24–013, 24–026,
24–027, 26–002, 26–004,
26–005, 26–011, 26–052
r.1(2) 24–014
r.4 .... 26–045, 26–046
r.5(3) 24–027
(7) 24–027
Ord.54 26–002
Ord.54.1(2)(f) 24–027
Ord.54.5(3) 26–027
Ord.54.17 24–045
1975 Tribunals and Inquiries (Discretionary Inquiries)
Order (SI 1975/1379) 9–043
1987 Social Security (Claims and
Payments) Regulations
(SI 1987/1968)
reg.37 16–009
1998 Civil Procedure Rules (SI
1998/3132)
Pt 1 26–043
Pt 3 26–043
r.3.1(2)(a) 26–045
r.3.4(2) 26–043
Pt 7 .... 26–013, 26–054
Pt 8 ...... 26–013, 26–053, 28–021
Pt 24 .... 26–013, 26–043

Pt.25 28–021
r.25.1(1)(a) 25–032
  (b) 25–030, 28–021
Pt 31 28–013
r.31.2 28–012
r.31.3 .... 26–050, 28–012
r.31.5(1) 26–050, 28–012
  (2) 26–050, 28–012
r.31.6 .... 26–050, 28–012
r.31.7(1) 26–050, 28–012
r.31.12 .... 26–050, 28–012
r.31.19(1) 28–005
  (8) 28–005
r.40.20 .... 25–020, 25–030
r.52.11(2) 15–007
r.52.15 26–053
  (4) 26–053
Pt 54 .... 26–002, 26–004, 26–049,
        26–052, 26–053, 26–054,
                26–056, 28–021
r.54.1(2)(a) 26–004
r.54.2 26–004
r.54.3(1) . 25–030, 25–037, 26–004
  (2) 26–004
r.54.4 ..... 26–040, 26–043, 26–053
r.54.5 ..... 26–045, 26–046, 26–053
  (1)(a) 26–046
r.54.6 26–053
r.54.6–9 26–043
r.54.7 26–053
r.54.8(2)(a) 26–053
  (b) 26–053
  (4) 26–053
r.54.9(1) 26–053
r.54.10 26–053
r.54.12(2) 26–053
  (3) 26–053
r.54.14 .... 26–053, 26–054
r.54.15 26–054
r.54.16 26–054
r.54.17 26–054
r.54.18 26–054
r.54.19(2) 25–013
  (3) 25–013
r.54.20 26–054
1999 National Assembly for Wales
      (Transfer of Functions)
      Order (SI 1999/672) 7–032
    Scotland Act 1998 (Con-
      sequential Modifications)
      (No.2) Order (SI 1999/
      1820) 7–013
    Local Government (Best
      Value)   Performance
      Plans and Reviews Order
      (SI 1999/3251) 5–021
2000 Town and Country Planning
      (Inquiries   Procedure)
      (England) Rules (SI 2000/
      1624) 9–042
    r.17(5) 13–015
    Town and Country Planning

        Appeals (Determination
          by Inspectors) (Inquiries
          Procedure)   (England)
          Rules (SI 2000/1625) 9–042
        r.19 9–039
    Town and Country Planning
        (Hearings   Procedure)
        (England) Rules (SI 2000/
        1626) 9–037, 9–038, 9–042
        r.13 9–040
    Town and Country Planning
        (Appeals)   (Written
        Representations Proce-
        dure) (England) Regula-
        tions (SI 2000/1628) 9–044
        r.5 9–044
        r.8 9–044
    Education (National Curricu-
        lum) (Modern Foreign
        Languages)   (Wales)
        Order (SI 2000/1980) .. 24–001,
                                      26–002
        r.3 26–045
    Scotland Act 1998 (Con-
        sequential Modifications)
        Order (SI 2000/2040) 7–013
    Civil Procedure (Amendment
        No.4) Rules (SI 2000/
        2092) . 24–027, 25–013, 26–002
2001 Local Government Best Value
        (Exclusion of Non-com-
        mercial Considerations)
        Order (SI 2001/909) 5–018
    Scotland Act 1998 (Con-
        sequential Modifications)
        Order (SI 2001/1400) 7–013
2002 Town and Country Planning
        (Enforcement) (Hearings
        Procedure)   (England)
        Rules (SI 2002/2684) 9–037
2003 Local   Government   (Best
        Value)   Performance
        Plans   and   Reviews
        (Amendment)   (England
        and Wales) Order (SI
        2003/662) 5–021
2004 Civil Procedure (Modification
        of Supreme Court Act
        1981) Order (SI 2004/
        1033)
        art.3 .... 25–001, 26–004
2004 Freedom of Information and
        Data Protection (Appro-
        priate Limit and Fees)
        Regulations   (SI   2004/
        3244)
        Reg.3 8–004
2005 Information Tribunal (Enfor-
        cement Appeals) Rules
        (SI 2005/14) 8–005
    Criminal Procedure Rules (SI
        2005/384)

Pt 25 28–011
Local Government (Best
    Value) Performance Indi-
    cators and Performance
    Standards (England)
    Order (SI 2005/598) 5–021
2006 Public Contracts Regulations
    (SI 2006/5) 5–028
    reg.3(1)(w) 5–028
    reg.47 5–030
Utilities Contracts Regula-
    tions (SI 2006/6) 5–028

2007 Regulatory Reform (Colla-
    boration, etc. between
    Ombudsmen) Order (SI
    2007/1889) 8–041
Tribunals, Courts and Enfor-
    cement Act (Commence-
    ment No.1) Order (SI
    2007/2709) 9–011
Proposed National Assembly
    for Wales (Legislative
    Competence) (No.3)
    Order 7–046

TABLE OF TREATIES AND CONVENTIONS

Treaties
1957   EC Treaty
    art.7 .... 10–002, 10–011
    art.10 10–032
    art.12 21–016
    art.13 21–018
    arts 17–18 21–016
    art.25 10–019
    art.28 .... 5–026, 10–030
    art.39 21–016
    art.43 .... 5–026, 10–020,
                    21–016, 29–057
    art.49 .... 5–026, 21–016
    art.52 10–011
    art.58 10–011
    art.81 11–004
    art.82 11–004
    art.119 21–017
    art.141 .... 10–021, 21–017
    art.189 10–006
    art.193 10–006
    art.194 10–006
    art.195 10–006
    art.202 10–003
    art.203 10–003
    art.207 10–003
    art.211 10–005
    art.213 10–004
    (1) 10–004
    art.214(2) 10–004
    art.215(2) 29–057
    art.219(2) 10–004
    art.221 10–011
    art.222 10–008
    art.225 10–008
    art.226 ... 10–016, 10–017, 10–019
    art.227 .... 10–016, 10–019
    art.228 10–017
    art.234 .... 10–012, 10–019,
                 10–024, 21–017
    art.249 ... 10–022, 10–023, 10–025

    art.251 10–009
    art.253 12–040
    art.272 10–006
    art.288(2) 29–057
1999   Treaty of Amsterdam
    art.13 21–018
2001   Treaty of Nice [2001] O.J.
    C80/1 10–003

Conventions
1950   European   Convention   on
    Human Rights
    art.2 .... 15–028, 18–023
    arts 2–12 18–003
    art.3 .... 15–026, 15–028,
                  18–023, 29–020
    art.4 21–008
    art.6 ..... 12–001, 12–013, 12–018,
             12–019, 12–035, 12–043,
             13–001, 13–012, 13–014,
             13–017, 13–018, 13–019,
             13–020, 15–007, 18–007,
             18–010, 18–049, 21–005,
             21–006, 24–025, 27–009,
             28–008, 29–019, 29–028
    (1) 12–018, 12–043,
           13–012, 13–013, 13–014, 13–
                   017, 13–019
    (2) 18–007
    (3)(c) 12–032
    art.8 .... 18–022, 18–023,
             18–038, 21–012, 21–013,
             29–027, 29–040
    art.9 18–045
    art.10 .... 18–032, 18–045
    art.11 18–032
    art.12 21–011
    art.13 29–020
    art.14 ... 18–003, 21–005, 21–006,
           21–007, 21–008, 21–009,
           21–011, 21–012, 21–013

arts 16–18 18–003
art.25 24–025
art.26 18–003
art.27(2) 18–003
art.29 19–012
art.30 19–012
art.31 18–003
art.34 .... 18–018, 19–012, 24–025
art.41 29–025

art.46 18–003
art.141 18–054
First Protocol
art.1 ..... 18–021, 20–049, 21–010
arts 1–3 18–003
Sixth Protocol
art.1 18–003
art.2 18–003
Eleventh Protocol 24–025

PART 1

THE ADMINISTRATIVE SYSTEM

CHAPTER 1

THE NATURE AND PURPOSE OF ADMINISTRATIVE LAW

1. INTRODUCTION[1]

There is, not surprisingly, considerable diversity of opinion concerning the nature and purpose of administrative law. Description and prescription are not easily separated. For some it is the law relating to the control of government power, the main object of which is to protect individual rights. Others place greater emphasis upon rules that are designed to ensure that the administration effectively performs the tasks assigned to it. Yet others see the principal objective of administrative law as ensuring governmental accountability, and fostering participation by interested parties in the decision-making process.

   None of these are right or wrong in some absolute sense. All are, however, incomplete. An adequate understanding of the nature and purpose of administrative law requires us to probe further into the way in which our society is ordered. It requires the articulation of the type of democratic society in which we live and some vision of the political theory which that society espouses. The role of more particular legal topics that constitute administrative law, such as natural justice and judicial review, can only be adequately assessed within such a framework.

   Concepts such as accountability, participation and rights do not possess only one meaning, which can be discerned by a purely "factual" inquiry. Nor can the place of such ideas be understood by pointing to their general connections with a democratic society. The very meaning and importance of such concepts will differ depending upon the *type* of democratic regime within which they subsist. Or to put the same point in a different way, every democratic society will have some ideas of rights, participation and accountability, but these will differ depending upon the nature of that society. An attempt to discuss particular topics without considering these

1-001

---

[1] Footnotes have been deliberately kept to a minimum within this chapter.

background ideas evidences a series of implicit assumptions about such ideas that are concealed and untested.

The legislature and the courts will both be important in determining the nature and shape of administrative law. It should never be forgotten that it is the legislature which enacts the policies which are directly constitutive of the administrative state. It will be the legislature which chooses whether these policies should be imbued with, for example, a market-oriented neo-liberal philosophy, or with one which is more social democratic in its orientation. In this sense the shape and nature of administrative law will be profoundly affected by the philosophy that underlies government policy. The courts also have a major influence on the nature of the subject. They will decide what particular constraints to impose on administrative action, and more generally on the overall purpose of judicial review. Administrative law, when viewed in this way, is always a combination of the political world, combined with the reactions of the judiciary.

2. Dicey, Unitary Democracy and the Ultra vires Principle

A. The Basis of the Model

i. Unitary democracy

1–002   It is a commonplace among administrative lawyers that Dicey is responsible for the subject having a "bad name" in this country. This is brought home to most law students early in their legal career when tackling the rule of law. Dicey's dislike of administrative law is readily apparent from the *Law of the Constitution*. We must, however, push further if we are to understand how Dicey's views have coloured administrative law. It is important to understand that Dicey based his view of administrative law on a certain view of democracy, which can be termed unitary. This is not a difficult idea and can be explained as follows.

First, all students are aware of the sovereignty of Parliament in the sense that Parliament is *omnicompetent*. It can in theory ban smoking in Paris, or repeal the grant of independence to former colonies. Less well known is an equally important aspect of sovereignty, which may be termed *parliamentary monopoly*: all governmental power should be channelled through Parliament in order that it might be subject to legitimation and over-sight by the Commons. There was a belief in the nineteenth century, albeit not universally shared, but held by Dicey, that the Commons could and did control the executive, *and* that all public power should be subject to legislative oversight.[2]

Second, Dicey used the rule of law to reinforce sovereignty in the sense of

---

[2] See the discussion below, para.1–003, and see A.V. Dicey, *Introduction to the Study of the Law of the Constitution* (Macmillan, 10th edn, 1959), 73, 83, 84, 433.

parliamentary monopoly.[3] The Diceyan rule of law had both a descriptive and a normative content. In *descriptive terms* it was assumed that the regular law predominated, that exercise of broad discretionary power was absent and that all people were subject to the ordinary law of the realm. All public power in fact resided with Parliament. In *normative* terms it was assumed that this was indeed a better system than that in France, where special rules and a distinct regime existed for public law matters.

Thus democracy was for Dicey unitary, in the sense that all public power was channelled through Parliament. This democratic system was also "self-correcting", in that Dicey believed that the Commons accurately reflected the will of the people and controlled the executive. The all-powerful Parliament would not therefore be likely to pass legislation which was contrary to the wishes of the electorate.

ii. Unitary democracy, the ultra vires principle and administrative law
It was this conception of democracy that provided the framework for administrative law. Dicey did not provide extensive discussion of this, principally because he misconceived the scope of administrative power that existed when he wrote. Notwithstanding this error, it was the conceptual foundation of unitary democracy, buttressed by the rule of law, which provided a fitting base to legitimate the judicial power of the courts. The connection can be expressed as follows.   **1–003**

It is readily apparent that the execution of legislation may require the grant of discretionary power to a minister or agency. Parliament may not be able to foresee all eventualities and flexibility may be required to implement the legislation. The legislature will of necessity grant power subject to conditions. For example *if* a house is unfit for habitation a minister may order its demolition. Herein lay the modern conceptual justification for judicial intervention. It was designed to ensure that those to whom such grants of power were made did not transgress the sovereign will of Parliament. If authority had been delegated to a minister to perform certain tasks on certain conditions, the courts' function was to check that only those tasks were performed and only where the conditions were present. For the courts not to intervene would have been to accord a legislative power to the minister or agency, by allowing them to "legislate" in areas not specified by the real legislature, Parliament. The less well known face of sovereignty, that of parliamentary monopoly, thus demanded an institution to *police* the boundaries Parliament had stipulated, and the ultra vires principle was the doctrinal tool used to achieve this end. This principle expresses two related ideas.

In a narrow sense it captured the idea that those to whom power has been granted should only exercise that power within their designated area: the agency must have the legal capacity to act in relation to the topic in question. An institution given power by Parliament to adjudicate on employ-

[3] Dicey, n.2, 188, 193.

ment matters should not take jurisdiction over non-employment issues. In a broader sense the ultra vires principle provided the justification for constraints upon the way in which the power given to the administrative agency was exercised. The agency must comply with rules of fair procedure, it must exercise its discretion to attain only proper and not improper purposes, it must act on relevant and not irrelevant considerations and it must not act unreasonably.

It would be mistaken to assume that the judiciary originally conceived of intervention in these terms. The origins of judicial review are complex, and are interwoven with the intricacies of the prerogative writs.[4] The motivation behind early judicial review resided principally in the desire to ensure the predominance of the High Court over "inferior jurisdictions", and to provide remedies to those whom the established judiciary felt had been unjustly or illegally treated by such authorities. In striving to attain these objectives the court could indeed often come into direct conflict with the legislative will.

1–004   Notwithstanding this continuing tension, the rationale for judicial review was slowly transformed in the nineteenth century. The twin rationales for early judicial review continued to exist. They were, however, supplemented by a growing tendency to relate the exercise of judicial power to the will of Parliament. The ultra vires principle became the justification for judicial intervention, and set the boundaries for that intervention. It did so in two distinct, albeit related, ways.

On the one hand, the judiciary began to justify the exercise of jurisdictional control more specifically and explicitly in terms of ensuring that the tribunal did not extend the area over which the legislature granted it jurisdiction. Conflicting cases were reconciled by reasoning that the legislature intended differing agencies to possess different amounts of power and that this was evident in the enabling legislation.[5] This explanation was generally unconvincing. Reference to the particular statutory grants of power in the conflicting cases gave no indication that the results could be reconciled by differences in legislative intent. The questionable nature of the reasoning did not destroy the utility of the conceptual tool. The courts would simply police the boundaries made manifest by the particular legislative grant of authority, preventing the agency from entering areas where Parliament had forbidden it to tread. The courts acquired a malleable tool through which to justify intervention with administrative behaviour.

On the other hand, the courts became more aware, in form at least, of the legitimate limits to the exercise of judicial power. If the administrative agency *was* within its assigned area, then it was performing tasks allocated

---

[4] S.A. de Smith, "The Prerogative Writs" (1951) 11 C.L.J. 40, and "Wrongs and Remedies in Administrative Law" (1952) M.L.R. 189; L. Jaffe and E. Henderson, "Judicial Review and the Rule of Law: Historical Origins" (1956) 72 L.Q.R. 345; E. Henderson, *Foundations of English Administrative Law* (Harvard University Press, 1963); A. Rubinstein, *Jurisdiction and Illegality* (Oxford University Press, 1975); P. Craig, "*Ultra vires* and the Foundations of Judicial Review" [1998] C.L.J. 63.
[5] See below, Ch.14.

to it by the legislature. It was not contravening the legislative monopoly possessed by Parliament, which had chosen to delegate this function to the agency. The courts should therefore be wary of substituting their view for that of the chosen agency, and many of the judicial limits on the way in which discretion could be used were justified as applications of statutory intent.[6]

The connection between this judicial approach and Dicey's rule of law was a natural one. The flexibility inherent in the idea of legislative intent preserved the veneer that the courts were simply applying the legislative mandate when controlling "inferior" jurisdictions. Dicey's rule of law added respectability to this exercise of power by entrenching the idea that it was natural, right and a matter of constitutional principle that the ordinary courts should be supreme and that the ordinary law should be all pervasive. The consequences of this model will now be assessed.

B. The Implications of the Ultra vires Model

i. Ultra vires: the form of judicial intervention
The model outlined above helped to shape the very form of judicial inter-   **1–005**
vention in the following way. There is a distinction between appeal and review. The former is concerned with the merits of the case, in the sense that the appellate court can substitute its own opinion for that of the initial decision-maker. Appeals can lie on fact and law, or simply upon law. Such rights of appeal are statutory, and the courts possess no inherent appellate jurisdiction. Review is, at least in theory, different from this. It is concerned not with the merits of the decision, but with its "validity", or with the "scope" of the agency's power. The courts' power of review is not based upon statute, but upon an inherent jurisdiction within the superior courts.

This inherent power was by no means novel, and the texts of early administrative cases were replete with the language of review and jurisdiction. The original rationale for this inherent jurisdiction was obviously linked to the rationale for judicial review: a judicial desire to control inferior agencies and to protect the individual from illegalities committed by them. Nonetheless the development of the traditional model in the 19th century served *both* to strengthen the rationale for this inherent jurisdiction, *and* to reinforce the division between review and appeal.

It achieved the former by linking the basis for intervention to the enforcement of the legislative will. All grants of power by parliament can be expressed in the following terms: if X exists, you may or shall do Y. For example, if an employee is injured at work a tribunal may or shall grant compensation. The inherent jurisdiction of the court was therefore strengthened by the insistence that it was simply deciding whether X existed, and what considerations could be taken into account when determining Y.

---

[6] See, Chs 17, 19.

The courts, it could now be argued, must possess this inherent jurisdiction to safeguard the legislative monopoly of Parliament.

It achieved the latter by insisting that when the court was enforcing the legislative will it was only undertaking review and not appeal. The court was simply determining the "validity" of agency behaviour. The merits were for the agency, which had been assigned the task by Parliament. This may all appear to be conceptually neat, if not elegant. It has however produced a host of problems, which will be examined more fully below.

ii. Ultra vires: the shape and scope of judicial intervention

1–006 The traditional model has had a profound effect upon the shape and scope of judicial intervention in three distinct ways.

First, it accorded centre stage to control by the courts of administrative agencies. This was regarded as the main purpose of administrative law. The vigorous assertion of the supremacy of the ordinary law was directed towards *controlling* or *containing* the bureaucratic organs of the state. Such agencies were viewed with implicit distrust, and judicial control was the principal means of containing agency power.[7]

A second consequence of the traditional model was to foster a *generalist* as opposed to a *functionalist* approach to administrative law, with a reluctance to admit of special regimes. The legacy of the rule of law was that all rules of the legal system should be equally applicable to all.

A third consequence was to *foster judicial activism* in the following sense. The basic thrust behind this approach was, as we have seen, that the ordinary courts and the ordinary law were superior, and that these organs would safeguard the legislative monopoly of Parliament by policing the boundaries of legislative intent through the ultra vires principle. Where there was a difference of opinion between the courts and an agency as to the meaning of one of these legislative conditions, the opinion of the reviewing court would be preferred, provided that this could be reconciled with review on grounds of "validity". The distinction between "validity" and the "merits" is, as we shall see,[8] an elusive one. Almost any scope of judicial intervention can be formally reconciled with the idea that the courts are thereby effectuating the intent of the legislature and simply intervening to determine the validity of the agency's decision.

iii. The range of protected interests: the ambit of natural justice and standing

1–007 The traditional ultra vires model has also had an impact upon the range of interests that are regarded as coming within the ambit of administrative law.

Administrative law has what may be regarded as certain *gateways*, methods of getting *into* the system. Thus the rules of natural justice tell us

---

[7] See also, C. Harlow and R. Rawlings, *Law and Administration* (Butterworths, 2nd edn, 1997), Ch.1.

[8] See, Chs 14, 19.

who is entitled to be heard before an agency makes its decision; and the rules of standing inform us as to who should be able to complain to the court that an agency has overstepped its powers. A notable feature of administrative law has been the insistence that only those who possessed private rights in the traditional sense of a cause of action in contract or tort, etc., were to be allowed into the system. The gateways were barred to those who did not possess such rights.[9]

There is no doubt that the preoccupation of the common law with traditional rights is a partial explanation of this phenomenon. However the judicial attitude fitted well with the traditional model. The judicial function was to police the boundaries of the legislative intent through the ultra vires principle, with the consequence that the individual's private autonomy was protected by confining the public body to its assigned area. The only types of private autonomy which the courts would recognise were however rights derived from contract, tort, etc. Only those who had such rights could use the gateways. The idea that the ordinary law was being applied by the ordinary courts was reinforced by this restriction on the range of protected interests. It strengthened the belief that the court was doing no more than applying standard notions of contract or tort to cases where the defendant happened to be a public body.

We should pause here to notice a tension inherent in the traditional model, which explains much of the complex case law on natural justice and standing: the twin objectives of policing the frontiers of legislative intent and protecting only traditional private rights could conflict. Legislation relating to matters such as licensing might not affect rights in the traditional sense. A disappointed applicant could not construct a case in contract or tort, etc. The court might, however, be eager to fulfil its policing role. Something has to give. *Either* the court gives up its policing role in this area, *or* it relaxes the definition of "right" and thereby widens the gateways available to the citizen. The courts sometimes did one and sometimes the other, hence the resulting complexity in the case law.[10]

iv. The type of procedural protection

The traditional model also had an influence upon the meaning that should **1–008** be given to "procedural rights". The twin elements of natural justice are a right to be heard and a right to an unbiased hearing. These are the rules the courts have generally imposed upon administrative agencies. They assume a method of decision-making which lawyers call adversarial adjudication. The parties will present their arguments to the relevant agency which will judge the matter.

The traditional model helped to shape this notion of process rights in the following way. If we assume, as the traditional model does, that the ordinary law is being applied by the ordinary courts to cases involving administrative

[9] See, Ch.24.
[10] See, Ch.24.

agencies, then it becomes natural to assume that the process rights which such agencies should have to follow will be the same as those used by the ordinary courts. The procedure in the courts is adversarial adjudication. Barristers present their arguments and do battle with their adversaries before an unbiased judge. Agencies should therefore have to comply with the same type of procedure. Three consequences follow from this reasoning.

First, it helps to explain the prevalence of the distinction between "administrative" and "judicial" proceedings, which is a prominent feature of some of the mid-20th case law.[11] If the procedure before an agency was to assume the form of adversarial adjudication then certain courts felt that this was only suitable if the agency was itself in some sense "judging" a matter between two opposing litigants.

Second, and more importantly, the traditional model helps us to understand the unwillingness of the courts to grant process rights in "legislative" contexts. Courts have been generally reluctant to interfere when an agency is making a rule of a generalised nature rather than engaging in individualised adjudication. The flaws in this reasoning will be examined later. The judicial response did, however, fit the "logic" of the traditional model. This was in part because it might be difficult to apply process rights designed for "judging", to a situation when someone was "legislating". It was in part because even to accept that any process rights might be necessary would be to challenge the foundation of the unitary vision of democracy. On this view, Parliament was the sole body which legislated. The public participated through the vote and then indirectly and vicariously through their MP. To admit that the agencies might make rules of a legislative nature and that people should be given process rights to participate in their formation, would be to challenge the whole idea that our democracy really was unitary. It would be to accept that bodies outside Parliament legislated, and that the ordinary parliamentary processes could not adequately control such norms.

The third consequence of modelling procedural rights after those of the ordinary courts has been to constrict experimentation with other types of process right.[12] If the courts always insist that the process rights before an agency are to be mirrored on those of the ordinary courts even if in a modified way, then it also follows that the agency is presumed to be in some way "judging" between two sides. The type of decision-making is adjudication and the species of process rights reflects this. Now we might decide that certain types of agency decision-making should not take the form of judging, but should rather, for example, be like arbitration, resort to chance or managerial discretion. Distinctive process rights which protect and reflect these types of decision-making will be required. The traditional model with its assumption that process rights must be like those of the ordinary courts impedes such experimentation.

---

[11] See, Ch.12.
[12] See, Ch.12.

v. Tort, contract and public bodies
The traditional model has moreover reinforced the demand that the   **1–009**
ordinary principles of tort and contract should be applied to public bodies.
Dicey attacked the French system for the way in which he perceived it as
giving advantageous treatment to public officials who committed a wrong.
The situation in England was different: the ordinary law applied to all and
special regimes did not exist. The Diceyan legacy forestalled reasoned discussion as to how far ordinary principles of tortious or contractual liability
ought to be modified when dealing with public bodies by insisting that any
such distinct regime would be contrary to the rule of law. When such discourse did surface in the case law it assumed a defensive, almost apologetic,
air. This has changed recently as the courts have become more willing to
articulate and assess what the justifiable, distinct needs of the public body
might in fact be.[13]

C. The Deficiencies of the Ultra Vires Model
Certain of the deficiencies of the traditional model have been touched on in   **1–010**
the preceding discussion. A more structured survey of these difficulties is
however warranted. At the most basic level the traditional view was flawed
because the premises about the way in which democratic society operated
were false. The idea of unitary democracy and legislative monopoly, in
which all public power was channelled through Parliament, and in which
Parliament controlled the executive, was flawed. There was a growing
awareness that the legislature did not in fact control the executive but vice-
versa. Legislation became the prerogative of the executive and parliamentary acquiescence was ensured by the managers of the party machine. There
was an increasing realisation that Parliament did not wield all public power,
and that many other institutions exercised some species of public authority.
These themes will be developed more fully later. Let us now consider their
general implications for the traditional model.

i. Mistake avoidance and the distrust of the administrative state
The traditional model was based upon a distrust of the administrative state.   **1–011**
The growth of administrative law was directly connected with the extension
of governmental functions relating to the poor, the unemployed, trade
regulation and the like. It became impossible to separate an evaluation of
the agencies applying these laws from a value judgment of the social policies
in the laws themselves. Those who disliked such social intervention,
including Dicey, tended to view the agencies applying such laws with suspicion. The predominance accorded to the "ordinary law" applied by the
"ordinary courts" was a means of controlling these agencies, and of
maintaining judicial supervision over the substantive policies they applied.
The paramount function of the courts was essentially negative, to ensure
that the agency did not make mistakes by exceeding the power granted to it.

---

[13] See, Ch.29.

These twin themes of mistake avoidance and distrust came to be challenged as a direct consequence of changing attitudes towards the social policies the agencies were applying. People perceived the positive contributions made by such policies. Academics such as Robson approached the study of administrative justice without "any ready-made assumption that every tribunal which does not at the moment form part of the recognised system of judicature must necessarily and inevitably be arbitrary, incompetent, unsatisfactory, injurious to the freedom of the citizen and to the welfare of society".[14] It was no longer taken for granted that the justice dispensed by the ordinary courts and the ordinary law was necessarily better than that of agencies. Nor was it felt that the sole object of administrative law was to ensure that the agency avoided making mistakes by overstepping its boundaries. A more positive desire that the agency should successfully fulfil the policy assigned to it became the focus of discussion and the courts were perceived as but one factor in fulfilling this objective.

ii. Form and scope of intervention: the indeterminacy of the ultra vires principle

1–012   The basis of the traditional model was that the courts would preserve the legislative monopoly of Parliament by ensuring that the agency remained within the area assigned to it by the legislature, and that the courts would achieve this through the ultra vires principle. Five problems can be identified, all of which relate to the indeterminacy of legislative intent.

The *first* problem is the difficulty of defining the scope of an institution's designated area. The flexibility inherent in the ultra vires concept preserved the veneer that the courts were simply obeying the legislative mandate, but it was precisely this flexibility that ultimately robbed the reasoning of conviction. Consider a simple statute stipulating that if an employee is injured at work then he or she shall receive compensation. In one obvious sense all these legislative conditions define the scope of the agency's power. There must be "an employee", "who is injured", "at work", before the agency can give any compensation. However to allow the reviewing court to substitute its opinion on all such matters would mean that the agency then only has power when the court agrees with the agency's findings, not otherwise. Any distinction between review, which goes to "validity", and appeal, which goes to the "merits", disappears. Courts have been aware of this conundrum and have defined jurisdictional error in differing ways, some broad, some narrow.[15] The central point for present purposes is that *almost any* such justification can be formally reconciled with legislative intent. It can always, for example, be argued that Parliament intended all questions of law to reside with the ordinary courts, or by way of contrast, that Parliament intended only that certain "preliminary" conditions be judicially reviewed. Legislative

---

[14] W. Robson, *Justice and Administrative Law, A Study of the British Constitution* (Macmillan, 1928), XV.
[15] See, Ch.14.

intent could legitimate almost all types of judicial control, and therefore lost its potency to legitimate any particular one. It is this very malleability of the ultra vires principle which led Sir John Laws to the conclusion that the principle is merely a tautology, in the following sense: that because the principle does not of itself indicate what is to count as a want of power, invocation of the principle amounts to saying no more than that the court will strike down what it chooses to strike down.[16] In the same vein he notes that the ultra vires principle is in reality a fig-leaf, enabling the courts to intervene in decisions without an assertion of judicial power which too nakedly confronts the established authority of the executive or other public bodies.

A *second* related problem is that the traditional model came under particular strain when the legislation seemed to preclude judicial interference. Imagine that our statute now reads that the minister's determination of the relevant issue should be *conclusive*. If the courts are simply enforcing the boundaries of legislative intent through the ultra vires principle, then their role should be limited in such instances. If they persist with review then the traditional model must be modified to accommodate the idea that the judiciary are not simply *implementing* legislative intent, but were also *supplementing* it, through the existence of certain judicially developed principles, which would be implicitly read into any legislation. This idea has considerable historical lineage,[17] but the content of the resulting principles can, as we shall see, be problematic.

The *third* difficulty with the ultra vires principle relates to the development   **1–013** of the law across time. Control over, for example, discretion has not remained static. It has altered and new forms of control have been added to the list. Let us imagine that the courts in 2009 recognise proportionality as an independent head of review. If they do so this will not be because legislative intent suddenly signalled in some miraculous fashion that this should be so. It will be because the courts decide that this should be added to existing heads of review. The result can be expressed through the language of ultra vires. It can in formal terms be stated that it will henceforth be ultra vires for an agency to exercise its discretion in a disproportionate manner. Any head of review can be rationalised in this manner. This should not, however, serve to conceal the obvious fact that it is the courts which decide on the appropriate heads of review, and that legislative intent is not the guiding principle in this respect.

The *fourth* difficulty concerns the relationship between direct and collateral attack. Claimants can challenge agency decisions either directly through judicial review, or collaterally through a defence to, for example, a criminal prosecution in which the validity of the order on which the prosecution is based is called into question. It would be possible in theory for the courts to determine the incidence of collateral attack by reference to

---

[16] Sir John Laws, "Illegality: The Problem of Jurisdiction", in M. Supperstone and J. Goudie (eds), *Judicial Review* (Butterworths, 2nd edn, 1997), Ch.4, p.3.
[17] See, e.g., the rationale for natural justice was sometimes expressed as the application of implied legislative intent, and sometimes as the courts supplying the omission of the legislature.

legislative intent. This is however difficult since the legislation normally provides no sure guidance on the matter. The courts' approach has been to decide on the availability of collateral challenge by considering issues of first principle concerning, for example, the injustice which could follow if the individual were not able to challenge a decision or order collaterally.[18]

A *final* difficulty relates to the changing nature of the legislation that the courts interpret. The growth of the welfare state led to the use of more open-textured legislation and the grant of wide discretionary powers. The task of interpreting legislative intent has become correspondingly more difficult.[19] If statutes require the courts to interpret phrases such as "public interest" and "individual need", then legislative intent may provide scant guidance as to how these broadly framed discretionary powers should be interpreted. The courts are forced to form their own view as to what considerations should be deemed to be relevant and what purposes can legitimately be pursued by the agency. Legislative intent becomes more indeterminate and its application in particular instances more contentious.

iii. The ambit of public law: the straining of the ultra vires principle

1–014   A further difficulty with the ultra vires principle concerns the range of institutions and the type of subject matter that are susceptible to judicial review.[20] The problem can be presented as follows.

The ultra vires principle is most readily applicable to *statutory powers* wielded by *traditional public bodies*. There are, as we have seen above, very real problems with applying the doctrine even in this context, but at the least it makes some intuitive sense to think of the courts confining such bodies within the ambit laid down in the empowering legislation. The courts have, however, as will be seen below,[21] expanded the scope of public law in a number of ways, which place the ultra vires principle under further strain. Two can be identified here.

On the one hand, the courts have applied the principles of judicial review to *non-statutory exercises of power by public bodies*. These principles have been held to be applicable to the prerogative and to certain forms of common law contracting power exercised by such public bodies. It is difficult to give real meaning to the ultra vires principle in these instances, because the power is not delineated in the same way as statutory grants of authority. It can of course be argued that any species of power must be subject to some outer limits. This may be so, but it is considerably more difficult to characterise the courts' role in these cases as delineating the ambit of parliamentary intent.

On the other hand, the courts have for some considerable time applied principles of a public law nature to *exercises of power by institutions which are not public bodies in the traditional sense, in circumstances where these*

---

[18] See below, Ch.23.
[19] R. Unger, *Law in Modern Society* (Free Press, 1976), 192–203.
[20] D. Oliver, "Is the *Ultra vires* Rule the Basis of Judicial Review?" [1987] P.L. 543.
[21] See, Ch.26.

bodies do not derive their power from statute. This has become more marked as of late because of the reforms in the law of remedies.[22] It would nonetheless be wrong to regard this as a recent development. The courts have applied these principles to such bodies ever since the time when it became meaningful to speak of judicial review and public law principles at all. Trade associations, trade unions and corporations with de facto monopoly power have, for example, been subject to some of the same principles as are applied to public bodies *stricto sensu*, since they often have the same degree of power as that possessed by a public institution. It is however difficult to apply the ultra vires concept to such bodies without substantially changing its meaning. These bodies do not derive their power from statute and therefore judicial control cannot be rationalised through the idea that the courts are delineating the ambit of Parliament's intent. The language of ultra vires can only be preserved by transforming the concept in the following way: the principles of judicial review are regarded as of generalised application to institutions that wield a certain degree of power and the principles are then read into the articles of association or other governing document under which the body operates.

iv. The defects in the private rights theme

We have seen that one characteristic of the traditional model was that the   **1–015**
gateways to administrative law were only to be open to those who possessed private rights in contract, tort, etc. This aspect of the traditional model has three related defects.

We have already touched on the first difficulty with this approach. If the private rights theme were to be taken literally it would mean that the courts could not police or monitor the boundaries of legislative intent, unless such rights were present. There are many areas of administrative law where legislation is passed which does not accord rights in contract, tort, etc., to the affected parties. Much licensing and social welfare legislation falls into this category. Courts faced with this legislation have often ignored the need for private rights, or have defined "rights" more expansively in their desire to exercise their policing role over such legislation.

The second difficulty with the private rights theme is equally important. Even if traditional private rights are present in a particular case, it would be mistaken to suppose that the case can be regarded simply as a private dispute, which an individual has with a defendant who happens to be a public body. Let us imagine that the public body has made a compulsory purchase order on John's property. John believes that the order is invalid. If he is correct there will be a trespass action, his private rights will be affected and he comes within the gateways of administrative law. However the case is not simply "about" John's private rights. *If* John wins his private rights will be vindicated. *Whether* he wins will however be dependent upon the validity of the compulsory purchase order. When contesting this issue, John will be

---

[22] See, Ch.26.

concerned with the scope of the planning legislation. The case is not just about John's private rights. It is about the legitimate ambit of the regulatory legislation in that area.[23]

The third defect in the private rights theme is that interests that are not rights may nonetheless be extremely important and should properly be the subject of administrative law. Legislation on social welfare, race relations, sexual equality, licensing and trade regulation, may seriously affect people even if the legislation does not accord them rights.

D. The Debate about the Ultra vires Principle

1–016 The challenge to the ultra vires principle has not gone unanswered. There has been a lively debate between defenders of the principle,[24] and those who believe that it cannot provide the real foundation for judicial review.[25] Limits of space preclude detailed examination of the contending arguments.[26] A number of points from this debate should however be noted since they are of general importance and have an impact on the subsequent discussion.

    (1)   The phrase "ultra vires" is indicative of action being beyond power. It does not, in and of itself, tell us whether an act is beyond power because the legislature has intended to place certain limits on an agency, or whether these limits are more properly regarded as a common law creation of the courts. It is this issue which divides the two camps in the debate about the foundations of judicial review.

---

[23] See, Ch.24.
[24] Sir William Wade & C. Forsyth, *Administrative Law* (Oxford University Press, 9th edn, 2004); C. Forsyth, "Of Fig Leaves and Fairy Tales: The *Ultra vires* Doctrine, the Sovereignty of Parliament and Judicial Review" [1996] C.L.J. 122; M. Elliott, "The Demise of Parliamentary Sovereignty? The Implications for Justifying Judicial Review" (1999) 115 L.Q.R. 119; M. Elliott, "The *Ultra vires* Doctrine in a Constitutional Setting: Still the Central Principle of Administrative Law" [1999] C.L.J. 129; C. Forsyth, "Heat and Light: A Plea for Reconciliation", in C. Forsyth (ed.), *Judicial Review and the Constitution* (Hart, 2000), Ch.18; M. Elliott, *The Constitutional Foundations of Judicial Review* (Hart, 2001); C. Forsyth and M. Elliott, "The Legitimacy of Judicial Review" [2003] P.L. 286.
[25] Oliver, n.20; *de Smith's Judicial Review* (Lord Woolf, J. Jowell, and A. Le Sueur, Sweet & Maxwell, 6th edn, 2007); Sir John Laws, n.16; P Craig, "*Ultra Vires* and the Foundations of Judicial Review" [1998] C.L.J. 63; D. Dyzenhaus, "Reuniting the Brain: The Democratic Basis of Judicial Review" (1998) 9 Pub. Law Rev. 98; P. Craig, "Competing Models of Judicial Review" [1999] P.L. 428; N. Bamforth, "*Ultra vires* and Institutional Independence", in C. Forsyth (ed.), *Judicial Review and the Constitution* (Hart, 2000), Ch.6; D. Oliver, "Review of Non-Statutory Discretions", in Forsyth (ed.) (2000), Ch.14; J Jowell, "Of Vires and Vacuums: The Constitutional Context of Judicial Review", in Forsyth (ed.) (2000), Ch.15; N. Barber, "The Academic Mythologians" (2001) 22 O.J.L.S. 369; P. Craig and N. Bamforth, "Constitutional Analysis, Constitutional Principle and Judicial Review" [2001] P.L. 763; P. Joseph, "The Demise of *Ultra Vires*— Judicial Review in the New Zealand Courts" [2001] P.L. 354; P. Craig, "Constitutional Foundations, the Rule of Law and Supremacy" [2003] P.L. 92.
[26] T.R.S. Allan, "The Constitutional Foundations of Judicial Review: Constitutional Conundrum or Interpretative Inquiry" [2002] C.L.J. 87, doubts the utility of the debate. For a response see, Craig, "Constitutional Foundations", n.25.

(2) The traditional ultra vires model, or specific legislative intent model, was based on the assumption that judicial review was legitimated on the ground that the courts were applying the intent of the legislature. The courts' function was to police the boundaries stipulated by Parliament. The ultra vires principle was regarded as both a neces- sary and sufficient basis for judicial intervention. It was necessary in the sense that any ground of judicial review had to be fitted into the ultra vires doctrine in order for it to be acceptable. It was sufficient in the sense that if such a ground of review could be so fitted into the ultra vires principle it obviated the need for further inquiry. On this view, the very doctrines which make up administrative law derived their legitimacy and content from the fact that the legislature intended them to apply in a particular way in a particular statutory context.

(3) Advocates of the common law model of illegality challenged these assumptions. They argued, as we have seen, that the ultra vires principle as articulated above was indeterminate, unrealistic, beset by internal tensions, and unable to explain the application of public law principles to bodies that did not derive their power from statute. Critics of the ultra vires principle are of course concerned to keep bodies within their assigned spheres. It is moreover self-evident that the enabling legislation must be considered when determining the ambit of a body's powers. This is not, however, the same thing as saying that the heads of review, their meaning or the intensity with which they are applied can be justified by legislative intent. The central issue is therefore how far these relevant legal rules and their application can be satisfactorily explained by reference to legislative intent.

(4) Proponents of the common law model argue that the principles of judicial review are in reality developed by the courts. They are the creation of the common law. The legislature will rarely provide indication as to the content and limits of what constitutes judicial review. When legislation is passed the courts will impose the controls which they believe are normatively justified on the grounds of justice, the rule of law etc. They will therefore decide on the appropriate procedural and substantive principles of judicial review that should apply to statutory and non-statutory bodies alike. Agency action that infringes these principles will be unlawful. If Parliament does not like these controls then it is open to it to make this unequivocally clear. If it does so the courts will adhere to such dictates. If Parlia- ment does manifest a specific intent as to the grounds of review the courts will also obey this, in the same way as they will obey such intent in other areas where the primary obligations are the creation of the common law. There is, in this sense, nothing odd or strange about a set of principles derived from the common law, which are then supplemented or complemented by specific legislative intent if

and when this is to be found. This is indeed the paradigm in areas such as contract, tort, restitution, and trusts. It has indeed been forcefully argued by Oliver[27] that the very principles of legality, rationality and procedural propriety are but part of a broader set of duties founded on "considerate decision making", which have been developed by the courts and apply to private as well as public decision making.

(5)   There is also a modified ultra vires model, or general legislative intent model. Supporters of the ultra vires doctrine have accepted some of the criticisms voiced by proponents of the common law model. They maintain, however, that ultra vires must still be the central principle of judicial review. It is argued that legislative intent *must* be found in order to vindicate judicial review, since to discard the ultra vires principle would entail a strong challenge to Parliamentary sovereignty, and would also involve the exercise of untrammelled power by the courts. They further maintain that legislative intent *can* be found to legitimate the exercise of judicial power. They argue in terms of general legislative intent. Parliament is taken to intend that its legislation conforms to the basic principles of fairness and justice which operate in a constitutional democracy. However, because Parliament itself cannot realistically work out the precise ramifications of this general idea it delegates power to the courts, which fashion the more particular application of this idea in accordance with the rule of law.

(6)   The claim that judicial review must be grounded in legislative intent, since to do otherwise would entail a strong challenge to the sovereignty of Parliament, is unfounded. There is nothing in the common law model that entails this conclusion. The common law model best reflects the historical foundation of judicial review, and the practice of the courts. It also captures the proper relationship in principle between sovereignty and the rule of law.[28] The modified ultra vires doctrine is, moreover, based on an implausible relationship between statute and the controls imposed pursuant thereto.

3. Rights, Legality and Abuse of Power

A. The Nature of the Model

1–017   The defects of the traditional model of public law have been presented above. Criticism of traditional orthodoxy is all very well, but we must put something in its place. An approach that has become more prevalent is to

[27] D. Oliver, *Common Values and the Public-Private Divide* (Butterworths, 1999).
[28] Craig and Bamforth, n.25.

argue for a rights-based conception of public law. This is based upon the imposition of certain standards of legality and is designed to prevent the abuse of power by public bodies *stricto sensu*, and by a range of other quasi-public or private bodies which possess a certain degree of power. On this view judicial intervention is no longer premised on the idea that the courts are simply applying the legislative will. Their role is to articulate principles, which should guide the exercise of administrative action and to interpret legislation in the light of these principles. It is, however, necessary to press further and to inquire more specifically as to the meaning of this approach, and the standards of legality to be applied.

B. The Meaning of a Rights-Based Approach

i. The protection of fundamental rights

A common element of a rights-based approach is that the courts should whenever possible interpret legislation and the exercise of administrative discretion to be in conformity with fundamental rights. The courts should construe legislation, and discretion exercised pursuant thereto, to be in conformity with fundamental rights. This can be achieved through, for example, the creation of strong judicial presumptions that legislation is not intended to interfere with these rights, combined with a more intensive, searching scrutiny which demands greater justification of discretionary decisions impinging upon such important interests. The courts have taken important steps in this direction,[29] and the passage of the Human Rights Act 1998 provides a more secure foundation for this approach.[30]

1–018

This approach requires some choice as to what are to count as fundamental rights *and* the more particular meaning ascribed to such rights. This is unavoidable. It is of course true that any democracy to be worthy of the name will have some attachment to particular liberty and equality interests. If, however, we delve beneath the surface of phrases such as liberty and equality then significant differences of view become apparent even among those who subscribe to one version or another of liberal belief. This leaves entirely out of account the issue as to how far social and economic interests ought to be protected. It also fails to take account of other visions of democracy, of a communitarian rather than liberal nature, which might well interpret the civil/political rights and the social/economic rights differently.[31]

ii. The protection of fundamental rights plus the articulation of principles of good administration

A second interpretation of a rights-based approach builds upon the first. Fundamental rights are to be protected in the above manner, but the courts

1–019

---

[29] See, Ch.17.
[30] See, Ch.18.
[31] P. Craig, *Public Law and Democracy in the United Kingdom and the United States of America* (Oxford University Press, 1990); W. Kymlicka, *Contemporary Political Philosophy: An Introduction* (Oxford University Press, 2nd edn, 2002).

should, in addition, openly articulate a number of procedural and substantive principles, such as: legality, procedural propriety, participation, openness, rationality, relevancy, propriety of purpose, reasonableness, legitimate expectations, legal certainty and proportionality. The object is to render the holders of power accountable.[32]

It should not, however, be assumed that uncertainties underlying criticism of the ultra vires principle will necessarily be absent in this new order. Ideas such as legality are just as malleable as those they replace. The existence of a principle of legality as a principle of good administration does not dictate its sphere of application. It does not determine whether the courts should always substitute their view on the meaning of every condition of jurisdiction of an agency. It does not provide any clue as to which of the conditions making up a body's area of power are to be treated as matters of law. It does not tell us how intensively the court should be reviewing the way in which discretion is exercised.[33] Moreover principles such as rationality, participation, openness, proportionality, procedural fairness and the like, can, as will be seen below, be interpreted differently depending upon the more general scheme into which they are to fit.

iii. A rights-based view of law and adjudication

1–020   A third possible meaning of a rights-based approach to public law draws more specifically upon a particular theory of law and adjudication. Any view of public law must be based upon some view, explicitly or implicitly, of law and the adjudicative process.[34]

Dworkin articulates a rights-based view of law and adjudication.[35] His theory is based on law as integrity, according to which, "propositions of law are true if they figure in or follow from the principles of justice, fairness and procedural due process that provide the best constructive interpretation of the community's legal practice".[36] It is integral to the Dworkinian approach that, subject to questions of fit, the court should choose between "eligible interpretations by asking which shows the community's structure of institutions as a whole in a better light from the stand-point of political morality".[37] On this view an individual will have a right to the legal answer which is forthcoming from the above test.

---

[32] The holders of power include public bodies, and some would go further and apply the principles to private bodies, which exercise a like degree of power.
[33] The only way in which the mere invocation of a term such as legality could possibly provide such answers is if that term were taken to incorporate the answers to these difficult issues concerning the respective competence of agencies and courts. This would, however, simply conceal these issues, or treat their resolution in a way thought to be self-evident, even though it manifestly is not.
[34] Craig, "Constitutional Foundations", n.25.
[35] *Taking Rights Seriously* (Duckworth, 1977), and *Law's Empire* (Fontana, 1986).
[36] Dworkin, *Law's Empire*, n.35, 225.
[37] Dworkin, *Law's Empire*, n.35, 256.

C. The Justifications for a Rights-Based Approach

The discussion thus far has set out the possible meanings of a rights-based   **1–021**
approach, but we must press further and consider the justifications for an
approach of this kind.

i. The courts, the legislature and constitutional democracy

The constitution assigns a role to the courts as well as the legislator and this   **1–022**
was perceived by those who laid the foundations for review.[38] In a constitutional democracy it is both right and proper for the courts to impose
limits on the way in which power is exercised. This was indeed the *traditional*
approach to the constraints imposed on public power in the seminal case law
which laid the foundations for judicial review. The courts imposed limits
that were felt to be normatively justified. Coke, Heath, Holt and Mansfield
based judicial review on the capacity of the common law to control public
power.[39] The principles of judicial review are therefore properly developed
by the courts in accord with the common law model set out above.

The legislature will rarely provide indication as to the content of judicial
review. The courts will impose the controls which constitute judicial review
which they believe are normatively justified on the grounds of justice, the
rule of law, etc. If the omnipotent Parliament does not like these controls
then it is open to it to make this unequivocally clear. If it does so the courts
will then adhere to such dictates. If Parliament does manifest a specific
intent as to the grounds of review the courts will also obey this, in just the
same way as they do in other areas where the primary obligations are the
creation of the common law. Rationalisations cast in terms of legislative
intent of the kind embodied in the ultra vires principle came much later. The
fact that the legislature can ultimately limit review, given traditional notions
of sovereignty, does not mean that the institution of review has to be
legitimated by reference to legislative intent in the absence of any such limits
being imposed.

The preceding argument can be reinforced by comparing public law and
private law. Proponents of the ultra vires principle maintain that controls on
public power must be legitimated by reference to legislative intent. In private
law, there is no such assumption. It is accepted that constraints on the
exercise of private power can and have been developed by the common law,
and there are numerous examples of this in contract, tort, restitution and
property law. There are consequential interesting differences in the sense of
legitimation that operates in the two areas. In public law, the traditional
ultra vires model sees legitimation in terms of the *derivation* of judicial
authority, flowing from legislative intent. The prime focus is not on the
content of the heads of review. This is in part a consequence of the fact that
the ultra vires doctrine is capable of vindicating virtually any chosen heads
of review. In private law, by way of contrast, we tend to think of legit-

---

[38] Sir Stephen Sedley, "Human Rights: A Twenty-First Century Agenda" [1995] P.L. 386 for a
powerful articulation that the courts should have the type of role being argued for here; P.
Craig, "Public Law, Political Theory and Legal Theory" [2000] P.L. 211.
[39] Craig, "*Ultra vires* and the Foundations of Judicial Review", n.25, 79–85.

imation in terms of the *content* of the common law norm which the courts have imposed, and more specifically about its *normative justification*. We ask whether certain constraints imposed on the exercise of private power in, for example, contract and tort, are sensible, warranted and justified in the light of the aims of the particular doctrinal area in question.

If controls on the existence of private power can be legitimated in this manner, then it is difficult to see why this should not also be true of controls on public power. Precisely which limits on public power are normatively justified is an inherently controversial issue, to which we shall return in due course. It should however be noted that invocation of the ultra vires principle never obviated or solved this inquiry, precisely because the content of the principle was indeterminate. It merely brushed the inquiry under the carpet with the pretence that the answer was to be found in some elusive legislative intent.

ii. The rule of law

1–023   Justification for some form of a rights-based approach might be founded on the rule of law. This however depends upon the meaning given to this constitutional concept.[40]

In one sense the rule of law is primarily a *formal* concept. It demands that there should be lawful authority for the exercise of power, *and* that individuals should be able to plan their lives on the basis of clear, open and general laws. On this hypothesis the rule of law is not the rule of the good law, and its dictates can be met by non-democratic societies.[41] On this view the rule of law cannot provide the foundation for particular substantive rights as such. The reason for restricting the concept in this way has been clearly articulated by Raz: if the rule of law is to be taken to demand certain substantive rights then it becomes tantamount to propounding a complete social and political philosophy and the concept would then no longer have a useful role independent of that political philosophy. Adherents of this formal model may well believe that individuals ought to have certain substantive rights, but argue that these rights should be articulated in their own terms: if you believe in justice and rights etc then argue for such concepts as such, against the background of the wealth of literature that openly addresses these issues.

A second sense of the rule of law is *substantive* in its orientation. The clearest formulation is to be found in Dworkin's work. He recognises that those who adhere to a formal conception of the rule of law care about the content of the law,[42] "but they say that this is matter of substantive justice, and that substantive justice is an independent ideal, in no sense part of the ideal of the rule of law".[43] His preferred version is what he terms the rights

---

[40] P. Craig, "Formal and Analytical Conceptions of the Rule of Law: An Analytical Framework" [1997] P.L. 467.
[41] J. Raz, "The Rule of Law and its Virtue" (1977) 93 L.Q.R. 195.
[42] R. Dworkin, *A Matter of Principle* (Harvard University Press, 1985), 11–12.
[43] Dworkin, *A Matter of Principle*, n.42, 11.

conception. On this view the moral and political rights possessed by individuals are to be recognised in positive law. They are to be enforced upon the demand of individual citizens through the courts. This conception of the rule of law does not distinguish, as does the formal conception, between the rule of law and substantive justice: "on the contrary it requires, as part of the ideal of law, that the rules in the book capture and enforce moral rights".[44] It should be recognised that this version of the rule of law directs us to the best theory of justice. Whether the best theory of justice is Kantian,[45] communitarian[46] or utilitarian is not in itself resolved by framing intervention in terms of the rule of law. Those who subscribe to the Dworkinian view may reach differing conclusions as to what the best theory of justice actually is.[47] My own preference is for this second sense of the rule of law.[48]

There is a third sense of the rule of law. Advocates of this view are unhappy with the purely formal version of the rule of law, but they are also mindful of the dangers of making the rule of law synonymous with some particular vision of substantive justice. They seek, therefore, to incorporate within the rule of law some substantive rights, while at the same time trying to avoid tying these too closely to any specific conception of justice.[49] It is however extremely difficult to specify some particular rights, and not others, that would be agreed to by proponents of differing conceptions of liberalism or democracy. The chosen list reflects the principles which would be agreed to by those who subscribe to a particular version of liberalism, and does not include principles which advocates of other conceptions of liberalism, or other political theories, would regard as equally, or more, important.[50]

A fourth sense of the rule of law sees the concept in terms of justified **1–024** authority. It is a process-based conception of the rule of law, in the sense that it accords pre-eminence to the values of accountability and participation. The focus is on public rational justification and on the "citizen as active participant in the legal order and not on the substance incorporated into law".[51] Space precludes a detailed examination of this approach. Suffice it to say that it is problematic for two related reasons.

It is clear that any theory of justice will entail some notion of participation and accountability. The very meaning accorded to participation and accountability will however vary depending upon the more general demo-

---

[44] Dworkin, *A Matter of Principle*, n.42, 11–12. Italics in the original.
[45] Sir John Laws, "Is the High Court the Guardian of Fundamental Constitutional Rights" [1993] P.L. 59; "Law and Democracy" [1995] P.L. 72; "The Constitution: Morals and Rights" [1996] P.L. 622.
[46] Lord Irvine, "Response to Sir John Laws" [1996] P.L. 636, 637.
[47] See, e.g., F. Michelman, "Foreword: Traces of Self-Government" (1986) 100 Harv. L.R. 4.
[48] P. Craig, "Constitutional Foundations, The Rule of Law and Supremacy" [2003] P.L. 92.
[49] See, e.g., T.R.S. Allan, *Law, Liberty and Justice* (1993), Ch.2, "The Rule of Law as the Rule of Reason: Consent and Constitutionalism" (1999) 115 L.Q.R. 221 and *Constitutional Justice, A Liberal Theory of the Rule of Law* (Oxford University Press, 2001).
[50] Craig, n.48, 96–102.
[51] D. Dyzenhaus, "Form and Substance in the Rule of Law: A Democratic Justification for Judicial Review", in Forsyth (ed.), n.24, 171.

cratic theory, or theory of justice, that is being espoused. This will be evident from the subsequent discussion within this chapter.

It is equally clear that process and substance interact. The idea that the rule of law can be explicated principally or solely in terms of participation and accountability is untenable because the meaning accorded to such ideas will be dependent upon, and resonate with, substantive principles. Thus it has been convincingly argued that no ostensibly process-based theory can avoid making substantive value judgments,[52] in part because many public law norms are manifestly substantive in nature, and in part because even allegedly procedural norms necessitate substantive choices. This is true in relation to both process writ small, or adjudicative process, and process writ large, or representative process.

iii. The Human Rights Act 1998

1–025   Justification for a rights-based approach to administrative law may also be grounded, in more concrete terms, in the Human Rights Act 1998 (HRA), which came into force on October 2, 2000. The HRA brought many of the rights contained in the European Convention on Human Rights (ECHR) into domestic law, so that they can be pleaded directly before our national courts. The HRA will be examined in detail below.[53]

It is clear that the HRA has implications for the orientation of administrative law in empirical terms: it is readily apparent from the case law post the HRA that a very significant number of judicial review cases are now pleaded on HRA grounds.

It is equally clear that the HRA has implications for administrative law in conceptual terms. The HRA requires the courts to read legislation in so far as is possible to be compliant with Convention rights, and provides for the issuance of a declaration of incompatibility where this is not possible. In this sense the HRA instantiates a novel relationship between courts and legislature, based on respect for human rights, albeit one that builds upon principles that the courts developed prior to the HRA. It is clear moreover that the courts have developed tools for more intensive judicial review under the HRA, through the use of proportionality as a ground for review. The HRA has therefore had a significant impact on the nature of judicial review by the emphasis thereby given to what has been termed the culture of justification.[54] This requires the primary decision-maker not merely to explain the challenged decision, but to proffer a reasoned argument, which the courts will scrutinise within the framework of proportionality to determine whether the limitation of the right was normatively justified.

---

[52] L. Tribe, "The Puzzling Persistence of Process-Based Constitutional Theories" (1980) 89 Yale L.J. 1063; P. Brest, "The Substance of Process" (1981) 42 Ohio St L.J. 131; R. Dworkin, "The Forum of Principle" (1981) 56 N.Y.U.L.Rev. 469.
[53] See, Ch.18.
[54] D. Dyzenhaus, "The Politics of Deference: Judicial Review and Democracy", in M. Taggart (ed.), *The Province of Administrative Law* (Hart, 1997), Ch.13; M. Taggart, "The Tub of Public Law", in D. Dyzenhaus (ed.), *The Unity of Public Law* (Hart, 2004), Ch.17.

D. A Critique

It is fitting at this juncture to consider a critique of a rights-based vision of   **1–026**
public law advanced by Poole in a series of articles.[55] He assigns the generic
label common law constitutionalism, CLC, to capture the views of a range
of theorists, including Sir John Laws, Allan, Oliver, Jowell and the present
author.

Poole discerns a number of related propositions that constitute common
law constitutionalism. These are that: a political community is ordered
according to a set of fundamental values; political decision-making is or
ought to be a matter of discovering what fundamental values require in
particular cases; the common law is the primary repository of the fundamental values of the political community; ordinary politics does not
necessarily connect with fundamental values; public law therefore consists of
a set of higher-order principles and rights; and decision-making in judicial
review is or ought to be value oriented.

The essence of his critique is as follows. Poole maintains that the nature
and practice of judicial review does not fit with the vision of public law
advanced by common law constitutionalists. Thus he maintains that participation within adjudication is perforce limited and is ill-adapted to consideration of a range of competing views; that judicial review is ill-suited to
consideration of polycentric disputes; that the arguments in judicial review
cases are relatively Spartan when compared to ordinary political debate;
that judicial review even in cases concerned with rights does not typically
involve considerations about fundamental values, but is more commonly
concerned with second order considerations concerning matters such as the
intensity of review.

His preferred vision of public law is one that focuses on legitimacy. In
instrumental terms, this is said to connote the idea that judicial review is
justified because of the fallibility in government decision-making. In non-
instrumental terms, it is said to capture the idea of trust in government.

E. A Response

It is of course perfectly right and proper for there to be debate, and the   **1–027**
issues that Poole raises should be taken seriously. It is important at the
outset to be mindful of a methodological concern. Poole's argument is
presented by drawing selectively from a number of writers, the assumption
being that all within the "CLC camp" agree with all the precepts that Poole
advances as being integral to CLC. This is certainly not true in the case of
the present author, and I doubt whether it is true of the others listed.

---

[55] T. Poole, "Back to the Future? Unearthing the Theory of Common Law Constitutionalism"
(2003) 23 O.J.L.S. 453; "Questioning Common Law Constitutionalism" (2005) 25 L.S. 142;
"Legitimacy, Rights and Judicial Review" (2005) 25 O.J.L.S. 697. See also, A Tomkins, *Our
Republican Constitution* (Hart, 2005), Ch.1. For a response, M. Cohn, "Judicial Activism in the
House of Lords: A Composite Constitutionalist Approach" [2007] P.L. 95.

i. The nature of common law constitutionalism

1-028   The depiction of common law constitutionalism is central to the critique thereof. A number of points can be made in this respect.

First, the picture painted of the authors who subscribe to CLC is incomplete, since there is no mention of their concern with accountability and legitimacy quite independently of judicial review. This is clear from the work of Jowell, Oliver and Craig. These authors do not just mention such matters, and then pass on to judicial review. They examine them in detail.[56] There is no sense in which they think that judicial review and the common law courts are the only relevant players when thinking about constitutionalism. Nor is there any inconsistency in having a view about the role of judicial review and the common law courts as one component in the search for accountability and legitimacy, while at the same time being properly aware of other important aspects of accountability and legitimacy that flow from institutional design, political controls, internal agency organisation and the plethora of other matters that these very authors have written about. This is not a zero sum game whereby attention being focused on judicial review implies in any way a lack of concern with other mechanisms for accountability and legitimacy.

Second, we need to think carefully about the role of fundamental values, legality and rights within public law, and to do so in the light of the role of courts in any area of the law. When the courts develop the common law of, for example, crime, contract, tort, and restitution they do so by articulating doctrine that is premised on certain assumptions about the important values that should be applicable within such areas. They make choices within the law of tort that are reflective of commitments to corrective or distributive justice; they develop doctrine within criminal law that is premised on conceptions of moral responsibility and justifiable excuse; and they mould contract law by considerations relating to matters such as consent, autonomy, bargain and the like. It is indeed difficult to imagine how such doctrine could otherwise be developed. It should therefore not be taken as somehow aberrant or unnatural for commentators to argue that a similar approach should infuse public law.

Third, the interrelationship between values and established doctrine within public law is not novel. It has in truth been a consistent theme within public law ever since its inception, and this is true irrespective of whether one chooses to try and rationalise this in terms of legislative intent or not. This is readily apparent if one reflects on standard features of public law doctrine. Thus, for example, the law concerning natural justice is premised on the instrumental and non-instrumental values that serve to explain why accord-

---

[56] See, e.g., J. Jowell, *Law and Bureaucracy, Administrative Discretion and the Limits of Legal Action* (Dunellen, 1975); J. Jowell and D. Oliver (eds), *The Changing Constitution* (Oxford University Press, 6th edn, 2007); D. Oliver. *Government in the United Kingdom: The Search for Accountability, Effectiveness and Citizenship* (Open University Press, 1991); D. Oliver, *Constitutional Reform in the UK* (Oxford University Press, 2003); D. Oliver and G. Drewry, *Public Service Reforms: Issues of Accountability and Public Law* (Pinter, 1996); P. Craig, *Administrative Law* (Sweet & Maxwell, 6th edn, 2008), Chs 2–11; P. Craig, *EU Administrative Law* (Oxford University Press, 2006), Chs 1–7.

ing a right to be heard before a decision is taken is so important; the law relating to nullity is grounded on the fundamental precept that where a public body takes a decision that is ultra vires it should, in principle, be retrospectively void; and development of the law relating to remedies in the 18th and 19th centuries was based on the value that relief should be granted where power was abused without too close an inquiry as to whether the defendant came within pre-existing categories of those subject to public law. The relationship between value and doctrine will often be piecemeal, in the sense that different, albeit related values, will underpin different doctrinal components of public law. It will also be evolutionary, in the sense that courts may well alter doctrine over time in the light of altered perceptions of the values that provide the foundation for that doctrine, as exemplified by developments in relation to areas such as error of law, error of fact and rationality review.

Fourth, what values should be regarded as fundamental, what rights **1–029** should be protected or what should be included within the rubric of legality, will be contestable. This is however endemic to all areas of the law. Public law is not special or exceptional in this respect. This is attested to by the vibrant debates about theory in contract, tort, restitution, crime and just about any other area of the law, where commentators discuss the values that do and should underpin the respective subjects. I do not believe that the values in public law are wholly self-evident, or axiomatic. Or to put the same point in a slightly different way, even if people agree on abstract concepts such as liberty, equality, property, security, citizenship and the like they may well have differing conceptions of such rights or values in particular contexts. Insofar as this separates me from some of the others regarded as being within the CLC camp so be it. My adherence to a conception of public law based broadly on rights, legality and abuse of power is not therefore premised on the pretence that the meaning ascribed to these concepts is uncontroversial. To the contrary, as is evident from the preceding discussion, and from that which follows in the remainder of this chapter, the more particular meaning accorded to such concepts may differ depending on the background political theory adopted. It is part of the continuing role of the commentator to reveal such premises and criticise them if that is felt to be warranted.

Finally, commitment to a conception of public law based broadly on rights, legality and abuse of power, or to one based on rights and fundamental values, does not in and of itself resolve important issues about the relationship between courts and legislature, and courts and executive in a constitutional democracy. It does not mean that courts are always right and the political branch wrong. It does not entail any "Whig reading of history", whereby the common law courts always got it "right". It does not "make the case" for US style constitutional review, whereby courts can invalidate legislation. Nor does it resolve the issue as to the extent to which courts should show some measure of deference or respect to legislative or executive choices.[57] The very fact that the interpretation of rights and values can be

---

[57] See below, Ch.18.

contestable, and that the legislature or executive may have a reasonable considered view, is I believe a relevant consideration in this respect. Some others within the CLC camp may disagree, and if that is so we differ.

We can now assess Poole's critique about the fit between the precepts of CLC as he articulates them and the practice of judicial review. Space precludes detailed treatment of these issues, but the following points can be made quite briefly.

ii. Common law constitutionalism and judicial review: participation

1–030 Poole argues that judicial review is essentially adjudicative and bipolar, and hence is ill-adapted to considering a range of competing points of view. It cannot therefore be a central forum for deliberating about matters relating to fundamental values and cannot match the republican model of active citizenship. There are three related points in this respect.

First, this argument elides the issue of participation in the initial agency decision, with judicial review before the court. CLC authors, or least some of them, favour the development of participatory rights before the initial agency, especially in the context of rule-making, precisely because it will enhance the republican ideal of deliberative discourse. They do not claim that this is the present law, but there is no reason in principle why such development should not occur, and indeed such participatory initiatives have been developed by the political branch of government.[58]

Second, most CLC authors do not claim that judicial review before the court itself presently comports with a model of republican discourse. It is true that Allan has said something to this effect, but his general line is against the idea of broadening standing rights, because he believes that this is inconsistent with the nature of the judicial process. Other CLC authors disagree. They argue that standing and intervention rights should be broadly construed. They do not claim that this position is perfectly embodied in the present law, especially in relation to intervention rights. Nor do they claim that even if it were that it would thereby reflect some perfect model of deliberative discourse. They accept that adjudication imposes limits. What some CLC authors maintain is that broadened participatory and intervention rights before the initial decision-maker, combined with relatively liberal standing and intervention rights before the courts, will enhance the deliberative, republican aspects of decision-making, albeit within the parameters necessarily imposed by the fact that we are within a judicial forum.

Third, Poole's argument is in any event premised upon a vision as to how decisions are made within the political forum, the premise being full consideration of the competing views on which the contested decision is made. It is true that some decisions may be made in this manner. It is equally clear that many are not. Many rules made by the administration or statutory instruments may receive little by way of scrutiny, and little in the way of

---

[58] See, Ch.22.

consideration of competing views. It is even more difficult to generalise about individualised decisions made by agencies, ministers, prison governors and the like, especially when, as will often be the case, the contested decision is actually made by an official.

iii. Common law constitutionalism and judicial review: polycentricity and the focus of judicial review

Poole argues that judicial review properly focuses on a particular issue, and is unsuited to the resolution of polycentric disputes, which will often better be considered in political terms. Three brief comments are warranted.   **1–031**

First, the authors associated with CLC accept that there are certain issues which are polycentric in nature and that courts are limited in their capacity to deal with these issues. The courts have recognised this too in certain cases.[59]

Second, having said this, there is an emerging sophisticated body of work elaborating the types of factor that should be taken into account in deciding on the appropriate intensity of review in cases concerned with resource allocation and social and economic rights.[60] The fact that a dispute is in some way polycentric does not therefore signal that it is or should be a no go area for the courts.[61]

Third, it should not in any event be assumed that the political process will conform to some perfect deliberative ideal when such matters are considered. There is a wealth of literature about how bureaucratic decision-making works, which emphasises its incremental nature and the limited capacity for more general overview of issues. This is moreover quite apart from the general literature on the political process at Westminster, with executive domination of the legislature.

iv. Common law constitutionalism and judicial review: the nature of argument in judicial review

Poole argues that the style of argument in judicial review is relatively   **1–032**
Spartan as compared to the richness of political debate, that it is restricted to certain well established categories, and that it cannot therefore conform to a deliberative ideal. Two brief comments are in order.

First, it can be accepted that there are differences between judicial review

---

[59] *R. v Cambridge Health Authority Ex p. B* [1995] 2 All ER 129; *R. (on the application of Walker) v Parole Board, R. (on the application of Wells) v Parole Board* [2007] EWHC 1835.
[60] S. Fredman, "Social, Economic and Cultural Rights", in D. Feldman (ed.), *English Public Law* (Oxford University Press, 2004), Ch.10; K. Syrett, "Opening Eyes to the Reality of Scarce Health Care Resources?" [2006] P.L. 664; J. King, "The Justiciability of Resource Allocation" (2007) 70 M.L.R. 197; A. Pillay, "Courts, Variable Standards of Review and Resource Allocation: Developing a Model for the Enforcement of Social and Economic Rights" [2007] E.H.R.L.R. 616; C. Newdick, "Judicial Review: Low-Priority Treatment and Exceptional Case Review" [2007] Med. L.R. 236; E. Palmer, *Judicial Review, Socio-Economic Rights and the Human Rights Act* (Hart, 2007).
[61] J. King, "The Pervasiveness of Polycentricity" [2008] P.L. 101.

and normal political argument. The former will be constrained both by the need for the argument to be fitted within one of the established heads of review, and by the fact that the grounds of review are themselves premised on certain assumptions about the relationship between courts and primary decision-makers, such as the injunction against substitution of judgment on matters of discretion that have been assigned to the primary decision-maker.

Second, this should not however lead us to assume that consideration of the particular issue before the court will necessarily be less searching or less rich than when the same issue was considered in the political process. Thus when legislation is passed there may well have been scant consideration as to whether a particular provision thereof conflicts with Convention rights, or some other precept of public law. Similarly when an executive decision is made that differentiates between groups the extent to which this has been preceded by searching analysis of the justification for the differential treatment may well vary. If such issues are adjudicated before the courts this may offer the opportunity for more in depth scrutiny of the reasons and justificatory arguments for the contested provision than occurred within the normal political process.

v. Common law constitutionalism and judicial review: the limited relevance of fundamental values

1–033 Poole argues that judges decide cases not by reflecting what fundamental values or rights require, but that even in cases concerned with rights the focus will often be on second-order considerations relating to the intensity or standard of judicial review, and in that sense on the authority of the court in relation to the primary decision-maker. This is said by Poole to undermine the CLC claim that public law should be conceived in terms of fundamental values.

It is unclear as to why Poole regards this as a difficulty for CLC authors of whatever persuasion. The inarticulate premise to his argument appears to be that any consideration of matters such as the appropriate intensity of review constitutes a diminution in some way of the precepts on which the CLC model is founded. The argument appears to be that any departure from substitution of judgment by the reviewing court in some way compromises adherence to a rights-based model of review, such that when courts engage in consideration of the appropriate meaning to be given to rationality or proportionality, or when they consider the extent to which they should accord deference to the primary decision-maker, this is somehow at odds with or diminishes the CLC view.

I do not accept this. It is true, as we shall see below,[62] that different authors broadly associated with CLC take different views as to when, for example, deference should be accorded to the primary decision-maker. This does not however mean that judicial engagement with this issue is contrary to the precepts on which the CLC model is based. It is, to the contrary,

---

[62] See, Ch.18.

natural within a regime of judicial review for the courts to focus on issues relating to the standard of review, as well as the meaning of the contested right or value, since the former may be a condition precedent to determination of the latter. Discourse concerning the standard of review that is felt to be appropriate is central within a regime of judicial review committed to rights, legality and the abuse of power, or rights and fundamental values. The answer, whatsoever it may be, will itself encapsulate certain important values indicative of the relationship between courts and the initial decision-maker.

We shall see below that in many instances the courts will substitute judgment on the meaning of speech, assembly, deprivation of liberty or the like, in which cases the focus will be squarely on the meaning of the contested right. In other instances, notably where the public body raises a defence that the limitation of the right came within grounds allowed by the ECHR, the courts will also engage in debate about the proper limits of their control in relation to the political branch of government, which will take place within the confines of the proportionality inquiry, although it is common even in such cases for the courts to make some determination about the meaning of the contested right. Both aspects of the inquiry are properly regarded as important within a model of review based on rights, legality and abuse of power, or rights and fundamental values.

vi. Legitimacy and judicial review

Poole's preferred foundation for public law is cast in terms of legitimacy. In **1–034** instrumental terms, this is said to connote the idea that judicial review is justified because of the fallibility in government decision-making. In non-instrumental terms, it is said to capture the idea of trust in government.

Space precludes comment on this idea, save for the following. This conception of legitimacy captures the same or a similar idea to that expressed earlier:[63] in a constitutional democracy it is both right and proper for the courts to impose limits on the way in which power is exercised in order to prevent abuse of that power.

4. PARTICULAR IMPLICATIONS OF THE MODEL—I: TRADITIONAL PLURALISM

It may be helpful to move beyond the propositions discussed above, and to **1–035** consider the differing implications which flow from the adoption of divergent background conceptions of our subject. We shall see that this produces distinct interpretations of rights, and of many other ideas, such as participation, rationality, control of power, and the proper scope for judicial review.

[63] See, para.1–022.

A. Intellectual Foundations

1–036   We have already seen that the traditional vision of administrative law was premised upon a particular view as to how our democracy functioned. This was termed unitary democracy, to express the idea that all public power was and should be channelled through Parliament, which body possessed a legislative monopoly. When practical necessity required the delegation of power to a minister or agency the purpose of administrative law was to ensure that the agency remained within its assigned area and therefore did not trespass upon the legislative monopoly of Parliament by exercising power outside of this sphere. This Diceyan view of administrative and constitutional law was challenged on the grounds that his vision of unitary democracy was both descriptively flawed and prescriptively questionable. Three strands of this challenge should be distinguished.

i. The pluralist critique of the unitary thesis

1–037   The first strand of the critique was advanced by writers in the late 19th and early 20th centuries who took an explicitly pluralist vision of democracy to replace the unitary view espoused by Dicey.[64] Their views differed, but central themes of their argument can nonetheless be delineated. They revealed the historical foundations of the unitary view of the state. The idea that sovereignty was indivisible appeared initially in the writings of, among others, Hobbes, as a defence against anarchy. Only if the state was all powerful could a breakdown in society be prevented; if groups or associations were rivals to the state then chaos would ensue. This political justification for the unitary state was unsurprising given the turmoil that occurred in the English civil war. This reasoning was reinforced in the 19th century by jurists like Austin who argued, in a more analytical vein, that it was simply not possible to have a sovereign whose power was limited. Dicey built on Austin. In a democracy where the people elected MPs who represented their views and controlled the executive, it was "right" that this central power should be all embracing. The pluralists then proceeded to challenge the unitary view in descriptive and prescriptive terms.

In *descriptive* terms, they contested the idea that all public power was wielded by the state. They pointed to pressure groups that shaped and constrained state action. Religious, economic and social associations exercised authority, and took part in decisions of a public character. "Legislative" decisions would often be reached by the executive, after negotiation with such groups, and would then be forced through Parliament.

In *prescriptive* terms, group power was applauded rather than condemned. The all powerful unitary state was dangerous. Liberty was best preserved by the presence of groups within the state to which the individual could owe allegiance. Decentralisation and the preservation of group autonomy were to be valued. This vision of political pluralism was com-

---

[64] See, e.g., H. Laski, *Studies in the Problem of Sovereignty* (Yale University Press, 1917), *Authority in the Modern State* (Yale University Press, 1919), and *Foundations of Sovereignty* (Allen & Unwin, 1921); J. Figgis, *Churches in the Modern State* (London, 1913); E. Barker, *Reflections on Government* (Oxford University Press, 1942).

plemented by a concern with the social and economic conditions within the state. There was a strong belief that political liberty was closely linked with social and economic equality. This influenced the pluralists' approach to the emergent regulatory welfare legislation passed in the early decades of the 20th century. Such legislation was viewed favourably, being one step in the alleviation of social and economic hardship and therefore of central importance to the effective operation of a pluralist democracy.

ii. The limited effectiveness of Parliamentary controls
A second strand of the challenge to the unitary vision of democracy was   **1–038**
implicitly, rather than explicitly, pluralist. It was argued that the unitary vision of democracy was flawed not just because public power was exercised by groups outside of the parliamentary process. It was also misleading because even those rules which were formally legitimated by Parliament were not properly scrutinised. Pressures of time, and executive dominance of the legislature, combined to ensure that legislative control over, for example, secondary legislation was minimal. Moreover, departmental policy choices made pursuant to the implementation of legislation might be inadequately thought through, with the consequence that there was no proper consideration of differing ways to attain legislative goals.[65]

If Parliament could not effectively control such matters then there should be other ways in which to legitimate and control the use of public power in society, such as citizen participation in the process of making agency rules. Whereas the unitary vision of democracy saw all public power as being legitimated through participation by MPs in Parliament, the pluralist vision was premised on the idea that power could be legitimated and constrained in more diverse ways, such as by citizen participation. It was not therefore surprising that the provision of consultation rights was an important part of the suggestions proffered by the early pluralists.

iii. The corporatist challenge
A third strand in the challenge to the unitary state was "corporatism",   **1–039**
which provided an explanation both of the form of pressure group action, and also the reasons for its existence.[66]

The *form* of interest group pressure under corporatist theory is best viewed as a modification of pluralism. The latter depicted the political process as one in which a relatively wide range of different groups would affect political decision-making. Such groups competed for political influ-

---

[65] See, e.g., I. Harden and N. Lewis, *The Noble Lie, The British Constitution and the Rule of Law* (Hutchinson, 1986).
[66] See, e.g., P. Schmitter and G. Lehmbruch (eds), *Trends Toward Corporatist Intermediation* (Sage, 1979); P. Schmitter and G. Lehmbruch (eds), *Patterns of Corporatist Policymaking* (Sage, 1982); A. Cawson, *Corporatism and Welfare* (Heinemann, 1982); R. Harrison (ed.), *Corporatism and the Welfare State* (Allen & Unwin, 1984); P. Birkinshaw, I. Harden and N. Lewis, *Government by Moonlight: The Hybrid Parts of the State* (Unwin Hyman, 1990).

ence and no particular group would enjoy a monopoly of representational status with the government. In corporatist theory a particular group or groups would be accorded a privileged representational status with the government, which would "licence" such a group to represent the interests of other less powerful groups within the same area. The privileged status accorded to the dominant group carried a "price", in the sense that such a group would accept certain controls or constraints on the range of demands which it advanced.

The *reasons* for this type of pressure group action were that the modern state was required to undertake a wide range of activities in order to correct defects in, or problems arising from, the capitalist system. Governments were forced to juggle with goals such as full employment, economic growth, the resolution of labour conflicts, inflation and the provision of protection for consumers and workers. The pursuit of these objectives necessitated discussion and collaboration with major interest groups, which achieved their dominant representational status for a number of reasons. The government perceived benefits in dealing with one bargaining agent. A relationship of trust could be built up, an understanding of the rules of the game and an assuredness that the organisation would promote an agreed policy among the relevant "constituency".

Corporatism undermined the unitary thesis by postulating the existence of groups which wielded public power outside of the normal parliamentary process, and helped us to understand how the alliance between such groups and the executive could bypass Parliament. A policy might be agreed between a dominant group and the executive, which was then forced through Parliament with little opportunity for comment. Or the executive and the relevant group might arrive at an understanding which never saw the parliamentary light of day at all, but remained in a non-statutory form.

B. Implications for Administrative Law

i. Accountability and the scope of administrative law

1–040   The traditional model encapsulated a particular vision of the accountability of the administrative state. The premise behind this model, which was explicit in Dicey's own work, was that Parliament controlled the executive, and was itself controlled by the electorate. Judicial control, based upon legislative intent and the application of the ordinary law, ensured that agencies remained within their designated area, and was all that was required to render the administrative state accountable. The pluralist model undermined this notion of accountability in two ways.

First, a natural corollary of the traditional notion of accountability was that the *scope* of administrative law was essentially only concerned with those bodies to which statutory or prerogative power had been given. It was only where such bodies were exercising delegated power that there was a danger of encroachment on the legislative monopoly of Parliament by such an agency going outside its assigned sphere. The pluralist model undermined this presupposition by its very insistence that other institutions exercised public power. Any realistic vision of administrative law would therefore have to decide how to treat such institutions.

Second, the pluralist model also undermined the idea that the traditional approach was *sufficient* to ensure accountability even within those areas where an agency had been given statutory power. Traditional theory, with its assumptions of electoral control over the legislature and legislative control over the executive, could comfortably reach the conclusion that keeping an agency within the area designated by legislative intent would ensure that the will of the people expressed through their elected representatives would triumph. This vision was challenged by the pluralist model, which recognised the power of the executive over the legislature, and the fact that policy often emerged as a result of accommodation between pressure groups and the executive. Even if we could accurately interpret legislative intent we could no longer presuppose that the will of the people expressed through their elected representatives would be fulfilled. All that we could conclude would be that the will of the executive forced through the legislature was being implemented.

ii. The gateways to administrative law: natural justice, standing and intervention

We have already seen why the traditional model tended to construe the "gateways" to administrative law narrowly. Supporters of the pluralist model would argue both that the existing gateways should be broadened, and that new types of gateway should be opened up. **1–041**

The rationale for *broadening* the gateways is easy to understand. The law relating to standing can be taken as an example. Standing determines the range of people who can seek judicial review of suspect agency action. The traditional model tended towards a narrow construction of standing. The public body exercised delegated power from Parliament and was the arbiter of the public interest in that area. An individual could only challenge such an agency decision, or so some cases held, where strict private rights were at stake. In such cases the individual was simply settling a private dispute in contract, tort, etc., which he had with the public body.

The pluralist model undermined this narrow construction. The public body might still be conceived as the arbiter of the public interest. It was, however, recognised that other private groups could wield "public" power and exercised influence over agency decisions. The thrust behind the pluralist argument was therefore that a third party should be able to come to court, even if no traditional private rights were affected, and ask the court to determine whether the result reached by the agency, in the light of representations from a particular group, really was in accord with the intent of the legislation.

The pluralist model would also suggest that the other principal gateway, that of natural justice, should be given a broader interpretation than under the traditional model. The traditional model was, as we have seen, reluctant **1–042** to admit of procedural rights in legislative contexts. A commitment to increased consultative rights would necessitate reversal of this idea, since such rights are required principally in those contexts where an agency is making rules of a legislative nature. If a statute does not accord such procedural rights, then, if we wish to develop the idea of participation, it will have to be through the ordinary courts supplying the omission of the legislature. The gateway of natural justice would have to be broadened to accommodate such a development.

There is a further reason why the natural justice gateway would be broadened. We have already seen that some cases held that only those with strict private rights should be afforded a hearing before an agency made its decision. The courts have, as we shall see, granted process rights even where no traditional substantive rights were present. The pluralist model would support this development. A prominent thread in pluralist thought stressed the interconnection between economic and political liberty, and viewed the governmental provision of, for example, social welfare benefits, as a step in this direction. Procedural protection should therefore apply before the distribution of such benefits was terminated.

The pluralist model would also indicate that there should be *new* gateways to administrative law, such as a right to intervene. There may be circumstances in which an interested group wishes to intervene in existing adjudicative proceedings before the agency itself. The gateways, as traditionally conceived, do not provide much assistance. The law of standing tells us who can challenge the agency decision before the reviewing court. Natural justice indicates who should be heard by the agency before it makes a decision, which relates to that individual in some fairly direct way. What one may require is an opportunity for an individual to intervene in proceedings before the agency itself, even if he or she is not immediately concerned. Public law adjudication may have far reaching implications, the effects of which are not confined to the nominal plaintiff and defendant. A group may wish to intervene because it feels that the actual parties to the action are not putting all the relevant arguments, or that the parties have reached an accommodation with the agency and that this does not reflect the public interest. Intervention rights may also be required where the agency has taken no action at all.

iii. Process rights: fostering participation

1–043   An important implication from the pluralist model might be that we ought to foster participation in administrative decision-making to a greater extent than we do at present. Rules are often made by agencies and the like. Sometimes they take the form of secondary legislation, on other occasions such rules emerge naturally from the process of bureaucratic decision-making. Traditional theory tells us that rules of a legislative nature should be legitimated through parliamentary scrutiny. This is, however, not terribly effective, and, in any event, there are many administrative rules which do not see the parliamentary light of day at all because they are not classified as statutory instruments.[67]

The pluralist model suggests that participation in the making of such rules by interested parties can help to secure their legitimacy. Our democracy is representative primarily because problems of time and scale preclude any more direct form of democracy in the complex modern world. However even representative democracy may be unable adequately to control all rules of a legislative nature. A direct form of input from the "bottom", in the form of citizen participation in the administrative process, can therefore help by making rule-making more directly democratic and hence accountable. The pluralist model provides support for this idea in a double sense.

In *descriptive terms*, proponents of this model acknowledge that some participation from external pressure groups already exists. The degree of such participation may however be uneven, and the participatory process may be dominated by particular powerful groups, who have favoured relationships with the public body. Pluralists may well therefore advocate more formal participatory rights in order that a wider variety of groups can be involved in the administrative process. In *prescriptive terms*, the pluralist model assumes that the decentralisation of public power which is fostered through the grant of such consultative rights is a "good thing". Liberty is best preserved by such dispersion of power, and the state is rendered more accountable by allowing an element of direct democracy within the administrative process.

iv. The scope of judicial review

The pluralist model has implications for the nature and intensity of judicial   **1–044**
review. It is more sympathetic to a functionalist approach towards such review, with the precepts of judicial review being tailored to the needs and nature of the particular area being reviewed.

The intensity of judicial review will be influenced by the need to ensure that participation rights are taken seriously. The basic premise is that the court should not simply substitute its view for that of the agency. There must however be some meaningful review because we have to ensure that the agency does not just go through the motions of listening to people. It may therefore be necessary for the courts to take a "hard look" at the reasoning process by which the agency reached its decision.[68] The courts should play a role in forcing the agency to be more thorough in its reasoning process, and in ensuring that the views of interested parties are adequately considered.

v. Remedies and the ambit of administrative law

In our earlier discussion we considered the impact of the pluralist model on   **1–045**
the "gateways" to administrative law, on those who could use the system.

---

[67] See, Ch.22.
[68] See, Ch.19.

There is a reverse side to this coin, which concerns the extent to which a pluralist model tells us something about those against whom public law principles should be applied.

On the traditional model public law remedies applied most naturally to those who derived their power from statute, or perhaps the prerogative. These bodies were given power by Parliament. It followed that only such bodies threatened the legislative monopoly of Parliament. Provided that they were kept within the ambit of their power this monopoly would be preserved. Public law remedies, such as the prerogative orders, were therefore only applicable to such bodies.

The pluralist model undermines this complacency. Parliament is not seen as possessing a monopoly of public power. Such power is also exercised by others, including interest groups on both the capital and labour sides of the market. The consequences of this are less easy to predict. We can drop the restrictive requirement that a body must derive its authority from statute before the public law remedies can "bite". Where we should go from there is less clear. It may be argued that any distinction between public and private law is impossible to draw, or more moderately, that which bodies should be subject to public law will have to be defined on an ad hoc basis.

5. Particular Implications of the Model — II: Market-Oriented Pluralism

A. Intellectual Foundations

1–046   Pluralism has both descriptive and prescriptive elements. The descriptive aspect of pluralism helps us to understand how governmental decisions are made within society and the role of non-elected groups in this process. The prescriptive aspect of pluralism seeks to delineate an appropriate role for the state in the light of these "facts". Writers have drawn radically differing conclusions from these facts, and these differing conclusions have significant ramifications for administrative law. Two differing visions of pluralism emerged.

There is the pluralism of those who in the early 20th century reacted against the unitary state postulated by Dicey. These pluralists were generally left of centre politically, and this was reflected in their policies. Their vision stressed the existence of group power, group rights and obligations, decentralisation and the interconnection between economic and political liberty, the latter requiring governmental intervention in order to secure such liberties for the individual. This approach was always subject to an inner tension between the desire for decentralisation, and the existence of the requisite central authority to enable the desired economic objectives to be fulfilled.

There is a more market based conception of pluralist democracy, manifest in governmental policy within the late 1970s and 1980s, which is closer to pluralism as understood in the United States.[69] The existence of group power that constrains and shapes governmental action is acknowledged, and there is a desire to decentralise decision-making by devolving many spheres of governmental activity to the market. The prescriptive role for the state was conceived differently from the earlier pluralist model, in part because the connection between economic and political liberty was seen from a different perspective. The market was viewed as the best "arbitrator" of many issues, and direct governmental regulation thereof was perceived as necessary only when there was market failure, the existence of which was narrowly defined. The sphere of legitimate governmental action was therefore closely circumscribed. There were however also tensions within this model. The thesis may well have been pluralist in admitting the existence of group power which constrains governmental action and, albeit more controversially, by devolving decision-making in certain areas to the market. In certain respects it produced, however, a more powerful centralised role for the government. The very fulfilment of the free market vision required, as we shall see, a strong central government. There was also a more overtly authoritarian element present within this philosophy, which served further to enhance the power of the centre.[70]

B. Implications for Administrative Law

An understanding of these two very different pluralist visions has implications for administrative law. The full ramifications of these differences cannot be examined here. The object is to demonstrate how concepts such as rights, citizenship, participation, and rationality, which constitute the newer model of administrative law, can assume very different meanings depending upon the background ideas against which they are read.   **1–047**

i. Rights, citizenship and society

Citizenship connotes the civil, political, social and economic rights individuals presently possess, or ought to possess, within society. Which rights individuals *presently have* will be affected by the particular theory of law and adjudication adopted. A positivist might give one answer to this question, based upon the existing corpus of statutory and common law materials. A follower of Dworkin might give a different answer if it is warranted by the application of that theory of law and adjudication. Which rights citizens *ought to have* has been one of the major preoccupations of political theory for at least 2000 years.   **1–048**

It is readily apparent that the conceptions of citizenship employed by the major political parties have differed significantly. The Conservative's

---

[69] P. Craig, *Public Law in the United Kingdom and the United States of America* (Oxford University Press, 1990), Chs 3, 4.
[70] See, e.g., R. Levitas (ed.), *The Ideology of the New Right* (Polity, 1986); R. Skidelsky (ed.), *Thatcherism* (Chatto & Windus, 1988); B. Jessop, K. Bonnett, S. Bromley and T. Ling, *Thatcherism* (Polity, 1988); S. Jenkins, *Accountable to None, The Tory Nationalization of Britain* (Penguin, 1995).

document did not deal with traditional civil and political rights at all, and emphasised the rights which consumers of services ought to have as against the service provider.[71] The documents produced by the Liberal Democrats[72] and the Labour party[73] in the early 1990s addressed a wider range of issues, which were political, social and economic in nature.

The differences in the conceptions of citizenship will therefore affect the interpretation accorded to a model of public law based upon rights, legality and the abuse of power. It will influence the particular construction given to a concept which all would agree should be part of the protected sphere of rights. It will also have a marked impact upon which rights are recognised at all. These points can be simply demonstrated.

All would agree that some concept of equality should feature within a list of protected rights, and that this should preclude differential treatment on the grounds of race, gender and the like. Disagreement centres upon the particular conception of equality that should be applied. Traditional pluralists tended to favour a conception of equality and distributive justice, which entailed state intervention to promote greater equality in the resources held by individual citizens. The more market based species of pluralism had a very different conception of distributive justice, which, on some versions at least, regarded existing property rights as sacrosanct holdings that should not be redistributed by the state. These differences of view concerning equality and distributive justice can have consequential implications for the legitimacy of state action which seeks, for example, to promote equality through affirmative action programmes.

The same theme is even more apparent when we consider which rights should fall within the protected sphere at all. Employment can be taken by way of example. Traditional pluralists, such as Laski, argued that society existed in order for citizens to realise their lives in the best possible manner. They saw a prominent connection between political and economic liberty.[74] This provided the foundation for analysis of the employment relationship: a citizen should have both the right to work, and certain rights while in work, including adequate wages and the ability to participate in the government of industry. Citizenship should not therefore stop at the factory gates, both because economic well-being was regarded as essential to political participation, and also because "ideas of political citizenship are as relevant in the economic as in the political arena",[75] in the sense that protection from arbitrary treatment is not something to be left at the beginning of work and "donned again at the end of a shift".[76] The market oriented pluralist adopted a very different view of the employment relationship. Market forces should be left to govern the employment field with little in the way of rights

---

[71] *The Citizen's Charter: Raising the Standard*, Cm. 1599 (1991).
[72] *Citizens' Britain: Liberal Democrat Policies for a People's Charter* (1991).
[73] *Citizen's Charter: Labour's Deal for Consumers and Citizens* (1991).
[74] Craig, n.69, Chs 5, 6.
[75] K. Ewing, "Citizenship and Employment", in R. Blackburn (ed.), *Rights of Citizenship* (Mansell, 1993), 117.
[76] Ewing, "Citizenship and Employment", n.75, 100.

to minimum terms or conditions of service; worker participation in the governance of the industry was not encouraged; and the collective rights of unions were closely circumscribed and subordinated in certain respects to the rights of the citizen as consumer.

ii. Process rights and participation

The two models also produce differing conclusions concerning both the incidence and objective of participation in agency decision-making. **1–049**

The *incidence* of participation is affected because both models find it necessary to place constraints on groups who are seen as opposed to the basic philosophy on which the model itself is based. An obvious example of this was the constraint placed on local authorities who were opposed to the market-oriented philosophy of the conservative government. The power of such groups was curbed and their participatory role was limited, because they were seen as jeopardising the political philosophy on which the model was based. The earlier pluralists also found it necessary to impose constraints on private property. Such power had to be restrained and the participatory role of those with property rights had to be diminished, because they jeopardised the philosophy which underpinned the aims of the pluralists.

The *objective* of granting participatory rights under the two models may also differ. The market-oriented pluralist granted such rights to those involved in the relevant activity, with the object of ensuring efficiency. Accountability was seen in market terms and granting participatory rights to "consumers" of the activity was justified on this basis. This was readily apparent in the Conservatives Citizen's Charter. The early pluralists viewed the objectives of participation rights more broadly. They were to enable the individual to participate in the process of government, and to foster the full development of the individual within society.

iii. The ambit of public law

Different conclusions are also apparent concerning the type of bodies which should be run by the state. The earlier pluralists required greater government intervention in order to secure the conditions of economic equality regarded as necessary for the attainment of political liberty. Nationalisation of industry, direct regulation of other aspects of economic life and economic redistribution of wealth were the consequences of this approach. Proponents of the market-oriented model viewed the connection between economic and political liberty very differently. Deregulation and privatisation were the consequences of this approach. Even where continuing regulation of a privatised industry was required, the aim was coloured by the market-oriented vision. The purpose was often to prevent an industry with monopolistic power from abusing its dominant position. **1–050**

The scope of public law was nonetheless contestable even *within* this newer market-oriented vision. It is clear that the courts have moved away from the previous formalism, which sought to limit the ambit of public law to those institutions which derived their power from statute or the pre-rogative. The precise metes and bounds of the wider application of public law principles are, however, still being worked out. Two separate, albeit related, questions must be distinguished when deciding upon these limits.

The first concerns the *nature of the bodies* which should be subjected to public law principles. Some would restrict this to bodies which have a connection with the state. Others would argue that principles of public law should apply to any institution which possesses power over the lives of others, irrespective of whether there is any formal connection with the state or not. Yet others adopt an intermediate position, the effect of which is that public law should be applied to bodies which possess some monopoly power over a sphere of activity, irrespective of whether the body with such power has any formal connection with the state.

The second question concerns the *nature of the principles* that should be applied to those bodies deemed to be part of public law. It might well be natural to think of *procedural* principles, such as those of fair hearings and the like, applying to bodies such as trade associations or unions, and indeed such principles have been applied to these bodies for some considerable time. If however we think it appropriate to bring within the ambit of public law large corporate undertakings which exercise monopoly power over a particular sphere of life then matters become more difficult. Would this mean that *all substantive* public law principles would be equally applicable to such bodies? Would the exercise of corporate discretionary judgment be open to attack on the basis that relevant considerations had not been taken into account, or on the grounds of proportionality?

6. PARTICULAR IMPLICATIONS OF THE MODEL—III: THE THIRD WAY

A. Intellectual Foundations

1–051   The victory of the Labour party, together with similar successes by social democratic parties on the continent, prompted a re-think of the options available to government at the end of the millennium. The preceding years had created the impression that the neoliberal, market-oriented vision of the Conservatives was the only viable way forward. This was all the more so given the collapse of socialist regimes in Eastern Europe. The Labour victory cast doubt on the idea that continued political success was in some way inevitable for those of the neoliberal persuasion. It also naturally prompted questions as to what New Labour would offer. The Labour party promised that their policies would be based on a "Third Way", which was neither old style socialism, nor the neoliberalism that had characterised Conservative policy.

Old style social democracy was based around a number of key ideas, including: state involvement in social and economic life, collectivism, Keynesian demand management, corporatism, full employment, strong egalitarianism, a comprehensive welfare state and internationalism.[77] The market-oriented neoliberalism of the New Right also had a number of defining characteristics, inter alia: minimal government, a belief in the market, moral authoritarianism, acceptance of inequality, the welfare state as a limited safety net, and nationalism.[78]

Giddens has described the central values of the Third Way as being: equality, protection of the vulnerable, freedom as autonomy, no rights without responsibilities, no authority without democracy, cosmopolitan pluralism, and philosophic conservatism.[79] In constitutional terms this manifests itself in a commitment to "democratizing democracy"[80] through decentralisation, devolution, greater transparency, increased efficiency, and mechanisms of direct democracy.[81] It also requires the reinvigoration of civil society and respect for local autonomy. The collapse of socialism as a form of economic management has meant that one of the principal divisions between left and right in politics has now gone. Capitalism is accepted as the basic form of economic organisation. There are, however, still real differences as to how far it should be regulated, and the centre-left still views equality and social justice as of paramount concern.[82]

This is but the barest outline of some of the values underlying the Third Way. This is not the place for any detailed evaluation of the claims made by its proponents. There have been critics of the Third Way, from both the left and right of the political spectrum, who are sceptical about this vision of society either from a theoretical or from an empirical perspective.[83] It should however be recognised that many of the policies implemented by the Labour government reflected the values of the Third Way, and provide more concrete evidence as to what it entails. These policies will be considered in detail within the relevant chapters of the book, but it is helpful to draw them together at this stage.

The major constitutional reforms introduced by the Labour government **1–052** are well known. Taken together the legislation on devolution, human rights, freedom of information, and reform of the House of Lords constitutes the most significant package of constitutional reform in the 20th century. The values enshrined in this legislation sit well with those which are part of the Third Way.

The major initiatives undertaken by the Labour government in relation to agencies, service delivery, regulation and local government are less well known. Certain features of these initiatives are worthy of note.

In economic terms, it is true that there is much which is a continuation of the previous government's thinking. Efficiency, contracting out to the

---

[77] A. Giddens, *The Third Way, The Renewal of Social Democracy* (Polity, 1998), 7.
[78] Giddens, *The Third Way*, n.77, 8.
[79] Giddens, *The Third Way*, n.77, 66.
[80] Giddens, *The Third Way*, n.77, 70.
[81] Giddens, *The Third Way*, n.77, 70–76.
[82] Giddens, *The Third Way*, n.77, 43–46.
[83] A. Giddens, *The Third Way and its Critics* (Polity, 2000), for an overview of some of these critiques, and a response to them.

market, benchmarking and the like are all still there. Advocates of the Third Way are, however, not opposed to market based reforms of central bureaucracy, nor are they against efficiency being used as an important criterion for institutional design. They do oppose the belief that market based solutions should always be regarded as best, and regard competitive based solutions as but one of the options which should be pursued. It is interesting to see these ideas being worked out in the Labour policies on, for example, service delivery and regulation. Compulsory competitive tendering has been abolished and replaced by a new approach based on Better Value, which has itself been recently modified. It is clear that efficiency and competition are still important considerations in the new order, but it is equally clear that they are not the sole considerations.

In broader social and political terms, it is clear that the Labour government's initiatives in relation to local government, the governance of London and the like are attempting to revitalise local government in a way which has not been done for many a year. There have been interesting and important innovations designed to enhance local autonomy, facilitate participation and render local government more effective. These reforms can properly be regarded as a concrete expression of some of the ideas found in more abstract terms in the literature on the Third Way. This is not to say that one should be complacent. More could undoubtedly be done, especially in relation to the development of social rights, including the constitutionalisation of such rights.[84]

B. Implications for Administrative Law

1–053   It is clear that the legislation enacted by the Labour government has had a profound impact on administrative law. Process rights have been enhanced in certain areas. Judicial review has, as we have seen, been fundamentally affected by the passage of the Human Rights Act 1998. The courts are also facing new challenges as a result of the legislation on devolution. The very success of the devolution experiment will be dependent in part on the attitude which the courts take to challenges to the competence of the Welsh Assembly or the Scottish Parliament. It will be for the courts to adjudicate on the freedom of information legislation. The judiciary will, moreover, face challenging issues in the legislation on service delivery, which is couched in broad, open textured terms.

7. Conclusion

1–054   It should be made clear that it is perfectly possible to proffer interpretations of a general approach based upon rights, legality and abuse of power other

---

[84] K. Ewing, "Social Rights and Constitutional Law" [1999] P.L. 104.

than those considered above. It might for example be argued that we should foster a participatory democracy, meaning some version of republicanism[85] or communitarianism, which has its origins in Athenian democracy. This is a specific democratic vision, with a certain view of the relationship of citizen and state. It has implications for rights, socio-economic conditions within society and for distributive justice. There are in certain respects connections between this theory and the Third Way discussed above. The virtues of rival theories will always be contested, as will the degree to which they are consonant with the way in which society is currently ordered.

---

[85] Tomkins, n.55.

CHAPTER 2

THE ADMINISTRATIVE SYSTEM: AN HISTORICAL PERSPECTIVE

1. INTRODUCTION

The institutions subject to administrative law include the executive, agen- **2–001**
cies, quangos, local authorities, tribunals, inquiries and inferior courts. This
list is not exhaustive.[1] The discussion which follows is not an exhaustive
historical analysis of each of these institutions. It is rather a sketch of some
of the main themes in their development. Details as to the workings of
government, agencies, local authorities and the like will be considered in
subsequent chapters.

An understanding of the antecedents of our administrative institutions is
important. It enables us to comprehend how the existing institutions have
developed and acts as a counterweight to the often unspoken assumption
that current difficulties are generated by the present or immediate past. The
20th century may well have produced some novel problems. Nevertheless,
there is an underlying continuity in the difficulties of administrative organisation, which can only be fully appreciated from an historical perspective.
There is, moreover, something faintly absurd about discussing administrative law with only the vaguest idea of how its subject-matter evolved.

2. THE 19TH CENTURY

A. Industrialisation and the Growth of Central Regulation

We have always had a somewhat messy system of administrative institu- **2–002**
tions. Bodies would be created to deal with particular problems as they

[1] This phrase is not intended to imply that the allocation of functions between institutions was
guided by some rational plan.

arose with little thought being given to any rational allocation of decision-making. Many administrative functions were, and are, performed by the local justices of the peace, while others were undertaken by institutions such as the Commissioners of Sewers, or Turnpike Trustees. The limited size and scope of central government in the 19th century must be kept very much in the forefront of one's mind. In 1833 the central departments of government employed 21,305 civilian officials of which the vast majority worked in the Revenue departments. The Home Office had a staff of 29, the Foreign Office 39, and the Board of Trade 25.[2] This was hardly the staff necessary for running a state which performed anything other than the minimum of governmental functions.

The size of central government in 1833 was not, however, simply a reflection of the more limited role played by the state in the 19th century. Political parties and pressure groups, albeit for differing and often contradictory reasons, favoured the limitation of central government.[3]

The Tories disliked expansion of central government, since this would often impinge upon the autonomy possessed by local squires and magistrates. Nor was this jealousy of local interests confined to the countryside. In areas controlled by Whigs there was a similar dislike of central influence encroaching upon local power. The Radicals had their own reasons for wishing the authority of central government to remain limited. Such expansion was often seen to be the vehicle for the creation of new sinecures and monetary waste.

In addition there were those who were influenced by the writings of Ricardo and Adam Smith. They expounded the doctrines of laissez-faire economics in contrast to the mercantilism of the 18th century. The new industrialists saw in such theories a conceptual basis on which to resist governmental encroachment upon private property, whether in the form of projected factory legislation limiting hours and conditions of work or in schemes for improving health.

Private groups also resisted expansion of central authority in areas that would involve a correlative diminution of their own power. Thus voluntary institutions, schools and hospitals provided further institutional pressure opposed to the growth of central government.

2–003   Despite this opposition there was a considerable expansion in the functions performed by central government in the period between 1830 and 1850. There was increased central regulation in four main areas: factories, the Poor Law, railways and public health.[4] The advocates of these reforms had different objectives. In the most general sense, however, the reforms were all the result of the growing industrialisation, which was such a mark

---

[2] D. Roberts, *Victorian Origins of the British Welfare State* (Yale University Press, 1960), 14–16.
[3] Roberts, n.2, 22–34. See also, W. Lubenow, *The Politics of Government Growth: Early Victorian Attitudes toward State Intervention 1833–1848* (David and Charles, 1971); Sir D.N. Chester, *The English Administrative System 1780–1870* (Oxford University Press, 1981).
[4] See Roberts, n.2, Chs 2–3, Lubenow, n.3, Chs 2–5, D. Fraser, *Evolution of the British Welfare State: A History of Social Policy since the Industrial Revolution* (Macmillan, 1973), Chs 1–4.

of the 19th century. For the administrative lawyer they are of particular interest because they gave rise to forms of administrative control, and debates over the appropriateness of public institutions that are still very much current today. A word about the reforms themselves is, therefore, necessary in order that the institutional question can be better understood.

Factory reform was the result of the efforts of Oastler, Ashley and Sadler. Oastler was the agent for a landowner in Yorkshire whose humanitarian instincts were severely shocked after witnessing the conditions in Bradford's textile mills. This prompted him to write a letter to the Leeds Mercury comparing the lot of the textile worker with that of the Negro slave. Oastler's tone is fierce.[5]

"[T]he very streets which receive droppings of an 'Anti-Slavery Society' are every morning wet by the tears of innocent victims of the accursed shrine of avarice, who are compelled (not by the coach-whip of the negro slave driver) but by the dread of the equally appalling throng or strap of the overlooker, to hasten, half-dressed, but not half-fed, to those magazines of British infantile slavery—the worsted mills in the town and neighbourhood of Bradford!!!"

Oastler was an Evangelical. So was Thomas Sadler who took up Oastler's cry in the House. Opposition to the demand for legislation on children in factories came from a variety of sources. The factory owners were, not surprisingly, averse to the scheme and sought support from the economic literature current at the time. Sadler was unmoved by such "scientific" reasoning, but his attempts to enact legislation were cut short by defeat in a Leeds election in 1832. Ashley took up the banner of reform. His own bill failed in 1832 but, largely as a consequence of a report produced by Sadler and the report of a subsequent commission headed by Edwin Chadwick, the Whig Government produced its own measure which was enacted as the Factory Act 1833.

While opposition to the passage of factory legislation had been strong, it did not equal the passions roused by the debate over the Poor Law. Prior to the 19th century the Poor Law was governed by the Poor Relief Act 1601. This legislation had been designed to deal differently with the aged or lunatic, the able-bodied unemployed and the able-bodied who had absconded from their own area. The idea was that the first group would be looked after, the second would be set to work and the third group would be punished. Administration was to be through the justices of the peace, who were authorised to appoint overseers of the poor. The latter would levy a rate on property in their area, which fund would then be used to carry out the functions connected with the three different groups. The system however came under pressure, most significantly because of unemployment in the late 18th century combined with bad harvests and rising prices, the result being that the wages of those in employment became deficient to meet basic needs.

---

[5] Fraser, n.4, 233.

2–004   The early decades of the 19th century witnessed increasing dissatisfaction with the old Poor Law. Two general themes lay behind the disquiet. The first was the cost. In the years 1817 to 1819 the Poor Law cost £8 million, or 12s per head of the population; by 1831 it was still £7 million or in excess of 10s per head. Moreover, the cost had not yielded the benefits of social stability.[6] The second pressure for reform came from those who believed that the old Poor Law was simply wrong, particularly the allowance system of which Speenhamland was an example. This was the age of Malthus and Ricardo. The former with his dire predictions about population growth exceeding food supplies gave ammunition to those who saw the Poor Law as encouraging hasty marriages and then providing support for their numerous offspring. Ricardo authored the wage fund theory under which only a fixed percentage of the national wealth could be expended on wages. It was then argued that the sums expended on poor relief could not be spent on wages, thereby creating an inexorable downward spiral in wages with more and more people being forced to become paupers.

The new Poor Law was born out of the Poor Law Report of 1834, the work of Edwin Chadwick and Nassau Senior. The workhouse test which emerged from the Report was to provide much material for later Victorian literature. For Chadwick, however, the logic of the argument was unassailable. The old Poor Law, and particularly the allowance system, had simply encouraged idlers who could have worked. Poor relief had to be rendered less attractive than any other option; only in this way could the truly needy, the pauper, be catered for. The workhouse test, the idea that relief would only be available in a workhouse, was simply an adjunct of this philosophy. The Poor Law should not be concerned with poverty as reflected in low wages, but with destitution.[7] It should be a deterrent to pauperism. The idea that there could be workers who through no fault of their own were rendered unemployed was recognised by the authors of the report, but it was treated as an exception, an extreme to be dealt with by private charity and not by government intervention. The Poor Law Amendment Act was passed in 1834.

Health was a third area subject to governmental intervention. Growing industrialisation brought an increasing realisation of the health hazards that attend the presence of large groups of people with inadequate sanitary facilities. It was the organising genius of Chadwick that provided the main impetus towards reform. During his time as Secretary of the Poor Law Commission Chadwick became aware that a certain proportion of the expenditure on poor relief was being devoted to the widows and offspring of those struck down by disease. For Chadwick the realisation of this connection demanded prophylactic measures to stem the root cause of disease.[8] His belief in the necessity for sanitary improvement found its most complete expression in the 1842 Report on the Sanitary Condition of the Labouring

---

[6] Fraser, n.4, 38.
[7] Fraser, n.4, 41–42.
[8] S. Finer, *The Life and Times of Edwin Chadwick* (Methuen, 1952), 155.

Population of Great Britain. The Report showed the clear correlation between living conditions and disease. The Chadwick Report was followed by the appointment in 1843 of a Royal Commission under the Duke of Buccleuch. The study undertaken by the Royal Commission confirmed many of the findings of the Chadwick Report, but went further in detailed and systematic investigation.

Despite the weight of evidence indicating the need for reform, opposition to change came from a number of sources, which rendered the 1848 Public Health Act much less effective than its advocates had initially hoped. The rationale for the opposition varied. Some objected to the cost involved. Whereas the Poor Law reforms had resulted in cost savings compared with the allowance system, implementation of the Public health programme would involve considerable expense. Expense moreover which would be borne in greater proportion by the wealthier inhabitants of an area. Arguments concerning interference with property rights thus became involved in the general debate. These concerns were overlaid by the continuing disagreement as to the correct division of function between central and local government. The spectre of a London based bureaucracy dictating how much expenditure local areas should incur was not pleasing to the bastions of the reformed municipal boroughs. As a result of these pressures the 1848 Public Health Act emerged as a shadow of the original proposals. The legislation suffered from being generally permissive rather than obligatory in character. It was to take another 30 years before the Public Health Acts 1872 and 1875 introduced obligations to be fulfilled by sanitary authorities across the nation. **2–005**

Pressures for governmental action did not come solely from considerations of health or welfare. New technology produced novel problems, one of the most important of which was the development of railways. The motives for state intervention were eclectic.[9] A principal reason for state action was the fear of monopoly and the ability to charge excessive prices which accompanied it. The competitive process would in its self-regulating manner normally be expected to break down monopolistic dominance and restore competitive equilibrium. In this, as in other areas, the magic wand of market forces appeared less than effective. This was partly due to the nature of the industry, with only one company serving on one route. The edge of the competitive process was further blunted by the frequency of price fixing engaged in by rival companies, thereby providing an example of Adam Smith's belief as to what occurred when businessmen met together. Gladstone was certainly less than sanguine as to the efficacy of the competitive process:[10]

"It was said, let matters . . . be allowed to go on as at present, and let the country trust to the effects of competition. Now, for his part, he would

---

[9] H. Parris, *Government and the Railways in Nineteenth Century Britain* (Routledge and Kegan Paul, 1965), Lubenow, n.3, Ch.4.
[10] Quoted in Lubenow, n.3, 129.

rather give his confidence to a Gracchus, when speaking on the subject of sedition, than give his confidence to a Railway Director, when speaking to the public of the effects of competition."

Fear of monopoly was but one reason prompting state intervention. Safety was another. A number of the problems were purely technical though of some concern to the ordinary traveller. Braking power, for example, was not the strong point of early railway transportation. Nor were track or signalling anywhere near pristine condition. Such mechanical problems were compounded by managerial decisions the correctness of which was not always immediately self-evident. To the problems of monopoly and safety was added that of over-speculation. The railway mania of the 1840s brought forth a rash of projects and speculation. Companies were often under-funded and exceeded their statutory borrowing limit. The result was the passage of a series of Acts in the 1840s and thereafter regulating various aspects of railway development, some of the details of which will be examined below.

Factory legislation, health, the Poor Law and railways represent four of the main areas in which the state intervened. They do not in any sense represent the totality of legislative intervention. A glance through Holdsworth[11] indicates the range and diversity of enactments passed at various times during the 19th century which regulated directly or indirectly wide areas of economic and social activity. There was legislation on mining, chimney sweeps, contagious animals, and building to name but a few. Trades such as chemists, doctors, peddlers and public houses were subject to increasing regulation. Both sides of industry, capital and labour, were the subject of legislative intervention albeit in very different ways.

B. The Machinery of Administration

i. The Board system

2–006 Until relatively recently it was common to think of new governmental functions being assigned to existing ministries, or to ministries created specifically for that purpose. The term ministry is used here to denote a department of state, where the power is vested in a single person who sits in one of the Houses of Parliament and is responsible to Parliament for departmental action. However ministerial government was not the standard procedure in the 19th century, or at least not in the first half thereof. The more common form of administration in the 18th and 19th centuries was the Board system. The precise structure and powers of Boards differed from area to area. What they possessed in common was a degree of independence from direct parliamentary control, although a minister might be answerable for part of their business.[12]

---

[11] *A History of English Law* (Methuen, 1965), Vol. 15 6–93.
[12] I have taken this formulation from F. Willson, "Ministries and Boards: some aspects of Administrative Development since 1832" (1955) 33 Pub. Adm. 43, 44.

The Board system was not an unusual form of administration in the 18th and early 19th centuries. It was an integral and accepted part of the machinery of government. A number of factors contributed towards its use.[13] For the Crown, the Board pattern possessed advantages over ministers. The latter could be too strong or too weak, either of which could be disadvantageous. Positions on Boards could be a useful source of patronage. They allowed greater continuity of policy, being less affected by the ebbs and flows of political change, and they were more flexible to the particular needs of decentralised administration. Developments within the constitutional balance of power did, however, place stresses on this form of organisation. As Parris states,[14]

"The system worked well so long as boards were responsible in fact as well as in name to the King. But once the executive became primarily responsible to parliament, the system came under strain. The result was a decline in the board pattern of administration and its supersession to a large degree by a ministerial pattern."

The reasons for the Boards' decline were part practical and part conceptual. Practical reasons for dissatisfaction were related to inefficiency. Large numbers on Boards could lead to ineffective management and waste. These practical problems were not, however, the prime cause for the decline in the use of Boards. Such difficulties could well be present if the administration were to be carried out by a ministry. The real cause of their decline was the altered constitutional position highlighted by the quotation from Parris. Parliament wished to control government action. At the least this required someone answerable in the House, a person responsible for the actions of the Board. This was particularly the case with controversial activities. When the Poor Law Commission was created in 1834 none of the Board members could sit in Parliament. Communication was naturally extremely difficult. Parliament became frustrated due to the absence of a person who could be rendered directly answerable. The Commissioners themselves suffered through having no direct way of defending themselves against personal attack or vilification. The Commission was, as a result, replaced by a ministry in 1847. The experience of Poor Law administration sent shock waves through other areas.

A middle way which was tried was to have one or more members of the Board with a seat in Parliament. This was adopted for the Board of Woods, Forests and Land Revenues, to be followed in the case of the General Board of Health. The experiment was not a noted success, largely because two crucial elements of the scheme were unclear: the relationship of the parlia-

[13] See generally, Roberts, n.2, Ch.4; Willson, n.12; H. Parris, *Constitutional Bureaucracy: The Development of British Central Administration since the Eighteenth Century* (Allen & Unwin, 1968), Ch.3.
[14] *Constitutional Bureaucracy* (1968), 83. See, G. Le May, *The Victorian Constitution: Conventions, Usages and Contingencies* (Duckworth, 1979), for a stimulating discussion of nineteenth century political development.

mentary member to the rest of the Board and the relationship with Parliament.

Dissatisfaction with this constitutional no man's land led to one of two results. The Board was either converted into a formal ministry, or a minister was made directly responsible for the activity of a Board. Gradually the paradigm of the modern ministry evolved: a minister running a department, and responsible to Parliament. The corollary was the development of civil service anonymity. This concept, with which we are now so familiar, only really developed in the mid-19th century. It was quite common, prior to that time, for civil servants to voice their views. This was not surprising when placed within the overall context of the Board system. It was the growth of individual ministerial responsibility for departmental policy that led the bureaucracy to develop its protective cloak.

A glance at the powers possessed by some of the Boards is, however, instructive. The Board system has revived this century. The problems presented by the range of powers exercised by these modern agencies have attracted public attention. A brief review of the powers held by the 19th-century Boards will help to place the modern problem in context. Reference will also be made to powers wielded by ministries where the comparison is apposite.

ii. Powers of Boards

2–007 Generalisation concerning the powers wielded by Boards is difficult. They were established to deal with diverse problems and the powers granted to them reflected that divergence. The difficulty is compounded by the need to distinguish between those powers granted to a Board and those which they actually exercised. The two could often differ substantially, with the Boards using powers which in a strict sense they did not possess. Given this diversity the matter is best approached by way of example, with comparisons being made to other institutions where appropriate.

The Poor Law Commission established under the Poor Law Amendment Act 1834 established a three-man Commission, which was independent of Parliament. As an example of a 19th-century Board it is particularly interesting, both in terms of the breadth of its powers and the limitations placed thereon. Its strengths lay in the fact that it could, in modern parlance, both make rules and adjudicate. It could make rules and regulations concerning the direction and management of the poor, the appointment of local officers and the government of workhouses. Breach of the rules could lead to a prosecution and an order of mandamus from the courts. General rules, defined as those applicable to more than one union at a time, had to be sanctioned by a Principal Secretary of State and by Parliament. However as Roberts makes clear the Commissioners adopted a technique which has been used by subsequent agencies in similar positions,[15]

---

[15] Roberts, n.2, 110.

"Special orders to a single union needed no such confirmation, a fact which the hard pressed commissioners anxious to avoid delay, exploited to the fullest, issuing general regulations individually as special rules."

After 1844 the powers were augmented to include the appointment of auditors, the granting of money to school teachers and medical officers, and the establishment of schools for pauper children. The wide range of powers possessed by the Commission led Roberts to state that it was the "prototype for the administrative bureaus of the future" with discretionary power to legislate and grant aid.[16]

Despite these extensive powers the Poor Law Commission's authority was limited in a number of ways. The legislation of 1834 reflected the Victorian balance between central and local government. The Commissioners could determine the qualification and duties of local Poor Law guardians, but the latter were elected by those eligible within that locality. The central Board could only alter the mode of appointment and order removal of the guardians with the consent of the rate-payers and property owners of a parish. It was the local guardians who appointed the paid officers who would actually administer the relief, subject to confirmation by the Poor Law Commission. Practical difficulties of enforcement must be added to legislative restriction of the Commission's powers. The Commissioners were entitled to appoint assistants to aid in the implementation of the legislation, but all too often the numbers were insufficient for the area assigned to them. Visits to local guardians but once a year were little deterrent to those unions that treated their inmates badly.

While the precise ambit of a Board or department's powers differed, they **2–008** nevertheless possessed certain features in common. Speaking of the 16 new departments with nation-wide responsibilities which existed in 1854 Roberts states,[17]

"All . . . could inspect local authorities and publish reports on them. Most could order prosecutions if local officials or industrialists violated those laws established for their regulation. Three of the central agencies could draw up and enforce their own rules and regulations, and nine of them could confirm the rules and regulations drawn up by local officials . . . Ten of the departments could hold hearings and pass judgments on matters in dispute, and three could license or certify local institutions, such as hospitals for the insane and prison cells for the criminal. Only three agencies enjoyed the power of dispensing grants of money to local authorities. Six could insist that local authorities keep registers of perti-

---

[16] Roberts, n.2, 110–111.
[17] N.2, 106. The 16 departments of which Roberts speaks are the Prison Inspectorate, the Mining Inspectorate, the Factory Inspectorate, the Anatomy Inspectorate, the Burial Inspectorate, the Poor Law Board, the General Board of Health, the Charity Commission, the Lunacy Commission, the Railway Department, the Merchant Marine Department, the Emigration Office, the Tithe, Inclosure and Copyhold Commission, the Department of Science and Art, the Ecclesiastical Commission, and the Education Committee.

nent information and almost all could demand that local authorities send in periodical releases on their activities."

Three more general points should be made to place matters in perspective. First, even where an addition to the administrative machinery was not a Board, but a sub-department of for example the Home Office, there was often nonetheless a good deal of independence in the administration of the policy in that area. The classic example of this is the working of the Home Office inspectorates. Factory, prison, mining and burial inspectors all came under the aegis of the Home Office.[18] Nineteenth-century papers of successive Home Secretaries are, however, replete with statements concerning the impossibility of the workload that this thereby thrust upon them. Even the tireless Palmerston despaired of ever reading the prison inspectors' reports.

Second, whether one is talking about Boards *stricto sensu*, or whether one is including some ministries too, it is clear that merely looking at the relevant statute to determine the ambit of their powers can be misleading. It is apparent, for example, that a number of Boards and ministries made and applied rules in circumstances where their ability to do so in general terms was debatable, or where the particular rule which they sought to enforce may well have been outside the ambit of their powers. The evidence for such rule-making, and its relevance for the modern debate over agencies, will be considered later.[19]

Third, while the precise reasons for the establishment of Boards in the 19th century and the expansion of agencies in the 20th might have differed, they did overlap in part. This bears testimony to the continuing problems of administrative organisation in a state which undertook an increasingly wide range of regulatory functions. To quote from Roberts once again,[20]

"The Victorians' experiments in semi-independent, non political boards reflected their fear that administrative decision would be made the handmaid of party bias or be caught in the maelstrom of factional politics. The Poor Law Commission was the classic and tragic example of such an attempt."

C. The Rationale for Administrative Growth

2–009   What were the main forces underlying the rapid administrative growth which characterised the 19th century? And how is this expansion to be squared with a view of that century as an age of laissez-faire? Opinions among historians continue to differ on this.

Some regard talk of an age of laissez-faire as misleading. For Holdsworth it possessed only peripheral relevance in matters of trade,[21] and Kitson

---

[18] See the useful diagrammatic representation in Roberts, n.2, 93–95.
[19] See below, Chs 4, 22.
[20] N.2, 133.
[21] *A History of English Law* (Methuen, 1965), Vol. 15, 6–93.

Clark believed that talk of a "period of laissez-faire" was unhelpful.[22] Whether it is meaningful to talk of an age of laissez-faire at all is something which continues to divide authorities on the subject.[23] Inextricably linked with this question is the relationship between Benthamite utilitarianism, laissez-faire and state intervention. For Dicey the utilitarian ideal of the greatest happiness of the greatest number was to be achieved by laissez-faire policies; the one implied the other. This verdict has been stood upon its head by subsequent authors, some of whom have gone so far as to see Benthamite theory as a direct catalyst of state intervention.[24] Others have followed Halevy's[25] lead in distinguishing between economic affairs, in which Utilitarianism presupposed a laissez-faire ideology, and social policy in which state intervention was necessary to secure the requisite harmony of interests.

While this is not the place to enter into a full discussion of these contending views each is in need of qualification. The Halevy approach presumes that one can see a reflection of his view in the type of reforms actually adopted in the mid-19th century. Yet while the Poor Law, factory inspection and public health had clear social implications, they also had economic reverberations, as the arguments of the advocates and opponents of these schemes makes apparent. Maintenance of the social-economic dichotomy is even more problematic when viewed against the background of, for example, price regulation of common carriers and public utilities. The polar opposite conclusions reached by Dicey and Brebner also appear too extreme. While Bentham's economic writings may have been based upon laissez-faire principles, he admitted exceptions, as indeed did the classical economists. For Bentham, while the basic premise might have been that the greatest good of the greatest number could be best attained without legislative meddling, this was not in the nature of an a priori truth, but more in the form of an empirical hypothesis. With the growing evils of industrialisation state intervention could well be necessary to attain the utilitarian aim.

Underlying the discussion thus far is an unspoken premise. This is that utilitarian ideology did in fact play a significant role in the administrative growth which characterised the 19th century. This premise has in itself been challenged by two different views, each of which ascribes minimal importance to the emergent doctrines of Utilitarianism.

MacDonagh[26] sees the expansion of government organs in much more **2–010** functional and less ideological terms. He develops a model of governmental growth which has five stages. In the first some social evil is exposed. This could be by the adventitious discovery of factory conditions by Oastler, the

[22] *An Expanding Society: Britain 1830–1900* (Cambridge University Press, 1967), 162.
[23] For a balanced account of the contending arguments see A. Taylor, *Laissez-faire and State Intervention in Nineteenth-Century Britain* (Macmillan, 1972).
[24] J. Brebner, "Laissez-faire and State Intervention in Nineteenth-Century Britain" (1948) 8 Journal of Economic History 59.
[25] *The Growth of Philosophical Radicalism* (Faber & Gwyer, 1928).
[26] "The Nineteenth-Century Revolution in Government: A Reappraisal" (1958) I The Historical Journal 52. See also, O. MacDonagh's, *A Pattern of Government Growth: The Passenger Acts and Their Enforcement, 1800–60* (MacGibbon & Kee, 1961).

outbreak of an epidemic, or a sudden tragedy such as the collapse of a mine. In some such way this brought the tragedy to the public attention, producing a demand in some quarters for change to end the intolerable situation. Support for legislative intervention was met by opposition, the result being a legislative measure much less efficacious than its original proponents had hoped. Stage two was a realisation that the original legislation, enacted as a result of this process of compromise, was indeed ineffective in its present form. The response was the grant of additional powers, the provision of summary legal procedures and most importantly, the development of an inspectorate to supervise the administration of the legislation. With the creation of an inspectorate (or some other form of executive enforcement) came stage three. Additional information became available as a result of inspectors' reports. An awareness of the problems at the grass roots evolved. This growing awareness led to demands for further legislation in order to close gaps that investigation had revealed, and also pressure towards a stronger, more centralised bureaucracy. The fourth stage witnessed a change of attitude by those who administered the system with the realisation that the "problems" with which they were dealing could not be solved once and for all. New legislation to plug loopholes in old was met by novel methods of circumventing the amended rules. Administration ceased to be a static concept and developed into a dynamic process. The final stage witnessed the further augmentation of the administration's powers, both in terms of the ability to impose penalties and to devise regulations. Investigation became more systematic and scientific, more professional.

The MacDonagh thesis has not gone unchallenged. Parris[27] tested the MacDonagh thesis against various types of administrative growth in the 19th century and found that the facts did not fit the model. He also disagreed with the role or lack of it that MacDonagh accorded to Benthamite ideology. As Parris pointed out, it is indeed difficult to discern how many people knew or were influenced by utilitarian thought. He argued moreover that MacDonagh overemphasised the anti-collective strain within Benthamism: the application of the principle of utility could lead to laissez-faire or state intervention depending upon the subject matter. For Parris, therefore, 19th-century government development should be seen as a function both of organic change and contemporary political and ideological thought, one of the main currents of which was Benthamism.[28]

No doubt the debate over the 19th-century revolution in government will continue. As with most such revolutions the rationale for its occurrence was probably eclectic as both Parris[29] and Fraser assert.[30] Administrative momentum, political ideology, laissez-faire and Utilitarianism all had their role to play, as did more fortuitous factors such as the political personalities

[27] "The Nineteenth-Century Revolution in Government: A Reappraisal Reappraised" (1960) III The Historical Journal 17.
[28] For a different view, see Lubenow, n.3.
[29] N.27.
[30] N.4, Ch.5.

comprising the government of the day and the presence of figures such as Chadwick and Simon.

D. Local Government

"A fundamental antithesis between centralisation and 'autonomous' decentralisation runs through the whole history of English government and its organisation. It is an antithesis that underlies every polity, but especially that of England, where the origin and building up of the nation give it an unparalleled importance. Indeed, among the primary causes which have governed the process of differentiating the early legal notions and institutions of the nation this conflict plays a leading part."[31]

2–011

We have already seen how the balance between central and local administration affected the shape and pattern of 19th-century reform. Thus far we have considered this development primarily from the perspective of the central government. The 19th century also witnessed fundamental reform in the character of local government. Many administrative functions were performed at local level. A closer look at the transformation of local government is therefore integral to an understanding of the overall pattern of administration.

The balance between central and local administration runs throughout our history; it is evident far earlier than the 19th century. The centralising tendencies of the Norman administration were offset to some extent by the creation of the office of justice of the peace under Edward III. These were appointees of the Crown drawn from the county or town over which they had jurisdiction. Originally their main role was to preserve the peace, but this was augmented by later legislation. An increasing range of regulatory activities were committed to their charge, such as the statutes of labourers and the supervision of the Poor Law.

The precise degree of control exercised by the central authority varied. Powers of appointment and dismissal of justices of the peace could be used to exert Crown influence. It was, however, the Tudors who attempted to extend central influence most forcefully. There were a number of different aspects of this policy. Privy Council supervision over the justices was increased, particularly by the Star Chamber. The traditional machinery of local administration was threatened by the creation of new local machinery more directly under the aegis of the centre, such as the Councils of the North. The grant of municipal charters of incorporation came to be used as a device through which the Crown exercised control over those sitting in Parliament. In the 16th century a large number of charters were granted to a narrow select body of the town. This was supposed to personify the bur-

---

[31] J. Redlich and F. Hirst, *The History of Local Government in England* (Macmillan, 2nd edn, 1970), 12. The book was originally printed in 1903. The second edition, with an introduction and epilogue by Keith-Lucas contains only Book I from the original work.

gesses, but in fact the main group of such burgesses was excluded from participation in government.[32] The select body could perpetuate itself by co-opting new members and thus began the reign of the narrow oligarchy in municipal life that was to persist until the 19th century. For the Crown the benefit resided in the greater ease with which the municipalities could be bribed or bullied into electing representatives to Parliament who would be subservient to the Crown.

2–012   Local autonomy increased in the 18th century. The events of the 17th century had profound effects upon the balance between central and local administration. The Star Chamber was abolished, the Bill of Rights (1689) was passed, parliamentary authority was increased and local power augmented. The legacy of earlier abuses however lived on. While the fate of Charles I, Charles II and James II added to the power of Parliament and reduced the central administration's hold on local authority, the corrupt nature of local politics continued unaltered. Nor is this surprising. As Redlich and Hirst observe,[33]

"Town franchises were preserved with all their anomalies and confusion. After two centuries of growth Select Bodies received Parliamentary recognition, and the municipal was confirmed by the political oligarchy. The reason is not far to seek. The ruling classes having conquered, as they thought the King, had no wish to see the basis upon which their own rule rested extended, or the balance of constitutional power again altered. They had come into a King's inheritance and they intended to enjoy it."

It was to be over 100 years before they were forced to share their legacy. The catalyst for change in municipal government was reform of the parliamentary franchise in the Reform Act 1832. The legislation was not radical in its immediate effects. Even after its passage less than 5 per cent of the populace could vote. Its main short-term effect was to bring the better off within the towns under the parliamentary franchise, by allowing the vote to the £10 householder. In the long term its impact was far greater. The old system of parliamentary franchise may have been illogical and unjust, but it was at least strengthened by the very weight of history. The post-1832 system, whatever its framers felt, was based on no real principle at all. It was difficult to think of reasons of principle why the £5 householder should not be admitted to the vote too.

Extension of the franchise produced ramifications in municipal government which came to fruition in the Municipal Corporations Act 1835. In 1833 a Royal Commission was appointed to investigate, inter alia, the defects in municipal corporations. The ills of municipal government were related with vigour. Specific examples of financial corruption were cited, as were the more general ills attendant upon a system in which power was concentrated in few hands and used for personal advantage. Inefficiency was

[32] Redlich and Hirst, n.31, 28-29.
[33] Redlich and Hirst, n.31, 37.

added to peculation. Because so many municipal corporations were poorly administered, independent boards had developed to provide particular services. This produced divided authority, jealousy and squabbling between the different bodies. Inefficiency in the provision of services at a local level might at least have been tolerated by central government. Local disorder would not. Considerable disquiet was voiced at the inability of the local authorities to prevent riots and preserve the peace.

It would, however, be mistaken to see the passage of the 1835 Act as solely derived from Whig desires to end corruption. The Municipal Corporations Act 1835 was at least as much concerned with party advantage. As Fraser explains,[34]

"Since the freemen and other ancient rights voters were to retain the Parliamentary vote for their lifetimes, and since the majority of corporate towns were still to return MPs, this left in the hands of the corporations considerable electoral power which, if past experience was followed, they were likely to use extensively and in a corrupt manner for the Tory interest in Parliamentary elections . . . The preservation of this electoral power would thus have frustrated the aims of the 1832 reform, and as The Times explained in 1833, 'the fact is that Parliamentary reform, if it were not to include Corporation reform likewise, would have been literally a dead letter.'"

The Municipal Corporations Act 1835 extended the vote to all those who had resided and paid rates in the borough for three years. One quarter of the council was comprised of aldermen who were elected by the council. Towns that were not yet incorporated could petition the Crown for a charter of incorporation. The effect of doing so was to render the 1835 Act applicable.

In conjunction with the Reform Act 1832, the Municipal Corporations Act 1835 laid the foundations for urban middle class involvement in the political life of the country. For the Whigs there was the hope of extending their power base, both through an alliance between the landed gentry and urban middle class, and through the removal of the old municipal corporations most of which were Tory. From the Tories there was a mixed response. Peel in the Commons presented little opposition to the 1835 Act. This was the Peel of the Tamworth manifesto, accepting the need to reform flagrant abuses. Lord Lyndhurst, leading the Tories in the House of Lords, was more strident, fearing that the removal of the old corporate bastions would herald the advent of democracy. For the Radicals it was hoped that the 1835 Act would be but the first step. Joseph Parkes, the Secretary to the Royal Commission, speaking of the recent reforms in the parliamentary and municipal franchises, puts the matter in dramatic apocalyptic terms.[35]

2–013

---

[34] *Power and Authority in the Victorian City* (Blackwell, 1979), 5.
[35] Quoted in Fraser, n.34, 16.

"The Tories are burked, no resurrection for them. The Whigs . . . are an unnatural party standing between the People and the Tory aristocracy chiefly for the pecuniary value of the offices and the vanity of power. Their hearse is ordered."

The limits of the 1835 reform must, however, be borne in mind. The counties remained untouched, to be ruled by the squirearchy for another 50 years. Even after the reform of municipal corporations there was still considerable diversity in the bodies which would impinge upon local life. Two reasons contributed towards this, both of which have been mentioned in differing contexts.

The first was that, because of the previous inefficiency of the unreformed boroughs, municipal functions from paving to lighting, and from cleaning to the supply of water, had been undertaken by other bodies, such as improvement commissioners. The 1835 Act did not unify these duties within the reformed corporations. It simply enabled the corporations to take over such jobs. Second, while the very reform of municipal government tended to bolster, potentially at least, local as opposed to central power, other legislation produced the opposite effect. The Poor Law Amendment Act 1834 with its centralised administration provides an example of this.

2–014   Reform of the counties was longer in coming. Attempts at reform in the 1840s came to nothing. The justice of the peace continued as the main administrative and judicial organ. As the number of duties imposed upon the justices expanded, so also did the sphere of their summary jurisdiction. The counties could not, however, remain unreformed forever. Legislation in 1867 and 1884 had extended the parliamentary franchise. The former conferred household suffrage upon the inhabitants of parliamentary boroughs and rid the voting system of many anomalies; the latter broadened the borough franchise by the addition of a service vote and extended to the counties the household suffrage that already existed in the boroughs.

The Local Government Act 1888 was the early vehicle for county reform and by the turn of the century the pattern of local government had taken on the following form. The metropolis had a two-tier system with the London County Council at the top and metropolitan boroughs providing the second tier. County boroughs, the larger towns, were single purpose authorities. The counties were slightly more complex. The county council was the main authority for the area. Beneath it there were three types of institution: non-county boroughs; urban districts; and rural districts. The last of these could have parish councils within its area, thereby providing a third tier of authority. This system was to remain with little change until 1972.[36]

While the local franchise had been considerably widened the actual powers possessed by the local authorities were never clearly spelled out. We have already seen how the Municipal Corporations Act 1835 merely

[36] For the present position, see Ch.6.

empowered the borough to take over functions performed by other institutions. As Fraser states,[37]

"The lack of a clear legal prescription for corporate activity is the most important single factor to weigh against the Webbs' notion of a municipal revolution in 1835. Without adequate powers the councils were unable to fulfil the promise of municipal reform."

Those powers were obtained either by use of the empowering provisions of general legislation or by obtaining the passage of local legislation. By the end of the 19th century Parliament was dealing with over 300 such Acts per year.[38] Underlying the vagueness as to the ambit of the local authorities' powers was the recurring theme of the balance between the centre and the parts. A desire to demonstrate that central control was not needed played a part in the welter of local Acts secured during this period.[39] This tension between centralisation and decentralisation has not disappeared. It is endemic in our political and social system. The debate as to the precise balance is, as we shall see, a continuing one.[40]

E. The Evolution of Statutory Inquiries

While the emergence of statutory inquiries can be traced back earlier than the 19th century, it is during that period that the inquiry procedure really developed. The agricultural and industrial revolutions increased the occasion for conflict between individual and individual, or individual and government, whether central or local. The inquiry procedure was one of the mechanisms for resolving this conflict.[41]

2–015

An early example of its use is to be found in relation to inclosures.[42] Inclosure of land was normally achieved by the passage of a private Act of Parliament. Inclosure Commissioners would be appointed to consider the facts of a particular scheme, and objections thereto. The Inclosure Act 1801 provided for the appointment of an ad hoc commission of inquiry. The meetings of the commission were to be advertised and the public could make objections to the scheme or parts of it. The normal private Bill procedure was modified by the General Inclosure Act 1845. This provided for an expedited form of procedure. Normally a private Bill would have to be considered by a Committee of each House. The provisional order procedure enshrined in the 1845 Act provided for an inquiry by a person who could investigate the matter at its actual physical location. The application for the provisional order was made to the appropriate government department

---

[37] N.34, 164.
[38] N.34, 165.
[39] N.34, 165–166.
[40] See, Ch.6.
[41] R. Wraith and G. Lamb, *Public Inquiries as an Instrument of Government* (Allen and Unwin, 1971), Ch.2.
[42] Wraith and Lamb, n.41, 17–21.

which would appoint the inspector. Normally, a public inquiry would be held before a provisional order was made.[43] Much time could be saved by this procedure.

Inquiries were used in other areas besides that of inclosure. Local government was one of the main spheres. The Public Health Act 1875 empowered the Local Government Board to hold such inquiries as they thought fit in relation to any matters concerning the public health in any place, or any matter in respect of which their sanction was required by the Act.[44] While the inquiry was utilised in the areas of inclosure and health to resolve conflicts between individual and individual, or individual and state, it was also used for other purposes. Accidents were investigated through the holding of an inquiry, when they occurred in areas such as railways, coal mining and factories to name but three.

It has, however, been the expansion of governmental control over the use of land which has provided the main impetus for the expansion of inquiries in the 20th century. The problems thereby created will be examined in due course.[45] The development of our administrative system in the present century must now be charted.

3. The 20th Century

A. The Birth of the Welfare State and the Development of the Tribunal System

2–016 In 1906 the Liberal landslide produced a majority of 356. The next five years were to witness the introduction of a range of measures often regarded as the basis for the Welfare State.[46] Protection of children was enshrined in the Children's Act 1908 to be followed closely by the introduction of old age pensions in the same year. It was, however, the gestation and ultimate passage of what became the National Insurance Act 1911 that was most significant in the long term.

It was through the combined energies of Lloyd George and Winston Churchill that this measure made its way onto the statute book. There was no shortage of ideas as to the path which reform ought to take. The Royal Commission on the Poor Law, which sat from 1905 to 1909, contained a plethora of opinion. Representatives of the Local Government Board wished for a reversion to the principles of 1834: relief should be based upon less eligibility, and there was alarm at the variety of relief services outside of

---

[43] Under the General Inclosure Act 1845 the procedure was somewhat different. The Assistant Commissioner would hold a meeting to hear objections, the Provisional Order would be made, and then a second meeting would be held for considering objections.
[44] Wraith and Lamb, n.41, 23–25.
[45] See, Ch.9.
[46] See generally, J. Hay, *The Origins of the Liberal Welfare Reforms 1906–1914* (Macmillan, 1975); Fraser, n.30, Ch.7.

the provisions of the Poor Law. While the Majority Report of the Commission did not accept this draconian view, the signatories believed that a remodelled Poor Law could be the basis for future development. Although the terms "Poor Law" and "guardian" were dropped for those of public assistance and public assistance committees, the essential idea that poverty was primarily a personal or moral, as opposed to a social or an economic problem, was adhered to. Beatrice Webb's Minority Report advocated, by way of contrast, the scrapping of the Poor Law entirely and its replacement by a strong Ministry of Labour and the expenditure of public money in times of cyclical depression.

As it transpired Lloyd George adopted neither view, and had strong ideas of his own. Insurance was the key to Lloyd George's scheme and the means of 'dishing the Webbs'. Like Bismarck before him, Lloyd George and the Liberals saw a social insurance scheme as the method of reducing the socialist threat. An insurance scheme possessed other advantages. It would reduce the financial burden placed upon the state as compared with a completely non-contributory plan. It would be more acceptable to the people, since it would be based upon contribution and hence entitlement. The moral stigma attached to the reluctant grant of relief that characterised the Poor Law had become deeply etched upon the country's mentality. Part I of the National Insurance Act 1911 established the foundations of health insurance with contributions from the state, employer and employee.

While Lloyd George was piloting the passage of the health and sickness provisions, Churchill and the young Beveridge were working on unemployment. The Labour Exchanges Act 1909 was intended as one half of a two-pronged attack upon the problem. The other half was once again insurance. This was encapsulated in Pt II of the National Insurance Act 1911, which provided for tripartite contributions from employer, employee and the state. Little controversy attended the passage of this part of the Act as compared with the health provisions contained in Pt I. A result which is somewhat ironic given the benefit of hindsight, since it was the unemployment provisions which were to be placed under most strain in the ensuing years.

2–017

This new legislation required administration. It is in the Liberal enactments of this period that the modern tribunal system has its real roots. Individual tribunals had of course existed earlier than this. However the reforms necessitated the development of an administrative and adjudicative mechanism on a scale different from that which had gone before.

A variety of machinery was established, the constant theme being that the ordinary courts were kept in the background, for a number of reasons. The cost of using the ordinary courts would often be disproportionate to the amounts involved and the number of potential disputes would simply overburden them. There was also the feeling that the courts were just not the appropriate mechanism.[47] Certain judicial decisions on the early factory

---

[47] B. Abel-Smith and R. Stevens, *Lawyers and the Courts: A Sociological Study of the English Legal System 1750-1965* (Heinemann, 1967), 111–121.

legislation, concerning hours of work for children, had emasculated the legislative intent by upholding the legality of the relay system. The judiciary had not been happy with their role as arbiters of the reasonableness of railway charges, while experience of appellate involvement in the Workmen's Compensation Acts 1897 and 1906 had been far from successful. Trade union feeling that the ordinary courts were unsympathetic to their position, as evidenced by a series of decisions in the early 1900s, also militated against their use. The Liberal measures were therefore designed to avoid using the ordinary courts either for first instance adjudication or appeal.

2–018   Reforms continued during the inter-war years. The Ministry of Health was created in 1919 and extension of state involvement in education was enshrined in the Education Act 1918. It was, however, the problem of unemployment and depression that increasingly concerned governments during the 1920s and 1930s. The theme during this period was the de facto modification of the insurance principle that underpinned the 1911 legislation. While this was extended in scope by the Unemployment Insurance Act 1920 the insurance principle came under strain. Rising unemployment caused the quid pro quo of contribution for entitlement to become warped. Increasingly the insurance fund came to bear the weight intended to be borne by the Poor Law. Further inroads into the insurance principle were made as a result of the Blanesburgh Report of 1927. The effect of its recommendations was to dilute the balance between contribution and entitlement. Benefits were no longer to be limited in time; they were no longer realistically seen as the equivalent of contributions. Provided some contributions had been made, benefits could be drawn on the basis of need.[48] The dichotomy between insurance based and non-insurance based assistance was however partially restored by the Unemployment Act 1934.

War brought further changes in its train, exemplified by the publication of the Beveridge Report in 1942. This Report became a major document for social reform. Insurance was set in the wider context of the eradication of the five evils: Want, Disease, Ignorance, Squalor and Illness. To this end the idea was to have a single weekly contribution which would provide cover for sickness, medical needs, unemployment, widows, orphans, old age, maternity, funeral benefits and industrial injury. Contributions and benefits were both to be flat rate and not earnings-related. Subsistence was all that was to be guaranteed. Herein lay the seeds of future difficulty, since post-war Britain did not think simply of avoiding starvation, but of maintaining accustomed living standards when earnings were interrupted.[49]

What emerged from the post-war Labour Government was a scheme which reflected the essentials of the Beveridge proposals, although the details of contribution levels differed. Industrial injuries were treated separately in the National Insurance (Industrial Injuries) Act 1946, the main difference being that benefits were earnings related. Other benefits were dealt

---

[48] Fraser, n.4, 171–174.
[49] Fraser, n.4, 202.

with in the National Insurance Act 1946. Contributions and benefits were both to be flat rate. Why on moral grounds work-based injury should be treated differently from that resulting from other causes is something which has puzzled many for a long time. Alongside the insurance system was the National Assistance Board designed to provide a non-contributory sum for those who had used up their insurance entitlement, or who had never qualified for any.

The emergence and generalisation of the social insurance and assistance principles brought with it a corresponding growth in the tribunal system, since it was by this mechanism that disputes concerning entitlement were to be resolved. It should not, however, be thought that developments in welfare policy constituted the only reasons for the growth of our administrative system. The government has implemented regulatory legislation in many areas, which has often been enforced outside the traditional court system. Rent and transport tribunals provide but two examples. Tribunals have also been established to provide protection for the citizen, such as the Mental Health Review Tribunal, while others enforced legislation affecting a specific, if large, group of people such as the industrial tribunals. Yet others were concerned with the competitive process such as the Monopolies and Mergers Commission. The list could be considerably extended. Indeed one of the difficulties of compiling such a list is that there is no accurate definition of what constitutes a tribunal. Nor is there any hard and fast rule as to why decision-making should be allocated to a body called a tribunal, or for that matter a commission or an authority rather than somebody else.

2–019

What should be stressed is that the growth of tribunals has not been the only developing part of our administrative system. There has of course been the expansion of the inquiry procedure flowing largely from the increase in state control over land use, planning and development. There has also been an increase in the use of quangos or agencies. They have one thing in common with tribunals: no one can quite define what should be included within the labels and what should not. A realisation that we were reverting to something approximating to the Board system, in the sense of establishing institutions making policy decisions with only indirect control from Parliament, did not escape all commentators. Willson, writing in 1955, noted that many of the newer regulatory functions undertaken by the state were given to such bodies.[50] An idea of the range and number of such institutions can be grasped by glancing through the appendices of the 1980 Report on Non-Departmental Public Bodies.[51] The reasons for the growth of agencies, and the problem attendant thereon, will be discussed below.[52] As a background to this discussion the reactions of government to the growth of administration will be considered through an examination of four of the major studies completed this century. The details of these reports are

[50] N.12, 55.
[51] Cmnd. 7797.
[52] See, Ch.4.

not of direct relevance. The interest lies rather in their perception of the problems to be solved and the government's reaction thereto.

B. Donoughmore, Franks, the 1980 Report and the 1988 Justice Report

2–020   The Committee on Ministers' Powers,[53] known as the Donoughmore Committee, produced a report the contents of which not unnaturally reflected the rationale for its establishment. The Committee had been constituted to look at two specific, but important areas, both of which reflected the concern at the extent of ministerial power.[54] These were delegated legislation and the making of judicial or quasi-judicial decisions by a minister or those under his control. Increasing use of broad delegations of power resulted in the acquisition of both legislative and adjudicative functions by the Executive. A powerful Committee[55] produced a report which contained suggestions for reform in both areas.

Just over 30 years later there appeared the Report of the Committee on Administrative Tribunals and Enquiries,[56] known as the Franks Report. The terms of reference were drawn quite specifically. The Committee was to examine the areas of tribunals and inquiries. Aside from decisions made in the ordinary courts this also put beyond the Committee's purview the broad area of decision-making where no formal procedure had been prescribed, a fact emphasised by the Committee itself.[57] What emerged from the Committee's investigations was a series of recommendations as to the constitution and working of tribunals and inquiries, many of which were enacted in the Tribunals and Inquiries Act 1958.[58] These were valuable reforms. It is the more general premises from which the Committee reasoned, which are of interest here. One of these was that tribunals should be seen as part of the machinery of adjudication.[59] This inadvertently contributed to the administrative lawyer's blindness to agencies, which cannot be so regarded. The Franks Report is not to blame for this. It was speaking about tribunals against the background of its terms of reference. Many though not all of such institutions can properly be regarded as part of the machinery of adjudication; formal statutory procedures for the resolution of social welfare claims, or rent disputes, etc. However, an indirect result of this categorisation was the implicit assumption that all of our administrative institutions could be fitted into the pigeon-holes "inquiry" or "tribunal", with those terms bearing their Franksian meaning.

The 1980 Report on Non-Departmental Public Bodies[60] contained useful factual information, combined with short summaries of the difficulties surrounding agencies and the like. The importance of this aspect of

---

[53] Cmd. 4060 (1932).
[54] See Lord Hewart, *The New Despotism* (Ernest Benn, 1929).
[55] It contained Laski, Holdsworth, Scott and Anderson to name but a few.
[56] Cmnd. 218 (1957).
[57] Cmnd. 218 (1957), paras 9–15.
[58] The reforms are considered in detail in Ch.9.
[59] Cmnd. 218 (1957), para.40.
[60] Cmnd. 7797(1980).

administrative law has been increased by recent developments in governmental policy. Privatisation and deregulation have indirectly added to the
number of such institutions. The desire to reduce the size of the central civil
service, and to administer policy through a variety of executive agencies, has
had an important impact in the same direction. These issues will be considered below.[61]

The Justice-All Souls Report[62] contained important recommendations on
particular topics, such as the duty to give reasons and the operation of
tribunals. It was, however, limited in its scope and in its approach. Thus, for
example, the problems generated by agencies were barely touched on; there
was no real discussion of how administrative agencies 'operated', or of their
relationship with government; and the significance of participation within
administrative decision-making was not considered.

The Labour government has produced a number of important policy
documents, dealing with the administrative system, including quangos, the
structure of local government and service provision. There are, moreover,
major changes to the administrative system as a consequence of devolution.
These matters are dealt with in detail below.[63]

---

[61] See below, Ch.4.
[62] *Administrative Justice, Some Necessary Reforms* (Oxford University Press, 1988). Report of
the Committee of the Justice—All Souls Review of Administrative Law in the United Kingdom.
[63] See below, Chs 4–7.

CHAPTER 3

PARLIAMENT AND THE EXECUTIVE

1. THE CHANGING PATTERN OF GOVERNMENT

The definition of government has always been somewhat problematic, but **3–001** these problems have been exacerbated by changes in the pattern of administration. The creation of executive agencies, contracting-out, privatisation, and the private financing of public projects have all served to make the definition of "government" more uncertain and to blur the line between the public and the private sector.

The present chapter will be concerned with Westminster, and the relationship between the House of Commons and the Executive. This will be followed by chapters on agencies, service provision and contracting out. There will be an analysis of governmental structures outside Whitehall, with separate chapters on devolution, local government and the European Union. The discussion of the administrative system will also focus on principles that are fundamental to good governance, including freedom of information, standards in public life and adequate complaints machinery. Tribunals and inquiries receive separate treatment. The analysis of the administrative system concludes with a case study of competition and regulation.

2. THE FOUNDATIONS OF EXECUTIVE POWER

3–002 What follows does not purport to summarise central government.[1] It does not attempt to set out systematically the method by which legislation is enacted, the role of the civil service or the various ways in which the Prime Minister can impose his or her will. Detailed exposition of such matters would be a work in itself. Some knowledge of the realities of central government is however vital for an understanding of administrative law.

This is in part because ministerial decisions have often been challenged in the courts. An understanding of the relationship between the executive and the legislature is necessary in order to be able to comprehend how such decisions have been made. It is in part because the issue as to whether administrative functions should be performed within traditional departments of government, or whether they should be "hived off" to an agency, has been the subject of much debate. This debate has been fuelled by governmental initiatives to reduce radically the size of the central civil service, and to assign more tasks to agencies. This raises, as we shall see,[2] problems concerning accountability.

However it should not be assumed that such problems are absent when decision-making is undertaken within traditional governmental departments. An understanding of the interrelationship of the executive and the legislature will enable us to appreciate the problems of accountability that exist even when decisions are made by "ordinary" governmental departments. We must therefore ensure that when we compare different institutional options we do so against a realistic rather than idealistic background. In the debate over agencies, their accountability must be juxtaposed to the constitutional reality not some paradigm long since disappeared.

[1] P. Norton, *The Commons in Perspective* (Martin Robertson, 1981), *The Constitution in Flux* (Blackwell, 1982); D. Kavanagh, *Thatcherism and British Politics: The End of Consensus?* (Oxford University Press, 1987); R. Rose, *Politics in England: Change and Persistence* (Macmillan, 5th edn, 1989); J. Griffith and M. Ryle, *Parliament, Functions, Practice and Procedure* (Sweet & Maxwell, 1989); P. Norton, *Does Parliament Matter?* (Harvester/Wheatsheaf, 1993); R. Rhodes and P. Dunleavy (eds), *Prime Minister, Cabinet and Core Executive* (Macmillan, 1995); C. Foster and F. Plowden, *The State under Stress: Can the Hollow State be Good Government?* (Open University Press, 1996); D. Oliver and G. Drewry (eds), *The Law and Parliament* (Butterworths, 1998); R. Brazier, *Constitutional Practice, the Foundations of British Government* (Oxford University Press, 3rd. edn, 1999); R. Hazell (ed.), *Constitutional Futures, A History of the Next Ten Years* (Oxford University Press, 1999); P. Dunleavy, A. Gamble, R. Heffernan, I. Holliday, and G. Peele (eds), *Developments in British Politics 6* (Palgrave, 2002); P. Norton, *Parliament in British Politics* (Palgrave, 2nd edn, 2005); P. Dunleavy, R. Heffernan, P. Cowley, C. Hay, *Developments in British Politics 8* (Palgrave, 2006); D. Kavanagh, *British Politics* (Oxford University Press, 5th edn, 2006); B. Jones, D. Kavanagh, M. Moran, and P. Norton, *Politics UK* (Longman, 6th edn, 2007).

[2] See below, Chs 4–5.

A. The Expansion of the Franchise and the Increase in the Area of Governmental Responsibility

"In the British Cabinet today is concentrated all political power, all   **3–003**
initiative in legislation and administration, and finally all public authority
for carrying out the laws in kingdom and empire. In the sixteenth century
and down to the middle of the seventeenth this wealth of authority was
united in the hands of the Crown and its privy council; in the eighteenth
century and the first half of the nineteenth Parliament was the dominant
central organ from which proceeded the most powerful stimulus to action
and all decisive acts of policy, legislation and administration; the second
half of the last century saw the gradual transfer from Crown and Parliament into the hands of the Cabinet of one after another of the elements
of authority and political power. This process took place side by side and
in organic connection with the passing of political sovereignty into the
hands of the House of Commons, supported as it now was by an electorate comprising all sections of the population."

This quotation, modern although it may sound, is taken from Josef Redlich
writing in 1905.[3] What caused this shift in the constitutional balance of
power?

The early part of the 19th century was one in which the functions of the
executive were limited, being principally concerned with the maintenance of
order, the raising of revenue and the conduct of foreign affairs. The idea that
the government had an obligation to carry out a set of domestic policies was
not yet acknowledged. Domestic legislation would normally receive its stimulus from the efforts of private members. The government of the day
might be persuaded to take up a particular measure, as with certain of the
Factory Acts, but it was normally after a private member had provided
the catalyst. It was often the adventitious discovery of an "evil", shocking
the nation, which produced the impetus for reform. This is not intended to
imply acceptance of the Cleopatra's nose theory of history, rather that early
19th century legislation was not as a rule devised, piloted and controlled by
the government.[4]

The reverse side of this same coin was the relative weakness of the party
system when it came to voting. Divisions were not along rigid party lines.
Labels such as Tory, Whig, Radical and Liberal contained a spectrum of
divergent views. Social and economic legislation of the early 19th century
would receive its support from those with widely differing views. The beliefs
of those ranged in opposition were similarly broad. Measures could of
course be promoted by the government, which would naturally attempt to

[3] *The Procedure of the House of Commons: A Study of Its History and Present Form* (Constable,
1908), i, 20, quoted in S. Walkland (ed.), *The House of Commons in the Twentieth Century*
(Clarendon, 1979), 247.
[4] A wider range of functions was undertaken by various commissions and boards, particularly
at the local level. See above, Ch.2.

ensure their passage. Party-based domestic legislation was not, however, the norm during this period.

It was, as Redlich observed, the development of the suffrage that was a main cause of the altered constitutional balance of power. As the electorate increased in size so it became necessary for governments to be able to appeal to a wider cross-section of the population. The Liberal Government's social welfare legislation of 1906 to 1911 was prompted in part at least by the perceived need to offer the "people" some tangible benefits. There were of course a number of other reasons leading to its passage, including developing social ideas, the desire to cut the ground from under the feet of the Fabians, and a real wish to cope with the problems of sickness, old age and unemployment. There was, nonetheless, an understandably distinct political motive, namely that many of those who would benefit could vote.

3–004   Herein lays the organic connection between the passing of political sovereignty into the hands of the House of Commons, and the passing of real power into the hands of the executive, of which Redlich spoke. The legitimacy of the House of Commons was strengthened by the extension of the suffrage. Somewhat paradoxically it was this very extension of the Commons' political base that strengthened the executive. The need to appeal to the expanded electorate was a powerful reason for the executive to bring within its purview a broader range of tasks than hitherto.

Political change is seldom a one-dimensional process. Factors affecting such development overlap and feed off each other. The fact that the government began to play an increasing role in the initiation, shaping and promulgation of domestic legislation helped to create, and was itself influenced by, a growing expectation that government could be looked on to remedy social and economic evils. The aspirations of the populace were continually increasing. Not only was government seen as having a social responsibility, but the nature of that responsibility was altering. In the realm of social policy, for example, the idea that the government had fulfilled its obligations by providing subsistence benefits was, by the middle of the 20th century, fast becoming outdated. As the fear of real destitution diminished, so the aim became one of preserving living standards in times of hardship caused by sickness, death or unemployment. A more positive social role for government was apparent in other areas too. Increases in educational opportunity and improved health standards were but two manifestations of the same theme.

Juxtaposed to this alteration in the government's social responsibility, was the executive's increasing role in the management of the economy. The macro-economic theories of Keynes indicated a positive role for government to rectify imbalances in the economic system.

The increase in executive involvement in an ever-broadening range of domestic policy was attended by changes in both the party system and the methods of legislation. If the government of the day was to secure the passage of its policies, then it had to control the legislative process and its own supporters more vigorously than it had done previously. It is to these developments that we should now turn.

B. The Centralisation of Legislative Initiative

Speaking of the change in the pattern of legislation during the late 19th and **3–005** early 20th centuries, Walkland states,[5]

> "In the case of the legislative process, this period essentially saw a nationalisation and centralisation of legislative initiative in the hands of the government, a massive supplementation of Private Bill procedure by government-introduced Public General Acts, and a marked diminution in the opportunities for private Members to legislate."

Three of the main causes of this centralisation of legislative initiative were the development of standing committees, the increasing discussion of legislation in cabinet committees, and the growth of delegated legislation.

Standing committees were used on limited occasions in the late 19th century,[6] but were viewed with suspicion. It was felt that the government should defend its measures, even as to points of detail, in a Committee of the Whole House. This was indeed the norm. Attempts to take the committee stage in standing committee were regarded as devices by which the government sought to escape criticism. This dislike of standing committees was fuelled by the oft-repeated sentiment that wholesale use of such committees would turn the Commons into a legislative machine, grinding out the maximum amount in the shortest possible time.[7] Despite these objections the use of standing committees has now become the normal way of considering the detail of legislation. Not surprisingly, increase in their use corresponded with periods in which the government had a large legislative programme. The two key periods were 1906 and 1945.

In 1906 a Procedure Committee recommended that all Bills, except finance, consolidated fund, and appropriation Bills, and Bills for confirming provisional orders, should be sent to a standing committee after second reading unless the House otherwise ordered. The Government supported these recommendations. Many backbenchers opposed them. It was to take four days of debate, during which the Government stood out against demands for amendment, before the recommendations of the 1906 Committee were accepted. Despite assurances by the Government that such committees would not be used for controversial measures, the ensuing years were to witness the sending of such minor matters as the National Insurance Act 1911 to a standing committee rather than a Committee of the Whole House.[8]

The use of standing committees received a significant boost as a result of **3–006** the Select Committee on Procedure, which was established in 1945. As in 1906, the principal reason for wishing to expedite parliamentary business

---

[5] "Government Legislation in the House of Commons," Walkland (ed.), n.3, 247.
[6] Walkland, n.3, 255.
[7] Walkland, n.3, 253.
[8] The existence of such committees did however benefit private Members' legislation, see Walkland, n.5, 25.

was the size of the Government's legislative programme. The Labour Government, returned to power in 1945, wished to implement measures, the technical complexity of which exceeded that of normal legislation. If this were to be possible the flow of parliamentary business had to be speeded up. The Select Committee's main brief was to consider ways in which the passage of public Bills could be accelerated. The Government accepted the Report. The Committee recommended the use of standing committees on all Bills, except those of major constitutional importance, the increase in the number of such committees, and the utilisation of the guillotine within the committees in order that the Government could be sure that its measures would not be unduly delayed.[9]

If the development of standing committees expedited the passage of business on the floor of the House, the centralisation of the legislative initiative within the executive was also affected by the increased sophistication of cabinet legislative planning. *Cabinet committees* were used by Liberal governments to settle the details of legislative proposals.[10] It was, however, the Second World War and its aftermath that saw the growing systematisation of legislative planning at cabinet level. A distinct Legislative Committee of the Cabinet with responsibility for, inter alia, planning a legislative programme existed in 1940. This idea was built on by the post-war Labour Government. The planning of the general legislative programme was assigned to a future legislation committee, with a distinct Legislation Committee, which would advise on the more technical aspects concerning the form of the legislation.[11] Bills could well go through several drafts before being presented to the House of Commons. Increased cabinet involvement in the drafting of legislation made the executive more certain as to the type of provision for which it sought legislative approval. It became rare for an amendment to be forced on a government against its will, whether in committee or elsewhere.[12] It is very much Cabinet committees, together with the Prime Minister's Office and the Cabinet Office, that are at the heart of executive policy formation in the modern day.[13] We shall see that many of the central initiatives relating to service delivery, regulatory reform and the like are directed from these offices.[14] There has, moreover, been increased recourse to what are termed "bilaterals", that is meetings between the Prime Minister and individual ministers, in which policy in a particular area is developed.[15]

The growth of *delegated legislation* has centralised the legislative initiative

---

[9] Walkland, n.5, 265–268.
[10] Walkland, n.5, 251–252.
[11] Walkland, n.5, 265–266.
[12] How rare is a matter of some debate, see Walkland, n.5, 287–288; J. Griffith, *Parliamentary Scrutiny of Government Bills* (1975).
[13] I. Holliday, "Executives and Administrations", in Dunleavy, Gamble, Heffernan, Holliday, and Peele (eds), n.1, Ch.6; M. Burch and I. Holliday, *The British Cabinet System* (Prentice Hall/ Harvester Wheatsheaf, 1996); M. Burch and I. Holliday, "An Executive Office in All But Name: The Prime Minister's and Cabinet Offices in the UK" (1999) 52 Parliamentary Affairs 32.
[14] See below, Chs 4, 5, and 11.
[15] Kavanagh, *British Politics: Continuities and Change*, n.1, Ch.11.

within the executive in a rather different way from either the development of standing committees or cabinet oversight. Delegated legislation is not a new phenomenon. The passage of a large volume of social and economic legislation led to an increase in the quantum of delegated legislation. The effect is to centralise the legislative initiative within the executive as a whole. It is the government, albeit acting through individual ministers, which decides when and whether to initiate such legislation, and effective legislative control is problematic.[16]

C. The Development of the Party System

The power of the executive was also markedly increased by the development 3–007
of the party system and the consequential control wielded by the government over its supporters in the House of Commons.

Parties are not a new phenomenon. They emerged in the late 18th and early 19th centuries. Even early parliamentary party organisation was designed to ensure that members adhered to the party line laid down by the party leaders.[17] The very existence of parties provided an avenue for the channelling of power from the legislature to the executive. It was, however, a combination of the extended suffrage and the expanded role of the state, which sowed the seeds of the rigid party discipline to which we are so accustomed today.

The expansion of the franchise in 1832 and in 1867 changed the nature of politics. Voters could not simply be bought. There were too many. An organisation outside Parliament was required in order to persuade and cajole voters into using their newly acquired rights for the benefit of a particular party. Promises for reform provided the carrot. But promises have, in theory, to be kept. A necessary if not sufficient condition for doing so was greater executive control within Parliament to ensure the passage of the requisite legislation. The point is put neatly by Norton,[18]

"Parties certainly had a profound impact upon Parliament: voters not only had to be contacted, they had to be promised something if their votes were to be forthcoming, and party promises could only be fulfilled if party nominees were returned in sufficient number to, and displayed voting cohesion in, the House of Commons; the consequence of this development was to be party government, with the parliamentary parties acting as a conduit for the transfer of power from Parliament to the executive."

The transition from the 19th to the 20th century simply exacerbated the problem. The role of the state developed partly as we have seen because of the extension of the franchise. This broadened range of functions placed

---

[16] See, Ch.22.
[17] P. Norton, "The Organisation of Parliamentary Parties," in Walkland (ed.), n.3, 9. See generally, R. Rose, *Do Parties Make a Difference?* (Macmillan, 2nd edn, 1984); P Norton, *Dissension in the House of Commons 1945–1974* (Macmillan, 1975).
[18] Norton, n.17, 8.

increasing strain upon parliamentary time. One response was reform of legislative procedures. Another was to tighten party discipline to ensure the passage of the expanded governmental programme. It should not be thought that MPs are continually being harassed by harridans called Whips. This would be to misrepresent reality. Whips perform valuable functions of communication and management as well as discipline. The government will, nevertheless, maintain a carefully calculated legislative programme, the Whip system will be applied to standing committees, the guillotine will be used to maintain impetus, and there will be considerable pressure on a Member not to vote against the government, especially on an important issue where the difference in numbers between government and opposition is finely balanced.

The party system not only centralised initiative and power in the executive as manifested in party voting cohesion, but also in the process of policy formation. As Johnson has noted,[19] policy is normally laid down by the executive when the party is in office, although on occasion the official leadership may defer to a particular powerful group because the executive fears to oppose them.

To this process of policy formulation may be added the impact of powerful interest groups outside Parliament. There is nothing wrong with extra-parliamentary groups having an effect on legislative programmes. It happens in all countries. What causes disquiet is the extent of this influence, and the way in which it serves to weaken further the power of the legislature over legislation.

3. THE ROLE OF THE LEGISLATURE

3–008   Whether we should be dismayed by the executive domination of the legislature depends on what we believe the latter's role to be. It could be argued that the legislature should primarily be a critic, a body to scrutinise the government rather than one that has any real hand in the legislative process. It might alternatively be thought that the House of Commons should still have a legislative role, which should be buttressed and strengthened at every opportunity. The two views are not antithetical. They do, however, judge the effectiveness of the House of Commons from different perspectives.[20]

---

[19] N. Johnson, *In Search of the Constitution, Reflections on State and Society in Britain* (Pergamon, 1977), 47. The extent to which this is so may differ as between the leading political parties.
[20] P. Norton, "Parliamentary Oversight", in P. Dunleavy, A. Gamble, I. Holliday, and G. Peele (eds) *Developments in British Politics 5* (MacMillan, 1997), Ch.8.

A. The Commons and Scrutiny

Control or influence over the substance of legislation is, says Ryle,[21] **3–009**
necessarily minimal; the government can always ensure that its policies
become law in much the way that it desires. The picture of the Commons as
critic is put forcefully by Ryle,[22]

"Thus much of the criticism of Parliament and particularly of the House
of Commons today, flows, I believe, from this fundamental mistake in
their perceived functions. Parliament is wrongly blamed for bad government because Parliament does not govern. To put it baldly: the government governs; Parliament is the forum where the exercise of government
is publicly displayed and is open to scrutiny and criticism. And the
Commons does not control the executive—not in any real sense; rather
the executive control the Commons through the exercise of their party
majority power."

This view of the House of Commons' role is essentially pragmatic: little
control is possible over the content of legislation, therefore the value of the
Commons must lie elsewhere. There is little doubt that critical scrutiny is a
valuable function for a legislature, and select committees are the most
important instrument in this respect.

i. Select committees: origins and development

Prior to 1914 such committees were used for a variety of purposes. Johnson **3–010**
lists four:[23] the investigation of alleged abuses, inquiries into areas of public
policy on which action was demanded, consideration of bills, and the continuing scrutiny of financial rectitude provided through the Public Accounts
Committee established in 1861. The use of such committees declined during
the inter-war years, but they were utilised more often, albeit somewhat
slowly at first, following the Second World War. Four main committees
carried on investigative work: the Public Accounts Committee, the Estimates Committee,[24] the Select Committee on Nationalised Industry[25] and
the Statutory Instruments Committee.

The development of select committees received two further boosts, the
first in the mid-1960s, the second in the late 1970s. Partly as a result of the
Report of the Procedure Committee of 1964–1965, and partly as a consequence of the feeling that the balance between the legislature and the
executive needed redressing, a number of select committees were established
in the late 1960s. The approach of the Government was, however, ad hoc:
no common theme runs through the committees that were established. Some

---

[21] "The Commons in the Seventies—A General Survey", in S. Walkland and M. Ryle (eds), *The Commons in the Seventies* (Fontana, 1977), 13–14.
[22] Walkland and Ryle, n.21, 12.
[23] "Select Committees and Administration", Walkland (ed.), n.3, 432.
[24] N. Johnson, *Parliament and Administration: The Estimates Committee 1945–65* (Allen & Unwin, 1966).
[25] D. Coombes, *The Member of Parliament and the Administration: The Case of the Select Committee on Nationalised Industries* (Allen & Unwin, 1966).

could be best categorised as dealing with a particular subject matter, others were based around the work of a department. Dissatisfaction with the disorganised pattern of select committees, coupled with the belief that greater coverage was required, led the Select Committee on Procedure to recommend a reshaping and extension of select committees along departmental lines.[26] These recommendations were put into effect in 1979, the result being that such committees now cover all major aspects of government.

ii. Select committees: early assessments

3–011   The effectiveness of such committees depends in part upon one's expectation. The strong argument for select committees was that their investigative and critical functions would enable Parliament to reassert real control over the government. A less ambitious view saw select committees as relatively impartial generators of advice and information, hoping to influence government because of their non-partisan approach.[27] It is doubtful whether the committees have played the stronger of these two roles. This is evident from research on their general work, the findings of which are reinforced by the limited impact of the committees in the area of financial scrutiny. Research on the departmental select committees indicated a number of reasons for their relatively limited impact.[28]

First, the committees did not have a role in the process by which the government framed its legislation. In this sense they were ancillary to the principal work of the House, though some select committees attempted to circumvent this limitation by examining matters which were likely to lead to legislation in the near future.[29]

Second, the committees did not have adequate resources, and operated with minimal support staff and a small budget.[30]

Third, it was inappropriate to conceive of the new committees as a "system", since they had different perceptions of their own function.[31] Thus some committees shied away from involvement with fundamental policy issues; others acted as advocates for particular pressure groups; and yet others engaged in more searching scrutiny of long term governmental objectives.

Fourth, the Memorandum for Guidance of Officials who appeared before the committees limited the information which civil servants should provide. Thus officials were instructed not to meet requests for information irrespective of the cost; not to disclose advice given to Ministers, nor

[26] *First Report from the Select Committee on Procedure* (HC 588; 1977–78).
[27] N. Johnson, "Select Committees as Tools of Parliamentary Reform: Some Further Reflections", Walkland and Ryle (eds), n.21, 195.
[28] G. Drewry (ed.), *The New Select Committees, A Study of the 1979 Reforms* (Oxford University Press, 1985). See also D. Englefield (ed.), *Commons Select Committees: Catalysts for Progress?* (Longman, 1984).
[29] A. Adonis, *Parliament Today* (Manchester University Press, 2nd edn, 1993), 166.
[30] Adonis, n.29, 165.
[31] P. Giddings, "What Has Been Achieved", Drewry (ed.), n.28, 368. See also, Sir D. Wass, "Checks and Balances in Public Policy Making" [1987] P.L. 181, 183, 192–193.

information concerning interdepartmental exchanges on policy issues; not to reveal discussions in Cabinet committees; and to confine their evidence, so far as possible, to questions of fact relating to existing governmental policy, and not to discuss alternative strategies.[32]

Fifth, the opportunities to debate the findings of select committees upon the floor of the House were limited. Between 1979 and 1988 only 25 per cent of the reports were debated, and only 13 out of 500 reports were the subject of any substantive motion, although some form of government response was often forthcoming.[33]

Finally, there was concern over the limited scrutiny of financial matters. **3–012** Scrutiny of expenditure in the Commons was severely limited.[34] The select committee structure replaced the Expenditure committee, the idea being that each committee scrutinises expenditure within its subject-matter area. Robinson argued that this impeded the development of any systematic critical approach to the scrutiny of public expenditure, and that there had not been "much enthusiasm" for financial scrutiny.[35] Moreover, when select committees did focus upon financial matters the nature of their inquiry differed.[36] Drewry echoed these sentiments and found that the record of departmental select committees in relation to financial scrutiny had been "decidedly patchy".[37] Some increase in legislative control over money already expended has, however, been provided by the National Audit Act 1983. The Comptroller and Auditor-General is an officer of the Commons, and can investigate the "economy, efficiency and effectiveness" with which departments and certain other public authorities discharge their functions.[38]

While there was therefore little evidence to support the strong role which it was hoped that select committees would play in reasserting parliamentary control over government, it would be mistaken to suppose that they have had no impact. Select committees have had an effect in a number of ways. They were able to affect governmental policy on certain issues before it has become too fixed. Their very existence led departments to be more rigorous in justifying their policy choices.[39] Civil service anonymity was "dented", notwithstanding the limitations on the advice they were allowed to offer.[40] They provided a forum for debate in which particular interest groups could offer their opinion on existing policies.[41] There was, moreover, evidence that

[32] G. Drewry, "Parliament", in P. Dunleavy, A. Gamble, I. Holliday, and G. Peele (eds), *Developments in British Politics 4* (Macmillan, 1993), 160–161.
[33] Adonis, n.29, 167.
[34] A. Robinson, "The House of Commons and Public Expenditure", Walkland and Ryle (eds), n.21, 129–130; A. Robinson, *Parliament and Public Spending* (Heinemann, 1978).
[35] "The Financial Work of the Select Committees", Drewry (ed.), n.28, 307–308.
[36] Drewry, n.28, 309–318. Some operated as balancing committees, scrutinising claims for extra spending against the costs which would be incurred. Others functioned as spending committees, supporting the dominant pressure groups and advocating higher expenditure in that area. Yet other committees operated "non-financially", in the sense that they devoted little time to public expenditure.
[37] "Parliament", n.32, 158.
[38] G. Drewry, "The National Audit Act–Half a Loaf" [1983] P.L. 531.
[39] Giddings, n.31, 370–371, 374, 377.
[40] G. Drewry, "The 1979 Reforms–New Labels On Old Bottles?", Drewry (ed.), n.28, 388–389.
[41] Giddings, n.31, 378–379.

the committees were now willing to tackle more controversial issues, such as the future of the NHS and privatisation, than hitherto.[42]

That there are limitations on the scrutiny function of Parliament is not surprising. They should be seen in the context of a more general problem underlying the concept of an effective critical role for Parliament. Changes in procedure are often thought of as "technical" alterations, which do not have any wider significance. It is assumed that alterations can be made without any substantive modification in the balance of power within the political system. A moment's reflection will show that this is not possible.[43] Our political system has been characterised by two major themes: the dominance of the executive, and an adversarial approach to politics. It is one in which government and opposition face each other in a partisan, gladiatorial combat each backed by its own legions.

Select committees run counter to both of these tenets: they seek to strengthen the power of Parliament as against the executive, and to proceed by a less partisan approach. The fundamental point is that a strengthening of Parliament must imply a consequential weakening of the executive's power for relatively untrammelled action, and a less partisan approach to politics in committees presumes either a dichotomy between policy and administration which is so elusive, or a distinction between the approach to politics on the floor of the House and that in committee. Some commentators believe that such a distinction may be emerging, with the committees operating more by way of consensus, with the members not unthinkingly accepting the party whips, with the prime aim being the objective scrutiny of governmental action rather than "the knee-jerk reflexes of Government and Opposition".[44]

iii. Select committees: reform initiatives

3–013 There is little doubt that the committees have increased the Commons' scrutiny of the executive as compared to the position prior to 1979. A survey of their work carried out by the Select Committee on Procedure[45] reached the conclusion that the system provided an improved framework for the sustained scrutiny of government departments. But if the select committees really are to have more than a limited impact then the executive will have to shed some of its powers, or to allow more than a symbolic genuflection to less partisan politics.

There have been a number of important reform initiatives in this area. The Select Committee on Liaison published a valuable Report in 1997[46] on select committees, in which it identified areas where reform would increase

---

[42] Adonis, n.29, 168.
[43] Johnson, n.23, 444–445.
[44] Adonis, n.29, 172.
[45] *The Working of the Select Committee System* (HC 19; 1989–90); D. Judge, "The Effectiveness of the Post-1979 Select Committee System: the Verdict of the 1990 Procedure Committee" (1992) 63 Pol. Q. 1.
[46] *First Report of the Select Committee on Liaison* (HC 323–I; 1997).

their effectiveness. The Report was premised on the assumption that scrutiny of the activities of the executive is one of the traditional and most important activities of a democratic Parliament, and that in a legislature such as our own this could only be effectively carried out through the select committee system.[47] Many of its suggestions were designed to redress the problems outlined earlier. Thus it recommended that such committees should have power to compel the attendance of any MP, including a minister, and that relevant documents should be laid before the select committee.[48] There should be a presumption that ministers accept requests from committees that individual named civil servants give evidence to them.[49] Departments should be under a duty to furnish documentation relevant to an inquiry without waiting for a specific request.[50] There should be provision for the recruitment of extra staff by a committee.[51] The work of Executive Agencies should be fully investigated by the committees, and the Heads of such agencies should be allowed to give evidence when invited to do so.[52] When Draft Bills are published the Department responsible should send them to the relevant committee.[53] The Select Committees should intensify their scrutiny of financial matters relating to the relevant Department.[54]

These themes were reiterated in Reports from the Select Committee on Modernisation,[55] and the Select Committee on Liaison.[56] Their principal recommendations were as follows. Nomination of members for departmental select committees should be independent, and should be entrusted to a Committee of Nomination. Departmental Select Committees should be accorded more resources to enable them to function effectively. There should moreover be a list of core tasks to be undertaken by such committees.

iv. Select committees: recent developments

A number of these reform initiatives have been taken forward, in particular the elaboration of core tasks to be undertaken by select committees. This is evident from the Report of the Select Committee on Liaison for 2005–2006.[57] Ten such core tasks have been elaborated, divided into four groups.

3–014

Objective A is to consider and comment on departmental policy. The four tasks included within this section are: to examine policy proposals from the UK Government and the European Commission; to identify and examine areas of emerging policy, or where existing policy is deficient, and to make

---

[47] HC 323–I; 1997, n.46, para.40.
[48] HC 323–I; 1997, n.46, paras 11 and 12.
[49] HC 323–I; 1997, n.46, para.13.
[50] HC 323–I; 1997, n.46, para.14.
[51] HC 323–I; 1997, n.46, para.23.
[52] HC 323–I; 1997, n.46, para.29, and Appendix 20.
[53] HC 323–I; 1997, n.46, para.32.
[54] HC 323–I; 1997, n.46, paras 34–36.
[55] *First Report of the Select Committee on Modernisation* (HC 224–I; 2002).
[56] *Second Report of the Select Committee on Liaison* (HC 692; 2002).
[57] *First Report of the Select Committee on Liaison* (HC 406; 2007).

proposals; to conduct scrutiny of any published draft Bill within the Committee's responsibilities; and to examine specific output from the department expressed in documents or other decisions. Objective B involves one task, which is the examination of expenditure by departments, agencies and non-departmental public bodies. Objective C is to consider administration by the department, and entails four tasks: examination of the department's Public Service Agreements, the associated targets and the statistical measurements employed; to monitor the work of the department's Executive Agencies, non-departmental public bodies and other associated public bodies; to scrutinise major appointments made by the department; and to examine the implementation of legislation and major policy initiatives. Objective D involves one task, which is the provision of reports that are suitable for debate in the House, Westminster Hall or relevant committees.

It seems clear that select committees are coming of age, and that scrutiny of expenditure has become more effective. This has been facilitated by the systematisation of the select committee's tasks, which may well expand to encompass post-legislative scrutiny.[58] It is equally clear that there are still some difficulties with select committees fulfilling their assigned tasks. Thus the Select Committee on Liaison was, for example, critical of the Government's failure to publish Bills in draft so that they could be considered by the relevant select committee: only three such bills out of a total of 58 were published in the 2005–2006 session.[59] The Select Committee on Liaison also expressed concern that some departments delayed their response to a select committee report in order to avoid a debate on the report in the House or Westminster Hall; and it expressed regret that the number of debates on committee reports had dropped from the two-thirds target recommended by the Modernisation Committee.[60]

B. The Commons and Legislation

3–015 Not all commentators accept that the legislative role of Parliament should be consigned to history. While recognising that the golden age of Parliament cannot be recaptured, proposals have been forthcoming for ways in which the impact of Parliament on the legislative process could be strengthened. The proposals are designed to allow more critical input from the floor of the House.[61] A number of reports have addressed this issue.[62]

---

[58] HC 406; 2007, n.57, para.105.
[59] HC 406; 2007, n.57, paras 14–17.
[60] HC 406; 2007, n.57, paras 55–56.
[61] The following are useful for evaluating the reforms discussed in this section, P. Cowley, "Legislatures and Assemblies", in Dunleavy, Gamble, Heffernan, Holliday, and Peele (eds), n.1, Ch.7; P. Norton, "Parliament in Transition", in R. Pyper (ed.), *British Government under Blair* (Macmillan, 1999).
[62] *Second Report of the Select Committee on Procedure* (HC 49; 1984–85); *Second Report of the Select Committee on Procedure* (HC 324; 1985–86); *Second Report of the Select Committee on Procedure* (HC 19–I; 1989–90).

i. Rippon Commission

The Rippon Commission[63] made a number of interesting proposals for improving Parliament's role in the legislative process. The initial assumption of the study was that Parliament did not "make the law" as such. This was done by the government. Parliament should nonetheless have proper facilities for scrutinising proposed legislative changes.[64] A number of more specific proposals were made, which would enhance Parliament's role in this respect.

3–016

Pre-legislative proceedings could be improved by making use of departmental select committees, which could comment upon White papers and other consultative documents. When a fuller inquiry into proposed legislation was merited then a select committee could be appointed specially for this purpose.[65]

Scrutiny of the actual Bill by the House should be divided into two stages. The first would be a *preliminary briefing stage*, which would operate after the Bill's first reading for more complex or important measures. This would be undertaken by a specially appointed select committee, "first reading committee", which should be free of ministers and opposition shadow ministers. It was hoped that such committees might work by the more consensual approach characteristic of departmental select committees. They would have the power to take evidence from civil servants, outside experts and the wider public. The committees would produce a report, drawing attention "to ambiguities in purpose or meaning, apparent problems in the application or implementation of the legislation, possible consequences of the proposed policies and other practical, technical or drafting points that have emerged".[66]

The second part of parliamentary scrutiny of a Bill would be the *formal committee* stage, which would continue to be undertaken by standing committees. The Rippon Commission noted the existing widespread dissatisfaction with the present standing committee procedures: many MPs regard the work of such committees to be a waste of time under the current arrangements; and the Opposition is frustrated because it can make so little impact on the Bill.[67] The Commission suggested that the norm should be for Bills to be referred to a *special standing committee*. These would examine witnesses and publish their evidence at the beginning of their examination of a Bill, before turning to the more formal debate and party discipline for the decision-taking processes on proposed amendments to the Bill.[68] Membership should include, wherever possible, those who were on the first reading committee, and those who were on a relevant departmental select committee. The special standing committees should carry out detailed scrutiny of

---

[63] *Making the Law, The Report of the Hansard Society Commission on the Legislative Process* (1992).
[64] *Making the Law*, n.63, para.310.
[65] *Making the Law*, n.63, paras 322–323.
[66] *Making the Law*, n.63, para.337.
[67] *Making the Law*, n.63, para.345. See also, J. Griffith and M. Ryle, *Parliament* (Sweet & Maxwell, 1989), 315–317.
[68] *Making the Law*, n.63, para.349. Such a system was used on five occasions between 1980–84.

the Bill, looking at practical problems of implementation and at matters where the Bill was unclear.[69] It should not, by way of contrast, be the function of these committees to debate major issues of policy, which had been dealt with on the floor of the House during the second reading, or could be raised during the Report stage after the committee had done its work.

ii. Select Committee on Modernisation

3–017   These issues have also been addressed in Reports of the Select Committee on Modernisation of the House of Commons.

The *1997 Report of the Select Committee* contained a wide-ranging examination of the legislative process,[70] and the Liaison Committee generally supported its conclusions.[71] The Report was premised on the assumption that legislation was a principal function of the House of Commons, and not the exclusive preserve of the executive.[72] It acknowledged the perceived defects of the present legislative regime. These included the absence of consultation with MPs prior to the introduction of a Bill, the patchy quality of consultation with outside interests, the Whitehall culture which measured legislative success by getting a Bill through Parliament unchanged, the adversarial and ineffective nature of standing committees, and the imbalance of legislative activity at different times of the year.[73]

The Report set out the essential criteria for reform.[74] These were that the government of the day should be assured of getting its legislation through in a reasonable time; that the opposition and MPs should have a full opportunity to discuss and seek to change provisions; that all parts of a Bill should be properly considered; that the time and expertise of MPs should be used to better effect; there should be full explanations provided on the meaning of the proposed legislation; there should, throughout the legislative process, be greater accessibility for the public; there should be balance throughout the legislative year; and that monitoring of legislation already enacted should be a vital part of Parliament's role. Many of the detailed issues considered in the Report are similar to those that were analysed by the Rippon Commission.

Thus, the Report of the Select Committee on Modernisation recognised that in principle *pre-legislative scrutiny* of Bills published in draft form was desirable, since it facilitated input from MPs before a measure had become

---

[69] *Making the Law*, n.63, para.351.
[70] *First Report of the Select Committee on Modernisation of the House of Commons, The Legislative Process* (HC 190; 1997).
[71] *First Report of the Select Committee on Modernisation of the House of Commons, The Parliamentary Calendar* (HC 60; 1998), Appendix 4.
[72] *First Report of the Select Committee on Modernisation of the House of Commons, The Legislative Process* (HC 190; 1997), para.1.
[73] HC 190; 1997, n.72, paras 4–12. See also, J. Griffith, "Standing Committees in the House of Commons", Walkland and Ryle (eds), n.21, 107; Wass, n.31, 193–194.
[74] *First Report of the Select Committee on Modernisation* (HC 190; 1997), n.72, para.14.

concretised into a formal Bill.[75] There were four possible institutional forms through which such scrutiny could occur: the existing departmental select committees; a new permanent structure of legislative committees; an ad hoc Select Committee; a Joint Committee of both Houses.[76]

The Select Committee's Report also followed the suggestion of the Rippon Commission that it should be possible to *refer some Bills to a committee for examination after the First Reading, but before the Second Reading*.[77] This would be particularly useful for those Bills that were not subject to pre-legislative scrutiny. In such instances, more especially where the Bill was complex, a reference to a committee after the First Reading would have the advantage that a minister would be more likely to be receptive to suggestions for change at this stage. The choice of committee to perform this task was the same as that for pre-legislative scrutiny.

There was much discussion of the *committee stage of a Bill*. It was acknowledged that greater use could be made of ad hoc select committees, and special standing committees.[78] It was nonetheless regarded as inevitable that most Bills would have to be routed through the existing Standing Committee procedure.[79] The Report accepted that many of the criticisms of such committees could only be properly addressed by a change of culture by those in the system, particularly ministers. A number of more technical changes were proposed to improve matters.[80]

3–018

The Select Committee's Report also adverted to *post-legislative scrutiny*. One of the "essential criteria of any effective legislative scrutiny system was a proper method of monitoring legislation which has come into force".[81] This task, which is already carried out in relation to some legislation, could properly be assigned to departmental select committees.

The *Select Committee on Modernisation's 2002 Report*[82] reiterated and developed many of the themes in the 1997 Report. The 2002 Report endorsed the importance of *pre-legislative scrutiny* of draft Bills, with this work normally being undertaken by a departmental select committee. Where it was not possible to produce a complete legal text the government should submit proposals for pre-legislative scrutiny based on a detailed statement of policy.[83] There should be consultations with other parties as to the broad shape of the *legislative agenda for that year*.[84] It should moreover be possible *to carry over a Bill* from one session to the next, thereby obviating more detailed scrutiny and avoiding the wastage of parliamentary resources. This would allow more bills to be considered by a Special

[75] HC 190; 1997, n.72, paras 20, 91.
[76] HC 190; 1997, n.72, paras 19–29.
[77] HC 190; 1997, n.72, paras 32, 93.
[78] HC 190; 1997, n.72, paras 42–46.
[79] HC 190; 1997, n.72, paras 47–49.
[80] HC 190; 1997, n.72, paras 48, 95–98.
[81] HC 190; 1997, n.72, para.54.
[82] *Second Report of the Select Committee on Modernisation, A Reform Programme* (HC 1168–I; 2002).
[83] HC 1168–I; 2002, n.82, paras 29–34.
[84] HC 1168–I; 2002, n.82, para.44.

Standing Committee.[85] The 2002 Report also contained recommendations for the timing of the working day. The House of Commons approved the Select Committee's Report.[86]

The preceding recommendations were reinforced in the *Select Committee on Modernisation's 2006 Report*.[87] It reiterated its belief in the value of pre-legislative scrutiny and like the Liaison Committee criticised the reduction in the number of draft Bills that had been considered in this manner. It also made important recommendations concerning the committee stage for public Bills. The Committee proposed that: special standing committees should be the norm for consideration of public Bills, with the power to take evidence; that special standing committees and standing committees should be renamed public bill committees; and that public bill committees should be one type of general committee.

iii. Continuity and change

3–019   It is readily apparent that the efforts to increase the effectiveness of Parliament's role in the legislative process have been continuing for some time. The continued pressure for change has borne fruit in certain respects. Thus the principle of pre-legislative scrutiny has been conceded by government, even if the number of times that it has been used has been disappointing more recently.[88] A number of the Select Committee's recommendations concerning the committee stage have now been enshrined in the relevant standing orders.[89] Thus the nomenclature has changed to public bill committee, which is one type of general committee. A Bill will, subject to limited exceptions, be referred to a public bill committee, which will normally have power to take evidence, and see papers and records.[90]

There have moreover been other developments designed to enhance the role of Parliament. Thus use has been made of Westminster Hall, to facilitate debate on issues for which there is insufficient time on the floor of the main House. It has been adjudged a modest success.[91] There has been consideration of the role of backbench MPs so as to revitalise the House of Commons.[92] The most significant such development, in principle at least, is that the Prime Minister expressed commitment in the Green Paper on the *Governance of Britain*[93] to reinvigorate democracy and limit executive

---

[85] HC 1168–I; 2002, n.82, para.38.
[86] HC Deb, col. 801, 29 Oct 2002.
[87] *First Report of the Select Committee on Modernisation, The Legislative Process* (HC 1097; 2006).
[88] A. Kennon, "Pre-legislative Scrutiny of Draft Bills" [2004] P.L. 477; J Smookler, "Making a Difference? The Effectiveness of Pre-legislative Scrutiny" (2006) 59 Parliamentary Affairs 522.
[89] *Standing Orders of the House of Commons* (2007), available at http://www.publications. parliament.uk/pa/cm200708/cmstords/105/105.pdf.
[90] Standing Orders 63, 84A.
[91] *Fourth Report of the Select Committee on Modernisation, Sittings in Westminster Hall* (HC 906; 2000); *Second Report of the Select Committee*, n.82, paras 97–99.
[92] *First Report of the Select Committee on Modernisation, Revitalising the Chamber, The Role of the Back Bench Member* (HC 337; 2007).
[93] *The Governance of Britain*, Cm. 7170 (2007).

power, by for example, moving royal prerogative powers to Parliament, and publishing the draft legislative agenda so that it can be considered by the Commons.[94]

4. Reform of the House of Lords

This is not the place for a detailed exegesis on the history of the House of Lords in its legislative capacity, nor of the varying attempts made at reform over the years. It is, however, appropriate to consider the current reforms, since they significantly alter the nature of the second chamber. **3–020**

The Labour manifesto contained a commitment to reform the House of Lords and to abolish the right of hereditary peers to sit and vote.[95] It proposed that this would be the first stage of reform to make the Lords more democratic and representative. The idea, as represented in the manifesto, was that the appointment of life peers would also be reviewed so as more accurately to reflect the proportion of votes cast at the previous election. Much has happened on this issue since Labour's first election victory,[96] but on the general point of principle, that hereditary peers should not be entitled to sit and vote, the government has remained firm. Thus the Prime Minister stated that,[97] "it cannot possibly be right that people sit as legislators in the Houses of Parliament on the basis that their birth makes them hereditary peers", and that "it is an absolute democratic scandal that hereditary Conservative peers outnumber the peers of the elected government of the day by three to one", thereby ensuring an in-built Tory majority in perpetuity.

The House of Lords Act 1999 implemented this aspect of the government's policy. It provides in s.1 that "no-one shall be a member of the House of Lords by virtue of hereditary peerage". This is subject to an exception contained in s.2, which allows 92 hereditary peers to remain. Section 3 removed disqualifications from hereditary peers, so that they can vote at elections for the Commons and be elected to that House.

This legislation was the first stage of the government's programme for reform of the Lords. A Royal Commission was established under Lord Wakeham to consider more comprehensive reform.[98] It recommended that the second chamber should bring a range of different perspectives to bear on the development of public policy, that it should be broadly representative, that it should act as one of the checks and balances in the constitution, and **3–021**

---

[94] *First Report of the Select Committee on Modernisation, Scrutiny of the Draft Legislative Programme* (HC 81; 2008).
[95] *New Labour: Because Britain Deserves Better* (1997), 32–33.
[96] House of Commons Research Paper 98/85, *House of Lords Reform: Developments since the General Election* (August 1998).
[97] HC Deb, Vol. 313, col. 366, June 3, 1998.
[98] Royal Commission on the Reform of the House of Lords, *A House for the Future*, Cm. 4534 (2000).

should provide a voice for the different parts of the UK. The Wakeham Commission recommended that the House of Lords should retain its existing powers under the Parliaments Acts 1911 and 1949. A new Constitutional Committee should be established to consider the constitutional implications of legislation, and keep the operation of the constitution under review, and a new Human Rights Committee should be set up to scrutinise the human rights' implications of legislation. The composition of the reformed second chamber was the most difficult issue addressed by the Commission. It rejected the view that the second chamber should be wholly or largely directly elected, or that it should be indirectly elected. It rejected also random selection and co-option. It recommended that a significant minority of members should be "regional", that others should be appointed by an Independent Appointments Commission, and that this same Commission should ensure that the politically affiliated members reflected an overall political balance of the country as expressed in voting at the most recent election.

The balance between elected and non-elected members of the second chamber continues to be the most controversial aspect of the reforms.[99] A White Paper on House of Lords' reform in 2007 proposed that the chamber should be 50 per cent elected and 50 per cent appointed.[100] Reaction to this suggestion was mixed, and in a subsequent free vote the Commons voted by a large majority for a wholly elected House of Lords, and also by a lesser margin supported a second chamber that was 80 per cent elected and 20 per cent appointed. It rejected other hybrid options. The Government now seems committed to moving forward with a second chamber that is either wholly or substantially elected, and the removal of the remaining hereditary peers.[101]

5. Conclusion

3–022   The tensions between the executive and Parliament will not magically disappear. They were manifest in the Arms to Iraq saga, and in the limited political consequences that followed from publication of the Scott Report.[102]

---

[99] Constitution Unit, *Reform of the House of Lords* (1996); Constitution Unit, *Rebalancing the Lords: The Numbers* (1998); R. Hazell, "Reforming the House of Lords: A Step by Step Guide", *Constitutional Reform in the United Kingdom: Practice and Principles* (University of Cambridge, Centre for Public Law, 1998), Ch.15; I. Richard and D. Welfare, *Unfinished Business: reforming the House of Lords* (Vintage, 1999).
[100] *The House of Lords: Reform*, Cm. 7027 (2007).
[101] *The Governance of Britain*, n.93, paras 129–138.
[102] *Report of the Inquiry into the Export of Defence Equipment and Dual-Use Goods to Iraq and Related Prosecutions* (HC 115; 1996); I. Leigh and L. Lustgarten, "Five Volumes in Search of Accountability: The Scott Report" (1996) 59 M.L.R. 695; D. Oliver, "The Scott Report" [1996] P.L. 357; A. Tomkins, "Government Information and Parliament: Misleading by Design or by Default?" [1996] P.L. 472; N. Lewis and D. Longley, "Ministerial Responsibility: The Next Steps" [1996] P.L. 490.

They are evident in the claims that ministers have willingly received leaked reports from select committees in advance of their publication in order the better to prepare their response. The tensions are apparent in the government's reaction to reports from departmental select committees.

There is nonetheless a sense that the scrutiny and legislative functions of Parliament should be and can be reinforced. There is an underlying connection between the proposals made concerning Parliament and scrutiny of government action, and Parliament and the legislative process. This is the desire to enhance Parliament's role *and* to reduce the extent to which the political system works in adversarial manner dominated by the executive. The desire for some less party-based scrutiny of governmental action and legislative proposals is a recurrent theme. This is a laudable objective. Whether it is realisable is another matter. It might be argued that in the absence of a major catalyst prompting a realignment of power between the executive and the legislature any change is bound to be marginal. Electoral reform that breaks the dominance of the two major parties might be such a catalyst,[103] but it is unlikely that this will be introduced by one of the two major parties. The very fact that backbench MPs have, in relative terms, been more willing recently to voice and vote their disapproval of government measures is however a positive development.

[103] P. Dunleavy, "The Constitution", Dunleavy, Gamble, Holliday and Peele (eds), n.20, Ch.1.

CHAPTER 4

AGENCIES AND NON-DEPARTMENTAL PUBLIC BODIES

The increasingly complex nature of "government" was noted earlier. The **4–001**
nature of this administrative diversity will be analysed in this chapter and
that which follows. The last thirty years has seen the most significant
reorganisation of the machinery of central government since the latter part
of the 19th century. A plethora of agencies and non-departmental public
bodies have been created. The reasons for this change, and the concerns
about the new institutional framework, will be considered within this
chapter.

1. EVOLUTION OF EXECUTIVE AGENCIES AND
NON-DEPARTMENTAL PUBLIC BODIES

A. Fulton, Hiving Off and Agencies
Until recently the civil service was still cast in the mould set by the **4–002**
Northcote-Trevelyan reforms of the mid-19th century. It was a unified and
uniform service in theory at least, and in most instances in reality too.
Governmental functions were organised in and through departments.

This was in contrast with the pattern of administration in the earlier part
of the nineteenth century when, as we have seen,[1] public functions were
often undertaken by boards, which operated outside the confines of
departments. The latter part of the nineteenth century witnessed the decline
in such institutions and the emergence of ministerial responsibility, with the
corollary of civil service anonymity.

By the 1960s strains had begun to appear in this organisational structure.
These became apparent in the Report of the *Fulton Committee*.[2] It stressed

[1] See above, Ch.2.
[2] *Report of the Committee on the Civil Service 1966–68*, Cmnd. 3638 (1968).

the need for improved efficiency within traditional departments, with a structure in which different units had clearly defined authority for which they could be held responsible. The Report also pressed for reassessment of the activities required to be undertaken directly within the department. Many activities might work better if they were "hived off" and run by bodies outside the departmental framework, albeit subject to overall ministerial guidance.

The proposals of the Fulton Committee were one of the catalysts for the hiving off of functions to newly created agencies. The Civil Aviation Authority was formed from the Department of Trade and Industry in 1971; the Manpower Services Commission, the Advisory and Conciliation and Arbitration Service (ACAS) and the Health and Safety Commission were split from the Department of Employment in 1974. These agencies were *regulatory* in nature, even though part of their brief might also include the giving of advice.

The general reasons for creating such agencies is neatly summarised in one study as follows:[3]

"First, there is the 'buffer' theory which sees them as a way of protecting certain activities from political interference. Second, there is the 'escape' theory which sees them as escaping known weaknesses of traditional government departments. Third, the 'corson' theory, following Mr. John Corson sees them as used to 'put the activity where the talent was,' which might be outside government departments. Fourth, there is the participation or 'pluralistic' theory which thinks it desirable to spread power. Fifth, there is the 'back double' theory. This is based on the analogy with a taxi-driver who finds the main streets too busy and therefore uses back streets—what are known to taxi drivers as 'back doubles.' The back double theory is that if governments, local authorities or other bodies find that they cannot do the things they want within the existing structure, they set up new organisations which make it possible to do them. Sixth, the 'too many bureaucrats' view, mainly an American one, suggests that if the public thinks a country has too many civil servants it can set up quasi-non-governmental organisations whose employees are not classified as civil servants."

These reasons are echoed in a consultation paper *Opening up Quangos*[4] by the Labour government. It listed the following reasons for the existence of quangos: the need to have bodies which are at arm's length from the government to carry out certain activities; the provision of expert guidance; the

---

[3] D. Hague, W. Mackenzie and A. Barker (eds), *Public Policy and Private Interests: The Institutions of Compromise* (MacMillan, 1975), 362. See also, the *Report on Non-Departmental Public Bodies*, Cmnd. 7797 (1980), paras 10–16 for a list of similar considerations; R. Baldwin and C. McCrudden, *Regulation and Public Law* (Weidenfeld & Nicolson, 1987), Ch.1. An additional reason for the creation of some agencies is that government can immunise itself from criticism in certain politically sensitive areas. In the public mind it will often be the "X commission" or the "Y authority" which receives the brunt of public disquiet.
[4] Cabinet Office (November 1997), Ch.2.

bringing of ordinary people into public life; the ability to respond quickly to matters which are of public concern; and the fact that such bodies facilitate a partnership between government and other interests.

B. Rayner, Ibbs and Executive Agencies

Various attempts at improving efficiency and effectiveness in the civil service followed the Fulton Committee Report.[5] It was however the establishment of the *Rayner Unit* in 1979, later known as the *Efficiency Unit*, by the Prime Minister after her election victory that was to sow the seeds for more major reform. Lord Rayner had run Marks & Spencer and was brought in by Mrs Thatcher to improve efficiency within the civil service. Rayner headed a small team that undertook a number of efficiency scrutinies of particular departmental activities. In this sense Rayner operated through the medium of the laser beam rather than the arc light.[6]

4–003

The scrutinies produced savings, and also acted as a catalyst for further change in the system. Thus it was a Rayner scrutiny of the Department of Employment that was the impetus for the establishment of MINIS, or Management Information Systems, designed to enable the minister to explore "who does what, why and what does it cost?"[7] The Efficiency Unit under Rayner also conceived what became known as FMI, Financial Management Initiative, although this was then put into operation by a different body, the Financial Management Unit.[8] As Hennessy notes,[9] the FMI was meant to be "fast breeder reactor which would achieve a permanent self-sustaining reaction the length and breadth of every Civil Service chain of command". All managers were intended to have a clear view of their objectives, well defined responsibility for making the best use of their resources, and the information, training and expertise necessary to exercise their responsibilities effectively.

Sir Robin Ibbs succeeded Lord Rayner as head of the Efficiency Unit and began by undertaking an overview of the achievements of the Rayner scrutinies.[10] This was followed by a more radical study, which culminated in the *"Next Steps" Report*.[11] The radical nature of its proposals led to it being concealed until after the 1987 election. The object of the study was to

---

[5] For an overview of the development of what are now termed Executive Agencies, http://www.civilservice.gov.uk/other/agencies/agencies_and_non_ministerial_depts/background_and_development/index.asp.

[6] P. Hennessy, *Whitehall* (Fontana, 1990), Ch.14; O. McDonald, *The Future of Whitehall* (Weidenfeld & Nicolson, 1991), Ch.1.

[7] G. Drewry and T. Butcher, *The Civil Service Today* (Blackwell, 2nd edn, 1991), 203–206.

[8] *Financial Management in Government Departments*, Cmnd. 9058 (1983); A. Gray, B. Jenkins, A. Flynn and B. Rutherford, "The Management of Change in Whitehall: The Experience of the FMI" (1991) 69 Pub. Adm. 41.

[9] *Whitehall*, n.6, 606.

[10] *Making Things Happen: A Report on the Implication of Government Efficiency Scrutinies* (1985).

[11] *Improving Management in Government: The Next Steps* (1988); D. Goldsworthy, *Setting Up Next Steps: A Short Account of the Origins, Launch, and Implementation of the Next Steps Project in the British Civil Service* (1991).

discover the achievements of the scrutiny exercises and FMI, and to decide what should be the next steps in civil service reform. The general conclusions of the study are aptly summarised by Hennessy.[12]

"Despite the real achievements of the Rayner years, it showed how little in the way of *real* financial and management responsibility had been devolved down the line; how meddlesome the Treasury and Cabinet Office remained; how dominant was the Whitehall culture of caution; how great was the premium on a safe pair of hands; and how rarely were proven managerial skills perceived as the way to reach the top of the bureaucratic tree."

The *Next Steps Report* proposed two fundamental changes, the implementation of which has continued to shape the structure of the bureaucracy. There should, on the one hand, be a split between service delivery and the making of policy, with a real devolution of power to executive agencies in the area of service delivery, which would cover approximately 95 per cent of civil service activity. There should, on the other hand, be an end to the fiction that the minister was responsible for everything done by officials in his or her own name.

4–004   The Report began to be acted upon in 1988–89. A project manager, Peter Kemp, was appointed to carry forward the Report's proposals, with reference to the creation of executive agencies responsible for service delivery. Government departments were required to review their activities and to consider five possibilities: abolition, privatization, contracting out, creating an agency, and preservation of the status quo. If the agency route was chosen then this would be taken forward by a Project Executive made up of representatives from Kemp's Project Team, the Treasury, the Efficiency Unit and the sponsoring department itself.

The Labour government continued the policy of what are now termed Executive Agencies.[13] Large parts of the civil service have been hived off and have agency status. As of June 2007 there were 86 agencies.[14] Examples of Executive Agencies include: the Defence Procurement Agency; the Driver and Vehicle Licensing Agency; the Planning Inspectorate; the Child Support Agency; the Central Statistical Office; the Patent Office; the Occupational Health Service; the Treasury Solicitor's department; the Pensions Service; the Meteorological Office; the Identity and Passport Service; HM Prison Service; Insolvency Service; the Medicines and Healthcare Products and Regulatory Agency and many others.

The existing mechanism for creation of an Executive Agency is as follows.[15] If following a business review the sponsor department considers that an Executive Agency is the most appropriate delivery agent, the

---

[12] *Whitehall*, n.6, 620. Italics in the original.
[13] Cabinet Office, *Next Steps Report 1997*, Cm. 3889 (1998).
[14] http://www.cabinetoffice.gov.uk/ministerial_responsibilities/executive_agencies/. This figure does not include Executive Agencies established in Wales, Scotland and Northern Ireland.
[15] Cabinet Office, *Executive Agencies, A Guide for Departments* (2006).

departmental minister makes a submission to Cabinet Office and the Treasury seeking agreement to the proposals. The "launch project" will address matters such as: the appointment of the Chief Executive, which is normally by open competition; the preparation of the Framework Document, the content of which is described in more detail below; and the preparation of an initial business plan, including key targets.

C. Non-Departmental Public Bodies

It is also important to have some idea about the public bodies that are not   **4–005**
Executive Agencies. The 2006 Report of Public Bodies[16] lists those public bodies that are not part of a government department, and carry out their functions to a greater or lesser extent at arm's length from central government. Non-ministerial departments and Executive Agencies are excluded from the directory, as they are departments or part of one.[17] Ministers are ultimately responsible to Parliament for the activities of the public bodies sponsored by their department and in almost all cases ministers make the appointments to their boards. Departments are responsible for funding and ensuring good governance of their public bodies.

The term "public body" is used to capture: Non-Departmental Public Bodies (NDPBs); Public Corporations; NHS Bodies; and Public Broadcasting Authorities (BBC and S4C). There are four types of Non-Departmental Public Body, which denote different funding arrangements, functions and kinds of activity.[18] There are *Executive NDPBs*, which are established by statute and carry out administrative, regulatory and commercial functions. They employ their own staff and are allocated their own budgets. *Advisory NDPBs* provide independent and expert advice to ministers on particular topics. They do not usually have staff, but are supported by staff from their sponsoring department. They do not usually have their own budget, as costs incurred come within the department's expenditure. *Tribunal NDPBs* have jurisdiction in a specialised field of law. They are usually supported by staff from their sponsoring department and do not have their own budgets. *Independent Monitoring Boards* were formerly known as "Boards of Visitors" of the prison system. Their duty is to satisfy themselves as to the state of the prison premises, their administration and the treatment of prisoners. The sponsoring department meets the costs.

In March 2006 there were 883 public bodies sponsored by UK Government departments. This figure was made up of 199 Executive NDPBs, 448 Advisory NDPBs, 40 Tribunal NDPBs (counted on the basis of tribunal systems rather than individual panels), 149 Independent Monitoring Boards (previously Boards of Visitors), 21 Public Corporations, the Bank of England, 2 Public Broadcasting Authorities and 23 NHS Bodies.

Examples of important Executive NDPBs are the: Civil Aviation

[16] Cabinet Office, *Public Bodies* (2006).
[17] Cabinet Office, *Public Bodies*, n.16, i.
[18] Cabinet Office, *Public Bodies: A Guide for Departments* (2006), Ch.2.

Authority; Commission for Racial Equality; Competition Commission; Health and Safety Executive; the Criminal Injuries Compensation Panel; Office of Communications; Office of Surveillance Commissioners; Gambling Commission; Criminal Cases Review Commission; Police Complaints Authority; Parole Board; Office of the Data Protection Commissioner; Arts Council; British Museum; Higher Education Funding Council; Audit Commission; Environment Agency; Legal Services Commission; Advisory Conciliation and Arbitration Service; Human Fertilisation and Embryology Authority; Economic and Social Research Council; and the Pensions Regulator.

D. Terminology

4–006 The names of the institutions that have been hived off from central government vary enormously: commission, directorate, agency, inspectorate, authority, service and office are all to be found. Nothing technical normally turns upon these differences. Various labels have been used to describe in more general terms the range of bodies discussed within this chapter.

The term *quango*, quasi-autonomous non-governmental organisation has been used in the past. It is however not the most useful term that could be devised, since many of these bodies are non-departmental, rather than non-governmental.[19]

The government itself distinguishes between *executive agencies* and *non-departmental public body* (NDPB).[20] Executive Agencies are those bodies created pursuant to the Next Steps initiative. They do not usually have their own legal identity, but operate under powers delegated from ministers and departments. They have a chief executive who reports to the minister against specific targets. NDPBs are, as we have seen, those bodies which have a role in the processes of national government, but are not a government department or part of one, and operate to a greater or lesser extent at arm's length from ministers.

While this distinction can be accepted as a starting point for analysis, it should not be pressed too far. Many of the same issues concerning accountability, transparency and the like are relevant to both sets of organisations.[21] Moreover, some NDPBs have the name "agency",[22] and many other NDPBs, which perform regulatory functions, would be regarded as agencies in other political systems, irrespective of their precise nomenclature.[23]

---

[19] *Report on Non-Departmental Public Bodies*, Cmnd. 7797 (1980), para.17; A. Barker, "Quango: A Word and a Campaign", in A. Barker (ed.), *Quangos in Britain* (MacMillan, 1982), 219–225.

[20] http://www.civilservice.gov.uk/other/agencies/guidance_for_departments/index.asp.

[21] Cabinet Office, *Opening up Quangos, A Consultation Paper* (November 1997), Ch.1, paras 2–4.

[22] See, e.g., Environment Agency, Food Standards Agency, Teacher Training Agency, Health Protection Agency, Oil & Pipelines Agency.

[23] See, e.g., Competition Commission, Civil Aviation Authority, Gambling Commission, Office of Communications, Commission for Racial Equality, Health and Safety Executive, Human Fertilisation and Embryology Authority, Qualifications and Curriculum Authority.

E. Conclusion

The developments from Fulton to Rayner to Ibbs do not follow in a series of **4–007**
logically inevitable steps. Few changes in the pattern of administration can
be viewed in this manner. Yet they are not unconnected either. Once the
drive for efficiency was on, and once the existing departmental structure had
been challenged, it was natural to consider whether it was desirable for
activities to be performed in-house. It became natural also to consider
whether the activity should continue to be performed by government at all;
whether it should be undertaken by an executive agency, rather than in-
house; or whether it should be done outside the department on a contracting-out basis, rather than by an executive agency. All three options
have been employed in differing contexts. It is for this reason that our
administrative landscape has become more complex.

It should, moreover, be emphasised that there are connections between
the administrative changes charted above and what has been termed the
"New Public Management" (NPM). The doctrinal components of NPM
include[24]: hands-on professional management in the public sector; standards
of performance; output controls; the break up of large bureaucratic structures; greater public sector competition; and greater discipline in resource
use.

These developments pose new challenges for public law, relating to
accountability, susceptibility to judicial review, and the appropriate procedural and substantive norms to be applied to such bodies. It is to these issues
which we must now turn.

2. Legal Status and Organisational Framework

It is, however, important to draw a distinction between the NDPBs and **4–008**
Executive Agencies because the legal and organisational framework differs
markedly in the two instances.

A. NDPBs

Executive NDPBs have separate legal identity and will normally be based **4–009**
upon statute, or on occasion the prerogative.[25] Most Executive NDPBs
require legislation, in order to confer functions on the body, and also for
reasons of government accounting.[26] The empowering legislation for bodies
such as the Civil Aviation Authority, the Competition Commission, the
Gambling Commission and the Office of Communications will normally

---

[24] C. Hood, "A Public Management for All Seasons?" (1991) 69 Pub. Adm. 3, 4–5.
[25] Cabinet Office, *Public Bodies: A Guide for Departments*, n.18, Ch.3.
[26] Public Bodies with their own legal personality do not generally enjoy Crown status. The
exceptions are the Health and Safety Commission, the Health and Safety Executive and the
Advisory, Conciliation and Arbitration Service, which are Crown bodies.

state the composition and powers of such bodies. Where the body is created by legislation it will usually be incorporated as a body corporate by the founding legislation. The staff of public bodies that have a separate legal personality are not civil servants.

Advisory NDPBs are, by way of contrast, normally set up by administrative action. Legislation is however required if the activity involves continuing government funding for which parliamentary authority is needed. It is moreover open to departments to decide if they wish to establish the body as part of the Crown, or as an unincorporated/incorporated body with a separate legal personality.

Tribunal NDPBs are normally statutory bodies, which are established to adjudicate on specific subject matter. While tribunals exercise their functions entirely independently, a government department will normally be responsible for providing administrative support.

The legislation or instrument creating the public body will commonly specify its functions and method of funding. It is common for the legislation or instrument to specify other powers, such as the power to: appoint staff, pay salaries, make pension provision, raise money by levies or charges, borrow and lend, take enforcement action, and acquire property. The legislation or instrument will normally impose obligations on the public body: to make suitable external audit arrangements, to report annually to Parliament, to be subject to investigation by the Parliamentary Commissioner for Administration, and to set fees and charges for services.

The legislation or instrument creating the NDPB will also indicate the role of the minister within the particular area. Thus the Cabinet Office Guidance to Departments when creating a public body states that departments should strike the balance between enabling the minister to fulfil his or her responsibilities to Parliament, and giving the public body the desired degree of independence. The precise balance will depend on the nature of the public body's functions and on the reasons for distancing these from government.[27] It will be common for the legislation or instrument to accord the minister power over appointment and dismissal of the chairman and board members. The legislation may also, for example, allow the minister to give statutory directions to the agency, or ministerial approval may be required before certain courses of action can be taken, or before borrowing above a certain limit is allowed.[28] Control may be exercised through non-legislative techniques, such as through conditions attached to the issue of grant-in-aid, or in a formal agreement between the department and the body.[29]

An action for judicial review will normally be brought against the public body in its own name, if an individual feels that the agency has exceeded its powers. Actions against bodies such as the Monopolies and Mergers Commission, the Commission for Racial Equality or the Gaming Board have been brought not infrequently. The relevant minister may also be a

[27] Cabinet Office, *Public Bodies: A Guide for Departments*, n.18, Ch.3, para.3.1.
[28] Cabinet Office, *Public Bodies*, n.18, Ch.3, para.5.
[29] Cabinet Office, *Public Bodies*, n.18, Ch.3, para.3.3.

party to any action if the applicant claims that ministerial powers granted under the legislation have been exceeded.[30]

B. Executive Agencies

The position with respect to Executive Agencies is markedly different.[31] **4–010**
They are part of the Crown. They do not usually have their own legal identity, but operate under powers delegated from ministers and departments. They have a Chief Executive who reports to the minister against specific targets. Most such agencies receive their funding from their parent department and, although they are required to publish and lay before Parliament separate accounts, these accounts are part of their parent department's accounts. Some Executive Agencies have become Trading Funds, and generate the cash they need to operate from their commercial business.[32] Other Executive Agencies are non-ministerial departments in their own right.[33]

Executive Agencies are given the task of carrying out executive functions within government, with emphasis being placed on ensuring delivery of specific outputs within a framework of accountability to ministers laid down in the Framework Document, which is published. While the details of such Framework Documents vary, the Cabinet Office recommends that they should contain:[34] a foreword by the minister; details of the Agency's size, location and functions; the Agency's aim and objectives; key target areas; the relationship between the minister, the Agency Chief Executive and senior officials in the parent department; the relations with the department accounting officer; the relationship with other bodies; arrangements for dealing with Parliamentary Questions and letters from MPs; the customer complaints procedure and the arrangements for handling Parliamentary Commissioner for Administration cases; the financial regime for the agency; the machinery for accounting, audit, monitoring and reporting, both within government and externally; the arrangements for producing accounts; the business and corporate planning framework; the arrangements for recruitment and pay; the method of recruitment and the basis of remuneration for the Chief Executive; appearance before the Public Accounts Committee and departmental select committees; the arrangements for risk management; and the arrangements for changing the Framework Document.

Executive Agencies do not normally have any separate legal status of their own,[35] and thus legal actions will in general have to be brought against the relevant minister under whose aegis the agency functions. It seems therefore that if an Executive Agency abuses its powers then it will be the relevant

---

[30] Baldwin and McCrudden, n.3.
[31] Cabinet Office, *Executive Agencies*, n.15.
[32] Government Trading Act 1990. See, e.g., HMSO, Companies House, Army Base Repair Organisation.
[33] Assets Recovery Agency, HM Land Registry, Ordnance Survey.
[34] Cabinet Office, *Executive Agencies*, n.15, Annex A.
[35] I. Harden, *The Contracting State* (Open University Press, 1992), 44, 46.

minister who will appear in any such action. The agency will simply be regarded as part of the parent department.[36]

3. NDPBs: Appointments, Accountability and Efficiency

4-011   The existence of bodies outside the normal departmental framework gives rise to a number of problems. The nature of these concerns can differ as between NDPBs and Executive Agencies created pursuant to the Next Steps initiative. Differential treatment between the two is also necessary because they are treated separately by government.[37] This section will therefore focus on issues concerning NDPBs; those concerning Executive Agencies will be addressed in the following section.

A. Appointments

4-012   There has in the past been concern about the process by which people are appointed to the NDPBs, more particularly about the power that this gives the minister in the sponsoring department. The Labour government recognised these concerns,[38] and reforms were implemented. The reality is that the appointment process is now highly regulated to ensure fairness and openness.

There is a Commissioner for Public Appointments, as a result of the First Nolan Report.[39] The Office of the Commissioner for Public Appointments (OCPA) supports the work of the Commissioner, a position which is independent of the government. The Commissioner's role is to regulate, monitor, report and advise on appointments made by UK Ministers and by members of the National Assembly for Wales to the boards of around 1,100 national and regional public bodies. Some bodies within Northern Ireland also fall under Commissioner's remit. Government departments are required to follow the Commissioner for Public Appointments Code of Practice when making ministerial appointments to the boards of public bodies.

The principles contained in the Code are that:[40] the ultimate responsibility for appointments is with ministers; selection should be based on merit; there should be independent scrutiny of appointments; appointments should respect equal opportunities; appointees must be committed to the values of public service and perform their duties with integrity; the principles of open

---

[36] *R. v Secretary of State for Social Services, Ex p. Sherwin* [1996] 32 B.M.L.R. 1.
[37] http://www.civilservice.gov.uk/other/agencies/index.asp; Cabinet Office, *Opening up Quangos, A Consultation Paper* (November 1997); Cabinet Office, *Quangos: Opening the Doors* (1998); Cabinet Office, *Quangos: Opening up Public Appointments* (1998).
[38] Cabinet Office, *Opening up Quangos, A Consultation Paper* (1997), Ch.1, para.8 I–j.
[39] *First Report of the Committee on Standards in Public Life*, Cm. 2850–I (1995).
[40] Office of the Commissioner for Public Appointments, *The Commissioner for Public Appointments Code of Practice for Ministerial Appointments to Public Bodies* (2005).

government must be applied to the appointments process; the appointments procedure must be proportionate, in the sense of appropriate for the nature of the post and its responsibilities. The Prime Minister, Gordon Brown, has moreover instituted a system whereby prospective appointees to become head of some NDPBs are subject to scrutiny by departmental select committee.

The Cabinet Office also publishes detailed guidance on making public appointments, which builds on that of the Commissioner, but goes into greater detail and applies to a wider range of appointments.[41] There is a website with details of vacancies in public bodies.[42] The Cabinet Office in addition provides detailed advice to departments about the arrangements for staffing of NDPBs, including a model code for staff of Executive NDPBs and a model code for contracts of employment for those in senior posts.[43]

B. Control and Accountability

Control and accountability have been major concerns in relation to NDPBs. Control refers to the way in which the parent department may influence or direct an agency. Accountability is concerned with the answerability of that institution to the public, either through Parliament or through some more direct means of public participation. Degrees of control and accountability need not necessarily go hand in hand. It may, for example, be desirable that the agency has significant independence in its decision-making. This may have been the principal reason for its establishment. While this would indicate relatively little direct control, it does not necessarily follow that accountability should be similarly minimal.[44]

4–013

It is not, however, difficult to perceive why the term accountability has been used to cover both control and the narrower sense of accountability mentioned here. The traditional notions of ministerial responsibility see accountability in its narrow sense as existing by and through normal departmental mechanisms to the minister and hence to Parliament. It is presumed that what the minister is answerable for he or she also controls, or should do at least in theory. In the case of agencies this presumption cannot always be maintained.

i. Control

Control can take two principal forms. It may be *ex ante*. This will be a function of *the degree of precision laid down in the enabling legislation*, primary or secondary, as to what is to be done, how it is to be achieved,[45] and the *type of relationship between the institution and the department responsible*

4–014

---

[41] Cabinet Office, *Making and Managing Public Appointments: A Guide for Departments* (4th edn, 2006), http://www.civilservice.gov.uk/publications/pa_guidance.asp.
[42] http://www.publicappts-vacs.gov.uk/(rxyae4veesywcnm1n00eji55)/Default.aspx.
[43] Cabinet Office, *Public Bodies: A Guide for Departments*, n.18, Ch.5.
[44] D. Keeling, "Beyond Ministerial Departments: Mapping the Administrative Terrain 1. Quasi-Governmental Agencies" (1976) 54 Pub. Adm. 161, 169.
[45] Hague, Mackenzie and Barker, n.3, 363–364.

for it. A wide discretion may be accorded to the organisation, because the problem is novel, or because the subject matter makes it difficult to delegate anything other than a broad discretion. As the Cabinet Office states, "the nature of the controls will depend both on the NDPB's functions, and on the closeness of supervision which ministers wish to exercise".[46]

This is developed further in the Cabinet Office guidance to departments concerning NDPBs.[47] It states that departments need to identify whether ministers need to retain control over certain aspects of the NDPB's activities. This includes matters such as whether questions of policy can be left to the NDPB acting in accordance with the responsibilities conferred by the governing instrument, or whether ministers will need to be able to direct or modify policy; whether the NDPB should be subject to guidance from the minister; whether the minister should have powers of direction; whether decisions in individual cases can be left to the NDPB, subject to appeal to the courts or a tribunal, or whether appeal to ministers is needed on some matters; whether the minister needs to retain some control over the level of fees charged by the NDPB; and whether the exercise of financial powers concerning borrowing or capital expenditure should be subject to ministerial approval or consent;

Control may also be exercised by *monitoring* the decisions reached by the institution. It is difficult to assess how closely departments exercise this type of control. The degree of monitoring will be partly dependent upon the composition of the particular organisation and the subject matter it is dealing with. Johnson concludes that executive control is blurred and spasmodic,[48] but points out that diffuse control is not necessarily a bad thing. Organisational theory indicates that there may well be certain institutions which function better where restraint is diffuse as opposed to a more rigid form of internal management control.[49]

ii. Accountability

4–015   It is in the realm of traditional accountability that most public disquiet has been focused. The discussion of the administrative machinery in the 19th century revealed the strains placed on the Board system by the growing desire of Parliament to have a person directly answerable in the House for its activities.[50] The resurgence of NDPBs has raised this same problem in a more acute form, since we are now accustomed to the idea of ministerial responsibility as the "constitutional norm". Accountability can operate in a number of ways. The Labour government's initiatives are a blend of accountability from the top, accountability from the bottom via public participation, and increased transparency.

---

[46] Cabinet Office, *Public Bodies: A Guide for Departments*, n.18, Ch.3, para.5.3.
[47] Cabinet Office, *Public Bodies: A Guide for Departments*, n.18, Ch.2, para.6, Ch.3, para.5.
[48] "Editorial: Quangos and the Structure of British Government" (1979) 57 Pub. Adm. 379, 388.
[49] (1979) 57 Pub. Adm. 379, 388–389.
[50] See above, Ch.2.

(1)   The NDPB will be *accountable to the minister, with the latter being responsible to Parliament.* Government practice is as follows. If a parliamentary question raises issues concerning the day to day operation of a NDPB then the relevant minister will refer the question to the Chief Executive Officer of the NDPB for a reply, and the reply will be printed. Where however the queries raised on a particular issue are numerous, or the subject of the query is sufficiently sensitive and/or high profile, then a ministerial response will be more appropriate.[51] Similar principles apply in relation to correspondence from MPs: ministers will answer correspondence relating to policies about sponsored bodies and the frameworks within such bodies operate, but issues concerning their day to day operation will normally be passed on to the Chief Executive of the NDPB.

(2)   Accountability may be secured through *select committees.*[52] Departmental select committees are entitled to examine the expenditure, administration and policy of the "associated public bodies" of the departments concerned, which is interpreted broadly to include those instances where there is a significant degree of ministerial responsibility for the body concerned.[53] The Chief Executive, as Accounting Officer, may also be summoned to the Public Accounts Committee. It is however unclear whether select committees are capable of comprehensive oversight of agencies, as opposed to having a more targeted impact upon particular issues.[54] Research on select committees would appear to substantiate these reservations.[55] The Labour government regards select committees as one way of enhancing accountability to the top. This is to be done partly by the select committee considering the annual report from the agency, and partly through involvement in the quinquennial reviews of the public bodies.[56]

(3)   Accountability can also be enhanced from the bottom, *through public participation* and the like. This is accepted by the government. The Cabinet Office guide states that "departments and public bodies should aim to consult their users and stakeholders on a wide range of issues by means of questionnaires, public meetings or other forms of consultation to ensure that they are responsive to and meeting the needs of their customers".[57] The government's Code of Practice on

---

[51] Cabinet Office, *Public Bodies: A Guide for Departments,* n.18, Ch.8, para.5.1.
[52] Suggested by the *Report on Non-Departmental Public Bodies,* Cmnd. 7797 (1980), paras 81–85.
[53] Cabinet Office, *Public Bodies: A Guide for Departments,* n.18, Ch.8, para.5.3.
[54] N. Johnson, "Editorial" (1979) 57 Pub. Adm. 379, 390; N. Johnson, "Accountability, Control and Complexity; Moving Beyond Ministerial Responsibility", in Barker (ed.), n.19, Ch.12.
[55] See above, Ch.3.
[56] *Quangos: Opening the Doors,* n.37, para.6.
[57] Cabinet Office, *Public Bodies: A Guide for Departments,* n.18, Ch.8, para.4.1.1.

Consultation is to be followed in all cases.[58] The Cabinet Office guide also enjoins NDPBs to establish complaints procedures.[59]

(4) Accountability will be fostered by *greater openness.* A number of proposals from the Labour government addressed this issue. Agencies were encouraged to hold open annual meetings,[60] to make reports available to the public[61] and to provide summary reports of their meetings.[62] Much of this is now reproduced in the Cabinet Office guidance to public bodies,[63] and NDPBs also come within the remit of the Freedom of Information Act 2000.

(5) The *Parliamentary Commissioner for Administration* (PCA) can also help to ensure accountability. A number of agencies have been brought within the PCA's jurisdiction,[64] and the Labour government has broadened the ambit of the bodies that the PCA can investigate.[65] While the PCA cannot provide systematic scrutiny of agency action, this reform is nonetheless to be welcomed.[66]

There is no simple solution to the problem of accountability. The general approach of the Labour government is to be welcomed, as is the willingness to conceive of accountability in the "round". Accountability can only be secured by considering it from the bottom as well as the top, and by making it a reality through proper regard for transparency.

C. Efficiency and Effectiveness

4–016   The efficiency and effectiveness of NDPBs is closely monitored, although the way in which this is done has altered.[67] The principal mechanism used to be quinquennial or financial, management and policy reviews, but these are no longer required by the Cabinet Office and the Treasury.

These have now been replaced by "landscape reviews", which are designed to produce better strategic alignment of objectives, improved targeting of services and customers and better governance arrangements across a department's entire delivery "landscape". These are complemented by "business reviews", which are concerned with the delivery of selected outcomes, as expressed, for example, through the targets set out in a Public Service Agreement. The focus is on the process of service delivery. There are also "light touch reviews" for smaller NDPBs. While there is no longer a

[58] Cabinet Office, *Public Bodies: A Guide for Departments,* n.18. For discussion of the Code, see below Ch.22.
[59] Cabinet Office, *Public Bodies: A Guide for Departments,* n.18, Ch.8, para.4.2.
[60] *Quangos: Opening the Doors,* n.37, para.20.
[61] *Quangos: Opening the Doors,* n.37, para.16.
[62] *Quangos: Opening the Doors,* n.37, para.23.
[63] Cabinet Office, *Public Bodies: A Guide for Departments,* n.18, Ch.8, para.3.
[64] e.g. Health and Safety Commission and Executive and the Office of Fair Trading.
[65] Cabinet Office, *Sweeping Extension of the Parliamentary Ombudsman's Jurisdiction,* February 10, 1999.
[66] Cabinet Office, *Public Bodies: A Guide for Departments,* n.18, Ch.8, para.4.3.
[67] Cabinet Office, *Public Bodies: A Guide for Departments,* n.18, Ch.9.

rigid requirement for departments to carry out these reviews every five years, they should be undertaken with "sufficient frequency to give the department confidence that the NDPB is delivering high quality services, efficiently and effectively and fits appropriately into the department's overall delivery structure".[68]

The review process will consider whether the function is required at all, and if so, whether the existing NDPB model is the best option for its delivery. The NDPB model is assessed alongside other options such as abolition, contracting-out, delivery in-house, merger or rationalisation, executive agency status, and privatisation.[69] When NDPB status has been confirmed as the most appropriate delivery mechanism, the review then looks at how services and functions could be provided more effectively in the future. Departments are encouraged to consider the following issues:[70] past performance, the relationship between the NDPB and the sponsoring department, possible efficiency savings and productivity gains, the relationship with customers, the suitability of the NDPB's aims and targets and whether the NDPB could benefit from partnership of some kind with another public body, or some alliance with those in the private sector.

4. EXECUTIVE AGENCIES: STAFFING, ACCOUNTABILITY AND EFFICIENCY

An important review of Executive Agencies was undertaken in 2002. The **4–017** Report on *Better Government Services, Executive Agencies in the 21st Century*[71] contains insights on Executive Agencies and their role in government. The Report made it clear that Executive Agencies are here to stay and that in general terms they had been a success. It nonetheless perceived a number of areas in which further improvement could be made. The recommendations have been acted on and will be integrated into the subsequent discussion.

A. Staffing
These agencies are staffed by civil servants, and approximately 70 per cent of **4–018** civil servants now work in such agencies. Agency Chief Executives will however be recruited through open competition.

The official response when agencies were created was to talk of a unified, but not uniform civil service, the message being that the structural diversity resulting from agencies would have ramifications for uniform conditions of pay, and conditions of service, which were the norm hitherto. HMSO, for

[68] Cabinet Office, *Public Bodies: A Guide for Departments*, n.18, Ch.9, para.1.5.
[69] Cabinet Office, *Public Bodies: A Guide for Departments*, n.18, 9–11.
[70] Cabinet Office, *Public Bodies: A Guide for Departments*, n.18, 12–15.
[71] HM Treasury and Office of Public Services Reform, *Better Government Services, Executive Agencies in the 21st Century* (2002).

example, introduced a new pay and grading structure tailored to meet its
business needs, and more flexibility in terms and conditions of service is very
much the order of the day.[72] The passage of the Civil Service (Management
Functions) Act 1992 has facilitated agency autonomy with respect to pay
bargaining and conditions of service.

The Report on *Better Government Services, Executive Agencies in the 21st
Century*[73] favoured flexibility that would enable agencies to recruit, pay and
promote staff in the light of local needs and labour markets. It also
recommended that more Executive Agencies explore the possibility of
gaining trading fund status, since this would help them to generate income.
This recommendation has been take up in the Cabinet Office *Guide on
Executive Agencies*, which provides that matters concerning agency pay,
terms and conditions of service and the like are normally delegated to the
Agency's Chief Executive, and that such matters should be allowed to vary
in accord with local employment conditions.[74]

These ramifications may well be greater than initially envisaged. The more
that Chief Executives are encouraged to develop pay structures which suit
their own agency, the less easy will it be for there to be a regular interchange
between the agency and the department itself. This is particularly so if
agency pay is determined in part by commercial criteria, while that at the
centre is held in check by political considerations.[75]

It should nonetheless be recognised that there has been a general change
in the way that pay and conditions of service are determined throughout
Whitehall. The Treasury has delegated pay bargaining to all departments,
many of which have further delegated this power to agencies within their
purview. Departments also have considerable freedom in relation to
recruitment to all grades below the senior civil service, and once again will
often give the same power to agencies.

B. Control and Accountability

i. Control

4–019   The degree of ministerial control will be largely dependent upon the specificity of the framework agreement, and this varies from area to area.[76] The
difficulty of sustaining the divide between policy consideration, undertaken
by the core department, and service delivery, done by the agency, should
however be acknowledged. It is not simply that these two activities can
naturally overlap. It is also that past experience with nationalised industries,
where a similar functional divide was meant to operate, is salutary. It taught
us that governments often meddled with day-to-day operations, while
staunchly resisting answering questions on the topic by claiming that such

---

[72] *Robertson v Department for the Environment, Food and Rural Affairs* [2005] I.C.R. 750.
[73] N.71.
[74] Cabinet Office, *Executive Agencies*, n.15, Annex A, para.28.
[75] Drewry and Butler, n.7, 234–237.
[76] McDonald, n.6, 54–55.

matters were not within its purview. We also learned that governmental guidance on more general issues of policy was often not forthcoming, or was subject to frequent revision.[77]

ii. Accountability
The problems of accountability have occupied more attention. The issue is   **4–020**
put succinctly by Drewry and Butcher.[78]

"The basic problem is quite simply stated but not at all easily resolved. How can ministers credibly cling to their virtual monopoly of account-ability to Parliament, via traditional models of ministerial responsibility that (according to Mrs Thatcher) were to remain unaltered by the *Next Steps*, in respect of agencies whose chief executives are expected to take managerial initiatives at arm's length from ministerial control?"

The Treasury and Civil Service Committee expressed concerns of this nat-ure,[79] but the government indicated that no change in the basic constitu-tional arrangements was required.[80] It is nonetheless clear that some modification in the traditional conception of ministerial accountability has been accepted.[81]

Agency Chief Executives are accountable to ministers.[82] The relevant minister is responsible for the policy framework within which each agency operates; for determining its strategic objectives; for setting its annual key financial and performance targets; and for approval of business plans. There should be at least one meeting per year between the Chief Executive and the minister. A senior member of staff within the department will normally act as a sponsor for the agency. The sponsor is a key link between the agency and the department, and will advise ministers on: the strategic direction of the agency in the context of wider departmental objectives; agree a frame-work for strategic performance management; advise ministers on their response to strategic performance information; and ensure that the agency has the power necessary to carry out its tasks. This regime has been developed in order to meet concerns expressed in the Report on *Better Government Services, Executive Agencies in the 21st Century*,[83] which argued that some Executive Agencies had become disconnected from their departments, with the consequence that the gulf between policy and delivery was thought to have widened.

The Agency Chief Executive is however responsible for the day to day management of the agency, and MPs are encouraged to deal directly with

---

[77] T. Prosser, *Nationalised Industries and Public Control* (Blackwell, 1986).
[78] n.7, 228.
[79] e.g. Eighth Report, 1987–88.
[80] *Government Reply*, Cm. 524 (1988).
[81] Cabinet Office, *Executive Agencies*, n.15, Annex A.
[82] Cabinet Office, *Executive Agencies*, n.15, Annex A, paras 11–12.
[83] n.71.

the Chief Executive on such matters, subject to the caveat that the minister retains the "right to intervene in the operations of the agency if public or parliamentary concerns justify it".[84] The Chief Executive will normally represent the Executive Agency before select committees on matters of day-to-day operations.[85]

This "compromise", reflecting as it does traditional British pragmatism, may be no bad thing. The minister is still there and responsible for matters of principle or general policy. In addition to this the Chief Executive of the Agency is visible and the objectives of the Executive Agency are publicly known. The existence of a person who can be called to account for operational agency failure is to be welcomed, more especially so because under the traditional regime prior to Executive Agencies it was often difficult to determine the detailed departmental goals, and who was responsible for them.[86]

> "Next Steps has enhanced accountability to Parliament through its requirements for Agencies to publish their framework documents, annual targets, annual reports and accounts and, where appropriate, their corporate and business plans. Agency Chief Executives are accounting officers and, as such, are answerable to the Public Accounts Committee for the use of the resources allocated to them."

4–021   There is nonetheless an interesting contrast between the approach to accountability of Executive Agencies and NDPBs. The approach taken to the accountability of NDPBs was laudable. The paper on *Quangos: Opening the Doors* and the more recent *Public Bodies: A Guide for Departments* recognised that accountability had to be viewed in the round. It acknowledged that there was an overtly *political* dimension to accountability, which was to be secured both from the top, through oversight by select committee and the like, and from the bottom, by facilitating participation, openness, and transparency. This was complemented by an *economic* dimension, which manifested itself in target setting, benchmarking and efficiency evaluation.

The approach taken to Executive Agencies has been subtly different. They are subject to separate guidance, primarily because they are regarded as part of central government.[87] There are however limits to this rationale, since the central reason for their establishment is the desire for agencies outside the traditional departmental norm, which would have considerable autonomy for operational aspects of service delivery. It is true that such agencies are still under the minister's aegis, but this is also true in certain respects of NDPBs. The continued distinction between the two types of agency may well have been the unwillingness to open Pandora's box. Executive Agencies were established on the premise that it was constitutional business as usual.

---

[84] Cabinet Office, *Executive Agencies*, n.15, Annex A, para.17.
[85] Cabinet Office, *Executive Agencies*, n.15, Annex A, para.32.
[86] *Next Steps, Briefing Note* (1992), para.20.
[87] Cabinet Office, *Executive Report on Non-Departmental Public Bodies 1998*, Cm. 4157 (1998), 2.

The recognition that they generated new constitutional and political concerns would run counter to this. If it were accepted that the broader concerns voiced about the political accountability of NDPBs applied also to Executive Agencies then the original premise behind the establishment of the latter would have been undermined. The incentive to treat NDPBs and Executive Agencies differently becomes more readily explicable when viewed in this way.

The consequence of this differential treatment is that it led in the case of Executive Agencies to a concentration on the economic dimension of accountability, and a downplaying of the more overtly political dimension.[88] It was assumed that the political dimension was adequately taken care of through traditional ministerial responsibility, combined with the content of Framework Documents. Insofar as the Charter initiatives addressed concerns relating to consultation and the like they did so from the perspective of the market citizen, rather than directly from the political perspective. It is almost as if this was regarded as the acceptable way to introduce such matters in relation to Executive Agencies, in that it could be done without thereby directly confronting change in the constitutional arrangements as a result of the Next Steps initiative.

There are however signs that the political dimension of accountability is becoming more openly acknowledged in relation to Executive Agencies. Thus the documentation concerning target setting by Executive Agencies emphasises that transparency and accountability are fundamental elements of the Government's approach to delivering better public services, and that targets and performance measurement are essential in this respect.[89] There is also considerable emphasis placed on consultation with delivery staff and those affected by the targets, and this is seen as part of a continuing relationship in which the organisation monitors the experience and satisfaction of customers and their changing needs.[90] This is to be welcomed, since the broader political concerns addressed in relation to NDPBs are equally relevant to many Executive Agencies.

C. Effectiveness

Measuring institutional effectiveness is always difficult, irrespective of whether the task is performed in-house or through an Executive Agency. It requires statistical evidence and criteria by which to use it. Statistical evidence may however be unreliable either because there is simply not enough data, or because the variables to be "computed" are too speculative.[91] The process of determining whether given objectives are being pursued

4–022

---

[88] See, e.g., *Next Steps Report 1997*, Cm. 3889 (1998). See also, K. Burgess, C. Burton and G. Parston, *Accountability for Results* (Public Services Productivity Panel, 2002).
[89] HM Treasury, Cabinet Office, National Audit Office, *Setting Key Targets for Executive Agencies: A Guide* (2003), 3.
[90] HM Treasury, Cabinet Office, National Audit Office, *Setting Key Targets*, n.89, 12–13.
[91] e.g. it may be unclear how those who are to be regulated will react to the proposed regulation and the costs of regulation may be affected by external factors (such as the costs of evasive techniques) which cannot be determined with accuracy.

effectively is even more difficult. The enabling legislation may be unclear as to what those objectives are, or they may clash *inter se*. There may be a choice as to the means to achieve the given end and what the "best choice" is may not be readily apparent. The area may be one in which it is inherently difficult to decide whether and how far the given end has in fact been successfully attained.[92]

It is clear that the government perceived a link between Executive Agencies and the attainment of the objectives in the Citizen's Charter.[93] The Charter established a number of principles which should operate in the context of governmental service delivery:[94] the setting of *standards* for service delivery; *openness* as to how the services are run; *consultation* with service users; *choice*, wherever possible, as to the services which are available; *value for money*; *remedies* when things go wrong. It is precisely because the Executive Agencies are so often in the front line of service delivery that the government attached considerable weight to the attainment of the Charter goals in this area. Official documents bore testimony to the zeal for demonstrating cost savings and better delivery of services.[95]

The Labour government renewed the Charter ideals. Its paper on *Service First, the New Charter Programme*[96] set out nine principles for public service delivery which highlighted the importance attached to accessibility, co-operation and credibility. The principles applied to all public services, central and local, including educational institutions, the NHS, non-departmental public bodies, and nationalised and privatised industries. The principles were: set standards of service; be open and provide full information; consult and involve; encourage access and the promotion of choice; treat all fairly; put things right when they go wrong; use resources effectively; innovate and improve; and work with other providers.

4–023   Things have now moved on. The government is still very much concerned with targets and the measurement of performance, but this is less linked to Charter initiatives than hitherto. The new strategy will be explicated more fully in the following chapter. Suffice it to say for the present, that departments now have Public Service Agreements, PSAs, in which they set out a clear commitment on what the public can expect for the money that they spend. These agreements are backed up by Service Delivery Agreements, in which departments explain how they will reach the targets elaborated in the PSAs.

The recommendations contained in the Report on *Better Government Services, Executive Agencies in the 21st Century* must be seen in the light of

---

[92] e.g. in the case of support for the Arts, or the prevention of sexual or racial discrimination
[93] See however G. Drewry, "Whatever Happened to the Citizen's Charter" [2002] P.L. 9 for the lower profile of the Charter in more recent years.
[94] Cm. 1599 (1991).
[95] *Improving Management in Government-The Next Steps Agencies*, Cm. 1760 (1991); *Improving Management in Government-The Next Steps Agencies*, Cm. 2111 (1992); *Next Steps, Briefing Notes* (1992–1998); *Next Steps Report 1997*, Cm. 3889 (1998).
[96] Cabinet Office (1998).

these more general developments.[97] Strategic performance monitoring was felt to be lacking in focus. There should be greater alignment between departmental and agency target setting. There should be a real linkage between high-level Public Service Agreements made by departments, and performance targets for agencies. Quinquennial reviews of agency performance should be abolished, and be replaced by business reviews of the entire process involved in securing a particular outcome. The government has acted on these recommendations. Landscape and business reviews are now conducted in relation to Executive Agencies, and the government has published detailed guidance on target-setting, designed to ensure greater alignment between the PSA made by the department and the targets set by the Executive Agency.[98]

5. AGENCIES: INSTITUTIONAL DESIGN AND LEGAL PRINCIPLE

Agencies raise a number of important issues of institutional design and legal principle. These issues are best approached initially through the study of different agencies in order to determine the legal problems they pose.[99] Some more general conclusions will be drawn thereafter.

4-024

A. The Civil Aviation Authority

Baldwin has shown how the CAA evolved as a result of dissatisfaction with its predecessor the Air Transport Licensing Board.[100] The ATLB operated like a traditional tribunal and suffered from three related defects: it failed to develop a working relationship with the Minister; it was unable to produce durable policies to guide its licensing decisions; and it lacked expertise. These criticisms were echoed by the Edwards' Committee on "Air transport in the seventies", which advocated the replacement of the ATLB by an

4-025

[97] n.71; See also, Report by the Comptroller and Auditor General, *Measuring the Performance of Government Departments* (HC 301; 2001)
[98] *Setting Key Targets for Executive Agencies*, n.89; National Audit Office, *Improving Service Delivery—The Role of Executive Agencies* (2003).
[99] Hague, Mackenzie and Barker, n.3; Baldwin and McCrudden, n.3; N. Lewis, "IBA Programme Contract Awards" [1975] P.L. 317; D. Bradley and R. Wilkie, "The Arts Council: The Case for an Organisational Enquiry" (1975) 53 Pub. Adm. 67; P. Giddings, "Parliament, Boards and Autonomy: The Case of Agricultural Marketing Boards" (1975) 53 Pub. Adm. 383; R. Baldwin, "A British Independent Regulatory Agency and the 'Skytrain' Decision" [1978] P.L. 57; M. Purdue, "The Implications of the Constitution and Function of Regional Water Authorities" [1979] P.L. 119; R. Baldwin, "A Quango Unleashed: The Abolition of Policy Guidance in Civil Aviation Licensing" (1980) 58 Pub. Adm. 287; G. Tyrrell, "The Politics of a Hived Off Board: The Advisory, Conciliation and Arbitration Service" (1980) 58 Pub. Adm. 225.
[100] R. Baldwin, *Regulating the Airlines, Administrative Justice and Agency Discretion* (Oxford University Press, 1985) and "Civil Aviation Regulation: From Tribunal to Regulatory Agency," Baldwin and McCrudden, n.3, Ch.8. See also the two articles by Baldwin, [1978] P.L. 57 and (1980) 58 Pub. Adm. 287.

agency, combining economic and safety regulation, air traffic control and the negotiation of traffic rights. Departmental licensing was rejected as an alternative because independent airline operators were unsure that they would obtain fair treatment from the Government.[101] To circumvent the constitutional problems flowing from the creation of an independent agency to control air transport licensing, it was proposed that the CAA be subject to guidance by the minister by way of written policy statements.

With some modification what emerged as the Civil Aviation Act 1971 followed the main thrust of the Edwards' Committee Report.[102] The Secretary of State for Trade was empowered to give guidance on policy.[103] The formation of these broad policies was not a one way operation. The CAA had an impact on the resulting statement of government policy through reports and consultation. In addition to such policy guidance from the department, the CAA structured its discretion through announcements and consultation.

The CAA was not the first regulatory agency to be given broad powers. The Poor Law Commission possessed a broad spectrum of powers, but Parliament's desire for more direct control and the controversial nature of the subject matter led to its downfall.[104] The creation of the CAA was based on appreciation of the benefits of administration outside of the departmental norm. There was nonetheless a desire to maintain some political control over the agency, to enable a minister to give it a clearer idea as to the manner in which its broad discretion should be exercised. The system of policy guidance was intended to achieve this end.

A result of the ministerial guidance indicating no competition on long haul routes was that the Laker "Skytrain" was told that it would not be allowed to operate. This was unfortunate because Laker had invested nearly £7 million on the strength of government representations that he would be granted the route. Laker took the Government to court. He argued that the policy guidance that led to the withdrawal of Laker Airways from the North American route was ultra vires. The Court of Appeal agreed.[105] It held that "guidance" had a limited role. The Secretary of State's power to give such guidance was contained in s.3(2) of the Civil Aviation Act 1971. The preceding s.3(1), set out four basic objectives that the CAA was to pursue. Guidance given pursuant to s.3(2) could not contradict the general statutory objectives laid down in s.3(1).[106] The Secretary of State's policy guidance was, said the Court of Appeal, attempting to do just that. It was therefore ultra vires.

4–026   The case raised a number of important legal issues. The precise way in which the policy guidance contradicted the statutory objectives was, for

---

[101] "Civil Aviation Regulation: From Tribunal to Regulatory Agency", Baldwin and McCrudden, n.3, 164–165.
[102] e.g. the negotiation of traffic rights was left to the Secretary of State.
[103] S.3(2).
[104] See above, Ch.2.
[105] *Laker Airways Ltd v Department of Trade* [1977] Q.B. 643.
[106] The Court of Appeal was influenced in reaching this conclusion by the power to give directions contained in s.4 of the 1971 Act which would override the objectives set out in s.3(1).

example, never made quite clear.[107] It is however the broader issue as to the relationship of the CAA and the Secretary of State that is relevant here. Baldwin argued persuasively that the court misconceived the role of the CAA[108] They treated it as if it were a traditional body with quasi-judicial functions which should be "protected" from executive interference, failing to perceive that it was a multi-faceted agency that was not intended to be independent of government.

The aftermath of the *Laker* decision is of interest.[109] The limitations placed upon the Secretary of State's power to issue policy guidance resulted in an increased structuring of discretion by the CAA itself. There is no inherent reason why the CAA should not be able to structure its discretion in this way.[110] This does not however touch the issue of principle, which is whether it is preferable to have some broad political control exercised through the mechanism of policy guidance. The debates on the Civil Aviation Bill 1979 reflected the two opposing views. The Government decided to drop the notion of policy guidance, the argument being that if an area was to be hived off it should be truly independent: "both hands should be taken off the wheel". Political control could, it was said, be maintained by alterations in the list of statutory criteria. The Opposition saw this as an abdication of legislative responsibility to a largely unaccountable body. Refining the list of statutory objectives would not solve the problem. Such criteria were often in conflict and had to be balanced.[111]

What the foregoing discussion of the CAA demonstrates is that issues of legal principle concerning decision-making by agencies can assume many forms. They can involve questions as to the proper levels of procedural constraint, or the scope of substantive review. Challenges framed in terms of ultra vires can, however, also raise fundamental questions as to the institutional structure of a particular agency. While such organisations cannot be forced into the traditional framework of ministerial responsibility for measures carried out within a department, this does not necessarily lead to a "both hands off the wheel" approach. Given the initial decision that air transport licensing should be hived-off, it is arguable that the institutional balance secured by the Civil Aviation Act 1971 was a desirable one.[112] The system of policy guidance enshrined therein went some way to preserve accountability, and to provide a more detailed clarification of inherently vague statutory standards.

---

[107] R. Baldwin, "A British Independent Regulatory Agency and the 'Skytrain' Decision" [1978] P.L. 57, 78–79.
[108] Baldwin, n.107, 78.
[109] It is set out in Baldwin, "A Quango Unleashed", n.99.
[110] See below, Ch.16.
[111] (1980) 58 Pub. Adm. 287, 293–294. See now the Civil Aviation Act 1980, ss.12, 13.
[112] The CAA itself did, however, have reservations about the guidance system, Baldwin, n.101, 167–168.

B. Nationalisation and the Public Corporation[113]

4–027   Public corporations have been the principal vehicle used in the nationalisation of industry. The reasons for such nationalisation have varied. They
include the belief that certain functions are vital to the nation and should
not be left in the hands of private enterprise; a desire to provide services
which the market would not sustain; a belief that natural monopolies should
be run by the state, to prevent the accumulation of excessive profits were the
industry to be left in private hands; and a political doctrine based on the
idea that the people should own the industrial assets of the nation, or at least
a proportion of them.

The principal institutional form used to realise these objectives was the
establishment of a public corporation.[114] The precise details of nationalisation statutes varied, but certain common features were evident.[115] The
general theme was that the industry should be autonomous in its day-to-day
administration, but that ministers should have power to determine overall
policy. This theme manifested itself in a number of ways: ministers possessed
the power of appointment to the boards of the industries; they could issue
general directions to these boards; ministerial sanction was required for
major development programmes and ministers exercised certain specific
powers over financial matters.

The ideal of day-to-day autonomy coupled with ministerial control over
long term planning was not a success. It was undermined from both sides.
Successive governments used nationalised industry to respond to short term
pressures. Long term planning was upset by ministerial pressure to buy
British, to resist wage increases, or to curtail a capital investment programme. Such pressure was exerted covertly, rather than through the power
to give directions. Governments were also notably lacking in the broad
policy directive envisioned by the enabling legislation.

There was moreover uncertainty as to the role that such industries should
play in the economy. Some saw them primarily as commercial enterprises, at
least to the minimal extent of balancing revenue and expenditure. Others
perceived their commercial role as largely secondary to their function as an
extended arm of government, to prevent regional unemployment, or to help
implement the broad aims of governmental policy. This did not make life
easy for those running the major corporations. Pushed from pillar to post
they were lambasted for poor commercial returns, while being cajoled by
government to achieve ends that ordinary commercial judgment would
reject.

The preceding uncertainty enabled successive ministers to use the formal

---

[113]   R. Robson, *Nationalised Industry and Public Ownership* (Allen & Unwin, 2nd edn, 1962); W.
Friedmann and J. Garner (eds), *Government Enterprise* (Stevens, 1970); W. Friedmann, *The
State and the Rule of Law in a Mixed Economy* (Stevens, 1971); W. Friedmann (ed.), *Public and
Private Enterprise in Mixed Economies* (Stevens, 1974); D. Coombes, *State Enterprise: Politics
or Business?* (Allen & Unwin, 1971); T. Prosser, *Nationalised Industries and Public Control*
(Blackwell, 1986).
[114]   Other techniques include the government taking a shareholding in an existing company.
[115]   e.g. Coal Industry Nationalisation Act 1946; Civil Aviation Act 1946; Transport Act 1946;
Gas Act 1948; Iron and Steel Act 1949.

statutory scheme as both a sword and a shield. Ministers used it as a sword to exercise influence, formally and informally, over the industry. They used it as a shield to protect them from embarrassing questions in Parliament. Such unwelcome interrogatories were often met by the response that the issue concerned day-to-day administration, and hence was outside the minister's responsibility.

The uncertainty as to the role such industries should play can be **4–028** demonstrated "schematically" by considering in temporal sequence a range of proposed "answers" to this question. The initial idea which permeated Labour thinking from 1945–1950 was that the change of ownership from private to public would remove the profit motive and enable nationalised industries to act as "high custodians of the public interest". The shift from private to public ownership did not however resolve, in and of itself, the task of defining the public interest. The imprecision in this phrase could enable managers and politicians alike to pursue their own objectives under the guise of acting in the national interest: "wolfish self-interest is all too easily cloaked in the public interest sheepskin".[116]

A second approach to the problem was evident in the White Papers of 1961 and 1967,[117] the latter of which strove to bring greater clarity to the objectives of nationalised industries. It advocated, inter alia, marginal cost pricing, set criteria for investment decisions, and proposed that non-commercial activities should be accounted for separately, with the government deciding whether to support such activities on cost–benefit criteria. This approach while reflecting a coherent policy proved to be of little effect. There "was no attempt to develop an adequate structure of incentives to encourage managers to act in the desired ways",[118] and consequently many ignored the pricing and investment guidelines. Moreover, the problem of ministers seeking to attain goals other than those stipulated in the White Paper was left unresolved. Not surprisingly they continued to do so.

A third approach was apparent in the 1978 White Paper and in Conservative policy subsequent thereto.[119] Financial target setting became the principal form of control, supplemented by performance indicators each industry was required to publish in order that sponsoring departments could assess efficiency.[120] The post-1978 framework of control relied most heavily upon external financing limits (EFL), which placed constraints upon the annual change of the net indebtedness of public corporations to the government. This served to restrict the difference between revenue and expenditure. The use of EFLs also highlighted the difficult situation of public corporations. EFLs were accorded such prominence principally because of governmental concern over macro-economic issues, such as the existence of

---

[116] J. Vickers and G. Yarrow, *Privatization, An Economic Analysis* (MIT Press, 1988), 130.
[117] *Financial and Economic Obligations of the Nationalised Industries*, Cmnd. 1337 (1961); *Nationalised Industries: A Review of Economic and Financial Objectives*, Cmnd. 3437 (1967).
[118] Vickers and Yarrow, n.116, 132.
[119] *The Nationalised Industries*, Cmnd. 7131 (1978); Vickers and Yarrow, n.116, 133–135; Prosser, n.113, 44–47, 54–74.
[120] Compare these themes to the policy espoused by the NEDO study of 1976, Prosser, n.113, 41–43.

fiscal deficit and the corresponding desire to control public sector borrowing. The tension between the exercise of commercial freedom, and the utilisation of public corporations as part of a broader governmental strategy was apparent once again.

C. Privatisation and Regulatory Control

4–029   A fuller analysis of the problems of regulating market power will be considered in a subsequent chapter.[121] It is, however, useful here to consider the agency structure established to oversee one particular privatisation, that of telecommunications.

The reasons for privatisation are, like those for nationalisation, eclectic.[122] They include the following: improving efficiency, reducing government involvement in industrial decision-making, widening share ownership, encouraging share ownership by employees, alleviating problems of public sector pay determination, reducing the public sector borrowing requirement and the enhancement of economic freedom.

The cogency of these reasons has been challenged.[123] For example, the argument that privatisation will enhance economic freedom has been criticised because it assumes that a private monopoly will be less threatening to such freedom than a statutory monopoly. The argument has also been criticised because it defines "freedom" in a limited way to mean the absence of government intervention in the market, thereby foreclosing the viability of a more active role for the state that might enhance economic liberty. Moreover the argument that privatisation augments economic freedom has to be qualified because, as we shall see, some privatised industries require regulatory control.

The contention that privatisation will improve efficiency has also been questioned.[124] The "conclusion" that nationalised industry performed inefficiently is contested. Any such conclusion is dependent upon the analysis of complex performance data, which must then take account of the managerial difficulties experienced by public corporations stemming from the lack of clarity as to their objectives. Furthermore, even if it is accepted that a change in ownership rights can have an effect upon incentives, behaviour and efficiency, by sharpening corporate incentives, the realisation of these benefits will "depend crucially upon the framework of competition and regulation in which the privatized firm is to operate".[125]

4–030   The problems posed by privatisation vary, but it is important to keep distinct two different situations. There has been the privatisation of large

---

[121] See below, Ch.11.
[122] Vickers and Yarrow, n.116, 157–160; J. Kay, C. Mayer and D. Thompson (eds), *Privatization and Regulation—the UK Experience* (Oxford University Press, 1986), Chaps 3, 4; C. Foster, *Privatization, Public Ownership and the Regulation of Natural Monopoly* (Blackwell, 1992), Ch.4; T. Prosser, *Law and the Regulators* (Oxford University Press, 1997), Ch.3.
[123] e.g. D. Heald and D. Steel, "Privatising Public Enterprises: An Analysis of the Government's Case", Kay, Mayer and Thompson, n.122, Ch.2.
[124] Kay, Mayer and Thompson, n.122, Chaps 5 and 6.
[125] Vickers and Yarrow, n.116, 7–44, 157–159.

companies, which do not possess undue market power. Firms such as British Aerospace, Britoil, and Cable and Wireless, operate in reasonably competitive industries. Once privatised, these corporations should be of no greater concern to public law than other large companies that have never been within public ownership.[126] These firms do not possess the requisite market power to necessitate a regulatory regime to control their prices. Such privatised companies do, however, often possess "special features", setting them apart from the normal corporation. The government may possess shareholdings in the company, there may be government directors and the articles of association may be structured to allow the government to prevent undesirable takeovers or changes in control.[127]

The other situation is where the privatised corporation does possess significant market power, and this requires the establishment of some regulatory regime to oversee it. The end result is a privatised firm or firms, which are controlled by an agency. The telecommunications industry can be taken as an example.

The Telecommunications Act 1984 brought about the first privatisation of a major public utility in this country. From 1912 until 1981 telecommunications were the responsibility of the Post Office, a state-owned monopoly. Legislation in 1981 separated telecommunications from postal services and established British Telecom as a public corporation.[128] The 1981 Act also allowed some liberalisation in the industry by, for example, abolishing BT's exclusive privilege to supply customer equipment, and by allowing the Secretary of State to license other firms to run telecommunications systems. The 1984 Act privatised BT and created a regulatory framework to oversee the industry.

Section 1 of the 1984 Act created the Director General of Telecommunications (DGT), who was appointed by the Secretary of State and s.2 abolished BT's exclusive privilege of running telecommunications systems. The duties of the Secretary of State and the DGT were set out in s.3. They were to act in the manner best calculated to secure the provision of telecommunications services, consonant with the demand for such services throughout the country. Eight broad guidelines structured the fulfilment of these duties. They included the promotion of: the interests of consumers, effective competition, efficiency and economy, research and development and the international competitiveness of United Kingdom firms supplying telecommunications services. Section 5 required operators of telecommunications systems to possess a licence. The DGT and the Secretary of

---

[126] This leaves open the more general issue as to how far corporate power generally should be the concern of public law.

[127] C. Graham and T. Prosser, "Privatising Nationalised Industries: Constitutional Issues and New Legal Techniques" (1987) 50 M.L.R. 16; C. Graham and T. Prosser, *Privatizing Public Enterprises, Constitutions, the State, and Regulation in Comparative Perspective* (Oxford University Press, 1991).

[128] British Telecommunications Act 1981.

State granted these under s.7.[129] Under s.12 the DGT could modify licence conditions, and s.13 empowered him to refer a matter to the Monopolies and Mergers Commission (MMC), which could decide whether the matter referred to would operate against the public interest. The DGT was empowered, by s.16, to make an order requiring compliance by the licensee. This could be enforced either by the DGT,[130] or by an action for breach of statutory duty.[131] The DGT also had other duties and powers, which included:[132] the investigation of complaints, and the publication of information to consumers. The DGT could exercise the powers of the Director General of Fair Trading to investigate anti-competitive practices or abuses of market power.[133] A number of comments on this system are warranted.

4–031   First, removing a firm from public ownership does not provide the answer as to the type of new regime that is to be established. If a privatised firm has significant market power then this can be addressed either structurally, or through regulation.[134] The former entails the breaking-up of the large firm. The latter involves monitoring the conduct of the dominant firm, with the added theme of introducing competitors via the issuing of new licences. The United Kingdom adopted the latter approach, the effectiveness of which depends upon two crucial issues, the criteria for regulation and the attitude of the regulator.

Second, the most important of the regulatory criteria relate to the price which the regulated industry can charge for its services. This will determine whether it is being "fair" to consumers. Deciding upon the correct formula is a complex issue.[135] Claims that privatisation would necessarily produce efficiency were crucially dependent upon the correct resolution of such issues.

Third, the success of the scheme is also dependent upon the energy, attitude and resources of the DGT. The DGT ran an agency called the Office of Telecommunications (Oftel). The breadth of the main empowering provisions of the legislation and the guidelines contained therein, gave the DGT considerable latitude. There is evidence that the DGT and Oftel avoided the danger of being "captured" by the firms being regulated, and that they pursued a fairly vigorous pro-competitive strategy.[136] However the effectiveness of Oftel was circumscribed by a number of factors. Regulatory control was dependent upon adequate information being available to the regulator, and the DGT complained that this was not forthcoming from BT on a regular basis. It was not clear initially that Oftel possessed the requisite resources to discharge the range of its functions adequately. Decisions by

---

[129] See also s.9, which created the separate category of public telecommunications systems. Such systems have the conditions of s.8 attached, which include a duty not to discriminate and required the operator of such a system to permit interconnection with other systems.
[130] Telecommunications Act 1984 s.18(8).
[131] Telecommunications Act 1984 s.18(6).
[132] Pt III of the Act.
[133] s.50. See now the Competition Act 1998 s.54 and Sch.10.
[134] Vickers and Yarrow, n.116, 212.
[135] Vickers and Yarrow, n.116, 213–216; Prosser, n.122, 66–71.
[136] Vickers and Yarrow, n.116, 217–241; Prosser, *Law and the Regulators*, 63–65.

the MMC pursuant to a reference by the DGT allowed BT to acquire other companies subject to conditions that are difficult to enforce. There is more evidence that BT "captured" the government rather than Oftel.[137] The government devised the privatisation "package". The change from public to private ownership was the principal concern, the promotion of competition being a secondary objective. The government made several policy decisions that favoured BT, including the choice of the pricing formula, and the limit upon licensees.

Fourth, it was partly in response to these problems, and partly because of the spirit of the Citizen's Charter, that the regulatory powers were increased by the Competition and Service (Utilities) Act 1992. The 1992 Act modified s.27 of the Telecommunications Act 1984. It empowered the DGT to make regulations prescribing the standards of performance that ought to apply in individual cases, with provision for the award of compensation if these were not met.[138] The DGT could, moreover, determine standards of overall performance in connection with the provision of the relevant services.[139] The 1992 Act also contained additional powers with respect to the information that the DGT could demand as to the levels of individual and overall performance.[140] Customers were to be given information about overall performance,[141] and complaints procedures were to be established by the telecommunications operators.[142] Specific provisions governed matters such as discriminatory pricing and billing disputes.[143]

Fifth, the regulatory system in this area has become increasingly complex as a result of a number of factors. There were EC initiatives in relation to telecommunications.[144] There was a growing emphasis on the role of the DGT as a specialist competition authority,[145] which was enhanced by the passage of the Competition Act 1998.[146] There was also greater attention to social aspects of regulation in this area. The principal focus of this has been on measures designed to secure or facilitate universal access, this being defined as affordable access to basic telecommunications services for all those reasonably requiring it regardless of where they live.[147]

Finally, while the regulatory regime has become more complex as a result of the factors mentioned above, the Communications Act 2003 has brought some greater measure of order into this area, at least insofar as the regulatory structure is concerned. The functions of the DGT, and other bodies concerned with telecommunications, have been transferred to OFCOM, the Office of Communications, which has overall regulatory responsibility for

---

[137] Vickers and Yarrow, n.116, 210–211, 235–236.
[138] Competition and Service (Utilities) Act 1992, s.1, adding a new s.27A to the Telecommunications Act 1984.
[139] Telecommunications Act 1984 s.27B.
[140] 1992 Act s.2, adding a new s.27C to the Telecommunications Act 1984.
[141] 1992 Act s.3, adding s.27D to the Telecommunications Act 1984.
[142] 1992 Act s.4, adding s.27E to the Telecommunications Act 1984.
[143] 1992 Act ss.5, 6.
[144] Prosser, n.122, 60–61.
[145] Prosser, n.122, 76–78.
[146] s.54 and Sch.10.
[147] Prosser, n.122, 78–83.

this area. The Communications Act 2003 has largely superseded previous legislation in this area.[148]

6. A CONSTITUTIONAL AND LEGAL FRAMEWORK FOR AGENCIES

4–032   While the diversity of institutions makes statements of principle difficult, consideration of constitutional and legal principle at a more general level is important. Problems of the same type recur in differing organisations. This is not to say that such bodies should be forced into some administrative straitjacket. There is, however, a significant spectrum running between the pure ad hoc and institutional rigidity.

The first issue concerns the divide between Executive Agencies and NDPBs. It may well be the case that we should simply accept these differences. They do, to some extent, reflect differing philosophies as to how far agencies should be independent from the traditional departmental structure: Executive Agencies have no separate legal foundation of their own, having been created by administrative reorganisation, unlike NDPBs. There are however tensions in relation to Executive Agencies, between the desire to foster agency autonomy and the preservation of departmental responsibility. This tension will not disappear and some of these agencies might be being accorded formal status in their own right. It is evident that current arrangements for any particular Executive Agency are not regarded as writ in stone, as witnessed by the fact that other ways of providing the relevant service, such as privatisation or contracting-out, are kept under review.[149] Given that this is so it might be decided that the optimum strategy would be to maintain an agency, but to accord it more formal status.

Second, it is important that there should be some general overseeing institution. The reality is that the Cabinet Office has undertaken this role, with input from the Treasury and the National Audit Office. There is clearly an advantage in having the oversight function for Executive Agencies and NDPBs performed by the same body. It is equally important that the body entrusted with this task has some real power within the government as a whole. The implementation of reforms on NDPBs was the more likely given that the proposals emanated from a body operating within the heart of government, rather than one, such as the Council on Tribunals, which exists on the periphery. There are potential dangers with this oversight strategy, since an institution such as the Cabinet Office may feel constrained as to what it can propose because of its very centrality within government. The Cabinet Office has however shown willingness to respond to suggestions as

---

[148] The Telecommunications Act 1984 has been largely superseded by the Communications Act 2003. The provisions of the Competition and Service (Utilities) Act 1992 concerning telecommunications have been superseded by the Communications Act 2003.
[149] Cabinet Office, *Executive Agencies*, n.15, paras 20–22.

to how the regime for Executive Agencies could be improved, as exemplified by the fact that it adopted the great majority of the suggestions contained in *Better Government Services, Executive Agencies in the 21st Century.*[150]

The third stage in the framework concerns the relationship of any such organisation with the parent department and Parliament. In the case of Executive Agencies, the relationship is defined by the Framework Document. The degree of detail will vary with respect to different agencies. The general aim is to foster agency autonomy for policy implementation, although recent initiatives have stressed the need for co- ordination between the agency and its sponsoring department. The issue of ministerial power over agencies is also present in relation to NDPBs. The enabling legislation should make it as clear as possible what degree of insulation or control the agency should have from the minister. The extent of any such control will obviously be dependent upon the nature of the area over which the agency exercises power: what is suitable for competition policy will not be the same as for funding of the Arts.

The last stage in the framework is control. This can have three meanings. **4–033** The extent of *legislative* control should have been answered by the terms of reference on which the institution was first established. Control may mean *quality* control, supervision over the effectiveness of the internal institutional structure and study as to how far the aims of the agency are being fulfilled. Control may also connote *judicial review*, which will be considered below. A general point about procedural and substantive review can, however, be made at this stage.

The procedural constraints imposed will reflect the purposes of the particular scheme. If, for example, it is felt that a high premium should be placed upon public participation then this may be reflected in rules as to notice and standing, and produce a procedure more akin to consultation than the adversary process. Trade-offs will, however, have to be made between the degree of participation and the time that this involves. The Citizen's Charter has had some impact on this issue, with its emphasis upon consultation with users of services, and the impetus it has given to the making of Charters applicable to particular substantive areas. The Citizen's Charter also provided the conceptual foundation for statutory changes in certain areas designed, inter alia, to increase the openness of the process, to improve citizen access to information and to enhance reasoned decision-making.[151]

Substantive judicial review should be sensitive to the nature of the organisation in question. If, for example, the institutional form makes it clear that the minister is intended to retain control over the general direction of policy then this should be respected. Judicial decisions should not operate from an inarticulate premise of organisational "independence" and "ministerial interference", which does not reflect the true division of roles between agency and minister. Where procedures have been designed for a

[150] n.71.
[151] e.g. Competition and Service (Utilities) Act 1992.

specific body they should not be struck down merely because they do not conform to the adversarial model which characterises adjudication in the ordinary courts.

CHAPTER 5

CONTRACT, SERVICE PROVISION AND GOVERNANCE

1. INTRODUCTION

Contract, which is the focus of the current chapter, is of increasing relevance **5–001**
for governance.[1] It should be made clear at the outset that this topic is
significant, large and that its very boundaries are contested. Contract and
contractual language have been used in areas as diverse as public procurement, service provision, contracting-out, the private finance initiative,
concordats between branches of government, Public Service Agreements
embodying obligations on departments, framework agreements between
departments and executive agencies, the control of deviance, unemployment
services, and education.

There are various taxonomies that might be used, a number of which are
considered in the stimulating modern literature.[2] A criterion might be
whether the contract is legally binding.[3] Thus, in terms of the subject matter
in the previous paragraph, in some instances the contracts are legally
binding, in others they are not. This is a significant distinguishing factor,
although even in the latter instance the contracts or agreements serve to
frame the obligations of the respective parties and may be backed by
sanctions that are real notwithstanding the fact that the contract is not
legally binding. An alternative suggested criterion is to distinguish between

---

[1] H. Street, *Governmental Liability* (Cambridge University Press, 1953), Ch.3; J.D.B. Mitchell,
Contracts of Public Authorities (LSE, 1954); C. Turpin, *Government Procurement and Contracts*
(Longman, 1989); S. Arrowsmith, *Civil Liability and Public Authorities* (Earlsgate Press, 1992);
I. Harden, *The Contracting State* (Open University Press, 1992); S. Arrowsmith, *The Law of
Public and Utilities Procurement* (Sweet & Maxwell, 2nd edn, 2005); A.C.L. Davies, *Account-
ability: A Public Law Analysis of Government by Contract* (Oxford University Press, 2001); P.
Vincent-Jones, *The New Public Contracting: Regulation, Responsiveness, Relationality* (Oxford
University Press, 2006); J.-B. Auby, "Comparative Approaches to the Rise of Contract in the
Public Sphere" [2007] P.L. 40.
[2] n.1.
[3] Davies, n.1, Ch.1.

public procurement, government by agreement and new public contracting, the last of which is used to characterise delegation of powers to public agencies in contractual arrangements whereby central government preserves control and power of intervention.[4] The choice of subject matter for inclusion within each of these categories may however well be contentious.

It is not possible within the confines of this chapter to consider all the varied instances in which contract or contractual language has been used. Contract is of relevance at varying points in administrative law. Thus, for example, the use of framework agreements in the context of Executive Agencies has been considered in the previous chapter,[5] while the susceptibility of contracts to judicial review,[6] and the extent to which contracts can be a fetter on the exercise of administrative discretion, will be considered within the appropriate sections of the book.[7]

The present chapter, while necessarily selective, will focus on certain important aspects of contract and governance. The discussion begins with the way in which procurement policy is framed. This is followed by analysis of contract and service provision by central government, and by local government, including the Private Finance Initiative. The focus then shifts to more general consideration of contract as a tool of government policy. The chapter concludes with detailed consideration of the legal rules governing the making of contracts, including constraints imposed by EU law.

2. Towards "Better Procurement": The Framing of Government Procurement Policy

5–002   Central government spends a very large sum of money on procuring the goods and services it requires. The principal purchasers of these goods and services have included the Ministry of Defence, the Property Services Agency, HMSO and the Department of Health. We shall consider the institutions that shape procurement policy, the guidelines they produce and the range of procurement options at the government's disposal.

A. Institutional Responsibility
5–003   A number of institutions have played a role in shaping procurement policy. The institutional structure of procurement has however altered as a result of a government review considered below.

Until recently it was the Treasury that exercised direct, overall responsibility for public procurement. This was not surprising given that department's role in the management of public expenditure. It was the Treasury

---

[4] Vincent-Jones, n.1, Ch.1.
[5] See above, para.4–010.
[6] See below, paras 26–023—26–024.
[7] See below, paras 16–022—16–034.

which would "distil and promulgate agreed principles",[8] and conduct necessary negotiations with the EC and industry. The principles that emerged from the Treasury would often take the form of guidance issued to departments on matters such as tendering procedures, the conditions to be included in the contract and project management.[9] Treasury guidance on procurement was focused around the Procurement Group (PG). The Cabinet Office was also involved with procurement through the Buying Agency. This was an Executive Agency that provided support for, inter alia, large-scale procurement through contract negotiation and facilities management.[10] Individual Departments had a section responsible for its own procurement requirements, and there was often a dialogue between the individual department and the Treasury.

There was a reorganisation of institutional responsibility for procurement, as a result of the Gershon review in 1999.[11] The review found, inter alia, that procurement strategy was fragmented across a number of different government departments and agencies. This resulted in the centre lacking the "clout" that it should have, given that central government, agencies and non-departmental public bodies spend very considerable sums on procurement. The review recommended the creation of a central body with overall responsibility for procurement. The Office of Government Commerce (OGC) was established in 1999. It is an independent office within the Treasury, and has its own chief executive.[12] The OGC reports to the Chief Secretary to the Treasury.

Further institutional reform is forthcoming as a result of the 2007 paper on *Transforming Government Procurement*.[13] The very fact that public sector procurement is £125 billion annually is indicative of the importance of the topic. The 2007 paper notes the achievements of the OGC, while at the same time laying the ground for further improvements in this area. There is to be a higher calibre OGC, which is to deliver improved standards, focused on driving better value for money from procurement on a whole-life costing basis. The Chief Executive will become the professional head of the Government Procurement Service (GPS). The government is to focus its top talent on the most complex and critical procurement projects, with a GPS that is flexible and able to focus resources where they can best be deployed. There is to be a new Major Projects Review Group to ensure that the most important and complex projects are subject to effective scrutiny at the key stages. Departments are to collaborate more in the purchase of goods and services to get better value for money. The OGC will have strong powers to: set the procurement standards departments need to meet; monitor departments' performance against them, ensuring that remedial action is taken

[8] Turpin, n.1, 62.
[9] Turpin, n.1, 64.
[10] Buying Agency, *Pathfinder Guides you through the Procurement Maze* (1998).
[11] *Review of Civil Procurement in Central Government* (1999).
[12] http://www.ogc.gov.uk/.
[13] HM Treasury, *Transforming Government Procurement* (2007), available at http://www.hm-treasury.gov.uk./media/E/6/government_procurement_pu147.pdf.

where necessary; and demand departmental collaboration when buying common goods and services. The OGC will also work closely with the Major Projects Review Group to ensure that the most complex projects are subject to high standards of scrutiny.

B. Guidelines on Procurement

5–004   The institutions responsible for procurement have always published guidelines to aid departments in the procurement process.

There are *general guidelines*, as exemplified by the *Procurement Policy Guidelines* produced by the Procurement Policy Unit.[14] The Labour government's general strategy has been to focus on "Better Procurement". The general guiding principle is value for money with due regard being given to propriety and regularity.[15] Value for money is defined as the optimum combination of whole-life cost and quality to meet the user's requirements.[16] Goods and services are to be acquired by competition unless there are convincing reasons to the contrary.[17] The guidelines emphasise that the award of contracts should rarely be based on price alone, and that value for money should be seen against other factors such as whole-life cost, quality and delivery against price.[18]

There is guidance in relation to *specific types of procurement*. This is exemplified by the guidance provided by the Procurement Group in relation to Construction projects. The Procurement Group prepared a number of detailed papers.[19] Value for money is once again the guiding theme and it is defined in the same way as in the preceding paragraph.[20] There were "approval gateways" at various stages of the project, the object being to ensure that the value for money approach could be confirmed by people independently of those managing the project.[21] There was also detailed guidance on matters such as risk management, value management, project assessment and the like.[22]

There are also *Model Conditions of Contract*. The Central Unit on Procurement, as it then was, produced detailed model conditions for procurement contracts.[23] It was not mandatory for departments to use such conditions, but they were strongly advised to incorporate them in their purchasing and supply manuals. The model conditions spanned over 40

[14] (November 1998).
[15] (November 1998) para.1.1.
[16] (November 1998) para.1.2.
[17] (November 1998) para.5.1.
[18] (November 1998) para.6.3.
[19] See, e.g., HM Treasury Procurement Group, *No.1: Essential Requirements for Construction Procurement* (1997); *No.2: Value for Money in Construction Procurement* (1997); *No.3: Appointment of Consultants and Contractors* (1997); *No.4: Teamworking, Partnering and Incentives* (1997); *No.5: Procurement Strategies* (1997).
[20] *Value for Money*, para.3.1.
[21] *Value for Money*, para.5.
[22] *Value for Money*, Appendix A.
[23] HM Treasury Central Unit on Procurement, *No.59D: Documentation: Model Conditions of Contract* (July 1997).

pages and went into great detail. They covered all matters relating to a procurement contract, including: the nature of the contract; the contract period; its commencement; matters relating to the provision of the services and payment; liabilities; compliance with legal obligations; control of the contract; default, breach and termination; and dispute resolution. The degree to which contracts made by public bodies involve standard conditions will obviously differ depending upon the type of public authority involved. It is, however, clear that standardised forms of contract have predominated in relation to contracts made by the government itself.[24]

The OGC now has central responsibility for procurement. It enunciated 10 key strategies. These include, achieving value for money through sharing knowledge about government commercial activity; securing improvements in the management of large, complex and novel projects; the facilitation of commercial relationships with suppliers that generate value for money; the promotion of effective competition for government business; and support for the wider public sector in achieving value for money. The OGC has taken over and developed many of the guides published by institutions that had responsibility for procurement hitherto. Thus the Procurement Policy Guidelines were updated.[25] The Gateway Process has been generalised. This considers projects at critical stages in their life cycle to determine whether they can successfully progress to the next stage.[26] The OGC also publishes a range of guidelines on best practice, successful delivery, project management and property and construction.[27]

C. The Range of Procurement Options

We have considered thus far the institutions that shape procurement policy **5–005** and the guidance they provide. It is equally important to realise that government has a range of procurement options at its disposal. Traditional procurement took the form of the government buying in the services it required. The activity would be run in-house, in the sense of within the relevant government department. The last 15 years have witnessed the proliferation of procurement strategies.

In institutional terms, the restructuring of government departments has meant that the procuring body may well be an agency rather than a central department of state. In strategic terms, there has, as will be seen, been an increasing emphasis placed on contracting-out service provision. In financial terms, new ways have developed, and old ways have been rediscovered, to finance the provision of government services. It is therefore now standard practice for government guidance to place emphasis on adopting the most effective procurement strategy for the type of project at hand. Thus the guidance on construction procurement listed the procurement strategies which could be used in this context. These include: the Private Finance

[24] Turpin, n.1, 105–111.
[25] Office of Government Commerce, *Procurement Policy Guidelines* (2001).
[26] http://www.ogc.gov.uk/ppm_documents_ogc_gateway.asp.
[27] http://www.ogc.gov.uk/Document_Library_procurement_documentsasp.

Initiative, a Private Developer Scheme, a Leased Building, Crown build, new build and refurbishment.[28]

D. Contract and Government Contracts

5–006   The eclectic nature of government contract principles is peculiarly English. The unwillingness to codify reflects our dislike of the rigidity that can be attendant upon such reform. There are clearly advantages in the flexibility of the present system and it would be wrong to assume a continuous state of conflict between government and prospective contractor. Standard terms can save costs, by saving the need for constant re-negotiation of basic contractual terms. They can, moreover, be easily reviewed and amended to take account of changing circumstances or the needs of a particular contract.

Street[29] suggested nonetheless that certain issues central to the contract such as agency, building, appropriations, supervision, direction and power to amend, should be enshrined in a Governments Contracts Act. Other less immutable terms should be applied to a contract by delegated legislation, thereby preserving a balance between flexibility, certainty and accessibility. Davies has also called for codification of the government's contracting power.[30]

Turpin, on the other hand, contends that the present system is not any less satisfactory than those in other countries which do recognise, in more formal terms, a separate body of government contract law.[31] He does, however, suggest that the revision of standard forms should only be undertaken after proper consultation with representative organisations of contractors, and that more substantial changes in the regime of government contracting should be open to wider public scrutiny.[32] This reflects the fact that "contract . . . is a kind of treaty by which the conditions of a relationship of interdependence between government and its suppliers are established", and this is "something of legitimate concern to the public".[33] Thus, while internal management systems are necessary to oversee the operation of government contracts, these must be supplemented by "arrangements for external political accountability that are proper to governmental functions in a parliamentary democracy".[34] The centralisation of procurement responsibility in the OGC will indirectly facilitate such control.

It is clear moreover that the ordinary principles of contract play only a limited role in this area. As Turpin states,[35] "the general law of contract, in

---

[28] HM Treasury Procurement Group, *No.1: Essential Requirements for Construction Procurement* (1997), 20, and *No.5: Procurement Strategies* (1997); OGC, *Procurement and Contract Strategies, Achieving Excellence in Construction Procurement Guide* (2007).
[29] *Governmental Liability*, n.1, 104–105.
[30] A. Davies, "Ultra Vires Problems in Government Contracts" (2006) 122 L.Q.R. 98, 104.
[31] *Government Procurement*, n.1, 114.
[32] *Government Procurement*, n.1, 114.
[33] *Government Procurement*, n.1, 258.
[34] *Government Procurement*, n.1, 260.
[35] *Government Procurement*, n.1, 104–105.

short, is only one of the elements, and not necessarily the most significant, by which the conduct of the parties to a government contract is regulated". A number of such contracts may be regarded as a "co-operative programme of work towards a still uncertain goal rather than as a precise definition of the contractor's obligation", and the legal liabilities that may exist under the contract "will not necessarily be decisive of the solution reached".[36]

3. Towards "Better Government": Contract and Service Provision by Central Government

The government has always had to make contracts in order to purchase the goods and services it requires. Recent years have, however, witnessed increased use of contractual language over a broader area.[37] We have already seen how contractual ideas influenced the relationship between Executive Agencies and their sponsoring departments, even though there is no real contract because the agency possesses no separate legal personality. Contractual themes have also had a marked impact upon other areas such as the Health Service.[38] What we will be principally concerned with in this section is the use of contracting-out as a method of providing public services, and the links between this and the regime for Executive Agencies.

5–007

A. Contracting-Out: The Initial Conservative Policy

The connection between the present topic and the discussion in the previous chapter should be made clear at the outset. The Conservative government's approach to institutional reform included not only the hiving-off of functions to agencies, but also contracting-out. When a department reviewed its existing activities it considered five options. The activity could be abolished, privatised, contracted-out, given to a Next Steps agency or the status quo could be maintained. Market Testing[39] was a key criterion for deciding between these options.[40] The process was taken very seriously by in-house teams whose activity was being market tested, since their jobs were often on the line. The previous chapter has discussed the implications of choosing the agency route. This chapter will focus on the consequences of adopting the contracting-out option.

5–008

---

[36] *Government Procurement*, n.1, 104.
[37] M. Freedland, "Government by Contract and Private Law" [1994] P.L. 86.
[38] D. Longley, *Public Law and Health Service Accountability* (Open University Press, 1992); Harden, n.1; Davies, n.1.
[39] *The Citizen's Charter, First Report*, Cm. 2101 (1992), 60–64, contains a detailed breakdown of market testing being carried out by different government departments and agencies.
[40] *The Government's Guide to Market Testing* (1993).

The *reasons for* contracting-out are said to be that:[41] public sector "in-house" monopolies are inefficient and this is reflected in low productivity; there is "open-ended" financial commitment to public sector "in-house" units and such units do not take sufficient account of costs; competition generates new ideas, techniques, etc.; and contractors can be penalised for defective performance and late delivery.

The *reasons against* contracting-out are said to be that: private contractors are unreliable, and may well default; contractors use low bids to eliminate the in-house capacity, thereby making the public body dependent on a private monopoly; competitive tendering entails monitoring costs; and private contractors in areas such as the Health Service can place patients at risk.

It should, moreover, be made clear that the contracting-out option applied *both* to activities performed in-house and to those for which agencies were responsible. This requires a word by way of explanation in order to avoid confusion. The five choices mentioned above applied to a *general* sphere of activity. It might, for example, be decided to create an agency for the payment of social welfare benefits, or for social welfare contributions. It might be decided to preserve some of the more general policy matters in the social welfare field in-house. Contracting-out as an option was considered for more *particular* activities *irrespective* of whether they were done by the agency or the department itself.

B. Contracting-Out: The Labour Strategy

5–009   A consistent theme in the Labour government strategy for service delivery has been the search for "better" government, or "better" quality in the provision of services. While the Labour government distanced itself from the more extreme implications of the previous government's market-oriented strategy, it adopted much of the same general strategic thinking.

This is exemplified by its approach towards service delivery at the central level, which was set out in its document on *Better Quality Services, Guidance for Senior Managers*.[42] The objective was said to be Better Government. It was made clear that competition was not the only option, and that value for money meant better quality services at optimal cost.[43] Twelve guiding principles were laid down, which were to be used when market testing and contracting-out. The most important of these were: development of modern, high quality, efficient, responsive and customer-focused central government services; partnerships with the private sector were encouraged; market testing and contracting-out to be used when they could be shown to offer better value for money; ministers to remain accountable for services contracted-out to the private sector; and staff were to be trained to carry out

---

[41] K. Hartley and M. Huby, "Contracting-Out Policy: Theory and Evidence", in J. Kay, C. Mayer and D. Thompson, *Privatization and Regulation—The UK Experience* (Oxford University Press, 1986), 289.
[42] (1998).
[43] *Better Quality Services*, paras 2–3.

market testing, contracting-out, benchmarking, restructuring and other means for achieving better value for money, in the sense of better quality services at optimal cost.

It was incumbent on each department to review all of its activities within a five-year period,[44] in order to decide which of the five options to pursue:[45] the service could be abolished if it was no longer needed; it could be restructured internally after benchmarking had been used to diagnose problems and ways of addressing them; the service could be contracted-out, after competition between external bidders; there could be market testing, which involved an in-house team bidding against external bidders; or the service could be privatised if it did not need to be undertaken by the government.

The Labour government's strategy for service delivery moved on in its second term in office. Service delivery in key areas such as health and education was central to the government's aims. This centrality was reflected in the creation of the Office of Public Services Reform (OPSR) and the Delivery Unit within the Prime Minister's Office. The strategy for service delivery was informed by the Prime Minister's four principles. There were to be *national standards*, through which tough targets are set for schools, hospitals, the police and local government. There was to be *devolution and delegation* to front line professionals to achieve these targets. The service providers were to have *flexibility* as to the manner in which to improve services. Consumers were to be afforded choice as to the type of public services that are delivered. These four principles were elaborated on by the OPSR in *Reforming our Public Services, Principles into Practice.*[46]

In Labour's third term of office, the work of the OPSR is now taken forward by the Cabinet Office itself, and more particularly by the Delivery Council, the Contact Council and the Strategy Unit, with assistance from the Economic and Domestic Secretariat.[47]

The Treasury is also integral to the attainment of service delivery goals. The Treasury administers Public Service Agreements, PSAs, which set out commitments to the public on what they can expect for their money, and which minister is responsible for delivery of the relevant target.[48] PSAs are underpinned by Delivery Agreements, DAs, in which government departments explain how they will achieve the targets laid down in the PSAs. The main elements within the DA establish who is responsible for delivering the agreement, how it will be achieved, how performance will be improved, how the department will focus on consumer needs, and the steps to be taken to improve policy-making. There are also Technical Notes, which set out how performance against PSA targets will be assessed. The preceding regime has now been complemented by the Service Transformation Agreement (STA), the aim of which "is to change public services so they more often meet the

---

[44] *Better Quality Services*, para.7.
[45] *Better Quality Services*, para.9.
[46] Office of Public Services Reform, (2002).
[47] http://www.cabinetoffice.gov.uk/public_service_reform.aspx.
[48] http://www.hm-treasury.gov.uk/documents/public_spending_reporting/public_service_performance/psp_index.cfm.

needs of people and businesses, rather than the needs of government, and by doing so reduce the frustration and stress of accessing them".[49]

C. Contracting-Out: Problems and Concerns

5–010 An appropriate place to begin is with the *issue of principle*: are there activities that should not be contracted-out? Should certain types of service only be run by the state *stricto sensu*? If so which services would be placed within this category, the police, adjudication, prisons? The latter have in fact already been contracted-out to some degree. So too have some aspects of the court process such as the movement of prisoners, as witnessed by the saga of Group 4 Security losing prisoners. What of services where confidentiality is at a premium, or does this not matter given that so much information is already available to private parties?

If an activity is contracted-out are there problems of *accountability*? The answer is both yes and no. Clearly the very fact that the activity has been contracted-out, rather than being privatised, means that the state has responsibility for its provision. This is particularly the case given that, as we have seen above, the types of activity which are contracted-out will often be integral to the service provided by the agency or the department. We should, moreover, be aware of the danger that a contractor who was intended only to "execute" a chosen policy, may come to have a real influence over the choice of policy itself. Furthermore, such contracts can be extremely valuable, and hence their disbursement can help to make or break fortunes and power in the corporate sector.[50]

Having said this it can be argued that these very contracts, like the framework documents used in agency creation, sharpen accountability by defining goals, setting targets and monitoring performance. This does not mean that we should be complacent about accountability in this context. Techniques have to be fashioned to fit the new order. An interesting suggestion has been to distinguish between three senses of accountability: programme, process and fiscal.[51] Programme accountability is concerned with the quality of the work being undertaken and whether it has achieved the goals required of it. Process accountability asks whether the procedures used to perform the research were adequate, while fiscal accountability investigates whether the funds were expended as stated. It is important to note in this respect that the Labour government's documentation on contracting-out and the Private Finance Initiative goes into considerable detail in its specification of the performance conditions to be met by those who contract with the government, and how risk is allocated between the government and the private supplier.

5–011 These techniques of control are not, however, self-executing. They require

---

[49] HM Government, *Service Transformation Agreements* (2007).
[50] B. Smith and D. Hague (eds), *The Dilemma of Accountability in Modern Government* (Macmillan, 1971).
[51] A. Robinson, "Government Contracting for Academic Research: Accountability in the American Experience", Smith and Hague (eds), n.50, Ch.3.

positive input from the government side. In order that programmes can be made accountable, government must be as clear as is possible in the terms of the contract as to what it requires of the contractor. Clarity as to the initial objectives of a scheme is a necessary condition for programme account-ability. It is not sufficient. Management within government must be capable of assessing the completed work. This requires personnel with the appro-priate skills and also the existence of criteria by which performance can be judged.[52] The Office of Government Commerce is mindful of these issues, and has addressed them through its key targets. Where the preceding techniques of control operate effectively contract can be a beneficial way of structuring administrative discretion. As Harden states,[53]

"Although contract is not a panacea for the problem of discretion, it does offer an opportunity to make real progress towards greater accountability by clearly identifying who is responsible for a policy, what it is, whether it is being carried out in practice and if not, why not."

At a more practical level there are *organisational* concerns. Can contracting-out function with sufficient *flexibility*, given that the demand for certain public services may fluctuate either due to exogenous market factors, or because of more radical shifts in governmental policy? How far does con-tracting-out produce problems of *integration*: are there difficulties of ensuring a coherent, integrated service when some parts of the whole are operated by private undertakings, while others are performed in-house? As Harden notes,[54]

"The public interest—i.e. the overall functioning of the public service in question—is not the responsibility of a single unitary organization, but instead emerges from the process of agreement between separate orga-nizations, none of which has responsibility for the public interest as a whole."

Closely related to the organisational concerns are those relating to *person-nel*. There are a number of different dimensions to this problem. There are the complexities involved with the Transfer of Undertakings Regulations where employees are transferred to a private firm. There is concerning about the morale of those within the department who fear the results of the market-testing exercise will be that they will lose their jobs, especially in circumstances where a recession may tempt the private bidder to tender at a very low price. There is concern about the impact of contracting-out on the broader work ethic of the public service. When work is contracted-out to private firms they will not normally have a "public service ethos", but will

---

[52] Smith, "Accountability and Independence in the Contract State", n.50, 34–35, 39–42.
[53] Harden, n.1, 71.
[54] Harden, n.1, 33.

be principally concerned with the interests of their shareholders. How important will any such change of attitude be?[55]

D. Contracting-Out: Contract Formation and Legal Principle

5–012   The agreements made as a result of contracting-out are legal contracts. There is a legally binding obligation between two entities with separate legal status. This raises a number of important issues of legal principle.

The first of these relates to the *creation* of the contract. We have already seen in outline the process whereby the government decides to market test an activity and then to hold a competition between the in-house unit and selected outside contractors. This procedure is subject to the Community law regime on public procurement, which has been extended to cover services.[56] There are important provisions relating to the competitive process, and the criterion for choosing to whom the contract should be awarded. Transparency is safeguarded by requirements as to publicity and reasoned decision-making. There will be more detailed examination of these rules below.[57]

A second point of importance concerns *the legal foundation for contracting-out*. Part II of the Deregulation and Contracting-out Act 1994 makes provision for the contracting-out of certain functions by government to bodies which will normally be private. Government departments have frequently contracted-out functions independently of this Act. The statute was passed in order to enable the body to which the power has been contracted-out to operate in the name of the minister, by analogy with the *Carltona* principle.[58] Section 69 enables functions which, by virtue of any enactment or rule of law, can be performed by an officer of a minister, to be contracted-out to an authorised party. Section 69(5)(c) makes it clear that the minister may still exercise the function to which the authorisation relates. Section 71 imposes certain limits upon the functions that can be contracted-out. Section 72(2) is designed to render the minister ultimately responsible for action taken by the body to which the power has been contracted-out, although the meaning of this particular section is not free from doubt. It is clear from s.72(3)(b) that s.72(2) does not apply in respect of any criminal proceedings brought against the person to whom the power has been contracted-out. The precise import of s.72(3)(a) is far less clear.[59] This states that s.72(2) does not apply "for the purposes of so much of the contract made between the authorised person and the Minister, office-holder or local authority as relates to the exercise of the function".

---

[55] D. Faulkner, "Public Services, Citizenship, and the State—The British Experience 1967–97", in M. Freedland and S. Sciarra (eds), *Public Services and Citizenship in European Law, Public and Labour Law Perspectives* (Oxford University Press, 1998), 42–44.
[56] Council Directive 92/50.
[57] See below, paras 5–024—5–030.
[58] See below, Ch.16.
[59] See below, para.16–010.

We are therefore faced with an increasingly complex picture in relation to **5–013** contracting-out as a whole. Contracting-out has been a feature of governmental policy for some time, and has often been undertaken without any statutory foundation. The Deregulation and Contracting-out Act is facultative not mandatory: a minister *may* provide for a function to be contracted-out using the provisions of the Act. There are therefore at least two tracks a department can follow if it wishes to contract-out. It can do so independently of the Act, or it can do so by promoting an order under the Act. The picture is rendered more complex by the existence of particular provisions for contracting-out in other legislation, which contain rules on contracting-out for specific services, such as prisons.

A third set of legal issues concerns the application of *public law principles* to contracted-out activities. If the department or agency is fulfilling a statutory function, whether this is framed as a duty or in discretionary terms, then it will be subject to normal public law principles. If it chooses to fulfil part of that statutory remit by contracting-out to a private undertaking then it would be contrary to principle for the citizens' protections to be reduced as result of this organisational choice. While the department or agency may still be subject to public law, it may in reality be difficult to show that it has broken such principles where the activity has been contracted-out.[60] It is therefore especially important to decide whether the private party to whom the activity has been contracted-out is also subject to public law. The courts have however been reluctant to hold that such private parties are subject to the Human Rights Act 1998,[61] or to the procedures for judicial review.[62] This is regrettable,[63] and the courts' reasoning will be examined below.[64]

The final important legal issue pertains to the ascription of *legal responsibility* for activities that have been contracted-out. Imagine that a tort is committed against an individual by a prison officer who works in a prison, the running of which has been contracted-out to a private firm. Who can the individual sue? No doubt the prison officer would be individually liable and the private employer would be subject to the normal rules on vicariously liability. But could any action be maintained against the department that had contracted-out the work? Would it have any legal responsibility? This might well be of importance if the private firm turns out to be not too solvent. The answer should depend upon the nature of the statutory duty/ discretion, the fulfilment of which has been contracted-out to the private firm. A court might interpret the governing statute as imposing a duty the legal responsibility for which could not ultimately be delegated to another. On this view it would be open to the department to contract-out the activity

---

[60] See, e.g., *R. v Servite Houses and the London Borough of Wandsworth Council Ex p Goldsmith and Chatting* (2000) 2 L.G.L.R. 997.
[61] *Poplar Housing and Regeneration Community Association Ltd v Donoghue* [2002] Q.B. 48; *R. v Leonard Cheshire Foundation (A Charity)* [2002] 2 All E.R. 936; *YL v Birmingham City Council* [2007] 3 W.L.R. 112.
[62] *Servite*, n.60.
[63] P. Craig, "Contracting-Out, The Human Rights Act and the Scope of Judicial Review" (2002) 118 L.Q.R. 551.
[64] See below, paras 18–024—18–025 and para.26–023.

if it wished to do so as a matter of organisational choice, but this would not necessarily serve to divest it of legal responsibility. It might alternatively decide that the department satisfied its legal responsibility if it took due care in the appointment of the independent contractor.[65]

4. Public Private Partnerships and the Private Finance Initiative: Contract and Service Provision by Central Government

5–014   The discussion thus far has focused upon the way in which services are delivered by central government, and the approaches of the Conservative and Labour governments to contracting-out. The discussion of service delivery would, however, be incomplete if it did not address Public Private Partnerships (PPPS) and the Private Finance Initiative (PFI).[66] Lest anybody should doubt the importance of this topic it is salutary to realise that as of March 2006 the capital value of PFI agreements in the pipeline was in excess of £26 billion.[67]

In terms of *history*, PFI dates back to 1992 and the statements of the Chancellor of the Exchequer, which were designed to encourage the provision of public services through the use of private capital funding. The PFI has been fully embraced by the Labour Government.[68] When it took office in May 1997 it launched a review of PFI, the Bates Review. This produced a number of recommendations to streamline the procedure, which were adopted by the government. There was a further review designed to improve the use of private sector finance in relation to public projects.[69] The Labour government reaffirmed its commitment to PFI in 2006, stating that it would play a "small but important role in the overall objective of delivering modernized public services".[70] It would continue to be used only where it could demonstrate value for money and was likely to continue to comprise around 10–15 per cent of total investment in public services.[71]

It is important to be clear about *the meaning of PPPS and PFI*. PPPS are a key element in the government's strategy for the delivery of modern, high quality public services, and promoting the UK's competitiveness.[72] They cover a range of business structures and partnership arrangements, from PFI to sale of equity stakes in state-owned businesses. PFI is therefore one

---

[65] *Quaquah v Group 4 Securities Ltd (No.2)* [2001] Prison L.R. 318. The case did not however involve contracting out pursuant to the 1994 Act.
[66] HM Treasury, *The Private Finance Initiative—Breaking New Ground* (1993); HM Treasury, *Private Opportunity, Public Benefit—Progressing the Private Finance Initiative* (1995).
[67] HM Treasury, *PFI: Strengthening Long Term Partnerships* (2006).
[68] Treasury Taskforce, *Partnerships for Prosperity—The Private Finance Initiative* (1997).
[69] See, e.g., Treasury Task Force, *Geoffrey Robinson Unveils Second Significant Projects List* (1998); Treasury Task Force, *Geoffrey Robinson Announces Second Review for the Private Finance Initiative* (November 1998).
[70] *Strengthening Long Term Partnerships*, n.67, 1.
[71] See also, HM Treasury, *PFI: Meeting the Investment Challenge* (2003).
[72] HM Treasury, *Public Private Partnerships: The Government's Approach* (2000).

species of PPPS. The idea is that the government decides between competing objectives, defines the standards required and safeguards the wider public interest.[73] The private sector brings the discipline of the market place, a focus on customer requirements, management expertise and innovation.[74]

Freedland has helpfully identified *three main species of PPPS*.[75] The first is where the private sector provides capital assets the use of which is then paid for by the public sector. This is exemplified by the private sector funding the building of a prison, offices, classrooms and the like, which are then rented by the relevant public body. The second is where a public service such as a bridge or a road is built by the private sector, which then is entitled to the tolls from those who use the service. Much of the public infrastructure in the 19th century was run in this fashion. There can, third, be areas where the asset provided by the private sector will be paid for partly by rent direct from the public body, and partly by payments made directly by the public. The more particular form of PPPS will vary depending upon the type of project in question.

It is clear that there are *two rationales* underlying PPPS and PFI. In micro-economic terms, "governments which are in general enthusiastic about privatisation and liberalisation of public services see advantage in private finance contracting because they believe that public services can in general be provided more efficiently by means of such contracting than by means of direct provision by public authorities".[76] In macro-economic terms, "such governments also perceive private finance contracting as a way of minimising or deferring immediate apparent public spending or borrowing requirements",[77] in much the same way that a private person will take a mortgage rather than pay cash for the house now. This is all the more attractive for government given that PFI deals augment public sector investment and stand alongside conventionally funded capital spending. The Treasury Task Force has described the general objective of PFI in the following terms.[78]

5–015

> "The Private Finance Initiative (PFI) has become one of government's main instruments for the delivery of high quality and cost effective public services. It presents those responsible for the provision of public services with the opportunity to procure those services, or the buildings and infrastructure within which to provide those services, while leaving the risks of asset and infrastructure ownership and maintenance with the private sector."

[73] HM Treasury, *Public Private Partnerships*, n.72, 10–11.
[74] HM Treasury, *Public Private Partnerships*, n.72, 11–12.
[75] n.76, 290–291.
[76] M. Freedland, "Public Law and Private Finance—Placing the Private Finance Initiative in a Public Law Frame" [1998] P.L. 288, 298–299.
[77] Freedland, n.76, 299.
[78] Treasury Task Force, *Introduction* (1997), 1.

The *administration of PPPS and PFI* is shared. Most major government departments will have a group responsible for PPPS projects coming within its remit. The Treasury, the Office of Government Commerce and Partnerships UK provide more general overview. Partnerships UK is itself a form of PPPS.[79] It is a public private partnership created in 2000, and is regarded as a private firm with a public interest mission. It was created to take over the work of the Treasury Task Force, which was the principal organising force behind PPPS, and many of its guides are still valid. Partnerships UK operates as a PPPS developer working in partnership with public bodies. Its objectives include the fast and efficient development of PPPS. If a particular PPPS project fails, then Partnerships UK loses money. If it succeeds Partnerships UK and the public body share the benefits. There is now an Operational Taskforce acting within Partnerships UK, to provide support and advice for public sector partners within operational PFI projects.

It should be made clear that *PFI agreements are real contracts, the terms of which are set out in considerable detail*. There is a standardised form of PFI contract.[80] The objectives of this document are to promote a common understanding as to the risks included in a standard PFI project; to engender consistency of approach and of pricing across a range of similar projects; and to reduce the time and costs of negotiation.[81] The standardised contract addresses in detail a whole range of issues that are central to PFI agreements. Guidance is provided as to the duration of the agreement, its commencement, incentives to timely service commencement, delay, service availability, service maintenance, performance monitoring, payment mechanisms, the effect of change in the law, the possibility of price variation and termination of the agreement. There are provisions giving the public body an option to purchase the capital asset on expiry of the contract term. Risk allocation is central in the standardised contract. It is apparent in relation to, for example, price variation and the effect of changes in the law.

There have been *concerns voiced about the government's strategy*. Freedland has pointed out two particular concerns in this respect. On the one hand, it is clear that the government has moved to a more pro-active stance in relation to the PFI. The Treasury has shifted from its more traditional stance of exercising regulatory control over capital spending, to positively promoting PPPS and PFI projects.[82] This may well be productive of tensions in the medium term.[83] On the other hand, there is the concern that risk transfer might result in the delegation to "private contractors of public decision-making powers affecting the interests and the welfare of citizens".[84] There is the related concern that it might result in private contractors "acquiring large commercial interests in the way that those decision-making

---

[79] http://www.partnershipsuk.org.uk/.
[80] HM Treasury, *Standardisation of PFI Contracts, Version 4* (2007).
[81] HM Treasury, *Standardisation of PFI Contracts*, n.80, para.1.2.1.
[82] n.76, 297–302.
[83] n.76, 299.
[84] n.76, 307.

powers are exercised, even though those powers remain, nominally at least, in the hands of the public authorities".[85]

5. TOWARDS "BEST VALUE": CONTRACT AND SERVICE PROVISION BY LOCAL GOVERNMENT

A. The Provision of Local Services: The Market and the Conservative Government's Approach

The Conservative government's approach to the provision of local services   **5–016** was, not surprisingly, imbued with the same market ethos that it applied to the provision of services by central government.[86] This was overlaid by measures designed to restrict local financial autonomy. This strategy was implemented in three main ways.

i. Competitive procedures

Local authorities had an obligation to employ competitive procedures in the   **5–017** award of their contracts. The Local Government Act 1972 s.135 requires such authorities to promulgate standing orders which make provision for competitive procedures to be used when contracts are awarded. There are, as would be expected, financial thresholds below which this obligation does not bite. The objectives are to ensure value for money and to help to prevent the improper allocation of valuable contracts.

ii. The exclusion of non-commercial considerations

The Conservative government enacted legislation aimed at preventing local   **5–018** authorities from taking non-commercial considerations into account when awarding contracts. Section 17 of the Local Government Act 1988 prevented public authorities[87] from taking into account non-commercial matters when exercising their power to make contracts relating to the supply of goods or services, or for the execution of public works. It is however open to the Secretary of State to make an order that a matter should cease to be a non-commercial consideration for the purposes of s.17 of the Local Government Act 1988.[88]

Non-commercial matters are defined in s.17(5). A public authority cannot take account of any of the following matters: the terms and conditions of

---

[85] n.76, 307.
[86] I. Leigh, *Law, Politics and Local Democracy* (Oxford University Press, 2000), Ch.10.
[87] As defined in Sch.2, to cover, *inter alia*, local authorities and development corporations Central government is not included.
[88] Local Government Act 1999 s.19; Local Government Best Value (Exclusion of Non-commercial Considerations) Order 2001 (SI 2001/909).

employment by contractors of their workers; whether the terms on which contractors contract with their sub-contractors constitute, in the case of contracts with individuals, contracts for the provision by them as self-employed persons of their services only; any involvement of the business activities of contractors with irrelevant fields of government policy; the conduct of contractors or their workers in industrial disputes; the country or territory or origin of supplies to, or the location in any country of the business activities of contractors; any political, industrial or sectarian affiliations of contractors or employees; the fact of financial support given to or withheld from an institution to which the public authority gives or withholds support; and use or non-use by contractors of technical or professional services provided by the authority under certain building legislation. Special provision was made for matters concerned with race relations.[89]

The legislation is fierce in respect of enforcement. If a public authority asks any question relating to a non-commercial matter, or includes such a matter in a draft contract, it will be deemed to have made its decisions on that forbidden ground.[90] It cannot, moreover, escape s.17 merely by "keeping quiet" and basing its decision on a non-commercial ground, because the disappointed contractor has a right to a reasoned decision as to why it was not chosen.[91] It may be difficult to formulate such reasons without revealing a "forbidden" consideration. The aggrieved contractor can seek judicial review of the public authority's decision, and also damages.[92] The damages remedy is limited to reliance type losses: expenditure reasonably incurred for the purpose of submitting the tender.[93]

The legislation is clearly premised upon the idea that contracts made by public authorities should be based solely upon commercial considerations, and was part of the more general Conservative ethos that the "market" should govern allocative decisions wherever possible. The principal difficulty with applying the legislation arises from the breadth of the non-commercial considerations. It is easy to envisage situations in which a public authority may wish to ask a question concerning one of the precluded matters precisely because it believes that it will affect the commercial viability of the tender submitted. If, for example, a contractor obtains supplies from, or is located in, a country that is politically unstable this will affect its ability to deliver the goods on schedule. Such an inquiry is, however, precluded by the legislation.[94]

5–019   The courts are faced with a difficult choice. They can apply s.17(5) "formalistically", refusing to listen to any such arguments, with the consequence that the authority will be prevented from choosing the bid that really was the best in commercial terms. They can, alternatively, hear such arguments, with the consequence that the peremptory force of s.17(5) will be

[89] Local Government Act 1988 s.18.
[90] Local Government Act 1988 s.19(10).
[91] Local Government Act 1988 s.20.
[92] Local Government Act 1988 s.19(7).
[93] Local Government Act 1988 s.19(8).
[94] Local Government Act 1988 s.17(5)(e).

weakened. Public authorities will then be able to argue that they are considering s.17(5) matters only in so far as they relate to the commercial viability of the tender.[95]

The soundness of the legislation is debatable, more especially because this may depend upon the particular type of non-commercial consideration.

The arguments *in favour of such legislation* are as follows. The ability to award contracts gives considerable power to public authorities. This power should, like other exercises of public power, not be used for improper purposes. If there were no restrictions upon an authority's contracting power it could pursue a policy that might have no legislative sanction, which might be unrelated to the primary objective for which the contracting power was granted. To allow authorities unrestricted freedom could also lead to regional variations in the criteria applied for the award of a contract, and these criteria might not be known to the prospective contractors. Covert blacklists might exist, and the "facts" which justified placing a firm on such a list might not be accurately or fairly determined. Central legislation which establishes contracting criteria serves, moreover, to facilitate the judicial task of deciding whether the conditions employed by a particular authority are valid or not, rather than leaving the matter to be dealt with through ad hoc applications of tests such as improper purposes or unreasonableness.[96]

A number of arguments can be made *against such legislation*, or against legislation as broad as s.17(5). Contracts made by public bodies should not be viewed solely as commercial bargains. The very power to grant contracts should be able to be used to advance socially desirable objectives, precisely because such authorities cannot and should not be politically neutral towards such matters. It may not always be possible to pass legislation that enshrines such objectives,[97] and even where this has been done, the use of contracting power may be an effective method of enforcing such legislative norms.[98] The existence of some regional variations in contracting criteria is on this view not a fact to be deplored, but rather a natural corollary of local autonomy, which should be respected. This should be upheld against the centralising tendencies of government legislation that establishes the criteria to be applied by all public authorities. This second view does not deny the need for some constraints on contracting power. It would clearly be wrong to blacklist a contractor because he or she held differing political views from that of the authority. Subject to such constraints it should, however, be open to an authority to decide, for example, to employ a local firm which will give employment to the area even if it does not submit the lowest tender. The line between pursuit of acceptable and unacceptable policies would then have to

---

[95] A further difficulty arises in relation to damages. It seems questionable in principle whether a contractor should be able to recover even reliance losses unless it can prove that but for the non-commercial consideration it would have been given the contract. The solution canvassed above, of assessing the chance of the contractor's success, could, however, be employed here.

[96] cf. *R. v Lewisham London Borough Council Ex p Shell UK Ltd* [1988] 1 All E.R. 938.

[97] T. Daintith, "The Executive Power Today: Bargaining and Economic Control," in J. Jowell and D. Oliver (eds), *The Changing Constitution* (Oxford University Press, 1985), Ch.8.

[98] See Religious and Political Discrimination and Equality of Opportunity in Northern Ireland, Report on Fair Employment, Cm. 237 (1987).

be determined upon an ad hoc basis through techniques such as propriety of purpose or unreasonableness.

iii. Contracting-out and compulsory competitive tendering

5–020 The market-oriented strategy of the Conservative government stretched beyond the commitment to ensuring that procurement was based upon commercial considerations. It extended to the decision whether a service should be performed "in house", or whether it should be "contracted-out" to a private undertaking. The objective was to further market-based practices in order to make sure that the activity was undertaken most efficiently, whether this was in-house or through a private firm.

The Local Government Planning and Land Act 1980, Pt III, made compulsory tendering a requirement for local authorities. The regime was extended by the Local Government Act 1988, the Local Government Act 1992 and secondary legislation. The 1988 Act s.2, imposed contracting-out obligations in relation to matters such as refuse collection, street cleaning, vehicle maintenance and some aspects of catering. This list was augmented as a result of powers exercised by the Secretary of State. Where a local authority was contemplating giving work of this kind to its own in-house labour organisation it had first to publicise the matter and call for bids from interested parties.[99] The local authority's labour organisation had to bid if it wished to retain the task. The local authority in reaching any decision could not act so as to restrict, distort or prevent competition. The Secretary of State had power to act against authorities that did not comply with the CCT competition rules. The exercise of this power was subject to judicial review, but the courts interpreted the Secretary of State's discretionary powers broadly.[100]

B. The Provision of Local Services: "Best Value" and the Labour Government's Approach

5–021 The Labour government moved away from CCT and towards a new principle for the provision of local services, based on "Best Value".[101] The essence of this idea is to be found in *Modernising Local Government: Improving Local Services through Best Value*.[102] The Best Value strategy is designed to secure the efficient and effective provision of local services, while preserving greater local autonomy and choice. It is premised on the idea that efficient and effective public services are an essential part of the fabric of a

---

[99] Local Government Act 1988 s.7.
[100] *R. v Secretary of State for the Environment Ex p London Borough of Haringey* [1994] C.O.D. 518.
[101] Vincent-Jones, n.1; P. Vincent-Jones, "Responsive Law and Governance in Public Services Provision: A Future for the Local Contracting State" (1998) 61 M.L.R. 362, and "Central-Local Relations under the Local Government Act 1999: A New Consensus" (2000) 63 M.L.R. 84.
[102] Department of the Environment, Transport and the Regions (1997).

healthy democracy,[103] and this is seen as part of a broader package of measures designed to re-invigorate local democracy. It was recognised that CCT had been beneficial in forcing authorities to consider how services could best be provided. The CCT regime was nonetheless abolished because it led to the neglect of service quality; the efficiency gains were uneven; it was inflexible; and because the compulsion which underpinned the system bred antagonism.[104]

The Best Value strategy is based on a number of principles.[105] These include the idea that Best Value is owed to local people both as taxpayers and users of local services, and that it is about quality as well as efficiency. Under the Best Value regime there was to be no presumption that services must be privatised, nor was there to be any compulsion to put services out to tender. There was however equally no reason to provide services in-house if other more efficient means were available. Central government would continue to set the basic framework for service provision, with local authorities being subject to targets and performance reviews.[106]

The Local Government Act 1999 enshrined the central elements of this strategy. Compulsory Competitive Tendering was abolished with effect from January 2, 2000,[107] and replaced by the concept of best value. Local authorities and a number of other public bodies are deemed to be best value authorities.[108] A best value authority (BVA) must make arrangements to secure continuous improvement in the way in which its functions are exercised, having regard to economy, efficiency and effectiveness.[109] It has a duty to consult when fulfilling this duty,[110] and this has been extended more recently in order to increase involvement by local people.[111]

The best value regime has been significantly modified and "softened" as a result of more recent legislation. The 1999 Act provided for a regime of performance indicators set by the Secretary of State by reference to which a BVA's performance could be measured and established performance standards to be met by BVAs.[112] It also stipulated that BVAs should conduct best value reviews in accordance with an order made by the Secretary of State specifying the matters to be taken into account.[113] The BVAs were in addition obliged to prepare a best value performance plan for each financial year, subject once again to guidance or an order made by the Secretary of

[103] *Modernising Local Government*, para 1.2.
[104] *Modernising Local Government*, para 1.5.
[105] *Modernising Local Government*, para 2.1.
[106] *Modernising Local Government*, paras 4.11–4.18.
[107] Local Government Act 1999 s.21.
[108] Local Government Act 1999 s.1.
[109] Local Government Act 1999 s.3(1).
[110] Local Government Act 1999 s.3(2).
[111] Local Government Act 1999 s.3A.
[112] Local Government Act 1999 s.4; Local Government (Best Value) Performance Indicators and Performance Standards (England) Order 2005 (SI 2005/598).
[113] Local Government Act 1999 s.5(1); Local Government (Best Value) Performance Plans and Reviews Order 1999 (SI 1999/3251); Local Government (Best Value) Performance Plans and Reviews (Amendment) (England and Wales) Order 2003 (SI 2003/662).

State who could specify matters that the BVA must include in its annual plan.[114] These plans were designed to provide a summary for local people of how far the BVA achieved its targets from the previous year, as compared to other BVAs. The best value performance plans were subject to audit.[115]

5–022   The Local Government and Public Involvement in Health Act 2007[116] has however significantly amended the Local Government Act 1999. The 2007 Act in effect removes certain obligations contained in the original 1999 Act from English local authorities. When the relevant provisions take effect they will remove the power of the Secretary of State to specify performance indicators and standards for best value authorities, and the duties of such local authorities to prepare best value reviews and performance plans will be abolished. The rationale for these changes was to reduce the regulatory burden that the 1999 Act had imposed on local authorities.[117]

It is important to understand that the schema put in place by the Local Government Act 1999 is but part of the overall strategy for improved service delivery by local authorities. There are other parts of this strategy.[118]

There are *Local Area Agreements*, LAAs,[119] whereby performance targets can be agreed between central and local government on all outcomes delivered by local government alone or in partnership. The Local Government and Public Involvement in Health Act 2007 places LAAs on a statutory footing.[120] It imposes a duty on all upper tier authorities to prepare an LAA, and a duty on named partners to co-operate in the agreement of targets in LAAs and to have regard to those targets in their work. From April 2008 there will be a new area-based grant that is not ring-fenced to provide local authorities and their partners with greater flexibility in the use of funding from central government.

There is the *Beacon Council Scheme*, whereby local authorities are encouraged to apply for recognition as beacon councils, in recognition of their excellence in relation to service delivery in specific areas.[121]

There are *Local Public Service Agreements*.[122] These agreements bear some analogy with the Public Service Agreements concluded by central government departments. The essence of the Local Public Service Agreements is that the local authority commits itself to certain targets that require performance over and beyond what would have been expected in the

---

[114] Local Government Act 1999 s.6(1).
[115] Local Government Act 1999 s.7.
[116] Local Government and Public Involvement in Health Act 2007 ss.139–140.
[117] Department for Communities and Local Government, *Strong and Prosperous Communities, The Local Government White Paper Implementation Plan: One Year On* (2007), paras 22, 26, 27.
[118] http://www.communities.gov.uk/localgovernment/performanceframeworkpartnerships/.
[119] http://www.communities.gov.uk/localgovernment/performanceframeworkpartnerships/localareaagreements/.
[120] Local Government and Public Involvement in Health Act 2007 ss.103–114.
[121] Office of the Deputy Prime Minister, *An Overview of the Beacon Council Scheme* (2002); http://www.communitiesgov.uk/localgovernment/efficiencybetter/deliveringefficiency/beacon scheme/.
[122] Department of Transport, Local Government and the Regions, *Local Public Service Agreements, New Challenges* (2001); Office of the Deputy Prime Minister, *Building on Success, A Guide to the Second Generation of Local Public Service Agreements* (2003).

absence of the agreement. The local authority thus undertakes to deliver improvements greater than would result simply from implementation of its best value review. The benefit for the local authority is that, if successful, it receives financial rewards from central government, either directly or indirectly.

The *Comprehensive Performance Assessment* (CPA) is central to the government's thinking about better local service delivery.[123] It is the link for, and apex of, the other initiatives considered above. The essence of the idea is to have a CPA for each local authority, which will draw together information on performance from different sources. Councils were classified as high-performing, striving, coasting, or poor-performing. Since 2004, the classification system has been modified, so that it is now based on "stars" with "4-star" being the highest rating.[124] High-performing councils will have greater autonomy over policy choices and the use of government grants. They will be free from the fear of capping and will have greater freedom to use income from sources such as fines. At the other end of the scale, poor-performing councils will be offered help to redress weaknesses, backed up by the threat of ministerial intervention should this not resolve the problem.

6. THE PRIVATE FINANCE INITIATIVE: CONTRACT AND SERVICE PROVISION BY LOCAL GOVERNMENT

The discussion of the provision of services by central government revealed **5–023** the interplay between the search for "better government" and the PFI. The same interplay is apparent at the local level between the search for "best value" and the PFI. While the Treasury has the principal oversight role in relation to PFI the initiative was carried forward in relation to local authorities by the Department of the Environment, Transport and the Regions (DETR), by the Office of the Deputy Prime Minister and now by the Department of Communities and Local Government.[125] The Office of the Deputy Prime Minister published a paper on *Local Government and the Private Finance Initiative*,[126] which set out general government thinking in this respect.

Partnerships between the public and the private sectors were said to be "central to the Government's aims of establishing first-class public services and infrastructure, and promoting economic growth and regeneration".[127] It echoed the tenor of the paper on Best Value by making it clear that there was no presumption that the public or private sector provided the better

---

[123] Department of Transport, Local Government and the Regions, *Strong Local Leadership—Quality Public Services*, Cm. 5327 (2001), Ch.3.
[124] Audit Commission, *CPA—The Harder Test Framework for 2007* (2007).
[125] http://www.local.communitiesgov.uk/pfi/index.htm.
[126] (1998).
[127] (1998) Preface, 1.

route for delivering these aims. What was required was a system that made the best use of both sectors in effective public/private partnerships (PPPS). The PFI was regarded as integral to such a system by facilitating access to private capital to fund facilities such as schools, roads, stations, museums, police stations and leisure centres. These were commonly known as DBFO schemes, Design, Build, Finance and Operate, where the risks relating to the funding and operation of a capital asset were transferred to the private sector.[128] Provided that there was a sufficient level of risk transfer, the capital investment undertaken by the private sector would not count against public sector capital spending limits.[129]

The precise nature of the PFI agreement will vary depending upon the project. However, as in the case of central government, there is a broad distinction to be drawn between those schemes where the private sector supplier undertakes a capital project which the local authority then pays for the use of, and those schemes where the private supplier is in effect granted a concession and recoups its money direct from charges to the public.[130] It is, however, also clear that the government favours flexibility when deciding upon the appropriate form for the PFI deal. This is exemplified by its encouragement of asset transfers to the contractor where this will reduce the direct costs of the project,[131] and of joint venture companies where these are felt to be the most appropriate form of the public/private partnership.[132]

The administration of PFI at the local level reflects the general interplay between central and local government in relation to finance. Many of the local projects that might be suited for PFI will only be viable if the local authority can secure additional revenue support from central government. Such support is intended to assist local authorities in meeting the service costs of the PFI agreement.[133] The promise of central government support is given in the form of a letter, which sets out a level of "PFI credits" issued for that project. PFI credits are a measure of the private sector investment which will be supported, and act as a promise that PFI grant can be claimed once the project is operational. The level of grant is then based on the level of PFI credits issued. Where no such support is needed then approval from central government is not normally required.

Where there is a need for central assistance there is a detailed mechanism for applications. Local authorities which put forward projects must have regard to four factors when making their applications:[134] value for money; the requirements of the Capital Finance Regulations; departmental policy priorities; and the project assessment considerations set out by the Project

---

[128] (1998) para.1.6.
[129] (1998) para.1.8.
[130] (1998) paras 2.5–2.7.
[131] (1998) para.5.18.
[132] (1998) paras 7.1–7.4.
[133] Local Government PFI Annuity Grant Determination (No.1) 2007 [No.31/597].
[134] *Local Government and the Private Finance Initiative*, n.126, paras 4.2–4.3.

Review Group (PRG). The PRG is central to this approval process.[135] Its members are drawn from the sponsoring government departments. Projects deemed worthy of support are awarded a PFI credit. The Treasury agrees annually with each government department a provisional allocation of PFI credits for projects in their service areas.

7. PUBLIC PROCUREMENT AND THE EC: CONTRACT AND SERVICE PROVISION BY GOVERNMENT

The principles considered thus far are those found in domestic law or policy. **5–024** There are, in addition, EC rules, which stipulate how certain types of contract should be advertised and made.[136] The rules are complex. They are, however, of great practical importance, and also raise interesting conceptual issues. An outline of the main provisions will, therefore, be provided within this section.

A. The Object of the EC Rules
One of the main objectives of the EC is to create a single market. Many of **5–025** the Treaty articles are directed towards this, by prohibiting, for example, trade barriers, tariffs, and quantitative restrictions on the free movement of goods within the Community. These provisions by themselves are not, however, sufficient to achieve the desired goal. Member States may inhibit free movement by more subtle means than tariff barriers.

They may, for example, discriminate against companies from other Member States that wish to tender for a contract, favouring instead their own domestic firms. This may be a particular problem during a recession when a country's instinct may be to put its own industry first, and perhaps second and third, at the expense of more Community-minded goals. This is of economic significance because public procurement has been estimated by the Commission to account for 15 per cent of the entire gross domestic product of the EC: if discrimination is not eradicated from this area then the hope of attaining a single market will always remain partially unfulfilled. With this in mind the Community institutions have applied Treaty norms to cases involving public procurement, and have passed directives which address the issue more specifically. These will be considered in turn.

---

[135] *Local Government and the Private Finance Initiative*, paras 4.7–4.8; Department of Transport, Local Government and the Regions, *Criteria for Assessing Schemes* (2002); http://www.local.communitiesgov.uk/pfi/pficredshtm.
[136] Turpin, n.1; Arrowsmith, *Civil Liability*, n.1, Ch.3 and *The Law of Public and Utilities Procurement*, n.1.

B. The Application of the Treaty

5–026   The articles of the Treaty will be applied to cases involving public procurement where relevant. This can be illustrated through three brief examples.

In *Commission v Ireland*[137] a water company called for tenders for a project, and specified an Irish national standard for pipes that was met by only one firm, which was also Irish. This was held to be prima facie in breach of what is now art.28 EC. This Article prohibits quantitative restrictions on the free movement of goods or measures which have an equivalent effect. A different specification of pipe might have been just as good for the job at hand and therefore the requirement in the tender document impeded free movement. The ECJ, in the *Du Pont* case,[138] invalidated a requirement of national legislation that obliged local authorities to obtain a minimum proportion of their supplies from a particular region. Articles 43 and 49 of the Treaty, which relate to freedom of establishment and freedom to provide services, can also be used in this context. Thus, in *Commission v Italy*[139] it was held that a national rule, whereby only those companies which had a majority of shares owned by the state could tender for certain government contracts, was in breach of these articles.

C. The Directives on Public Procurement

i. The Community directives

5–027   Notwithstanding the application of the Treaty provisions it has long been acknowledged that more detailed regulation of these areas was needed. To this end the Community enacted directives on Public Works and Public Supplies, which have been in force in the UK since 1973 and 1978 respectively.[140] These directives were later strengthened: Directive 93/37 for Public Works,[141] Directive 93/36 for Public Supplies,[142] Directive 92/50 for Public Services,[143] Directive 89/665 for Public Sector Remedies,[144] and Directive 93/38 governed Utilities.[145] The current regulatory regime is embodied in two Directives dating from 2004,[146] the first of which relates to public works

---

[137] Case 45/87, [1988] E.C.R. 4929.
[138] Case 21/88, *Du Pont de Nemours Italiana SpA v Unita Sanitaria Locale, No.2 di Carrara* [1990] E.C.R. I–889.
[139] Case 3/88, [1989] E.C.R. 4035.
[140] Office of Government Commerce, *EC Public Procurement: State of Play—December 2001* (2001).
[141] [1993] O.J. L199/54.
[142] [1993] O.J. L199/1.
[143] [1992] O.J. L209/1.
[144] [1989] O.J. L395/33.
[145] [1993] O.J. L199/84.
[146] R. Williams, "The New Procurement Directives of the European Union" (2004) 13 P.P.L.R. 153; S. Arrowsmith, "Implementation of the New EC Procurement Directives and the *Alcatel* Ruling in England and Wales and Northern Ireland: A Review of the New Legislation and Guidance" (2006) 15 P.P.L.R. 86.

contracts, public supply contracts, and public service contracts,[147] while the second Directive deals with contracts made by utilities.[148]

ii. Application in the UK

Directives dictate the ends that must be reached, while leaving the means to the Member States.[149] The Community directives on public procurement have been given effect in the UK through secondary legislation,[150] as exemplified by the Public Contracts Regulations 2006,[151] and the Utilities Contracts Regulations 2006.[152] This legislation will, in line with the *Von Colson*[153] principle, have to be construed so as to effectuate the objects of the directives. Space precludes a detailed examination of the entirety of this legislation. The main provisions of the Public Contracts Regulations 2006 will be taken by way of example.

5–028

The principal objectives of the Community rules in this area are: to ensure that public contracts above a certain value are advertised, thereby enabling all those in the Community who are interested to tender for them; to prohibit the use of technical specifications in the contract documents which could favour domestic firms; to mandate procedures for the award of the contract; and to stipulate the substantive criteria for award of the contract itself.

The Public Contracts Regulations apply to *contracting authorities*, which include:[154] ministers of the Crown; government departments; the House of Commons and the House of Lords; local authorities; and fire and police authorities. Regulation 3(1)(w) extends the definition of contracting authorities to include corporations, or groups of individuals, which or who act together for the specific purpose of meeting needs in the public interest, not having an industrial or commercial character, where they are financed wholly or mainly by another contracting authority, or are subject to management by another contracting authority, or more than half of the members are appointed by another contracting authority.[155]

---

[147] Directive 2004/18/EC of the European Parliament and of the Council of March 31, 2004 on the coordination of procedures for the award of public works contracts, public supply contracts and public service contracts [2004] O.J. L234/114.
[148] Directive 2004/17/EC of the European Parliament and of the Council of March 31, 2004 coordinating the procurement procedures of entities operating in the water, energy, transport and postal services sectors [2004] O.J. L134/1.
[149] See below, Ch.10.
[150] The Office of Government Commerce is responsible for implementation, http://www.ogc.gov.uk/procurement_policy_and_application_of_eu_rules_guidance_on_the_2006_regulations_.asp.
[151] The Public Contracts Regulations 2006 (SI 2006/5).
[152] The Utilities Contracts Regulations 2006 (SI 2006/6).
[153] Case 14/83, *Von Colson & Kamaan v Land Nordrhein-Westfalen* [1984] E.C.R. 1891.
[154] SI 2006/5 reg.3.
[155] Bodies such as the Health and Safety Executive, the Advisory, Conciliation and Arbitration Service, the National Rivers Authority and the Commission for New Towns have been held to meet these criteria.

A *public contract* is held to cover[156] public works contracts, public supply contracts and public service contracts.[157] The regulations then define each type of contract. Thus a public works contract is defined as a contract in writing for consideration, for the carrying out of work or works for a contracting authority, or under which the contracting authority engages a person to produce the specified work.[158] The regulations only apply if the contract is worth more than a certain amount,[159] but there are provisions designed to prevent the contracting authority from dividing contracts in order to avoid the bite of the regulatory scheme.[160] Subject to this threshold, the regulations pertain whenever a contracting authority offers a public contract other than one which is expressly excluded from the operation of the regulations.

There are detailed rules which relate to the *technical specifications* permitted in the tender document, the object being to avoid discrimination against non-domestic companies by the specification of standards which can be more easily met by the domestic operator.[161]

5–029   A central part of the regulations concerns *procedures*. There are four such procedures.[162] Under the *open procedure* any interested party can submit a bid; under the *restricted procedure* only those selected by the contracting party can do so; under the *negotiated procedure* the authority negotiates the terms of the contract with one or more persons who are selected by it; while under the *competitive dialogue procedure* a limited number of parties are invited to engage in the competitive dialogue, which is used for complex contracts. The open and restricted procedures are regarded as the norm, and there are limits as to when the other two procedures can be used. Notice of intent to seek offers in relation to public works must be publicised in the Official Journal. There are further detailed rules which specify when a contractor may be excluded from the tendering process, such as in the event of bankruptcy. The contracting authority is entitled to consider the economic and financial standing of the contractor.

The regulation then designates the criteria to be used when *awarding* the contract. This must be on the basis either of the tender which offers the lowest price, or the offer which is the most economically advantageous, taking account of, inter alia, considerations of price, period for completion, running costs, environmental considerations, functional and aesthetic considerations, profitability and technical merit.[163] If the contracting authority intends to apply the economically advantageous test all the criteria must be stated in the contract documentation. It may be lawful to specify a policy objective the contractor should comply with, provided that this is itself

---

[156] SI 2006/5 reg.2(1). Works contracts relating to utilities are dealt with under the separate utilities regulation, and there are exceptions for public works involving state security.
[157] SI 2006/5 reg.2(1), subject to exceptions reg.6.
[158] SI 2006/5 reg.2(1).
[159] SI 2006/5 reg.8.
[160] SI 2006/5 reg.8(11).
[161] SI 2006/5 regs 9–10.
[162] SI 2006/5 reg.12.
[163] SI 2006/5 reg.30.

compatible with Community law. But compliance with such an objective is not relevant to the assessment of that contractor's technical capacity to do the work, nor is it part of the actual criteria for deciding upon the award of the contract.[164]

Once the contract has been awarded the regulations impose a duty to provide *reasons* as to why a particular contractor has been chosen.[165] This duty is owed to any unsuccessful contractor who requests a reasoned explanation. There is, in addition, an obligation to furnish a more general dossier, which indicates the procedure adopted, the successful applicant, and the reasons for this choice.

A defect of the earlier provisions on public procurement concerned **5–030** enforcement, and the lack of effective *remedies*. This problem was addressed by Directive 89/665, the Remedies or Compliance Directive, and provisions to effectuate these obligations were incorporated in the relevant UK regulations. This is dealt with, in the context of public works, by reg.47. This provides that the duties under the regulation and under Community law are owed to contractors. A breach of such duties is not a criminal offence, but it does sound as an action for breach of duty, presumably breach of statutory duty, in civil law. The aggrieved contractor must first tell the contracting authority of the apprehended breach of duty and the intention to bring the action.[166] The court has a number of options: it may issue an interim order, which, in effect, halts the contract award procedure; it may set aside the decision by the contracting authority and it can award damages to the contractor.[167] However, if a contract has already been entered into pursuant to the contested decision then damages is the only available remedy.[168] The court cannot, therefore, set aside a contract made in breach of the regulations.

The precise *measure of damages* is unclear. The problem for the aggrieved contractor is that it may be uncertain how far a breach of the regulations affected its chances of winning the contract. It may be equally questionable whether it would have made profits from the contract. A possible solution would be to use doctrines developed within contract law to cope with uncertain losses, and to allow those who would have had a reasonable chance of success to recover a percentage of the likely profit.[169]

---

[164] Case 31/87, *Gebroeders Beentjers BV v State of the Netherlands* [1988] E.C.R. 4635.
[165] SI 2005/6, reg.32.
[166] The action must be brought within 3 months from the date when the grounds for bringing it first arose, unless the court believes that there are good reasons for extending the time, SI 2006/5 reg.47(7).
[167] *Harmon CFEM Facades (UK) Ltd v Corporate Officer of the House of Commons* (2000) 2 L.G.L.R. 372.
[168] SI 2006/5, reg.47(8)–(9).
[169] S. Arrowsmith, "Enforcing the EC Public Procurement Rules: The Remedies System in England and Wales" (1992) 1 P.P.L.R. 92; *Chaplin v Hicks* [1911] 2 K.B. 786; *Hotson v East Berkshire Health Authority* [1987] 1 A.C. 750; H. Leffler, "Damages Liability for Breach of EC Procurement Law: Governing Principles and Practical Solutions" (2003) 12 P.P.L.R. 151; M. Bowsher and P. Moser, "Damages for Breach of the EC Public Procurement Rules in the United Kingdom" (2006) 15 P.P.L.R. 195.

The remedies set out are without prejudice to any other powers of the court.[170] This leaves open the possibility of an application for judicial review,[171] and a damages action for breach of the Treaty or norms made thereunder. Both of these issues will be considered below.[172]

8. CONTRACT, SERVICE PROVISION AND GOVERNANCE

5–031 The discussion thus far has been concerned with the framing of government procurement policy and the way in which this operates at the central and local level. It is now appropriate to stand back and consider in more general terms the implications of these developments for governance.

A. Contract as an Instrument of Policy

5–032 Governments and public bodies disburse extremely large sums through their grant of contracts, and have in the past used such power to attain policy goals other than the provision of goods or services. The power to award contracts has been used to further the Fair Wages Resolution,[173] and policies such as "Buy British". Bargaining has also been a not uncommon feature in the planning context, and the award of contracts has been used as a device to secure compliance with anti-inflation policy.[174] The presently declared policy is that procurement power should not be used in this manner,[175] but it is important nonetheless to consider the relevant legal issues.

The legality of such action has always been debatable, and legal control may be exerted in a variety of ways. Judicial review may be applied in certain circumstances to the exercise of public contractual power. The precise metes and bounds of judicial review in this context will be considered below.[176] Statute imposes constraints upon the considerations that public bodies can take into account when awarding contracts, as we have seen in relation to local government. There are, in addition, the Community controls over public procurement, flowing from the EC Treaty and directives. The Treaty itself imposes constraints upon the types of policies which

---

[170] SI 2006/5 reg.47(8).
[171] See however, *Cookson & Clegg v Ministry of Defence* [2005] EWCA Civ. 811; S.H. Bailey, "Judicial Review and Public Procurement Regulations" (2005) 14 P.P.L.R. 291.
[172] See below, Chs 26, 29.
[173] O. Kahn-Freund, "Legislation through Adjudication, The Legal Aspect of Fair Wages Clauses and Recognised Conditions" (1948) 11 M.L.R. 269, 429.
[174] J. Jowell, "Bargaining in Development Control" (1977) J.P.L. 414; and "Limits of Law in Urban Planning" (1977) CLP 63; R. Ferguson and A. Page, "Pay Restraint; The Legal Constraints" (1978) 128 N.L.J 515; T. Daintith, "Regulation by Contract: The New Prerogative" (1979) C.L.P. 41; T. Daintith, "Legal Analysis of Economic Policy" (1982) 9 Jnl Law & Soc. 191; A. Page, "Public Law and Economic Policy: The United Kingdom Experience" (1982) 9 Jnl Law & Soc. 225.
[175] Procurement Policy Unit, *Procurement Policy Guidelines* (1998), para.2.4.
[176] See below, Ch.26.

governments can pursue through their contracting power. It is clear, for example, that "Buy British" policies are illegal under EC law, as an impediment to the free movement of goods.[177] The directives, which apply to a wide range of bodies concerned with the award of contracts for works, supply and services, have, moreover, further restricted the degree to which contracting power can be used to attain other socio-political goals.

B. The Source and Nature of Executive Power

Daintith has produced important work on this issue.[178] He distinguishes two **5–033** ways in which government can seek to attain its goals.[179] It can do so through what he terms *imperium*, which is manifest in the ordinary command of law. It can also do so through *dominium*, which is the use made by government of its power to disburse benefits to those who comply with governmental objectives. There can be limitations and disadvantages in seeking to pursue objectives through the use of imperium. It may be impracticable to draft the necessary legislation, which may be lengthy, complex and uncertain in its impact. Pursuit of objectives through dominium can, by way of contrast, have positive attractions. Where expenditure requires statutory authorisation the legislation will often leave a broad measure of discretion to the implementing body. Dominium power can also be used in other ways, such as bargaining and informal agreement. This can facilitate short-term experimentation with policy choices and obviate the need for legislative authorisation. Daintith admits that constitutional problems can occur as a result of the use of dominium power, such as when third parties are affected by agreements of which they had no knowledge, or in areas where an individual had no real choice as to whether to enter such an agreement.[180]

There is no ready-made solution which will determine the appropriate legal response to the many and varied instances in which dominium power is used as opposed to the more formal exercise of governmental power through imperium.[181] There are a number of options at our disposal. These could include process rights for third parties, and indeed for those more directly involved in the bargaining. There could be an obligation to make the transactions more transparent, open and public to those affected by them. There could, as a matter of principle, also be intervention designed to safeguard the legislative process itself, by, for example, stipulating that if the executive wishes to achieve certain policy objectives then it must obtain specific legislative authorisation. This is not as strange as it might appear, since much of the history of judicial control over prerogative power has been

---

[177] Case 249/81, *Commission v Ireland* [1982] E.C.R. 4005.
[178] "The Techniques of Government", in J. Jowell and D. Oliver (eds), *The Changing Constitution* (Oxford University Press, 3rd edn, 1994); "Regulation by Contract: The New Prerogative" (1979) CLP 41; "Legal Analysis of Economic Policy" (1982) 9 Jnl Law & Soc. 191.
[179] "The Techniques of Government", n.178, 213–219.
[180] "The Techniques of Government", n.178, 228–229.
[181] "The Techniques of Government", n.178, 236.

concerned with just this issue: placing limits upon the policies the executive can pursue without Parliamentary authority. The options at our disposal are, therefore, varied. Their suitability will no doubt depend upon the more particular type of dominium power that is at stake. The importance of the issue should not, however, be doubted.

C. The Blurring of the Public/Private Divide and the Responsibility for Policy Formation

5–034   The discussion in the preceding sections has shown the way in which the public/private divide has become blurred as result of the new initiatives concerning service provision. The line between policy formation and policy execution is always fragile, and becomes even more so as a result of financing methods which consciously lay emphasis on public–private partnerships and the like. There have undoubtedly been developments that have constrained the use of dominium as a technique of government policy.[182]

It is, however, equally the case that the increased emphasis on innovative financing of service provision means, at the most fundamental level, that what "government" delivers by way of services will be increasingly dependent on what the market is willing provide. It also raises broader issues about the ethics of public service, and how these are being transformed as a result of these developments.[183]

9. MAKING THE CONTRACT: GENERAL PRINCIPLES

A. Capacity to Contract

i. Crown

5–035   Ministers are often granted a power to conclude contracts by a statute, but in addition the Crown possesses a common law power to contract.[184] It is debatable whether this power should be seen as part of the prerogative.[185] Whatever label is attached, the Crown's contracting power is unconstrained by restrictions as to subject-matter or person.[186]

ii. Ministers of the Crown

5–036   The contractual *capacity* of Ministers of the Crown, and other Crown agents, requires separate treatment. It is clear that a minister will normally possess the *authority* to make a contract on behalf of the Crown. This will be

---

[182] "The Techniques of Government", n.178, 229–235.
[183] Faulkner, n.55; N. Lewis and D. Longley, "Ethics and the Public Service" [1994] P.L. 596.
[184] *Bankers Case* (1700) 90 E.R. 270. Turpin, n.1, 83–84; Arrowsmith, *Civil Liability*, n.1, 53–54.
[185] Daintith, "Regulation by Contract", n.178, 42–43.
[186] cf. *New South Wales v Bardolph* (1934) 52 C.L.R. 455, 496.

examined below. What is of relevance here is the question of whether a minister possesses *capacity* to make contracts in his or her own name.

It could be argued either that such agents have no independent contractual capacity, in the sense that the Crown is the only entity which is a party to the contract. It could be argued that while the primary liability rests with the Crown, the minister may also be a party to the contract. It might also be argued that ministers do have an independent contractual capacity within their area of responsibility, in the same way as any other artificial legal entity. On this view, while they can contract on behalf of the Crown, they can also choose to make a contract to which the Crown is not a party, and for which the Crown bears no liability.[187]

There is some authority that a minister or other Crown agent can choose to contract in his or her own name, even in relation to those functions which are carried out on behalf of the Crown, and that whether this has occurred depends upon the intent of the parties.[188] The principal motivation behind these cases was, however, to allow plaintiffs to sue without the necessity of using the Petition of Right procedure: this procedure was only necessary in actions against the Crown, not when suits were brought against individual ministers.

Other cases have adopted a different approach. In *Town Investments*,[189] certain rent legislation only gave protection from rent increases where the tenant and the occupier were the same person. The Department of the Environment (DOE) organised accommodation for other Departments and had negotiated a lease, but the building was occupied by a different Department. The landlord sought to argue that the tenant and occupier were not one and the same, that the DOE had power to make the lease in its own name and hence that the protective rent legislation did not apply. The House of Lords rejected the argument. Acts of government done by ministers were acts done by the Crown, and the Crown was to be treated as one entity. Although there are ambiguities in the judgments, the general thrust is that ministers do not possess an independent contractual capacity.

A ministerial office may be created at common law or by statute. If the minister's office is one which exists at common law then the minister will, it seems, possess the contractual capacity of the Crown. Thus, a contract made will be valid even if it is outside the specific terms of a statute, unless a court construes the statute as imposing a limit on contractual power in the area covered by the enabling instrument. Where a minister is a purely statutory creation the argument for restricting the contracting power by the ultra vires principle is, in theory, stronger. However, as seen above, the effect of *Town Investments*[190] appears to be that the contractual capacity and authority of a specific minister merges with that of the Crown. It is unclear whether this

5–037

---

[187] Arrowsmith, *Civil Liability*, n.1, 56–59.

[188] *Graham v Public Works Commissioners* [1901] 2 K.B. 781; *International Railway Co v Niagara Parks Commission* [1941] A.C. 328.

[189] *Town Investments v Department of the Environment* [1978] A.C. 359.

[190] *Town Investments*, n.189.

will always be the case, but certain dicta suggest an affirmative answer.[191] On this view any contract made by the minister in a public capacity will bind the Crown, and it would also seem to be the case that the minister has no separate contractual capacity as such, unless this is specifically conferred by statute. Other jurisdictions have, however, not adopted this approach,[192] nor as will be seen below, does it sit easily with the approach of our own courts in other areas. Three comments may be made on the foregoing.

First, it is doubtful whether anything should turn upon whether the minister's office existed at common law or was the creation of a statute. There is no reason in principle why there should be any difference in their respective contractual capacities.

Second, the argument for saying that the minister possesses the contractual capacity of the Crown is that the Crown in its governmental capacity operates through individual ministers or other Crown servants. It has to do so. It is, therefore, thought to be unrealistic to speak of the Crown in a governmental sense that is divorced from those servants. However, our courts have recognised that ministers and departments can be regarded as separate from the Crown. This is commonly acknowledged in judicial review proceedings where the orthodox view is that the prerogative orders will not lie against the Crown itself, but will lie against individual ministers.[193] Thus in the context of such proceedings, it has been recognised that ministers can act in an *official* capacity separate from the Crown itself. The statute will be construed as giving powers to a particular minister to be exercised in his or her own name as *persona designata*, and not as agent for the Crown.[194] The "logic" of merging the capacity of the minister with that of the Crown is not pursued remorselessly in this context.[195] It is clear, therefore, that on some occasions our courts have chosen to regard the Crown and its ministers as one and indivisible, while on others they have accepted that they can be treated as separate entities for many important purposes.[196] It has indeed been persuasively argued that the way in which the law treats the Crown differs significantly as between administrative law and contract, such that in the former there is a tendency to disaggregate the powers of different ministers, whereas in the latter the tendency has been to aggregate government into a unified whole.[197]

Third, given that this is so, a preference for one of these theories should not be allowed to dictate a conclusion that is unacceptable in substantive terms. For example, even if one does subscribe to the *Town Investments'* approach, and believes that the contractual capacity of the minister merges with that of the Crown, this should not enable clear delimitations of a

[191] *Town Investments*, n.189, 380–382, 400.
[192] *JE Verrault & Fils v Quebec* [1971] S.C.R. 41; *Meates v Attorney-General* [1979] 1 N.Z.L.R. 415.
[193] Whether this orthodoxy is in fact correct is questionable, see below, para.28–017.
[194] *M v Home Office* [1994] 1 A.C. 377.
[195] Many statutes such as the Ministers of the Crown Act 1975 are, however, premised upon the hypothesis that a minister accepts rights and obligations in his or her own name.
[196] See also, *Department for Environment Food and Rural Affairs v Robertson* [2005] I.C.R. 750.
[197] J. McLean, "The Crown in Contract and Administrative Law" (2004) 24 O.J.L.S. 129.

minister's contracting power laid down in a statute to be circumvented by reliance on some more general contractual power of the Crown. Where such a limit is clearly expressed or can be implied then, by analogy with the case law on the royal prerogative, such a limit should be respected and enforced.[198]

iii. Statutory bodies

Authorities which are not Crown agents and which derive their powers from statute are subject to the limitations imposed by the legislation. Thus, a contract that is beyond the limits imposed by the statute will be ultra vires.[199] This is exemplified by the decision in *Hazell*.[200] A local authority was held to have no power to enter into speculative interest rate swap transactions, which would result in profits or losses depending upon movements in interest rates.

5–038

The scope of such a public body's contractual capacity will, therefore, be dependent upon the construction of the relevant statute. However, many such bodies are granted broad powers to facilitate the carrying out of their tasks: for example s.111 of the Local Government Act 1972 empowers local authorities to do anything which is calculated to facilitate the discharge of any of its functions, or is incidental thereto. Moreover, the courts have held that a power to contract may be implied as an incidence of other powers the particular body has been given.[201] The Local Government Act 2000 s.2, accords to local authorities the power to do anything they consider is likely to achieve the promotion or improvement of the economic, social or environmental well-being of their area.

B. The Authority of an Agent

The public body must have capacity to make the contract, and the agent must have been authorised to do so. Special problems can occur when such an agent purports to act on behalf of a public authority.

5–039

i. The extent of the agent's authority: general

In a contract made between two private parties an agent can bind the principal if the agent has authority, actual or ostensible.[202] There are, however, difficulties in applying these principles to the situation where a public body makes a contract through an agent. These problems will be

5–040

---

[198] *Att-Gen v De Keyser's Royal Hotel Ltd* [1920] A.C. 508.
[199] *Att-Gen v Manchester Corporation* [1906] 1 Ch 643; *Att-Gen v Fulham Corporation* [1921] 1 Ch.44.
[200] *Hazell v Hammersmith and Fulham London Borough Council* [1992] 2 A.C. 1.
[201] *Att-Gen v Great Eastern Railway* (1880) 5 App. Cas. 473, 478.
[202] See generally, *Bowstead and Reynolds on Agency* (Sweet & Maxwell, 18th edn, 2006).

considered in the discussion of representations, and reference should be made to that discussion.[203] The principles can be briefly reiterated here.

Actual authority may be given by the terms of a statute, and it may be excluded where the legislation stipulates that an individual cannot bind the authority in a certain transaction. The fact that the authority has purported to delegate to a particular officer will not legitimate the contract if the statute makes it clear that the function must be performed by a different party. Ostensible authority exists in the situation where a representation is made by the principal that the agent has authority to deal with a certain type of transaction, or perhaps where an agent in that position would normally do so. However, ostensible authority cannot validate a transaction that is ultra vires the public body itself, nor can it validate a delegation of authority to an agent where this is prohibited by the relevant statute. The harsh results of this doctrine will be considered below, and the reforms suggested there are equally apposite here.[204]

These principles apply in general to Crown servants and agents. Thus it will normally have to be shown that a minister possesses actual or ostensible authority to enter into a contract of the type in question. These principles have been applied to servants of the Crown who are not ministers.[205] The only difference between such servants and ministers of the Crown is that the latter are likely to have a broader remit of authority than the former.[206]

ii. Breach of warranty of authority

5–041   In normal circumstances if an agent is duly authorised to make a contract then the principal will be liable but the agent will not. Where, however, the agent possesses no authority he or she can be sued for breach of warranty of authority.

There is some case law indicating that this action will not lie against a servant who makes a contract on behalf of the Crown. Thus, in *Dunn*[207] the plaintiff was engaged for three years by the defendant on behalf of the Crown. He was dismissed prior to the end of his term and claimed breach of an implied warranty of authority by the defendant. The action failed, but the case is not conclusive authority that such an action could never succeed.

The reasons given for the decision differed. Charles J. believed that such an action would be against public policy,[208] while the Court of Appeal preferred to rest its decision on the fact that there had been no breach.[209] The reasoning based upon public policy is unconvincing. It is difficult to see why

[203] See below, paras 20–032–20–033; *R. (on the application of BAPIO Action Ltd) v Secretary of State for the Home Department* [2008] 2 W.L.R. 1073, para.28.
[204] See below, Ch.20.
[205] *Attorney General for Ceylon v AD Silva* [1953] A.C. 461.
[206] Unless one were to read the *Town Investments* case to mean that ministers always had the authority of the Crown generally, but this would be an extreme application of the merger theory applied in that case.
[207] *Dunn v MacDonald* [1897] 1 Q.B. 401, 555.
[208] *Dunn v MacDonald*, n.207, 404–406.
[209] *Dunn v MacDonald*, n.207, 556–558.

the agent acting on behalf of the Crown should be in any better position than any other agent.[210]

C. Parliamentary Appropriation

Given the breadth of the Crown's power to contract, the legislature must have power to refuse an appropriation to pay for a contract of which it disapproves made by the executive.[211]   **5–042**

It was at one time thought that unless an express appropriation of money had been made the contract would be invalid and null. This belief was derived from dicta by Shee J.,[212] and Viscount Haldane.[213] However, it is clear from later cases that Viscount Haldane regarded the absence of the requisite appropriation as making the contract unenforceable, as there was no res against which to enforce it, rather than making the contract null.[214] The view that the absence of appropriation goes to enforceability and not validity is supported by fully reasoned authority in Australia,[215] which also establishes that the appropriation does not have to be specifically directed towards a particular contractual expense.

The meaning of "enforceability" is not entirely clear. It is unclear what the result is if the necessary funds are not appropriated. In *Bardolph*, Evatt J. at first instance, stated that failure to vote the funds would relieve the Crown from performance, the voting being an implied condition of the contract.[216] This comes perilously close to regarding appropriation as a condition of validity by the backdoor. On appeal, the High Court disagreed with this part of Evatt J.'s judgment, finding that the lack of appropriation did not relieve the Crown from its obligation to perform.[217]

Enforceability could have one of two other meanings. One suggestion is that it should bear the same interpretation as in the Statute of Frauds.[218] There are, however, difficulties in transferring the meaning of unenforceable from a statute concerned with ensuring written evidence for certain transactions, to the different context of the absence of the requisite parliamentary appropriation.[219] Another suggestion is that enforceability is best seen as a condition to the satisfaction of judgment, rather than as to the enforceability of the claim itself. The difficulty with this view is that it amounts to saying

[210] Street, n.1, 93 makes the further points that the representation may well have been one of law rather than fact and that the plaintiff may not, on the facts, have relied upon it.
[211] Street, n.1, 84–90.
[212] *Churchward v R.* (1865) L.R. 1 Q.B. 173, 209, Cockburn C.J. was clearly of a different opinion, 200–201.
[213] *Commercial Cable Co v Government of Newfoundland* [1916] 2 A.C. 610, 617.
[214] *Commonwealth of Australia v Kidman* [1926] 32 A.L.R. 1, 2–3; *Att-Gen v Great Southern and Western Ry Co of Ireland* [1925] A.C. 754.
[215] *New South Wales v Bardolph* (1934) 52 C.L.R. 455.
[216] *New South Wales v Bardolph*, n.215, 483–484.
[217] *New South Wales v Bardolph*, n.215, 497–498, 508–510.
[218] Street, *Governmental Liability*, n.1, 91–92.
[219] e.g. would the distinction between law and equity operate here, and would the doctrine of part performance with its specialised meaning be regarded as an exception to the unenforceability?

no more than that there is no legal right to execute judgment against Crown property which is the general rule for all judgments against the Crown.

Appropriation Acts are, in any event, drawn broadly at present and thus the above problems are unlikely to occur.

D. Proceedings against the Crown

5–043   In claims brought against public authorities there is, in general, no problem about who to bring an action against or how: public bodies can be sued in their own name. Where the defendant is the Crown the position is different. The petition of right developed as a mechanism whereby actions, including those for breach of contract, could be brought against the Crown.[220]

The Crown Proceedings Act 1947 abolished the petition of right and certain other forms of procedure. Under s.1 any claim against the Crown which could have been enforced, albeit subject to fiat, by petition of right (or under any of the more specialised statutory liabilities prior to the Act) can now be enforced without the fiat, as of right. The defendant is either the appropriate government department or the Attorney-General. It is clear, therefore, that the substantive areas covered by the old petition of right will still provide the actual scope of actions that can be brought against the Crown. However, apart from actions in tort (and salvage) the coverage of the petition of right appears to be comprehensive. Two qualifications are necessary.

First, the Act is only applicable in relation to the United Kingdom government.[221] A claimant seeking redress against the Crown for other areas is dependent upon the petition of right procedure. It has been held that even this pre-1947 procedure is unavailable and that the repeal of the Petitions of Right Act 1860 is total. This conclusion is debatable.[222] Second, it is unclear whether the Crown can be sued personally. It was, prior to 1947, possible to bring a petition of right but this, as stated, has been abolished and s.40(1) states that nothing in the 1947 Act shall apply to proceedings by or against the sovereign in his private capacity. It may, however, be that the petition of right survives to the extent of allowing such actions.

E. Crown Service

i. The existence of a contract

5–044   There are special problems with the law relating to Crown service, which has been much criticised.[223] An initial issue to be resolved is whether Crown

---

[220] See below, paras 29–045—29–046.
[221] Crown Proceedings Act 1947 s.40(2)(b),(c).
[222] *Franklin v Att-Gen* [1974] Q.B. 185, 201. The 1947 Act states that nothing in it shall affect proceedings against the Crown relating to non-UK claims This saving should, in this respect, preserve the 1860 Act.
[223] S. Fredman and G. Morris, *The State as Employer, Labour Law in the Public Services* (Mansell, 1989).

servants have any actual contract of service at all. This issue has come before the courts on a number of occasions.

The argument that Crown servants do not have any contract of service as such is based, in part, on the fact that they can be dismissed at will. However, as noted by Lord Atkin in *Reilly*,[224] the existence of a power to dismiss such servants at will is not inconsistent with the existence of a contract prior to that dismissal. In *Bruce*,[225] May L.J. held that there was nothing unconstitutional about civil servants being employed by the Crown pursuant to a contract of service, and that this would be consistent with the modern view of the position of the civil servants vis-à-vis the Crown. However, he went on to hold that prior to 1985 the Crown did not intend that civil servants should have such contracts. The point arose once again in *McClaren*,[226] where a prison officer claimed that the introduction of a new shift system constituted a breach of contract, or of his conditions of service. It was held that it was at least arguable that the relationship between the Home Office and prison officers was a contractual one. The willingness to think of Crown servants as having a contract of service is also apparent in *Nangle*,[227] where the court affirmed the view taken in *Bruce* that the Crown does possess the capacity to make a contract with its staff. It went on to hold that a contract had been created on the facts, and that there was a strong presumption in favour of an intention to create legal relations.

These decisions are to be welcomed. There is no sound reason in the modern day why civil servants should not be employed under a contract of service. It is true that the regime has been based upon the assumption that no such contract existed.[228] It is true also that provision has been made for resolving disputes between the Crown and its staff within this framework, and that statutory protections of varying kinds have been extended to Crown servants.[229] The recognition that Crown servants have a contract of employment would, nonetheless, go some way to demystifying the relationship between the Crown and its employees, and to undermining the idea that such employees should be treated very differently from others. This does not, however, necessarily mean that they should be treated in the identical manner as those in private employment, as the following extract from Fredman and Morris demonstrates.[230]

"We would argue that the major difference is that, while private employers are free to act unless constrained by the law, public employers derive their authority from prerogative or statute. There is a 'public'

---

[224] *Reilly v King* [1934] A.C. 176, 180.
[225] *R. v Civil Service Appeals Board Ex p Bruce* [1988] ICR 649. The point was not taken before the Court of Appeal, [1989] I.C.R. 171.
[226] *McClaren v Home Office* [1990] I.C.R. 824.
[227] *R. v Lord Chancellor's Department Ex p Nangle* [1991] ICR 743, but not for members of the armed forces, *Quinn v Ministry of Defence* [1997] P.I.Q.R. 387.
[228] Fredman and Morris, n.223, 61–70.
[229] Equal Pay Act 1970 s.1(8); Sex Discrimination Act 1975 s.85(2); Race Relations Act 1976 ss.75, 76; Disability Discrimination Act 1995 s.64.
[230] *The State as Employer*, n.223, 66.

dimension to the way in which the civil service and the rest of the public services are administered, which means that the State owes duties to the general public as well as its workforce. It is necessary to find a balance between these interests. To declare that civil servants have no contract is to give too little emphasis to the rights of the individual employee; but simply to reverse this and declare that they do have contracts is to ignore the public duties of the Crown."

ii. Dismissal of Crown servants

5–045 One of the main areas in which Crown employees have been in a disadvantageous position concerns dismissal. In *Dunn*,[231] a consular agent was appointed for three years and dismissed before the end of that period. His claim for damages for wrongful dismissal was denied, the court stating that Dunn's office was held at pleasure. This rule was applied by way of analogy with the dismissibility of military servants, the policy being the necessity for the Crown to be able to rid itself of a servant who might otherwise act detrimentally to the interests of the state. There are obvious flaws in this reasoning. While some Crown servants in senior positions might represent a danger of this type, it is difficult to envisage this being so for the majority of such servants. More important is the fact that this reasoning only goes to preclude specific performance of the contract, not to the award of damages.

The rule of dismissibility at pleasure can be excluded by statute.[232] It is less clear whether it can be excluded by the terms of the contract itself, and if so what terms are capable of doing so.[233] In a sequel to the *Dunn* case the Court of Appeal found that a provision for a fixed term would not in itself prevent dismissibility at pleasure.[234] There are however indications in the case law that appropriate terms in the contract can exclude the general rule,[235] for example, where there is provision for a fixed term and for power to determine for cause.[236] However, a number of authorities support the conclusion that dismissibility at pleasure can only be excluded by statute, and that any contractual term purporting to exclude this rule will be disregarded.[237] The reasoning in these latter cases is not convincing,[238] but they have not been overruled.

---

[231] *Dunn v Queen* [1896] 1 Q.B. 116.
[232] *Gould v Stuart* [1896] A.C. 575.
[233] G Nettheim, "*Dunn v The Queen* Revisited" [1975] C.L.J. 253.
[234] *Dunn v Macdonald* [1897] 1 Q.B. 401, 555.
[235] *Shenton v Smith* [1895] A.C. 229.
[236] *Reilly v King* [1934] A.C. 176; *Robertson v Minister of Pensions* [1949] 1 K.B. 227.
[237] *Rodwell v Thomas* [1944] K.B. 596; *Riordan v War Office* [1959] 1 W.L.R. 1046, [1961] 1 W.L.R. 210.
[238] In neither case are the authorities relied on convincing for establishing the propositions laid down. As pointed out above, the provision for a fixed term in the *Dunn* case appears to have been held not to be inconsistent with a power to dismiss at pleasure, rather than a clog upon such power. See also, *Terrell v Secretary of State for the Colonies* [1953] 2 Q.B. 482.

iii. Arrears of pay

Until 1943 it was believed that a civil servant would be entitled to salary **5–046** accrued at the date of dismissal.[239] The point had not, however, been fully argued in any case and in *Lucas*[240] Pilcher J. reached the opposite conclusion. The reasoning is, with respect, unconvincing. Starting from the premise that a Crown servant is dismissible at pleasure, Pilcher J. reached the conclusion that therefore arrears of pay were irrecoverable, which is a non sequitur. As Lord Atkin stated in *Reilly*, a right to terminate the contract at will is not inconsistent with the existence of a contract prior to termination.[241] The decision in *Lucas* has been cogently criticised by the Privy Council,[242] which refused to follow it. It is to be hoped that other courts will adopt the same approach.[243]

iv. Statutory protection

In the context of Crown service the maxim that the common law will supply **5–047** the omission of the legislature has been reversed: it is statute which has provided protection. The common law has not been overruled, but rendered less important by the passage of legislation concerning unfair dismissal.[244] The legislation, now contained in the Employment Rights Act 1996, provides that an employee has the right not to be unfairly dismissed[245] and the legislation sets out what constitutes dismissal. Remedies for unfair dismissal are either a monetary award or an order for reinstatement or re-engagement. The general scheme of the legislation relating to unfair dismissal applies to Crown employment,[246] which means employment under or for the purposes of a government department, or any officer or body exercising on behalf of the Crown functions conferred by any enactment. The most important general exception, apart from the military, is for national security.[247] Civil servants also have the benefit of the Equal Pay Act 1970,[248] and the Sex Discrimination Act 1975.[249] It should however be borne in mind that executive agencies and contracting-out have had important implications for employment practices in public services.[250]

---

[239] *R. v Doutre* (1884) 9 App. Cas. 745; *Sutton v Att-Gen* (1923) 39 T.L.R. 294.
[240] *Lucas v Lucas* [1943] P. 68; *Mulvenna v The Admiralty* 1926 S.C. 842; D. Logan, "A Civil Servant and his Pay" (1945) 61 L.Q.R. 26.
[241] [1934] A.C. 176. *cf. IRC v Hambrook* [1956] 2 Q.B. 641.
[242] *Kodeeswaran v Att-Gen of Ceylon* [1970] A.C. 1111, 1123.
[243] *cf.* Crown Proceedings Act 1947 s.27.
[244] Employment Protection (Consolidation Act) 1978, Pt V.
[245] Employment Rights Act 1996 s.94.
[246] Employment Rights Act 1998 s.191. See also, Public Interest Disclosure Act 1998, s.10.
[247] Employment Rights Act 1998 s.193, as amended by Employment Relations Act 1999 Sch.8.
[248] Equal Pay Act 1970 s.1(8).
[249] Sex Discrimination Act 1975 s.85.
[250] M. Freedland, "Law, Public Services and Citizenship—New Domains, New Regimes?", in M. Freedland and S. Sciarra (eds), *Public Services and Citizenship in European Law, Public and Labour Law Perspectives* (Oxford University Press, 1998), Ch.1; G. Morris, "Fragmenting the State: Implications for Employment Practices in Public Services" [1999] P.L. 64.

F. The Effect of an Unlawful Contract

5–048   The precise effects of a contract that is beyond the capacity of the relevant body are not entirely clear. The common law rule was that the unlawful contract was unenforceable against the corporation that made it.[251] The principal rationale behind this rule was to prevent corporate funds from being disbursed for an unauthorised purpose, to the detriment of the shareholders and creditors of the company. The common law position has now been amended by statute, which, in general, allows such agreements to be enforced against the company.

Whether the common law rule applies to unlawful contracts entered into by a public body is not entirely clear. If they are unenforceable then this can cause real hardship to the contractor who may lose any expected profits on the transaction, and may be unable to recover expenses incurred in preparing to perform the contract.

Credit Suisse[252] is the leading authority. The defendant local authority established a company to assist with the financing of a leisure pool complex, with the intention that the company could obtain finance outside the statutory controls imposed on local authority borrowing. The plaintiff bank loaned the company £6 million and the local authority entered into a contract of guarantee to repay the money in the event that the company was wound up. The company did fail, and the bank sought to enforce the guarantee. The local authority resisted the claim on the ground that it lacked the statutory power to make the contract. The Court of Appeal recognised the unfairness of the local authority relying on its own illegality in order to evade its contractual obligations,[253] but held that the contract was void and unenforceable since the local authority had no power to make it.

Neill L.J. pointed to the distinction drawn in company law between acts beyond the capacity of the company, which were wholly void, and those which were within the capacity of the company but involved a misuse of power. In the latter instance the enforceability of the transaction would depend upon whether the third party had notice of the excess of power.[254] He considered whether a similar distinction could apply in relation to acts done by public authorities. Neill L.J. recognised that the concept of ultra vires had been expanded in *Anisminic*, but acknowledged that in public law cases the courts exercised a broad discretion as to whether a remedy should lie even though an ultra vires act had occurred. The bank argued that the courts should exercise a similar discretion where the decision was ultra vires not for lack of statutory capacity, but for some other reason, and drew on the analogies from company law. Neill L.J. rejected the argument. The ultra vires decisions of local authorities could not be classified into categories of invalidity and any error in the *Anisminic* list resulted in the decision being void. This conclusion is with respect open to question. The bank was not

---

[251] *Ashbury Carriage and Iron Co v Riche* (1875) L.R. 7 H.L. 653.
[252] *Credit Suisse v Allerdale Borough Council* [1997] Q.B. 306; *Credit Suisse v Waltham Forest LBC* [1997] Q.B. 362.
[253] This was also recognised in *Stretch v West Dorset District Council* (2000) 2 L.G.L.R. 140.
[254] *Rolled Steel Products (Holdings) Ltd v British Steel Corporation* [1986] Ch.246, 302.

seeking to argue that there should be different categories of invalidity, but whether, *assuming that the act was invalid*, there could be any discretion as to the granting of the remedy.

Hobhouse L.J. was even more forceful. Public law was only relevant for determining the ambit of the local authority's powers. When it was decided that the local authority had no power, the effect of that lack of capacity was dealt with by private law, and the broad remedial discretion exercised by courts in judicial review actions was irrelevant. This line of argument is also open to question. The reasoning assumes that it is meaningful to categorise the case along the public law–private divide in this manner.

The central issue in cases of this nature is the extent to which a public **5–049** body which lacks the power to contract, or which even though it has such a power has used it for an improper purpose, should be bound by the contract it has made. The resolution of this issue is not easy, since we wish both to protect citizens against illegal government action and also to protect the public purse from the effects of illegal government conduct.[255] It should be noted at the outset that reliance by a public body on the ultra vires nature of its own action may constitute a breach of Convention rights, more particularly the right to property.[256]

We should in any event accept that the courts possess a remedial discretion in such cases akin to that exercised in judicial review actions. To deny the existence of any such discretion by rigid demarcations between public law, where such discretion exists, and private law, where it does not, is unhelpful. It may be that the courts will be less minded to exercise such discretion so as to enforce an invalid contract where the invalidity goes to the very contractual capacity of the public body, and that it may be more willing to exercise it when the invalidity relates to cases where the body possesses the power but exercises it improperly. A remedial discretion should nonetheless exist in both instances. The extent to which the other contracting party had notice that the transaction was in excess or abuse of the public body's power could then be a factor affecting the exercise of this discretion. If this solution is felt to be too radical then it should at the least be accepted that the courts have the remedial discretion in cases concerned with excess of power as opposed to lack of capacity *stricto sensu*.[257]

These problems will be less likely to occur as a result of the Local Government (Contracts) Act 1997. The Act was passed in order to allay fears about the *Credit Suisse* judgment and the inhibiting effect that this was having on banks lending to local authorities. The banks were unwilling to do so if they might be unable to recoup the loan in the event that the contract was found to be ultra vires.[258]

---

[255] P. Cane, "Do Banks Dare to Lend to Local Authorities?" (1994) 110 L.Q.R. 514.
[256] *Stretch v United Kingdom* (2004) 38 E.H.R.R. 12.
[257] See also, Arrowsmith, *Civil Liability*, n.1, 64–65. For detailed consideration of the problems surrounding recovery in the *Hazell* case [1992] 2 A.C. 1 see, M. Loughlin, "Innovative Financing in Local Government: The Limits of Legal Instrumentalism—Pt. II [1991] P.L. 568.
[258] A. Davies, "Ultra Vires Problems in Government Contracts" (2006) 122 L.Q.R. 98, 115–122, makes a number of valuable suggestions for improvements to the legislation.

Section 1(1) provides that every statutory provision conferring or imposing a function on a local authority confers power on the local authority to enter a contract with another person for the provision of assets or services, for the purposes of discharging that function. Section 1(2) in effect empowers the local authority to make financial arrangements with a bank, etc. which has loaned money to a party other than the local authority itself, as exemplified by the facts of *Credit Suisse* itself.

Section 2 makes provision for the certification of a contract. The certification signifies that the local authority had power to make the contract, and the certificate is not invalidated by anything in the certificate that is inaccurate or untrue.[259] The certification protects the contract from challenge in private law proceedings.

It is however still possible to argue that the contract was ultra vires in proceedings for judicial review and audit review.[260] Where the court finds that the contract was ultra vires then it is empowered to find that the contract should nonetheless have effect, having regard to the consequences for the financial position of the local authority, and for the provision of services to the public.[261] The enforceability of contract discharge terms is preserved in the event that the contract is found to be ultra vires.[262] Where the contract has been found to be of no effect, but there are no discharge terms, there is provision for a damages remedy for a sum equivalent to that which would be given where there was a repudiatory breach by the local authority.[263]

---

[259] Local Government (Contracts) Act 1997 s.4.
[260] Local Government (Contracts) Act 1997 s.5.
[261] Local Government (Contracts) Act 1997 s.5(3).
[262] Local Government (Contracts) Act 1997 s.6.
[263] Local Government (Contracts) Act 1997 s.7.

Chapter 6

LOCAL GOVERNMENT, LOCAL GOVERNANCE AND DEMOCRACY

1. The Changing Pattern of Local Government

The development of local authorities in the 19th century has already been charted. There will be no attempt to provide a comprehensive legal guide to these authorities within the discussion that follows. This is a specialist field with a wealth of literature.[1]

    6–001

An understanding of local government is, however, essential, since such authorities are among the principal decision-makers in the public law sphere. Moreover, as we shall see, their powers have been transformed. This transformation means that it is no longer possible to define *local government* merely by describing the present pattern of *local authorities* and their respective powers. Many of their traditional responsibilities have been transferred to *agencies*, which are often subject to central control, while others have been *contracted-out* to private contractors. It is this development which has led some commentators to distinguish between formal and

[1] For a legal analysis see, S. Bailey, *Cross on Principles of Local Government Law* (Sweet & Maxwell, 3rd edn, 2004). For a broader view see, J. Griffith, *Central Departments and Local Authorities* (Allen & Unwin, 1966); D. Hill, *Democratic Theory and Local Government* (Allen & Unwin, 1974); H. Elcock, *Local Government* (Methuen, 1982); A. Alexander, *Local Government in Britain since Reorganisation* (Allen & Unwin, 1982); M. Elliott, *The Role of Law in Central-Local Relations* (1981); G. Jones (ed.), *New Approaches to the Study of Central-Local Government Relationships* (Gower, 1980); M. Loughlin, D. Gelfand and K. Young (eds), *Half a Century of Municipal Decline 1935–1985* (Allen & Unwin, 1985); G. Jones and J. Stewart, *The Case for Local Government* (Allen & Unwin, 2nd edn, 1985); M. Goldsmith, *New Research in Central-Local Relations* (Gower, 1986); M. Loughlin, *Local Government in the Modern State* (Sweet & Maxwell, 1986); D. King and J. Pierre (eds), *Challenges to Local Government* (Sage, 1990); G. Stoker, *The Politics of Local Government* (Macmillan, 2nd edn, 1991); M. Loughlin, *Legality and Locality, The Role of Law in Central-Local Government Relations* (Oxford University Press, 1996); D. King and G. Stoker (eds), *Rethinking Local Democracy* (Macmillan, 1996); I. Leigh, *Law, Politics and Local Democracy* (Oxford University Press, 2000).

informal local government,[2] while others speak in terms of a shift from local government to local governance.[3]

The following section will, therefore, chart the powers of local authorities. The range of other bodies with responsibilities at the local level will be considered thereafter. The Labour government made a number of important changes to the pattern of local governance and these will be incorporated into the discussion. The final section will consider more generally the issue of central–local relations and democracy.

2. LOCAL AUTHORITIES: STRUCTURE, ORGANISATION, POWERS AND FINANCE

A. Structure

6–002   The pattern of local authorities established by the end of the 19th century was to continue largely unchanged until 1972. In the period after the Second World War there was however increasing disquiet. The shape of local government was felt to be outdated and ill-adapted to the demographic and technological development that occurred in the post-war period. This sentiment was voiced most strongly by Richard Crossman in 1965, who was then Minister of Housing and Local Government. In 1966 a Royal Commission was established under the chairmanship of Lord Redcliffe-Maud.[4] The Report of the Royal Commission identified a number of key problems: the division between town and country, that between boroughs and counties, the allocation of responsibility within counties, the small size of some local authorities, and the relationships between local authority and the public, and local authority and government.

The response of the Royal Commission to these perceived difficulties was, in short, to reverse conventional thinking about decision-making at the local level. The traditional pattern was based on the assumption that single-tier authorities would be suited to the larger urban areas and that a two-tier structure was required in other contexts. This thinking was directly challenged. For the future the Redcliffe-Maud Report proposed that unitary authorities should be the norm. These would cover urban and rural areas, normally focused around the main towns. The unitary principle would be departed from only in those large urban conurbations where to adhere rigidly to the single-tier principle would make the authority unwieldy and remote from the community. In such conurbations a two-tier structure was recommended.

[2] D. King, "Government Beyond Whitehall: Local Government and Urban Politics", in P. Dunleavy, A. Gamble, I. Holliday and G. Peele (eds), *Developments in British Politics 4* (Macmillan, 1993).
[3] P. John, "Local Governance", in P. Dunleavy, A. Gamble, I. Holliday and G. Peele (eds), *Developments in British Politics 5* (Macmillan, 1997), Ch.13; G. Stoker, "Introduction: Normative Theories of Local Government and Democracy", in King and Stoker, n.1, Ch.1.
[4] Cmnd. 4040 (1969).

The Labour government was largely in favour of the Royal Commission's proposals with some modifications. It accepted the unitary concept.[5] The Conservative Party was, however, in favour of the two-tier principle. The return of that party to government in 1970 ensured the demise of the Redcliffe-Maud proposals. The Conservative Party's proposals[6] represented a reversion to the two-tier principle, and their plan was enacted as the Local Government Act 1972.[7]

There were four different types of local government. The first was the metropolitan county of which there were six, divided into 36 metropolitan districts. Second, there were 39 non-metropolitan counties with 296 districts. Both types of county could have parishes beneath the districts. Third, in London there was the Greater London Council, under which existed 32 London boroughs. Fourth, Wales had eight counties, 37 districts, and communities below these. Boundary Commissions, one for England and one for Wales, were constituted by the 1972 Act.[8] Both Commissions have the duty to review district and county areas within 10 to 15 years, or otherwise as the Secretary of State may direct.

This pattern of local authority organisation was radically revised, with the abolition of the metropolitan county councils (MCCs) and the Greater London Council (GLC). The Conservative government argued that such authorities should be abolished because they had limited operational responsibilities, because their expenditure had been excessive, and because they sought to establish a role that was not really required. It was argued that reform would "streamline" the cities, save money, and provide a simpler system. The cogency of these arguments was challenged by studies commissioned by the MCCs. Evidence as to likely cost savings was not readily apparent, and the argument concerning simplicity was undermined by the very institutional changes that were to replace the MCCs and the GLC. The Local Government Act 1985 abolished the MCCs and the GLC. Some of their functions were transferred to district or borough councils.[9] Others were assigned to new joint authorities composed primarily of members from the relevant district or borough councils.[10] The decision to abolish the MCCs and the GLC appears to have been motivated rather more by the desire to dismantle large authorities that had been predominantly Labour, rather than by the objective of improving local government in large conurbations.[11]

6–003

The present structure of local authorities varies from area to area. In some there are two layers or tiers, a district council and a county council; in others there is just one, a unitary authority. In London each borough is a unitary authority, with the Greater London Authority, the Mayor and Assembly,

[5] *Reform of Local Government in England*, Cmnd. 4276 (1970).
[6] *Local Government in England*, Cmnd. 4584 (1971).
[7] It did not take effect until April 1, 1974.
[8] Local Government Act 1972 ss.46, 53.
[9] e.g. planning, highways and waste disposal.
[10] e.g. police, fire and civil defence and passenger transport.
[11] S. Leach and C. Game, "English Metropolitan Government since Abolition: An Evaluation of the Abolition of the English Metropolitan County Councils" (1991) 69 Pub. Adm. 141.

providing strategic, city-wide government.[12] There can in addition be a town or parish council, covering a much smaller area.

Structural reviews will be used to decide whether or not a single, all-purpose council, rather than two councils, would better reflect the interests of local communities and lead to more effective local government. These reviews were undertaken by the Local Government Commission (LGC) established under the Local Government Act 1992. The LGC has now been replaced by Boundary Committees. The Boundary Committee for England was established in April 2002, and it is a committee of the Electoral Commission. The Boundary Committee may recommend the creation of one or more new unitary authorities or the division of an existing authority into one or more new authorities.[13]

The detailed provisions by which an area where there are two tiers of local government can be reorganised so that there is a single tier of local government, and the process by which the boundaries of local government areas can be altered, are now regulated by the Local Government and Public Involvement in Health Act 2007.[14]

B. Internal Organisation

6–004 The internal structure of local authorities changed as a result of new initiatives contained in the DETR's[15] White Paper on *Modern Local Government, In Touch with the People*.[16] The traditional committee structure still used by most councils was said to lead to "inefficient and opaque decision making", with significant decisions being taken behind closed doors by political groups or by a small group within the majority group.[17] Councillors were felt to be unproductive, since they spent too much time in meetings when the decisions had already been taken elsewhere.[18] Leadership was said to be lacking, and people often did not know who was taking the decisions.[19] The cure for this malaise was the separation of roles as between the local authority executive and the backbench councillors. This separation was said to enhance efficiency, transparency and accountability.[20] The executive is to propose the policy framework and implement policies within the agreed framework. The backbench councillors are to represent their constituents, share in the policy and budget decisions of the full council, suggest policy improvements and scrutinise the executive.[21]

---

[12] *A Mayor and Assembly for London: The Government's Proposals for Modernising the Governance of London* (1998); Greater London Authority Act 1999; Greater London Authority Act 2007.
[13] http://www.boundarycommittee.org.uk/our-work/structuralreviews.cfm.
[14] Local Government and Public Involvement in Health Act 2007 ss.1–23.
[15] Department of the Environment, Transport and the Regions.
[16] Cm. 4014 (July 1998).
[17] Cm. 4014 (July 1998) para.3.4.
[18] Cm. 4014 (July 1998) para.3.5.
[19] Cm. 4014 (July 1998) paras 3.6–3.7.
[20] Cm. 4014 (July 1998) para.3.14.
[21] Cm. 4014 (July 1998) paras 3.13, 3.39, 3.41–3.44.

These ideas were enshrined in the Local Government Act 2000,[22] but have been amended by the Local Government and Public Involvement in Health Act 2007. The following analysis deals with local authorities in England. There are now two principal ways in which this new division of roles can be introduced for local authorities in England, although it is open to the Secretary of State to prescribe, within certain limits, other forms of executive organisation.[23] A local authority must submit proposals to the Secretary of State as to which of the forms of executive arrangements described below it wishes to adopt. The local authority must consult the local electors and other interested persons. If it chooses to adopt the option involving an elected mayor it must hold a local referendum.[24] Detailed guidance has been published as to the workings of the new regime.[25]

There can be a *directly elected mayor plus a cabinet*.[26] The mayor is elected by the whole electorate and then forms a cabinet from among the councillors. The mayor acts as the political leader for the community, proposing policy for approval by the council and steering implementation by the cabinet through council officers. The elected mayor may discharge any of the executive functions,[27] or can arrange for those functions to be discharged by the executive, another member of the executive, a committee of the executive, or an officer of the authority.[28] There are however provisions allowing, for example, the mayor to exercise the relevant function even where arrangements have been made for the exercise of that function to be undertaken by a different person.[29]

The second option is to have a *leader and cabinet executive*.[30] A councillor   **6–005** is elected leader of the executive by the local authority. Two or more councillors are appointed to the executive by the executive leader. The executive arrangements can make provision for the allocation of any executive function to the executive, any member of the executive, any committee of the executive, and any officer of the executive.[31] There are once again provisions allowing, for example, the executive leader to exercise the relevant function even where arrangements have been made for the exercise of that function to be undertaken by a different person.[32]

There is also provision for the *local authority executive to take such form as may be prescribed by the Secretary of State in regulations*, subject to

[22] Leigh, n.1, 230–246.
[23] Local Government Act 2000 ss.11(5)–(6), 12.
[24] Local Government Act 2000 ss.25–27.
[25] Department for Communities and Local Government, *New Council Constitutions, Guidance to English Authorities* (2006); http://www.communitiesgov.uk/localgovernment/360902/ constitutionsandethics/constitutionalarrangements/newcouncilconstitutions/.
[26] Local Government Act 2000 s.11(2).
[27] Local Government Act 2000 s.14(2)(a).
[28] Local Government Act 2000 s.14(2)(b).
[29] Local Government Act 2000 s.14(6).
[30] Local Government Act 2000 s.11(2A).
[31] Local Government Act 2000 s.14(2).
[32] Local Government Act 2000 s.14(6).

criteria specified in the Act itself.[33] There are detailed provisions concerning the variation of executive arrangements by local authorities.[34]

The Local Government Act 2000 makes provision for overview and scrutiny committees. These committees can review and scrutinise decisions taken by the executive, and they can require members of the executive to appear before them to answer questions.[35] The Act contains provisions as to which meetings of the executive are held in public and which in private.[36] Local authorities are required to have a constitution,[37] containing such information as the Secretary of State may direct. The Secretary of State has said that the constitution should, inter alia, describe clearly the way in which the local authority conducts its business and should be readily available to the public.[38]

The provisions for London are in the same vein with a directly elected mayor and a directly elected assembly.[39] They are enshrined in the Greater London Authority Act 1999.[40] The Mayor has the main executive responsibility. He or she is responsible for general planning, the establishment of the budget, the running of new transport and economic development bodies, and improvements to the environment. It is for the Assembly to question the Mayor on his or her actions, and to agree or suggest changes to the Mayor's overall budget and plans. In general terms the GLA has responsibility, in varying degrees, for transport, economic development, the environment, planning, the police, fire authorities, culture and health.

It is clear that the government regards these as more than mere organisational changes. They are designed to reinvigorate local democracy by providing for more efficient, accountable and transparent local government. The broader impact of these initiatives will be considered below.[41]

C. Functions and Powers

6–006   The functions of local government have altered considerably over the last 100 years. Four periods can be broadly identified.

The modern role of local authorities has its origins in the problems attendant upon industrialisation and urbanisation in the 19th century. This necessitated collective action to provide a variety of goods and services, and local authorities were perceived as well placed to undertake this task.[42] Some of these services were "public goods": services which the market either would not provide at all or would do so only inefficiently. Others were

---

[33] Local Government Act 2000 ss.11(5)–(6), 12.
[34] Local Government Act 2000 ss.33A–33O.
[35] Local Government Act 2000 s.21.
[36] Local Government Act 2000 s.22.
[37] Local Government Act 2000 s.37.
[38] Local Government Act 2000 (Constitutions) (England) Direction 2000; *New Council Constitutions*, n.25.
[39] *A Mayor and Assembly for London: The Government's Proposals for Modernising the Governance of London* (1998).
[40] See also Greater London Authority Act 2007.
[41] See below, paras 6–014—6–016.
[42] Loughlin, *Local Government in the Modern State*, n.1, 4.

trading services, which the private market could provide, but only with the attendant risk of private monopoly profit. Yet other services were redistributive, being designed to benefit certain groups within society, such as by the provision of social welfare.[43]

The second period is characterised by the relative decline in the importance of trading services and the relative increase in the importance of providing redistributive services. In 1885 the latter accounted for only 23 per cent of local authority expenditure, whereas by 1975 this had risen to 65 per cent.[44]

The third period was characterised by changing perceptions as to the proper functions of local authorities as a result of Conservative policy in the late 1970s and 1980s. The general theme was that the functions of local authorities should be opened up to market forces, and should be judged by the criteria of market efficiency. Local authority services should be provided in accordance with what are essentially individualistic principles for action rather than any overriding conception of collective good.[45] A range of devices was employed to this end. These included direct competition with private industry for the provision of services, contracting-out service provision, the sale of local authority assets, and the encouragement of market accountability to consumers.[46]

Thus legislation such as the Local Government Act 1988[47] specified a **6–007** number of services which local authorities were required to put out to competitive tendering. The Housing and Building Control Act 1984 extended the policy of selling off council houses to tenants. The Education Reform Act 1988 reduced local authority control over schooling. The Local Government Act 1992 empowered the Audit Commission to require local authorities to supply information to enable it to make comparisons based upon cost, economy, efficiency and effectiveness, between the standards of performance of different bodies. Other legislative initiatives were aimed at forcing local authorities to privatise further areas, such as municipal airports, and to sell off other municipal property. King brings out the change in the role of local authorities.[48]

"Instead of envisaging local government as an institution representing a local community and its local tradition, it is to be designed as an institution responsible for overseeing service provision. Local government is thought of as an enabling institution and not one of direct service delivery . . . This new role maximises efficiency and profit criteria in local government. It treats citizens as customers of government services.

[43] Loughlin, *Local Government in the Modern State*, n.1, 4–5.
[44] Loughlin, *Local Government in the Modern State*, n.1, 6.
[45] Loughlin, *Local Government in the Modern State*, n.1, 170.
[46] Loughlin, *Local Government in the Modern State*, n.1, 167–171.
[47] The list of services to which competitive tendering applies has been increased by the Local Government Act 1992 s.8.
[48] "Government Beyond Whitehall", n.2, 204.

Furthermore, local authorities are viewed as purchasers rather than providers of services."

The fourth period covers local authorities' functions as seen in the light of the Labour government's approach to this area. The White Paper on *Modern Local Government, In Touch with the People*,[49] must be read in conjunction with the papers on *Modernising Local Government: Improving Local Services through Best Value*[50] and *Local Government and the Private Finance Initiative*.[51] The latter two papers have been considered in the chapter on service provision.[52] The general approach to local authority services has been maintained in the 2006 White Paper *Strong and Prosperous Communities*.[53] The essence of the overall approach can be set out here.

The Labour strategy for the powers of local authorities is less doctrinaire than that of the previous Conservative government. The market is not always perceived as the best way to secure service provision. However, while the Conservative strategy has been toned down, and while the Labour approach is designed to be less confrontational, it is also clear that the Labour government accepted that service provision should be by the "most effective, economic and efficient means available".[54] The Best Value strategy, enshrined in the Local Government Act 1999, as amended by the Local Government and Public Involvement in Health Act 2007, is designed to secure the efficient and effective provision of local services, while preserving greater local autonomy and choice. Efficient and effective public services are seen as an essential part of the fabric of a healthy democracy.[55]

The attainment of Best Value is seen as being about quality as well as efficiency. There is no presumption that services must be privatised, nor is there any compulsion to put services out to tender, but there is no reason to provide services in-house if other more efficient means are available. Competition is only one tool in assessing Best Value, but it is clear that it is an important tool. It is equally clear that partnerships between the public and the private sectors are central to the Government's aims of establishing first-class public services and infrastructure, and promoting economic growth and regeneration. The Private Finance Initiative, which is designed to facilitate such partnerships, has been applied vigorously at the local level.[56]

D. Finances

6–008 The system of local authority finances is complex and only the most general outline can be provided here.

---

[49] Cm. 4014 (July 1998).
[50] 1997.
[51] September 1998.
[52] See above, Ch.5.
[53] Department of Communities and Local Government, (October, 2006). http://www.communitiesgov.uk/publications/localgovernment/strongprosperous2.
[54] *Modern Local Government*, para.7.1.
[55] *Modernising Local Government*, para.1.2.
[56] See above, para.5–023.

i. Resources

Local authorities do not have their own source of revenue derived from local **6–009** income tax. The traditional basis of local authority revenue was the rates, which were levied upon property owners,[57] combined with income from charges and fees. These sources of revenue were supplemented by grants from central government.

A radical change was brought about by the Local Government Finance Act 1988, which replaced the rating system with the community charge/poll tax. The objective was to increase the financial accountability of local authorities. The rating system imposed the financial burden upon property owners. It was argued that many who lived in an area could happily support expensive local policies, secure in the knowledge that they would not have to bear the financial burden if they were not liable to pay rates. The poll tax was to be levied on all those who lived in an area, subject to certain exceptions, at a flat rate.

The political debacle caused by the poll tax is well known. The poll tax was replaced by the council tax in the Local Government Finance Act 1992. The tax is made up of both a personal and a property element, although each household only receives one bill. Properties are valued through a banding system, so those houses in the same band should receive the same bill. The Labour government retained the council tax, subject to a property revaluation.[58] An obvious problem of any system based upon property values is that the financial returns are susceptible to fluctuation with movements in the value of property.

ii. Grants and curbs on spending: history

Local authorities only ever derived part of their funds from rates, the poll **6–010** tax or the council tax. Grants from central government provide approximately 80 per cent of their funds. It is important to understand a little history of this area in order to appreciate the present position.

In historical terms the basic grant was the Rate Support Grant (RSG),[59] the main objective of which was to provide some degree of equalisation between the financial resources and expenditure requirements of different local authorities. The method of calculating the RSG was felt to be complex and prone to encourage higher spending by local authorities. A new mechanism for calculating the grant was therefore introduced in 1980.[60] The technique for calculating the grant is complex, and cannot be examined here. The essential idea was however to provide a simpler, more equal system of grant allocation and one which removed incentives for "excessive spending". Expenditure above the level of the grant would have to be

[57] Rating and Valuation Act 1925; Local Government Act 1948; Rating and Valuation Act 1961; Local Government Act 1966.
[58] *Modern Local Government, In Touch with the People*, paras 5.21–5.25.
[59] Local Government Act 1974.
[60] Local Government, Planning and Land Act 1980 ss.54–62; Local Government Finance Act 1987 ss.1–5.

funded from the rates (or the poll tax, etc.). It was argued that such expenditure would indicate that the local authority was seeking to provide a higher level of service than was necessary, or that it was being inefficient. These arguments are of questionable validity, as is the claim that the new method of calculation is simpler.[61]

This attempt to curb local expenditure also proved relatively ineffective because many local authorities chose not to cut the provision of services, but to raise the additional revenue from rates.[62] This led to the Rates Act 1984, which empowered the Secretary of State to limit the rating level of local authorities. The Act gave broad discretionary power to the Secretary of State,[63] and this was used to "rate-cap" a number of authorities.

Local authorities attempted to use certain creative accounting devices to enhance local financial independence, and to make ends meet when income fell short of expenditure. The best known of these devices was the "swaps" transaction, which was held to be ultra vires by the House of Lords.[64]

The rationale for such controls over local authority current expenditure was questionable. The main foundation of the government's argument was that this was necessary for the success of its macro-economic strategy, which entailed control of public expenditure and hence local authority expenditure. Whether this justified the measures adopted is however contested.[65]

iii. Grants and curbs on spending: current position

6–011   The present position is as follows.[66] The Spending Review determines the total level of grant to local authorities, for the following three years. Government grants and business rates together are known as Aggregate External Finance (AEF). The annual Local Government Finance Settlement is concerned with the distribution of Formula Grant, which is made up of Revenue Support Grant, redistributed business rates and the Police Grant. Formula Grant totalled £25 billion in 2006/07 and £26 billion in 2007/08. Formula Grant is part of AEF. Councils also fund their spending by raising Council Tax. The Formula Grant is distributed by formula through the Local Government Finance Settlement. There are no restrictions on what local government can spend it on. Specific formula grants are distributed outside the main settlement. Some of these are known as ring-fenced grants, which control council spending. These usually fund particular services or

[61] Loughlin, *Local Government in the Modern State*, n.1, 25–35, 38–39.
[62] Loughlin, *Local Government in the Modern State*, n.1, 38–49.
[63] Rates Act 1984 s.2; Local Government Finance Act 1987 ss.6, 7, 8.
[64] *Hazell v Hammersmith and Fulham London Borough Council* [1992] 2 A.C. 1; M. Loughlin, "Innovative Financing in Local Government: The Limits of Legal Instrumentalism" [1990] P.L. 372, [1991] P.L. 568.
[65] Loughlin, *Local Government in the Modern State*, n.1, 20–22.
[66] Office of the Deputy Prime Minister, *A Guide to the Local Government Finance Settlement* (2006).

initiatives that are a national priority. Other specific formula grants are unfenced and are sometimes called targeted grants.[67]

To work out each council's share of Formula Grant the government calculates the Relative Needs Formula (RNFs). The RNFs are mathematical formulae that include information on the population, social structure and other characteristics of each authority. The Relative Resource Amount, RRA, is a negative figure, and takes account of the fact that areas that can raise more income locally require less support from government to provide services. The negative RRA is balanced against the positive proportion calculated for each authority by the Relative Needs Amount.

The Labour government signalled a shift in thinking about curbs on local authority expenditure.[68] It acknowledged that central government has a strong interest in local government's taxation and spending decisions, in part because of its desire to ensure best value and in part because a significant proportion of local spending is financed by the national taxpayer.[69] Labour's strategy is based on a balance between local financial accountability, and the existence of reserve powers for central government to intervene where necessary. It abolished what it regarded as "crude and universal capping".[70] The central government's reserve powers have been structured more flexibly.[71] The repeal of the previous capping legislation and the introduction of a more discriminating system to regulate local authority expenditure are key features of the Local Government Act 1999.[72]

Government also exercises control over capital expenditure. Prior to 1980 **6–012** local authorities required loan sanction from central government for specific projects. Before the Labour government took office, there were a number of separate service-specific funding mechanisms used to allocate capital resources to councils. The trend had been towards an increasing use of allocations for restricted purposes, with a corresponding reduction in block allocations that could be used flexibly to meet a range of spending priorities.[73]

The Labour government introduced the idea of a single capital pot. The single capital pot constituted a cross-service allocation for the bulk of central government capital support to councils. The idea was to allow councils to take greater responsibility for the internal allocation of their resources among services.[74] Resources from the pot were allocated to councils partly on need, and partly on a competitive assessment of councils'

[67] Local Government Act 2003 ss.31–33 give a broad power to a Minister of the Crown to make grants to local authorities.
[68] *Modern Local Government, In Touch with the People*, Ch.5.
[69] *Modern Local Government, In Touch with the People*, para.5.3.
[70] *Modern Local Government, In Touch with the People*, para.5.7.
[71] *Modern Local Government, In Touch with the People*, para.5.11.
[72] Local Government Act 1999 Sch.1, introducing a new Pt IVA to the Local Government Finance Act 1992. Fourteen local authorities were capped in 2004–05, and nine in 2005–06.
[73] *Modern Local Government, In Touch with the People*, para.9.6.
[74] *Modern Local Government, In Touch with the People*, para.9.7.

capital strategies and their performance in delivering them.[75] This must now be seen in the light of the Local Government Act 2003, which allows local authorities to raise finance for capital expenditure, without government consent, where they can afford to service the debt without government support, subject to certain reserve powers for government to set limits on borrowing and credit.

The financial controls considered above, which aim to control and limit expenditure in advance, are supplemented by the existence of the audit which reviews past expenditure decisions. The Audit Commission oversees local authority spending. The auditor appointed by the Commission will ensure that the authority's records are in order and that proper arrangements have been made for securing economy and efficiency in the use of resources.[76] There are also powers to surcharge and disqualify those who expend money in breach of the law.

3. LOCAL GOVERNANCE: AGENCIES AND SERVICE DELIVERY

6–013 The statutory changes introduced by the Conservative government, combined with an increasing emphasis on contracting out and the like, have led to the creation of a variety of agencies that are responsible for certain important functions which affect the local community. Thus John, writing in 1997, provided the following list of bodies with responsibility for service provision at the local level:[77]

(1) Companies/management buyouts supplying contracted out services such as waste collection.

(2) Private or semi-public bodies providing services purchased by local authorities, such as nursing homes.

(3) Hospital trusts.

(4) New central government agencies administering new or formerly local government functions, such as urban development corporations and Housing Action Trusts.

(5) Partnership organisations such as Business Links.

(6) Micro agencies formerly under the umbrella of the local authority, such as schools running their own budgets, or schools which opted out of local authority control.

---

[75] *Modern Local Government, In Touch with the People*, para.9.10; Department for Transport, Local Government and the Regions, *Local Government Finance, Single Capital Pot Guidance 2002*.

[76] Audit Commission Act 1998.

[77] John, "Local Governance", n.3, 255–256.

(7) Existing public agencies that have been given an enhanced new role, such as housing associations.

(8) Regional officers of central government reorganised into government offices for the regions in 1995 (GORs).

(9) Decentralised offices of Next Steps Agencies.

(10) Voluntary associations.

(11) Revitalised business organisations, such as larger Chambers of Commerce.

(12) Large private sector companies with a renewed interest in local public decisions.

(13) The privatised public utilities, such as water companies.

(14) New or rejuvenated regional organisations.

It is important to look a little more closely at two examples of these types of bodies.

The Local Government, Planning and Land Act 1980 laid the foundation for urban development corporations. UDCs were intended to regenerate a particular urban environment. To this end they had powers to acquire land within their area, to build factories, housing and other infrastructure facilities. Funds were acquired in part from central government and in part from private sources. The relevant minister nominated the boards of UDCs. UDCs were subject to a number of criticisms. There was said to be insufficient integration of their work with that of the local authority in whose area they functioned. It was unclear whether they were really accountable, since central government control over UDCs constituted accountability only in a formal sense. It was uncertain how successful they were, since it was difficult to obtain reliable figures and equally difficult to assess the quality of the improvements said to have been made.[78] UDCs have now been wound up.

The second example is from the field of regional development. The Regional Development Agencies Act 1998 established a development agency for each region of England.[79] The members are appointed by the Secretary of State. Regional development agencies (RDAs) are to further economic development and regeneration; promote business efficiency, investment and competitiveness; promote employment; enhance the development of the relevant skill for employment; and contribute to the achievement of sustainable development.[80] The RDA may do anything which it considers expedient for its purposes, but it can only give financial assistance, sell land

[78] King, "Government Beyond Whitehall", n.2, 208.
[79] Department of Trade and Industry, *Supplementary Guidance for the Regional Development Agencies' Regional Economic Strategies* (2002); http://www.berr.gov.uk/regional/regional-dev-agencies/index.html.
[80] Regional Development Agencies Act 1998 s.4.

for less than the going rate, or form a corporate body if the Secretary of State consents.[81] The Secretary of State can, however, delegate functions to the RDA, subject to certain limitations imposed by the Act.[82]

4. CENTRAL–LOCAL RELATIONS AND DEMOCRACY

6–014   The previous discussion indicated how much influence the central government wields over local authorities. How much influence it should wield is quite another matter. The whole debate on central–local relations can only be touched upon here. It involves a number of fundamental issues, such the balance between efficiency and democracy, between uniformity of standard and diversity, and the meaning to be attached to participation. In historical terms there have been two opposing views of central–local relations, that which sees the latter as a mere agent of the former, and that which accords the two a more equal or autonomous status.

The agency view was adopted by some at least of the Utilitarians. For Chadwick the prime consideration was efficiency with a presumption of uniformity. This was reflected in the administrative structure of the Poor Law, and public health. A strong central authority was desired and concessions to local autonomy were grudgingly accepted. The utilitarian approach must also be seen in its temporal setting. Municipal corporations were only just being reformed. Little faith could be placed in the corrupt oligarchies, which had not yet come to conceive of themselves as trustees of public funds. Most municipal functions were still performed independently of the municipal corporation by improvement commissioners and the like. It is unsurprising that Chadwick was wary of local power.

The modern heirs of the agency view add notions of equality and pragmatism to that of efficiency.[83] Divergent treatment of the same problem in different areas is regarded as unjust. Benefits and services should not depend upon the fortuity of where one lives, more especially because the poorer areas will be those with greater needs and smaller sources of independent revenue from the rates, etc. Pragmatism is used to buttress arguments from equality. The major sums involved in local authority financing, in terms of revenue and borrowing, necessitate centralised control in the form of loan sanctions, government grants and the like. A coherent economic policy would be impossible without such restraints.

The structural expression of the agency view has tended in the past towards relatively large unitary authorities. Fewer authorities providing the combined services a local community requires with the maximum economies of scale, has been thought to be the ideal. While admitting the benefits of

---

[81] Regional Development Agencies Act 1998 s.5.
[82] Regional Development Agencies Act 1998 s.6.
[83] D. Hill, *Democratic Theory and Local Government* (Allen & Unwin, 1974), Ch.5.

local democracy and participation, the proposals of the Redcliffe-Maud Report[84] reflected a preference for the unitary model. More modern advocates of the agency view have, however, to some extent moved away from the preference for large unitary authorities. This is in part because of the "dangers" that large power structures outside of central government were felt to pose, and in part because of the very desire to remove functions from local authorities and place them with a plethora of other institutions either in the public or private sector.

The agency concept also manifests itself in the types of power that are left with local authorities. The totality of these may well be diminished if it can be shown to be preferable for functions to be administered from the centre, or by an institution separate from the traditional local authority.

The agency view was vehemently opposed in the 19th century by Toulmin   **6–015**
Smith for whom the parish was sacred. Opponents of the agency view do not however have to rely solely upon the Victorian sentimentality of a Toulmin Smith. The argument for more equal treatment between the centre and the local authorities can stand on stronger ground than that. This second view of central–local relations challenges certain key tenets of the agency approach. Notions of representative democracy may provide no sure guide as to the degree of freedom to be accorded to different levels of government, both of which have been duly elected.[85] It has however been argued that a strong democratic case can be made for local government as compared with the alternative, which is local administration accountable upwards to an elected minister, and downwards to customers.[86] When criteria such as accountability, responsiveness and representativeness are applied to these two modes of governance a system of local democracy is clearly to be preferred.

The argument from equality is tendentious, or at least founded upon a contentious premise. It can be argued that if a duly elected local authority chooses to administer benefits and services differently from some other authority then that choice should within bounds be respected. What those bounds are is the main focus of the debate. The agency view tends to set narrow limits reflecting a predisposition for centrally determined standards uniformly applied. The alternative view would allow greater latitude to the local body, although subject to some constraints. While central government would ensure that minimum standards for a particular service were adhered to, greater choice over and beyond this would remain with the local authority than that allowed by advocates of the agency view.

Opponents of the agency model have also taken a different view as to the structure of local authorities and the ambit of their powers. Large unitary authorities were opposed because of the distancing effect that this produced. People no longer perceived of such authorities as "local", but as simply another arm of government with its seat appearing remote from the

---

[84] Cmnd. 4040 (1969).
[85] Griffith, n.1, 507–508.
[86] D. Beetham, "Theorising Democracy and Local Government", in King and Stoker, n.1, Ch.2.

community. Two-tier authorities were preferred. Greater community participation was advocated and found expression in the addition of a further limb to the hierarchy, that of neighbourhood councils. Involvement of the local populace in community decision-making was encouraged. This could take the form of co-option of local people onto council committees dealing with particular matters. It could, more radically, become allied with movements for tenants' rights and social welfare pressure groups.

6–016 The distinction between the two views of central–local relations has no doubt been presented in an overly black and white fashion. Shades of grey clearly exist. It should not, moreover, be thought that the two views discussed here represent the only perspectives on central–local relations. Theories abound. Some argue that the relationship is more accurately characterised as one of exchange, in which the central and the local authorities bargain with each other to maximise their respective positions. Others articulate a more complex model, which denies a straightforward dichotomy between central and local authorities. They emphasise the fact that the centre is a collection of different units, as are the local authorities. Yet other approaches seek to advance the debate by placing it within a more general conceptual frame.[87] Each of these theories focuses upon distinct facts. They place varying weights on the sum total of facts that constitute the central–local relationship.[88]

It is, however, readily apparent from the preceding discussion that central control over local authorities increased considerably under the Conservative government, and that this changed the way in which the two spheres of government interrelated. Local authorities were perceived as agents of central government. Their expenditure was controlled by the executive. The manner in which they conducted their operations was imbued with the central government's market-based perspective. The ambit of their powers was curtailed as more of their functions were given to the private sector or local agencies. Participation in local authority decision-making was not perceived as being beneficial in the sense of facilitating the development of the individual, or as being an integral aspect of partaking in civic life. When people participated they did so in a "market-role" as "consumers" of local services.[89]

This strategy had an effect upon the legal dimension of central–local relations. Traditionally the statutes that gave power to local authorities were generally phrased in broad, open-textured terms. It is true that there might well be central supervisory powers to prescribe standards, central control through an inspectorate, or default powers, which enabled a minister to take over the functions of a local authority if it was failing to perform its duties.[90] Notwithstanding this framework, central–local relations were generally governed by bargain, negotiation and administrative practice, rather than

---

[87] King and Stoker, n.1.
[88] See, e.g., R. Rhodes, *Beyond Westminster and Whitehall, The Sub-Central Governments of Britain* (Routledge, 1988).
[89] This is equally true of the participation which is fostered by the Citizen's Charter initiatives.
[90] Griffith, n.1.

resort to formal legal machinery.[91] The latter provided the framework for the bargain rather than being determinative of the particular outcome.[92]

The Conservative government's legislation in the late 1970s through to **6–017** the mid-1990s changed this approach. It placed an increasingly large number of more specific duties upon local authorities and sought to curb expenditure by local government. The result was that central–local relations became more politicised, in the sense that a previous general mutuality as to objectives was questioned. The relations also became more juridified, in the sense that the law assumed a more significant role in defining the boundaries of central–local power, and in resolving conflicts between the two levels of government.[93] The role of law was transformed from that of providing a facilitative framework, into one where it operated as a tighter regulatory regime whereby central control over local authorities was imposed.[94] The earlier facilitative legislation was designed to provide "a flexible structure enabling norms to emerge through working practices",[95] whereas the regulatory mode of legislating had as its object the specification of the norms which would regulate the central–local relationship. This transformation required the passage of an increasing amount of detailed legislation. It forced the courts to adjudicate on a range of issues which had not hitherto been felt suitable for legal resolution,[96] while being hampered by limitations of judicial review concerning fact finding, discovery and cross-examination.[97]

The Labour government's initiatives signalled a shift away from much that characterised the Conservative government's approach to central–local relations. This is apparent from the paper *Modern Local Government, In Touch with the People*,[98] and other relevant government documents. The general tenor and approach of these documents was to revitalise local government and to enhance local democracy. There will be those who take issue with the suggestions made to achieve this end. This should not, however, serve to mask the general objective, which has now found expression in the Local Government Act 2000, the Local Government Act 2003, the 2001 White Paper on *Strong Local Leadership, Quality Public Services*,[99] and the 2006 White Paper on *Strong and Prosperous Communities*.[100]

The changes in the organisational pattern of local government, as expressed through the division between the executive and legislative arm

[91] Loughlin, *Legality and Locality*, n.1, 365.
[92] R. Rhodes, *Control and Power in Central-Local Government Relations* (Gower, 1981).
[93] Loughlin, *Local Government in the Modern State*, n.1, Ch.9; J. Gyford, "The Politicization of Local Government", in Loughlin, Gelfand and Young, n.1, Ch.4.
[94] Loughlin, *Legality and Locality*, n.1, 367.
[95] Loughlin, *Legality and Locality*, n.1, 381.
[96] Loughlin, *Legality and Locality*, n.1, 368.
[97] Loughlin, *Legality and Locality*, n.1, 405–407.
[98] Cm. 4014 (July 1998).
[99] Office of the Deputy Prime Minister (2001).
[100] Department of Communities and Local Government, (October, 2006). http://www.communitiesgov.uk/publications/localgovernment/strongprosperous2.

thereof, are designed to foster accountability, transparency and efficiency.[101] There is increased emphasis on empowerment of local communities, involving greater choice for local communities in the way local services are designed and delivered, combined with increased duties on local authorities to inform and consult.[102] London has a central governing authority once again. A new ethical framework has been devised for those in local politics.[103] Financial controls from the centre continue to exist, but the controls are more discriminating.[104] The general principle underlying service provision is Best Value, which has been considered above.[105] The Best Value approach may still result in services being provided by agencies, firms or organisations outside of local government. In this sense we still have both local government and local governance. The market is however viewed in less doctrinaire terms than under the Conservative government. The Compulsory Competitive Tendering regime was abolished because it led to the neglect of service quality; the efficiency gains were uneven; it was inflexible; and because the compulsion which underpinned the system bred antagonism. The Local Government Act 1999, which gives effect to the Best Value regime, allows local authorities more leeway, while still preserving the possibility of central intervention, and the local area agreements, LAAs, are designed to enhance flexibility and choice in relation to service provision.

Time will tell how far these and other changes serve to reinvigorate local government. There is clearly still more to be done in terms of reinvigorating local communities, increasing their freedom as to how to deploy resources and improving their accountability, as recognised by the Lyons Inquiry.[106] It is however refreshing to see recognition of local government as an important institution within a modern democratic polity.

---

[101] *Strong Local Leadership*, n.99, para.3.14.
[102] *Strong and Prosperous Communities*, n.53; http://www.communitiesgov.uk/communities/communityempowerment/communityempowermentcommitments/.
[103] Local Government Act 2000 Pt III.
[104] Local Government Act 1999 Sch.1.
[105] Local Government Act 1999 Pt I. See above, Ch.5.
[106] Lyons Inquiry into Local Government, *Place-Shaping: A Shared Ambition for the Future of Local Government* (2007).

CHAPTER 7

DEVOLUTION, SCOTLAND AND WALES

The Government of Wales Act 1998 and the Scotland Act 1998 brought **7–001** about major changes in the pattern of government for the UK as a whole. Taken together with devolution of power in Northern Ireland, regional development agencies for England and reforms in the pattern of local government, they constitute a significant change in the structure of political authority for the UK as a whole.[1] This chapter will focus on devolution to Scotland and Wales. Limits of space preclude treatment of Northern Ireland.

1. SCOTLAND

A. The Background

The history of Scottish nationalist and separatist sentiment is far too rich **7–002** and diverse to be captured here, and no attempt will be made to do so.[2] This brief background will, therefore, simply provide a chronology of some of the more important developments relating to the governance of Scotland.

A Secretaryship for Scotland and a Scottish Office were established in 1885 with responsibility for a number of areas, including education, health,

---

[1] The reports pursuant to the Devolution Monitoring Programme run by the Constitution Unit provide an invaluable picture of the reality of devolution, available at http://www.ucl.ac.uk/constitution-unit/research/devolution/devo-monitoring-programme.html.

[2] H. Drucker and J. Gordon Brown, *The Politics of Nationalism and Devolution* (Longman, 1980); C. Harvie, *Scotland and Nationalism: Scottish Society and Politics 1707–1994* (Routledge, 1994); J. Mitchell, *Strategies for Self-Government* (Polygon, 1996); V. Bogdanor, *Devolution in the United Kingdom* (Oxford University Press, 1999), Ch.4; N. Walker, "Beyond the Unitary Conception of the United Kingdom Constitution?" [2000] P.L. 384; N. Burrows, *Devolution* (Sweet & Maxwell, 2000); R. Hazell and R. Rawlings (eds), *Devolution, Law Making and the Constitution* (Imprint Academic, 2005); A. Trench (ed.), *The Dynamics of Devolution: The State of the Nations 2005* (Imprint Academic, 2005); A. Trench, *Devolution and Power in the United Kingdom* (Manchester University Press, 2007).

the poor law, local government, police, prisons, roads and public works. The following year the all-party Scottish Home Rule Association was set up. The Scottish Secretary became a full Secretary of State in 1926, and in 1939 responsibility for Scottish affairs of a number of departments was vested directly in him.

It was the upsurge in the fortunes of the Scottish National Party in the late 1960s, combined with economic factors such as the discovery of North Sea oil, which placed the future shape of the United Kingdom on the political agenda. There was a growing sense that the Westminster Parliament did not adequately address the concerns of those in Scotland. We have already seen in the discussion of Wales the impact this had on the setting up of the Royal Commission on the Constitution. The Labour government of 1974–1979 enacted the Scotland Act 1978, which provided for devolution of power. The referendum in Scotland was in favour of the measure, but not by the majority required for the Act to become effective. The Act was then repealed by the Conservative government on taking power in 1979.

The Conservative government under Margaret Thatcher had no interest in the devolution of power. When the Conservatives were re-elected in 1987 the Campaign for a Scottish Assembly created a group to draw up plans for a constitutional convention. The committee published a report in 1988, entitled *A Claim of Right for Scotland*, which recommended, inter alia, that a scheme should be drawn up for a Scottish Assembly. These plans gained further support because of a growing sense of Scottish alienation, since the Conservatives who dominated Westminster politics had a steadily declining share of the Scottish vote. The Scottish Constitutional Convention (SCC) held its first meeting in 1989. All parties were invited to attend, but the Conservatives declined, and the SNP, after taking part in the preparations for the Convention then withdrew. When the Conservatives were re-elected again in 1992 the SCC established a Scottish Constitutional Commission to work out the details of their proposals. The Commission reported in 1994, and its work was incorporated in the SCC's report presented in 1995. The document, entitled *Scotland's Parliament, Scotland's Right*, contained detailed proposals for a Scottish Parliament. The return of a Labour government in 1996 brought the possibility of devolution onto the Westminster political agenda.[3]

B. The Composition of the Scottish Parliament

7–003　　Section 1 of the Scotland Act 1998 (SA)[4] establishes the Scottish Parliament, elections for which were held on May 6, 1999, with the Parliament and the

---

[3] N. Walker, "Constitutional Reform in a Cold Climate: Reflections on the White Paper & Referendum on Scotland's Parliament", in A. Tomkins (ed.), *Devolution and the British Constitution* (Key Haven, 1998), Ch.6.

[4] See generally, C. Himsworth and C. Munro, *The Scotland Act 1998* (Sweet & Maxwell, 2nd edn, 2000); C. Himsworth and C. O'Neill, *Scotland's Constitution: Law and Practice* (Lexis Nexis, 2003).

Executive taking up their powers on July 1, 1999. Ordinary general elections for the Scottish Parliament are held every four years.[5]

A member is returned for each constituency under the simple majority system,[6] and the constituencies are the parliamentary constituencies that operate for elections to the Westminster Parliament, plus the Orkney Islands and the Shetland Islands.[7] MSPs are also elected from regions under the additional member system of proportional representation.[8] There are eight regions, which are those used for elections to the European Parliament, and seven members are returned for each region.[9] Electors will therefore vote for both a constituency member and regional members.[10]

Entitlement to vote is based on those who would be entitled to vote as electors in local government elections in an electoral area which falls wholly or partly within the constituency, provided that the person is registered in the register of local government electors at an address within the constituency.[11]

C. The Formal Operation of the Scottish Parliament

We shall consider below how the Scottish Parliament and Executive have fared in practice.[12] The discussion within this section will concentrate on the formal allocation of powers and offices.

A Presiding Officer of the Scottish Parliament, plus two deputies, are appointed from the elected members.[13] There is also a Clerk for the Parliament appointed by the Scottish Parliamentary Corporate Body.[14] This Corporate Body is composed of the Presiding Officer and four MSPs.[15] The Corporation is to provide the Parliament with the property, services and staff required for the Parliament's purposes,[16] and it has power to do anything it considers necessary or expedient for the discharge of its functions.[17]

The proceedings of the Parliament are regulated by standing orders,[18] which may or must make provision for a range of matters, including[19]: preserving order in the Parliament; withdrawal of members' rights and privileges; the reporting of parliamentary proceedings; and the way in which

7–004

---

[5] SA s.2(2). Extraordinary general elections can be held on a different date if two thirds of the total number of Members of the Scottish Parliament (MSP) vote for a dissolution, or where a First Minister has not been nominated within the period specified in the legislation, SA, s.3(1).
[6] SA s.1(2).
[7] SA Sch.1, para.1.
[8] SA s.1(3).
[9] SA Sch.1, para.2.
[10] SA s.6.
[11] SA s.11(1).
[12] See below, paras 7–025—7–026.
[13] SA s.19.
[14] SA s.20.
[15] SA s.21(2).
[16] SA s.21(3).
[17] SA Sch.2, para.4(1).
[18] SA s.22(1); *Standing Orders of the Scottish Parliament* (2007), available at http://www.scottish.parliament.uk/business/so/sto-c.htm.
[19] SA Sch.3.

committees function. Proceedings of the Parliament are to be held in public, except so far as the standing orders dictate otherwise.[20] There is a Register of Members' Interests, which is to be open for public inspection.[21]

The Scottish Executive is composed of the First Minister, such ministers as he or she appoints, and the Lord Advocate and Solicitor General for Scotland.[22] They are known collectively as the Scottish Ministers,[23] they can hold property,[24] and appoint persons to be members of the Scottish Administration.[25] The First Minister is appointed by Her Majesty from among the members of the Scottish Parliament,[26] but the nomination for the position comes from the Parliament itself.[27] Ministerial appointments made by the First Minister must also be approved by Her Majesty, but the First Minister must secure the agreement of Parliament before tendering names.[28]

D. The Powers of the Scottish Parliament: Legislative Powers

i. Devolution strategies

7–005   The Scottish Parliament has been given power to make primary laws. Before examining its legislative powers it may be helpful to say something more general about techniques for the devolution of legislative power. There are in essence two approaches that can be adopted. The central government can devolve all its power to the other body, with the exception of reserved matters. It can, alternatively, devolve specified matters, with the corollary that all other matters remain within the power of the central authority. Both strategies have been employed in the past in the UK. The Government of Ireland Act 1920 adopted the first of these approaches, the Scotland Act 1978 the second.

It is tempting to think that the first approach will be more generous to the body to which power is devolved. There is no a priori reason why this should be so. The method used is in this sense neutral,[29] although there may well be symbolic differences between the two approaches. The reason why this is so is that even if the first approach is adopted so much turns on the list of reserved matters. One only has to compare the list of such matters contained in the Government of Ireland Act 1920, and the Scotland Act 1998, for this to be apparent. The list of reserved powers contained in the former Act is relatively short, and relatively general. The list contained in the Scotland Act 1998 is very long, contains general reservations and a plethora of much more detailed specific reservations.

---

[20] SA Sch.3 para.3(1).
[21] SA s.39.
[22] SA s.44(1).
[23] SA s.44(2).
[24] SA s.59.
[25] SA s.51.
[26] SA s.45.
[27] SA s.46(1).
[28] SA ss.47(1)–(2). The same regime applies for the appointment of Scottish Law Officers, s.48.
[29] Constitution Unit, *Scotland's Parliament, Fundamentals for New Scotland Act* (1996).

Where the list of devolved *or* retained powers is long and complex it is difficult for the lay person to know for certain whether action really is within the power of the body to which authority has been devolved. The Scotland Act 1978 adopted the second strategy of providing a very detailed, complex list of devolved powers, on the assumption that all else remained with the central authority. It provoked the following comment from MacCormick.[30]

"One fears that only lawyers and Civil Servants, but by no means all of them, will be able to work out or give reliable advice on the full meaning of the affirmations as qualified by the negations. Beyond doubt, this complexity and difficulty of comprehension is a defect of the Act. It infringes the principle of intelligibility of law, a principle most to be prized in constitutional enactments."

When reading the material that follows it would be well to reflect on whether this same sentiment might not apply to the Scotland Act 1998.[31]

ii. Legislative powers: sections 28 and 29(1)

With these thoughts in mind we can now turn to the 1998 Act and consider **7–006** the legislative powers it accords. The Scottish Parliament is given the power by s.28 SA to make primary laws, which are known as Acts of the Scottish Parliament. Standing orders must make provision for general debate on a Bill. There must be an opportunity for MSPs to vote on its general principles, for the consideration of, and the opportunity to vote on, the details of a Bill, and for a final stage at which a Bill can be passed or rejected.[32] The Parliament's legislative capacity is presumptively general. It is however qualified in two ways.

First, s.28 does not affect the power of the Westminster Parliament to make laws for Scotland.[33] Second, the legislative competence of the Scottish Parliament is bounded, and s.29(1) provides that an "Act of the Scottish Parliament is not law so far as any provision of the Act is outside the legislative competence of the Parliament". The meaning of this section is not beyond doubt. It could be interpreted to mean that if any provision of the challenged Act is outside the Parliament's legislative competence then the Act itself is not law. This would be very draconian. It is also not the most natural reading of the relevant words.[34] The better interpretation of s.29(1) is that the challenged Scottish Act is only not law so far as the provisions are ultra vires. The remainder of the Act that is untainted remains good law. It should nonetheless be realised that in practice there may be occasions where

---

[30] "Constitutional Points", in D. Mackay (ed.), *Scotland: The Framework for Change* (Harris, 1979), 53–54.

[31] See, however, the more positive tone of N. MacCormick, "Sovereignty or Subsidiarity? Some Comments on Scottish Devolution", in Tomkins, n.3, Ch.1.

[32] SA s.36(1); *Standing Orders of the Scottish Parliament* (2007), rule 9.5.

[33] SA s.28(7).

[34] I. Jamieson, "Challenging the Validity of an Act of the Scottish Parliament: Some Aspects of *A v Scottish Ministers*" [2002] S.L.T. 71.

the invalidity of certain provisions of an Act will prevent the remainder from being a viable and effective piece of legislation.

iii. Limits to legislative power: section 29(2)

7–007   Section 29(2) defines the bounds of the Scottish Parliament's competence. The member of the Scottish Executive who is in charge of a Bill must, on or before the introduction of the Bill in the Parliament, state that in his or her view the provisions of the Bill would be within the legislative competence of the Parliament.[35] The Presiding Officer must also do so.[36] Section 29(2) states that a provision is outside the Parliament's competence if[37]:

> "(a)   it would form part of the law of a country or territory other than Scotland, or confer or remove functions exercisable otherwise than in or as regards Scotland,
> (b)   it relates to reserved matters,
> (c)   it is in breach of the restrictions in Schedule 4,
> (d)   it is incompatible with any Convention rights or with Community law,
> (e)   it would remove the Lord Advocate from his position as head of the systems of criminal prosecution and investigation of deaths in Scotland."

Whether a provision of an Act of the Scottish Parliament relates to a reserved matter is to be determined by reference to the purpose of the provision having regard, inter alia, to its effects in all the circumstances.[38] There have been a number of challenges to Scottish legislation on the ground that it is incompatible with Convention rights.[39]

iv. Limits to legislative power: section 29(2)(b) and Schedule 5

7–008   Section 29(2)(b) requires further explanation because it leads to the list of reserved matters, which is set out in Sch.5. This Schedule, which is divided into three parts, is very lengthy and therefore only the broad outlines of its provisions can be described here. It should be noted that s.29(2)(b) states that a matter is outside the competence of the Scottish Parliament if it *relates* to reserved matters. The Scottish Parliament is prevented from

---

[35] SA s.31(1).
[36] SA s.31(2).
[37] SA s.29(2).
[38] SA s.29(3). See also, s.29(4) which touches on the this same issue.
[39] *Starrs v Ruxton* 2000 S.L.T. 42; *Adams v Scottish Ministers* [2002] U.K.H.R.R. 1179; *Anderson v Scottish Ministers* [2003] 2 A.C. 602; *Brown v Stott* [2003] 1 A.C. 681; *HM Advocate v McIntosh (Robert) (No.1)* [2003] 1 A.C. 1078; *Montgomery v HM Advocate* [2003] 1 A.C. 641; *Mills (Kenneth Anthony) v HM Advocate (No.2)* [2004] 1 A.C. 441; *HM Advocate v R.* [2004] 1 A.C. 462; *Flynn (Patrick Anthony) v HM Advocate (No.1)* [2004] H.R.L.R. 17; *DS v HM Advocate* [2007] H.R.L.R. 28; *Friend v Lord Advocate* [2007] U.K.H.L. 53; *Somerville v Scottish Ministers* [2007] U.K.H.L. 44.

legislating in a way that "relates" to any of the very broad range of matters considered below. The inhibiting effect this might have on the Scottish Parliament's legislative power can be appreciated by looking at the Schedule itself.

Part I deals with General Reservations and lists a number of matters that are outside the competence of the Scottish Parliament. Important aspects of the *Constitution* are one such category[40]: the Crown, including succession to the Crown and a regency; the Union of the Kingdoms of Scotland and England; the Parliament of the United Kingdom; the continued existence of the High Court of Justiciary as a criminal court of first instance and of appeal; and the continued existence of the Court of Session as a civil court of first instance and of appeal. The prerogative and other executive functions are not, however, reserved matters.[41] A second general reservation relates to the *registration and funding of political parties*.[42] The *conduct of foreign affairs*, including relations with the EC, other international organisations, and the regulation of international trade, is not surprisingly another reserved matter.[43] The other general reservations relate to, *the public service, defence and treason*.[44]

Part II of Sch.5 deals with Specific Reservations.[45] A glance at this part of the Act makes one realise that it will be difficult for the Scottish Parliament to determine with certainty whether it has legislative competence or not. This may lead to legal challenge to test the correctness of the Parliament's judgment on these matters.

Part II contains a large number of reserved heads, which are listed as "Head A—Financial and Economic Matters", "Head B—Home Affairs", "Head C—Trade and Industry" and so on, there being eleven such heads in total.[46] Each of these Heads is then sub-divided into a number of sections labelled in the case of, for example Trade and Industry, which is Head C, from C1–C15. The list of the sub-divisions which apply for Trade and Industry relate to: business associations; insolvency; competition; intellectual property; import and export control; sea fishing; consumer protection; product standards, safety and liability; weights and measures; telecommunications and wireless telegraphy; Post Office, posts and postal services; Research Councils; designation of assisted areas; Industrial Development Advisory Board; and the protection of trading and economic interests.

The legal advisor's task of indicating whether the Scottish Parliament has competence or not is made more difficult by the style of drafting used in Pt **7–009**

---

[40] SA Sch.5 Pt I para.1.
[41] SA Sch.5 Pt I para.2(1).
[42] SA Sch.5 Pt I para.6.
[43] SA Sch.5 Pt I para.7(1). The implementation of international obligations, including those flowing from EC law and the ECHR, is not a reserved matter, Sch.5, para.7(2).
[44] SA Sch.5 Pt I paras 8–10.
[45] It is also the case that Sch.4, para.1, prevents the Scottish Parliament from modifying certain legislative provisions including, *inter alia*, the Human Rights Act 1998.
[46] The other Heads are: Energy, Transport, Social Security, Regulation of the Professions, Employment, Health and Medicines, Media and Culture and Miscellaneous.

II. On some occasions the reserved heads are set out at a high level of generality, without mentioning any particular existing statute. On other occasions the reserved heads will specify a particular section of a particular statute which is off-limits for the Scottish Parliament. On yet other occasions it will stipulate that the subject matter dealt with by an entire statute is outside the legislative competence of the Scottish Parliament. The format of Pt II is further complicated by the fact that any of these styles are often accompanied by exceptions, which allow the Scottish Parliament to legislate within the area thus stipulated, by interpretative statements designed to clarify the reach of the reserved head, and by illustrations aimed at clarifying the meaning of generally worded statements. These differing techniques will not infrequently be used within the same sub-division.[47]

Part III of Sch.5 has a more institutional focus. This is somewhat strange given that the Schedule is about "Reserved Matters": it is difficult to see how an institution as such can be a reserved matter. The gist of this Part of the Schedule is nonetheless to reserve certain bodies, or to clarify which bodies are not reserved. Thus, for example, a body mentioned by name in Pt II of Sch.5 is a reserved body, as is the Commission for Racial Equality, the Equal Opportunities Commission and the Disability Rights Commission.[48] The effect of being denoted as such a body is to reserve its constitution, and its functions. Thus it is outside the bounds of the Scottish Parliament's power to pass any legislation which would interfere with the constitution or functions of these bodies.

The force of s.29(2)(b) and Sch.5 are reinforced by section 29(2)(c). This latter section brings Sch.4 into play, para.2(1) of which states that an Act of the Scottish Parliament cannot modify, or confer power by subordinate legislation to modify, the law on reserved matters. It is clear that the "law on reserved matters" covers any enactment whose subject matter is reserved, which is comprised in an Act of Parliament or subordinate legislation made thereunder. It also covers any rule of law that is not contained in an enactment where the subject matter is a reserved matter.[49] There is an exception where the modification is incidental to a provision that does not relate to the reserved matter, provided that the modification does not have a greater effect on reserved matters than is necessary to give effect to the purpose of the provision.[50] It is however open to the Scottish Parliament to restate the law.[51]

The judicial approach to Schs 4 and 5 was captured by Lord Hope in the *DS* case,[52] where he stated that an attempt by the Scottish Parliament to widen the scope of its legislative competence as defined in those schedules would be met by the requirement that any provision which could be read in

[47] See, e.g., Sch.5, Pt II, sections D1, E1, E3, and F1.
[48] SA Sch.5 Pt III, para.3.
[49] SA Sch.4 para.2(2).
[50] SA Sch.4 para.3(1).
[51] SA Sch.4 para.7(1).
[52] *DS*, n.39, para.23.

such a way as to be outside competence must be read as narrowly as was required for it to be within competence.

E. The Powers of the Scottish Parliament: The Powers of the Executive

The Scottish Ministers that comprise the Scottish Executive are accorded power in four ways by the Scotland Act. **7–010**

First, specific statutory functions can be conferred on the Scottish Ministers by name through any enactment.[53] Such statutory functions are to be exercisable on behalf of Her Majesty, and can be exercised by any member of the Scottish Executive.[54]

Second, the SA makes a general transfer to the Scottish Ministers of functions hitherto exercised by a Minister of the Crown.[55] The functions transferred are[56]: those prerogative and other executive functions which are exercisable on behalf of her Majesty by a Minister of the Crown; other functions conferred on a Minister of the Crown by a prerogative instrument; and functions conferred on a Minister of the Crown by any pre-commencement enactment.[57] The Scottish Ministers are therefore prima facie given the powers exercised by Ministers of the Crown in relation to Scotland. Subordinate legislation can adapt the functions previously exercised by a Minister of the Crown in order to facilitate the transfer.[58] These functions are however only transferred in so far as they are exercisable within "devolved competence".[59] The exercise of a function will be outside a devolved competence if it would be outside the legislative competence of the Scottish Parliament itself.[60] What this means of course is that the executive cannot act so as to circumvent the limits placed on the legislative competence of the Parliament,[61] and that Scottish ministers cannot act incompatibly with Convention rights or Community law.[62] This is entirely logical given the general scheme of the SA. It inexorably follows that all the difficulties in interpreting the boundaries of legislative competence charted above will apply whenever the executive itself seeks to act, irrespective of the form the act takes.

Third, notwithstanding the generality of the transfer of functions described in the preceding paragraph, the SA stipulates that the functions under certain statutes are to be exercisable by a Minister of the Crown as

---

[53] SA ss.52(1), 52(7).
[54] SA ss.52(1)–(3).
[55] SA s.53(1).
[56] SA s.53(2).
[57] This provision, s.53(2)(c), is subject to Sch.4, paras 12–14.
[58] SA s.106.
[59] SA s.53(1).
[60] SA ss.54(2)–(3).
[61] *Somerville*, n.39, para.14.
[62] SA s.57(2).

well as the Scottish Ministers.[63] There is moreover a power to make an Order in Council which would provide for a function which had been transferred to the Scottish Executive to be exercised by a Minister of the Crown instead, or by a Minister of the Crown concurrently with a member of the Scottish Executive, or by a member of the Scottish Executive only with the agreement, or after consultation with, a Minister of the Crown.[64]

Finally, an Order in Council can be passed providing for the transfer of additional functions to Scottish Ministers.[65]

F. The Powers of the Scottish Parliament: Subordinate Legislation

7–011   The discussion thus far has concentrated on the making of Acts of the Scottish Parliament and the powers of the executive. The SA also makes provision for the passage of subordinate legislation, which involves the exercise of power by the legislature and the executive.

i. Subordinate legislation and earlier enactments: the scope of the power

7–012   The position here is clear. Where any pre-commencement enactment, prerogative instrument or other instrument or document contain references to a Minister of the Crown these are to be read as including references to the Scottish Ministers.[66] The power of the Scottish Ministers to make such legislation is premised on the assumption that it is within their devolved competence.[67]

ii. Subordinate legislation made under the Scotland Act: the scope of the power

7–013   The Scotland Act gives extensive power to make subordinate legislation in a wide variety of circumstances. Four situations are of particular importance.

First, as we have already seen, the Act provides for both specific and general transfer of functions to Scottish Ministers which were previously exercised by a Minister of the Crown, and these functions clearly include the making of subordinate legislation.[68]

Second, s.104 allows subordinate legislation to make such provision as the person making it considers necessary or expedient in consequence of any provision made by or under any Act of the Scottish Parliament.

Third, s.105 provides that subordinate legislation may modify any pre-commencement enactment, prerogative instrument, or any other instrument or document, as appears necessary or expedient to the person making the legislation in consequence of the SA. It seems clear from the definition of

---

[63] SA ss.56–57; *Somerville*, n.39; *Napier v Scottish Ministers* [2004] U.K.H.R.R. 881; *Potter v Scottish Prison Service* [2007] C.S.I.H. 67; *X v Scottish Ministers* [2007] C.S.I.H. 45; *B, Petitioner* [2007] C.S.O.H. 73.
[64] SA s.108.
[65] SA s.63.
[66] SA s.117.
[67] SA s.118(1).
[68] SA ss.52, 53, 54.

"pre-commencement enactment"[69] that this term includes primary legislation passed before the SA. This therefore means that s.105 constitutes a broad "Henry VIII" clause allowing earlier primary legislation to be modified by secondary legislation.[70] The subordinate legislation made under s.105 is however subject to scrutiny by the Westminster Parliament.[71]

Finally, a further important "Henry VIII" power is to be found in s.107. This in effect allows subordinate legislation to be used to cure defects in an Act of the Scottish Parliament, or exercise of power by the Scottish Executive, which has been found to be ultra vires. The "curative" subordinate legislation, if made without a draft having been approved by resolution of each House of Parliament, is subject to annulment pursuant to a resolution of either House.[72]

iii. Subordinate legislation made under the Scotland Act: who has the power?
The SA therefore gives extensive powers to make subordinate legislation. It **7–014** is, however, not entirely clear who has power to make such legislation. Section 112 states that if no other provision is made as to the person by whom the power is exercisable, it shall be exercisable by Her Majesty by Order in Council or by a Minister of the Crown by order. This is not problematic in relation to the specific or general transfer of functions to Scottish Ministers, since the relevant sections of the Act clearly authorise them to make subordinate legislation. However, other sections of the SA which authorise the making of subordinate legislation, such as 104, 105 and 107, do not provide any further definition as to who can exercise the power, and therefore s.112 is operative in such instances. The key issue is whether the Scottish Ministers can exercise these powers.

It might be argued that Scottish Ministers are Ministers of the Crown and therefore come within s.112(1). The arguments in favour of this approach are as follows. The Scottish Ministers are appointed by, and hold office at, Her Majesty's pleasure.[73] Section 117 provides that any pre-commencement enactment, or prerogative instrument, *and any other instrument or document*, shall be read as if references to a Minister of the Crown were, or included,

---

[69] SA s.53(3). The matter is not entirely free from doubt for two reasons. First, although the definition of pre-commencement enactment given in s.53(3) is stated to be a definition for the purposes of the Act, the context of s.53(3) is in relation to the transfer of power to the Scottish ministers, which is very different from the modification of earlier legislation. Second, the definition of "enactment" contained in s.126 may be narrower. This definition is itself problematic. We are told that the term "enactment" includes, *inter alia*, "an enactment comprised in, or in subordinate legislation under, an Act of Parliament whenever passed or made". It is not clear whether the phrase "an enactment comprised in an Act of Parliament" is intended to mean a section of such legislation, or whether it has some other meaning. In any event the use of the same word, enactment, to describe both legislation, such as an Act of the Scottish Parliament, and a section of an Act of the Westminster Parliament is confusing to say the very least.
[70] See, e.g., Scotland Act 1998 (Consequential Modifications) (No.2) Order (SI 1999/1820); Scotland Act 1998 (Consequential Modifications) Order (SI 2000/2040); Scotland Act 1998 (Consequential Modifications) Order (SI 2001/1400).
[71] SA Sch.7 paras 1(2), 2, applying the Type G procedure to such subordinate legislation
[72] SA Sch.7 para.1(2).
[73] SA ss.45, 47.

references to the Scottish Ministers. It might be argued that the italicised words resolve the matter. This would be so if these words could be read so as to include the Scotland Act itself. Scottish Ministers come within the definition provided in the general legislation on this issue.[74] The reference to "Her Majesty's Government" within this definition might be read as excluding other parts of Her Majesty's possessions (such as the remaining dependencies), but it is taken to include Northern Ireland.[75] Given that this is so, there is no reason why it should not also include Scotland. The Scottish Ministers do, moreover, fit the summary of Minister of the Crown provided in the academic literature.[76]

There are however arguments the other way, which suggest that Scottish Ministers are not regarded as Ministers of the Crown. Most important in this respect is the fact that the Act, at a number of relevant points, expressly treats Ministers of the Crown and Scottish Ministers separately.[77] The very breadth of the subordinate legislative powers contained in ss.104–107 also indicates that only a minister from the Westminster Parliament should exercise them.

The reality in practice is that statutory instruments made pursuant to ss.104–105 SA are signed by the relevant Whitehall minister, who is normally the Secretary of State for Scotland or an Under Secretary of State. The statutory instruments will commonly deal with modifications to Westminster legislation consequent upon Scottish Acts of Parliament. This does not in itself preclude Scottish Ministers seeking to promote an Order in Council, which is the other option mentioned in s.112(1); the Scottish Minister would be the person who drafted and presented the subordinate legislation for approval to Her Majesty by Order in Council.[78]

iv. Subordinate legislation made in pursuance of the Scotland Act: the procedure

7–015 The procedural rules applicable to the making of subordinate legislation are complex, and only an outline can be provided here. It is important to distinguish broadly between two types of situation.

First, there is the situation where a function has been transferred to a Scottish Minister, and this includes the power to make subordinate legislation. The Scotland Act provides that where the making of subordinate legislation under the pre-commencement enactment required the laying of the measure before the Westminster Parliament, and for the annulment or approval of it by resolution of either or both Houses of Parliament, then the

---

[74] Ministers of the Crown Act 1975 s.8(1) which provides that: "In this Act. . .'Minister of the Crown' means the holder of an office in Her Majesty's Government in the United Kingdom, and includes the Treasury, the Board of Trade and the Defence Council".
[75] R. Brazier, *Ministers of the Crown* (Oxford University Press, 1996), 24.
[76] Brazier, n.75, 30–31.
[77] See, e.g., SA, ss.52(6), 53(1), 60(1), 106(1), 108(1), 112(5).
[78] The standard practice is for statutory Orders in Council to be drafted by the relevant government department, which would, of course normally be a Whitehall department, Sir C. Allen, *Law and Orders* (Stevens, 3rd edn, 1965), 90–91.

reference to the Westminster Parliament is to be taken to be a reference to the Scottish Parliament.[79] In essence therefore the mode of approving such legislation which applied when it was made at Westminster is carried across to Scotland.

Second, there are many situations where the Scotland Act allows subordinate legislation to be made in relation to powers conferred by the Act itself. Detailed rules are stipulated as to the procedure for the passing of such legislation. Schedule 7 sets out 11 different procedures that can apply to the making of subordinate legislation under the SA. It then dictates which procedure is to apply to each of the stated sections of the Act. The procedures vary considerably as to what is required. The common theme is, however, that approval in some form must be gained from the Westminster Parliament as well as from the Scottish Parliament. The procedures in Sch.7 therefore apply to subordinate legislation that is of some real importance, and such legislation requires the approval of each House of Parliament, or is subject to annulment in pursuance of a resolution of either House.[80]

G. The Powers of the Scottish Parliament: Money

In the period leading to the passage of the Scotland Act 1998 much was made of the fact that the Scottish Parliament would have the ability to vary the rate of income tax. This power has been enshrined in the legislation.[81] This will not however lead to any radical increase in the Parliament's revenue base. The basic rate of income tax can only be varied by plus or minus three pence in the pound, and even if this is used to the maximum it will only yield an additional £400–500 million pounds. This is not a great deal when set against the fact that the total budget is of the order of £31 billion in 2007–2008. This assumes that the Parliament exercises the power so as to increase basic rates of taxation. Any such move will, in relative terms, be costly to administer.[82]

7–016

Leaving aside the power to vary income tax the Scottish Parliament has no revenue-raising power and will be dependent on block transfers from central government.[83] In the past these block transfers have been allocated to the Secretary of State for Scotland who has had considerable autonomy as to the distribution of this money as between different programmes. This distributional autonomy now lies with the Scottish Parliament.[84] It is, nonetheless, questionable whether it will be able to exercise very much real autonomous policy choice. This is in part because the aggregate block grant

---

[79] SA s.118(2).
[80] SA Sch.7 para.1, applying the Type G procedure in such instances.
[81] SA s.73.
[82] R. Hazell and R. Cornes, "Financing Devolution: The Centre Retains Control", in R. Hazell (ed.), *Constitutional Futures, A History of the Next Ten Years* (Oxford University Press, 1999), 207–208.
[83] HM Treasury, *Funding of the Scottish Parliament, National Assembly for Wales and the Northern Ireland Assembly, A Statement of Funding Policy* (5th edn, 2007), available at http://www.hm-treasury.gov.uk/media/2/2/pbr_csr07_funding591.pdf .
[84] *Scotland's Parliament*, Cm. 3658 (1997), paras 7.1–7.4.

is still determined by central government, and there may be pressure to reduce the amount of the grant to Scotland, which is, in relative terms, funded better than many other parts of the UK. It is in part a consequence of the way in which changes in the level of the grant are decided.[85] These are determined in accordance with the Barnett formula, under which Scotland, Wales and Northern Ireland receive a population-based proportion of changes in planned spending on comparable United Kingdom Government services in England. Change in each devolved administration's spending allocation is determined by the quantity of the change in planned spending in departments of the United Kingdom Government, the extent to which the relevant United Kingdom programme is comparable with the services carried out by each devolved administration and each country's population proportion.[86] This necessarily means that changes in expenditure decisions in England will have consequential effects for Scotland, and may well limit the room for policy variation by the Scottish Parliament. An example provided by Hazell and Cornes makes this clear.[87]

"Suppose that a future government in London wishes to cut income tax, and introduces tax incentives for private health insurance which enable it to reduce spending on the health service in England. Under the Barnett formula this would lead automatically to a proportionate cut in the block grants for Scotland, Wales and Northern Ireland; but they might want to retain their levels of health spending. The funding formula should be able to allow for policy variation, and to cope with differing concepts of the public sector in different parts of the country."

H. Political Challenge to the Competence of the Scottish Parliament

7–017 The Scotland Act contains provisions enabling the Secretary of State to intervene in certain cases. Two sections of the Act are of particular importance in this respect.

Section 35 allows the Secretary of State to make an order prohibiting the Presiding Officer from submitting a Bill for Royal Assent if it contains provisions which he or she has reasonable grounds to believe would be incompatible with any international obligations, or the interests of defence or national security. The Secretary of State can also make such an order where the Bill has provisions which modify the law as it applies to reserved matters, and which he or she has reasonable grounds to believe would have an adverse effect on the operation of the law as it applies to reserved matters. Reasons must be given for making such an order.

---

[85] R. Hazell, "Intergovernmental Relations: Whitehall Rules OK?", in R. Hazell (ed.), *The State and the Nations, The First Year of Devolution in the United Kingdom* (Imprint Academic, 2000), 175–179.

[86] HM Treasury, n.83, Ch.4.

[87] Hazell and Cornes, n.82, 203.

Section 58 contains a parallel power for the Secretary of State to intervene on the same grounds in relation to subordinate legislation made by the Scottish Executive.[88] In such instances the Secretary of State may by order actually revoke the legislation. This section also empowers the Secretary of State to direct that action proposed to be taken by the Scottish Executive, which would be incompatible with international obligations, is not taken, or to direct that such action is taken where that is required to give effect to an international obligation.[89]

I. Judicial Challenge to the Competence of the Scottish Parliament

The SA places significant limitations on the legal competence of the Scottish   **7–018** Parliament. The corollary is the need for legal rules that indicate when a challenge can be made. Schedule 6, which is made operative by s.98, is central in this respect. It defines "devolution issue" to mean,[90]

"(a) a question whether an Act of the Scottish Parliament or any provision of an Act of the Scottish Parliament is within the legislative competence of the Parliament,

(b) a question whether any function (being a function which any person has purported, or is proposing, to exercise) is a function of the Scottish Ministers, the First Minister or the Lord Advocate,

(c) a question whether the purported or proposed exercise of a function by a member of the Scottish Executive is, or would be, within devolved competence,

(d) a question whether a purported or proposed exercise of a function by a member of the Scottish Executive is, or would be, incompatible with any of the Convention rights or with Community law,

(e) a question whether a failure to act by a member of the Scottish Executive is incompatible with any of the Convention rights or with Community law,

(f) any other question about whether a function is exercisable within devolved competence or in or as regards Scotland and any other question arising by virtue of this Act about reserved matters."

Section 101 provides important guidance for courts faced with devolution issues. The effect is to impose an interpretative obligation on courts to try and read Acts and Bills of the Scottish Parliament, and subordinate legislation, as being intra vires rather than ultra vires. Where any provision of such a measure could be read so as to be ultra vires, s.101(2) states that it is to be read as narrowly as possible as is required for it to be within

[88] SA s.58(4).
[89] SA ss.58(1)–(2).
[90] SA Sch.6 para.1.

competence,[91] if such a reading is possible.[92] The Scotland Act contains detailed rules as to the different types of legal challenge.

i. The resolution of devolution issues: direct reference to the Privy Council

7–019 A devolution issue may be resolved through direct reference to the Privy Council. There are three types of case where this can occur.

First, there can be *pre-enactment scrutiny*. The Advocate General, the Lord Advocate or the Attorney-General may refer the question, whether a Bill or any provision of a Bill would be within the legislative competence of the Parliament, to the Judicial Committee of the Privy Council, henceforth to be the Supreme Court,[93] for a decision.[94] The Presiding Officer must not submit a Bill for Royal Assent at any time when such a law officer is entitled to make a reference, or where the reference has been made, but the Privy Council has not yet disposed of the matter.[95] Decisions made by the Privy Council are binding in all legal proceedings, other than proceedings before the Privy Council itself.[96] If the Privy Council decides that the Bill is ultra vires then the Presiding Officer cannot submit it for Royal Assent in its unamended form.[97] Special provision is made for cases which might be referred by the Privy Council to the European Court of Justice.[98]

Second, there is the possibility of a direct reference to the Privy Council *from existing proceedings*. Law officers must be notified of a devolution issue which arises in particular proceedings, and they are entitled to take part in the proceedings so far as they relate to the devolution issue.[99] The Lord Advocate, the Advocate General, the Attorney-General and the Attorney-General for Northern Ireland may require the court or tribunal to refer the devolution issue to the Privy Council.[100]

Third, there can be a direct reference of a devolution issue *which is not the subject of existing proceedings*. The same law officers can exercise this power.[101]

---

[91] "Competence" is defined in relation to an Act of the Scottish Parliament, or a Bill, to mean the legislative competence of the Parliament; in relation to subordinate legislation it is defined to mean the powers conferred by the SA s.101(3).
[92] *Somerville*, n.39.
[93] Such cases will be heard by the Supreme Court, when it becomes operational, Constitutional Reform Act 2005 Sch.9, para.96.
[94] SA s.33(1). Such a reference can be made within four weeks beginning with the passing of the Bill, and any period of four weeks beginning with the subsequent approval of the Bill in accordance with standing orders which are made, s.33(2).
[95] SA s.32(2).
[96] SA s.103(1).
[97] SA s.32(3).
[98] SA s.34.
[99] SA Sch.6, paras 5–6, 16–17, 26–27. Which Law officers must be notified depends on where the proceedings initially arise, Scotland, England and Wales or Northern Ireland.
[100] SA Sch.6 para.33.
[101] SA Sch.6 paras 34–35.

ii. The resolution of devolution issues: institution of proceedings by a law officer

The Scotland Act allows the relevant law officer to institute proceedings for **7–020** the determination of a devolution issue. The Lord Advocate will normally be the defendant in such actions.[102] The law officers have the power to require the devolution issue to be referred to the Privy Council, as described above, but may choose not to exercise this power.

iii. The resolution of devolution issues: reference to other courts

The discussion thus far has focused on the role of the law officers in **7–021** enforcing the limits to the Scottish Parliament's power. It is, however, readily apparent that devolution issues may arise in the course of proceedings involving individuals, or between an individual and a public body. The Act clearly contemplates such actions.[103] It makes provision in such instances for the referral of devolution issues from one court to another. Proceedings which raise devolution issues may occur in Scotland itself, in England and Wales or in Northern Ireland. The SA establishes a reference system for all three jurisdictions. The description which follows applies in relation to England and Wales.

In non-criminal proceedings, magistrates' courts can refer devolution issues to the High Court.[104] Other courts may refer such issues to the Court of Appeal.[105] In criminal cases, a court, other than the Court of Appeal or the House of Lords, can refer a devolution issue to the High Court, in the case of summary proceedings, or the Court of Appeal in the case of proceedings on indictment.[106] Tribunals from which there is no appeal must refer to the Court of Appeal, and may make a reference in other instances.[107]

The Court of Appeal can refer any devolution issue which comes before it, other than on a reference as described above, to the Privy Council.[108] Where a devolution issue arises in judicial proceedings in the House of Lords it must be referred to the Privy Council, unless the House decides that it would be more appropriate in all the circumstances for it to hear the issue.[109]

Appeals from the High Court or the Court of Appeal on devolution issues lie to the Privy Council. Leave is required for such an appeal from the High Court or Court of Appeal, or from the Privy Council.[110]

---

[102] SA Sch.6 paras 4, 15, 25.
[103] SA Sch.6 paras 4(3), 15(3), 25(3).
[104] SA Sch.6 para.18.
[105] SA Sch.6 para.19, with the exception of magistrates' courts, the Court of Appeal or the House of Lords, or the High Court where acting under para.18.
[106] SA Sch.6 para.21.
[107] SA Sch.6 para.20.
[108] SA Sch.6 para.22.
[109] SA Sch.6 para.32.
[110] SA Sch.6 para.23.

iv. The resolution of devolution issues: decision made by the court immediately seized of the matter

7–022 The court immediately seized of the matter has the power to refer the matter in the manner described above. It does not have the duty to do so, subject to being compelled to make a reference by the intervention of a law officer requiring the case to be referred to the Privy Council.

v. Devolution issues which "arise": the relevance of the general law on collateral challenge

7–023 The Scotland Act is framed in terms of devolution issues "arising".[111] The paradigm case is one of direct challenge, but devolution issues may also arise indirectly. There will be collateral challenges where, for example, the Assembly is enforcing a piece of subordinate legislation and the applicant claims that it is ultra vires, and should not therefore be enforced. Recent decisions of the courts have been more liberal in allowing collateral challenge, although there are still some uncertainties.[112] This raises the interesting question as to how far these general rules concerning collateral challenge and vires issues will apply in this context. The courts' more liberal attitude to collateral challenge should mean that if the general legal rules on collateral challenge are applied, claimants will normally be able to raise vires issues indirectly as well as directly.

vi. The result of finding that the Scottish Parliament acted outside its competence

7–024 The Scotland Act makes provision as to what should occur if an Act of the Scottish Parliament, or subordinate legislation, is found to be ultra vires.

In political terms, the SA contains a broad "Henry VIII" clause allowing the passage of subordinate legislation to amend an Act of the Scottish Parliament, or other subordinate legislation, which has been found to be ultra vires.[113] The subordinate legislation which performs this corrective function will, however, be subject to scrutiny by the Westminster Parliament.[114]

In legal terms, the SA empowers a court or tribunal which has decided that an Act of the Scottish Parliament, or subordinate legislation, is ultra vires, to make an order removing or limiting any retrospective effect of that decision, or suspending the effect of that decision for any period and on any conditions to allow the defect to be corrected.[115] The court, in deciding whether to make such an order, must take into account, inter alia, the extent to which persons who are not party to the proceedings would otherwise be

---

[111] SA Sch.6.
[112] See below, Ch.26.
[113] SA, s.107.
[114] SA Sch.7 para.1(2).
[115] SA s.102(2).

adversely affected.[116] The appropriate law officer must be given an intimation that such an order might be made, and can then join the proceedings for this issue.[117]

J. Scottish Devolution: Some Reflections

Time will tell whether devolution to Scotland has the effect of weakening   **7–025**
separatist claims, or whether it proves to be but the first step towards a more
formal separation from the rest of the UK. Political, intergovernmental,
economic and legal considerations will be of importance in this respect.

In *political terms*, the Scottish Parliament was initially run by a coalition
between the Scottish Labour Party and the Scottish Liberal Democrat
Party. However 2007 saw the SNP take office, albeit as a minority government, together with the election of a nationalist First Minister, Alex
Salmond. The Scottish Executive was rebranded in September 2007 as the
Scottish Government, although the former term, enshrined in the Scotland
Act 1998, remains the strict legal appellation. It remains to be seen whether
Scottish devolution is a "motorway without exit to an independent state".
These were the evocative words of Tam Dalyell,[118] although experience from
other countries demonstrates that the grant of autonomy may invigorate an
existing union, and not lead to its destruction.[119]

The SNP Scottish government has however published a White Paper on
constitutional reform, *Choosing Scotland's Future: A National Conversation*,[120] in which it canvassed three choices: retention of the devolution
scheme defined by the Scotland Act 1998, with the possibility of further
evolution in powers; redesigning devolution by adopting a specific range of
extensions to the current powers of the Scottish Parliament and Scottish
government, possibly involving fiscal autonomy, but short of progress to full
independence; extending the powers of the Scottish Parliament and Scottish
government to the point of independence.

The SNP Scottish government was, not surprisingly, in favour of the third
option, which would involve repeal of the 1707 Anglo-Scottish Union.
Much of the White Paper was nonetheless devoted to discussion of the
powers that could be devolved to Edinburgh without thereby dissolving the
UK. It advocated transfer of further powers in areas such as economic and
fiscal policy, employment and trade union law, social security and pensions,
broadcasting, anti-terrorism and firearms law, energy and climate change
policy. The opposition parties were vocal in their condemnation of the

---

[116] SA s.102(3).
[117] SA s.102(4).
[118] R. Hazell and B. O'Leary, "A Rolling Programme of Devolution: Slippery Slope or Safeguard of the Union?", in Hazell, n.82, 23.
[119] Hazell, n.82, 23–26.
[120] *Choosing Scotland's Future: A National Conversation. Independence and Responsibility in the Modern World* (August 2007), available at, www.scotland.gov.uk/Publications/2007/08/13103747/0.

nationalist agenda, but were willing to engage in debate about the best way for devolution to develop.[121]

7–026   In *intergovernmental terms*, the relationship between Scotland, Wales and Westminster is ordered through a Memorandum of Understanding,[122] (MOU) and accompanying Concordats. The MOU is not legally binding,[123] but it is of central importance for establishing the relations between the bodies to whom power has been devolved and Westminster. The MOU provides for communication and consultation between the different administrations, co-operation on areas of mutual interest, and exchange of information. A Joint Ministerial Committee (JMC) has been established to consider, inter alia, non-devolved matters that impinge on devolved responsibilities, and vice versa, the respective treatment of devolved matters in different parts of the UK, and disputes between the administrations. The JMC meets in plenary session once a year, and in sectoral areas, dealing with Europe, Health, the Knowledge Economy and the European Union. The MOU is supplemented by individual Concordats between the Scottish Executive and UK government departments,[124] and between the National Assembly for Wales and such departments. There are also Concordats on issues that cut across particular departments, such as European Union Policy,[125] and International Relations. Intergovernmental mechanisms for resolving conflict and co-ordinating policy are essential in the new order,[126] and similar mechanisms exist in other countries.[127] The intergovernmental machinery was however little used in 2007–2008, in part at least because of frosty relations between the Scottish Government and Westminster.[128]

In *economic terms*, much turns on what happens to the aggregate block grant and whether the Barnett formula is changed. As things stand, the room for policy variation by the Scottish Parliament is limited.[129] This may increase the sense of frustration felt in Scotland and fuel the demands for further reform. This frustration was certainly evident in the introduction to the 2007 Budget and Spending Review by John Swinney, the Scottish Secretary for Finance.[130] To be balanced against this is the fact that Scotland has done relatively well in funding terms, as compared to parts of England.

---

[121] Jack McConnell, Annabel Goldie and Nicol Stephen, "Statement on Independence" (August 13, 2007), available at, http://news.bbc.co.uk/1/hi/scotland/6944185.stm.
[122] *Memorandum of Understanding and Supplementary Agreements between the United Kingdom Government, Scottish Ministers, the Cabinet of the National Assembly for Wales and the Northern Ireland Executive Committee*, Cm. 5240 (2001).
[123] Cm. 5240 (2001), n.122, para.2.
[124] A list of such concordats is available at http://www.scotland.gov.uk/About/concordats.
[125] G. Clark, "Scottish Devolution and the European Union" [1999] P.L. 504.
[126] R. Cornes, "Intergovernmental Relations in a Devolved United Kingdom: Making Devolution Work", in Hazell, n.82, Ch.9; R. Rawlings, "Concordats of the Constitution" (2000) 116 L.Q.R. 257.
[127] J. Poirier, "The Functions of Intergovernmental Agreements: Post-Devolution Concordats in a Comparative Perspective" [2001] P.L. 134.
[128] A. Trench, "Intergovernmental Relations", in C. Jeffrey (ed.), *Scotland Devolution Monitoring Report* (Constitution Unit, January 2008), 61.
[129] A. Trench, "Finance", in Jeffrey (ed.), n.128, 82.
[130] Available at http://www.scotland.gov.uk/News/Releases/2007/11/14081839.

There are nonetheless moves within the Scottish administration to review finance and the Barnett formula.[131]

In *legal terms*, much will turn on the way in which the courts treat challenges to the competence of the Scottish Parliament. The law officers are however likely to be wary of using their power to refer to the Privy Council where a clash between an Act of the Scottish Parliament and a reserved matter is not relatively clear. This is borne out by the Memorandum of Understanding, which states that a reference to the Privy Council on a vires issue will be seen "very much as a matter of last resort".[132] The emphasis is squarely placed on resolving problems through discussion. The very fact that the matter being challenged is an Act of the Scottish Parliament is moreover likely to make the courts wary of finding that its provisions are ultra vires. This is all the more so given the presence of the interpretative obligation contained in the SA, encouraging the courts to give a narrow reading to a provision in Scottish legislation in order to render it legal. The way in which the courts interpret the word "relates" in s.29(2)(b) will be crucial, as will the latitude which the courts allow to the Scottish Parliament through the exception for measures which have only an incidental effect on reserved matters.

It is inevitable nonetheless that the Scottish Parliament will, when framing legislation, have to be aware of the "judge over its shoulders". The Parliament's legal advisers will have to scrutinise Scottish Bills carefully to ensure that they do not impinge on reserved matters. This is equally true of actions of the Scottish Executive. If the courts interpret the list of reserved matters broadly, and give a wide reading to the word "relates", there is a danger that the Scottish Parliament and Executive will feel that their powers are cramped in embryo. The reality thus far is however that most legal challenges raising devolution issues have been concerned with claims that ECHR rights have been infringed,[133] and there has been little litigation concerning the list of reserved matters. The courts have however affirmed that the Scottish Parliament is a creature of statute, and must therefore remain within the limits of its powers. If it does not do so the courts will intervene.[134] The fact that the member of the Scottish Executive in charge of the Bill states that, in his view, it is within the competence of the Scottish Parliament, and that this is affirmed by the Presiding Office, are mere statements of opinion, which do not bind the courts.[135]

[131] Trench, n.129, 87–88.
[132] MOU, n.122, para.26.
[133] See cases in n.39; S.Tierney, "Convention Rights and the Scotland Act: Re-defining Judicial Roles" [2001] P.L. 38; B. Winetrobe, "Scottish Devolved Legislation and the Courts" [2002] P.L. 31.
[134] *Whaley v Lord Watson of Invergowrie* [2000] S.L.T. 475.
[135] *Anderson*, n.39, para.7.

2. WALES

A. The Background

7–027   Proposals for some form of devolution to Wales are not new, but go back
for approximately 100 years.[136] While Gladstone could claim that the distinction between England and Wales was unknown to our constitution, it
was during his period in office that the issue of home rule for Wales began to
emerge. It was no coincidence that this occurred when the franchise was
extended in 1867 and 1884, since this brought politics to many in Wales for
the first time. By the early 1890s Lloyd George was urging home rule for
Wales. This early initiative failed because the Welsh liberals themselves were
divided on the issue, because these divisions grew with the industrialisation
of South Wales, and because this very industrialisation led to the collapse of
the Liberal Party.[137]

   The post-war years saw the growing recognition of Wales as a separate
area of concern within central government. In 1951 a Minister for Welsh
Affairs was established, in 1957 a separate Minister of State was appointed
as the first full-time Minister for Wales, and in 1964 this post was upgraded
to Secretary of State, with the holder being given a place in the Cabinet.

   The attitude of the Labour Party during the 1960s and 1970s was mixed.
It derived considerable support from Wales, which inclined it to take Welsh
concerns seriously, but it also had a strong belief in the need for nationalisation and economic planning, both of which inclined it towards centralisation. A catalyst for central action during this period was the success of
the Scottish National Party, which had achieved this largely at the expense
of the Labour Party.

   A Royal Commission on the Constitution was established, initially under
Lord Crowther, and then under Lord Kilbrandon.[138] The Commission
reported in 1973, shortly before Labour returned to power in 1974. There
was a good deal of disagreement among the members of the Commission,
although they were united in rejecting separation, federalism or the status
quo. A number of different devolution options were suggested.

7–028   The response of the Labour government was to opt for a minimal form of
devolution for Wales. The proposed Assembly was to have executive powers
only, with no power to raise revenue. This model was the basis of the Wales
Act 1978. The entry into force of the Act was, however, predicated on
approval in a referendum by 40 per cent of those who were eligible to vote.
This approval was never forthcoming. The voters rejected the idea of a
Welsh Assembly by four to one.

   Labour returned to power in 1996 after 17 years of Conservative rule. The
Labour Party was committed to devolution as part of its more general
project of constitutional reform. Devolution to Wales was enshrined in the

[136] Constitution Unit, *An Assembly for Wales* (1996).
[137] Constitution Unit (1996), n.136, para.6.
[138] *Report of the Royal Commission on the Constitution, 1969–1973*, Cmnd. 5460 (1973).

Government of Wales Act 1998.[139] A referendum was held in 1997, and on this occasion the voters were in favour of a Welsh Assembly. The margin was, nonetheless, perilously thin. It turned on approximately 7,000 votes out of 1,100,000. The yes vote was 50.3%, the no vote 49.7 per cent, and the turn out a meagre 50.1 per cent.

The GWA 1998 however only provided for executive devolution. The National Assembly for Wales in effect assumed the responsibilities hitherto exercised by the Secretary of State for Wales. In 2002 those exercising executive powers on behalf of the National Assembly adopted the title "Welsh Assembly Government", and appointed a Commission under the chairmanship of Lord Richard to review the operation of devolution in Wales. The Richard Report recommended, inter alia, that the Assembly should be able to make primary legislation for Wales.[140] This was the catalyst for the White Paper on *Better Governance for Wales*,[141] which laid the foundations for the Government of Wales Act 2006, GWA. This legislation now provides the framework for Welsh devolution. Relations between the Welsh Assembly and Welsh Assembly Government, and the UK government continue to be regulated through the Memorandum of Understanding considered above.[142]

B. The Assembly

i. Composition

Section 1 GWA 2006 established the National Assembly for Wales. Ordinary elections for the return of the Assembly normally take place every four years.[143] The Assembly consists of one member for each Assembly constituency, and members for each Assembly electoral region.[144] Voters have two votes.[145] The constituency vote is given for the candidate for an Assembly constituency, election is based on the simple majority system,[146] and Assembly constituencies are the parliamentary constituencies for Wales.[147] The electoral region vote is given for a registered political party that has submitted a list of candidates for the electoral region in which the Assembly constituency is included, or an individual who is a candidate to be

7–029

---

[139] For a valuable account of the early operation of the 1998 Act, R. Rawlings, "The New Model Wales" (1998) 25 J.L.S. 461; R. Rawlings, *Delineating Wales: Constitutional, Legal and Administrative Aspects of National Devolution* (University of Wales Press, 2003).

[140] *Report of the Richard Commission on the Powers and Electoral Arrangements of the National Assembly for Wales* (2004); R. Rawlings, *Say Not the Struggle Naught Availeth: The Richard Commission and after* (Centre for Welsh Legal Affairs, University of Wales, 2004); T. Jones and J. Williams, "The Legislative Future of Wales" (2005) 68 M.L.R. 642.

[141] Cm. 6582 (2005); R. Rawlings, "Hastening Slowly: The Next Phase of Welsh Devolution" [2005] P.L. 824.

[142] N.122; http://new.wales.gov.uk/about/constitutional/memofunderstanding/?lang = en.

[143] GWA 2006 s.3(1).

[144] GWA 2006 s.1(2).

[145] GWA 2006 s.6.

[146] GWA 2006 s.6(4).

[147] GWA 2006 s.2(1).

an Assembly member for that region.[148] There are five electoral regions, each of which returns four members.[149] Voting for electoral regions is based on the additional member system of proportional representation.[150] The result is an Assembly of 60 members, 40 of whom are elected from Assembly constituencies, the other 20 from regions.

ii. Operation

7–030 The procedure of the Assembly is regulated by standing orders.[151] The GWA 2006 mandates a number of important procedural and substantive principles as to the operation of the Assembly. Thus, for example, the English and Welsh languages are to be treated equally,[152] and the Assembly is instructed, when conducting its business, to have due regard to the principle that there should be equality of opportunity for all people.[153] Proceedings of the Assembly are to be held in public.[154] There is an Ombudsman to investigate complaints. There has to be a register of interests of Assembly members, which is open to the public.[155]

The Assembly elects from among its members a Presiding Officer and a Deputy Presiding Officer, who cannot in general be from the same party.[156] There is also a Clerk of the Assembly,[157] and an Assembly Commission, the latter being responsible for ensuring that the Assembly has the requisite staff, services and property.[158] Provision is made for Assembly committees.[159]

C. The Executive

i. Composition

7–031 The GWA 2006 differs from the GWA 1998 in relation to executive power. The scheme in the GWA 1998 was in effect that the executive was constituted as a committee of the Assembly,[160] although there was much in the legislation to suggest that it acted like a cabinet.

The GWA 2006 by way of contrast makes distinct provision for a Welsh Assembly Government. The government consists of the First Minister, Welsh Ministers, Deputy Welsh Ministers and the Counsel General to the Welsh Assembly.[161] The First Minister, who must be a member of the

---

[148] GWA 2006 s.6(3).
[149] GWA 2006 ss.2(2), 2(4).
[150] GWA 2006 s.6(5).
[151] GWA 2006 s.31; *Standing Orders of the National Assembly of Wales* (2007).
[152] GWA 2006 s.35(1).
[153] GWA 2006 s.35(2).
[154] GWA 2006 s.31(5).
[155] GWA 2006 s.36.
[156] GWA 2006 s.25.
[157] GWA 2006 s.26.
[158] GWA 2006 s.27.
[159] GWA 2006 ss.28–30.
[160] GWA 1998 ss 53–56.
[161] GWA 2006 s.45.

Assembly, is appointed by the Queen, after being nominated by the Assembly,[162] and holds office at Her Majesty's pleasure.[163] It is then for the First Minister to appoint the Welsh Ministers from among the Assembly members,[164] with an upper limit of 12 such appointments.[165]

ii. Functions

The GWA 2006 specifies distinct functions for the Welsh Assembly Government. Thus Welsh Ministers have those functions conferred on them by the 2006 Act itself or by any other enactment or prerogative instrument. Many such functions were transferred to the National Assembly for Wales under the GWA 1998, and were effectively exercised by the members of the executive.[166] Under the GWA 2006 executive functions are transferred directly to the Welsh Government.

7–032

When a function is conferred on Welsh Ministers it can be exercised by any of the ministers.[167] There is a mechanism for the transfer to the Welsh ministers, or specifically to the First Minister or to the Counsel General, of functions in relation to Wales which are exercisable by a Minister of the Crown, or for the concurrent exercise of those functions by Welsh Ministers and the Minister of the Crown.[168] Welsh Ministers can be designated under s.2(2) of the European Communities Act 1972 to implement Community obligations.[169] The Welsh Ministers are moreover accorded a broad power to do anything which they consider is appropriate to achieve the promotion of the economic, social or environmental well-being of Wales, [170] and power to take appropriate action in relation to culture, such as buildings of historical or architectural interest.[171] The GWA 2006 also makes provision for liaison mechanisms between the Welsh Assembly Government and local authorities, the voluntary sector and business interests in Wales.[172]

The GWA 2006 imposes obligations as well as powers on the Welsh Assembly Government. Thus it is enjoined to: create a code for regulatory impact assessments; to make arrangements to ensure that their functions are exercised with due regard for equality of opportunity for all people; to adopt a strategy for how it is to promote the Welsh language; and to make a

---

[162] GWA 2006 s.47(1).
[163] GWA 2006 s.46.
[164] GWA 2006 s.48. The appointment of the Counsel General and Deputy Welsh Ministers are dealt with in ss.49–50.
[165] GWA 2006 s.51.
[166] A list of such Transfer of Functions Orders is available at http://new.wales.gov.uk/publications/accessinfo/decisionreport/governmentdrs/governmentdrs2007/1936166/?lang=en The first TFO transferred UK Minister of the Crown functions to the National Assembly for Wales under some 350 Acts and 32 Statutory Instruments, The National Assembly for Wales (Transfer of Functions) Order 1999 (SI 1999/672).
[167] GWA 2006 s.57.
[168] GWA 2006 s.58.
[169] GWA 2006 s.59.
[170] GWA 2006 s.60.
[171] GWA 2006 s.61.
[172] GWA 2006 ss.72–75.

scheme for sustainable development.[173] The Welsh Ministers are also obliged to comply with Community law,[174] and cannot exercise any of their powers if they violate Convention rights.[175] There is further provision dealing with compliance with international obligations.[176]

D. Powers

7–033   The GWA 2006 has enhanced the lawmaking powers of the Assembly, but these still fall short of those accorded to the Scottish Parliament. The schema in the GWA 2006 is as follows.

i. Assembly Measures

7–034   Under the GWA 2006, Pt 3, The Assembly is given power to make laws, which are termed Measures of the National Assembly for Wales,[177] although this does not affect the power of the Parliament of the United Kingdom to make laws for Wales.[178] An Assembly Measure can, in principle, make any provision that could be made by an Act of Parliament.[179] An Assembly Measure is not law so far as any of its provisions fall outside the Assembly's legislative competence.[180] A provision of an Assembly Measure is within the Assembly's legislative competence in two types of case.

First, the provision of an Assembly Measure must relate to one or more of the matters specified in Pt 1 of Sch.5, and not apply outside Wales.[181] Second, a provision of an Assembly Measure may alternatively fall within the Assembly's competence if it provides for the enforcement of a provision that is within the Assembly's competence, or it is otherwise appropriate for making such a provision effective, or it is otherwise incidental to, or consequential on, such a provision.[182]

A provision which satisfies one of the two preceding conditions will nonetheless fall outside the Assembly's legislative competence if: it breaches any of the restrictions in Pt 2 of Sch.5, subject to exceptions in Pt 3 of that Schedule; it extends otherwise than only to England and Wales; or it is incompatible with Convention rights or with Community law.[183]

---

[173] GWA 2006 ss.76–79.
[174] GWA 2006 s.80.
[175] GWA 2006 s.81.
[176] GWA 2006 s.82.
[177] GWA 2006 s.93.
[178] GWA 2006 s.93(5).
[179] GWA 2006 s.94(1).
[180] GWA 2006 s.94(2).
[181] GWA 2006 s.94(4).
[182] GWA 2006 s.94(5).
[183] GWA 2006 s.94(6).

The nature of this legislative competence requires a further word by way of explanation. The general fields specified in Sch.5 Pt 1, are broad, and include many prominent areas of governmental activity.[184] The GWA 2006 does not however generally confer new legislative powers on the Assembly, but creates a mechanism whereby this can occur. Thus if the Assembly wishes to be able to legislate on, for example, child care, fostering and adoption, or social care for young persons, it will have to promote what is termed a legislative competence order, LCO.[185] This is a statutory instrument which must be approved by the Assembly and the Westminster Parliament.[186] The content of the LCO constitutes an amendment to Sch.5 Pt 1, stating that the general field of, for example, social welfare should now have certain "matters" specified to enable the Assembly to legislate in relation to child care, fostering and adoption etc., each of which will be specified as a separate matter on which the Assembly has legislative competence.[187] If the LCO is approved the Assembly Measures passed thereafter on that topic partake of the nature of laws pursuant to GWA 2006 s.93.[188]

An alternative way in which the Assembly can be given power over certain "matters" to enable it to enact Assembly Measures is for a statute enacted by the Westminster Parliament to accord it such power. The statutory provisions will take the form of amendments to the GWA 2006 Sch.5, by specifying the "matters" within the relevant field over which the Assembly can then enact Assembly Measures.[189]

ii. Assembly Acts

The GWA 2006 also makes provision for more far-reaching law-making power for the Assembly. The GWA 2006, Pt 4, makes provision for the Assembly to have primary legislative powers across the broad range of the subjects in Pt 1 of Sch.7, without the need for further recourse to Parliament. Thus if Pt 4 of the 2006 GWA becomes operative there would be no need to seek authorisation for a particular exercise of legislative competence in the manner described above in relation to Assembly Measures, and Pt 3 of the GWA 2006 would become redundant.

In order for Pt 4 of the GWA 2006 to become operative there must be a

7–035

---

[184] Agriculture, fisheries, forestry and rural development; ancient monuments and historic buildings; culture; economic development; education and training; environment; fire and rescue services and promotion of fire safety; food; health and health services; highways and transport; housing; local government; National Assembly for Wales; public administration; social welfare; sport and recreation; tourism; town and country planning; water and flood defence; Welsh language.

[185] National Assembly for Wales, *A Guide to the Legislative Process in the National Assembly for Wales* (2007), available at http://www.assemblywales.org/guide_to_the_legislative_process-2.pdf.

[186] GWA 2006 s.95.

[187] For examples of LCOs being considered, see http://www.assemblywales.org/bus-home/bus-legislation/bus-leg-legislative-competence-orders/bus-legislation-lco-2007-3.htm.

[188] The procedure for enactment of Assembly Measures is set out in GWA 2006 ss.97–102.

[189] See, e.g., Local Government and Public Involvement in Health Act 2007 s.235, Sch.17; Further Education and Training Act 2007 s.27.

referendum.[190] The Order in Council providing for such a referendum must be approved by two-thirds of the Assembly and both Houses of Parliament. If this were to occur and the referendum voted in favour of the change, the Assembly would then have primary legislative powers so as to be able to make law on all subjects within its devolved fields, as delineated in Sch.7, subject to the conditions listed in ss.107–108 GWA 2006.

However by way of contrast to the Scotland Act 1998, the GWA 2006 defines the scope of the Assembly's legislative powers after a referendum by listing the subjects in relation to which the Assembly would be able to make law, rather than only listing those areas outside its legislative competence. Assembly legislation made in exercise of this "primary" legislative power will be known as Acts of the National Assembly for Wales.[191]

iii. Subordinate legislation

7–036   We should also consider powers in relation to subordinate legislation, which will be made pursuant to an Act of Parliament, or in due course to an Assembly measure. It should be remembered, as stated above, that many functions were transferred to the National Assembly pursuant to Transfer of Functions Orders.[192] The GWA 1998 provided for the transfer of functions of the Minister of the Crown in relation to Wales to the Assembly.[193] The GWA 2006 now accords the power to make such subordinate legislation to the Welsh ministers and there are transitional provisions specifying that Assembly functions over such legislation are transferred to the Welsh ministers.[194] The subordinate legislation will normally be subject to either the affirmative procedure, requiring Assembly approval before it takes effect, or the negative procedure, requiring the Assembly to active steps to annul the measure.[195] The scrutiny is undertaken by the Subordinate Legislation Committee.

iv. The Assembly and other bodies

7–037   Certain provisions from the GWA 1998 were not repealed by the GWA 2006. Thus s.28 GWA 1998 grants the Assembly power by order to transfer one or more of the statutory functions of a body specified in Sch.4. The section in effect allows the transfer of functions to another of the bodies listed in the Schedule, sometimes requiring the consent of the body that loses out, on other occasions not making this a requirement.[196] The section also sanctions the transfer to a local authority, or to the Assembly itself.[197]

---

[190] GWA 2006 s.103, Sch.6.
[191] GWA 2006 ss.107–108.
[192] n.166.
[193] GWA 1998 s.22.
[194] GWA 2006 Sch.11 para.30, subject to para.31.
[195] For relevant measures, see http://www.assemblywales.org/bus-home/bus-legislation/bus-legislation-sub.htm.
[196] GWA 1998 s.28(1)(a)–(b).
[197] GWA 1998 s.28(1)(c)–(d).

E. Judicial Challenge

The Assembly and Welsh Government have limited powers and the GWA 2006 makes provision for legal challenge in order to ensure that they do not stray beyond their respective powers.[198] The rules are contained in Sch.9 para.1(1) of which defines the phrase "devolution issue" to mean— **7–038**

"(a) a question whether an Assembly Measure or Act of the Assembly, or any provision of an Assembly Measure or Act of the Assembly, is within the Assembly's legislative competence,

(b) a question whether any function (being a function which any person has purported, or is proposing, to exercise) is exercisable by the Welsh Ministers, the First Minister or the Counsel General,

(c) a question whether the purported or proposed exercise of a function by the Welsh Ministers, the First Minister or the Counsel General is, or would be, within the powers of the Welsh Ministers, the First Minister or the Counsel General (including a question whether a purported or proposed exercise of a function is, or would be, outside those powers by virtue of section 80(8) or 81(1)),

(d) a question whether there has been any failure to comply with a duty imposed on the Welsh Ministers, the First Minister or the Counsel General (including any obligation imposed by virtue of section 80(1) or (7)), or

(e) a question of whether a failure to act by the Welsh Ministers, the First Minister or the Counsel General is incompatible with any of the Convention rights."

It is possible that there will be attempts to challenge competence where there is no real foundation for the argument. The GWA 2006 makes provision for this eventuality by providing that a devolution issue shall not be taken to arise in any proceedings merely because it is raised by one of the parties. The court or tribunal can disregard the issue if the claim is frivolous or vexatious.[199]

A devolution issue may arise in proceedings that are begun in England and Wales, Scotland, or Northern Ireland. The GWA makes provision for all these jurisdictional possibilities. The discussion will concentrate on the rules that apply where a devolution issue arises in England and Wales. The applicable rules where the case is heard in Scotland or Northern Ireland are not different in principle. There are a number of different ways in which devolution issues can come before the courts.

---

[198] For discussion of analogous provisions under the GWA 1998, P. Craig and M. Walters, "The Courts, Devolution and Judicial Review" [1999] P.L. 274.
[199] GWA 2006 Sch.9 para.2.

i. Direct reference to the Supreme Court

7–039 A devolution issue can be resolved by direct reference of the matter to what will become the Supreme Court. This can occur in three types of case.

First, there is the possibility of *pre-enactment challenge and scrutiny*. The Attorney-General or the Counsel General may, pursuant to Sch.9 para.30(1), refer to the Supreme Court any devolution issue which is not the subject of civil or criminal proceedings. Paragraph 30(2) states that where a reference is made under para.30(1) by the Attorney-General in relation to a devolution issue which relates to the proposed exercise of a function by the Welsh Ministers, the First Minister or the Counsel General, the Attorney-General must notify the Counsel General of that fact, and the function must not be exercised by the Welsh Ministers, the First Minister or the Counsel General in the manner proposed during the period beginning with the receipt of the notification and ending with the reference being decided or otherwise disposed of.

Second, it is clear that there can be *post-enactment challenge even where the devolution issue has not arisen in independent proceedings*. This follows from the wording of para.30(1). Thus the Assembly may have passed certain subordinate legislation, which is later felt to have exceeded the bounds of its powers under a Transfer of Functions Order. The matter can be referred to the Supreme Court by the Attorney-General or Counsel General, even though the subordinate legislation has not been contested in any other proceedings.

Third, it is open to the *Attorney-General or Counsel General to require a court or tribunal to transfer a case to the Supreme Court*. Paragraph 29(1) of Sch.9 authorises the Attorney-General or Counsel General to require any court or tribunal to refer to the Supreme Court any devolution issue which has arisen in any proceedings before it to which he is a party. Courts and tribunals are under an obligation to give notice of devolution issues that arise in any proceedings to the Attorney-General and the Counsel General.[200] The person or body given notice is entitled to take part in the proceedings so far as they relate to the devolution issue.[201]

ii. Institution of proceedings by a law officer

7–040 The GWA allows the Attorney-General or Counsel General to institute proceedings for the determination of a devolution issue.[202] The law officer has the power to require the devolution issue to be referred to the Supreme Court, as described above, but may choose not to exercise this power.

iii. Reference through other courts

7–041 A devolution issue can also arise before a court that is empowered by the GWA to refer the matter on to another court. The relevant rules distinguish

[200] GWA 2006 Sch.9 para.5(1).
[201] GWA 2006 Sch.9 para.5(2).
[202] GWA 2006 Sch.9 para.4.

between civil and criminal proceedings. The rules discussed within this section relate to referral. It is the devolution issue that is referred to the higher court. Once this matter has been decided the case returns to the lower court for final resolution of the case. There will, however, be cases where the resolution of the devolution issue will be conclusive for the entire dispute.

The rules on civil proceedings are that a magistrate's court may refer a devolution issue to the High Court.[203] A court may refer a devolution issue that arises in civil proceedings to the Court of Appeal,[204] but this does not apply to a magistrates' court, the Court of Appeal or the Supreme Court, nor to the High Court taking a reference from a magistrates' court pursuant to para.6.[205] Civil proceedings are defined by the Act to mean any proceedings other than criminal proceedings.[206] It therefore includes proceedings for judicial review.

If the devolution issue arises in criminal proceedings then a court, other than the Court of Appeal or the Supreme Court, may refer the issue to the High Court in the case of summary proceedings, or to the Court of Appeal if the proceedings are on indictment.[207]

It is open to the Court of Appeal to refer a devolution issue that has come before it other than by way of reference from a lower court on to the Supreme Court.[208] This option will be open to it where the devolution issue emerges in proceedings before the Court of Appeal itself.

The discussion thus far has concentrated on courts. Tribunals are treated somewhat differently. A tribunal from which there is no appeal must refer the devolution issue to the Court of Appeal. Where there is an appeal from the tribunal's findings it has discretion to refer, but does not have a duty to do so.[209]

Provision is made for an appeal against a determination of a devolution issue by the High Court or the Court of Appeal when a reference has been made to those courts in the manner described above. The appeal lies to the Supreme Court, but only with the permission of the court concerned, or failing such permission, with special permission from the Judicial Committee.[210]

iv. Decisions made by the court immediately seized of the matter
The provisions described above give courts discretion whether to refer a **7–042** devolution issue. They do not have the duty to do so. The court before which the issue is raised is therefore entitled, subject to the discussion below,

---

[203] GWA 2006 Sch.9 para.6.
[204] GWA 2006 Sch.9 para.7(1).
[205] GWA 2006 Sch.9 para.7(2).
[206] GWA 2006 Sch.9 para.1(2).
[207] GWA 2006 Sch.9 para.9.
[208] GWA 2006 Sch.9 para.10.
[209] GWA 2006 Sch.9 para.8.
[210] GWA 2006 Sch.9 para.11.

to decide the case for itself. Thus the High Court exercising its judicial review jurisdiction may well feel able to resolve devolution issues,[211] and be wary, moreover, of overburdening the Court of Appeal through too ready an exercise of the referral power. The discretion of the court seized of the matter to hear the case is qualified to the extent that the Attorney-General or Counsel General may, as discussed above, require the case to be referred to the Supreme Court.

v. The relevance of the general law on collateral challenge

7–043   Schedule 9 GWA 2006 is framed in terms of devolution issues "arising" before a particular court. It is clear that such issues may arise directly, as in the context of a judicial review action. There will, subject to the normal rules on such actions, be no difficulty about raising the vires of action by the Assembly or Welsh Government in this manner.

Devolution issues may also arise indirectly. There will be collateral challenges where, for example, the applicant claims that subordinate legislation being applied against him is ultra vires, and should not therefore be enforced. Recent decisions of the courts have been more liberal in allowing collateral challenge, although there are still some uncertainties.[212] The courts' more liberal attitude to collateral challenge should mean that if the general legal rules on collateral challenge are applied, claimants will normally be able to raise vires issues indirectly as well as directly.

vi. The effect of a finding that the Assembly or Welsh Government lacked power

7–044   The GWA 2006 deals with acts of the Assembly or the Welsh Government that are ultra vires in a number of ways.

The Secretary of State has broad powers to initiate the making of a statutory instrument, which can modify any enactment or instrument that lies beyond the legislative competence of the Assembly.[213] There is a further broad power to remedy ultra vires acts by Order in Council.[214]

The GWA 2006 also makes provision for what is to happen if a court or a tribunal decides that the Assembly or Welsh Government did not have the power to make the relevant measure. The basic assumption behind s.153 is that the decision of the court or tribunal finding the lack of power renders the measure retrospectively null. Section 153(2) empowers the court or tribunal to make an order removing or limiting any retrospective effect of the decision, or suspending the effect of the decision for any period and on any conditions to allow the defect to be corrected. In deciding whether to make such an order the court or tribunal is to have regard to, inter alia, the extent

---

[211] See, e.g., *South Wales Sea Fisheries Committee v National Assembly for Wales* [2001] EWHC Admin 1162.
[212] See below, Ch.26.
[213] GWA 2006 s.150.
[214] GWA 2006 s.151.

to which persons who are not parties to the proceedings would otherwise be adversely affected by the decision.[215] When considering making such an order the court etc. must give notice of that fact to the relevant law officer, unless they are already party to the proceedings. They can join the proceedings so far as they relate to the making of the order.[216]

F. Welsh Devolution: Some Reflections

It is clear that Welsh devolution has evolved since 1998, and that the foundations of the 2006 legislation differ from those of the GWA 1998.   **7–045**

The GWA 1998 conferred formal powers on the Assembly, and not on the individual members of the Executive Committee.[217] Notwithstanding this, the GWA inclined strongly towards a cabinet model, with the executive role being taken by the Executive Committee. The provisions of the Act were premised on this Committee taking such a role, and the extensive powers to delegate authority to it served to reinforce this. The cabinet image of the Executive Committee was fostered by the National Assembly Advisory Group (NAAG), the recommendations of which fostered the image of the Executive Committee as Assembly cabinet.[218] The standing orders reinforced the cabinet model.[219] Rawlings captures the shift of power when speaking of the rapid emergence of a "virtual parliament" in Wales and the de facto development inside the corporate body of a divide between the executive in the guise of the Welsh Assembly Government and the representative institution as a whole.[220] He notes moreover that when viewed in this way the architectural proposals in the White Paper that set the ground for the 2006 GWA were largely derivative in nature, "whereby London plays catch up with, as well as usefully building on, the institutional dynamics in Cardiff, so giving them formal legal recognition".[221]

The 2006 GWA represents a step forward in terms of Welsh devolution, albeit a somewhat hesitant one. The Assembly and the Welsh Assembly Government are formally separated. The Assembly is accorded law-making power via the technique of Assembly Measures described above, and potentially can be accorded fuller law making competence to pass Assembly Acts. The Welsh Assembly Government assumes in formal terms many of the traditional executive functions within a devolved body, and is accorded power over subordinate legislation, subject to scrutiny by the Assembly. It remains to be seen how this new schema works in practice.

The early indications are that there is not going to be any flood of legislative competence orders being promoted by the Assembly, in order to

---

[215] GWA 2006 s.153(3).
[216] GWA 2006 ss.153(4)–(6).
[217] GWA 1998 s.22.
[218] National Assembly Advisory Group, *Report to the Secretary of State for Wales* (August 1998), Section 2, paras 7, 19, 21 32.
[219] *Standing Orders of the National Assembly of Wales* (2002).
[220] R. Rawlings, "Law Making in a Virtual Parliament", in R. Hazell and R. Rawlings (eds), *Devolution, Law Making and the Constitution* (Imprint Academic, 2005).
[221] Rawlings, n.141, 825.

increase the scope of Assembly legislative competence and enable it to pass Assembly Measures in the relevant areas. There were, at the time of writing, six such orders under consideration.[222] It should nonetheless be recognised that once such an order is approved the Assembly then possesses legislative competence to pass Assembly Measures on that topic thereafter, and in that sense each LCO that is approved by the Assembly and by the Westminster Parliament augments the overall area in which the Assembly can legislate. It should also be noted that Westminster legislation has fleshed out Sch.5, specifying "matters" within fields such as education and local authorities over which the Assembly can then enact Assembly Measures.[223]

7–046   The impact of any particular LCO in expanding the legislative competence of the Assembly will be markedly affected by the breadth of definition of the "matters" that are thereby brought within the Assembly's competence. These may be broadly or narrowly defined. An example of relatively broad definition is the proposed LCO on vulnerable children,[224] which specifies eight "matters" to come within the general field of social welfare. These are: safeguarding children from harm and neglect; fostering and adoption; social care for children and the persons who care for them; social care for young persons; co-operation between those who look after vulnerable children; strategic planning by local authorities in relation to the well-being of children and young persons; continuance, dissolution or creation of, and conferral of functions on, an office or body concerned with safeguarding and promoting the well-being of children or young persons; and the promotion of equality between children and young persons in relation to their well-being. It is clear that if this LCO is approved by the Assembly and Westminster Parliament it will effectively bring a broad area of social policy concerning all facets of child care within the remit of the Assembly, thereby enabling it to pass Assembly Measures. A further example of relatively broad definition of "matters" over which the Assembly can then enact Assembly Measures is to be found in relation to local authorities.[225]

The provisions of the GWA 2006 enabling legislative competence to be enhanced therefore clearly have potential. This should not however mask the current reality that the principal legislative business continues to be the passage of subordinate legislation, which is under the control of the Welsh Assembly Government, subject to scrutiny by the subordinate legislation committee. The great majority of this subordinate legislation is moreover subject to the negative resolution procedure,[226] which thereby limits the reality of Assembly control.

The likely use to be made of the law-making powers in the 2006 GWA

---

[222] http://www.assemblywales.org/bus-home/bus-legislation/bus-leg-legislative-competence-orders.htm.

[223] n.189.

[224] Proposed National Assembly for Wales (Legislative Competence) (No.3) Order 2007 (Relating to Vulnerable Children).

[225] Local Government and Public Involvement in Health Act 2007 s.235, Sch.17.

[226] http://www.assemblywales.org/bus-home/bus-legislation/bus-legislation-sub.htm.

should now be seen in the light of the policy statement issued by the coalition Labour and Plaid Cymru government.[227] They expressed a joint commitment to use the GWA 2006 provisions to the full under Pt 3, and to proceed with a referendum for full law-making powers under Pt 4, as soon as practicable, at or before the end of the Assembly term. Both parties agreed to campaign for a successful outcome to such a referendum. They agreed also to set up an all-Wales Convention within six months. A group from both parties would be commissioned to set the terms of reference and membership of the Convention based on wide representation from civic society. Both political parties would then take account of the success of the bedding down of the use of the new legislative powers already available and "assess the levels of support for full law-making powers necessary to trigger the referendum".[228]

---

[227] An Agreement between the Labour and Plaid Cymru Groups in the National Assembly, *A Progressive Agenda for the Government of Wales* (2007), 6.
[228] *A Progressive Agenda for the Government of Wales*, n.227, 6.

CHAPTER 8

INFORMATION, STANDARDS AND COMPLAINTS

The flourishing of a healthy democracy, in which governmental organs are **8–001** accountable for their actions, will always depend upon a range of factors. There are nonetheless certain factors that generally enhance accountability, irrespective of the specific nature of the institution in question.

This chapter will examine three such matters: access to information, standards in public life and complaints machinery, principally in the form of the Ombudsman model. These issues are central to the relationship between government and governed. Access to information is vital if there is to be an informed public, which can participate in public life and hold the government to account. Standards of propriety are equally essential, since if they are not adhered to then public trust in the soundness of governmental policy will suffer. Mechanisms whereby individuals can voice complaints outside of the traditional court system have come to play an increasingly important role in monitoring the administration of government policy.

There is a micro and macro perspective to the issues addressed in this chapter. The former focuses primarily on the position of the specific individual, whether this is as seeker of information, target of a complaint of breach of standards, or applicant who seeks redress for maladministration. The macro perspective looks to more systemic concerns and seeks to address them. In the context of access to information, this may be the desire to combat a culture of secrecy and to foster citizen participation in public life. In relation to standards of government, it will be apparent in initiatives designed to imbue an ethical code among those in power, and to structure appointments so as to maximise transparency and opportunity. In the context of complaints machinery, it becomes apparent in the debate as to whether the Parliamentary Commissioner for Administration should be able to conduct more general administrative audits, as well as being able to respond to individual applicants.

1. Freedom of Information: Rationale and Background

A. The Rationale for Freedom of Information

8–002   Access to information and openness is of crucial importance in ensuring the accountability of government. We have not until recently had any general freedom of information legislation such as exists within many other countries.[1] It is important to consider both the reasons for such legislation, and its effectiveness.

The most prominent *reasons* for freedom of information legislation are as follows. First, and most fundamental, it is felt that access to information concerning governmental decision-making is central to the idea of a democratic society. Government should be accountable for its action, and this is difficult if it has a "monopoly" over the available information. Second, individual citizens should be able to know the information held about them in order to check its correctness and the uses to which it is put. Third, public disclosure of information will, it is hoped, improve decision-making.

The *effectiveness* of any such legislation is dependent upon a number of variables. We need to consider the range of *exceptions* contained in the legislation, and the way in which these are interpreted. The effectiveness of such legislation will also be dependent on the *way it is administered*. Thus the original American legislation was modified in 1974 to meet problems arising from agency delay in responding to requests for documents. The amended legislation set time limits within which the documents must be produced, and subjected officials who arbitrarily withheld information to disciplinary proceedings. The cost of using the system, and the way in which the material is presented to the individual, will also be important in determining the utility of the scheme.[2]

B. The Move towards Freedom of Information Legislation in the UK

8–003   Legislation to ensure freedom of information was long overdue in this country.[3] Specific statutes had some impact,[4] but these were no substitute for more general legislation of the kind that exists in many other countries.[5]

---

[1] P. Birkinshaw, *Freedom of Information, The Law, the Practice and the Ideal* (Butterworths, 3rd edn, 2001); P. Birkinshaw, *Government and Information: The Law Relating to Access, Disclosure and Their Regulation* (Tottel, 3rd edn, 2005).

[2] Birkinshaw, *Freedom of Information*, n.1, Ch.2.

[3] Birkinshaw, *Freedom of Information*, n.1, Ch.3.

[4] Data Protection Act 1984; R. Austin "The Data Protection Act 1984: The Public Law Implications" [1984] P.L. 618; Local Government (Access to Information) Act 1985; P. Birkinshaw, *Open Government, Freedom of Information and Local Government* (Local Government Legal Society Trust, 1986); Access to Personal Files Act (1987); Data Protection Act 1998.

[5] The related, but distinct, topic concerning the extent to which a government employee can reveal information obtained in confidence cannot be examined here. See, Y. Cripps, "Disclosure in the Public Interest; The Predicament of the Public Sector Employee" [1983] P.L. 600; *Att.-Gen v Guardian Newspapers Ltd (No.2)* [1990] 1 A.C. 109.

The Campaign for Freedom of Information published a draft Bill designed to provide general access to information.[6] Various arguments were nonetheless advanced against a Freedom of Information Act. It was argued that such legislation was unnecessary; that it would interfere with the effectiveness of government; that it would somehow subvert the ordinary democratic process; and that it would be too costly.[7] These arguments were unconvincing. For example, in relation to the contention that such legislation would interfere with the efficiency of government, Birkinshaw states,[8]

"Quite frankly, this argument has no support from the evidence of those countries where FOI operates. Organizing sections of the administration to facilitate responses to requests from citizens for information about their government and its operations is a small price to pay for treating citizens as citizens and not as subjects."

The Conservative government evinced some concern for greater openness and transparency, as exemplified by the Citizen's Charter, which had openness as one of its central principles: there should be no secrecy about how public services are run, how much they cost and whether they are meeting their standards.[9] This theme was taken up in the White Paper on *Open Government*,[10] which built upon the Charter initiatives.[11] It established a Code of Practice on Access to Government Information. The Code of Practice[12] was applicable to all departments, agencies and authorities within the jurisdiction of the Parliamentary Commissioner for Administration (PCA). It allowed access to facts and analysis which the government considered relevant and important when framing major policy proposals and decisions; explanatory material on departments' dealings with the public, including rules and procedures; the reasons for decisions; and information relating to the running of the public services. This access was qualified by exceptions relating to matters such as defence, security and international relations, internal policy discussion, and effective management of the public service. The Parliamentary Commissioner for Administration adjudicated on complaints relating to breach of the Code. The Code did not however establish any general legal right to access to government information.

---

[6] M. Frankel, *A Freedom of Information Act for Britain* (Campaign for Freedom of Information, 1991).

[7] P. Birkinshaw, "Citizenship and Privacy", in R. Blackburn (ed.), *Rights of Citizenship* (Mansell, 1993), 43–47; Birkinshaw, *Freedom of Information*, n.1, Ch.4.

[8] Birkinshaw, *Freedom of Information*, n.1, 46.

[9] *The Citizen's Charter, Raising the Standard*, Cm. 1599 (1991), 5.

[10] Cm. 2290 (1993).

[11] P. Birkinshaw, "'I only ask for information'—The White Paper on Open Government" [1993] P.L. 557.

[12] Home Office, *Open Government, Code of Practice on Access to Government Information* (2nd edn, 1997).

2. The Freedom of Information Act 2000

8–004 The Labour government came to power committed to legislation on freedom of information, and published a White Paper on the subject.[13] The legislation took longer to emerge than was initially thought, and it was vigorously criticised for taking a more limited view of freedom of information than the White Paper.[14] Different sections of the Act come into force at different times.

Section 1(1) of the Freedom of Information Act 2000 (FOIA) established the *basic right*. It provides that any person making a request for information to a public authority is entitled to be informed in writing by the public authority whether it holds information of the description specified in the request, and if that is the case to have that information communicated to him. This is termed the duty to confirm or deny. The public authority must comply with the request promptly and in any event, subject to exceptions, within 20 days from the date of the request.[15] The basic right is however qualified by other provisions of the FOIA. Thus s.1(3) states that where a public authority reasonably requires further information to identify and locate the information, and has told the applicant of that requirement, the authority is not obliged to comply with s.1(1) unless it is supplied with that information. The basic right is further qualified by s.2. This, in effect, excludes it in relation to the exempted categories listed in Pt II of the FOIA. This is so either where a provision of Part II confers absolute exemption, or where, in all the circumstances of the case, the public interest in maintaining the exemption outweighs the public interest in disclosing whether the public authority holds the information, or in disclosing that information.[16] The force of the basic right is further limited by the fact that a fee may be charged,[17] and the public authority may refuse to supply information where the cost of compliance would exceed the "appropriate limit".[18] There are also provisions dealing with vexatious or repeated requests.[19]

The FOIA applies to *public authorities*, s.3. The term public authority is broadly defined. It covers any body listed in Sch.1. The list is extensive, and can be amended by the Secretary of State. The term public authority also covers publicly-owned companies.

Public authorities have a duty to maintain *publication schemes*, which must be approved by the Information Commissioner.[20] The duty requires

---

[13] *Your Right to Know, The Government's Proposals for a Freedom of Information Act*, Cm. 3818 (1997).

[14] Birkinshaw, *Freedom of Information*, n.1, Ch.6.

[15] Freedom of Information Act 2000 s.10.

[16] Information Commissioner's Office, *Freedom of Information Act, Awareness Guide No 3, The Public Interest Test* (2007), available at http://www.ico.gov.uk/what_we_cover/freedom_of_information/guidance.aspx.

[17] Freedom of Information Act 2000 s.9.

[18] Freedom of Information Act 2000 s.12; the basic figure is £600, Freedom of Information and Data Protection (Appropriate Limit and Fees) Regulations 2004 (SI 2004/3244), reg 3.

[19] Freedom of Information Act 2000 s.14.

[20] Freedom of Information Act 2000 s.19.

public authorities to adopt and maintain a scheme relating to the publication of information by that authority. The scheme must specify classes of information that the authority publishes, the manner in which this is to be done, and whether a fee is to be charged. The Information Commissioner may approve model publication schemes.[21]

Part II of the FOIA specifies the categories of *exempt information*, thereby qualifying the basic right in s.1. Information that is reasonably accessible by other means is exempted, as is information intended for future publication.[22] There are exemptions for information held by security bodies, and information required for the purposes of safeguarding national security.[23] There are other exemptions dealing, inter alia, with defence, international relations, relations within the UK, the economy, investigations conducted by public authorities, law enforcement, court functions, audit functions, parliamentary privilege, the formulation of government policy, and the disclosure of information that would be prejudicial to the effective conduct of public affairs, personal information and information given in confidence. It is readily apparent that the efficacy of any scheme for freedom of information will depend in part on the range of exemptions. The list of exemptions contained in the FOIA is long. A number of the exemptions, such as that dealing with the formulation of government policy, are very broad. Moreover, the general formula used in the FOIA is that information can be withheld if its disclosure would, or would be likely to, prejudice the interest specified in the exempt category. This is by way of contrast to earlier formulations, where the criterion had been "substantial prejudice". The breadth of the exemptions is compounded, as we shall see below, by the "enforcement override" that the Act accords to certain public bodies.

8–005

The freedom of information scheme is *administered* by the Information Commissioner,[24] IC, and the Information Tribunal,[25] IT.[26] The Ministry of Justice has overall responsibility for policy in this area. The IC has a number of general duties to promote the observance by public authorities of the requirements of the FOIA.[27] The IC also has more specific enforcement functions. The IC, having received a complaint, can decide that a public authority has not complied with its duty under s.1.[28] Where this is so, the IC can serve an enforcement notice on the public authority,[29] which can be further enforced through contempt proceedings in the High Court.[30] There

[21] Freedom of Information Act 2000 s.20.

[22] Freedom of Information Act 2000 ss.21–22.

[23] Freedom of Information Act 2000 ss.23–24.

[24] http://www.ico.gov.uk/.

[25] http://www.informationtribunal.gov.uk/; The Information Tribunal (Enforcement Appeals) Rules 2005 (SI 2005/14).

[26] Freedom of Information Act 2000 s.18.

[27] Freedom of Information Act 2000 ss.47–49.

[28] Freedom of Information Act 2000 ss.50–51.

[29] Freedom of Information Act 2000 s.52. The IC issued an enforcement notice in relation to discovery of information about the Attorney-General's advice concerning military intervention in Iraq, available at http://www.ico.gov.uk/what_we_cover/freedom_of_information/enforcement.aspx.

[30] Freedom of Information Act 2000 s.54.

are provisions for appeals from the IC to the IT.[31] The IC's enforcement power is however subject to an important limitation. It is open to certain bodies, including government departments, to override the IC. An accountable person within such a body can attest that in relation to the provision of exempt information, he has reasonable grounds to believe that there was no breach of s.1.[32] This means that the IC's assessment of whether the disclosure of information in an exempt category would be prejudicial to the relevant interest is subject to departmental override.

3. STANDARDS OF CONDUCT IN PUBLIC LIFE

A. Cash, Sleaze and Concerns: The Development of the Administrative Machinery

8–006   Over the last 15 years we have seen the emergence of administrative institutions designed to regulate the standards of conduct in public life. The origin of this machinery is interesting.[33] In 1994 the Committee of Privileges published a Report on what became known as cash for questions, the practice whereby an MP would table a question in the House of Commons in return for payment. The Committee not surprisingly took a dim view of this practice.[34] Concerns over standards of conduct in public life were further fuelled by other issues that occurred at this time. There was the dubious practice whereby one MP would table amendments to Bills before the House in the name of other MPs without their consent. There was the general sense that "sleaze" had infected government, and there was a feeling that ministers and civil servants had not always behaved with due propriety in the Matrix Churchill affair which led to the Scott Inquiry.

These concerns led to the establishment in 1994 of the Committee on Standards in Public Life under the chairmanship of Lord Nolan, a Law Lord. This is a standing committee of the House of Commons the work of which will be examined below. Suffice it to say for the present that it developed a programme for inquiry into standards in public life, but the Committee did not look into individual cases. The first report from the Nolan Committee contained a number of recommendations relating to the conduct of MPs and the like. It was the catalyst for the House of Commons to establish a Select Committee on Standards in Public Life to consider the Nolan Report. The House of Commons accepted most of the recommendations from the Select Committee. This in turn led to the creation of a new Select Committee on Standards and Privileges, which took over the role of the Select Committee on Privileges and Members' Interests.

---

[31] Freedom of Information Act 2000 ss.57–61.
[32] Freedom of Information Act 2000 s.53.
[33] D. Oliver, "Standards of Conduct in Public Life—What Standards?" [1995] P.L. 497.
[34] Committee of Privileges, *Complaint Concerning an Article in the "Sunday Times" of July 10, 1994 relating to the Conduct of Members* (HC 351; 1994–95).

It also led to the establishment of a Parliamentary Commissioner for Standards (PCS), and a Commissioner for Public Appointments (CPA).

The regulation of standards in public life is now to be found in the work of the Committee on Standards, the Select Committee on Standards and Privileges, the PCS and the CPA. The interrelationship between these bodies is itself interesting. The Committee on Standards focuses on standards at the macro level, and does not consider individual cases. The PCS and the Select Committee will consider issues at the macro level, but they will also investigate specific allegations of a breach of standards. We shall begin by looking more closely at the important work of the Committee on Standards in Public Life.

B. The Committee on Standards

There has always been much in the constitutional life of the UK that has been regulated not by statute, but by convention, practice and the rules of the game. The work of the Committee on Standards exemplifies this tradition.[35] Its original terms of reference in 1994 were to examine current concerns about standards of conduct of all holders of public office, including arrangements relating to financial and commercial activities. It was to make recommendations as to any changes that might be required to ensure the highest standards of propriety in public life.

8–007

The Committee's First Report[36] was wide ranging. It began by identifying "seven principles of public life", which were to apply to all those who worked in the public sphere: selflessness, integrity, objectivity, accountability, openness, honesty and leadership.[37] It recommended that there should be Codes of Conduct drawn up by public bodies, which incorporated these principles, and that such internal systems for the maintenance of standards should be supported by external scrutiny. It felt also that more should be done by way of education to inculcate and reinforce standards of conduct in public bodies. These general recommendations were complemented by more detailed proposals relating to various parts of government.

In relation to MPs, the proposals were directed principally at the probity of contacts between MPs and those outside the House. The Report recommended that there should be full disclosure by MPs of their consultancy agreements and payments, and that the Register of Members' Interests should be more informative. A Parliamentary Commissioner for Standards should be appointed, who would have responsibility for advising and guiding MPs on their conduct.

In relation to ministers, the Report recommended that allegations of misconduct made against a particular minister should be investigated promptly. A minister should not, on leaving office, take up a position with a

---

[35] http://www.public-standards.gov.uk/.
[36] *First Report from the Committee on Standards in Public Life*, Cm. 2850 (1995).
[37] *Sixth Report of the Committee on Standards in Public Life, Reinforcing Standards*, Cm. 4557 (2000).

company for a period of time if there had been official dealings with that company while he was still in office.

There were numerous recommendations related to quangos or executive non-departmental public bodies. These were directed principally at the manner of appointment to such bodies, the need for appointments to be made on merit, the importance of inculcating principles of propriety into those who worked in such bodies and greater transparency.

8–008   Jaundiced political observers might have expected that the Report would have been left to gather dust like many other such initiatives. The reality has proven otherwise, and many of the proposals have been acted on. To be sure this was because the government was willing to accept them. This is, in a reductionist sense, a condition of almost any change within our political system. It should not mask the difficulty the government would have faced if it had tried to reject the proposals totally. Nor should it mask the astuteness of those who framed the Report. Each of the recommendations had a mark, A, B or C, attached thereto. These signified respectively recommendations that the Committee believed could be implemented immediately, those which should be implemented by the end of the year, and those on which progress would be re-examined in the latter part of the following year. The strategy of including "timed action points", which was clearly redolent of practice in the business sector, made it all the more difficult for the government of the day to resist given its attachment to the market ethos.

Most of the recommendations that related to MPs and the House of Commons were accepted. A new Select Committee on Standards and Privileges was established, the PCS was created, there was a new Code of Conduct[38] and the Register of Interests was revitalised. The government also accepted albeit with some modifications the principles which applied to ministers.[39] It acknowledged that ministers should behave according to the highest standards, that they should ensure that there was no conflict between their public duties and their private interests, and that public resources should not be used for party political purposes.

It should moreover be recognised that the recommendations from the Nolan Committee had an impact on other governmental initiatives. The comments made in the Committee's First Report were one of the catalysts for the more extensive reforms on quangos.[40] A later Report from the Committee[41] on standards of conduct in local government provided the foundation for the government's proposals for a new ethical framework within local politics.[42]

The terms of reference of the Committee on Standards in Public Life were

---

[38] *The Code of Conduct together with the Guide to the Rules Relating to the Conduct of Members* (HC 688; 1996).
[39] *The Government's Response to the First Report from the Committee on Standards in Public Life*, Cm. 2931 (1995).
[40] Cabinet Office, *Opening Up Quangos: A Consultation Paper* (1997).
[41] *Third Report of the Committee on Standards in Public Life: Standards of Conduct in Local Government in England, Scotland and Wales*, Cm. 3702 (1997).
[42] Department of the Environment, Transport and the Regions, *Modern Local Government, In Touch with the People*, Cm. 4014 (1998), Ch.6.

extended in November 1997 so as to enable it to review issues in relation to the funding of political parties, and to make recommendations for change. The Committee, under the chairmanship of Lord Neill, produced a valuable Report on the funding of political parties.[43] The majority of the recommendations, as well as other provisions, were incorporated in the Political Parties, Elections and Referendums Act 2000. Later reports from the Committee have dealt with important topics such as the boundaries between ministers, special advisers and civil servants,[44] and review of the Electoral Commission.[45]

C. The Parliamentary Commissioner for Standards and the Select Committee on Standards and Privileges

The office of Parliamentary Commissioner for Standards (PCS)[46] was created in 1995 as a result of recommendations from the Committee of Standards. The principal responsibilities of the office are: overseeing the Register of Members' Interests; providing confidential advice to individual MPs and the Select Committee on Standards and Privileges about the interpretation of the Code of Conduct and Guide to the Rules relating to the Conduct of Members[47]; preparing guidance and providing training for MPs on matters of conduct, propriety and ethics; monitoring the operation of the Code of Conduct and Guide to the Rules and, where appropriate, proposing possible modifications to the Committee; receiving and investigating complaints about Members who are allegedly in breach of the Code of Conduct and Guide to the Rules, and reporting the findings to the Committee. A valuable summary of the work of the first PCS, Sir Gordon Downey, is to be found in an appendix to a Report of the Select Committee.[48]

8–009

The Select Committee on Standards and Privileges has a number of functions. It is to consider specific matters relating to privileges referred to it by the House.[49] It is to oversee the work of the PCS, including arrangements proposed by the PCS in relation to the register of Members' Interests.[50] The Select Committee will also consider any matter relating to the conduct of MPs which is drawn to its attention by the PCS, including specific

---

[43] *Fifth Report of the Committee on Standards in Public Life: The Funding of Political Parties in the United Kingdom*, Cm. 4057 (1998).
[44] *Ninth Report of the Committee on Standards in Public Life: Defining the Boundaries within the Executive, Ministers, Special Advisers and the Permanent Civil Service*, Cm. 5775 (2003).
[45] *Eleventh Report of the Committee on Standards in Public Life: Review of the Electoral Commission*, Cm. 7006 (2007).
[46] http://www.parliament.uk/about_commons/pcfs.cfm.
[47] *The Code of Conduct together with the Guide to the Rules Relating to the Conduct of Members* (HC 351; 2005), available at http://www.publications.parliament.uk/pa/cm/cmcode.htm.
[48] *Nineteenth Report of the Select Committee on Standards and Privileges: Retirement of the Parliamentary Commissioner* (HC 1147; 1998).
[49] See, for example, the *Ninth Report*, n.50, dealing with restrictions on the initiation of parliamentary proceedings in relation to matters where the MP has a pecuniary interest.
[50] *Ninth Report of the Select Committee on Standards and Privileges: Public Access to Registers of Interest* (HC 437; 1997).

complaints about alleged breach of any applicable Code of Conduct, and make any recommendation as may be necessary for modification of the Code.

The precise nature of the relationship between the PCS and the Select Committee has given rise to debate, particularly with respect to appeal procedures. The Select Committee produced a Report that attempted to clear the ground on this issue.[51] In most cases the PCS will receive and investigate a complaint and report his findings to the Select Committee as to whether the rules have been broken. The Select Committee then reviews the PCS's procedures and evidence, reaches a conclusion as to whether the rules have been broken, assesses the gravity of the breach and recommends what penalty should be imposed.[52] The imposition of any penalty is then a matter for the House itself.

8–010   The initial investigation is undertaken by the PCS. If he is of the opinion that there is no case to answer then this will normally be upheld by the Committee, which will not report the matter to the House.[53] If the PCS finds that there is a case to answer it will be considered by the Committee. This does not usually give rise to any difficulty, but there are instances where issues of fact may be seriously in dispute. The Select Committee rejected the suggestion that in such instances a sub-committee of the Select Committee should investigate the matter. Its view was in that in serious cases the PCS might invite the Committee to appoint a legally qualified assessor who would assist in the investigation and share responsibility for its findings.[54]

The Select Committee then considered what appellate procedures should apply in cases where there were disputes as to the facts. It felt that the PCS should inform the subject of the complaint of the factual findings in sufficient detail for the latter to decide whether to appeal on this ground.[55] The nature of the appeal before the Select Committee was contested. Some were in favour of the Committee exercising a limited review on grounds akin to those in judicial review cases. Others advocated a full re-hearing by the Committee. The Committee itself felt that the nature of the appeal should be determined by it according to the circumstances of the case, and accepted that there would be some instances where a re-hearing was appropriate.[56] There were also differences of view expressed as to whether the Committee or some other body should hear any appeal. The Select Committee was once again of the opinion that it depended on the nature of the appeal. If this was akin to a judicial review then it felt that the Committee itself could undertake the task. Where, however, the appeal was more in the nature of a re-hearing it believed that the appointment of an ad hoc tribunal was the best solution.[57]

---

[51] *Twenty First Report of the Select Committee on Standards and Privileges: Appeal Procedures* (HC 1191; 1998).
[52] *Twenty First Report*, n.51, para 5.
[53] *Twenty First Report*, n.51, para 10.
[54] *Twenty First Report*, n.51, para 16.
[55] *Twenty First Report*, n.51, para 19.
[56] *Twenty First Report*, n.51, para 24.
[57] *Twenty First Report*, n.51, paras 25–32.

This Report of the Select Committee raises broader issues of interest and importance. The existing regime is premised on internal self-regulation by the House. There is however clearly a tension between this and the need to ensure procedural rectitude. The Select Committee was mindful of the need to comply with the requisites of procedural fairness, but wary lest this led to the over-judicialisation of the process and the surrender of ultimate competence to an external body. It was for this reason that on the key issues relating to appeal procedures and the choice of an internal or an external appellate body the Committee ended up treading such a fine line. Whether it proves possible to maintain this line remains to be seen.

D. Local Authorities and Standards of Conduct

The Local Government Act 2000 Pt III, introduced important new statutory provisions regarding the conduct of members of local government. The Secretary of State is empowered to issue model codes of conduct[58] and has done so.[59] Local authorities are under an obligation to have a code of conduct,[60] and individual members must undertake to comply with it.[61] Local authorities must create a Standards Committee, which is to promote and maintain high standards by members, and to assist them to observe the authority's code of conduct.[62] There is a Standards Board for England that can, inter alia, issue guidance to local authorities on matters relating to conduct of members.[63] Ethical standards officers investigate complaints,[64] and may refer a case to a tribunal drawn from members of an Adjudication Panel.[65]

8–011

4. THE PARLIAMENTARY COMMISSIONER FOR ADMINISTRATION

A. General

In the late 1950s there was increasing concern over the operation of the administration. The Crichel Down affair, which was a catalyst for the establishment of the Franks Committee, proved to be outside the terms of

8–012

---

[58] Local Government Act 2000 s.50, subject to amendments made by Local Government and Public Involvement in Health Act 2007 s.183.
[59] See, e.g., the Local Authorities (Model Code of Conduct) (England) Order 2001 (SI 2001/3575); Local Authorities (Model Code of Conduct) Order 2007 (SI 2007/1159); *R. (on the application of Richardson) v North Yorkshire CC* [2004] 1 W.L.R. 1920; *Scrivens v Ethical Standards Officer* [2005] EWHC 529.
[60] Local Government Act 2000, s.51.
[61] Local Government Act 2000 s.52; *Livingstone v Adjudication Panel for England* [2006] H.R.L.R. 45.
[62] Local Government Act 2000 ss.53–55.
[63] Local Government Act 2000 s.57.
[64] Local Government Act 2000 ss.59–67.
[65] Local Government Act 2000 ss.75–76.

reference of that Committee. In 1961, Justice[66] published a report, which made two suggestions. There were recommendations for the establishment of a General Tribunal to deal with a miscellaneous group of appeals. This suggestion was not adopted. The report also considered the possibility of machinery to deal with maladministration, that is, decisions taken with bias, negligently, unfairly, etc. While the courts could tackle some of these, others might not be reviewable or such control might be inappropriate. The inspiration for the subsequent proposals was the Ombudsman in Scandinavian countries, an independent and impartial person who would investigate complaints of maladministration made by members of the public.

Largely as a result of those recommendations the Parliamentary Commissioner Act 1967 was passed, appointing a Parliamentary Commissioner for Administration,[67] (PCA).[68] The PCA is appointed by the Crown and holds office for the period for which he or she is appointed, which cannot be more than seven years. He or she may be removed from office as a result of an address from both Houses of Parliament.

The idea of having an Ombudsman to provide a check on maladministration has taken hold in other areas. The work of the Health Service Commissioner, and the Local Government Commissioners will be considered below.[69] There is a PCA[70] and a Commissioner of Complaints for Northern Ireland,[71] and provision has been made for investigative machinery in relation to the Scottish Parliament and the Welsh Assembly.[72] There is now an Ombudsman in important areas such as[73]: Pensions,[74] Financial Services,[75] Energy Supply,[76] Estate Agents,[77] Prisons and Probation,[78] Telecommunications,[79] There was a Legal Services Ombudsman,[80]

---

[66] The Whyatt Report, *The Citizen and the Administration: the Redress of Grievances* (1961).

[67] F. Stacey, *The British Ombudsman* (Clarendon, 1971); R. Gregory and P. Hutchesson, *The Parliamentary Ombudsman* (Allen & Unwin, 1975); F. Stacey, *Ombudsmen Compared* (Oxford University Press, 1978); M. Seneviratne, *Ombudsmen in the Public Sector* (Open University Press, 1994); G. Drewry, "The Ombudsman: Parochial Stopgap or Global Panacea?", in P. Leyland and T. Woods (eds), *Administrative Law Facing the Future: Old Constraints & New Horizons* (Blackstone, 1997), Ch.4.

[68] http://www.ombudsman.org.uk/.

[69] See below, paras 8–036—8–039.

[70] Parliamentary Commissioner (Northern Ireland) Act 1969; http://www.ni-ombudsman.org.uk/.

[71] Commissioner of Complaints Act (Northern Ireland) 1969; http://www.ni-ombudsman.org.uk/.

[72] Scotland Act 1998 s.91; Public Services Ombudsman (Wales) Act 2005, as amended by the Government of Wales Act 2006.

[73] For a full list, see http://www.ombudsman.org.uk/contact_us/if_we_cannot_help.html.

[74] http://www.pensions-ombudsman.org.uk/.

[75] See, e.g., http://www.financial-ombudsman.org.uk/; R. James and M. Seneviratne, "The Building Societies Ombudsman Scheme" (1992) 11 C.J.Q. 157; A. Mowbray, "Ombudsmen: the Private Sector Dimension", in W. Finnie, C. Himsworth and N. Walker (eds), *Edinburgh Essays in Public Law* (Edinburgh University Press, 1991), 315–334.

[76] http://www.energy-ombudsman.org.uk/links/index.php.

[77] http://www.oea.co.uk/.

[78] http://www.ppo.gov.uk/.

[79] http://www.otelo.org.uk/.

[80] Courts and Legal Services Act 1990; R. James and R. Seneviratne, "The Legal Services Ombudsman: Form versus Function?" (1995) 58 M.L.R. 187.

but this function is now to be performed by the Office for Legal Complaints.[81]

B. Who can be Investigated?

The PCA is empowered to investigate complaints relating to any action, subject to the limitations mentioned below, which is taken by or on behalf of a government department or other authority to which the Act applies, where the action taken is in the exercise of administrative functions of that department or authority.[82]

8–013

The departments and other authorities to which the Act applies are listed in Sch.2, which can be altered by Order in Council. Reference to a department or other authority is taken to include a reference also to the ministers, members or officers of the department.[83] The list of bodies within the PCA's jurisdiction has been expanded, and includes many agencies and non-departmental public bodies.

Agencies created independently of the Next Steps initiative will normally have to be added to Sch.2 to be within the PCA's remit. Executive Agencies are, as we have seen, part of the parent department and do not have any formal separate identity. Given that this is so they would be within the PCA's ambit of authority by virtue of his jurisdiction over the department itself.

Somewhat more difficult is the position of firms to whom work has been contracted-out. The 1967 Act does, however, talk of administrative functions being carried out by or *on behalf of* departments.[84] Firms to whom work has been contracted-out are acting on behalf of the department and should therefore be regarded as within the 1967 Act. This is the view taken by the PCA, and it is surely correct as a matter of principle.[85]

C. What can be Investigated?

i. Administrative, legislative and judicial functions

The complaint must relate to action taken in the exercise of administrative functions of that department, body or agency. This could be said to exclude judicial or legislative functions.

8–014

Thus, the question arises as to whether, for example, the making of delegated legislation is within the PCA's jurisdiction. The Attorney-General, in evidence before the Select Committee,[86] expressed the view that the making of a statutory instrument is a legislative process and hence outside

---

[81] Legal Services Act 2007 ss.114–115, 159.
[82] Parliamentary Commissioner Act 1967 ss.4(1), 5(1).
[83] Parliamentary Commissioner Act 1967 s.4(8).
[84] Parliamentary Commissioner Act 1967 s.5(1).
[85] Parliamentary Commissioner for Administration, Annual Report 1992, 2.
[86] *Report from the Select Committee on the Parliamentary Commissioner for Administration* (1968–1969; HC 385).

the PCA's jurisdiction, and that this applied equally to the preliminary stages of the making of the instrument. When the instrument has been made, the Attorney-General felt that the PCA could receive complaints about its operation and ensure that the relevant department was keeping the matter under review, but that the actual content of the rules could not be questioned. This appears to be the position adopted by the PCA Where a statutory order is not a statutory instrument, the PCA's powers appear to be wider, allowing an investigation of maladministration in the administrative process leading to the actual making of the order.[87]

Judicial functions in the sense of the work of tribunals or courts are not in any event within the PCA's powers. It should not, however, be supposed that any matter with a judicial flavour will be excluded. Public inquiries have, for example, been the subject of the PCA's attention.

ii. Administrative functions and maladministration

8–015 Provided that the action is taken by a body listed in the Act, and the action is taken in the exercise of administrative functions, the PCA is empowered to investigate claims of injustice resulting from maladministration, which have been referred by a Member of Parliament.[88]

The term maladministration is not defined in the Act.[89] A sense of what the legislature intended is to be derived from the Crossman catalogue which included bias, neglect, inattention, delay, incompetence, ineptitude, arbitrariness and the like. The PCA himself has defined maladministration to mean poor administration or the wrong application of rules.[90] Examples include: avoidable delay; faulty procedures or failure to follow correct procedures; not telling the individual about appeal rights; unfairness, bias or prejudice; giving misleading or inadequate advice; refusing to answer reasonable questions; discourtesy; mistakes in handling claims; and not offering an adequate remedy where one is due.[91]

In reality the defects most commonly found in the context of executive administrative action are failing to provide information, misapplication of departmental rules, misleading advice, unjustifiable delay and inconsiderate behaviour. The PCA criticises discretionary administrative action most often because a relevant consideration has not been taken into account, or the evidence has not been properly collated prior to making the decision.

---

[87] Given that the decision whether a rule becomes a statutory instrument is often fortuitous, the wisdom of this dichotomy is questionable. See further on this, Ch.22.

[88] Parliamentary Commissioner Act 1967 s.5(1). See also ss.5(1A)–(1C), which contain special provisions for dealing with complaints relating to failure to perform a duty in relation to victims under the Domestic Crime, Violence and Victims Act 2004 ss.32, 35–44.

[89] G. Marshall, "Maladministration" [1973] P.L. 32.

[90] Parliamentary Commissioner for Administration, *About the Ombudsman* (1998).

[91] See also, *R. v Parliamentary Commissioner for Administration, ex P. Balchin* [1997] C.O.D. 146, where Sedley J. held that maladministration included bias, neglect, inattention, delay, incompetence, ineptitude, perversity, turpitude and arbitrariness.

iii. Administrative functions, maladministration and principles of good administration

The PCA has more recently published *Principles of Good Administration.*[92] It is clear that these principles are intimately linked with a finding of maladministration. Thus as Ann Abraham, the PCA states,[93]

8–016

"This document gives our views on the key Principles of Good Administration. We want to be open and clear with both complainants and public bodies within the Ombudsman's jurisdiction about the sorts of behaviour we expect when public bodies deliver public service, and the tests we apply in deciding whether maladministration and service failure have occurred."

Six such principles are elaborated. The first such principle is termed *"getting it right"*, which embraces the following: acting in accordance with the law and with due regard for the rights of those concerned; acting in accordance with the public body's policy and guidance (published or internal); taking proper account of established good practice; providing effective services, using appropriately trained and competent staff; and taking reasonable decisions, based on all relevant considerations.

The second principle is *"being customer focused"*, which covers: ensuring that people can access services easily; informing customers what they can expect and what the public body expects of them; keeping to its commitments, including any published service standards; dealing with people helpfully, promptly and sensitively, bearing in mind their individual circumstances; and responding to customers' needs flexibly, including, where appropriate, co-ordinating a response with other service providers.

The third principle of good administration is *"being open and accountable"*. This demands that the relevant public body should be: open and clear about policies and procedures, ensuring that information, and any advice provided, is clear, accurate and complete; state its criteria for decision making and giving reasons for decisions; handle information properly and appropriately; keep proper and appropriate records; and take responsibility for its actions.

8–017

The fourth such principle requires that the public body should act *"fairly and proportionately"*. This entails: treating people impartially, with respect and courtesy; treating people without unlawful discrimination or prejudice, and ensuring no conflict of interests; dealing with people and issues objectively and consistently; and ensuring that decisions and actions are proportionate, appropriate and fair.

The fifth and penultimate principle is *"putting things right"*. Thus the public body should: acknowledge mistakes and apologise where appropriate; put mistakes right quickly and effectively; provide clear and timely information on how and when to appeal or complain; and operate an

---

[92] Parliamentary and Health Service Ombudsman, *Principles of Good Administration* (2007).
[93] *Principles of Good Administration*, n.92, 1.

effective complaints procedure, which includes offering a fair and appropriate remedy when a complaint is upheld.

The final principle is entitled *"seeking continuous improvement"*, which requires that the relevant body should: review policies and procedures regularly to ensure that they are effective; ask for feedback and use it to improve services and performance; and ensure that the public body learns lessons from complaints and uses these to improve services and performance.

iv. Administrative function, maladministration and the merits

8–018 The PCA is not authorised to question the merits of a decision taken without maladministration by a government department or other authority in the exercise of discretion vested in that department or authority.[94]

The precise purpose of this provision is not entirely clear. On one view, it seems merely to restate the requirement from s.5(1), that maladministration is a condition precedent to the exercise of the PCA's jurisdiction, without telling us anything further about what maladministration means. On another view, it indicates that the maladministration must reside in the procedure by which the decision was made.

It was this interpretation which was adopted by the first PCA. He drew a distinction between the procedure leading to a decision and the decision itself. The latter he regarded as outside his competence, even if it resulted in manifest hardship to the complainant. The Select Committee regarded this interpretation as over-restrictive,[95] and the PCA subsequently broadened his perspective.

A similar caution initially constrained the PCA in relation to departmental rules and regulations. The Select Committee, once again, encouraged a broader interpretation,[96] enabling the PCA to consider the effect of statutory instruments and the action taken to review their operation, with a wider jurisdiction in relation to rules which were not statutory instruments.

It is nonetheless important to realise that complaints about the content of government policy or legislation are not within the remit of the PCA: the former is for the government, the latter for Parliament.[97]

v. Maladministration and political response

8–019 The recent decision in *Bradley*[98] casts significant light on the relationship between a finding of maladministration made by the PCA and the

[94] Parliamentary Commissioner Act 1967 s.12(3).
[95] *Second Report from the Select Committee on the Parliamentary Commissioner for Administration* (HC 350; 1967–1968), para 14.
[96] *Report from the Select Committee on the Parliamentary Commissioner for Administration* (HC 385; 1968–1969), para 11; *First Report of Parliamentary Commissioner for Administration* (HC 49; 1974–1975), para 63.
[97] Parliamentary Commissioner for Administration, *About the Ombudsman* (1998).
[98] *R. (on the application of Bradley) v Secretary of State for Work and Pensions* [2008] EWCA Civ. 36.

subsequent political response. A number of people had lost all or part of their final salary pensions when their occupational pension schemes were wound up. The PCA made various findings of maladministration by the Secretary of State, who rejected all but one of those findings. The claimant sought judicial review of the Secretary of State's decision to reject the PCA's findings. The first of the PCA's findings of maladministration related to whether official information concerning the security that members of final salary schemes could expect was inaccurate and misleading.

The Court of Appeal held that the 1967 Act could not be construed to require the body whose conduct was the subject of investigation to accept the findings of maladministration. Parliament had not enacted such a provision in the legislation. The Secretary of State, acting rationally, was therefore entitled to reject a finding of maladministration and prefer his own view. However, the decision to reject the PCA's findings in favour of his own view was itself subject to rationality review by the courts. The Secretary of State had to have a reason for rejecting the PCA's findings and the Secretary of State was not entitled to reject those findings merely because he preferred another view which could not be characterised as irrational. The court concluded that it was irrational for the Secretary of State to reject the PCA's finding that the official information was incomplete and potentially misleading and quashed the Secretary of State's decision in that respect.

D. Matters Excluded from the PCA's Jurisdiction

The PCA's jurisdiction is limited in a number of ways. The principal limitations are as follows.   **8–020**

i. Section 5(2): PCA and courts

Section 5(2) prevents the PCA from investigating any action in respect of which the person aggrieved has or had a right of appeal, reference, or review to, or before, a tribunal constituted by, or under, any enactment or by prerogative, and any action in respect of which the person aggrieved has or had a remedy by way of proceedings in any court of law. This prohibition is subject to an exception where the PCA is satisfied that it would not be reasonable to expect the claimant to resort to such a remedy.[99]   **8–021**

Section 5(2) raises issues of general interest as to the role the PCA is and should be performing. These will be considered in the next section. For the present, it is sufficient to say that there has, despite s.5(2), been overlap between the courts' jurisdiction and that of the PCA. This is particularly so as the courts have expanded the ambit of judicial review.

---

[99] D. Foulkes, "Discretionary Provisions of the Parliamentary Commissioner Act" (1971) 34 M.L.R. 377.

ii. Section 5(3) and Schedule 3: Excluded Matters

8–022 The second type of exclusion is contained in s.5(3). This prevents the PCA from investigating any action or matter described in Sch.3 of the Act. This Schedule covers a wide range of matters.

(1) Actions certified by a minister to affect relations between the United Kingdom government and any other government or international organisation.

(2) Subject to limited exceptions, action taken, in any country or territory outside the United Kingdom, by or on behalf of any officer representing or acting under the authority of Her Majesty in respect of the UK, or any other officer of the UK government.

(3) Action taken in connection with the administration of the government of any country or territory outside the United Kingdom which forms part of Her Majesty's dominions or in which Her Majesty has jurisdiction.

(4) Action taken under the Extradition Act 2003.

(5) Action taken by or with the authority of the Secretary of State for the purposes of investigating crime or of protecting the security of the State, including action so taken with respect to passports.

(6) The commencement or conduct of civil or criminal proceedings before any court of law in the UK, or proceedings before any international court or tribunal, or under relevant legislation concerning the armed forces.

(7) Action taken by any person appointed by the Lord Chancellor as a member of the administrative staff of any court or tribunal, so far as that action is taken at the direction, or on the authority (whether express or implied), of any person acting in a judicial capacity or in his capacity as a member of the tribunal.

(8) Action taken by any member of the administrative staff of a relevant tribunal, so far as that action is taken at the direction, or on the authority (whether express or implied), of any person acting in his capacity as a member of the tribunal.[100]

(9) Any exercise of the prerogative of mercy.

(10) Action taken on behalf of the minister by certain health authorities.

(11) Action relating to contractual and commercial transactions, whether in the UK or elsewhere, other than the acquisition of land whether compulsorily or by agreement, and the disposal of surplus land thus acquired.

---

[100] There is an analogous provision relating to the Criminal Injuries Compensation Scheme.

(12) Personnel matters, which encompasses both civil and military services, and cases where the government has power to take, determine
or approve action.

(13) The grant of honours, awards or privileges by the Crown.

The two areas where there has been most pressure for reform have been the
exemptions for contractual/commercial matters and personnel. There have
been a number of arguments against any change. The existence of other
machinery for scrutiny of these areas, and the idea that the PCA is concerned with the relationship of the government and the governed and not
with the government as employer or trader, provide the main arguments
against reform. Neither of these reasons is convincing.[101]

iii. Matters within the remit of devolved jurisdictions
The Parliamentary Commissioner Act 1967 has been amended[102] so as to   **8–023**
ensure that the PCA does not investigate matters that fall within the remit of
the devolved administrations in Scotland and Wales, both of which have
their own Ombudsmen regimes.

E. The Complainant and the Procedure

i. Who can complain
Section 6(1) spells out who can complain. In essence, it provides that   **8–024**
complaints can be made by any individual or body of persons, whether
incorporated or unincorporated. Complaints cannot however be made by
local authorities, nationalised industries, or other bodies appointed by a
minister or by a government department. These exclusions are designed to
emphasise the character of the PCA as someone who arbitrates between the
government and the governed, but who does not hear complaints by one
department against another. The complaint must be made by the person
aggrieved, or a personal representative. It must be submitted to a Member
of Parliament within 12 months from the date on which the person
aggrieved first had notice of the matters alleged in the complaint, but the
PCA has discretion to allow a claim to proceed outside that time limit.[103]
The complainant must either be resident in the United Kingdom, or the
complaint must relate to action taken while he or she was present in the
United Kingdom.[104]

---

[101] Sir C. Clothier, "The Value of an Ombudsman" [1986] P.L. 204, 210–211.
[102] Parliamentary Commissioner Act 1967 ss.4(3A), 4(3B), 5(5A), 5(5B).
[103] Parliamentary Commissioner Act 1967 s.6(3).
[104] Parliamentary Commissioner Act 1967 s.6(4), subject to the qualifications in s.6(5). See also,
Parliamentary Commissioner (Consular Complaints) Act 1981.

ii. The MP filter

8–025   The complaint must be addressed initially to a Member of Parliament.[105]
This is in contrast to the position in a number of other countries where the
individual is allowed direct access to the Ombudsman. This has always been
rejected in the United Kingdom. The PCA is viewed as an adjunct to Parliament. He aids Parliament in the performance of its traditional function of
protecting the citizen, but is not intended to be an independent citizen
protector. The argument against allowing direct access has been bolstered
by more practical considerations. It is felt that in a country with a large
population direct access would place an impossible burden upon the PCA.
The disadvantages in not allowing direct access have partly been overcome
by a system whereby the PCA passes on to the relevant MP a complaint
which he receives directly from the public, stating that he is willing to
consider the case should the MP wish him to do so. This allows the MP to
function as a filter, but avoids the necessity of outright rejection of the claim
by the PCA It would nonetheless be preferable if individuals could have
direct access to the PCA.[106]

iii. The investigation

8–026   The PCA has considerable choice as to the method of investigation[107] and
possesses wide powers in relation to the obtaining of evidence. There is in
effect a three-stage procedure, which is divided into screening, investigation
and report.[108]

Screening serves principally to remove those cases where the PCA lacks
jurisdiction. Where the PCA proposes to investigate he must afford the
principal officer of the department or authority concerned, and any other
person alleged to have taken or authorised the action complained of, an
opportunity to comment upon the allegations. Investigations are conducted
in private, but the PCA has a broad discretion as to the type of information
required, the persons who are questioned, and whether any person may be
represented by counsel, solicitor or otherwise in the investigation.[109] Provision is made for the payment of expenses to the complainant, or to a person
involved in the investigation.[110] An investigation by the PCA does not,
however, invalidate or suspend action taken by an authority.[111]

The PCA can require the minister, or any other person with information
relevant to the investigation, to furnish it to him. The PCA has the same

---

[105] Parliamentary Commissioner Act 1967 s.5(1); L. Cohen, "The Parliamentary Commissioner
and the 'M.P. Filter' " [1972] P.L. 204.
[106] Justice, *Our Fettered Ombudsman* (1977), paras 24–31; Justice/All Souls Review, *Administrative Justice—Some Necessary Reforms* (Oxford University Press, 1988), 90.
[107] The PCA also has discretion as to whether to investigate or not, s.5(5); *Re Fletcher's
Application* [1970] 2 All E.R. 527.
[108] Cabinet Office, *The Ombudsman in Your Files* (1996).
[109] Parliamentary Commissioner Act 1967 s.7(1), (2).
[110] Parliamentary Commissioner Act 1967 s.7(3).
[111] Parliamentary Commissioner Act 1967 s.7(4). Except in so far as the person aggrieved has
been removed from the UK, he must, if the PCA so directs, be brought back to the UK, subject
to such conditions as the Secretary of State may direct, for the purposes of the investigation

powers as a court with respect to the attendance of witnesses, including the administration of oaths, and the production of documents.[112] No obligation to maintain secrecy, whether derived from any enactment or any rule of law, applies to the disclosure of information for the purposes of an investigation under the Act, nor can the Crown claim Crown privilege in respect of such documents.[113] Information related to the Cabinet or Cabinet committees cannot, however, be furnished. A certificate issued by the Secretary of the Cabinet with the approval of the Prime Minister certifying that any document does so relate is conclusive of the matter.[114]

The PCA must furnish a number of reports at various stages of the investigatory procedure. A report must be sent to the MP who requested the investigation, stating the result, or the reasons why the investigation cannot be undertaken.[115] Where an investigation is conducted a report shall also be sent to the principal officer of the department concerned.[116] If, having made a report finding maladministration, it appears to the PCA that the injustice will not be remedied, he may lay before each House of Parliament a special report on the case.[117] An annual general report must be laid before each House, and the PCA may submit other reports if he thinks fit.[118]

F. Remedies

i. Remedial awards and compliance

The PCA has no formal power to award a remedy. The investigation will in general not even have a suspensory effect upon the action under investigation.[119] If the recommendations are not complied with a special report can be submitted to Parliament,[120] and there is, as we saw above, the possibility of judicial review to challenge the rejection of the PCA's findings.[121] The PCA's reports have however in practice led to a wide range of remedies. This is apparent from any of the annual reports.

8–027

Thus the Annual Report for 2006–2007 states that all the recommendations made during the year were accepted, or were being considered by the body or practitioner complained about.[122] The nature of the "remedy" varied. In some instances, it took the form of an apology. In others it took

---

[112] Parliamentary Commissioner Act 1967 s.8(1), (2).
[113] Parliamentary Commissioner Act 1967 s.8(3). There are however provisions to prevent the PCA disclosing information to any person where it would be contrary to interests of the state. This does not prevent the PCA himself from seeking such documents, s.11(3).
[114] Parliamentary Commissioner Act 1967 s.8(4).
[115] Parliamentary Commissioner Act 1967 s.10(1).
[116] Parliamentary Commissioner Act 1967 s.10(2), and to any other person who is alleged to have taken or authorised the action complained of.
[117] Parliamentary Commissioner Act 1967 s.10(3).
[118] Parliamentary Commissioner Act 1967 s.10(4).
[119] Parliamentary Commissioner Act 1967 s.7(4).
[120] Parliamentary Commissioner Act 1967 s.10(4).
[121] *Bradley*, n.98.
[122] Parliamentary and Health Service Ombudsman, *Annual Report 2006–7, Putting Principles into Practice* (HC 838; 2007), 60–61.

the form of action to prevent recurrence of the problem, by, for example, a review of or changes to procedures, staff training or change in departmental practice. In yet others it took the form of action to remedy the failure identified, or reconsideration of the decision. In many instances the recommendation was for financial compensation for loss, inconvenience or distress.

The PCA has also had an impact on certain more high profile cases.[123] The Sachsenhausen case[124] concerned the distribution of money provided by the German government to compensate those who had been victims in the Sachsenhausen concentration camp. The sum was distributed by the UK government, but money was withheld from 12 people who claimed that they fell within the relevant criteria. The PCA investigated the matter and found that there had been maladministration. The government gave compensation even though the original sum given by the German government had already been distributed.

Another example of a high profile case is the Barlow Clowes affair.[125] The Barlow Clowes investment business collapsed in 1988 leaving many investors with substantial losses. The business had been licensed by the Department of Trade and Industry under the relevant legislation. The PCA found that there had been maladministration by the DTI, and although the government did not accept these findings it did provide ex gratia compensation for up to 90 per cent of the losses.

ii. Remedial principles

8–028　The PCA has now developed certain remedial principles, which are intended to guide government departments and public bodies.[126] The underlying principle is that the service provider restores the complainant to the position they would have been in if the maladministration or poor service had not occurred. If that is not possible, the service provider should provide appropriate compensation. The object of the principles is to secure suitable and proportionate remedies for complainants. The remedial principles are consciously based on the organizing framework provided by the principles of good administration set out above.

Thus *"getting it right"* entails putting right cases of maladministration or poor service that have led to injustice or hardship, and considering all relevant factors when deciding the appropriate remedy. The principle of *"being customer focused"* means apologising for and explaining the maladministration or poor service, understanding people's expectations and needs,

---

[123] The PCA will not always be successful in this regard, see, for example, the saga concerning compensation for World War II internees, http://www.ombudsman.org.uk/improving_services/special_reports/pca/internees05/index.html; and that concerning occupational pensions, http://www.ombudsman.org.uk/pdfs/pensions_report_06.pdf .

[124] *Third Report of the Parliamentary Commissioner for Administration* (HC 54; 1967–68).

[125] R. Gregory and G. Drewry, "Barlow Clowes and the Ombudsman-Part I" [1991] P.L. 192; "Barlow Clowes and the Ombudsman-Part II" [1991] P.L. 408.

[126] Parliamentary and Health Service Ombudsman, *Principles for Remedy* (2007), available at http://www.ombudsman.org.uk/pdfs/principles_remedy.pdf.

dealing with people professionally and sensitively, and providing remedies that take account of people's individual circumstances. The ideal of being *"open and accountable"* requires the relevant body to be open and clear about how it decides remedies, to operate a proper system of accountability and delegation in providing remedies, and to keep a clear record of what it has decided in relation to remedies and why.

The injunction to *"act fairly and proportionately"* means offering remedies that are fair and proportionate to the complainant's injustice or hardship, providing remedies to others who have suffered injustice or hardship as a result of the same maladministration or poor service, where appropriate, and treating people without bias, unlawful discrimination or prejudice. The principle of *"putting things right"* requires that the complainant and, where appropriate, others who have suffered similar injustice or hardship, should where possible be returned to the position they would have been in if the maladministration or poor service had not occurred. If that is not possible, there should be compensation. The final principle, which entailed *"seeking continuous improvement"*, meant that lessons should be learned from complaints to ensure that maladministration or poor service did not recur, and that information concerning complaints should be used to improve services.

G. Workload

An overview of the current workload of the PCA can be gleaned from the **8–029** Annual Report for 2006–7.[127] The following picture emerges.

The number of contacts made with the PCA did not change markedly over the previous year, but the overall number that were recorded as "enquiries" was lower, because repeated contacts about the same complaint were no longer recorded as separate enquiries. Considerably fewer cases were accepted for investigation in 2006–2007 than in 2005–2006. This was in part because there was a more robust process for deciding whether the PCA could and should accept a case for investigation, the aim being to ensure that decisions to accept cases for investigation were correct in law, as well as being consistent, speedy and strategic. The drop in the number of cases accepted for investigation was also in part explicable because of PCA policy that the complainant should where possible make use of local complaints procedures.

Thus before the PCA takes a case for investigation it will ensure that the complaint is properly within its remit; that the body complained about has not been able to resolve it; that there is evidence of maladministration leading to unremedied injustice; and that there is a reasonable prospect of a worthwhile outcome to the investigation. It is nonetheless clear that while the overall number of investigations has reduced, the PCA's overall workload remains substantially unchanged, since more work is being done at the enquiry stage.

In terms of actual figures, the PCA dealt with over 14,000 enquiries

---

[127] n.122, 57–59.

during the year. 4,400 (31 per cent) were requests for information and approximately 9,800 (69 per cent) were requests to investigate. 17 per cent of the requests to investigate were accepted; 28 per cent were made improperly; 23 per cent were deemed to be premature; 18 per cent were outside the PCA's remit; and 3 per cent were withdrawn. The PCA decided not to investigate in a further 11 per cent of cases, because, for example, there was no evidence of maladministration. 34 per cent of the complaints investigated in 2006–2007 were upheld in full (the figure for 2005–2006 being 37 per cent); 28 per cent were upheld in part (30 per cent in 2005–2006); and 38 per cent were not upheld (33 per cent in 2005–2006).

H. The Select Committee on the PCA

8–030   The Select Committee on Public Administration examines the PCA's reports laid before the House. It provides a focal point for parliamentary attention on the work of the PCA. It has also been of value in two more direct ways. The Select Committee encouraged the PCA to adopt a broad view of his powers, and it exerted political pressure to ensure departmental compliance with the PCA's recommendations.[128]

In 1993 the Select Committee conducted a wider inquiry into the powers, work and jurisdiction of the PCA.[129] It recommended, inter alia, that: the legislation should be amended so as to specify exclusions from, rather than inclusions within, the PCA's jurisdiction; the retention of the MP filter; speedier handling of complaints; examples from the PCA's reports should be distributed to government departments in order to provide guidance as to good administrative practice; and that the PCA should on occasion be able to conduct a broader ranging administrative audit of a particular body. The government was supportive of some of these recommendations, but rejected others, such as that regarding the conduct of broader ranging administrative audits.[130]

I. Judicial Review and the PCA

8–031   It is clear that the PCA can be subject to judicial review in relation to decisions made concerning matters which are appropriate for investigation, and the proper manner of the investigation. The court will not readily be persuaded to interfere with the PCA's exercise of discretion, more especially given the broad terms in which this discretion is cast by ss.5(5) and 7(2) of

---

[128] R. Gregory, "The Select Committee on the Parliamentary Commissioner for Administration 1967–1980" [1982] P.L. 49; Public Administration Select Committee, *The Ombudsman in Question: The Ombudsman's Report on Pensions and its Constitutional Implications* (HC 1081; 2006).

[129] *First Report from the Select Committee* (HC 333; 1993–94).

[130] P. Giddings and R. Gregory, "Auditing the Auditors: The Select Committee Review of the Powers, Work and Jurisdiction of the Ombudsman 1993" [1994] P.L. 207; P. Giddings, R. Gregory and V. Moore, "Auditing the Auditors: Responses to the Committee's Review of the United Kingdom Ombudsman System 1993" [1995] P.L. 45.

the Act.[131] Controls based on for example reasons and relevancy will nonetheless be applied to determinations made by the PCA.[132]

J. The Role of the PCA

The role of the ombudsman has developed considerably since the office was first introduced. The scope of bodies within the PCA's jurisdiction has been expanded, and we have seen the creation of Commissioners for health and local government. The idea of an ombudsman has taken hold more generally and has been applied in areas such as banking and insurance.[133] The role of the PCA is still however a matter for debate.[134] There are at least three ways in which the PCA can be viewed.

8–032

i. The PCA and remedying of individual grievances

The first is to see the PCA's main task as the remedying of individual grievances caused by neglect, bias, or inattention within the administration. In performing this role, the PCA operates as an adjunct to Parliament, aiding that body in the protection of the individual. The MP filter, the absence of the power to award remedies, and the duty to report to Parliament, all reinforce this perspective.

8–033

This picture of the PCA sees the job as primarily concerned with the avoidance of mistakes. The jurisdictional divide between the courts and the PCA serves to emphasise this. Each is responsible for ensuring the avoidance of mistakes within its own sphere of responsibility, and this is so even accepting that there is some overlap in this respect. There is no doubt that correction of individual grievances constitutes an important aspect of the PCA's work. It is facilitated by the adoption of a two-track system, with a more and less intensive type of investigation depending upon the nature of the complaint. The existence of a fast track procedure will, hopefully, make the system more attractive to MPs who make the references.[135]

ii. The PCA, enhanced remedial power, and small claims administrative court

A second way in which the PCA could be viewed preserves the mistake avoidance approach, but seeks to expand the existing jurisdiction. There are suggestions that citizens should have direct access to the PCA, and that the discretion to take cases even if they are within the jurisdiction of the ordinary courts should be generously exercised. Some advocate this as a

8–034

---

[131] *R. v Parliamentary Commissioner for Administration Ex p. Dyer* [1994] 1 W.L.R. 621.
[132] *R. v Parliamentary Commissioner for Administration Ex p. Balchin* [1997] C.O.D. 146; *R. v Parliamentary Commissioner for Administration Ex p. Balchin (No.2)* [2000] 2 L.G.L.R. 87; *R. (on the application of Balchin) v Parliamentary Commissioner for Administration (No.3)* [2002] E.W.H.C. 1876.
[133] Mowbray, n.75, 315–334.
[134] C. Harlow and R. Rawlings, *Law and Administration* (Butterworths, 2nd edn, 1997), Ch.13.
[135] R. Gregory and J. Pearson, "The Parliamentary Ombudsman after Twenty-Five Years" (1992) 70 Pub. Adm. 469, 492–496.

means of obtaining the expeditious and cheap disposition of justice. There are in addition suggestions that the PCA should have remedial power, directly or indirectly. The PCA would be able to give remedies in his own capacity, or be able to apply to the court for the grant of relief. The image of the PCA as a small claims administrative court emerges.

The attractions of this second approach are obvious, but it is problematic. The suggestion that the PCA should be a form of small claims court would involve a fundamental reorientation of the PCA's original role. This is not a logical bar to proceeding further, but is worth stating nonetheless. The effects of such a change need to be thought through. It is clear that any such move would entail the transformation of the PCA into a judicial figure with a bureaucratic hierarchy. Benefits of the present system, particularly those of informality of procedure and negotiated settlement, would be lost or placed in jeopardy. There would be a tendency for the process to become adversarial in nature. Procedures would become more rigid. Many of these comments apply with equal force to suggestions that the PCA should have the power to award a remedy. Such a power is bound to generate demands for more formal hearings before being condemned, the right to representation, and other safeguards normally associated with judicial proceedings.[136]

The suggestion that the PCA should liberally exercise the discretion to hear complaints that are within the courts' purview[137] also has important ramifications. There is bound to be some overlap between the PCA and the courts. The nature of administrative law precludes rigid statements that a matter is or is not within the purview of the courts. The reason for caution is the danger of there being two inconsistent views upon the same subject matter, or the application of the same view in an inconsistent manner.

There is a link between this point and the possibility of the PCA applying to a court for the award of a remedy. If the PCA did have this power and also liberally interpreted the discretion to take cases that could come before the court, we would be faced with the following conundrum. Let us assume that in some cases the PCA might reach a result inconsistent either with the judicial principle applied in an area or, while consistent with the principle, applied it in a way in which a court would not. The PCA approaches the court claiming maladministration. Either the court accepts the charge and grants the remedy, in which case the dual system of jurisprudence would be a reality, or the court would look to the substance of the charge and reassess whether maladministration had taken place. If the court re-examined the matter and found that the action called maladministration could not be thus dubbed because, for example, estoppel should not bind the Crown, then the dual system of jurisprudence would be avoided, but a cumbersome and partial form of review would have taken its place.

It might be argued that these fears are misconceived because the courts

---

[136] And note the reservations about such a system expressed by Clothier, n.101, 210.
[137] A. Bradley, "The Role of the Ombudsman in Relation to the Protection of Citizen's Rights" [1980] C.L.J. 304, 331–332.

and the PCA are doing different things. The courts are concerned with the limits of jurisdiction and the principles on which discretion should be exercised, while the PCA focuses on principles of good administration. We are in danger of allowing form to blind us from substance. Whether, for example, a representation should bind is the substantive question. The conclusion may be expressed in the affirmative or negative. To imagine that there is no conflict if the conclusions are reached under different labels called ultra vires or good administration is short-sighted. We are back once again with a dual system of jurisprudence or, to put it more neutrally, a dual set of values being applied to the same problem.

iii. The PCA, remedying of individual grievances and improved administration
If this second view of the PCA is felt to be problematic, the office could still **8–035** be expanded in a third direction. Proponents of this view accept the limited mistake avoidance role of the PCA, outlined as the first view, but advocate an expansion of the jurisdiction in a different direction. This is to ask the PCA to draw attention to lessons that should be learned from individual cases in order to improve administrative practice generally.[138] This would not mean neglect of individual cases. It would be an additional task. The investigation of individual cases would be, as Harlow says,[139] a catalyst for discovering more general administrative deficiencies. This could be particularly helpful given that MPs do not at present seem to pay undue regard to the PCA's role in addressing individual grievances.[140]

It is clear that the PCA already fulfils this general function to some degree, as a glance at any of the annual reports will confirm. Problems in individual cases lead to the discovery of a more general concern, and result in recommendations for changing the administrative practice that gave rise to the initial problem.[141] The Select Committee has emphasised that the PCA may have a role in assessing whether an agency's performance has matched up to the standards laid down in the Citizen's Charter.[142] It has, moreover, been accepted that reports of good administrative practice should be circulated to departments, and that departments should provide a response to a finding of maladministration, indicating the steps taken to rectify the situation.[143] The publication in 2007 of the *Principles of Good Administration* and the *Principles for Remedy* fit well with this vision of the PCA. They are designed, as we have seen, to provide general guidance to individual departments and bodies concerning good administrative practice, with the hope that adherence to these precepts will reduce the incidence of

[138] C. Harlow, "Ombudsmen in Search of a Role" (1978) 41 M.L.R. 446.
[139] Harlow, n.138, 452.
[140] G. Drewry and C. Harlow, "A Cutting Edge? The Parliamentary Commissioner and M.P.s" (1990) 53 M.L.R. 745; A. Bradley, "Sachsenhausen, Barlow Clowes-And Then?" [1992] P.L. 353.
[141] Gregory and Pearson, n.135, 480–484.
[142] Second Report of the Select Committee on the PCA, *The Implications of the Citizen's Charter for the Work of the PCA* (HC 158; 1991–92).
[143] Giddings, Gregory and Moore, n.130, 47.

administrative deficiency and individual error. The PCA has moreover signalled that in the forthcoming years more attention will be given to the ways in which public services can be improved by learning from individual complaints.[144]

The breadth of any formal PCA report will nonetheless be limited by the nature of the complaint made.[145] Governments have moreover not accepted that the PCA should be able to carry out administrative audits. The Select Committee made a suggestion along these lines in 1977, but the government rejected it.[146] A more recent suggestion by the Select Committee[147] that the PCA should have the capacity to carry out administrative audits suffered the same fate.[148] The rationale for the government's attitude was in part that other bodies already undertake this type of task. The principal reason for rejecting this suggestion was however that the PCA's independence when conducting individual investigations could be compromised where the complaint related to a department which the PCA had approved in such an audit.[149] The force of this objection can however be questioned. The fact that the PCA had, for example, given a clean bill of health to the general procedures applied by a particular department would not necessarily imply that the department was incapable of maladministration in a specific case. There is nothing inconsistent between sound standard operating procedures and mistakes in the application of such procedures in a particular instance.

5. The Health Service Commissioners

8–036   The National Health Service Reorganisation Act 1973 created two Health Service Commissioners, one for England and the other for Wales. The PCA holds the office for England, as well as the office created by the 1967 Act. Scotland was provided with a Commissioner by the Health Service (Scotland) Act 1972.

The Health Service Commissioner (HSC) can investigate Strategic Health Authorities, certain Special Health Authorities, National Health Service trusts managing a hospital, or other establishment or facility, in England, Primary Care Trusts, and NHS foundation trusts.[150] Persons are subject to

---

[144] http://www.ombudsman.org.uk/improving_services/index.html.
[145] *R. (on the application of Cavanagh) v Health Service Commissioner* [2006] 1 W.L.R. 1229.
[146] *Review of Access and Jurisdiction* (HC 615; 1977–78), The Select Committee argued that the PCA should have some capacity to undertake audits where investigation of individual complaints revealed a more general problem. This was not accepted by the government, *Observations by the Government on Review of Access and Jurisdiction*, Cmnd. 7449 (1977–78).
[147] *First Report from the Select Committee* (HC 33; 1993–94).
[148] *Fifth Report from the Select Committee* (HC 619; 1993–94).
[149] Giddings, Gregory and Moore, n.130, 48.
[150] Health Service Commissioners Act 1993 s.2.

investigation by the HSC if: they were at the time of the action complained of persons (whether individuals or bodies) providing services under a contract entered into by them with a Primary Care Trust under the National Health Service Act 2006; persons (whether individuals or bodies) undertaking to provide in England general ophthalmic services or pharmaceutical services under that Act; individuals performing in England primary medical services or primary dental services in accordance with arrangements made under the 2006 Act; individuals providing in England local pharmaceutical services in accordance with arrangements made under a pilot scheme established under the 2006 Act. The HSC can also investigate persons who provide services under arrangements with health service bodies or family health service providers.[151]

The matters that the HSC may investigate are an alleged failure in a service provided by the authority, an alleged failure by an authority to provide a service that it was meant to provide, and any other action taken by or on behalf of an authority. The complainant must allege that injustice or hardship has been suffered in consequence of the first two heads of failure, and that there has been maladministration in connection with the third type of matter referred to.[152] Maladministration in this context connotes avoidable delay, not following proper procedures, rudeness or discourtesy, not explaining decisions, or not answering complaints fully or properly.

The jurisdiction of the HSC was expanded in 1996. Before then the exercise of clinical judgment was excluded from his jurisdiction and this was a principal reason for the rejection of complaints. This has now been changed,[153] and the Commissioner can investigate complaints about the exercise of clinical judgment, and the actions of family health service practitioners. He can also investigate complaints about the operation of the NHS complaints procedure. These changes have had a significant effect on the Commissioner's case-load, and on the way in which such cases are processed.[154] The HSC's Annual Report for 2001–2002 made it clear that since 1996 the majority of complaints are about clinical care and treatment,[155] and this theme was reiterated in the Annual Report for 2006–2007.[156]

The matters excluded from the jurisdiction of the HSC are similar to those excluded from the general jurisdiction of the PCA. Thus, he cannot investigate matters which are within the jurisdiction of the courts or a tribunal, subject to the same discretion to proceed as he ordinarily has.[157]

A difference between the PCA's jurisdiction under the 1967 Act and the legislation relating to health is that direct access is allowed under the latter

8–037

---

[151] Health Service Commissioners Act 1993 s.2B.
[152] Health Service Commissioners Act 1993 s.3.
[153] Health Service Commissioners (Amendment) Act 1996 s.6.
[154] Health Service Commissioner, Annual Report 1997–98.
[155] Health Service Commissioner, Annual Report 2001–2002 (HC 887; 2001–2002).
[156] n.122, 28.
[157] Other matters which are excluded are personnel matters relating to pay, discipline, etc., contractual or commercial transactions, except in relation to the provision of services for patients, disciplinary actions of an executive council or family practitioner committee.

legislation. The reason is that MPs do not occupy the same constitutional position with respect to the health service as they do in connection with ordinary departments. A condition precedent to direct access is, however, that the complainant first brings the matter to the notice of the health authority or relevant practitioner, which must be allowed a reasonable opportunity to respond to the complaint. Complainants are also encouraged to have recourse to the HealthCare Commission before approaching the HSC.[158]

The Select Committee on Public Administration will receive the annual report of the HSC. It will review the report, making suggestions for improvements where it feels they are warranted. It will also put pressure on government to act in relation to deficiencies revealed by the HSC's report. The government takes such reports from the select committee seriously and responds to the criticisms contained therein.[159]

6. LOCAL COMMISSIONERS

A. Scope of Authority

8–038 The 1967 Act did not include complaints against local authorities. This had long been a source of criticism, which was remedied by the Local Government Act 1974.[160] Two Commissions for local administration were established, one for England and one for Wales.[161] The work is done by local commissioners who are appointed by the Crown. There are now three commissioners for England who deal with complaints from different parts of the country.

The local commissioners can investigate complaints against any local authority except town or parish councils, and this includes committees, members and officers.[162] Police authorities, education appeal panels and many bodies providing local services are also within the remit of the local commissioners. Access to the local commissioner was originally indirect, the complaint being referred initially to a member of the local authority. Since 1988 individuals have been given a right of direct access to the local commissioner.[163]

---

[158] http://2007ratings.healthcarecommission.org.uk/homepage.cfm.
[159] See, e.g., *Select Committee on Public Administration—Second Report* (HC 352; 1998), and the government's response reported in *Select Committee on Public Administration—Fifth Report* (HC 1055; 1998).
[160] Amendments are pending under the Local Government and Public Involvement in Health Act 2007 ss.168, 169.
[161] Scotland has its own system, Local Government (Scotland) Act 1975 Pt II.
[162] Local Government Act 1974 ss.25, 34(1).
[163] Local Government Act 1988 s.29 Sch.3 para 5.

The complainant must allege that injustice has been suffered as a consequence of maladministration and allow the local authority a reasonable opportunity to investigate and reply to the complaint.[164] Exclusions exist similar to those governing the jurisdiction of the PCA. Thus, cases where there is a remedy before a court or tribunal are excluded, as are cases subject to an appeal to a minister.[165] There is a discretionary exception to this prohibition, which is the same as that in the 1967 Act.[166] There are important exclusions for cases where the complaint affects all or most of the inhabitants of the authority's area,[167] and for certain other types of case.[168]

The procedure for investigation is similar in certain respects to that of the **8–039** PCA.[169] Copies of the report must be sent to the complainant, the local authority and the member who originally referred it. The report must be made available for public inspection for a period of three weeks.[170] The procedural powers of the local commissioners were reinforced in 1989.[171] Once an adverse report has been made the local authority is under a duty to respond to it within three months. If no such action is forthcoming, or the commissioner is not satisfied with the proposed course of action, the local commissioner must make a further report setting out these facts and making further recommendations about remedying the injustice. If the local authority still proves recalcitrant, or has not taken the necessary action, then it can be forced to issue a statement in the press containing the local commissioner's proposals and any reasons why they have not taken action. A minister of the Crown or a local authority may by written notice prevent any disclosure of information or documents if such disclosure would be contrary to the public interest.[172] A local commissioner will make an annual report. There is, in addition, an obligation on each of the Commissions as a whole to report annually to the local authorities.[173]

In 2001–2002 there were 18,300 new complaints, and 19,055 complaints were decided. In 34.3 per cent of all complaints that were not premature or outside their jurisdiction, the complainants obtained remedies as a result of

---

[164] Local Government Act 1974 s.26(5); *R. v Local Commissioner for Administration Ex p. Bradford Metropolitan Council* [1979] Q.B. 287; *R v Commissioner for Local Administration Ex p. Eastleigh Borough Council* [1988] Q.B. 855; M. Jones, "The Local Ombudsmen and Judicial Review" [1988] P.L. 608.

[165] Where a person has successfully sought judicial review, it is not possible to have resort to the local ombudsman to seek compensation, *R. v Commissioner for Local Administration Ex p. H* [1999] C.O.D. 382.

[166] Local Government Act 1974 s.26(6). See, *R. v Commissioner for Local Administration Ex. P. Croydon London Borough Council* [1989] 1 All E.R. 1033.

[167] Local Government Act 1974 s.26(7). Other exclusions are investigation or prevention of crime, contractual or commercial transactions, personnel matters, educational matters.

[168] Local Government Act 1974 s.26(8) Sch.5.

[169] The decision in *Re a Complaint against Liverpool City Council* [1977] 1 W.L.R. 995 has been bypassed by the Local Government, Planning and Land Act 1980, s.184. This brings the provisions of the Local Government Act 1974 s.32(3) into line with those of the Parliamentary Commissioner Act 1967 s.11(3).

[170] Local Government Act 1974 s.30.

[171] Local Government and Housing Act 1989 s.26, amending s.31 of the Local Government Act 1974.

[172] Local Government Act 1974 s.32(3).

[173] Local Government Act 1974 s.23.

using the local government ombudsmen. In 2004–2005 18,487 complaints were decided. A significant number, 4,713 were regarded as premature, and 2,405 were held to be outside the jurisdiction of the local commissioners. They also exercised their discretion not to pursue the complaint in 2,892 cases. A local settlement was reached in 2,875 cases, maladministration was found in 167 cases, and no such maladministration was held to exist in 5,407 cases.

B. The Commissioners, Internal Complaints Procedures and General Advice to Local Authorities

8–040 A complainant will only have to resort to the local ombudsman if the local authority does not redress a grievance. This is an obvious proposition, but it is important nonetheless. Our focus should not therefore be exclusively upon the local commissioner, but also upon internal grievance procedures used by local authorities.

Valuable work on this has been done by Lewis and others at Sheffield.[174] They found that less than 50 per cent of local authorities had general complaints procedures, that those with such procedures did not advertise their existence and that few systematically monitored complaints with a view to checking on service quality. Their recommendations included a statutory duty to have a complaints procedure, the appointment of a complaints officer, and the adoption of a code of good administrative practice.[175] Other studies, such as that by the Public Law project, have also cast doubt on the efficacy of local complaints procedures.[176] The Local Government Act 2000 has gone some way to meet these concerns.[177]

8–041 The Commission for Local Administration has published guidance on this issue. Its paper on *Running a Complaints System*[178] placed considerable emphasis on the virtues of having a good complaints system, and provided practical guidance on the principles required for it to be effective. A good complaints system must be accessible, simple to use, speedy, objective, confidential, and comprehensive.[179] There should be three stages in the handling of a complaint. The initial response would be from a service provider within the department, there would then if necessary be an investigation by a more senior officer or an internal complaints officer, with the final resort to someone outside the department concerned.[180] A system that

---

[174] N. Lewis, M. Seneviratne and S.Cracknell, *Complaints Procedures in Local Government* (Centre for Criminological and Socio-Legal Studies, University of Sheffield, 1987); C. Crawford, "Complaints, Codes and Ombudsmen in Local Government" [1988] P.L. 246.
[175] Local Government and Housing Act 1989 s.31 makes provision for a National Code of Local Government Conduct.
[176] Public Law Project, *Review of the Local Government Ombudsman* (1996), 14.
[177] Local Government Act 2000 ss.49–67.
[178] Commission for Local Government in England, *Guidance on Good Practice 1* (2002).
[179] *Guidance on Good Practice*, n.178, para 20.
[180] *Guidance on Good Practice*, n.178, paras 27–31.

combines a mechanism for internal complaints with the possibility of external scrutiny may well be the way forward.[181]

The Sheffield study also contained interesting suggestions about the role of the local commissioners. Some of these, such as direct access, have been implemented. Other recommendations include: modification of the jurisdictional limits; allowing the local commissioners to investigate on their own initiative, rather than waiting for a complaint; enabling them to comment on issues where many people are affected; shifting away from the concern with maladministration as such, in part because the word carries an unfortunate connotation, and in part because it acts as a barrier to a more wide ranging role which would allow the local ombudsmen to investigate more general failure in the administrative system.[182] The study did not, however, favour judicial enforcement in the event that a local authority did not comply with the commissioner's recommendations. This role for the courts has been advocated,[183] but such a change would render the investigative process more formal. If local authorities know that a report of the local commissioner could produce legal liability, even indirectly, they are likely to demand more extensive rights to controvert his findings.[184]

The Commission for Local Administration has published a number of papers to provide more general guidance to local authorities on a range of matters. Statutory provisions serve to reinforce this aspect of the CLA's role, by encouraging the giving of general advice on good administrative practice.[185] Most notable in this respect are the papers on good administrative practice, remedies and devising a complaints system.

The paper on *Good Administrative Practice*[186] extrapolates from the commissioners' work in individual cases and sets out 42 principles or axioms of good administration. Some of the principles reflect legal requirements, such as keeping within the allowable legal limits, not acting for improper purposes, taking account of relevant considerations, giving reasons and the like. Other principles may not be formally required by the law, but are clearly desirable in the interests of good administration. The formulation of policies which set the general criteria for decision making within a particular area, and the communication of these policies to customers, are of this nature. Yet other principles are designed to ensure that the internal administrative process within the local authority is structured in the optimum manner. The existence of adequate systems for staff to follow in

---

[181] See generally, N. Lewis and P. Birkinshaw, *When Citizens Complain, Reforming Justice and Administration* (Open University Press, 1993).

[182] Local Government and Housing Act 1989 s.23 modifies s.23 of the Local Government Act 1974 s.23 by allowing the local commissioners to give general advice to local authorities about good administrative practice.

[183] As recommended in *Administrative Justice, Some Necessary Reforms* (Oxford University Press, 1988), 128–129.

[184] See the comments by local authority officers reported in the Justice Study, n.183 127–128. See also, the Sheffield study, *Complaints Procedures*, n.174, 39; C. Himsworth, "Parliamentary Teeth for Local Government Ombudsmen" [1986] P.L. 546; G. Marshall, "Ombudsmanaging Local Government" [1990] P.L. 449.

[185] Local Government Act 1974 s.23(12A).

[186] Commission for Local Government in England, *Guidance on Good Practice 2* (2001).

dealing with particular areas of activity, the maintenance of adequate records and the monitoring of progress in dealing with a problem exemplify this type of principle.

The paper on *Remedies*[187] provides a very helpful overview about the commissioners thinking on this issue. The guiding principle is, as is the case with the PCA, that the remedy should place the complainant in the position he would have been in had the maladministration not occurred.[188] It is clear that practical action to redress the grievance, such as repairs to a council house, or the provision of special educational needs, is regarded as the first line of attack.[189] Financial compensation becomes of greater relevance where the practical action is not possible, where loss has been suffered in the interim, or where the very essence of the complaint is a failure to pay money.[190] The paper provides detailed guidance on the type of compensation which is awarded, dealing with issues such as loss of value, lost opportunity, loss of non-monetary benefit and the like.[191]

7. Ombudsman: Looking to the Future

8–042 The PCA and the Local Commissioners have argued for overhaul of the existing system. They advocated a modern, unified Ombudsman scheme dealing with central and local government, and health. The Cabinet Office undertook a review in 2000.[192] It proposed a major overhaul of the present system, the creation of an integrated system for the ombudsmen sector in England, and the removal of the MP filter. A further consultation took place in 2005 albeit narrower in scope.[193] The latter consultation led to passage of a Regulatory Reform Order, which facilitates collaboration and joint investigation between the PCA, HSC and Local Commissioners where the subject matter of the complaint falls within the remit of more than one jurisdictional area.[194]

---

[187] Commission for Local Government in England, *Guidance on Good Practice 6* (2005).
[188] *Guidance on Good Practice*, n.187, para 7.
[189] *Guidance on Good Practice*, n.187, paras 15–18.
[190] *Guidance on Good Practice*, n.187, paras 19–21.
[191] *Guidance on Good Practice*, n.187, paras 24–48.
[192] Cabinet Office, *Review of the Public Sector Ombudsmen in England* (2000); M. Seneviratne, "'Joining Up' the Ombudsmen—The Review of the Public Sector Ombudsmen in England" [2000] P.L. 582.
[193] Cabinet Office, *Reform of Public Sector Ombudsmen Services in England* (2005).
[194] The Regulatory Reform (Collaboration etc. between Ombudsmen) Order 2007 (SI 2007/1889).

CHAPTER 9

TRIBUNALS AND INQUIRIES

1. TRIBUNALS: RATIONALE AND NATURE

A. Introduction

Tribunals have been part of our administrative landscape for some con-   **9–001**
siderable time.[1] General and specific legislation has, as we shall see, affected
their operation. The Tribunals, Courts and Enforcement Act 2007 has
however produced far-reaching changes in the organisation of tribunals and
the way in which they function. The impact of the legislation will be fully
considered in the course of the subsequent discussion.

B. Reasons for their Creation

The reasons for the creation of tribunals have been considered in the his-   **9–002**
torical discussion.[2] A word or two more is warranted at this juncture. It is
important to realise that a number of differing arguments have been used to
justify assigning tasks to tribunals. Three such arguments can be distinguished here.

First, tribunals are often preferred to courts because they have the
advantages of speed, cheapness, informality and expertise. These advantages
are of particular importance in areas involving mass administrative justice,
such as the distribution of social welfare benefits. It would, moreover, be
extremely difficult for the ordinary courts to cope with the large increase in
case load if these matters were assigned to the ordinary judicial process. The
creation of a tribunal system can also alleviate problems for the courts,

---

[1] R. Wraith and P. Hutchesson, *Administrative Tribunals* (Allen & Unwin, 1973); J. Farmer,
Tribunals and Government (Weidenfeld & Nicolson, 1974); P. Birkinshaw, *Grievances, Remedies
and the State* (Sweet & Maxwell, 2nd ed, 1994); R. Rawlings, *Grievance Procedure and
Administrative Justice. A Review of Socio-Legal Research* (1987).
[2] See above, paras 2–016—2–019.

which can become inundated by judicial review applications within a particular area.[3]

Second, a rather different type of argument was that the ordinary courts might not be sympathetic to the protection of the substantive interests contained in the legislation that laid the foundation of the welfare state at the turn of the century, and that therefore the matter should be assigned to a tribunal instead.

A third and more radical argument sees the creation of some tribunals as a symbolic means of giving the appearance of legality in a particular area in order to render more palatable unpopular changes in the substantive benefits to which individuals were entitled. Thus Prosser[4] has argued that appeals machinery introduced in the Unemployment Assistance Act 1934 was designed to defuse opposition to cuts in benefits by directing it into channels where it could be controlled and have a minimal effect.

These differing reasons may well have force in different contexts. What is readily apparent is that tribunals have been set up in many areas. There are, for example, tribunals dealing with industrial matters, financial services, mental health, immigration, social security, revenue and child support to name but a few, and new tribunals are often created. The government classifies tribunals as non-departmental public bodies (NDPBs), and the 2006 Report on Public Bodies listed 40 Tribunal NDPBs, counted on the basis of tribunal systems, rather than individual panels.[5]

C. The Nature of Tribunals

9–003   The definition of what constitutes a tribunal is no easy matter. The name is not conclusive. The Council of Tribunals supervised bodies called authorities, commissions and committees, as well as tribunals. It is clear therefore that we must look beyond the label attached, and have regard to the substance or nature of the body. It is possible to articulate a number of "properties" that a tribunal should possess, and then test to see how many do in fact possess them.[6] These properties could be: the ability to make final, legally enforceable decisions, subject to review and appeal; independence from any department of government; the holding of a public hearing judicial in nature; the possession of expertise; a requirement to give reasons; and the provision of appeal to the High Court on points of law. However few of the tribunals listed in the Tribunals and Inquiries Act 1992 possessed all of these features.[7]

The Tribunals, Courts and Enforcement Act 2007 will however have a marked impact on this issue. The Act, as we shall see, provides for the

---

[3] Sir Harry Woolf, "Judicial Review: A Possible Programme for Reform" [1992] P.L. 221, 228.
[4] T. Prosser, "Poverty, Ideology and Legality: Supplementary Benefit Appeal Tribunals and their Predecessors" (1977) 4 British Jnl of Law and Soc. 44; L. Bridges, "Legality and Immigration Control" (1975) 2 British Jnl of Law and Soc. 221, 224.
[5] Cabinet Office, *Public Bodies 2006* (2006), ii.
[6] Farmer, n.1, 185–186.
[7] Farmer, n.1, 186–187.

establishment of a First-tier Tribunal and an Upper Tribunal. The functions previously performed by most central government tribunals will be transferred to the newly created Tribunals under the 2007 Act, thereby reducing the number of separate tribunal jurisdictions that existed hitherto.

It should in any event be recognised that while tribunals may differ from the courts in the way in which they operate, the difference is one of degree rather than kind.[8] Studies have shown[9] that, for example, while not bound by precedent in the same way as the superior courts, tribunals will often follow and build on past decisions.[10] Nor is this necessarily something to be deprecated. Consistency of treatment and rational development of principles are important.

2. TRIBUNAL REFORM: FRANKS AND LEGGATT

A. The Franks Report

i. The Committee's remit
In the 1950s there was growing concern as to the range and diversity of **9–004** tribunals, uncertainty as to the procedures they followed, and worry over the lack of cohesion and supervision. The catalyst for the establishment of the Franks Committee[11] was however the Crichel Down affair. This received wide publicity, but as it was an example of ad hoc high-handed administrative behaviour it was not within the brief given to the Franks Committee.

This brief was limited in two important ways. The Committee was not to consider decisions made in the ordinary courts. It was only to discuss those areas in which a decision was reached after a formal statutory procedure had been followed, thereby excluding the "one-off" high-handed administrative action, and informal decision-making.

ii. The recommendations
The Franks Committee proceeded on the assumption that tribunals should **9–005** be regarded as part of the machinery of adjudication, and not as part of the machinery of the administration,[12] and that tribunal procedure should be open, fair and impartial.[13]

---

[8] See, e.g. K. Whitesides and G. Hawker, *Industrial Tribunals* (Sweet & Maxwell, 1975); J. Evans, *Immigration Law* (Sweet & Maxwell, 2nd edn, 1983); L. Dickens et al, *Dismissed: A Study of Fair Dismissal and the Industrial Tribunal System* (Blackwell, 1985); J. Peay, *Tribunals on Trial: A Study of Decision-Making under the Mental Health Act 1983* (Clarendon, 1989); J. Baldwin, N. Wikeley and R. Young, *Judging Social Security: The Adjudication of Claims for Benefit in Britain* (Clarendon, 1992).
[9] Wraith and Hutchesson, n.1, Ch.10; Farmer, n.1, Ch.7.
[10] T. Buck, "Precedent in Tribunals and The Development of Principles" (2006) 25 C.J.Q. 458.
[11] Report of the Committee on Administrative Tribunals and Enquiries, Cmnd. 218 (1957).
[12] Cmnd. 218 (1957), para.40.
[13] Cmnd. 218 (1957), para.42.

"In the field of tribunals openness appears to us to require the publicity of proceedings and knowledge of the essential reasoning underlying the decisions; fairness to require the adoption of a clear procedure which enables parties to know their rights, to present their case fully and to know the case which they have to meet; and impartiality to require the freedom of tribunals from the influence, real or apparent, of Departments concerned with the subject matter of their decisions."

The Franks Report contained a series of valuable general recommendations concerning the constitution and procedure of tribunals.[14]

As to *constitution*, the Committee stated that the Lord Chancellor should appoint chairmen of tribunals, and the Council on Tribunals should appoint other members. Chairmen should normally have legal qualifications and should always do so in the case of appellate tribunals.

Detailed recommendations were made concerning *procedure*. The Council on Tribunals should formulate procedure for particular tribunals, the aim being to combine orderly procedure with an informal atmosphere. The citizen should be aware of the right to apply to a tribunal and should know in good time before the hearing the case to be met. Tribunal hearings should be public except where there were considerations of public security, intimate personal or financial circumstances had to be disclosed, or the hearing was a preliminary investigation of a case involving professional reputation. Legal representation before tribunals should normally be allowed. Tribunals should be empowered to award costs, to take evidence on oath and to subpoena witnesses. Decisions should be as fully reasoned as possible, and a written notice of the decision should be sent to the parties as soon as possible after the hearing. Final appellate tribunals should publish selected decisions and circulate them to lower tribunals.

The Report also contained recommendations on *appeal* and *judicial review*. As to the former, the Committee advocated an appeal on fact, law and merits from a first instance tribunal to an appellate tribunal, except where the tribunal of first instance was particularly well qualified. There should not, on principle, be an appeal from a tribunal to a minister. As to review, the Committee recommended that no statute should contain words purporting to oust the remedies of certiorari, prohibition and mandamus.

In addition to judicial control by review and appeal, the Committee urged that bodies called the Council on Tribunals for England and Wales and the Scottish Council be established. Their main functions would be to advise on the detailed application to tribunals of the general principles contained in the Franks Report.

iii. Implementation

9–006 Many of the measures recommended by the Franks Committee were enacted in the Tribunals and Inquiries Act 1958, replaced by the Tribunals

[14] The recommendations are summarised in Cmnd. 218 (1957), Ch.31.

and Inquiries Act 1992. Other recommendations were implemented by changes in administrative practice.

The Council on Tribunals was established with a membership of not more than 15 and not less than 10.[15] Its functions were advisory, and it was instructed to keep under review the constitution and working of the tribunals listed in a schedule to the Act. In addition it could report on any matter referred to it by the government. It had power to make general recommendations concerning the membership of those tribunals listed in the schedule and it had to be consulted prior to the enactment of any new procedural rules pertaining to them.[16]

Other recommendations enacted were the right to a reasoned decision, subject to the condition that it was requested on or before the giving or notification of the decision,[17] and the restrictive construction to be placed upon clauses which purported to exclude judicial review.[18] The list of tribunals subject to the legislation can be augmented by ministerial order, as has been done.

In some areas however less was achieved than advocated by the Franks Committee. Appeals to the High Court were limited to questions of law, excluding questions of fact and the merits,[19] and the procedure for the appointment of chairmen and members of tribunals diverged from that recommended by the Franks Committee.

B. The Leggatt Report

In May 2000 the Lord Chancellor appointed Sir Andrew Leggatt to **9–007** undertake a review of tribunals. The Leggatt Report, *Tribunals for Users— One System, One Service*,[20] is the most important investigation of tribunals since the Franks Report, and its recommendations were far-reaching.

i. The tribunals service

The Leggatt Report recommended the creation of a Tribunals Service, **9–008** which should be an executive agency of the Lord Chancellor's Department.[21] This should be a national organisation with a strong local presence, structured along regional lines. The Tribunals Service should set out in a Charter the standards of service that users can expect, as well as indicating what should occur if those standards have not been met.

---

[15] Tribunals and Inquiries Act 1992 ss.1, 2. There is provision for a Scottish Committee of the Council.
[16] Tribunals and Inquiries Act 1992 s.8.
[17] Tribunals and Inquiries Act 1992 s.10.
[18] Tribunals and Inquiries Act 1992 s.12.
[19] Tribunals and Inquiries Act 1992 s.11.
[20] Report of the Review of Tribunals by Sir Andrew Leggatt: *Tribunals for Users—One System, One Service*, 16 August 2001, www.tribunals-review.org.uk.
[21] *Tribunals for Users*, n.20, paras 5.3–5.4.

ii. The tribunals system

9–009 The recommendations made in relation to the tribunal system as a whole were equally important. The reality is that we did not have anything that could be called a tribunals "system". Individual tribunals were created on an ad hoc basis, and while they might share procedural rules, and some organisational features, there was no system running through tribunals as a whole.

The Leggatt Report sought to remedy this. It proposed that the Tribunals System should be divided into subject-matter Divisions, with new tribunals allocated to Divisions by Practice Direction.[22] First-tier tribunals should be grouped into eight Divisions to deal with disputes between citizen and state, and one to deal with disputes between parties. There should be a single route of appeal for all tribunals, to a single appellate Division. First-tier tribunals would consider each case on its merits and their decisions would not create binding precedent. Appellate tribunals could, following the practice of the Social Security Commissioners, designate binding cases. The Presidential system should be generalised. There would be a Senior President for the Tribunals System who would be a High Court judge. There would also be Presidents for the appellate divisions, and for the nine first-tier divisions. The Tribunals System should be directed by a Tribunals Board.

There should be a right of appeal on law, by permission, from first to second-tier tribunals, and from the latter to the Court of Appeal. The appellate body would have power to quash the original determination, remit it for reconsideration, grant declaratory relief, or decline to grant relief where there was no substantial prejudice.

The establishment of this comprehensive system of appeals led the Leggatt report to recommend the exclusion of judicial review in relation to decisions of first-tier tribunals, if the rights of appeal had not been exhausted. The Leggatt Report also recommended that the decisions of second-tier tribunals should be excluded from the supervisory jurisdiction of the High Court. This was in part because such tribunals would often be headed by a High Court judge, who would develop knowledge and expertise in the area. It was therefore felt to be inappropriate to subject such decisions to review by another judge of equal status. It was in part because there would, in any event, be a right of appeal on a point of law to the Court of Appeal.

iii. Operation of the tribunals system

9–010 The Leggatt Report contained a wealth of important recommendations as to how the tribunal system should operate. The tribunal system should be *independent*, in the sense that there should be separation between the ministers and other authorities whose policies and decisions are tested by tribunals, and the minister who appoints and supports them. The tribunal system should be *coherent*, in the sense that the citizen should be presented

---

[22] *Tribunals for Users*, n.20, paras 6.3–6.4.

with a single, overarching structure, which gives access to all tribunals. The system should be *user friendly*. There should be ready access to information about how to bring a case before a tribunal, and this information could be provided by the initial decision-maker as well as the tribunal.

3. TRIBUNALS: THE TRIBUNALS, COURTS AND ENFORCEMENT ACT 2007

The Leggatt Report was the most important document published about **9–011** tribunals. It led to a government White Paper,[23] and many of the Leggatt recommendations were incorporated in the Tribunals, Courts and Enforcement Act 2007 (TCE).[24]

A. Senior President of Tribunals

The TCE Act, s.2, creates the office of Senior President of Tribunals, who is **9–012** appointed on the recommendation of the Lord Chancellor.[25] The Act creates a number of specific powers and duties for the Senior President.

(1) The Senior President's concurrence in relation to the chambers structure for the First-tier Tribunal and the Upper Tribunal (and any change in it), s.7(1).

(2) The Senior President may, with the concurrence of the Lord Chancellor, make provision for the allocation of functions between chambers, s.7(9).

(3) A duty to report to the Lord Chancellor on matters which the Senior President wishes to bring to the attention of the Lord Chancellor and matters which the Lord Chancellor has asked the Senior President to cover, s.43.

(4) Power to make practice directions, s.23.

(5) The right to be consulted on the making of fees orders, s.42(5).

(6) The concurrence of the Senior President in relation to the making of orders prescribing the qualifications required for appointment of members of the First-tier Tribunal, Sch.2 para.2(2) and the Upper Tribunal, Sch.3 para.2(2).

(7) The Senior President has power to request a judge of the First-tier Tribunal or the Upper Tribunal to act as a judge of those tribunals, Sch.2 para.6(2), Sch.3 para.6(2).

[23] *Transforming Public Services: Complaints, Redress and Tribunals*, Cm. 6243 (2004).
[24] The provisions of the TCE Act 2007 came into affect at different times, The Tribunals, Courts and Enforcement Act (Commencement No.1) Order 2007 (SI 2007/2709).
[25] The details of the appointment process are set out in TCE Act 2007 Sch.1.

(8) The duty to maintain appropriate arrangements for training, welfare and guidance of judges and other members, Sch.2 para.8, Sch.3 para.9.

There is power to delegate most of these functions.[26] The Senior President of Tribunals must, in carrying out these functions, have regard to the need for tribunals to be accessible, the need for proceedings before tribunals to be fair, to be handled quickly and efficiently, and the need for members of tribunals to be experts in the subject-matter of the relevant area. The Senior President of Tribunals should also have regard to the need to develop innovative methods of resolving disputes.[27]

B. First-Tier Tribunal and Upper Tribunal

9–013 The government's response to the Leggatt recommendation for a single tribunal system was to create two new, generic tribunals, the First-tier Tribunal and the Upper Tribunal, into which existing tribunal jurisdictions could be transferred.

Thus the TCE Act s.3, provides for the creation of a First-tier Tribunal and an Upper Tribunal, each consisting of judges and other members, and presided over by the Senior President of Tribunals.[28] It is intended that the Upper Tribunal will primarily, but not exclusively, be an appellate tribunal from the First-tier Tribunal. The intent is that not only existing, but new tribunal jurisdictions will be fitted into this framework, such that in the future, when Parliament creates a new appeal right or jurisdiction, it will not have to create a new tribunal to administer it. The Upper Tribunal is a superior court of record, like the High Court and the Employment Appeal Tribunal. The TCE Act makes detailed provision for appointment of judges and other members of the First-tier Tribunal and Upper Tribunal.[29] The First-tier and Upper Tribunals are empowered to appoint assessors,[30] award costs and expenses,[31] and monetary awards made by the Tribunals are enforceable through the courts.[32]

The Act also provides for the establishment of "chambers" within the two tribunals so that the many jurisdictions that will be transferred into the tribunals can be grouped together appropriately. Each chamber will be headed by a Chamber President.[33] The rationale for this is that the pre-existing tribunals dealt with very different subject matter. These are now to be replaced by just two tribunals, the First-tier Tribunal and the Upper Tribunal. It would dilute expertise if the new system was organised on the basis that all judges and members could deal with all kinds of case. Thus the

[26] TCE Act 2007 s.8.
[27] TCE Act 2007 s.2(3).
[28] They can sit anywhere in the UK, TCE Act 2007 s.26.
[29] TCE Act 2007 ss.4–5, Schs 2–3.
[30] TCE Act 2007 s.28.
[31] TCE Act 2007 s.29.
[32] TCE Act 2007 s.27.
[33] TCE Act 2007 s.7, Sch.4.

chambers system enables jurisdictions to be grouped so that similar work is dealt with by judges and members with the relevant skills. The chambers system is intended to be flexible and is likely to evolve over time, in response to, inter alia, the transfer of functions of other tribunals to the First-tier or Upper Tribunals, and the creation of new areas of appeal, such as the regulation of gambling.

C. Transfer of Functions to First-tier Tribunal and Upper Tribunal

The transfer of jurisdictions to the First-tier Tribunal and the Upper Tri-   **9–014**
bunal is central to the regime of the TCE Act. The new tribunals will exercise the jurisdictions currently exercised by the tribunals listed in the TCE Act Sch.6, Pts 1 to 4. This constitutes most of the tribunal jurisdictions administered by central government. Government policy is that in the future, when a new tribunal jurisdiction is required to deal with a right of review or appeal it will be given to these new tribunals. The Lord Chancellor is given power, subject to certain constraints, to amend the list of tribunals in Sch.6.[34]

Some tribunals have been excluded from the new structures because of their specialist nature, and tribunals run by local government have been excluded for the present because of their different funding and sponsorship arrangements.

There are also tribunals that will share a common administration, and the leadership of the Senior President of Tribunals, but whose jurisdictions will not be transferred to the new tribunals. They are the Asylum and Immigration Tribunal, the employment tribunals and the Employment Appeal Tribunal.[35]

The detailed provisions for the transfer of functions are set out in the TCE Act s.30. The Lord Chancellor is empowered to provide that a function of a tribunal listed in Schedule 6 should be transferred to the First-tier tribunal, the Upper Tribunal, the employment tribunals or the Employment Appeal Tribunal. The aim is that the adjudicative functions that are currently undertaken by a wide range of tribunals can be consolidated into the new tribunals, the employment tribunals and Employment Appeal Tribunal.[36]

The Lord Chancellor is given certain supplementary powers consequent upon the transfer of function. Thus the Lord Chancellor can, for example, provide by order for the abolition of a tribunal whose functions have been

---

[34] TCE Act 2007 s.37.

[35] The rationale is that the AIT has a unique single-tier structure (as prescribed by the Nationality, Immigration and Asylum Act 2002, as amended by the Asylum and Immigration (Treatment of Claimants etc) Act 2004), which would not fit into the new structure established by the TCE Act 2007. The employment tribunals and the Employment Appeal Tribunal were excluded because of the nature of the cases that come before them, which involve one party against another, unlike most other tribunals which hear appeals from citizens against decisions of the State.

[36] Functions that are within the sphere of devolved administrations are, subject to certain exceptions, not transferred, TCE Act 2007 s.30(5)–(8). However the TCE Act 2007 ss.32–34, provides for the possibility of appeal to the Upper Tribunal in relation to Wales, Scotland and Northern Ireland, when the relevant function has not been transferred to the First-tier Tribunal.

transferred under the TCE Act section 30,[37] and he can provide for members
of the "old" tribunal who are judicial office holders to have a new office
within either the First-tier Tribunal or the Upper Tribunal.[38] The TCE Act
also provides for the transfer to the Lord Chancellor of the administrative
functions of other ministers in relation to tribunals listed in Sch.6.[39] When
such power has been transferred it cannot be revoked by another order
under TCE Act s.35, or under the Ministers of the Crown Act 1975.[40] The
rationale for this is to ensure that judiciary-related functions are performed
by the Lord Chancellor, thus securing the independence of tribunals from
the departments that were responsible for them.[41] This theme is further
reinforced by s.36 of the TCE Act, which enables the Lord Chancellor by
order to transfer power to make procedural rules for certain tribunals to
himself or to the Tribunal Procedure Committee.

The courts will in any event protect the independence of tribunals. Thus in
the *Brent* case[42] the court held that where Parliament had created an arm's
length relationship between a department/local authority and a tribunal it
was unacceptable for the former to collapse the distinction between
administration and adjudication by the use of ministerial guidance.

**D. First-Tier Tribunal and Upper Tribunal: Self-Review, Appeal and Judicial
Review**

9–015 The TCE Act contains an interesting and novel array of mechanisms for
checking decisions made by the First-tier Tribunal and the Upper Tribunal.

i. Self-review

9–016 The speedy and efficient discharge of tribunal business is central to the TCE
Act 2007. This serves to explain the powers contained in ss.9 and 10 of the
TCE Act to allow the First-tier Tribunal and the Upper Tribunal to review
their own decisions.

Thus s.9 of the TCE Act empowers the First-tier Tribunal to review a
decision made by it, unless it is an excluded decision,[43] and subject to limits
that may be laid down in Tribunal Procedure Rules. The First-tier Tribunal's power is exercisable of its own initiative, or by a person who has a right
of appeal in respect of the decision. When the power of review is exercised
the First-tier Tribunal can: correct accidental errors in the decision or in a
record of the decision; amend reasons given for the decision; or set the
decision aside. If the First-tier Tribunal sets a decision aside, it must either
re-decide the matter, or refer it to the Upper Tribunal. If the latter occurs,

---

[37] TCE Act 2007 s.31(1).
[38] TCE Act 2007 s.31(2).
[39] TCE Act 2007 s.35.
[40] TCE Act 2007 s.35(8)-(9).
[41] See also, Constitutional Reform Act 2005 s.19 and Sch.7.
[42] *R. (on the application of S (a child)) v Brent LBC* [2002] A.C.D. 90.
[43] TCE Act 2007 s.11(5).

the Upper Tribunal can make any decision which the First-tier Tribunal could make if the First-tier Tribunal were deciding the matter. A decision of the First-tier Tribunal can not be reviewed more than once, and if the Tribunal has decided that an earlier decision should not be reviewed under s.9(1) it may not then change its mind.

The TCE Act s.10, contains analogous provisions, which empower the Upper Tribunal to review its own decisions. The only salient difference is of course that if the Upper Tribunal decides to set aside its own earlier decision, then it must re-decide the matter itself.

ii. Appeal of First-tier Tribunal decisions to the Upper Tribunal
A party to a case generally has a right of appeal on a point of law from the **9–017** First-tier Tribunal to the Upper Tribunal.[44] The right of appeal is subject to permission being given, by either the First-tier Tribunal or the Upper Tribunal. There is however no right of appeal against a decision which is "excluded", and the list of "excluded decisions" is set out in TCE Act s.11(5). The Lord Chancellor is empowered to specify who may or may not be treated as being a party to a case for the purposes of making an appeal from the First-tier Tribunal to the Upper Tribunal.

The effect of the TCE Act is therefore that appeal rights will in general remain as they are now when jurisdictions transfer to the new tribunal. Thus where there is a right of appeal, it will also exist after transfer. Where decisions could not be appealed, the transfer of the jurisdiction to the First-tier Tribunal will give rise to new rights of appeal, unless an order excluding such rights is made under s.11(5)(f), which empowers the Lord Chancellor to characterise a decision of a First-tier Tribunal as an excluded decision.[45]

The TCE Act s.12, specifies the powers of the Upper Tribunal when it decides that an error of law has been made by the First-tier Tribunal. The TCE Act s.12(2) states that the Upper Tribunal may "but need not" set aside the decision of the First-tier Tribunal. Thus if the Upper Tribunal decides that the error of law does not invalidate the decision of the First-tier Tribunal it can let that decision stand.

If it does set aside the decision the Upper Tribunal then has two options. It can remit the case back to the First-tier Tribunal with directions for its reconsideration, and the Upper Tribunal may direct that a different panel reconsiders the case, and give procedural directions in relation to the case. The alternative option is for the Upper Tribunal to make the decision which it considers should have been made, and in doing so it can take any decision that could have been taken if the First-tier Tribunal were remaking the decision. The Upper Tribunal can also make findings of fact.

---

[44] TCE Act 2007 s.11.
[45] The Lord Chancellor's power in this respect is limited by TCE Act 2007 s.11(6).

iii. Appeal of Upper Tribunal decisions to the Court of Appeal

9–018   The TCE Act s.13, provides for a right of appeal to the relevant appellate court[46] on any point of law arising from a decision made by the Upper Tribunal, other than an excluded decision.[47] The right is subject to permission being granted by the Upper Tribunal, or the relevant appellate court on an application by the party. The time limits within which such appeals can be made are to be specified in rules of court made by the Civil Procedure Rules Committee.

The Lord Chancellor may by order make provision for a person to be treated as being, or to be treated as not being, a party to a case for the purposes of the right to appeal. It is also open to the Lord Chancellor by order[48] to restrict appeals to the relevant appellate court to cases where the Court of Appeal or the Upper Tribunal considers that the proposed appeal would raise some important point of principle or practice, or that there is some other compelling reason for the appeal to be heard.[49] This restriction of second appeals applies where the prospective appellant has already had the case considered by both the First-tier Tribunal and the Upper Tribunal.[50]

The TCE Act s.14, specifies the powers of the relevant appeal court in deciding an appeal under s.13. If the appeal court finds an error on a point of law it may "but need not"[51] set aside the decision of the Upper Tribunal. This is analogous to the power of the Upper Tribunal when hearing appeals from the First-tier Tribunal. If the appeal court does set aside the decision it has two options.

It can remit the case to the Upper Tribunal with directions for its reconsideration.[52] It can stipulate that the reconsideration should be undertaken by persons other than those who made the decision subject to appeal, and it can give procedural directions for the handling of the case. If the case remitted to the Upper Tribunal concerns an appeal that it heard from, for example, the First-tier Tribunal, as will commonly be so, then it is open to the Upper Tribunal to remit the case to the First-tier Tribunal for reconsideration in accord with the directions given by the appeal court.[53]

The appeal court can alternatively re-make the decision itself. If it does so it can make any decision which the Upper Tribunal could make if the Upper Tribunal were re-making the decision, and may make such findings of fact as it considers appropriate.

[46] TCE Act 2007 s.13(12), which may be the Court of Appeal for England and Wales, the Court of Session for Scotland or the Court of Appeal for Northern Ireland.
[47] TCE Act 2007 s.13(8).
[48] TCE Act 2007 s.13(6). The exercise of the power under the subsection is subject to the affirmative resolution procedure, s.49.
[49] The criteria are the same as those applied by the Court of Appeal in considering second appeals from the High Court or county court, Access to Justice Act 1999 s.55(1).
[50] TCE Act 2007 s.13(7).
[51] TCE Act 2007 s.14(2).
[52] TCE Act 2007 s.14(2)(b)(i), or, where the decision of the Upper Tribunal was on an appeal or reference from another tribunal or some other person, to the Upper Tribunal or that other tribunal or person, with directions for its reconsideration.
[53] TCE Act 2007 s.14(5).

iv. Appeal and the meaning of "law"

The appeal rights considered above are dependent upon there being a question of law.[54] The existing jurisprudence on the meaning of "law" for the purposes of appeal will therefore still be relevant.   **9–019**

There has been considerable discussion of the *analytical distinction* between law and fact. Distinctions can be made between primary facts, what people saw, heard, did, etc., and the application of a statutory term to these facts, which is a question of law. Numerous cases avowedly support this division.[55] It is, however, unclear whether the meaning of any statutory term is itself a question of law and hence susceptible to appeal. Denning L.J. held that where a layman, albeit one instructed on the relevant legal principles, could declare the inferences from the primary facts, the conclusion reached would be one of fact. Where however to reach a correct conclusion from the primary facts required a thoroughgoing legal knowledge then that conclusion would be one of law.[56]

The distinction between law and fact will also be affected by *functional or pragmatic considerations*, as manifested by the desire of the court to intervene or not. The very difficulty of analytically separating law from fact will allow the courts to apply the label which best fits their aim of intervention or not, as the case may be. This is the key to understanding a number of the cases within this area.

It is moreover important to distinguish two issues that can arise in this area: whether the alleged error involves a question of law, and the test the courts use to determine whether there has been an erroneous construction of this legal term. The courts may simply substitute their view as to what the meaning ought to be, or they may apply a less rigorous standard, which demands only that the construction was reasonable and based on some evidence.[57]

A leading decision on the meaning of law for the purposes of an appeal is the judgment of Lord Radcliffe in *Edwards v Bairstow*.[58] Bairstow alleged that the General Commissioners for income tax had made an error of law in finding that a transaction to which he was a party was not "an adventure in the nature of trade" for tax purposes. Lord Radcliffe began by stating unequivocally that the disputed phrase involved a question of law, the meaning of which had to be interpreted by the courts. The law did not however give a precise meaning to that phrase. It was clearly susceptible to a range of meanings.[59]   **9–020**

---

[54] The Tribunal and Inquiries Act 1992 s.11, accorded a right of appeal to a party who was "dissatisfied in point of law" with the decision reached by certain specified tribunals

[55] *Farmer v Cotton's Trustees* [1915] A.C. 922, 932; *British Launderers' Research Association v Hendon Rating Authority* [1949] 1 K.B. 462, 471; *Woodhouse v Peter Brotherhood Ltd* [1972] 2 Q.B. 520, 536; *R. v Barnet LBC Ex p. Nilish Shah* [1983] 2 W.L.R. 16, 24; *ACT Construction Ltd v Customs and Excise Commissioners* [1981] 1 W.L.R. 49, [1981] 1 W.L.R. 1542.

[56] *British Launderers'*, n.55, 471–472.

[57] *Global Plant Ltd v Secretary of State for Social Services* [1972] 1 Q.B. 139.

[58] [1956] A.C. 14, 33–36.

[59] [1956] A.C. 14, 33.

"[T]he field so marked out is a wide one and there are many combinations of circumstances in which it could not be said to be wrong to arrive at a conclusion one way or the other. If the facts of any particular case are fairly capable of being so described, it seems to me that it necessarily follows that the determination of the Commissioners . . . to the effect that trade does or does not exist is not 'erroneous in point of law'."

Thus far Lord Radcliffe demonstrated clearly the distinction highlighted above. The meaning of trade was a legal question, but there might be no error of law given the standard applied by the above quotation. The role of the court was, in his Lordship's own terms, to lay down the limits within which it would be permissible to say that a trade existed in the meaning of the legislation.

What followed was somewhat more difficult, since Lord Radcliffe labelled cases in which the facts warranted a determination either way as questions of degree, and therefore as questions of fact. This was, with respect, a confusing label to apply. A legal issue does not cease to be such either because it is open to a range of possible meanings or, a fortiori, because there was no error. The reason for denying an appeal where these conditions are present is simply to say that there is a point of law, but that there has been no error in construction, and therefore the appeal fails.

9–021   Lord Radcliffe's judgment was, nonetheless, based on the assumption that the courts did not necessarily have to substitute judgment. The court would, said his Lordship, intervene if there were anything *ex facie* which was bad law and which affected the determination. There would also be an error of law if, in the absence of any misconception appearing *ex facie*, the facts found were such that no person acting judicially and properly instructed to the relevant law could have reached the determination under appeal. Such a case should best be described as one in which the true and only conclusion contradicted the determination actually made.[60] The decision arrived at by the Commissioners was overturned for this reason. A number of other cases have followed this approach.[61]

The courts have, on other occasions, adopted an approach closer to substitution of judgment, as exemplified by *Woodhouse*.[62] The case involved calculation of continuity of employment for the purposes of redundancy payments, which entailed questions as to the transfer of business assets. It was argued that the meaning of the latter term was one of fact and degree. Lord Denning M.R. disagreed.[63] The primary facts were not in dispute. The

[60] [1956] A.C. 14, 36.
[61] e.g. *Marriott v Oxford and District Co-operative Society Ltd (No.2)* [1969] 1 W.L.R. 254; *Global Plant*, n.57, 154–156; *Central Electricity Generating Board v Clwyd County Council* [1976] 1 W.L.R. 151, 160; *O'Kelly v Trusthouse Forte plc* [1984] Q.B. 90; *Shaw (Inspector of Taxes) v Vicky Construction Ltd* [2002] S.T.C. 1544; *New Fashions (London) Ltd v Revenue and Customs Commissioners* [2006] S.T.C. 175; *Salaried Persons Postal Loans Ltd v Revenue and Customs Commissioners* [2006] S.T.C. 1315; *Wood v Holden (Inspector of Taxes)* [2006] 1 W.L.R. 1393; *Zurich Insurance Co v Revenue and Customs Commissioners* [2007] EWCA Civ. 218.
[62] *Woodhouse v Peter Brotherhood Ltd* [1972] 2 Q.B. 520.
[63] [1972] 2 Q.B. 520, 536–537.

issue concerned the correct meaning of a statutory term, and this was a question of law. This then raised the issue as to the test to be applied to determine whether there had been an error of law. Lord Denning M.R. cited the *Edwards* case, and Lord Radcliffe's formulation that if a tribunal reached a conclusion that could not reasonably be drawn, then it would be wrong in law. Lord Denning, however, paraphrased this to mean something rather different: if the tribunal drew the wrong conclusion from the primary facts it would be wrong in law. The gentle change in the linguistic formulation transformed the test to be applied.[64]

These examples demonstrate the pragmatic approach in operation at both levels mentioned above: as to whether the appeal raises a question of law at all, and as to the standard to be applied in determining whether there has been an error. The influences guiding the judicial choice with respect to both topics are not difficult to discern. Where matters of real technical legality or broad principle[65] are involved the courts will veer towards substitution of judgment. They will be influenced in addition by the comparative qualifications of the courts and the tribunal for resolving the question posed, and also by the need to provide a uniform answer in an area where a number of tribunals are interpreting the same term differently. There may, by way of contrast, be a large area in between technical legality and broad principle in which the court is content to allow the decision-maker the degree of latitude provided by Lord Radcliffe's test in the *Edwards*[66] case. There is no reason why we should not continue to use both standards: the range of institutions in relation to which there is a right of appeal on law makes any attempt to force them all under one standard inappropriate.

v. Judicial review by the Upper Tribunal

The inherent powers of judicial review are vested in the High Court. The **9–022** TCE Act is however innovatory in that it has vested judicial review powers in the Upper Tribunal.

The TCE Act s.15(1), empowers the Upper Tribunal to grant mandatory, prohibiting and quashing orders, and a declaration and an injunction, in the circumstances described below. The Upper Tribunal can also grant restitution or monetary relief, if satisfied that the High Court would have done so.[67] The relief granted by the Upper Tribunal has the same effect as that granted by the High Court on an application for judicial review, and is enforceable in the same way. The Upper Tribunal must apply the principles of judicial review developed by the High Court. Applications under s.15 are subject to the same hurdles as they would be if judicial review were sought

---

[64] *Instrumatic Ltd v Supabrase Ltd* [1969] 1 W.L.R. 519; *British Railways Board v Customs and Excise Commissioners* [1977] 1 W.L.R. 588; *Farmer*, n.55; *ACT Construction*, n.55.
[65] e.g. *Ransom v Higgs* [1974] 1 W.L.R. 1594, 1610–1611.
[66] [1956] A.C. 14, 36.
[67] TCE Act 2007 s.16(6).

before the High Court. Thus, permission is required,[68] the applicant must have a sufficient interest in the matter to which the application relates, and there are provisions concerning undue delay.[69]

The circumstances in which the Upper Tribunal can exercise powers of judicial review are set out in TCE Act s.18, which specifies four conditions. The first condition[70] is that the application does not seek anything other than the relief that the Upper Tribunal is able to grant under s.15(1), a monetary award under s.16(6), interest and costs. The second condition[71] is that the application does not call into question anything done by the Crown Court, the rationale being that it would be anomalous for a tribunal, a superior court of record, to have supervisory powers over another superior court of record. The third condition[72] is that the application falls within a class specified for the purposes of s.18(6), in a direction given in accordance with the Constitutional Reform Act 2005.[73] The direction is made by or on behalf of the Lord Chief Justice with the concurrence of the Lord Chancellor. The final condition[74] relates to the status of judge presiding at the hearing of the application.[75]

If these conditions are not met the judicial review application is transferred to the High Court.[76] If all four conditions are met then an application for judicial review made to the High Court must be transferred to the Upper Tribunal.[77] If all conditions are met apart from the third, the High Court may nonetheless decide to transfer the case to the Upper Tribunal if it appears just and convenient to do so. Thus even if the case does not fall within a class of case designated for the Upper Tribunal by a direction, the High Court has a discretion to transfer it to the Upper Tribunal, subject to the caveat that this does not apply to matters concerning immigration and nationality. There are separate provisions dealing with Scotland.[78]

If the Upper Tribunal makes a quashing order it can in addition remit the matter to the court, tribunal or authority that made the decision, with a direction to reconsider the matter and reach a decision in accordance with the findings of the Upper Tribunal. It can alternatively substitute its own decision for the decision in question, provided that the decision was made by a court or tribunal, the decision was quashed for error of law, and without

---

[68] Refusal of permission by the Upper Tribunal can be appealed to the Court of Appeal, TCE Act s.16(8).
[69] TCE Act 2007 s.16.
[70] TCE Act 2007 s.18(4).
[71] TCE Act 2007 s.18(5).
[72] TCE Act 2007 s.18(6).
[73] Constitutional Reform Act 2005 Sch.2 Pt 1.
[74] TCE Act 2007 s.18(8).
[75] He or she must be either a judge of the High Court or the Court of Appeal in England and Wales or Northern Ireland, or a judge of the Court of Session, or such other persons as may be agreed from time to time between the Lord Chief Justice, the Lord President, or the Lord Chief Justice of Northern Ireland, as the case may be, and the Senior President of Tribunals.
[76] TCE Act 2007 s.18(3), (9).
[77] TCE Act 2007 s.19, inserting a new s.31(A) into the Supreme Court Act 1981.
[78] TCE Act 2007 ss.20–21.

the error, there would have been only one decision that the court or tribunal could have reached.[79]

vi. Judicial review of the First-tier and Upper Tribunal by the High Court
The discussion in this section thus far has been concerned with the new statutory regime established by the TCE Act 2007. This will have implications for traditional judicial review before the High Court.   **9–023**

First, a claimant may seek judicial review of a decision made by the First-tier Tribunal before the High Court. Such a claim will fail if the matter is one which satisfies all the conditions for the Upper Tribunal to exercise judicial review, since it must then be transferred to the Upper Tribunal. It will also fail where the High Court decides that even if the third condition is not met that it is just and convenient for the judicial review application to be heard by the Upper Tribunal.

Second, a claimant who seeks judicial review of a decision by a First-tier Tribunal before the High Court may also be turned down because the High Court decides that the claimant should exercise his or her statutory appeal rights to the Upper Tribunal. There is an extensive case law on the circumstances in which statutory appeal rights must be used rather than judicial review.[80] It is likely, given the overall regime of the TCE Act, that the High Court will insist that the claimant use the statutory appeal from the First-tier to the Upper Tribunal and thence onward to the Court of Appeal. This is likely to be so even where the case does not fall within the judicial review jurisdiction of the Upper Tribunal, since it may well still come within its general statutory jurisdiction to hear appeals on points of law from the First-tier Tribunal.

Third, there is the case where a claimant seeks judicial review by the High Court of a decision on appeal made by the Upper Tribunal. The policy of the TCE Act is that, subject to an order made by the Lord Chancellor, any onward appeal should be to the Court of Appeal, and then only where the Court of Appeal or the Upper Tribunal considers that the proposed appeal would raise some important point of principle or practice, or that there is some other compelling reason for the appeal to be heard, where the claimant has already had the case considered by both the First-tier Tribunal and the Upper Tribunal.[81] The High Court is unlikely to allow this policy to be circumvented by allowing the claimant to bring a judicial review action against the Upper Tribunal to the High Court. An action for judicial review may, by way of contrast, be countenanced where there are doubts as to whether it would come within the statutory appeal regime at all.

The final scenario is where the Upper Tribunal has exercised its judicial review powers in accord with the TCE Act s.15, and the claimant wishes to contest this finding. The logic of the TCE Act s.15, is that the decision and

---

[79] TCE Act 2007 s.17.
[80] See below, Ch.26.
[81] TCE Act 2007 s.13(7).

relief given by the Upper Tribunal correspond to relief given by the High Court on an ordinary application for judicial review and are enforceable in the same manner. If therefore a claimant is dissatisfied with the judicial review decision made by the Upper Tribunal then recourse should be had to the Court of Appeal, in the same way as if the initial judicial review decision had been made by the High Court.

E. Tribunal Procedure Rules

i. The position prior to the TCE Act

9–024 Tribunals have traditionally had their own procedural rules, and rule-making normally vested in the Lord Chancellor or Secretary of State, subject to consultation with the Council on Tribunals.[82] The Council sought to balance uniformity with the need to design procedures to cope with the special problems of a particular tribunal.[83]

The most obvious procedural norm which applies *before the hearing* is that an individual must know of the right to apply to a tribunal. It is however relatively clear that although the individual was normally informed of this, there was no uniform way in which it occurred. In some areas there was a statutory obligation to inform, in others it could be left to established practice, while in yet other areas the individual was left to discover the right to apply. The other crucial factor in order that tribunals can be accessible is that individuals have the means to use them. There is no general provision for legal aid to all tribunals. It seems clear that absence of the financial means to secure assistance hampers individuals who appear before tribunals.[84]

Procedural rules are also relevant during the *hearing process* itself. Whether an individual has a right to a hearing, and what this entails, will be decided by a combination of statute and the principles of natural justice.[85] These will also determine particular aspects of the hearing process. The rules of evidence have, for example, been relaxed in their application,[86] and the tribunal is allowed to rely on its own knowledge in addition to the evidence tendered before it.[87] In most instances a party before a tribunal can be

---

[82] Tribunals and Inquiries Act 1992 s.8.
[83] *Model Rules of Procedure for Tribunals*, Cm. 1434 (1991). The Model Rules of Procedure were revised in 1999 to take account, *inter alia*, of the Human Rights Act 1998; N. Brown, "Tribunal Adjudication in Britain: Model Rules of Procedure" (1993) Special Number E.R.P.L. 287.
[84] A valuable survey of this aspect of tribunals is to be found in, *Administrative Justice, Some Necessary Reforms* (Oxford University Press, 1988), 225–251.
[85] See below, Ch.12.
[86] *R. v Deputy Industrial Injuries Commissioner Ex p. Moore* [1965] 1 Q.B. 456.
[87] *R. v City of Westminster Assessment Committee Ex p. Grosvenor House (Park Lane) Ltd* [1941] 1 K.B. 53; *Crofton Investment Trust Ltd v Greater London Rent Assessment Committee* [1967] 2 Q.B. 955; *Metropolitan Properties Ltd (FGC) v Lannon* [1969] 1 Q.B. 577.

represented by a lawyer if he or she so chooses, as was recommended by the Franks Report.[88]

A number of procedural principles are of relevance *after the hearing*. An important procedural innovation introduced as a result of the Franks Report was the requirement that a tribunal provide reasons for its decision.[89] This obligation only applies to those institutions listed in the Act, and only becomes operative when the individual requests a statement, which request must be tendered on or before the giving or notification of the decision. Once given the reasons are deemed to form part of the record.[90] There are exceptions to these general provisions. Thus reasons need not be given where a decision is made in connection with a scheme or order of a legislative and not an executive character.[91] A statement of reasons can be withheld on grounds of national security,[92] or if the request for reasons is from one who is not primarily concerned with the decision where to furnish those reasons would be contrary to the interests of the person who is primarily concerned.[93] The Lord Chancellor also possesses the power to dispense with the need for a tribunal to give reasons where he is of the opinion it would be impracticable or unnecessary for the tribunal to do so.[94] Certain tribunals are also exempted from any duty to give reasons in relation to decisions made in the exercise of their executive functions.[95]

Where the obligation to give reasons applies the court has made it clear that the reasons must deal with the substantial points that have been raised, and must not be too vague.[96] Lord Brown in the *Porter* case summarised the matter as follows.[97]

"The reasons for a decision must be intelligible and they must be adequate. They must enable the reader to understand why the matter was decided as it was and what conclusions were reached on the 'principal important controversial issues', disclosing how any issue of law or fact was resolved. Reasons can be briefly stated, the degree of particularity required depending entirely on the nature of the issues falling for decision. The reasoning must not give rise to a substantial doubt as to whether the decision-maker erred in law, for example by misunderstanding some relevant policy or some other important matter or by failing to reach a rational decision on relevant grounds. But such adverse inference will not readily be drawn. The reasons need refer only to the main issues in the dispute, not to every material consideration."

[88] Cmnd. 218 (1957), para.87.
[89] Tribunals and Inquiries Act 1992 s.10.
[90] Tribunals and Inquiries Act 1992 s.10(6).
[91] Tribunals and Inquiries Act 1992 s.10(5)(b).
[92] Tribunals and Inquiries Act 1992 s.10(2).
[93] Tribunals and Inquiries Act 1992 s.10(3).
[94] Tribunals and Inquiries Act 1992 s.10(7).
[95] Tribunals and Inquiries Act 1992 s.14.
[96] *Re Poyser and Mills' Arbitration* [1964] 2 Q.B. 467. They can, however, be brief, *Westminster City Council v Great Portland Estates* [1985] A.C. 661.
[97] *South Buckinghamshire DC v Porter (No.2)* [2004] 1 W.L.R. 1953, para.36.

The legal consequence of failure to provide the required reasons is not entirely clear. Some authorities have held that such a failure itself constitutes an error of law,[98] while others have held that inadequate reasons do not per se constitute an error of law, and will lead to invalidity only if they furnish evidence of such an error.[99] Sedley J. signalled that this issue should be reconsidered, so that the law in this respect could be brought into line with that on judicial review.[100] However Lord Brown in *Porter*[101] more recently held that a "reasons challenge will only succeed if the party aggrieved can satisfy the court that he has genuinely been substantially prejudiced by the failure to provide an adequately reasoned decision".

ii. The position under the TCE Act

9–025　The TCE Act s.22, is intended to produce greater consistency in the development of procedure. Tribunal Procedure Rules are to be made by the Tribunal Procedure Committee. It is to exercise this power with a view to securing the objectives specified in the TCE Act s.22(4), that: justice is done; the tribunal system is accessible and fair; proceedings are handled quickly and efficiently; the rules are both simple and simply expressed; and that the rules where appropriate confer on members of the First-tier Tribunal, or Upper Tribunal, responsibility for ensuring that proceedings before the tribunal are handled quickly and efficiently. The Senior President of Tribunals is also empowered to make Practice Directions concerning practice and procedure of the First-tier Tribunal and the Upper Tribunal.[102]

The details concerning the making of procedural rules are set out in the TCE Act Sch.5. Pt 1 makes provision for what the tribunal procedural rules may contain, relating to, inter alia, time limits, the extent to which matters may be decided without a hearing and whether a hearing may be public or private, proceedings without prior notice, representation, evidence and witnesses, use of information, and arbitration. Schedule 5 Pt 2 is concerned with the creation of the Tribunal Procedure Committee, and Pt 3 with the process by which the procedural rules are made. The Committee is required to consult before rules are made. The Lord Chancellor's powers are limited. He can allow or disallow the rules, and can specify a purpose that the rules must attain. Sch.5 Pt 4 gives the Lord Chancellor power to amend, repeal or revoke any Act in pursuance of a rule change, this being based analogously on the provisions in the Civil Procedure Act 1997. An order exercising this power is subject to the affirmative resolution procedure.

The existence of the Tribunal Procedure Committee is very likely to

---

[98] *Poyser*, n.96; *Givaudan v Minister of Housing and Local Government* [1967] 1 W.L.R. 250.
[99] *Mountview Court Properties Ltd v Devlin* (1970) 21 P. & C.R. 689; *Crake v Supplementary Benefits Commission* [1982] 1 All E.R. 498; *S (A Minor) v Special Educational Needs Tribunal* [1996] 1 All E.R. 171; *Yeoman's Row Management Ltd v London Rent Assessment Committee* [2002] EWHC 835; G. Richardson, "The Duty to Give Reasons: Potential and Practice" [1986] P.L. 437, 450–457.
[100] *R. v Northamptonshire County Council Ex p. Marshall* [1998] C.O.D. 457, 458.
[101] *Porter*, n.97, para.36.
[102] TCE Act 2007 s.23.

produce greater consistency in procedural rules, more especially because the number of separate tribunals has been reduced as a result of the TCE Act. Insofar as there is a need for different procedural rules for different subject matter areas this can be accommodated by tailoring procedural rules to the chambers that deal with them. Some of the previous law will still be of relevance under the new regime. Thus the rules of natural justice will continue to be applicable under the TCE Act. The procedural rules devised by the Tribunal Procedure Committee can be tested for conformity with the guiding principles set out in TCE Act s.22(4), and with the principles of natural justice. The duty to give reasons contained in the Tribunals and Inquiries Act 1992 s.10, was not repealed by the TCE Act, but it may nonetheless be superseded in due course: the procedural rules under the TCE Act will hopefully contain a duty to give reasons and in any event many of the tribunals to which the 1992 Act applies will cease to exist, their functions being taken over by the First-tier Tribunal and the Upper Tribunal.

It is to be hoped that the Tribunal Procedure Committee will be willing to **9–026** draw on both adversarial and inquisitorial models of procedure when devising the procedural rules. We are strongly wedded to the adversary system in this country, which forms the basis for adjudication in the superior courts, and is the norm for the tribunal system. The assumptions that underlie the adversarial system may nonetheless be absent in certain areas. An implicit premise behind the adversarial system is that the two opponents are equal, save for natural inequalities of intellect and experience. Battle is waged and the judge, in the position of umpire, will decide. This premise may not be sustainable in relation to certain types of tribunals, such as those concerned with social welfare and immigration. The very fact that the adversarial system tends to see parties in the position of "plaintiff" and "defendant" may well be inappropriate in some areas. Public law litigation will moreover often raise a wider public interest, over and beyond that of the particular parties before the tribunal.[103]

It may well, therefore, be appropriate for tribunals to take a more "active" role.[104] Some tribunals have power to require the attendance of witnesses or the production of documents,[105] while others, particularly those dealing with land and property, have powers of inspection and examination. Care should be taken to ensure that this does not develop into what has been termed accusatory inquisition,[106] where the individual feels under attack from the tribunal itself. We should nonetheless be willing to fashion procedures that draw on the best from both the adversarial and inquisitorial

[103] A. Chayes, "The Role of the Judge in Public Law Litigation" (1976) 89 Harv. L.R. 1281; cf. L. Fuller, "The Forms and Limits of Adjudication" (1978) 92 Harv. L.R. 353, 382–384.
[104] For the limits of a tribunal's obligation to assist an unrepresented applicant see, *Chilton Saga Holidays plc* [1986] 1 All E.R. 841; *R v Criminal Injuries Compensation Board Ex p. Pearce* [1994] C.O.D. 235; *R. v Criminal Injuries Compensation Board Ex p. Milton* [1996] C.O.D. 264.
[105] G. Ganz, *Administrative Procedures* (Sweet & Maxwell, 1974), 31–32; Wraith and Hutchesson, n.1, 146–147.
[106] Ganz, n.105, 35; G. Richardson and H. Genn, "Tribunals in Transition: Resolution or Adjudication?" [2007] P.L. 116.

system. The blanket rejection of anything that savours of an inquisitorial role for any tribunal is unwarranted. The idea that better justice can never be achieved by a procedure adopted by a large number of civilised jurisdictions smacks of the parochial and insular.

When fashioning procedures a balance should also be struck between formality and informality. The site of the hearing, the absence of the accoutrements of judicial office, and the presence of lay members on the adjudicating panel, all tend to produce a less formal, more relaxed atmosphere than in an ordinary court.

There are nonetheless real limits to informality as the valuable work of Genn has shown.[107] She identified four factors that constrain the degree of informality of the proceedings. The *complexity of the subject* matter may militate against an approach that is too informal. Many issues in, for example, social welfare cases are complex because of the statutory material. *Procedural informality should not be confused with substantive informality*. The fact that the procedure itself is informal may lead the claimant to believe that the substantive outcome is to be decided on a similarly informal basis. This will often not be so where the statute prescribes specific criteria if the claimant is to succeed. *Unrepresented applicants are often at a disadvantage in tribunal proceedings*, notwithstanding the efforts of the tribunal to put the person at their ease. The disadvantage is often a consequence of the applicant believing that the whole matter could be dealt with by a quiet chat, tailoring any solution to the applicant's own personal circumstance, and not realising the constraints which the legislation place upon the tribunal's discretion. Finally, the *tribunal may be less able to assist an unrepresented claimant than has been commonly thought in the past*. The standard picture is of a tribunal composed of those with expertise in the area who are capable of aiding the individual, particularly if he or she is unrepresented. Such assistance may be less forthcoming, because of constraints of time, because the tribunal may not know what questions would best help the applicant, and because the more adversarial are the proceedings the more reluctant are tribunal members to get involved on one side of the case.

F. Mediation and Alternative Dispute Resolution

9–027　It is increasingly common for mediation and other forms of alternative dispute resolution to be used in the justice system. The TCE Act s.24, provides the statutory basis for mediation. It enables staff appointed for the First-tier and Upper Tribunals to act as mediators in relation to disputed matters in proceedings before the First-tier or Upper Tribunal. It is however made clear by s.24(1) that mediation is to take place only by agreement between the parties, and that where they fail to mediate, or where mediation between the parties fails to resolve disputed matters, the failure is not to affect the outcome of the proceedings.

---

[107] "Tribunals and Informal Justice" (1993) M.L.R. 393.

G. The Tribunals Service, Administrative Support and Staffing

The TCE Act s.39, imposes an obligation on the Lord Chancellor to ensure   **9–028**
that there is an efficient and effective system of tribunal administration. This
duty applies to the First-tier Tribunal, the Upper Tribunal, employment
tribunals, the Employment Appeal Tribunal and the Asylum and Immigration Tribunal.

This duty is complemented by the TCE Act s.40, which empowers the
Lord Chancellor to provide staff, services and accommodation for tribunals.
Civil servants can be employed as tribunal staff. Certain functions can be
contracted-out, but not those that involve making judicial decisions or
exercising any judicial discretion, and even the contracting-out of administrative functions has to be legitimated by an order authorising the Lord
Chancellor to do so.

Following the recommendations of the Leggatt Report, a Tribunals
Service was created in 2006 as an Executive Agency of the Ministry of
Justice.[108] The Tribunals Service strategic plan for 2007–2008[109] listed its
strategic objectives as to: deliver effective services within the tribunals; focus
on customers and the wider community; make efficient use of available
resources and infrastructure; build the Tribunals Service capacity to deliver
by unlocking the potential of its staff; and to work effectively in partnership
with the judiciary and others.

The Tribunals Service proposed a number of reforms to meet these
objectives over the next five years. These included: implementing a new
delivery model centred on a network of multi-jurisdictional hearing centres
and administrative support centres; implementing the provisions of the
Tribunals, Courts and Enforcement Act; implementing a new regional
management structure with streamlined corporate services; consolidating
the provision of IT services and case management systems to improve
communications and management information and provide a base from
which to move towards electronic case processing and e-services for customers; and introducing proportionate dispute resolution processes that will
provide greater choice for users and reduce the number of cases reaching a
full hearing.

H. Oversight: The Administrative Justice and Tribunals Council

The TCE Act s.44, establishes the Administrative Justice and Tribunals   **9–029**
Council, AJTC,[110] to oversee the system of tribunals and inquiries, and s.45
abolishes the Council on Tribunals, which previously performed the oversight role. The intention was that the Council on Tribunals would be
transformed into the AJTC.

---

[108] http://www.tribunalsgov.uk/.
[109] Tribunals Service, *Strategic Business Plan for 2007–08: Delivering the Future, One System,
One Service* (2007), available at http://www.tribunalsgov.uk/Documents/Publications/
strategicbusinessplan0708.pdf.
[110] http://www.ajtc.gov.uk/index.htm.

i. The Council on Tribunals

9–030 A brief word about the Council on Tribunals will help in understanding the shift to the AJTC. The establishment of an institution to keep under review the organisation of the tribunal system developed out of evidence tendered to the Franks Committee by academics.[111] The Franks Committee agreed that such an institution should be established and proposed two councils, one for England and Wales, the other for Scotland.[112] They were to be concerned with the procedure, constitution, and organisation of tribunals; they should be consulted prior to the creation of any new tribunal; and they should have responsibility for the appointment of lay members. What emerged in the subsequent legislation was more limited. There was only one Council, albeit with provision for a Scottish Committee, appointment of lay members remained with departments, and the Council's role in the procedural area was reduced. The Franks' Committee proposed that the Council would formulate procedural rules, but the legislation accorded it only a consultative role. The Council was thus an advisory as opposed to executive body, although its advisory role did encompass keeping under review the general constitution and working of the tribunals brought within the legislation.[113]

The effectiveness of the Council was questioned. It made a real contribution towards the clarity of procedural rules where it was consulted,[114] produced a valuable set of model procedural rules for tribunals,[115] and made important recommendations concerning the organization and independence of tribunals.[116] Success in other fields was more limited. The government was under no statutory obligation to consult the Council about proposed legislation creating or affecting tribunals. The Council was often not consulted adequately or at all, and it was often dissatisfied with the reaction to its suggestions. There was dissatisfaction with its powers.[117]

ii. The Administrative Justice and Tribunals Council

9–031 The detailed workings of the new AJTC, which is a non-departmental public body, are set out in the TCE Act Sch.7, which is divided into four parts.

Part 1 is concerned with the *membership* of the AJTC and its committees. The AJTC has a minimum of 10 and a maximum of 15 members and the Parliamentary Commissioner for Administration, PCA. The members, other than the PCA are appointed by the Scottish Ministers, the Welsh

---

[111] Professors W.A. Robson and H.W.R. Wade.
[112] Cmnd. 218 (1957), paras 131–134.
[113] D. Foulkes, "The Council on Tribunals: Visits, Policy and Practice" [1994] P.L. 564.
[114] The Annual Reports 1999/2000 and 2000/2001 contain representative examples of the work of the Council.
[115] n.83.
[116] *Tribunals, Their Organisation and Independence*, Cm. 3744 (1997).
[117] H.W.R. Wade and C.F. Forsyth, *Administrative Law* (Oxford University Press, 9th edn, 2004), 924–926; D. Foulkes, *Administrative Law* (7th edn, 1990), 164–168; H. Street, *Justice in the Welfare State* (Sweet & Maxwell, 2nd edn, 1975), 63; C. Harlow and R. Rawlings, *Law and Administration* (Butterworths, 2nd edn, 1997), 469–471.

Ministers and the Lord Chancellor, each with the concurrence of the others. The members hold and leave office in accordance with the terms on which they were appointed. The Chairman is a member of the AJTC and is nominated by the Lord Chancellor after consulting the Scottish and Welsh Ministers. There is provision for Scottish and Welsh Committees of the AJTC.[118]

The *functions* of the AJTC are dealt with in Pt 2 of Sch.7. The AJTC is to formulate an annual programme of work[119] and must make an annual report to the Lord Chancellor, the Scottish Ministers and the Welsh Ministers.[120] The AJTC has functions in relation to the administrative justice system, tribunals and statutory inquiries. These will be considered in turn.

Thus the AJTC is instructed[121]: to keep the administrative justice system under review; consider ways to make the system accessible, fair and efficient; advise the Lord Chancellor, the Scottish and Welsh ministers and the Senior President of Tribunals on the development of the system; refer proposals for changes in the system to those persons, and make proposals for research into the system. The "administrative justice system" is defined to cover the overall system by which decisions of an administrative or executive nature are made in relation to particular persons, including: the procedures for making such decisions; the law under which such decisions are made; and the systems for resolving disputes and airing grievances in relation to such decisions.[122]

The AJTC's responsibility in relation to tribunals is as follows.[123] It is to keep listed tribunals under review and report on those tribunals and also on any matter that the AJTC thinks is of special importance. The AJTC is also to consider and report on any matter referred to it by the Lord Chancellor, Scottish Ministers and Welsh Ministers. The AJTC may also scrutinise and comment on legislation that is extant or proposed, including procedural rules, relating to tribunals. The "listed tribunals" include the First-tier Tribunal, the Upper Tribunal and any other tribunal that an authority who has responsibility for a tribunal provides is to be a listed tribunal for the purpose of Sch.7.[124] The AJTC reports to the Lord Chancellor and also to the Scottish and Welsh Ministers if the report relates to Scotland and/or Wales.[125]

---

[118] TCE Act 2007 Sch.7 paras 4(2) and 7(2): each Committee is to consist of the Parliamentary Commissioner for Administration, the Public Services Ombudsman for each jurisdiction, the members of the AJTC appointed under para.1(2) by the Scottish or Welsh Ministers and a specified number of other persons who are not members of the AJTC appointed by the Scottish or Welsh Ministers. These must be consulted on any matter that relates solely to their jurisdiction before the Council is authorized to report on it. The committees can make reports to the AJTC on their own motion in relation to matters specified in paras 18 and 19.

[119] TCE Act 2007 Sch.7 para.20.
[120] TCE Act 2007 Sch.7 para.21.
[121] TCE Act 2007 Sch.7 para.13(1)–(2).
[122] TCE Act 2007 Sch.7 para.13(4).
[123] TCE Act 2007 Sch.7 para.14.
[124] TCE Act 2007 Sch.7 para.25.
[125] TCE Act 2007 Sch.7 para.17.

9–032   The AJTC also has responsibility for statutory inquiries.[126] It is to keep under review, and report on, the constitution and working of statutory inquiries, both generally and in relation to any particular statutory inquiry or type of inquiry; it is to consider and report on any other matter that relates to statutory inquiries in general, to statutory inquiries of a particular description or to any particular statutory inquiry, which the AJTC determines to be of special importance; and it is to report on any particular matter referred to it concerning such inquiries referred to it by the Lord Chancellor, the Welsh Ministers and the Scottish Ministers.[127] The AJTC reports to the Lord Chancellor and also to the Scottish and Welsh Ministers if the report relates to Scotland and/or Wales.[128]

The AJTC's role in the making of *procedural rules* is dealt with in Pt 3 of Sch.7. The AJTC must be consulted on procedural rules made for a listed tribunal by a Minister of the Crown, a Scottish Minister or a Welsh Minister.[129] This duty does not apply to procedural rules made by the Tribunal Procedure Committee in relation to a listed tribunal,[130] the rationale being that a member of the AJTC sits on the Tribunal Procedure Committee.

Matters of *interpretation and definition* are dealt with by Sch.7 Pt 4. This includes the definition of "listed tribunal" which, as we have seen, means the First-tier Tribunal, the Upper Tribunal or any tribunal that the Lord Chancellor, Scottish Ministers or Welsh Ministers requests to be listed for the purpose of Sch.7.[131] The latter part of this definition enables the AJTC's oversight responsibilities to cover tribunals that are inside and outside the new tribunal system.

The expanded jurisdiction accorded to the AJTC by way of comparison to the Council on Tribunals is to be welcomed. The limits of the power accorded to the AJTC should nonetheless be borne in mind. Thus there is for example no obligation to consult the AJTC on legislation that affects tribunals, although the AJTC has power to scrutinise and comment on such legislation.[132] Moreover the definition of administrative justice[133] is focused on the overall system by which decisions of an administrative or executive nature are made in relation to particular persons. It is clear therefore that the making of decisions by a minister, Executive Agency or non-departmental public body that affect a particular individual would come within the brief of the AJTC.

It remains however to be seen how far the AJTC will feel able to extend its remit to rulemaking by, for example, Executive Agencies and non-departmental public bodies, and how far it will feel able to comment on more general issues concerning the accountability of such agencies and bodies.[134]

---

[126] TCE Act 2007 Sch.7 para.15.
[127] TCE Act 2007 Sch.7 para.16.
[128] TCE Act 2007 Sch.7 para.17.
[129] TCE Act 2007 Sch.7 para.24(1).
[130] TCE Act 2007 Sch.7 para.24(2).
[131] TCE Act 2007 Sch.7 para.25.
[132] TCE Act 2007 Sch.7 para.14(2).
[133] TCE Act 2007 Sch.7 para.13(4).
[134] See Ch.4.

Much depends on how the AJTC chooses to interpret the phrase "overall system" in the TCE Act.[135] It would be regrettable if the jurisdiction of the AJTC were to be limited to administrative justice conceived narrowly in terms of individual adjudication, more especially since the line between adjudication and rulemaking can be a fine one, and because an agency may use both strategies to develop policy in its area. There are institutions in other legal systems that undertake more extensive oversight,[136] and this would be beneficial in this country.[137] It is encouraging that the AJTC's initial statements about its strategic objectives are broadly framed.[138]

4. STATUTORY INQUIRIES

A. The Background

The historical antecedents of the inquiry procedure have already been   **9–033**
related.[139] It was, however, the 20th century that saw the expansion in the use of inquiries, most particularly in the context of land and housing. A variety of purposes are served by the inquiry procedure, the two most important of which are as a mechanism of appeal and as a means for airing objections. An example of the former is the system of appeal against the refusal of planning permission by a local authority, while objections to the siting of a road, or building, provide examples of the latter. Inquiries may also be used as a form of post-mortem to investigate an accident, or a breach of governmental secrecy, or as a method of preliminary investigation into the viability of a proposal.[140]

At the most general level inquiries are used to collect and collate information, or to serve as a vehicle for the resolution of conflicts. They may of course do both. Insofar as they serve the latter function they are used for the most part in circumstances where it is felt desirable that political control be maintained by vesting the ultimate decision in a minister. Decisions concerning the siting of a new town, the approval of a slum clearance order, or the confirmation of a road building scheme, involve considerations of policy, which should be decided by those who are politically accountable. It will not be the minister who makes the initial decision and very often officials will render decisions in the minister's name. The process of government would grind to a halt were it to be otherwise. The minister will, however,

---

[135] TCE Act 2007 Sch.7 para.13(4).
[136] e.g. Australia: Administrative Review Council established by the Administrative Appeals Tribunal Act 1975 s.48; USA: Administrative Conference of the United States, Administrative Conference Act 1964 s.51.
[137] Sir Harry Woolf, "Judicial Review: A Possible Programme for Reform" [1992] P.L. 221, 235–236.
[138] http://www.ajtc.gov.uk/about/strategic-objectives.htm.
[139] See above, para.2–015.
[140] R. Wraith and G. Lamb, *Public Inquiries as an Instrument of Government* (Allen & Unwin, 1971), 14–15, 305–306.

make the final choice in circumstances that are especially contentious or important.

B. The Franks Committee

i. The recommendations

9–034   Prior to 1957 there was increasing public disquiet not just with tribunals, but also with inquiries. Issues concerning cost and delay were overlaid by a sense of frustration at the secrecy surrounding the whole procedure. The report of the inspector who held the inquiry would normally not be made public, and there was a feeling that the administration was very much just "going through the motions".

Witnesses who gave evidence before the Committee were divided as to the role of inquiries. One group saw inquiries as part of the process of administration, as an extension of departmental decision-making in specific areas, which should be relatively free from controls other than those imposed by Parliament. A different view was expressed by those who saw the inquiry as akin to a judicial process in which the inspector who undertook the hearing was in the position of a judge. The corollary of this latter approach was that the procedures by which the inquiry was run should be modelled upon the judicial process, at least to the extent that this entailed the decision being taken directly on the evidence presented at the inquiry.[141] The Franks Committee rejected both positions.[142]

"Our general conclusion is that those procedures cannot be classified as purely administrative or purely judicial. They are not purely administrative because of the provision for a special procedure preliminary to the decision—a feature not to be found in the ordinary course of administration—and because this procedure, as we have shown, involves the testing of an issue, often partly in public. They are not on the other hand purely judicial, because the final decision cannot be reached by the application of rules and must allow the exercise of wide discretion in the balancing of public and private interest. Neither view at its extreme is tenable, nor should either be emphasized at the expense of the other."

Instead of attempting to model the inquiry procedures upon either of the preceding views the Franks Committee drew up a series of recommendations which attempted to balance the conflicting interests. What emerged were proposals concerning the pre-inquiry stage, the procedure at the inquiry, and post-inquiry practice.[143]

9–035   As to the practice *before the inquiry*, the Committee recommended that the public authority should be required to make available in good time a

[141] Cmnd. 218 (1957), paras 263–264.
[142] Cmnd. 218 (1957), para.272.
[143] These are summarised at 96–98 of the Franks Committee Report.

written statement giving full particulars of its case. The minister who had the ultimate power of decision should whenever possible provide a statement of the policy relevant to the particular case, but should be free to direct that the statements be wholly or partly excluded from discussion of the inquiry. Where this policy changed after the inquiry the letter conveying the ministerial decision should explain the change and its relation to the decision.

As to procedure *at the inquiry*, it was recommended that the initiating authority should be required to explain its proposals fully and support them by oral evidence, and that in principle the procedure should be public. A code of procedure should be formulated by the Council on Tribunals, which should be made statutory; rules of evidence should be relaxed; the inspector should have power to subpoena witnesses and should have a wide discretion in controlling the proceedings.

Post-inquiry procedure was mainly concerned with the inspector's report and the consequent ministerial decision. It was proposed that the inspector's report be divided into two parts comprising a summary of the evidence, finding of facts and inferences of fact on the one hand, and reasoning from those facts, including application of policy on the other. The whole report should then accompany the minister's letter of decision, and there should be provision for a person to suggest corrections of fact. When the minister made the final decision he or she should be required to submit to the parties concerned any factual evidence obtained after the inquiry, while the decision itself should set out in full the findings and inferences of fact and the reasons for the decision.

Apart from proposals concerning procedure there was also an important recommendation that the main body of inspectors should be placed under the control of the Lord Chancellor, while being allowed to be kept in contact with policy developments in the departments responsible for inquiries.

ii. Implementation

The Franks Committee Report was warmly received and justly so. A **9–036** number of its proposals were taken up rapidly by the Government and the Tribunal and Inquiries Bill duly appeared before Parliament. What however became apparent at the Committee stage was that the Bill actually said very little about inquiries. It was mainly concerned with tribunals. As a result of pressure in the House of Lords, the Government introduced a new sub-paragraph, which became s.1(1)(c) of the Tribunals and Inquiries Act 1958. This provided that the Council on Tribunals was to consider and report on such matters as might be referred to it, or as the Council itself should determine to be of special importance, with respect to administrative procedure involving an inquiry.[144] The Council's powers with respect to inquiries were therefore somewhat different to those concerning tribunals. While it had no power to keep such inquiries under review, as it did with tribunals, it did have power to intervene on its own initiative in more specific

---

[144] See now Tribunals and Inquiries Act 1992 s.1(1)(c).

terms than in connection with tribunals.[145] Again however, as with tribunals, the powers of the Council were advisory rather than executive.

Despite the extension of the Council's role in relation to inquiries as a result of the Committee stage of the Bill, most of the changes advocated by the Franks Committee were implemented by administrative practice and not by statute. Many of these recommendations were put into effect, but two important proposals were rejected by the government: those related to placing the inspectorate under the Lord Chancellor, and the requirement that the minister should make available a statement of policy prior to the inquiry. The procedure that now applies will be a mixture of law and administrative practice. The precise details will differ in different areas, but the general principles are the same. It is to these that we must now turn.

C. Inquiries: Practice and Procedure

i Procedure before the inquiry

9–037   A number of statutory instruments have been enacted, drafted by the Lord Chancellor's office pursuant to the Tribunals and Inquiries Act 1992 s.9.[146] These will normally be drafted in conjunction with the appropriate department. Others have emanated directly from, for example, the Ministry of Housing and Local Government. The details of these rules differ, but there are a large number of points in common.

Thus there are provisions concerned with procedure prior to the inquiry covering both the length of notice that must be given of the holding of the inquiry, and also a statement of reasons of the case that has to be met. The precise length of notice varies; in some areas it is 21 days; in others 28 days; and in yet others 42 days. There will in addition be rules requiring, for example, an acquiring authority acting under compulsory purchase legislation to provide facilities for the inspection of relevant documents and plans.

ii. Procedure at the inquiry

9–038   The procedure at the inquiry is, as recommended by the Franks Committee, very much left in the hands of the inspector,[147] subject to the rules of natural justice.[148] Legal rules of evidence do not, for example, apply[149] and the inspector is often given power to enforce the attendance of persons and the production of documents. The inspector will also have the power to take evidence on oath.

---

[145] A point made by Wraith and Lamb, n.140, 222.
[146] See, e.g., Town and Country Planning (Hearings Procedure) (England) Rules 2000 (SI 2000/1626); Town and Country Planning (Enforcement) (Hearings Procedure) (England) Rules 2002 (SI 2002/2684).
[147] SI 2000/1626, n.146, r.11.
[148] See, e.g., *Edwards v Environment Agency* [2007] Env. L.R. 9.
[149] *Miller (TA) Ltd v Minister of Housing and Local Government* [1968] 1 W.L.R. 992.

Bushell demonstrates the breadth of the discretion accorded to the decision-maker.[150] A public local inquiry was held to consider objections to a road building scheme. At the time of the inquiry procedural rules concerning highway inquiries had not yet come into force. A key element in the Department's case for the new motorways was projected traffic flow, the statistical basis of which was derived from a publication known as the "Red Book". Objectors at the inquiry sought to challenge the accuracy of the Red Book's predictions, but the inspector refused to allow them to cross-examine the Department's witnesses as to the reliability of the Red Book. He did, however, allow the objectors to call their own evidence as to the need for motorways. The objectors sought to quash the decision of the minister confirming the scheme, on the ground, inter alia, that the denial by the inspector of a right to cross-examine was in breach of natural justice and wrong in law. The House of Lords found for the minister.

The majority decided that in the absence of statutory rules prescribing the conduct of the inquiry, the procedure to be followed was a matter for the discretion of the minister and inspector. This was subject to the general safeguard that the procedure be fair to all concerned, including the general public and supporters of the scheme. In deciding what was a fair procedure the court should not be tied to the ordinary model of civil litigation between private parties. Lord Diplock put this point most strongly.[151]

> "To 'over-judicialise' the inquiry by insisting on observance of the procedures of a court of justice which professional lawyers alone are competent to operate effectively in the interests of their clients would not be fair. It would, in my view, be quite fallacious to suppose that at an inquiry of this kind the only fair way of ascertaining matters of fact and expert opinion is by the oral testimony of witnesses who are subjected to cross-examination on behalf of parties who disagree with what they have said. Such procedure is peculiar to litigation conducted in courts that follow the common law system of procedure; it plays no part in the procedure of courts of justice under legal systems based upon the civil law. . . . So refusal by an inspector to allow a party to cross-examine orally at a local inquiry a person who has made statements of facts or has expressed expert opinions is not unfair *per se*."

Whether refusal to allow cross-examination was unfair depended upon all the circumstances of the case. These included: the nature of the topic on which the opinion was expressed, and the forensic competence of the proposed cross-examiner. The court would also consider the inspector's view as to whether the cross-examination would enable him to make a report more useful to the minister than it otherwise would have been, and that this justified the extra cost in time thereby expended.

The most important of these factors for the majority was the nature of the

---

[150] *Bushell v Secretary of State for the Environment* [1981] A.C. 75.
[151] [1981] A.C. 75, 97.

topic itself. The majority distinguished between general government policy, which would clearly not be suitable for discussion at a local inquiry, an example being the desirability of having a nation-wide set of motorways, and a matter such as the exact line that a road should follow, which would be amenable to local discussion.[152] Midway between these there was a "grey area" in which the suitability of a point for cross-examination could well be debatable. The validity of the Red Book's methodology was treated as akin to a matter of government policy and therefore not suitable for local discussion and cross-examination. It was not that the majority saw these technical matters as of the same order as the decision to have a nation-wide set of motorways. Rather that the techniques for determining traffic need involved a wider range of issues than could appropriately be considered at a local inquiry.[153]

The rules governing procedure in any particular area will also delineate those who have a right to appear. In general such a right is only accorded to those who have some legal interest at stake, while allowing the inspector discretion to admit others.[154] This discretion is normally exercised liberally, but such third parties may nevertheless be placed at a disadvantage as compared with those who do have a right to appear. They may not, for example, have a right to see a statement of the authority's case, nor does evidence obtained outside of the inquiry have to be disclosed to them. It was however held in *Hamsher* that a person admitted at the discretion of the inspector was entitled to a fair hearing and that this entailed being enabled to know the nature of the opposing party's case,[155] while in *Jory* it was held that fairness required that such a party should be informed of proposed amendments to planning conditions in the same way as other parties to the case.[156]

iii. Procedure after the inquiry: inspectors' reports

9–039   Procedure consequent upon the inquiry raises a number of important issues, one of the most controversial of which has been whether the inspector's report ought to be published or not. An inspector will be appointed to conduct a wide range of inquiries. Typically the situation will be one in which a local authority proposes to acquire land, to clear an area of slums. Having passed a resolution to that effect it will have to advertise the matter in the local press, as well as informing those whose property rights are affected so that they have an opportunity to object. If such objections are

---

[152] [1981] A.C. 75, 97–98, 108–109, 121–123. See also, *R. v Secretary of State for Transport Ex p. Gwent County Council* [1987] 2 W.L.R. 961.
[153] cf. Lord Edmund-Davies, dissenting 116–117, who felt that the Red Book was not a matter of government policy and should have been amenable to cross-examination.
[154] See, e.g., SI 2000/1626, n.146, r.9.
[155] *R. (on the application of Hamsher) v First Secretary of State* [2004] EWHC 2299, paras 20–21. See also, *Local Government Board v Arlidge* [1915] A.C. 120, 147; *Wednesbury Corporation v Ministry of Housing and Local Government (No.2)* [1966] 2 Q.B. 275, 302.
[156] *Jory v Secretary of State for Transport, Local Government and the Regions* [2002] EWHC 2724.

forthcoming then the appropriate minister will be obliged to establish an inquiry presided over by an inspector. It is this report which will then be confirmed or not by the minister.

The Franks Committee received much evidence on the publication of these reports.[157] The arguments for publication were primarily fairness and acceptability. A main cause of public dissatisfaction had been a feeling of secrecy shrouding the whole inquiry procedure, a sense which publication of the reports would have done much to dispel. Greater knowledge would bring a greater acceptance, since the public would be more aware of the policies underlying the decisions being made. A number of arguments were put against publication. It was argued that the inspector's report was but one of the considerations which the minister should take into account, and that to publish it alone would be to accord it an unwarranted primacy, creating a misguided impression as to its relative importance. In addition, it was felt that inspectors would be less frank if their reports were to be published and that there was not in fact a widespread demand to see the reports.

The Franks Committee came down firmly in favour of publication,[158] and this has been the general practice since 1958. In some instances the statutory instruments make provision for this,[159] in others publication is dependent upon departmental practice. None of the fears voiced by those opposed to publication appear to have transpired and public confidence in the inquiry procedure has undoubtedly been increased by this reform.

iv. Procedure after the inquiry: extrinsic evidence

We have seen that one of the arguments against publication of the inspec- **9–040** tors' reports was that they were but one of the sources relied on by the minister when reaching a decision. What types of extrinsic evidence the minister does and should be enabled to take into account is a difficult problem, as exemplified by the Essex Chalkpit case of 1961.

A company had been refused planning permission to dig and work chalk, this decision being upheld by an inspector, on the basis that the proposed development would injuriously affect neighbouring landowners. The company appealed to the minister who consulted the Ministry of Agriculture, experts from which stated that the development of the land could take place without any injurious affect upon the neighbours provided that an appropriate process was used. On receipt of this evidence the minister upheld the appeal even though the objectors to the scheme had had no opportunity for comment on the new evidence.

An appeal to the courts having failed,[160] the objectors complained to the

---

[157] Cmnd. 218 (1957), paras 327–346. The hearing will normally be in public, Planning Inquiries (Attendance of Public) Act 1982.
[158] Cmnd. 218 (1957), para.344.
[159] See, e.g., Town and Country Planning Appeals (Determination by Inspectors) (Inquiries Procedure) (England) Rules 2000 (SI 2000/1625), r.19.
[160] *Buxton v Minister of Housing and Local Government* [1961] 1 Q.B. 278.

Council on Tribunals. The Council criticised the way in which the case had been handled. It recommended that if a minister differed from an inspector on a finding of fact, because of fresh evidence, or because a new issue had arisen which was not one of government policy, then the parties should be notified and be allowed to comment thereon. This has become the established practice and is enshrined in some of the statutory instruments governing the procedure at inquiries.[161] Difficulties can however still arise when distinguishing between findings of fact and matters of opinion.[162]

Natural justice will also impose limits upon the receipt of extrinsic evidence. Thus in the *Bushell*[163] case it was accepted that the Minister could not, after the close of the inquiry, hear one side rather than the other, or receive evidence from third parties without allowing comments thereon. There is, however, a distinction between evidence from such sources and advice from within the department itself.

In the *Bushell* case a further ground of complaint was that after the close of the inquiry, but before the report was made, the Department revised their methods of computing traffic needs, the result being a prediction of slower traffic growth than originally forecast. The objectors asked the minister to reopen the inquiry but he declined, saying that he would look at their representations as part of his continuous consideration of the Department's proposals. In his decision the minister stated that, despite the change in the criteria for traffic need, he still felt that the inspector's recommendation should be upheld. The House of Lords rejected the argument that the minister had acted wrongfully by confirming the inspector's report without allowing the objectors an opportunity to comment on undisclosed information. The minister was, said Lord Diplock,[164] perfectly in order in consulting his own department for advice on whether to confirm the recommendations. He did not have to disclose this advice to objectors, nor did he have to allow them to comment thereon. Viscount Dilhorne and Lord Lane placed the matter rather more generally on the ground that such consultation involved no breach of natural justice in the circumstances of the case.[165]

---

[161] See, e.g., SI 2000/1626, n.146, r.13.
[162] *Luke (Lord) v Minister of Housing and Local Government* [1968] 1 Q.B. 172; *Murphy and Sons Ltd v Secretary of State for the Environment* [1973] 1 W.L.R. 560; *Darlassis v Minister of Education* (1954) 52 L.G.R. 304.
[163] [1981] A.C. 75, 102.
[164] [1981] A.C. 75, 102–103.
[165] [1981] A.C. 75, 110 and 123–124. See also, *Steele v Minister of Housing and Local Government* (1956) 6 P. & C.R. 386, 392. Compare however *Edwards*, n.148.

v. Procedure after the inquiry: reasons
An obligation to provide reasons is imposed by s.10(1)(b) of the Tribunals   **9–041**
and Inquiries Act 1992. The section provides for the giving of reasons where
the minister notifies any decision taken by him after the holding by him or
on his behalf of a statutory inquiry, or taken by him in a case in which a
person concerned could (whether by objecting or otherwise) have required
the holding of such a statutory inquiry, where an individual requests the
reasons for the decision, on or before the giving or notification of the
decision.

The provisions of the Act operate in the same way and subject to the same
qualifications as in the case of tribunals. A decision will be quashed if the
reasons given are obscure, too vague, or confused.[166]

vi. Inquiry rules of procedure: an example
We have already seen that the Lord Chancellor can enact procedural rules,   **9–042**
pursuant to s.9 of the Tribunals and Inquiries Act 1992. A number of the
more specific aspects of these rules have been touched upon in the previous
discussion. It is nonetheless helpful to consider such rules as they have been
made in a specific area. Planning appeals will be taken by way of example.[167]
The Planning Inspectorate is now an Executive Agency.[168]

The procedure begins with a *notice* from the Secretary of State addressed
to the local planning authority that an inquiry is to be held in connection
with an appeal made to the Secretary of State. The local planning authority
must then tell the Secretary of State the name of any statutory party who
has made representations to them about the matter under appeal. A similar
obligation lies on the Secretary of State. The date for the inquiry will then be
fixed, and the Secretary of State will identify the inspector who will handle
the matter.

The local planning authority and the appellant must then serve their
respective *statements of case* on each other, the Secretary of State and other
statutory parties. The statement of case will contain the principal submissions to be made at the inquiry.

---

[166] *Iveagh (Earl) v Minister of Housing and Local Government* [1964] 1 Q.B. 395; *Givaudan & Co
Ltd v Minister of Housing and Local Government* [1967] 1 W.L.R. 250; *French Kier Developments
Ltd v Secretary of State for the Environment* [1977] 1 All E.R. 296; *Barnham v Secretary of State
for the Environment* (1985) 52 P. & C.R. 10; *Reading Borough Council v Secretary of State for the
Environment* (1985) 52 P. & C.R. 385.
[167] The Town and Country Planning (Inquiries Procedure) (England) Rules 2000 (SI 2000/
1624), govern certain planning applications and appeals decided by the Secretary of State; The
Town and Country Planning Appeals (Determination by Inspectors) (Inquiries Procedure)
(England) Rules 2000 (SI 2000/1625), govern certain appeals decided by an inspector appointed
by the Secretary of State where the inspector makes the decision in the name of the minister;
Town and Country Planning (Hearings Procedure) (England) Rules 2000 (SI 2000/1626). Most
appeals are in fact decided by an inspector. See, Sir D. Heap, *An Outline of Planning Law* (Sweet
& Maxwell, 11th edn, 1996), Ch.13; L. Blundell and G. Dobry's, *Planning Applications, Appeals
& Proceedings* (Sweet & Maxwell, 5th edn, 1996), Ch.6; V. Moore, *A Practical Approach to
Planning Law* (Oxford University Press, 2005); R. Duxbury, *Telling and Duxbury's Planning
Law and Procedure* (Oxford University Press, 13th edn, 2006).
[168] http://www.planning-inspectorate.gov.uk/pins/index.htm.

There will generally be a *pre-inquiry* meeting in order to facilitate the efficient and expeditious resolution of the problem, where the inquiry is expected to last for eight days or more, and such an inquiry can be held in respect of shorter inquiries where it is felt to be necessary.

Those who are *entitled to appear* at the inquiry itself are: the appellant, the local planning authority, any other local authority in whose area the land is situated, any person who, in effect, claims proprietary rights over the land in question, and any other person who has served a statement of case under the relevant rules. Other parties are allowed to appear at the discretion of the inspector. A lawyer can represent those who are entitled or permitted to appear.

The *procedure at the inquiry* is determined by the inspector who will have discretion as to matters such as the calling of evidence and cross-examination. However the appellant, the local planning authority and certain other parties entitled to appear as of right, have the right to call evidence. The inspector may receive written representations from any person before the inquiry, provided that disclosure is made at the inquiry itself.

The *procedure after the inquiry* is that the inspector will make the decision. This will be given in writing and be supported by reasons. The report must be given to all those entitled to appear at the inquiry, who did appear, and also to those who, having appeared at the inquiry, then asked to be notified of the inspector's decision. The report will go to the minister, who may disagree with the inspector's report either because he takes a different view on a matter of fact, or because of fresh evidence which is not a matter of government policy. If the former occurs those taking part in the inquiry are to be afforded an opportunity of making written representations within 21 days. If the latter takes place then those who participated in the inquiry can either make written representations or request that the inquiry should be re-opened within the 21-day period.

vii. Limitations: discretionary inquiries

9–043 An important limitation on the scope of the legislation on tribunals and inquiries is that the term statutory inquiry was originally defined to include only those inquiries held in pursuance of a statutory duty. This excluded the important class of inquiries the holding of which was at the discretion of the minister, such as inquiries held under the general powers of the Education Act 1944[169] and the Highways Act 1980.[170] The Tribunals and Inquiries Act 1966 dealt with this unsatisfactory situation by empowering the Lord Chancellor to make orders designating certain groups of inquiries as subject to the Tribunals and Inquiries Act 1958.[171] Designating orders have been made pursuant to this power.[172]

---

[169] Education Act 1944 s.93.
[170] Highways Act 1980 s.302.
[171] Tribunals and Inquiries Act 1992 ss.16(1)(b), 16(2) makes the designated inquiries subject to the Act. The provisions concerning the giving of reasons do not, however, apply unless the designating order specifically so directs, s.10(4).
[172] e.g. SI 1967/451; SI 1975/1379; SI 1983/1287.

*viii. Related types of decision-making: decisions by appointed persons and
written representations*

An inquiry conducted by an inspector who then sends proposals to the **9–044**
minister may well be the "standard" or "normal" method of proceeding.
There are, however, a number of related procedures, which have the central
theme of preserving decision-making in the hands of those who are politically accountable, while allowing some degree of public participation.

These techniques are designed to expedite the process of reaching a
decision as compared with the full panoply of an inquiry. Serious delays
over planning appeals led to legislation empowering the Secretary of State to
designate certain classes of appeal that could be heard and decided by a
person whom he had appointed. Flexibility in procedure was increased by
making statutory provision for such appeals to be decided on written
representations if both parties agreed.[173] Even within areas in which the final
decision resides with the Secretary of State the parties may agree to have
their case settled on the basis of purely written representations.[174] Pressures
of time have rendered the written representation procedure an attractive one
for the parties, and over 80 per cent of all planning appeals are decided in
this way. The main disadvantage of this procedure was that third parties had
no opportunity to participate,[175] but the current regulations afford such
parties the opportunity to take part in the appeal process.[176]

ix. Related types of decision-making: planning inquiry commissions

If the increase in the number of decisions reached by written representation **9–045**
reflects one development in the planning sphere, the planning inquiry
commission reflects another. While the former is a response to the demand
for quicker and cheaper decisions, the latter demonstrates the need for
planning machinery to consider problems on a level which the previous
institutions did not allow.

Under the Town and Country Planning Act 1990 s.101, a planning
inquiry commission can be established. It will be used in circumstances
where there are considerations of regional or national importance
demanding a special inquiry, or where novel technical or scientific questions
are involved that cannot adequately be resolved without some such
mechanism. The Commission will proceed in two stages, the first being a
general investigation, the second a local inquiry conducted by one of the
members of the Commission. The former will be in the nature of a roving,

---

[173] Town and Country Planning Act, 1990 s.79(7) Sch.6; The Town and Country Planning
(Appeals) (Written Representations) (England) Regulations 2000 (SI 2000/1628). The Tribunals
and Inquiries Act 1992 still applies Heap, n.167, 201–205.
[174] M. Purdue, *Cases and Materials on Planning Law* (Sweet & Maxwell, 1977), 218–221; Wraith
and Lamb, n.140, 198–200.
[175] Council on Tribunals, Annual Report 1966, paras 89–91; Heap, n.167, 204–205.
[176] The Town and Country Planning (Appeals) (Written Representations) (England) Regulations 2000 (SI 2000/1628), rr.5, 8.

unrestricted investigation, comparable to a Royal Commission, to be used in circumstances such as the development of a new airport.[177]

D. The Inquiries Act 2005

i. The position pre-2005

9–046 Inquiries have in the past been ordered on a variety of issues, such as the first inquiry into the expansion of Stansted airport, and the inquiry into the "Arms to Iraq" affair.[178] A number of these inquiries did not have a statutory base. They were used for a variety of purposes,[179] including the Crichel Down affair,[180] which was a catalyst for the establishment of the Franks Committee, though paradoxically the type of behaviour in this case was not within the Committee's terms of reference.

There were also inquiries made pursuant to the Tribunals of Inquiry (Evidence) Act 1921, which was passed to provide a procedure for investigating allegations of improper behaviour by certain officials in connection with armaments contracts.[181] It was used mainly to investigate similar allegations of misconduct by ministers, civil servants or other organs of government. Thus the leaking of budget secrets[182] and the bribing of a junior minister were both the subject of such an inquiry,[183] as were the circumstances surrounding the spying activities of Vassall.[184] The powers possessed by such tribunals of inquiry came to the forefront of the public eye during the Vassall inquiry, the catalyst being the imprisoning of three journalists for contempt of court[185] after failing to disclose the sources of stories which they had written about the Vassall affair.

In 1965 a Royal Commission was established to review the operation of such inquiries.[186] It made 50 recommendations designed to safeguard the operation of such inquiries, focusing in particular on the absence of procedural checks.

ii. The Inquiries Act 2005

9–047 More recently in 2004 the Government published a consultation paper on inquiries and this was the catalyst for the passage of the Inquiries Act 2005 and the consequent repeal of the Tribunals of Inquiry (Evidence) Act 1921.

The Inquiries Act 2005 is intended to provide a comprehensive statutory

---

[177] Town and Country Planning Act 1990 Sch.8.
[178] *Inquiry into the Export of Defence Equipment and Dual-Use Goods to Iraq and Related Prosecutions* (HC 115; 1995–96).
[179] Wraith and Lamb, n.140, 202–212.
[180] Report of the Inquiry by Sir Andrew Clarke QC, Cmd. 9176 (1954).
[181] Wraith and Lamb, n.140, 212–217.
[182] Cmd. 5184 (1936).
[183] Cmd. 7616 (1948).
[184] Cmnd. 2009 (1962).
[185] The Tribunal of Inquiry could not itself punish for contempt, but it did certify the journalists before the High Court.
[186] Report of the Royal Commission on Tribunals of Inquiry, Cmnd. 3121 (1966).

framework for inquiries set up by ministers to look into matters of public concern. A minister may cause an inquiry to be held where it appears to him that particular events have caused, or are capable of causing, public concern, or there is public concern that particular events may have occurred.[187] There is power to convert actual or pending inquiries created independently of the 2005 Act into inquiries that come within its remit.[188] An inquiry panel is not to rule on, and has no power to determine, any person's civil or criminal liability, but it is not to be inhibited in the discharge of its functions by any likelihood of liability being inferred from facts that it determines or recommendations that it makes.[189]

Appointment to the inquiry panel is made by the relevant minister, and the Act requires appointments to be suitable, possess the requisite expertise and that they should be impartial.[190] It is for the minister to set out the terms of reference of the inquiry, which may be amended. The terms of reference cover: the matters to which the inquiry relates; any particular matters where the inquiry panel is to determine the facts; whether the inquiry panel is to make recommendations; and any other matters relating to the scope of the inquiry specified by the minister.[191]

The chairman of the inquiry has control over its procedure and conduct, subject to provisions of the 2005 Act or rules made there under.[192] In making any decision as to the procedure or conduct of an inquiry, the chairman must act with fairness and with regard also to the need to avoid any unnecessary cost, whether to public funds, witnesses or others. It is open to the chairman to take evidence on oath, and administer oaths. The inquiry has the power to compel production of evidence.[193] The inquiry chairman must report its conclusions to the minister,[194] and subject to certain qualifications the report is published and laid before Parliament.[195]

The default position is that members of the public should be able to attend, and obtain or view a record of evidence put before the inquiry.[196] Restrictions can however be placed on public access where this is required by any statutory provision, enforceable Community obligation or rule of law. Restrictions can also be placed on public access where the minister or chairman considers this conducive to the inquiry fulfilling its terms of reference or to be necessary in the public interest. In making such a determination the minister or chairman must have regard to: the extent to which any restriction on attendance, disclosure or publication might inhibit the allaying of public concern; any risk of harm or damage that could be avoided or reduced by any such restriction; any conditions as to

[187] Inquiries Act 2005 s.1.
[188] Inquiries Act 2005 s.15.
[189] Inquiries Act 2005 s.2.
[190] Inquiries Act 2005 ss 8–9.
[191] Inquiries Act 2005 s.5.
[192] Inquiries Act 2005 s.17.
[193] Inquiries Act 2005 s.21.
[194] Inquiries Act 2005 s.24.
[195] Inquiries Act 2005 ss.25–26.
[196] Inquiries Act 2005 s.18.

confidentiality subject to which a person acquired information that he is to give, or has given, to the inquiry; and the extent to which not imposing any particular restriction would be likely to cause delay or to impair the efficiency or effectiveness of the inquiry, or otherwise to result in additional cost, whether to public funds, witnesses or others.[197]

The Inquiries Act 2005 is to be welcomed insofar as it introduces regularity into the conduct of inquiries set up as a result of public concern about a particular matter. The government intends that the Act should be the mechanism for holding such inquiries and this too is to be welcomed. It remains to be seen how chairmen of inquiries exercise their power to set inquiry procedure, although such decisions would be subject to judicial review for compliance with the precepts of natural justice. It will also be important to monitor the way in which the rules allowing restriction on public access are interpreted and applied.

E. Supervision

i. The Administrative Justice and Tribunals Council

9–048   The Tribunals and Inquiries Act 1992 s.1(1)(c) gave the Council on Tribunals power to consider and report on such matters as were referred to them, or as the Council deemed to be of special importance. The Council also had to be consulted by the Lord Chancellor when the latter made procedural rules for inquiries, an obligation which did not attach to procedural rules made by other ministers. The Council's powers were therefore advisory and not executive. It was nonetheless of value in a number of ways, by receiving complaints from individuals concerning specific problems encountered at inquiries, by publication of special reports on particular aspects of tribunal procedure, and through its comments on draft legislation concerning inquiries.[198]

We have already seen in the earlier discussion that the Tribunals, Courts and Enforcement Act 2007 abolished the Council on Tribunals and replaced it with the Administrative Justice and Tribunals Council.[199] The AJTC has responsibility for statutory inquiries.[200] It is to keep under review, and report on, the constitution and working of statutory inquiries, both generally and in relation to any particular statutory inquiry or type of inquiry; it is to consider and report on any other matter that relates to statutory inquiries in general, to statutory inquiries of a particular description or to any particular statutory inquiry, which the AJTC determines to be of special importance; and it is to report on any particular matter concerning such inquiries referred to it by the Lord Chancellor, the Welsh Ministers and the Scottish Ministers.[201] The AJTC reports to the Lord Chancellor and also to the

---

[197] Inquiries Act 2005 s.19.
[198] Wraith and Lamb, n.140, 236.
[199] TCE Act 2007 ss.44–45.
[200] TCE Act 2007 Sch.7 para.15.
[201] TCE Act 2007 Sch.7 para.16.

Scottish and Welsh Ministers if the report relates to Scotland and/or Wales.[202]

ii. *The Parliamentary Commissioner for Administration*

The Parliamentary Commissioner was a member of the Council on Tribu-   **9–049**
nals,[203] and is a member of the new AJTC.[204] In his own capacity, when
investigating complaints of maladministration, he has had occasion to
examine matters arising from public inquiries such as delay and cost. This
overlap between the Council/AJTC and the Commissioner may not be neat,
but it is beneficial given the more extensive powers of investigation possessed by the latter.

iii. *Judicial review*

Principles of judicial review are applied to inquiries. The application of these   **9–050**
principles will be considered below.

F. Planning Inquiries, the Government and the Public

Lawyers tend to have a limited interest in inquiries, once they are satisfied   **9–051**
that the procedures are fair. To some extent this is because inquiries present
the lawyer with less familiar issues, as compared to those that arise in
relation to tribunals. The uncertainties as to inquiry procedure are reflected
in the way in which we do or do not, as the case may be, consider some of
the fundamental questions that arise in this area. What rights should third
parties have at inquiries? How much time should be expended on consultation with interested parties? To what extent should we allow discussion
of policy at inquiries? How costly are these procedures and what do we
mean when we speak of an efficient process of decision-making? The
answers will, explicitly or implicitly, be based upon the perceived aim of the
law in this area. There is nothing surprising about this. Indeed it would be
odd if the situation were otherwise. What is less immediately obvious is that,
in determining what those purposes are, we may have to make value judgments, the implications of which go over and beyond the particular area in
question.

That this is so is brought out by McAuslan's study of planning law.[205] The
author identified three different ideologies, which helped to shape the law in
this area. The first saw the aim of the law as to protect private property,
which was termed the traditional common law approach to the legal role.
The second conceived the purpose of the law as to advance the public

---

[202] TCE Act 2007 Sch.7 para.17.
[203] Parliamentary Commissioner Act 1967 s.1(5).
[204] TCE Act 2007 Sch.7 para.1(1).
[205] *The Ideologies of Planning Law* (1980). On planning law in general see Heap, n.167; P.
McAuslan, *Land, Law and Planning* (Weidenfeld and Nicolson, 1975); Purdue, n.174; M. Grant,
Urban Planning Law (Sweet & Maxwell, 1983); Moore, n.167; Duxbury, n.167.

interest, even as against traditional property rights. This was called the orthodox public administration approach to the legal role. The third ideology was that the function of the law was to aid the cause of public participation in decision-making, which might be in opposition to the other two approaches. This ideology was labelled the populist approach.[206] Which of these approaches predominated could impact on the answers to the central questions posed above.

This is readily apparent by looking further at McAuslan's study. The essence of the argument was that the first two approaches towards planning were dominant, albeit in varying degrees, that participation was much genuflected to in theory, but pushed into third place in practice. The author demonstrated this in a number of areas,[207] two of which may be taken as examples.

The relevant legislation on planning was, until 2005,[208] contained in the Town and Country Planning Act 1990, which imposed an obligation on the local planning authority to make a survey of its area, including size, composition and distribution of the population, and the principal physical and economic features of the area.[209] The survey was then forwarded to the Secretary of State, together with what was known as a unitary development plan for metropolitan areas and a structure plan for non-metropolitan areas. These plans consisted of a written statement which formulated the local planning authority's policy and general proposals for development and other use of the land in that area, together with a statement as to how that development related to development in neighbouring areas.[210] Local plans were designed to fill in the details of the wider ranging policies considered in the structure plan.[211] Public participation took place both before and after submission of the plans to the Secretary of State.[212]

9–052   In 1966 the Skeffington Committee had been established specifically to consider and report on the best method of ensuring publicity for and public participation in the formative stages of drawing up plans for an area. The Committee reported in 1968.[213] It recommended that there should be pauses in the plan-making process to enable the public to comment, and that the local planning authority should arrange meetings for local groups to consider planning issues. Alternative choices should be put forward and community involvement with the project should be encouraged. These recommendations must, however, be seen in the light of the Committee's

---

[206] *The Ideologies of Planning Law*, n.205, 2.
[207] *The Ideologies of Planning Law*, Chs 1–2. I am indebted to McAuslan's study for the material which appears in this example. See also, C. Harlow and R. Rawlings, *Law and Administration* (Weidenfeld and Nicolson, 1984), Chs 14, 15.
[208] The relevant legislation is now, Planning and Compulsory Purchase Act 2004.
[209] Town and Country Planning Act 1990 s.11 applied to metropolitan areas, s.30 to non-metropolitan areas
[210] Town and Country Planning Act 1990 ss.12, 31.
[211] Town and Country Planning Act 1990 s.36.
[212] Town and Country Planning Act 1990 ss.13, 20, 33, 35, 39–42.
[213] People and Planning, Report of the Committee on Public Participation in Planning (1969).

conclusion that responsibility for the making of the plan lay with the elected representatives and that their role should not be diminished.

It was three years before the Government responded to the proposals of the Skeffington Committee. A circular was sent to the local authorities setting out the Government's attitude.[214] The general impression left by this document was that discretion should remain with local authorities as to implementation of the Committee's proposals. Juxtaposed to this general theme were warnings about the time and cost that participation could entail, which were particularly evident in the way in which the circular addressed the Skeffington proposals concerning stages of participation. As McAuslan states,[215]

"The overall impression given by the circular is that the Skeffington Committee had been a little over enthusiastic . . . and that the hard headed realism and discipline of costs and time, very much administrative concerns, were to be determining factors in public participation in plan-making. Only by placing the organisation and implementation of participation firmly under the jurisdiction of local authorities and reminding them of their statutory obligations, as opposed to the Report's recommendations, were these overriding concerns likely to be met."

Consultation prior to the submission of the unitary development or structure plan to the minister was intended to be but part of the participation by the public. It was to be complemented by examination of the plan before it was approved by the Secretary of State.[216] The nature and degree of any such participation was, however, firmly placed in the hands of the Secretary of State. The legislation left no doubt that the scope of any examination into the structure plan would be decided upon by the Secretary of State. There was no general duty to consult or to consider the views of interested parties.[217] This reflection of the public interest ideology of planning, with that interest being decided upon by the government of the day, was further reinforced by the non-statutory code of practice, which provided guidance as to the nature of the examination. The code made it clear that the conduct of the examination would be kept firmly in the hands of the Secretary of State, who would choose which matters would be considered at the examination, and who would be entitled to take part in the discussion.

The second example of the conflicting ideologies underlying the planning sphere can be seen in the public local inquiry pursuant to a refusal of planning permission. The very idea of, or necessity for, an inquiry prior to the refusal of planning permission[218] was a natural outgrowth of the common law's protection of private property. If property belonged to you and

[214] Department of the Environment, Circular No.52/72.
[215] *Ideologies of Planning Law*, n.205, 23.
[216] *Ideologies of Planning Law*, 39–45.
[217] 1990 Act ss.20, 35.
[218] McAuslan, *Ideologies*, n.205, 45–55; Wraith and Lamb, n.140, 253–264.

someone wished to prevent you using it as you chose an appeal should be provided.[219] Despite this the actual inquiry procedure prior to the Franks Committee reflected the predominance of the public interest perspective: the absence of procedural rules, the secrecy surrounding inspector's reports, and the closed nature of the government policy all contributed towards this. With the reforms of the Franks Committee came a shift in the ideology underlying the inquiry. The pendulum was realigned to take greater account of private property rights through the grant of procedural safeguards prior to, at, and after the inquiry. What is of interest is that, as commentators have observed, provisions originally enacted to protect the interests of property owners have been used by third parties to widen the scope of the inquiry. The "pure milk" of planning doctrine that the inquiry was limited to the appellant, the local authority and the minister has been rendered out of date by administrative practice. The inspector, having general discretion over the procedure at the inquiry, can and normally will admit those without a legal right to attend. Interest groups will use the inquiry to advance arguments over and beyond the facts of the particular case, and once admitted to the inquiry such third parties may for some purposes at least be in as good a position as those with legal rights.[220] Notwithstanding these advances of the public participation ideology, third parties still stand in a somewhat uneven position.[221]

The preceding two examples may be supplemented by a third drawn from developments in planning. Partnership between the public and the private sector in land development has been fostered, and there have been moves to expedite the planning process, to enable such joint schemes to proceed more rapidly.[222] Local authorities have been encouraged by central government to "play the roles of facilitator and underwriter of the profitability of private development proposals".[223] Bargains may be negotiated in secret to facilitate particular developments, with the consequence that "public participation is squeezed out, and policy conflict internalized within the local authority".[224]

9–053   What these examples show is that the type of procedure at the inquiry, the very type of inquiry itself, and the substantive rights accorded to participants will depend directly on the prevailing ideology in the particular area. We cannot resolve questions as to third party rights, or the inquisitorial as opposed to adversarial method of investigation, without implicitly if not explicitly adopting one of these perspectives.

Thus the private property approach to planning would tend to favour an adversarial procedure akin in broad nature to the common law model of

---

[219] Town and Country Planning Act 1990 Pt III.
[220] See, e.g. *Turner v Secretary of State for the Environment* (1973) 28 P. & C.R. 123.
[221] Report of the Council on Tribunals on the position of third parties at planning appeal inquiries, Cmnd. 1787 (1962).
[222] e.g. enterprise zones, Local Government, Planning and Land Act 1980 s.179, and Town and Country Planning Act 1990 ss.88–90; simplified planning zones, Town and Country Planning Act 1990 ss.82–87.
[223] M. Loughlin, *Local Government in the Modern State* (Sweet & Maxwell, 1986), 157.
[224] M. Grant and P. Healey, "The Rise and Fall of Planning," in M. Loughlin, M. Gelfand, K. Young (eds), *Half a Century of Municipal Decline 1935–1985* (Allen & Unwin, 1985), 185.

adjudication, with its rules of examination and cross-examination. Substantive rights would be restricted to the property owner being affected, and the issues that could be raised at an inquiry would be confined to the case at hand.

The public interest approach to planning would gravitate towards a less formal, more inquisitorial style of procedure. The government of the day is regarded as the embodiment and guardian of the public interest, and should be relatively free to pursue the procedures of its choosing, subject to certain elementary concepts of fairness. This view finds expression in *Bushell*,[225] and especially the judgment of Lord Diplock. The substantive rights accorded are limited, as the example of the structure plan shows. Policy is retained firmly in the hands of the government of the day, and the public interest as thereby defined takes prominence over private property and the views of those participating in the decision-making.

The public participation ideology would require more modifications to our institutional mechanisms. The inquiry procedure would be modified to enable a wider variety of views to be taken into account at the formative stages of, for example, a structure plan or unitary development plan. Consultation would be a continuing process and would take place after the plan has been submitted to the Secretary of State. As seen both pre- and post-submission consultation has taken place, but the reins are kept firmly in hand by local and central government. A real commitment to the public participation ideology would entail an increase in the rights of the participator and a corresponding diminution in the control and discretion of the government. In some areas the procedure would cease to be either inquisitorial or adversarial, but be more in the nature of consultation, discussion, with broader community involvement.

The portrayal of these different ideologies is of course somewhat stark. A system of planning may well be a balance between them. Yet this is not to deny the formative influence that each can have on the type of procedures adopted and the nature of the rights granted to those entitled to participate. It is not therefore surprising that lawyers find inquiries involving them in territory with which they are less familiar. Answers to apparently more straightforward issues such as those of costs and delay, let alone those of third party rights and the questioning of government policy, cannot however be formulated without addressing our minds to these complex problems.[226]

---

[225] [1981] A.C. 75, 92–104.
[226] M. Purdue, R. Kemp and T. O'Riordan, "The Government at the Sizewell B Inquiry" [1985] P.L. 475, and "The Layfield Report on the Sizewell B Inquiry" [1987] P.L. 162, for an interesting account of the problems presented by the large public inquiry.

CHAPTER 10

THE EUROPEAN UNION

The discussion thus far has focused upon the principal domestic institutions **10–001**
relevant for administrative law. To stop there would, however, be to give a
misleading picture, since many important "public" decisions are now made
not in Whitehall, but in Brussels.[1] This chapter will therefore examine the
European Union and its significance for administrative law.

There will be a description of the principal Community institutions, which
will be followed by a discussion of the legislative process. There will then be
an analysis of the main Community legal doctrines that are of relevance.
Subsequent chapters of the book will include more detailed discussion of
particular points of Community law doctrine. The relevant Treaty provisions concerning the institutions and legislative process may well change if
the Lisbon Treaty is duly ratified and comes into effect.[2]

1. THE INSTITUTIONS

There are five principal institutions mentioned in art.7 EC, which are **10–002**
entrusted with carrying out the tasks of the Community. They are the
European Parliament, the Council, the Commission, the Court of Auditors
and the Court of Justice. The structure and powers of the Council, the
Commission, the European Parliament, the European Council and the
European Court of Justice (ECJ) will be described here.

---

[1] P. Craig and G. de Búrca, *EU Law, Text, Cases and Materials* (Oxford University Press, 4th
edn, 2007); Wyatt and Dashwood's, *European Union Law* (Sweet and Maxwell, 5th edn, 2006);
D. Chalmers, C. Hadjiemmanuil, G. Monti and A. Tomkins, *European Union Law* (Cambridge
University Press, 2006).
[2] P. Craig, "The Treaty of Lisbon: Process, Architecture and Substance" (2008) 33 E.L.Rev.
137.

A. The Council

10–003 Article 203 EC states that the Council shall consist of a representative of each Member State at ministerial level, who is authorised to commit the government of that state. The members of the Council are, therefore, politicians as opposed to civil servants, but the politician can be a member of a regional government where this is appropriate. It is common for meetings of the Council to be arranged by subject-matter. Article 203 also provides for the Presidency of the Council to be held by each Member State in turn for six months.

The work of the Council is prepared by the Committee of Permanent Representatives (COREPER), which is dealt with in art.207 EC. COREPER is staffed by senior national officials and it operates at two levels. COREPER II consists of permanent representatives who are of ambassadorial rank, and deals with matters such as external relations. COREPER I is composed of deputy permanent representatives and is responsible for more technical issues. COREPER plays an important part in EC decision-making, in part because it sets the agenda for Council meetings. The agenda is divided into Parts A and B: the former includes those items which COREPER has agreed can be adopted by the Council without discussion; the latter will cover topics which do require discussion.

The powers of the Council are described in art.202 EC, albeit in a rather vague manner. The Council is to: "ensure the co-ordination of the general economic policies of the Member States"; it is to "have power to take decisions"; and it can delegate to the Commission powers to implement the rules which the Council has laid down.

The Treaty of Nice (TN) was designed to modernise the institutional structure of the EC, pending enlargement. Institutional reform of the Council occupied more of the IGC's time than any other topic. The negotiations centred on the extension of qualified majority voting, with battles being fought in relation to each relevant Treaty article. There were also lengthy discussions concerning the weighting of votes, and the number required for a qualified majority. Conclusions on these issues are to be found in documents attached to the TN.[3]

B. The Commission

10–004 While the Council represents the interests of the Member States, the Commission is independent of national concerns. The Commissioners are persons whose "independence is beyond doubt", and they "shall neither seek nor take instructions from any government or from any other body", art.213. The Commission operates under the guidance of its President, whose organisational powers have been strengthened by the TN reforms, and the Commissioners take decisions by majority vote.[4]

Article 213, as amended by the Protocol on Enlargement in the TN,

---

[3] TN, Protocol on Enlargement of the Union, coupled with Declaration 20 on Enlargement.
[4] Art.219(2) EC.

stipulates that from January 1, 2005 there shall be one Commissioner from each Member State, and that the Council, acting unanimously, can alter the number of members of the Commission. However, when the Union reaches 27 Member States art.213(1) is further modified, such that the number of Commissioners is less than the number of Member States. It is for the Council acting unanimously to decide on the precise number of Commissioners and, acting on the principle of equality, to adopt a rotation system.

The method of choosing Commissioners has been altered, with the consequence that, from 1995, the Parliament has more say in the process than hitherto. Under art.214(2) EC the governments of the Member States, after consulting the European Parliament, nominate the person they intend to be President of the Commission. These governments, together with the nominee for President, then nominate those who are intended to serve as Commissioners. All such nominees are then subject to a vote of approval by the European Parliament, after which they are appointed by common accord of the Member State governments. Their term of office is five years, and this term can be renewed. The main amendment introduced by the TN is that the Member State decisions are reached by qualified majority. This is in contrast to the position hitherto when they were made by common accord. The change was made because of the prospective enlargement of the EU: to require common accord in a Community with 27 states could well be impossible.

The permanent officials who work in the Commission, and who form the Brussels bureaucracy, are organised into Directorates General covering the major differing subject matter areas, and these will be headed by a Commissioner. The Commissioners will, in addition, have their own personal staff (or *cabinet*), which consists partly of national and partly of Community officials.

The powers of the Commission are set out in art.211 EC. In order to **10–005** ensure the proper functioning of the Community the Commission is to: ensure that the Treaty and attendant measures are applied; formulate recommendations or deliver opinions on matters dealt with in the Treaty if requested to do so, or if the Commission thinks that it is necessary; have its own power of decision and take part in the shaping of measures taken by the Council and by the European Parliament in the manner provided for in the Treaty; and exercise the powers conferred on it by the Council.

It is important to realise that the Commission has a whole array of powers, which are judicial, administrative, executive and legislative in nature. The Community institutional structure is not characterised by any rigid doctrine of separation of powers, and the Commission is at the heart of many Community initiatives.

One of the most important aspects of its powers concerns the legislative process itself. The common format in the Treaties is for the Council to act on a proposal from the Commission when making legislation that fills out the Treaty articles themselves. In this sense the Commission has a right of initiative, which places it in the forefront of the development of Community policy.

C. The European Parliament

10–006 The European Parliament has been transformed since the inception of the Community. It was originally known as the Assembly, and the change of name was brought about by the Single European Act (SEA), which was signed in 1986, and ratified in 1987. The European Parliament was originally indirectly elected from the parliamentary institutions of the Member States, and direct elections occurred in 1979. The powers of the European Parliament have, moreover, been continually increased in subsequent revisions of the original Treaty. The method of electing Members of the European Parliament (MEPs) from Great Britain has been modified.[5]

Article 189 EC provides that the overall number of MEPs should not exceed 732, with the possibility for this to be temporarily exceeded in the case of accession of new Member States during 2004–2009. The number of MEPs returned for most existing Member States was reduced, in order to "make room" for the new members of the Community.

MEPs sit in party-political groupings, rather than along national lines. These groupings correspond to those to be found within the states, including Conservatives/Christian Democrats, Labour/Socialist and more centrist parties. This form of political organisation undoubtedly enhances the sense that there is a *European* Parliament. However, as the Parliament increases its power there can be expected to be greater pressure from particular national constituencies to represent their interests and these interests will not always be identical across the same political party.

The European Parliament has three different types of power: budgetary, legislative and supervisory. The European Parliament plays an important role in the budgetary process within the Community, particularly with respect to non-compulsory expenditure. This process is complex and is dealt with in art.272 EC. The legislative powers of the European Parliament have been increased significantly over the last 30 years, and will be considered within the next section. There are a number of ways in which the European Parliament exercises supervisory control, and these have been increased by amendments introduced by the TEU: it can establish a temporary Committee of Inquiry to consider alleged contraventions or maladministration in the administration of Community law, except where the matter is sub judice;[6] Community citizens can petition the Parliament on a matter which affects them directly[7]; and provision is made for an Ombudsman to investigate maladministration.[8]

D. The European Council

10–007 The European Council consists of the Heads of State or Governments of the Member States, together with the President of the Commission. It came into

[5] European Parliamentary Elections Act 1999.
[6] art.193 EC.
[7] art.194 EC.
[8] art.195 EC.

existence in 1974, and regular meetings have been held ever since. Formal recognition was accorded by art.2 of the SEA, and Article 4 TEU states that the purpose of the European Council is to provide the necessary impetus for the development of the Union, and the definition of its guidelines.

The European Council emerged to deal with important problems that could only be resolved at the highest governmental level, such as crises over Member States' budgetary contributions, the consequences of the collapse of Communism in Eastern Europe, or the timetable for the Community's development, such as the steps towards economic and monetary union. The decisions reached by the European Council are, therefore, of considerable consequence for the speed and direction of Community change.

E. The European Court of Justice

The European Court of Justice (ECJ) has, as will be seen below, played a vital role in the development of the Community. There is one judge from each Member State, and they are appointed for six years renewable. The Judges elect a President of the ECJ for a period of three years, and the post is renewable. The ECJ can decide cases either in plenary session, or in Chambers. **10–008**

The ECJ is assisted by Advocates General.[9] The post has no real analogy within the common law system. After the parties have submitted their arguments, and before the Court delivers its judgment, the Advocate General will present an impartial Opinion on both fact and law to the Court. It is not formally binding on the Court, but will often be influential.

In addition to the ECJ there is now a Court of First Instance, (CFI), which was established pursuant to the SEA. Its existence is regulated by art.225 EC. It was created to relieve the ECJ's workload. More recently judicial panels have been created on specific topics, such as staff disputes.

2. THE LEGISLATIVE PROCESS

The EC legislative process is complex, with different legislative procedures applicable in different contexts. Detailed examination of these procedures cannot be undertaken here.[10] What follows is an outline of the relevant principles. The distinguishing characteristic of the different legislative procedures is, principally, the degree of power which the European Parliament has in each of these processes. The European Parliament was given the smallest role in the legislative process in the Rome Treaty, and subsequent Treaty modifications have increased its role. **10–009**

It is important to dispel any thought of identifying a single body as the

---

[9] art.222 EC.
[10] Craig and de Búrca, n.1, Ch.4.

"legislature" for the Community as a whole. The players which comprise the legislature for the purpose of Community law vary. It should, however, be recognised that "some" measure of order has now been instilled into the legislative process as a result of the Treaty of Amsterdam (ToA). While the number of legislative procedures has not in itself been altered by the ToA, much important legislation is now governed by the co-decision procedure contained in art.251 EC.

The exercise of delegated legislative power by the Community institutions will be considered separately as part of the general discussion of delegated legislation and rulemaking.[11]

It is not possible within the confines of this chapter to consider the complex literature on the "democratic deficit" which is said to beset the Community's decision-making process.[12]

3. The Legal Order: Supremacy and Direct Effect

10–010　　The ECJ has had a marked impact on the development of the Community and has been a major force in securing greater Community integration. Two of its most important contributions have been concerned with supremacy and direct effect.

A. Supremacy

10–011　　It is readily apparent that there will be clashes between Community law and national law. These will often be inadvertent, simply the result of an "absence of fit" between complex Community provisions on a topic and those subsisting within national law. More intentional recalcitrance on the part of the Member States will be less common, though it is not unknown. Some rules must exist for such cases. Not surprisingly the ECJ has held that EC law is supreme in the event of any such conflict.

This principle was first enunciated in *Costa v ENEL*[13] where the ECJ responded to an argument that its preliminary ruling would be of no relevance to the case at hand because the Italian courts would be bound to follow national law. It held,

"By creating a Community of unlimited duration, having . . . powers stemming from a limitation of sovereignty, or a transfer of powers from

[11] See below, Ch.22
[12] An overview of some of the relevant issues can be found in Craig and de Búrca, n.1, Ch.4, and more detailed discussion can be found in P. Craig, "The Nature of the Community: Integration, Democracy and Legitimacy", P. Craig and G. de Búrca (eds), *The Evolution of EU Law* (Oxford University Press, 1999), Ch.1.
[13] Case 6/64, [1964] E.C.R. 585, 593.

the States to the Community, the Member States have limited their sovereign rights, albeit within limited fields, and thus have created a body of law which binds both their nationals and themselves."

The Community's supremacy was given added force by the ECJ's ruling in the *Simmenthal* case,[14] where the Court made it clear that Community law would take precedence even over national legislation which was adopted after the passage of the relevant EC norms. The existence of Community rules rendered automatically inapplicable any contrary provision of national law, *and* precluded the valid adoption of any new national law which was in conflict with the Community provisions.[15]

"It follows from the foregoing that every national court must, in a case within its jurisdiction, apply Community law in its entirety and protect rights which the latter confers on individuals and must accordingly set aside any provision of national law which may conflict with it, whether prior or subsequent to the Community rule."

The supremacy of Community law was felt to pose particular problems for legal systems such as our own, which are wedded to the idea of Parliamentary sovereignty. The leading decision is *Factortame*.[16] The applicants were companies incorporated under UK law, but the majority of the directors and shareholders were Spanish. The companies were in the business of sea fishing and their vessels were registered as British under the Merchant Shipping Act 1894. The statutory regime governing sea fishing was altered by the Merchant Shipping Act 1988. Vessels that had been registered under the 1894 Act had to register once again under the new legislation. Ninety-five vessels failed to meet the criteria in the new legislation, and they argued that the relevant parts of the 1988 Act were incompatible with what were arts 7, 52, 58, and 221 of the EC Treaty. The UK government responded by advancing two arguments.

First, it was argued that nothing in Community law prevented a Member State from defining for itself who was to be regarded as a national of that state, and that the relevant sections of the 1988 legislation were doing no more than that. Second, the government contended that the 1988 legislation was not in fact in breach of Community law.

Whether the 1988 statute was in fact in breach of EC law was clearly a **10–012** contentious question. The UK courts agreed that a reference should be made to the ECJ under what was art.177 EC (now art.234). The question that remained for decision in the first *Factortame* case concerned the status of the 1988 Act pending the decision on the substantive issue by the ECJ. This decision might not be forthcoming for some time and if the applicants could not fish in this intervening period they might well go out of business.

[14] *Amministrazione delle Finanze dello Stato v Simmenthal Spa* (106/77) [1978] E.C.R. 629.
[15] [1978] E.C.R. 629 para.21.
[16] *R. v Secretary of State for Transport Ex p. Factortame Ltd* [1990] 2 A.C. 85.

The applicants sought therefore either for the 1988 Act to be "disapplied" pending the ECJ's substantive decision. Or if the Act remained in force to prevent them from fishing, then the government should have to give an undertaking to provide compensation should the ultimate decision given by the ECJ be in the applicants' favour. Lord Bridge gave the judgment of the House of Lords and reasoned as follows.

First, his Lordship rejected the applicant's argument that the 1988 Act should be disapplied pending the final determination by the ECJ. An Act of Parliament was presumptively valid, and this presumption would only be displaced if a challenge to the Act was upheld. A court might exercise its discretion to refuse to grant an order to enforce a disputed legislative measure in circumstances where it was necessary to invoke the court's jurisdiction in order to secure the enforcement of the legislation. However, the position was different here since the government did not require such assistance from the court: the government was simply refusing to register the applicants under the 1988 Act.

Second, Lord Bridge decided that in any event there was no jurisdiction under English law to grant interim injunctions against the Crown. This aspect of the case is considered in detail below.[17]

Third, Lord Bridge then considered the applicants' argument that the absence of any interim relief against the Crown was itself a violation of Community law. The applicants argued that there was an overriding principle of Community law, which imposed an obligation on the national court to secure effective protection of rights having direct effect under Community law where a seriously arguable claim was advanced to be entitled to such rights, and where the rights claimed would in substance be rendered nugatory, or would be irremediably impaired if not effectively protected during the interim period which would elapse pending determination of a dispute as to the existence of those rights. Lord Bridge was unsure whether this was indeed required by EC law, but since the point was clearly important a preliminary ruling was requested from the ECJ. The ECJ was therefore in effect being asked to rule on whether a "gap" in the availability of administrative law remedies in UK law was itself a breach of EC law, at least insofar as this "gap" affected actions which had an EC element to them.

10–013   The ECJ decided for the applicants,[18] and reasoned from the earlier judgment in *Simmenthal*.[19] In that case the ECJ held that provisions of Community law rendered "automatically inapplicable" any conflicting provision of national law. The *Simmenthal* decision had given a broad construction to the idea of a "conflicting provision" of national law, interpreting it to cover any legislative, administrative or judicial practice that might impair the effectiveness of Community law.[20] With this foundation the ECJ in the *Factortame* case concluded that,[21]

[17] See below, Ch.28.
[18] *R. v Secretary of State for Transport Ex p. Factortame Ltd* (213/89) [1990] E.C.R. I-2433.
[19] n.14.
[20] [1978] E.C.R. 629, paras 22 and 23.
[21] [1990] E.C.R. I-2433, para.21.

"[T]he full effectiveness of Community law would be just as much impaired if a rule of national law could prevent a court seised of a dispute governed by Community law from granting interim relief in order to ensure the full effectiveness of the judgment to be given on the existence of the rights claimed under Community law. It follows that a court which in those circumstances would grant interim relief, if it were not for a rule of national law is obliged to set aside that rule."

The case then returned to the House of Lords to be reconsidered in the light of the ECJ's preliminary ruling, *Factortame Ltd (No.2)*.[22] Their Lordships accepted that, at least in the area covered by EC law, interim relief would be available against the Crown.[23] The present discussion will focus upon the House of Lords' approach to sovereignty and the EC.

Factortame (No.2) contains dicta by their Lordships on the more general issue of sovereignty. The final decision on the substance of the case involved a potential clash between norms of the EC Treaty itself, combined with EC rules on the common fisheries policy, and a *later* Act of the UK Parliament, the Merchant Shipping Act 1988. The traditional idea of sovereignty in the UK has been taken to mean that if there is a clash between a later statutory norm and an earlier legal provision the former takes precedence. The strict application of this idea in the context of the EC could obviously be problematic, since the ECJ has held that Community law must take precedence in the event of a clash with national law.

Earlier UK cases had taken a variety of approaches to the issue of a potential clash between the two legal systems. Some authorities appeared to stick to the traditional orthodoxy of giving precedence to national law.[24] Others applied a rule of construction, under which it would be assumed that Parliament had not intended there to be any inconsistency between UK law and EC law, unless Parliament had expressly stated its intent to derogate from the norms of Community law. The dicta of the House of Lords in *Factortame (No.2)* are therefore clearly of importance. Lord Bridge had this to say.[25]

"Some public comments on the decision of the Court of Justice, affirming the jurisdiction of the courts of the member states to override national legislation if necessary to enable interim relief to be granted in protection of rights under Community law, have suggested that this was a novel and dangerous invasion by a Community institution of the sovereignty of the United Kingdom Parliament. But such comments are based on a misconception. If the supremacy within the European Community of Community law over the national law of member states was not always inherent in the EEC Treaty it was certainly well established in the

---

[22] *R. v Secretary of State for Transport Ex p. Factortame Ltd (No 2)* [1991] 1 A.C. 603.
[23] Ch.28.
[24] P. Craig, "Sovereignty of the United Kingdom Parliament after *Factortame*" (1991) 11 Y.B.E.L. 221, 240–243.
[25] [1991] 1 A.C. 603, 658–659.

jurisprudence of the Court of Justice long before the United Kingdom joined the Community. Thus, whatever limitation of its sovereignty Parliament accepted when it enacted the European Communities Act 1972 was entirely voluntary. Under the terms of the 1972 Act it has always been clear that it was the duty of a United Kingdom court, when delivering final judgment, to override any rule of national law found to be in conflict with any directly enforceable rule of Community law. Similarly, when decisions of the Court of Justice have exposed areas of United Kingdom statute law which failed to implement Council directives, Parliament has always loyally accepted the obligation to make appropriate and prompt amendments. Thus there is nothing in any way novel in according supremacy to rules of Community law in areas to which they apply and to insist that, in the protection of rights under Community law, national courts must not be prohibited by rules of national law from granting interim relief in appropriate cases is no more than a logical recognition of that supremacy."

10–014 It is clear that Lord Bridge was speaking in broad terms about the general relationship between EC law and UK law. His dictum represents a general statement concerning the priority of Community law over national law in the event of a clash between the two. The foundation for this reasoning is essentially contractarian: the UK knew when it joined the EC that priority should be accorded to EC law, and it must be taken to have contracted on those terms. If, therefore, "blame" was to be cast for a loss of sovereignty then this should be laid at the feet of Parliament and not the courts.

Lord Goff, who gave the leading judgment of the House of Lords, said less on this particular issue than did Lord Bridge. However, even Lord Goff did state, in the course of deciding whether to grant interim relief to the applicants, that the applicants had strong grounds for "challenging the validity" of the provisions relating to residence and domicile in the UK legislation.[26]

Space precludes detailed analysis of *Factortame (No.2)* on the traditional concept of sovereignty.[27] It is clear that our courts are now willing to disapply even a primary statute where it comes into conflict with Community law.[28] At the very least the *Factortame* decision means that the concept of implied repeal, under which inconsistencies between later and earlier norms were resolved in favour of the former, will no longer apply to clashes concerning Community and national law. If Parliament wishes to derogate from its Community obligations then it will have to do so expressly and unequivocally. Whether our national courts would then choose to follow the

---

[26] [1991] 1 A.C. 603, 674.
[27] Craig, n.24; Sir William Wade, "Sovereignty—Revolution or Evolution?" (1996) 112 L.Q.R. 568; T.R.S. Allan, "Parliamentary Sovereignty: Law, Politics and Revolution" (1997) 113 L.Q.R. 443; N. MacCormick, *Questioning Sovereignty, Law, State and Practical Reason* (Oxford University Press, 1999), Ch.6; P. Craig, "Britain in the European Union", in J. Jowell and D. Oliver (eds), *The Changing Constitution* (Oxford University Press, 6th edn, 2007), Ch.4.
[28] *Equal Opportunities Commission v Secretary of State for Employment* [1994] 1 W.L.R. 409.

latest will of Parliament, or whether they would argue that it is not open to our legislature to pick and choose which obligations to subscribe to while still remaining within the Community, remains to be seen.

B. Direct Effect

The doctrine of Community law supremacy has been a cornerstone of a Community legal order. The ECJ's other principal contribution has been the doctrine of direct effect. In order to appreciate its importance, it is necessary to understand why it was introduced.

10–015

i. *The limits of public enforcement*

The concept of direct effect allows individuals to bring actions in their own names within national courts in order to vindicate rights secured to them by the Treaty. It is in this sense a species of *private enforcement*. Whether the framers of the original EC Treaty intended individuals to be able to bring such actions is debatable. It is nonetheless clear that the Treaty obligations have to be enforced in some manner, and the principal mechanism for doing so was through *public enforcement*, art.226 EC. One of the principal rationales for the introduction of direct effect was to supplement public enforcement of Community law with private enforcement, because of the weaknesses of the former.

10–016

Under art.226 the Commission has the responsibility of bringing Member States who have failed to comply with the Treaty before the ECJ. Article 227 allows a Member State to bring another Member State to the ECJ, provided that it first submits the issue to the Commission. There are six principal limits to this manner of enforcing EC norms, each of which is cured, or at the least alleviated by, the development of direct effect.

The first, and most obvious, difficulty created by this approach is that it thereby effectively places the entire burden of policing EC law on the Commission, since one Member State will rarely sue another. This entails a considerable *workload* for the Commission, which has a plethora of other responsibilities quite separate from that of "prosecutor". Private actions, rendered possible by direct effect, complement the enforcement role of the Commission by sanctioning claims brought by individuals in their own capacity.[29]

A second difficulty with public enforcement is closely related to the first. *Knowledge* of the existence of a breach is a condition precedent for an enforcement action. This knowledge could be acquired by the Commission itself, but this would be an extremely complex process given the size of the Treaty and the volume of legislation made thereunder. This would be so

[29] Another way of putting the same point is that direct effect creates a large number of "private attorney-generals", who operate not only to vindicate their own private rights, but also to ensure that the norms of the EC Treaty are correctly applied by the Member States. Enforcement of the Treaty is thereby shared and the Commission is no longer solely responsible for this important task.

even if, as is the case, individuals can inform the Commission of a possible Treaty violation. Direct effect alleviates this problem. An individual who believes that a wrong has been done by a Member State contrary to the EC Treaty is in the optimal position to know the facts to which the alleged violation relates, and has a strong incentive to take steps to have the matter tested.

The third limit of public enforcement is that it is *only available against a Member State*. While an individual may wish to assert rights against the state, there may also be many instances where the appropriate defendant is another individual or a corporation, such as actions involving, for example, competition law or discrimination. Direct effect imposes obligations on private parties, subject to the limits mentioned below, and allows such actions to be brought before the national courts.

10–017   The fourth difficulty with relying on public enforcement per se is the *conflict of interest* problem. There is an extensive literature concerning agency capture, the situation in which an agency comes to associate with the interests of those which it was established to regulate. There is little evidence of this occurring within the EC, where the Commission has pursued the objectives of the Community vigorously, even where this has met with opposition from Member States. Notwithstanding this strident approach, the Commission may be vulnerable to a conflict of interest, and the result may be similar, albeit less dramatic, to agency capture. The reason is as follows. The Commission, as we have seen, possesses a wide range of powers, legislative as well as judicial. This can lead to tension. An important legislative initiative may be under consideration in the Council, with the consequence that the Commission may be wary of pursuing an action against a Member State lest the latter should manifest its displeasure by rendering the passage of the legislation more protracted. If the legislation is important, and the wrongdoing is of less significance, the temptation to ignore the latter, or to pursue it less vigorously, may be great, even though the breach may be of import to the particular group affected by it. It is difficult to determine how often the Commission has been placed in this conundrum, since it is unlikely to admit that its decision has been affected in this manner. At the very least it can be said that a system which relies exclusively on public enforcement, and in which the "prosecutor" also exercises legislative powers, will be prone to this type of tension. The introduction of direct effect eases this tension dramatically. It is now the individual who is bringing the action. The individual is not, and cannot be, subject to the same pressures as the Commission.

The fifth shortcoming with the regime of public enforcement concerns *remedies*. These have inherent limitations. Article 228 EC as originally formulated stipulated that a Member State found to be in breach of the Treaty should take the necessary measures to comply with the ECJ's judgment. This clearly imposes an obligation on the State, but it sounds principally as a breach of an international obligation derived from the Treaty. If the State should continue to prove recalcitrant there was, until the TEU, little more that could realistically be done, short of bringing a further action.

The ECJ now has the power to fine a Member State pursuant to art.228. Notwithstanding this, direct effect provides a particularly effective way to secure a remedy. This is because the action begins and ends in the national courts, and national governments are more likely to adhere to a judgment given directly from within their own system. This much is well known. The impact of direct effect at the remedial level is, however, more significant than this. The ECJ, while leaving some choice of remedy to the national courts, has made it clear that the remedy must provide an effective protection for the right in question.[30] The more precise implications of this will vary depending on the nature of the issue. At the most general level the ECJ has demanded that national courts should, in effect, treat as done what ought to be done. Thus if, for example, a state has imposed a tariff that is inconsistent with Community law and has levied money pursuant thereto, then the national court should treat the tariff as invalid and return the money. It is for the national court to decide whether to invalidate the tariff, or disregard it in the instant litigation.

The final stumbling block with public enforcement is of a more symbolic nature. It has already been seen how such a system could be creative of tensions between Member States and the Commission in particular cases. At a more general level the approach in art.226 produces a *public relations problem*. The preamble to the Treaty speaks of laying the foundations "of an ever closer union among the peoples of Europe". This theme has always been close to the heart of the federalist-minded Commission. Vigorous enforcement of existing Treaty norms against Member States is not formally inconsistent with this long term goal. It does nonetheless not look "quite right" that a Community which is meant to be moving towards a closer social and political union should have countless cases in which one organ of the Community is continually suing its constituent members. Direct effect therefore possessed a significant symbolic advantage. EC norms could be enforced without there being endless cases in which the Commission was directly suing the states. The reality was, as reality is, unchanged. Actions brought by individuals were still about states whose compliance with EC law was imperfect. However the concept of direct effect served to ensure that this did not appear as a direct confrontation between the Commission and the Member States.

ii. Direct effect and the empowerment of the individual

The discussion thus far has concentrated on the way in which direct effect alleviated the problem attendant upon public enforcement of EC norms. The discussion would, however, be incomplete if it were to rest there. Direct effect has made a positive contribution to the development of EC law quite independently of this. Granting rights to individuals, which they can enforce in their own name, transformed the very nature of the EC treaty. No longer

10–018

---

[30] For detailed discussion of EC jurisdiction in relation to remedies, see Craig and de Búrca, n.1, Ch.9.

would the Treaty be viewed solely as the business of nation states in the manner of many other international treaties.

It was to be a form of social ordering in which individuals were involved in their own capacity. They were no longer to be passive receptors who had to await action taken on their behalf by other organs of the Community. They were now accorded rights that they could enforce in their own name. This was a necessary step in the transformation of the Community from a compact between states, which was principally economic in nature, to that vision glimpsed at in the preamble of the Treaty "a closer union among the peoples of Europe". It represented the first step in the judicial contribution towards the building of a more federal Europe.

iii. Van Gend en Loos

10–019 The seminal case in the development of the concept of direct effect was *Van Gend en Loos*.[31] Dutch importers challenged the rate of duty imposed on a chemical imported from Germany. They argued that a reclassification of the product under a different heading of the Dutch tariff legislation had led to an increase in the duty and that this was prohibited under art.12 EC (now art.25), which prohibits the imposition of any new customs duties on imports and also precludes any increase in existing rates. The Dutch court asked the ECJ whether art.12 gave rise to rights which could be invoked by individuals before their national courts.

The details of the arguments advanced by Holland, Germany and Belgium differed, but their general tenor was the same. The major theme was that provisions already existed through which EC law could be enforced, and these were to be found in arts 169 and 170 (now arts 226 and 227). This theme was complemented by a second, the substance of which was that the Treaty was simply a compact between states, to be policed in the manner dictated by the Treaty itself. If a Member State was in breach of the Treaty then it should have to face the consequences at the hands of another state, or at the hands of the organ explicitly accorded the task of policing the Treaty, the Commission. To afford individuals the right to initiate actions within national courts would be to alter the nature of the obligations accepted by the signatories.

Three strands of reasoning are apparent in the ECJ's judgment. The first demonstrates the use of a purposive and teleological approach which has become such a characteristic of the ECJ's jurisprudence. The core of the judgment opens with reference to the general aims and spirit of the Treaty, the objective being to deny the very basis of the Member States' reasoning. The EC was *not* simply to be viewed as a compact between nations. The "interested parties" included the people, a fact which was affirmed by the preamble and by the existence of institutions charged with the duty of making provisions for those individuals. It was this crucial conceptual starting point which laid the foundation for the now famous passage from

---

[31] *Van Gend en Loos v Nederlandse Administratie der Belastingen* (26/62) [1963] E.C.R. 1.

the judgment. The ECJ depicted the Community as a new legal order for the benefit of which states have limited their sovereign rights, with the consequence that individuals have rights and could be regarded as subjects of the Community.

The second strand in the ECJ's judgment was designed to buttress the first by drawing upon the Treaty to substantiate the conclusion that individuals could proceed before national courts. The ECJ utilised art.177 (now art.234), which is concerned with the reference of questions on Community law by national courts to the ECJ. This provision was said to indicate that the states acknowledged that Community law had an authority which could be invoked by their nationals before national courts.

The third, and final, aspect of the ECJ's reasoning focused on the particular articles of the Treaty in the case. The argument sought to show that art.12 was a natural candidate for enforcement in this manner. Thus the ECJ stressed the *negative* nature of the obligation, the fact that it was *unconditional*, and that its *implementation was not dependent on any further measures* before being effective under national law. It was thereby able to conclude that the very nature of this prohibition made it ideally suited to produce direct effects in the legal relationship between Member States and their subjects.

iv. Expansion of direct effect: Treaty articles
The years following the decision in *Van Gend en Loos* witnessed the application of the concept to a growing range of Treaty articles. The Court itself was keen to expand the concept given its advantages. In applying direct effect to other Treaty articles the ECJ began to relax the conditions for its application. Direct effect was applied in circumstances where it could not be said that the Treaty article in question created a negative obligation which was legally perfect, in the sense that no further action was required by the Community or the Member States, and no real residue of discretion existed. The concept was applied to Treaty Articles dealing with broad areas of regulatory policy, which were as much social as economic.

The *Reyners* case[32] provides a simple example. The plaintiff was a Dutch national educated in Belgium, who obtained a Belgian legal qualification. He was, however, unable to practice because of a Belgian law which restricted this right to those of Belgian nationality. Dispensation from the nationality condition could be granted, but the plaintiff had been unsuccessful in such applications. He therefore sought to argue that the Belgian law was inconsistent with art.52 EC (now art.43) on freedom of establishment.

A number of Member States contended that this article could not have direct effect because it represented simply a statement of general principle, which had not yet been fleshed out by the secondary legislation in the manner envisaged by the Treaty. The Community and the Member States

10–020

---

[32] *Reyners v Belgian State* (2/74) [1974] E.C.R. 631.

were required to take further action before this part of the Treaty fulfilled the conditions for direct effect to operate. It was not therefore for "the courts to exercise a discretionary power reserved to the legislative institutions of the Community and the Member States".[33]

The ECJ did not accept this argument. It based its reasoning upon an interpretation of the purpose of the relevant chapter taken as a whole. Viewed in this light primacy of position was accorded to the prohibition of discrimination contained in art.52 itself. The further legislation was perceived as a way of effectuating this goal, but the absence thereof was not to be allowed to impede one of the fundamental legal provisions of the Community.

The ECJ may well have been correct in deciding that art.52 should have direct effect even in the absence of these norms being promulgated. This should not however blind us to the fact that the original conditions for direct effect were modified and that this was necessitated by the difference in the type of Treaty article in question. Article 52, when placed within the relevant chapter of the Treaty, could not be regarded as complete and legally perfect in the same sense in which this phrase was used in relation to, for example, art.12. This is so even if one accepts the analysis of the ECJ.

10–021   Article 52, and the provisions on freedom of establishment, expressly contemplated further action by the legislative organs of the Community and by the Member States in order to effectuate the social and economic aims of this part of the Treaty. The very regime of freedom of establishment involves a complex array of legislative norms in order that these aims can be achieved.

The requisite Community legislation pursuant to art.52 had not been enacted in large part because Member States were unwilling to make the compromises to allow this to happen. The choice was clear. Either these spheres of policy could be left unfulfilled. Or the ECJ, through direct effect, could ensure that the basic principles within these areas should be enforced and developed through the judicial process.[34]

The same theme is evident in other important ECJ decisions, such as the seminal *Defrenne* case.[35] Sabena employed Defrenne as an air hostess. Her contract stated that she should retire at 40. She sought to argue that the conditions of her employment were discriminatory and contrary to art.119 EC (now art.141), insofar as they were less favourable than those applicable to male stewards who performed the same task. The fact that the tasks performed by female hostesses and male stewards were identical was not disputed.

The ECJ acknowledged the central importance of art.119 from an economic and a social perspective. It recognised that the complete implementation of the article might well involve "the elaboration of criteria

---

[33] [1974] E.C.R. 631 648–649.
[34] J. Weiler, "The Community System: The Dual Character of Supranationalism" (1981) 1 Y.B.E.L. 267; P. Craig, "Once Upon a Time in the West: Direct Effect and the Federalization of EEC Law" (1992) 12 O.J.L.S. 453.
[35] *Defrenne v Sabena* (43/75) [1976] E.C.R. 455.

whose implementation necessitates the taking of appropriate measures at Community and national level".[36] This was not, however, to be a bar to giving direct effect to the Article. Direct and overt discrimination could be identified solely through art.119 itself. Direct effect could operate in relation to such forms of discrimination, even if the proscription of more indirect and disguised forms of discrimination could only be identified by reference to explicit implementing provisions of a Community or national character.

Article 119, like art.52, provides the general aim for a complex sphere of regulatory social and economic policy. It could not be regarded as complete and legally perfect in the same manner as, for example art.12, without radically distorting the meaning of that phrase. It was clear that art.119 required, as the Court recognised, further measures at both Community and national level in order for the aims to be fulfilled. Not all the requisite measures had been promulgated in the stipulated time. As with *Reyners*, the ECJ introduced direct effect to provide an alternative method through which the principles of equal pay could be furthered, at least in the area of direct discrimination.

v. Expansion of direct effect: Regulations
The discussion thus far has concentrated on the application of direct effect to Treaty provisions. The ECJ, however, also made it clear that the concept could apply to legislation enacted pursuant to the Treaty itself, such as regulations. The definition in art.249 EC states: "A regulation shall have general application. It shall be binding in its entirety and directly applicable in all Member States".

10–022

In *Leonosio v Italian Ministry of Agriculture and Forestry*,[37] (known affectionately as *Slaughtered Cow*), the applicant sought to rely on two Community regulations under which she was entitled to receive a premium if she slaughtered a dairy cow. The relevant Italian authority was awaiting the necessary allocation of funds before it could pay over the money. The ECJ held that the regulation conferred rights on individuals, which they could use in national courts, and that the absence of the requisite allocation of funds was no excuse.

It is moreover clear that the Member State cannot alter the content of the relevant Community norm. Thus in *Amsterdam Bulb*[38] the ECJ held that the direct application of a Community regulation meant that its entry into force was "independent of any measure of transformation into national law",[39] and that states were precluded from adopting "any measure which would conceal the Community nature and effects of any legal provision from the persons to whom it applies".[40]

---

[36] [1976] E.C.R. 455 473.
[37] Case 93/71, [1973] C.M.L.R. 343.
[38] *Amsterdam Bulb v Produktschap voor Siergewassen* (50/76) [1977] E.C.R. 137.
[39] [1977] E.C.R. 137 146.
[40] Loc.cit.

vi. Expansion of direct effect: directives

10–023 According to art.249, directives are binding as to the result to be achieved while leaving the choice of form and methods to the Member States. Moreover, while regulations are binding on all states, directives are only binding on the specific Member States to whom they are addressed.

Directives have proved to be a particularly useful device for legislating in an enlarged Community. Many areas of Community policy concern complex topics ranging from products liability to the environment, and from the harmonisation of company law to the free movement of capital. The "normal" methods of legislating are ill-suited to these spheres. Regulations, as noted above, are intended to be directly applicable in the Member States without being transformed into national laws. This requires that the content of the legislation be written with sufficient clarity and specificity to pass into national systems without more ado. It also requires that the norm is capable of so entering many different legal systems, some of which have a common law foundation, others of which have a civil law base, and where differences abound even within these two groupings. It may well be the case that some regulations are written more loosely than indicated above, and that certain directives are imbued with considerable specificity. Notwithstanding this fact, directives are invaluable precisely because without this doctrinal form it would be more difficult to legislate in many important areas.

The application of direct effect to directives has proven to be more controversial than in the context of regulations. This is in part because directives clearly require further action on the part of the Member States, and because they leave the states with some measure of discretion as to methods of implementation. The reluctance to admit that directives can have direct effect is also in part because art.249 states that regulations are directly applicable, while not using this phraseology in relation to directives. The ECJ has nonetheless held that directives are capable of having direct effect. The Court has used three arguments to justify this conclusion.

Firstly, there is an argument from *general principle*, the essence of which is that it would be inconsistent with the binding effect of directives to exclude the possibility that they can confer rights. The mere fact that regulations were deemed to be directly applicable, and hence capable of conferring rights, should not be taken to mean that other Community norms could never have the same effect.[41]

10–024 The second argument is derived from art.234. This article allows questions concerning the interpretation and validity of Community law to be referred by national courts to the ECJ. The Court concluded that questions relating to directives can therefore be raised by individuals before national courts.[42]

The third reason for according direct effect to directives, in some instances at least, is the *estoppel* argument. Given that the peremptory force of directives would be weakened if individuals could not rely on them before

---

[41] *Van Duyn v Home Office* (41/74) [1974] E.C.R. 1337, para.12.
[42] Loc.cit.

national courts, a Member State which has not implemented the directive "may not rely, as against individuals, on its own failure to perform the obligations which the directive entails".[43]

Provided, therefore, that the directive is sufficiently precise, that the basic obligation is unconditional and that the period for implementation has passed, an individual can derive enforceable rights from a directive.

The decision in *Van Duyn*[44] provides an apt example. The applicant was a Dutch woman who wished to take up employment with the Church of Scientology. Article 48 EC (now art.39) protects the free movement of workers within the Community, subject to exceptions based upon public policy. The UK sought to exclude the applicant on the ground that it believed that the Church was socially undesirable, even though it did not prevent its own nationals from working there. The ECJ considered whether an individual could rely on Directive 64/221, which specified in greater detail the circumstances in which foreign nationals could be excluded on grounds of public policy, public security or public health. More specifically, the applicant sought an interpretation of art.3(1) of the Directive, which provided that exclusionary measures must be based solely on the personal conduct of the individual concerned. The ECJ held that this provision had direct effect.

vii. Directives: horizontal and vertical direct effect

While the ECJ has been willing to give direct effect to directives it has, however, held that they only have vertical as opposed to horizontal direct effect. Treaty articles and regulations give individuals rights enforceable both against the state, vertical direct effect, and against private parties, horizontal direct effect. Directives only have vertical direct effect.

10–025

The seminal case is *Marshall*.[45] The Southampton Area Health Authority operated different retirement ages for men and women, and the applicant claimed that this was in breach of Directive 76/207 on equal treatment. The ECJ reiterated its previous holding that directives were capable of having direct effect. It held that a directive could not, however, impose obligations on individuals, but only on the state, either qua state or qua employer. It reached this conclusion because of the wording of art.189 (now art.249): the binding nature of the directive existed only in relation to "each Member State to which it is addressed".

There are differing opinions on the correctness of, and rationale for, this ruling. The arguments cannot be fully explored here.[46] It is doubtful whether the actual argument advanced by the ECJ is correct. It is true that art.249 talks of directives being binding on the state to which they are addressed. To

---

[43] *Pubblico Ministero v Ratti* (148/78) [1979] E.C.R. 1629, para.22.
[44] Case 41/74, [1974] E.C.R. 1337.
[45] *Marshall v Southampton & South West Hampshire Area Health Authority (Teaching)* (152/84) [1986] E.C.R. 723; *Faccini Dori v Recreb Srl* (C-91/92) [1994] E.C.R. I-3325.
[46] See, e.g., Advocate General Reischl in *Ratti* (148/78) [1979] E.C.R. 1629, 1650; Advocate General Slynn in *Becker v Finanzamt Munster-Innenstadt* (8/81) [1982] E.C.R. 53, 81.

infer from this that they cannot impose duties on individuals is more questionable. The relevant wording of art.249 is simply expressive of the fact that states are the primary addressees of the obligation contained in the directive. It is they who have the correlative duty to take the requisite measures to effectuate the ends stipulated therein. This does not necessarily mean that individuals should not be under an obligation flowing from a directive. A similar argument was rejected in the *Defrenne* case.[47]

If there is a more meaningful argument against giving directives horizontal direct effect then it is based on legal certainty. The essence of the argument is that private individuals should not be placed in unreasonable doubt concerning the nature of their obligations. Given that directives require national implementing legislation this uncertainty might occur if individuals were required to scrutinise differing texts both at national and Community level in order to find out what the law was. There are, however, two limits to this argument.

10–026   On the one hand, it will not always have force even in its own terms. The articles of many directives may be suited to application between private parties, without encountering any problems of legal certainty. Directive 76/207 on equal treatment can be taken as an example. Article 3(1) of the Directive prohibits discrimination on grounds of sex in relation to access to employment, and art.5 bans such discrimination in relation to working conditions. The state is then instructed to take a range of measures to implement the directive. These include measures to ensure that terms in contracts of employment which are contrary to the Directive will be declared null and void. Even if the state has not taken these measures there would seem to be no reason not to impose duties on individuals. The obligations contained in the Directive are clear. An employer who continues to discriminate on these grounds should not be allowed to shelter behind the fact the state has been tardy in fulfilling its duties to implement the Directive.

On the other hand, it is not immediately obvious why the objection based upon legal certainty is thought to be relevant in the context of directives when no such objection is raised in the context of the primary Treaty provisions themselves. Many such articles have been interpreted expansively by the ECJ. These articles have horizontal direct effect, and no one has raised the objection of legal certainty. This is so even though there are often conflicting national norms on precisely the same issue, and even though it may not be easy for an individual to know in advance whether there will in fact be any clash between the requirements of Community law and national law.

Even though directives only have vertical direct effect the force of this limitation has been weakened in four ways: by an expansive definition of the state, by the development of the doctrine of indirect effect, by the creation of what has been termed "incidental" horizontal direct effect, and by damages actions against the state for loss caused by non-implementation of a

[47] Case 43/75, [1976] E.C.R. 455.

directive. The first three of these will be examined within the remainder of this section, the fourth in the section which follows.

viii. Directives: the scope of vertical direct effect

Given that directives only have vertical and not horizontal direct effect it is clearly important to define the ambit of the state for these purposes. The ECJ has given an expansive interpretation to this concept. **10–027**

In *Foster*[48] the applicant wished to rely upon the Equal Treatment Directive 76/207, because she had been compulsorily retired earlier than male employees. The defendant was British Gas, and the question was whether it was to be treated as part of the state for these purposes. The ECJ held that the directive could be relied upon against any body, whatever its legal form, which has been made responsible, pursuant to a measure adopted by the state, for providing a public service under the control of the state, and has for that purpose special powers over and beyond those which normally apply as between individuals.[49]

The correctness of this expansive definition may be questioned. It may well be accepted that bodies such as British Gas should be treated as part of the state for certain purposes, given the nature of its powers and the service which it is providing. What is less obvious is whether it should be so treated for this purpose, *given* the reasoning in *Marshall* itself. The premise underlying *Marshall* must be that the state as the addressee of the directive is meant to implement it. Yet bodies such as British Gas plainly have no powers in this respect, nor can estoppel-type arguments meaningfully apply against such institutions. It will often only be central government which has the authority to execute the directive. It is, of course, true that other bodies may well be in a position to abide by a directive or not as the case may be. But this is equally true for purely private parties as it is for bodies such as British Gas. There is no more or less reason to apply a directive against such bodies than against any other corporation. It is difficult to escape the conclusion that the expansive definition of the state given in *Foster* is an indirect way of circumventing the holding in *Marshall* itself.

ix. Directives: indirect effect

The other way in which the force of the *Marshall* limitation has been blunted has been through the development of the doctrine known as indirect effect. **10–028**

The concept is associated with the important decision in *Von Colson*.[50] The applicants relied upon the provision of a directive in order to argue that the quantum of relief provided by German law in cases of discrimination was too small. The ECJ held that these provisions were not sufficiently

---

[48] *Foster v British Gas* (C-188/89) [1990] E.C.R. I-3133.
[49] D. Curtin, "The Province of Government: Delimiting the Direct Effect of Directives in the Common Law Context" (1990) 15 E.L.Rev. 195.
[50] *Von Colson and Kamann v Land Nordrhein-Westfalen* (14/83) [1984] E.C.R. 1891.

precise to have direct effect. It went on, however, to hold that national courts had an obligation to interpret national law so as to be in conformity with the directive. The purpose of the directive was to provide an effective remedy in cases of discrimination, and if states chose to fulfil this through the provision of compensation then this should be adequate in relation to the damage suffered. National courts should, therefore, construe their own national law with this in mind.

This principle of construction was applied and extended in *Marleasing*.[51] The case was concerned with Council Directive 68/151 which contained rules on safeguards for the establishment of companies within the Community. The plaintiff claimed that one of the defendant companies had been established "without cause" and that it was established to perpetrate a fraud. The plaintiff sought a declaration that the contract establishing the defendant corporation should be held void, and sought to found this claim on a provision of Spanish law. The defendant resisted the claim on the ground that art.11 of Directive 68/151, which listed the grounds on which the nullity of a company could be ordered, did not include lack of cause among these grounds. The Directive had not yet been implemented in Spain, but the Spanish court nonetheless asked the ECJ whether art.11 could be said to be directly applicable, so as to preclude a declaration of nullity of a public company on a ground other than one set out in that article.

The action was between private corporations, and the ECJ reiterated the holding that a directive could not, in itself, impose obligations on individuals, citing the *Marshall* case as authority.[52] However, the ECJ qualified this by drawing on *Von Colson*. It held that the authorities of the Member States have an obligation to effectuate the ends stipulated in a directive, and that this obligation is binding on all authorities in the state, including the courts. It followed that in applying national law, whether *passed before or after* the directive, a national court was required to interpret national law *in every way possible* so as to be in conformity with the directive. From this it followed that the Spanish court should so interpret their national law so as not to order the nullity of a company on a ground not listed in art.11 of the Directive.

10–029   While the ruling of the ECJ preserves its previous position, that there is no horizontal direct effect for directives, its findings on the interpretative duties of the national courts go a considerable way to according directives a measure of "indirect" direct effect. Thus, although an individual cannot, in a literal sense, derive rights from a directive in an action against another individual, it is possible to plead the directive in such an action, in the manner exemplified by the defendant in the present case. Once the directive has been placed before the national court, then the interpretative obligation derived from *Von Colson*, and built upon in *Marleasing*, comes into operation. Where the directive encapsulates precise obligations, and where

---

[51] *Marleasing SA v La Commercial International De Alimentation SA* (C-106/89) [1990] E.C.R. 4135.
[52] [1990] E.C.R. 4135, para.6.

the national court is minded to interpret national law in the required fashion, this "indirect" species of enforcement of a directive as between individuals will have the same results as if the directive had been accorded horizontal direct effect.

There is little doubt but that indirect effect offers a way to circumvent the holding in *Marshall*, or to reach similar results in many instances, albeit by a different route. There is also little doubt that the interpretative obligation creates real problems of its own.[53]

On the one hand, it places national courts in some difficulty in deciding how far they can go in reconciling national legislation with Community norms while still remaining within the realm of interpreting, as opposed to rewriting or overruling national norms. On the other hand, it raises questions of legal certainty for individuals which are, paradoxically, more problematic than if directives had been given horizontal direct effect. Individuals will now have to decide or guess how far their national courts might feel able to go in reconciling national law with differently worded Community legislation. If directives did have horizontal direct effect then at least the individual would know that in the event of any inconsistency between the two norms Community law would trump national law.

Our own courts have, on the whole, shown themselves to be willing to construe national law in the light of the directive in the event of any inconsistency between the two,[54] particularly where the national law was passed to effectuate the directive.[55] The courts have shown more ambivalence where the relevant national law was not promulgated to carry out the directive.[56]

x. Directives: "incidental" horizontal direct effect

The jurisprudence in this area has become even more complex as a result of **10–030** cases in which the ECJ has been willing to accord some measure of effect to a directive in actions between private individuals.

This is exemplified by the *CIA Security* case.[57] CIA Security claimed that the defendants had libelled it by asserting that its alarm systems had not been approved, as required by Belgian legislation. CIA accepted that it had not sought approval under the national legislation, but argued that this legislation was itself in breach of art.30 (now art.28). This was because the Belgian legislation had not been notified to the Commission as required by Directive 83/189, which imposed an obligation on states to notify the Commission of any new national provision which could limit the free movement of goods. The ECJ held that failure to comply with the directive

[53] G. de Búrca, "Giving Effect to European Community Directives" (1992) 55 M.L.R. 215.
[54] *Webb v EMO Cargo* [1995] 4 All E.R. 577.
[55] *Litster v Forth Dry Dock* [1990] 1 A.C. 546. See however *White v White* [2001] 2 All E.R. 43.
[56] *Duke v GEC Reliance* [1988] 1 A.C. 618.
[57] *CIA Security International SA v Signalson SA and Securitel SPRL* (C-194/94) [1996] E.C.R. I-2201.

meant that the non-notified national legislation could not be enforced against individuals.

C. Direct Effect: Rights and Remedies

10–031 The discussion thus far has focused upon the extent to which Community law creates rights which are enforceable by individuals in their own national courts. Rights demand remedies. How far EC law has an impact upon the remedies that are available at the national level is a complex topic. A brief outline will be given here.[58]

The ECJ's early stance is exemplified by *Rewe v Hauptzollamt Kiel*[59] where it was held that, while national courts were under an obligation to use all available national remedies to aid the enforcement of Community law, they were not bound to create new remedies for this purpose. However, in *San Giorgio*[60] the Court held that a Member State could not render claims for the repayment of charges, which were levied in breach of Community law, subject to procedural requirements which made that recovery virtually impossible.

The reconciliation of these two authorities was by no means easy. It was felt that a litigant could only claim a form of relief in aid of Community law rights if national law allowed that relief to be granted between the parties in proceedings before the court in question. If it did not do so then recourse was to be had to the legislature to fill the gap. However, if national law did allow the relief claimed to be granted between the parties by the court before which the proceedings were instituted, it was the duty of that court to make that relief available in aid of Community law, and to disregard any substantive restrictions or procedural conditions of national law which are either discriminatory, or deprive the Community right of useful effect.

Indications that Community law might well require greater modifications in the regime of national remedies are to be found in the *Factortame* litigation. Prior to the House of Lords' decision in the second *Factortame* case[61] UK law did not allow interim injunctive relief against the Crown. It did not permit that relief to be granted between the parties in proceedings before the court in question. The ECJ's decision in *Factortame*[62] had, nonetheless, held that such relief should be available in principle, and that its absence was itself a breach of Community law. The requirements of Community law as to the national remedies for the protection of Community rights were, therefore, more stringent than had previously been thought.

10–032 The principle underlying the *Factortame* litigation was that provided the type of relief sought by the applicant is recognised by national law, in this instance the injunction, the fact that it was not previously available against the Crown would be regarded as an example of ineffective protection of

[58] Craig and de Búrca, n.1, Ch.9.
[59] Case 158/80, [1981] E.C.R. 1805, 1838.
[60] *Amministrazione delle Finanze dello Stato v San Giorgio* (199/82) [1983] E.C.R. 3595.
[61] *R. v Secretary of State for Transport , ex p Factortame Ltd (No.2)* [1991] 1 A.C. 603.
[62] *R. v Secretary of State for Transport Ex p. Factortame Ltd* (C–213/89), n.18.

Community rights, with the consequence that the national law must be changed. Other ECJ decisions evince the same concern that the remedy provided by the Member State must constitute effective relief for breach of the right in issue.[63] Later ECJ jurisprudence has, however, been somewhat less interventionist and allowed greater room for national remedial rules to continue to apply.[64]

The case law considered thus far was concerned primarily with the extent to which EC law would intervene in relation to the adequacy of the remedies currently provided by Member States for breach of Community law. In the *Francovich* case[65] the ECJ, however, created a remedy in damages for breach of EC law. This was conceived as a Community remedy in its own right, and not simply as an option which a particular Member State might or might not choose to embrace. The applicant claimed damages from the Italian government for losses suffered as a result of the non-implementation of a directive designed to safeguard workers when a firm became insolvent. The ECJ held that the principle of state liability for harm caused to individuals by breaches of Community law for which the state can be held responsible was inherent in the system of the Treaty. The full effectiveness of Community rights would be impaired if no such right to compensation existed.[66] This argument from first principle was buttressed by reference to art.5 EC (now art.10), which required Member States to take all appropriate measures to ensure the fulfilment of Community obligations. This included the obligation to nullify the unlawful consequence of a breach of Community law.[67]

The ruling in *Francovich* left open numerous issues concerning the nature of the damages remedy. Many of these were clarified in *Brasserie du Pecheur* and *Factortame*.[68] A bare outline of the decision will be given at this juncture. More detailed treatment can be found in the discussion on damages actions against the state.[69] The principle of state liability in damages was held to be general in nature and existed irrespective of whether the Community norm which had been broken was directly effective or not. Liability could be imposed irrespective of which organ of the state was responsible for the breach, the legislature, the executive or the judiciary. The ECJ set out the criteria to determine when the state could incur liability. Where a Member

[63] *Cotter and McDermott v Minister for Social Welfare and Attorney General* (C-377/89) [1991] E.C.R. I-1155; *Marshall v Southampton and South West Area Health Authority (No.2)* (C-271/91) [1993] E.C.R. I-4367.

[64] *Steenhorst-Neerings v Bestuur van de Bedrijfsvereniging voor Detailhandel, Ambachten en Huisvrouwen* (C-338/91) [1993] E.C.R. I-5475; Case C-66/95, *R. v Secretary of State for Social Security Ex p. Sutton* [1997] E.C.R. I-2163.

[65] *Francovich v Italian Republic, Bonifaci v Italian Republic* (C-6 and 9/90) [1991] E.C.R. I- 5357; M. Ross, "Beyond *Francovich*" (1993) 56 M.L.R. 55; D. Curtin, "State Liability under Private Law: A New Remedy for Private Parties" [1992] I.L.J. 74; J. Steiner, "From Direct Effects to *Francovich*" (1993) 18 E.L.Rev. 3; P. Craig, "*Francovich*, Remedies and the Scope of Damages Liability" (1993) 109 L.Q.R. 595.

[66] *Francovich*, n.65, paras 32–35.

[67] *Francovich*, n.65, para.36.

[68] *Brasserie du Pecheur SA v Germany, R. v Secretary of State for Transport Ex p. Factortame Ltd* (C-46 and 48/93) [1996] E.C.R. I-1029.

[69] See below, Ch.29.

State acted in an area in which it had some measure of discretion, comparable to that of the Community institutions when implementing Community policies, the conditions for liability in damages must, said the ECJ, be the same as those applying to the Community itself.[70] The right to damages was dependent upon three conditions: the rule of law infringed must have been intended to confer rights on individuals; the breach of this rule of law must have been sufficiently serious; there must have been a direct causal link between the breach of the obligation imposed on the state and the damage which was sustained by the injured parties.

4. THE IMPACT OF COMMUNITY LAW

10–033 It is clear that many public law cases will be concerned with the application of Community law principles at the national level. National agencies and institutions are under a duty to apply the principles laid down in the Treaty and the norms made pursuant thereto. If they do not do so then an action can be maintained. This will be brought either by way of the public law procedures, or an ordinary action will be used. In reading the materials in this book one should, moreover, be aware of the fact that Community law can have an impact in four different ways.

First, and most obviously, are the instances in which EC law dictates the result in a particular area, and takes precedence over national law.

Second, there are instances where EC law has a "spillover" effect for the resolution of analogous problems of a purely domestic character. Thus, the fact that interim injunctive relief had to be available against the Crown in the Community law context, operated as a catalyst for the rethinking of this issue within domestic law, in part at least because it looked odd for the remedy to be available in the one context but not the other.

Third, Community law can be a spur for more general doctrinal development in our regime of public law. The development, for example, of proportionality as a ground for review is due, in no small measure, to the fact that it exists as such within Community law.

Finally, the existence of the Community has had the effect of bringing the public law systems of the differing European countries closer together. This is due in part to the fact that EC law draws its inspiration from the laws of the Member States. It is due also to the fact that the very existence of the Community has fostered a growing awareness of the mutual dependence of its component parts. This has led to an increased interest in understanding the ways in which civilian and common law systems tackle the same problem.

---

[70] For discussion of the principles governing the liability of the Community itself in damages under art.288(2), see Craig and de Búrca, n.1, Ch.16.

CHAPTER 11

A CASE STUDY: COMPETITION AND REGULATION

The institutions directly covered by administrative law have been considered   **11–001**
in the previous chapters. It is, however, helpful to consider the operation of
the administrative process in more detail, and this chapter will do so in
relation to competition policy and the regulation of utilities and market
power. These areas are particularly well suited to such an analysis. They
demonstrate how the choice of regulatory machinery has been affected by
political considerations. They exemplify many of the procedural and substantive issues with which administrative law has to grapple. They are also
areas of importance given the market-based approach to regulation.

1. COMPETITION: WHETHER TO REGULATE

Competition policy is concerned with controlling firms within the market in   **11–002**
order that they do not harm the competitive process. Central examples of
such behaviour are cartels and monopolies. Cartels are agreements by rival
companies to fix prices or divide the market, with the consequence that
fewer goods will be available to consumers at a higher price than if normal
market conditions prevailed. Monopoly power can enable a company to
raise price and restrict output with the consequence that it can reap
"abnormal" profits. The possession of such power may also enable its
holder to drive other firms from the market or prevent their initial entry.

 The common law did exercise some control over these areas, but this was,
by the end of the 19th century, almost wholly ineffectual in promoting
competition. For example, the interpretation accorded to the restraint of
trade doctrine meant that the preservation of competition was not the prime
objective. Reluctance to interfere with a bargain even if the direct consequence was to injure the economic interest of another reached its high
point in the case law on conspiracy. A price-fixing and market-allocation

scheme, backed up by exclusionary tactics employed against those unwilling to submit, was held not to be an illegal conspiracy at common law.[1] The 19th century did, however, see some statutory regulation of monopoly power. Thus it was common for utility services to be regulated by the Board of Trade, which would oversee the rates to be charged.

It was nonetheless some considerable time before Parliament attempted any more comprehensive control of market power.[2] The reasons for the absence of intervention were eclectic. Three may be mentioned here.

First, it was felt that there was no urgent case for legislation dealing with market power.[3] Second, the First World War had fostered a climate of co-operation between firms, which was regarded as beneficial.[4] Third, the failure of post-war prosperity, the depression, business failure and unemployment, brought forth cries of "ruinous competition". The feeling that the market mechanism had failed, and that collusion was "good", was fostered by the idea of rationalisation, one tenet of which was that large firms were more efficient and therefore should be encouraged.

The eventual passage of legislation after the Second World War owed its origins partly to a change in attitude towards competition, and partly to other governmental policies canvassed during this period. Thus, some within government began to feel that industry would have to become more efficient, and that cartels were an impediment to this development. This view was given added force by the White Paper on employment policy.[5] It was argued that the object of securing full employment could be jeopardised by monopoly power and cartels, both of which could lead to higher prices and restricted output, thereby hampering employment prospects.[6]

2. COMPETITION: WHO SHOULD REGULATE?

11–003 The first general, modern piece of legislation was passed in 1948, the Monopolies and Restrictive Practices (Inquiry and Control) Act. We have seen in the previous chapters that the choice of regulatory institution is often influenced as much by short-term political arguments as by any attempt to devise an optimum, rational administrative strategy. The choice of regulatory institutions for competition policy provides a good example of this. Five stages can be identified.

The initial allocation of regulatory power was to an agency, the Monopolies and Restrictive Practices Commission (MRPC). It was felt that a

[1] *Mogul SS Co Ltd v McGregor Gow* [1892] A.C. 25; *Sorrell v Smith* [1925] A.C. 700.
[2] Some governmental initiatives occurred after the First World War, e.g. Committee on Trusts, Cmd. 9236 (1918).
[3] Committee on Trade and Industry, Cmd. 3282 (1929).
[4] L. Hannah, *The Rise of the Corporate Economy* (Methuen, 1979), 32–33.
[5] Cmd. 6527 (1944).
[6] G. Allen, *Monopoly and Restrictive Practices* (Allen & Unwin, 1968), 62.

body outside of the normal departmental framework would be better suited to the investigatory nature of the work, and this institutional choice facilitated the involvement of non-civil servants who possessed specialist expertise. These are, as we have seen, both common reasons for establishing an agency.[7]

The second stage came in 1956. The Restrictive Trade Practices Act 1956 was passed to deal specifically with the problems of cartels, and the Restrictive Practices Court (RPC) was established to adjudicate upon the area. The shift from a system of discretionary administration via an agency, to a judicial regime that purported to apply "black-letter" legal rules, is particularly interesting. It was motivated principally because of industry's dissatisfaction with the operation of the MRPC. The selection of an industry for investigation was regarded as arbitrary, firms which appeared before the MRPC felt themselves to be on trial, and corporations said that they had little idea as to which types of behaviour were suspect. The legislators responded by enacting a statute framed in formalistic, legal terms, which purported to clarify the type of proscribed behaviour. A court was created to adjudicate upon the matter, as opposed to a court-substitute tribunal, because it was thought that such a body would gain the respect of industry more easily.

The third stage saw the expansion of the functions of the Monopolies Commission. This body was retained to investigate issues concerning monopoly power after 1956. Its powers were augmented by two major legislative developments. The Monopolies and Mergers Act 1965 added merger regulation to its jurisdiction, and the body was henceforth called the Monopolies and Mergers Commission (MMC). The Competition Act 1980 gave the MMC power to investigate certain anti-competitive practices, which were defined in broad, open textured terms. In exercising its powers in relation to monopolies, mergers or anti-competitive practices, the MMC worked with the Office of Fair Trading (OFT). It was the Director General of Fair Trading (DGFT) who made[8] a monopoly reference to the MMC, or a reference concerning an anti-competitive practice.[9] Merger references were dealt with rather differently, and the DGFT advised the Secretary of State as to whether a reference should be made to the MMC.[10] The OFT was an agency with responsibilities for consumer protection as well as competition policy.[11]

The fourth stage in the choice of institutions to administer competition policy was the rejection of a composite, single authority to oversee the area. The division between cartel policy, regulated by the OFT and the RPC, and the remainder of competition policy which was within the jurisdiction of the

---

[7] See above, Ch.4.
[8] Fair Trading Act 1973 s.50. A government minister can also refer, s.51.
[9] Competition Act 1980 s.5.
[10] Fair Trading Act 1973 s.76.
[11] I. Ramsay, "The Office of Fair Trading: Policing the Consumer Market-Place," in R. Baldwin and C. McCrudden (eds), *Regulation and Public Law* (Weidenfeld & Nicolson, 1987), Ch.9.

OFT and the MMC, was always of doubtful validity. The inability of one authority to consider all anti-competitive aspects of a problem made little sense. The division of authority also produced a large volume of complex legislation dealing with these distinct areas. The issue came to a head during the discussion that led to the Competition Act 1980. It was unclear whether this new area should be assigned to the MMC or the RPC, or whether there should be a new authority with jurisdiction over all areas of competition policy.[12] In the end the new powers were assigned to the MMC, and plans for a single competition authority were not pursued. The reasons for rejecting this bolder option were not convincing,[13] and the result was the continuance of an administrative strategy that was over-complex and outdated.

The fifth stage saw the acceptance of the bolder option. The Competition Act 1998 radically revised the UK's approach to competition policy. The specific legislation on restrictive trade practices ceased to have effect,[14] as did certain provisions of the legislation concerning anti-competitive practices.[15] The basic institutional structure of the new legislation is that decision-making is shared between the DGFT, the Competition Commission and the Competition Appeal Tribunal. The Competition Commission replaced the Monopolies and Mergers Commission.[16] There have been consequential changes to the legislation as a result of reforms in the Community regime of competition law.[17] The present regime is a much more rational decision-making structure than that which previously existed. The force of this change will be even more apparent when we consider the criteria that apply to determine whether there has been a competition violation, which as we shall see, have become more economics focussed.

3. COMPETITION: HOW TO REGULATE

A. Effectiveness and the Choice of the Legislative Criterion

11–004　Any legal system that regulates competition has to decide whether to frame its legislation in terms of legal form or economic effects. The essence of this choice is easily explained. There are many types of cartels. They can be agreements to fix price, divide the market, share information or boycott

---

[12] *Review of Restrictive Trade Practices Policy*, Cmnd. 7512 (1979).

[13] P. Craig, "The Monopolies and Mergers Commission: Competition and Administrative Rationality," Baldwin and McCrudden, n.11, Ch.10. A later government report indirectly undermined much of the reasoning contained in the earlier report: *Review of Restrictive Trade Practices Policy*, Cm. 331 (1988).

[14] Restrictive Trade Practices Acts 1976 and 1977, Restrictive Practices Court Act 1976 and the Resale Prices Act 1976. See, Competition Act 1998 s.1.

[15] Competition Act 1980 ss.2–10. See, Competition Act 1998 s.17.

[16] Competition Act 1998 ss.45–46.

[17] Competition Act 1998 and Other Enactments (Amendment) Regulations 2004 (SI 2004/1261).

third parties. They can be contracts under which one party will accept a certain type of product, such as beer or petrol, only from a particular supplier, as in the case of contracts covered by the restraint of trade doctrine.[18]

An approach based upon legal form attempts to set out in black-letter legal terms the types of agreement to be caught. This was, until recently, the strategy in the legislation on cartels.[19] There are, however, two difficulties with this approach. It was introduced, as we have seen, partly under pressure from industry, which wished to have a more "certain" system than that which had preceded it. Legal form was intended to provide this. There are, however, certain key terms within any such legislation, such as whether activity "restricts" competition, which prove impossible to define purely "legally" without producing absurd results. An economic analysis is required. The other difficulty is that companies making illegal agreements will attempt to conceal the fact that they are dividing the market by, for example, an elaborate exchange of information about production. Legislation based on legal form encourages such "escape" devices.[20]

An approach based upon economic effects uses economic criteria to determine whether the legislation will "bite". Such legislation tends to be much shorter, and focuses upon the economic effects of an agreement irrespective of the way in which it is "dressed up" by the parties. This is the approach used in the EC and the USA, and it was exemplified by the Competition Act 1980 in this country.

We have already seen that one of the general issues when assessing regulatory agencies is their effectiveness. If legislation does not use the most appropriate criterion there is little hope that the regulatory scheme will be successful. There was increasing consensus that form-based legislation did not work,[21] and that it was not sensible to base one part of the regulatory strategy upon a criterion of legal form, and another upon a test of economic effects.

The Competition Act 1998 marked a major shift in policy by using a general criterion of economic effect. The approach based on legal form, which dominated thinking in relation to restrictive agreements, has gone. The basic rationale behind the new legislation is to bring the criteria for domestic competition policy into line with that which applies in the EC. Articles 81 and 82 EC govern anti-competitive agreements and abuse of a dominant position respectively. The wording of these Articles has been used as the basis for these matters within domestic law. Thus section 2(1) of the 1998 Act borrows directly from art.81, while s.18 of the 1998 Act adopts the language of art.82.

---

[18] e.g. *Esso Petroleum Co Ltd v Harper's Garage (Stourport) Ltd* [1968] A.C. 269.
[19] Restrictive Trade Practices Act 1976.
[20] e.g. *Re Cadbury Schweppes Ltd and J. Lyons & Co Ltd's Agreement* [1975] 1 W.L.R. 1018.
[21] A later government report was more favourable to an effects system: *Review of Restrictive Trade Practices Policy*, Cm. 331 (1988).

B. Procedure and Procedural Rights

11–005 The earlier discussion touched upon the choice between adversarial and inquisitorial procedures that an agency might adopt.[22] Competition policy provides an apt illustration of these differing approaches.

The procedure before the RPC was essentially adversarial. Cartels within the ambit of the legislation had to register, and the DGFT then had a duty to take proceedings before the RPC.[23] In the subsequent trial the RPC heard arguments from the DGFT and the firms concerned as to whether the agreement should be allowed to stand because it was claimed to be beneficial to the public interest.[24]

The procedure before the MMC was more inquisitorial and investigative in nature. When the MMC received a monopoly reference from the DGFT it would collect information concerning the industry. An oral hearing might be held to ascertain the facts. It would then consider the impact of the monopoly upon the public interest. The firms involved would be sent a "public interest letter", and they could make representations to the MMC about it. A public interest hearing would then be held at which the firms could present their arguments. It was clear that the MMC had to comply with natural justice.[25] It was also clear that its procedure did not fit the traditional adversarial mould. The MMC did not sit as an "umpire" to hear the arguments from opposing sides. It carried out investigative work of its own, it possessed technical staff to assess financial evidence, it had its own view as to what constituted the public interest in a particular area, and it had considerable latitude in devising its own procedures.[26] Monopoly references of the kind mentioned here are not fundamentally altered by the Competition Act 1998.[27]

The procedures under the Competition Act 1998 represent an interesting blend of the inquisitorial and the adversarial. It is common for those who make agreements which they know or think might be in breach of s.2 to conceal them. If the legislation is to be effective there must therefore be adequate investigative powers. The Director's powers are modelled on those of the European Commission, which makes the initial determination of a competition violation in the EC. The DGFT is given extensive powers to investigate to see whether there is an anti-competitive agreement or an abuse of a dominant position.[28] The DGFT's decisions can then be appealed to the Competition Commission (CC),[29] with a further appeal on limited grounds to the Court of Appeal.[30] The procedure before the appeal tribunals will be

---

[22] See above, paras 9–025—9–026.
[23] Restrictive Trade Practices Act 1976 s.1(2)(c), subject to s.21.
[24] Restrictive Trade Practices Act 1976 ss.10, 19.
[25] *Hoffmann-La Roche & Co v Secretary of State for Trade and Industry* [1975] A.C. 295.
[26] Fair Trading Act 1973 s.81(2).
[27] Competition Act 1998 ss.66–67 Sch.10.
[28] Competition Act 1998 ss.25–31.
[29] Competition Act 1998 s.46.
[30] Competition Act 1998 s.49.

more traditionally adversarial, although even here there is discretion as to the way in which the hearing is conducted.[31]

C. Defining the Public Interest: Rule-Making and Discretion

The question whether regulatory agencies should proceed through the application of rules/policy guidelines, or through the exercise of ad hoc discretion, is of particular interest to administrative lawyers.[32]

11–006

Competition policy provides an interesting example of this general problem. The legislation allowed the MMC to take into account a wide variety of factors in determining the public interest including[33]: maintaining effective competition; promoting the interests of consumers; reducing costs; developing new products; maintaining the balanced distribution of industry and employment in the United Kingdom; and encouraging overseas competitiveness. This broad list seemed to dictate that the MMC should proceed by way of ad hoc discretion and this was indeed generally the case.

It was, however, argued that a more rule-based system should be applied in for example the area of mergers, for the following reason.[34] Economic analysis might indicate that mergers could produce welfare benefits, in terms of economies of scale. These could in theory be balanced against the disadvantages from having a larger firm as the result of the merger, which would have more market power and greater ability to raise price and restrict output. Such cost-benefit analysis is, however, difficult and time consuming, and the necessary data is often not available. It was argued that the best approach was therefore to proceed by way of rules, rather than through ad hoc discretion. A rule might, for example, prohibit all mergers leading to a market share in excess of 50 per cent.

The preceding argument was nevertheless based upon an important implicit premise. If the reduction of competition was regarded as the principal factor within the public interest analysis, then it might well be possible to devise rules accordingly. Where the range of factors felt to be relevant was broader, then the problems of rule definition became more intractable. Thus, if the effects of a merger on unemployment, the balance of payments, regional policy and the like are felt to be of integral importance, then the possibility of formulating appropriate "rules", while still yielding predictability of result is questionable.[35]

The balance between rules and discretion can be relevant in a number of other areas within competition policy. This is readily apparent by considering the Competition Act 1998. In substantive terms, there is, for

---

[31] Competition Act 1998 Sch.8, para.9.
[32] See below, Ch.16.
[33] Fair Trading Act 1973 s.84.
[34] M. Crew and C. Rowley, "Antitrust Policy: Economics versus Management Science" Moorgate and Wall Street, Autumn 1970; M. Howe, "Antitrust Policy: Rules or Discretionary Intervention" Moorgate and Wall Street, Spring 1971; M. Crew and C. Rowley, "Antitrust Policy: The Application of Rules" Moorgate and Wall Street, Autumn 1971.
[35] The 1969 and 1978 Merger Guidelines took a broad range of factors into account, but how much "guidance" they actually provided is debatable.

example, the device of the block exemption. Agreements that are prima facie
caught by s.2 can be exempted if certain conditions are present. The grant of
individual discretionary exemptions is however time consuming for the
competition authorities and can lead to uncertainty for the parties. The
approach taken in the EC has been to promulgate block exemptions, which
are designed to exempt categories of agreements that fulfil certain criteria.
This option is open under the 1998 Act.[36] The balance between rules and
discretion can also be of relevance on the procedural level. Thus the DGFT
is given power to make a wide variety of rules relating to matters such as the
procedure to be followed when dealing with an application, the documents
to be provided and the way in which agreements should be notified.[37]

D. Defining the Public Interest: Politics, Policy and Justiciability

11–007   Governments have differed as to the way in which the public interest "list"
ought to be interpreted. These differences had a considerable impact on the
operation of the OFT and the MMC, because the Secretary of State had
power both in the initiation of references to the MMC, and at the remedial
level. Two views of the "public interest" can be contrasted.

The Labour Party of the 1970s believed that, for example, merger policy
should be based upon a relatively thorough consideration of the list of
public interest factors mentioned in the legislation. The MMC should weigh
the economic costs and benefits to competition, industrial efficiency, and the
balance of payments, against the wider social costs and benefits to workers
and consumers in each merger reference. Such an assessment had to be
qualitative as well as quantitative.

The Conservative Party's attitude differed. Their market-based philosophy meant that they attached prime importance to competition within the
public interest list. Other factors, such as the possible effects upon
employment, were not regarded as the principal concerns of the OFT and
MMC.[38] This approach also favoured quicker investigative mechanisms in
order to determine whether behaviour was in fact injurious to competition.[39]

It would be wrong to assume that the government could in a literal sense
dictate to the MMC the type of view it should adopt on the meaning of the
"public interest". It would also be wrong to assume that the fact that the
government exercised power in this respect was "wrong". The legislation
upon competition was structured to leave discretion and ultimate control in
the hands of the minister. Competition, like planning, was regarded as an
area that should not be completely divorced from political considerations
and one where some executive control was required. No conclusion can be
reached about the effectiveness of a regulatory institution without some
prior idea as its purpose. The object of competition policy has been crucially

[36] Competition Act 1998 ss.6–9.
[37] Competition Act 1998 s.51 Sch.9 para.2.
[38] See, *Charter Consolidated Ltd, Anderson Strathclyde Ltd*, Cmnd. 8771 (1982); *R. v Secretary of State for Trade Ex p. Anderson Strathclyde Plc* [1983] 2 All E.R. 233.
[39] Competition Act 1980.

bound up with the political question concerning the meaning of the public interest. Indeed attempts to divorce such matters more thoroughly from the political arena have produced arguments that they are not readily justiciable.

This was a recurring theme in the operation of the RPC, which had to consider whether a cartel should be exempted under the "gateways". These were broad. It could, for example, be argued that removal of the restrictive agreement would deny specific and substantial benefits to users of goods. It was doubtful whether a court was best suited to resolving such issues, and questionable whether they should be divorced from the political arena.[40]

E. Enforcement

If a regulatory strategy is to be successful then it must be enforced. The choice of enforcement mechanisms will often throw considerable light upon the regulatory regime itself, and this is certainly the case with competition policy. Two features have characterised the enforcement process in this area: the emphasis upon negotiation, and upon public as opposed to private enforcement. These will be considered in turn.

11–008

Regulatory systems often have formal enforcement powers that mask a more informal process of negotiation between the parties. Competition policy placed negotiation expressly at the forefront of its regulatory strategy. The DGFT was instructed to seek undertakings pursuant to an adverse report from the MMC under the Fair Trading Act 1973.[41] Under the Competition Act 1980 the whole emphasis was on negotiation between the DGFT and the firm under investigation.[42] More formal powers existed should the negotiating strategy prove unsuccessful,[43] but they were regarded as a long stop. This same theme is apparent in the Competition Act 1998. The DGFT has significant formal enforcement powers, including the ability to impose interim measures and to fine.[44] The legislation nonetheless places much emphasis on reaching a solution without recourse to such formal measures. Thus the first step in the "enforcement process" will be directions issued by the DGFT as to how the infringement can be brought to an end by, for example, modifying an agreement or conduct.[45] The importance given to the "negotiated solution" reflects the belief that this will be more effective than a formal legal sanction, and that the latter can be difficult to devise and enforce in this area.

Competition policy in the UK has traditionally evinced a strong preference for public as opposed to private enforcement. With few exceptions, the enforcement process has been concentrated in the hands of the DGFT

---

[40] e.g. R. Stevens and B. Yamey, *The Restrictive Practices Court* (Weidenfeld & Nicolson, 1965); A. Hunter, *Competition and the Law* (Allen & Unwin, 1966).
[41] Fair Trading Act 1973 s.88.
[42] Competition Act 1980 ss.4, 8, 9, 10.
[43] e.g. Fair Trading Act 1973 ss.56, 73.
[44] Competition Act 1998 ss.35–36.
[45] Competition Act 1998 ss.32–33.

and the Secretary of State. Individuals have had little role to play. They may serve as a catalyst for the initiation of an investigation, but they are not generally viewed as a separate means of enforcement in their own right.

This stands in stark contrast to competition policy in, for example, the EC and the USA where private actions assume a far more prominent role.[46] Changes to the EC competition regime have however accorded national courts and national competition authorities a more prominent role in enforcement in this area, with consequential implications for private enforcement.[47]

F. Accountability and Control

11–009 The general concern over the accountability and control of agencies has been considered above.[48] Two aspects of this problem can be considered here: ministerial control and judicial control.

Ministerial control is evident at varying points within the system. Under the Fair Trading Act 1973 the relevant minister possesses powers to initiate a reference to what is now the CC. Such consent is necessary before any merger reference can take place at all. The minister can stop certain types of reference from being considered further. It is the minister who has the power to order formal sanctions where negotiation has failed. He or she can also exert more general influence over the pattern of competition policy dependent upon the political party's interpretation of the public interest. Ministerial influence continues to be present under the Competition Act 1998. Thus the Secretary of State may modify the list of agreements excluded from the Act,[49] and similar powers exist in relation to abusive conduct.[50] The DGFT has to secure the Secretary of State's approval for a block exemption.[51] How far such control is warranted is a contentious issue. The fact that decisions concerning the public interest may be felt to warrant some political oversight does not immunise particular ministerial decisions from criticism.

Judicial review has generally played a limited role in this area. This may seem surprising: given that companies have no continuing "client" relationship with the OFT and MMC, there would be no risk of upsetting future relations by seeking judicial review. The explanation lies principally in the broad discretion possessed by the OFT and the MMC, both in the decision whether to investigate, and also in determining whether behaviour is in the

---

[46] See generally, K. Elzinga and W. Breit, *The Antitrust Penalties* (Yale University Press, 1976).
[47] P. Craig and G. de Búrca, *EU Law, Text, Cases and Materials* (Oxford University Press, 4th edn, 2007), 999–1002.
[48] See above, Ch.4.
[49] Competition Act 1998 s.3.
[50] Competition Act 1998 s.19.
[51] Competition Act 1998 s.6.

public interest. There are, however, instances where the actions of the MMC, OFT and the Secretary of State have been challenged.[52]

G. The Importance of Competition Policy

The effectiveness of competition policy has become increasingly important as a result of the privatisation programme. The privatisation of utilities led to the creation of new regulatory bodies to oversee such industries. A Director General, the Secretary of State and what is now the CC run these new regulatory structures. Two important consequences flow from such developments.

11–010

First, the degree of prominence or importance given to the promotion of competition by the different Director Generals may well differ. They are given a duty framed in broad terms, which is then "guided" by a wide range of factors, including the promotion of consumer interests, effective competition, and the encouragement of research and development. The prominence each Director General accords to the promotion of effective competition may therefore differ.

Second, the extra burdens these developments have placed upon the CC means that there is an even greater need to ensure that its resources are properly used. References have in the past been made by the OFT which could, by no stretch of the imagination, be regarded as vital to the basic competitive structure of the industry concerned. If competition policy is to cope with the demands placed upon it by privatisation then a more sensitive use of the CC may well be required.

4. Utilities and Market Power: Whether to Regulate

There are many activities that are regulated in varying ways. The focus of the ensuing analysis will be on the regulation of utilities, but it is important at the outset to have some idea of the more general rationales for regulation. The literature identifies two broad rationales for regulation.

11–011

A. The Public Interest Rationale for Regulation

On one view regulation in certain areas is justified on public interest grounds.[53] The market will decide the incidence of many activities within

11–012

---

[52] See, however, *R. v Monopolies and Mergers Commission Ex p. Elders IXL Ltd* [1987] 1 W.L.R. 1121; *R. v Monopolies and Mergers Commission Ex p. Mathew Brown plc* [1987] 1 W.L.R. 1235; *R. v Secretary of State for Trade and Industry Ex p. Lonrho Plc* [1989] 1 W.L.R. 525.
[53] A. Ogus, *Regulation, Legal Form and Economic Theory* (Oxford University Press, 1994), Ch.3; B. Morgan and K. Yeung, *An Introduction to Law and Regulation, Text and Materials* (Cambridge University Press, 2007), Ch.2.

capitalist societies. This is, in many respects, the default position. Individual consumer choice will determine the demand and supply of goods, and the prices at which they are sold. Markets allow individuals to express their preferences for certain products, and in this sense enhance individual autonomy. The ordinary competitive process also enhances allocative efficiency within society. A standard rationale for regulation is where there is market failure, and this can occur in a number of different ways.

A classic example of market failure is the *natural monopoly*. The market model is premised on competition. If this cannot operate then the assumptions underlying the model cannot be fulfilled. If the impairment of the competitive process is relatively short term it can be dealt with by the competition authorities. Thus as we have seen cartels and abuses of monopoly power are the standard fare of such authorities. It is, however, also apparent from the earlier discussion on agencies that regulatory regimes can be established to control privatised firms with market power.[54] This regulatory control can subsist in addition to that provided under competition law. There may be a desire to regulate the detailed pricing policy of the monopolist and the terms on which it will deal with its customers. There may be concern over the way in which it can hinder new entry into the industry. There may be fears over the quality of service provided by the dominant firm. This is particularly so in relation to natural monopolies where it is less costly for production to be carried out by one firm rather than many. As Breyer has stated,[55]

"The most traditional and persistent rationale for governmental regulation of a firm's prices and profits is the existence of a 'natural monopoly.' Some industries, it is claimed, cannot efficiently support more than one firm. Electricity producers or local telephone companies find it progressively cheaper (up to a point) to supply extra units of electricity or telephone service. These 'economies of scale' are sufficiently great so that unit costs of service would rise significantly if more than one firm supplied service in a particular area. Rather than have three connecting phone companies laying separate cables where one would do, it may be more efficient to grant one firm a monopoly subject to governmental regulation of its prices and profits."

A second example of market failure arises in relation to what are known as *public goods*. Such goods have two characteristics[56]: consumption by one person does not leave less for others to consume, and it is impossible or too costly for the supplier to exclude those who do not pay for the service. National defence is an oft-cited example of a public good. There are also what are termed "impure" public goods, which may well be bought in the

---

[54] See above, paras 4–029—4–031.
[55] S. Breyer, *Regulation and its Reform* (Harvard University Press, 1982), 15. The validity of the traditional economic rationale for regulating such forms of monopoly power has, however, been questioned, Breyer, 16–19.
[56] Ogus, n.53, 33.

market, but which require regulatory intervention in order to correct a degree of market failure. Thus, while the primary beneficiary of education is the immediate recipient, it is generally acknowledged that others within society benefit from having a better-educated workforce.[57]

A third public interest rationale for regulatory intervention exists where an activity creates *externalities* for others. The classic example is the firm that pollutes a river when making its product. There are strong arguments for making the firm internalise the full costs of its operation, including the harm caused to the river. Private law, in the form of nuisance actions and the like, may well help to achieve this end. Another way of doing so is through regulation in the form of, for example, environmental standards.[58] The existence of such externalities may also have an impact beyond state boundaries. A strong theme running through the literature on integration is that the EU developed in part to meet the problems caused by such international externalities.[59]

A fourth important reason for regulatory intervention is *to correct information deficits*, or to address circumstances where there is a strong asymmetry in information. This idea is captured by Ogus.[60]

"The market system of allocation is fuelled by an infinite number of expressions of . . . preferences. However, the assertion that observed market behaviour in the form of expressed preferences leads to allocative efficiency depends crucially on two fundamental assumptions: that decision-makers have adequate information on the set of alternatives available, including the consequences to them of exercising choice in different ways; and that they are capable of processing that information and of 'rationally' behaving in a way that maximizes their expected utility. A significant failure of either assumption may set up a prima facie case for regulatory intervention."

B. The Private Interest Rationale for Regulation

The idea that regulation is intended to serve the public interest has been contested.[61] It has been argued by those within the public choice literature that much, if not all, regulation is designed to serve the private interests of certain groups within society. **11–013**

The intellectual ancestors of public choice were pluralists, who emphasised the group nature of politics and stressed that the public interest was nothing more than the outcome of the current group exchange. Public choice theorists brought more finely tuned tools of economic analysis to the political forum in order to explain the behaviour of political markets, but

[57] Ogus, n.53, 34–35.
[58] Ogus, n.53, 35–38.
[59] P. Craig, "The Nature of the Community: Integration, Democracy and Legitimacy", in P. Craig and G. de Búrca (eds), *The Evolution of EU Law* (Oxford University Press, 1999), Ch.1.
[60] *Regulation*, n.53, 38.
[61] Ogus, n.53, Ch.4; Morgan and Yeung, n.53, Ch.2.

agreed on many points with the conclusions reached by the earlier pluralist writers.[62] The public choice theorists based their analysis on methodological individualism,[63] and while they were willing to accept that individuals could have selfish or altruistic preferences, they were also of the view that there was no conception of the public interest separate from the results of individual choice.[64] Collective action was a means of reducing the costs of purely private or voluntary action. Individuals would engage in such action where the costs thereby saved outweighed the transaction costs, combined with the costs of loss of autonomy, in the sense of the consequential risk that the individual might have to accept a decision which he or she disliked. The fact that collective political decisions took place over time generated vote-trading, with each individual's vote possessing an economic value for which a market would develop in the same way as with any other commodity.

On this view the very existence of regulation was seen as a function of the demands of interest groups which would benefit from the measure, coupled with the responses of those, normally politicians, who had power to deliver the measure. Proponents of this thesis argued that producer groups would normally be stronger, more coherent and better financed than other groups, and that therefore most regulation could be expected to benefit industry directly or indirectly.[65]

Public choice theorists believed that the role of the state should be narrowly confined for a number of reasons. They felt that private markets were better at reaching optimal decisions than political markets. They argued strongly that much regulatory legislation was a front to mask wealth-transfer and rent-seeking behaviour by particular interest groups. Rent in this context is the difference between the revenue from producing a product and the cost of production. The very process of competition will eliminate the rent. Public choice theorists contended that regulation, such as that limiting entry into a profession, was often designed to protect the existing incumbents from competition, allowing them to retain monopoly rents rather than passing them onto the consumer. Public choice theorists also disapproved of regulation because they felt that governmental intervention via redistributive policies was illegitimate, since it offended against

[62] J. Buchanan and G. Tullock, *The Calculus of Consent* (University of Michigan Press, 1962); J. Buchanan, *The Limits of Liberty: Between Anarchy and Leviathan* (University of Chicago Press, 1975); J. Buchanan, *Freedom in Constitutional Contract* (Texas A & M, 1978); J. Buchanan, *Liberty, Market and State: Political Economy in the 1980s* (Wheatsheaf Books, 1986); G. Brennan and J. Buchnanan, *The Reason of Rules* (Cambridge University Press, 1985). See also, I. McLean, *Public Choice: An Introduction* (1987); D. Mueller, *Public Choice* (Cambridge University Press, 1979).
[63] Although they fully accepted that individuals would be likely to operate through pressure groups because of the gains in terms of power which individuals could attain by so grouping together, Buchanan and Tullock, *The Calculus of Consent*, n.62, 286–287.
[64] Buchanan and Tullock, n.62, 32, 122–124, 125–130, 209.
[65] G. Stigler, "The Theory of Economic Regulation" (1971) 2 Bell Jnl Econ. 3; R. Posner, "Theories of Economic Regulation" (1974) 5 Bell Jnl Econ. 335; S. Peltzman, "Towards a More General Theory of Regulation" (1976) 19 Jnl Law & Econ. 211.

individual entitlements.[66] The descriptive and normative assumptions that underlie public choice have been contested.

In descriptive terms, it has, for example, been argued that the equation between individual behaviour in the marketplace and the political arena is not self-evidently correct. Even if the assumption is accepted it still leaves open the issue of how market-place behaviour itself should be perceived. At one extreme is the view that elected officials and individuals seek to maximise a specific wealth function. At the other is the non-falsifiable view that seeks to incorporate all ideological and other variables within an individual's utility function. On this latter view behaviour and motivation are flattened and reduced to an economic calculus, which often amounts to little more than the tautological observation that people who understand the consequences of their actions "will do things that make them as well off as they can be".[67]

The normative aspect of public choice has proven to be equally contentious.[68] The methodology is self-avowedly contractarian, but there are crucial differences in the use of this methodology when compared to the work of Rawls. It is highly debatable, to say the very least, whether a vision of politics that seeks to legitimate legislation on the basis of group bargain is consistent in normative terms with the theory of justice postulated by public choice theorists. The norms which public choice theorists regard as emerging from their contractarian foundations are questionable. Their arguments for the restriction of wealth transfers on the ground that they offend entitlements are weak.

C. Natural Monopoly: Regulation or Structural Adjustment

The preceding discussion has revealed why some form of regulation of natural monopoly has been felt necessary. But should we not be approaching the problem by breaking up the monopolies? If we choose not to do so what more specifically should the regulator be trying to do? How far should the regulator attempt to enhance competition in other ways and what other objectives should be pursued? We will consider these issues in turn.   **11–014**

Let us begin with the argument that the monopolies should in fact be broken up, with a corresponding increase in competition. This is an option, but it is not always the most desirable one. Breaking up the monopoly may not lead to greater efficiency. The monopoly may possess economies of scale, which would not be available to smaller units. It may, moreover, be more efficient to organise a particular economic activity within one

---

[66] See, e.g., Brennan and Buchanan, n.62, Chs 6–8; Buchanan, *Liberty, Market and State*, n.62, Chs 12, 13, 15, 22, 23; Buchanan, *The Limits of Liberty*, n.62.
[67] M. Kelman, "On Democracy Bashing: A Skeptical Look at the Theoretical and Empirical Practice of the Public Choice Movement" (1988) 74 Virg. L. Rev. 199, 206.
[68] P. Craig, *Public Law and Democracy in the United Kingdom and the United States of America* (Oxford University Press, 1990), 84–90.

corporate unit rather than through a number of smaller firms.[69] While it
would be theoretically possible for all economic activity to be undertaken by
individuals who contract with one another, this may not be efficient because
the individuals may not have the knowledge through which to make the
rational calculation as to the best course of action in all circumstances. As
Foster notes,[70]

> "It is because of lack of information and bounded rationality—that is an
> inability to weigh all factors relevant to making a rational decision
> between all feasible alternatives—that firms develop as alternative ways of
> completing a set of transactions."

It is not therefore surprising that when a firm is experiencing difficulties in
devising satisfactory contracts it may well take on the activity itself.[71] The
reverse side of the same coin is the problem encountered if the monopoly is
broken up: how far can the transactions, which were previously internalised,
be undertaken "contractually between the divorced parties?"[72]

If the break up of a monopoly is not always the most desirable solution
what then should the regulator be trying to do when regulating the firm?
Some economists argue that regulation is in fact unnecessary even in the
absence of competition. They contend that natural monopolies can be kept
efficient by ensuring that there is free entry into the particular market.
Others disagree. They believe that regulation of such markets is both
necessary and desirable in order to attain a number of objectives. These
include the prevention of predatory behaviour,[73] the control of excess
monopoly profits and the detection of organisational inefficiency in firms
with monopoly power. There is moreover the aim of fostering competition
by allowing other firms to use the distribution network of the monopolist, or
what is known as competition through interconnection.[74] These rationales
for regulatory intervention have been the subject of vigorous debate between
economists,[75] but the existence of regulatory regimes to oversee the privatised industries indicates that governments in the UK have accepted some of
these arguments.

---

[69] O. Williamson, *Markets and Hierarchies* (Free Press, 1975).
[70] *Privatization, Public Ownership and the Regulation of Natural Monopoly* (Blackwell, 1992),
147.
[71] Foster, *Privatization*, n.70, 148.
[72] Foster, *Privatization*, n.70, 150.
[73] This is, in essence, behaviour designed to drive would-be competitors out of the market in
order to preserve the monopolist's power.
[74] Foster, *Privatization*, n.70, 1–13 and Ch.5.
[75] e.g. there is considerable disagreement as to whether predation is in reality a problem at all,
and as to whether the difficulties of defining it render regulatory cure worse than the disease.
Compare, R. Bork, *The Antitrust Paradox* (Basic Books, 1978), Ch.7, with Foster, *Privatization*,
n.70, 163–167.

D. Whether to Regulate: The Government's Approach to Regulation

An understanding of the economic theory behind regulation is important. It   **11–015**
is equally important to understand the government's approach to
regulation.

Responsibility for regulatory matters now lies with the Department for
Business, Enterprise and Regulatory Reform, BERR.[76] The Better Regulation Executive, BRE, has principal responsibility in this respect and is
located within the BERR. It is the BRE that has overall responsibility for
the government's commitments to regulate only when necessary; setting
exacting targets for reducing the cost of administering regulations; and
rationalising the inspection and enforcement arrangements for both business
and the public sector. To this end the BRE scrutinises new policy proposals
from departments and regulators; speeds up the legislative process to make
it easier for departments to take through deregulatory measures; and works
with departments and regulators to reduce existing regulatory burdens.

The BRE is assisted by the Better Regulation Commission, BRC. It is an
independent advisory body, which provides advice on the reduction of
unnecessary regulatory and administrative burdens; and also helps to ensure
that regulation and its enforcement are proportionate, accountable, consistent, transparent and targeted.[77]

Proposed regulations are subject to a Regulatory Impact Assessment
(RIA), now termed an Impact Assessment, through which costs and benefits
of the regulation can be calculated. The IA requires that the purpose and
effect of the measure be specified, that the options listed above have been
considered, that the benefits of the measure be identified, that the costs for
business and other bodies be estimated, and that there should be consultation with those affected.[78]

The emphasis placed on assessing whether regulation is warranted at all
and on regulatory simplification[79] has been carried over into legislation. The
Deregulation and Contracting Out Act 1994 gave the government broad
powers to dispense with, or amend, any provision that had the effect of
imposing a burden on business, where it would be possible, without
removing any necessary protection, to remove or reduce the burden. This
was replaced by the Regulatory Reform Act 2001, and it has now been
overtaken by the Legislative and Regulatory Reform Act 2006.

The LRRA 2006 includes two order-making powers which a minister can
use to amend primary legislation. The first allows a minister to make a
Legislative Reform Order, LRO, for the purpose of removing or reducing
burdens. The second allows a minister by LRO to ensure that regulatory

---

[76] http://www.berr.gov.uk/ Hitherto responsibility lay with the Regulatory Impact Unit, which
was located in the Cabinet Office.
[77] http://www.brc.gov.uk/about_us.aspx The BRC is the successor to the Better Regulation
Task Force.
[78] Cabinet Office, *Good Policy Making: A Guide to Regulatory Impact Assessment* (2000);
BERR, *Impact Assessments*, http://bre.berr.gov.uk/regulation/ria/index.asp; J. Black, "Tensions in the Regulatory State" [2007] P.L. 58.
[79] Cabinet Office, *Administrative Burdens—Routes to Reduction* (2006); Department for Business, Enterprise & Regulatory Reform, *Next Steps on Regulatory Reform* (2007).

functions are exercised so as to comply with the five principles of good regulation. These mandate that regulatory activities should be carried out in a way that is transparent, accountable, proportionate, consistent, and targeted only at cases in which action is needed. The 2006 Act allows LROs to amend primary legislation, and in that sense it contains a "Henry VIII" clause.[80] The Act proved to be controversial because of the breadth of these powers, notwithstanding the fact that such statutory instruments are subject to a special procedure.[81]

E. Utilities Regulation: Political, Economic and Social Considerations

11–016 The remainder of the analysis will focus in particular on the regulation of utilities. The earlier discussion might have given the impression that the only force at work in this area was economics. This would be mistaken, both in relation to the initial privatisation process, and in relation to the way in which the utility regulators now operate. These will be considered in turn.

If we consider the *privatisation process itself*, it should not be assumed that the privatised industries in the UK, such as British Telecom and Gas, were necessarily preserved as monopolies because of their potential for enhanced efficiency. When these public corporations were privatised it would have been possible to enhance competition by the "structural remedy" of breaking up, for example BT, rather than opting for the "regulatory remedy" which was chosen.[82] The preference for the latter appears to have had more to do with political strategy, than with alleged benefits of enhanced efficiency which might follow from the preservation of a monopoly. As Vickers and Yarrow state,[83]

"The objective of promoting the well being of B.T. was favoured by those in Government wishing to maximise the proceeds from the sale of B.T. shares, their merchant bank advisers, and of course the management of B.T. Especially in view of the Government's evident desire to privatize B.T. speedily, good relations with B.T. management were imperative, and they came to have considerable influence."

The interplay between different forces is equally marked when we consider the general way in which the *regulators supervising the utilities now operate*. It has been argued forcefully by Prosser[84] that the enabling legislation that governs the privatised utilities, and the way in which this has been interpreted by the relevant regulatory authorities, shows that three different tasks are being performed in this area.

The first is the regulation of monopoly itself, which is most evident in the constraints imposed by the regulator on the prices that can be charged by

---

[80] See below, Ch.22.
[81] See below, Ch.22.
[82] J. Vickers and G. Yarrow, *Privatization, An Economic Analysis* (MIT Press, 1988), 121.
[83] Vickers and Yarrow, n.82, 235–236.
[84] *Law and the Regulators* (Oxford University Press, 1997), Ch.1.

the regulated entity. The second is what is termed regulation for competition. This is designed to create the conditions for competition to exist and to police it to ensure that it continues to exist. This is exemplified by the grant of licences to firms other than the dominant firm in the area, and the fixing of conditions for the interconnection of competing but interdependent systems. The third task being undertaken by the regulator is social regulation. Here the regulatory rationale is not primarily economic, but social, and is linked to concepts of public service. It is exemplified by provisions made for the securing of universal service by some utilities. The regulatory principles applied by the regulators are therefore "not limited to those concerned with the maximization of economic efficiency . . . but include those based on more egalitarian or rights-based arguments".[85] This development has been fuelled in part by EU law, which requires Member States to impose universal service obligations on certain service providers.[86] We shall return to these important arguments in the course of the ensuing analysis.

F. Utilities Regulation: The Broader Context

The discussion in the previous section leads naturally on to the broader   **11–017**
context within which the privatisation of utilities has occurred. It is important to recall at this juncture the earlier discussion about the changing nature of the public–private divide.[87] The privatisation of utilities has been but part of a broader development.

This has led to the creation of what Freedland has termed a public-service sector,[88] which is distinct from both the purely public and the purely private sectors. The essential characteristic of the public-service sector is that the state no longer assumes direct responsibility for the provision of certain services, but nonetheless retains certain secondary responsibility in these areas. This secondary responsibility is manifested through, for example, the creation of regulatory regimes to oversee the activities of the privatised utilities.

An equally important feature of the public-service sector is that the citizen has a relationship both with the service provider, who has the primary responsibility for the delivery of the service, and the state itself, which retains a secondary responsibility within the relevant area. The relationship therefore becomes trilateral rather than bilateral.

---

[85] *Law and the Regulators*, 30–31.
[86] See, e.g., Communications Act 2003 ss.65–72; T. Prosser, *The Limits of Competition Law, Markets and Public Services* (Oxford University Press, 2005).
[87] See above, Ch.4.
[88] "Law, Public Services, and Citizenship—New Domains, New Regimes", M. Freedland and S. Sciarra (eds), *Public Services and Citizenship in European Law, Public and Labour Law Perspectives* (Oxford University Press, 1998), Ch.1.

5. UTILITIES AND MARKET POWER: WHO SHOULD REGULATE?

11–018   The choice of "regulator" for market power has altered considerably over the last 200 years. Five differing institutions have undertaken the regulatory mantle.

A. The Common Law and the Courts
11–019   The common law has exercised influence over corporations with monopoly power. Two areas are of principal interest, one which is well known, the other far less so.

The area that is relatively well known is the law of monopolies *stricto sensu*. Somewhat paradoxically this was the less important of the two areas in which the common law courts exercised control over market power. Such control existed, but the leading cases had as much to do with other issues, as they did with the adverse economic effect of market power. Thus in *Darcy v Allen*[89] it was held that a royal grant of a patent to manufacture and import playing cards was void if it created a monopoly. Two main themes pervade the court's judgment: the desire to protect the right to work which would be weakened should the patent be allowed to stand, and the desire not to allow the Crown prerogative powers of this novel form. It would therefore be mistaken to allow such classic cases on the law of monopolies to create the impression that the common law courts were zealous in their control of market power per se. Nor should one believe that the right to work precluded the existence of any monopoly power. As Letwin states,[90]

> "The common-law right to work was predicated on an economic system that would protect the established trades from competition, whether from foreign workmen, improperly qualified English workmen, overly aggressive guilds, or domestic monopolists. The right to work was protected by giving each guild a monopoly, and Darcy's grant was condemned not because it was a monopoly and therefore necessarily bad, but because it was a bad monopoly."

The other area in which the common law courts exercised influence is less well known. It was almost forgotten, but it is of considerable importance. The courts held that the common law imposed an obligation on those who had market power to charge no more than a reasonable price for their goods. The courts in effect were imposing a common law based species of price regulation on those who wielded monopoly power, and they reasoned through the rationale for doing so from first principles.

---

[89] (1602) 11 Co. Rep. 84, (*The Case of Monopolies*).
[90] W. Letwin, *Law and Economic Policy in America: The Evolution of the Sherman Antitrust Act* (Random House, 1965), 28–29. The court in *Darcy v Allen* did, however, take note of the potential for monopoly power to lead to price increases

In *Allnutt*[91] the question was whether the London Dock Company, which by licence from Parliament possessed a monopoly to receive certain wines, could lawfully exclude from the docks a cargo owner who refused to pay their schedule of charges. Lord Ellenborough reasoned as follows.[92] While a man could fix his own price for the use of his property, he could not do so where the public had a right to resort to the premises and to make use of them. Where a person had the benefit of a monopoly this entailed a correlative responsibility, the consequence of which was that he could charge no more than a reasonable price for the service offered. The monopoly itself could be either "legal" or "factual": it could result from the grant of an exclusive licence from Parliament, or it could exist because, on the facts, the provider of the service controlled the entirety of the space available for the warehousing of the goods. The statute, which required that the goods be warehoused in the Dock Company's premises, was not passed solely for the benefit of the Company, but also for the benefit of trade and the public. The latter purposes could be defeated if the Dock Company was at liberty to charge any price it chose.

Similar reasoning is evident in other areas where monopoly power existed. **11–020** In *Pawlett*[93] the corporation possessed the right to hold two fairs each year. It customarily received a "toll" of 2d on the sale of certain items at the fair. The defendant refused to pay the toll. The court held that where the word toll was found in a charter it should be taken to mean reasonable toll. It was not open to the King to allow a corporation to charge an unreasonable toll, and any such excess charge could be recovered in a legal action. The principle underlying such cases is the same as that expounded above. The grantee of rights to a market or fair was the holder of an exclusive privilege. The grant was not merely for his benefit, but for the benefit of the public and the trade. It could be defeated if any price whatsoever could be charged.[94]

This reasoning receives further support from that used in the context of common callings. There is abundant authority for the proposition that those who exercise a common calling can charge only a reasonable price for their services.[95] The history of common callings is complex and cannot be fully developed here. The origin of the term common calling was simply one that was available to the public generally, "a holding out". There could therefore be common carriers, common innkeepers, and common millers. Those who exercised a common calling had a duty to serve at a reasonable price. Historically this obligation appears to have evolved due to economic and

---

[91] *Allnutt v Inglis* (1810) 12 East 527.
[92] *Allnutt v Inglis* (1810) 12 East 527, 538–539. See also, *Bolt v Stennett* (1800) 8 T.R. 606.
[93] *Corporation of Stamford v Pawlett* (1830) 1 C. & J. 57, 400.
[94] See also, *Gard v Callard* (1817) 6 M. & S. 69; *Wright v Bruister* (1832) 4 B. & Ald. 116; *Att-Gen. v Horner* (1912) 107 L.T. 547; *Duke of Newcastle v Worksop Urban District Council* [1902] 2 Ch.145, 161; *Nyali v Att-Gen* [1955] 1 All E.R. 646, 651, [1956] 2 All E.R. 689, 694; B. McAllister, "Lord Hale and Business Affected with a Public Interest" 43 Harv L. Rev. 759 (1929-30); P. Craig, "Constitutions, Property and Regulation" [1991] P.L. 538.
[95] *Harris v Packwood* (1810) 3 Taunt 263; *Thompson v Lacy* (1820) 3 B. & Ald. 283; *Ashmole v Wainwright* (1842) 2 Q.B. 837, 845; *Peek v North Staffs Ry Co* (1862) 11 H.L.C. 473; *Great Western Railway v Sutton* (1869) L.R. 4 H.L. 226, 237–238.

social conditions. In times of social hardship, such as the period following the Black Death, it could be possible for surviving tradesmen to exact "any price they pleased".[96] The obligation to serve at reasonable rates was intended to counteract this potential for abuse of market power. As the law developed the types of industry that retained the label "common" tended to be those with a monopoly character, such as railways and public utilities.

It would therefore be mistaken to regard the common law as having had no regulatory role within this area. There is moreover a link between common law regulation by the courts and departmental regulation: the two formed an intersecting web as will be apparent from the subsequent discussion.

B. Departmental Regulation

11–021 The pattern of administrative development in the 19th century has already been reviewed and one aspect is of particular relevance here.[97] Many administrative functions during this period were undertaken neither by central nor local government. They were often performed by corporations, which had special statutory authority insofar as this was necessary to enable them to carry out their tasks. The provision of most utilities, such as water, lighting, canals, railways and roads, was carried on in this way even after the reform of the municipal corporations. Moreover such bodies normally possessed a large degree of market power. A considerable amount of time was spent in the Commons on the legislation that empowered the statutory undertakings to perform these tasks. For example, in 1844 there were 248 Railway Bills, which necessitated a system of Commons' committees in order to oversee their passage. It also led to the introduction of certain "Model Bills" concerned with issues such as the compulsory purchase of land, and railway development, which were intended to ensure greater uniformity in the types of measures which emerged.[98] The growing need to pave roads in order to render them suitable for increased use by heavier wheeled traffic was the motivation behind the turnpike trusts, and by 1830 there were 1,100 in existence.[99] Once again each such turnpike trust derived its power from a local Act of Parliament, subject to supervision pursuant to more general Turnpike Acts. Improvement Commissioners, who derived their authority from a local Act of Parliament, often undertook the provision of municipal lighting and cleansing.

The rates to be charged for services by those who possessed a degree of monopoly power granted to them by statute had to be regulated. A common technique was for direct departmental supervision of the "tariff" which the statutory undertaking proposed to charge. This was used, for example, in

[96] Arterburn "The Origin and First Test of Public Callings" (1926–27) 75 Univ of Penn. L. Rev. 411, 421.
[97] Ch.2.
[98] Sir N. Chester, *The English Administrative System 1780–1870* (Oxford University Press, 1981), 118–119.
[99] Chester, n.98, 326.

relation to roads and canals. The trustees or commissioners would forward to the Board of Trade a detailed list of the prices they intended to levy, specifying, for example, that the toll to be charged for a wagon of certain size and weight which journeyed from Oxford to Woodstock would be Xd. The Board of Trade would have to approve such charges before they could be lawfully levied. Direct departmental price regulation in areas of market power was, therefore, quite common.

We can now understand the link between common law and departmental price regulation. The former was utilised particularly in those circumstances where direct departmental price regulation was absent. This could be for one of two reasons: either the area might be one over which no such departmental supervision had yet been established; or it might be an area where the type of supervision exercised by the department was difficult to operate. This latter point requires explanation. Departmental supervision normally operated through scrutiny of a relatively fixed series of possible charges: so much per mile, per weight, etc. There could be areas where this type of advance delineation of charges might not be possible, principally because the variables that could affect the price were more complex. It was such areas in which the common law proscription that "unreasonable charges" should not be levied remained of particular relevance.[100]

C. Regulation by Tribunal or Board

The importance of Boards within the 19th-century administrative landscape   **11–022**
was considered above.[101] They provided a further institutional technique through which to regulate entrepreneurial behaviour. Railway regulation within the last century can be examined by way of a brief example.[102]

Prior to 1840 the main regulatory body was the Railway Commission. Although its formal powers were limited it had the authority to certify that a railway was "complete" before it could commence operations. It could attach conditions to its certificate, and was willing to use this as a mechanism for requiring minimum standards of service by the railways. Failure to abide by the conditions of the certificate led to its revocation, and the Commission published criteria for judging applications.[103] From the 1840s significant responsibility was transferred to the railway department of

---

[100] The common law insistence upon the reasonableness of prices charged by public utilities has been of particular importance in the US, see W. McCurdy, "The Power of a Public Utility to Fix Its Rates in the Absence of Regulatory Legislation" 38 Harv. L. Rev. 202 (1924–25); *Smyth v Ames* 169 U.S. 466 (1898); *Texas & Pacific Ry. v Abilene Cotton Oil Co* 204 U.S. 426 (1906). The common law authorities were also of seminal importance in determining the constitutionality of later attempts at statutory regulation of price, *Munn v Illinois* 94 U.S. 113 (1877). See, M. Finkelstein, "From *Munn v Illinois* to *Tyson v Banton*, A Study in the Judicial Process" 27 Col. L. Rev. 769 (1927).
[101] See above, Ch.2.
[102] H. Parris, *Government and the Railways in Nineteenth Century Britain* (Routledge, 1965); Foster, n.70, Chs 1, 2.
[103] H. Arthurs, *"Without the Law," Administrative Justice and Legal Pluralism in Nineteenth Century England* (University of Toronto Press, 1985), 120, 124.

the Board of Trade.[104] The department however suffered a political set-back in 1844–1845 and this combined with concern over railway speculation led to the establishment of an independent Railway Commission in 1846.[105] This body was to be short-lived: the railway boom collapsed, the Commission was dissolved and its powers reassigned to the Board of Trade.

Experimentation with differing institutional devices to regulate railways continued in the 1850s with the assignment of responsibility to the common law courts, where "it languished for almost twenty years, hostage to the notion that all adjudication is properly the business of the courts".[106] A further turn of the institutional wheel occurred in 1873. A new Railway and Canal Commission was established with a range of activities including the fixing of tolls, fares and routes. The Commission was also meant to ensure that the public could use the facilities with as much ease as possible.[107] The Commissioners had power to inspect property, require the production of documents and the giving of testimony, and could use assessors with technical knowledge.[108] Notwithstanding these powers the Commission established in 1873 was not a noted success, with one critic observing that it had "the power enough to annoy the railroads, and not power enough to help the public efficiently".[109] A new Railway and Canal Commission was set up in 1888, and although it enjoyed some early success, it, like its predecessors, turned out to be an ineffective regulatory mechanism. Control over the rates charged by railways was assigned to the Railway Rates Tribunal in 1921, and in 1947 the railways were nationalised.

D. Public Ownership

11–023   The nationalisation of the railways provides a suitable point of transition to the option of public ownership. Earlier discussion has revealed how the choice of regulatory institution has been influenced by the political beliefs of those who operate the system. Thus, the very demise of the board system was caused by the growing insistence that there should be a member of the executive directly answerable in the Commons for major spheres of administrative activity.[110] Certain changes in the institutions to regulate the railways were motivated by the wish for more direct legislative control.

The shift towards public ownership provides a further exemplification of this theme. While the reasons for nationalisation were eclectic, one prominent rationale was that major repositories of market power should be within state ownership in order that excess profits should not be left in private hands, and in order to ensure that the industry operated in the public interest. The general difficulties that beset the nationalised industries have

---

[104] Railways Regulation Act 1840.
[105] Commissioners of Railways Act 1846.
[106] Arthurs, n.103, 126.
[107] Regulation of Railways Act 1873.
[108] Arthurs, n.103, 128.
[109] Arthurs, n.103, 129.
[110] See above, Ch.2.

been considered above.[111] What is particularly relevant here is the fact that public ownership of a firm with market power does not, in and of itself, mean that the firm will necessarily be operated in such a way as to further the public interest.[112] This point can be understood by considering the gas industry prior to privatisation.

The industry was nationalised by the Gas Act 1948, and there were 12 area boards that were largely autonomous as regards the manufacture and supply of gas. Operations were later centralised[113] with a single public corporation assuming responsibility for the activities covered by the 12 area boards. As Vickers and Yarrow state,[114]

"By the 1970's the policy framework for the industry had been brought into line with that pertaining in telecommunications and electricity generation: there was a single national firm, protected from competition by statutory entry barriers and regulated by a department of central government. The underlying rationale for this approach was the familiar argument that the core activities of gas transmission and distribution constituted a natural monopoly, and that the operation of more than one firm in the market would therefore lead to cost inefficiencies. To protect consumers from the effects of the resulting market power, it was considered desirable that the industry should be publicly owned and controlled."

The transfer of the industry to public ownership did not, however, necessarily serve to ensure that the consumers really were protected. Two important aspects of the operation of the British Gas Corporation were open to serious question.

First, British Gas was granted sole rights to purchase gas from other producers. The ostensible reason was to prevent the accumulation of excessive profits by such producers, but it is highly questionable whether the award of this privileged position to British Gas was the optimum method of achieving this goal.[115] Second, research indicates that British Gas was in fact selling its product at too low a price.[116] Consumers can be harmed by paying too little as well as by being overcharged. If the former occurs the product is rendered "artificially" attractive as compared with other possible fuels. Too much is consumed at the inaccurate low price, with the consequence that resources within society are allocated inefficiently. Irrespective therefore of the problems caused by ad hoc governmental interference with public corporations, the retention of ownership in public hands did not always lead to the accrual of public benefit.

---

[111] See above, paras 4–027—4–028.
[112] Foster, n.70, Ch.3.
[113] Gas Act 1972.
[114] n.70, 255.
[115] This statutory privilege was terminated by the Oil and Gas (Enterprise) Act 1982.
[116] Vickers and Yarrow, n.82, 256–257.

E. Privatisation and Agencies

11–024   If the move towards public ownership was motivated by the political beliefs of its advocates, this was equally true of the shift towards privatisation. The general reasons for this shift have been considered above, as have some of the difficulties that face the regulatory organisations.[117]

The decision as to "who" should regulate market power has come down firmly in favour of agencies. This strategy bears some analogy to the regimes which existed in the 19th century, where a private firm with market power would be regulated by a commission or board.[118] Experience from this period also indicates that the efficacy of such regulatory devices will depend crucially both on the degree of market power wielded by the private firm, and the range of regulatory powers granted to the board or commission.

These two factors will be central to the analysis that follows. This will be concerned with "how" market power is controlled under the present regime of privatised industry plus regulatory agency.

6. Utilities and Market Power: How to Regulate

A. Selling State Assets: Constitutional Implications

11–025   The privatisation programme entailed the sale of assets that had previously been within public ownership in the form of nationalised industries.[119] This is a trite proposition, but one which is important nonetheless. The fact that the assets were public raises a legitimate public interest in seeing that they were disposed of on beneficial economic terms; or at the very least that the public coffers did not end up being under-compensated on the sale of public property.

The government employed two main methods for the sale of public assets, offers for sale and tender offers. The former involved offering shares to the public at a price fixed in advance of the sale; the latter entailed inviting bids at or above a stated minimum price, with the final price being established once all the bids had been received. Offers for sale were used more widely than tender offers, largely because they were simpler to operate. The latter are, however, probably more accurate economically, since they do not require a precise estimate of the value of the firm to be made prior to the sale itself. This is advantageous because most assets sold to the public did not have a previously quoted value, and there was therefore a relative scarcity of information on which to base estimates of value. The tender offer procedure

---

[117] See above, paras 4–029—4–031.
[118] See above, Ch.2.
[119] See T. Daintith and M. Sah, "Privatisation and the Economic Neutrality of the Constitution" [1993] P.L. 465, for a discussion of constitutional constraints relevant to privatization in a range of countries

which "permits the market to establish the valuation therefore has sub-stantial appeal".[120]

Whether the proceeds from the sales would have been significantly improved by greater reliance on tender offers may be debatable. However, few would argue that the public coffers received the real value of the assets sold. As Mayer and Meadowcroft state,[121]

"Whatever one's views about the desirability of a programme of priva-tization, considerable concern must be felt about the techniques that have been employed in implementing the programme to date. As set out at the beginning of this article there are three primary considerations that may have influenced the form of the asset sales: extent of ownership, costs of sale, and disruption to markets. Certainly on the first two there is little evidence that objectives have been met: costs have been high, primarily as a consequence of underpricing of assets, and large personal shareholdings have only been maintained for very short periods. Furthermore, there would appear to be a simple way of avoiding high costs by staggering sales, which would also diminish financing disruptions to equity markets."

It might be felt that this under-valuation of state assets was "unfortunate", but that it did not have constitutional or legal implications. This assumption bears testimony to the way in which we think in "pigeon holes", and the limited nature of our constitutional constructs. Let us imagine the converse situation in which the state is nationalising assets held by private indivi-duals. If those assets were "forcibly" acquired at a value significantly less than that determined by the market, lawyers would immediately be aware of the appropriate legal rhetoric to employ. There would be talk of interference with private rights, expropriation without proper compensation and infringement of private autonomy.[122] The situation in which the state decides to sell public property, and does so at a price which is too low, prompts no such automatic legal response. No conception of "public property rights" comes readily to hand.

The distinctive manner in which we respond to these similar situations   **11–026**
provides a good example of Daintith's thesis concerning the exercise of dominium powers.[123] The legal response where the government can be said to "own" something, whether money or other assets, is far more muted than it is where the government operates so as to command others to do some-thing with their property. In the former situation the government is

---

[120] C. Mayer and S. Meadowcroft, "Selling Public Assets: Techniques and Financial Implica-tions", in J. Kay, C. Mayer and D. Thompson (eds), *Privatization and Regulation—the U.K. Experience* (Oxford University Press, 1986), 325.
[121] Kay, Mayer and Thompson, n.120, 339.
[122] Whether an effective legal remedy could be provided would depend upon the form of the governmental action: the sovereignty of parliament would serve to protect such governmental action if it was enshrined in a statute. It would now be possible to make a challenge under the Human Rights Act 1998 and secure a declaration of incompatibility under ss.3–4.
[123] "Legal Analysis of Economic Policy" (1982) 9 Jnl Law & Soc. 191.

implicitly treated like a private individual and can dispose of "its" property on the terms it thinks best. If the bargain is bad so be it.

The very fact that we draw a "legal blank" where the Government undervalues state assets is reflective of the limited nature of our constitutional concepts. It is clear that such concepts can be utilised in the context of privatisation, as experience from France indicates. The Conseil Constitutionnel applied constitutional provisions to the sale of state holdings. While it held that the basic law on privatisation did not infringe the Constitution it attached a number of important conditions to the privatisation process. As Prosser states,[124]

"A central issue was the pricing of the enterprises to be privatized. The deputies had argued that it would be unconstitutional to sell enterprises below their true value as this would breach constitutional principles of equality and would give vendors an unfair advantage; indeed it was argued that the obligation to sell by 1991 could have precisely this effect, and could also lead to transfers to foreigners threatening national independence. The Conseil accepted that both the Constitutional principle of equality and the protection for rights of property in the Declaration of the Rights of Man prohibited the sale of public goods to private parties at a price below their value; these principles applied to the property of the state as well as to that of private individuals."

The French government anticipated this response of the court and proposed that an independent body of experts should undertake the valuation work. A Privatisation Commission was established that valued the assets to be sold. The minister established the actual sale price, but it could not be below that recommended by the Commission.[125]

The absence of a written constitution, combined with the characterisation of public assets as government property, to be disposed of like an ordinary private sale, renders it difficult to reach the same conclusion in this country. There are, however, threads of legal reasoning which point in a more interventionist direction. Thus the courts have, for example, held that local authorities owe a fiduciary duty towards their ratepayers in the way in which they manage local funds.[126] The application of this concept has been criticised. However if such a concept exists it is difficult on principle to see why an analogous idea should not apply to central government's duties towards taxpayers. A sensible and sensitive use of such a concept could provide the basis for the development of public property rights better suited to the needs of the age.

---

[124] *The Privatization of Public Enterprises in France and Great Britain, The State, Constitutions and Public Policy*, EUI Working Paper No. 88/364 (1988), 37. See more generally, C. Graham and T. Prosser, *Privatizing Public Enterprises, Constitutions, the State and Regulation in Comparative Perspective* (Oxford University Press, 1991).
[125] *The Privatization of Public Enterprises*, n.124, 38–39.
[126] See below, para.17–011.

B. The Regulatory Regime: Legal Powers and Legal Constraints, the Initial Regime for Gas

The law both empowers and constrains. This, like the proposition that **11–027** began the previous section, is trite. It is also important, and particularly so in the context of the regulatory mechanisms. The success of regulatory machinery will be crucially dependent upon the degree of monopoly power that resides with the privatised firm, and the powers accorded to the regulator. The greater the degree of monopoly power statutorily preserved to the privatised company, the more necessary it is for the regulator to have effective supervisory powers, since the firm will be relatively immune from the discipline of the market. The legal structure under which the firm is privatised will therefore be of considerable importance. The legal rules will both empower and constrain the privatised corporation, and will also empower and constrain the regulatory agency. The effectiveness of the new scheme will be dependent upon these respective powers. This is evident from the earlier discussion of the telecommunications industry,[127] but it can be demonstrated by considering privatisation of the gas industry.

Historically the major activities of the gas industry were[128]: the production of natural gas, which was mostly from off-shore fields; transmission of the gas to landing points; transmission of the gas to regional take-off points; local distribution of gas to customers' premises; the sale of gas; and the sale and installation of gas appliances. Prior to privatisation the British Gas Corporation had a monopoly in the third, fourth and fifth of these tasks, and also enjoyed a statutory exclusive right to buy gas produced by other companies.

The industry was fully privatised by the Gas Act 1986, the principal provisions of which were as follows. Section 1 empowered the Secretary of State to appoint the Director General of Gas Supply, who appointed the staff of the Office of Gas Supply (Ofgas). The Gas Consumers' Council, a watch-dog body for consumers, was established by s.2. British Gas's monopoly privilege in relation to the supply of gas through pipes was abolished by s.3, and this opened the possibility for alternative suppliers to sell their product to customers. Section 4 established guidelines for the DGGS and the Secretary of State in pursuit of their functions. These included: protecting the interests of consumers in relation to the prices charged and the other terms of supply; promoting efficiency by gas suppliers and users; preventing dangers which can arise from gas transmission; and enabling persons to compete effectively in the supply of gas which, in relation to any premises, exceeds 25,000 therms a year. Section 7 empowered the Secretary of State to authorise a "public gas supplier" to supply the product to any premises within a designated area, but s.7(9) precluded such an authorisation in any area which was within 25 yards from the main of another public gas supplier. Given that British Gas is an authorised public gas supplier, this had the effect of preventing a new gas supplier from

---

[127] See above, paras 4–030—4–031.
[128] Vickers and Yarrow, n.82, 248.

emerging to challenge British Gas in the ordinary domestic sales market. Section 8 did, however, allow the Secretary of State to authorise other persons to supply gas where, inter alia, the supply was expected to exceed 25,000 therms per annum. The effect of this was to allow competition in the provision of gas to large commercial customers. Subsequent legislation empowered the Secretary of State to modify or remove the 25,000-therm condition.[129] Section 19 empowered the DGGS to grant an applicant the right to use a pipeline owned by a public gas supplier.

11–028   The legal powers and constraints applied to British Gas and the DGGS left little doubt that the former emerged in a strong position as a result of the original legislation. This can be understood by reflecting on their respective powers and duties. British Gas was empowered in three important ways by the 1986 legislation.

First, the law sanctioned the continued existence of British Gas as a single corporation post-privatisation. The assets of the previously nationalised industry were transferred to a successor corporation.[130] The possibility of restructuring the industry prior to privatisation was therefore not pursued. Such a course would have been feasible, and could have been achieved by the creation of 12 separate regional gas companies, together with an enterprise that would operate the transmission system.[131] This restructuring would have increased competition within the system.[132] It would have lowered the barriers to entry and facilitated the task of other gas producers who wished to become direct sellers of gas to, for example, large industrial concerns. It would have reduced the exclusive purchasing power of British Gas, since each of the regional companies would have had to compete in the purchase of supplies from other gas producers. It would have improved regulatory control, for although each distribution company would still have had monopoly power within its own region, Ofgas "would have been able to draw on information from several independent sources, opening up the possibility of yardstick competition".[133]

The failure to pursue such a policy of regionalisation, despite its competitive advantages, was the result of various political factors.[134] A restructuring of the industry would have slowed down the privatisation process, with the consequence that the receipts from the sale would have accrued to the revenue authorities at a date that was less advantageous to the government, given its concerns over the public sector borrowing targets. The management of the British Gas Corporation was hostile to any such restructuring. It was possible that short-term gas prices would have increased to the consumer, which was disadvantageous in electoral terms, even though restructuring the industry and installing greater competition

---

[129] Competition and Service (Utilities) Act 1992 s.37.
[130] Gas Act 1986 ss.49–61.
[131] E. Hammond, D. Helm and D. Thompson, "British Gas: Options for Privatization", in Kay, Mayer and Thompson, n.120, Ch.13.
[132] Vickers and Yarrow, n.82, 268–269.
[133] Vickers and Yarrow, n.82, 269.
[134] Vickers and Yarrow, n.82, 270–271.

would have yielded greater medium- and long-term efficiency. The decision not to reorganise the industry has been termed a response to interest group pressure from management and consumers in which short-term electoral considerations took precedence over longer-term economic efficiency.[135] There is no doubt that this decision coloured the privatisation process, and that the dominance of the privatised corporation was augmented by other legal powers it was accorded. It is to these that we should now turn.

Second, the original legal regime established by the Gas Act 1986, served to insulate the dominant privatised firm from new competitors. As noted above, s.7(9) effectively precluded new entrants into the market for the domestic sale of gas, although, as seen, later legislation modified this. There were, moreover, significant difficulties to be faced by the new entrant who attempted to supply to larger industrial concerns. British Gas had access to low price gas and could probably undercut potential new entrants, or even engage in disguised "predatory pricing" to deter a new competitor. Furthermore, control over the pipeline network provided British Gas with certain tactical advantages. New entrants had to negotiate for the transfer of their gas, "thus providing the incumbent with advance notice of its rival's intentions and giving the former time to offer more favourable terms to the targeted customer".[136] This was all the more important given that the proscriptions in the legislation on giving undue preference to any person did not it seems apply to sales to industrial concerns. British Gas could therefore price as it chose in relation to these concerns.[137]

Third, given that the privatised industry was not restructured, and given the difficulties faced by new entrants into the industry, the pricing formula for gas supplies to tariff customers[138] was of particular importance. The details of the formula were complex and cannot be examined here, but one detailed study concluded that the "pricing constraints imposed on British Gas can hardly be described as stringent".[139]

The powers given to the DGGS and to Ofgas were not strong when **11–029** juxtaposed to those possessed by British Gas. The DGGS could impose conditions on the grant of authorisation to a public gas supplier.[140] These conditions could then be modified either by agreement with the supplier,[141] or the DGGS could make a reference to the Monopolies and Mergers Commission. The MMC could specify the ways in which modification of the authorisation could remedy any possible harmful effects on the public

[135] Vickers and Yarrow, n.82, 271.
[136] Vickers and Yarrow, n.82, 275.
[137] The obligation not to show undue preference was contained in Gas Act 1986 s.9(2), but only applied to the supply of gas "to persons entitled to a supply". The effect of s.10(5) was that a public gas supplier was under no obligation as such to supply gas to any premises in excess of 25,000 therms per year, which effectively removed the force of s.9(2) from sales to major gas users such as large industry. The only limit on this freedom was the general provisions of competition law.
[138] Tariff customers are, in essence, those within the market who receive less than 25,000 therms per year, Gas Act 1986 s.14. Large industrial concerns are therefore not included
[139] Vickers and Yarrow, n.82, 265.
[140] Gas Act 1986 s.7(7).
[141] Gas Act 1986 s.23.

interest which was being caused by the gas supplier.[142] The DGGS also had power to secure compliance with the authorisation conditions,[143] and to investigate complaints made to him by the Gas Consumers' Council and certain interested parties.[144] He had to keep under review the general provision of gas supplies and could publish information and advice to customers.[145] Notwithstanding this array of legal powers the original regulatory mechanism was relatively weak for the following reasons.

First, the DGGS could not alter the legal structure of the 1986 Act itself and this placed British Gas in a strong monopolistic position which, for the reasons given above, it was difficult for competitors to assail. Second, an important factor in determining the effectiveness of the DGGS was the degree of access to information concerning costs, etc. from British Gas. The DGGS had statutory power to require information,[146] but the provisions of the authorisation granted to British Gas concerning its accounting did not place the DGGS in a strong position. The company had to prepare separate accounts for its gas supply business, but this was defined very broadly and covered the bulk of its activities. It was therefore "difficult to assess whether or not British Gas is willing to make its transmission grid available to third party suppliers on reasonable terms, since there is no requirement to treat the transmission system as a separate cost centre".[147] It was also difficult more generally to monitor the efficiency of the firm. The relationship between the initial DGGS and the industry was adversarial,[148] and the general conclusion reached by Vickers and Yarrow was not encouraging:[149]

"We conclude that the most fundamental weaknesses of U.K. regulatory policy are associated with an excessively short-term view of the underlying economic issues. The Government has been content to focus upon the initial post-privatization period, leaving many fundamental issues unresolved . . . What has happened is that one of the major deficiencies of the U.K. control system for nationalized industries—preoccupation with short-term political issues—has been duplicated in the policy framework set for the regulated privately owned gas industry."

C. The Regulatory Regime: Legal Powers and Legal Constraints, the Modified Regime for Gas

11–030   The regulation of the gas industry has moved on since the initial legislation. The adversarial relationship between the regulator and British Gas led to references to the MMC. The MMC review laid the groundwork for later government proposals concerning the increase in competition in the

---

[142] Gas Act 1986 ss.24, 26.
[143] Gas Act 1986 ss.28, 29, 30.
[144] Gas Act 1986 s.31.
[145] Gas Act 1986 ss.34, 35.
[146] Gas Act 1986 s.38.
[147] Vickers and Yarrow, n.82, 263.
[148] Prosser, n.84, 95–96.
[149] Vickers and Yarrow, n.82, 278.

domestic market for gas. The MMC proposed the divestment by British Gas of its trading business by 1997, to be followed by the opening up of the domestic market over a five-year period.[150] The government decided that it would be sufficient if the trading business was separated from its other activities, but decided also that competition in the domestic market should be introduced more rapidly. Meanwhile, British Gas came to the conclusion that it would separate into two companies, TransCo International dealing with transport and production, and British Gas Energy dealing with supply, retail and service.

The Gas Act 1995 was passed, inter alia, to facilitate the changes mentioned in the preceding paragraph. The Utilities Act 2000 amended the Gas Act 1986. It is this version of the 1986 Act that provides the governing criteria for the gas industry. The separate regulatory authorities for gas and electricity have been replaced by Ofgem, which protects consumer interests by promoting competition and regulating monopoly. It must have regard to the need to secure that all reasonable demands for gas are met, and must, inter alia, have regard to the interests of those who are disabled or chronically sick, those who are of pensionable age, those with low incomes, and those who live in rural areas. Ofgem and the Secretary of State must carry out their respective functions in the manner best calculated to promote efficiency and economy on the part of the gas companies. They must promote the efficient use of gas, secure viable long-term energy supply, and protect the public from the dangers arising from gas. The Secretary of State is required to issue guidance on social and environmental matters, which Ofgem must take into account when discharging its duties. There is also a Gas and Electricity Consumer Council.[151]

It is clear that the emphasis has shifted to what Prosser has aptly termed regulation for competition.[152] This is evident in the emphasis placed on the protection of consumers through competition wherever this is appropriate.[153] It is apparent in the fact that the areas held by persons holding gas transportation licences are not exclusive,[154] and by the duty imposed on gas transporters to facilitate competition in the supply of gas.[155]

The regime also contains elements of social regulation. The scheme introduced in 1995 brought new issues of social regulation to the fore, most notably provisions designed to prevent "cherry-picking". The licence conditions issued to gas suppliers were structured so as to minimise any attempt to restrict supply to the most profitable customers within a particular area, or to exclude supply from those who are old, disabled or of pensionable age.[156]

---

[150] *Gas*, Cm. 2314 (1993).
[151] This is to be replaced by the new National Consumer Council: Consumers, Estate Agents and Redress Act 2007.
[152] n.84, 104–106.
[153] Utilities Act 2000 s.9, amending Gas Act 1986 s.4AA.
[154] Utilities Act 2000 s.76, amending Gas Act 1986 s.7.
[155] Utilities Act 2000 s.79, amending Gas Act 1986 s.9.
[156] n.84, 108–110.

Thus, as Prosser states,[157] the "regulation of suppliers to enforce licence requirements concerning social obligations is likely to become more, not less important" over time. This has been borne out by the obligation to have regard to the position of the disabled, old, etc., and the obligation to give guidance on social and environmental matters, contained in the Utilities Act 2000.

D. The Regulatory Regime: Institutional Design

11–031   The discussion thus far has focused upon the regulatory regime established for the gas and the telecommunications industries.[158] It is now necessary to stand back from the detail of these two areas and consider some of the more general preconditions for effective regulatory control.

An appropriate starting point is the importance of *information*. As Foster notes, "a state of unbalanced or asymmetric information benefits the regulated by comparison with not only the regulator, but also actual and potential competitors and customers".[159] Regulated bodies have a number of tactics to reduce the effectiveness of the regulatory machinery. They may produce too little information; they may give too much in a form that is unclear or opaque; or they may offer the desired information too slowly.[160] An effective regulatory scheme requires the production of relevant information on a periodic basis, set against the background of clear objectives as to why the information is needed.[161] The information should, moreover, be geared to the detection of the types of offences the regulatory regime hopes to control.[162]

A second aspect of effective regulatory control concerns the *objectives* of the regulatory regime. The powers of the regulatory authorities are set out in broad terms, coupled with the more specific proscription of certain types of activity, such as discriminatory pricing. It is clear that a significant part of the remit of the regulatory bodies is economic in nature, whether in the form of protecting consumers from excessive prices or potential competitors from predation. It may be less apparent how far non-economic considerations should feature as part of the regulator's objectives, such as regulating pricing in a way which is geared towards those with low incomes. There are difficulties with this type of regulation. Thus Foster has argued that it may be more difficult to monitor the data in relation to social offences; there may be a conflict between the pursuit of economic and non-economic goals; non-economic goals can themselves conflict; and the greater the number of divergent aims which are being pursued the more difficult might it be to develop a coherent overall strategy.[163] However, as Prosser has shown, it is

---

[157] n.84, 109–110.
[158] For telecommunications, see above, paras 4–029—4–031.
[159] *Privatization*, n.70, 226.
[160] *Privatization*, n.70, 235–236.
[161] *Privatization*, n.70, 236–238.
[162] *Privatization*, n.70, 250–254.
[163] *Privatization*, n.70, 316–323.

clear that the regulators do in fact engage in social regulation, and that this is so even where an element of competition has been introduced into the provision of the relevant service.[164] The social facet of the regulator's task is expressly provided for in the Utilities Act 2000, in relation to gas and electricity. The social dimension of regulation has more generally been developed as a result of initiatives from EU law, concerned with universal service obligations and the like.[165]

A third aspect of the institutional design of a regulatory system is that it should minimise the possibility of *regulatory failure*. This term can cover a number of differing scenarios. It may mean that the regulated industry is no longer capable of sustaining profitable trading because the regulatory controls do not, for example, allow it to adapt to new market circumstances such as inflation. It may mean that the regulator is no longer capable of properly fulfilling his or her remit because of governmental interference with the regime, or because there are inadequate powers in the original legislation.

A more general cause of regulatory failure is *regulatory capture*, in the sense that the regulator is captured by the very industries being regulated. We have touched on this issue in the preceding discussion.[166] The Chicago School developed a well-known version of regulatory capture.[167] The essence of the argument is that the monopolist in an industry about to be regulated has a real economic incentive to influence the content of the legislation, since the regulatory regime will constrain what the monopolist can do with its monopoly profits. This same incentive will also lie behind attempts by the monopolist to influence the regulator once the regulatory regime has been established. The monopolist will predictably be willing to expend a great amount of its monopoly profits upon influencing the regulator in order to retain at least some of these profits.

11–032

The Public Choice School provides a somewhat different account of regulatory capture or bias.[168] The theory draws analogies between markets for ordinary goods and the making of legislation, which is conceived of as a political market. The content of the legislation will reflect the contesting pressures of the differing interest groups who are concerned with the topic. On this view "trade continues until the marginal value to the politicians and regulator of the obligation assumed by the regulated industry equals its marginal financial cost to the industry".[169]

The theoretical and empirical assumptions underlying these models have been contested. We should nonetheless structure the regulatory regime so as to minimise the likelihood of this occurring. Foster has provided a number

---

[164] n.84, Chs 3–7.
[165] n.86.
[166] See above, para.11–013.
[167] n.65.
[168] n.62; G. Becker, "A Theory of Competition among Pressure Groups for Political Influence" (1983) 98 Quarterly Jnl of Econ. 371.
[169] Foster, *Privatization*, n.70, 387.

of helpful pointers in this regard.[170] There should be an independent regulator who retains discretion to interpret regulatory offences. Formal court procedures should be avoided since these are likely to favour the regulated industry, but there should be appropriate procedural rights, which safeguard the interests of affected parties. Appeals on the merits should be provided in some instances, but preferably to another regulatory agency which has appropriate expertise. The more firms there are within an industry, the less likely will it be that the regulator will be captured by any one firm. There should be the possibility of input from other interested parties, including consumers, since they will act as some counterweight to the power of the regulated industry itself. The scope of any ministerial power should be defined as clearly as possible, in order that the regulated industry is not tempted to by-pass the regulator and seek to capture the Minister instead.

11–033   The final aspect of a coherent regulatory strategy is to ensure that the regulatory authority observes the requisite *procedural and substantive norms* expected of other public agencies.[171]

In procedural terms, this means that the basic principles of fair procedure apply to decisions made by such bodies, whether in the setting of prices, the grant of licences or the adjudication of offences under the 1992 legislation to be discussed below. This does not mean that such agencies should necessarily have to operate in accordance with the full rigours of the ordinary adversarial/adjudicative conception of fair procedure, modelled as it is upon ordinary court processes.[172] Procedural justice is a more flexible concept, which can be tailored to the needs of the particular area. It is clear that some agencies have adopted ideas of informal adjudication and rule-making used by US agencies, as mandated by the Administrative Procedure Act 1946.[173] This is particularly true in the context of telecommunications where the DGT employed sophisticated regulatory procedures designed to elicit the views of a wide range of people when making regulations relating to price controls and conditions of fair trading. There was a double consultation exercise with a timetable for the receipt of views from interested parties.[174] It is equally clear that not all other regulatory agencies have been as forthcoming in this respect. There is much to be said for Prosser's suggestion that the procedural obligations imposed by the APA in the United States should be required here.[175] This links in more generally with concerns for participation in the administrative process.[176]

In substantive terms, the agencies that oversee the regulated industries are subject to the ordinary principles of judicial review.[177] There is in addition a form of internal appeal on a number of issues, such as when a licence

---

[170] *Privatization*, n.70, 413.
[171] Graham and Prosser, n.124, Ch.7.
[172] See below, Ch.12.
[173] Foster, *Privatization*, n.70, 274–275.
[174] Prosser, *Law and the Regulators*, n.84, 84–86.
[175] Prosser, *Law and the Regulators*, n.84, 277–286.
[176] See below, Ch.22.
[177] See below, Ch.26.

condition is to be changed. The application of the principles of judicial review will be dependent on the structure and content of the enabling legislation. This will provide the background for determining which considerations are deemed to be relevant, and whether agency action is reasonable. We have already seen that the UK agencies undertake social regulation to varying degrees. There may well be lessons to be learned in this respect from experience in France and Italy. Prosser has provided a valuable analysis of the more structured way in which social goals of equality, impartiality, consumer choice and consumer participation have been written into the enabling legislation in, for example, Italy.[178] There has been "a fuller recognition of the plurality of regulatory goals through the establishment of a relatively sophisticated case law dealing with the social requirements of public service, and suggestions that there is something different about basic services linked to citizenship".[179] It is, moreover, important to place this issue into its broader context. The substantive norms applied by regulatory agencies necessarily raises wider issues as to the way in which we conceptualise public-sector service delivery.[180] This issue has been considered above and reference should be made to that discussion.

E. The Regulatory Regime: The Limits of Public Law

It is clear, as noted above, that the principles of administrative law can apply to the activities of the regulatory agencies themselves.[181] It also seems clear that the exercise of monopoly powers by a local authority in administering an ancient market is susceptible to judicial review concerning the level of rents which can lawfully be charged.[182] **11–034**

More interesting and controversial is the issue as to whether these procedures and principles could be used directly against the privatised bodies themselves. This raises the vexed topic as to the scope of "public law" for the purposes of remedies.[183] It requires us to judge how far those procedures are appropriate to a corporation which is nominally private, with some degree of monopoly power, which is buttressed directly and indirectly by a statute.

It is readily apparent from the earlier discussion that the courts have in the past found little difficulty in subjecting such institutions to rules that differ from those of the ordinary "private" corporation.[184] It might well be argued that any complainant would have to exhaust the "internal" remedial options before seeking judicial review. The force of this argument would

---

[178] *Law and the Regulators*, n.84, 287–292.

[179] *Law and the Regulators*, n.84, 292.

[180] M. Freedland and S. Sciarra (eds), *Public Services and Citizenship in European Law, Public and Labour Law Perspectives* (Oxford University Press, 1998).

[181] For problems which can arise from the government's continued share holdings in some privatized corporations, C. Graham and T. Prosser, "Privatising Nationalized Industries: Constitutional Issues and New Legal Techniques" (1987) 50 M.L.R. 16.

[182] *R. v Birmingham City Council Ex p. Dredger and Paget* [1993] C.O.D. 340.

[183] See below, Ch.26.

[184] See above, paras 11–019—11–020.

depend upon whether the complaint fell within the relevant internal procedures, and also upon the general law governing the relationship between
the pursuit of judicial review and the availability of alternative remedies.
The possibility of using judicial review was mooted by Sir Gordon Borrie,
who had a wealth of experience as Director General of Fair Trading.[185]

> "Is it satisfactory . . . that neither private individuals or bodies nor (in
> many instances) public officials can bring to bear on private centres of
> power the kind of legal challenge in the courts that has been so effective as
> the challenges to the exercise of local government power by way of
> application for judicial review in recent decades? The lack of any possi-
> bility for the industrial customers of British Gas or even for a public
> official such as the Director General of Fair Trading to take British Gas
> to court to challenge their exercise of monopoly power meant that a
> reference to the Monopolies and Mergers Commission, which the custo-
> mers had no right to initiate themselves and which could result only in
> recommendations for government action, was the only possible way of
> pursuing the matter."

F. The Regulatory Regime: The Citizen's Charter and Subsequent Legislation

11–035 Some of the force of Sir Gordon's complaint has now been addressed by
legislation, which applies principles contained in the Citizen's Charter: the
Competition and Service (Utilities) Act 1992.[186]

Part I of this legislation amends the existing statutes through which utilities were privatised[187] and imposes standards of performance and service to
customers. The details of the legislation vary with respect to telecommunications, gas, water and electricity. The description given below
focuses principally upon gas by way of example.[188]

The Director of the agency is empowered to make regulations prescribing
standards of performance that ought to be achieved by designated operators
in *individual* cases.[189] The regulations require the consent of the Secretary of
State, and can only be made after consulting the operators and parties likely
to be affected by the regulations. Compensation is payable to any person
who is affected by failure to meet the specified standard. The Director will
adjudicate on a dispute as to whether the standards have been met, and any
order takes effect as if it were a judgment of a county court. The Director is

---

[185] "The Regulation of Public and Private Power" [1989] P.L. 552, 560–561.
[186] This Act has been amended by the Utilities Act 2000 ss.90–96 in relation to gas and
electricity.
[187] Telecommunications Act 1984; Gas Act 1986; Electricity Act 1989; Water Industry Act
1991.
[188] The Competition and Service (Utilities) Act 1992 has been amended in significant respects.
Thus the provisions relating to telecommunications have been repealed and replaced by provisions in the Communications Act 2003.
[189] Competition and Service (Utilities) Act 1992 s.11, modifying the Gas Act 1986 s.33A.

also empowered to determine *overall* standards[190] of performance for the industry.[191]

The Director is instructed to collect *information* with respect to compensation paid by designated operators in individual cases, and with respect to overall levels of performance.[192] Failure to provide the information is punishable by a fine. The Director is to publish the information provided at least once a year. There are provisions dealing with more particular issues such as discriminatory pricing, billing disputes and deposits.

Penalties can be imposed for breach of the relevant conditions, and compliance may be made part of the licence conditions under which the firm operates. Where this is so breach of these conditions can lead to an order for compliance by the Director and a subsequent action brought either by the Director or by another for breach of statutory duty. The Regulatory Enforcement and Sanctions Bill 2007 will, if enacted, further enhance the range of sanctions that can be imposed by regulators.

The link between these provisions and the general aims of the Citizen's Charter is readily apparent. The importance of the 1992 legislation in attaining these goals was brought out further in the First Report on the Citizen's Charter, which identified progress the utilities had made towards complying with the statutory requirements on performance and standards.[193]

The Competition Act 1998 added important powers to the armoury of the regulatory agencies. Section 54 of the Act in effect provides that the Directors of the agencies responsible for telecommunications, gas, electricity, water and rail, have concurrent powers, within their assigned area, to enforce the provisions relating to agreements and abuse of a dominant position.[194] This means that the Director of the relevant agency, who best knows the area, can apply the new legislation on competition. This serves to reinforce the agencies' powers in regulating for competition.

7. Conclusion

No attempt will be made to summarise the entirety of the preceding arguments. What this discussion demonstrates is that administrative law principles must be seen as but part of a larger picture concerned with the institutional design of administrative systems. The "whether", "who" and "how" questions that have formed the framework of this chapter could be applied to any substantive area that is of concern to administrative law.   **11–036**

---

[190] See, e.g., with respect to gas, Competition and Service (Utilities) Act 1992 s.11, modifying the Gas Act 1986 s.33B.
[191] See further Utilities Act 2000 ss.90–91.
[192] See, e.g., with respect to gas, Competition and Service (Utilities) Act 1992 ss.12–13, modifying the Gas Act 1986 ss.33C–D; Utilities Act 2000 s.94.
[193] Cm. 2101 (1992), 20–23.
[194] Competition Act 1998 Sch.10.

PART 2

JUDICIAL REVIEW

CHAPTER 12

NATURAL JUSTICE: HEARINGS

1. INTRODUCTION

A. Historical Development

The phrase natural justice encapsulates two ideas: that the individual be **12–001**
given adequate notice of the charge and an adequate hearing (*audi alteram
partem*), and that the adjudicator be unbiased (*nemo judex in causa sua*).[1]
The former will be dealt with in this chapter; the latter in that which follows.

The development of the *audi alteram partem* principle has, like many
other legal concepts, been eclectic. An early group of cases was concerned
with deprivation of offices,[2] requiring notice and a hearing prior to the
deprivation. Another somewhat later group involved the clergy: penalties or
disciplinary measures to which the clergy were subjected had to be preceded
by notice and a hearing.[3]

In the 19th century the *audi alteram partem* principle was applied to a
wide variety of bodies, private as well as public. Clubs,[4] associations[5] and
trade unions[6] were included within its ambit. The increase in the regulatory
role of public authorities provided a further opportunity for the generalised
application of the maxim. Thus in *Cooper v Wandsworth Board of Works*[7] it
was held that demolition powers vested in the defendant Board were to be
subject to notice and hearing requirements. The omission of positive words

[1] See generally, J. Mashaw, *Due Process in the Administrative State* (Yale University Press, 1985); D. Galligan, *Due Process and Fair Procedures* (Oxford University Press, 1996).
[2] *Bagg's Case* (1615) 11 Co. Rep. 93b; *R. v Chancellor of the University of Cambridge* (1723) 1 Str. 557; *Osgood v Nelson* (1872) L.R. 5 H.L. 636; *Fisher v Jackson* (1891) 2 Ch. 824. See generally, Galligan, n.1, Ch.5.
[3] *Capel v Child* (1832) 2 Cr. & J. 588; *Bonaker v Evans* (1850) 16 Q.B. 163; *R v North Ex p. Oakey* [1927] 1 K.B. 491; *cf. R. v Canterbury (Archbishop) Ex p. Morant* [1944] K.B. 282.
[4] *Dawkins v Antrobus* (1881) 17 Ch. D. 615; *Fisher v Keane* (1878) 11 Ch. D. 353.
[5] *Wood v Woad* (1874) L.R. 9 Ex. 190; *Lapointe v L'Association de Bienfaisance et de Retraite de la Police de Montreal* [1906] A.C. 435.
[6] *Abbott v Sullivan* [1952] 1 K.B. 189; *Lawlor v Union of Post Office Workers* [1965] Ch. 712.
[7] (1863) 14 C.B. (N.S.) 180.

in the statute requiring a hearing was not conclusive, since the justice of the common law would supply the omission of the legislature.[8] The generality and flexibility of the *audi alteram partem* maxim, were brought out by Lord Loreburn.[9] He stated that the maxim applied to "everyone who decides anything," while recognising that the manner in which a person's case was heard did not necessarily have to be the same as an ordinary trial.

The principles of natural justice have in general been developed at common law by the courts. Statutes may nonetheless specify aspects of procedural rights as they apply in specific areas. The Human Rights Act 1998 (HRA) has introduced a further source of procedural rights, flowing from art.6 of the European Convention of Human Rights. Article 6 is of increasing relevance in this area, and it will be integrated into the discussion throughout this and the subsequent chapter.

B. The Rationale for Procedural Rights

12–002　Justifications for process rights in adjudication vary. One rationale emphasises the connection between procedural due process and the substantive justice of the final outcome. All rules are designed to achieve a particular goal, for example that liquor licences should only be granted to those of good character. Giving a person a hearing before deciding to refuse a licence can help to ensure that this goal is correctly applied. Procedural rights perform an *instrumental* role, in the sense of helping to attain an accurate decision on the substance of the case.[10] Other rationales focus upon *non-instrumental* justifications for procedural rights. Formal justice and the rule of law are enhanced, in the sense that the principles of natural justice help to guarantee objectivity and impartiality.[11] Procedural rights are also seen as protecting human dignity by ensuring that the individual is told why she is being treated unfavourably, and by enabling her to take part in that decision.[12]

These twin rationales for the existence of procedural rights have been recognised by the judiciary. *Doody*[13] was concerned with whether prisoners given a life sentence for murder should be told the reasons relating to the length of their imprisonment. Lord Mustill stated that a prisoner would wish to know why the particular term was selected, "partly from an obvious human desire to be told the reason for a decision so gravely affecting his future, and partly because he hopes that once the information is obtained he

---

[8] (1863) 14 C.B. (N.S.) 180, 194; *Hopkins v Smethwick Local Board of Health* (1890) 24 Q.B.D. 713.

[9] *Board of Education v Rice* [1911] A.C. 179, 182.

[10] e.g. J Resnick, "Due Process and Procedural Justice," in J. Pennock and J. Chapman (eds), *Due Process* (Nomos, 1977), 217.

[11] H.L.A. Hart, *Concept of Law* (Clarendon Press, 1961), 156, 202. See also J. Rawls, *A Theory of Justice* (Oxford University Press, 1973), 235.

[12] e.g. F. Michelman, "Formal and Associational Aims in Procedural Due Process," in *Due Process,* n.10, Ch.4; Mashaw, n.1, Chs 4–7. For a detailed discussion of the relationship between the two rationales for process rights which is sceptical about the dignitarian rationale see, Galligan, n.1, 75–82.

[13] *R. v Secretary of State for the Home Department Ex p. Doody* [1994] A.C. 531, 551.

may be able to point out errors of fact or reasoning and thereby persuade the Secretary of State to change his mind, or if he fails in this to challenge the decision in the courts". The non-instrumental and instrumental justifications for procedural protection are readily apparent in this quotation.

In reading the material which follows two important points should be borne in mind. First, the content of natural justice which should be applicable in any particular instance may well vary depending upon whether one accords primacy to instrumental or non-instrumental considerations.[14] Second, the traditional approach has been to model procedural rights by analogy to ordinary court procedure; the principles of natural justice reflect an adversarial-adjudicative conception of process rights. Process rights can however, as we shall see,[15] be fashioned in other ways which may be both better suited to the needs of particular areas, *and* also better attain the instrumental and non-instrumental values which process rights are designed to serve.

2. LIMITATION OF THE PRINCIPLE

The breadth of the *audi alteram partem* principle was limited in the first half of this century. This occurred in a number of ways.　**12–003**

A. Administrative v Judicial

It is evident from the 19th-century cases that the right to a hearing was　**12–004** invoked in a number of areas that could properly be called administrative. In so far as the term judicial was used it was automatically implied whenever a decision was made which affected a person's rights in a broad sense.[16] Despite this the courts began to draw a dichotomy between administrative and judicial decisions, to take a narrow view of what constituted a judicial or quasi-judicial decision and to require this as a condition precedent for the application of a right to a hearing.

For example in *Errington*[17] it was argued that the Minister was in breach of natural justice by conferring with the local authority and receiving further evidence from it after the close of a public inquiry. The Court of Appeal found that there had been a breach, but the phrasing of the judgment was nonetheless restrictive. Maugham L.J. stated that if the minister acted administratively natural justice would not apply, that the minister was in

[14] See, paras 12–025—12–026.
[15] See, paras 12–044—12–047.
[16] e.g. *Hopkins v Smethwick Local Board of Health* (1890) 24 Q.B.D. 713. The courts did not define precisely what type of right would have to be affected before natural justice could apply. The case law indicates that it was not confined to Hohfeldian rights, nn.2–6. See below, para.12–006, for the way in which the courts have interpreted rights more narrowly.
[17] *Errington v Minister of Health* [1935] 1 K.B. 249.

fact acting quasi-judicially, but only because the situation was "triangular" in that the minister was deciding a *lis inter partes* between the local authority and objectors.[18] In cases where the *lis* had not yet been joined the applicant was less successful.[19]

B. Rights and Remedies

12–005   The detailed study waits to be written on the way in which developments in the law of certiorari affected the law on natural justice. The problem can be briefly stated as follows. It was thought that for certiorari to be available there would have to be not just a determination affecting the rights of individuals, but also a superadded duty to act judicially.[20] This view has now been overturned.[21] However, while it held sway it was interpreted on occasion to mean not just that there had been a breach of natural justice with no remedy available. The courts went further and said that natural justice itself was not applicable.[22] One of the reasons given in *Ridge v Baldwin* by Lord Reid for the demise of natural justice was the misunderstanding over the scope of certiorari.[23]

C. Rights v Privileges

12–006   Closely allied to the previous reasons for the limitation of natural justice was the distinction drawn between rights and privileges. In *Nakkuda Ali* one of the reasons the Privy Council denied the application of natural justice was because the cancellation of a licence was characterised as the withdrawal of a privilege and not the determination of a right,[24] and in *Parker*[25] the cab licence which was withdrawn was just a "permission".

D. Statutory Hearings and Inquiries

12–007   The application of natural justice in the context of inquiries has already been touched upon in discussing the administrative–judicial dichotomy. A further example of the limited application of natural justice in this area may be given. In *Arlidge*[26] the House of Lords considered whether an individual

[18] [1935] 1 K.B. 249, 270–273. See also, *Local Government Board v Arlidge* [1915] A.C. 120.
[19] *Offer v Minister of Health* [1936] 1 K.B. 40; *Frost v Minister of Health* [1935] 1 K.B. 286. See also, *R. v Metropolitan Police Commissioner Ex p. Parker* [1953] 1 W.L.R. 1150, 1153–1154; *Nakkuda Ali v Jayaratne* [1951] A.C. 66; *R. v Leman Street Police Station Inspector Ex p. Venicoff* [1920] 3 K.B. 72.
[20] *R. v Legislative Committee of the Church Assembly Ex p. Haynes-Smith* [1928] 1 K.B. 411, 415 interpreting *R. v Electricity Commissioners Ex p. London Electricity Joint Committees Co (1920) Ltd* [1924] 1 K.B. 171, 205.
[21] *Ridge v Baldwin* [1964] A.C. 40, 72–76.
[22] *Nakkuda Ali v Jayaratne* [1951] A.C. 66, 75–77; *Parker*, n.19, 1153; *R. v St. Lawrence's Hospital Statutory Visitors Ex p. Pritchard* [1953] 1 W.L.R. 1158.
[23] [1964] A.C. 40, 72–76.
[24] [1951] A.C. 66, 77–78.
[25] *Parker*, n.19, 1153; *R. v Leman Street Police Inspector Ex p. Venicoff* [1920] 3 K.B. 72.
[26] *Local Government Board v Arlidge* [1915] A.C. 120.

should have an oral hearing before the Local Government Board, and whether the person should be entitled to see the report of the hearing inspector in the context of a statutory scheme to determine whether a closing order on a house should be rescinded.

Lord Haldane L.C. upheld the general principles in the *Rice* case, but refused access to the housing inspector's report or to the Board itself: when a matter was entrusted to a department of state or similar body, Parliament should be taken, subject to contrary intent, to have meant that it could follow its own procedure, which would enable it to work with efficiency. When, therefore, the Board was entrusted with appeals this did not mean that any particular official should undertake the task, nor was the Board bound to disclose the report any more than minutes made on the paper before a decision was arrived at.[27] Much of this is uncontroversial in principle, but the failure to disclose the report was a severe set-back in the evolution of inquiry procedures which has taken long to heal.[28]

3. THE PRINCIPLE REVIVED

A. Ridge v Baldwin

While some cases limited the *audi alteram partem* principle,[29] there were nonetheless indications in England,[30] Australia,[31] Canada[32] and New Zealand[33] of a less rigid application of the principle.   **12–008**

However the application of natural justice was at a low ebb prior to the decision of the House of Lords in *Ridge v Baldwin*.[34] Their Lordships held that a chief constable who was dismissable only for cause was entitled to notice of the charge and an opportunity to be heard before being dismissed. The importance of the case lies in the general discussion of the principles of natural justice, especially by Lord Reid.

His Lordship reviewed the 19th-century case law that showed the broad application of natural justice and then considered why the law had become confused. Lord Reid gave three reasons. The first was that natural justice could have only a limited application in the context of the wider duties or discretion imposed upon a minister, but the courts had, unfortunately,

[27] [1915] A.C. 120, 132–134.
[28] For the position now, see Ch.9.
[29] A further reason for the non-applicability of the rules of natural justice was said to be if the decision-maker was acting in a disciplinary manner *Ex p. Fry* [1954] 1 W.L.R. 730, 733 though *cf.* the reasoning of the appeal court, 736. See now *Buckoke v Greater London Council* [1971] 1 Ch. 655, 669; *R. v Board of Visitors of Hull Prison Ex p. St. Germain* [1979] Q.B. 425, 445, 455.
[30] e.g. *Hoggard v Worsborough Urban District Council* [1962] 2 Q.B. 93.
[31] e.g. *Delta Properties Pty. Ltd v Brisbane City Council* (1956) 95 C.L.R. 11, 18–19.
[32] e.g. *Alliance des Professeurs Catholiques de Montreal v Labour Relations Board of Quebec* [1953] 2 S.C.R. 140.
[33] e.g. *New Zealand Licensed Victuallers' Association of Employers v Price Tribunal* [1957] N.Z.L.R. 167, 203–205.
[34] [1964] A.C. 40.

applied these limits to other areas where the constraints were unnecessary.[35] The second reason was that the principle had received only limited application during the war. Special considerations that might be pertinent during wartime should not affect the ambit of natural justice now. The third was the confusion between rights and remedies evident in the requirement of a superadded duty to act judicially for certiorari, and the way that this had stilted the development of natural justice.[36]

For Lord Reid, the judicial element should rather be inferred from the nature of the power and its effect on the individual. Lord Morris of Borth-y-Gest also based his judgment on the 19th-century jurisprudence.[37] For Lord Hodson[38] the absence of a *lis inter partes* was not decisive, nor was the characterisation of the act as judicial, administrative or executive.[39]

Their Lordships therefore revived the principles of natural justice in two connected ways. They rediscovered the 19th-century jurisprudence, which had applied the principle to a broad spectrum of interests and a wide variety of decision-makers. They disapproved of impediments created in the 20th century: the requirements of a *lis inter partes* and a superadded duty to act judicially were said to be false constraints.

However little positive guidance is to be found in the case as to when natural justice should apply. The closest to any general formulation is that the applicability of natural justice will be dependent on the nature of the power exercised and its effect upon the individual concerned. It is therefore unsurprising that in the years following *Ridge* the courts were faced with many cases concerned not just with the content of natural justice, but with the criterion for its applicability.

B. Natural Justice and Fairness

12–009   The years since *Ridge v Baldwin* saw the development of new terminology. The case law is replete with mention of "fairness", or a "duty to act fairly". The terms were initially used by Lord Parker C.J. in *Re HK*.[40] Since then their use has varied. Some courts treat these terms in an omnibus fashion: natural justice is said to be but a manifestation of fairness.[41] In other cases the courts will apply natural justice to judicial decisions, and reserve a duty to act fairly for administrative or executive determinations.[42] It is not

---

[35] [1964] A.C. 40, 71–72.

[36] [1964] A.C. 40, 72–78. His Lordship expressly disapproved Lord Hewart C.J.'s requirement of a superadded duty to act judicially which had been developed in the *Church Assembly* case and disapproved also of *Nakkuda Ali* in so far as that case supported the requirement.

[37] [1964] A.C. 40, 120–121.

[38] [1964] A.C. 40, 127–132.

[39] Lord Devlin based his judgment primarily upon the application of the police regulations, [1964] A.C. 40, 137–141; Lord Evershed dissented, [1964] A.C. 40, 82–100. His Lordship's judgment will be considered in Ch.23.

[40] [1967] 2 Q.B. 617, 630.

[41] e.g. *Wiseman v Borneman* [1971] A.C. 297, 308–309; *McInnes v Onslow-Fane* [1978] 1 W.L.R. 1520, 1530; *O'Reilly v Mackman* [1983] 2 A.C. 237, 276.

[42] e.g. *Re HK (an infant)* [1967] 2 Q.B. 617, 630; *Pearlberg v Varty* [1972] 1 W.L.R. 534, 550; *Bates*, n.56, 1378.

uncommon for different members of the same court to be in agreement as to the contents of the procedural duty, but to differ as to whether they describe this as resulting from natural justice or fairness.[43] There are differing views as to the significance of the development of fairness.

One view sees the development of fairness as a corollary of the expansion of procedural rights post *Ridge v Baldwin*. Thus Megarry V.C. in *McInnes*[44] stated that natural justice was a flexible term, which imposed distinct requirements in different cases. It was capable of applying to the whole range of situations encapsulated by the terms "judicial", "quasi-judicial", "administrative", or "executive". However, the further that one moved away from any thing resembling a "judicial" or "quasi-judicial" situation, the more appropriate it became to use the term fairness rather than natural justice. On this view the distinction between the terms natural justice and fairness is linguistic rather than substantive. The former can cover all cases, but it is felt to be more appropriate to use the term fairness in the context of, for example, company inspectors or immigration officers.

Some commentators take a different view, seeing a broader significance in the shift from natural justice to fairness.[45] It is argued that the basis of natural justice was the desire of the ordinary courts to maintain control over adjudication, and to impose their own procedures on those subject to judicial control. The necessity for the function to be characterised as "judicial" before procedural constraints were imposed was said to be integral to this approach, because only bodies exercising such functions were suited to adjudicative procedures. A corollary of this view was that the content of the rules of natural justice could be relatively fixed and certain. The shift to a broader notion of fairness is said to alter fundamentally the basis of procedural intervention: it can no longer be restricted to adjudicative settings, and there can no longer be fixed standards for determining whether there has been a breach of procedural fairness. The courts are forced to engage in a difficult balancing operation, taking into account the nature of the individuals' interest and the effect of increased procedural protection upon the administration.

There are however difficulties with this argument. First, the *premise* is that natural justice stemmed from a judicial desire to maintain control over adjudication. While this may have formed part of the rationale for natural justice, the major reason for the development of the doctrine was the protection of property rights and interests akin thereto.[46]

Second, the argument that the term "judicial" was used to ensure that only those bodies *suited to adjudicative procedures* should be subject to natural justice is not sound. That term was automatically held to be satisfied

---

[43] e.g. *Re Pergamon Press Ltd* [1971] Ch.388, 399–400 (Lord Denning M.R., "fairly"), 402–403 (Sachs L.J., "natural justice"), 407 (Buckley L.J., "not a judicial function").

[44] *McInnes*, n.41.

[45] M. Loughlin, "Procedural Fairness: A Study in Crisis in Administrative Law Theory" (1978) 28 U. Tor. L.J. 215; R. Macdonald, "Judicial Review and Procedural Fairness in Administrative Law" (1979–1980) 25 McGill L.J. 520, (1980–1981) 26 McGill L.J. 1.

[46] See the cases on officers and the clergy nns.2–3 which were particularly influenced by this consideration

when the effects on the interests of the individual were felt to be serious enough to warrant procedural protection, and this was so whether the context was deprivation of an office, expulsion from a trade association, the destruction of one's property, or the loss of something which would juridically be termed a privilege.[47] Indeed, in cases where the remedy sought was not certiorari there was often no mention of the "judicial" requirement at all. It is, moreover, mistaken to view the 20th-century cases that limited natural justice through the judicial–administrative dichotomy as doing so primarily because of a feeling that those categorised as administrative would be unsuited to adjudicative procedures. This may have been a factor, but the case law dealing with aliens, licensing and discipline[48] reflects much more a judicial conclusion that the substantive interests at stake were not worthy of judicial protection.[49]

12–010   Third, the *application* of natural justice, prior to the introduction of fairness, was never uniform. Courts often explicitly or implicitly balanced the interests of the individual with the effects on the administration in deciding where the line should be drawn on many issues concerning the content of natural justice.[50]

What is undoubtedly true is that natural justice has resulted in adjudicative types of procedural constraints. Process rights are modelled on those of the ordinary courts, and any balancing is undertaken within this context.[51] Whether the introduction of the term fairness causes any modification in this respect depends upon the meaning accorded to that term.[52]

One interpretation would see fairness as simply fitting into an adjudicative framework, and not necessitating the development of non-adjudicative procedures. On this view the courts would determine what adjudicative procedures are required in particular areas. In some it may approximate to the full panoply of procedural safeguards, including notice, oral hearing, representation, discovery, cross-examination, and reasoned decisions. In others it may connote considerably less. There will be a broad spectrum in between. This is indeed how the system generally works at present. The term fairness can be used to cover all such instances, or the term natural justice can be used for that part of the spectrum that requires a relatively wide range of procedural checks. In so far as fairness is used within the traditional adjudicative framework the balancing involved therein may be different in degree, but not in kind from that which has always been

---

[47] See cases nns.1–8.

[48] *Nakkuda Ali*, n.22; *Parker*, n.19; *Venicoff*, n.19.

[49] The thesis holds up best in the context of statutory inquiries, where the nature of the subject matter did influence the courts in reaching the conclusion that it was not suitable for fully adjudicative procedures, and in the unwillingness to accord procedural rights in "legislative" contexts.

[50] See, e.g. *Board of Education v Rice* [1911] A.C. 179, 182, where Lord Loreburn L.C. openly acknowledges the necessity for flexibility in the operation of the procedural safeguards; *Russell v Duke of Norfolk* [1949] 1 All E.R. 109, 118. See also the cases on, e.g. notice, hearing and representation, below paras 12–027—12–032.

[51] See above, para.12–002, and below, para.12–044, for further consideration of this point.

[52] The shift in terminology from natural justice to fairness does not, of itself, demand any particular one of these meanings.

undertaken within natural justice itself. Lord Loreburn L.C. might well question whether there is really a difference in degree.

The *other interpretation* would see the emergence of fairness as having a broader implication. Adjudication is only one form of decision-making with its own distinctive procedure. Mediation, arbitration, contract and managerial direction are other forms of decision-making, and each possesses its own procedural norms. A general concept of procedural fairness could, therefore, lead the courts into developing procedural forms other than classical adjudication. If this transpires then fairness will have a substantial effect on the procedural due process.

The discussion now turns to the way in which fairness is presently used in an adjudicative context. This will be followed at the end of the chapter by a look at some of the broader possible implications of fairness, and the way in which that term might aid in the development of procedural forms other than classical adjudication.

4. APPLICABILITY OF PROCEDURAL PROTECTION[53]

Any legal system will have criteria for determining the applicability of procedural protection, whether this is cast in the language of "natural justice" or a "duty to act fairly". There are a range of options in this regard. **12–011**

A. Categorisation: Administrative v Judicial v Legislative
A legal system might decide to render the applicability of procedural protection dependent upon categorisation of the nature of the function performed by the body subject to judicial review. This is apparent in the use of the administrative–judicial dichotomy to determine the applicability of natural justice in some cases prior to *Ridge*. Categorisation of this type has however been disapproved of explicitly in the post-*Ridge* case law.[54] The nature of the decision may well be taken into account in determining the *content* of natural justice, but it has little if any utility over and beyond this, for the following reason. **12–012**

The rationale for rendering the applicability of natural justice dependent upon such classification would be certainty and predictability: if a case fell within one category certain results would follow. It is however notoriously difficult to decide whether a case should be categorised as judicial,

---

[53] The phrase procedural protection is used instead of natural justice because this section will be examining types of procedural checks in addition to those of traditional natural justice.
[54] e.g. *R. v Gaming Board for Great Britain Ex p. Benaim and Khaida* [1970] 2 Q.B. 417, 430; *O'Reilly v Mackman* [1983] 2 A.C. 237, 279.

administrative, executive, etc. Moreover, the presumption is that once the characterisation has been made the content of natural justice is fixed and certain: all administrative matters will be subject to the same rules, as will all judicial or quasi-judicial. Yet the variety of matters comprehended within the terms "administrative", "quasi-judicial", or "executive" is vast, however sensitively they are defined, and therefore the same procedural rules may not be appropriate for all cases within the category.[55]

The discussion thus far has concentrated upon the distinction drawn between administrative and judicial decisions. The courts have however held that rules of a legislative nature are not generally subject to natural justice.[56] The exceptions to this proposition will be considered below.[57] Whether such protection should apply raises broader questions concerning the way in which delegated legislation and rules of a legislative nature are made, and also the type of remedy available.

B. Rights, Interests and Legitimate Expectations

12–013   A legal system must necessarily have some criterion for deciding whether procedural protection is applicable. It is common for legal systems to focus on the nature of the applicant's interest. The general approach used by our courts is to consider whether there is some right, interest or legitimate expectation such as to warrant the applicability of procedural protection.[58] The common law meaning of these terms will be explained, followed by examination of the jurisprudence under Article 6 of the ECHR.

i. Rights

12–014   The term right in this context will clearly cover instances in which the challenged action affects a recognised proprietary or personal right of the applicant. Thus, if, for example, the public body's action impinges upon a person's real property, process rights will be required for the action to be legal.[59] This has been equally the case in respect of personal property, and process rights will be applicable where a job is regarded as an office and a species of personal property.[60] Some form of hearing right will also be demanded if the action affects the personal liberty of the individual, more particularly if that action entails some actual loss of liberty.[61] Thus in the post-*Ridge* era the courts have insisted that procedural fairness applies to

---

[55] See the similar point made by Lord Wilberforce in *Wiseman v Borneman* [1971] A.C. 297, 317.
[56] *Bates v Lord Hailsham* [1972] 1 W.L.R. 1373; *R. v Devon County Council Ex p. Baker* [1993] C.O.D. 138. cf. *R. v Liverpool Corporation Ex p. Liverpool Taxi Fleet Operators' Association* [1972] 2 Q.B. 299.
[57] See below para.12–028.
[58] See, e.g., *Schmidt v Secretary of State for Home Affairs* [1969] 2 Ch.149.
[59] As in the situation exemplified by *Cooper*, n.7.
[60] See the cases in n.2.
[61] See, e.g., *R. v Parole Board Ex p. Wilson* [1992] 1 Q.B. 740.

disciplinary actions that impact on liberty interests, or adversely affect the individual.[62]

ii. *Interests*

The term interest is looser than that of right, and has been used as the basis **12–015** for some type of hearing even where the individual would not be regarded in law as having any actual substantive entitlement or right in the particular case.[63] Many of the cases concerning natural justice in the context of clubs, unions and trade associations provide examples of the courts demanding that process rights be accorded in circumstances where the applicant has an interest as such, rather than any substantive entitlement.[64] The application of natural justice or fairness in the context of, for example, licensing and aliens is also based upon the individual possessing an interest as opposed to a right *stricto sensu*.[65]

The willingness to accept that interests that fall short of rights *stricto sensu* can trigger the applicability of procedural protection is clearly right in principle. The technical distinction between rights and privileges should not be determinative of the applicability of procedural protection. Many interests may be extremely important to an individual even though they would not warrant the label "right" or "Hohfeldian right".[66] The absence of a substantive right to a particular benefit should not lead to the conclusion that procedural rights are inapplicable,[67] although it might have some impact on the content of the applicable procedural rights. The absence of substantive protection may indeed render procedural rights even more important, a point made cogently by Lord Wilberforce in *Malloch*.[68] Thus the mere fact that, for example, in the employment area, an office is held at pleasure should not lead to the denial of procedural protection. This is more

---

[62] *Taylor v National Union of Seamen* [1967] 1 W.L.R. 532; *R. v Aston University Senate Ex p. Roffey* [1969] 2 Q.B. 538; *Glynn v Keele University* [1971] 1 W.L.R. 487; *St. Germain*, n.29; *R. v Board of Visitors of Hull Prison Ex p. St. Germain (No.2)* [1979] 1 W.L.R. 1401; *Leech v Parkhurst Prison Deputy Governor* [1988] A.C. 533. For general discussion see, G. Richardson, *Law, Process and Custody: Prisoners and Patients* (Weidenfeld and Nicolson, 1993); M. Loughlin and P. Quinn, "Prisons, Rules and Courts: A Study in Administrative Law" (1993) 56 M.L.R. 497. In the case of students this is subject to the jurisdiction of the Visitor, *Thomas v University of Bradford* [1987] A.C. 795; *Oakes v Sidney Sussex College, Cambridge* [1988] 1 W.L.R. 431, although the courts will exercise limited supervisory review over the Visitor, *Page v Hull University Visitor* [1993] A.C. 682; P. Smith, "The Exclusive Jurisdiction of the University Visitor" (1981) 97 L.Q.R. 610.
[63] The dividing line between rights and interests can be problematic precisely because the definition of what constitutes a right is itself contentious.
[64] See cases nn.4–6.
[65] See, e.g., *Gaming Board*, n.54, 430; *R. (on the application of Quark Fishing Ltd) v Secretary of State for Foreign and Commonwealth Office* [2002] E.W.C.A. Civ 1409.
[66] See further, C. Reich, "The New Property" (1964) 73 Yale L.J. 733.
[67] In this respect Lord Denning's reasoning in *Schmidt v Secretary of State for Home Affairs* [1969] 2 Ch.149, which equated, on the facts of the case, the absence of the right to stay in the UK longer than the prescribed period, with the absence of procedural protection, is open to criticism. Compare the reasoning of Lord Phillips M.R. in *R. (on the application of L) v Secretary of State for the Home Department* [2003] 1 All E.R. 1062, para.30.
[68] [1971] 1 W.L.R. 1578, 1595–1598. See also, *Stevenson v United Road Transport Union* [1977] I.C.R. 893.

especially so because the dividing line between officers who can be dismissed for cause[69] and those who can be dismissed at pleasure can be hard to draw,[70] as can the line between an office and a pure master–servant relationship.[71]

iii. Legitimate Expectation

12–016 The concept of legitimate expectations adds to those of right and interest in three different ways.[72]

First, the court may decide that the interest, although not presently held, is important enough that an applicant should not be refused it without having some procedural rights. In this sense the courts are protecting *future interests*. The courts make a normative judgment that a consequence of applying for a substantive interest is that some procedural protection is warranted. Thus, in *McInnes*[73] Megarry V.C. held that there was a class of case in which the applicant could be said to have a legitimate expectation that an interest would be granted. This was where the applicant was a licence holder who was seeking the renewal of a licence, or where a person was already elected to a position and was seeking confirmation of the appointment from a different body. Precisely which future interests should be deserving of this procedural protection may be contestable.[74]

A second way in which the concept of legitimate expectation adds to the ideas of right and interest is where there is a clear and unequivocal *representation*.[75] Where this condition is satisfied a representation generating a legitimate expectation can be of importance in two types of case.

---

[69] Traditionally, the availability of natural justice in the employment context depended upon the nature of the employment relationship. If there is what is regarded by the law as an office then public law remedies are available to protect its holder who is entitled to natural justice. The individual can thus regain the office if dismissed without a hearing, *Bagg's Case* (1615) 11 Co. Rep. 93b; *R. v Chancellor of the University of Cambridge* (1723) 1 Str. 557; *Fisher v Jackson* (1891) 2 Ch.824; *Ridge v Baldwin* [1964] A.C. 40, 66; *R. v East Berkshire Health Authority Ex p. Walsh* [1985] Q.B. 152; *R. v Secretary of State for the Home Department Ex p. Benwell* [1985] Q.B. 554. Where the office was held at pleasure then the presumption was that no procedural protection was applicable.

[70] For an early example of the absence of procedural protection where offices are held at pleasure, see *R. v Darlington School Governors* (1844) 6 Q.B. 682, though the courts often evaded the rule *Willis v Childe* (1851) 13 Beav 117.

[71] Contrast *Cooper v Wilson* [1937] 2 K.B. 309 and *Ridge v Baldwin* [1964] A.C. 40 (police are office-holders) with *Barber v Manchester Regional Hospital Board* [1958] 1 W.L.R. 181 (consultant surgeon) and *Vidyodaya University Council v Silva* [1965] 1 W.L.R. 77 (university teacher, not office holders). Compare further *Walsh*, n.69, and *Benwell*, n.69.

[72] C. Forsyth, "The Provenance and Protection of Legitimate Expectations" (1988) 47 C.L.J. 238; P. Elias, "Legitimate Expectation and Judicial Review", in J. Jowell and D. Oliver (eds), *New Directions in Judicial Review*, (Sweet & Maxwell, 1988), 37–50; P. Craig, "Legitimate Expectations: A Conceptual Analysis" (1992) 108 L.Q.R. 79.

[73] *McInnes*, n.41.

[74] Megarry V.C., in *McInnes*, held that even a pure applicant would be entitled to a measure of procedural protection, in that the deciding authority should reach its decision without bias and without pursuing a capricious policy.

[75] *R. v Falmouth and Truro Port Health Authority Ex p. South West Water Ltd* [2001] Q.B. 445; *R. (on the application of Galligan) v Chancellor, Masters and Scholars of the University of Oxford* [2002] A.C.D. 33.

On the one hand, there may be cases in which the representation provides the foundation for the procedural rights, even though in the absence of the representation it is unlikely that the substantive interest would, in itself, entitle the applicant to natural justice or fairness. In this type of case the *interest* of the applicant, by itself, would not warrant procedural protection. It is the *conduct* of the public body, through its representation, which provides the foundation for the procedural protection. In *Att-Gen of Hong Kong v Ng Yuen Shiu*[76] it was held that although the rules of natural justice or fairness might not generally be applicable to an alien who had entered the territory illegally, a person could claim some elements of a fair hearing if there was a legitimate expectation of being accorded such a hearing. Such an expectation could arise if, as was the case, the government had announced that illegal immigrants would be interviewed with each case being treated on its merits, albeit there being no guarantee that such immigrants would be allowed to remain in the territory. The point is well captured by Elias, who states that, [77]

"[I]t was only the legitimate expectation arising from the assurance given by the Government that enabled the court to intervene on behalf of the illegal immigrant: his status as an illegal immigrant would not of itself have created any entitlement to a hearing."

On the other hand, the representation that gives rise to the legitimate expectation may *augment* the applicant's procedural rights, as exemplified by the *Liverpool Taxi* case.[78] In that case the council had pursued a policy of limiting the number of licensed taxis to 300. The applicants were repeatedly assured that the figure would not be increased without their being consulted, but the council did so nonetheless. It is unclear whether the court believed that the applicants would have had any procedural rights in the absence of the initial council assurances.[79] It is, however, clear that the content of the applicants' procedural rights were enhanced by the representations. Thus, Lord Denning M.R. stated that the council ought not to depart from the undertaking, "except after the most serious consideration and hearing what the other party has to say and then only if they are satisfied that the overriding public interest requires it".[80] Roskill L.J. held that the council could not resile from their undertaking, "without notice to and representations from the applicants", and only after "due and proper consideration of the representations of all those interested".[81]

12–017

---

[76] [1983] 2 A.C. 629.
[77] "Legitimate Expectation and Judicial Review", n.72, 41.
[78] *R. v Liverpool Corporation Ex p. Liverpool Taxi Fleet Operators' Association* [1972] 2 Q.B. 299.
[79] Lord Denning M.R. believed that they would have some such rights, [1972] 2 Q.B. 299, 307–308, Roskill L.J. left the matter open, [1972] 2 Q.B. 299, 311.
[80] [1972] 2 Q.B. 299, 308.
[81] [1972] 2 Q.B. 299, 311. See also, *R. v Secretary of State for Health Ex p. United States Tobacco International Ltd* [1992] Q.B. 353, 370. *Cf. R. v Devon County Council Ex p. Baker* [1993] C.O.D. 138.

The third way in which legitimate expectations can arise is closely related to, but distinct from, the second. This is where the defendant institution has established criteria for the application of policy in a certain area, an applicant has relied on these criteria, and the defendant then seeks to apply different criteria. In *Khan*[82] the applicant sought to adopt his brother's child from Pakistan. The Home Office, while stating that there was no formal provision for this in the immigration rules, provided a circular stating the criteria used by the Home Secretary. The applicant sought entry clearance for the child on the basis of these criteria, but was refused, and the Home Office indicated that different tests had been used. The court found for the applicant. Parker L.J. held that while there was no *specific* undertaking in this case, the principle from *Liverpool Taxi* was nonetheless applicable. Thus if the Home Secretary stipulated certain *general* entry conditions he should not be allowed to depart from them "without affording interested persons a hearing and then only if the overriding public interest demands it".[83] A new policy could be implemented, but the recipient of the letter which set out the previous policy must be given the opportunity to argue that the "old" policy be applied to the particular case. More recently, in the *Guardians ad Litem* case[84] the court held that self-employed guardians had a legitimate expectation, based on the defendant's conduct and statements, that they would be consulted before changes in their terms of engagement.

iv. Article 6(1) ECHR: "Civil Rights and Obligations"

12–018   The discussion thus far has focused upon the applicability of procedural protection in accordance with the criteria employed at common law. This must, however, now be seen in the light of art.6 of the European Convention of Human Rights (ECHR). The Human Rights Act 1998 (HRA) incorporated Convention rights into domestic law, including art.6. The courts have an obligation to interpret legislation to be in accord with these rights,[85] and acts of public authorities that are incompatible with the rights are unlawful.[86] Section 2 of the HRA provides that the national courts must take into account the jurisprudence of the Strasbourg institutions, although they are not bound by it. The Human Rights Act will be considered in detail below,[87] but it is appropriate to consider the implications of Article 6 at this juncture. Article 6(1) applies to both civil and criminal cases alike.

---

[82] *R. v Secretary of State for the Home Department Ex p. Asif Mahmood Khan* [1984] 1 W.L.R. 1337.

[83] [1984] 1 W.L.R. 1337, 1344. See also, *R. v Rochdale Metropolitan Borough Council Ex p. Schemet* [1993] C.O.D. 113. Reliance is required to sustain an action of this nature, *R. v Lloyds of London Ex p. Briggs* [1993] C.O.D. 66.

[84] *R. (on the application of National Association of Guardians Ad Litem and Reporting Officers v Children and Family Court Advisory and Support Service* [2001] EWHC Admin 693.

[85] HRA s.3.

[86] HRA s.6.

[87] See below, Ch.18

"In the determination of his civil rights and obligations or of any criminal charge against him, everyone is entitled to a fair and public hearing within a reasonable time by an independent and impartial tribunal established by law. Judgment shall be pronounced publicly but the press and the public may be excluded from all or part of the trial in the interests of morals, public order or national security in a democratic society, where the interests of juveniles or the protection of the private life of the parties so require, or to the extent strictly necessary in the opinion of the court in special circumstances where the publicity would prejudice the interests of justice."

It is the first sentence of art.6(1) that is of crucial importance for our purposes, since it imposes a duty to provide a hearing where the conditions mentioned therein are present. The initial trigger for the application of art.6(1) is the existence of "civil rights and obligations". It is important to be clear about the meaning of this phrase.

The *intent of the framers of the ECHR in using this phrase is by no means clear*. On one view, the phrase "civil rights and obligations" was originally intended to cover those rights and obligations that would, in Continental legal systems, be adjudicated upon by the civil courts. These were in essence rights and obligations in private law.[88] On another view, it has been argued that studies of the drafting history of art.14 of the International Covenant on Civil and Political Rights, which was used as the model for art.6 of the ECHR, offer a strong indication that it was not the intent to restrict the scope of art.6 to determinations of rights and obligations of a private law character.[89]

The existence of a civil right is for the autonomous determination of the European Court of Human Rights (ECtHR). It is not resolved solely by the classification adopted by the national legal order. Both the Commission and the ECtHR have stressed that the interpretation of this phrase cannot be answered exclusively by reference to categorisations used in domestic law. While these will be taken into account, they will not be determinative, and the ECtHR will make its own autonomous judgment as to whether a dispute involves civil rights and obligations.[90]

The phrase *civil rights and obligations has been interpreted broadly* by the Strasbourg organs so as to include[91]: disputes concerning land use[92];

---

[88] *Feldbrugge v Netherlands* (1986) 8 E.H.R.R. 425, 444, paras 19–21; *Runa Begum v Tower Hamlets LBC* [2003] 2 A.C. 430, para.28.

[89] P. van Dijk and G. van Hoof, *Theory and Practice of the European Convention on Human Rights* (Kluwer Law International, 3rd edn, 1998), 393.

[90] *Golder v UK* (1975) 1 E.H.R.R. 524, 536.

[91] Jacobs and White, *The European Convention on Human Rights* (Oxford University Press, 3rd edn, C. Ovey and R. White, 2002), 144–150; P. Van Dijk, "The Interpretation of 'Civil Rights and Obligations' by the European Court of Human Rights—One More Step to Take", in F. Matscher and H. Petzold (eds), *Protecting Human Rights: The European Dimension: Studies in Honour of Gerard J. Wiarda* (Carl Heymans Verlag, 2nd edn, 1990), 131–143.

[92] *Ringeisen v Austria* (1979–80) 1 E.H.R.R. 455; *Sporrong and Lonnroth v Sweden* (1983) 5 E.H.R.R. 35; *Zander v Sweden* (1994) 18 E.H.R.R. 175; *Skarby v Sweden* (1990) 13 E.H.R.R. 90.

monetary claims against public authorities[93]; applications for, and revoca-
tions of, licences[94]; claims for certain types of social security benefit[95]; and
disciplinary proceedings leading to suspension or expulsion from a profession.[96] The rationale for this jurisprudence is, in part, that administrative
decision-making can determine or affect rights and obligations in private
law. It is in part that public law rights may closely resemble rights in private
law.

12–019   There is nonetheless *considerable uncertainty about the outer limits of "civil
rights", with distinctions drawn by the ECtHR that are difficult to justify in
normative terms.* Van Dijk and van Hoof attest to the lack of clarity and
certainty in the Strasbourg case law.[97] They point also to distinctions drawn
that have little normative justification. This is especially so insofar as the
ECtHR has reasoned from the existence of discretion on the part of public
authorities, to the absence of a civil right for the purposes of art.6.[98] The line
between a substantive entitlement and a discretionary benefit is notoriously
difficult to draw. It is not moreover a valid normative criterion on which to
base the existence of procedural protection.[99] The distinction drawn by the
ECtHR between rights that the individual has as a private person, and those
possessed as a citizen, the latter not being regarded as civil rights for the
purposes of art.6, is also deeply problematic.[100] Lord Hoffmann, echoing the
sentiments of Laws L.J., stated that "an English lawyer tends to see all
claims against the state which are not wholly discretionary as civil rights and
to look with indifference upon the casuistry that finds the need to detect
analogies with private law".[101]

The *difficulties as to the meaning of civil rights and obligations are apparent
in the UK jurisprudence on art.6.* Space precludes a detailed examination of
the case law,[102] but two examples will convey the difficulty faced by the
courts.[103] In *Husain*,[104] the applicant sought judicial review for the withdrawal of financial asylum support. It was accepted that some social security
payments were to be classified as civil rights,[105] but that this was not so in
relation to discretionary social welfare benefits. The court was consequently
required to decide on which side of the line the applicant's claim fell, a task
that was not easy. In *Begum*, the claimant was offered housing as a homeless

[93] *Editions Periscope v France* (1992) 14 E.H.R.R. 597.
[94] *Benthem v Netherlands* (1986) 8 E.H.R.R. 1; *Pudas v Sweden* (1988) 10 E.H.R.R. 380.
[95] *Feldbrugge*, n.88; *Deumeland v Germany* (1986) 8 E.H.R.R. 448; *Salesi v Italy* (1998) 26
E.H.R.R. 187; *Mennitto v Italy* (2002) 34 E.H.R.R. 1122.
[96] *Le Compte, van Leuven and de Meyere v Belgium* (1982) 4 E.H.R.R. 1; *H v Belgium* (1988) 10
E.H.R.R. 339; *Madan v General Medical Council* [2001] EWHC Admin 577.
[97] Van Dijk and van Hoof, n.89, 404.
[98] Van Dijk and van Hoof, n.89, 405.
[99] P. Craig, "The HRA, Article 6 and Procedural Rights" [2003] P.L. 753.
[100] Van Dijk and van Hoof, n.89, 405; *Ferrazzini v Italy* (2002) 34 E.H.R.R. 45.
[101] *Runa Begum*, n.88, para.69.
[102] Craig, n.99.
[103] See also, *R. (on the application of Wright) v Secretary of State for Health* [2007] EWCA Civ
999.
[104] *R. (on the application of Hamid Ali Husain) v Asylum Support Adjudicator* [2001] EWHC
Admin 852.
[105] *Feldbrugge*, n.88; *Deumeland*, n.95.

person, but refused it on the ground that the area in which it was situated suffered from drugs and racism. In the Court of Appeal,[106] Laws L.J. held that a right was by definition something to which the individual had an entitlement, and that a discretionary benefit that a public authority could give or refuse as it wished could not be the subject of a right. He acknowledged however that the definition of right was broader than the common law conception of cause of action. He acknowledged also that the administration of the regime under the Housing Act 1996 Pt VII, required the authority to resolve a series of matters on a spectrum between the wholly objective and the wholly subjective. In such circumstances the issue of whether there was a civil right could not be answered by a sharp criterion. Laws L.J. found that although there was discretion, the applicant possessed a civil right under the housing legislation for the purposes of art.6. The House of Lords in *Begum*[107] left open the issue as to whether the applicant had a civil right for the purposes of art.6. Their Lordships recognised that the Strasbourg jurisprudence had extended the meaning of civil right beyond private rights *stricto sensu*. They acknowledged that the local authority had some discretion under the relevant statutory provisions, but this did not necessarily preclude the existence of a civil right for the purposes of art.6. When the statutory criteria for providing accommodation were met, the local authority were under a duty to provide it, even though they had some discretion as to the manner in which this would be done. In this sense, the applicant's interest was, in terms of the Strasbourg case law, personal, economic and flowed from specific statutory rules.

Applicants seek to use art.6 in domestic courts primarily in order to argue that the decision-maker was not independent and impartial as required by that article. The courts are fully aware of this connection. Thus in *Begum*, Lord Hoffmann was willing to accept for the sake of argument that the applicant had a civil right for the purpose of art.6. He made it clear however that he would be willing to reconsider this point if the Strasbourg court required a more intrusive form of judicial review, pursuant to the requirement of an independent and impartial tribunal, than he felt was warranted in this type of case.[108] Lord Bingham was equally cognisant of the connection between the definition of civil right and the obligation to provide an independent and impartial tribunal.[109] The case law on this will be considered within the following chapter, since it is connected to the issue of bias. Suffice it to say for the present, that the wording of art.6 threatens to embroil the courts in complex disputes as to the meaning of civil right, with the consequence that the obligation to provide an independent and impartial tribunal will often be unpredictable and turn on distinctions that have little or no normative foundation.[110]

[106] *Runa Begum v Tower Hamlets LBC* [2002] 2 All E.R. 668, paras 23–24.
[107] *Runa Begum*, n.88.
[108] *Runa Begum*, n.88, para.69.
[109] *Runa Begum*, n.88, para.35.
[110] Craig, n.99.

5. THE CONTENT OF PROCEDURAL PROTECTION: BALANCING

12–020 Any legal system will have to decide how to determine the content of procedural protection, assuming that some such protection has been held to be
applicable. There are a number of options. At one end of the spectrum is the
all-embracing procedural code, which addresses such matters in detail. At
the other end of the spectrum are ad hoc judicial decisions, with the courts
deciding on a case by case basis. There are various options in between. The
courts may develop a general formula through which to determine the
content of process rights.[111] Legislation may stipulate the content of process
rights for hearings of a certain type, for example those that are more formal
in nature.[112] The content of hearing rights can alternatively be determined by
a mixture of ad hoc case law, combined with sector-specific legislation that
applies the courts' precepts and fleshes them out.

We have no general procedural code to determine the detailed content of
procedural rights, although sector-specific legislation operates in particular
areas. The courts therefore generally undertake a balancing test to determine the content of procedural rights required in a particular case.

A. Balancing: The Factors taken into Account
12–021 The courts take account of a wide variety of factors within this balancing
test. These include the nature of the individual's interest; the type of decision
being given; whether it is final or preliminary; the type of subject-matter;
and how far it is felt necessary to supplement statutory procedures, to name
but a few. None of these will be determinative alone. In more general terms,
the result is arrived at after balancing three types of factor: the individual's
interest; the benefits to be derived from added procedural safeguards; and
the costs to the administration, both direct and indirect, of complying with
these procedural safeguards.

The more important the individual interest, the greater the procedural
protection. Thus in *Wilson*[113] the court was concerned with whether the
applicant who was given a discretionary life sentence should be told of the
reasons why the Parole Board had refused to recommend his release on
licence. In deciding that the applicant should be entitled to information of
this kind the court was strongly influenced by the fact that the liberty of the
subject was involved.[114] This justified departure from previous authorities,
which had held that this information did not have to be disclosed.

The balancing process is exemplified by *Re Pergamon Press Ltd.*[115]

---

[111] See, e.g., the approach adopted in relation to the content of constitutional due process in the
USA, *Mathews v Eldridge* 424 U.S. 319 (1976).
[112] This is the methodology for formal adjudication and formal rulemaking under the
Administrative Procedure Act 1946 in the USA.
[113] *Wilson*, n.61.
[114] See also cases where livelihood is at stake, *R. v Life Assurance and Unit Trust Regulatory
Organisation Ltd Ex p. Ross* [1993] 1 Q.B. 17; *United States*, n.81, 370.
[115] [1971] Ch.388. See also, *Maxwell v Department of Trade* [1974] Q.B. 523.

Inspectors had been appointed to investigate two companies under the control of Robert Maxwell. The directors were unwilling to respond to questions unless given a number of assurances, and on condition that a judicial type inquiry was conducted. When the inspectors refused to give all the detailed assurances the directors claimed a breach of natural justice. The Court of Appeal found for the inspectors. Although they were under a duty to act fairly, they had not broken this duty. While the potentially serious effect of the report required some procedural protection, this was weighed against the interest of the administration in ensuring confidentiality, added to which were the factors of speed and the preliminary nature of the proceedings.

The *GCHQ*[116] case exemplifies judicial "balancing" within a very different **12–022** context. Their Lordships decided that past practice in the operation of GCHQ generated a legitimate expectation that those who worked there would be consulted before any important changes were made in the terms and conditions of their employment. The government decision that workers at GCHQ could no longer belong to national trade unions, which was reached without prior consultation, was prima facie in breach of natural justice. Considerations of national security were, however, held to outweigh those of procedural fairness. The court accepted the view of the executive that to give prior notice of their intentions would run the risk of actions that would disrupt the intelligence services. Whether this approach to considerations of national security was too deferential will be considered in more detail below.

The way in which the nature of the affected interest can impact on the procedural rights accorded is evident in licensing cases. Thus in *McInnes*,[117] Megarry V.C. held that in the case of forfeiture the individual was entitled to an unbiased tribunal, notice and a hearing, whereas in the case of an application less was required. Since nothing had been taken away the duty in such a case was to reach an honest conclusion without bias and not in pursuance of a capricious policy.[118] Renewal of a licence fell into an intermediate category. Here the individual might have a legitimate expectation that the licence would be renewed. These cases were, said Megarry V.C., to be treated as closer to forfeiture than to those of initial application.[119]

These distinctions should not however be allowed to become over-rigid. There may well be areas where the interest at stake in an application for a licence is considerably more important than that involved in a forfeiture or failure to renew in a different context. Moreover, the duty owed to the applicant may well be higher in certain areas than that indicated by Megarry

---

[116] *Council of Civil Service Unions v Minister for the Civil Service* [1985] A.C. 74. GCHQ is the Governmental Communications Headquarters responsible for the security of military and official communications and the provision of signals intelligence to the government.
[117] *McInnes*, n.41.
[118] *McInnes*, n.41, 1532–1535.
[119] *McInnes*, n.41, 1520, 1529. See also, *R. v Calgary Ex p. Sanderson* (1966) 53 D.L.R. (2d) 477; *R. v Secretary of State for the Environment Ex p. Brent London Borough Council* [1982] Q.B. 593, 642–643.

V.C. This was recognised in *Quark Fishing*,[120] where it was accepted that elements of procedural fairness could be required even in application cases, especially where the licence constituted a valuable commodity. The public body could be required to afford the applicant the opportunity to make representations, and to provide information on which the decision was founded.

B. Balancing: Preliminary Hearings—An Example

12–023 The application of natural justice to preliminary hearings or investigations has tended to produce polarised arguments: the public body arguing that procedural rules have no place in this context, and the individual asserting that they should apply in their full vigour.[121] The courts have adopted an intermediate position, where some element of fairness is required, but not the full vigour of natural justice. There are, as Lord Wilberforce stated, many types of prima facie or preliminary determination and the requirements of fairness in one area may be unsuited to another.[122] The actual content of natural justice or fairness will depend upon a range of factors: the proximity between the initial investigation and the final decision; the construction of the statute; the importance of the subject matter for the individual; and the need for administrative efficiency.

Thus, in *Wiseman v Borneman*[123] the Inland Revenue Commissioners believed that s.28 of the Finance Act 1960 concerning share transactions was applicable to the case before them. The taxpayer objected and entered a statutory declaration setting out his reasons. The Commissioners still believed that the Act applied and referred the statutory declaration, a certificate and counter-statement setting out their views on the taxpayer's statutory declaration, to a tribunal, which would decide whether there was a prima facie case for proceeding. The taxpayer claimed that he should be entitled to see the counter-statement. The House of Lords, while accepting that some elements of natural justice could apply to investigations and preliminary determinations, held that an opportunity to see the counter-statement was not required: no final decision was being made and if the taxpayer could comment on the counter-statement the Commissioners would wish to comment on those comments, thereby producing an endless succession of exchanges, bringing the administration to a standstill.[124]

C. Balancing: The Issue of Causation

12–024 An important issue is whether the applicability of procedural protection can be affected by the likelihood that the hearing would make a difference to the

---

[120] n.65.
[121] *Wiseman*, n.55.
[122] *Wiseman*, n.55, 317.
[123] n.55.
[124] *Wiseman*, n.55, 308, 310, 315, 319–320; *Pearlberg*, n.42; *Pergamon*, n.43, 399–400; *Maxwell*, n.115, 534.

result reached in the particular case. There are a number of authorities holding that this should be irrelevant.[125] This is surely correct. The path of the law is, as Megarry J. stated,[126] strewn with examples of unanswerable charges that were completely answered. A reviewing court is, moreover, not in a good position to calculate whether a hearing would have made a difference.[127] Some decisions have come out strongly against taking into account whether the hearing would have made any difference, and this is to be welcomed.[128] Other courts have, however, looked to the causal link between the existence of a hearing and the final outcome. This has manifested itself in three ways.

First, a court may regard the likelihood of the hearing making a difference as a reason for denying the existence of natural justice or fairness. In *Cinnamond*[129] a number of minicab drivers had been repeatedly prosecuted by the BAA for touting for passengers at the airport. The BAA prohibited the drivers from entering the airport except as bona fide passengers. The drivers sought a declaration that the ban was invalid arguing, inter alia, that the ban was in breach of natural justice, since they had not been given an opportunity to make representations before the ban was imposed. Lord Denning M.R. stated that where there was no legitimate expectation of being heard there was no requirement for a hearing. Because the drivers had a long record of bad behaviour and convictions no such expectations were held to exist.

Second, the likelihood of the hearing making a difference may influence the discretionary power to grant a remedy. In *Glynn*[130] the court found that there had been a breach of natural justice by the failure to give a hearing to a student who had been disciplined. A remedy was refused, the court holding that nothing the student could have said could have affected the decision reached.

A third way in which the courts have moved from considerations of procedural form to substance, is by interpreting the concept of fairness as allowing them to consider, in a general sense, whether the decision reached was fair and reasonable. This issue arose indirectly in *Evans*.[131] The House of Lords explicitly disapproved of statements made in the Court of Appeal that

---

[125] *General Medical Council v Spackman* [1943] A.C. 627, 644; *Annamunthodo v Oilfield Workers' Trade Union* [1961] A.C. 945, 956; *Ridge v Baldwin* [1964] A.C. 40; *R v Thames Magistrates' Court Ex p. Polemis* [1974] 1 W.L.R. 1371, 1375; *R. v Board of Visitors of Hull Prison Ex p. St. Germain (No.2)* [1979] 1 W.L.R. 1401, 1411–1412; *Waite v United Kingdom* (2003) 36 E.H.R.R. 54, paras 58–59.
[126] *John v Rees* [1970] Ch.345, 402.
[127] The point is put powerfully by Lord Morris of Borth-y-Gest in *Ridge* [1964] A.C. 40, 127.
[128] *R. v Chief Constable of the Thames Valley Police Forces Ex p. Cotton* [1990] I.R.L.R. 344; Sir Thomas Bingham, "Should Public Law Remedies be Discretionary?" [1991] P.L. 64, 72–73.
[129] *Cinnamond v British Airports Authority* [1980] 1 W.L.R. 582; *Malloch v Aberdeen Corporation* [1971] 1 W.L.R. 1578, 1595, 1600.
[130] *Glynn*, n.62.
[131] *Chief Constable of North Wales Police v Evans* [1982] 1 W.L.R. 1155; in *R. v Secretary of State for the Environment Ex p. Brent London Borough Council* [1982] Q.B. 593, 645–646 the argument that the hearing would make no difference and therefore should not be required was expressly rejected. Ackner L.J. quoted the passage from *John v Rees* [1970] Ch.345, 402 with approval.

a court could exercise a general power to consider whether the decision reached was fair and reasonable. It was firmly stated that where review was based upon breach of natural justice, the court should only be concerned with the manner in which the decision was reached, and not with the correctness of the decision itself.[132]

Where review is based upon procedural grounds the applicability of such protection should not be placed in jeopardy by the court second-guessing whether a hearing would have made a difference. The weight of authority is firmly against such an approach, and arguments of principle firmly support the predominant approach of the case law.

D. Balancing: The Nature of the Balancing Process

12–025   A number of comments upon the balancing process are warranted. *First*, it is clear that balancing necessitates not only an identification of the individual's interest, but also some judgment about how much we *value* it, or the *weight* which we accord to it. Thus to take some position, as Megarry V.C. did in *McInnes*,[133] as to whether the renewal of a licence is a "higher" interest than an initial application, is not to engage in rigid conceptualism, but is rather a necessary step in reaching any decision. Provided that we do not assume that all renewal cases warrant more protection than all initial application cases, irrespective of the nature of the subject matter, then such ranking is both necessary and helpful.

Second, valuing the other elements in the balancing process, the social benefits and costs of the procedural safeguards may be problematic. This is not simply a "mathematical" calculus. Deciding what are the relevant costs and benefits is itself a hard task.[134]

Third, the existence of judicial balancing should not lead us to conclude that all such balancing is necessarily premised on the same assumptions. The premises which underpin an essentially law and economics approach to natural justice or fairness, may be far removed from those which underlie a more rights-based approach to process considerations.[135]

A law and economics approach to judicial balancing is apparent in the following extract from Posner.[136]

> "[W]hile most lawyers consider that the question whether there is a right to a trial-type hearing in various administrative contexts, such as the exclusion of aliens . . . turns on some irreducible concept of 'fairness', the economic approach enables the question to be broken down into

---

[132] [1982] 1 W.L.R. 1155, 1160–1161, 1174–1175. *cf.* the reasoning in *Cheall v APEX* [1983] 2 A.C. 180, 190.
[133] *McInnes*, n.41. See also, Judge Friendly, "Some Kind of Hearing" 123 U Pa LR 1267 (1975).
[134] e.g. J. Mashaw, "The Supreme Court's Due Process Calculus for Administrative Adjudication in *Mathews v Eldridge*: Three Factors in Search of a Theory of Value" (1976) 44 U. Chi. L.R. 28, 47–48.
[135] Compare, e.g., R. Posner, "An Economic Approach to Legal Procedure and Judicial Administration" 2 J. Legal Studies 399 (1973), and Mashaw, n.1.
[136] *Economic Analysis of Law* (Little Brown, 2nd edn, 1972), 430.

objectively analysable, although not simple, inquiries. We begin by asking, what is the cost of withholding a trial-type hearing in a particular
type of case? This inquiry has two branches: first, how is the probability of
an error likely to be affected by a trial-type hearing? . . . Second, what is
the cost of an error if one occurs? . . . Having established the costs of
error, we then inquire into the costs of the measures—a trial-type hearing
or whatever—that would reduce the error costs. If those direct costs are
low . . . then adoption can be expected to reduce the sum of error and
direct costs and thus increase efficiency."

This particular species of balancing focuses principally upon an instrumental connection between process rights and the correct determination on
the substance of the case. The process rights are accorded insofar as they
constitute an efficient mechanism for ensuring the correctness of the substantive outcome. There are connections between this mode of thought and
utilitarianism, which can be traced back to Bentham.[137]

This approach to judicial balancing has, however, been criticised. There   **12–026**
are problems of implementing a calculus of this kind. Thus, Mashaw has
pointed out that balancing of this kind "has an enormous appetite for data
that is disputable, unknown, and, sometimes, unknowable",[138] and that "the
accounting task that a thorough analysis of social costs and benefits would
impose on the Court is simply too formidable".[139] Moreover, the "dynamic
effects of procedural change are unpredictable".[140] The approach moreover
risks undervaluing concerns relating to process rights that are not directly
related to the accuracy of the decision-making.[141] It is also inconsistent to
test procedural rules by some pure utilitarian calculus in circumstances
where one believes that a person has a substantive entitlement of some
kind.[142] Some balancing must, nonetheless, be undertaken. To denominate
certain interests as rights for the purposes of procedural protection, and to
take no account of other factors in determining the nature of this protection,
is implausible given that the costs of such protection have to be borne by
society. This has been recognised by Dworkin, who notes that in both the
criminal and civil process the individual is provided with less than the
optimum guarantee of accuracy, and that "the savings so achieved are
justified by considerations of the general public welfare".[143] As Mashaw
states,[144]

"[W]e cannot sustain a vision of the world in which rights ring out true
and clear, unencumbered by the consideration of conflicting claims of

---

[137] Mashaw, n.1, 104–108.
[138] Mashaw, n.1, 115.
[139] Mashaw, n.1, 127.
[140] Mashaw, n.1, 127.
[141] Mashaw, n.1, 113. See also, the literature above nn.11–12.
[142] R. Dworkin, *A Matter of Principle* (Harvard University Press, 1985), 79–84.
[143] R. Dworkin, n.142, 74.
[144] Mashaw, n.1, 154–155.

others to scarce resources. It is the fundamentally compromised nature of social life that interest balancing recognizes and confronts."

It is important therefore to consider what species of judicial balancing *would* be countenanced by those who disapprove of "pure" cost–benefit analysis, and yet at the same time recognise that society cannot provide an absolute level of procedural protection, which pays no heed to cost considerations. Dworkin advances one such approach.[145] He draws a distinction between the bare harm suffered by an individual who is punished, and the further injury suffered when the punishment is unjust, simply by virtue of that injustice. This injustice factor is termed moral harm.[146] The importance of this element is brought out in the following extract.[147]

"People are entitled that the injustice factor in any decision that deprives them of what they are entitled to have be taken into account, and properly weighted, in any procedures designed to test their substantive rights. But it does not automatically follow either that they do or do not have a right to a hearing of any particular scope or structure. That depends on a variety of factors, conspicuously including those the Court mentioned in *Mathews*.[148] The Court was wrong, not in thinking those factors relevant, but in supposing that the claimant's side of the scales contained only the bare harm he would suffer if payments were cut off. . . . The claimant's side must reflect the proper weighting of the risk of moral harm, though it may well be that the balance will nevertheless tip in the direction of denying a full adjudicative hearing anyway."

It may be contentious whether a court has weighted the injustice factor appropriately. This does not undermine the importance of the point. It *is* very difficult to reconcile a view of the law as comprising, in part at least, substantive rights or entitlements, while at the same time being content with a view of procedure based on some pure utilitarian cost–benefit calculus. The recognition that there is an injustice factor will help to ensure that the balancing, necessary though it may be, does not undervalue the nature of the individual's interest.[149] It can in fact be argued that the Dworkinian approach does not go far enough, because Dworkin restricts its use to those cases where the individual possesses a substantive right, and as Galligan has persuasively argued this restriction is unwarranted.[150]

---

[145] Dworkin, n.142, Ch.3.
[146] Dworkin, n.142, 80.
[147] Dworkin, n.142, 100–101.
[148] The case is *Mathews v Eldridge* 424 U.S. 319 (1976), in which the Supreme Court of the United States held that the availability of procedural rights would depend upon the following factors: the interest of the individual; the risk of any erroneous deprivation of that interest through the procedures actually used, and the probable value of additional procedural safeguards; and the governmental interest, including the costs imposed by the additional procedural requirement.
[149] See also, Mashaw, n.1, Chs 4–7.
[150] "Rights, Discretion and Procedures", in C. Sampford and D. Galligan (eds), *Law, Rights and the Welfare State* (Croom Helm, 1986), 139–141; Galligan, n.1, 104–107.

6. CONTENT OF PROCEDURAL PROTECTION: SPECIFIC PROCEDURAL NORMS

A. Notice

As Lord Denning said,[151] if "the right to be heard is to be a real right which   **12–027**
is worth anything, it must carry with it a right in the accused man to know
the case which is made against him". Thus, it is contrary to natural justice to
inform an individual of only one complaint if there are two,[152] or to find the
person guilty of a different offence from the one that she was actually
charged with.[153] Similarly, it was held to be contrary to natural justice to
confirm an order on facts that the individual had no opportunity to show to
be erroneous.[154] The right to notice extends also to giving the individual a
reasonable amount of time in which to prepare the case.[155]

The importance of the right to notice was reaffirmed more recently in
Anufrijeva.[156] The claimant was an asylum seeker, whose income support
was terminated after the Home Secretary rejected her asylum application.
This determination was not however communicated to the claimant. Lord
Steyn held that notice of a decision was essential in order to enable the
person affected to be able to challenge it. It was an "application of the right
of access to justice", which was a "fundamental and constitutional principle
of our legal system".[157] The rule of law required that a constitutional state
should accord to individuals the right to know of a decision before their
rights could be affected. The "antithesis of such a state was described by
Kafka: a state where the rights of individuals are overridden by hole in the
corner decisions or knocks on doors in the early hours".[158] Lord Steyn
acknowledged that there could be exceptional cases where notice was not
possible, such as with arrests and search warrants, but held that the present
case fell within the ambit of the general rule requiring notice. The right to
notice was a fundamental right and could therefore only be excluded by
Parliament expressly or by necessary implication. He concluded that Parliament had not done so in the relevant legislation.

---

[151] *Kanda v Government of Malaya* [1962] A.C. 322, 337; *Att-Gen v Ryan* [1980] A.C. 718;
Hadmor Productions Ltd v Hamilton [1982] 2 W.L.R. 322. *cf. R v Secretary of State for the
Home Department Ex p. Santillo* [1981] Q.B. 778.
[152] *Board of Trustees of the Maradana Mosque v Mahmud* [1967] 1 A.C. 13, 24–25.
[153] *Lau Luit Meng v Disciplinary Committee* [1968] A.C. 391.
[154] *Fairmount Investments Ltd v Secretary of State for the Environment* [1976] 1 W.L.R. 1255,
1260, 1265–1266. See also, *R. v Deputy Industrial Injuries Commissioner Ex p. Jones* [1962] 2
Q.B. 677, 685; *Sabey & Co Ltd v Secretary of State for the Environment* [1978] 1 All E.R. 586; *R.
v Secretary of State for the Environment Ex p. Norwich City Council* [1982] Q.B. 808; *Mahon v
Air New Zealand Ltd* [1984] A.C. 808; *R. (on the application of X) v Chief Constable of the West
Midlands Police* [2004] 2 All E.R. 1.
[155] *R. v Thames Magistrates' Court Ex p. Polemis* [1974] 1 W.L.R. 1371, 1375; *R. v Grays
Justices Ex p. Graham* [1982] Q.B. 1239.
[156] *R. (on the application of Anufrijeva) v Secretary of State for the Home Department* [2004] 1
A.C. 604.
[157] *Anufrijeva*, n.156, para 26.
[158] *Anufrijeva*, n.156, para 28.

While the courts have jealously protected an individual's right to notice,[159] they have on occasion interpreted it in a limited manner.[160] In the *Gaming Board*[161] case the Court of Appeal held that applicants for a gaming licence should have the opportunity to respond to the negative views formed by the Gaming Board. The Board did not however have to quote "chapter and verse", nor did it have to disclose the source of its information if it would be contrary to the public interest, nor did the reasons for the refusal have to be given.[162] In *Breen*[163] a majority of the Court of Appeal held that a disciplinary committee of a trade union did not have to tell a shop steward why they had refused to endorse his election. In *McInnes*[164] it was held that the council of the Boxing Board of Control did not have to give an applicant for a manager's licence an outline of its objections to him. The test adopted in both cases was that the decision-maker should not capriciously withhold approval.[165]

There is a tension underlying these decisions between the right to notice and the absence of any general duty to give reasons. In the context of, for example, an application for a licence, there is no "charge". Where the applicant has made repeated unsuccessful requests the person may wish to know why a licence has not been granted. This is, however, tantamount to requiring the giving of reasons, a point made explicitly by Megarry V.C. in *McInnes*.[166] Whether reasons should be given will be considered below.[167]

B. Consultation

12–028 The circumstances in which consultation is required will be considered in detail when considering rule-making, and reference should be made to that discussion.[168]

Suffice it to say for the present that statute may impose a duty to consult and that where it does so the public body must supply sufficient information to those being consulted to enable them to tender advice,[169] a sufficient opportunity to tender that advice before the mind of the authority becomes

---

[159] *In re Hamilton* [1981] A.C. 1038; *R. v Chichester Justices Ex p. Collins* [1982] 1 W.L.R. 334; *R. v Diggines Ex p. Rahmani* [1985] Q.B. 1109; *R. v Secretary of State for the Home Department Ex p. Al-Mehdawi* [1990] 1 A.C. 876; *R. v Bolton Justices Ex p. Scally* [1990] 1 Q.B. 537.

[160] *R. (on the application of M) v Secretary of State for Constitutional Affairs and the Lord Chancellor* [2004] 2 All E.R. 531.

[161] n.54, 430–432.

[162] cf. *R. v Kent Police Authority Ex p. Godden* [1971] 2 Q.B. 662; *Denton v Auckland City* [1969] N.Z.L.R. 256.

[163] *Breen v Amalgamated Engineering Union* [1971] 2 Q.B. 175, 195, 200.

[164] *McInnes*, n.41.

[165] There is some indication that more would have to be disclosed to the applicant if a charge was made against the person, *Breen*, n.163, 200; *McInnes*, n.41, 1534, or if the refusal constituted a slur against the applicant or deprived the individual of a statutory right, *McInnes*, 1535.

[166] n.41, 1532.

[167] How much the applicant is entitled to know may also depend upon what stage the proceedings are at: *Maxwell v Department of Trade* [1974] Q.B. 523.

[168] See, Ch.22.

[169] *R. (on the application of Edwards) v Environment Agency (No.2)* [2006] EWCA Civ 877; *R. (on the application of Smith) v East Kent Hospital NHS Trust* [2002] EWHC 2640.

unduly fixed and the consultation must be taken conscientiously into account when making the final determination.[170]

There is no general duty to consult imposed by the common law where the order is of a legislative nature.[171] The courts will however impose a duty to consult where the claimant can show that there is a legitimate expectation of being consulted. Thus where a public authority issues a promise, makes a representation or adopts a practice indicating how it will act in a given area, the law requires the promise or practice to be honoured unless there is good reason not to do so. This includes instances where the promise, representation or practice relates to the fact that there will be consultation before a decision is made.[172] Thus in the recent *Greenpeace* case[173] a government White Paper on energy policy indicated that the Government was not minded to support "new nuclear build" and stated that there would be full public consultation before the Government reached any decision to change its policy. A consultation exercise was held and the government decided that it would support some element of "new nuclear build". The court held that there was a legitimate expectation that consultation would occur and that the consultation process that took place was seriously flawed for a number of reasons.

The potential implications of this case are far-reaching. If a government department or agency formally announces that it will engage in consultation on a particular policy matter then it is arguable that this will in itself create a legitimate expectation that such consultation will occur, and allow the courts to adjudicate on the adequacy of the consultation exercise. This could open the door to judicial review of the adequacy of consultation exercises that are undertaken pursuant to the government's Code of Practice on Consultation.[174]

C. The Hearing

Two of the most important aspects of the hearing are the type of hearing required and the rules of evidence that will apply.

12–029

---

[170] *R. v Brent London Borough Council Ex p. Gunning* (1985) 84 L.G.R. 168; *R. v Secretary of State for Social Services Ex p. Association of Metropolitan Authorities* [1993] C.O.D. 54; *R. v British Coal Corporation and Secretary of State for Trade and Industry Ex p. Price* [1993] C.O.D. 482; *R. (on the application of Wainwright) v Richmond upon Thames LBC* [2001] EWCA Civ 2062; *R. (on the application of Partingdale Lane Residents Association) v Barnet LBC* [2003] EWHC 947.

[171] *Bates v Lord Hailsham* [1972] 1 W.L.R. 1373, 1378; *R. (on the application of BAPIO Action Ltd) v Secretary of State for the Home Department* [2007] EWCA Civ 1139, paras 33–47.

[172] e.g. *Att-Gen. of Hong Kong v Ng Yuen Shiu* [1983] 2 A.C. 629; *R. v Liverpool Corporation Ex p. Liverpool Taxi Fleet Operators' Association* [1972] 2 Q.B. 299; *R. v Secretary of State for the Home Department Ex p. Khan* [1985] 1 All E.R. 40; *Council of Civil Service Unions v Minister for the Civil Service* [1985] A.C. 374, 408–409; *R. v Secretary of State for the Home Department Ex p. Ruddock* [1987] 1 W.L.R. 1482; *R. (on the application of Niazi) v Secretary of State for the Home Department* [2007] EWCA Civ 1495.

[173] *R. (on the application of Greenpeace Ltd) v Secretary of State for Trade and Industry* [2007] EWHC Admin 311; J. Thornton, "Greenpeace and the Law of Consultations" (2007) J.P.L. 975.

[174] See para.22–021 for discussion of the Code.

i. The Type of Hearing

12–030 While hearings will normally be oral, there is no fixed rule that this must be so.[175] An oral hearing will however be required where this is necessary for the applicant to be able to present his case effectively to the tribunal or body making the decision, more especially when a liberty interest is at stake.[176]

The courts will, moreover, avoid construing a statute so as to dispense with a hearing completely. A statute empowering a public body to dispense with a hearing will, for example, be interpreted to allow oral hearings to be omitted. There are some cases that appear to hold that natural justice may not require a hearing.[177] These statements must be treated with great reserve. While the type of hearing may differ within different areas, and while it might vary depending upon, for example, the stage the proceedings have reached or the nature of the interest being asserted, to go further than this would be contrary to principle. To assert that, quite apart from the above factors, natural justice could be satisfied even though there was nothing in the nature of a hearing at all would be to denude the concept of all content.

It is axiomatic that the hearing should accord the affected party the opportunity to respond to allegations made against him, the corollary being that the evidence against him should be made known to the affected party.[178] Courts will therefore lean strongly against allowing a tribunal to decide a matter without giving the individual a chance to see the opposing case and have his own considered.[179] There may also be a breach of natural justice where the tribunal referred in its decision to an authority that the parties did not have the opportunity to address, provided that the authority was central to the decision and that a material injustice resulted.[180]

The application of these basic precepts can however be contentious, as is evident from *Roberts*.[181] The claimant challenged the decision of the Parole Board that certain sensitive material placed before it by the Home Office should be withheld from the claimant and his solicitor, and that it should only be disclosed to a specially appointed advocate, who would represent the claimant at a closed hearing of the Parole Board. The case provoked sharp division of opinion in the House of Lords. The majority held that this procedure was prima facie compatible with natural justice, and within the powers of the Parole Board. Lord Bingham and Lord Steyn dissented. They held that the procedure was incompatible with the principle that the affected

---

[175] e.g. *R v Amphlett (Judge)* [1915] 2 K.B. 223; *Kavanagh v Chief Constable of Devon and Cornwall* [1974] Q.B. 24; *Att-Gen v Ryan* [1980] A.C. 718.

[176] *R. (on application of Smith) v Parole Board* [2005] 1 All E.R. 755.

[177] *Roffey*, n.62; 552, 556; *Breen v Amalgamated Engineering Union* [1971] 2 Q.B. 175. The requirement that a party must have an opportunity to present her case will not apply with full force if the public body has to act in an emergency, *R. v Secretary of State for Transport Ex p. Pegasus Holdings (London) Ltd* [1988] 1 W.L.R. 990.

[178] *Official Solicitor v K* [1965] A.C. 201; *Re D (Minors) (Adoption Reports: Confidentiality)* [1996] A.C. 593, 603–604, 615; *Wilson*, n.61, 751–752; *Doody*, n.13, 562.

[179] *R. v Housing Appeal Tribunal* [1920] 3 K.B. 334; *Re Wilson* [1985] A.C. 750; *R. v Birmingham JJ Ex p. Lamb* [1983] 1 W.L.R. 339; *R. v Central Criminal Court Ex p. Boulding* [1984] Q.B. 813; *Wright*, n.103.

[180] *Sheridan v Stanley Cole (Wainfleet) Ltd* [2003] 4 All E.R. 1181.

[181] *Roberts v Parole Board* [2005] 2 A.C. 738.

party should have the opportunity to respond to allegations made against him, the corollary being that the evidence should be made known to the affected party.[182] They held moreover that the Parole Board had no power to adopt such a procedure, and that the principle of legality meant that statutes should be interpreted as not interfering with fundamental rights, in this context the right to a fair hearing.[183]

An individual can waive the right to a hearing,[184] but this option will not always be open. Thus, in *Hanson*[185] it was held that where the matter was one in which there was a wider public interest it might not be possible for one party to withdraw without the assent of the other once the proceedings had begun. Even if both parties agreed the issue might not be withdrawn if the tribunal objected. However, where an individual has lost the opportunity to present the case through the fault of her own advisers this could not constitute a breach of natural justice.[186]

ii. Rules of Evidence

The strict rules of evidence do not have to be followed.[187] Diplock L.J. set **12–031** out the following general principles. The tribunal is not restricted to evidence acceptable in a court of law; provided that it has some probative value the court will not reassess its weight. Where there is an oral hearing, written evidence submitted by the applicant must be considered, but the tribunal may take account of any evidence[188] of probative value from another source provided that the applicant is informed and allowed to comment on it. An applicant must also be allowed to address argument on the whole of the case.[189]

These general principles are, however, subject to the following reservation. The overriding obligation is to provide the applicant with a fair hearing and a fair opportunity to controvert the charge.[190] This may in certain cases

---

[182] *Roberts*, n.181, paras 16–18, 88–97.
[183] *Roberts*, n.181, paras 25, 93.
[184] *R. v Deputy Industrial Injuries Commissioner Ex p. Moore* [1965] 1 Q.B. 456, 489–490. The onus placed on the individual to request a hearing may well be inappropriate.
[185] *Hanson v Church Commissioners* [1978] Q.B. 823.
[186] *R. v Secretary of State for the Home Department Ex p. Al-Mehdawi* [1990] 1 A.C. 876.
[187] *Moore*, n.184, 476–477, 486–490; *Mahon*, n.154, 820–821.
[188] For the extent to which personal knowledge and impression can be used, *R. v City of Westminster Assessment Committee Ex p. Grosvenor House (Park Lane) Ltd* [1941] 1 K.B. 53; *Crofton Investment Trust Ltd v Greater London Rent Assessment Committee* [1967] Q.B. 955, 967; *Wetherall v Harrison* [1976] Q.B. 773.
[189] *Mahon*, n.154, 820–821; *R. (on the application of Afzal) v Election Court* [2005] EWCA Civ 647. It is doubtful whether there is a right to cross-examination in all cases, *Kavanagh v Chief Constable of Devon and Cornwall* [1974] Q.B. 624; *Bushell v Secretary of State for the Environment* [1981] A.C. 75; *R. v Commission for Racial Equality Ex p. Cottrell and Rothon* [1980] 1 W.L.R. 1580; *Chilton v Saga Holidays Plc* [1986] 1 All E.R. 841; *R. v Secretary of State for the Home Department Ex p. Tarrant* [1985] Q.B. 251, 288–289; *Public Disclosure Commission v Isaacs* [1989] 1 All E.R. 137; *R. (on the application of N) v M* [2006] EWCA Civ 1789, para.39; *R. (on the Application of JB) v Haddock (Responsible Medical Officer)* [2006] EWCA Civ 961, para.64.
[190] *R. v Board of Visitors of Hull Prison Ex p. St. Germain (No.2)* [1979] 1 W.L.R. 1401, 1408–1412.

require not only that the applicant be informed of the evidence, but that the individual should be given a sufficient opportunity to deal with it,[191] more especially when a public consultation has taken place.[192] This may involve the cross-examination of the witnesses whose evidence is before the hearing authority in the form of hearsay. Where there are insuperable difficulties in arranging for that evidence to be questioned it should not be admitted in evidence, or the hearing authority should exclude it from their consideration.

D. Representation

12–032 The position as to whether an individual can choose a representative, including a lawyer, is as follows.[193]

First, there appears to be no absolute right to such representation.[194] Legal representation may be counterproductive, unnecessary or overly cumbersome in cases where a matter must be speedily resolved, and hence the courts have resisted claims that there should be a *right* to such representation. This must however now be seen in the light of the decision in *Ezeh*,[195] where the ECtHR held that a person charged with a criminal offence who does not wish to defend himself in person must be able to have recourse to legal assistance of his own choosing, and that the denial of legal representation constituted a breach of the second limb of art.6(3)(c) of the Convention.

Second, the courts have, however, emphasised that tribunals possess *discretion* as to whether to allow such representation, and are willing to review the manner in which the discretion is exercised. A tribunal controls its own procedure, and this provides the foundation from which it can permit such representation.[196] Consideration of the statutory scheme within a particular area may convince the court that representation by a lawyer should on construction be excluded.[197] However, the courts are in general reluctant to exclude the possibility of such legal representation *in toto* within a particular area.[198] In exercising their discretion whether to permit such representation, tribunals should take the following factors into account[199]: the seriousness of the charge or penalty; whether any points of law are likely

[191] *Smith*, n.176.
[192] *Edwards*, n.169; *Smith*, n.169.
[193] J. Alder, "Representation Before Tribunals" [1972] P.L. 278; Galligan, n.1, 361–369.
[194] *Enderby Town Football Club Ltd v Football Association Ltd* [1971] Ch.591, 605; *Fraser v Mudge* [1975] 1 W.L.R. 1132, 1133, 1134; *R. v Secretary of State for the Home Department Ex p. Tarrant* [1985] Q.B. 251, 270–272, 295–296; *R. v Board of Visitors of H.M. Prison, The Maze Ex p. Hone* [1988] 1 A.C. 379.
[195] *Ezeh and Connors v United Kingdom* (2002) 35 E.H.R.R. 28.
[196] *Tarrant*, n.194, 273.
[197] *Maynard v Osmond* [1977] Q.B. 240, 253, 255.
[198] In *Enderby Town*, n.194, Lord Denning M.R. thought that a rule which sought to exclude the possibility of legal representation might be an unlawful fetter on discretion See also, 609, *per* Fenton Atkinson L.J.
[199] *Tarrant*, n.194, 284–286; *R. v Secretary of State for the Home Department Ex p. Anderson* [1984] Q.B. 778; *Hone*, n.194.

to arise; the capacity of a person to present their own case; procedural difficulties; the need for speed in reaching a decision; and the need for fairness as between the individual and the officers concerned.

Third, there does not appear to be any general right to attend a hearing as the friend or adviser of the individual directly concerned. Whether such a right exists depends on the nature of the tribunal in question. Any such tribunal does, however, possess the discretion to allow the individual to be assisted by such an adviser.[200]

E. Reasons

i. The importance of reasons

There are a number of advantages to be secured by insisting upon reasons for decisions.[201] First, reasons can assist the courts in performing their supervisory function. Substantive review based on relevancy, propriety of purpose or proportionality is much easier to apply if the agency's reasons are evident. Second, an obligation to provide reasons will often help to ensure that the decision has been thought through by the agency. Third, the provision of reasons can help to ensure that other objectives of administrative law are not frustrated. If, for example, we decide to grant consultation rights in certain areas, then a duty to furnish reasons will make it more difficult for the decision-maker merely to go through the motions of hearing interested parties without actually taking their views into account. Finally, it is arbitrary to have one's status redefined without an adequate explanation of the reasons for the action. The provision of reasons can, by way of contrast, increase public confidence in the administrative process and enhance its legitimacy. A duty to provide reasons can, therefore, help to attain both the instrumental and non-instrumental objectives that underlie process rights.

12–033

The disadvantages of a duty to provide reasons are said to be that it can stifle the exercise of discretion and overburden the administration. It is doubtful whether these objections are convincing. EC law has a general duty to provide reasons embodied in art.253 EC, which applies to the making of regulations as well as decisions.[202] This has been a requirement since the Community was first created and there is no indication that it has

---

[200] *Tarrant*, n.194, 282–283, 298.
[201] M. Akehurst, "Statements of Reasons for Judicial and Administrative Decisions" (1970) 33 M.L.R. 154; G. Flick, "Administrative Adjudications and the Duty to Give Reasons—A Search for Criteria" [1978] P.L. 16; D. Galligan, "Judicial Review and the Textbook Writers" (1982) 2 O.J.L.S. 257; G. Richardson, "The Duty to Give Reasons: Potential and Practice" [1986] P.L. 437; P. Craig, "The Common Law, Reasons and Administrative Justice" [1994] C.L.J. 282; Sir Patrick Neil, "The Duty to Give Reasons: The Openness of Decision-Making", in C. Forsyth and I. Hare (eds), *The Golden Metwand and the Crooked Cord* (Oxford University Press, 1998), 161–184.
[202] P. Craig, *EU Administrative Law* (Oxford University Press, 2006), 381–384.

overburdened the administration or stifled the exercise of discretion. The experience from Australia points to the same conclusion.[203]

There is no general duty to give reasons in English law, although the common law is moving in that direction. While statutory and common law rules impose a duty to provide reasons in certain circumstances, the absence of any general duty is still a gap in our procedural protection.[204] The historical origins of the rule that there is no general duty to provide reasons are obscure.[205] In so far as they are based upon analogy with the position of courts of law, this reasoning is being undermined, as the judiciary increasingly require some statement of reasons within judgments.[206]

An obligation to furnish reasons in a particular case may be imposed by statute, the common law, or EC law. These will be considered in turn.

ii. Reasons and statute: general

12–034   Statutory intervention owes much to the Franks Committee, which recommended the giving of reasons.[207] This was enacted in the Tribunals and Inquiries Act 1958,[208] which requires the tribunals listed in the Act to give a statement, written or oral, of the reasons for a decision, if requested by the individual. The statute also applies to ministerial decisions subsequent to statutory inquiries. In addition, primary and secondary legislation has imposed a duty to give reasons in specific situations.[209]

The stringency of the duty to provide reasons will depend upon the statutory language and the context. The reasons given must be adequate, intelligible and deal with the substantial points that have been raised. They must enable the individual to assess whether the decision can be challenged.[210] Yet the courts have also held that an alleged deficiency in the

---

[203] Neil, n.201, 163–164.
[204] For a survey of the practice in other countries, see Report of the Committee of Justice-All Souls Review of Administrative Law in the United Kingdom, *Administrative Justice, Some Necessary Reforms* (Oxford University Press, 1988), 46–68. See also, *R. v Secretary of State for the Home Dept Ex p. Harrison* [1988] 3 All E.R. 86; *R. v Civil Service Appeal Board Ex p. Bruce* [1989] I.C.R. 171.
[205] *Administrative Justice,* n.204, 29–32.
[206] e.g. *Eagil Trust Co Ltd v Piggott-Brown* [1985] 3 All E.R. 119; *R. v Harrow Crown Court Ex p. Dave* [1994] C.O.D. 99; *R. v Winchester Crown Court Ex p. Morris* [1996] C.O.D. 104; *Flannery v Halifax Estate Agencies (t/a Colleys Professional Services)* [2000] 1 W.L.R. 377; *R. v Denton* [2001] 1 Cr. App. R. 16; *English v Emery Reimbold & Strick Ltd* [2002] 1 W.L.R. 2409; *Butler v Thompson* [2005] EWCA Civ 864; *Cunliffe v Fielden* [2006] Ch.361.
[207] Cmnd. 218 (1957), paras 98, 351.
[208] Tribunals and Inquiries Act 1958 s.12(1), replaced by the Tribunals and Inquiries Act 1992 s.10(1).
[209] See, e.g. *R. v Minister of Housing and Local Government Ex p. Chichester RDC* [1960] 1 W.L.R. 587; *Givaudan & Co Ltd v Minister of Housing and Local Government* [1967] 1 W.L.R. 250; *Brayhead (Ascot) Ltd v Berkshire County Council* [1964] 2 Q.B. 303; *French Kier Developments Ltd v Secretary of State for Environment* [1977] 1 All E.R. 296; *R. v Secretary of State for the Home Department Ex p. Dannenberg* [1984] Q.B. 766; *Bone v Mental Health Review Tribunal* [1985] 3 All E.R. 330; *R. v Mental Health Review Tribunal Ex p. Pickering* [1986] 1 All E.R. 99; *Westminster City Council v Great Portland Estates Plc* [1985] A.C. 661.
[210] *Re Poyser and Mills's Arbitration* [1964] 2 Q.B. 467,478; *Westminster City Council v Great Portland Estates plc* [1985] A.C. 661, 673; *R. v City of Westminster Ex p. Ermakov* [1996] C.O.D. 391.

provision of reasons will only lead to the decision being quashed if the applicant has been substantially prejudiced.[211] Moreover, the preponderant view appears to be that a mere failure to comply with the duty to provide reasons does not, of itself, provide grounds for appeal on a point of law. The decision will only be quashed if the reasons as stated actually furnish evidence of such an error.[212] Sedley J. has however signalled that this issue should be reconsidered, so that the law in this respect could be brought into line with that on judicial review.[213] It is moreover open to the court to refer an inadequately reasoned decision back to the original decision-maker.[214]

iii. Reasons and statute: the HRA and the ECHR

The general relevance of the ECHR for the content of procedural norms will be considered below. Article 6 ECHR will have implications for the provision of reasons in circumstances where there are civil rights and obligations. While there is no express requirement to give reasons the ECtHR regards this as implicit in the obligation to provide a fair hearing. Reasons do not have to be given on every single point, but they must be sufficient to enable a party to understand the essence of the decision in order to be able to exercise any appeal rights.[215] The Privy Council recognised in *Stefan*[216] that the advent of the HRA, which brought art.6 into domestic law, would therefore require the courts to pay close attention to the giving of reasons in cases involving civil rights and obligations.

12–035

iv. Reasons and the common law: indirect techniques for securing the provision of reasons

There is no general common law duty to give reasons,[217] but there are none the less a number of ways in which the common law has imposed such a duty in particular instances.

A first method of indirectly requiring reasons is to contend that the absence of reasons renders any right of appeal or review nugatory, or that it makes the exercise of that right more difficult. This reasoning was originally developed in the context of appeal as illustrated by *Wrights' Canadian*

12–036

---

[211] *Save Britain's Heritage v Secretary of State for the Environment* [1991] 1 W.L.R. 153. It is not clear whether this was intended as a general proposition, or as one restricted to the planning context which was in issue in the case.

[212] *Mountview Court Properties Ltd v Devlin* (1970) 21 P. & C.R. 689; *Crake v Supplementary Benefits Commission* [1982] 1 All E.R. 498; *R. v Legal Aid Area No.8 (Northern) Appeal Committee Ex p. Angel* [1990] C.O.D. 355; *S (A Minor) v Special Educational Needs Tribunal* [1996] 1 All E.R. 171; Richardson, n.201, 450–457.

[213] *R. v Northamptonshire County Council Ex p. Marshall* [1998] C.O.D. 457, 458.

[214] *Emery Reimbold*, n.206; *Adami v Ethical Standards Officer of the Standards Board for England* [2005] EWCA Civ 1754.

[215] *Helle v Finland* (1998) 26 E.H.R.R. 159; *Van de Hurk v The Netherlands* (1994) 18 E.H.R.R. 481.

[216] *Stefan v General Medical Council* [2000] H.R.L.R. 1.

[217] *Minister of National Revenue v Wrights' Canadian Ropes Ltd* [1947] A.C. 109, 123; *Gaming Board*, n.54, 431; *McInnes*, n.41, 1532; *R. v Civil Service Appeal Board Ex p. Cunningham* [1991] 4 All E.R. 310.

Ropes.[218] Wrights' Canadian Ropes Limited complained that the minister should have allowed claims for expenses to be set off against tax. The Privy Council held that although the Minister was not bound to disclose his reasons, he could not thereby render the company's right of appeal nugatory. The Court could look at the facts before the minister, and if those were insufficient in law to support his determination then the Court would deem that it must have been arbitrary. The same approach has been adopted in later cases.[219]

If this line of argument were applied to the courts' powers of review it would lead to a general right to a reasoned decision.[220] The exception would have devoured the principle. There are some indications of such a development. *Doody*[221] was concerned with life sentences for murder, and whether the Secretary of State should tell the prisoner the reasons why he was deciding on a certain period of time for imprisonment. Lord Mustill, giving the judgment of the court, reiterated the orthodoxy that there was no general duty to provide reasons. However, he also found that there was a duty to give reasons in this instance, and one rationale for this conclusion was that the reasons would facilitate any judicial review challenge by the prisoner, who might wish to argue that the Secretary of State had erred in departing from the sentence originally recommended by the judges.

A *second way* in which the courts have indirectly imposed a requirement to give reasons is by labelling the result reached in their absence as arbitrary. This approach was adopted in *Padfield*,[222] but the scope of this exception to the general rule was limited by *Lonrho*.[223] It was claimed, inter alia, that the Secretary of State should have referred a merger between AIT (Lonrho's rivals), and the House of Fraser to the Monopolies and Mergers Commission. It was argued that in the absence of convincing reasons for not having done so, the decision not to refer should be regarded as irrational. Their Lordships disagreed. They held that if there was no duty to provide reasons in a particular instance, then their absence could not, of itself, provide any support for the suggested irrationality of the decision. The only significance of the absence of reasons was that if all known facts appeared to point overwhelmingly in favour of a decision other than that reached, then the decision-maker could not complain if the court drew the inference that there was no rational reason for the decision actually taken.

A *third way* in which the courts can indirectly inquire into the reasoning process is by examining the evidence the decision-maker used to arrive at the

---

[218] *Wrights' Canadian Ropes*, n.217. If there were sufficient material to support the determination the court would not interfere merely because it would have reached a different conclusion, *Wrights' Canadian Ropes*, n.217, 123.

[219] *Norton Tool Co Ltd v Tewson* [1973] 1 W.L.R. 45, 49; *Alexander Machinery (Dudley) Ltd v Crabtree* [1974] I.C.R. 120, 122; *Bone* [1985] 3 All E.R. 330; *Dannenberg*, n.209, 775–776; *Flannery*, n.206.

[220] *R. v Knightsbridge Crown Court Ex p. International Sporting Club (London) Ltd* [1982] 2 Q.B. 304, 314–315; *R. v Immigration Appeal Tribunal Ex p. Khan* [1983] Q.B. 790.

[221] *Doody*, n.13, 564. See also, *R. v Commissioners of Customs and Excise Ex p. Tsahl* [1990] C.O.D. 230, 231.

[222] *Padfield v Minister of Agriculture, Fisheries and Food* [1968] A.C. 997.

[223] *Lonrho Plc v Secretary of State for Trade and Industry* [1989] 2 All E.R. 609.

jurisdictional findings. The court can then assess whether that evidence justified the findings made.[224]

A *fourth exception* to the general rule that there is no duty to provide reasons has been touched upon already: if a public body has created a legitimate expectation that it will act in a certain manner then this may lead to the imposition of a duty to provide reasons as to why it has departed from the course of action which was expected of it.[225]

v. Reasons and the common law: the direct link with procedural fairness
The common law techniques described above provided some indirect basis   **12–037**
for the provision of reasons. The courts have also imposed a duty to provide reasons more directly, by linking the provision of reasons to fairness itself. The court will consider the nature of the decision-maker, the context in which it operates and whether the provision of reasons is required on grounds of fairness.

This was the approach in *Cunningham*.[226] Lord Donaldson M.R. reaffirmed previous orthodoxy by making it clear that there was no general duty to provide reasons. However, he imposed such a duty on the Civil Service Appeal Board, which had given the applicant far less compensation for unfair dismissal than he would have received under the normal employment protection legislation. The duty was imposed because the CSAB was held to be a judicial body performing functions analogous to those of an industrial tribunal. The latter would have to provide reasons, and fairness demanded that so too should the CSAB. The same approach is evident in later cases. Thus, in *Wilson*,[227] Taylor L.J. based his decision that the applicant should be entitled to know the reasons why the Parole Board was not recommending him for release, on the general ground of natural justice. This method is also apparent in *Doody*.[228] Lord Mustill noted the recent tendency to greater transparency and openness in the making of administrative decisions, and gave an alternative rationale for his judgment to that considered above. His Lordship stated that the statutory scheme should be operated as fairly as possible in the circumstances, and that one should ask whether the refusal to give reasons was fair. On the facts of the case he thought not, since the prisoner had a real interest in understanding how long might be the term of imprisonment and why this particular period was imposed.[229]

The general trend of the case law has been for the courts, while accepting that there is no general duty to provide reasons, none the less to demand

---

[224] *Secretary of State for Education and Science v Tameside Metropolitan Borough Council* [1977] A.C. 1014; *Mahon*, n.154, 832–833; *R. v Sykes* (1875) 1 Q.B. 52; *R. v Thomas* [1892] 1 Q.B. 426.
[225] See above, paras 12–016—12–017.
[226] *R. v Civil Service Appeal Board Ex p. Cunningham* [1991] 4 All ER 310.
[227] *Wilson*, n.61.
[228] [1994] 1 A.C. 531.
[229] See also, *R. v Dairy Produce Quota Tribunal and Minister for Agriculture, Fisheries and Food Ex p. Cooper* [1993] C.O.D. 277.

them on the facts of the particular case,[230] and to justify this in the light of the reasoning in *Cunningham, Wilson, Doody,* and the *Dental Surgery* case.[231]

In *Matson*[232] the applicant complained that he had not been told the reasons why the Court of Aldermen had not confirmed his election. The Court of Appeal held that it must do so. It was influenced by the fact that the applicant had been duly elected, that the Court of Aldermen's verdict was a matter of public record, and that it had made suggestions during an interview with the applicant which indicated that it felt that he was unsuited for the post, but without saying why. In *Hickey*[233] the Home Secretary had ordered substantial police inquiries in order to decide whether to refer a case of a person who had been convicted to the Court of Appeal. The court held that he must allow the affected individuals to make effective representations concerning the material revealed by his inquiries before deciding whether or not to make the referral. In the *Fayed* case[234] the applicants were seeking naturalisation as British citizens. Their application was refused without reasons being given, and s.44 of the British Nationality Act 1981 expressly provided that reasons did not have to be given. Lord Woolf M.R. held, however, that while reasons as such did not have to be given, s.44 did not exclude the right to notice, which was a separate aspect of natural justice. This right to notice was then used as the conceptual foundation for an obligation to provide the applicants with sufficient information in order for them to understand the essence of what troubled the Home Secretary. In *Stefan*[235] the Privy Council decided that the General Medical Council was under a common law duty to provide reasons when suspending a practitioner indefinitely, even though there was no express or implied statutory duty to do so.

12–038   In some cases the court has however denied a duty to give reasons. In the *Institute of Dental Surgery* case[236] the applicants sought judicial review of the decision by the Higher Education Funding Council which rated the Institute for research purposes at a lower level than the Institute believed was correct. The Institute challenged the rating on the grounds that reasons for the

---

[230] There are numerous examples, see, e.g., *R. v Criminal Injuries Compensation Board Ex p. Cobb* [1995] C.O.D. 126; *R. v Secretary of State for the Home Department Ex p. Pegg* [1995] C.O.D. 84; *R. v Secretary of State for the Home Department Ex p. Hickey (No.2)* [1995] C.O.D. 164; *R. v City of London Corporation Ex p. Matson* [1997] 1 W.L.R. 765; *R. v Secretary of State for the Home Department Ex p. Follen* [1996] C.O.D. 169; *R. v Secretary of State for the Home Department Ex p. Murphy* [1997] C.O.D. 478; *R. v Secretary of State for the Home Department Ex p. McAvoy* [1998] C.O.D. 148; *R. (on the application of Wooder) v Fegetter* [2002] 3 W.L.R. 591.
[231] *R. v Higher Education Funding Council Ex p. The Institute of Dental Surgery* [1994] 1 W.L.R. 242. See also, *R. v Bristol City Council Ex p. Bailey* [1995] C.O.D. 347; *R. v Royal Borough of Kensington and Chelsea Ex p. Grillo* (1995) 28 H.L.R. 94; *R. (on the application of Asha Foundation) v Millennium Commission* [2003] EWCA Civ 88.
[232] *Matson*, n.230.
[233] *R. v Secretary of State for the Home Department Ex p. Hickey (No.2)* [1995] C.O.D. 164.
[234] *R. v Secretary of State for the Home Department Ex p. Fayed* [1997] 1 All E.R. 228.
[235] *Stefan*, n.216; *Madan*, n.96.
[236] n.231. In *Fegetter*, n.230, it was held that the *Dental Surgery* case might now be decided differently on its facts, but see *Millenium Commission*, n.231.

assessment were not provided and that this was unfair. Sedley J. rejected the application, on the grounds, inter alia, that where what was sought to be impugned was *no more* than an exercise of informed academic judgment, fairness alone would not require reasons to be given.

Notwithstanding this decision on the facts, the judgment indicates the progress the common law has made in this area. The judgment accepts that reasons should be given either when the interest at stake is so important that fairness demands the provision of reasoned explanation, or where the decision appears to be aberrant. Of particular importance is Sedley J.'s view that where reasons ought to have been given, but have not been forthcoming, this in itself constitutes a breach of an independent legal obligation with the consequence that the impugned decision is a nullity. It was not necessary to establish that the failure to provide the reasons established some other head of review, such as irrationality or irrelevancy.

Lord Chief Justice Bingham in *Murray*[237] distilled certain principles concerning the duty to give reasons from earlier decisions. His Lordship stated that there was at present no general duty to give reasons, and that the public interest might outweigh the advantages of giving reasons in a particular case. He held that certain factors militated against the giving of reasons: it could place an undue burden on the decision-maker; demand the articulation of inexpressible value judgments; and offer an invitation to the captious to comb the reasons for grounds of challenge. Lord Bingham recognised however that there was a perceptible trend towards greater transparency in decision-making. He acknowledged that there were significant factors in favour of giving reasons: it could concentrate the mind of the decision-maker; demonstrate to the recipient that this was so; show that the issues had been properly addressed; and alert the individual to possible justiciable flaws in the process. Where a body had power to affect individuals a court would therefore readily imply procedural safeguards in addition to any stipulated in the relevant statute if they were necessary to ensure the attainment of fairness. If a just decision could not be given without the provision of reasons then they should be given, and so too where the decision appeared to be aberrant. In deciding whether reasons should have been given, the court would take into account the absence of any right of appeal, and the role reasons can play in detecting the kind of error which would entitle the court to intervene by way of review. The fact that a tribunal was carrying out a judicial function was a consideration in favour of the giving of reasons, particularly where personal liberty was concerned.

The courts have made great strides in this area. There is, moreover, little doubt that the criteria laid down in *Murray* will afford any later courts with ample opportunity to justify the imposition of a duty to give reasons should they so wish. It would none the less be desirable to shift the focus still further. The general rule should be that reasons should be given, subject to exceptions where really warranted. The jurisprudence of our courts is

---

[237] *R. v Ministry of Defence Ex p. Murray* [1998] C.O.D. 134.

coming close to this proposition, as evident from the dictum of Lord Clyde, giving judgment for the Privy Council in *Stefan*. He stated that while there was no general duty to give reasons there was a strong argument for the view that "what were once seen as exceptions to a rule may now be becoming examples of the norm, and the cases where reasons are not required may be taking on the appearance of exceptions".[238] It would do much to simplify and clarify matters if the legal rule could be expressed in this way.

vi. Reasons, statute and common law: "late evidence of reasons"

12–039 A number of cases have considered whether a body that is under a duty to provide reasons should be able to adduce evidence as to the reasons that were given, where the original statement of reasons was inadequate.[239] The position appears to be as follows.

Where there is a statutory duty to provide reasons as part of the notification of the decision, the adequacy of the reasons is itself a condition of the legality of the decision. In such cases it will be very exceptional for a court to accept subsequent evidence of the reasons.

The court will also be cautious about accepting late reasons in other cases. It will take account of a number of factors in this regard. The court will consider whether the new reasons are consistent with the original reasons, merely seeking to elucidate them. It will decide whether the later reasons have been advanced to support the original decision, or whether they are in reality an attempt to support that decision on different grounds. The court will consider whether the decision-maker would have been expected to state in the original decision the reason that he or she was seeking to adduce later.

vii. Reasons and EC law

12–040 In EC law there is a duty to give reasons based on art.253 EC. The extent of the duty will depend upon the nature of the relevant act and the context within which it was made.[240] The duty is principally imposed upon the Community organs themselves, but it can apply to national authorities where they are acting as agents of the Community for the application of EC law.[241]

There is also authority for the proposition that where a fundamental Community right is in issue, such as the right to free movement of workers,

---

[238] *Stefan*, n.216, 10.
[239] *Angel*, n.212; *R. v Westminster City Council Ex p. Ermakov* [1996] 2 All E.R. 302; *R. v Northamptonshire County Council Ex p. D* [1998] E.L.R. 291; *R. (on the application of Alletta Nash) v Chelsea College of Art and Design* [2001] EWHC Admin 538; *Leung v Imperial College of Science, Technology and Medicine* [2002] A.C.D. 100; *R. (on the application of Hereford Waste Watchers Ltd) v Herefordshire CC* [2005] EWHC 191.
[240] *Craig*, n.202; *Beus* (5/67) [1968] E.C.R. 83; *Germany v Commission* (24/62) [1963] E.C.R. 63; *Meroni v High Authority* (9/56) [1958] E.C.R. 133.
[241] *Wachauf v Germany* (5/88) [1989] E.C.R. 2609.

this can generate a duty to give reasons by the relevant national authorities.[242] Thus where a Member State seeks to deny a particular worker free movement by claiming, for example, that his qualification for the job is not accepted by that state, the competent national authority must inform the person of the reasons for the refusal, in order that the applicant can decide with full knowledge of the relevant facts whether there is any point in attempting to seek legal redress.

F. Appeals and Rehearing

An important issue is the extent to which a defect of natural justice can be cured by an appeal within the administrative hierarchy or by a rehearing by the original body. The authorities were reviewed by the Privy Council in *Calvin.*[243] It was argued that a breach of natural justice at the original hearing conducted by racing stewards could not be cured by an appeal to a committee of the Australian Jockey Club since there would be nothing to appeal against, the first decision being a nullity. Lord Wilberforce reviewed the authorities and adopted a tripartite distinction.

12–041

First, where the rehearing was by the same body or some more complete form of it the general rule was that defects at the original hearing could be cured.[244] Second, there were cases where after considering the whole hearing structure in its particular context a fair hearing might be required at the original stage and on appeal.[245] This second proposition was not however an absolute one. His Lordship posited a third situation where, looking again at the whole context, it could be seen whether the end result was fair despite some initial defect. This would depend, inter alia, on the type of appeal process: for example, if the appeal body was only entitled to a transcript from the original decision then the later hearing would probably be inadequate.[246] The facts of *Calvin* itself were said to fall into category three. The stewards' inquiry had to make a quick decision. Any defect in natural justice at that stage would be cured by the hearing before the full committee of the Jockey Club.

G. Deciding Without Hearing

How far is the decision-maker allowed to determine a matter without a hearing? The answer depends upon the enabling legislation, the type of

12–042

---

[242] *Unectef v Heylens* (222/86) [1987] E.C.R. 4097, para.15.
[243] *Calvin v Carr* [1980] A.C. 574.
[244] [1980] A.C. 574, 592. *De Verteuil v Knaggs* [1918] A.C. 557; *Ridge v Baldwin* [1964] A.C. 40, 79. Presumably this would be subject to a caveat to cover cases where failure to give an initially fair hearing prejudiced the individual in a way that could not be cured by the later rehearing.
[245] [1980] A.C. 574, 592–593. An example of this is *Leary v National Union of Vehicle Builders* [1971] Ch.34, otherwise the individual could be deprived of "two cracks of the whip", since the appeal would be the first fair hearing, *per* Megarry J., 48–58. See also, *Roffey*, n.177; *Wright*, n.103.
[246] [1980] A.C. 574, 593. *Annamunthodo v Oilfields Workers' Trade Union* [1961] A.C. 945 and *Pillai v Singapore City Council* [1968] 1 W.L.R. 1278 were treated as contrasting examples of a case where a defect was not cured on appeal and one where it was.

function being performed, and the nature of the decision-maker. Thus, it is accepted that if a minister is made the deciding authority the decision will often have to be made through officers, who will collect the material and the officer may even make the decision in the minister's name.[247]

In other areas the general principle is that the greater the judicial element involved, the more likely it is that the decision-maker must also hear.[248] Investigation may well be undertaken by a sub-committee, but the deciding authority must then be appraised of that material. Whether the material thus collected can be summarised, and whether all those on the deciding authority must possess all the papers[249] will depend on the nature of the function being performed and the language of the enabling statute.

Evans[250] provides an example of what may be required. A probationer constable sought, inter alia, an order of certiorari to quash the decision of the Chief Constable that he should resign or be discharged. The Chief Constable had decided to dispense with his services because of a report made on the probationer constable, which led the Chief Constable to believe that he was not fitted to be a member of the police force. The investigation had been conducted by the deputy Chief Constable. Delegation of the inquiry was allowed provided that a number of conditions were met. The ultimate decision must be made by the Chief Constable. The delegate must tell the constable the nature of the complaint against him and allow him an opportunity to comment upon it before the final decision was taken by the Chief Constable. It seems that the Chief Constable must also show the report to the constable and invite his comments before reaching his final decision. On the facts of the case the rules of natural justice had been broken because the constable had had no opportunity to comment upon the allegations made against him.

H. The ECHR and the Content of Procedural Rights

12–043   We have already considered the relevance of art.6(1) ECHR in relation to determining the applicability of procedural rights. We must now consider art.6(1) in relation to the content of such rights. The ECtHR has stressed a number of elements as integral to the requirement of a fair hearing pursuant to art.6.[251]

There must be access to a court.[252] There must be procedural equality or what is often termed "equality of arms". This implies that each party must be afforded a reasonable opportunity to present his case, including his

---

[247] *Local Government Board v Arlidge* [1915] A.C. 120.

[248] *Barnard v National Dock Labour Board* [1953] 2 Q.B. 18; *Vine v National Dock Labour Board* [1957] A.C. 488; *Jeffs v New Zealand Dairy Board* [1967] 1 A.C. 551, 568, 569; *R. v Race Relations Board Ex p. Selvarajan* [1975] 1 W.L.R. 1686.

[249] *Selvarajan*, n.248, 1695–1696, 1698; *R. v Commission for Racial Equality Ex p. Cottrell and Rothon* [1980] 1 W.L.R. 1580, 1589.

[250] *Chief Constable of the North Wales Police v Evans* [1982] 1 W.L.R. 1155, 1161, 1165. This issue was only considered by Lord Hailsham and Lord Bridge.

[251] Jacobs and White, n.91, 155–170.

[252] *Golder v UK* (1979–80) 1 E.H.R.R. 524.

evidence, under conditions that do not place him at a substantial disadvantage in relation to his opponent.[253] There is a right to a hearing within a reasonable time.[254] There must be some proper form of judicial process, which will often take the form of an adversarial trial where the parties have the opportunity to have knowledge of, and comment on, the observations and evidence adduced by the other side.[255] The requirement that there be a fair hearing will not always mean that the applicant must be present in person, but this should be so where personal character, or manner of life, are relevant to the subject matter of the case. While there is no express requirement to give reasons the ECtHR regards this as implicit in the obligation to provide a fair hearing. Reasons do not have to be given on every single point, but they must be sufficient to enable a party to understand the essence of the decision in order to be able to exercise any appeal rights.[256]

7. Fairness: Non-Adjudicative Procedures

i. The relationship between decision-making and procedure
The discussion thus far has been concerned with the applicability and content of procedural fairness, where the norms applied have been developed against the background of adversarial adjudication. It is time now to consider non-adjudicative procedures.

    12–044

> "This whole analysis will derive from one simple proposition, namely that the distinguishing characteristic of adjudication lies in the fact that it confers on the affected party a peculiar form of participation in the decision, that of presenting proofs and reasoned arguments for a decision in his favour. Whatever heightens the significance of this participation lifts adjudication towards its optimum expression. Whatever destroys the meaning of that participation destroys the integrity of adjudication itself."

Thus wrote Fuller[257] in a paper published after his death, on which he had worked for over 20 years. Fuller laid down what he conceived to be the forms and limits of adjudication. The precise nature of these need not be rehearsed here, although they will be touched upon in the course of discussion. What is of immediate importance is the realisation, often lost sight

---

[253] *Dombo Beheer BV v The Netherlands* (1994) 18 E.H.R.R. 213.
[254] *Attorney General's Reference (No.2 of 2001)* [2004] 2 A.C. 72; *Eastaway v Secretary of State for Trade & Industry* [2007] EWCA Civ 425.
[255] *Ruiz-Mateos v Spain* (1993) 16 E.H.R.R. 505.
[256] *Helle v Finland* (1998) 26 E.H.R.R. 159.
[257] "The Forms and Limits of Adjudication" 92 Harv. L.R. 353, 364 (1978). See also J. Allison, "The Procedural Reason for Judicial Restraint" [1994] P.L. 452 for an examination of Fuller's ideas and their relevance for public law and the adversarial process; Galligan, n.1, Chs 8 and 9.

of when discussing procedure, that adjudication is but one form of decision-making. It is clear that our procedural rules are sown in an adjudicative framework.[258] The rules of natural justice are related directly or indirectly to the idea of presenting proofs and reasoned argument. Thus, to give an obvious example drawn from Fuller[259] participation through reasoned argument loses its meaning if the arbiter of the dispute is insane or hopelessly prejudiced. Similar connections clearly exist in relation to matters such as notice. The development of fairness within our jurisprudence has not generally caused us to depart from the adjudicative framework within which we operate.

While attention has been paid to the modification of adjudicative procedures to meet the requirements of a particular area, there has been little thought directed to the broader question of whether adjudication is the correct decision-making process on which to be fashioning procedures. The vital point, brought out forcefully by Fuller, is that just as adjudication is distinguished by the form of participation that it confers, so are other types of decision-making, and just as the nature of adjudication shapes the procedures relevant to its decisional form, so do other species of decision-making. Nine modes of decision-making are listed by Fuller: mediation; property; voting; custom; law officially declared; adjudication; contract; managerial direction; and resort to chance.

12–045   In each of these instances the relationship between the type of decision-making, and the procedural rules attendant thereon, can be presented in the following manner. The procedural rules will be *generated* by, and will *protect* the integrity of, the type of decision-making in issue. For example, adjudication is one species of decision-making. The rule against bias is generated by this type of decision-making. It would be inconsistent with our idea of what judging means to allow the decision to be made by one who was biased. In this sense, the procedural rule is there to protect the integrity of what we mean by adjudication. It is equally the case that if we demand that an agency uses adjudicatory process rights then we are indirectly forcing it to make its decisions by adjudication rather than by some other means.

The relevance of this can be simply stated. There may well be situations when the procedures modelled on adjudication are not the most effective or appropriate, and where safeguards developed against the backdrop of a different type of decision-making may be more efficacious and apposite. The emergence of fairness may help us towards a realisation of this. The point is well put by Macdonald,[260]

"Rather than ask what aspects of adjudicative procedures can be grafted onto this decisional process reviewing tribunals must ask: what is the nature of the process here undertaken, what mode of participation by

---

[258] This does not mean that the principal aim of natural justice was to impose uniform adjudicative procedures.
[259] (1978) 92 Harv. L.R. 353, 364.
[260] "Judicial Review and Procedural Fairness in Administrative Law: II" (1980–1981) 26 McGill L.J. 1, 19.

affected parties is envisioned by such a decisional process, and what specific procedural guidelines are necessary to ensure the efficacy of that participation and the integrity of the process under review?"

It may well be the case that the very concept of adjudication as applied to disputes between private individuals has to be modified in its application to litigation involving public bodies. This does not negate the point being made by Fuller and MacDonald: it may still be the case that a different decisional form is more appropriate in a particular area.[261] Two brief examples of this idea may be given.

ii. Example 1: Statutory Inquiries

Let us first take statutory inquiries. They have always presented a problem for the application of natural justice.[262] The courts have been troubled by the very nature of the decision-making process, bifurcated as it is between the inspector and the minister. By their nature such inquiries do not fit one of the requisites of classical adjudication, which has been termed strong responsiveness.[263] This expresses nothing more than the notion that the decision should proceed from the proofs and arguments advanced by the parties. The position of the minister, and the broad range of policy considerations that must be taken into account, precludes this. This same fact prevents the minister from being an impartial adjudicator. Despite this lack of harmony between the facts and the ideal, the courts have traditionally seen the procedures for such inquiries against an adjudicative backdrop. It is true that they have recognised that the minister cannot be impartial in the way that a judge would be.[264] It is true also that the courts afford considerable latitude to the public authority in devising its own procedures.[265] Nevertheless, these are seen as modifications within the traditional adjudicatory framework.

What these modifications indicate, however, is that this decisional paradigm may not be the most appropriate. As the quotation from Fuller makes clear, whatever destroys the meaning of participation that characterises adjudication, destroys the integrity of adjudication itself. Moreover, it is

12–046

---

[261] A. Chayes, "The Role of the Judge in Public Law Litigation" 89 Harv. L.R. 1281 (1976); M. Eisenberg, "Participation, Responsiveness and the Consultative Process" 92 Harv. L.R. 400, 426–431 (1978); L. Fuller, "Mediation: Its Forms and Functions" (1971) 44 S Cal. L.R. 305.
[262] e.g. *Errington*, n.17; *Offer*, n.19; *Franklin v Minister of Town and Country Planning* [1948] A.C. 87.
[263] Eisenberg, n.261, 411–412.
[264] *R. (Alconbury Developments Ltd) v Secretary of State for the Environment, Transport and the Regions* [2001] 2 W.L.R. 1389.
[265] *Bushell v Secretary of State for Environment* [1981] A.C. 75; *R v Secretary of State for Transport Ex p. Gwent County Council* [1987] 2 W.L.R. 961.

arguable that classical adjudication is in general unsuited to the resolution of what are termed polycentric problems,[266] which may form the subject-matter of statutory inquiries. Judicial realisation that the full implications of the adjudicative model cannot be applied in this area is of, course, beneficial. A broad notion of procedural fairness may, however, demand more. It may require us to rethink the type of decision-making process from which we are deriving our procedures. Statutory inquiries may be better seen as a form of mediation or consultation. Some of the legislation in the planning sphere reflects such an approach.[267] If inquiries, or some of them,[268] were to be viewed in this light then the courts could help to devise procedural rules to fit *this* type of decision-making. What those rules are would be derived from the type of participation demanded by that decisional process. Some of these may overlap with characteristics found in adjudication, others may not.[269]

iii. Example 2: Social Welfare

12–047 The field of social welfare provides a second example of the theme under discussion. Claimants for social welfare provisions have not always been in a good position so far as procedural protection is concerned. There has been a tendency to regard such provisions as government largesse to be dispensed at the unfettered will of the public body. This view has been more manifest in the USA[270] than in this country, although we have not entirely escaped the same phenomenon. The response has been to bolster the procedural checks attendant upon the disbursement of such benefits. These safeguards are framed in an adjudicative fashion, albeit one which is significantly modified to take account of the circumstances. It may however be that this type of procedural check is not the most effective in this area. A number of reasons contribute towards this.

First, giving claimants appeal rights with a hearing before a higher tribunal ignores the factual background from which such cases spring. There will often be a continuing relationship between the claimant and the original officer, which the former is unlikely to want to sully by taking appellate action. To this must be added the nature of the claimants themselves, who may not fully comprehend the mechanics of such an appeal process.[271]

---

[266] Put simply, this is a problem in which one part interacts with a number of others so that a change in any one will produce ramifications in the whole: the decision of the team captain to move X from centre-back to half-back may necessitate alteration in the whole team. See Fuller, n.257, 384–405; Chayes, n.261; Eisenberg, n.261, 426–431. For a critical view, see, J. King, "The Pervasiveness of Polycentricity" [2008] P.L. 101.

[267] See above Ch.9.

[268] In particular those dealing with more major schemes.

[269] Fuller, n.261; M. Eisenberg, "Private Ordering Through Negotiation, Dispute Settlement and Rule-Making" (1976) 89 Harv. L.R. 637.

[270] C. Reich, "The New Property" (1964) 73 Yale L.J. 773; "Midnight Welfare Searches and the Social Security Act" (1963) 72 Yale L.J. 1347; "Individual Rights and Social Welfare: The Emerging Issues" (1965) 74 Yale L.J. 1245; "The Law of the Planned Society" (1966) 75 Yale L.J. 1227. The Supreme Court strengthened the procedural rights of such claimants in *Goldberg v Kelly* (1970) 397 U.S. 254.

[271] J. Handler, "Controlling Official Behaviour in Welfare Administration" (1966) 54 Cal. L.R. 479; M. Adler and A. Bradley, *Justice, Discretion and Poverty* (Professional Books, 1975).

Second, the adversary nature of the adjudicative process may not be well suited to this area. The idea of "opponents" and the "winner take-all" attitude inherent in it is not necessarily the best form of decision-making for social welfare cases.[272] What this suggests is that a different type of decision-making with correspondingly different procedures may be more relevant. A mixture of consultation and internal management control might well prove a better starting point.[273]

It should, however, be noted that other commentators have expressed reservations about the extent to which informal procedures can be successful, and have also pointed to the benefits of a broadly adjudicative appeal regime.[274]

We should nonetheless be prepared to think more broadly about what procedural protection connotes. Procedures developed against a backdrop of adjudication may well be the most appropriate in certain areas. They may not however be equally suited to all the institutions that comprise administrative law. What is equally important is that other types of procedural norms may, in certain circumstances better effectuate the twin rationales for process rights. Procedures developed in the context of consultation may, for example, better attain the instrumental and non-instrumental aims that underlie process rights.[275]

8. Conclusion

The courts have not been idle since the landmark decision in *Ridge v Baldwin*.[276] While many of the subsequent developments are to be welcomed continuing analysis is required to determine whether the content of the rules in general, and their application to particular areas, is being pitched at the "right" level. There is, for example, a cogent argument for the recognition of a general duty to provide reasons, while improvements in the context of employment relationships and aliens could be made. More thought should also be given to understanding the general nature of the balancing process that operates within fairness. The extent to which this should be viewed as a utilitarian calculus of some kind, or whether a more dignitarian approach should be pursued, is of considerable importance.

The concluding comments thus far have been directed towards the application and content of natural justice and fairness seeing both of these terms against an adjudicative framework. This is how they operate at present. Procedures derived from a backdrop of adjudication may not,

12–048

---

[272] G. Ganz, *Administrative Procedures* (Sweet & Maxwell, 1974), 35.
[273] J. Mashaw, *Bureaucratic Justice* (Yale University Press, 1983).
[274] N. Wikeley and R. Young, "The Administration of Benefits in Britain: Adjudication Officers and the Influence of Social Security Appeal Tribunals" [1992] P.L. 238.
[275] See above, para.12–002.
[276] [1964] A.C. 40.

however, be the most appropriate or effective in particular areas. Other decisional forms, whether they be mediation or managerial direction, may be better in certain contexts. The recognition and development of other types of decision-making, with the procedures necessarily consequent upon them, is one of the important tasks for the administrative lawyer, just as important as the workings of fairness within the traditional adjudicative context.

CHAPTER 13

NATURAL JUSTICE: BIAS AND INDEPENDENCE

1. INTRODUCTION

The second limb of natural justice is that decisions should be made free from **13–001**
bias or impartiality.[1] The issue can arise in two main contexts. The decision-
maker might have some interest of a pecuniary or personal nature in the
outcome of the proceedings. There are in addition problems where the
decision-maker is interested in the result of an inquiry or investigation, not
in any personal sense, but because the institution that is represented wishes
to attain a certain objective. Discussion of these two problems will be followed by consideration of the test for establishing bias.

The Human Rights Act 1998 has added a further dimension to this
inquiry. Article 6 of the European Convention on Human Rights (ECHR)
establishes a right to a fair trial. The relevance of art.6 for the applicability
and content of procedural rights has been considered in the previous
chapter. The present discussion will focus on another important aspect of
art.6. This is the requirement that the hearing should be by "an independent
and impartial tribunal established by law".

2. BIAS: PERSONAL INTEREST

A. Pecuniary Interest

The courts have long insisted that any pecuniary interest disqualified the **13–002**
decision-maker be he high or low. Thus, in *Dimes*[2] the House of Lords
reversed a decision made by the Lord Chancellor, Lord Cottenham, when

---

[1] D. Galligan, *Due Process and Fair Procedures* (Oxford University Press, 1996), 437–450.
[2] *Dimes v Grand Junction Canal Co Proprietors* (1852) 3 H.L.C. 759.

the latter had affirmed decrees by the Vice-Chancellor in relation to a company in which the Lord Chancellor held some shares. No imputation of any actual bias was made against Lord Cottenham, but it was held that the principle that no man can be a judge in his own cause must be sacred.[3] The courts have consistently held that if there was a pecuniary interest it was not necessary to go on to consider reasonable suspicion or real likelihood of bias.[4] It is therefore important to establish what will constitute a pecuniary interest.

Blackburn J. held that any pecuniary interest, however small, will be sufficient.[5] Some qualification is however required to the breadth of this statement. If the pecuniary interest is not personal to the decision-maker then the matter will fall to be considered as a challenge on the grounds of favour.[6] Moreover, if the alleged pecuniary interest is extremely remote,[7] or based upon contingencies that are unlikely to materialise,[8] then the matter will similarly be treated as a challenge on the grounds of favour. Subject to these qualifications, the prohibition of pecuniary interest seems to be an absolute one and is not further qualified by any requirement that the interest be substantial.[9]

B. Other Personal Interests

13–003   Other types of personal interest may disqualify the decision-maker if the courts find that the interest gave rise to a reasonable suspicion or real danger of bias. In this area much will be dependent upon the factual nexus between the decision-maker and one of the other parties involved in the dispute. Family relationship,[10] business connections, and commercial ties,[11] are examples of the interests that can disqualify the decision-maker, as is membership of an organisation interested in the dispute.[12] It may, on occasion, be someone other than the actual adjudicator who has been involved. Nevertheless, provided that he has, or may appear to have, an

---

[3] *Dimes*, n.2, 793–794.
[4] e.g. *R. v Rand* (1866) L.R. 1 Q.B. 230; *Leeson v General Council of Medical Education and Registration* [1889] 43 Ch. D. 366.
[5] *R. v Hammond* (1863) 9 L.T. (N.S.) 423; *R. v Rand* (1866) L.R. 1 Q.B. 230, 232.
[6] In the *Rand* case those challenged were two justices who were trustees for a hospital and friendly society, respectively, which bodies had funds invested in a corporation which had applied to the justices.
[7] *R. v McKenzie* [1892] 2 Q.B. 519.
[8] *R. v Burton Ex p. Young* [1897] 2 Q.B. 468.
[9] e.g. *R. v Gaisford* [1892] 1 Q.B. 381, the interest of a ratepayer was held to be a pecuniary interest.
[10] e.g. *Metropolitan Properties (FGC) Ltd v Lannon* [1969] 1 Q.B. 577.
[11] e.g. *R. v Barnsley Licensing JJ Ex p. Barnsley and District Licensed Victuallers Association* [1960] 2 Q.B. 167; *R. v Hendon Rural District Council Ex p. Chorley* [1933] 2 K.B. 696; *R. v Chesterfield Borough Council Ex p. Darker Enterprises Ltd* [1992] C.O.D. 466.
[12] *Leeson*, n.4; *Allinson v General Council of Medical Education and Registration* [1894] 1 Q.B. 750.

influence on the decision given, then that will be sufficient to render the determination invalid.[13]

3. BIAS: INSTITUTIONAL

A. Prosecutor and Judge

A somewhat different way in which bias can manifest itself is when the   **13–004**
prosecutor of an offence is also the judge.

This may happen *directly* as in *Shaw*,[14] where the sanitary committee of a town council instructed the town clerk to prosecute a person and one of the justices before whom he was prosecuted was a member of that committee. The court held that the decision could not stand.[15]

The matter may also arise *indirectly* in situations in which the decision-maker belongs to an organisation that initiated the proceeding, but where he himself has taken no part in the decision to prosecute. In *Leeson*,[16] the General Medical Council had disqualified a doctor for infamous misconduct in a prosecution brought by the Medical Defence Union, an organisation designed to uphold the character of doctors and to suppress unauthorised practitioners. Two of the twenty-nine who held the inquiry were members of the Medical Defence Union, but not of its managing body. The court found that, looked at in substance and fact, the two Medical Defence Union members on the General Council were not accusers as well as judges and that they could not reasonably be suspected of bias.[17] The court may also overturn a decision if it is felt that, for example, a justice has pre-judged the matter before hearing the full case.[18]

This can be contrasted to the ruling in *Pinochet Ugarte (No.2)*.[19] The applicant was the former head of state of Chile. He challenged a decision of

---

[13] e.g. *R. v Sussex Justices Ex p. McCarthy* [1924] 1 K.B. 256 (clerk to the justices was member of a solicitor's firm acting for one of the parties in a collision out of which the prosecution of the other party arose); *Cooper v Wilson* [1937] 2 K.B. 309 (chief constable who had purported to dismiss a policeman sits with the Watch Committee when they hear the policeman's case); *R. v Kent Police Authority Ex p. Godden* [1971] 2 Q.B. 662 (in deciding whether a policeman should be compulsorily retired a report should not be sought from a psychiatrist who had already formed an adverse view of the person); *R. v Barnsley Metropolitan Borough Council Ex p. Hook* [1976] 1 W.L.R. 1052 (market manager in the position of a prosecutor should not give evidence to a committee in the absence of the accused). *cf. R. v Frankland Prison Board of Visitors Ex p. Lewis* [1986] 3 W.L.R. 61.
[14] *R. v Lee Ex p. Shaw* [1882] 9 Q.B.D. 394.
[15] See also, *R. v Gaisford* [1892] 1 Q.B. 381; *R. v Pwllheli JJ Ex p. Soane* [1948] 2 All E.R. 815; *Frome United Breweries Co Ltd v Bath Justices* [1926] A.C. 586; *Roebuck v National Union of Mineworkers (Yorkshire Area) (No.2)* [1978] I.C.R. 676.
[16] n.4; *Re S (A Barrister)* [1981] Q.B. 683.
[17] See also, *Allinson*, n.12; *Burton*, n.8; *cf. Law v Chartered Institute of Patent Agents* [1919] 2 Ch.276.
[18] *R. v Romsey JJ Ex p. Gale* [1992] C.O.D. 323.
[19] *R. v Bow Street Metropolitan Stipendiary Magistrate Ex p. Pinochet Ugarte (No.2)* [2000] 1 A.C. 119; T. Jones, "Judicial Bias and Disqualification in the *Pinochet* case" [1999] P.L. 391; Sir D. Williams, "Bias; the Judges and the Separation of Powers" [2000] P.L. 45.

the House of Lords that he could be extradited in respect of acts committed while he was still head of state. The foundation for the challenge was that one of the Law Lords who had heard the matter, Lord Hoffmann, was the director and chairperson of Amnesty International Charity Ltd (AICL), a body which had been incorporated to carry out the charitable work of Amnesty International (AI). AI had been given leave to intervene in the contested proceedings and had argued that Pinochet should be extradited. The House of Lords made it clear that there was no allegation of any actual bias against Lord Hoffmann, but held that the earlier decision could nonetheless not stand. The principle that a judge was automatically disqualified from hearing a matter in his own cause was, said their Lordships, not restricted to cases where the judge had a pecuniary interest in the outcome, but applied also to cases where the judge's decision would lead to the promotion of a cause in which the judge was involved with one of the parties. This did not preclude judges from sitting on cases concerning charities which they were involved with, and they would normally only have to recuse themselves, or disclose the position to the parties, where they had an active role as trustee or director of a charity which was closely allied to, and acting with, a party to the litigation.[20] In the instant case Lord Hoffmann was a director of a charity closely related to AI, in a case where AI had argued directly for a particular result, and therefore the original decision could not be allowed to stand.

The difficulty presented here is more acute in the context of governmental agencies that have responsibility both for adjudication and prosecution, a combination more normal in the USA than in this country. In response to this problem the 1946 Federal Administrative Procedure Act s.5(c) established an internal separation of function between decider and prosecutor.[21]

B. Institutional Opinion

13–005 Overlapping with, but nevertheless separate from the mixture of function between prosecutor and judge, is the fact that administrators of a particular scheme may well have "strong views" or "preconceived ideas" concerning the issue before them.[22] This may be of a discretionary or regulatory nature and while these elements should not exclude proscriptions against bias they are likely to modify their application. Administrators may have guidelines to help them to interpret a broadly worded statute, the application of which should not in itself constitute bias. Clear pre-judgment of a case is to be disapproved of, but the success of a piece of legislation may well be dependent upon the administrator enforcing the institution's policies with

---

[20] *Leeson*, n.4; *Allinson*, n.12; *Meerabux v Attorney General of Belize* [2005] 2 A.C. 513.
[21] S. Breyer, R. Stewart, C. Sunstein and M. Spitzer, *Administrative Law and Regulatory Policy, Problems, Text and Cases* (5th edn, 2002), Ch.7.
[22] A valuable discussion can be found in G. Flick, *Natural Justice* (Butterworths, 1979), 122–129.

some rigour. Indifference to the end in view, even if it were possible, might well be undesirable.[23]

Seen against this background the decision in *Franklin*,[24] although influenced by the judicial conservatism of the time, would probably not be different today. The House of Lords stated that the Minister had a duty to give genuine consideration to a report of an inspector concerning the siting of a new town at Stevenage and to consider objections to that position. It was held that reference to bias was out of place in this context. However, while the result might well be the same, the reasoning of the Court of Appeal is to be preferred: complete impartiality could not be expected and the term impartiality when used in the context of a minister making a decision such as the siting of a new town, would not necessarily be the same as when applied to a magistrate deciding a case of nuisance.

While complete impartiality cannot always be expected in such a case, natural justice may still require that a minister hear representations. In the *Brent LBC* case,[25] the applicant local authorities claimed that they should be entitled to make representations to the Minister as to the way in which he should exercise his powers concerning local authority grants. Representations had been made prior to the passage of the legislation, but the court held that the Minister was still under a duty to act fairly in the way in which he exercised his discretion under the legislation. He should, therefore, have listened to representations made after the Act received the Royal Assent, but before he actually exercised his discretion. The court accepted that the Minister would not be expected to hear such representations as if he were a judge. The Minister would not be expected to approach the matter with an empty mind, but his mind should, in the words of the court, at least be ajar.

The problem adverted to above can also manifest itself at local as well as at central level. Thus, it has been held that licensing justices are not precluded from hearing an appeal for a licence, even though some of them had been concerned with an earlier application: the nature of the licensing function required those with local knowledge to form a policy for their area which they could have regard to when hearing individual applications, and the limited number of licensing justices meant that they might, on occasion hear an appeal when they had been concerned with an earlier application.[26]

---

[23] See the Committee on Ministers' Powers, Cmd. 4060 (1932), 78.
[24] *Franklin v Minister of Town and Country Planning* [1948] A.C. 87; *Turner v Allison* [1971] N.Z.L.R. 833. An expression of opinion by the adjudicator will not constitute bias, *R. v London County Council, Re The Empire Theatre* (1894) 71 L.T. 638; *R. v Nailsworth Licensing Justices Ex p. Bird* [1953] 1 W.L.R. 1046.
[25] *R. v Secretary of State for the Environment Ex p. Brent London Borough Council* [1982] Q.B. 593.
[26] *R. v Crown Court at Bristol Ex p. Cooper* [1990] 2 All E.R. 193. See also, *Darker Enterprises Ltd v Dacorum Borough Council* [1992] C.O.D. 465.

4. Bias: The Test for Bias

A. Past Confusion

13–006 There has been considerable confusion concerning the test for determining bias in cases other than those concerning pecuniary interest. Two tests were espoused by the courts, that of "real likelihood of bias", and that of "reasonable suspicion of bias".[27] In the 19th-century cases the former test held sway: if there was no pecuniary interest the court inquired whether there was a real likelihood of bias.[28] However in *McCarthy*,[29] Lord Hewart C.J. said that a reasonable suspicion of bias was sufficient to quash the determination. The tide appeared to be shifting back to the higher test for in two prominent cases the courts expressly adopted that criteria and disapproved of Lord Hewart C.J."s formulation.[30] Certainty was not however to last for in *Lannon* Lord Denning M.R. "rescued" Lord Hewart's reasonable suspicion test.[31] The root of the confusion for later cases was that Lord Denning M.R. began by approving the Hewart test and ended by talking of real likelihood. Not surprisingly later cases found *Lannon* difficult to interpret.[32]

B. From Gough to Porter

i. The Porter test

13–007 The House of Lords attempted to clarify the law in *Gough*.[33] It held that the same test should be applied in all cases of apparent bias, whether concerned with justices, tribunals, jurors, arbitrators and coroners. It held, in terms of the *degree of bias*, that the test should be whether there was a real danger of bias on the part of the relevant member of the tribunal, etc., in the sense that he might unfairly regard with favour or disfavour the case of the party under consideration by him. In terms of the *perspective from which bias should be viewed*, it was not necessary, said Lord Goff, to formulate the test in terms of the reasonable man, both because the court personified the reasonable man; and because the court had to ascertain the relevant circumstances from the evidence which might not be available to the ordinary observer.

This test was however criticised by courts in other common law jurisdictions, on the ground that it tended to emphasise the court's view of the facts and to place inadequate emphasis on the public perception of the

---

[27] R. Cranston, "Disqualification of Judges for Interest, Association or Opinion" [1979] P.L. 237; H. Rawlings, "The Test for the Nemo Judex Rule" [1980] P.L. 122.
[28] e.g. *Rand*, n.4; *R v Sunderland JJ.* [1901] 2 K.B. 357.
[29] *R. v Sussex Justices Ex p. McCarthy* [1924] 1 K.B. 256, 259.
[30] *R. v Camborne JJ Ex p. Pearce* [1955] 1 Q.B. 41; *Barnsley Licensing*, n.11.
[31] *Metropolitan Properties (FGC) Ltd v Lannon* [1969] 1 Q.B. 577, 598–600, 606.
[32] *Hannam v Bradford Corporation* [1970] 1 W.L.R. 937; *R. v Altrincham JJ Ex p. Pennington* [1975] Q.B. 549.
[33] *R. v Gough* [1993] A.C. 646; *R. v HM Coroner for Inner West London Ex p. Dallaglio and Lockwood Croft* [1994] 4 All E.R. 139.

incident being challenged.[34] The House of Lords indicated that it might review the test in *Gough*.[35] The Court of Appeal undertook such a review,[36] and its approach, with some modification, was confirmed in *Porter*.[37] This review was precipitated by continuing uncertainty over the correctness of the test, and its compatibility with the criterion used by the Strasbourg Court, which considered whether there was an objective risk of bias in the light of the circumstances identified by the court.[38]

The test adopted in *Porter* was whether, having regard to the relevant circumstances, as ascertained by the court, the fair-minded and informed observer, having considered the facts, would conclude that there was a real possibility that the tribunal was biased.[39] Courts have applied this test in subsequent cases.[40] Thus in *Davidson* it was held that a risk of apparent bias arose where a judge was called upon to rule judicially on the effect of legislation that he had drafted or promoted during the Parliamentary process.[41]

The courts have, on occasion, found that there was no bias according to this test by attributing quite detailed knowledge of the workings of the judicial system,[42] and the substantive law,[43] to the "fair-minded and informed observer". This renders it more difficult for the claimant to succeed. It was moreover held in *Condron*[44] that how the person to whom words were addressed had interpreted them was not determinative. The question was whether the fears expressed by the complainant were objectively justified. There was, said the court, a clear distinction between a legitimate predisposition towards a particular outcome and an illegitimate predetermination of the outcome. The court therefore rejected a claim of bias in relation to a casual statement by a member of the Welsh Assembly, prior to the hearing on the matter, that he was minded to agree with the report of a planning inspector concerning a mining operation to which the claimant objected.

---

[34] See, e.g., *Webb v R.* (1994) 181 C.L.R. 41.
[35] *Pinochet Ugarte (No.2)*, n.19, 136.
[36] *In re Medicaments and Related Classes of Goods (No.2)* [2001] 1 W.L.R. 700.
[37] *Porter v Magill* [2002] 2 A.C. 357.
[38] *Piersack v Belgium* (1982) 5 E.H.R.R. 169, 179–180; *Pullar v UK* (1996) 22 E.H.R.R. 391, 402–403.
[39] *Porter*, n.37, paras 102–103.
[40] *Taylor v Lawrence* [2002] 3 W.L.R. 640; *Lawal v Northern Spirit Ltd* [2002] I.C.R. 486; *Taylor v Williamsons (A Firm)* [2002] EWCA Civ 1380; *Hart v Relentless Records Ltd* [2002] EWHC 1984; *Jones v DAS Legal Expenses Insurance Co Ltd* [2003] EWCA Civ 1071; *Lawal v Northern Spirit Ltd* [2004] 1 All E.R. 187; *R. (on the application of Carroll) v Secretary of State for the Home Department* [2005] 1 W.L.R. 688; *Gillies v Secretary of State for Work and Pensions* [2006] 1 W.L.R. 781; *El Farargy v El Farargy* [2007] EWCA Civ 1149.
[41] *Davidson v Scottish Ministers (No.2)* [2004] H.R.L.R. 34.
[42] *Taylor v Williamsons*, n.40.
[43] *Hart*, n.40.
[44] *R. (on the application of Condron) v National Assembly for Wales* [2006] EWCA Civ 1573.

ii. The bodies subject to the Porter test

13–008   There is still some uncertainty as to whether the test in *Porter* will apply to all types of decision-maker. The test as formulated in *Gough* applied to the bodies specified in that judgment: justices, tribunals, jurors, arbitrators and coroners. The test as reformulated in *Porter* was framed in terms of tribunals. It is clear however that the House of Lords in *Porter* regarded itself as modifying the test as laid down in *Gough*, and therefore the *Porter* test covers at least the same range of bodies as in *Gough*.

This still leaves open the issue as to whether a different test might apply when bias is alleged against a body other than one in the above list. It has in the past been suggested that administrative decisions made by a local authority, which necessarily has an interest in the outcome, should only be overturned for bias when it acted in such a way prior to its decision that it could not properly have exercised its discretion, taking due account of its interest in the proceedings.[45]

These cases should however be read in the light of *Kirkstall*.[46] The case concerned alleged bias by members of an urban development corporation in relation to planning. Sedley J. acknowledged that members of an elected or appointed body might well take up office with publicly stated views on policy issues. This was acceptable provided that the prior view was legitimate, and provided that it did not amount to predetermination of the matter. The issue of predetermination was, however, separate from that of bias. An allegation of bias would be determined by the normal test, which is now that laid down in *Porter*.

It is likely that the courts will follow this approach. The general test for bias will be that laid down in *Porter*.[47] The test can be applied so as to take account of the different situations of for example a tribunal and a local authority. It will still be open for an applicant to claim that the decision of a local authority should be open to challenge on the ground of predetermination.

5. Bias: Exceptions

A. Necessity

13–009   The normal rules against bias will be displaced where the individual whose impartiality is called in question is the only person empowered to act. Thus

---

[45] *R. v St. Edmundsbury Borough Council Ex p. Investors in Industry Commercial Properties Ltd* [1985] 1 W.L.R. 1157; *R. v Sevenoaks District Council Ex p. Terry* [1985] 3 All E.R. 226; *Darker Enterprises Ltd v Dacorum Borough Council* [1992] C.O.D. 465; *R. v Chesterfield Borough Council Ex p. Darker Enterprises* [1992] C.O.D. 466.

[46] *R. v Secretary of State for the Environment and William Morrison Supermarkets Plc Ex p. Kirkstall Valley Campaign Ltd* [1996] 3 All E.R. 304. See also *R. (on the application of Ware) v Neath Port Talbot CBC* [2007] EWHC 913.

[47] This approach fits moreover with cases such as *Condron*, n.44, which applied the *Porter* test to the Welsh Assembly, and with *R. (on the application of Georgiou) v Enfield LBC* [2004] EWHC Admin 779, which applied the *Porter* test to a local authority.

in the *Dimes*[48] case it was held that the Lord Chancellor's signature on an enrolment order which was necessary in order for the case to proceed to the House of Lords, was unaffected by his shareholding in the company because no other person was empowered to sign. Similarly, in *Phillips*[49] it was held that the Governor of a colony could validly assent to an Act of Indemnity which protected, inter alia, his own actions because the relevant Act had to receive this signature.

B. Statute

Parliament has made statutory exceptions to the rule against bias, allowing justices to sit who have some type of interest in the subject-matter of the action.[50] The courts have construed such statutory provisions strictly.[51] Thus in *Shaw*[52] s.258 of the Public Health Act 1872, which enabled a justice of the peace to sit even though a member of a local authority, was held not to protect him where he acted in a prosecutorial and adjudicatory capacity. In other areas statute may, for example, create an offence to take part in a decision on a matter in relation to which a person has a pecuniary interest, and yet will allow acts thus made to remain valid.[53]

13–010

C. Waiver

It is permissible for an individual to waive the interests of an adjudicator,[54] and the courts were quick to infer such a waiver.[55] Later courts have been more reluctant to so infer, particularly where the applicant did not know of the right to object at that stage. In order for a waiver to be valid the party waiving the right had to be aware of all the material facts and the consequences of the choice open to him and should be given a fair opportunity to reach an unpressured decision.[56] This restriction on waiver is to be welcomed. Such a surrender of rights should not be inferred lightly. It is in fact open to question whether it should be allowed at all, at least in certain types of cases. The premise behind the ability to waive is that it is only the individual who is concerned, and thus if that person "chooses" to ignore the fact that the adjudicator is an interested party then so much the worse for the

13–011

---

[48] (1852) 3 H.L.C. 759, 787.
[49] *Phillips v Eyre* (1870) L.R. 6 Q.B. 1. See also *Re Manchester (Ringway Airport) Compulsory Purchase Order* (1935) 153 L.T. 219; *Jeffs v New Zealand Dairy Production and Marketing Board* [1967] 1 A.C. 551; *cf. Wilkinson v Barking Corporation* [1948] 1 K.B. 721.
[50] See, e.g. Justices Jurisdiction Act 1742.
[51] *Frome United Breweries Co. Ltd v Bath Justices* [1926] A.C. 586.
[52] n.14; *cf. Soane*, n .15.
[53] Local Government Act 1972 ss.82, 94, 97. Similar provisions in licensing legislation have been strictly construed, *Barnsley Licensing Justices*, n.11. It is unclear whether actual bias would have to be shown in order to circumvent the statutory provisions, see Rawlings, n.27, 125–126.
[54] *Nailsworth Licensing Justices*, n.24.
[55] *R. v Williams Ex p. Phillips* [1914] 1 K.B. 608.
[56] *R. v Essex Justices Ex p. Perkins* [1917] 2 K.B. 475; *Pinochet Ugarte (No.2)*, n.19; *Smith v Kvaerner Cementation Foundations Ltd (General Council of the Bar intervening)* [2007] 1 W.L.R. 370.

applicant. However there may well be a wider interest at issue, in that it may be contrary to the public interest for decisions to be made where there may be a likelihood of favour to another influencing the determination.

6. THE HRA AND THE ECHR

A. Article 6(1): The ECHR Legal Requirements

13–012 The Human Rights Act 1998 brought many Convention rights into domestic law. This includes art.6 ECHR, which provides the guarantees of a fair trial. Article 6(1) provides that,

> "In the determination of his civil rights and obligations or of any criminal charge against him, everyone is entitled to a fair and public hearing within a reasonable time by an independent and impartial tribunal established by law. Judgment shall be pronounced publicly but the press and the public may be excluded from all or part of the trial in the interests of morals, public order or national security in a democratic society, where the interests of juveniles or the protection of the private life of the parties so require, or to the extent strictly necessary in the opinion of the court in special circumstances where the publicity would prejudice the interests of justice."

The previous chapter considered the impact of art.6 on the applicability and content of process rights.[57] The present discussion is concerned with the requirement that there should be an "independent and impartial tribunal established by law".

It is clear from the Strasbourg jurisprudence that in deciding whether a body is independent regard will be had to the manner of its appointment, its term of office, the existence of guarantees against outside pressure, and whether the body presents an appearance of independence.[58] A decision of a court or tribunal will not satisfy this requirement if, for example, some other authority is able to decide whether or not the judgment of the court or tribunal should be implemented,[59] nor where the court or tribunal is biased. The requirement of "independence" also means that the decision-maker should be independent from the parties and the executive.[60] This has important consequences for decisions made by, for example, local

[57] See above, paras 12–018—12–019, 12–043.
[58] *Bryan v UK* (1996) 21 E.H.R.R. 342; *Kingsley v UK* (2001) 33 E.H.R.R. 288, (2002) 35 E.H.R.R. 177; *Stefan v UK* (1998) 25 E.H.R.R. CD 130.
[59] *Van de Hark v The Netherlands* (1994) 18 E.H.R.R. 481.
[60] *Ringeisen v Austria* (1979–80) 1 E.H.R.R. 455.

authorities and government departments, since these will normally not satisfy this requirement.[61]

It is clear also from the Strasbourg jurisprudence that this requirement of independence does not have to be satisfied at every stage of the decision-making process. Where an administrative body does not comply with the duty imposed by art.6 it must be subject to the control of a judicial body that does so comply.[62] It has been recognised by both the Commission and the European Court of Human Rights (ECtHR) that many initial decisions are made by local authorities or government departments. The compatibility of such decision-making with art.6 then depends upon whether there are adequate appeal rights, or judicial review, to a judicial body that has "full jurisdiction" and provides the guarantees of art.6(1). The Article does not require that the appellate or review body has the power to substitute judgment on issues of expediency or the merits.[63] The ECtHR will, when assessing the sufficiency of review or appeal, consider the subject-matter in issue within its entire statutory context.

Thus in the context of an appeal from an inspector's decision in the planning sphere,[64] the ECtHR found that a planning inspector was not independent for the purposes of art.6, because of the minister's power over his determinations. It held that the sufficiency of review would be judged taking account of factors such as the subject-matter of the decision, the manner in which that decision was arrived at, and the content of the dispute. The Strasbourg Court stressed in *Bryan* the "safeguards" attendant on the procedure before the inspector. These were the quasi-judicial nature of the decision-making process, the duty to exercise independent judgment, the fact that the inspector made decisions in accord with principles of openness, fairness and impartiality and the requirement that the inspector must not be subject to any improper influence.[65] It was sufficient that the High Court had power to overturn findings of fact if they were irrational. This was the limit of what could be expected given the specialised nature of the subject-matter, and the nature of the preceding inquiry.

B. Article 6(1) in Domestic Courts: Fairness and Waiver

The centrality of the requirement that the tribunal should be independent and impartial was vividly emphasised in *Millar*.[66] The defendants were convicted by temporary sheriffs in Scotland. In another case it was held that temporary sheriffs were not independent and impartial for the purposes of art.6(1). The convicted parties contended, in reliance on that case, that their prosecutions had been unlawful, since the Lord Advocate had no power to

13–013

---

[61] See, e.g., *Tre Traktorer AB v Sweden* (1991) 13 E.H.R.R. 309; *Benthem v Netherlands* (1986) 8 E.H.R.R. 1; *Bryan*, n.58.

[62] *Albert and Le Compte v Belgium* (1983) 5 E.H.R.R. 533.

[63] *Kaplan v UK* (1994) 76A D.R. 90; *ISKON v UK* (1994) 76A D.R. 90. See, however, *W v UK* (1987) 10 E.H.R.R. 29.

[64] *Bryan*, n.58.

[65] *Bryan*, n.58, para.46.

[66] *Millar v Dickson (Procurator Fiscal, Elgin)* [2002] 1 W.L.R. 1615.

do an act incompatible with a Convention right. It was argued by way of defence that the accused had in fact received fair trials, since the critical issue under art.6(1) was the fairness of the proceedings as a whole.

The Privy Council held that the right of accused in criminal proceedings to be tried by an independent and impartial tribunal could not be compromised, unless validly waived by the accused. The appearance of independence and impartiality was just as important as whether those qualities existed in fact. A claim that art.6(1) had been breached could not, therefore, be met by asking whether the proceedings overall had been fair. An accused could moreover only be held to have waived art.6(1) by a voluntary, informed and unequivocal election by a party not to claim a right, or raise an objection.

C. Article 6(1) in Domestic Courts: Planning and the Distinction between Policy and Fact-Finding

13–014   The impact of art.6(1) on the freedom of the legislature to choose who should make decisions in the planning sphere was a central issue in *Alconbury*.[67] It was alleged that the role of the Secretary of State for the Environment, Transport and the Regions (SSETR) in making decisions relating to different pieces of legislation was inconsistent with art.6(1) ECHR. One case[68] involved decisions by the minister to call in applications for planning permission.[69] The local council normally decides planning applications, but the minister however has the power to call in such applications and to make the decision himself. Another case[70] involved what is known as a recovered appeal against a refusal of planning permission.[71] The SSETR decided that he should hear and determine the appeal against the refusal of planning permission, instead of the inspector. The third case[72] was concerned with proposed highway orders, and related compulsory purchase orders, in connection with a scheme to improve the A34/M4 junction.

The Minister accepted that he was not an independent tribunal for the purposes of art.6. He argued, however, that the decision-making process as a whole, including judicial review, complied with art.6. He relied on the *Bryan* case,[73] where the Strasbourg Court held that an inspector did not constitute an independent tribunal because the minister could revoke the inspector's power. It found nonetheless that the courts' powers of appeal and review were sufficient to ensure that the decision-making process as a whole complied with art.6. The minister argued in the alternative that if the whole process did not comply with art.6 then the court should expand its

[67] *R. (Alconbury Developments Ltd) v Secretary of State for the Environment, Transport and the Regions (SSETR); R. (Holding & Barnes Plc) v SSETR.; SSETR v Legal and General Assurance Society Ltd* [2003] 2 A.C. 295.
[68] *Holding and Barnes.*
[69] Town and Country Planning Act 1990, s.77.
[70] *Alconbury Developments Ltd.*
[71] Town and Country Planning Act 1990, ss.78, 79.
[72] *Legal and General.*
[73] *Bryan*, n.58.

powers of judicial review pursuant to ss.3 and 6 HRA, so as to make it do so.

The Divisional Court found for the claimants.[74] The House of Lords overturned this decision.[75] Their Lordships accepted that the minister was not an impartial tribunal as required by the Convention. They held however that the decision-making process taken as a whole was compatible with the Convention, since there was sufficient review of legality through judicial review. Two issues were central to this part of the case: the role and position of the minister, and the sufficiency of control by way of review.

On the first issue, *the role and position of the minister*, there was a marked difference of view between the Divisional Court and the House of Lords. Both courts regarded the legality of the ministerial power to make policy, and adjudicate thereon, as the nub of the issue. The premise of the Divisional Court's judgment was that this duality of function was wrong. It felt that the minister made important policy decisions in these areas, and also adjudicated on individual matters, without there being sufficient safeguards to prevent him acting in his own self-interest when making such decisions.[76] The premise of the House of Lords' judgment was precisely the opposite. Their Lordships felt that the ministerial role was quite proper. Lord Slynn refused to accept that a policy-maker could not be a decision-maker, or that the final decision could not be that of a democratically elected person or body.[77] Lord Nolan held that a degree of central control was essential to orderly planning. Parliament had entrusted this task to the minister, who was accountable to it. To substitute for the minister an "independent and impartial body with no electoral accountability would not only be a recipe for chaos: it would be profoundly undemocratic".[78] Lord Clyde stated that once "it is recognised that there should be a national planning policy under a central supervision, it is consistent with democratic principle that the responsibility for that work should lie on the shoulders of a minister answerable to Parliament".[79] Lord Hutton noted that the minister would be answerable to Parliament for the exercise of his power.[80] Lord Hoffmann was most forceful in this respect. He accepted, with the Divisional Court, that the minister was not an independent and impartial tribunal. Lord Hoffmann however strongly disagreed with the lower court that it was objectionable in terms of art.6 that the minister should be judge in his own cause where his policy was in play. For Lord Hoffmann, the question was not whether he should be a judge in his own cause, but whether he should be regarded as a judge at all.[81] His Lordship was clear that he should not be

13–015

---

[74] *R. (on the Application of Holding and Barnes Plc) v Secretary of State for the Environment, Transport and the Regions* (2001) 3 L.G.L.R. 21.
[75] n.67.
[76] *Alconbury*, n.74, para.56.
[77] *Alconbury*, n.67, para.48.
[78] *Alconbury*, n.67, para.60.
[79] *Alconbury*, n.67, para.141. See also, paras 142–144, 159.
[80] *Alconbury*, n.67, para.176.
[81] *Alconbury*, n.67, para.124.

thought of in this way: the minister's constitutional role was to formulate and apply government policy.[82]

The differing views on the propriety of the minister's role had a marked affect on the second issue, which was the *sufficiency of the controls provided by judicial review*. We have seen that the Strasbourg jurisprudence stipulated that the requirements of art.6 could be met either if the initial decision-maker was independent and impartial, or if there was control by a judicial body with full jurisdiction, which provided the guarantees of art.6.[83] In *Alconbury* the Divisional Court found that the "safeguards" mentioned in *Bryan* were insufficient where the minister, rather than the inspector, made the decision. This was because he was free to make his own decision after taking account of internal legal and policy elucidation.[84] Given that this was so the lower court felt that restricted review was not sufficient to make the decision-making process as a whole compatible with art.6.[85]

The House of Lords reached the opposite conclusion. Lord Slynn emphasised the detailed procedural rules that applied when the minister made a decision on a called in planning application, or recovered appeal. These rules were pertinent when the minister differed from the inspector on a matter of fact, or took into account new evidence, and was disposed to disagree with the inspector. He was required to notify persons entitled to appear at the inquiry, to give reasons for his differences with the inspector and to allow written representations.[86] It was this, combined with the rules on judicial review, which Lord Slynn felt to be determinative in concluding that the procedure as a whole was compatible with art.6.[87] Lord Clyde examined the factors mentioned in *Bryan*, which were relevant to the sufficiency of control exercised by way of review. He considered the subject matter of the dispute, the manner in which the decisions were taken, and the content of the dispute. His conclusion was that, judged by these criteria, judicial review was sufficient to ensure that the decision-making process as a whole complied with art.6.[88] Lord Hutton was of the opinion that the principles in *Bryan* could be applied to the instant case, notwithstanding that the minister rather than the inspector made the decision.[89]

13–016   It was Lord Hoffmann who considered this issue in most depth. He held that the lower court had seriously misunderstood the relevance of the "safeguards" mentioned in *Bryan*, by finding that they were necessary before appeal or review could satisfy art.6 whatever the issues actually were.[90] This was, he said, the opposite of what had been intended in *Bryan* itself. Where the question was one of policy or expediency these

---

[82] *Alconbury*, n.67, para.127.
[83] *Albert*, n.62. See also *R. (Kehoe) v Secretary of State for Work and Pensions* [2004] Q.B. 1378.
[84] *Alconbury*, n.74, para.94.
[85] *Alconbury*, n.74, para.95.
[86] Town and Country Planning (Inquiries Procedure) (England) Rules 2000 r.17(5).
[87] *Alconbury*, n.67, paras 16–19, 49–56.
[88] *Alconbury*, n.67, paras 155–60.
[89] *Alconbury*, n.67, paras 188–89.
[90] *Alconbury*, n.67, para.116.

"safeguards" were irrelevant. The reason why judicial review was sufficient in such cases had nothing to do with the "safeguards", but depended on respect for the ministerial decision on matters of expediency. The fact that the parties were not privy to departmental processes of decision-making was "no more than one would expect",[91] given that the constitutional role of the minister in formulating and applying government policy required the advice and assistance of civil servants. It was only where findings of fact, and evaluation of fact, were in issue that the safeguards were essential for the acceptance of limited review of fact by the appellate tribunal.[92] In this respect the procedural rules on planning, combined with controls on fact-finding through judicial review, were sufficient to satisfy art.6.[93]

The application of art.6 in the context of planning has continued to give rise to problems. The discussion in cases after *Alconbury* focused on whether the requirements of art.6 are satisfied where the initial decision is not made by a planning inspector, as was the case in *Alconbury* itself, but by a local planning authority. This issue arose in *Kathro*,[94] where the applicants argued that the grant of planning permission by the local authority did not comply with art.6, notwithstanding that the authority's decisions were subject to judicial review. It was accepted that such a planning authority was not independent for the purposes of art.6. The issue before the court was whether the procedure taken as a whole, including judicial review, was nonetheless compliant with art.6. Richards J. concluded that the finding in *Alconbury* that the decision-making process was compatible with art.6 was based to a significant extent on the fact-finding role of the inspector, with its attendant procedural safeguards. There was, said Richards J., no equivalent to these safeguards in the decision-making process of the local planning authority. There was a right to make representations, and submit evidence, and persons could be heard orally by the relevant committee. There was however "nothing like a public inquiry, no opportunity for cross-examination and no formal procedure for evaluating the evidence and making findings of fact".[95] This considerably reduced the scope for effective scrutiny of the planning decision by way of judicial review.

The issue came before the court again in *Friends Provident*,[96] in the context of a challenge to the grant of planning permission by the local council for a large retail complex in Norwich. It was accepted that the local council was not independent for the purposes of art.6. It was argued that the only way for the procedure to be compatible with art.6 was for the Secretary of State to call in the planning application, and establish a public inquiry presided over by an inspector. Forbes J. disagreed. He recognised that a

---

[91] *Alconbury*, n.67, para.127.
[92] *Alconbury*, n.67, para.117.
[93] *Alconbury*, n.67, para.128. See also, *R. (on the application of Aggregate Industries UK Ltd) v English Nature* [2002] A.C.D 67, para.12.
[94] *R. (on the application of Kathro, Evans, Evans, Grant, Llantwit Fadre Community Council) v Rhondda Cynon Taff County Borough Council* [2002] Env. L.R. 15.
[95] *Kathro*, n.94, para.28.
[96] *Friends Provident Life & Pensions Ltd v Secretary of State for Transport, Local Government and Regions* [2002] 1 W.L.R. 1450.

decision made by a local authority, combined with judicial review, might not comply with art.6 where there were contested issues of primary fact.[97] He felt however that the principal issue in the present case was the retail impact assessment that was made as part of the planning decision. This did not, said Forbes J., "give rise to the type of investigation of fact which requires the safeguards attaching to a public inquiry before an independent inspector" in order to be in compliance with art.6, since that assessment was principally a matter of "local planning judgment, policy and expediency".[98]

D. Article 6(1) in Domestic Courts: Housing and the Re-evaluation of the Policy/Fact-Finding Distinction

13–017   It would be mistaken to think that the impact of art.6 has been confined to the planning sphere. The courts have had to grapple with it in other areas, such as housing. The courts' general approach was to apply the distinction between policy and fact-finding, developed in the planning cases, to this area.[99]

This approach will have to be reappraised in the light of the House of Lords' decision in *Begum*.[100] The claimant was offered housing as a homeless person, but refused it on the ground that the area in which it was situated suffered from drugs and racism. Her decision to decline the offer was reviewed by an officer of the local authority, who found that the offer was suitable. She appealed to the county court, which found that the failure of the local authority to refer the matter to an independent tribunal constituted a breach of art.6. The House of Lords held to the contrary.

Lord Hoffmann gave the main judgment in the House of Lords. He agreed that the reviewing officer did not constitute an independent and impartial tribunal for the purposes of art.6, since she was an employee of the local authority, and hence could not be independent when deciding whether it had discharged its duty to the applicant. The live issue was, therefore, whether this was cured by the right of appeal to the county court, so as to satisfy art.6. The county court's jurisdiction was in substance the same as that of the High Court in judicial review. It was however acknowledged that the county court could not make fresh findings of fact. The applicant argued that this meant that it could not satisfy art.6: when a case turned on contested facts it was necessary either that the appellate body should have full jurisdiction to review the facts, or that the primary decision-making process should have sufficient safeguards to make it virtually judicial.[101] Reliance was placed[102] on a dictum of Lord Hoffmann in *Alconbury*,[103] that the safeguards mentioned in *Bryan* would be required in relation to the

---

[97] *Friends Provident*, n.96, para.93.
[98] *Friends Provident*, n.96, para.94.
[99] *Runa Begum v Tower Hamlets LBC* [2002] 2 All E.R. 668; *R. (on the application of the Personal Representatives of Beeson) v Dorset CC* [2002] EWCA Civ 448.
[100] *Runa Begum v Tower Hamlets LBC* [2003] 2 A.C. 430.
[101] *Begum*, n.100, para.37.
[102] *Begum*, n.100, para.39.
[103] *Alconbury*, n.67, para.117.

evaluation of facts. Lord Hoffmann in *Begum* stated that this was an incautious remark,[104] and adopted a rather different approach to the policy/fact distinction that he had articulated in *Alconbury*.

Lord Hoffmann held that the rule of law required that decisions made **13–018** about private rights, and breaches of the criminal law, must be entrusted to the judicial branch of government. This basic principle did not yield to utilitarian considerations that it would be cheaper to have such matters decided by administrators. The possibility of an appeal could not compensate for the lack of independence and impartiality on the part of the primary decision-maker.[105] Matters were however different in relation to social welfare or regulatory functions, such as licensing or the grant of planning permission. In these areas regard could be had to considerations, such as efficient administration, democratic accountability and the sovereignty of Parliament. It was, in particular, legitimate for Parliament not to over-judicialise dispute procedures. It would therefore not be appropriate to require that findings of fact should be made by a body other than the primary decision-maker; there did not need to be a mechanism for independent findings of fact or full appeal.[106]

This left open the issue as to precisely how the shortcomings of the reviewing officer, who did not satisfy art.6, were cured by having regard to the entire procedure, including the role of the county court. Lord Hoffmann's response was that even though there did not need to be a mechanism for independent findings of fact, or full appeal, the overall procedure had to be lawful and fair.[107] This was to be determined in part by the procedure attendant upon the initial decision. Thus, even though the reviewing officer might not be independent for the purposes of art.6, the rules regulating the way in which such reviews were conducted would be relevant for the purpose of deciding whether the overall process was lawful and fair. The other safeguard to be taken into account in this respect was the supervisory power of the county court judge, which was, as stated above, akin to judicial review. Lord Hoffmann acknowledged that it was open to such a court to adopt a more intensive scrutiny of the rationality of the reviewing officer's decision, by considering whether it had been made on a misunderstanding or ignorance of an established and relevant fact, or where rights were at stake by using proportionality.[108] Lord Hoffmann nonetheless declined to say that this was necessary. He held that where no human rights other than Article 6 were engaged then conventional judicial review would suffice.[109]

Space precludes a detailed examination of the implications, positive and normative, of the above jurisprudence.[110] Suffice it to say for the present that while the desire not to over-judicialise the administrative process may be

---

[104] *Begum*, n.100, para.40.
[105] *Begum*, n.100, para.42.
[106] *Begum*, n.100, paras 43–47.
[107] *Begum*, n.100, para.47.
[108] *Begum*, n.100, para.49.
[109] *Begum*, n.100, para.50.
[110] P. Craig, "The HRA, Article 6 and Procedural Rights" [2003] P.L. 753.

laudable, the approach adopted in *Begum* may nonetheless be problematic. It will require, in terms of positive law, the drawing of difficult lines between cases involving private rights, and social/regulatory schemes. This may be especially difficult in circumstances where some aspects of a single area, such as enforcement of planning notices, are held to be akin to cases of private rights, while others, such as planning permissions, are not.[111] It raises moreover important normative issues as to the type of procedural protection that should apply in cases involving private rights, and social/regulatory policy.

E. Article 6(1) in Domestic Courts: Developments since Begum

13–019   It is in any event clear that the reasoning in *Begum* may have to be re-evaluated in the light of subsequent case law by the ECtHR and its application by UK courts.

The relevant ECtHR decision is *Tsfayo*.[112] The applicant for housing and council tax benefit failed to submit her benefit renewal form in time. Her claim was rejected by the Council because she had failed to show "good cause" why she had not claimed benefits earlier. Her appeal to the Housing Benefit Review Board was dismissed. She sought judicial review on the grounds that the HBRB was not an independent and impartial tribunal. The ECtHR reviewed the authorities and gave two reasons for deciding that there had been a violation of art.6(1), notwithstanding the availability of judicial review.[113]

First, the decision-making process was significantly different from that in earlier cases such as *Kingsley*, *Bryan* and *Runa Begum*. In those cases, the issues to be determined required a measure of professional knowledge or experience and the exercise of administrative discretion pursuant to wider policy aims. In *Tsfayo* by way of contrast the HBRB was deciding a simple question of fact, whether there was "good cause" for the applicant's delay in making a claim. This was moreover not merely incidental to the reaching of broader judgments of policy or expediency, which it was for the democratically accountable authority to take. Second, the HBRB was not merely lacking in independence from the executive, but was directly connected to one of the parties to the dispute, since it included five councillors from the local authority which would be required to pay the benefit if it was awarded. The ECtHR concluded that the HBRB's procedures were not adequate to overcome this fundamental lack of objective impartiality.

The implications of *Tsfayo* were apparent in the Court of Appeal decision in *Wright*.[114] The Care Standards Act 2000 introduced a listing system for the protection of vulnerable adults. Care workers who were included on the lists were prevented from working as carers of vulnerable adults. Under s.82(4) if the Secretary of State felt that it might be appropriate for the

---

[111] *Begum*, n.100, paras 41–42.
[112] *Tsfayo v UK* [2007] L.G.R. 1; J Howell Q.C., "*Alconbury* Crumbles" [2007] J.R. 9.
[113] *Tsfayo*, n.112, paras 46–47.
[114] *R. (on the application of Wright) v Secretary of State for Health* [2007] EWCA Civ 999.

worker to be included on the list from information submitted with the reference, he had to include the worker provisionally in the list pending a determination of the reference. The evidence was that the Secretary of State took several months between receiving a reference and making the decision required in s.82(4). An aggrieved worker could, inter alia, try to convince the Secretary of State that the listing was unjustified. The issue was whether the provisional listing procedure was compatible with art.6 ECHR.

The Court of Appeal held that it was not. It followed, said Dyson L.J., from *Tsfayo* that in deciding whether judicial review could cure an earlier breach of process rights, it was important to have regard to the nature of the earlier breach. The more serious the failure to accord a hearing by an independent and impartial tribunal, the less likely it was that this could be cured via judicial review.[115] In the instant case the failure to accord care workers the opportunity to make any representations before inclusion on the Secretary of State's list constituted denial of one of the fundamental elements of the right to be heard and this could not be made good via subsequent judicial review. The Secretary of State should therefore be required to give care workers the opportunity to make representations before inclusion on the list, unless this would expose vulnerable adults to the risk of harm.

7. A COMMON LAW REQUIREMENT OF "AN INDEPENDENT AND IMPARTIAL TRIBUNAL"

The discussion thus far has focused on the traditional concept of bias **13–020** developed at common law, and the requirement for an independent and impartial tribunal that flows from art.6 of the ECHR. There is however authority for the proposition that the latter is also a requirement of the common law. The Court of Appeal held this to be so in the *Medicaments* case,[116] although the claim in that case related to bias rather than structural independence.

The issue of independence came more squarely before the court in *Bewry*.[117] The case was concerned with housing benefit, and whether the Housing Benefit Review Board, which included members of the council that had rejected the initial application, was independent. Moses J. considered the existence of a common law right to an independent and impartial tribunal because the facts occurred before the HRA came into force. He held that the "right of review of a determination of statutory entitlement is akin to the right of access to a court and carries with it a right to an independent

---

[115] *Wright*, n.114, para.105.
[116] *Medicaments*, n.36, para.35.
[117] *R. (on the application of Bewry) v Norwich City Council* [2002] H.R.L.R. 2.

and impartial review".[118] The common law therefore provided no lesser protection than the ECHR.[119] This reasoning fits with the general stance of the courts prior to the HRA, where they made it clear that the common law protected the rights contained in the ECHR.[120]

It might be thought that the common law recognition of this right was no longer of importance, now that the HRA has come into force. This conclusion would be premature. The protection afforded by art.6 only applies where there is a civil right. Moses J.'s formulation of the common law requirement of an independent and impartial tribunal is that it applies in cases of statutory entitlement. There is however no reason in principle why the common law requirement should necessarily be limited to cases where the applicant has a right. It may be fortuitous whether the legislation is framed in terms of a right, or the grant of discretion. It may be debatable whether the statutory language should be read as conferring a right or discretion. The normative arguments in favour of an independent and impartial tribunal are, moreover, strong even where the public body has been accorded discretion. The absence of a substantive right should not lead to the conclusion that this important procedural guarantee is inapplicable.

---

[118] *Bewry*, n.117, para.29, relying on *Medicaments*, n.36, para.35, and *R. v Secretary of State for the Home Department Ex p. Saleem* [2001] 1 W.L.R. 443, 457–458.
[119] The reasoning in *Bewry* was questioned in *R. (McLellan) v Bracknell Forest BC* [2002] Q.B. 1129, paras 75–78, but these doubts appear to relate to the application of the common law principle, rather than its existence.
[120] See below, Ch.17.

CHAPTER 14

JURISDICTION AND ERROR OF LAW

1. INTRODUCTION

The problem that concerns us now can be expressed as follows. A tribunal is **14–001** given authority to decide upon a particular issue. If a furnished tenancy exists the tribunal may adjudicate on the rent. If a person is unfairly dismissed she may be awarded compensation. All such grants of authority may be expressed in the following manner: if X exists the tribunal may or shall do Y. X may consist of a number of different elements, factual, legal and discretionary. An individual wishes to complain of the tribunal's findings. In what circumstances should the court say that the tribunal has exceeded its power?

Judicial review has traditionally dealt not with the correctness of the findings as such, but with their legality. For a full rehearing of the merits, appeal, a creature of statute, is required. The inherent power of the courts to review the findings of a tribunal has, by way of contrast, been concerned with ensuring that the decision-maker remains within its jurisdiction. Whether the distinction between review and appeal is sustainable will be considered in due course.

There is a real difficulty in deciding which matters should be regarded as jurisdictional. If review is drawn too *narrowly* then the spectre is raised of the tribunal becoming a power unto itself, of it adjudicating upon matters widely different from those that the legislature intended, and yet being free from control. The Albert Hall is deemed to be a furnished tenancy and a rent set for it. However, if review is drawn too *broadly* it will approximate to appeal on the merits. Almost every finding made by the tribunal will be binding only if judged right by the reviewing court. The grant of jurisdiction to a tribunal or other decision-maker has, in the past, been thought to involve a power to come to a decision which in the opinion of a reviewing court may well be wrong. If the scope of review becomes too broad this is effectively destroyed. How far any such latitude still exists will be considered below.

14–002   The conceptual basis for judicial review over the conditions of jurisdiction has already been examined,[1] and reference should be made to that discussion when reading what follows. In essence the courts' control over jurisdiction was premised upon the assumption that they were thereby effectuating the will of Parliament. They were ensuring that the tribunal or authority remained within the boundaries of what Parliament intended it to examine by ensuring that those conditions were present. However, there are two problems with this conceptual basis for judicial intervention.

First, it furnished little guidance as to the *extent* of control over the conditions of jurisdiction. The dilemma is evident from the preceding example. In a certain sense, all the elements which comprise X, condition the tribunal's power to decide upon Y. The statute says, explicitly or implicitly, if X you may or shall do Y. However, to accept that the reviewing court should be the ultimate arbiter of the meaning of all the elements comprising the X factor would cause review to become very like appeal. Such an approach moreover presumes that the meaning to be ascribed to all elements which comprise the X factor is to be determined by the reviewing court in preference to the tribunal. There are, as we shall see, objections to accepting that this should always be so.

The second problem with the traditional conceptual basis of review is, as we shall see, that it is no longer self-evident that the courts use it. Error of law is the organising principle in the more recent case law.

This chapter will begin by examining the various theories about jurisdiction. There will then be an analysis of the case law from both the 19th and 20th centuries. The final part of the chapter will consider some of the broader policy arguments concerning the scope of review.

Devolution raises important issues concerning the jurisdictional competence of the Welsh Assembly and the Scottish Parliament. Because these issues are integrally related to the overall scheme of devolution for Wales and Scotland they are considered within the earlier chapter dealing with this topic.[2]

2. THEORIES OF JURISDICTION

14–003   A general word concerning the theories will be helpful in understanding what follows, and should be borne in mind when reading the detailed analysis.

The first two theories attempted to draw the following distinction. Errors which related to the *type* or *kind* or *scope* of case into which a tribunal could inquire were regarded as jurisdictional; errors which related to the *truth* or

---

[1] See Ch.1.
[2] See above, Ch.7, and P. Craig and M. Walters, "The Courts, Devolution and Judicial Review" [1999] P.L. 274.

detail of the findings that it made were categorised as non-jurisdictional. The line between the two was said to provide the justification for judicial review. The court only intervened when the tribunal was outside the "scope" assigned to it by the legislature. The judiciary would not intervene if the tribunal had simply made an error within its assigned area, since this would eradicate the distinction between review of legality and appeal. The first two theories drew this distinction in different ways, and, as we shall see, the dichotomy may not be capable of being drawn satisfactorily at all.

An analysis of theories based on the jurisdictional/non-jurisdictional distinction is important, since it is impossible to understand the current law without some understanding of the case law which preceded it, and of the theories upon which that case law was based. The following analysis is not predicated upon the assumption that the courts which employed the jurisdictional/non-jurisdictional distinction always used it in a purely logical manner. It is readily apparent that some courts used the very ambiguity inherent in that dichotomy in an instrumental fashion: the decision whether to label an X factor as jurisdictional or non-jurisdictional was influenced by a judicial desire to intervene or not as the case may be. Examination of the theories is nonetheless important. It would be wrong to assume that all or even most judges viewed the distinction in a purely instrumental fashion. It is manifestly clear from a reading of the case law that many believed that a real division could be drawn in analytical terms.

The more recent approaches, by way of contrast, largely ignore any distinction between scope and truth/detail. Judicial intervention is based on error of law as the organising principle. While this approach, by rejecting the distinction between jurisdictional and non-jurisdictional errors of law, avoids the difficulties created by the earlier theories it is not unproblematic. Thus, as we shall see, there are crucial issues of classification to be resolved, such as the division between law and fact. There are also important policy issues which require discussion, such as whether the courts are always better suited to resolve issues of law than are the tribunals which they are reviewing.

A. Collateral Fact Doctrine
Until relatively recently the most widely accepted theoretical explanation of which issues should be held to go to jurisdiction was the collateral or preliminary or jurisdictional fact doctrine. It has a long historical lineage, but the most sophisticated explanation was that given by Diplock L.J.,[3] as he then was. The exposition is more easily understood if broken down into a number of stages.

14–004

---

[3] *Anisminic Ltd v Foreign Compensation Commission* [1968] 2 Q.B. 862, 887–905. *cf.* Lord Diplock's view in *Re Racal Communications Ltd* [1981] A.C. 374.

i. Preliminary questions and merits

14–005 A decision is "correct" if it is made by that person within the legal system to whose opinion on the existence of fact or law effect will be given by the executive. A tribunal is given power on the existence of certain conditions. There are certain preliminary questions that it must decide before it can proceed to the merits. These include matters such as whether the tribunal was properly constituted and whether the case was of a kind referred to in the statute. The tribunal must make an initial determination on such matters, but its decision is not conclusive. If the court on review believes that the requisite situation spoken of in the statute did not exist then the conclusion reached by the tribunal will be a nullity. Such preliminary questions can involve *fact, law* or *discretion.*

ii. The ambit of the preliminary question

14–006 The crucial issue is therefore the ambit of the preliminary or collateral question. The nature of this dilemma can best be described as follows. Let us revert to the example used before of a tribunal having power to decide whether a furnished tenancy exists. The existence of a furnished tenancy may be expressed as follows.

$$f \, (a, \, b, \, c, \, d \, \ldots \, n) \, = \, \text{furnished tenancy.}$$

This equation is merely convenient shorthand. The elements within the bracket constitute the furnished tenancy; or, conversely, the term furnished tenancy is a shorthand description of the presence of those elements. Thus, here "a" would represent the need for time certain in a lease, "b" the intent of the parties, "c" the fixtures and fittings required to render the tenancy furnished. These factors can be law, fact, mixed fact and law or discretion. The letter "f" is simply shorthand for indicating that a furnished tenancy will be determined by the elements within the bracket. This picture is a simplified one. The position will often be more complex. It is very common for a statute to say if X1, X2, X3 exist the tribunal may or shall do Y. X2 and X3 would, like X1, be shorthand descriptions presuming the existence of elements within the bracket.

What the preliminary or collateral fact doctrine sought to do was to distinguish those elements within the bracket which could be regarded as conditioning the power of the tribunal to go on and consider the merits from the merits themselves.[4] The fundamental problem was that in an everyday sense all the elements relating to X, or, to X1, X2, X3, could be said to condition jurisdiction. The enabling statute always, explicitly or implicitly, states, if X1, X2, X3 exist, you may or shall do Y. Yet, if X1, X2, and X3, and all the elements constituting them, were always held to be jurisdictional

---

[4] The word merits requires further explanation. As used within the collateral fact doctrine this did not mean only what I have termed the Y question, the question of what is, in fact, a fair rent given the existence of a furnished tenancy. Courts which employed the doctrine accepted that there could be matters on the X level which were not jurisdictional and the term merits included these items.

in a legal sense, the dividing line between review and appeal would be emasculated. The tribunal would have power to give only the right answer, this being the answer which accorded with the opinion of the reviewing court.

Diplock L.J. attempted to solve this conundrum by drawing the following distinction: a misconstruction of the enabling statute describing the *kind* of case into which the tribunal was meant to inquire would go to jurisdiction, but misconstruing a statutory description of the *situation* that the tribunal had to determine would, at most, be an error within jurisdiction.

The problem is that this line is impossible to draw with any certainty or accuracy, because the definition of "kind" or "type" is *inevitably* comprised of descriptions within the statute of the "situation" which the tribunal has to determine. The former represents the sum, the latter the parts. This is simply demonstrated. If one were asked to produce a summary of the *kind* of case into which the tribunal was intended to inquire one would do so by looking at the *situations* which the tribunal had to determine as mentioned in the statute. These situations consist of the statutory terms in the enabling legislation. Thus, in a case such as *Anisminic* one would say, inter alia, that if there was property in Egypt, which belonged to a British national or successor in title at the relevant dates, which had been seized, the FCC should award compensation. The *kind* of case is comprised of the *situations described in the statute* which the tribunal has to determine.[5]

The distinction between *kind* or *type* on the one hand, and *truth* or *detail* or *situation* on the other, proved illusory. There was no predictability as to how a case would be categorised before the court pronounced on the matter. There was also no ex post facto rationality that could be achieved by juxtaposing a series of cases and asking why one case went one way and another was decided differently.[6]

B. Limited Review

With these difficulties in mind let us approach a second theory of review put forward by Gordon.[7]   **14–007**

---

[5] The distinction may be capable of being drawn at a more philosophical, abstract level, but it does not provide any workable criterion for judicial intervention. See further, *Blanchard v Control Data Canada Ltee* [1984] 2 S.C.R. 476, 14 D.L.R. (4th) 289, 300.

[6] In *Anisminic* [1968] 2 Q.B. 862, 904–905, Diplock L.J. found that the error was, at most, one within jurisdiction. It did not relate to the "kind" of case into which the FCC could inquire. No real indication is given as to why the error was categorised in this way. See, further, the examples given in D. Gordon, "The Relation of Facts to Jurisdiction" (1929) 45 L.Q.R. 458.

[7] "The Relation of Facts to Jurisdiction" (1929) 45 L.Q.R. 458; "Observance of Law as a Condition of Jurisdiction" (1931) 47 L.Q.R. 386, 557; Conditional or Contingent Jurisdiction of Tribunals" (1959–1963) 1 U.B.C.L.Rev. 185; "Jurisdictional Fact: An Answer" (1966) 82 L.Q.R. 515; "What did the Anisminic Case Decide?" (1971) 34 M.L.R. 1. See also P. Hogg, "The Jurisdictional Fact Doctrine in the Supreme Court of Canada; *Bell v Ontario Human Rights Commission*" (1971) 9 Osgoode Hall L.J. 203.

i. Relative rather than absolute facts

14–008   If a tribunal is given jurisdiction over a certain topic the question is whether the facts relating to that topic exist in the opinion of the tribunal. Thus, if a tribunal is given jurisdiction over assault the question is whether an assault exists in the opinion of that tribunal. Any tribunal might err in a finding that it makes: no tribunal is infallible. But so long as the tribunal decides the question assigned to it by the law, its relative opinion will bind, subject to appeal. Jurisdiction must involve the power to make a wrong as well as a correct decision.

ii. The limits

14–009   There must be a limit to a tribunal's jurisdiction, but that limit was determined *not* by the truth or falsehood of its findings, but by their scope or nature. It was sufficient that the charge was laid in the correct form. Thus, jurisdiction was determined at the commencement not at the conclusion of the inquiry.

Gordon was scathing of the collateral fact doctrine for three reasons. First, every Act of Parliament says that if a certain state of facts exists the tribunal may do a certain thing; those facts were always for the relative decision of the tribunal.[8] Second, it was unrealistic to divide the matters which a tribunal had to decide into preliminary and essential: all elements within the statement, "if X", in some way condition the jurisdiction to proceed to do Y. Third, it was impossible to reconcile the cases which used the collateral fact doctrine. No rhyme or reason could be found as to why the courts called a fact preliminary in one case but not in another.

iii. Criticism of the Gordon theory

14–010   There are a number of difficulties with the Gordon theory. It may, for example, be hard to decide when an inquiry commences. It may also be that this limited review is unacceptable on policy grounds. The policy issues will be discussed in detail later. For the present, attention will be focused on the most crucial part of the theory, the distinction between scope and truth.

For Gordon it was fallacious to say that if a tribunal blundered in its estimation of the factors involved in a subject-matter properly before it, and thereby misconceived the questions that it should consider, that it thereby exceeded its jurisdiction. The subject-matter of the tribunal's inquiry might involve decisions on a number of issues, but each of these was not a subject-matter by itself. Any error was only an error within jurisdiction.

This can best be understood by reverting to our previous example concerning a furnished tenancy, which could be expressed as,

$$f\,(a, b, c, d \ldots n) = \text{furnished tenancy.}$$

---

[8] This is made in response to the statement by Farwell L.J. in *R. v Shoreditch Assessment Committee Ex p. Morgan* [1910] 2 K.B. 859, 880 that no tribunal of limited jurisdiction can have unlimited power to determine the extent of those limits.

The elements in the bracket represent the need for time certain, intent of the parties, amount of fixture and fittings, etc. The premise underlying Gordon's argument was that scope or subject-matter meant simply the assertion of the existence of a furnished tenancy by the tribunal. Any blunder concerning *a, b, c,* etc., would, at most, be an error within jurisdiction. What Gordon sought to do, therefore, was to avoid the pitfalls of the collateral fact doctrine by, in effect, erecting a brick wall between the words furnished tenancy and the bracket. The court was not allowed to peer inside at the meanings assigned to those elements, except to find a non-jurisdictional error.

There is clearly an element of circularity in the argument in that it presumes that the subject-matter is properly before the tribunal, a presumption which can only be made if subject-matter is defined purely in terms of furnished tenancy itself. Whether this assumption is properly made depends ultimately upon one's conception of meaning and on questionable premises concerning legislative intent.

The *conception of meaning* is raised in that the Gordon argument was **14–011** premised on a formal separation between the term furnished tenancy, which went to scope, and the elements within the bracket which constituted it. An error relating to scope would be jurisdictional and thus, if the wrong term was used instead of furnished tenancy, a court should intervene. Mistakes concerning elements within the bracket were, however, regarded differently, being non-jurisdictional at most. Since however the words furnished tenancy are only a shorthand description of the presence of the elements, factual and legal, within the bracket, to regard an error relating to these words as jurisdictional, but mistakes concerning *a, b, c* or *d* as not, makes little sense.

People may well disagree as to whether, for example, an assault has in fact occurred. But to argue from this that we can divorce the term furnished tenancy or assault from the elements within the bracket is a non sequitur. It would mean accepting that an assault could exist without any of the elements which comprise that term. No one would, for example, have to be placed in fear for their bodily safety. One cannot, in other words, argue from the premise that people may disagree as to whether a person was in fact placed in fear for their bodily safety, to the conclusion that a decision-maker can have untrammelled power to decide whether such an apprehension is indeed a constituent part of the offence at all. To do so would have quite fundamental consequences for the way in which we use language. The words furnished tenancy or assault would be empty vessels into which anything could be poured. The formal incantation of such words would suffice for the tribunal to remain within the scope of its authority. They could be applied to anything regardless of whether it was an Oxford College, or for that matter an oak tree or my dog.

The thesis is also based on *questionable assumptions concerning legislative intent*. It might be argued that the content of the bracket constituting the term furnished tenancy or employee or assault should, itself, be for the relative opinion of the tribunal. It is, however, doubtful in the extreme whether one can assume that the legislature *always* intended the tribunal to be the arbiter as to what the contents of the bracket ought to be. This might happen in a particular area. There is nothing to prevent the legislature preferring a tribunal's interpretation of the term, for example, employee, to that of the reviewing court. Greater recognition of this would be valuable. Gordon's argument is however dependent upon showing not just that this might happen, but that it *must* happen. There is no reason why this should be so. Even if the tribunal's view of the meaning of a particular term were to be preferred, the formal separation of the term furnished tenancy from the contents of the bracket would still be unwarranted.[9]

C. Extensive Review: The Academic Argument

14–012   A theory of extensive review has been advanced by Gould.[10] A similar approach is evident in the courts' more recent jurisprudence, and represents the current case law. Gould's argument will be considered within this section, while the related ideas in the case law will be analysed in the following section.

i. Preliminary questions and substance

14–013   Gould's argument was as follows. Any tribunal had two questions to answer. First, there was a preliminary question, which was whether the question it was asked to answer was a question it was empowered to answer. This could not be decided finally by the tribunal itself. A decision that jurisdiction existed was always a logically necessary precondition to the exercise of jurisdiction: because it was logically prior to the exercise of jurisdiction, it could not in itself be part of the exercise of jurisdiction. It was not therefore a question on which the tribunal could go right or wrong. Secondly, the substance of the matter or the merits was for the tribunal itself.

Thus far, Gould provided a restatement of the collateral or preliminary fact doctrine. He sought however to provide a logical answer to the question that had previously been unsolved: what matters *are* collateral or preliminary?

ii. The content of the preliminary question

14–014   The factors which came within the first category were those which must exist independently of the substance to be decided. These factors were given: their meaning could not be altered by the tribunal itself. It was not that they were

---

[9] Imagine that the content of such a term is assigned to the tribunal. Once the tribunal has decided that the bracket should contain certain elements, then everything said earlier would still apply. The only way out of this conundrum would be to argue, not only that the contents of the bracket are for the tribunal, but that it can alter these at will, and put any other contents in their place at any time. We are however in danger of losing all touch with reality by postulating such a scenario.

[10] B. Gould, "Anisminic and Jurisdictional Review" [1970] P.L. 358; H Rawlings, "Jurisdictional Review after Pearlman" [1979] P.L. 404.

facts in the absolute. Gould, like Gordon, agreed that they were relative. However, they were for the relative opinion of the reviewing courts, *not* the tribunal. These factors were all legal rules and concepts, because such rules must have a given meaning established by the courts. A coherent theory of jurisdiction seems to have been produced. The basis for judicial intervention becomes clear and worrisome problems of jurisdictional versus non-jurisdictional errors of law are left behind. All legal terms within our bracket would go to jurisdiction.

iii. Criticisms of the Gould theory
The key to the theory is obviously the cogency of the argument that all **14–015** issues of law are "given", to be determined by the courts. Three reasons can be extracted from the argument as to why this should be so.

(1) Parliamentary intent
Legal issues are "given", Gould argued, because Parliament intended them **14–016** to be decided by the ordinary courts. This argument could be regarded as a *rebuttable* presumption, but then the inexorable logic of the theory would break down. It could not be said that legal rules were always to be determined by the ordinary courts. The argument must therefore be based upon an *irrebuttable* presumption as to parliamentary intent. This might be derived from constitutional theory or judicial practice.

There are difficulties with the argument based on *constitutional theory*. Parliament is sovereign and in theory it can give the task of determining the meaning of a term to, for example, a tribunal or inferior court. It manifests an explicit intent to do so when it places a privative clause in a statute empowering a tribunal. The courts, it is true, will interpret these clauses and have construed them to mean that jurisdictional errors are not protected.[11] It is equally true that Lord Diplock has stated[12] that the normal presumption is that Parliament intends questions of law to be decided by the courts, but his Lordship did not state that this was an irrebuttable presumption. This presumption has been repeated in the *Page* case, but their Lordships were equally clear that this was not, in all cases, to be viewed as an irrebuttable presumption. It should moreover be emphasised that allowing a tribunal to give the precise meaning to a statutory term does not entail the absence of judicial control, since the courts could still review the rationality of the tribunal's interpretation.

We can now turn to *judicial practice*. It could be argued that Gould's irrebuttable presumption finds support in the fact that the judiciary has arrogated to itself the ultimate decision on all questions of law. However the courts have not for the last 300 years recognised, nor have they acted upon, a logic which renders all questions of law jurisdictional. To the contrary,

---

[11] See generally, Ch.27.
[12] *Re Racal Communications Ltd* [1981] A.C. 374; *O'Reilly v Mackman* [1983] 2 A.C. 237.

review has differed over time, but it is indisputable that the judiciary accepted that non-jurisdictional errors of law could exist. A number of courts gave substantial latitude to the decision-maker. The judicial approach has altered in recent years, as the courts have taken authority over most legal questions. It is therefore difficult to build an *irrebuttable* presumption upon 30 years' judicial practice, in the light of the contrary position that prevailed hitherto.[13]

There is, as already noted, now a rebuttable presumption that all questions of law should be for the ordinary courts. The authority supporting this view will be examined below. Whether that view should be sustained will, however, be dependent upon a value judgment as to whose opinion on the meaning of a term should be preferred. It is not to be derived from an allegedly logical a priori argument that all legal questions are "given".

(2) The impossibility argument

14–017 It would not, said Gould, be possible to talk of error of law at all unless such elements had a "given" meaning, because such language implied a departure from a criterion laid down by the courts. This is to confuse cause and effect. When the legal meaning of a term is given to, or arrogated by the courts, then of course the phrase "error of law" implies a deviation from that standard. It cannot provide the *reason why* all matters of law should have an interpretation provided by the ordinary courts. If the interpretation of the point is not given to the ordinary courts then the error will not be an error of law at all; the criterion laid down by the tribunal will be the accepted standard.

The possibility of the latter occurring is not contrary to the rule of law. Many legal terms could have one of a number of possible meanings, each of which is reasonable. Words or phrases such as "furnished tenancy", "successor in title", "course of employment", "trade dispute", "boat" and "resources", are open to a spectrum of possible meanings, a number of which may be reasonable. The statement that the tribunal has made an "error of law" means that the construction placed upon the term by the court is preferred to that of the tribunal. Parliament might however prefer the precise construction adopted by the specialist tribunal to that given by the generalist court. This is more especially so since, as will be seen below, it is quite possible to maintain control in such situations without the judiciary substituting their view for that of the tribunal. The courts might review the rationality of the tribunal's interpretation, rather than simply substituting their own preferred interpretation.

---

[13] The argument presented within this section assumes a variety of guises. It should not, however, be confused with the principle that the courts always have jurisdiction to declare the law unless that jurisdiction is specifically excluded by Parliament. This principle finds its application in the construction of privative clauses and alternative remedies, and is designed to preserve the *possibility* of judicial review. It says nothing as to the *scope* of review.

(3) The uniformity argument

A third argument is that it is only by giving the legal meaning of a term to **14-018**
the courts that uniformity can be achieved, as opposed to a number of
inferior bodies giving diverse interpretations of the same term.

The limits of this argument should be noted. It will not apply to tribunals
with an internal hierarchy, the top of which can impose a uniform meaning,
nor will it necessarily apply where there is only one tribunal in an area. The
need for uniformity is greatest where there are a number of parallel tribunals
deciding the same point. Uniformity should be achieved by providing an
appeal rather than by distorting review to become appeal, or by insisting
that the particular meaning adopted by one of the set of tribunals should be
applied consistently by those in a similar position.

D. Extensive Review: The Judicial Argument

Arguments for more extensive review have been made by the courts. The **14-019**
case law will be examined below, but it is important to assess the arguments
underlying the courts' jurisprudence.

i. Review for error of law

Judicial indications that the courts would no longer follow the collateral fact **14-020**
doctrine have been apparent for some time.[14] These indications were confirmed by the House of Lords in the *Page* case.[15] A detailed analysis of the
case will be provided below. The present discussion will be confined to the
more general assumptions which underlie the decision.

Lord Browne-Wilkinson gave the leading judgment, and reasoned as
follows.[16] He held that the effect of the *Anisminic* case was to render obsolete
the distinction between errors of law on the face of the record, and other
errors of law, by extending the doctrine of ultra vires. Thenceforward it was
to be taken that Parliament had only conferred a decision-making power on
the basis that it was to be exercised on the correct legal basis: a misdirection
in law when making the decision rendered it ultra vires. The general rule was
that any (relevant) error of law could be quashed. The constitutional basis
of the courts' power was that the tribunals' unlawful decision was *ultra vires*.
In general, the law applicable to an administrative institution was the
ordinary law of the land. Therefore, "a tribunal or inferior court acts *ultra
vires* if it reaches its conclusion on a basis erroneous under the general
law".[17] It is clear from the judgment that the presumption, (that any error of
law is open to review), is rebuttable, and it also appears to be the case that

---

[14] *Anisminic* [1969] 2 A.C. 147, *Re Racal Communications Ltd* [1981] A.C. 374, and *O'Reilly v
Mackman* [1983] 2 A.C. 237.
[15] *R. v Hull University Visitor Ex p. Page* [1993] A.C. 682.
[16] Lord Slynn and Lord Mustill dissented on other grounds, but agreed with the majority on
this general issue, [1993] A.C. 682, 705–706.
[17] *Page*, n.15, 702.

the strength of this presumption might vary depending upon the nature of the institution being reviewed.[18]

ii. Assessment

14–021   It is necessary to distinguish between four different aspects of the reasoning used in the *Page* decision.

First, there is the disapproval cast upon the collateral fact doctrine. This is to be welcomed. The difficulties with that doctrine have already been discussed, and it is high time that it was discarded.

Second, there is the replacement of that doctrine with the test that all errors of law are open to scrutiny. The similarities between this approach and Gould's are readily apparent. It is not therefore surprising that some of the concerns expressed in the context of the Gould theory should be equally relevant here. *If Page* is taken to mean that in relation to *any* of the X factors which involve *any* element of law the court will substitute its view for that of the tribunal, then it is problematic. The courts will become embroiled in the minutiae of disputed interpretations as to what many, or all, of the X conditions mean in any particular context. Moreover, such an approach is based upon the presumption that the courts' particular interpretation of phrases such as "employee", "course of employment", "boat" or "resources" is necessarily to be preferred to that of the agency; *and* that substitution of judgment is the only way to exercise control over such agency interpretations. Neither of these assumptions is well founded. The courts' particular interpretation of such terms may not necessarily be better than that of the agency, *and* adequate control may be maintained through a different standard of review.[19]

Third, although Lord Browne-Wilkinson based judicial intervention upon the ultra vires principle, this should not serve to conceal the fact that the principle now has a different meaning than previously. When that principle was the basis for intervention under the collateral fact doctrine, the assumption was that there was a distinction to be drawn between jurisdictional and non-jurisdictional errors. The former would result in the decision being regarded as ultra vires and void, because the tribunal had acted *outside* its jurisdiction. The latter were errors *within* jurisdiction and would only be open to attack if the error was one of law on the face of the record. However, the ultra vires principle as used in *Page* bears a different meaning. Any error of law may lead to the decision being regarded as ultra vires, because the tribunal reached its conclusion on a basis that is erroneous under the general law. It has indeed been argued by Sir John Laws that once the distinction between jurisdictional and non-jurisdictional errors is discarded, there is no longer any need or purpose for the ultra vires principle as such, since the courts are in reality simply intervening to correct errors of

---

[18] *Page*, n.15, 702–704.
[19] See below, paras 14–040—14–045.

law.[20] So why do the courts persist, as in *Page*, in employing the principle? On one view it provides a legitimating device for the exercise of the courts' power. Rather intervene by saying that the tribunal has acted ultra vires, than on the simple ground of error of law per se. Sir John Laws captures this idea.[21]

> " 'Ultra vires' is, in truth, a fig-leaf; it has enabled the courts to intervene in decisions without an assertion of judicial power which too nakedly confronts the established authority of the Executive or other public bodies. . .The fig-leaf was very important in *Anisminic*; but fig-leaf it was. And it has produced the historical irony that *Anisminic*, with all its emphasis on nullity, nevertheless erected the legal milestone which pointed towards a public law jurisprudence in which the concept of voidness and the ultra vires doctrine have become redundant."[22]

Fourth, and finally, there is a duality latent in the meaning given to the ultra vires principle by Lord Browne-Wilkinson.[23] One reading of this principle sees it as being based on legislative intent, in the sense that Parliament intended that all errors of law should be open to challenge. It is this version of the principle which is evident when his Lordship stated that Parliament "had only conferred the decision-making power on the basis that it was to be exercised on the correct legal basis",[24] with the consequence that a misdirection in law when making the decision rendered it ultra vires. A rather different reading of the ultra vires principle is, however, to be found later in the judgment. Ultra vires is equated with the general law of the land, which clearly includes the common law. On this view the ultra vires principle is no longer based exclusively on legislative intent. It simply becomes the vehicle through which the common law courts develop their controls over the administration. [25]

> "[T]he constitutional basis of the courts' power to quash is that the decision of the inferior tribunal is unlawful on the grounds that it is *ultra vires*. In the ordinary case, the law applicable to a decision made by such a body is the general law of the land. Therefore, a tribunal or inferior court acts *ultra vires* if it reaches its conclusion on a basis erroneous under the general law."

---

[20] "Illegality: The Problem of Jurisdiction", in M. Supperstone and J. Goudie (eds), *Judicial Review* (Butterworths, 1992), Ch.4.
[21] "Illegality", n.20, 67.
[22] By laying the foundation for the idea that all errors of law can be reviewed.
[23] P. Craig, "Ultra Vires and the Foundations of Judicial Review" [1998] C.L.J. 63, 79–80; Sir John Laws, "Illegality", n.20, Ch.4,19–4.20.
[24] [1993] A.C. 682, 701.
[25] [1993] A.C. 682, 702F.

iii. The distinction between law and fact

14–022 Precisely *how* extensive the *Page* test of review proves to be will depend upon the meaning accorded to the phrase "error of law", and it is to this that we should now turn.

The traditional case law on judicial review provides little guidance as to whether a certain issue is one of law or fact. This was in part because the judicial attitude towards the scope of review was, until recently, premised upon either the collateral fact doctrine or the theory of limited review. Both theories applied equally to issues of law and fact. Thus, provided that the court categorised the issue as collateral it would substitute judgment, whether the issue was one of fact or law.[26] The lack of guidance as to the law/fact distinction is also explicable in part because the cases are commonly concerned with the interpretation of terms such as boat, resources, employee, successor in title, furnished tenancy, structural alteration, and the like. The decision whether to categorise such issues as law or fact is a matter on which judicial and academic opinion differs.

The shift to the idea that all errors of law are jurisdictional means that the distinction between law and fact will be of more significance. Much of the literature has been generated by cases concerned with appeal and not review. Appeal will often only be allowed on questions of law, and not on questions of fact. The case law upon this point has already been discussed.[27] There are three themes which run through the literature upon the law/fact distinction, which are often not distinguished.

The first is that there may well be disagreement as to whether, on analytical grounds, a question should be deemed to be one of law or fact.[28] Thus both the case law and the academic commentary display considerable diversity of opinion on whether, for example, the application of statutory terms to facts always involves a question of law or not. Should the meaning to be ascribed to a statutory term such as employee, trade, boat or successor in title always be regarded, in analytical terms, as a question of law? On *analytical* grounds the answer is probably in the affirmative.[29]

14–023   Second, it is, however, clear that the courts have not always adopted this

---

[26] It may well be the case that the courts felt less inclined to intervene in relation to matters which were purely factual, but the juridical basis of intervention was never premised upon the need to distinguish between law and fact. The only real occasion for distinguishing between law and fact was when the court intervened to quash an error of law on the face of the record.

[27] See paras 9–019—9–021; W. Wilson, "A Note on Fact and Law" (1963) 26 M.L.R. 609 and "Questions of Degree" (1969) 32 M.L.R. 361; E. Mureinik, "The Application of Rules; Law or Fact?" (1982) 98 L.Q.R. 587; J. Beatson, "The Scope of Judicial Review for Error of Law" (1984) 4 O.J.L.S. 22; T. Endicott, "Questions of Law" (1998) 114 L.Q.R. 292; R. Williams, "When is an Error not an Error? Reform of Jurisdictional Review of Error of Law and Fact" [2007] P.L. 793; L. Jaffe, "Judicial Review: Question of Law" (1955) 69 Harv. L.R. 239; L. Jaffe, "Judicial Review: Question of Fact" (1955) 69 Harv. L.R. 1020.

[28] *Moyna v Secretary of State for Work and Pensions* [2003] 1 W.L.R. 1929.

[29] See paras 9–019—9–021, and the articles by Wilson and Mureinik, n.27; *R. v Barnet London Borough Council Ex p. Nilish Shah* [1983] 2 A.C. 309; *ACT Construction Ltd v Customs and Excise Commissioners* [1981] 1 W.L.R. 49, aff'd [1981] 1 W.L.R. 1542. For a different view, see Endicott, n.27, who argues that there can be an analytical approach which does not lead to this conclusion. This argument does, however, explicitly build pragmatic considerations into the analytical approach.

approach. The labels law and fact have been attached depending upon whether the courts wished to intervene or not. The courts have not, therefore, always reached their conclusion on analytical grounds; often these conclusions are expressive of a pragmatic desire to intervene or not in a particular case.

Third, the courts have often acted upon questionable assumptions as to the conclusions which follow from the attachment of one label or the other. Thus some courts have reasoned that if an issue is deemed to be one of law then this must *inevitably* involve substitution of judgment on their part. Conversely where a statutory term is open to a spectrum of reasonable interpretations then it must be a question of fact.[30] This conclusion is controversial. A legal issue does not cease to be such simply because the term in question is open to a range of possible meanings.

The effect of the thesis that all errors of law are jurisdictional will, therefore, be crucially dependent upon which approach the courts adopt. If they pursue a rigid *analytical* approach then it is likely to result in many, if not all, of the constituent elements which comprise the "if X" question being labelled as questions of law. The construction of most statutory terms would be characterised as a question of law. If, in addition, the judiciary then substitute their opinion as to the precise meaning that each of these terms should bear for that of the initial decision-maker, the result will be an extensive form of review.

This is not the only possible approach for the courts to adopt. They could interpret the word law in a more *pragmatic* or *policy oriented* sense. The application of certain statutory terms might be deemed questions of fact. Or the courts could characterise the application of a statutory term as a question of law, but accept that it does not have to have only the one meaning which the court itself would accord to it. Provided that the authority adopts a meaning which is reasonable or has a rational basis the courts could accept that interpretation, even if it did not accord with the precise meaning which they would have ascribed. We will return to this matter after considering the case law on the scope of review.

E. Conclusion

Two conclusions can be drawn from all this. The first is that the line between scope and truth/detail is not capable of furnishing a satisfactory guide as to what should, and what should not, be regarded as jurisdictional. The second point is equally important. The scope of jurisdictional review is not self-defining. It is not capable of being answered by linguistic or textual analysis of the statute alone, however assiduously that is performed. The critical question, the answer to which underlies any statement concerning jurisdictional limits, is whose relative opinion on which matters should be held to be authoritative? All of the theories encapsulate a view about this, although it is often not openly expressed. The answer to this decisive question resides not

14–024

---

[30] *Edwards v Bairstow* [1956] A.C. 14, 33–36.

in a logic which compels, for example, that all questions of law must always to be for the courts or the tribunal. Such logic is flawed. A response must ultimately be based upon a value judgment, the precise content of which will not necessarily always be the same. We shall consider this in more detail after examining the case law.

3. CASE LAW HISTORY

14–025 The present attitude of the courts towards judicial review cannot be adequately understood unless some idea is conveyed of 18th- and 19th-century case law. This history shows clearly the differing views taken by the courts as to how far they should be reviewing tribunals and other inferior bodies.

A. Limited Intervention

14–026 A number of leading authorities supported only limited review. To revert to our example of the equation, they were saying that if the subject-matter lies within the tribunal's jurisdiction, the factors within the bracket constituting that subject-matter would not be reassessed. In *Bolton*[31] magistrates found that the plaintiff had occupied a parish house as a pauper and that a formal notice to quit had been served on him, and directed constables to enforce the notice. The applicant sought certiorari. He wished to show by affidavit evidence that he had not occupied the house qua pauper, but had paid rates and carried out repairs, and that he had not therefore been chargeable on the parish during the period of his occupation.

Lord Denman C.J. made the following distinction. Where the charge laid before the magistrate did not constitute the offence over which the statute gave him jurisdiction, affidavit evidence could be introduced. So too could it where the charge was insufficient, but had been misstated. In both cases, extrinsic evidence could be introduced to show a want of jurisdiction. However, where the charge had been well laid before the magistrate, on its face bringing itself within his jurisdiction, any error would be only an error within jurisdiction. The question of jurisdiction depended not on the truth or falsehood of the charge, but upon its nature and was determinable at the commencement not at the conclusion of the inquiry. The limit of the inquiry must be whether the magistrates had jurisdiction, supposing the facts alleged in the information to be true. The magistrates' return contained all that was needed to give them jurisdiction over the subject-matter: occupation of a parish house belonging to the hamlet and service of a notice to quit. The

---

[31] *R. v Bolton* (1841) 1 Q.B. 66, 72–74. See also, *Brittain v Kinnaird* (1819) 1 B. & B. 432, 442; *Ackerley v Parkinson* (1815) 3 M. & S. 411; *Wilson v Weller* (1819) 1 B. & B. 57; *Fawcett v Fowlis* (1827) 7 B. & C. 396; *R. v Justices of Cheshire* (1838) 8 Ad. & E. 398; *Re Baines* (1840) Cr. & Ph. 31; *Cave v Mountain* (1840) 1 M. & G. 257.

application for certiorari was therefore rejected. There were many examples of the same approach.[32]

B. Collateral or Preliminary Fact Cases

There were also numerous cases that applied the collateral fact doctrine. **14–027** Certain facts were required to be proven to the satisfaction of the reviewing court before the magistrate or tribunal could go right or wrong.

An early example can be seen in *Nichols*.[33] The plaintiff lived in Totteridge and was evaluated for the poor rates by the assessors for Hatfield. In a trespass action the plaintiff's case was upheld. Hatfield and Totteridge were separate places and the one could not levy rates for the other. A number of similar cases concerned with the Poor Laws followed.[34]

What had been implicit in the above cases was made explicit in *Bunbury*.[35] The plaintiff brought an action in debt against the defendant owner of the land, claiming the amount due as being for tithes. The defendant argued that part of the land was exempt from tithes, but an assistant tithe commissioner denied this. The defendant claimed that the determination was an excess of jurisdiction. Coleridge J. found for the defendant, his reasoning being as follows,[36]

"Now it is a general rule, that no court of limited jurisdiction can give itself jurisdiction by a wrong decision on a point collateral to the merits of the case upon which the limit to its jurisdiction depends; and however its decision may be final on all particulars, making up together that subject-matter which, if true, is within its jurisdiction, and, however necessary in many cases it may be for it to make a preliminary inquiry, whether some collateral matter be or be not within the limits, yet, upon this preliminary question, its decision must always be open to inquiry in the superior Court."

The existence of land subject to a tithe was a point collateral to the decision of the assistant tithe commissioner. There were many similar cases.[37]

---

[32] See cases in n.31. See also *Mould v Williams* (1844) 5 Q.B. 469; *Allen v Sharp* (1848) 2 Ex. 352; *R. v Buckinghamshire JJ* (1843) 3 Q.B. 800; *R. v Wilson* (1844) 6 Q.B. 620; *R. v Wood* (1855) 5 El. & Bl. 49; *Revell v Blake* (1872) 7 C.P. 300; *Usill v Hales* (1878) 3 C.P.D. 319; *R. v Whitfield* (1885) 15 Q.B.D 122; *R. v Justices of the Central Criminal Court* (1886) 17 Q.B.D. 598.

[33] *Nichols v Walker* (1632–1633) Cro. Car. 394.

[34] *Milward v Caffin* (1778) 2 Black. W. 1330; *Lord Amherst v Lord Somers* (1788) 2 T.R. 372; *Weaver v Price* (1832) 3 B. & Ad. 409; *Governors of Bristol Poor v Wait* (1834) 1 A. & E. 264; *Fernley v Worthington* (1840) 1 Man. & G. 491. See also, cases on title, *Thompson v Ingham* (1850) 14 Q.B. 710, 718; *Dale v Pollard* (1847) 10 Q.B. 505; *Chew v Holroyd* (1852) 8 Ex. 249.

[35] *Bunbury v Fuller* (1853) 9 Ex. 111.

[36] *Bunbury*, n.35, 140.

[37] e.g. *R. v Badger* (1856) 6 El. & Bl. 138; *R. v Stimpson* (1863) 4 B. & S. 301; *Ex p. Vaughan* (1866) L.R. 2 Q.B. 114; *Elston v Rose* (1868) L.R. 4 Q.B. 4; *Ex p Bradlaugh* (1878) 3 Q.B.D. 509.

C. Attempts at Reconciliation

14–028   It is clear that there cannot be any reconciliation on the basis that some judges preferred more limited, while others opted for more extensive review.[38] The most common strategy was to say that both groups of cases were equally valid and that differences turned on the legislative instrument.[39]

Thus in *R. v Commissioners for Special Purposes of Income Tax*[40] Lord Esher M.R. distinguished between two types of tribunal. There were tribunals which had jurisdiction if a certain state of facts existed but not otherwise; it was not for the inferior tribunal to determine conclusively upon the existence of such facts. There could, however, be a tribunal which had jurisdiction to determine whether the preliminary state of facts existed; here it would be for the inferior tribunal to decide upon all the facts.

This reconciliation was one of form rather than substance. It is impossible by juxtaposing the legislative instruments in these cases to determine why one case should fall within one category rather than the other. All statutes in effect say if X exists, you may or shall do Y. The answer as to who is to determine X, (and the factors constituting X), is dependent upon which theory of jurisdiction is accepted. The two groups of cases discussed above reflect different answers to that question, and Lord Esher's analysis simply reiterates ex post facto that divergence. The analysis does not provide us with an ex ante tool to determine which group a case should fall into. This is not to say that a statute might not assign the relative meaning of "if X", as between courts and tribunals, differently in diverse areas. It is to say that whether it has done so cannot be determined by asking whether the statute requires a certain state of facts to exist before a decision is reached: all statutes always do this.

4. THE CURRENT CASE LAW

A. The Impact of *Anisminic*

14–029   The passing of the Victorian age, significant in so many spheres, brought no great change in this area. There is no magic in the divide between the 19th and 20th centuries so far as the scope of judicial review is concerned. There were still cases advocating only limited review.[41] These were the heirs of

---

[38] e.g. Lord Denman C.J. decided *R. v Bolton* (1841) 1 Q.B. 66 and *Governors of Bristol Poor v Wait* (1834) 1 A. & E. 264; Coleridge J. decided *R. v Buckinghamshire JJ* (1843) 3 Q.B. 800 and *Bunbury v Fuller* (1853) 9 Ex. 111: and see Coleridge J. *arguendo* in *Thompson v Ingham* (1850) 14 Q.B. 710, 713.

[39] For a different, and unsuccessful, attempt at reconciliation, see *Thompson v Ingham* (1850) 14 Q.B. 710, 718.

[40] (1888) 21 Q.B.D 313. See also, *Colonial Bank of Australasia v Willan* (1874) L.R. 5 P.C. 417.

[41] e.g. *R. v Mahony* [1910] 2 I.R. 695; *R. v Bloomsbury Income Tax Commissioners* [1915] 3 K.B. 768; *R. v Nat Bell Liquors Ltd* [1922] 2 A.C. 128; *R. v Swansea Income Tax Commissioners* [1925] 2 K.B. 250; *R. v Minister of Health* [1939] 1 K.B. 232; *Tithe Redemption Commission v Wynne* [1943] K.B. 756.

Brittain and *Bolton*. There were also decisions which adopted a more interventionist attitude,[42] using the collateral or preliminary fact doctrine. These were the descendants of *Bunbury*. It was still difficult to determine which matters should be characterised as collateral or preliminary, and it was admitted that there could be errors of law within jurisdiction which, if they appeared on the face of the record, would be quashed.[43]

The scope of review must now be seen in the light of *Anisminic*.[44] The plaintiff was an English company which owned property in Egypt prior to 1956. In November 1956 the property was sequestrated by the Egyptian authorities, and in April 1957 the sequestrator sold the property to TEDO, an Egyptian organisation. Anisminic put pressure on their customers not to buy ore from TEDO, as a result of which an agreement was reached in November 1957 whereby the plaintiff sold the mining business to TEDO for £500,000. In February 1959 a Treaty was made between the United Kingdom and the United Arab Republic which provided for the return of sequestrated property, except property sold between October 1956 and August 1958. A sum of £27,500,000 was paid by the United Arab Republic in final settlement of claims to property which was not being returned. Orders in Council were then passed setting out the conditions for participation in the fund.

The Foreign Compensation Commission, the FCC, found that Anisminic did not qualify. The Foreign Compensation (Egypt) (Determination and Registration of Claims) Order 1962[45] stated in art.4(1)(b)(ii) that the applicant and the successor in title should be British nationals on October 31, 1956 and February 28, 1959. The FCC interpreted this to mean that they had to inquire whether there was a successor in title and, if so, whether the person qualified under art.4(1)(b)(ii). TEDO was a successor in title according to the FCC and was not a British national at the relevant dates, therefore the plaintiff failed. The plaintiff claimed that the nationality of the successor in title was irrelevant where the claimant was the original owner. Anisminic therefore sought a declaration that the determination was a nullity.

The House of Lords[46] found for the plaintiffs. Lord Reid stated that **14–030** jurisdiction in a narrow sense meant only that the tribunal be entitled to enter upon the inquiry. There were, however, a number of ways in which, having correctly begun the inquiry, the tribunal could do something which rendered its decision a nullity. Misconstruction of the enabling statute so that the tribunal failed to deal with the question remitted to it, failure to take account of relevant considerations, and asking the wrong question were, said Lord Reid, examples of this.[47] The plaintiff's construction of

---

[42] e.g. *R. v Fulham, Hammersmith and Kensington Rent Tribunal Ex p. Zerek* [1951] 2 K.B. 1; *R. v Fulham, Hammersmith and Kensington Rent Tribunal Ex p. Hierowski* [1953] 2 K.B. 147.
[43] *R. v Paddington North and St. Marylebone Rent Tribunal Ex p. Perry* [1956] 1 Q.B. 229.
[44] *Anisminic Ltd v Foreign Compensation Commission* [1969] 2 A.C. 147.
[45] SI 1962/2187.
[46] [1969] 2 A.C. 147. The case was also concerned with privative clauses. This problem is considered in Ch.27.
[47] [1969] 2 A.C. 147, 171.

successor in title was correct and the decision by the FCC was a nullity. Lord Reid's judgment significantly broadened the potential scope of review. A court, if it wished to interfere, could always characterise an alleged error as having resulted from asking the wrong question, or having taken account of irrelevant considerations. Three observations are warranted.

The first is as follows. "Asking the wrong question" or "irrelevancy" tell one that an error has been made, but they do not tell one whether the error was jurisdictional.[48] The step from "asking the wrong question", to the error being regarded as jurisdictional, presupposes that any "condition" to the exercise of jurisdiction becomes jurisdictional. The implicit assumption is that questions of law are for the ordinary courts. The tribunal must give what the reviewing court regards as the correct meaning to the statutory terms, *before* the tribunal can be properly within the sphere of its jurisdiction. Concepts such as "asking the wrong question" simply function as the vehicle through which the court can substitute its views on the meaning of the relevant statutory term for that of the tribunal. Applying such reasoning in its full rigour reduces the division between jurisdictional and non-jurisdictional error to vanishing point. To revert to our earlier terminology: given that all tribunals are delegated power in the form of if X1, X2, X3, you may or shall do Y, everything relating to X becomes potentially jurisdictional. Where the enabling legislation is complex this means that a large number of matters must be "got right" in the opinion of the reviewing court before the tribunal can go right or wrong.

The second point to note is that the language of judicial intervention should not serve to conceal the "basic" nature of the issue at stake in cases such as *Anisminic*. This issue is the meaning to be ascribed to one of the X conditions. The language of "asking the wrong question" and the like is simply an indirect way for the court to express the conclusion that it believes that a different construction of the term in question should be substituted for that adopted by the agency.

The third point concerns the scope of the decision. Notwithstanding the broad potential for jurisdictional error, Lord Reid reaffirmed the continued existence of errors of law within jurisdiction.[49] This is difficult to reconcile with the general tenor of his Lordship's judgment. Later case law has, as will be seen, drawn out the implications of *Anisminic* more fully, and held that the case did indeed eradicate the distinction between jurisdictional and non-jurisdictional error.

Lord Pearce and Lord Wilberforce both reached their conclusions in similar way.[50] The tribunal had a limited authority, the corollary of which was the power of the reviewing court to keep the tribunal within its assigned area. It was for the court to determine the true construction of a statute

---

[48] A point made by Diplock L.J. in the Court of Appeal [1968] 2 Q.B. 862, 904–905. See also *R. v Furnished Houses Rent Tribunal for Paddington and St. Marylebone Ex p. Kendal Hotels Ltd* [1947] 1 All E.R. 448, 449; *R. v Paddington North and St Marylebone Rent Tribunal Ex p. Perry* [1956] 1 Q.B. 229, 237–238.
[49] [1969] 2 A.C. 147, 174.
[50] [1969] 2 A.C. 147, 194–195, 207–210.

delineating that area. Lack of jurisdiction could arise in various ways, inter alia, absence of a condition precedent to the tribunal's jurisdiction, irrelevancy, and asking the wrong question. Lord Pearson agreed that if there had been an error it would have been jurisdictional, but found no such mistake.[51] Lord Morris of Borth-y-Gest dissented. His Lordship realised the implications of the majority judgments and pointed out that the Order "bristled" with words requiring statutory construction. It could not, said his Lordship, be the case that any misconstruction of any of these terms would involve a jurisdictional error.[52]

B. From *Anisminic* to *Racal*

It was to be over a decade before the House of Lords engaged in further detailed scrutiny of this area, which it did in the *Racal* case considered below. In the meantime the decision in *Anisminic* provided a broad armoury for later courts. If a court wished to categorise an error as jurisdictional it could do so by using the "wrong question" or "irrelevant consideration" formula. However, the courts could choose whether to utilise this armoury. If the court did not wish to intervene it could achieve this result by saying that there was no error at all, by characterising the error as one within jurisdiction, or by defining jurisdiction itself more narrowly than in *Anisminic*. Two cases may be contrasted by way of example.

14–031

In *Moore*,[53] the claimant sought certiorari on the basis that the Supplementary Benefits Commission had misinterpreted the meaning of the term "resources" for the purposes of calculating entitlement to supplementary benefits. Lord Denning M.R. found that the interpretation of the Commission was correct, but made it clear that he did not wish the legislation to become a hunting ground for lawyers whereby the court, on review, would have to interpret every minute point of law.

This may be contrasted with Lord Denning M.R.'s decision in *Pearlman*.[54] The question was whether the installation of central heating was "an improvement made by the execution of works amounting to a structural alteration" within the Housing Act 1974. Lord Denning held that the line between errors of law which went to jurisdiction and those within jurisdiction was a fine one, and that the characterisation would often be dependent upon whether the court wished to intervene. Distinctions between errors within and errors going to jurisdiction should be discarded. Any error of law should be held to be jurisdictional if the case depended upon it.[55]

---

[51] [1969] 2 A.C. 147, 220–222.
[52] [1969] 2 A.C. 147, 182–190.
[53] *R. v Preston Supplementary Benefits Appeal Tribunal Ex p. Moore* [1975] 1 W.L.R. 624; *R. v Industrial Injuries Commissioner Ex p. Amalgamated Engineering Union (No.2)* [1966] 2 Q.B. 31; *Re Allen and Mathews Arbitration* [1971] 2 Q.B. 518.
[54] *Pearlman v Keepers and Governors of Harrow School* [1979] Q.B. 56; *ACT Construction Ltd v Customs and Excise Commissioners* [1981] 1 W.L.R. 49, the point was not touched on in the House of Lords [1982] 1 All E.R. 84.
[55] [1979] Q.B. 56, 69–70.

C. The Uncertainty of *Racal*

14–032 Despite the observations of the Master of the Rolls, it was too early yet to build a pyre on which to consign conventional doctrine to its timely or untimely end. The courts continued to equivocate as to whether the traditional approach should be maintained. Put more accurately, individual judges may have been clear as to their preferences, but those preferences did not always coincide.

This is clear from *Re Racal Communications Ltd.*[56] Lord Diplock, with whom Lord Keith agreed, drew a tripartite distinction as to the scope of review.[57] First, administrative tribunals or authorities were subject to the full rigours of the *Anisminic* judgment: the parliamentary intent was presumed, subject to a clear contrary indication, to be that questions of law were to be decided by the courts. The distinction between errors within jurisdiction and errors going to jurisdiction was, for practical purposes, abolished, and any error of law would automatically result in the tribunal having asked itself the wrong question. The resultant decision would be a nullity. Second, inferior courts were, however, subject to a different test. It would depend upon the construction of the statute whether Parliament intended questions of law to be left to an inferior court. There was no presumption that it did not so intend. The third category was the High Court. These courts were not subject to judicial review at all which only applied to administrative authorities and inferior courts. Appeal was the only corrective for a mistake by a High Court judge.

There was, however, little support in the other judgments either for Lord Diplock's tripartite standard of review, or for the extensive review which his Lordship advocated for administrative institutions.[58] Lord Salmon confined himself to saying that *Anisminic* was only relevant for tribunals, commissioners and inferior courts of law.[59] His Lordship drew no distinction as to the scope of review for inferior courts and administrative institutions. Nor did Lord Salmon follow through the reasoning from *Anisminic* to reach the conclusions arrived at by Lord Diplock. Lord Edmund-Davies[60] similarly arrived at a narrower conclusion than Lord Diplock, and expressly disapproved of Lord Denning M.R.'s reasoning in *Pearlman*[61] which had purported to destroy the distinction between jurisdictional and non-jurisdictional error. Nor did Lord Edmund-Davies draw any demarcation between administrative institutions and inferior courts for the purposes of review. Lord Scarman said nothing general about the scope of review for administrative institutions and inferior courts and drew no dichotomy between them.

---

[56] [1981] A.C. 374. On appeal from *Re A Company* [1980] Ch.138.
[57] [1981] A.C. 374, 381–382.
[58] The headnote in the Official Law Reports is misleading. The second part gives the impression that a majority of their Lordships accepted Lord Diplock's view as to the scope of review for inferior courts. This is not borne out by the passages referred to in the judgments of Lord Salmon or Lord Edmund-Davies.
[59] [1981] A.C. 374, 386.
[60] [1981] A.C. 374, 389–390.
[61] [1979] Q.B. 56, 69–70.

D. The Impact of *Page*

It was to be over a decade before the House of Lords, (though not the Privy Council), had another detailed look at the issue. Decisions in the period between *Racal* and *Page* did little to establish a uniform judicial approach to the scope of review. Some decisions, such as *South East Asia Fire*,[62] persisted with the traditional collateral fact doctrine, rejecting arguments that the distinction between jurisdictional and non-jurisdictional error had been discarded. Others, such as *O'Reilly*,[63] stated that the result of *Anisminic* was to render unnecessary the continued distinction between errors of law going to jurisdiction, and errors of law within jurisdiction. Yet other cases accepted in principle review for error of law which flowed from *Anisminic* and *O'Reilly*, but then qualified it in varying ways, emphasising, for example, that such review was only a presumption which could be rebutted by having regard to the language of the relevant statute.[64]

The decision of the House of Lords in *Page*[65] is now the leading authority. Page was a lecturer at Hull University who was made redundant. He argued that the terms of his appointment did not allow termination of his employment on this ground. The University Visitor dismissed the argument, and Page then sought judicial review of the Visitor's decision. Much of the case turned upon particular issues concerning the reviewability of the Visitor. However, there were also more general observations concerning the scope of jurisdictional review, which can be summarised as follows.

First, Lord Browne-Wilkinson, who gave the leading judgment, held that *Anisminic*, combined with Lord Diplock's dictum in *O'Reilly*, had rendered obsolete the distinction between errors of law on the face of the record and other errors of law, and had done so by extending the ultra vires doctrine. Thenceforward, it was to be taken "that Parliament had only conferred the decision making power on the basis that it was to be exercised on the correct legal basis: a misdirection in law in making the decision therefore rendered the decision *ultra vires*".[66] In general therefore, "any error of law made by an administrative tribunal or inferior court in reaching its decision can be quashed for error of law".[67]

Second, the constitutional foundation for the court's power was, said his Lordship, the ultra vires doctrine. This was so for the following reason. In an ordinary case,[68] the law applicable to a decision made by such a body was

---

[62] *South East Asia Fire Bricks Sdn Bhd v Non-Metallic Mineral Products Manufacturing Employees Union* [1981] A.C. 363, disapproving of Lord Denning M.R.'s dictum in *Pearlman* [1979] Q.B. 56, 69–70, and approving of the dissenting judgment of Geoffrey Lane L.J., [1979] Q.B. 56, 76.

[63] *O'Reilly v Mackman* [1983] 2 A.C. 237. See also *Council of Civil Service Unions v Minister for the Civil Service* [1985] A.C. 374, 410–411.

[64] *R. v Registrar of Companies Ex p. Central Bank of India* [1986] Q.B. 1114, 1175–1176.

[65] *R. v Hull University Visitor Ex p. Page* [1993] A.C. 682.

[66] *Page*, n.65, 701. Lord Slynn and Lord Mustill dissented in relation to certain aspects of the case concerning the Visitor. However, on the general point concerning the scope of review for error of law they were of the same view as the majority, *Page*, n.65, 705–706.

[67] *Page*, n.65, 702. See also, *R. v Bedwelty Justices Ex p. Williams* [1997] A.C. 225.

[68] The Visitor was regarded as being in a special position in this respect, since he was not applying the general law, but a special domestic legal regime.

the general law of the land. A tribunal or inferior court would, therefore, be acting ultra vires if it reached a decision that was erroneous under the general law.[69]

Third, it was, however, only *relevant* errors of law which would lead to the decision being quashed or declared null. The error had to be one which affected the actual making of the decision and affected the decision itself. The mere existence of an error of law at some earlier stage of the proceedings would not vitiate the decision itself.[70]

Finally, the case is unclear as to whether varying presumptions still exist for administrative bodies on the one hand, and for inferior courts on the other. A distinction does still appear to exist. Lord Browne-Wilkinson cited the relevant dicta from Lord Diplock in *Racal*, and then reasoned on the assumption that differing presumptions still existed in the two situations.[71] Moreover, the reasoning of Lord Griffiths was also based upon the continued vitality of the distinction.[72]

E. The Impact of *South Yorkshire Transport*

14–034   Before drawing any more general conclusions about the impact of the *Page* case it is necessary to consider the decision in *South Yorkshire Transport Ltd.*[73]

The Secretary of State had power under the Fair Trading Act 1973 s.64(1)(a), to refer a merger to the Monopolies and Mergers Commission (MMC) where it appeared to him that the two or more enterprises ceased to be distinct and that as a result the supply of over 25 per cent of the services of any description "in a substantial part of the United Kingdom" would be carried on by one person. The MMC investigated a merger between two companies that operated bus services within an area which was 1.65 per cent of the total UK, and which contained only 3.2 per cent of the total population. The companies claimed that the investigation should be set aside because the jurisdictional condition relating to a "substantial part of the UK" had not been fulfilled. Lord Mustill gave the House of Lords' judgment for the MMC. He reasoned as follows.

First, the term "substantial" was open to a range of possible meanings, ranging from "not trifling" to "nearly complete". In between these two senses of the term there were many others which drew colour from the statutory context in which they were found.[74]

---

[69] [1993] A.C. 682, 702.
[70] [1993] A.C. 682, 702, explaining *R. v Independent Television Commission Ex p. TSW Broadcasting Ltd* (1992) *Independent* 27 March. See also, *R. (on the application of Warren) v Mental Health Review Tribunal London & North East Region* [2002] A.C.D. 84.
[71] *Page*, n.65, 703–704. cf. *R. v Greater Manchester Coroner Ex p. Tal* [1985] Q.B. 67, 82–83, where Goff L.J. assumed that differential tests for review would not operate depending upon the nature of the decision-maker.
[72] *Page*, n.65, 693–694.
[73] *R. v Monopolies and Mergers Commission Ex p. South Yorkshire Transport Ltd* [1993] 1 W.L.R. 23; *R. (on the application of BBC) v Information Tribunal* [2007] 1 W.L.R. 2583.
[74] *South Yorkshire Transport Ltd*, n.73, 29.

Second, it was up to the court to decide where along the "spectrum of possible meanings"[75] the term was to be placed. Once the court had pronounced upon this matter the fact that the chosen meaning was formerly part of a range of possible meanings on which opinions might legitimately differ became simply a matter of history.[76]

Third, the criterion which was chosen might, however, itself be so imprecise that different decision-makers, could rationally reach different conclusions when applying it to the facts of a given case.

> "In such a case the court is entitled to substitute its opinion for that of the person to whom the decision has been entrusted only if the decision is so aberrant that it cannot be classed as rational: *Edwards v. Bairstow* . . . The present is such a case. Even after eliminating inappropriate senses of "substantial" one is still left with a meaning broad enough to call for the exercise of judgment rather than an exact quantitative measurement."[77]

F. Summary

The present law may be summarised as follows. How satisfactory this position is will be examined below.   **14–035**

(1) The courts will review any error of law, and will, in general, no longer employ distinctions between jurisdictional and non-jurisdictional error. When an error has been made the court will normally substitute its view for that of the body subject to review. There appear to be five qualifications to this basic proposition.

(2) The error of law must be relevant or material in the sense discussed above.

(3) The varying presumption as to legislative intent still appears to operate depending upon the type of institution being reviewed. If the institution subject to review is a tribunal or other administrative body, then the presumption will be that Parliament did not intend that body to be the final arbiter on issues of law. If, however, the institution subject to review is an inferior court then there is no presumption that Parliament did not intend questions of law to be left to that court.[78]

---

[75] *South Yorkshire Transport Ltd*, n.73, 30.
[76] *South Yorkshire Transport Ltd*, n.73, 32.
[77] *South Yorkshire Transport Ltd*, n.73, 32.
[78] However, even in this latter instance it appears to be the case that, for example, a legislative finality clause, which purports to render a decision of an inferior court final and conclusive, will only be interpreted to protect that body from errors of law within jurisdiction, *Page* [1993] A.C. 682, 703.

(4)   In *Sivasubramaniam* the Court of Appeal held that judicial review
      was in principle still available in relation to decisions of county
      courts, notwithstanding the existence of a statutory appeal proce-
      dure.[79] The court however affirmed that in general claimants should
      pursue the regime of appeal laid down by statute, subject to the
      exceptional possibility of judicial review on grounds of absence of
      jurisdiction. Thus pre-*Anisminic* conceptions of absence of jurisdic-
      tion may be relevant in relation to this type of case.

(5)   The court will not necessarily substitute its judgment for that of the
      agency in circumstances like those in the *South Yorkshire Transport*
      case. In such a case the reviewing court will define the actual
      meaning that the statutory term is to have, but where that particular
      meaning is itself inherently imprecise the court will only intervene if
      the application of the term is so aberrant as to be irrational.

(6)   The courts continue to regard the grant of a remedy as discretionary,
      and will not necessarily grant the remedy merely because an error of
      law has been committed during, for example, an inquest.[80]

G. Error of Law within Jurisdiction

14–036   In addition to review for jurisdictional error, the courts have, in the past,
maintained control over errors of law within jurisdiction if they appeared on
the face of the record. Indeed certiorari appears to have developed to
control this very type of error.[81] Control over such errors declined during the
latter half of the 19th century,[82] and was only "rediscovered" 100 years
later.[83] This control could only be exercised if the defect appeared on the
face of the record. The courts construed this broadly to include the documents which initiated the proceedings, the pleadings and the adjudication.[84]
The reasons for the decision might also be held to be part of the record.[85]

---

[79]   *R. (on the application of Sivasubramaniam) v Wandsworth County Court* [2003] 1 W.L.R. 475;
R. (on the application of Sinclair Gardens Investments (Kensington) Ltd) v Lands Tribunal [2005]
EWCA Civ 1305.
[80]   *R. v Inner South London Coroner Ex p. Douglas-Williams* [1999] 1 All E.R. 344, 347, citing *R.
v Greater Manchester Coroner Ex p. Tal* [1985] Q.B. 67, 83. It should however be noted that the
court was influenced in framing its judgment in this manner by the legislation relating to
coroners which specifies that a new inquest should not be held unless it is necessary or desirable
in the interests of justice.
[81]   A. Rubinstein, *Jurisdiction and Illegality* (Oxford University Press, 1965), Ch.4.
[82]   The primary reason was the passage of the Summary Jurisdiction Act 1848 which authorised
a truncated form of record in which the charge, evidence and reasoning to support it were no
longer required to be set out in criminal convictions, *R. v Nat Bell Liquors Ltd* [1922] 2 A.C.
128, 159.
[83]   *R. v Northumberland Compensation Appeal Tribunal Ex p. Shaw* [1951] 1 K.B. 711, [1952] 1
K.B. 338.
[84]   *Shaw* [1952] 1 K.B. 338, 352.
[85]   *R. v Medical Appeal Tribunal Ex p. Gilmore* [1957] 1 Q.B. 574; *Baldwin and Francis Ltd v
Patents Appeal Tribunal* [1959] A.C. 663; *R. v Knightsbridge Crown Court Ex p. International
Sporting Club (London) Ltd* [1982] Q.B. 304; *R. v Chertsey JJ Ex p. Franks* [1961] 2 Q.B. 152.

Statute also played a part in broadening the ambit of the record. The Tribunals and Inquiries Act 1958, s.12 initiated a right to reasoned decisions which were to be treated as part of the record, but only in the sphere covered by the Act.

The revival of this head of review was greeted enthusiastically. Whether it continued to survive was simply another way of asking whether the traditional collateral fact doctrine would continue to be used by the courts. This question has just been considered. Although the House of Lords in *Anisminic*[86] affirmed the continued existence of non-jurisdictional errors of law, we have seen that the *Page*[87] case discarded the distinction between jurisdictional and non-jurisdictional error. A separate category of error of law within jurisdiction will, therefore, very largely become redundant.

The only instances where error of law within jurisdiction might still be of relevance[88] are where there is a finality clause *and* the court believes that Parliament might have intended that the decision-maker should be the final arbiter on questions of law. In such circumstances the finality clause might well immunise the decision from attack if there is an error of law within jurisdiction. This is equally true if the common law has recognised that decisions of, for example, University Visitors are final and conclusive. Provided that the University Visitor has jurisdiction in the narrow sense to consider the relevant matter, the courts will not interfere further and will not review errors of law committed within jurisdiction.[89]

H. Statutory Review

A number of statutes contain provisions allowing review only within a limited period, commonly being six weeks. The effect of the six weeks' time limit will be considered within the general context of exclusion of remedies.[90] What falls to be considered now is the effect of a specific statutory formula which allows challenge within the six-week period on certain grounds.[91] The statute will normally establish two grounds of review. These are that the order impugned is not within the powers of the Act, or that any requirement of the Act has not been complied with. If the latter is the ground of attack, there is often the additional requirement that the interests of the applicant have been substantially prejudiced.

There has been considerable difference of judicial opinion as to the construction of these clauses. Part of the difficulty lies in the developments in the ordinary common law of judicial review. If such statutory clauses were ever intended to reflect the common law, (and this is not clear), the distinction between the two heads of review now makes little sense given the

14–037

---

[86] [1969] 2 A.C. 147.
[87] *Page* [1993] A.C. 682, 701.
[88] *Page*, n.87, 703.
[89] *Page*, n.87, 702–703; *R. (on the application of Ferguson) v Visitor of the University of Leicester* [2003] EWCA Civ 1082; *R. (on the application of Varma) v Duke of Kent* [2004] E.L.R. 616.
[90] See Ch.27.
[91] This formula is common in legislation on housing and land use.

expansion of non-statutory review. Moreover, the very existence of the two heads of control has, in itself, exacerbated the confusion as judges have sought to find a function for each of the terms.

This can be seen in *Smith v East Elloe Rural District Council*[92] where there were a number of views as to the meaning of "not within the powers of this Act." Lord Reid[93] held that bad faith and unreasonableness were outside the statute completely and therefore could be impugned even after six weeks. A similar result was reached by Lord Somervell[94] who was of the opinion that fraud did not go to jurisdiction and could be challenged at any time. The majority decided that challenge for fraud was precluded after six weeks. Lord Morton went on to construe the statutory terms extremely narrowly as permitting challenge only if express statutory requirements were violated.[95]

The sensible interpretation would be to read the phrase, "not within the powers of this Act" so as to include any of the traditional heads of ultra vires, and there is authority for this position.[96] Later courts have given the formula a broad interpretation. It has been held to encompass not only traditional forms of jurisdictional error, but also no evidence, and any error of law.[97] The puzzles of *East Elloe* will therefore probably be quietly forgotten.

Despite this broad formulation, the courts still continue to use the second limb of the formula: "a requirement of the Act has not been complied with".[98] It may well be best that this should be confined to the challenge of directory provisions, allowing a court to quash an order if non-compliance with such provisions has caused substantial prejudice to the applicant.

5. THE TEST FOR REVIEW: POLICY CONSIDERATIONS

A. Clearing the Deck: The Demise of the Collateral Fact Doctrine and Limited Review

14–038 The demise of the collateral fact doctrine is to be welcomed. It was always arbitrary and uncertain in its application. The difficulty of distinguishing between the *kind* of case which a tribunal had to determine, and the statutory description of the *situation* which the tribunal had to decide, was the

---

[92] [1956] A.C. 736.
[93] [1956] A.C. 736, 763.
[94] [1956] A.C. 736, 772.
[95] [1956] A.C. 736, 755.
[96] *Webb v Minister of Housing and Local Government* [1965] 1 W.L.R. 755, 770 (Lord Denning M.R.). See cases, n.97.
[97] *Ashbridge Investments Ltd v Minister of Housing and Local Government* [1965] 1 W.L.R. 1320; *Coleen Properties Ltd v Minister of Housing and Local Government* [1971] 1 W.L.R. 433; *Gordondale Investments Ltd v Secretary of State for the Environment* (1971) 70 L.G.R. 158; *Peak Park Planning Board v Secretary of State for the Environment* (1980) 39 P. & C.R. 361.
[98] *Gordondale Investments Ltd* (1971) 70 L.G.R. 158; *Miller v Weymouth Corporation* (1974) 27 P. & C.R. 468.

root cause of the problem.[99] It was not possible to predict in advance the way in which a case would be categorised, nor was there any ex post facto rationality to explain why cases were categorised in different ways.

The Gordon thesis of limited review was also unsatisfactory. It was analytically flawed,[100] and was unacceptable on policy grounds. While the spectre of the Albert Hall being deemed a furnished tenancy haunts the annals of legal literature rather than the real world, we nonetheless require more control than allowed by Gordon's commencement theory.

B. Judicial Control and Agency Autonomy: Remembering the Past when Constructing the Future

It is important to pause at this point and consider a simple, but funda- **14–039** mental, question. Why did the courts persist with the collateral fact doctrine and limited review for so long? What were they trying to achieve? No answer is to be found in the modern case law. The judges in cases such as *Racal* and *Page* simply regard the distinctions between jurisdictional and non-jurisdictional error as esoteric and unnecessary. The implicit message is that the earlier decisions failed to realise that such distinctions were not needed, and that the judiciary could now discard them and impose more far-reaching controls. This is, with respect, to do a disservice to the older jurisprudence.

It is clear from a reading of this case law that the courts did not feel that they were bound by some a priori logic to employ either of the discredited theories. They fully acknowledged the possibilities open to them when devising the tests for jurisdictional control. The truth is that they adopted the collateral fact doctrine or the theory of limited review because they believed that these best captured the appropriate balance between judicial control and agency autonomy.[101] The courts did not believe that that they should be substituting judgment on every issue of law which comprised the "if X" question, since this would emasculate autonomy over issues which had been assigned to the agency by Parliament. They realised also that some judicial control was clearly required. The collateral fact doctrine and limited review were the tools used by these courts to preserve control, while giving some leeway to agency autonomy.

It is true, as we have seen, that these tests were defective. We are, however, in danger of discarding the tests and forgetting the rationale for them. We do not of course have to accept the balance between judicial control and agency autonomy adopted by earlier courts, but we should not forget that there is an issue here at all. Courts in other common law jurisdictions are, as we shall see, fully cognisant of this underlying policy issue. This should be borne in mind when considering the modern jurisdictional criterion of error of law.

---

[99] See above, paras 14–005—14–006.
[100] See above, paras 14–010—14–011.
[101] P. Craig, "Jurisdiction, Judicial Control and Agency Autonomy", in I. Loveland (ed.), *A Special Relationship, American Influences on Public Law in the UK* (Oxford University Press, 1995), Ch.7.

C. The Modern Law: Review for Errors of Law

14–040 The effect of *Anisminic*, as interpreted in *Racal*, *O'Reilly* and *Page*, is that all errors of law become open to review. Four comments on this test are warranted.

First, the suggestion that this scope of review is logically demanded is not convincing.[102] There is no a priori reasoning which indicates that the courts' view on the meaning of an "if X" issue should necessarily and always be preferred to that of the agency or inferior court. The answer resides not in some logically compelled statement as to whose opinion should count, but in a normative judgment as to whose relative opinion on a particular matter we wish to adopt.

Second, if we adopt the view that all errors of law are reviewable, in the sense that the court will substitute its view for that of the decision-maker, *and* we interpret error of law in the analytical sense discussed above,[103] there is a real danger that a valuable aspect of administrative autonomy will be eliminated.[104] The typical case arises over a contested interpretation of one of the statutory terms which the tribunal has to interpret. The courts tend to regard misconstruction of many of these terms as errors of law, the effect being that the court will substitute its view for that of the tribunal. However terms such as "resources", "employee", or "structural alteration" may be capable of having a spectrum of possible meanings depending upon the overall scope and policy of the legislation. It is difficult to believe that the ordinary courts' particular interpretation of all of these terms will necessarily always be better than that of the tribunal. The latter is established partly because of the expertise it can develop, and this expertise is not related solely to fact finding. Whether "course of employment" in a particular statute should include a tea break or the trip to work may be better decided by a tribunal staffed with a lawyer chairman and "wing" members representing the interests of trade unionists and employers rather than the ordinary courts.[105] Adequate control can be maintained, as will be seen below, through a rationality test.

Third, these problems would be mitigated if the courts were to interpret the term law in a more pragmatic, functional or policy-oriented way, taking into account the desirability of interfering with the agency decision, and the relative abilities of the court and the agency for deciding the question in issue. It is, however, clear that if the courts gave this construction to the term law they would be applying a very different thesis from that originally conceived by Gould and applied more recently by the courts. As Beatson stated,[106] "a system that uses the pragmatic approach is not using the concept of error of law as an organizing principle" as such, but rather as a

---

[102] See above, para.14–016.
[103] See above, paras 14–022—14–023.
[104] See also, J. Black, "Reviewing Regulatory Rules: Responsibility to Hybridisation", in J. Black, P. Muchlinski and P. Walker (eds), *Commercial Regulation and Judicial Review* (Hart, 1998), Ch.6.
[105] See the similar point made by J. Beatson, "The Scope of Judicial Review for Error of Law" (1984) 4 O.J.L.S. 22, 40–42.
[106] Beatson, n.105, 43.

facade behind which to weigh the relative competence of court and agency. They would in fact be applying a test for review not dissimilar to the one to be examined within the next section. The decision in the *South Yorkshire Transport* case[107] goes some way in this direction, but only to a limited extent. Their Lordships made it clear that they would decide upon the meaning of the open textured statutory term, while accepting that if that meaning was itself imprecise then the court would only intervene if the agency's decision was so aberrant as to be irrational.

The final comment concerns the issue of how far the nature of the decision-maker should affect the scope of review. We have seen that Lord Diplock in *Racal*[108] drew a distinction between the scope of review for tribunals and inferior courts. The latter would be subject to less extensive review than would tribunals and other administrative institutions. The continued vitality of this distinction appears to have been accepted by the House of Lords in *Page*.[109] There are difficulties with this distinction. It is often fortuitous whether a new institution is called a "court" or a "tribunal". The types of functions allocated between them may be equally haphazard. Moreover, while it is possible to give undue weight to expertise, it is also possible to underrate its significance. Many administrative institutions possess qualifications which render them just as capable of giving conclusive judgments on legal issues, or issues of mixed fact and law, as are the inferior courts. This is more particularly so given that tribunals are very likely to have a specialised, as opposed to a general jurisdiction. This enables them to develop expertise within their own area in a way which is more difficult for a generalist inferior court. The rationale for the distinction drawn by Lord Diplock has been further undermined by the regime instituted by the Tribunals, Courts and Enforcement Act 2007. Thus the Upper Tribunal created by this Act is a superior court of record and moreover exercises judicial review functions as well as operating as an appeal body from the First-tier Tribunal.[110]

D. A Middle Way: Rightness and Rational Basis

It is important to consider whether it is possible for control be achieved **14–041** without the court automatically substituting judgment for that of the tribunal, and without allowing the tribunal to have unlimited power. It is instructive in this respect to examine experience from other common law jurisdictions.

The leading decision on this issue in the United States is *Chevron*.[111] In that case the Supreme Court drew the following distinction. *If* a court reviewing an agency's construction of a statute decided that Congress did have a specific intention on the precise question in issue then that intention

---

[107] [1993] 1 W.L.R. 23.
[108] [1981] A.C. 374, 382–383.
[109] See above, paras 14–033, 14–035.
[110] See above Ch.9.
[111] *Chevron USA Inc v NRDC* 467 U.S. 837 (1984).

should be given effect to. The court will substitute judgment for that of the agency and impose the meaning of the term Congress had intended.[112] *If*, however, the reviewing court decided that Congress had not directly addressed the point of statutory construction, the court did *not* simply impose its own construction on the statute. Rather, if the statute was silent or ambiguous with respect to the specific issue, the question for the court was whether the agency's answer was based on a permissible construction of the statute. In answering this question the reviewing court might uphold the agency finding even though it was not the interpretation which the court itself would have adopted, and even though it was only one of a range of permissible such findings that could be made.[113] Moreover, the Supreme Court also held that the delegation to an agency of the determination of a particular issue might well be implicit rather than explicit, and that in such instances "a court may not substitute its own construction of a statutory provision for a reasonable interpretation made by the administrator of an agency".[114] *Chevron* therefore established a two-part test. Cases which fall under part one will result in substitution of judgment by the reviewing court; cases which fall under part two will result in a less intensive standard of review, that of reasonableness or rational basis.

It is clear that judges possess considerable discretion when deciding whether a case comes within part one or part two of the *Chevron* formula. This is inevitable. What is less readily apparent is that there has been disagreement among the judiciary as to the meaning which should be ascribed to the two parts of test, especially part one.[115] In *Cardozo-Fonseca*[116] the Supreme Court decided that the meaning of a particular statutory term was clear within the first limb of the *Chevron* test because the Court could divine its meaning through the normal tools of statutory construction. This provoked a powerful separate opinion from Justice Scalia. He felt that the approach of the majority would radically undermine the purpose of the *Chevron* formula, given that a Court could always then hold that the meaning of a statutory term was clear through the use of "normal tools of statutory construction". By way of contrast in *Rust*[117] Chief Justice Rehnquist interpreted the first limb of *Chevron* to apply only where the

---

[112] See also, *Etsi Pipeline Project v Missouri* 484 U.S. 495, 517 (1988); *Pittston Coal Group v Sebben* 488 U.S. 105, 113 (1988); *Bowen v Georgetown University Hospital* 488 U.S. 204, 212 (1988); *Adams Fruit Company, Inc v Ramsford Barrett* 494 U.S. 638, 649 (1990); *Department of the Treasury* 494 U.S. 922 (1990); *Dole v United Steelworkers of America* 494 U.S. 26, 43 (1990); *NRDC v Defense Nuclear Facilities Safety Board* 969 F 2d 1248, 1250–1251 (DC Cir1992).
[113] 467 U.S. 837, 842–843 (1984).
[114] 467 U.S. 837, 844. See also, *NLRB v United Food and Commercial Workers Union, Local 23, AFL-CIO* 484 U.S. 112, 123 (1987); *Mississippi Power v Moore* 487 U.S. 354, 380–382 (1988); *Sullivan v Everhart* 494 U.S. 83, 89 (1990); *Pension Benefit Guaranty Corporation v LTV Corporation* 496 U.S. 633, 648 (1990); *Department of the Treasury, Internal Revenue Service v Federal Labour Relations Authority* 494 U.S. 922, 928 (1990); *Armstrong World Industries, Inc v Commissioner of Internal Revenue* 974 F. 2d 422, 430 (3rd Cir 1992); *West v Sullivan* 973 F. 2d 179, 185 (3rd Cir 1992).
[115] S. Breyer, R. Stewart, C. Sunstein and M. Spitzer, *Administrative Law and Regulatory Policy, Problems, Text and Cases* (Aspen law & Business, 5th edn, 2002), 268–414.
[116] *Immigration and Naturalization Service v Cardozo-Fonseca* 480 U.S. 421 (1986).
[117] *Rust v Sullivan* 111 S. Ct. 1759 (1991).

Congressional meaning of the term really was evident on the face of the statute. If this was not so then the matter would fall to be determined under the rationality part of the formula.

A good example of a case pre-dating *Chevron* which applied a rationality **14–042** test is *Hearst Publications*.[118] Hearst published newspapers and refused to bargain collectively with a union representing newsboys who distributed the papers on the streets. Hearst argued that the newsboys were not "employees" within the relevant legislation; the Board claimed that they were. Justice Rutledge examined the evil which the statute was designed to cure and decided that it encompassed people outside the traditional common law classification of an employee. There could be differences of opinion as to which workers should be termed "employees" for the purposes of the statute. There were "myriad forms of service relationship" within the economy.[119] The Board's determination would, said the court, be accepted if it had warrant in the record and a reasonable basis in law, judged in the light of the overall statutory objective. The court did not simply substitute its own view because Congress had assigned the task primarily to the agency which, because of its greater experience, placed it in a better position to resolve the matter than the Court. Other cases adopted the same approach.[120]

The tendency in recent case law appears however to be in favour of less deference and toward greater reliance on the "plain" meaning of statutory terms.[121] This has led to more cases being characterised as falling within part one of the *Chevron* test, even if there is sharp disagreement within the Supreme Court as to what the relevant statutory terms actually mean.[122] The law has moreover been complicated by the difficult ruling in the *Mead* case,[123] which limits the circumstances in which the *Chevron* approach is deemed applicable.

The UK jurisprudence, as exemplified by the *South Yorkshire Transport* case,[124] allows some room for a rational basis test, but only to a very limited degree. Under the rational basis test as applied in cases such as *Hearst* and *Chevron* the agency's interpretation of the statutory term itself will be accepted if it is within the spectrum of possible rational interpretations which such a term could bear. By way of contrast the *South Yorkshire* case leaves this choice with the court which will determine the meaning which the

---

[118] *National Labour Relations Board v Hearst Publications, Inc* 322 U.S. 111 (1944).
[119] *Hearst Publications*, n.118, 126.
[120] *Rochester Tel Corp v United States* 307 U.S. 125 (1939); *Gray v Powell* 314 U.S. 402 (1941); *SEC v Chenery Corp* 332 U.S. 194 (1947); *Ford Motor Co v NLRB* 441 U.S. 488 (1979); *Ford Motor Credit Co v Milhollin* 444 U.S. 555 (1980); *FEC v Democratic Senatorial Campaign Committee* 454 U.S. 27 (1981); *Mississippi Power and Light Company v Mississippi, ex rel. Moore* 108 S. Ct. 2428, 2442–2444 (1988).
[121] Breyer, Stewart, Sunstein and Spitzer, *Administrative Law*, n.115, 359–361; *MCI Telecommunications Corp v American Telephone & Telegraph Co* 512 U.S. 218 (1994); *Brown v Gardner* 513 U.S. 115 (1994); *Food and Drug Administration v Brown & Williamson Tobacco Corporation* 529 U.S. 120 (2000).
[122] See, e.g., *Brown & Williamson Tobacco*, n.121.
[123] *U.S. v Mead Corporation* 533 U.S. 218 (2001); *Alaska Department of Environmental Conservation v Environmental Protection Agency* 540 U.S. 461 (2004).
[124] [1993] 1 W.L.R. 23.

statutory term should bear. It is only where the term, as defined by the reviewing court, is still inherently imprecise, that a rational basis test will be applied to test whether the agency's interpretation can withstand scrutiny.

E. A Middle Way: The Pragmatic and Functional Approach

14–043 The Canadian courts have also engaged in extensive analysis of the proper standard of judicial review. The case law is rich and complex.[125] It is clear that the courts will on some occasions use a correctness test, while on others they will employ a test of reasonableness.

It is clear from the Supreme Court's decision in *Pushpanathan*[126] that a number of factors will be taken into account when deciding on the applicability of these standards of review. These include: the existence or not of a privative clause and the nature of any such clause; the relative expertise of the decision-maker and the court; the purpose of the legislation and of the particular contested provision; and the nature of the problem, more especially whether it is one of law, fact or involves elements of both. The term "jurisdictional" is "now simply a label for a legislative provision that, following the application of the pragmatic and functional approach, a court determines must be answered correctly".[127]

It is evident that the approach of the Canadian courts has ebbed and flowed and that while some judges favour a test based of correctness, others prefer one which allows greater latitude for agency interpretation, as expressed through some form of reasonable test.[128]

---

[125] Madame Justice L'Heureux-Dube, "The 'Ebb' and 'Flow' of Administrative Law on the 'General Question of Law' ", in M. Taggart (ed), *The Province of Administrative Law* (Hart, 1997), Ch.14; D. Brown and J. Evans, *Judicial Review of Administrative Action in Canada* (Canvasback Publishing, 1998), Ch.14; D. Mullan, "Establishing the Standard of Review: The Struggle for Complexity?" (2003) 17 Can. J. Admin. Law & Prac. 59; D. Mullan, *Administrative Law: Cases, Text and Materials* (Emond-Montgomery, 5th edn, 2003); G. Huscroft, "Judicial Review from *CUPE* to *CUPE*: Less is not Always More", in G. Huscroft and M. Taggart (eds), *Inside and Outside Canadian Administrative Law, Essays in Honour of David Mullan* (University of Toronto Press, 2006), 296–326.

[126] *Pushpanathan v Canada (Minister of Citizenship and Immigration)* [1998] 1 S.C.R. 982; *Dr Q v College of Physicians and Surgeons of British Columbia* [2003] 1 S.C.R. 226; *Voice Construction Ltd v Construction & General Workers Union* [2004] 1 S.C.R. 609. The recent decision in *Dunsmuir v New Brunswick* 2008 SCC 9 reduced the tests for review to correctness and reasonableness, abolishing the previous distinction between reasonableness *simpliciter* and patent unreasonableness.

[127] Huscroft, n.125, 297; *Pushpanathan*, n.126, para.28; Brown and Evans, *Judicial Review*, n.125, Ch.14: 2531; *Union des Employes de Service, Local 298 v Bibeault* [1988] 2 S.C.R. 1048; *Public Service Alliance of Canada v Attorney General of Canada* [1991] 1 S.C.R. 614.

[128] Madame Justice L'Heureux-Dube, n.125, Compare, e.g., La Forest J. in *Canada (Attorney General) v Mossop* [1993] 1 S.C.R. 554, 584–585, and La Forest J. in *Gould v Yukon Order of Pioneers* [1996] 1 S.C.R. 571, 600–601, with Wilson J. in *National Corn Growers' Assn v Canada Import Tribunal* [1990] 2 S.C.R. 1324, 1353, and L'Heureux-Dube J. in *Mossop* [1993] 1 S.C.R. 554, 599.

F. The Middle Way: Concerns

i. Constitutional principle

It might be felt that the approaches considered above are inconsistent with **14–044** the juridical basis of judicial review. The inherent power of the courts to ensure that inferior jurisdictions remain within their assigned ambit has always, it may be argued, related to the legality of the findings that can be made and not their correctness. It might be thought that to adopt the approaches considered here would fundamentally alter the rationale for judicial review.

This will not withstand examination. The line between legality and correctness has always been hard to define. The distinction was maintainable while the courts applied a very limited form of review, and to a lesser extent, when they moved towards the collateral fact doctrine. Any attempt at continued demarcation became impossible once the courts moved to a theory of extensive review for error of law, which bases judicial intervention on a criterion of correctness and substitution of judgment.

We can of course continue to talk in jurisdictional terminology. We can say that a tribunal's jurisdiction is conditional on it making no errors of law. It is, however, this very flexibility of the jurisdiction concept which, if pushed too far, contains the seeds of its own destruction, or at least redundancy. To regard the jurisdictional cloak as a vital precondition justifying judicial intervention, while allowing the categories of jurisdictional error to multiply, simply conceals reality. It provides a fragile mask for avoiding awkward questions. The conceptual basis of judicial review, that the courts are thereby enforcing the legislative will by ensuring that the authority remains within the limits of its assigned area, has never provided any sure guide as to the appropriate scope for review. Almost any answer that we give to this question can, if we so wish, be formally accommodated within the language of jurisdiction. It is high time that we assessed the desirability of judicial intervention in its own terms.

ii. Certainty

It might be felt that the approaches considered above would produce **14–045** uncertainty. It is important in this respect to distinguish between different senses of uncertainty.

First, uncertainty might relate to the difficulty of predicting which test for review, rational basis or rightness, would be adopted in any particular case. This objection can, in one sense, be conceded. If the courts developed the idea that all errors of law are jurisdictional, defined the word law in a purely analytical way so that it embraced any application of a statutory term and substituted judgment on the meaning of that term, then a prospective applicant would be clear that the courts would intervene using that standard. This is, however, to say no more than that the presence of only one arbiter on the meaning of the jurisdictional conditions produces more certainty than a division of responsibility. The courts would decide all questions of law using that word in the sense described above. This certainty would mean reducing the competence of the initial decision-maker to a mere fact-finder, denying any weight to its opinion on the interpretation of the constituent parts of the X question, and embroiling the courts in the minutiae of all the elements which comprise the conditions of jurisdiction.

A second meaning of the term certainty relates to the *probability* that the court would *uphold* the finding of the initial decision-maker. This is the issue of most practical concern to the applicant. It may be very difficult for even the most experienced adviser to predict whether the reviewing court will accept that the interpretation of a term adopted by the initial decision-maker was right. Within those areas covered by the rational basis part of a test there would be greater certainty. A criterion of reasonableness or rational basis is obviously a narrower standard of review. Other things being equal, there is a greater chance that the original decision will be upheld as having a rational basis, even if the interpretation is not the precise one which the court itself would have chosen.

The concern for certainty could, third, mean that a claimant would be uncertain as to whether, on a rational basis test, an administrative authority would apply the *same meaning* to a term that it had used previously, or whether it would adopt a different interpretation. This has not been a problem in the USA or Canada. It could in any event be met by developing principles of consistency under which an authority should not change the interpretation accorded to a term, even if the second interpretation is reasonable, without due notice.

G. Conclusion

14–046 It is clear that a number of factors affect the judicial choice in the USA as to whether to use a test of rightness or rational basis in a particular case, including the extent to which the court sympathises with the agency's result, the type of agency under review and the nature of the invalidity alleged. If, for example, the alleged error relates to the construction of a term with which the courts are familiar then this will tend towards substitution of judgment, whereas more specific or technical matters will normally lead to a greater degree of discretion being granted to the agency, the legal conclusion being expressed in the form of the rational basis test. It should, moreover, be made clear that a test of rightness will clearly be adopted for certain types of jurisdictional error. If the allegation is that the tribunal was improperly constituted, or that it made an order which it was not empowered to make, arguments concerning rational basis are irrelevant.[129]

It might well be argued, in a cynical vein, that if we adopted such an approach the courts would manipulate the labels. The label rational basis would simply be reflective of a conclusion already reached that the court did

---

[129] Nor is there any suggestion that the test should be applied in the context of procedural error, i.e. if the rules of natural justice have been breached, the decision should not be upheld on the basis that the substantive decision has some rational basis.

not wish to intervene. A test of rightness would indicate the opposite conclusion. It might be argued further that the courts can do the same under
our present test by deciding whether an alleged defect should be characterised as an error of law.

There is undoubtedly some truth in this observation, but the point can be
overplayed. It is true that legal labels can be used to express a conclusion
already reached, rather than to dictate the result which should be arrived at.
To infer that the labels that we use are irrelevant is a non sequitur, because
the labels fashion the result which the court believes it ought to reach. Under
our approach which holds that all errors of law are jurisdictional, the courts
can choose to abstain by defining an issue as one of fact and not law. Yet,
the basic thesis that all issues of law should be for the ordinary courts, and
that this is the only way to maintain control over agencies, will itself shape
the conclusion which the court believes to be correct. In the United States
the courts can and will choose as between rational basis and rightness
depending, inter alia, on whether they are in accord with the interpretation
reached by the agency. However, the labels used also react with and influence the result which these courts believe to be correct. The labels tell us that
the courts in the USA, and other countries, believe that control over
agencies can be maintained without always substituting judgment and that
there is nothing absurd in accepting that the agency's choice as to the precise
meaning should govern, subject to constraints of rationality.

The rightness/rational basis approach is not without its problems, but it
does focus on the relevant issues directly: whose opinion on the existence
and meaning of a statutory term should be accepted, that of the agency or
that of the courts? Once we rid ourselves of the dual notions that some
magic divides jurisdictional and non-jurisdictional questions, *and* that all
matters of law have one inexorably correct meaning which must *always* be
supplied by the courts, we are in a position to make a reasoned choice. This
choice allows us to accord primacy to the authority's interpretation, while
still preserving judicial control. Given the diversity of tribunals, commissions, authorities, ministers and inquiries which constitute our administrative system, it would be surprising if we did not conclude that in some
instances the rational basis test was preferable and in others a test of substitution of judgment.

This approach would, moreover, enable us to recapture the point of
principle which was apparent to the 18th- and 19th-century courts, but
which has been largely forgotten more recently: jurisdiction centres around
the correct balance between judicial control and agency autonomy.

CHAPTER 15

REVIEW OF FACT AND EVIDENCE

1. INTRODUCTION

The previous chapter considered the scope of review for errors of law. We **15–001** saw, in the course of that discussion, that the divide between issues of law and fact could be contentious. This nonetheless still leaves open the test for judicial review of questions of fact and the related issue of how far the courts will review evidentiary material.

The extent to which facts were susceptible to review or appeal was, until recently, unclear, notwithstanding the inherent importance of the issue.[1] There were numerous cases dealing in one way or another with review and appeal for fact, but there was little in the way of any systematic and principled judicial guidance as to when facts ought to be susceptible to judicial scrutiny.

There were a number of reasons why this was so. It was in part because of the very malleability of the categories of judicial review, with the consequence that courts could on an ad hoc basis choose to catch factual error through a category such as relevancy if they were so inclined. It was in part because courts intervened in relation to factual error where they felt that this was warranted, without too close an inquiry as to whether such intervention was justified in the light of the existing case law. It was in part also because judicial indications that the scope of review for fact might be broader than hitherto perceived tended to be given as dicta in cases where this was not the main issue before the court.

---

[1] T. Jones, "Mistake of Fact in Administrative Law" [1990] P.L. 507; M. Kent, "Widening the Scope of Review for Error of Fact" [1999] J.R. 239; P. Craig, "Judicial Review, Appeal and Factual Error" [2004] P.L. 788; R. Williams, "When is an Error not an Error? Reform of Jurisdictional Review of Error of Law and Fact" [2007] P.L. 793.

Text writers tended to advocate expansion and consolidation of this head of review.[2] It was nonetheless surprising given the importance of the issue that the courts had not attempted to address in a principled manner the criteria for judicial review and appeal in relation to facts. The Court of Appeal in *E v Secretary of State for the Home Department*[3] has now attempted to bring some order into this area and the reasoning of the court will be examined below.

The discussion will begin by considering the variety of situations covered by the general category of mistake of fact. This will be followed by detailed analysis of the reasoning in the *E* case. The remainder of the chapter will consider the limits of judicial intervention in relation to factual claims, with particular emphasis being given to the respective roles of the court and initial decision-maker in relation to factual findings, and to the criteria for the admissibility of fresh evidence to prove factual error.

2. The Meaning of Mistake of Fact

15–002   It may be helpful at the outset to consider the meaning of mistake of fact. There has been considerable academic discussion of the divide between law and fact for the purposes of appeal and judicial review.[4] This focus is readily explicable given the expansion in review for error of law. There has however been less attention paid to the meaning of mistake of fact. It has for the most part been treated as a "residual unitary category" embracing cases where there is no error of law. It is however clear that the category of mistake of fact includes a plethora of different situations. The simple paradigm is of a mistake relating to a primary fact, in the sense of an error pertaining to the existence of something said, done or perceived. Closer examination reveals a more complex spectrum of situations entailing factual error. What follows does not purport to be an exhaustive list. It draws out from the case law the variety of situations that are to be found within the general category of mistake of fact.

We can begin with the paradigm where a *simple factual finding made by the decision-maker is challenged as being incorrect*. This covers the type of case where the initial decision was premised on the existence of certain relatively simple or straightforward primary facts, such as whether a person was in a certain place at a certain time, or whether two towns were separate

---

[2] P. Craig, *Administrative Law* (Sweet and Maxwell, 5th edn, 2003), 502–510; S. de Smith, Lord Woolf and J. Jowell, *Judicial Review of Administrative Action* (Sweet and Maxwell, 5th edn, 1995), paras 5–091–5–096; H.W.R. Wade and C. Forsyth, *Administrative Law* (Oxford University Press, 8th edn, 2000), 266–268, 278–285.
[3] [2004] Q.B. 1044. See also *R. (Iran) v Secretary of State for the Home Department* [2005] EWCA Civ 982.
[4] See above, paras 9–019—9–021.

with the consequence that one could not levy rates for poor relief on inhabitants of the other.[5]

This leads on to cases involving *more complex factual findings, which require a greater degree of evaluative judgment.* Thus in *Kibiti* the applicant sought asylum, and the Immigration Appeals Tribunal made a finding that there was a civil war in the Congo at the relevant time.[6] This was important because it had an impact on the test for persecution used when deciding on asylum applications.[7] Kibiti argued that the IAT had erred factually, because there was no civil war in the Congo, but the court found against him, holding that the evidence available to the IAT amply justified its factual finding. *Turgut*[8] provides another good example. The applicant claimed that he faced a real risk of persecution and ill-treatment if returned to Turkey, since he was a Turkish Kurd who had evaded the draft. It is clear that the decision on this factual issue required a considerable degree of evaluative judgment, prompting the court to discuss the respective roles of the court and the Secretary of State in relation to the assessment of the relevant factual evidence.[9]

There is then a category of case where *the primary decision-maker factually misinterpreted or misunderstood evidence presented at the hearing.* The *Haile* case[10] exemplifies this type of case. The essence of the complaint, upheld by the court, was that the special adjudicator in an asylum case had found against the applicant, inter alia, because he, the adjudicator, had mixed up the names of two organisations in Ethiopia. The special adjudicator had thought that the applicant was referring to membership of a body called the EPRF, when in fact the applicant was referring to the EPRP. The adjudicator felt that certain evidence adduced on behalf of the applicant was not credible, on the assumption that it referred to the EPRF, whereas it actually referred to the EPRP and when read in that way the evidence presented made sense. **15–003**

We can move on to a fourth type of case where the *decision-maker makes a mistake of fact by failing to take account of crucial evidence when it made its initial decision.* The prime modern example is the *CICB* case.[11] The Criminal Injuries Compensation Board denied the applicant's claim for compensation in ignorance of the report by a police doctor that lent weight to her allegations that she had been sexually assaulted, and in reliance on a statement from a member of the police force that ran counter to the findings of the police doctor.

There is a fifth type of case where the *decision is made on certain factual assumptions and the applicant seeks to show, sometimes through the admission*

---

[5] *Nichols v Walker* (1632–1633) Cro. Car. 394; *Milward v Caffin* (1778) 2 Black W. 1330; *Lord Amherst v Lord Somers* (1788) 2 T.R. 372; *Weaver v Price* (1832) 3 B. & Ad. 409; *Governors of Bristol Poor v Wait* (1834) 1 A. & E. 264; *Fernley v Worthington* (1840) 1 Man. & G. 491.
[6] *Romain Kibiti v Secretary of State for the Home Department* [2000] Imm. A.R. 594.
[7] *Adan v Secretary of State for the Home Department* [1999] 1 A.C. 293.
[8] *R. v Secretary of State for the Home Department Ex p. Turgut* [2001] 1 All E.R. 719.
[9] See also *K v Secretary of State for the Home Department* [2006] EWCA Civ 1037.
[10] *R. (on the application of Haile) v Immigration Appeal Tribunal* [2002] I.N.L.R. 283.
[11] *R. v Criminal Injuries Compensation Board Ex p. A* [1999] 2 A.C. 330.

of fresh evidence, that these factual assumptions were mistaken. This was in essence the claim in *Tameside*.[12] The Secretary of State had intervened in the local authority's education plans because he did not believe that the relevant school selection procedures could be applied within the required time, and therefore the local authority was acting unreasonably so as to justify his intervention. The House of Lords held that this assumption was not made out on the facts of the case. This was also the nature of the claim in the *E* case.[13] The decision of the Adjudicator and the IAT was based in part on the factual assumption that membership of the Muslim Brotherhood would not render E liable to persecution, more especially since his involvement had been at a low level. E sought to rely on subsequent evidence in the form of two reports revealing that membership of the Muslim Brotherhood would lead to a serious risk of detention and torture. The same was true in the related case of *R* who claimed asylum on the ground that he was a convert from Islam to Christianity and would therefore face persecution if he was returned home. His claim was rejected because the Adjudicator and the IAT felt that he did not have a well-grounded fear of persecution since the Taliban were no longer in power. He argued that the IAT should have taken into account a report from April 2003, which indicated that apostates were still at risk of persecution or death.[14]

There is a sixth category, which is closely related to, but distinct from, the fifth. This is where *the initial decision was made on certain general factual assumptions about for example the degree of risk faced by a certain category of persons, but these general assumptions are then modified in the light of later evidence.* Thus in *Polat*[15] the claimant was a Turkish Kurd who sought asylum. The IAT rejected the claim and based its decision on the assumption that such a person could not succeed unless he could show something more than that the Turkish authorities would have a record of his involvement in or sympathy for a separatist organisation. Later information came to light which caused the IAT in a subsequent case to modify its view about the risks faced by this category of person, such that suspected membership of, or support for, a separatist organisation would result in the person being handed over to the Turkish anti-terror branch, with the attendant risk of torture.

15–004 It is important moreover to appreciate that the category of *jurisdictional facts may cut across the preceding categories.* Jurisdictional facts are those that relate to the existence of the public body's power over the relevant area. Thus, as we saw in the previous chapter, a statute will always stipulate certain preconditions for the exercise of the agency's power. In a simple paradigm it will state that if an employee is injured at work then compensation can or should be granted. The statutory conditions thus laid down

---

[12] *Secretary of State for Education and Science v Tameside MBC* [1977] A.C. 1014.
[13] n.3; See also, *A v Secretary of State for the Home Department* [2003] I.N.L.R. 249; *R. (on the application of Bagdanavicius) v Secretary of State for the Home Department* [2003] EWCA Civ 1605.
[14] n.3.
[15] *Bulent Polat v Secretary of State for the Home Department* [2003] EWCA Civ 1059.

may be factual, legal or discretionary in nature. A classic factual pre-condition is that a person should be of a particular age to qualify for a benefit; a simple legal stipulation is provided by the meaning of the term employee; a discretionary precondition is where the statute provides that if a minister has reasonable grounds to believe that a person is a terrorist then he may be detained. Claims of factual error can arise in all three types of case. It might be argued that the agency simply got the applicant's age wrong because it confused the applicant with a different person. It might be claimed that the agency misapplied the legal meaning of the term employee to the facts of the applicant's case. It might be contended that the minister did not on the facts have sufficient material to sustain a reasonable ground for believing that the applicant was a terrorist.

It should also be recognised that *factual issues can occur in the context of rulemaking*. The discussion thus far has been concerned with the various meanings of factual error in the context of individual determinations. It is of course perfectly possible for an applicant to contest the factual basis behind a rule promulgated by an agency or the factual assumptions that underlie an agency policy determination. The relationship between courts and agency in such instances will be considered more fully below.

3. *E v Secretary of State for the Home Department*

A. The Facts

The decision of the Court of Appeal arose out of two joined cases concerned with immigration and asylum.   **15–005**

In one of the cases E, an Egyptian national, who had lived outside Egypt all his life, came to the UK in 2001 from Bangladesh and claimed asylum. He argued that if he were required to return to Egypt he would be at risk of detention and torture, because he was a sympathiser with the Muslim Brotherhood and because his family were involved in its activities. His application for asylum was refused by the Home Secretary, and this was confirmed by the Adjudicator and by the IAT. The decision of the Adjudicator and the IAT was based in part on the factual assumption that membership of the Muslim Brotherhood would not render him liable to persecution, more especially since his involvement had been at a low level. E sought to rely on subsequent evidence in the form of two reports revealing that membership of the Muslim Brotherhood would lead to a serious risk of detention and torture. The IAT refused permission to appeal to the Court of Appeal, stating that the IAT could only decide a case on the evidence before it at the time of hearing, and the reports relied on by E were not before the tribunal when it made its decision.

In the other case R was an Afghan national who came to the UK in 2001 and claimed asylum on the ground that he was a convert from Islam to Christianity and would therefore face persecution if he was returned home.

His claim was refused principally because the Adjudicator and the IAT felt that he did not have a well-grounded fear of persecution since the Taliban were no longer in power. The IAT hearing was held in April 2003, but the decision was not promulgated until August 2003. R sought permission to appeal to the Court of Appeal. He claimed that the IAT should have taken into account a report from April 2003, which indicated that apostates were still at risk of persecution or death. The IAT refused permission to appeal, holding that the relevant report was not in fact available until May 2003, and that it decided the case on the material available at the time.

B. Judicial Review, Appeal and Fact

15–006 The essence of E and R's claim was that the IAT had erred by not admitting the relevant evidence, and that this could be appealed even where, as under this statutory regime, the right of appeal was limited to questions of law. Carnwath L.J. gave the judgment of the Court of Appeal. The relevant aspects of the judgment may be presented as follows.

Carnwath L.J. considered the relationship between appeals on law and judicial review. He proceeded on the assumption that there should be no material difference as to whether the case reached the Court of Appeal as an application for judicial review or an appeal on a point of law. There had been a general assimilation of the various forms of review, statutory and common law, such that "it has become a generally safe working rule that the substantive grounds for intervention are identical".[16] The main practical dividing line was therefore between instances where appeal or review was accorded on fact and law, and those where it was confined to law.

The key issue was therefore whether a decision reached on an incorrect basis of fact could be challenged on an appeal limited to points of law.[17] Given that Carnwath L.J. had already decided that the operative reach of appeal and review for questions of law was materially the same, this meant that the resolution of this issue would have general implications for judicial review as well as appeal. It meant also that Carnwath L.J. could draw on the judicial review jurisprudence relating to errors of fact.

To this end Carnwath L.J. analysed the existing jurisprudence concerning judicial review for factual error. He noted that there were differing views as to the existence and scope of this ground of review.[18]

The narrower view was that judicial review for error of fact only existed in limited circumstances. Thus Buxton L.J. was of the view that leaving aside special considerations that might apply, albeit for different reasons, in the formalised context of planning, and asylum, there was no general right to challenge the decision of a public body on fact alone.[19] Buxton L.J. endorsed the earlier observations of Watkins L.J. who had stated that mistake of fact could vitiate the decision where the fact was a condition precedent to an

---

[16] *E*, n.3, para.42; see also, para.50.
[17] *E*, n.3, para.44.
[18] *E*, n.3, paras 44–60.
[19] *Wandsworth LBC v A* [2000] 1 W.L.R. 1246.

exercise of jurisdiction, where the fact was the only evidential basis for the decision, or where the fact related to a matter that had, expressly or impliedly to be taken into account. There was however no power of judicial review on grounds of error of fact outside of these categories.[20]

There was also authority for a broader view of the courts' jurisdiction to review for error of fact. Thus Scarman L.J. in *Tameside* held that misunderstanding or ignorance of an established and relevant fact could be a ground for review.[21] Lord Wilberforce in the House of Lords in *Tameside* stated that if a judgment required, before it could be made, the existence of certain facts, then while the evaluation of those facts was for the minister, the court could inquire whether the facts existed and had been taken into account, whether the judgment was made on a proper self-direction as to those facts, and whether irrelevant facts had been taken into account.[22] There were also a number of planning cases in which the courts had intervened where there was factual error.[23] More recent support for the broader view was evident in the House of Lords. In the *CICB* case[24] Lord Slynn was willing to characterise a failure to take account of certain factual evidence as justifying judicial review on the grounds of unfairness. It was Lord Slynn once again who alluded to the courts' powers over fact finding in *Alconbury*,[25] stating that they could quash for misunderstanding or ignorance of an established and relevant fact.[26] Lord Clyde noted that fact could be subject to review where the decision-maker was mistaken or where account had been taken of irrelevant facts,[27] while Lord Nolan was willing to countenance review of fact at least where the factual finding had no justifiable basis.[28]

Carnwath L.J.'s conclusion from existing authority was that cases concerned with factual error could be dealt with under a separate ground of review based on fairness.[29] In categorising matters in this way he chose to follow Lord Slynn's approach in the *CICB* case.[30] Carnwath L.J. held that this was a convincing explanation of the cases where decisions had been set aside for mistake of fact[31] and stated that if this was felt to take fairness beyond the traditional confines of procedural irregularity it was going no further than the use of fairness in previous cases.[32] He concluded that mistake of fact

15–007

---

[20] *R. v London Residuary Body*, July 24, 1987.
[21] *Tameside*, n.12, 1031–1032.
[22] *Tameside*, n.12, 1047.
[23] *Hollis v Secretary of State for the Environment* (1984) 47 P. & C.R. 351; *Jagendorf v Secretary of State and Krasucki* [1985] J.P.L. 771; *Simplex GE (Holdings) Ltd v Secretary of State for the Environment* (1989) 57 P. & C.R. 306.
[24] *Ex p. A*, n.11, 343–346.
[25] *R. v Secretary of State for the Environment Ex p. Alconbury* [2003] 2 A.C. 295, para.53.
[26] This was relevant in deciding whether the courts' powers were sufficient for the purposes of art.6 of the European Convention on Human Rights.
[27] *Alconbury*, n.25, para.169.
[28] *Alconbury*, n.25, para.62.
[29] n.3, para.63.
[30] n.11.
[31] n.3, para.64.
[32] n.3, para.65, citing *HTV Ltd v Price Commission* [1976] I.C.R. 170 and *R. v IRC Ex p. Preston* [1985] A.C. 835.

giving rise to unfairness was a separate head of challenge in an appeal on a point of law "at least in those statutory contexts where the parties share an interest in co-operating to achieve the correct result",[33] asylum being regarded as one such area. There would, said Carnwath L.J., normally be four requirements to show the requisite unfairness and hence justify setting aside a decision for mistake of fact.[34]

"First, there must have been a mistake as to an existing fact, including a mistake as to the availability of evidence on a particular matter. Secondly, the fact or evidence must have been 'established', in the sense that it was uncontentious and objectively verifiable. Thirdly, the appellant (or his advisers) must not have been responsible for the mistake. Fourthly, the mistake must have played a material (not necessarily decisive) part in the Tribunal's reasoning."

The judgment then considered the circumstances in which evidence could be admitted to prove the mistake of fact. The reasoning thus far had established that the courts could, subject to the above conditions, intervene where there was a mistake of fact. It is however readily apparent that the applicant might need to present evidence to prove the relevant error. Carnwath L.J. analysed the conditions in which such evidence could be admitted. The court has discretion under the CPR to admit new evidence.[35] This is however generally subject to the principles in *Ladd v Marshall*,[36] which established that for fresh evidence to be admitted it must be shown that it could not with reasonable diligence have been obtained for use at the trial, that if the evidence had been given it would probably have had an important influence on the result of the case, and that it was credible, albeit it did not have to be incontrovertible. Carnwath L.J. analysed the extent to which these principles should be relevant in public law cases. He distinguished between two different types of case.

15–008   There were, on the one hand, cases where the courts had admitted fresh evidence without reference to the principles in *Ladd v Marshall*. This was explicable, said Carnwath L.J., because the cases turned on the legality of a ministerial decision, where the evidence was not available when the minister made the initial determination *and* where the Minister was regarded as having a continuing responsibility over the matter.[37] *Launder*[38] and *Simms*[39] were seen as examples of such cases. Carnwath L.J. did not regard them as controlling in relation to cases dealing with a body with finite jurisdiction, such as the IAT.[40]

---

[33] n.3, para.66.
[34] n.3, para.66.
[35] CPR 52.11(2).
[36] [1954] 1 W.L.R. 1489.
[37] n.3, paras 73–75.
[38] *R. v Secretary of State for the Home Department Ex p. Launder (No.2)* [1997]1 W.L.R. 839, 860–861.
[39] *R. v Secretary of State for the Home Department Ex p. Simms* [2000] 2 A.C. 115, 127.
[40] n.3, paras 74–75, 77.

There were, on the other hand, cases dealing with challenges to decisions made by tribunals such as the IAT, where the applicant sought to introduce fresh evidence in order to prove the factual error. Some courts had been willing to admit such evidence, notwithstanding the fact that the error could have been spotted by the applicant's advisers at the time of the decision by the IAT, such as in the *Haile*[41] case. Carnwath L.J. held that the principles in *Ladd* should be treated as the starting point, albeit with discretion to depart from them in exceptional circumstances, and the *Haile* case should be seen as an instance where this was warranted.[42] He was mindful of the dangers of statutory appeals on law or judicial review being used too readily as a mechanism for the re-evaluation of factual matters, and this was the rationale for the emphasis accorded to the principles in *Ladd* within public law.

The Court of Appeal decided that it was within the powers of the IAT to reopen its decision to take account of evidence that existed before its decision, where the evidence was only drawn to its attention when an application to appeal was made. The IAT should however be satisfied that there was a risk of serious injustice because of evidence that had been overlooked at the hearing.[43] The case was therefore remitted to the IAT to reconsider in the light of the principles laid down by the Court of Appeal in this case.

4. THE TEST FOR MISTAKE OF FACT: FOUNDATIONS

The test for judicial intervention on the grounds of mistake of fact developed in the *E* case represents a compromise between two pairs of rival considerations.   **15–009**

There is, on the one hand, the obvious tension between the primary role of the initial decision-maker in relation to the findings of fact, and the desire of the courts to be able to provide relief in some instances through review or appeal where a factual error occurred. There is, on the other hand, the tension resulting from the limitation of appeals in certain areas to questions of law. This rendered it necessary to produce a ground of intervention in relation to mistake of fact which could be couched in terms of error of law. It will perforce be difficult to reconcile these competing considerations, and there will doubtless be differences of opinion as to whether the test in the *E* case achieves this. It will be argued that the Court of Appeal was on the right lines for the following reasons.

---

[41] *Haile*, n.10.
[42] n.3, paras 81–82, 91.
[43] n.3, paras 35, 97–98.

A. The Overview was Necessary

15–010 The test in the *E* case brings a degree of order to an area that was lacking
hitherto. It was regrettable that the pre-existing law on appeal and review
for mistake of fact was so unclear. This was especially so given the practical
importance of the topic for courts and litigants alike. Thus, as Carnwath
L.J. noted, there were widely differing views expressed as to the scope of
review for mistake of fact, but in practice administrative court judges tended
to set aside decisions on this ground when justice so required.[44] A judgment
seeking to instil some order and principle into this area was therefore timely.

B. The Conceptual Foundation for Judicial Intervention

15–011 The conceptual foundation for judicial intervention in relation to mistake of
fact, unfairness and error of law, is explicable. It would in principle have
been perfectly possible, if there had not been the need to accommodate
appeals on questions of law, to justify judicial review squarely on mistake of
fact leading to unfairness, without the necessity of conceptualising this as an
error of law. There has long been intervention in relation to factual matters
within judicial review. The issue has always been the scope of this head of
judicial review, rather than its existence.[45]

It should however be remembered that the Court of Appeal had already
decided that the substantive grounds of intervention should be the same in
relation to statutory appeals limited to law and judicial review.[46] This is
important in understanding why it chose unfairness as the conceptual
foundation for judicial intervention when a mistake of fact occurred that
satisfied the four parts of the guidance.[47] The choice of this label was
motivated in part by the need to ensure that intervention for mistake of fact
could be accommodated within the remit of appeals limited to questions of
law and within the general framework of judicial review. It was therefore
necessary to construct a rationale that could be couched in terms of error of
law, and it was the unfairness resulting from the mistake of fact that provided the requisite link.

It might be argued that where the legislature limited appeals to questions
of law this reveals an intention not to allow appeals in relation to facts. This
issue must be squarely addressed. It is however the very meaning of law that
is in issue. It cannot simply be assumed, a priori, that factual error can never
lead to an error of law, since that would be to presume the answer to the
question at issue.

The reality is that the conception of "legality" within judicial review is in
effect used as a label to cover a variety of more specific grounds of challenge
relating to the rule of law. The courts have on a number of previous

---

[44] n.3, para.52.
[45] Thus, for example, the courts intervened in relation to facts that conditioned the existence of
the public body's power over a certain area without any need to depict such intervention as an
error of law.
[46] n.3, paras 42, 50.
[47] n.3, paras 63, 66.

occasions forged the link between factual mistake and error of law in order to facilitate judicial intervention.[48] In that sense the reasoning in the *E* case was following a well trodden path. It was simply more specific as to which aspect of error of law, unfairness, was engaged.

Judicial review for "illegality" embraces a wide range of situations. Thus there are classic errors of law in the sense that the public body has, in the opinion of the reviewing court, misconstrued the meaning of a legal term in the empowering legislation. Illegality also covers matters such as action for improper purposes, and the taking account of irrelevant considerations, or the failure to take account of relevant considerations. These are treated as species of illegality because they involve statutory construction to delimit the ambit of the public body's power. The line between failing to take account of relevant considerations and factual error may however be a fine one, which explains why relevancy has in the past been used as a surrogate doctrinal device through which to deal with factual mistake. The denomination of factual error leading to unfairness as giving rise to an appeal on a point of law is not therefore so odd when the category of legal error is viewed in this manner.

15–012

It is true, as recognised by the Court of Appeal, that unfairness when used in this context went beyond its traditional role as an aspect of procedural irregularity.[49] The response was that its application in this context went no further than its use in previous cases such as *HTV*[50] and *Preston*.[51] The Court of Appeal did not say that the cases on mistake of fact and unfairness were the same as *HTV* and *Preston*.[52] The argument was that the use of fairness as the ground for intervention in relation to mistake of fact was warranted because it went no further than its use in these cases, and that in both types of case the unfairness could occur even though there was no fault on the part of the public body.

This can be accepted. It should nonetheless be acknowledged that fairness plays only a limited role in relation to mistake of fact. It is not a matter to be proven independently of the four requirements laid down by the Court of Appeal. It is rather the necessary consequence of finding that those requirements are met. If they are then the requisite unfairness will exist. While the role played by the concept of fairness is therefore limited, it should also be recognised that other conceptual labels to legitimate judicial intervention could also be problematic, in the sense that they would not

---

[48] *R. v Deputy Industrial Injuries Commissioner Ex p. Moore* [1965] 1 Q.B. 456, 488; *Ashbridge Investments Ltd v Minister of Housing and Local Government* [1965] 1 W.L.R. 1320, 1326; *Coleen Properties Ltd v Minister of Housing and Local Government* [1971] 1 W.L.R. 433; *General Electric Co Ltd v Price Commission* [1975] I.C.R. 1; *R. v Secretary of State for the Environment Ex p. Ostler* [1977] Q.B. 122, 123; *Mahon v Air New Zealand* [1984] A.C. 808, 821; *R. v Bedwelty Justices Ex p. Williams* [1997] A.C. 225; *Reid v Secretary of State for Scotland* [1999] 2 W.L.R. 28, 54.

[49] n.3, para.65.

[50] *HTV*, n.32.

[51] *Preston*, n.32.

[52] Those cases were concerned with the unfairness that could result from the public body's attempt to resile from representations on which the representee had detrimentally relied.

necessarily cover the differing types of situation within which factual error could arise.[53]

C. Difficulties with the Pre-Existing Narrow View

15–013   The pre-existing narrow view of intervention for mistake of fact was difficult to apply, and increasingly out of step with other developments in judicial review. If the courts intervene in relation to mistake of fact then the criteria for when they do so should in so far as possible be coherent and clear. This was unfortunately not so on the pre-existing narrow view.

It will be recalled that on this narrow view mistake of fact could vitiate the decision where the fact was a condition precedent to an exercise of jurisdiction, where the fact was the only evidential basis for the decision, or where the fact related to a matter that had, expressly or impliedly to be taken into account. There was on this view no power of judicial review for error of fact outside of these categories. The difficulty with this approach is the extent to which the categories denominated where intervention for mistake of fact was countenanced were really separable from other instances of factual error.

Thus the category of jurisdictional fact assumes that there is a clear divide in the powers accorded to a public body between those factual matters that can be regarded as jurisdictional and other factual matters that condition the exercise of power that are not to be so regarded. The reality is that this divide is difficult if not impossible to draw in any principled manner. Insofar as the jurisdiction of a public body is defined by a series of statutory conditions, some of which relate to facts, it is well-nigh impossible to decide in a principled manner that some of these factual conditions should be treated as jurisdictional, while others should not. The reality is that all such factual jurisdictional conditions operate so as to condition the ability of the primary decision-maker to be able to proceed to the substance of the case.[54] The real issue will always be the degree of control wielded by the courts over such factual findings, whether they choose to substitute judgment or to accord some greater degree of autonomy to the findings of fact made by the initial decision-maker.

There were similar problems with the category of intervention where the fact was the only evidential basis for the decision. It may well be difficult to decide whether the contested fact really was the only evidential basis for the decision. Even if this could be determined it still leaves open the issue of principle, as to why the courts should not be able to intervene where the fact was not the only evidential basis for the decision, but nonetheless had a marked causal impact thereon.

The final category for review of fact allowed by the narrow view, viz, that the fact related to a matter that had expressly or impliedly to be taken into

---

account, provided the courts with a flexible tool to allow intervention or not as they chose, but it did little to enhance certainty.

5. THE TEST FOR MISTAKE OF FACT: THE CRITERIA IN THE *E* CASE

The guidance given in the *E* case avoids the difficulties attendant upon the narrow view of judicial review for mistake of fact set out above and provides the foundation for future development in this area.

15–014

A. Mistake as to Existing Fact including Mistake as to Availability of Evidence

The first limb of the guidance in the *E* case makes it clear that intervention is possible in principle for all species of mistake of existing fact, including mistake as to availability of evidence on a particular matter, subject to the other criteria that make up the test. This is especially important in the light of the different types of case which come within the general umbrella of mistake of fact. The demarcation of types of factual error that are susceptible to review/appeal, and those that are not, would involve protracted litigation concerning the boundaries of the respective categories leading to uncertainty of the kind that bedevilled the jurisprudence prior to the *E* case.

15–015

Such demarcation would moreover only serve a valid purpose if the distinctions between different types of factual error made sense in normative terms. It is however not at all self-evident that, for example, a factual error materially affecting the way in which discretion is or is not exercised is less deserving of judicial attention than a factual error relating to the conditions establishing the jurisdiction of the public body. This is more especially so where the factual error relating to the exercise of discretion can have an impact on the applicant's human rights.

It is however important to emphasise that there must be a mistake as to an *existing* fact. This is exemplified by *Kaydanyuk*.[55] The applicant sought asylum, but his application was denied. The IAT took note of a report from a psychiatrist to the effect that the applicant was suffering from depression and that deportation would increase the risk that he would commit suicide. His state of mind declined sharply when he learned that his application for asylum had been turned down. He argued that the IAT's determination was based on a mistake of fact, in the sense that his real state of mind only became apparent after the IAT's determination. The Court of Appeal disagreed and held that the applicant did not succeed in overcoming the first part of the test: the IAT had taken full account of the medical report, which

---

[55] *Kaydanyuk v Secretary of State for the Home Department* [2006] EWCA Civ 368, paras 20–21.

included the risk of suicide, and the increase in this risk after its decision did not mean that the decision was based on any mistake of existing fact.

This can be contrasted with the *L* case.[56] The Special Educational Needs and Disability Tribunal decided that a child with autism should be educated at school A rather than school B. The decision was based in part on the assumption that school B was to be closed, whereas the reality was that there was a proposal that it should be closed. Jack J. held that this constituted a mistake as to existing fact and therefore allowed the appeal by the local authority.

B. The Fact or Evidence must be Uncontentious and Objectively Verifiable

15–016 The second limb of the guidance is that the fact or evidence must have been established, in the sense that it was uncontentious and objectively verifiable. It is clear from the judgment[57] that the Court of Appeal had in mind a case such as *CICB*,[58] where the fact was established, this being the failure to mention the police doctor's report, and hence if attention had been drawn to the point the correct position could have been shown by objective and uncontentious evidence. The requirement that the fact or evidence must be uncontentious has been the ground for rejecting a number of claimants in later cases.[59]

The requirement that the fact or evidence should be objectively verifiable is not problematic in principle. The difficulty resides rather with the requirement that the fact or evidence should be uncontentious. This could be interpreted in varying ways. Thus, for example, it might be contended that a fact is contentious because it requires evaluation, as opposed to mere "observation", and hence there could be disagreement about the resulting evaluation. It might alternatively be contended that a fact is contentious because it is not crucial or reliable to the initial determination. These alternative constructions will be examined in turn.

i. Contentious and Complex

15–017 It would be regrettable if the term uncontentious were interpreted so as to exclude review/appeal of more complex factual findings that require evaluation as opposed to mere observation. This narrow construction would mean that only simple errors of primary fact, falling into the first of the categories articulated above,[60] would suffice to raise this head of review/ appeal. If the term "uncontentious" is interpreted this strictly it will severely limit the number of cases where applicants can seek to have factual errors redressed. It could exclude more complex cases where the factual determination requires evaluative judgment, on the ground that such evaluative judgment might well be "contentious". This would be regrettable, since

---

[56] *R. (on the application of L) v London Borough of Wandsworth* [2006] EWHC 694.
[57] n.3, paras 63, 66.
[58] n.11.
[59] See, e.g., *W v Staffordshire CC* [2006] EWCA Civ 1676, paras 25–26.
[60] See above, para.15–002.

there are many cases that fall within this and the other categories articulated above.

It is moreover questionable how far this very narrow construction of the term "uncontentious" is compatible with earlier case law. It is clear from case law prior to the *E* case that the courts engaged in review or appeal of fact in cases where the facts could not, in reality, be regarded as uncontentious in the very narrow sense of the term. This is exemplified by cases such as *Kibiti*,[61] *Turgut*,[62] and *Polat*.[63]

This is also clear from the earlier case law dealing with review of subjectively worded statutory conditions. If the statute states that the "Minister may intervene if he thinks it necessary or desirable", there may be no term, such as successor in title, or resources, which the courts can insist should bear a certain meaning. The courts therefore sought to ensure that the decision-maker had some reasonable grounds for the action and reviewed the facts and evidence on which the Minister acted. They initially exercised this control where there was no evidence to support the finding that was made.[64] This control was extended to cover cases where, for example, a Minister reached a decision to which on the evidence he could not reasonably have come.[65] The control was further reinforced in *Tameside*,[66] where the Secretary of State was empowered to give directions if he was satisfied that the local education authority was acting unreasonably. Lord Wilberforce stated that,[67]

"If a judgment requires, before it can be made, the existence of some facts then, although the evaluation of those facts is for the Secretary of State alone, the court must inquire whether those facts exist, and have been taken into account, whether the judgment has been made upon a proper self-direction as to those facts, whether the judgment has not been made upon other facts which ought not to have been taken into account. If those requirements are not met, then the exercise of judgment, however bona fide it may be, becomes capable of challenge."

The factual and evidentiary issues raised in many of these cases could not readily be regarded as "uncontentious" in the very narrow sense of that term considered above. The courts nonetheless exercised control over these determinations. It would therefore be regrettable if the term "uncontentious" were to be construed too narrowly in the jurisprudence post the *E* case.

[61] n.6.
[62] n.8. See also more recently, *K*, n.9.
[63] n.15.
[64] *R. v London Residuary Body Ex p. Inner London Education Authority*, *The Times*, July 26, 1987; *R. v Secretary of State for Education Ex p. Skitt* [1996] C.O.D. 31; *R. v Bedwelty Justices Ex p. Williams* [1997] A.C. 225. cf. *R. v Nat Bell Liquors Ltd* [1922] 2 A.C. 128, 151–154.
[65] See n.48: *Ashbridge Investments*; *Coleen Properties*; *General Electric*; *Ostler*. See also, *Allinson v General Medical Council* [1894] 1 Q.B. 750, 760; *Lee v Showmen's Guild of Great Britain* [1952] 2 Q.B. 329, 345.
[66] n.12.
[67] *Tameside*, n.12, 1047. See also, *Mahon*, n.48, 832–833; *Alconbury*, n.25, para.53; *R. v Criminal Injuries Compensation Board Ex p. A* [1999] 2 A.C. 330, 344.

ii. Contentious and reliable

15–018   It may however be that the requirement that the fact should be uncontentious relates to the extent to which it is crucial and reliable to the initial determination, rather than complexity. This appears to be the meaning accorded to it by Brooke L.J., giving the judgment of the Court of Appeal in *Shaheen*.[68] He expressed concern about a prior case, *Cabo Verde*,[69] where the court held that there was a mistake of fact because the IAT had made its asylum determination on the basis that the applicant was badly treated in Angola, whereas subsequent evidence indicated that he was in Portugal at the relevant time. In *Shaheen* Brooke L.J. expressed his concern in the following terms.[70]

> "We seem to be in danger, in this area, of slipping from the identification of an uncontentious and objectively verifiable fact such as the prior existence of crucial and reliable documentary evidence into a willingness to re-open appeals for error of law merely because a witness has been subsequently found who could have made a witness statement challenging the factual conclusions that were reached by the original decision-maker in ignorance of such evidence."

There may well be a valid concern that controls over fact and evidence do not lead to initial decisions being challenged on questionable or spurious grounds. It is nonetheless necessary to disaggregate two related, albeit distinct, issues.

The first is whether the fact or evidence is uncontentious and objectively verifiable, which clearly entails that it is reliable, and perhaps also that it is crucial to the initial determination, although this latter element is also captured by the fourth limb of the test.

The second issue is whether fresh evidence should be admitted. The approach in the *E* case to the admissibility of evidence to prove the mistake was considered above, and will be analysed below. Now it may well be that the fresh evidence could with reasonable diligence have been obtained when the initial determination was made, or that it is not credible, in which case it should be rejected on these grounds. If however this is not so then it should be admitted to prove the initial mistake and the matter remitted to the primary decision-maker.[71]

---

[68] *Shaheen v Secretary of State for the Home Department* [2005] EWCA Civ 1294. See also *R. (Iran)*, n.3, para.50.
[69] *Cabo Verde v Secretary of State for the Home Department* [2004] EWCA Civ 1726.
[70] n.68, para.28.
[71] In *Shaheen*, n.68, Brooke L.J. distinguished between cases where an appeal court was satisfied, on new evidence, that a minister or an inferior body or tribunal took a decision on the basis of a belief as to the existence of a material fact that was now demonstrated beyond peradventure to be wrong, and those situations where it took its decision in the mistaken belief that there was in fact no apparently cogent evidence to refute a material finding it had made, *ibid* para.20. This distinction is, with respect, difficult to apply.

C. Responsibility for the Mistake

The third limb of the guidance is that the applicant or his advisers should   **15–019**
not have been responsible for the mistake. This clearly makes good sense. It
prevents the applicant from taking advantage of his or her own wrongdoing
and provides a potent incentive for the applicant to disclose the full and
accurate facts when the initial determination was made.

D. The Mistake should have Played a Material Part in the Tribunal's Reasoning

The final requirement is that the mistake should have played a material,   **15–020**
albeit not necessarily decisive, part in the tribunal's reasoning.[72]

E. The Admissibility of Fresh Evidence

The full impact of the E case can only be understood when the four-part   **15–021**
guidance is read in tandem with the approach to the admissibility of fresh
evidence. It is clear that the Court of Appeal wished to keep a tighter rein on
the admissibility of fresh evidence in public law than had been so in some of
the previous case law. The rationale for this was readily apparent.

The Court of Appeal in E had opted for a relatively liberal and expanded
category of appeal and review for mistake of fact. This perforce creates the
potential for an increase in the number of cases argued on this ground, and
serves to explain the approach to the admissibility of fresh evidence. The
Court of Appeal was clearly concerned about the impact of too great a
liberality in this respect, when viewed against the expansion of appeal and
review for mistake of law.

Thus it held that the principles in *Ladd v Marshall*[73] should be treated as
the starting point, albeit with discretion to depart from them in exceptional
circumstances.[74] It was clearly mindful of the dangers of statutory appeals
on law or judicial review being used too readily as a mechanism for the re-
evaluation of factual matters,[75] and this was the rationale for the emphasis
accorded to the principles in *Ladd* within public law.

Similar concerns about the admissibility of fresh evidence, and the consequential implications for the efficiency of the appellate process and finality
in public law were voiced by Auld L.J. in *Bagdanavicius*.[76] Auld L.J. opined
that it might soon be time for Parliament or the courts to take a "more
comprehensive and principled look at both forensic processes with a view to
reshaping their structures and jurisdictions so that the form and substance
of what the courts are doing bears some resemblance to each other".[77]

The admissibility of fresh evidence in later cases will depend in part on

---

[72] See, e.g., *Montes v Secretary of State for the Home Department* [2004] EWCA Civ 404.
[73] n.36.
[74] n.3, paras 81–82, 91.
[75] E, para.85.
[76] n.13.
[77] n.13, para.72.

how the courts apply the principles in *Ladd* in a public law context and the extent to which they are willing to exercise discretion to depart from them in particular situations. There is but little doubt that the exercise of such discretion will quite properly be affected by the nature of the case, and that courts will be more willing to exercise such discretion in cases where life and liberty are at stake.

In cases dealing with a body with finite jurisdiction, such as the IAT, the principles in *Ladd* were to be treated as the starting point. Thus in *Montes*[78] an application for fresh evidence to be considered was rejected on the ground that it could have been obtained with reasonable diligence for use at the hearing before IAT, and that in any event the evidence was unlikely to have led to any different conclusion. By way of contrast in *Gungor*[79] Collins J. held that it would be dangerous to rely merely on the fact that the evidence would have been available at the time of the initial hearing as entitling it to be disregarded, and it should have been considered whether such evidence might have affected the result.

The admissibility of fresh evidence will also depend in part on how later courts choose to interpret the divide between different types of cases, this being central to the judgment on this point. Carnwath L.J. distinguished the preceding type of case from that concerned with the legality of a ministerial decision, where the evidence was not available when the Minister made the initial determination *and* where the Minister was regarded as having a continuing responsibility over the matter.[80] *Launder*[81] and *Simms*[82] were regarded as examples of cases within this second category. The crucial element in this latter group of cases seems to be the continuing responsibility of the Minister over the matter. It is this which serves to explain the greater willingness to admit evidence that was not available when the initial decision was made. It will be for later courts to decide when this reasoning can be applied to decisions made by other public bodies.

6. The Role of the Reviewing Court in the Determination of Factual Error

15–022   The decision in *E* establishes four requirements for the applicant to show the requisite unfairness and hence justify setting aside a decision for mistake of fact. The first requirement of the test assumes that there has been a mistake of fact. It does not however resolve the role of the reviewing court in

---

[78] *Montes*, n.72; *AM (Iran) v Secretary of State for the Home Department* [2006] EWCA Civ 1813.
[79] *R. (on the application of Gungor) v Secretary of State for the Home Department* [2004] EWHC 2117.
[80] n.3, paras 73–75, 77.
[81] n.38.
[82] n.39.

assessing whether the factual error has actually occurred. This is a crucial issue that was not directly addressed in the *E* case, and it will be considered within this section.

A. The Standard of Proof Required in Relation to Facts

It is axiomatic that the existence or not of a factual error may well be **15–023** dependent on the standard of proof demanded in relation to the relevant facts. It is right and proper for the reviewing court to determine the standard of proof required for the establishment of facts by the primary decision-maker.

The *Khawaja* case[83] provides a clear example. The House of Lords held that an illegal entrant under the Immigration Act 1971 could cover a person who had obtained leave to enter by deception or fraud, as well as a person who had entered by clandestine means. Their Lordships then considered the standard of proof required of the immigration officer if his decision on the facts that a person had entered by deception was to be upheld. The House of Lords held that it was insufficient for the immigration officer to show that he had some reasonable grounds for his action. The standard should be higher when a power to affect liberty was in issue. An immigration officer would have to satisfy a civil standard of proof to a high degree of probability that the entrant had practised such deception. The court would determine whether that standard of proof had been met.

Rehman[84] provides a more controversial example of the interrelationship between the meaning of the statutory term, and the standard of proof required to satisfy the existence of that term on the facts of the case. R was a Pakistani national with temporary leave to stay in the UK, who had applied for indefinite leave to remain. The Home Secretary, acting on the advice of the security service, decided that R's activities were intended to further the cause of a terrorist organisation abroad. The Home Secretary therefore refused his application to remain in the UK, and decided instead that R's departure from the UK would be conducive to the public good in the interests of national security. The House of Lords held that the term national security could, as a matter of law, cover not only direct threat to the UK, but also action against a foreign state that might indirectly affect the security of the UK. It held that preventative or precautionary action could be taken in these circumstances.

The House of Lords then considered the standard of proof that should apply to determine whether R's actions constituted a threat to national security as defined above. The Special Immigration Appeals Commission had applied a test of a "high civil balance of probabilities". The House of Lords disagreed. It held that in determining whether there was a real possibility of activity harmful to national security, the Home Secretary did not have to prove this according to a high civil degree of probability in the

---

[83] *R. v Secretary of State for the Home Department Ex p. Khawaja* [1984] A.C. 74.
[84] *Secretary of State for the Home Department v Rehman* [2002] 1 All E.R. 122.

manner akin to a trial. While there had to be past proven action relied on as
grounds for deportation, the Home Secretary was also entitled to have
regard to R's potential action, in accord with the preventative principle. The
court should, moreover, give considerable weight to the Home Secretary's
assessment in this regard, since he was in the best position to determine what
national security required.

B. The Reviewing Court Should Not in General Engage in *De Novo* Review of Facts

15–024   The court should therefore as a matter of principle establish the standard of
proof required of the primary decision-maker in relation to matters of fact.
The court should not however generally be making its own *de novo* decision
about the existence of those facts.

The court should not in general regard itself as the primary fact-finder,
nor as a general rule should it substitute its judgment about the relevant
factual matter for that of the initial fact-finder. The court is not well-
equipped or well-placed to undertake *de novo* review. The finding and
evaluation of facts is quintessentially a matter accorded to the initial decision-maker, who will normally have dealt with many such cases and hence
have developed an understanding and expertise in the relevant area that a
generalist court cannot match. It would moreover be inappropriate for the
courts to exercise *de novo* judgment in circumstances where the initial
decision-maker has conducted an oral hearing, and evaluated the cogency of
witnesses, which process the reviewing court will rarely wish or be able to
replicate. If it did so with any degree of frequency and proceeded to make a
de novo judgment in cases where the factual issues were complex then this
would moreover seriously overburden the courts.

If the reviewing court is to engage in *de novo* review this must be justified
by the special circumstances of the case before it. This could be so where it is
felt that the fact finding procedures used by the primary decision-maker are
inadequate,[85] or where the facts relate to matters over which the courts have
expertise greater than that of the body being reviewed.

The courts should not however engage in *de novo* review merely because
the allegation relates to a factual matter that conditions the existence of the
public body's power. The rationale for caution can best be expressed
through an example. It may well be that the power of an agency is conditioned on the existence of, inter alia, a "trade dispute". The court stipulates
the legal meaning that this term should bear, and it is then for the agency to
decide on the facts whether such a dispute exists or not. This finding is
contested before the courts. It is important in this respect to disaggregate
two related issues that can arise in such cases.

It is generally accepted that the courts can receive evidence to affirm or
controvert the finding of fact made by the agency.[86] If the evidence was not

[85] *Citizens to Preserve Overton Park v Volpe* 401 U.S. 402, 415 (1971).
[86] *Eshugbayi Eleko v Government of Nigeria* [1931] A.C. 662, 670–72.

before the agency that made the initial decision, but the court admits it and finds it compelling then to that extent the court will be making its own judgment on the relevant factual matter.

The applicant may however simply argue before the reviewing court that the facts which were before the agency did not warrant the finding of a trade dispute. There is in such instances no reason why the reviewing court should substitute its own independent assessment of the facts for that of the agency. It can properly recognise the agency's expertise in relation to the factual matter, while maintaining judicial control, through a test which is less intrusive than substitution of judgment. It can, for example, deploy a substantial evidence test or a rationality test and decide whether the factual finding made by the agency is sustainable according to this standard of review.[87]

This has indeed been recognised by the courts. Thus in *Rolls*[88] it was held that Parliament must have intended that if the local authority applied the correct test in law to determine the meaning of the word "gypsy", the question of whether particular persons were as a matter of fact gypsies within this test was pre-eminently a matter for the local authority, subject to review on *Wednesbury* grounds of unreasonableness. A similar conclusion was reached in *Begum*[89] concerning the duties of a local authority in the housing context. It was held that a decision by a local authority that a person lacked the capacity to make an application for housing, because he could not understand or act on the offer of accommodation, could only be challenged if it could be shown to be *Wednesbury* unreasonable. We see the same reasoning in *Moyna*,[90] where the claimant sought a disability allowance because she was so severely disabled that she could not prepare a main cooked meal for herself. The House of Lords set out the legal meaning of the statutory term and then held that whether facts fell within the legal category thus defined was a question of fact for the tribunal. It could therefore only be overturned by an appellate body limited to questions of law if the tribunal's conclusions fell outside the bounds of reasonable judgment.

C. The Reviewing Court's Options when Engaged in Factual Scrutiny: Sufficiency of Evidence or Rationality

It should be recognised that there will be cases of relatively simple factual **15–025** error where there is no meaningful issue concerning the role of the court vis-à-vis the initial decision-maker in relation to the determination of the factual error. The existence of the factual error will be uncontentious. Thus in the *CICB* case there was no doubt that the relevant doctor's report had not been placed before the Board.[91] Similarly in the *Haile* case[92] it was clear that the

[87] *Universal Camera Corp v NLRB* 340 U.S. 474 (1951).
[88] *Rolls v Dorset County Council* [1994] C.O.D. 448.
[89] *R. v Tower Hamlets London Borough Council Ex p. Begum* [1993] A.C. 509.
[90] *Moyna v Secretary of State for Work and Pensions* [2003] 1 W.L.R. 1929.
[91] n.11.
[92] n.10.

special adjudicator had confused the names of the relevant organisations in Ethiopia.

There will however be other cases concerned with the assessment of more complex factual issues, requiring evaluative judgment, where the court will have to decide, explicitly or implicitly, the extent to which it should be making its own *de novo* judgment about the relevant factual matter, and the extent to which it should be acting in a more supervisory capacity. If it chooses to act in a more supervisory capacity then it can deploy a substantial evidence test or rationality scrutiny.

The substantial evidence test is used extensively in the USA in relation to the assessment of more formal factual findings resulting in a record of the proceedings. The courts will uphold the agency finding if there is substantial evidence in the record as a whole, even if the court might not have made those findings if it had been the initial decision-maker.[93] There must be such relevant evidence as a reasonable mind might accept as adequate to support a conclusion.[94] The courts might, alternatively, use a test for review couched in terms of rationality or arbitrariness. Such tests have been deployed in the USA in relation to factual findings resulting from less formal adjudicatory proceedings, and in relation to informal rule-making, the argument being that criteria framed in terms of rationality or arbitrariness are better suited to situations where there is no formal record. There is however considerable support for the view that tests of rationality and arbitrariness tend to converge with the substantial evidence test, in the sense that a finding unsupported by substantial evidence is regarded as arbitrary.[95]

15–026 It should be recognised that there will be differences of view as to the application of the substantial evidence test and that of rationality/arbitrariness in particular instances, and that these differences will themselves be reflective of different views about the degree of deference that should be accorded to the initial fact finder in the specific case.[96] It should be acknowledged also that factual review in relation to rule-making may involve particular difficulties. This is in part because the consequences of invalidation will be more dramatic, in the sense that it might involve the overturning of an agency rule that has been many years in the making. This is in part because there is a danger in the courts being over zealous in their deployment of this head of review, requiring a degree of factual certainty or probability for a rule that might not be attainable in the light of the existing scientific or technical data. Caution in this respect is therefore warranted. There is no magical way of avoiding this problem, but awareness of the danger will go some way towards preventing its occurrence.

The role of the court in relation to the initial decision-maker was at the

---

[93] A. Aman and W. Mayton, *Administrative Law* (West Publishing, 2nd edn, 2001), 453–460; *Universal Camera*, n.87.

[94] *Consolidated Edison Co v NLRB* 305 U.S. 197, 229 (1938).

[95] *Associated Industries v US Dept of Labor* 487 F. 2d 342, 350 (2d Cir 1973); *Association of Data Processing Service Organizations, Inc v Board of Governors of the Federal Reserve System* 745 F. 2d 677, 683 (DC Cir 1984).

[96] See, e.g., *Allentown Mack Sales and Service v National Labor Relations Board* 522 U.S. 359 (1998).

forefront of the decision in *Turgut*.[97] The applicant was a Turkish Kurd, who had evaded the draft in Turkey, and sought asylum in the UK. The special adjudicator found him to be lacking in credibility and rejected the claim. The applicant argued nonetheless that he should be given exceptional leave to remain in the UK, because any young Turkish Kurd who evaded the draft would be subject to a real risk of ill-treatment or torture if returned home. The forced return would therefore be a violation of art.3 ECHR.

The Court of Appeal considered whether it should have the role of primary fact-finder, and decide for itself on all the available material whether the applicant was subject to the risk in question, or whether the court was still exercising an essentially supervisory jurisdiction, albeit heightened because of the human rights context. Simon Brown L.J. concluded that the court was not the primary fact-finder: it was not for the court to form its own independent view of the facts which would then necessarily prevail over that of the Secretary of State.[98] The courts' role was to subject the Secretary of State's decision to rigorous examination by considering the underlying factual material to see whether or not it compelled a different conclusion. While the court was not therefore the primary fact-finder, it would not accord any special deference to the Secretary of State's conclusion on the facts. This was in part because of the human rights' context; in part because the court was hardly less well placed than the minister to make the assessment once it had the material before it; and in part because of the possibility that the minister might, albeit unconsciously, have underplayed the risk.

The same tension is apparent in other cases, even if it features less explicitly in the court's judgment. Thus in *Kibiti* the court decided that there was ample evidence on which the IAT could have concluded that there was civil war in the Congo, rather than making its own primary judgment on the point.[99]   **15–027**

It is surely right that the courts' role in these types of case should be supervisory for the reasons discussed above, while accepting that the supervisory review may be more or less intensive depending on the nature of the factual inquiry before the court.

It should also be recognised that the precise role of the court will perforce be influenced by the relevant statutory language. Thus in *Tameside*[100] the Minister could only intervene and give directions if the local authority was acting unreasonably. The factual allegations concerning the viability of conducting the selection procedures within the specified time were therefore assessed within this statutory frame. The minister had to show in the light of the factual issues concerning the selection procedures that the local authority was acting so unreasonably that no local authority would have attempted to organise their schooling in such a manner. The House of Lords held that he had failed to demonstrate that this was so.

---

[97] n.8.
[98] *Turgut*, n.8, 728–729.
[99] n.6.
[100] n.12.

D. The Reviewing Court's Role in Relation to Factual Error only Apparent in the Light of Fresh Evidence

15–028   The role of the court vis-à-vis the initial decision-maker in relation to fact finding raises particular considerations where the factual error is only apparent in the light of fresh evidence. The reviewing court may choose to remit the case to the initial decision-maker to consider it again. This was the approach adopted by the Court of Appeal in the *E* case.[101] The nature of the remission should be carefully noted. The Court of Appeal decided, as we have seen, that the IAT had the power to consider the fresh evidence and to decide whether that evidence justified a re-hearing of the case. It therefore remitted the matter to the IAT to consider, in the light of the principles enunciated by the Court of Appeal concerning the admissibility of fresh evidence, whether the new material warranted a re-hearing.[102] However before remitting the case to the IAT the Court of Appeal took a look at the fresh evidence in order to decide whether there was something that might have affected the IAT's original findings.

There are however other cases where, having decided to admit the fresh evidence, the reviewing court will then make the determination itself, rather than remit the case to the initial decision-maker, more especially when it feels that the fresh evidence admits only one possible conclusion. Thus in the *A* case[103] the applicant claimed asylum and argued also that return to Jamaica would be in violation of arts 2 and 3 ECHR. She had informed on a gang member who had killed her daughter, was threatened by other gang members and moved to a different part of Jamaica. She was not however safe or welcome in those areas, because the structure of the social order was such that inhabitants of one part of Jamaica were not welcome in another area. She was harassed, sexually and non-sexually. The IAT concluded that she could settle in a different area of Jamaica. The applicant presented fresh evidence that this was not feasible, and that she would continue to be at serious risk of harm from the original gang. The Court of Appeal admitted the fresh evidence, decided that it admitted of only "one sensible interpretation",[104] which was supportive of the applicant, found in her favour and declined to remit the matter to the IAT.

The approach in the *E* case should be the "default position". The court should remit the case to the original decision-maker to decide whether the new material should be admitted in the light of the principles developed by the courts for the admission of such evidence. It is the original decision-maker who will often be best placed to decide whether the new material really does warrant a re-hearing, given its greater familiarity with the details of the contested decision, as well as decisions in related cases. The court should therefore be cautious about departing from this default position and should only do so where the fresh evidence that has been admitted really does only allow of one sensible interpretation.

[101] n.3.
[102] *E*, n.3, paras 95–98.
[103] n.13, paras 21–34.
[104] n.13, para.33.

7. Conclusion

There is no doubt that the full implications of the judgment in the *E* case will **15–029** only be worked out through subsequent case law. It is especially important that the courts remain mindful of the respective roles of courts and initial decision-makers in deciding whether a factual error has occurred. There are, as seen above, well developed tests for maintaining judicial control over facts without the courts thereby assuming the role of primary fact-finder. Developed public law jurisprudence should contain accessible and principled guidance on a matter as important as mistake of fact, and the decision in the *E* case is therefore timely. It remains to be seen whether the test in the *E* case is applied to all errors of fact. However, even if the courts make some distinction between jurisdictional facts and other facts the point made above and earlier in the chapter concerning reviewability and the standard of such review is still important: the existence of judicial review for this species of fact does not mean that the courts should necessarily substitute judgment on such matters, and they may well maintain control through a test based on sufficiency of evidence of rationality, as they have done in some past cases.[105]

[105] See above, para.25–024. See also, paras 15–025–15–027.

CHAPTER 16

FAILURE TO EXERCISE DISCRETION

1. INTRODUCTION

A. Discretion: Types of Constraint

It was said at the inception of the previous chapter that all grants of power **16–001** to public bodies could be broken into two parts: if X exists, you may or shall do Y. This chapter will be principally concerned with the judicial constraints imposed upon the Y level. Discretion may also exist on the X level, in the conditions which determine the scope of the tribunal's jurisdiction.

This is not the place for a jurisprudential analysis on the nature of discretion.[1] Discretion for the purposes of this and related chapters will be defined as existing where there is power to make choices between courses of action or where, even though the end is specified, a choice exists as to how that end should be reached. There are three principal ways in which such discretion can be controlled. This chapter, and those which follow, will deal with these topics.

First, the courts can impose controls on the *way in which* the discretion has been exercised, with the objective of ensuring that there has been no *failure* to exercise the discretion. Limitations on delegation, and on the extent to which an authority can proceed through policies or rules, are the two main controls of this type.

Second, constraints can be placed upon an administrative authority in order to ensure that there has been no *misuse of power*. The judiciary can impose substantive limits on the power of an administrative body on the ground that it is thereby ensuring that the body does not act *illegally*, outside the remit of its power.

Third, the courts can develop principles to make sure that the

---

[1] D. Galligan, *Discretionary Powers, A Legal Study of Official Discretion* (Oxford University Press, 1986).

administrative authority does not misuse its power by acting *irrationally*, thereby placing substantive limits on the power of that authority.

B. Discretion: The Rationale for Intervention

16–002 The conceptual rationale for judicial intervention in this area is, as will be seen, in a state of flux.

The *traditional rationale* has already been examined.[2] When the courts intervene to control the X factor they do so in purported fulfilment of the legislative will, by delineating the boundaries of one institution's powers from that of another. A public body adjudicating on furnished tenancies cannot trespass on the territory of a different body dealing with unfurnished tenancies. The rationale for judicial intervention on the Y level has always been more indirect. The authority is within its assigned area, in the sense that it is, for example, properly adjudicating on furnished tenancies. The issue now is as to the rationale for judicial control over, for example, the fair rent that should be charged for such premises. Traditional theory posited the link with sovereignty and with the ultra vires doctrine in the following manner: Parliament only intended that such discretion should be exercised on relevant and not irrelevant considerations, or to achieve proper and not improper purposes. Any exercise of discretion which contravened these limits was ultra vires. The ease with which the judicial approach can be reconciled with sovereignty demonstrates the limits of the ultra vires concept as an organising principle for administrative law. Almost any such controls can be formally squared with legislative intent.

It is in part because of this that the more *modern conceptual rationale* bases judicial intervention on rather different grounds. Legislative intent and the will of Parliament are still regarded as relevant, but the judicial controls are seen as being as much concerned with *supplementing* legislative intent as with *implementing* it. On this view the judicial role is to fashion and enforce *principles of fair administration*.[3] The implications of this will become apparent in the discussion which follows.

2. DELEGATION

A. General Principles

16–003 The general starting point is that if discretion is vested in a certain person it must be exercised by that person. This principle finds its expression in the maxim *delegatus non potest delegare*. It is important, however, to bear in mind that the maxim is expressive of a principle and not a rigid rule.

---

[2] See above, Ch.1.
[3] See above, Ch.1. Sir Harry Woolf, *Protection of the Public—A New Challenge* (Sweet & Maxwell, 1990), 122–124.

Whether a person other than that named in the empowering statute is allowed to act will be dependent upon the entire statutory context. The nature of the subject-matter, the degree of control retained by the person delegating, and the type of person or body to whom the power is delegated, will all be taken into account.[4]

Thus, in *Allingham*[5] the court held that it was unlawful for a wartime agricultural committee, to which powers concerning cultivation of land had been delegated by the Minister of Agriculture, to delegate to an executive officer the choice of which particular fields should be subject to a certain type of cultivation. In *Ellis*[6] a condition imposed by the licensing committee of a county council that it would not allow films to be shown unless certified for public exhibition by the Board of Film Censors, was held invalid as involving a transfer of power to the latter.[7] There are numerous other instances where the courts have found that an unlawful delegation occurred.[8]

The type of power that is delegated will be of importance, though not conclusive. Thus, the courts are reluctant to allow further delegation of delegated legislative power.[9] Similarly, the courts are reluctant to sanction the delegation of judicial power. In *Barnard*,[10] the National Dock Labour Board had lawfully delegated powers, including those over discipline, to the local Boards. The latter purported to delegate these to the port manager who suspended the plaintiff from work. This was held to be unlawful, the court stressing that a judicial function could rarely be delegated. In a subsequent case the House of Lords reached the same conclusion, though emphasising that there was no absolute rule that judicial or quasi-judicial functions could never be delegated; the golden rule was always to consider the entire statutory context.[11]

B. Agency and Delegation

The relationship between agency and delegation is difficult and the case law is often contradictory. It is best therefore to approach the matter by considering first principles and juxtaposing these to the decided cases.

16–004

---

[4] J Willis, "Delegatus non Potest Delegare" (1943) 21 Can. B.R. 257.

[5] *Allingham v Minister of Agriculture* [1948] 1 All E.R. 780.

[6] *Ellis v Dubowski* [1921] 3 K.B. 621.

[7] See *Mills v London County Council* [1925] 1 K.B. 213 where the opposite result was reached because the county council retained the power to review the decision made by the Film Censors; *R. v Greater London Council Ex p. Blackburn* [1976] 1 W.L.R. 550; *R. v Police Complaints Board Ex p. Madden* [1983] 1 W.L.R. 447.

[8] See, e.g. *Jackson, Stansfield & Sons v Butterworth* [1948] 2 All E.R. 558; *H Lavender & Son Ltd v Minister of Housing and Local Government* [1970] 1 W.L.R. 1231; *Ratnagopal v Attorney General* [1970] A.C. 974. Compare *R. (on the application of Ealing LBC) v Audit Commission* [2005] EWCA Civ 556.

[9] *King-Emperor v Benoari Lal Sarma* [1945] A.C. 14; P. Thorp, "The Key to the Application of the Maxim 'Delegatus non Potest Delegare' " (1972–1975) 2 Auck U.L.J. 85.

[10] *Barnard v National Dock Labour Board* [1953] 2 Q.B. 18.

[11] *Vine v National Dock Labour Board* [1957] A.C. 488. Terminology or "categories" can, however, still be important. The questionable decision in *R. v Race Relations Board Ex p. Selvarajan* [1975] 1 W.L.R. 1686 was influenced by labelling the proceedings administrative.

i. The creation of agency and delegation

16–005   Both delegation and agency involve an authorisation that someone may act
on behalf of another. The types of things which may be delegated are, as we
have seen, limited. A glance at the leading treatise on agency indicates that
limits also exist on the capacity of an agent. An agent can perform any act
on behalf of a principal which the principal could execute, except for the
purpose of executing a right, or power, or performing a duty imposed on the
principal personally, the exercise of which requires discretion or skill, or
where the principal is required by statute to do the act personally.[12]
Although the ability to delegate and to appoint an agent are both limited,
there is a difference as to presumption. Where public bodies possess powers
the presumption is that the power should be exercised by the person named
in the statute, though this is of course rebuttable. Where private parties are
concerned the norm is that a principal should be able to appoint an agent,
subject to the limits mentioned above.

This difference in presumption is, however, of importance and failure to
comprehend it has led the courts into error. The error is the belief that
principles of agency can "cure" an unlawful delegation. In *Lever Finance*[13] a
planning officer represented to a developer that minor changes in a building
plan were not material. The developer proceeded to build the houses, the
residents complained, the developer applied for planning permission for the
modifications and his application was rejected by the planning committee,
the body duly authorised to make the decision. Lord Denning M.R. held
that the public body was estopped from contesting the representation made
by its planning officer who had acted within the scope of his ostensible
authority. It was clear from the statutory context that any delegation to the
planning officer would have been ultra vires.[14] This cannot somehow
magically be circumscribed by calling the officer an agent who acts within
his ostensible authority. If the initial delegation to the officer would have
been unlawful that is an end to the matter. This cannot be cured by saying
that the officer possessed apparent authority, since one of the necessary
conditions to make the parent responsible for the acts of its agent is that the
parent was not deprived, inter alia, of the capacity to delegate authority of
that kind to the agent.[15]

Denning L.J. stated the correct position in the *Barnard* case. It was argued
that the unlawful delegation to the port manager could be cured by ratification of the Labour Board. Denning L.J. rejected this, stating that the
effect of ratification is to make the action equal to a prior command.
However, since a prior command in the form of delegation would have been
unlawful, so also would ratification.[16]

A second example may be taken from cases concerning local authorities.

---

[12] *Bowstead and Reynolds on Agency* (Sweet & Maxwell, 18th edn, 2006), para.2–017.
[13] *Lever Finance Ltd v Westminster (City) London Borough Council* [1971] 1 Q.B. 222.
[14] P. Craig, "Representations by Public Bodies" (1977) 93 L.Q.R. 398, 404–408.
[15] *Freeman & Lockyer v Buckhurst Park Properties (Mangal) Ltd* [1964] 2 Q.B. 480, 506.
[16] [1953] 2 Q.B. 18, 39–40. See also, *Western Fish Products Ltd v Penwith District Council* [1981]
2 All E.R. 204.

A number of cases have raised the problem of a delegate who takes certain action, for example, to institute legal proceedings, without prior approval. The authority whose approval is required then purports to ratify the action already undertaken.[17] Two issues are relevant and have not always been distinguished. One is whether ratification could occur at the stage the proceedings had reached. The other is whether the officer instituting the proceedings was capable of doing so at all; whether that task could ever have been validly delegated to that person.

ii. Delegation and retention of authority by the delegator

There has been uncertainty as to whether the person delegating retains **16–006** power concurrently with the delegate, in the way that a principal retains power with an agent. There is authority supporting this view.[18]

However Scott L.J. in *Locker*[19] reached the opposite conclusion. The Minister of Health had delegated power to the Corporation or their town clerk to requisition property subject to certain conditions, which were not complied with on the facts of the case, thereby rendering the requisition by the Corporation inoperative. Scott L.J. stated that the relationship between the Minister and Corporation or town clerk was not one of principal/agent, that there had been a sub-delegation of legislative power and that this divested the Minister of any concurrent power unless he had expressly reserved such power to himself.[20] In the absence of any such reservation a later attempt by the Minister himself to requisition the property was inoperative.

The case has been criticised by writers[21] and doubted in the courts. In *Roberts*,[22] Denning L.J., on similar facts, stated that the town clerk was an agent of the Ministry, that the delegation, whether general or specific, was not a legislative act, and that it did not divest the government of its powers. The *Locker* case was said to turn on the inability of the Minister to ratify the acts of an agent who had exceeded the assigned authority.

The relevant authorities were however more recently reviewed in *Robertson*.[23] Burton J. held that he was bound by the decision in *Locker*. He held moreover that he preferred the proposition that the ordinary consequence of delegation was divestment of the delegator of the powers delegated, unless there was an express or implied retention of some or all of the powers, whether with or without a provision for notice to the delegate,

[17] *Firth v Staines* [1897] 2 Q.B. 70; *R. v Chapman Ex p. Arlidge* [1918] 2 K.B. 298; *Bowyer, Philpott & Payne Ltd v Mather* [1919] 1 K.B. 419; *Warwick Rural District Council v Miller-Mead* [1962] Ch.441.
[18] *Huth v Clark* (1890) 25 Q.B.D 391; *Gordon Dadds & Co v Morris* [1945] 2 All E.R. 616, 621. *cf Battelley v Finsbury Borough Council* (1958) 56 L.G.R. 165.
[19] *Blackpool Corporation v Locker* [1948] 1 K.B. 349, Asquith L.J. agreed with Scott L.J.
[20] *Locker*, n.19, 365, 367–368, 377.
[21] R. Jackson, "County Agricultural Executive Committees" (1952) 68 L.Q.R. 363, 375–376.
[22] *Lewisham Borough Council v Roberts* [1949] 2 K.B. 608, 621–622.
[23] *Robertson v Department for the Environment, Food and Rural Affairs* [2004] I.C.R. 1289. The matter was not considered in depth by the Court of Appeal, *Robertson v Department for the Environment, Food and Rural Affairs* [2005] EWCA Civ 138, para.41.

rather than the proposition that the delegator retained power unless something was stated to the contrary. This was so irrespective of whether the power delegated was administrative or legislative in nature. The principal rationale for Burton J.'s position was that the possession of concurrent authority by delegator and delegee could lead to uncertainty and that it would not normally be appropriate for the delegator to go off and do for himself what had just been delegated.

C. Government Departments

i. General principles

16–007 It is accepted that where powers are granted to a minister that they can be exercised by the department. This is known as the *Carltona* principle.[24] It is clearly sensible since it would be impossible for the minister personally to give consideration to each case. The minister need not personally confer the authority for the official to act. It may be granted in accordance with departmental practice,[25] but it is unclear whether it is necessary for the officer to act explicitly on behalf of the minister.[26] There are judicial indications that the delegation of power should be subject to a requirement that the seniority of the official exercising a power should be of an appropriate level having regard to the nature of the power in question.[27] The ability to delegate may be limited where the empowering statute explicitly states that the minister in person must perform certain functions.[28]

It is uncertain whether, apart from this, there is a class of case in which the minister must personally direct his or her mind to the issue. It has been stated that such a distinction would be impossible to apply and that it is not established by the case law.[29] Some other cases dealing with personal liberty such as deportation[30] and fugitive offenders[31] left the matter more open. However, it has now been held by the House of Lords in the *Oladehinde* case[32] that the power to deport can be delegated to immigration inspectors who were of a suitable grade and experience, provided that this did not conflict with the officers' own statutory duties.

Where civil servants are acting on behalf of ministers the better view is

---

[24] *Carltona Ltd v Commissioners of Works* [1943] 2 All E.R. 560.
[25] *Carltona*, n.24; *Lewisham Borough Council v Roberts* [1949] 2 K.B. 608; *R. v Skinner* [1968] 2 Q.B. 700; *Re Golden Chemical Products Ltd* [1976] Ch.300; *Bushell v Secretary of State for the Environment* [1981] A.C. 75; *R. v Secretary of State for the Home Department Ex p. Oladehinde* [1991] 1 A.C. 254; D. Lanham, "Delegation and the Alter Ego Principle" (1984) 100 L.Q.R. 587.
[26] *Woollett v Minister of Agriculture and Fisheries* [1955] 1 Q.B. 103, 120–121.
[27] *DPP v Haw* [2007] EWHC 1931, para.29.
[28] *R. v Secretary of State for the Home Department Ex p. Oladehinde* [1991] 1 A.C. 254, 303; *Haw*, n.27, para.33.
[29] *Re Golden Chemical Products Ltd* [1976] Ch.300, 309–310.
[30] *R. v Superintendent of Chiswick Police Station Ex p. Sacksteder* [1918] 1 K.B. 578, 585–586, 591–592.
[31] *R. v Governor of Brixton Prison Ex p. Enahoro* [1963] 2 Q.B. 455, 466.
[32] [1991] 1 A.C. 254.

that there is no delegation as such at all. The responsible officer is the alter ego of the minister who maintains responsibility before Parliament.[33]

ii. The application of Carltona to other public bodies

It has been held that the *Carltona* principle is not limited to government   **16–008**
departments. In *Birmingham Justices*,[34] Sedley L.J. held, contrary to earlier indications,[35] that the *Carltona* principle was not dependent on the particular status of civil servants as the alter ego of the minister. The principle could also allow a Chief Constable to discharge functions through an officer for whom he was answerable. This was so provided that the function could, consistently with the statute, be delegated, and provided also that a suitable person was entrusted with the task.

This approach was affirmed in *Haw*.[36] Lord Phillips C.J. stated that the *Carltona* principle could apply to the exercise of prerogative powers that were not conferred by statute. Where powers were conferred on a minister by statute, the *Carltona* principle would apply to those powers unless the statute, expressly or by implication, provided to the contrary. Where a statutory power was conferred on an officer who was a creature of statute, whether that officer had the power to delegate depended upon the interpretation of the relevant statute or statutes. Where the responsibilities of the office created by statute were such that delegation was inevitable, there would be an implied power to delegate. In such circumstances there would be a presumption, where additional statutory powers and duties were conferred, that there was a power to delegate unless the statute conferring them, expressly or by implication, provided to the contrary.

iii. Government departments and Executive Agencies

The decision in *Sherwin*[37] provides guidance as to how the preceding prin-   **16–009**
ciples will apply where the relevant power has been de facto exercised by an Executive Agency, as opposed to a civil servant within the parent department.

Regulation 37 of the Social Security (Claims and Payments) Regulations 1987 gave the Secretary of State power to suspend the payment of a benefit where there was an appeal pending on a point which affected payment of that benefit. Regulation 37A gave the Secretary of State the same suspensory power where another case was being used as a test case on the same point. A decision to suspend payment had to be made within one month. The applicant's benefit was suspended by a District Manager of the Benefit Agency in Birmingham, and this was an Executive Agency operating within

---

[33] See, e.g., *R. v Skinner* [1968] 2 Q.B. 700, 707; *Nelms v Roe* [1970] 1 W.L.R. 4, 8.
[34] *R. (on the application of the Chief Constable of the West Midlands Police) v Birmingham Justices* [2002] EWHC 1087.
[35] *Nelms*, n.33.
[36] *Haw*, n.27, para.33.
[37] *R. v Secretary of State for Social Services Ex p. Sherwin* (1996) 32 B.M.L.R. 1

the Department of Social Security. It was argued on behalf of the applicant that notice was not given within the requisite period of one month, because the District Manager of the Agency could not be said to speak for the minister within the context of the *Carltona* principle.[38] The Divisional Court disagreed, holding that the *Carltona* principle could indeed apply notwithstanding that the officer who made the decision operated within an Executive Agency.

This decision clearly has much to recommend it. These agencies do not have any separate legal status, and powers are still formally vested in the name of the minister. Given that this is so the policy underlying the *Carltona* principle can be seen to have continuing force in this context: the minister cannot literally be expected to address his or her mind to each such decision and must, of necessity, act through officials. Moreover, the result serves to ensure that it will be the minister who will continue to have ultimate legal responsibility for the decision which has been taken.

The creation of Executive Agencies has, however, created a tension in this area. These agencies are, as we have seen, designed to have authority over operational matters.[39] They are meant to function de facto more independently from the minister, as compared to the situation when all matters are carried on in-house within a unitary government department. The idea of the framework agreement, the appointment of a Chief Executive and the growing autonomy which these agencies have over pay and conditions, are all factors that serve to reinforce this sense of separation. The particular framework agreement which governed this area expressly emphasised the idea that there was a delegation of operational autonomy to this agency.[40] There is therefore a tension between this institutional scheme and the idea that a decision taken by an official in such a case can really be regarded as one taken on behalf of the Secretary of State.

iv. Government Departments and contracting-out

16–010 The application of the *Carltona* principle to situations where power has been contracted-out to a private undertaking is both legally clearer and also more alarming at the same time as a result of the Deregulation and Contracting Out Act 1994. Part II of this legislation makes provision for the contracting-out of certain functions by government to bodies which will normally be private. It should be made clear that government departments have frequently contracted-out functions independently of this Act. The statute was passed in order to enable the body to which the power has been contracted-out to operate in the name of the minister, by analogy with the *Carltona* principle.

Section 69 enables functions which, by virtue of any enactment or rule of law, can be performed by an officer of a minister, to be contracted-out to an

---

[38] n.24.
[39] See above, Ch.4.
[40] See, e.g., para.4 of the Framework Agreement.

authorised party.[41] Section 69(5)(c) makes it clear that the minister may still exercise the function to which the authorisation relates.

Section 71(1) imposes certain limits upon the functions which can be contracted-out. Thus a function is excluded from ss.69 and 70 where: its exercise would constitute the exercise of jurisdiction of any court or of any tribunal which exercises the judicial power of the State; or its exercise, or a failure to exercise it, would necessarily interfere with or otherwise affect the liberty of any individual; or it is a power or right of entry, search or seizure into or of any property[42]; or it is a power or duty to make subordinate legislation.

Section 72(2) is designed to render the minister ultimately responsible for action taken by the body to whom the power has been contracted-out, although the meaning of this particular section is not free from doubt. It is clear from s.72(3)(b) that s.72(2) does not apply in respect of any criminal proceedings brought against the person to whom the whom the power has been contracted out. The precise import of s.72(3)(a) is far less clear. This states that s.72(2) does not apply "for the purposes of so much of the contract made between the authorised person and the Minister, office-holder or local authority as relates to the exercise of the function". It is as, Freedland states,[43] difficult to know what is meant by a rule which says that where a contract brings about the treatment of the acts or omissions of one party as those of the other, that treatment nevertheless does not occur "for the purposes of" so much of the contract as relates to the exercise of the function. One reading of this section would enable the Minister to plead the terms of the contract against third parties in order to show that the act or omission of the contractor should not be seen as that of the Minister, although this would emasculate s.72(2).

It is readily apparent from the discussion of the legislation while it was in the House of Commons that the government regarded these sections as merely technical amendments involving no issue of principle as such. They were depicted as minor changes designed to facilitate contracting-out by sweeping away unnecessarily restrictive distinctions as to what had to be done by civil servants as opposed to outside contractors.[44] It is nonetheless difficult to regard these changes with such equanimity for two reasons.

On the one hand, although Pt II of the legislation is entitled "Contracting-Out" s.69 is actually framed so as to empower an outside body to exercise the functions of the minister. The donee of the power is not simply the alter ego of the minister, but the actual repository of the statutory power.[45]

On the other hand, the very idea that one can transfer the *Carltona* type principle and apply it to private bodies to which power has been contracted-

[41] Deregulation and Contracting Out Act 1994 s.70 contains provisions concerning local authorities.
[42] This is subject to exceptions listed in Deregulation and Contracting Out Act 1994 s.71(3).
[43] M. Freedland, "Privatising *Carltona*: Part II of the Deregulation and Contracting-Out Act 1994" [1995] P.L. 21, 25.
[44] Freedland, n.43, 22.
[45] Freedland, n.43, 24–25.

out is itself contentious. In formal legal terms this can of course be done, given that Parliament is sovereign and has passed the 1994 legislation which stipulated this result. This should not, however, serve to mask the substantive shift in thinking which has occurred in this area. The point is captured well by Freedland,[46]

> "One cannot read the unanimous judgment of the Court of Appeal in the *Carltona* case without concluding that it would have been unthinkable to that court that their doctrine could be extended so that the functions of a Minister could be exercised by a private sector employee linked to the minister only by a chain of contracts and not by any public service relationship. They would have been amazed that the Minister could be expected on the one hand to seek and maintain a commercial relationship with an outside contractor, while on the other hand treating that contractor as the very embodiment of himself. It requires some ingenuity thus to treat somebody as standing in one's shoes, yet at the same time to keep that person at arm's length."

D. Statutory Power

16–011 Power to delegate will often be granted by statute, a prominent example of this being the Local Government Act 1972 authorising local authorities to discharge any of their functions by committees, officers, or acting jointly with other local authorities.[47] Similar powers exist in other areas such as planning.

3. Fettering of Discretion: Rules, Policies and Discretion

16–012 Unlawful delegation is one way in which a public body may be held to have failed to exercise its discretion. A second is where the public body adopts a policy which precludes it from considering the merits of a particular case. Two related issues will be separated in the discussion which follows. First, given that a public authority does have a policy or rule, what test should the courts apply in determining whether such a general policy should be allowed to stand; and if it does uphold the policy/rule, what further consequences should ensue, in terms of, for example, allowing participation in the rule-making process? Second, if a public body does not have a rule or policy, how far can and should the courts go in actually encouraging the agency to make such rules? The words policy and rule will be used interchangeably for the present.

---

[46] Freedland, n.43, 25.
[47] Local Government Act 1972 ss.101, 102; *R. v Secretary of State for the Environment Ex p. Hillingdon London Borough Council* [1986] 1 W.L.R. 192, affirmed [1986] 1 W.L.R. 807.

A. An Existing Rule or Policy: The Present Law

i. General principles
A public body endowed with statutory discretionary powers is not entitled   **16–013**
to adopt a policy or rule which allows it to dispose of a case without any
consideration of the merits of the individual applicant who is before it. In
Corrie[48] the court quashed a decision refusing the applicant permission to
sell pamphlets at certain meetings. The decision had been taken in reliance
upon a council bylaw that nothing was to be sold in parks. Darling J. stated
that each application must be heard on its merits. There could not be a
general resolution to refuse permission to all.[49] This does not mean that a
public body is precluded from having any general policy/rule at all. A
general policy is allowed provided that due consideration of the merits of an
individual case takes place, and provided that the content of the policy is
intra vires.[50]

Most discretionary power will be accorded by statute. The position in
relation to common law discretionary power is less clear. In *Elias*[51] the
claimant who had been interned by the Japanese was denied access to the
UK Government's ex gratia compensation scheme, because only civilian
internees who had been born in the UK or one of whose parents or
grandparents had been born in the UK were eligible to receive payment. She
argued, by way of analogy with the case law on statutory discretion, that the
Secretary of State had unlawfully fettered his common law power by
refusing to consider whether to make an exception to the criteria for
compensation.

The Court of Appeal rejected the analogy.[52] It held that it was lawful to
formulate a policy for the exercise of statutory discretionary power, but the
person who fell within the statute could not be completely debarred, and
continued to have a statutory right to be considered by the person entrusted
with the discretion. These considerations did not, said the court, apply in the
case of an ordinary common law power, since it was within the power of the
decision-maker to decide on the extent to which the power was to be
exercised when, for example, setting up a scheme. It might be decided that
there should be no exceptions to the criteria in the scheme, and that "bright
line" criteria should determine eligibility for payments from public funds.
Such criteria should not be regarded as a fetter on an existing common law

---

[48] *R. v London County Council Ex p. Corrie* [1918] 1 K.B. 68.
[49] *Corrie*, n.48, 73; *R. v Flintshire County Council Licensing (Stage Plays) Committee Ex p. Barrett* [1957] 1 Q.B. 350; *Att-Gen, ex rel. Tilley v London Borough of Wandsworth* [1981] 1 W.L.R. 854.
[50] See, e.g., *Boyle v Wilson* [1907] A.C. 45; *R. v Torquay Licensing Justices Ex p. Brockman* [1951] 2 K.B. 784; *Merchandise Transport Ltd v British Transport Commission* [1962] 2 Q.B. 173, 186, 193; *R. v Commissioner of Police of the Metropolis Ex p. Blackburn* [1968] 2 Q.B. 118, 136, 139; *R. v Commissioner of Police of the Metropolis Ex p. Blackburn (No.3)* [1973] Q.B. 241; *R. v Tower Hamlet London Borough Council Ex p. Kayne/Levenson* [1975] 1 Q.B. 431, 440, 453.
[51] *R. (on the application of Elias) v Secretary of State for Defence* [2006] 1 W.L.R. 3213.
[52] *Elias*, n.51, paras 191–192.

discretionary power to decide each application according to the circumstances of each individual case

This may well be true in relation to the facts of the *Elias*. There could however be instances where common law discretionary power is exercised, where a policy is expressed as to how the power is to be exercised and where the nature of that policy does not preclude consideration of circumstances that do not fall within the ambit of the policy.

ii. The weight to be given to the policy/rule

16–014 In relation to the exercise of statutory discretionary power, the courts have not always been uniform in deciding on the weight which the public body is to be allowed to accord to its policy or rule.[53] The dominant line of authority allows the body to apply its rule provided only that the individual is granted the opportunity to contest its application to the particular case.

Thus, in the *Kynoch* case Bankes L.J.[54] contrasted two situations, the former being permissible, the latter not. It was lawful for an authority to adopt a policy, to intimate to the applicant what that policy was, and to tell that person that it would apply the policy after a hearing, unless there was something exceptional in the case. It was, however, not permissible for the authority to make a determination not to hear any application of a particular character. A similar approach was adopted in *British Oxygen*.[55] The Board of Trade exercised its discretion under the Industrial Development Act 1966 not to give grants towards expenditure of less than £25. BOC had spent a large sum on gas cylinders, the individual cost of which was however only £20 and it sought a declaration that the Board of Trade's practice was unlawful. Lord Reid disagreed. His Lordship stated that while anyone possessing a discretion could not shut his ears to an application, and while there might be cases where it should listen to arguments that its "rules" should be changed, an authority was entitled to have a policy. This policy would have evolved over many similar cases and might well have become so precise that it could be called a rule. That was acceptable provided that the authority was willing to listen to anyone who had something new to say.[56]

There are, however, some cases which allow only a more minor role to be played by the policy. It is allowed to be but one relevant factor used by the public body in arriving at its determinations. Thus in *Stringer*[57] Cooke J. reviewed the legality of a policy which restricted planning permission for

[53] D. Galligan, "The Nature and Function of Policy within Discretionary Power" [1976] P.L. 332, 346–355. The article contains a valuable analysis.
[54] *R. v Port of London Authority Ex p. Kynoch Ltd* [1919] 1 K.B. 176, 184; *Boyle v Wilson* [1907] A.C. 45, 57.
[55] *British Oxygen Co Ltd v Board of Trade* [1971] A.C. 610.
[56] *British Oxygen*, n.55, 625; *Cumings v Birkenhead Corporation* [1972] 1 Ch.12; *R. v Tower Hamlets London Borough Council Ex p. Kayne-Levenson* [1975] 1 Q.B. 431; *Kilmarnock Magistrates v Secretary of State for Scotland* (1961) S.C. 350; *R. v Secretary of State for the Environment Ex p. Brent London Borough Council* [1982] Q.B. 593, 640–642; *R. v Chief Constable for the North Wales Police Area Authority Ex p. AB and DC* [1997] C.O.D. 395; *R. (on the application of S) v Chief Constable of South Yorkshire* [2002] 1 W.L.R. 3223.
[57] *Stringer v Minister of Housing and Local Government* [1970] 1 W.L.R. 1281, 1297–1298.

developments which could interfere with the Jodrell Bank telescope. He held that the general policy could stand provided that it did not inhibit the taking account of all issues relevant to each individual case which came up for determination.[58]

The preponderance of authority favours the less restrictive approach,[59] and the reasons for preferring this will be examined below. The difference between the two approaches is brought out well by Galligan.[60]

> "The implications of this more restrictive approach are that not only must an authority (a) direct itself to whether in the light of the particular situation a predetermined policy ought to be altered, but also (b) must refrain from regarding a policy as anything more than one factor amongst others to take into account. In other words a policy may not become a norm which, subject only to (a) determines the outcome of particular decisions."

iii. Control over the substance of the policy

It is clear on authority[61] and on principle that the policy must be one which is legitimate given the statutory framework within which the discretion is exercised. It must be based upon relevant considerations and must not pursue improper purposes.[62] These controls are necessary since otherwise a public authority could escape the normal constraints upon the exercise of discretion by framing general policies. Thus in *Venables*[63] it was held that the governing statute required the Home Secretary to have regard to the interests of a child offender when sentencing, and therefore that it was unlawful for him to adopt a policy which failed to take this into account.

However, the extent of control that the courts should be exercising is more questionable, in particular when the courts demand evidence and facts for hypotheses which are not susceptible to such clear-cut analysis. Thus, while one could test factually whether the Jodrell Bank telescope would function less efficiently if planning permission were granted for houses, it is much less easy to test assumptions such as whether amusement arcades have a socially deleterious effect upon young people. The courts have, however,

16–015

---

[58] *H Lavender & Son Ltd v Minister of Housing and Local Government* [1970] 1 W.L.R. 1231, 1240–1241; *Sagnata Investments Ltd v Norwich Corporation* [1971] 2 Q.B. 614.
[59] See, e.g., *R. v Rochdale Metropolitan Borough Council Ex p. Cromer Ring Mill Ltd* [1982] 3 All E.R. 761; *R. v Eastleigh Borough Council Ex p. Betts* [1983] 2 A.C. 613, 627–628; *Re Findlay* [1985] A.C. 318, 334–336. *cf. R. v Windsor Licensing Justices Ex p. Hodes* [1983] 1 W.L.R. 685; *R. v Secretary of State for the Environment Ex p. Brent London Borough Council* [1982] Q.B. 593, 640–642; *P v Hackney LBC* [2007] EWHC 1365.
[60] [1976] P.L. 332, 349.
[61] See, e.g., *British Oxygen Co Ltd v Board of Trade* [1971] A.C. 610, 623–624; *Cumings v Birkenhead Corporation* [1972] 1 Ch.12, 37–38; *R. v London Borough of Lambeth Ex p. Ghous* [1993] C.O.D. 302.
[62] See, Ch.17.
[63] *R. v Secretary of State for the Home Department Ex p. Venables* [1998] A.C. 407.

struck down decisions in pursuance of policies of the latter type for just this reason.[64] To insist on the type of factual "back-up" which the majority demanded in the *Sagnata* case is excessive.[65]

iv. Rules and process rights

16–016   The existence of a rule or policy which is upheld by the courts raises three important questions concerning process rights.

First, the individual may wish to argue that the policy *should not be* applied to the particular case. There is authority for the view that such an applicant should be informed of what the policy entails, this being necessary if there is to be any effective right to challenge it.[66] The extent of this right is unclear. There may, depending on the circumstances, be a right to a hearing of some type. It is, however, unclear whether the individual will be entitled to an oral hearing,[67] although this will be so if the applicant were normally entitled to this degree of protection. Equally it is not certain whether the individual can only challenge the application of the policy in the instant case, or whether the substance of the policy itself can be questioned. The latter issue can clearly be raised at the stage of judicial review, the question being whether the individual can raise the matter before the authority itself.[68]

The second situation is the converse of the first. The individual may wish to argue that an established policy *should be* applied to the particular case, while the public body may wish to change its policy or resile from it. The law will be analysed in more detail when considering substantive principles which constrain agency discretion.[69] The general position can be summarised as follows.

(1)   If a public body has made a representation to a specific individual or group of individuals that a particular policy will be followed, or that they will be informed before any such change in policy takes place, then the individuals will be entitled to comment before any such

---

[64] *Sagnata Investments Ltd v Norwich Corporation* [1971] 2 Q.B. 616. There is a marked difference in approach between Lord Denning M.R. (dissenting) and Edmund Davies and Phillimore L.JJ.

[65] It should be borne in mind that the test should be not what evidence a social scientist with full research grant and expertise, etc., could produce, but what evidence would be available to the Corporation, apart from the general feeling that such places were a bad influence on the young.

[66] See, e.g., *Kynoch* [1919] 1 K.B. 176, 184; *R. v Torquay Licensing Justices Ex p. Brockman* [1951] 2 K.B. 748, 788; *R. v Criminal Injuries Compensation Board Ex p. Ince* [1973] 1 W.L.R. 1334, 1344–1345.

[67] In the *British Oxygen* case Lord Reid stated that the hearing did not have to be oral, [1971] A.C. 610, 625.

[68] Contrast *Boyle v Wilson* [1907] A.C. 45, 57, where the court doubted whether the applicant could challenge the policy itself, with *British Oxygen*, where Lord Reid thought that there were instances where this was possible, [1971] A.C. 610, 625. The latter view is supported by *Ince*, n.66, 1344.

[69] See, Ch.20.

change occurs, or before there is a departure from that policy.[70] The change in policy may, moreover, only be countenanced for the instant case if the public interest so demands.

(2) If an individual has in the past enjoyed a benefit or advantage which could legitimately be expected to continue, that person may be entitled to a statement of reasons for the change of position, and an opportunity to be consulted thereon.[71]

(3) The principle of consistency creates a presumption that a public body will follow its own policy. If it seeks to depart from that policy then there must be good reasons for the departure and these must be given to the applicant.[72]

(4) The existence of any legitimate expectation, whether arising from a representation or past practice, will be a matter of construction. Thus in *Khan*,[73] Parker L.J. held that a Home Office circular concerning adoption procedure for foreign children generated a legitimate expectation that the procedures would be followed. The Minister could not depart from them without affording the applicants a hearing and then only if the public interest demanded it. In *Robson*,[74] a council decided to allow those who opposed or supported the grant of planning permission to address the relevant committee. It was held that the council was bound to operate this policy properly and fairly within its own terms. In the recent *Greenpeace* case[75] a government White Paper on energy policy indicated that the Government was not minded to support "new nuclear build" and stated that there would be full public consultation before the Government reached any decision to change its policy. A consultation exercise was held and the government decided that it would support some element of "nuclear new build". The court held that there was a legitimate expectation that consultation

---

[70] See, e.g., *Att-Gen. of Hong Kong v Ng Yuen Shiu* [1983] 2 A.C. 629; *R. v Liverpool Corporation Ex p. Liverpool Taxi Fleet Operators' Association* [1972] 2 Q.B. 299; *R. v Secretary of State for the Home Department Ex p. Khan* [1985] 1 All E.R. 40; *Council of Civil Service Unions v Minister for the Civil Service* [1985] A.C. 374, 408–409; *R. v Secretary of State for the Home Department Ex p. Ruddock* [1987] 1 W.L.R. 1482; *R. v Secretary of State for the Home Department Ex p. Gangadeen* [1998] C.O.D. 216; *R. (on the application of Niazi) v Secretary of State for the Home Department* [2007] EWCA Civ 1495. *Cf. R. v Falmouth and Truro Port Health Authority Ex p. South West Water Ltd* [2001] Q.B. 445.
[71] See, e.g., *CCSU* [1985] A.C. 374, 408–409; *Khan*, n.70; *Ruddock*, n.70; *R. v Birmingham City Council Ex p. Dredger* [1993] C.O.D. 340. Cases may be difficult to classify as type (i) or (ii) particularly where, as in *Khan* or *Ruddock*, there is a circular in question This could be regarded either as a representation, or as the past practice justifying the legitimate expectation.
[72] *R. v Secretary of State for the Home Department Ex p. Urmaza* [1996] C.O.D. 479; *R. v Secretary of State for the Home Department Ex p. Gangadeen* [1998] C.O.D. 216.
[73] [1985] 1 All E.R. 40.
[74] *R. v Alnwick District Council Ex p. Robson* [1998] C.O.D. 241.
[75] *R. (on the application of Greenpeace Ltd) v Secretary of State for Trade and Industry* [2007] EWHC 311.

would occur and that the consultation process that took place was seriously flawed for a number of reasons. However, in *Findlay*[76] a change of policy concerning parole was not held to infringe the legitimate expectations of certain prisoners, notwithstanding the fact that they would, under the previous policy, have expected earlier release. The content of the prisoners' legitimate expectations was held to be that their cases would be individually considered under whatever policy the Minister sought fit to adopt.

(5) The content of the duty to consult held to flow from the legitimate expectation may also depend upon the circumstances. The applicant may, as in *Khan*, be allowed to argue why the pre-existing policy should continue to be applied to the instant case. The duty may, however, be more extensive, and the applicant may be enabled to contest the soundness of the new policy itself. Thus, in *Dredger*,[77] stall-holders were held to have a legitimate expectation of being consulted about a major change in rental policy for market stalls. This was held to entail consultation rights very similar to those set out in the *Gunning* case. The council had to provide details of its proposals; the applicants were to be given sufficient time to respond; the council had to listen to the applicants' responses with an open mind; and these responses had to be taken into account when reaching a final decision.

(6) It is doubtful whether there is a duty to consult derived from the duty to act fairly, which applies independently of any legitimate expectation based on a prior representation or a prior practice of consultation.[78] Thus in *Kelly*,[79] the applicant, who was blind, complained that there had been a failure to consult before the BBC closed a local radio station that was of particular importance to people such as himself. The application failed because there was nothing in the BBC's charter, or other relevant documentation, which suggested that there was any promise, undertaking or representation by the BBC that it would consult about the future of local radio, and hence nothing to establish an arguable case based on legitimate expectations.

---

[76] [1985] A.C. 318, 338. See also, *R. v Secretary of State for the Home Department Ex p. Hargreaves* [1997] 1 All E.R. 397.
[77] *R. v Birmingham City Council Ex p. Dredger* [1993] C.O.D. 340.
[78] There are some indications in the Court of Appeal in *R. v Devon County Council Ex p. Baker* [1995] 1 All E.R. 73, that such a duty might exist. However Popplewell J. in the same case [1993] C.O.D. 138 denied the existence of any such obligation Hutchison J in *Dredger*, n.77, held that no duty to consult could be based on the duty to act fairly, in the absence of a legitimate expectation.
[79] *R. v BBC Ex p. Kelly* [1998] C.O.D. 58. See also, *R. v Secretary of State for Education Ex p. London Borough of Southwark* [1994] C.O.D. 298.

The third aspect of process rights and rules is the most general. We have seen that the traditional position has been that the courts do not in general apply the principles of natural justice or fairness to legislative proceedings: there is no general right to participate in rule-making.[80] The arguments concerning this issue will be considered in more detail below.[81]

B. No Existing Rule or "Insufficient" Rules

i. The debate over rules v discretion
The discussion thus far has focused upon the appropriate judicial response to a situation where an agency has made rules. There is, however, an important literature concerning the extent to which an agency should be encouraged to make rules rather than proceeding by way of individual discretionary decisions. Davis was responsible for much of the early work in this area.[82]

16–017

He begins by making clear the importance of discretionary action: while informal adjudication may be more important than formal adjudication, the former is only one part of discretionary action taken as a whole. Discretion is a vital tool in society for the individualisation of justice, and no society has existed in which discretion has been absent. Writers[83] who have expressed a yearning for a purely rule-based government from which discretion has been expunged, what Davis terms the extravagant version of the rule of law, were postulating an ideal which has and could never be attained by any country. Although Davis therefore rejects the extravagant rule of law doctrine, the purpose of the book is to argue that, while discretion may be indispensable, there is "too much of it".[84] He suggests two principal ways in which unnecessary discretion can be curtailed.

The first is to eliminate unnecessary discretionary power or *confine* it within necessary bounds.[85] This can be achieved by encouraging administrators to make standards and rules which will clarify vague legislative criteria. Courts should require an administrative agency to achieve this within a reasonable time. The agency should not feel hesitant about making rules for fear that they will involve too broad a generalisation, for Davis argues that such rules may be limited to the resolution of a narrow spectrum of cases. Development of agency policy through rule-making is felt to be preferable to such development being brought about through adjudication, because it allows more consultation and participation by interested parties.

[80] See above, para.12–012.
[81] See Ch.22.
[82] K.C. Davis, *Discretionary Justice, A Preliminary Inquiry* (Louisiana State University Press, 1969), and *Discretionary Justice in Europe and America* (University of Illinois Press, 1976).
[83] F. Hayek, *The Road to Serfdom* (University of Chicago Press, 1944) and *The Constitution of Liberty* (University of Chicago Press, 1960).
[84] Davis, *Discretionary Justice, A Preliminary Inquiry*, n.82, Chs 1–2.
[85] Davis, n.82, Ch.3.

16–018   The second method of controlling discretion is to ensure that it is *struc-tured*.[86] Whereas confining discretion seeks to keep it within certain boundaries, structuring discretion is aimed at controlling the way in which discretionary power is exercised within those boundaries. Davis suggests a number of ways in which this can be achieved: open plans, open policy statements and rules, open findings, open reasons, open precedents and fair procedure. The overall aim is not to eliminate discretion. It is to find the optimum degree of structuring in respect of each discretionary power.

Structuring of discretion is not the only technique of control that is advocated. Discretion should also be *checked*. A variety of such checks can be used, supervision by superiors, administrative appeals and judicial review being just three.

A number of other writers have pursued similar themes, albeit with modifications. For example, Jowell[87] tabulates the merits and demerits of rules. The former include the clarification of organisational aims, thereby rendering it less likely that an official will take a decision based upon improper criteria, and that rules will be more exposed to public scrutiny, thereby rendering the administration more accountable. There are, more-over, the benefits of like cases being treated alike and the possibility of greater public participation in the formulation of goals. The defects of rules are familiar, including in particular the legalism and rigidity that can be attendant upon them.[88] Despite such disadvantages other writers have joined the call for more structuring of discretion.[89]

Reservations have, however, been expressed. It has been argued that where the issue is inherently subjective, such as that of "need" within social welfare, rules are unsuitable for resolution of the question. Another area where rules are said to be of limited value is that in which the problem is polycentric with a number of interacting points of influence such that alteration of one variable produces an effect on all the others.[90] A similar point is made by those who argue that agencies may not make rules because the issues are highly complex or controversial, with the consequence that the agency does not yet feel able to commit itself, or wishes to gain more experience before doing so.[91]

---

[86] Davis, n.82, Ch.4.
[87] J. Jowell, *Law and Bureaucracy, Administrative Discretion and the limits of Legal Action* (Dunellen, 1975), Ch.1.
[88] Jowell, n.87, 22; "For example, a parking meter will not show understanding or mercy to the person who was one minute over the limit because he was helping a blind man across the street." See also J. Jowell, "Legal Control of Administrative Discretion" [1973] P.L. 178.
[89] C. Reich, "The New Property" (1964) 73 Yale L.J. 733.
[90] Jowell, n.87, Ch.5.
[91] D. Shapiro, "The Choice of Rulemaking or Adjudication in the Development of Adminis-trative Policy" (1965) 78 Harv. L.R. 921; G. Robinson, "The Making of Administrative Policy: Another Look at Rule-Making and Adjudication and Administrative Procedures Reform" (1970) 118 U. Pa. L.R.; R. Baldwin and K. Hawkins, "Discretionary Justice: Davis Recon-sidered" [1984] P.L. 570.

ii. Organisations, the decision-making process, rules and discretion

Any assessment of the relative merits of rules and discretion will often be **16–019** based, implicitly or explicitly, upon assumptions as to how bureaucracies are structured, how they operate, and the decision-making process which operates therein. Some understanding of the literature within this area will therefore be of help in the debate about rules and discretion.

Interest in organisational structure emerged earlier this century with the work of the "classical" school of scientific management, the object being to discover the most efficient method of performing an assigned task, and the type of command structure most likely to achieve the purposes of the organisation.[92] The work of the scientific school was directed initially at private industry, but was viewed with increasing interest by governments who sought to apply such ideas to public functions.[93]

Weber focused more directly upon the public sector when constructing his "ideal-type" bureaucracy.[94] The main attributes of a Weberian bureaucracy were that[95]: duties should be distributed in a fixed way as official duties; officers should be hierarchically ordered, being responsible to the person above, and responsible for those below; the institution should apply abstract rules to particular cases; the official should operate "without hatred or passion", neutrally applying the given rules; and advancement and dismissal should be objectively assessed. All aspects of the Weberian scheme were designed to ensure the objective, efficient pursuit of the task assigned to the agency.[96] Whether they do in fact achieve this is more debatable. For example, reserved detachment could hinder the development of ésprit de corps, while the insistence on conformity could engender rigidity and inhibit the rational exercise of judgment.[97]

More modern theory has reacted against the "mechanistic" aspects of earlier analysis. One strand has emphasised the role of more complex motivational considerations which operate on the individual.[98] Another, more promising strand, has been the development of systems theory as a

---

[92] H. Fayol, *General and Industrial Management* (Pitman, 1949); F. Taylor, *Scientific Management* (Harper, 1947).
[93] R. Brown and D. Steel, *The Administrative Process in Britain* (Methuen, 2nd edn, 1979), 156–157.
[94] M. Weber, *The Theory of Social and Economic Organisation*, transl. by Henderson and Talcott Parsons (Free Press, 1947), 302–313; M. Weber: *Essays in Sociology* (Oxford University Press, 1946), 196–245.
[95] For a succinct summary, see P. Blau and M. Meyer, *Bureaucracy in Modern Society* (Random House, 2nd edn, 1971), 18–23.
[96] e.g. the application of rules "without passion or hatred" is aimed at the exclusion of favouritism or bias.
[97] Blau and Meyer, n.95, 23–24. See also, the criticisms and qualifications of the Weberian approach in M. Crozier, *The Bureaucratic Phenomenon* (University of Chicago Press, 1964); T. Burns and G. Stalker, *The Management of Innovation* (Tavistock, 2nd edn, 1966); M. Meyer, *Change in Public Bureaucracies* (Cambridge University Press, 1979).
[98] See, e.g., J. March and H. Simon, *Organisations* (John Wiley & Son Ltd, 1958), Ch.3; C. Argyris, *Personality and Organisation* (Harper, 1957).

response to the perceived limitations of the earlier approaches. Drawing analogies from the biological sciences, organisations are perceived as systems which have inputs, process those inputs and produce outputs.[99] The processing of inputs will have technical, social and structural aspects, all of which will combine to determine the shape which the organisation takes. Structural influences would, for example, be whether work was organised in terms of specific client groups or on geographical criteria. Social influences would include the organisation's own perception of its primary goals. The outputs would encompass the rules and regulations, etc. produced by the organisation. These will have to satisfy the demands placed upon the organisation by government, client groups, and affected parties; if they do not the institution will become endangered.

16–020   Systems theory has important ramifications for the rules/discretion debate. Lawyers tend to view decisions as relatively simple and discrete.[100] A more realistic picture would view them as "complex, subtle and woven into a broader process"[101]: they result from a variety of intersecting inputs each of which may itself be a complex variable. This more realistic view of decision-making has three important consequences for the debate on rules and discretion.

First, if we decide that a certain administrative area should be more "rule based", then we must be aware that this can lead to problems of displacement. An attempt to limit discretion in one part of the system can lead to its re-emergence elsewhere; "squeeze in one place, and, like toothpaste, discretion will emerge at another".[102] Rendering sentencing more rule based may, for example, increase the pre-trial discretion exercised by prosecutors since a person knows that if there is a guilty plea on a certain charge, there will necessarily be a particular sentence.[103]

Second, the Davis thesis emphasises what may be termed the external aspect of discretion: the potential for arbitrary action if agencies possess broad, unstructured discretionary power. However, organisational theory would also emphasise the internal aspect of discretion: systems theory stresses that the execution of a programme may be materially affected by the "managerial structures which are built and sustained in connection with it".[104] If discretion is permitted in the building of such an organisation, this may well affect the shape of the policy which emerges. To enshrine the external aspect of discretion, through its formulation into rules, without any regard for the internal aspect could simply reinforce existing imbalances. Thus if the internal organisational structure of an agency has been so

[99] See, e.g., Sir J. Bourn, *Management in Central and Local Government* (Pitman, 1979); Brown and Steel, n.93, 167–169; P. Self, *Administrative Theories and Politics: An Inquiry into the Structure and Processes of Modern Government* (Allen & Unwin, 1973), 48–50; W. Evan, *Organisation Theory: Structures, Systems and Environments* (John Wiley & Son Ltd, 1976).
[100] Baldwin and Hawkins, n.91, 580–586.
[101] Baldwin and Hawkins, n.91, 580.
[102] Baldwin and Hawkins, n.91, 582.
[103] Baldwin and Hawkins, n.91, 582–583. See also, 576–577.
[104] P. Selznick, *TVA and the Grass Roots* (University of California Press, 1949), 67; Brown and Steel, n.93, 193–194.

constructed that the inputs and outputs favour particular interests, a requirement that the agency should make rules to confine the external aspect of its discretion could simply reinforce these existing imbalances.[105]

Third, and perhaps most fundamentally, attention to organisational structure is vital because the nature of this structure will necessarily be dependent upon the purpose which regulation is designed to serve in that area. The identification of that purpose will affect the balance between rules and discretion. This can be simply demonstrated. The structure of an organisation distributing benefits for disability will depend upon the objective behind such a scheme. One such objective has been termed "professional treatment", the idea being that decisions which are made should provide support or therapy viewed from the perspective of a particular professional culture.[106] Given this model, "the incompleteness of facts, the singularity of individual context, and the ultimately intuitive nature of judgment are recognised, if not exalted".[107] In such a system considerations of hierarchy and rules would have little role to play. To insist upon the structuring of discretion could undermine the very purpose of regulation.

iii. Conclusion

It is readily apparent that the optimum balance between rules and discretion will vary from area to area. Only careful analysis of particular regulatory contexts can reveal that balance. Given that this is so, suggestions that the courts should force or persuade agencies to develop rules should be treated with reserve. The judiciary are not in a good position to assess whether the complex arguments for and against rule-making should lead to an increase in the prevalence of such rules within a particular area.   **16–021**

4. FETTERING OF DISCRETION: CONTRACTS AND THE EXERCISE OF DISCRETION

A. The Problem

The discussion within the previous section was concerned with the situation where a public body has discretion and the extent to which it can nonetheless use rules to determine the application of the relevant policy. We have seen that the courts have been willing to allow such rules to stand provided that they do not unduly fetter the exercise of the discretion accorded to the public body.   **16–022**

---

[105] Such rules might make existing biases more overt and hence more open to attack. It is more likely that they would be built into the system and become the accepted way of administering it, but not be apparent on the face of the rules. Such rules need not appear absurd or even openly biased, see, e.g. the subtle but real prejudices at work within the TVA in favour of wealthier farming interests, Selznick, n.104, Chs 3–5.

[106] J. Mashaw, *Bureaucratic Justice* (Yale University Press, 1983), 25–27.

[107] Mashaw, n.106, 27–28. See generally, P. Craig, "Discretionary Power in Modern Administration", in M. Bullinger (ed), *Verwaltungsermessen im modernen Staat* (1986), 79–111.

A similar problem can arise where there is a clash between a discretionary power or duty and a contractual obligation which the public body has undertaken. More general issues concerning contracts and public bodies have been considered in an earlier chapter.[108] The present discussion focuses on this particular issue of contract and the fettering of discretion. A public body, whether a statutory corporation, governmental department, or local authority, has a variety of statutory powers and duties to perform. The issue that concerns us is the effect of a clash between such a power or duty and an existing contractual obligation that the public body has with a private individual.[109] The courts have to decide when the contractual obligation will be declared ineffective as a fetter on the statutory power of duty. If it is declared ineffective it has to be decided whether the private individual should have any claim to compensation. These issues will be examined in turn.[110]

B. The Incompatibility Test

16–023   It is clear that a public body cannot escape from a contract merely because it has made a bad bargain.[111]

i. The incompatibility test

16–024   The problem presented above is not a new one. The emergence of the Welfare State and the growth of bodies rendering a public service have merely increased its incidence. The problem was posed clearly in the 19th-century case of *Leake*.[112] The court had to decide whether certain land vested in commissioners responsible for drainage could be dedicated to the public as a highway, it having been thus used for 25 years. Parke J. expounded a test based upon compatibility. If the objects prescribed by the statute were incompatible with the land being dedicated as a highway then the commissioners could not in law do such a thing. However, if such use by the public was not incompatible with the statutory purposes then the dedication could take place. On the facts no incompatibility was found to exist.

This test clearly has much to commend it. If the rule were that no contract could stand if it were hypothetically to be a fetter on another of the body's powers then very few contracts could subsist. This would be disadvantageous to the public body as well as the contractor, since the former needs to make contracts where it might be acting qua an ordinary

---

[108] See above, Ch.5.
[109] H. Street, *Governmental Liability* (Cambridge University Press, 1953), Ch.3; J.D.B. Mitchell, *Contracts of Public Authorities* (University of London, 1954); S. Arrowsmith, *Civil Liability and Public Authorities* (Winteringham, 1992), 72–79; A. Davies, "Ultra Vires Problems in Government Contracts" (2006) 122 L.Q.R. 98.
[110] Some of the cases concern, as will be apparent, proprietary rights rather than simple contracts.
[111] *Att-Gen v Lindegren* (1819) 6 Price 287; *Municipal Mutual Insurance Co Ltd v Pontefract Corporation* (1917) 33 T.L.R. 234; *Commissioners of Crown Lands v Page* [1960] 2 Q.B. 274.
[112] *R. v Inhabitants of Leake* (1833) 5 B. & Ad. 469.

commercial undertaking. A balance is required between the necessity for the public body to make contracts, fairness to the contractor, and the need to ensure that the contracts thus made do not stifle other statutory powers. Parke J.'s incompatibility test achieved this by allowing the contract to stand unless it was incompatible with another statutory power or duty.

ii. Development of the test

Cases after *Leake* may be divided into two groups. The first group concerns decisions which may well have been correct on the facts: the contract may indeed have been incompatible with the statutory power. However, the language in these cases was suggestive of a stricter test, to the effect that whenever a statutory power and a contract touched upon the same subject-matter the latter would inevitably be void. For example, in *Ayr Harbour*[113] trustees were concerned with the management of a harbour and were empowered by statute to take certain lands to carry out specified works. They acquired part of Oswald's land and took a restrictive covenant that they would allow access from his remaining land to the harbour, thereby reducing the amount of compensation that they would have to pay. The House of Lords held that the covenant could not stand. Where the legislature had conferred powers to take land compulsorily, now or in the future, a contract purporting to bind them not to use those powers was void. It may well have been that the covenant could be seen as a sterilisation of the "statutory birthright" given to the trustees and hence incompatible with the statute. The court did not, however, speak in terms of incompatibility, the cases cited used a stricter test[114] and *Ayr Harbour* became the cornerstone of any counsel's arguments that a public body should be freed from a private law obligation. Other cases gave the same impression of a test stricter than that in *Leake*, or at least of the application of that test with undue strictness.[115]

The second group of cases reaffirmed the incompatibility test and applied it less strictly. The Court of Appeal confirmed that a public body or statutory undertaking could grant an easement,[116] or take a restrictive covenant,[117] provided that these were not incompatible with the statutory powers. It emphasised that it could be disadvantageous for a public body not to be able to do so since a potential vendor would be less likely to agree to a sale. Decisions of the House of Lords were to follow. In *Birkdale District Electricity Supply*[118] Lord Sumner refused to hold ultra vires a contract by Birkdale Electricity Supply that it would not increase the price for electricity higher than that charged by Southport Corporation. His

---

[113] *Ayr Harbour Trustees v Oswald* (1883) 8 App. Cas. 623.
[114] *Mulliner v Midland Railway* (1879) 11 Ch.D. 611.
[115] *York Corporation v H Leetham & Sons Ltd* [1924] 1 Ch.557. The decision in the *Amphitrite* [1921] 3 K.B. 500, discussed in the context of Crown liability, could be mentioned here also.
[116] *South Eastern Ry Co v Cooper* [1924] 1 Ch.211.
[117] *Stourcliffe Estates Co Ltd v Bournemouth Corporation* [1910] 2 Ch.12.
[118] *Birkdale District Electricity Supply Co Ltd v Southport Corporation* [1926] A.C. 355.

Lordship held that the contract was not incompatible with a statutory
power to charge what it wished up to a certain maximum. The *Ayr Harbour*
case was distinguished as being concerned with proprietary rights and
Leetham[119] was disapproved.

This more lenient approach was firmly endorsed in the *British Transport
Commission* case.[120] The question before their Lordships was whether a
footpath across an accommodation bridge could be dedicated to the public.
This was opposed by the railway authority, which argued that statutory
powers enabled it to discontinue the bridge and therefore the footpath
across it could not be dedicated to the public. Viscount Simonds, giving the
leading judgment, endorsed the incompatibility test of *Leake*, and found
that there was no incompatibility on the facts of the *British Transport
Commission* case. He said of *Ayr Harbour*, which was relied on by the
railway authorities, that "it was in fact an example of incompatibility not a
decision to the effect that incompatibility does not supply a test". [121]

iii. The determination of incompatibility: reasonable foresight

16–025   The incompatibility test was firmly established in the *British Transport
Commission* case. Compatibility is to be judged by reasonable foresight: is it
reasonably foreseeable that a conflict will arise between the contract and the
statute? The existence of a mere possibility that this might occur at some
future date is insufficient.[122] Whether incompatibility exists in a particular
case will therefore be in part a factual question,[123] and in part dependent on
construction of the relevant legislation. In *Kilby*[124] the legislation was decisive, the court holding that where a statute specifically stated that the local
authority's contractual tenancies could be varied by unilateral notice, a
system which circumscribed that power by giving to tenants' representatives
an absolute veto was incompatible with the statute.

Two factors which have been held to be relevant in the determination of
incompatibility do, however, require further mention.

iv. The determination of incompatibility: contract and property rights

16–026   In the *Birkdale* case[125] Lord Sumner made certain statements which could be
interpreted to mean that only where the contract created something akin to

---

[119] *Leetham*, n.115.
[120] *British Transport Commission v Westmoreland County Council* [1958] A.C. 126.
[121] *Westmoreland*, n.120, 143; Lord Radcliffe, 152–153.
[122] *Westmoreland*, n.120, 144.
[123] Examples of application of the incompatibility test are *Ransom and Luck Ltd v Surbiton
Borough Council* [1949] Ch.180; *Marten v Flight Refuelling Ltd* [1962] Ch.115; *Triggs v Staines
Urban District Council* [1969] 1 Ch.10. The incompatibility test will also be applied to attempts
by the private contractor to imply a term into a contract which is incompatible with a statutory
power, *Board of Trade v Temperly Steam Shipping Co Ltd* (1927) 27 Ll. L. Rep. 230; *William
Cory and Son Ltd v London Corporation* [1951] 2 K.B. 476; *Commissioners of Crown Lands v
Page* [1960] 2 Q.B. 274.
[124] *R. (on the application of Kilby) v Basildon DC* [2007] EWCA Civ 479.
[125] [1926] A.C. 355.

a property right would it be deemed to be incompatible with the statutory power.

Thus when distinguishing the *Ayr Harbour* case his Lordship said that in that case the trustees were, by the covenant, forbearing to acquire all that the statute intended them to acquire; they were sterilising part of their birthright. This was distinguished from a mere contract, even if in perpetuity. Thus, Lord Sumner believed that if the trustees had covenanted with Oswald to allow him to moor his barges in perpetuity at any wharf the decision could have been different. It was on this ground also that the *Leetham* case was criticised: there the contract was only concerned with trading profit, not the land itself.[126]

While the possibility of incompatibility is increased if the right is proprietary rather than contractual, it is doubtful whether the distinction should be taken any further than that. There may well be cases where even though there is no proprietary right there is a clear incompatibility between the contract and the statutory power.

v. The determination of incompatibility: "valid exercises of statutory power"

In *Dowty Boulton Paul*[127] the defendant corporation had conveyed to an aircraft company a plot of land for the erection of a factory in 1936, together with the right of the company to use the municipal airport for business purposes for 99 years, or so long as the corporation should maintain the airport as a municipal airport, whichever should be the longer. The conveyance also stated that, without prejudice to the Corporation's powers to deal with the airport, they should not, in exercise of their powers, unreasonably affect the plaintiff's rights. The corporation changed its mind in 1970, wishing to use the area for housing, and therefore refused to renew the licence for the airfield. The plaintiff relied on its lease and the corporation argued that this was ultra vires as fettering its statutory powers to provide housing.

Pennycuick V.C. found for the plaintiff, and reasoned as follows. The cases on incompatibility were concerned with attempts to fetter in advance the future exercise of statutory powers otherwise than by the valid exercise of a statutory power. They were not concerned with the position where a statutory power had been validly exercised creating a right extending over a term of years. The existence of that right excluded other statutory powers in relation to the same subject-matter, but it could not be held to be a fetter upon the future exercise of powers.[128]

If this means that whenever a contract or lease is created in pursuance of one statutory power it can never be incompatible with a second statutory power then it must be wrong. A moment's reflection will show that it is quite possible for one statute to give a public body a general power of leasing

16–027

---

[126] [1926] A.C. 355, 371.
[127] *Dowty Boulton Paul Ltd v Wolverhampton Corporation* [1971] 1 W.L.R. 204.
[128] The case was decided differently, on other grounds, in *Dowty Boulton Paul Ltd v Wolverhampton Corporation (No.2)* [1976] Ch.13.

land, etc. the lease so granted becoming incompatible with a later statutory power.

16–028   The point is well illustrated by *Blake*.[129] The corporation had acquired land for a park under a statute of 1875 and claimed that the beneficial ownership was, for rating purposes, in the public. This was contested by the valuation officer who argued that such a dedication would be incompatible with the Local Government Act 1933, which allowed a local authority to grant leases. The corporation could not do this *vis-à-vis* the park if the beneficial ownership was in the public. Devlin L.J. rejected the valuation officer's argument, but did not reason in the same manner as Pennycuick V.C.. Where two statutory powers might conflict they had, said Devlin L.J., to be construed. Here the power to lease in the 1933 Act was subordinate to that in the 1875 Act. However, Devlin L.J. could envisage a situation in which the plaintiff's argument did work. There could be circumstances in which the 1933 Act would predominate, for example where the Act contained a specific provision allowing the leasing of parkland, on which hypothesis the beneficial ownership could not be in the public.

Devlin L.J.'s approach must be correct. The two statutory powers must be construed, and a decision must be made as to whether the later in time really does render incompatible what was done under the earlier power. It cannot be presumed that the grant of a lease under the first statutory power is immune from the effect of a later statute. The latter may, as in Devlin L.J.'s example, contain provisions that mandate an outcome inconsistent with the exercise of the earlier statutory power.

There may however be cases where the later statute simply contains a broad discretion and the public body seeks to exercise this in a manner that is inconsistent with the contract or property right created pursuant to the earlier statutory power. In such instances Davies has argued persuasively that the court should be able to evaluate whether it is really necessary to disrupt the contract in order to exercise the later statutory discretion. The courts could use a proportionality test, require the public body to identify the public interest goal promoted by the exercise of the later statutory power, and decide whether this constituted an overriding public interest sufficient to justify the disruption to the contractor.[130]

C. Compensation

16–029   If a contract is found to be incompatible with a statutory power or duty should it merely be declared null, or ultra vires? Or should the contractor be entitled to some form of compensation? There are three possible ways in which compensation could be awarded.

---

[129] *Blake (Valuation Officer) v Hendon Corporation (No.1)* [1962] 1 Q.B. 283; *R. v Hammersmith and Fulham London Borough Council Ex p. Beddowes* [1987] Q.B. 1050. Compare *Kilby*, n.124.
[130] Davies, n.109, 110.

i. Damages for breach of contract

It has been argued that the incompatibility test only tells us that a contract **16–030** which is incompatible with a statutory power should not be specifically enforced. It does not mean that the contractor should not obtain damages for breach of the contract.

This argument is, however, flawed. A condition precedent to the grant of damages for breach of a contract is that there has been a breach. A party is failing to do something which it has expressly or impliedly promised to do. It is however difficult to identify any breach of a promise by the public body in these cases. The loss caused to the private contractor flows from the exercise by the public body of its other powers or duties. This is simply a manifestation of the fact that such bodies act both commercially and as public authorities.

An allegation of breach of contract would therefore have to be framed such that the public body was promising expressly or impliedly that it would do nothing in its public role that was incompatible with such a contract. Such a promise is clearly unrealistic and would never be made by a public authority. An express promise would certainly be ultra vires and thus a fortiori no such promise could be implied.[131]

ii. Frustration

A second possible way of granting compensation would be to say that the **16–031** contract had been frustrated. There are, however, a number of difficulties.

First, it is not clear whether on normal principles the contract would be held to be frustrated. For example, in the *Cory* case, although the corporation had conceded frustration the point was not argued, and it is unclear whether the contract would have been frustrated since the essence of the claim was simply that it was now less profitable to do the work.

Second, the compensation available under the Law Reform (Frustrated Contracts) Act 1943 might not be adequate or appropriate.

Third, the suggestion that the public body's action in this type of case should be deemed self-induced frustration is misconceived.[132] The premise behind this concept is that a party cannot rely on frustration brought about by its own conduct, act or election. The party will still be liable to perform the contract or pay damages for breach, because it has deliberately, or perhaps negligently, without legal constraint, brought about the event in question. A public body has no freedom in this sense. It has either exercised a statutory duty with which the contract is incompatible, or it has decided intra vires to exercise its statutory powers in a particular way with the same result. The action, unlike that of the private individual, is done under these legal constraints and thus cannot be deemed self-induced frustration.[133]

---

[131] *William Cory and Son Ltd v London Corporation* [1951] 2 K.B. 476; *Commissioners of Crown Lands v Page* [1960] 2 Q.B. 274, 291.
[132] C. Harlow, " 'Public' and 'Private' Law: Definition without Distinction" (1980) 43 M.L.R. 241, 248–249.
[133] The argument from self-induced frustration is simply a damages action by the backdoor.

The fourth difficulty is perhaps the most important. Underlying the frustration solution is the idea that the contract should be at an end, and that neither the public body nor the private party have any interest in its continuity. This was felt to be the case by Lord Sumner in *Birkdale*.[134] This assumption is not sound, in many cases at least.

16–032   The *Cory* case[135] provides a good example. The plaintiffs in 1936 made a contract with the defendant corporation to dispose of its refuse. In 1948 the defendant, qua Port of London Health Authority, made bylaws which caused refuse disposal to be more expensive. Cory claimed that this was a breach of contract, arguing that the 1936 contract contained an implied term that the defendant would not do anything which made the contract more onerous. This argument was, as seen above, rejected.

The essence of the plaintiff's argument was that it had offered a price presuming that certain costs would be involved and that these costs had risen due to the bylaws. If Cory could not make any profit at all it would be forced into liquidation. This was of no concern to Lord Sumner since a different company would undertake refuse collection. Yet, presuming that Cory was a reasonably efficient firm, any other firm which tendered for the contract would set its price taking full account of the more expensive nature of the job resulting from the 1948 bylaws. The defendant corporation did, therefore, have an interest in the continuity of performance of the task. The simplest solution would be to allow Cory to revise their price upwards to take account of the greater costs incurred.

On the actual facts of the *Cory* case it appeared that Cory had made a bad bargain from which it was seeking to escape. The general point being made, that a public body may well have an interest in the continuity of the relationship, is nonetheless still important. If the firm undertaking the refuse collection *had* made a reasonable bargain, which was only rendered unreasonable by regulations that applied solely to that firm, then a remedy allowing revision of the price would be beneficial.

iii. A specialised remedy

16–033   The particular problems created by public authority contracts, where the public body may be acting in a "public" and a "private" role, is the key to understanding the remedy which should be given. Normal contract principles have as their premise the necessity for one party to show that the other has committed a wrong in order to found a claim for a breach of contract. X has broken its promise so that Y can now claim damages. This does not work here. A public body cannot promise not to exercise its statutory or common law powers so as not to interfere with one of its contracts. The exercise of such powers is lawful and cannot be hindered by the threat of an action for breach of contract. However, this may be hard upon the private contracting party who may have suffered considerable loss. What is required

---

[134] [1926] A.C. 355, 374–375.
[135] [1951] 2 K.B. 476.

is a remedy which recognises the legality of the public body's action, but which nevertheless accepts that compensation should be payable.

Such remedies exist in France, which recognises administrative contracts as a separate entity.[136] The central idea is the predominance of the public interest. The realisation that in certain circumstances the public body may in its public role be required to take action which is detrimental to the other contracting party, and can to this end suspend or vary the contract. Three remedies are of a particular interest.

Imprévision is similar to frustration subject to two important differences. It is based upon the continuity of the relationship and not necessarily its termination. It does not require that the contract should have become legally or physically incapable of being performed, and applies when circumstances upset the economic substance of the contract, rendering it more difficult than contemplated, over and beyond the normal risk. The contractor, when this occurs, may, for example, continue to perform the contract, but at a revised rate.

The second and perhaps most interesting of the three is a remedy called *fait du prince*. An unforeseeable loss may be shared by the two parties, and the contractor can obtain an indemnity for increased costs. This applies where the contract is affected by something done by the public body itself in its public role which renders the bargain less profitable. The remedy may constitute an indemnity for the private party or an authorisation to increase the charge. *Fait du prince* will not apply where the loss is caused by legislation affecting all people equally.

A third doctrine, *supervision*, allows the administration to modify the contractual terms in the public interest, but it has to pay an indemnity to the other party if, on the facts, that is the fair balance.

The flexibility provided by the French remedies is to be envied. Recognising the specialised nature of the problem, specialised solutions have been found. English law, by way of contrast, is inadequate in this respect. While the rules developed as to when a contract should fall are now satisfactory, the consequences are not. Epithets such as ultra vires, void or null tend to be attached as if some initial invalidity always existed thereby providing an excuse not to grant compensation. This does not bear examination.[137] Care must be taken to ensure that the person contracting with the public body is not placed in a better position than the party to a purely private contract. However, where action taken by a public authority does not affect people generally then a remedy akin to *fait du prince* would be most welcome.[138]

It is true, as we have seen,[139] that the standard form contracts made by the

---

[136] Mitchell, n.109, Ch.4; N. Brown and J. Bell, *French Administrative Law* (Clarendon Press, 5th edn, 1998), 202–210.
[137] In *Dowty Boulton Paul* [1971] 1 W.L.R. 204 a decision by a local authority that it now wished to use the land for housing could not be said to render the prior lease of that land for 30 years void *ab initio*.
[138] On the actual facts of *Cory* the plaintiffs should probably not be granted such compensation since it is difficult to see how they were in any worse position than anyone else who would be affected by the new byelaws.
[139] See, Ch.5.

government go some way to achieving the same result, by allowing the government to vary the contract unilaterally and by recognising that it may have to break the original bargain, subject to adjustments in the recompense paid to the contractor. It would, nonetheless, be of assistance if these principles were recognised in relation to public contracts generally, and enshrined in legal doctrine.

D. The Position of the Crown

16–034   The problems arising when a public body acts in a dual capacity, as a contracting party and as the holder of statutory powers, is not altered by the public body being the Crown. The same principles outlined above should be applied, both as to when any contract should fall, and as to whether compensation should be granted. Rowlatt J.'s decision in the *Amphitrite*[140] does, however, suggest a stricter test.

Neutral ship owners, aware of the danger of their ships being detained in British ports, obtained undertakings from the British government that if the ship carried a particular type of cargo it would not be detained. The ship was nevertheless detained and the ship owners sought damages. Rowlatt J. denied the claim. It was, he said, competent for the Crown to bind itself by an ordinary commercial contract, but the present agreement was not a contract. It was an arrangement whereby the government purported to say what its future executive action would be, and was an expression of intent and not a contract. Rowlatt J. characterised matters in this way because he felt that the government could not fetter its future executive action, which had to be determined by the needs of the community. Reliance was placed upon the cases concerning Crown service.

The case has been criticised in later authorities,[141] and ignored in at least one case to which it might have been applied.[142] On principle the judgment of Rowlatt J. is too extreme. It can be accepted that the Crown, like any other public body, cannot enter into a contract that would be incompatible with its executive powers. However, the judgment implies that any contract that in any way fetters the discharge of any executive power must fall, or be deemed not to be a contract at all. This, like the judgment in the *Ayr Harbour* case, is unnecessarily draconian. The position of the Crown should be brought into line with that of other public bodies and the incompatibility test should be applied.

---

[140] [1921] 3 K.B. 500.
[141] *Robertson v Minister of Pensions* [1949] 1 K.B. 227; *Howell v Falmouth Boat Co* [1951] A.C. 837.
[142] *Steaua Romana* [1944] P. 43.

CHAPTER 17

ABUSE OF DISCRETION

1. ILLEGALITY AND IRRATIONALITY

The courts have, ever since the origins of judicial review, exercised control to **17–001** prevent the abuse of discretionary power. It is important to realise that there are essentially two differing *levels* at which the judicial controls can operate.

The courts can, on the one hand, intervene because the tribunal has, for example, used its discretionary power for a purpose not allowed by the legislation at all. They can, on the other hand, intervene because the tribunal, while able in principle to use its power to reach a certain end, has done so in a manner felt to be unreasonable, irrational, or disproportionate. Lord Diplock's distinction in *GCHQ*[1] between review based upon illegality and that based upon irrationality captures this idea. This chapter will be concerned with controls that relate to illegality, while controls pertaining to irrationality will be considered in later chapters.

It should be acknowledged that it may not always be easy to distinguish between the two levels. Courts and commentators may differ as to whether a particular case should be placed within one or the other of these divisions. The reason is that statutes conferring broad discretionary powers do not have neat corners, nor is the process of statutory construction self-executing. Challenges based on illegality, may, therefore, not be easy to distinguish from those based upon irrationality. Moreover, the court may, in determining the permitted ambit of a broad discretionary power, utilise substantive principles.

While the main focus of control was at the first level the impression could be maintained that the courts were applying legislative intent, in the sense of delineating the purposes for which such discretionary power could legitimately be used. If the controls at the second level are expanded then it becomes much more difficult to preserve this rationale for judicial

[1] [1985] A.C. 374, 410–411.

intervention. The courts' role shifts inevitably towards ensuring principles of fair administration.

The discussion of illegality within this chapter will be structured in the following manner. The next three sections will address the basic structure of the *Wednesbury* test, the types of power that can be judicially controlled and the intensity of judicial review. There will then be a discussion of the constraints that relate directly to illegality. Until recently these were principally of common law origin, and focused on the purpose for which the power was exercised, the relevancy of the considerations which were taken into account and the like. The Human Rights Act 1998 (HRA) has added a new, important, head of statutory illegality and this will be analysed in the following chapter.

2. Reasonableness: The Two Meanings

17–002　　The distinction drawn above concerning the levels of review is apparent in the two senses of unreasonableness found in the oft-cited judgment of Lord Greene M.R. in the *Wednesbury* case.[2] The corporation was empowered to grant licences for Sunday entertainment subject to such conditions as it thought fit. A picture house was licensed subject to the condition that no children under 15 be admitted. This condition was challenged as unreasonable and ultra vires. Lord Greene M.R. stressed that the court should not substitute its view for that of the corporation, and then proceeded to examine what the term unreasonable meant in this context. Two meanings of the term unreasonable emerged from his judgment.

The first can be called the "umbrella sense". Unreasonable was used as a synonym for a host of more specific grounds of attack, such as taking account of irrelevant considerations, acting for improper purposes and acting *mala fide*, which, as Lord Greene M.R. said, tend to run into one another. The second meaning may be termed the "substantive sense" of unreasonableness: a decision may be attacked if it is so unreasonable that no reasonable public body could have made it. To prove this would require something quite extreme. Lord Greene M.R. gave the example of a teacher being dismissed because of red hair.

The role of unreasonableness in its substantive sense was conceived of as a safety net to be used after tests such as relevancy or purpose.[3] The court looked first to see whether, for example, the body had acted for improper purposes. If it had not the decision might still be struck down if it was unreasonable in the substantive sense. The two senses of the term unreasonable reflected, therefore, the two levels at which judicial control could take place that were mentioned above.

---

[2] *Associated Picture Houses Ltd v Wednesbury Corporation* [1948] 1 K.B. 223, 228–230.
[3] *Wednesbury*, n.2, 233–234.

It is evident that neither of Lord Greene M.R.'s constructions of the term reasonable accord with the dictionary meaning of that word. The special interpretation of the term reasonableness was warranted by the constitutional position of the courts.[4] They should not intervene simply because they believed that a different way of exercising discretionary power would be more reasonable than that chosen by the public body. This would be to substitute a judicial view as to, for example, the most appropriate way in which to allocate aid, or to disburse licences, for that of the public body. Hence the controls over the substantive ends that can be pursued by an administrative authority are expressed in terms of relevancy, purpose or unreasonableness in its substantive sense. By phrasing control in these terms, the courts preserve the impression that they are thereby only fulfilling the legislative will. They will not dictate which result should be reached, but they will impose limits on which ends cannot be pursued.

However, what are relevant considerations or proper purposes will often not be self-evident. Decisions about these factors will themselves involve social and political value judgments. Moreover the boundary line between this form of intervention and more direct substitution of opinion by the judiciary may well become blurred.

3. The Types of Power that can be Controlled

It is important to understand the types of power that can be controlled by the courts. Certain points are clear.   17–003

A. Statutory Power

The UK courts have not traditionally held it to be within their power to invalidate primary legislation, this being regarded as inconsistent with parliamentary sovereignty, although there are dicta countenancing the possibility that primary statute might be judicially challenged in certain exceptional cases.[5] The courts will however exercise control over primary legislation in certain instances.   17–004

Thus it is open to the courts to interpret primary legislation in the manner that best fits with the precepts of judicial review. Primary statutes can moreover be challenged for compatibility with EU law. They are subject to the Human Rights Act 1998, in that the courts have a duty to interpret legislation to be compatible with the Convention rights mentioned in the Act. The courts have in addition heard a claim that primary legislation was

---

[4] This point is brought out forcefully in *Pickwell v Camden London Borough Council* [1983] Q.B. 962. See also, *Council of Civil Service Unions v Minister for the Civil Service* [1985] A.C. 374, 410–411.
[5] *R. (on the application of Jackson) v Attorney General* [2006] 1 A.C. 262, paras 101–102.

not properly made in accordance with the Parliament Acts, and that the Parliament Act 1949 was invalid.[6]

Delegated or secondary legislation is subject to judicial review.[7] So too is discretionary power exercised pursuant to a statute; indeed, the majority of cases are of this nature.

B. Prerogative Power

17–005   It is now clear that prerogative powers are subject to judicial review. The previously traditional view was that the courts would control the existence and extent of prerogative power, but not the manner of exercise thereof,[8] although there were some dicta supporting a wider review power.[9]

This position was modified by the *GCHQ*[10] case. Their Lordships emphasised that the reviewability of discretionary power should be dependent upon the subject-matter, and not whether its source was statute or the prerogative. Certain exercises of prerogative power would, because of their subject-matter, be less justiciable, and Lord Roskill compiled the broadest list of such forbidden territory.[11] Thus, in the actual case their Lordships held that although the Minister had to adduce evidence that the decision to ban national unions at GCHQ was based on considerations of national security, the question of whether such considerations outweighed the prima facie duty of fairness was for the Minister himself to decide.[12] Subject to this important caveat, their Lordships were willing, albeit in varying degrees,[13] to consider the manner of exercise of prerogative power, as well as adjudicating on its existence and extent. The success of such a challenge might be affected by the ground of attack,[14] as well as the nature of the subject-matter.

---

[6] *Jackson*, n.5.

[7] See below, Ch.22.

[8] *Case of Monopolies* (1602) 11 Co. Rep. 84b; *Prohibitions del Roy* (1607) 12 Co. Rep. 63; *Burmah Oil Co Ltd v Lord Advocate* [1965] A.C. 75; *Att-Gen. v De Keyser's Royal Hotel Ltd* [1920] A.C. 508; *Chandler v DPP* [1964] A.C. 763; P. Craig, "Prerogative, Precedent and Power", in C. Forsyth and I. Hare (eds), *The Golden Metwand and the Crooked Cord, Essays in Honour of Sir William Wade* (Oxford University Press, 1998), 65–91.

[9] *Chandler*, n.8, 809–810 (Lord Devlin); *Laker Airways Ltd v Department of Trade* [1977] Q.B. 643 (Lord Denning MR).

[10] *Council of Civil Service Unions*, n.4, 417–418.

[11] *Council of Civil Service Unions*, n.4, 418. The making of treaties, the defence of the realm, the dissolution of Parliament, the appointment of ministers, as well as other areas where the subject-matter was not justiciable.

[12] *Council of Civil Service Unions*, n.4, 402–403, 406–407, 412–413, 420–421, unless *semble* the Minister's decision was one which no reasonable Minister could make, 406. See also, *R. v Secretary of State for the Home Department Ex p. Ruddock* [1987] 1 W.L.R. 1482, where the court emphasised that the evidence concerning national security must be cogent and that the court could, if necessary, hear such evidence in camera; *R. v Secretary of State for Foreign and Commonwealth Affairs Ex p. Everett* [1989] 2 W.L.R. 224.

[13] Thus Lord Fraser and Lord Brightman reserved the question, not directly raised by the case, of whether the direct exercise of prerogative power would be subject to review, [1985] A.C. 374, 398, 423–424. See however *R. (on the application of Bancoult) v Secretary of State for Foreign and Commonwealth Affairs* [2007] EWCA Civ 498.

[14] Lord Diplock stated that an applicant would be more likely to succeed if alleging illegality or procedural impropriety, as opposed to irrationality, *Council of Civil Service Unions*, n.4, 411; C. Walker, "Review of the Prerogative: The Remaining Issues" [1987] P.L. 62.

Later courts have however been prepared to reassess the extent to which any particular prerogative subject-matter is immune from review, and the general trend has been to reduce such islands of immunity. Thus in *Bentley*,[15] it was held that the prerogative of mercy was subject to judicial review, and the court could stipulate the types of consideration which could be taken into account when exercising this power. In *Abbasi*,[16] the court held that it was no answer to a claim for judicial review to say that the source of the power of the Foreign Office was the prerogative, since it was the subject-matter that was determinative. In *Bancoult*,[17] Sedley L.J. opined that a number of the examples given by Lord Roskill might be regarded as questionable in the modern day and that the grant of honours for reward, the waging of a war of manifest aggression or a refusal to dissolve Parliament could well call in question immunity based purely on subject-matter. The prerogative power of colonial governance, the power in issue in *Bancoult*, was not wholly immune from judicial review.

Later cases also indicate judicial willingness to exercise some review even over broadly framed prerogative power. Thus in *Bancoult* while the court accepted that review of the prerogative power concerning the peace, good order and governance of a colony might be limited, immunity would only attach to prerogative measures lawfully enacted and rationally capable of addressing the peace, order and good government of the colony.[18]

There have moreover been important political developments relating to prerogative power. Thus in the White Paper on the *Governance of Britain*[19] the Prime Minister stated that changes would be made to many of the principal prerogative powers, in order to place them on a statutory basis and increase parliamentary scrutiny and control over what has hitherto been executive discretionary power.

C. Common Law Discretionary Power

There is some debate as to whether public bodies possess discretionary **17–006** powers which are neither statutory nor prerogative in nature, but which are more properly to be classified as common law discretionary powers.[20] For example, the power to contract can be regarded as an inherent common law power of this nature. The courts may be uncertain as to how to classify certain powers. Thus in *Elias* the court appeared to conceptualise a ministerial ex gratia compensation scheme as a common law discretionary power

---

[15] *R. v Secretary of State for the Home Department Ex p. Bentley* [1994] Q.B. 349.
[16] *R. (on the application of Abbasi) v Secretary of State for Foreign and Commonwealth Affairs* [2002] EWCA Civ 1598, para.106.
[17] *Bancoult*, n.13, para.46.
[18] *Bancoult*, n.13, para.47.
[19] Cm. 7170 (2007), paras 14–51; Draft Constitutional Renewal Bill 2008, Cm. 7342.
[20] B.V. Harris, "The 'Third Source' of Authority for Government Action" (1992) 109 L.Q.R. 626; M. Freedland, "Public Law and Private Finance—Placing the Private Finance Initiative in a Public Law Frame" [1998] P.L. 288; B.V. Harris (2007) 123 L.Q.R. 225.

separate from the prerogative, although there were also statements that appeared to regard the ministerial power as part of the prerogative.[21]

Insofar as there is this further type of power the trend of the case law is, as seen in the context of the prerogative, to base reviewability upon the subject-matter of the power and not its source. Thus in *Elias* the court duly considered the claim that there had been a fettering of ministerial power in relation to the ex gratia compensation scheme, and was willing to do so irrespective of whether this was conceptualised as a common law discretionary power or a prerogative power.[22]

This is surely right as a matter of principle. The courts quite rightly broke down previous barriers between review of statutory and prerogative discretionary power, and held that review should be dependent on the subject matter rather than the source of the power. Insofar as a separate category of common law discretionary power is recognised then it too should be subject to the same precepts.

There has been greater uncertainty as to the extent to which the courts are willing to review contracting power, and the relevant case law has been affected by the extent to which the courts have been willing to conclude that a public body exercising such power is exercising a public function.[23]

D. Non-statutory Bodies

17–007   The courts have also imposed controls on the way in which power is exercised by bodies that are not the creature of statute. The law in this area has been driven principally by developments relating to remedies, and its precise metes and bounds are still being worked out. There will be a detailed consideration of this within the chapter on remedies.[24]

4. INTENSITY OF REVIEW

17–008   It is important to understand that judicial review can vary in intensity. It is becoming increasingly common for courts to adopt a variable standard of review, the intensity of which alters depending upon the subject matter of the action. Terms such as irrationality or proportionality can be applied with differing degrees of rigour or intensity. This feature has become more marked as the courts have shown a greater willingness to protect individual rights, employing more intensive review in such instances. This can be briefly demonstrated by contrasting two decisions.

---

[21] *R. (on the application of Elias) v Secretary of State for Defence* [2006] 1 W.L.R. 3213, paras 185, 193.
[22] *Elias*, n.21, para.193.
[23] See below, paras 26–025—26–026.
[24] See, Ch.26.

In the *Brind* case,[25] to be considered fully below, a number of their Lordships made it clear that if the exercise of discretionary power impinged upon a fundamental right then the courts would require an important competing public interest to be shown in order to justify this intrusion.

By way of contrast in the *Hammersmith* case,[26] the House of Lords reviewed charge capping by the Secretary of State, which the applicant local authorities claimed was in breach of the relevant statute. Lord Bridge held that while the court could intervene if the Secretary of State had acted illegally, that is for improper purposes, or on irrelevant considerations, it should, in this sphere of economic policy, be very wary of review based upon irrationality unless there was some manifest absurdity or bad faith. When reading the material which follows one should, therefore, consider not simply whether we should or should not utilise a particular concept, such as proportionality, in our armoury of judicial review, but also the intensity with which this tool should be applied in differing contexts.

Various considerations will necessarily influence the judiciary in deciding on the intensity of review in any particular case.[27] This issue will be considered more fully in subsequent chapters. Suffice it to say for the present that we should be cautious about generalisations in this regard. Thus it has, for example, been common for the courts to exhibit wariness when reviewing decisions that can have implications for resource allocation, or where they may involve socio-economic interests. While there are some legitimate concerns in this respect, we should nonetheless be wary of regarding such matters as beyond the purview of the courts. There is a sophisticated literature analysing in detail the issues that pertain to such cases, with recommendations with regard to the appropriate intensity of review.[28]

5. ILLEGALITY: COMMON LAW CONSTRAINTS

The courts have, ever since the origins of judicial review, exerted control **17–009** over the discretion exercised by tribunals, agencies and the like, in order to

---

[25] *R. v Secretary of State for the Home Department Ex p. Brind* [1991] 1 A.C. 696.
[26] *R. v Secretary of State for the Environment Ex p. Hammersmith and Fulham London Borough Council* [1991] 1 A.C. 521.
[27] See, e.g., *IBA Healthcare Ltd v Office of Fair Trading* [2004] I.C.R. 1364, paras 90–101; *R. (on the application of Carson) v Secretary of State for Work and Pensions* [2006] 1 A.C. 173, paras 15–17, 55–60; *R. (on the application of Al Rawi) v Secretary of State for Foreign and Commonwealth Affairs* [2006] EWCA Civ 1279.
[28] S. Fredman, "Social, Economic and Cultural Rights", in D. Feldman (ed.), *English Public Law* (Oxford University Press, 2004), Ch.10; K. Syrett, "Opening Eyes to the Reality of Scarce Health Care Resources?" [2006] P.L. 664; J. King, "The Justiciability of Resource Allocation" (2007) 70 M.L.R. 197; A. Pillay, "Courts, Variable Standards of Review and Resource Allocation: Developing a Model for the Enforcement of Social and Economic Rights" [2007] E.H.R.L.R. 616; C. Newdick, "Judicial Review: Low-Priority Treatment and Exceptional Case Review" [2007] Med. L.R. 236; E. Palmer, *Judicial Review, Socio-Economic Rights and the Human Rights Act* (Hart, 2007).

prevent power from being misused or abused. Thus in *Rooke's Case*,[29] Commissioners of Sewers had repaired a river bank and taxed R for the whole amount despite the fact that other landowners had benefited from the work. The Commissioners had discretion as to the levying of the money, but the court struck their decision down: the discretion was to be exercised according to reason and law and it was unreasonable for R to bear the whole burden.

A. Improper Purposes

17–010   The law reports abound with examples of the courts striking down discretionary decisions where the discretion has been used for an improper purpose. A public body with power to construct lavatories could not use that power in order to build a subway under a street[30]; deportation could not be used to achieve extradition[31]; the Home Secretary could not use his powers to revoke television licences where people had bought a new licence early in order to avoid a price increase[32]; a local authority had no power to enter into speculative financial swap transactions[33]; and a local authority could not use its power to dispose of land to promote the electoral advantage of the dominant party on the council.[34]

The courts will determine the purpose of a particular statute as a matter of construction. While they generally maintain that they are only keeping the authority within the boundaries of its power and not substituting their view, the dividing line can be a fine one.

For example, planning authorities may grant planning permission unconditionally, or subject to such conditions as they think fit. A number of cases have turned on the legality of such conditions. The general position adopted has been that the conditions must fairly and reasonably relate to the permitted development.[35] In applying this test the courts have upheld fairly broad conditions,[36] but they have also struck down a number by using concepts that are open to debate. Thus, the court held invalid conditions attached to the grant of a caravan site licence which required, inter alia, site rents to be agreed with the council and security of tenure to be provided for caravan owners.[37] The House of Lords found that the legislation only allowed terms to be attached that related to the use of the site, and not to the

---

[29] (1598) 5 Co. Rep. 99b; *Hetley v Boyer* (1614) Cro. Jac. 336; *R. v Askew* (1768) 4 Burr. 2186; *Leader v Moxon* (1773) 2 W. Bl. 924.
[30] *Westminster Corporation v L & NW Ry* [1905] A.C. 426; *Galloway v London Corporation* (1866) L.R. 1 H.L. 34.
[31] *R. v Governor of Brixton Prison Ex p. Soblen* [1963] 2 Q.B. 243.
[32] *Congreve v Home Office* [1976] Q.B. 629.
[33] *Hazell v Hammersmith and Fulham London Borough Council* [1992] 2 A.C. 1.
[34] *Porter v Magill* [2002] 2 A.C. 357.
[35] *Pyx Granite Co Ltd v Ministry of Housing and Local Government* [1958] 1 Q.B. 544, 572, affirm'd [1960] A.C. 260; *Newbury District Council v Secretary of State for the Environment* [1981] A.C. 578.
[36] e.g. *Fawcett Properties Ltd v Buckingham County Council* [1961] A.C. 636.
[37] *Chertsey Urban District Council v Mixnam Properties Ltd* [1965] A.C. 735.

types of contract the site owner could make with the caravan owners. In reaching this conclusion the court argued that freedom of contract was a fundamental right, and that if Parliament intended to empower a third party to make conditions which affected the provisions of a contract between others then this should be expressed in clear terms.[38] In other cases the courts have relied on the principle that private rights of property should not be taken without compensation unless there exists clear authority in the statute.[39]

This is not to say that either of the above decisions was necessarily wrong. The balance between presumptions as to freedom of contract and the protection of private property rights unless due compensation is paid, and the overall direction of the planning system is a complex one on which opinions may differ. There is, however, no doubt that the denomination of a purpose as proper or improper in such circumstances raises issues of political and social choice, which do not cease to be so by being expressed in the language of vires. Later authority has held that planning law is of a "public character", and that the courts should not introduce private law principles unless these are expressly authorised by parliament or are necessary to give effect to the legislative purpose.[40]

Cases raising such issues are not restricted to the planning field. In *Roberts*,[41] Poplar Council had decided to pay their low grade workers £4 per week. The relevant statute empowered the council to pay such wages as it thought fit.[42] Despite this the House of Lords found that the payment was excessive: the statute was to be read subject to an implied condition that the wages should be reasonable, which was to be judged by the current rates payable in the industry. Anything above this was a gratuity, and the advancement of a social purpose, such as payment of a minimum wage, was unlawful.[43]

The decision in *Bromley* provides a further example of the difficulties **17–011** entailed when determining the purposes for which a statutory power can be used.[44] The Transport (London) Act 1969 s.1, imposed upon the GLC a duty to develop policies that promoted the provision of integrated, efficient and economic transport facilities for Greater London. The London Transport Executive (LTE) was to implement these policies. Under the Act the LTE was required, so far as was practicable, to make up any deficit incurred

---

[38] *Mixnam Properties Ltd*, n.37, 763–764.
[39] *Minister of Housing and Local Government v Hartnell* [1965] A.C. 1134. But *cf. Kingston London Borough Council v Secretary of State for the Environment* [1973] 1 W.L.R. 1549.
[40] *Pioneer Aggregates (UK) Ltd v Secretary of State for the Environment* [1985] A.C. 132, 140–141; *R. v St Edmunsbury Borough Council Ex p. Investors in Industry Commercial Properties Ltd* [1985] 1 W.L.R. 1157.
[41] *Roberts v Hopwood* [1925] A.C. 579. See, however, *Pickwell*, n.4.
[42] Metropolis Management Act 1855 s.62.
[43] See also, *Prescott v Birmingham Corporation* [1955] Ch.210; *Taylor v Munrow* [1960] 1 W.L.R. 151; *Bromley*, n.44.
[44] *Bromley London Borough Council v Greater London Council* [1983] 1 A.C. 768. See *R. v London Transport Executive Ex p. Greater London Council* [1983] Q.B. 484, in which a revised fares reduction scheme was held to be lawful.

in one accounting period within the next such period.[45] The legislation empowered the GLC to take such action as was necessary and appropriate in order to enable the LTE to comply with this obligation.[46] The GLC also had power to make grants to the LTE for any purpose.[47]

The GLC decided to implement a resolution, which had been included by the majority group in their manifesto, to reduce fares by 25 per cent. To this end, the GLC issued a supplementary precept for rates to all London boroughs. The money thereby obtained would be paid by the GLC to the LTE as a grant, in order to enable the latter to balance its accounts. An indirect result of the reduction of the fares was that the GLC would lose approximately £50 million of the rate support grant. Bromley London Borough Council sought certiorari to quash the supplementary rate, arguing that it was either beyond the powers of the GLC under the 1969 Act, or that it was an invalid exercise of discretion under that legislation.

The House of Lords upheld this claim. Their Lordships recognised that the power to make grants contained within s.3 conferred a wide discretion, and that such grants could be made to supplement the revenue received by the LTE from fares. This discretion was, however, limited. The LTE's basic obligation was to run its operations on ordinary business principles, which the fare reduction contravened. The GLC could not use its grant making powers to achieve a social policy that was inconsistent with these obligations. Reduction of the fares was also invalid because it involved a breach of the fiduciary duty owed by the GLC to the ratepayers. The effect of the 25 per cent reduction in fares would be to place an inordinate burden on the ratepayers, particularly because this would be accompanied by a known loss of rate support grant. Nor could the GLC defend its policy on the basis that it possessed a mandate to lower fares. Those who were elected were representatives and not delegates. They could not regard themselves as irrevocably bound by their manifesto.

The case is interesting in many respects.[48] The statutory language was, Lord Diplock admitted,[49] sometimes opaque and elliptical, and this is reflected in the fact that although the House of Lords reached a unanimous conclusion, their Lordships differed in their interpretation of the legislation. Because of the intricacy and ambiguity of the statute, all of their Lordships, explicitly or implicitly, adopted a purposive approach to its construction. Two aspects of that approach will be examined here, the fiduciary duty owed to the ratepayers, and the argument based upon the election manifesto.

17–012   The idea that a local authority owes a fiduciary duty to its ratepayers is by

---

[45] s.7(3)(b).
[46] s.7(6).
[47] s.3(1).
[48] J. Dignan, "Policy-Making, Local Authorities and the Courts: the 'GLC Fares' Case" (1983) L.Q.R. 605; M. Loughlin, *Local Government in the Modern State* (Oxford University Press, 1986), Ch.3.
[49] [1983] 1 A.C. 768, 822–823.

no means new,[50] but it was not subjected to a thorough judicial investigation. The idea seems self-evident: a local authority occupies a position of trust, or a fiduciary duty, in relation to the ratepayers whose money it is using, and who are the beneficiaries of the services being provided. Closer analysis reveals a shakier foundation.[51] Ratepayers do not provide all, or even the major proportion of, local authority revenue. Central government grants furnish the main source of such funds. Control through the fiduciary duty operates, moreover, in an asymmetrical fashion. It serves to quash expenditure deemed to be in breach of this duty, but does not impose any obligation to spend money that is being unreasonably withheld.[52] This is a reflection of a more general characteristic of review, which is that it is geared towards the avoidance of mistakes. Effectiveness and mistake avoidance are treated as synonymous, which is often overly simplistic. Furthermore, given that ratepayers were, as their Lordships admitted, only one part of those to whom the local authority owed duties, it was then necessary to determine the balance between their interests and those of others in local society. This was a difficult determination to make and it is arguable that the determination actually made by the elected representatives should have been allowed to stand. This leads directly onto the argument based on the manifesto.

The response of the House of Lords to the argument based upon the election manifesto is, in many ways, incontrovertible. A person who is elected is not a delegate of those who voted, but rather a representative who must act in the best interests of all the constituents. The representative cannot be irrevocably bound to fulfil election promises. This is unexceptionable in itself, but it does not sit easily with the views expressed by the House of Lords in the *Tameside*[53] case. In that case their Lordships placed much emphasis upon the fact that the local authority had a virtual mandate to retain certain grammar schools in the area. It was a significant factor to be taken into account when assessing the reasonableness of the local authority's conduct in attempting to allocate children to the correct school.

It would be a simple world in which an authority always acted for one purpose only. Complex problems can arise where one of the purposes is lawful and one is regarded as unlawful. The courts have used various tests to resolve this problem. First, what was the true purpose for which the power was exercised? Provided that the legitimate statutory purpose was achieved it is irrelevant that a subsidiary object was also attained.[54] Second, what was the dominant purpose for which the power was exercised?[55] Third, were any of the purposes authorised? This has less support in the case law than the

---

[50] *Roberts*, n.41; *Prescott*, n.43.
[51] Note, Griffiths (1982) 41 C.L.J. 216.
[52] D. Williams, "The Control of Local Authorities," in J. Andrews (ed.), *Welsh Studies in Public Law* (University of Wales Press, 1970), 132–133.
[53] *Secretary of State for Education and Science v Tameside Metropolitan Borough Council* [1977] A.C. 1014.
[54] *Westminster Corporation*, n.30; *R. v Brixton Prison Governor Ex p. Soblen* [1963] 2 Q.B. 243.
[55] *R. v Immigration Appeals Adjudicator Ex p. Khan* [1972] 1 W.L.R. 1058; *R. v Greenwich London Borough Council Ex p. Lovelace* [1991] 1 W.L.R. 506.

previous two tests. Fourthly, if any of the purposes was unauthorised and this had an effect upon the decision taken, it will be overturned as being based upon irrelevant considerations.[56]

B. Relevancy

17–013   The second principal method of controlling the exercise of discretion is relevancy: a decision will be declared ultra vires if it is based upon irrelevant considerations or if relevant considerations are not taken into account. Relevancy overlaps with control maintained through improper purposes and a number of the cases could be classified under one section or the other.

In exercising control based upon relevancy, the courts have, for example, defined the types of considerations which licensing justices can take into account. These included the character and needs of an area,[57] but not the terms on which an applicant conducted the business, if those terms did not affect the applicant's fitness to hold the licence.[58] Control of a like kind is maintained over other areas such as education,[59] housing,[60] the police,[61] the mentally disordered,[62] sentencing[63] and nationalised industry,[64] although the courts have been more reluctant to specify the considerations deemed to be relevant in conduct of foreign relations.[65]

While the courts will intervene if a relevant consideration has not been taken into account, they will not generally have regard to the weight it has been accorded, this being seen as the function of the primary decision-maker.[66] The courts can however have regard to such matters where the weighing was *Wednesbury* unreasonable, or where there was evidence that the decision-maker had fettered its discretion.

An important issue that has arisen in a number of cases is whether a local authority is allowed to take account of shortage of resources when deciding how to fulfil its statutory duties.[67] In *Barry*[68] the House of Lords considered

---

[56] *Hanks v Minister of Housing and Local Government* [1963] 1 Q.B. 999, 1016, 1020, 1037; *R. v Inner London Education Authority Ex p. Westminster City Council* [1986] 1 W.L.R. 28; *R. v Broadcasting Complaints Commission Ex p. Owen* [1985] Q.B. 1153.

[57] *Sharp v Wakefield* [1891] A.C. 173.

[58] *R. v Hyde* [1912] 1 K.B. 645; *R. v Bowman* [1898] 1 Q.B. 663; *R. v Wandsworth Licensing JJ Ex p. Whitbread and Co Ltd* [1921] 3 K.B. 487; *R. v Birmingham Licensing Planning Committee Ex p. Kennedy* [1972] 2 Q.B. 140.

[59] *Sadler v Sheffield Corporation* [1924] 1 Ch.483; *Short v Poole Corporation* [1926] Ch.66.

[60] *Bristol District Council v Clark* [1975] 1 W.L.R. 1443; *Cannock Chase District Council v Kelly* [1978] 1 W.L.R. 1; *Victoria Square Property Co Ltd v Southwark London Borough Council* [1978] 1 W.L.R. 463.

[61] *R. v Commissioner of Police of the Metropolis Ex p. Blackburn* [1968] 2 Q.B. 118; *Blackburn (No.3)* [1973] Q.B. 241.

[62] *Retarded Children's Aid Society Ltd v Barnet London Borough Council* [1969] 2 Q.B. 22.

[63] *R. v Secretary of State for the Home Department Ex p. Venables* [1998] A.C. 407.

[64] *South of Scotland Electricity Board v British Oxygen Co Ltd* [1956] 1 W.L.R. 1069, [1959] 1 W.L.R. 587.

[65] *R. (on the application of Al Rawi) v Secretary of State for Foreign and Commonwealth Affairs* [2007] 2 W.L.R. 1219.

[66] *Tesco Stores Ltd v Secretary of State for the Environment* [1995] 1 W.L.R. 759.

[67] See the literature in n.28.

[68] *R. v Gloucestershire County Council Ex p. Barry* [1997] A.C. 584.

whether the availability of resources could be taken into account under the Chronically Sick and Disabled Persons Act 1970 s.2(1). This provided that if a local authority was satisfied that it was necessary to make arrangements in order to meet the needs of a chronically sick or disabled person then it was the duty of that authority to make those arrangements. The applicant had been provided with cleaning and laundry services pursuant to this provision, but the local authority withdrew these services due to cuts in the funding provided by central government. A majority of the House of Lords held that, as a matter of construction, the needs of such a person for services could not sensibly be assessed without having some regard for the costs of providing them.

The same issue arose in *Tandy*.[69] The House of Lords decided as a matter **17–014** of construction that the question of "suitable education" for the purposes of the Education Act 1993, s.298, was to be determined solely by reference to educational considerations, in the sense that the education had to be efficient and suitable for the child's age and ability. Resources were not relevant to this determination, although they were of relevance when choosing between different ways of making such provision. Lord Browne-Wilkinson distinguished the *Barry* case. He held that the statutory provision in *Barry* was somewhat strange in that it imposed a duty to meet the "needs" of disabled persons, even though the lack of the benefits enumerated in the section could not possibly give rise to "need" in any stringent sense of the word. The 1970 Act had, moreover, not provided any guidance as to how such needs were to be assessed. Given that this was so it was not, he said, surprising that the House of Lords had held that resources could be taken into account. In *Tandy* by way of contrast the statute imposed an immediate obligation to make arrangements for "suitable education", which was defined by objective criteria.

The courts have had to decide whether the availability of resources is a relevant consideration under other social welfare legislation, or how statutory provisions with resource implications should be exercised, and have generally made their decisions by way of construction of the particular statute.[70] Where the statute is construed as imposing a specific duty for the benefit of particular individuals the court will be considerably less willing to listen to arguments concerning limited resources, but there can be significant differences of view by judges in the same case as to whether the statute can be regarded as imposing duties and the precise content of such obligations.[71] The issue concerning resources can also arise in the context of a challenge to the rationality of administrative action.[72]

The stringency with which the courts have applied the criterion of

---

[69] *R. v East Sussex County Council Ex p. Tandy* [1998] A.C. 714.
[70] *R. v Sefton Borough Council Ex p. Help the Aged Ltd* [1997] 4 All E.R. 532; *R. v Norfolk County Council Ex p. Thorpe* [1998] C.O.D. 208; *R. v Bristol City Council Ex p. Penfold* [1998] C.O.D. 210; *R. (on the application of G) v Barnet LBC* [2004] 2 A.C. 208; *R. (on the application of Spink) v Wandsworth LBC* [2005] 1 W.L.R. 2884; *R. (on the application of Conville) v Richmond upon Thames LBC* [2006] 1 W.L.R. 2808;
[71] See, e.g., *R. (on the application of G) v Barnet LBC*, n.70.
[72] *R. (on the application of Rogers) v Swindon NHS Primary Care Trust* [2006] 1 W.L.R. 2649.

relevancy has varied in different areas,[73] and there has been an unwillingness to declare invalid administrative decisions simply because the applicant could point to one "relevant" factor which the authority did not take into account. This is particularly so where it is felt that the consideration did not have a causal effect upon the authority's determination and where the decision being impugned was not determinative of rights, such as a decision by a local authority to refer a landlord to a rent tribunal.[74]

The denomination of a consideration as relevant or irrelevant may involve the court in substituting its own views for those of the administration, a danger appreciated by Diplock L.J. in *Luby*.[75] The Housing Act 1957 s.111, vested the management of local authority houses in the Corporation and gave it power to charge reasonable rents. The policy of the defendant was to fix rents for the houses as a whole at an aggregate sum necessary to balance the cost of the loan capital and repairs. There was no differential applied whereby tenants paid rent according to their means. After a series of rent increases L complained that the basis of assessment was invalid as it did not take account of his personal circumstances, and resulted in him having to pay an unreasonable rent. Diplock L.J. rejected the claim. The court should not, he said, substitute its view for that of the Corporation. The latter was applying a social policy on which reasonable men could differ: it had decided against differential rating and this was not a decision so unreasonable that no reasonable corporation could come to it. Any deficit in housing revenue would have to be made good from the general rate fund. The choice of rent structures involved, therefore, a weighing of the interests of tenants as a whole, including impoverished tenants, with those of the general body of ratepayers.

C. Bad Faith

17–015 The concept of bad faith has remained either largely in the region of hypothetical cases,[76] or has been treated as synonymous with improper purposes or relevancy.[77] It is indeed difficult to conceive of bad faith that would not automatically render applicable one of the two traditional control mechanisms. This is not to say that spite, malice or dishonesty may not exist. They clearly can.[78] It is to question the necessity of its being a separate method of control.[79]

---

[73] *Re Fletcher's Application* [1970] 2 All E.R. 527n
[74] *R. v Barnet and Camden Rent Tribunal Ex p. Frey Investments Ltd* [1972] 2 Q.B. 342; *R. v Secretary of State for Social Services Ex p. Wellcome Foundation Ltd* [1987] 1 W.L.R. 1166.
[75] *Luby v Newcastle-under-Lyme Corporation* [1964] 2 Q.B. 64; *R. (on the application of Western Riverside Waste Authority) v Wandsworth LBC* [2005] EWHC 536.
[76] *Smith v East Elloe Rural District Council* [1956] A.C. 736, 770.
[77] *Westminster Corporation*, n.30; *Webb v Minister of Housing and Local Government* [1965] 1 W.L.R. 755, 784.
[78] *Roncarelli v Duplessis* (1959) 16 D.L.R. (2d) 689.
[79] It may be easier to evade a clause excluding judicial review if the allegation is of bad faith, *Lazarus Estates Ltd v Beasley* [1956] 1 Q.B. 702, 712–713, 722. cf. *R. v Secretary of State for the Environment Ex p. Ostler* [1977] Q.B. 122, 138–139.

6. HUMAN RIGHTS: THE COMMON LAW BACKGROUND

The Human Rights Act 1998 has, as will be seen in the next chapter, created **17–016** a new statutory head of illegality and requires public authorities to comply with the rights laid down in the European Convention of Human Rights. This is an important statutory innovation. Before examining the statute in detail it is necessary to understand how far the common law protected fundamental rights, since there may be situations in which the common law regime is still of relevance.[80]

On the traditional theory of sovereignty Parliament is omnipotent. This constitutional orthodoxy has, moreover, been taken to mean that talk of fundamental rights within our system is simply a misnomer: what we have are residual liberties. This may represent the traditional position. It ceased, however, accurately to reflect the reality of the common law jurisprudence.

A. The Common Law Jurisprudence

It is clear that our courts had, even prior to the Human Rights Act 1998, **17–017** begun to give a special status to fundamental rights and to engage in more searching scrutiny in such instances.

i. Heightened rationality review

In *Brind*,[81] the Home Secretary had issued directives under the Broadcasting **17–018** Act 1981 requiring the BBC and the IBA to refrain from broadcasting certain matters by persons who represented organisations which were pro- scribed under legislation concerning the prevention of terrorism. The ambit of this proscription was limited to direct statements made by the members of the organisations. It did not, for example, prevent the broadcasting of such persons on film, provided that there was a voice-over account paraphrasing what had been said. The applicant's claim based directly on the European Convention of Human Rights failed for reasons considered in the next chapter. The decision none the less contained interesting dicta on the rele- vance of rights at common law. Lord Bridge, having noted the absence of any code of rights in domestic law, then had this to say.[82]

"But . . . this surely does not mean that in deciding whether the Secretary of State, in the exercise of his discretion, could reasonably impose the restriction he has imposed on the broadcasting organisations, we are not perfectly entitled to start from the premise that any restriction of the right to freedom of expression requires to be justified and nothing less than an important competing public interest will be sufficient to justify it."

[80] M. Hunt, *Using Human Rights Law in English Courts* (Hart, 1997).
[81] *R. v Secretary of State for the Home Department Ex p. Brind* [1991] 1 A.C. 696.
[82] *Brind*, n.81, 748–749.

Lord Bridge went on to say that while the primary judgment as to whether the public interest warranted the restriction imposed rested with the Minister, the court could exercise a secondary judgment by asking whether a reasonable minister could reasonably make that judgment on the material before him.[83] Lord Templeman reasoned in a similar manner. He held that freedom of expression was a principle of every written and unwritten democratic constitution; that the court must inquire whether a reasonable minister could reasonably have concluded that the interference with this freedom was justifiable; and that in "in terms of the Convention" any such interference must be both necessary and proportionate.[84]

The courts went further in other cases. They took the important step of aligning the position at common law with that under the ECHR. In the *Spycatcher* case[85] Lord Goff, in delineating the ambit of the duty of confidentiality, stated that he saw no inconsistency between the position under the Convention and that at common law. The dictum of Lord Goff was used in the *Derbyshire* case.[86] Their Lordships held that, as a matter of principle, a local authority should not be able to maintain an action in its own name for defamation, since this would place an unwarranted and undesirable limitation upon freedom of speech. Lord Keith, giving judgment for the House, reached this conclusion on the basis of the common law and echoed Lord Goff's statement that there was no difference in principle between the common law and the Convention.

17–019   The "green light" given by the House of Lords was not lost on lower courts. It became normal for there to be searching scrutiny in rights-based cases.[87] In *Leech*[88] the court considered the validity of a rule that allowed a prison governor to read letters from prisoners and stop those which were inordinately long or objectionable. The court held that the more fundamental the right which had been interfered with, the more difficult was it to imply any such rule-making power in the primary legislation.

The same approach was evident in *Smith*,[89] where there was a challenge to the policy of prohibiting gay men and women from serving in the armed forces. Sir Thomas Bingham M.R. held that the more substantial the interference with human rights, the more the court would require by way of justification before it would accept that the decision was reasonable.[90]

In *McQuillan*[91] the applicant challenged the legality of an exclusion order

---

[83] *Brind*, n.81, 749.

[84] *Brind*, n.81, 750–751.

[85] *Att-Gen v Guardian Newspapers (No.2)* [1990] 1 A.C. 109, 283–284.

[86] *Derbyshire County Council v Times Newspapers Ltd* [1993] A.C. 534.

[87] See, e.g., *R. v Broadcasting Complaints Commission Ex p. Granada Television Ltd* [1995] C.O.D. 207; *R. v Secretary of State for the Home Department Ex p. Norney* (1995) 7 Admin. L.R. 861; *R. v Secretary of State for the Home Department Ex p. Moon* [1996] Imm. A.R. 477; *R. v Secretary of State for Social Security Ex p. Joint Council for the Welfare of Immigrants* [1997] 1 W.L.R. 275; *R. v Chief Constable for the North Wales Police Area Authority Ex p. AB and DC* [1997] 3 W.L.R. 724.

[88] *R. v Secretary of State for the Home Department Ex p. Leech* [1994] Q.B. 198.

[89] *R. v Ministry of Defence Ex p. Smith* [1996] Q.B. 517.

[90] *Ex p. Smith*, n.89, 554.

[91] *R. v Secretary of State for the Home Department Ex p. McQuillan* [1995] 4 All ER 400.

prohibiting him from entering Great Britain on the ground that he was or had been involved in acts of terrorism. He maintained that he was no longer a member of a terrorist organisation and that his life was in danger if he continued to live in Northern Ireland. The Home Secretary was not persuaded and refused to revoke the exclusion order. Sedley J. recognised that freedom of movement, subject only to the general law, was a fundamental value of the common law.[92] The power given to the Home Secretary to restrict this freedom, not by modifying the general law, but by depriving certain persons of the full extent of this right, was a draconian measure, which could be justified only by a grave emergency. It was for this reason that the courts would scrutinise the minister's reasoning closely and "draw the boundaries of rationality tightly around his judgment".[93] This was equally true in relation to the right to life. This too was recognised and protected by the common law and "attracted the most anxious scrutiny by the courts of administrative decision-making".[94]

ii. The principle of legality and the interpretation of legislation

The courts also created a priority rule, to the effect that legislation will not **17–020** be held to allow an interference with a common law constitutional right unless this was sanctioned by Parliament.

Thus in *Witham*[95] Laws J. held that access to the court was a constitutional right and that the executive could only abrogate that right if it was specifically permitted to do so by Parliament. Laws J. accepted that Parliament might expressly limit this right, but stated that he could not conceive of anything short of this which would convince the court that the right had been limited by implication. The class of case where the right might be limited by necessary implication was a class with no members.[96]

A similar approach is apparent in *Simms*.[97] Legislation was to be read subject to a principle of legality, which meant that fundamental rights could not be overridden by general or ambiguous words. This was, said Lord Hoffmann, because there was too great a risk that the full implications of their unqualified meaning might have passed unnoticed in the democratic process. In the absence of express language or necessary implication to the contrary, the courts would therefore presume that even the most general words were intended to be subject to the basic rights of the individual. Parliament had, therefore, to squarely confront what it was doing and accept the political cost. Lord Hoffmann left open the possibility that a fundamental right could be overridden by necessary implication, as well as

---

[92] [1995] 4 All E.R. 400, 421–422.
[93] [1995] 4 All E.R. 400, 422.
[94] [1995] 4 All E.R. 400, 422D.
[95] *R. v Lord Chancellor Ex p. Witham* [1998] Q.B. 575, 585–586.
[96] *Cf. R. v Lord Chancellor Ex p. Lightfoot* [1999] 2 W.L.R. 1126.
[97] *R. v Secretary of State for the Home Department Ex p. Simms & O' Brien* [2000] 2 A.C. 115; *R. (on the application of Morgan Grenfell & Co Ltd v Special Commissioner of Income Tax* [2003] 1 A.C. 563; *R. (on the application of Anufrijeva) v Secretary of State for the Home Department* [2004] 1 A.C. 604.

by express words. It seems clear that he would only accept that this was so in extreme cases, and this is the import of the phrase "necessary implication". Viewed in this way his approach was very similar to that of Laws J.

B. The Secondary Literature

17–021   The case law considered above was complemented by a rich secondary literature, which was all the more significant given that many of the contributions were from judges. Different strands of reasoning are apparent in this literature.

One such strand was that the courts should recognise and employ a general presumption against interference with human rights, which was grounded in the common law. Thus Lord Browne-Wilkinson[98] argued that the presumption should apply not only when there was ambiguity in the domestic provisions, but also where there was just general statutory language.[99] Sir John Laws[100] drew a distinction between reliance upon the European Convention as a legal instrument *stricto sensu*, and reliance upon the content of the Convention as a series of propositions that were either already inherent in our law, or could be integrated into it by the judiciary through the normal process of common law adjudication. It was not for the courts themselves to incorporate the Convention, since that would be to trespass upon the legislature's sphere. The courts could, however, legitimately pursue the latter approach and consider the Convention jurisprudence as one source for charting the development of the common law. The standard of review would, moreover, be higher or more intensive in rights-based cases.[101]

> "[T]he greater the intrusion proposed by a body possessing public power over the citizen in an area where his fundamental rights are at stake, the greater must be the justification which the public authority must demonstrate. . . . It means that the principles [of review] are neither unitary nor static; it means that the standard by which the court reviews administrative action is a variable one. It means, for example, that while the Secretary of State will largely be left to his own devices in promulgating national economic policy . . . the court will scrutinise the merits of his decisions much more closely when they concern refugees or free speech."

The argument in a second strand of this literature went further. There were suggestions that the courts would not always feel constrained to obey the will of Parliament in areas concerned with fundamental rights, or with the

---

[98] "The Infiltration of a Bill of Rights" [1992] P.L. 397, 404.
[99] [1992] P.L. 397, 406.
[100] "Is the High Court the Guardian of Fundamental Constitutional Rights?" [1993] P.L. 59.
[101] [1993] P.L. 59, 69.

basic structures of a democratic society. Lord Woolf[102] argued that if Parliament were to do the unthinkable and seek to abolish or radically curtail the courts' power of review, then the courts too "would also be required to act in a manner which would be without precedent".[103] There were, in his Lordship's view, limits to the supremacy of Parliament, which it was the courts' duty to identify and uphold. The existence of rights-based limits to the sovereignty of Parliament also featured in the work of Sir John Laws.[104] The survival of democracy in which rights are respected and enshrined "requires that those who exercise democratic, political power must have limits set to what they may do: limits which they are not allowed to overstep".[105] Democratic power cannot therefore be absolute. The effective protection of basic rights, and also the essential structural workings of a democracy, such as free and regular elections, necessitates a higher order law, which cannot be abrogated by Parliament.[106] Lord Steyn voiced similar sentiments in the *Jackson* case,[107] stating that the Diceyan idea of absolute supremacy of Parliament was out of place in the modern UK. The supremacy of Parliament might, said Lord Steyn, still be regarded as the general principle of our constitution. It was however a construct of the common law, which had been created by the courts. It was not therefore unthinkable that circumstances might arise where the courts would have to qualify that principle, such as where the legislature attempted to abolish judicial review or the ordinary role of the courts.

A third strand in this rich vein of literature is to be found in the writings of Sir Stephen Sedley.[108] He did not subscribe to the idea of a higher order law against which the legality of governmental action was to be tested.[109] He believed however that the reinvigoration of judicial review was motivated, in part at least, by the desire of the judiciary to repair dysfunction in the democratic process, and to fill "lacunae of legitimacy in the functioning of democratic polities".[110] This led to a refashioning of our constitutional order, away from the traditional Diceyan paradigm of parliamentary sovereignty, and towards a "bi-polar sovereignty of the Crown in Parliament and the Crown in its courts, to each of which the Crown's ministers are answerable—politically to Parliament, legally to the courts".[111] For Sir Stephen Sedley it was equally important to realise that the government of the day had no separate sovereignty: the sharpest of all lessons from Eastern Europe was that "it is when state is collapsed into party that democracy founders".[112]

---

[102] "Droit Public-English Style" [1995] P.L. 57.
[103] [1995] P.L. 57, 69.
[104] "Law and Democracy" [1995] P.L. 72.
[105] [1995] P.L. 72, 81.
[106] [1995] P.L. 72, 84–85. See also, Sir John Laws, "The Constitution, Morals and Rights" [1996] P.L. 622 and "The Limitations of Human Rights" [1998] P.L. 254.
[107] *Jackson*, n.5, para.102.
[108] "Human Rights: A Twenty-First Century Agenda" [1995] P.L. 386.
[109] [1995] P.L. 386, 389–390.
[110] [1995] P.L. 386, 388.
[111] [1995] P.L. 386, 389.
[112] [1995] P.L. 386, 389.

CHAPTER 18

THE HUMAN RIGHTS ACT AND JUDICIAL REVIEW

1. INTRODUCTION

This is not the place for a detailed examination of the articles of the European Convention on Human Rights, ECHR. There are a number of specialised works that deal with this topic.[1] The aim of this chapter is rather to consider the impact of the Human Rights Act 1998 (HRA) on judicial review. The more general impact of the HRA on the nature of judicial review has been considered in an earlier chapter, and reference should be made to that discussion.[2] It should nonetheless be emphasised at the outset of this chapter that the advent of the HRA has had a marked impact more generally on the practice and nature of judicial review. It has impacted on the practice of judicial review in the sense that a significant number of such cases involve some HRA argument. It has had a significant impact on the nature of judicial review by the emphasis thereby given to what has been termed the culture of justification.[3] This requires the primary decision-maker not merely to explain the challenged decision, but to proffer a reasoned argument, which the courts will scrutinise within the framework of proportionality to determine whether the limitation of the right was normatively justified. The nature of this adjudicative process will be examined within the course of this chapter.

18–001

---

[1] P. Van Dijk and G. Van Hoof, *Theory and Practice of the European Convention of Human Rights* (Kluwer, 3rd edn, 1998); C. Gearty (ed.), *European Civil Liberties and the European Convention on Human Rights* (Kluwer, 1997); Jacobs and White, *European Convention on Human Rights* (Oxford University Press, 4th edn, C. Ovey and R. White, 2006); M. Janis, R. Kay and A. Bradley, *European Human Rights Law: Text and Materials* (Oxford University Press, 3rd edn, 2008); D. Harris, M. O'Boyle, C. Warbrick, *Law of the European Convention of Human Rights* (Oxford University Press, 2nd edn, 2007); A Mowbray, *Cases and Materials on the European Convention on Human Rights* (Oxford University Press, 2nd edn, 2007).
[2] See above, para.1–025.
[3] D. Dyzenhaus, "The Politics of Deference: Judicial Review and Democracy", in M. Taggart (ed.), *The Province of Administrative Law* (Hart, 1997), Ch.13; M. Taggart, "The Tub of Public Law", in D. Dyzenhaus (ed.), *The Unity of Public Law* (Hart, 2004), Ch.17.

The chapter is structured in the following manner. The discussion begins with the genesis of the HRA. This is followed by analysis of the HRA provisions, ss.3 and 4 HRA, concerning the interpretation of legislation and the issuance of a declaration of incompatibility if the court feels unable to read legislation to be compatible with Convention rights. The discussion then turns to s.6 HRA, which renders it illegal for a public authority to act incompatibly with Convention rights. The focus then shifts to the difficult issue of the standard of review under the HRA, and the chapter concludes by consideration of the relevant principles of EC law concerning rights.

2. The Genesis of the Human Rights Act 1998

A. The Status of the European Convention on Human Rights prior to the HRA

18–002   Prior to the enactment of the Human Rights Act 1998 (HRA) the European Convention on Human Rights (ECHR) could be relied upon in our courts in limited circumstances.[4] *Brind* established that there was no presumption that statutory discretion should be exercised in conformity with the Convention.[5] There was, however, a growing list of instances in which the courts regarded it as acceptable to have regard to the ECHR[6]: it could be used as an aid in the construction of primary legislation where there was an ambiguity[7]; as an aid in the interpretation of legislation enacted as a result of an adverse judgment from the European Court of Human Rights[8]; it could be of assistance in determining the ambit of common law rights[9]; it could be a factor that shaped the exercise of judicial discretion[10]; courts began to take increasing notice of the ECHR when determining irrationality claims in cases concerned with rights[11]; some case law to suggested that it could, in certain contexts, be regarded as a relevant consideration[12]; and the ECHR jurisprudence could also be applied in and by our courts through EC law.[13]

B. The HRA: "Bringing Rights Home"

18–003   It was nonetheless felt to be both wrong and embarrassing that applicants should be forced to have recourse to the Convention institutions in

---

[4] M. Hunt, *Using Human Rights Law in English Courts* (Hart, 1997); M. Beloff and H. Mountfield, "Unconventional Behaviour? Judicial Uses of the European Convention of Human Rights in England and Wales" [1996] E.H.R.L.R. 467.
[5] *R. v Secretary of State for the Home Department Ex p. Brind* [1991] 1 A.C. 696.
[6] Lord Bingham, HC Deb July 3, 1996, col. 146.
[7] *Garland v British Rail Engineering Ltd* [1983] 2 A.C. 751, 771; *R. v Chief Immigration Officer, Heathrow Airport Ex p. Bibi* [1976] 1 W.L.R. 979, 984, 988.
[8] *R. v Secretary of State for the Home Department Ex p. Norney* (1995) 7 Admin. L.R. 861.
[9] *Derbyshire County Council v Times Newspapers Ltd* [1993] A.C. 534.
[10] *Att-Gen v Guardian Newspapers (No.2)* [1990] 1 A.C. 109, 283–284.
[11] See, e.g., *R. v Ministry of Defence Ex p. Smith* [1996] Q.B. 517.
[12] *R. v Secretary of State for the Home Department Ex p. Chahal* [1993] Imm. A.R. 362.
[13] See below, para.18–057.

Strasbourg. The Government's objective in enacting the Human Rights Act 1998 was to "bring rights home", thereby allowing our courts to adjudicate directly on ECHR rights.[14] To this end s.1 HRA lists the "Convention rights" which can be used in litigation in our courts pursuant to the Act. They are arts 2–12 and 14 of the ECHR, arts 1–3 of the First Protocol, and arts 1 and 2 of the Sixth Protocol as read with arts 16–18 of the Convention. The articles are set out in Sch.1 of the HRA. The HRA came into force on October 2, 2000.[15]

Section 2 provides that a court or tribunal determining a question which has arisen under the HRA in connection with a Convention right must take into account any: judgment, decision, declaration or advisory opinion of the European Court of Human Rights (ECtHR); opinion of the Commission given in a report adopted under art.31 of the ECHR; decision of the Commission in connection with art.26 or 27(2) of the ECHR; or decision of the Committee of Ministers taken under art.46 of the ECHR.

The courts are not therefore bound by the jurisprudence of the Strasbourg institutions. They have an obligation to take this into account so far as they believe that it is of relevance to the proceedings before them. It is clear moreover that English courts continue to apply domestic rules of precedent, with the consequence that if a judge feels that a decision is inconsistent with Strasbourg authority he has to follow the binding precedent, but can give leave to appeal as appropriate.[16]

There is undoubtedly a tension in this respect.[17] If the courts depart significantly from Strasbourg case law it will be open to a claimant to argue before the ECtHR that the domestic interpretation of Convention rights is

---

[14] S. Grosz, J. Beatson and P. Duffy, *Human Rights, The 1998 Act and the European Convention* (Sweet & Maxwell, 2000); R. Clayton and H. Tomlinson, *The Law of Human Rights* (Oxford University Press, 2000); T. Campbell, K. Ewing, and A. Tomkins (eds), *Sceptical Essays on Human Rights* (Oxford University Press, 2001); F. Klug, *Values for a Godless Age: The Story of the UK's New Bill of Rights* (Penguin, 2000); J. Jowell and J. Cooper (eds), *Understanding Human Rights Principles* (Hart, 2001); D. Feldman, *Civil Liberties and Human Rights in England and Wales* (Oxford University Press, 2nd edn, 2002); J. Wadham, H. Mountfield and A. Edmundson, *Blackstone's Guide to the Human Rights Act 1998* (Oxford University Press, 3rd edn, 2003); Lord Lester and D. Pannick (eds), *Human Rights Law and Practice* (LexisNexis, 2nd edn, 2004); C. Gearty, *Principles of Human Rights Adjudication* (Oxford University Press, 2004); H. Fenwick, G. Phillipson, R. Masterman (eds), *Judicial Reasoning under the UK Human Rights Act* (Cambridge University Press, 2007); H. Fenwick, *Civil Liberties and Human Rights* (Taylor and Francis, 4th edn, 2007).
[15] The extent to which the HRA can have an impact on matters prior to this date has proven to be controversial, *R. v Benjafield* [2001] 3 W.L.R. 75; *R. v Lambert* [2002] 2 A.C. 545; *R. v Kansal (No.2)* [2002] 2 A.C. 69; *R. (on the application of Hurst) v HM Coroner for Northern District London* [2007] 2 A.C. 189.
[16] *Kay v Lambeth LBC* [2006] 2 A.C. 465; *Leeds City Council v Price* [2005] 1 W.L.R. 1825.
[17] R. Masterman, "Section 2(1) of the Human Rights Act 1998: Binding Domestic Courts to Strasbourg?" [2004] P.L. 725; R. Masterman, "Taking the Strasbourg Jurisprudence into Account: Developing a 'Municipal Law of Human Rights' under the Human Rights Act" (2005) 54 I.C.L.Q. 907.

not in accord with the ECHR.[18] Laws L.J. expressed the counter consideration in *Begum*.[19] He stated that the courts' task under the HRA was not simply to add on the Strasbourg learning to the corpus of English law, as if it were an adjunct taken from an alien source. The task was rather to develop a municipal law of human rights by the incremental method of the common law, case by case, taking account of the Strasbourg jurisprudence as required by s.2 of the HRA.

3. LEGISLATION: THE INTERPRETATIVE OBLIGATION AND THE DECLARATION OF INCOMPATIBILITY

A. The Statutory Provisions

18–004   The framers of the HRA were not in favour of what might be termed "hard constitutional review" such as exists in some other countries where the courts can strike down legislation that is incompatible with fundamental rights. This degree of judicial power was felt to be unsuitable for the UK with its traditions of parliamentary sovereignty. The HRA therefore encapsulates a "softer" form of constitutional review in relation to the scrutiny of legislation.[20]

Before any legislation is passed the relevant Minister must comply with the obligation in s.19 HRA.[21] This stipulates that a Minister of the Crown in charge of a Bill in either House of Parliament must, before the second reading of the Bill, make a statement to the effect that in his view the provisions of the Bill are compatible with Convention rights.[22] This is known as a "statement of compatibility".[23] The Minister can, alternatively, make a statement to the effect that although he is unable to make a statement of compatibility the government wishes the House to proceed with the Bill.[24]

If legislation is challenged s.3 HRA provides that "so far as it is possible to do so, primary legislation and subordinate legislation must be read and given effect in a way which is compatible with the Convention rights". This interpretative obligation applies to any legislation whenever enacted.[25]

---

[18] *R. (Alconbury Developments Ltd) v Secretary of State for the Environment, Transport and the Regions (SSETR)* [2003] 2 A.C. 295, para.26, Lord Slynn; *R. (on the application of Anderson) v Secretary of State for the Home Department* [2003] 1 A.C. 837, para.18, Lord Bingham; *R. (on the application of Amin) v Secretary of State for the Home Department* [2004] 1 A.C. 653, para.44, Lord Bingham.

[19] *Begum v Tower Hamlets LBC* [2002] H.R.L.R. 24, para.17; *R. (on the application of ProLife Alliance) v British Broadcasting Corporation* [2002] 3 W.L.R. 1080, paras 33–34.

[20] P. Craig, "Constitutional and Non-Constitutional Review" [2001] C.L.P. 147.

[21] N. Bamforth, "Parliamentary Sovereignty and the Human Rights Act 1998" [1998] P.L. 572, 575–582.

[22] D. Feldman, "Parliamentary Scrutiny of Legislation and Human Rights" [2002] P.L. 323.

[23] HRA s.19(1)(a).

[24] HRA s.19(1)(b).

[25] HRA s.3(2)(a).

Section 3 does not, however, affect the validity, continuing operation or enforcement of any incompatible primary legislation,[26] or of any incompatible secondary legislation if, leaving aside any possibility of revocation, primary legislation prevents the removal of the incompatibility.[27]

Where a court is satisfied that primary legislation is incompatible with a Convention right then it can, pursuant to s.4 HRA, make a declaration of that incompatibility.[28] It can also do so in relation to secondary legislation where, leaving aside any possibility of revocation, the primary legislation prevents removal of the incompatibility.[29] The courts that can make such a declaration are however limited by the HRA, with the lowest court being the High Court.[30] This may well be problematic, particularly because challenges to legislation may factually originate in lower courts or tribunals.[31]

The declaration of incompatibility does not affect the validity, continuing operation or enforcement of the provision in respect of which it has been given, and is not binding on the parties to the proceedings in which it is made.[32] The Crown is accorded the right to notice where a court is considering whether to make a declaration of incompatibility and a Minister of the Crown is entitled to be joined as a party to the proceedings.[33]

While a declaration of incompatibility does not, in itself, affect the **18–005** validity of the challenged legislation, it does, however, trigger s.10 HRA, which applies where a declaration of incompatibility has been made and any appeal rights have either been exhausted, attempted or are not intended to be used. Section 10 can also apply where it appears to a Minister that primary legislation is incompatible with the ECHR as a result of a ruling by the European Court of Human Rights in a case concerning the UK. In either of these circumstances s.10(2) states that if "a Minister of the Crown considers that there are compelling reasons for proceeding under this section, he may by order make such amendments to the legislation as he considers necessary to remove the incompatibility".

The HRA therefore gives a power to amend the offending legislation through secondary legislation. It is, in this sense, an example of a Henry VIII clause, which will be considered when discussing delegated legislation.[34] The justification for such a power in this context is that the aim is the speedy

---

[26] HRA s.3(2)(b).
[27] HRA s.3(2)(c).
[28] HRA ss.4(1) and 4(2).
[29] HRA ss.4(3) and 4(4). See A. Bradley, "The Impact of the Human Rights Act 1998 upon Subordinate Legislation Promulgated before October 2, 2000" [2000] P.L. 358; R. Allen and P. Sales, "Joint Note for the Court of Appeal in *R. v Lord Chancellor Ex p. Lightfoot*" [2000] P.L. 361.
[30] The courts which can make such a declaration are: the House of Lords (and for the future the Supreme Court), the Judicial Committee of the Privy Council, the Court Martial Appeal Court, in Scotland the High Court of Justiciary sitting otherwise than as a trial court or the Court of Session, in England and Wales or Northern Ireland, the High Court or Court of Appeal, and in certain instances the Court of Protection, HRA s.4(5).
[31] I. Leigh and L. Lustgarten, "Making Rights Real: The Courts, Remedies and the Human Rights Act" [1999] C.L.J. 509.
[32] HRA ss.3(2) and 4(6).
[33] HRA s.5.
[34] See below, Ch.22.

removal of legislative provisions that offend the rights protected by the HRA.

The remedial orders made under section 10 can amend or repeal primary or secondary legislation, including legislation other than that which contains the incompatible provisions.[35] The orders can also be retrospective.[36] The orders are statutory instruments,[37] and are therefore subject to the general provisions of the Statutory Instruments Act 1946.[38] A remedial order is subject to the affirmative resolution procedure and must be approved by resolution of each House of Parliament made after the end of the period of 60 days beginning with the day on which the draft was laid.[39] The order cannot be made until the end of the 60-day period, and this is intended to provide an opportunity for representations to be made to the Minister about the measure. This process is facilitated by the existence of an obligation on the Minister to provide information[40] about the nature of the incompatibility, and a statement of the reasons for proceeding under s.10. Where representations have been made during this period, they must be summarised, and details given of any changes made to the draft order as a result of the representations.[41] There are exceptions to the need to secure parliamentary approval in cases of urgency.[42]

B. Legislative History

18–006   It is clear that the interpretation accorded by the courts to the key words of s.3 will be crucial. The courts are instructed by s.3 that "so far as it is possible to do so" legislation must be read and given effect in a way which is compatible with the Convention rights.[43] The more the courts are willing to construe legislation to be in conformity with Convention rights, the less they will need to issue declarations of incompatibility. A strident approach to the interpretation of s.3 means that the courts retain the matter in their own hands. Parliamentary choice as to whether to comply with a declaration of incompatibility will, by definition, not arise where no such declaration is issued.

The legislative history of s.3 provided little by way of firm guidance to the meaning of s.3.[44] The Lord Chancellor was of the opinion that the HRA gave the courts the strongest jurisdiction possible, to enable them to

---

[35] HRA Sch.2, para.1(2).
[36] HRA Sch.2, para.1(1)(b).
[37] HRA s.20.
[38] See, Ch.22.
[39] HRA Sch.2, para.2(a).
[40] HRA Sch.2, para.5.
[41] HRA Sch.2, para.3.
[42] HRA Sch.2, paras 2(b), 4.
[43] See above, Ch.10 for consideration of the interpretative obligation flowing from EU law; *Von Colson and Kamann v Land Nordrhein-Westfalen* (14/83) [1984] E.C.R. 1891; *Marleasing SA v La Commercial International De Alimentation SA* (C-106/89) [1990] E.C.R. 4135.
[44] F. Klug, "The Human Rights Act 1998, *Pepper v Hart* and All That" [1999] P.L. 246, 252–55.

interpret legislation whenever possible so as to be compatible with the Convention.[45] It was not necessary to find an ambiguity.[46] In relation to statutes passed after the HRA, Parliament should be presumed to legislate compatibly with the Convention, and the courts should only find the contrary where it was impossible to construe a statute in that way.[47] The Home Secretary however noted that the courts should not contort the meaning of statutory language so as to produce implausible meanings.[48]

C. Judicial Interpretation of Section 3: Early Case Law

It is clear from the early case law that judges accorded somewhat differing **18–007** interpretations to section 3. This is evident from *R. v A.*[49] It was argued that s.41 of the Youth Justice and Criminal Evidence Act 1999 violated art.6 of the Convention. Section 41 severely restricted the cross-examination of a rape victim about her sexual conduct, which might otherwise be of relevance to a defence based on consent. The House of Lords held that s.41 must be read subject to s.3 of the HRA, and that the test for the admissibility of such evidence should be whether it was so relevant to the issue of consent that to exclude it would endanger the fairness of the trial and thus be in breach of art.6. Lord Steyn held that s.3 required the courts to "subordinate the niceties of the language in s.41(3) to broader considerations of relevance".[50] He reached that conclusion on certain assumptions about the meaning of s.3.[51]

> "[T]he interpretative obligation under section 3 . . . is a strong one. It applies even if there is no ambiguity in the language in the sense of the language being capable of two different meanings. . . . The White Paper made clear that the obligation goes far beyond the rule which enabled the courts to take convention rights into account in resolving any ambiguity in a legislative provision. . . . Parliament specifically rejected the legislative model of requiring a reasonable interpretation. Section 3 of the 1998 Act places a duty on the court to strive to find a possible interpretation compatible with convention rights. Under ordinary methods of interpretation a court may depart from the language of the statute to avoid absurd consequences: s.3 goes much further. Undoubtedly, a court must always look for a contextual and purposive interpretation: s.3 is more radical in its effect. It is a general principle of the interpretation of legal instruments that the text is the primary source of interpretation: other sources are subordinate to it. . . . Section 3 of the 1998 Act qualifies this general principle because it requires a court to find an interpretation

---

[45] *Hansard*, HL Debs, November 24, 1997, col. 795.
[46] Lord Irvine, "The Development of Human Rights in Britain under an Incorporated Convention on Human Rights" [1998] P.L. 221, 228.
[47] *Hansard*, HL Debs, November 18, 1997, cols 535, 547.
[48] *Hansard*, HC, June 3, 1998, cols 421–22.
[49] *R. v A* [2002] 1 A.C. 45.
[50] *R. v A* [2002] 1 A.C. 45, para.45.
[51] *R. v A* [2002] 1 A.C. 45, para.44. Italics in the original.

compatible with convention rights if it is possible to do so. . . . In accordance with the will of Parliament as reflected in s.3 it will sometimes be necessary to adopt an interpretation which linguistically may appear strained. The techniques to be used will not only involve the reading down of express language in a statute but also the implication of provisions. A declaration of incompatibility is a measure of last resort. It must be avoided unless it is plainly impossible to do so. If a *clear* limitation of convention rights is stated in *terms*, such an impossibility will arise. . . . There is, however, no limitation of such a nature in the present case."

Lord Hope gave a somewhat more cautious reading of s.3, as is evident in the following quotation.[52]

"The rule of construction which s.3 lays down is quite unlike any previous rule of statutory interpretation. There is no need to identify an ambiguity or absurdity. Compatibility with convention rights is the sole guiding principle. That is the paramount object which the rule seeks to achieve. But the rule is only a rule of interpretation. It does not entitle the judges to act as legislators. As Lord Woolf CJ said in *Poplar Housing* . . . s.3 of the 1998 Act does not entitle the court to legislate; its task is still one of interpretation. The compatibility is to be achieved only so far as this is possible. Plainly this will not be possible if the legislation contains provisions which expressly contradict the meaning which the enactment would have to be given to make it compatible. It seems to me that the same result must follow if they do so by necessary implication, as this too is a means of identifying the plain intention of Parliament."

There were in the early case law instances where *the courts saved legislation from incompatibility through s.3.* They "read in" provisions, normally by implying words in a statute, or "read down" legislation, by according it a narrower interpretation to ensure that it remained valid.[53] The line between these two techniques may however be a fine one. In *R. v A*, the House of Lords in effect modified the test for the admissibility of evidence contained in the primary legislation, by reading words into the statute.[54] In *Lambert* the House of Lords read down s.28 of the Misuse of Drugs Act 1971 that imposed a reverse burden of proof.[55] The ordinary meaning of s.28 was that it imposed the legal burden of proof on the accused, but the House of Lords decided that it should be construed, pursuant to s.3, as imposing only an evidential burden, so as to render it compatible with art.6(2) of the Convention.

There *were also other decisions where the courts were unable to "save the*

---

[52] *R. v A* [2002] 1 A.C. 45, para.108. See also, *R. v Lambert* [2002] 2 A.C. 545, paras 79–81; *Re S (children: care plan)* [2002] 2 A.C. 291, para.40.
[53] R. Clayton, "The Limits of What's 'Possible': Statutory Construction under the Human Rights Act" [2002] E.H.R.L.R. 559, 562–563.
[54] n.49.
[55] *R. v Lambert* [2002] 2 A.C. 545.

legislation" through s.3 and issued declarations of incompatibility.[56] This is exemplified by *Matthews.*[57] The court held that the Crown Proceedings Act 1947 s.10, which prevented in certain circumstances an action in tort against the Crown by a serviceman, did not infringe art.6 ECHR, because a serviceman had no civil right that engaged this Article. Counsel for the claimant argued, drawing on *R. v A*,[58] that the court should read down section 10, by adding a sentence the effect of which was that the section would not be used unless the Secretary of State was satisfied that the injury occurred in warlike conditions. The court rejected this argument, in part because Convention rights were not engaged. Lord Phillips M.R. held moreover that it would be beyond the courts' power under s.3 HRA to imply such a clause, since the fundamental alteration of the scope of s.10 would amount to legislation by the court, which was not permissible.[59] The reluctance to rewrite legislation is evident once again in *Roth*.[60] The court considered the Immigration and Asylum Act 1999 Pt II. It provided for fixed penalties on hauliers who intentionally or negligently allowed a person to gain illicit entry to the UK, and imposed a reverse burden of proof. The court found the scheme to be inconsistent with Convention rights. It could not be saved by s.3, since a radically different approach would be required to comply with the Convention.[61] This would entail a fundamental re-orientation of the roles of the minister and the court under the scheme, such that the "rewritten scheme would not be recognisable as the scheme which Parliament intended".[62]

D. Judicial Interpretation of Section 3: *Ghaidan v Godin-Mendoza*

The judicial approach to s.3(1) HRA must now be seen in the light of the **18–008** House of Lords' decision in *Ghaidan v Godin-Mendoza*.[63] The case concerned differential treatment of homosexual couples by way of comparison with heterosexual couples in relation to the legal ability to succeed to a tenancy when one partner died. The House of Lords found that the legislation was discriminatory, but held that it could be read so as to be compatible with Convention rights. Their Lordships also took the opportunity to provide more general guidance on the interpretation of s.3(1). The following principles emerged from the case.

---

[56] See, in addition to the cases discussed, *Wilkinson v The Commissioners of Inland Revenue* [2002] S.T.C. 347; *Hooper v Secretary of State for Work and Pensions* [2002] EWHC 191; *D v Secretary of State for the Home Department* [2002] EWHC 2805; *Poplar Housing & Regeneration Association Ltd v Donoghue* [2002] Q.B. 48; *R. (on the application of H) v Mental Health Review Tribunal for the North and East London Region* [2002] Q.B. 1.
[57] *Matthews v Ministry of Defence* [2002] 3 All E.R. 513.
[58] n.49.
[59] *Matthews*, n.57, para.76. The point was not considered in the House of Lords, *Matthews v Ministry of Defence* [2003] 1 A.C. 1163.
[60] *R. (on the application of International Transport Roth GmbH) v Secretary of State for the Home Department* [2003] Q.B. 728.
[61] *International Transport Roth GmbH*, n.60, para.66.
[62] *International Transport Roth GmbH*, n.60, para.156.
[63] *Ghaidan v Godin-Mendoza* [2004] 2 A.C. 557.

First, it is clear that the application of s.3 is not dependent upon the presence of ambiguity in the legislation being interpreted. Thus, even if, construed according to the ordinary principles of interpretation, the meaning of the legislation is not in doubt, s.3 may none the less require the legislation to be given a different meaning.[64]

Second, it followed that s.3 could require the court to depart from the unambiguous meaning the legislation would otherwise bear.[65] It followed also that while the natural starting point was the wording used by Parliament, this was not determinative. In the words of Lord Nicholls,[66]

"[O]nce it is accepted that section 3 may require legislation to bear a meaning which departs from the unambiguous meaning the legislation would otherwise bear, it becomes impossible to suppose Parliament intended that the operation of section 3 should depend critically upon the particular form of words adopted by the parliamentary draftsman in the statutory provision under consideration. That would make the application of section 3 something of a semantic lottery. If the draftsman chose to express the concept being enacted in one form of words, section 3 would be available to achieve Convention-compliance. If he chose a different form of words, section 3 would be impotent."

Thirdly, it was therefore open to the court to read in words which changed the meaning of the enacted legislation, so as to make it Convention-compliant, and could modify the meaning of primary and secondary legislation, subject to the constraint that this constituted a "possible" interpretation of the legislation.[67]

Fourth, there were however limits to the use of s.3(1). Thus the courts should not adopt a "meaning inconsistent with a fundamental feature of legislation"[68]; the meaning imported "must be compatible with the underlying thrust of the legislation being construed"[69]; any word implied must "go with the grain of the legislation"; and the courts should moreover not use s.3 to adopt an interpretation of legislation for which they were ill-equipped, such as where the interpretation would bring about far-reaching change of a kind that was best dealt with by Parliament.

18–009   These features were said in *Ghaidan*[70] to explain and justify prominent previous decisions, *Re S* and *Bellinger*, in which the courts had concluded that the legislation could not be made Convention-compliant through s.3.

---

[64] *Ghaidan*, n.63, paras 29, 44, 67.
[65] *Ghaidan*, n.63, para.30.
[66] *Ghaidan*, n.63, para.31. See also para.49, Lord Steyn.
[67] *Ghaidan*, n.63, para.32.
[68] *Ghaidan*, n.63, para.33. See, e.g., *R. (on the application of Anderson) v Secretary of State for the Home Department* [2003] 1 A.C. 837.
[69] *Ghaidan*, n.63, para.33.
[70] *Ghaidan*, n.63, paras 34, 49, 114.

Re S[71] was concerned with the Children Act 1989 s.38. The Court of Appeal had, pursuant to s.3 HRA, read into s.38 of the 1989 Act a wider discretion to make an interim care order, and introduced a new procedure by which certain essential elements of a care plan would be identified and elevated to a starred status; it would then be open for a court to check whether the starred elements were being fulfilled. Lord Nicholls, giving judgment for the House of Lords, held that the starring system could not be justified under s.3 HRA. Parliament had under the 1989 Act entrusted local authorities, not the courts, with the responsibility for looking after children who were subject to care orders. The starring system departed substantially from that system, and constituted an amendment of the 1989 Act, not its interpretation: a "meaning which departs substantially from a fundamental feature of an Act of Parliament is likely to have crossed the boundary between interpretation and legislation".[72]

In *Bellinger*[73] the applicant contended that legislation was contrary to Convention rights because it precluded a post-operative transsexual from being regarded as a woman for the purposes of marriage. The House of Lords held that the legislation could not be interpreted to be in accord with Convention rights by using s.3 HRA, because such recognition of the validity of the marriage would represent a major change in the law relating to gender reassignment which would have far reaching ramifications, necessitating extensive enquiry and the widest possible consultation. The issues were ill-suited for judicial determination and were pre-eminently a matter for Parliament, more especially since the government had said that it would introduce primary legislation on the subject.

E. Judicial Interpretation of Section 3: The Post-*Ghaidan* Case Law

There may inevitably be differences of view as to the application of the criteria in *Ghaidan*. The reasoning in that case has nonetheless been the touchstone for courts in later cases.   **18–010**

Thus in *Sheldrake*[74] the House of Lords concluded that s.11(2) of the Terrorism Act 2000, which placed on the defendant the burden of proving that the relevant organisation was not proscribed, was intended by Parliament to place the legal burden of proof on the defendant. Their Lordships held however that there was a real risk that a person who was innocent of any blameworthy conduct, but who was unable to establish a defence under s.11(2), might fall within s.11(1), thereby resulting in a clear breach of the presumption of innocence and an unfair conviction. They therefore, pursuant to s.3 HRA, read down s.11(2) so as to impose on the defendant an evidential burden only, even though that was not Parliament's intention when enacting the subsection.

---

[71] *Re S (children: care plan)* [2002] 2 A.C. 291.
[72] *Re S*, n.71, para.40.
[73] *Bellinger v Bellinger* [2003] 2 A.C. 467.
[74] *Sheldrake v DPP* [2005] 1 A.C. 264.

The judicial willingness to interpret legislation to be compatible with Convention rights is also apparent in other cases.[75] In *Hammond*[76] legislation allowed for the determination of the minimum term to be served by a prisoner serving a mandatory life sentence to be decided by the judge without an oral hearing. The House of Lords held that this was incompatible with the right to a fair trial in art.6 ECHR, but it was willing, following a concession made by the government, to accept that the legislation should be read subject to an implied condition whereby the judge could allow an oral hearing where this was necessary to ensure fairness and compliance with art.6. In *Wright*[77] legislation designed to protect vulnerable adults included a listing system whereby care workers who were placed on the list were prevented from working with such adults. The legislation was held to be prima facie in breach of art.6 ECHR, since those placed on the list were not accorded any right to make representations concerning the correctness of their inclusion on the list. The Court of Appeal nonetheless read the legislation subject to s.3 HRA and interpreted it so as to require the Secretary of State to give the care worker an opportunity to make representations before he was included in the list, unless the resultant delay in giving such an opportunity would expose vulnerable adults to the risk of harm.

It would nonetheless be mistaken to conclude that the statutory language can always be interpreted consistently with Convention rights. Where the court believes that this is not possible, it will issue a declaration of incompatibility under s.4 HRA. This is exemplified by *A v Secretary of State for the Home Department*.[78] The UK Government, as part of the response to the situation post 9/11, enacted the Anti-terrorism, Crime and Security Act 2001, s.23 of which provided for the detention of non-nationals if the Home Secretary believed that their presence in the United Kingdom was a risk to national security and he suspected that they were terrorists who, for the time being, could not be deported because of fears for their safety or other practical considerations. The House of Lords held that s.23 was discriminatory and disproportionate, since it did not apply to United Kingdom nationals who might pose the same threat, and issued a declaration of incompatibility.

---

[75] See also, *R. (on the application of O) v Crown Court at Harrow* [2007] 1 A.C. 249; *Secretary of State for the Home Department v MB* [2007] 3 W.L.R. 681.
[76] *R. (Hammond) v Secretary of State for the Home Department* [2006] 1 A.C. 603.
[77] *R. (on the application of Wright) v Secretary of State for Health* [2007] EWCA Civ 999.
[78] [2005] 2 A.C. 68. See also, *R. (on the application of Wilkinson) v Inland Revenue Commissioners* [2005] 1 W.L.R. 1718; *R. (on the application of Clift) v Secretary of State for the Home Department* [2007] 1 A.C. 484.

F. Reflections on the Courts' Jurisprudence

There have unsurprisingly been differences in the academic literature on the **18–011** construction that should be accorded to s.3 HRA.[79] These differences have primarily been concerned with the central issue of how far the courts should go in reading legislation so as to make it compatible with Convention rights. The following points should be borne in mind in this respect.

First, it should be noted at the outset that there are two senses of legislative intention at play in the case law. There is the legislative intent expressed in the particular piece of legislation that is said to be incompatible with Convention rights. There is also the legislative intent expressed in s.3 HRA itself, that such legislation, whether enacted before or after the HRA, should insofar as possible be read so as to be compatible with Convention rights. It should also be noted that the most natural reading of the injunction contained in s.3 HRA is to accord the courts with more latitude to interpret legislation to be in accord with Convention rights than would flow from the ordinary principles of statutory interpretation.[80]

Second, the House of Lords' decision in *Ghaidan*[81] is now the leading authority on what can and cannot be achieved via s.3 HRA. The House of Lords adopts a position that is midway between the radical view of Lord Steyn, which seemed to indicate that s.3 could resolve all cases by reading down the primary legislation or reading in provisions, save where it contained a clear limitation on Convention rights, and the more cautious view of Lord Hope set out above. Thus their Lordships make clear in *Ghaidan* that s.3 can be used in the absence of legislative ambiguity, the corollary of which is that the legislation may be interpreted in a manner different from the unambiguous meaning of the wording used. The wording of the statute is not therefore conclusive, and the court inclines against a purely linguistic or semantic approach, expressing its willingness to read down and read in

---

[79] See, e.g., G. Marshall, "Interpreting Interpretation in the Human Rights Bill" [1998] P.L. 167; D. Pannick, "Principles of Interpretation of Convention Rights under the Human Rights Act and the Discretionary Area of Judgment" [1998] P.L. 545; G. Marshall, "Two Kinds of Compatibility: More about Section 3 of the Human Rights Act 1998" [1999] P.L. 377; Lord Lester of Herne Hill, "The Art of the Possible: Interpreting Statutes under the Human Rights Act" in University of Cambridge Centre for Public Law, *The Human Rights Act and the Criminal Justice and Regulatory Process* (1999); F. Bennion, "What Interpretation is 'Possible' under Section 3(1) of the Human Rights Act 1998?" [2000] P.L. 77; C. Gearty, "Reconciling Parliamentary Democracy and Human Rights" (2002) 118 L.Q.R. 248; R. Clayton, "The Limits of What's 'Possible': Statutory Construction under the Human Rights Act" [2002] E.H.R.L.R. 559; G. Phillipson, "(Mis)-reading Section 3 of the Human Rights Act" (2003) 119 L.Q.R. 183; C. Gearty, "Revisiting Section 3(1) of the Human Rights Act" (2003) 119 L.Q.R. 551; R. Ekins, "A Critique of Radical Approaches to Rights Consistent Statutory Interpretation" [2003] E.H.R.L.R. 641; D. Nicol, "Statutory Interpretation and Human Rights after *Anderson*" [2004] P.L. 274; A. Kavanagh, "Statutory Interpretation and Human Rights after *Anderson*: A More Contextual Approach" [2004] P.L. 537; A. Kavanagh, "The Elusive Divide between Interpretation and Legislation under the Human Rights Act 1998" (2004) 24 O.J.L.S. 259; A. Kavanagh, "Unlocking the Human Rights Act: The 'Radical' Approach to Section 3(1) Revisited" [2005] E.H.R.L.R. 259; A. Young, "Ghaidan v Godin-Mendoza: Avoiding the Deference Trap" [2005] P.L. 23; A. Kavanagh, "The Role of Parliamentary Intention in Adjudication under the Human Rights Act 1998" (2006) 26 O.J.L.S. 179.

[80] Grosz, Beatson and Duffy, n.14, Ch.3.

[81] n.63.

provisions in order to render the legislation compatible with Convention rights. This aspect of the reasoning in *Ghaidan* is however tempered by the limits imposed by their Lordships: the courts should not adopt a meaning that was inconsistent with the fundamentals of the legislation being reviewed, nor should they use s.3 to adopt an interpretation of legislation for which they were ill-equipped, such as where the interpretation would bring about far-reaching change of a kind that was best dealt with by Parliament. There will doubtless still be differences of view in particular cases as to whether s.3 HRA as interpreted in *Ghaidan* can render legislation compatible with Convention rights. That is inevitable. *Ghaidan* nonetheless provides welcome guidance in this respect, more especially because the midway approach is more nuanced than that in previous cases.

Third, it should also be recognised that the interpretation of s.3 HRA has a marked impact on the relationship between the courts and the legislature. The more cases that are resolved through s.3, the fewer that will be returned to the legislature, since there will be no need to make a declaration of incompatibility. The desire to accord primacy to s.3 in the remedial scheme of the HRA, with the consequence that the declaration of incompatibility becomes a matter of last resort,[82] should not however be pressed too far. We should, for example, be wary of allowing s.3 as interpreted in *Ghaidan* to be used where it would involve a significant revision of the statutory scheme, since the impact of such revisions on the workability of the scheme as a whole may be profound and Parliament may be best placed to revise the legislation to comply with the court's judgment, should it be minded to do so, which it normally will. We should also be mindful of the cautionary words of Sir Jack Beatson.[83]

"Words that are read in, added, or read down are not made part of the statute by s 3, but they have a stronger force than the product of ordinary statutory interpretation because it is accepted that those words can change the meaning of the statute. It must be recognised that, quite apart from any complexity and difficulty of understanding caused by the nature of the subject matter or the drafting technique used, we are going to have statutes that simply do not mean what the words say. That is, it is submitted, not good for the law because it increases its opacity. What is the solution? One possibility . . . is that where s 3 has been used to read and give effect to a statute in a way that is Convention compliant but changes the meaning of the enacted words, textual amendments should be made to the statute. But this would only be a solution if the state provides an updated version of our statutes. Without that, we must recognise that the quest for transparency and clarity faces a considerable obstacle, an obstacle that has nothing to do with drafting styles."

---

[82] *Ghaidan*, n.63, para.46, Lord Steyn.
[83] Sir Jack Beatson, "Common Law, Statute and Constitutional Law" [2006] Stat. L.Rev. 1, 13–14.

4. ACTS OF PUBLIC AUTHORITIES: A NEW HEAD OF ILLEGALITY

A. Section 6(1) HRA
The other main legal innovation introduced by the HRA is to be found in **18–012**
s.6(1), which provides that it is "unlawful for a public authority to act in a
way which is incompatible with a Convention right".[84] The significance of
s.6(1) should be made clear at the outset.

Section 6(1) creates a new statutory head of illegality for breach of a
Convention right. It is a free-standing statutory ground of challenge. We
have already seen that the common law had increased the protection of
rights. It was not, however, possible at common law to go to court and
argue that administrative action was unlawful simply because there had
been a breach of a right. The breach of a right might, by way of contrast,
signal more intensive review under the *Wednesbury* test, or it might convince
the court that a relevant consideration had not been taken into account.

It is now possible to argue that an act of a public authority is unlawful
because it is incompatible with a Convention right. The force of the preceding statement, and of the contrast with the position at common law,
must, however, be qualified for the following reason. Section 6(1) only
renders the act of the public authority unlawful *if* there has been a breach of
a Convention right. Much will therefore turn on the standard of review
which the courts use when deciding whether a Convention right has been
broken.

It should be recognised that many cases will be brought under s.6 rather
than ss.3 and 4. It was ss.3 and 4 that received most attention when the
HRA was being framed, because the subject matter of the action concerned
primary legislation, with all the attendant concerns about sovereignty.
Applicants will, however, often be most concerned about their own particular case and about the availability of some concrete remedy. They will
therefore be inclined to use s.6 whenever this is possible. The importance of
s.6(1) for claimants is further enhanced because s.6(6) states that an "act"
for these purposes includes also a failure to act, albeit not a failure to
legislate. This means that the courts will have the power to compel public
authorities to take positive action.[85] This is all the more significant when
read in conjunction with the fact that the state may, under the jurisprudence
of the ECtHR, be responsible for the violation of a Convention right by
another private party.[86]

---

[84] See, *R. (on the application of Al-Skeini) v Secretary of State for Defence* [2007] 3 W.L.R. 33
and *R. (on the application of Quark Fishing Ltd) v Secretary of State for Foreign and Commonwealth Affairs (No.2)* [2006] 1 A.C. 529 for consideration of the territorial scope of s.6
HRA.
[85] See, e.g., *Rose v Secretary of State for Health, Human Fertilisation and Embryology Authority*
[2002] UKHRR 1329, paras 45, 49–51.
[86] A. Clapham, *Human Rights in the Private Sphere* (Oxford University Press, 1993), Ch.7.

B. Section 6(2) HRA

18–013   Section 6(1) HRA is qualified by s.6(2) HRA, which is designed to prevent legislation from being indirectly attacked under s.6(1), since the proper method of challenging such legislation is through ss.3 and 4. Section 6(2) provides that:

> "(2) Subsection (1) does not apply to an act if—
>
> (a)   as the result of one or more provisions of primary legislation, the authority could not have acted differently; or
>
> (b)   in the case of one or more provisions of, or made under, primary legislation which cannot be read or given effect in a way which is compatible with the Convention rights, the authority was acting so as to give effect to or enforce those provisions."

i. An Example: Wilkinson

18–014   The interpretation of s.6(2) HRA can be exemplified by *Wilkinson*.[87] The claimant was a widower who if he had been a widow would have received a widow's bereavement allowance by way of deduction from his liability for income tax under s.262 of the Income and Corporation Taxes Act 1988. He argued that the failure to pay such an allowance constituted discrimination under the ECHR. Lord Hoffmann, giving judgment for the Law Lords, held that s.262 of the 1988 Act only authorised the payment of the allowance to widows and not widowers, and that it could not be read so as to include the latter,[88] and that this was so even in the light of the approach to s.3 HRA taken in *Ghaidan*. It followed that the IRC were protected by s.6(2)(a) of the HRA, since they were required by the 1988 Act to pay the benefit to women and had no power to pay the equivalent benefit to men.

The courts will nonetheless construe the protection afforded by s.6(2) narrowly. Thus it was held in *Bono*[89] that it protects the public authority only where the primary legislation cannot be read or given effect in a way that is compatible with Convention rights. It does not give protection in relation to subordinate legislation where there is some incompatibility, but that is not the necessary consequence of the primary legislation.[90]

ii. The relationship between sections 6(2)(a) and 6(2)(b): Hooper

18–015   The relationship between ss.6(2)(a) and 6(2)(b) was considered in *Hooper*.[91] The claimants argued that the provision of certain benefits to widows and not widowers was in breach of arts 14 and 8 ECHR. The claim was brought not under s.3 HRA, but under s.6, since they wished to secure the benefits,

---

[87]   *Wilkinson*, n.78.
[88]   *Wilkinson*, n.78, paras 17–18.
[89]   *R. (on the application of Bono) v Harlow DC* [2002] 1 W.L.R. 2475, para.34.
[90]   See also, *R. (on the application of H) v Secretary of State for Health* [2006] 1 A.C. 441.
[91]   *R. (on the application of Hooper) v Secretary of State for Work and Pensions* [2005] 1 W.L.R. 1681.

which any declaration of incompatibility made under s.3 could not have given them. The House of Lords held that there was objective justification for the differential treatment so far as it concerned widow's pensions. In relation to the payment of other benefits, the widow's payment and the widowed mother's allowance, the Secretary of State argued by way of defence that the claim under s.6(1) could not succeed because of s.6(2)(b).

Their Lordships agreed that the general purpose of s.6(2) was to prevent the foundational principles in the HRA from being undermined. The premise of the HRA is that if primary legislation cannot be interpreted to be compatible with Convention rights, then Parliament is given the option of revising the legislation so as to bring it into line with the demands of the Convention. That is the logic of ss.3 and 4 HRA. The purpose of s.6(2) is therefore to prevent this from being undermined by applicants who seek to challenge as unlawful an act of the relevant minister made pursuant to the primary legislation said to be inconsistent with the HRA.[92] There was nonetheless disagreement between Lord Hope and Lord Brown about the interrelationship between ss.6(2)(a) and (b).

For *Lord Hope*, the key to the two limbs of s.6(2) was the distinction between duty and discretion. Section 6(2)(a) captured the situation where the legislation imposed a duty to act. Thus if an authority could not have acted differently because of one or more provisions of primary legislation the disputed act could not be regarded as unlawful under s.6(1), and the claimant would have to challenge the primary legislation directly under s.3. It thus covered the situation where the "authority is obliged to act in the manner which the legislation lays down even if the legislation requires it to act in a way which is incompatible with a Convention right".[93]

Lord Hope held that s.6(2)(b) by way of contrast captured the situation where the authority has discretion derived directly or indirectly from primary legislation, which cannot be read or given effect in a way that is compatible with Convention rights.[94] In such cases, the discretion could not be read to be compatible with Convention rights, and the exercise of that discretion in an instant case could not therefore be challenged under s.6(1). The proper mode of attack would be to challenge the primary legislation itself under s.3.[95]

Lord Brown agreed with Lord Hope as to the general purpose of s.6(2) HRA, this being to safeguard the sovereignty of Parliament by preventing an act or failure to act under legislation that could not be read compatibly with Convention rights under s.3 from being declared unlawful under s.6(1).[96] He regarded the case as falling squarely within s.6(2)(a): Parliament intended the benefits to be payable only to widows, the legislation could not

---

[92] *Hooper*, n.91, paras 51, 70, 92, 105.

[93] *Hooper*, n.91, para.71.

[94] Lord Hope *Hooper*, n.91, paras 72–73 gave the following cases as examples: *R. (on the application of Alconbury Developments Ltd) v Secretary of State for the Environment, Transport and the Regions* [2003] 2 A.C. 295 and *R. v Kansal (No.2)* [2002] A.C. 69, paras 86–88.

[95] *Hooper*, n.91, para.73.

[96] *Hooper*, n.91, para.105.

be read so as to include widowers,[97] and the Secretary of State could not have acted differently.[98]

Lord Brown however disagreed about the interpretation of s.6(2)(b). He accepted that it would provide a defence where the discretion could never be exercised in a manner that was Convention compliant and therefore the primary legislation would be set at naught. He held however that this was different from cases where the nub of the argument was that the power must always be exercised in order to be Convention compliant. It was said Lord Brown generally accepted in many cases that discretion must be exercised in a particular way in order to be compliant with Convention rights and there was no suggestion that s.6(2)(b) would be applicable in such circumstances. It should not then make a difference if the statutory discretion was one that had to be exercised in every case in order to ensure Convention compliance.[99] The fact that this converted a power into a duty was said Lord Brown no bar in this respect since this was often required to ensure Convention-compliant decision-making.

iii. The relationship between sections 6(2)(a) and 6(2)(b): conclusions

18–016   The difference of opinion as to the reach of s.6(2)(b) made no difference in the instant case since, as seen above, Lord Brown decided that s.6(2)(a) was applicable. It is nonetheless worth dwelling on the difference of view between Lord Hope and Lord Brown, since it has significant repercussions for the ambit of s.6(2)(b).

Lord Hope's view was premised on a symmetrical reading of s.6(2)(b), in the sense that he held that it was applicable either where it would not be possible to exercise the discretion in a manner compliant with Convention rights, or where the discretion had to be exercised in order to be compliant with such rights. In either eventuality s.6(2)(b) would provide a defence to an action under s.6(1), and the applicant would have to proceed via ss.3 and 4 HRA.

Lord Brown's view was premised on a denial of this symmetry. He accepted that s.6(2)(b) provided a defence where the power could not be exercised without breaching Convention rights, since otherwise the primary legislation would be set at naught. He held however that matters were different in relation to cases where the discretion had to be exercised. The effect of this reading of s.6(2)(b) is that it would rarely apply so as to provide a defence to exercise of discretionary power. It would have to be compliant with Convention rights and if it was not so the defendant could not take the benefit of s.6(2)(b). Similarly, if compliance with Convention rights could only be secured by always exercising the discretion, then this should be done

---

[97] *Hooper*, n.91, para.122.
[98] *Hooper*, n.91, para.124.
[99] *Hooper*, n.91, para.118.

and it would not be open to the defendant to rely on s.6(2)(b) by way of defence.[100]

The reasoning in *Hooper* should also be seen in the light of the subsequent decision in *Morris*.[101] Sedley L.J., having considered the judgment in *Hooper*, held that where a statutory provision could not be read to be compatible with Convention rights then it fell prima facie within s.6(2) HRA. This did not however prevent a public authority from using other statutory powers that it possessed, although it was not under a duty to do so, provided that it did not use such alternate powers solely as the means to circumvent the provisions of the statute that were not compatible with the HRA.

C. Acts of Public Authorities: The Scope of Section 6

i. Two types of public authority

The scope of s.6 HRA is clearly important.[102] Section 6(1) provides that it is unlawful for a public authority to act in a way which is incompatible with a Convention right. Section 6(3) provides that a public authority includes: "a court or tribunal" (s.6(3)(a)), and "any person certain of whose functions are functions of a public nature" (s.6(3)(b)). It does not include either House of Parliament or a person exercising functions in connection with proceedings in Parliament.[103] The definitional guidance is augmented by s.6(5), which states that in relation to a particular act, a person is not a public authority by virtue only of s.6(3)(b) if the nature of the act is private. Private action by a private body is not therefore within the remit of the HRA, subject to what will be said below concerning the horizontal effect of the HRA.

18–017

These definitional sections draw a distinction between core public bodies *stricto sensu*, such as government departments, which are always within the ambit of s.6 whatever the nature of the act complained of, and other hybrid bodies which are only caught because certain of their functions are of a public nature within s.6(3)(b). This is important because bodies caught by virtue of s.6(3)(b) can argue, based on s.6(5), that they are not within the HRA if the nature of the act was private.

The distinction between core public authorities, which are bound by the HRA in respect of everything they do, and hybrid public authorities, which

---

[100] This conclusion was only qualified in so far as the defendant could show that the way in which the discretion was to be exercised in the particular case would be inconsistent with the demands of the primary legislation, with the conclusion then being, as in Lord Brown's reasoning in *Hooper*, that the defendant would have a defence under s.6(2)(a). This does not alter the fact that the conversion of a discretion into a duty that had invariably to be exercised in order to be compliant with convention rights did not bring the case within s.6(2)(b).

[101] *R. (Morris) v Westminster City Council* [2005] 1 W.L.R. 505.

[102] D. Oliver, "The Frontiers of the State: Public Authorities and Public Functions under the Human Rights Act" [2000] P.L. 476; G. Morris, "Public Employment and the Human Rights Act 1998" [2001] P.L. 442.

[103] The qualification to this for the House of Lords acting in a judicial capacity contained in HRA, s.6(4) will be repealed by the Constitutional Reform Act 2005 Sch.9 para.66(4) when the House of Lords in its judicial capacity is replaced by the Supreme Court.

are bound by the HRA in respect of their public but not their private functions, is apparent in the debates on the Bill in Parliament, and in subsequent case law.

Thus in relation to the debates in Parliament, the Home Secretary stated that it would not be possible to list all the bodies to which the HRA would be applicable, and that a non-exhaustive definition of a public authority was adopted in s.6. He then added that "obvious public authorities, such as central Government and the police are caught in respect of everything they do", and that "public—but not private—acts of bodies that have a mix of public and private functions are also covered".[104]

18–018　　　This distinction has been recognised in the subsequent case law. Thus in *Aston Cantlow*[105] their Lordships accepted the distinction between core and hybrid public authorities. Lord Nicholls stated that a core public authority was bound by the HRA in respect of "everything it does", [106] as did Lord Rodger;[107] Lord Hope stated that core public bodies were public authorities "through and through" [108] with the consequence that s.6(5) did not apply to them, the assumption being that everything done by such an authority constituted a public function for the purposes of the HRA[109]; and Lord Hobhouse held that core public authorities were those bodies all of whose functions were of a public nature, so that s.6 applied to all of their actions.[110] Hybrid public authorities by way of contrast were only bound by the HRA in relation to functions of a public nature. Similarly in *YL*[111] Lord Neuberger held that a core public authority was bound by s.6 in relation to "every one of its acts whatever the nature of the act concerned",[112] with the consequence that there was no need to distinguish between private and public acts or functions of a core public authority. A hybrid public authority was however only bound by s.6 in relation to an act which was not private in nature, and which was pursuant to or in connection with a function which was public in nature.

This twin-track approach does moreover seem to fit with that adopted by the ECtHR. It has applied the Convention to state institutions *stricto sensu* even where it has been argued that the challenged action concerned the exercise of power by the State *qua* employer rather than *qua* legislator or executive, and it rejected the contention that the Convention could not impose obligations on the State which were not incumbent on private employers.[113]

It is interesting to reflect further on the rationale for subjecting all actions

[104] HC Debates, February 16, 1998, col. 775.
[105] *Aston Cantlow and Wilmcote with Billesley Parochial Church Council v Wallbank* [2004] 1 A.C. 546.
[106] *Aston Cantlow*, n.105, para.7.
[107] *Aston Cantlow*, n.105, para.144.
[108] *Aston Cantlow*, n.105, para.35.
[109] *Aston Cantlow*, n.105, para.41.
[110] *Aston Cantlow*, n.105, para.85.
[111] *YL v Birmingham City Council* [2007] 3 W.L.R. 112.
[112] *Aston Cantlow*, n.105, para.131. See also para.129.
[113] *Swedish Engine Drivers' Union v Sweden* (1979) 1 E.H.R.R. 617; *Schmidt and Dahlstrom v Sweden* (1979) 1 E.H.R.R. 632.

of core public authorities to the HRA. It might be felt that such bodies never do anything that could be regarded as private. This empirical claim is debatable. It might, alternatively, be argued that bodies which are "so public" should set an example and that acts which might be felt to be private if performed by others should none the less be subject to the HRA when undertaken by a core public authority. This is an interesting normative claim that might well be warranted. It should, however, be openly acknowledged. A third possible rationale might be a mix of the previous two. It might be felt that there are "not many" acts of such bodies which would be classified as private, *and* that it would not be good if these bodies were to seek to evade the HRA in such instances, since this would send the wrong message about the government's overall commitment to the legislation.

ii. The test for core public authorities
It follows from the above that there must be some criterion for dividing   **18–019**
between core and hybrid public authorities. The case law provides guidance in this respect, both as to the criteria that should be used and as to the criteria that are not appropriate or determinative.

The principal criterion that has been used by the courts to determine the meaning of core public authority is whether the relevant body is, in the words of Lord Nicholls, "governmental in a broad sense of that expression",[114] such that the government is answerable for the relevant body under the ECHR. Lord Nicholls gave by way of example government departments, local authorities, the police and the armed forces. Underlying this classification were factors such as the "possession of special powers, democratic accountability, public funding in whole or in part, an obligation to act only in the public interest, and a statutory constitution".[115] The judicial interpretation of core public authority has not surprisingly been influenced by the consequences of inclusion within this category: the core public authority is bound by the HRA in respect of all its actions and it cannot itself enjoy Convention rights.[116] The latter consideration has inclined the courts to be cautious about defining core public authority too broadly. They have concluded that, for example, non-governmental organisations should not generally be regarded as falling within the category of core public authorities, since this would thereby deny them the benefit of Convention rights, more especially because such organisations are included within the list of those who are allowed to bring actions before the ECtHR under art.34 ECHR.[117]

The courts have also provided guidance as to the criteria that should not be determinative of the category of core public authority. Thus the case law on the amenability of a body to judicial review is properly regarded as not

[114] *Aston Cantlow*, n.105, para.7.
[115] *Aston Cantlow*, n.105, para.7.
[116] *Aston Cantlow*, n.105, para.8.
[117] *Aston Cantlow*, n.105, paras 8, 47, 87.

being conclusive, since that case law has been developed for different purposes.[118] The courts have also made it clear that case law concerning the meaning of the "state" which has been developed by other courts is of limited utility in answering the salient issues under the HRA. The ECJ's jurisprudence concerning the meaning of the "state" for the purposes of deciding whether a directive can be enforced against a particular body, has therefore been said to provide limited assistance for the purposes of the definitional issues that arise under the HRA.[119] This must surely be correct. The purpose of the inquiry undertaken by the ECJ is very different from that under the HRA. The ECJ's case law is concerned with whether such bodies are sufficiently public to be regarded as part of the state for the purposes of vertical direct effect, with the consequence that a directive can be pleaded against them.[120] The issue here is as to which bodies should be regarded as "obviously public", with the consequence that they should be bound in all their activities, public or private, by the HRA.

iii. The test for hybrid public authorities

18–020   The courts have also furnished guidance concerning the category of hybrid public authorities, indicating the relevant criteria and those that are not determinative.

It is clear that the dominant approach is to consider a range of factors in order to decide whether the function being performed by the body can be regarded as public and hence render that body subject to the HRA as regards that function. This is apparent from the judgment of Lord Nicholls in *Aston*.[121]

> "What, then, is the touchstone to be used in deciding whether a function is public for this purpose? Clearly there is no single test of universal application. There cannot be, given the diverse nature of governmental functions and the variety of means by which these functions are discharged today. Factors to be taken into account include the extent to which in carrying out the relevant function the body is publicly funded, or is exercising statutory powers, or is taking the place of central government or local authorities, or is providing a public service."

A similar approach is evident in later cases. Thus in *YL* Lord Bingham echoed Lord Nicholls' reasoning, and listed factors that should be taken into account in construing "public function" in s.6(3)(b) HRA.[122] These included: the role and responsibility of the state in relation to the subject

---

[118] *Aston Cantlow*, n.105, paras 52, 87.
[119] *Aston Cantlow*, n.105, paras 55, 87.
[120] P. Craig and G. de Búrca, *EU Law, Text, Cases and Materials* (Oxford University Press, 4th edn, 2007), 284–287.
[121] *Aston Cantlow*, n.105, para.12.
[122] *YL*, n.111, paras 5–11. Lord Bingham dissented on the facts, but that does not undermine the force of his observations as to the approach to be adopted to deciding on the meaning of a hybrid public authority.

matter in question; the nature and extent of the public interest in the function in question; the nature and extent of any statutory power or duty in relation to that function; the extent to which the state, directly or indirectly, regulates, supervises and inspects the performance of that function, taking into account the extent to which it imposes penalties on those who fail to meet the requisite standards; the extent to which, whether directly or indirectly, the state was willing to pay for the function that is in issue; and the extent of the risk that improper performance of the function might violate an individual's Convention rights. A factor-based approach was also endorsed by Baroness Hale,[123] Lord Mance,[124] Lord Scott,[125] and Lord Neuberger.[126]

The courts have also indicated factors that should not be regarded as determinative or particularly helpful in deciding whether a body should be regarded as a hybrid public authority, such as the amenability of bodies to judicial review and the EU case law on the definition of the "state" for the purposes of direct effect of directives.[127]

iv. The application of the test for hybrid public authorities

The very fact that a range of factors are taken into account in deciding **18–021** whether a body falls within s.6(3)(b) HRA inevitably means that there will be differences of view as to the application of those factors in a particular case.

This is exemplified by *Aston Cantlow*. The parochial church council served a notice on the defendants to repair the chancel of the parish church. The defendants resisted payment, alleging, inter alia, that the notice infringed its rights under art.1 of the First Protocol. The Court of Appeal concluded that the parochial church council could be regarded as within the HRA, either because it was a core public authority, or at the very least that it fell within the category of hybrid public authority.[128]

The House of Lords however held that the parochial church council could not be regarded as falling in either category.[129] It concluded that although the Church of England had special links with central government and performed certain public functions, it was essentially a religious organisation and not a governmental organisation, and parochial church councils were part of the means whereby the Church promoted its religious mission and discharged financial responsibilities in respect of parish churches. The functions of parochial church councils were primarily concerned with pastoral and administrative matters within the parish and were not wholly of a public nature, and therefore they were not core public authorities under

[123] *YL*, n.111, paras 64–72.
[124] *YL*, n.111, para.91.
[125] *YL*, n.111, para.64.
[126] *YL*, n.111, paras 154–160.
[127] *Aston Cantlow*, n.105, paras 52, 55, 87; *YL*, n.111, para.12.
[128] *Aston Cantlow PCC v Wallbank* [2002] Ch.51.
[129] *Aston Cantlow*, n.105.

s.6(1). The fact that the public had certain rights in relation to their parish church was not sufficient to characterise the actions of a parochial church council in maintaining the fabric of the parish church as being of a public nature, so that when the plaintiff took steps to enforce the defendants' liability for the repair of the chancel, it was not performing a function of a public nature, which rendered it a hybrid public authority under s.6(3)(b).

v. The application of the test for hybrid public authorities: contracting out

18–022 The meaning accorded to s.6(3)(b) has been especially problematic in cases where a public body has contracted out the provision of certain services.

This is exemplified by the *Donoghue* case.[130] A housing association had been created by a local authority, which had transferred to it a substantial proportion of the local authority's housing stock. The relevant issue was whether the housing association was a public authority for the purposes of s.6 HRA. Lord Woolf C.J. gave the judgment of the Court of Appeal and reasoned as follows.[131]

> "The fact that a body performs an activity which otherwise a public body would be under a duty to perform cannot mean that such a performance is necessarily a public function. A public body in order to perform its public duties can use the services of a private body. Section 6 should not be applied so that if a private body provides such services, the nature of the functions are inevitably public. If this were to be the position, then when a small hotel provides bed and breakfast accommodation as a temporary measure, at the request of a housing authority that is under a duty to provide that accommodation, the small hotel would be performing public functions and required to comply with the Human Rights Act 1998. That is not what the Human Rights Act 1998 intended. . . . Section 6(3) means that hybrid bodies, who have functions of a public and private nature are public authorities, but *not* in relation to acts which are of a private nature. The fact that through the act of renting by a private body a public authority may be fulfilling its public duty, does not automatically change into a public act what would otherwise be a private act . . . ."

Lord Woolf set out a list of factors to determine whether a body such as the housing association should be regarded as a public authority for the purposes of the HRA[132]: the existence of statutory authority could mark out the act as being public; so too could the extent of control over the function exercised by a body that was a public authority; and the more closely enmeshed were the prima facie private acts with the activities of a public body, the more likely they were to be treated as public. However the mere

---

[130] *Poplar Housing and Regeneration Community Association Ltd v Donoghue* [2002] Q.B. 48.
[131] *Poplar Housing*, n.130, 67. Italics in original.
[132] *Poplar Housing*, n.130, 69.

fact that a public regulatory authority supervised the acts would not suffice in this respect. The housing association was, judged by these criteria, deemed to be performing a public function and subject to the HRA: the housing association had been created by the local authority, members of the local authority sat on its board, and it was subject to guidance by the local authority. The housing association was therefore subject to the HRA, and Convention rights. The court, however, held that there was no breach of art.8 of the ECHR.

The Court of Appeal considered the issue again in the *Leonard Cheshire* case.[133] The appellants were long-term patients in a home run by the Leonard Cheshire Foundation (LCF), and sought judicial review of LCF's decision to close the home. They argued that they had been promised a "home for life" in their current accommodation, that the decision to close the home was in breach of art.8 ECHR, and that this was so even though alternative accommodation in community based units would be provided. The majority of the residents had been placed there by the social services departments of their local authority or by their health authority. The placements were paid for by the authorities and were made pursuant to statutory powers.[134] The legislation made it clear that the accommodation could be provided either "in house", by the local authority itself,[135] or it could be contracted out to third parties.[136]

Lord Woolf C.J. gave the court's judgment, and adhered to the approach in *Donoghue*. If the local authority itself provided accommodation, it would be performing a public function. This would also be so where it made arrangements for the accommodation to be provided by LCF. This did not however mean that LCF should be regarded as performing a public function so as to come within the HRA.[137] Lord Woolf then considered the factors, set out in *Donoghue*, to determine whether the LCF should be regarded as a public authority for the purposes of the HRA.[138] He concluded that it should not. The mere fact of public funding by the local authority for the accommodation was not determinative of whether the functions were public or private.[139] There was, said Lord Woolf, no other evidence of there being a public flavour to the functions of LCF or LCF itself, which did not exercise statutory powers in caring for the appellants.[140]

The reasoning and result in *Leonard Cheshire* were challenged before the House of Lords in *YL*.[141] The claimant, who was 84, suffered from Alzheimer's disease. The defendant council had a statutory duty under the

18–023

---

[133] *R. v Leonard Cheshire Foundation (A Charity)* [2002] 2 All E.R. 936.
[134] The National Assistance Act 1948 s.21(1), required the local authority to provide accommodation for the claimants, being people who by reason of age, illness or disability were in need of care and attention that was not otherwise available to them.
[135] National Assistance Act 1948 ss.21(4) and (5).
[136] National Assistance Act 1948 s.26.
[137] *Leonard Cheshire*, n.133, para.15.
[138] *Leonard Cheshire*, n.133, paras 16–28.
[139] *Leonard Cheshire*, n.133, para.35(i).
[140] *Leonard Cheshire*, n.133, para.35(ii).
[141] *YL*, n.111.

National Assistance Act 1948 to make arrangements for providing her with residential accommodation,[142] and it chose to fulfil that duty, as it was allowed to,[143] by contracting with the second defendant company, an independent provider of health and social care services, for the claimant to be placed in one of its care homes, which accommodated both privately funded residents and those whose fees were paid by the council in full or in part. The claimant's fees were paid by the council, save for a small top-up fee paid by her relatives. The company subsequently sought to terminate the contract for her care and remove her from the home. The claimant argued that the company fell within s.6(3)(b) HRA and that its actions were in breach of arts 2, 3 and 8 ECHR.

The majority of the House of Lords rejected the claim. The reasoning was complex, but its essence was as follows. The majority distinguished between the function of a local authority in making arrangements pursuant to the 1948 Act for those in need of care and accommodation who were unable to make such arrangements for themselves, and that of a private company in providing such care and accommodation under contract with the authority, on a commercial basis rather than by subsidy from public funds. They then held that the actual provision of such care and accommodation by the private company, as opposed to its regulation and supervision pursuant to statutory rules, was not an inherently public function and thus fell outside s.6(3)(b). Thus while the claimant retained public law rights as against the local authority that had arranged the accommodation, she did not have Convention rights as against the care home.

There was however a powerful dissent by Lord Bingham and Baroness Hale, who reasoned as follows. The duty imposed on the local authority by the 1948 legislation could be discharged either by arranging for residential care itself, or by doing so through another local authority or a voluntary organisation, such as the second defendant. These were "alternative means by which the responsibility of the state may be discharged".[144] They rejected the distinction, which was crucial to the majority's reasoning, between arranging for and providing such accommodation. The intent of Parliament was that residential care should be provided. It was this duty that had to be performed, and the means by which it was done were not important.[145] The factors listed by Lord Bingham as indicative of a "public function" undertaken by a hybrid public authority all inclined to the conclusion that the second defendant fell within this category.[146] As Lord Bingham concluded,[147]

"When the 1998 Act was passed, it was very well known that a number of functions formerly carried out by public authorities were now carried out

---

[142] National Assistance Act 1948 s.21.
[143] National Assistance Act 1948 s.26.
[144] *YL*, n.111, para.16.
[145] *YL*, n.111, para.16.
[146] *YL*, n.111, paras 65–72, as applied by Baroness Hale.
[147] *YL*, n.111, para.20.

by private bodies. Section 6(3)(b) of the 1998 Act was clearly drafted with this well-known fact in mind. The performance by private body A by arrangement with public body B, and perhaps at the expense of B, of what would undoubtedly be a public function if carried out by B is, in my opinion, precisely the case which section 6(3)(b) was intended to embrace. It is, in my opinion, this case."

vi. The application of the test for hybrid public authorities and contracting out: an assessment

The application of s.6(3)(b) HRA to cases where a public body contracts out   **18–024**
the performance of its duties remains highly problematic in the light of the decision in *YL* and the dissent is to be preferred. The reasons are as follows.[148]

First, it is important at the outset to remember that s.6(3)(b) may be applicable either in cases where there is no contracting out, such as *Aston Cantlow*, or in cases where this does feature on the facts of the case, such as *YL*. This has implications for the test to determine "public function" for the purposes of s.6(3)(b). It may well be right to apply the "list of factors" approach developed in *Aston Cantlow* to the former situation, precisely because there is no single criterion that can be used to determine whether a nominally private body should be subject to the HRA. It is however questionable whether the "list of factors" approach should be relevant to cases of the former kind, where there is contracting out. If it is decided that a core public authority is performing a public function pursuant to a statutory duty or power cast upon it, then that should be decisive. The nature of the function does not change if the task is contracted out to a body that is nominally private. That is the essence of the quotation from Lord Bingham set out above, and it is surely correct. The same point can be put in a different way. The fact that a core public authority is bound under the HRA in respect of all its actions, does not preclude us from deciding that, as will very commonly be the case, its action in a particular instance is properly to be regarded as the fulfilment of a public function cast upon it in the public interest by legislation. Where this is so the fact that it contracts out the performance of the task to a private body does not alter its nature: if it was properly regarded as a public function when performed by the public authority itself, then it should be so regarded when the same task is performed by the body to whom the power has been contracted out.

Second, this conclusion is reinforced by principle. It cannot be correct as a

---

[148] P. Craig, "Contracting Out, the Human Rights Act and the Scope of Judicial Review" (2002) 118 L.Q.R. 551; M. Sunkin, "Pushing Forward the Frontiers of Human Rights Protection: The Meaning of Public Authority under the Human Rights Act" [2004] P.L. 643; C. Donnelly, "*Leonard Cheshire* Again and Beyond: Private Contractors, Contract and Section 6(3)(b) of the Human Rights Act" [2005] P.L. 785; H. Quane, "The Strasbourg Jurisprudence and the Meaning of a 'Public Authority' under the Human Rights Act" [2006] P.L. 106; Joint Committee on Human Rights, Ninth Report, *The Meaning of Public Authority under the Human Rights Act* (HL 77, HC 410, 2006–7); C. Donnelly, *Delegation of Governmental Power to Private Parties, A Comparative Perspective* (Oxford University Press, 2007), Ch.6.

matter of principle for the availability of Convention rights to be dependent upon the fortuitous incidence as to how the core public authority chooses to discharge its functions. It is increasingly the case that public authorities contract out some of the duties cast upon them. There may be good reasons for this. The choice whether to do so should not however place in jeopardy the applicability of Convention rights, since this would make the protections secured by the HRA a lottery.

18–025   Third, the preceding arguments can be tested against the facts of *YL* itself. The statutory duty cast on local authorities by the National Assistance Act 1948 to make arrangements for providing accommodation for those who could not do so for themselves for reasons of age, infirmity, disability, etc. was, as recognised by Baroness Hale, part of the post-war Beveridge social welfare reforms.[149] It was quite clearly a public function, imposed in the public interest. It did not change its nature in any respect by the fact that it could be fulfilled through a voluntary organisation. The distinction that lies at the heart of the majority judgment between making arrangements for such accommodation, and the provision of such accommodation, is, with respect, not supported either by the words of the statute,[150] or by the legislative intent underlying the statutory scheme. The clear legislative intent was, as Lord Bingham noted, that residential care should be provided, while leaving choice as to the means by which this was done.[151] The dissent is to be preferred. This is so whether one applies the "list of factors" approach to conclude that the second defendant was performing a public function, or whether, as argued above, one reaches the same conclusion by saying that the local authority was performing a public function in the public interest, such that when the task was contracted out the second defendant was also performing a public function and hence bound by the HRA.

Fourth, the majority in *YL* were concerned that if the HRA were to be applicable to the instant case then there would be inequality between those who were resident in care homes as a result of the local authority fulfilling its statutory duties, and others who resided in a purely private capacity. There is some force in this argument. The counter argument is however that the schema of the HRA as applied to this type of case means that there will always be some possible equality issue. Thus the actual decision reached in *YL* means that there will be differential treatment in terms of the HRA between the infirm, ill, etc. who are housed in local authority accommodation, who would take the benefit of Convention rights, and those who are housed in accommodation pursuant to a contracting out scheme, who would be denied such rights.

Finally, legislative intervention may now be required in order to reform

---

[149] *YL*, n.111, para.49.
[150] The actual wording of the National Assistance Act 1948 s.21(1) is that the local authority shall "make arrangements for providing". This is simply reflective of the fact that the local authority has choice under the legislation as to how the duty should be fulfilled. It does not mean that there is no duty in relation to the provision of the accommodation. This reading does not fit with the legislative scheme and is inconsistent with, for example, s.21(4).
[151] *YL*, n.111, para.16.

the law on this issue. A Private Members' Bill has been introduced to do this. The Human Rights Act (Meaning of Public Authority) Bill adopts the formulation proposed by the Joint Committee on Human Rights[152] and defines "function of a public nature" to include a "function performed pursuant to a contract or other arrangement with a public authority which is under a duty to perform that function". It remains to be seen whether the Bill receives the support of the government.

D. Acts of Public Authorities: The Horizontal Effect of the Human Rights Act

i. Vertical and horizontal impact: general theory
Any legal system that protects fundamental rights will have to decide how far those protections are to apply.[153] The traditional sphere of application for such protections is "vertical", operating between state and individual. An important issue is how far they can apply "horizontally" as between private individuals, or between a public body acting in a private capacity and an individual.

18–026

The view that protections for rights should only apply vertically is premised, as Hunt has argued, on a "rigid distinction between the public and private sphere and presupposes that the purpose of fundamental rights protection is to preserve the integrity of the private sphere against coercive intrusion by the state".[154] Legal relations between individuals are, by way of contrast, seen as part of private autonomy, with the consequence that the choices individuals make about how to live their lives and deal with each other should not be dictated by the state.

The alternative view that rights-based protections should apply even as between private parties is premised ultimately on the hypothesis that all legal relations are constituted by the state, in the sense that the law itself is constructed and supported by the state.[155] Viewed from this perspective, choices are constantly being made and expressed through legal rules as to the limits on private freedom of action. Legal rules, derived both from statute and the common law, frequently impose limits on private choice whether in the sphere of contract, tort, property or restitution.

---

[152] n.148, para.150. The effects of *YL*, n.111, albeit not the more general reasoning, will be reversed if the Health and Social Care Bill 2008 s.139 becomes law.
[153] M. Hunt, "The 'Horizontal Effect' of the Human Rights Act" [1998] P.L. 423; B. Markesinis, "Privacy, Freedom of Expression and the Horizontal Effect of the Human Rights Bill: Lessons from Germany" (1998) 114 L.Q.R. 47; Sir W. Wade, "The United Kingdom's Bill of Rights", *Constitutional Reform in the United Kingdom: Practice and Principles* (University of Cambridge Centre for Public Law, 1998), Ch.6; G. Phillipson, "The Human Rights Act, 'Horizontal Effect' and the Common Law: A Bang or a Whimper" (1999) 62 M.L.R. 824; I. Leigh, "Horizontal Rights, the Human Rights Act and Privacy: Lessons from the Commonwealth" (1999) 48 I.C.L.Q. 57; N. Bamforth, "The Application of the Human Rights Act 1998 to Public Authorities and Private Bodies" [1999] C.L.J. 159; Sir R. Buxton, "The Human Rights Act and Private Law" (2000) 116 L.Q.R. 48; Sir W. Wade, "Horizons of Horizontality" (2000) 116 L.Q.R. 217; A. Young, "Remedial and Substantive Horizontality: The Common Law and *Douglas v Hello! Ltd* [2002] P.L. 232.
[154] Hunt, n.153, 424.
[155] Clapham, n.86.

When the matter is viewed in this light the formal divide between the public and private sphere begins to crumble. The issue becomes which types of restraint on private action are felt to be normatively warranted. When seen in this way it becomes far more difficult to argue that rights-based protections should have no application in the private sphere, more especially since power which is nominally private may be just as potent as power which is formally public. It should be stressed at this juncture that even if constitutional rights are applied horizontally this does not preclude differences in the way in which they would be interpreted in public and private contexts.

ii. Vertical and horizontal impact: the HRA

18–027 It might be thought that while this discussion is interesting in the abstract it has no immediate application here, since we have seen from the preceding discussion that s.6 HRA only applies to public authorities. It might be thought that the legislature has made a choice and has limited the HRA to vertical relations between citizen and state. The matter is not, however, so straightforward.

It should be noted at the outset that ss.3 and 4 HRA can be relied on in actions between private parties. The obligation in s.3 to read and give effect to legislation in a manner that is consistent with Convention rights is general in scope and can be applied to the interpretation of legislation in actions between private parties.[156]

Subject to this, the general view is that the HRA does not have "direct horizontal effect". It is not open to a private party in an action against another private party simply to go to court and contend that action by the private defendant is unlawful for violation of Convention rights. The wording of s.6 HRA, limited as it is to public authorities, precludes such an independent cause of action between private parties.[157]

It is also generally accepted that the HRA does not thereby preclude all horizontal effect. To the contrary, the text and the legislative history reveal that, at the least, some element of "indirect horizontal effect" is intended by the legislation. The textual indication of this is to be found in the inclusion of courts and tribunals as public authorities in s.6(3). Such bodies are bound by the obligation in s.6(1) to act compatibly with Convention rights.[158] The text takes us only so far. It does not in itself indicate that courts and tribunals are under this obligation when deciding purely private disputes between private parties. That this was the framers' intention is, however, clear from consideration of the legislative history. Hunt[159] has shown that the government rejected an amendment to the Bill designed to prevent it from having any horizontal effect. The amendment would have altered s.6(1) so as to prevent it from applying where "the public authority is a court or a

---

[156] See, e.g., *Ghaidan*, n.63; *CGU International Insurance Plc v Astrazeneca Insurance Co Ltd* [2006] EWCA Civ 1340.
[157] The argument for direct horizontality is put by Wade, n.153.
[158] *Hammerton v Hammerton* [2007] EWCA Civ 248.
[159] Hunt, n.153, 440.

tribunal and the parties to the proceedings before it do not include any public authority". The Lord Chancellor's response in rejecting the amendment was unequivocal. He stated that it was right as a matter of principle for the courts to have the duty to act compatibly with the Convention not only in cases involving other public authorities, but also in developing the common law in deciding cases between individuals.[160]

It is therefore important to consider what is meant by "indirect horizontal effect" in cases between private individuals. Canadian and German jurisprudence both indicate that the values and principles enshrined in the protection of rights may have an influence on the rules applicable as between private parties.[161] These values can therefore be used to help shape the development of, for example, the common law rules in a particular area of private law.[162] Strong and weak versions of indirect horizontality have been identified.[163] Under a model of strong horizontality, the courts are under a duty to develop the common law so as to be compatible with Convention rights, and should link the common law very closely with the rights as interpreted by the Strasbourg institutions. Under a model of weak indirect horizontality, the courts have a power to develop the common law so as to be compatible with Convention rights, and have greater latitude in allowing the common law to develop differently from the precise jurisprudence of the Strasbourg institutions.[164]

18–028

Hunt has articulated a view about the possible impact of the HRA on private relations that is more extensive than encapsulated by "indirect horizontal effect".[165] Drawing on case law from South Africa,[166] he posits a view about the effect of such rights on private parties, which is different from both direct and indirect horizontal effect. On this view fundamental rights are applicable to "all law", irrespective of the parties to the action. This does not thereby destroy private autonomy, since it is still open to a particular individual to conduct his affairs as he chooses, however unpleasant the criteria may be. What it does mean is that the law will not protect these bigoted choices where they conflict with protected rights.

The indications thus far are that the courts are adopting some version of indirect horizontality. Thus in the *Douglas* case,[167] the claimants sought an injunction against *Hello!* magazine, because it had published pictures of their wedding, which they had promised exclusively to another magazine. The court, while refusing to grant the injunction, accepted that s.6 HRA

---

[160] HL Deb, November 24, 1997, col. 783.
[161] Hunt, n.153; Markesinis, n.153.
[162] It follows that even if a public authority successfully brings itself within s.6(5), and claims that it is not bound by s.6(1) because the nature of the act was private, it will still be open to the court to consider the values underlying the Convention rights in any "private litigation" between it and another party.
[163] Young, n.153; Phillipson, n.153.
[164] Young, n.153, 236.
[165] Hunt, n.153, 434–435, 441–442.
[166] *Du Plessis v Du Klerk* 1996 3 S.A. 850, 914–915, *per* Kriegler J.
[167] *Douglas v Hello! Ltd* [2001] Q.B. 967.

required the court to have regard to art.8 ECHR when considering a common law claim to privacy as between private parties.[168]

E. Proceedings and Standing under Section 6

18–029 The forum in which claims under the HRA can be brought is dealt with in ss.7 and 9 HRA. Section 7(1) provides that:

> "A person who claims that a public authority has acted (or proposes to act) in a way which is made unlawful by section 6(1) may—
>
> (a) bring proceedings against the authority[169] under this Act in the appropriate court or tribunal, or,
> (b) rely on the Convention right or rights concerned in any legal proceedings,
>
> but only if he is (or would be) a victim of the unlawful act."

Section 7(3) makes it clear that the standing criterion of being a victim operates when the proceedings are brought by way of judicial review. The phrase "appropriate court or tribunal" within s.7(1)(a) means such court or tribunal as may be determined in accordance with rules[170] to be made by the Secretary of State or the Lord Chancellor.[171] The phrase "legal proceedings" within s.7(1)(b) includes proceedings brought by or at the instigation of a public authority, and an appeal against the decision of a court or tribunal.[172] Proceedings brought under s.7(1)(a) in respect of a judicial act[173] may be brought only by exercising a right of appeal, or by way of judicial review, or in such other forum as may be prescribed by rules.[174] This does not, however, affect any rule of law, which prevents a court from being the subject of judicial review.[175]

The time limits are specified in s.7(5). Where proceedings are brought under s.7(1)(a) they must be commenced before the end of one year beginning with the date on which the act complained of took place, or such longer period as the court or tribunal considers equitable having regard to all the circumstances.[176] This is however expressly made subject to any rule imposing a stricter time limit in relation to the procedure in question. The

---

[168] *Douglas*, n.167, paras 111, 167; *Berezovsky v Forbes (No.2)* [2001] E.M.L.R. 45, para.10; *In Re A Local Authority (Inquiry: Restraint on Publication)* [2004] 2 W.L.R. 926; Compare however *Wainwright v Home Office* [2004] 2 A.C. 406; *Money Markets International Stockbrokers Ltd (in liquidation) v London Stock Exchange Ltd* [2002] 1 W.L.R. 1150, paras 137–140.
[169] This covers a counterclaim or similar proceeding, HRA s.7(2).
[170] HRA s.7(2).
[171] HRA s.7(9).
[172] HRA s.7(6).
[173] Defined as a judicial act of a court, including an act done on the instructions, or on behalf, of a judge, HRA s.9(5).
[174] HRA s.9(1).
[175] HRA s.9(2).
[176] See, e.g., *Cameron v Network Rail Infrastructure Ltd (formerly Railtrack Plc)* [2007] 1 W.L.R. 163.

effect of this proviso is that if, for example, the procedure chosen is the application for judicial review then the time limit applicable to such proceedings will operate.

It is clear from s.7(1) that Convention rights can be used "offensively" as covered by s.7(1)(a), whereby the individual instigates the action based on the infringement of s.6(1). Convention rights can also be used "defensively" as covered by s.7(1)(b), where the action is brought against an individual by a public authority and the former relies on a breach of s.6(1) by the authority as a defence. It should be noted that the limitation period set out in s.7(5) only applies to "offensive" actions. Where the individual relies on a breach of Convention rights by way of defence pursuant to s.7(1)(b) he will often have no control over the timing of the action. Nor may he necessarily have been aware of the possible s.6(1) illegality until the public authority sought to enforce an order against him, which he believes to violate Convention rights.[177]

Many s.6(1) actions will be brought by way of application for judicial review and will be linked with other possible heads of illegality. The implications which this has for the operation of the ordinary judicial review procedure will be considered below.[178]

The test for standing in relation to s.6(1) is, as stated above, that the person must be a victim of the unlawful act. A person will only be deemed to be a "victim" if he would be a victim for the purposes of art.34 ECHR as interpreted by the ECtHR.[179] This criterion is certainly different in formal terms from that which applies in ordinary judicial review applications, where the test is one of sufficiency of interest. This was a cause of some disquiet during the passage of the Bill. The meaning of the term victim in the jurisprudence of the ECtHR will be discussed within the general context of standing.[180]

If it should transpire that a s.6(1) action is not allowed to proceed, because the applicant is not deemed to be a victim, then it should be remembered that the courts can always fall back on their common law jurisprudence. This has been set out above, and there is nothing in the HRA that overrules this body of doctrine. If, therefore, a public interest group, which complained of a violation of a Convention right was held not to be a victim for the purposes of the HRA, it could argue that the challenged action was ultra vires in accord with the common law protections for fundamental rights.

F. The Remedies for Breach of Section 6

Section 8(1) HRA provides that "in relation to any act (or proposed act) of **18–030** a public authority which the court finds is (or would be) unlawful, it may grant such relief or remedy, or make such order, within its powers as it

---

[177] Similar considerations affect judicial review actions, see below, para.26–014.
[178] See below, para.26–012.
[179] HRA s.7(7).
[180] See below, para.24–025.

considers just an appropriate". The courts are therefore given a wide discretion concerning remedies. A declaration that the act of the public authority was unlawful, or an order to quash the act, will be the normal remedy. The appropriate relief may well be an order of prohibition or an injunction to prevent an unlawful act from being committed, since s.8(1) expressly contemplates a remedy being granted where a proposed act would be unlawful. The fact that s.6(6) defines an act to include a failure to act means that mandatory orders, whether in the form of mandamus or a mandatory injunction, may also be ordered where the court believes that this is just and appropriate.

Section 8(1) contains the proviso that the remedy must be within the powers of the court that makes it, and s.8(6) defines court to include a tribunal. We have seen that actions for breach of s.6(1) may be brought before an appropriate court or tribunal.[181] It may well be that a particular tribunal lacks the power to award certain types of remedy. This issue is addressed by s.7(11). It states that the Minister who has power to make rules in relation to a particular tribunal may by order add to the relief or remedies which the tribunal may grant, or the grounds on which it may grant them, to the extent to which he considers this necessary to ensure that the tribunal can provide an appropriate remedy for the purposes of a s.6(1) action.

The application of s.8(1) to cases where the defendant public authority is a court or tribunal poses interesting problems. The acts of superior courts are not amenable to judicial review and therefore there would be no power to issue certiorari to such a body. The decision of the offending court could be set aside on appeal, on the ground of error of law.

The HRA also provides for the possibility of a remedy in damages. This will be considered in more detail in the general discussion of damages liability.[182] The bare outline of the relevant provisions will be given here. Section 8(1) is framed broadly enough to include such a remedy, and this is clearly contemplated by the legislation since s.8(2) then stipulates that "damages may be awarded only by a court which has power to award damages, or to order the payment of compensation in civil proceedings". While damages can be given for breach of s.6(1) the intention is that they should be awarded only where other relief cannot afford just satisfaction to the claimant. This is the import of s.8(3).

"No award of damages is to be made unless, taking account of all the circumstances of the case, including—

    (a)   any other relief or remedy granted, or order made, in relation to the act in question (by that or any other court), and

    (b)   the consequences of any decision (of that or any other court) in respect of that act,

---

[181] HRA s.7(1)(a).
[182] See below, Ch.29.

the court is satisfied that the award is necessary to afford just satisfaction to the person in whose favour it is made."

5. THE STANDARD OF REVIEW

The discussion thus far has been concerned with ss.3–4 and 6 HRA. There is however an important issue that has not yet been touched upon, which is the standard of judicial review that is applied by the courts under the HRA. This has generated, as will be seen, significant case law and academic comment, which will be considered within this section.   **18–031**

A. ECHR Precepts

It is helpful to begin with the Convention precepts that shape the issues   **18–032**
placed before domestic courts. The paradigm circumstance in which this issue arises is where the court decides that there has been a prima facie interference with a Convention right, and the defendant then argues that this was warranted on the facts of the case.

It will be for the national court to decide whether the interference was "in accordance with the law", or "prescribed by law" as demanded by various Convention articles. It is clear from the Strasbourg jurisprudence that compliance with these phrases requires not only that there must be some proper source of law authorising the interference, but also that it has the quality of "law". It must be adequately accessible to the citizen, it must be sufficiently clear so that the individual can foresee the consequences of his action and it must not leave excessive discretion to the public authorities.[183]

The national court may then have to decide whether the limitation on a Convention right serves a legitimate aim. Many articles of the ECHR allow for restrictions of the rights protected therein, but only on specified grounds. Thus, for example, art.10 concerning freedom of speech, and art.11 concerning freedom of assembly and association, not only require that any restriction be prescribed by law, but also that it falls within the specified list of recognised exceptions.

It will then be for the national court to determine whether the interference with the right was proportionate. Even if it can be argued that a restriction on speech can be linked to, for example, the protection of health or morals, the ECHR specifies that any such restriction only be such as is "necessary in a democratic society" for the protection of the relevant interest. In the *Sunday Times* case[184] the ECtHR made it clear that while the word

---

[183] *Sunday Times v UK* (1979) 2 E.H.R.R. 245; *Winterwerp v The Netherlands* (1979) 2 E.H.R.R. 387; *Kruslin v France* (1990) 12 E.H.R.R. 547; *Groppera Radio v Switzerland* (1990) 12 E.H.R.R. 321. See, e.g., *Regina (Wardle) v Crown Court at Leeds* [2002] 1 A.C. 754.
[184] *Sunday Times*, n.183, paras 59, 62, 65; *Silver v UK* (1983) 5 E.H.R.R. 347, para.97; *Olsson v Sweden* (1988) 11 E.H.R.R. 259.

"necessary" was not synonymous with indispensable, nor did it have the flexibility of expressions such as "admissible", "useful", "reasonable" or "desirable". The word necessary implied a "pressing social need". Any interference had to be proportionate to the legitimate aim being pursued and this had to be judged not in the abstract, but by whether the interference was necessary having regard to the facts and circumstances prevailing in the case before it. The application of this test will of course be affected by the nature of the right that is in issue in the instant case.

The Strasbourg institutions apply a "margin of appreciation" when reviewing the compatibility of state action with Convention rights. The doctrine is associated with cases such as *Handyside*.[185] The ECtHR held that in determining whether interference with a protected right was "necessary in a democratic society" some deference would be given to the state authority, which would be in a better position than the international judge to determine the needs within its own country. The margin of appreciation doctrine is a settled feature of the ECHR jurisprudence. The justification for the doctrine is integrally connected with the supranational nature of the ECHR. The doctrine helps to define the relationship between a supranational court and national authorities, including national courts. The rationale for the doctrine is premised on the assumption that what might be necessary to attain the stated interests might vary from state to state even within democratic societies, and that the distance of the ECtHR from local circumstance as compared to the national executive means that some deference should be accorded to the latter. Viewed in this way the margin of appreciation is recognition of subsidiarity inherent in the ECHR system.[186]

B. The Domestic Concept of Deference/Discretionary Area of Judgment/ Respect

18–033   Having surveyed the applicable precepts flowing from the ECHR, we can now consider the way in which our courts have fashioned the standard of review. A number of points have become clear in the HRA jurisprudence.

i. The ECHR margin of appreciation has not been adopted

18–034   It is clear that our courts have not adopted the margin of appreciation doctrine developed by the ECtHR. The twin rationales for the Strasbourg doctrine set out above are not appropriate where Convention rights are applied by domestic courts. It would, as Sir John Laws stated, be inapt to the administration of the Convention in the domestic courts for the very reason that they are domestic. They will not be subject to an "objective

---

[185] *Handyside v UK* (1979) 1 E.H.R.R. 737, para.48.
[186] R. Ryssdal, "The Coming of Age of the European Convention on Human Rights" [1996] E.H.R.L.R. 18, 24–25, 27.

inhibition generated by any cultural distance between themselves and the state organs impleaded before them".[187]

ii. A domestic concept of deference

It is clear however that our courts recognised early within their jur- **18–035**
isprudence a domestic concept of deference within the HRA.[188]

Lord Hope in *Kebilene*[189] held that the margin of appreciation doctrine was not available to national courts under the HRA for the reasons considered above. He held that national courts should however recognise that difficult choices might have to be made between the rights of the individual and the needs of society. It followed that in some circumstances the courts should acknowledge an area of judgment "within which the judiciary will defer, on democratic grounds, to the considered opinion of the elected body or person whose actual decision is said to be incompatible with the Convention".[190] Such an area of judgment would more readily be found where the Convention required a balance to be struck, or where the case raised issues of social and economic policy. It would be less likely to be found where the right was unqualified, or where the rights were of high constitutional importance which the courts were well placed to assess.[191]

The importance of deference, and its limits, was brought out forcefully by Lord Hoffmann in *Alconbury*.[192] He stated that "in a democratic country, decisions as to what the general interest requires are made by democratically elected bodies, or persons accountable to them".[193] On some occasions Parliament would be able to lay down the general policy in advance through legislation. In others areas it was not possible to formulate general rules, and the question of what the general interest required would have to be decided on a case by case basis, as with planning. In these latter areas Parliament will delegate decision-making to ministers, or local authorities, thereby preserving the democratic principle. In such instances the "only fair method of decision is by some person or body accountable to the electorate".[194] The HRA "was no doubt intended to strengthen the rule of law but not inaugurate the rule of lawyers".[195] There were however limits to deference. Certain basic individual rights "should not be capable in any circumstances of being overridden by the majority, even if they think that the public

---

[187] Sir John Laws, "The Limitations of Human Rights" [1998] P.L. 254, 258. See also, D. Pannick, "Principles of Interpretation of Community Rights under the Human Rights Act and the Discretionary Area of Judgment" [1998] P.L. 545, 548–549.
[188] *Brown v Stott (Procurator Fiscal, Dunfermline)* [2003] 1 A.C. 681; *R. (on the application of Marper) v Chief Constable of South Yorkshire* [2002] EWCA Civ 1275; *Lambert*, n.52; *Holder v Law Society* [2003] 1 W.L.R. 1059.
[189] *R. v DPP Ex p. Kebilene* [2000] 2 A.C. 326.
[190] *Kebilene*, n.189, 380.
[191] *Kebilene*, n.189, 380.
[192] *R. (Alconbury Developments Ltd) v Secretary of State for the Environment, Transport and the Regions* [2003] 2 A.C. 295.
[193] *Alconbury*, n.192, para.69.
[194] *Alconbury*, n.192, para.70.
[195] *Alconbury*, n.192, para.129.

interest so requires".[196] These were rights which belonged to individuals "simply by virtue of their humanity, independently of any utilitarian calculation".[197] The protection of these rights from majority decision required an independent and impartial tribunal, which would decide whether the legislation infringed the right in question. If it did then the legislation must, said Lord Hoffmann, either be declared invalid, as in the United States, or it must be declared incompatible with the governing human rights instrument, as under the HRA.

The significance of deference/respect is apparent once again in the *Countryside Alliance* case,[198] in which it was alleged that the Hunting Act 2004, which prohibited the hunting of wild mammals with dogs, constituted an infringement of certain Convention rights. The House of Lords concluded that art.1 of the First Protocol was engaged, since the 2004 Act limited the use that an owner could make of his land. It nonetheless held that the restriction was proportionate and in reaching this conclusion accorded the legislature a wide margin of discretionary judgment in reaching this conclusion on a controversial matter of social policy. Lord Bingham acknowledged that the mere fact that Parliament had enacted the statute did not conclude the issue as to whether there was a violation of Convention rights. However he was also duly mindful of the dangers of subverting the democratic process if "on a question of moral and political judgment, opponents of the Act achieve through the courts what they could not achieve in Parliament".[199]

iii. Factors taken into account by the courts

18–036   It is readily apparent from the preceding analysis that the courts will take into account a range of factors in deciding on the appropriate level of deference, discretionary area of judgment or respect to accord to primary decision-maker.

In *Roth* Laws L.J. articulated four principles that would more generally guide the courts.[200] The first was that greater deference would be paid to an Act of Parliament than to a decision of the executive or subordinate measure. The second principle was that there was more scope for deference where the Convention itself required a balance to be struck, much less so where the right was stated in terms which were unqualified, although even in the latter instance there could be room for differences of view as to how the requirements of a particular Convention right could be met. Third, greater deference will be due to the democratic powers where the subject-matter in hand was peculiarly within their constitutional responsibility, such as defence of the realm, and less when it was more particularly within the

---

[196] *Alconbury*, n.192, para.70.
[197] *Alconbury*, n.192, para.70.
[198] *R. (on the application of Countryside Alliance) v Attorney General* [2007] 3 W.L.R. 922.
[199] *Countryside Alliance*, n.198, para.45. Compare however the approach taken by Baroness Hale, paras 124–126.
[200] *Roth*, n.60, paras 83–87.

constitutional responsibility of the courts, which were concerned with maintenance of the rule of law. The final principle was that greater or lesser deference would be due according to whether the subject matter was more readily within the actual or potential expertise of the democratic powers or the courts. It was for this reason that government decisions in the area of macro-economic policy were relatively remote from judicial control.

It is moreover perfectly possible for the courts to accord differing degrees of deference to distinct issues that arise in the same case. This is exemplified by *A v Secretary of State for the Home Department*,[201] the facts of which were set out above.[202] It will be remembered that the case was concerned with government measures taken to combat terrorism post 9/11. Two issues came before the House of Lords. In relation to whether there was a risk of terrorist attacks at some future date, which was the foundation for an order derogating in certain respects from Convention rights, the House of Lords characterised the issue as pre-eminently political in character and gave great weight to the judgment of the executive and Parliament. In relation however to the alleged violation of Convention rights through statutory provisions that treated nationals and non-nationals unequally, the House of Lords engaged in more intensive review, more especially because the right to liberty was at stake. Their Lordships did not regard themselves as precluded by the doctrine of deference from examining the proportionality of a measure taken to restrict such a right and held that the relevant statutory provisions violated Convention rights.

iv. Terminology

There have nonetheless been differences of view within the judiciary as to the label that best captures the courts' approach to review under the HRA. It is clear from the preceding discussion that the label "deference" has been used by a number of courts. So too has the phrase "discretionary area of judgment".[203]

Lord Hoffmann in *Prolife* was however unhappy about the language of deference, since he believed that it had overtones of servility.[204] It was, said Lord Hoffmann, necessary in a society based upon the rule of law and the separation of powers, to decide which branch of government had decision-making power and what the legal limits of that power were. That was a question of law to be decided by the courts. The inevitable consequence was that the courts themselves would often have to decide the limits of their own decision-making power.[205]

18–037

---

[201] [2005] 2 A.C. 68.
[202] See above, para.18–010.
[203] See, e.g., *R. (on the applications of P and Q and Q.B.) v Secretary of State for the Home Department* [2001] 1 W.L.R. 2002; *Samaroo v Secretary of State for the Home Department* [2001] UKHRR 1150; *R. (on the application of Farrakhan) v Secretary of State for the Home Department* [2002] Q.B. 139.
[204] *R. (on the application of ProLife Alliance) v BBC* [2004] 1 A.C. 185, paras 75–76.
[205] *ProLife Alliance*, n.204, para.76.

"But it does not mean that their allocation of decision-making power to the other branches of government is a matter of courtesy or deference. The principles upon which decision-making powers are allocated are principles of law. The courts are the independent branch of government and the legislature and executive are, directly and indirectly respectively, the elected branches of government. Independence makes the courts more suited to deciding some kinds of questions and being elected makes the legislature or executive more suited to deciding others. The allocation of these decision-making responsibilities is based upon recognised principles. The principle that the independence of the courts is necessary for a proper decision of disputed legal rights or claims of violation of human rights is a legal principle. It is reflected in article 6 of the Convention. On the other hand, the principle that majority approval is necessary for a proper decision on policy or allocation of resources is also a legal principle. Likewise, when a court decides that a decision is within the proper competence of the legislature or executive, it is not showing deference. It is deciding the law."

More recently in *Huang* Lord Bingham expressed some impatience with prolonged discussion about due deference, discretionary area of judgment, democratic accountability, relative institutional capacity and the like.[206] He stated that giving weight to factors legitimately taken into consideration by the initial decision-maker was not properly described as deference. It was rather "performance of the ordinary judicial task of weighing up the competing considerations on each side and according appropriate weight to the judgment of a person with responsibility for a given subject matter and access to special sources of knowledge and advice", which was "how any rational judicial decision-maker is likely to proceed".[207]

Different judges and indeed commentators may well have preferences as to the language that should be used when the courts undertake review under the HRA. It is however doubtful whether anything logically follows from the choice of this terminology, at least insofar as judicial practice is concerned. Thus the mere fact that a particular court chooses to use the language of deference does not in itself indicate that it is likely to leave more leeway to Parliament or the executive than if it had adopted the approach of Lord Hoffmann or Lord Bingham, since so much depends on how it weights the factors that incline in favour of or against deference on the facts of the case.

The same point can be put from the opposite perspective, by taking Lord Bingham's approach by way of example. It is doubtful whether the considerations that have been central to judicial and academic debates about due deference, respect, discretionary area of judgment and the like, would not re-enter by the back door, having been excluded from the front. Thus the very decision as to what constitutes giving "appropriate weight" to the

[206] *Huang v Secretary of State for the Home Department* [2007] 2 A.C. 167, para.14.
[207] *Huang*, n.206, para.16.

judgment of the initial decision-maker, and the "special sources of knowledge and advice" that warrant giving weight to the view of that person, is likely to generate the same debate as currently exists when deciding on the meaning of "due deference" or "discretionary area of judgment".

C. Proportionality under the HRA: Daly

The standard of review under the HRA is clearly important and the courts **18–038** have adopted proportionality as the appropriate standard. The issue of deference/discretionary area of judgment/respect will moreover normally be considered within the framework of the proportionality analysis.[208]

Daly[209] is the leading authority. The applicant challenged the policy, made pursuant to s.47(1) of the Prison Act 1952, whereby a prisoner could not be present during a search of his cell, when prison officers examined legally privileged correspondence. He argued that this infringed his common law right to communicate confidentially with his legal adviser, and art.8 ECHR.

Lord Steyn clarified the test for review under the HRA, and this was reaffirmed by the House of Lords in *Shayler*.[210] Lord Steyn referred to the judgment in *Mahmood*[211] and observed[212] that this formulation was cast in terms of heightened scrutiny under the *Wednesbury* test, in the manner laid down in cases such as *Smith*.[213] This heightened level of scrutiny had been held to be insufficient by the Strasbourg Court in *Smith and Grady*.[214] This was because it effectively excluded any consideration by the national court of whether the interference with the applicant's rights answered a pressing social need or was proportionate to national security or public order. Lord Steyn held[215] that there was a material difference between the heightened scrutiny test, and one framed in terms of proportionality. While Lord Steyn accepted that many cases would be decided the same way under either test, he acknowledged that the intensity of review would be greater under proportionality. This was so for two reasons.

Proportionality could, said Lord Steyn, require the reviewing court to assess the balance struck by the decision-maker, not merely whether it was

[208] See, cases in n.203. See also, *R. (on the application of Ponting) v Governor of HMP Whitemoor, and Secretary of State for the Home Department* [2002] EWCA Civ 224; *R. (on the application of E) v Ashworth Hospital Authority* [2001] EWHC Admin 1089; *R. (on the application of L) v Manchester City Council* [2001] EWHC Admin 707; *R. (on the application of Hirst) v Secretary of State for the Home Department* [2002] 1 W.L.R. 2929; *R. (on the application of X) v Headteachers and Governors of Y School* [2007] H.R.L.R. 20; *R. (on the application of Animal Defenders International) v Secretary of State for Culture, Media and Sport* [2007] H.R.L.R. 9.

[209] *R. (on the application of Daly) v Secretary of State for the Home Department* [2001] 2 A.C. 532.

[210] *R. v Shayler* [2003] 1 A.C. 247, para.33.

[211] *R. (Mahmood) v Secretary of State for the Home Department* [2001] 1 W.L.R. 840, 857. See also, *R. v Secretary of State for the Home Department Ex p. Isiko* [2001] H.R.L.R. 15, paras 30–31.

[212] n.209, para.26.

[213] *R. v Ministry of Defence Ex p. Smith* [1996] Q.B. 517.

[214] *Smith and Grady v United Kingdom* (1999) 29 E.H.R.R. 493, para.138.

[215] n.209, para.26.

within the range of reasonable decisions. The proportionality test could, second, oblige the court to pay attention to the relative weight accorded to relevant interests, in a manner not generally done under the traditional approach to review. The proper intensity of review was, said Lord Steyn, guaranteed by the twin requirements that the limitation of the right was necessary in a democratic society, in the sense of meeting a pressing social need, and really was proportionate to the legitimate aim being pursued.[216]

Two points should be made by way of clarification concerning the standard of review articulated in *Daly*.

18–039   First, it is clear that the courts do substitute judgment on certain issues under the HRA. This is so in relation to the meaning of many of the Convention terms that arise before the courts pursuant to the HRA. Thus the courts decide for themselves what constitutes speech, an assembly or one of the plethora of other interpretative issues that arise under the legislation.[217] The *Daly* proportionality test will however apply as the standard of review in the paradigm case where the public authority argues that the restriction of a right was necessary in the interests of a democratic society on one of the grounds specified in the relevant article.

Second, there is no inconsistency in principle in having proportionality as a test for review, and recognising that deference/respect or a discretionary area of judgment will impact on how proportionality is applied in a particular case. The legal test to be applied as the standard of review, and the effect of deference/respect/discretionary area of judgment on the application of that standard, are distinct issues.

This is evident from decisions made by the Strasbourg Court itself. The legal test to be applied is that the limitation, which must relate to one of the legitimate grounds in the relevant article, is prescribed by law, and is necessary in a democratic society. Proportionality will be relevant when deciding whether the limitation really was necessary in a democratic society.[218] If it were not proportionate then it would not be deemed necessary. Proportionality will also be pertinent when deciding whether the burden imposed on the individual was excessive. For the Strasbourg Court, deference, cast in terms of the margin of appreciation, will come into play in deciding whether this legal test has been met or not.

These issues are also germane when our courts make decisions under the HRA. The legal test to be applied is laid down in *Daly*. Lord Steyn explicitly recognised the link between proportionality and the decision as to whether the restriction was necessary in a democratic society. Deference, insofar as the courts choose to accord it on the facts of a particular case, will be germane when deciding on the application of this legal test. It will be taken into account within the three stages of the proportionality inquiry. The classic formulation is whether the measure was necessary to achieve the

---

[216] n.209, para.27.
[217] See, e.g., *Secretary of State for the Home Department v JJ* [2008] 1 All E.R. 613; *Secretary of State for the Home Department v E* [2008] 1 All E.R. 699.
[218] D. Feldman, "Proportionality and the Human Rights Act 1998", in E. Ellis (ed), *The Principle of Proportionality in the Laws of Europe* (Hart, 1999), 117–144.

desired objective, whether it was suited to doing so, and whether it nonetheless imposed excessive burdens on the individual.[219]

D. Proportionality under the HRA: The Role of the Court and the Initial Decision-Maker

Daly therefore established proportionality as the test for review. The precise role of the courts in the proportionality analysis has however been the subject of discussion in subsequent cases in the House of Lords, notably in *Denbigh*,[220] *Huang*,[221] and *Miss Behavin' Ltd*.[222] It is important to disaggregate a number of related issues that affect this inquiry. **18–040**

i. The court makes the final determination concerning proportionality

This may sound like a statement of the obvious, but it is nonetheless worth clearing the ground by making this point clear: it is for the reviewing court to make the ultimate decision as to whether the impugned action violates the proportionality principle. Thus as Lord Bingham stated in *Denbigh* proportionality must be judged objectively by the court.[223] This was echoed by Lord Hoffmann, Lord Mance and Lord Neuberger in *Miss Behavin'*, who made it clear that it was for the court to decide whether the challenged action infringed a Convention right, including in this respect the proportionality analysis.[224] We see the same point at work more generally in the insistence in *Denbigh* and *Miss Behavin'* that the key consideration is not whether the initial decision-maker properly considered the rights-based issue, but whether the substantive result reached was in accord with Convention rights, including in this respect proportionality.[225] **18–041**

ii. The weight accorded to the view of the initial decision-maker: prior categorization

The fact that the ultimate decision as to compliance with proportionality resides with the court does not however tell us in itself how much weight will be accorded to the view of the initial decision-maker when the court is making its ultimate decision. This issue is itself one for the ordinary courts to decide. It will properly be for the ordinary courts to determine how far **18–042**

---

[219] In *Daly*, n.209, para.27, Lord Steyn relied on the formulation of Lord Clyde in *de Freitas v Permanent Secretary of Ministry of Agriculture, Fisheries and Housing* [1999] 1 A.C. 69, 80. Lord Clyde formulated the three-part test in terms of whether the objective was sufficiently important to justify limiting a fundamental right, whether the measures designed to achieve the objective were rationally connected to it, and whether the means used to impair the right were no more than necessary to accomplish the objective.

[220] *R. (on the application of Begum) v Denbigh High School Governors* [2007] 1 A.C. 100.

[221] *Huang*, n.206. See also, *Machado v Secretary of State for the Home Department* [2005] EWCA Civ 597.

[222] *Belfast City Council v Miss Behavin' Ltd* [2007] 1 W.L.R. 1420.

[223] *Denbigh*, n.220, para.30.

[224] *Miss Behavin'*, n.222, paras 13, 44, 88.

[225] *Denbigh*, n.220, paras 28, 29, 31, 68; *Miss Behavin'*, n.222, paras 13–14, 31, 44, 88, 89.

the views of the initial decision-maker should be taken into account in this respect.

The courts may approach this task by distinguishing different types of case, to which different standards of proportionality review are applicable. These differential standards will be indicative, inter alia, of the weight to be attached to the views of the primary decision-maker. Consider in this respect the following categories that are commonly found in legal systems that use proportionality as a test for review.

The *courts might decide in certain instances that they should undertake de novo the relevant inquiry*. The courts in such instances make the decision as if they were the initial or primary decision-maker and substitute their judgment on the relevant issue. The breadth of the *de novo* inquiry will be for the court to determine. It can in theory extend to factual, legal and discretionary issues. How far it extends will depend in part on the rationale for this extensive judicial oversight, which might be the importance of the subject matter, the nature of the particular legislative scheme, or structural defects in the initial decision-making process. Where this form of judicial oversight is felt to be appropriate the reviewing court may, for example, decide for itself the proportionality calculus attendant upon breach of a Convention right.

This can be exemplified by *Huang*.[226] It is important to recognise that the case was concerned with appeal rather judicial review, and with the respective roles of bodies concerned with immigration decisions. The issue before the House of Lords was the role to be played by appellate immigration authorities when hearing appeals on ECHR grounds against a decision of the primary decision-maker refusing leave to enter or remain in the UK under the Immigration and Asylum Act 1999. Lord Bingham, giving judgment for the House of Lords, held that the best interpretation of the empowering legislation was that the appellate immigration authority should not merely exercise a secondary reviewing function, in order to decide whether the primary decision-maker acted irrationally or contrary to procedural propriety. The appellate immigration authority should rather decide for itself whether the impugned decision was lawful or not.[227]

18–043   It is clear from Lord Bingham's judgment that he regarded the appellate immigration authorities as deciding the relevant issue *de novo*, or something closely proximate thereto. Thus the appellate immigration authority was to establish the relevant facts for itself, in the light of circumstances that might well have changed since the initial decision. The appellate immigration authority was regarded as better placed than the primary decision-maker to investigate the facts, test the evidence and the genuineness of the applicant's concerns about return to her country.[228] It was then for the appellate immigration authority in the light of these facts to consider and weigh the

[226] *Huang*, n.206.
[227] *Huang*, n.206, para.11.
[228] *Huang*, n.206, para.15.

factors that could affect whether the refusal of leave to enter or remain in the UK was compatible with Convention rights.[229]

A more common approach is for the courts to adopt a strict form of judicial review. This is the traditional approach in rights-based cases. The court inquires whether the limitation placed on the right is really necessary, often, but not always, demanding that it be the least restrictive in all the circumstances, and if it is not then it is deemed to be disproportionate. The extent to which weight will be accorded to the views of the initial decision-maker in reaching this conclusion will be explored below. Suffice it to say for the present that while review according to this standard is searching and intensive it does not preclude the court from taking account of the views of the initial decision-maker when deciding whether this version of the proportionality test is met or not.

It is also common for legal systems that adopt proportionality to accord it a different meaning in those cases where the initial decision is concerned with discretionary social and economic choices. In such instances the initial decision will often only be overturned if it can be shown to be manifestly disproportionate, as exemplified by the jurisprudence of the ECJ considered in the following chapter. Where it is accorded this meaning it will still be for the reviewing court to decide whether the initial decision meets proportionality interpreted in this manner. The views of the initial decision-maker will perforce be of considerable importance in making this determination, since the test demands that the claimant shows that the initial decision was manifestly disproportionate.

It is therefore readily apparent that the judicial determination to accord proportionality a distinctive meaning for different types of case will necessarily have implications for the weight attached to the views of the initial decision-maker. The different standards of proportionality review are themselves reflective of a prior judicial determination that has implications as to how far the views of the primary decision-maker should be of relevance when the court makes its decision as to whether the test for review is met on the facts of the case.

iii. The weight to be accorded to the view of the initial decision-maker: the HRA

We can now move forward to understand the difficulties that beset resolution of this issue in relation to decisions made under the HRA. The nature of this difficulty can be explicated here and explained in more detail below. A legal system may well opt for prior categorisation in the manner set out above and decide that, for example, HRA cases should be subject to a strict form of proportionality review. However the variety of cases that can arise as rights-based determinations may nonetheless lead the courts to accord

18–044

---

[229] *Huang*, n.206, paras 11, 13, 16.

different degrees of weight to the views of the initial decision-maker in different types of case. Thus as Baroness Hale stated,[230]

> "The concept of what may be 'necessary in a democratic society' has to take into account the comparative importance of the right infringed in the scale of rights protected. What may be a proportionate interference with a less important right might be a disproportionate interference with a more important right. The concept of what is 'necessary in a democratic society' also has to accommodate the differing importance attached to certain values in different member states."

The extent to which the courts are willing to accord some discretionary area of judgment to the initial decision-maker will be a key factor in this respect. Prior categorisation will therefore only get you so far, and will only tell you so much, about the extent to which the views of the initial decision-maker should be taken into account; there may still be latitude for differences in this respect *within* a particular category, as well as *between* categories. It is clear from the courts' judgments that a number of factors are taken into account in deciding on the discretionary area of judgment accorded to the primary decision-maker. These factors are taken into account when applying the proportionality test. They include the nature of the Convention right, the extent to which the issues require consideration of social, political and economic factors, the extent to which the court has expertise, whether the rights claimed are of especial importance, the democratic status of the primary decision-maker, and the nature of the subject matter area in which the decision has been taken.[231] The point made in this paragraph can now be explained more fully with the help of the case law.

It is clear that our courts have made a judicial choice in favour of searching scrutiny under the HRA. They have adopted Lord Steyn's view of proportionality as articulated in *Daly*.[232] The intensity of review is, as noted by Lord Bingham in *Denbigh*,[233] more searching than that previously applicable under the heightened *Wednesbury* test. We have moreover already seen judicial statements in HRA cases that it is for the court to make the decision about proportionality in accord with this test.[234] We have therefore a clear articulation of the type of strict proportionality scrutiny to be applied in this type of case, combined with judicial affirmation that it is the court that will make that ultimate determination.

18–045   This does not however preclude the court from according weight to the views of the primary decision-maker, even within the framework of this version of the proportionality test. This is exemplified by *Denbigh*. A school banned the wearing of Muslim dress in the form of the jilbab, while allowing

---

[230] *Countryside Alliance*, n.198, para.124.
[231] *Samaroo*, n.203; *Farrakhan*, n.203; *Ponting*, n.208; *Langley v Liverpool City Council* [2005] EWCA Civ 1173; *Miss Behavin'*, n.222; *Denbigh*, n.220; *Countryside Alliance*, n.198.
[232] *Daly*, n.209.
[233] *Denbigh*, n.220, para.30.
[234] See above nn.223–225.

a different form of Muslim dress, the shalwar kameeze. It was argued that this constituted an infringement of art.9 ECHR, safeguarding freedom of religion. The House of Lords held, inter alia, that the school ban on the jilbab was proportionate within the framework of the *Daly* test. Their Lordships made the ultimate decision on proportionality, but took account of the school's views on the dress code that was most appropriate for their pupils. Thus Lord Bingham noted that different schools had different uniform policies, influenced by the composition of their student population and each school had to decide what uniform would best serve its wider educational purposes.[235] Lord Hoffmann applied the proportionality analysis in accord with the discretionary area of judgment applicable to the circumstances of the case: Parliament had left the decision about uniforms to individual schools and it was the school that was best placed to weigh and consider the factors that should influence its particular choice of uniform.[236] For Baroness Hale the school's choice of dress code was devised to meet the social conditions prevailing in that area at that time and was a proportionate response to the need to balance social cohesion and religious diversity.[237]

The same point can be exemplified in relation to *Miss Behavin'*. A local authority decided pursuant to statutory licensing powers that the appropriate number of licensed sex shops in a particular locality should be nil. The claimant argued that this decision infringed the right of free speech protected by art.10 ECHR. The House of Lords found against the claimant. In relation to the proportionality analysis, Lord Hoffmann emphasised that the key issue was whether the local authority's action infringed the Convention right, not the reasoning process that it adopted. He nonetheless held that the licensing of sex shops was an area of social control in which the Strasbourg Court accorded Member States a wide margin of appreciation and that this translated at domestic level to a broad power of judgment entrusted to local authorities; provided that the local authority exercised that power rationally and in accord with the statute, it would require unusual facts for it to amount to a disproportionate restriction on Convention rights.[238] Baroness Hale held that when the court was deciding whether there was a breach of Convention rights, it was bound to acknowledge that the local authority was much better placed than the court to decide whether the right of sex shop owners to sell pornography should be restricted for the protection of the rights of others or the protection of health and morals. It would therefore be difficult for the court to overturn that balance when it had been made expressly by the local authority. Where there was no indication that the local authority had undertaken that balance, the court had no alternative but to strike the balance itself, but even then it would give due weight to the "judgments made by those who are in much closer touch with the people

---

[235] *Denbigh*, n.220, para.33.
[236] *Denbigh*, n.220, paras 63–65.
[237] *Denbigh*, n.220, paras 97–98.
[238] *Miss Behavin'*, n.222, para.16.

and the places involved than the court could ever be".[239] Lord Mance took a similar view. He held that it was for the court itself to assess the proportionality of the challenged decision,[240] and then considered the inter-relationship between this precept and judicial recognition of a discretionary area of judgment afforded to the initial decision-maker. The existence of this area of judgment necessarily meant, said Lord Mance, that there could be decisions "which a court would regard as proportionate, whichever way they went".[241] Where however the decision-maker had not addressed its mind to Convention values then the court would be deprived of its considered opinion on Convention issues, with the consequence that he, like Baroness Hale, concluded that the court would have to strike the balance for itself, but nonetheless "giving due weight to such judgments as were made by the primary decision-maker on matters he or it did consider".[242] Lord Neuberger reasoned in a similar manner.[243]

iv. Conclusion

18–046   The following conclusion can be drawn. The court will make the ultimate decision on whether there has been a breach of a Convention right, including the proportionality issue which is integral to the final decision as to whether there has been a violation of the relevant Convention right. The proportionality analysis will be undertaken in accord with Lord Steyn's approach in *Daly*.

It will however still be open for the reviewing court to give weight to the views of the primary decision-maker insofar it believes that they should be accorded some deference/respect, or that the issue falls within the primary decision-maker's discretionary area of judgment.

The weight given by the court to the view of the primary decision-maker will also be influenced by the extent to which the latter addressed Convention issues when it made its deliberation, as is evident from the reasoning of Baroness Hale, Lord Mance and Lord Neuberger in *Miss Behavin'*. Thus while the House of Lords in *Denbigh* and subsequent cases disapproved of the process approach articulated by Brooke L.J. in the Court of Appeal in *Denbigh*,[244] it is nonetheless clear that there will be a greater likelihood of the public body's decision being regarded as proportionate if it consciously addressed the Convention issues when making its decision. In that sense, while the House of Lords rejected Brooke L.J.'s formulaic process-based approach, a public body would still be advised that the chances of its

---

[239] *Miss Behavin'*, n.222, para.37.
[240] *Miss Behavin'*, n.222, para.44.
[241] *Miss Behavin'*, n.222, para.46.
[242] *Miss Behavin'*, n.222, para.47.
[243] *Miss Behavin'*, n.222, para.91.
[244] *R. (on the application of Begum) v Denbigh High School Governors* [2005] 1 W.L.R. 3372, para.81.

decision being treated as proportionate will be greater if it has addressed a number of the issues articulated by Brooke L.J.[245]

E. The Standard of Review: The Academic Debate

There has been considerable academic commentary on proportionality and the HRA,[246] and more generally on the concept of deference.[247] It is not possible within the confines of this chapter to do justice to all of the varied positions staked out in this rich literature. The discussion will therefore focus on some of the principal contending lines of argument.

18–047

i. Constitutional and institutional competence

Jowell has articulated an important distinction between constitutional and institutional competence that has been influential in the subsequent debates.[248] He argued that while it was legitimate for courts in certain

18–048

[245] See also, R. Gordon, "Structures or Mantras? Some New Puzzles in HRA Decision-Making" [2006] J.R. 136.

[246] D. Feldman, "Proportionality and the Human Rights Act 1998", in E. Ellis (ed.), *The Principle of Proportionality in the Laws of Europe* (Hart, 1999), 117–144; J. Jowell, "Beyond the Rule of Law: Towards Constitutional Judicial Review" [2000] P.L. 671; M. Elliott, "The Human Rights Act 1998 and the Standard of Substantive Review" [2001] C.L.J. 301; R. Clayton, "Regaining a Sense of Proportion: The Human Rights Act and the Proportionality Principle" [2001] E.H.R.L.R. 504; I Leigh, "Taking Rights Proportionately: Judicial Review, the Human Rights Act and Strasbourg" [2002] P.L. 265; M. Fordham and T. de la Mare, "Identifying the Principles of Proportionality, in J. Jowell and J. Cooper (eds), n.14, 27–89; S. Attrill, "Keeping the Executive in the Picture: A Reply to Professor Leigh" [2003] P.L. 41; Lord Woolf, "On the Occasion of the Opening of the Judicial Year at the European Court of Human Rights", January 23, 2003, 3–4; Lord Irvine, "The Human Rights Act Two Years On: An Analysis", November 1, 2002, 6–9; C. Knight, "Proportionality, the Decision-maker and the House of Lords" [2007] J.R. 221.

[247] Dyzenhaus, n.3; P. Craig, "The Courts, the Human Rights Act and Judicial Review" (2001) 117 L.Q.R. 589; R. Edwards, "Judicial Deference and the Human Rights Act" (2002) 65 M.L.R. 859; Lord Hoffmann, "Separation of Powers" [2002] J.R. 137; J. Jowell, "Judicial Deference and Human Rights: A Question of Competence", in P. Craig and R. Rawlings (eds), *Law and Administration in Europe, Essays in Honour of Carol Harlow* (Oxford University Press, 2003), Ch.4; J. Jowell, "Judicial Deference: Servility, Civility or Institutional Capacity" [2003] P.L. 592; F. Klug, "Judicial Deference under the Human Rights Act 1998" [2003] E.H.R.L.R. 125; M. Hunt, "Sovereignty's Blight: Why Contemporary Public Law Needs the Concept of 'Due Deference'", in N. Bamforth and P. Leyland (eds), *Public Law in a Multi-Layered Constitution* (Hart, 2003), Ch.13; T. Allan, "Common Law Reason and the Limits of Judicial Deference", in D. Dyzenhaus (ed.), *The Unity of Public Law* (Hart, 2004), Ch.11; L. Tremblay, "The Legitimacy of Judicial Review: The Limits of Dialogue Between Courts and Legislatures" (2005) 3 I-CON 617; R. Clayton, "Judicial Deference and 'Democratic Dialogue': The Legitimacy of Judicial Intervention under the Human Rights Act" [2004] P.L. 33; Lord Steyn, "Deference: A Tangled Story" [2005] P.L. 346; T. Hickman, "Constitutional Dialogue, Constitutional Theories and the Human Rights Act" [2005] P.L. 306; D. Nicol, "Law and Politics after the Human Rights Act" [2006] P.L. 722; T. Allan, "Human Rights and Judicial Review: A Critique of 'Due Deference'" [2006] C.L.J. 671; Lord Justice Dyson, "Some Thoughts on Judicial Deference" [2006] J.R. 103; R. Clayton, "Principles for Judicial Deference" [2006] J.R. 109; M. Beloff, "The Concept of 'Deference in Public Law'" [2006] J.R. 213; T. Poole, "The Reformation of English Administrative Law", LSE Working Papers 12/2007; T. Hickman, "The Courts and Politics after the Human Rights Act: A Comment" [2008] P.L. 84; J. King, "Three Approaches to Judicial Restraint", forthcoming.

[248] Jowell, "Judicial Deference and Human Rights", n.247.

instances to defer to the legislature or executive on grounds of institutional competence, they should not do so on the mistaken belief that they lacked constitutional competence.[249]

> "Institutional competence refers to the *capacity* of a body to make the relevant decision. The question asked is whether the court's structures and procedures equip it to decide the matter better than the body being reviewed. Factors to be taken into account in answering this question include the respective expertise of the two institutions, access to information and so on. *Constitutional competence*, on the other hand refers to the *authority* of the body to decide the relevant question. The question asked is whether the body is authorized to take the relevant decision under the constitutive rules and principles which allocate decision-making power to bodies (including the courts) exercising public functions in a democracy."

It is central to this thesis that democracy is conceived in terms of individual rights as well as majority rule, with the courts being accorded the task of delineating the boundaries of legislative and executive power in a rights-based democracy.[250] Under the HRA regime, Jowell argues that the courts should not be regarded as constitutionally disabled from making difficult decisions in relation to Convention rights, nor should they in any sense be constitutionally required to defer to Parliament or the executive on such matters.[251] Jowell nonetheless accepts that there may well be reasons of institutional competence, such as lack of expertise, lack of investigative techniques, or limits to the adversarial process, that would justify the courts deferring to the legislature or executive on a particular matter.[252] Three comments can be made about this thesis.

First, the distinction between constitutional and institutional competence is important and Jowell must surely be right to insist that the courts should not defer on the former ground. The very nature of the HRA regime, which is itself embodied in an Act of Parliament, legitimates rights-based judicial review undertaken by the courts to ensure that legislative and executive action is in accord with Convention rights. It follows that there should not be any "islands of immunity" which are regarded as off limits on the alleged ground that the courts are not constitutionally competent to undertake any form of judicial review.

Second, courts and commentators alike may nonetheless disagree as to whether there are institutional features that justify deference or a discretionary area of judgment in a particular case. This is inevitable given the nature of the institutional features listed above and the range of rights that are protected by the ECHR. We should however press a little further to understand the nature of this disagreement.

---

[249] Jowell, n.247, 73. Italics in the original.
[250] Jowell, n.247, 74.
[251] Jowell, n.247, 74–75, 80.
[252] Jowell, n.247, 80–81.

Thus there may be agreement that expertise or the limits of the adversarial process are relevant institutional factors to be taken into account in deciding whether to defer, but courts or commentators may differ as to the application of such factors in a particular case, or they may differ as to how much deference is warranted in the light of such factors.

There may also be disagreement as to whether a particular factor should **18–049** "count" as going to institutional competence at all, and if so how much it should count. Perhaps the most difficult issue in this respect is the fact that the meaning of rights may often be controversial, in the sense that there is often room for reasonable disagreement as to how rights should be interpreted in any particular instance.[253] Whether and to what extent this should be regarded as a factor that can legitimately be taken into account under the guise of institutional competence is itself contestable. We need to tread carefully here. If the very fact that the interpretation of rights can often be contestable were to be regarded as a reason in and of itself for deferring to the executive or legislature then we would in effect be admitting a concept of constitutional competence by the back door, and generally disabling the courts from performing the very task assigned to them by the HRA. That would neither be warranted nor desirable.[254] We should at the same time be wary of veering too far in the opposite direction and disregard the contestability of rights interpretation in adjudication under the HRA. It should be a legitimate, but not determinative, consideration in deciding whether to overturn the considered view of the legislature or the executive as to how to balance the demands of conflicting rights, or the meaning to be accorded to a particular right. This is more especially so since, as is apparent from adjudication under the HRA, there is often significant disagreement even within the courts on such matters.

Third, the difficulties posed by substantive rights adjudication may however be alleviated to some degree by placing proper emphasis on the procedural dimension of such claims. Hunt[255] and Clayton[256] have both emphasised this aspect of rights-based claims. The defendant, whether it is in relation to legislation or an executive act, should be required to give a properly reasoned explanation as to why it adopted the challenged act. This facilitates subsequent judicial review. It enables the courts to apply the proportionality analysis more fully cognizant of the factors that played into the contested decision, and allows the court to evaluate the evidentiary basis of those reasons.[257]

The importance of reasoned justification within the HRA is exemplified

---

[253] J. Waldron, *Law and Disagreement* (Oxford University Press, 1999).
[254] *RJR McDonald v Canada Attorney General* [1995] S.C.R. 199, paras 135–136, McLachlin J.
[255] Hunt, "Sovereignty's Blight", n.247.
[256] Clayton, "Principles for Judicial Deference", n.247.
[257] A reading of the leading cases on, for example, arts 8–11 reveals the close attention paid by the ECtHR to the reasons given by the national authorities to determine whether they could be said to meet the criterion of pressing social need. Many cases are decided at this point, with the ECtHR deciding that the reasons advanced by the state do not suffice to show a pressing social need

by *Ponting*.[258] The claimant, who was a prisoner, was pursuing various legal actions, and argued, inter alia, that a prison rule that limited his use of a computer to the evening violated his right of access to court, in breach of art.6 ECHR. The rationale for the prison rule was that a prisoner had to be available for work during the day, but the claimant was not in fact employed within the prison at that time, and argued that, in any event, three hours access to the computer was too limited. Schiemann L.J. and Arden L.J. upheld the rule as proportionate, given the margin of discretion accorded to the prison authorities in respect of running the prison.[259] Clarke L.J. also accepted that the prison governor had a discretionary area of judgment, but held that it was incumbent on him to provide the evidence explaining his reasons, since "in the absence of such evidence, it is difficult if not impossible for the court to carry out the intensity of review referred to by Lord Steyn".[260] Clarke L.J. concluded that, even taking account of the governor's discretionary area of judgment, he had not provided sufficient evidence of the reasons for the blanket refusal to allow a prisoner to work on a computer during the day. Clarke L.J. felt that the limitation was therefore disproportionate and hence unlawful. *Daly* was explicitly premised on the assumption that proportionality would require the courts to consider the balance struck by the decision-maker, not merely whether it was within the range of reasonable decisions, and that it would oblige the court to pay attention to the relative weight accorded to relevant interests, in a manner not generally done under the traditional approach to review. Where the procedural component of deference is generously interpreted in favour of the primary decision-maker the court may, as Clarke L.J. stated,[261] lack the evidence that is essential for more intensive proportionality review.

ii. Democratic dialogue

18–050 Another strand of the academic literature emphasises the notion of democratic dialogue between courts, legislature and executive within the HRA.[262] It is clear that the concept of democratic dialogue can bear different meanings both generally and when applied to a regime such as the HRA.[263] The following discussion will focus on the concept of democratic dialogue within the confines of the HRA. It may be helpful to disaggregate a number of related points.

First, an element of democratic dialogue is built into the HRA through ss.3 and 4. If the court feels unable to interpret the contested legislation so as to be compatible with Convention rights then it issues a declaration of incompatibility. This does not affect the validity of the legislation and it is

---

[258] *Ponting*, n.208.
[259] *Ponting*, n.208, paras 36, 113–115.
[260] *Ponting*, n.208, para.80.
[261] *Ponting*, n.208, para.80.
[262] Clayton, "Judicial Deference and 'Democratic Dialogue'", n.247; Clayton, "Principles for Judicial Deference", n.247; Hickman, "Constitutional Dialogue", n.247.
[263] Hickman, "Constitutional Dialogue", n.247.

for Parliament to decide whether to amend the legislation so as to render it compatible with Convention rights. This can be regarded in dialogic terms: the courts proffer an interpretation of the challenged legislation that is found to be incompatible with Convention rights, which is the catalyst for Parliament to rethink its initial view embodied in the original legislation and modify it in the light of the court's judgment. Clayton, speaking of democratic dialogue, states,[264]

> "The value of the concept is that it draws attention to a critical structural feature of the HRA. It articulates the fact that a judicial pronouncement routinely prompts a response from those whose decision is being reviewed. The need for courts to defer to Parliament or the executive is less compelling once it is acknowledged that the HRA envisages that the other branches of government will have a second bite of the cherry."

Second, we should however be careful about the *opportunities* for democratic dialogue contained in this structural reading of the HRA. In relation to primary legislation, Parliament will only be accorded a second bite of the cherry if the court makes a declaration of incompatibility under s.4 HRA. If the court chooses to give a broad interpretation to s.3 HRA, and to regard this as the primary remedial mechanism with resort being had to s.4 HRA in relatively rare cases, then Parliament will simply not have the opportunity to respond. It is true that Parliament will always have the possibility of enacting new legislation if it so chooses, which is expressive of a different view than that contained in the court's original judgment. This does not however alter the substance of the point being made here, which is that in structural terms dialogue of the kind being envisioned is premised on Parliament having the opportunity within the framework of the HRA to respond to the judicial decision. This limit on democratic dialogue is even more apparent in relation to court decisions made under s.6 HRA. There is, subject to s.6(2) HRA, nothing equivalent to s.4 HRA. Thus once the court finds that the challenged action is contrary to Convention rights it is deemed illegal under s.6 HRA, with no opportunity for the other branch of government to have a second bite of the cherry within the framework of the HRA. To be sure the judicial finding may prompt another branch of government to rethink the policy that led to the challenge; it might alternatively be the catalyst for new legislative action. This does not alter the nature of the point being made, which is that the HRA provides no institutionalised mechanism for other branches of government to respond to determinations made pursuant to s.6.

Third, even where there are opportunities for democratic dialogue it is equally important to be mindful about the *nature* of this dialogue. This is apparent from the debate concerning democratic dialogue in Canada. The idea of democratic dialogue has been developed in the Canadian jurisprudence and has been deployed to measure legislative responses to

[264] Clayton, "Principles for Judicial Deference", n.247, 125.

judicial decisions under the Canadian Charter.[265] There has however been debate about what constitutes democratic dialogue, with some contending that legislative repeal of the offending enactment should not count as dialogue for these purposes,[266] while others object more generally that dialogue theory makes no attempt to assess matters qualitatively, but simply identifies legislative responses, whatsoever they may be.[267] Dialogue theory has also been challenged on grounds relating to the very nature of the envisioned dialogue.[268] Thus it has been argued that the proponents of dialogue theory conceive of it as one in which the court is free to interpret the Charter, with the "legislature required to adopt the court's interpretation and act within such parameters as the Court allows".[269] It has been argued that this is not dialogue, but "top–down constitutionalism",[270] to be contrasted with a vision of democratic dialogue in which the court would respect and be influenced by the legislature's interpretation of the Canadian Charter.

iii. A critique of deference

18–051   It is fitting to end with a general critique of a doctrine of deference advanced by Allan,[271] who takes issue with Hunt. The latter argued that adjudication under the Human Rights Act should be informed by a concept of due deference, the essence of which was that judicial non-interference with legislative or executive decisions had to be earned or justified by the primary decision-maker openly demonstrating the justifications for the decisions they reached and demonstrating why those decisions were worthy of curial respect.[272]

Allan is however unhappy with any "doctrine" of deference, and deprecates judicial attempts, such as those of Laws L.J.,[273] to adumbrate principles to guide the extent to which deference will be accorded. Allan moreover rejects the idea that the courts should be swayed by the greater expertise or democratic credentials of the primary decision-maker, seeing such factors as external to the intrinsic quality of the decision that is under review. He accepts that the courts should cede to Parliament and government an appropriate sphere of decision-making protected from judicial interference,

---

[265] P. Hogg and A. Bushell, "The *Charter* Dialogue between Courts and Legislatures (or perhaps the Charter isn't such a bad thing after all)" (1997) 35 Osgoode Hall L.J. 75; P. Hogg, A. Bushell-Thornton, and W. Wright, "*Charter* Dialogue Revisited—Or 'Much Ado About Metaphors'" (2007) 45 Osgoode Hall L.J. 51.

[266] C. Manfredi and J. Kelly, "Six Degrees of Dialogue: a response to Hogg and Bushell" (1999) 37 Osgoode Hall L.J. 513; P. Hogg and A. Thornton, "Reply to Six Dialogues" (1999) 37 Osgoode Hall L.J. 529.

[267] G. Huscroft, "Rationalizing Judicial Power: The Mischief of Dialogue Theory" (2008), available at *http://ssrn.com/abstract=1083685*.

[268] G. Huscroft, "Constitutionalism from the Top Down" (2007) 45 Osgoode Hall L.J. 91; A. Petter, "Taking Dialogue Theory Much Too Seriously (Or Perhaps *Charter* Dialogue Isn't Such a Good Thing After All)," (2007) 45 Osgoode Hall L.J. 147; Huscroft, n.267.

[269] Huscroft, n.267, 2.

[270] n.268.

[271] Allan, "Human Rights and Judicial Review", n.247.

[272] Hunt, "Sovereignty's Blight", n.247.

[273] *Roth*, n.60, paras 83–87.

but insists that the boundaries of that sphere must be determined by the circumstances of the particular case, with the consequence that judges should defer only to the extent that the reasons proffered are persuasive. For Allan, a doctrine of due deference is therefore regarded as either empty or pernicious.[274]

> "It is empty if it purports to implement a separation of powers between the courts and other branches of government; that separation is independently secured by the proper application of legal principles defining the scope of individual rights or the limits of public powers. A doctrine of deference is pernicious if, forsaking the separation of powers, correctly conceived, it permits the abdication of judicial responsibility in favour of reliance on the good faith or good sense or special expertise of public officials, whose judgments about the implications of rights in specific cases may well be wrong. . . . . A judge who allows his own views on the merits of any aspect of the case to be displaced by the contrary view of public officials—bowing to their greater expertise or experience or democratic credentials—forfeits the neutrality that underpins the legitimacy of constitutional adjudication."

A number of comments can be made about Allan's argument. First, there is a sense in which he is attacking a straw man. He is undoubtedly correct that deference should not be regarded as some trump, such that the mere mention of "democratic credential" leads the court to refrain from judicial review, or accept without more the view taken by the legislature or executive. It is however difficult to see who maintains such a position. This is not the view taken by Hunt, who makes it manifestly clear that any deference has to be earned by the nature of the reasons advanced by the primary decision-maker, whether that is the legislature or the executive. Nor is it the view generally taken by the courts when they have used concepts such as deference or discretionary area of judgment. Now it may well be the case that a particular commentator may question whether the court that took account of such reasons proffered by the legislature or the executive reached the correct conclusion. That is however inevitable given the subject matter of rights adjudication.

Second, Allan disaggregates the intrinsic quality of the decision reached from "external factors" concerning the status of the primary decision-maker, repeatedly iterating that a bad decision in terms of human rights cannot be cured by the good intentions, expertise or democratic credentials of the primary decision-maker. Now it is certainly true that the courts have made it clear in cases such as *Denbigh* or *Miss Behavin'* that the status or procedural rectitude of the primary decision-maker will not save a decision that is substantively defective. That is correct as a matter of principle. Those cases however also demonstrate that in deciding whether there is an infringement of rights at all, deference or respect should, where appropriate,

---

[274] Allan, "Human Rights and Judicial Review", n.247. 675–676.

be accorded to the primary decision-maker. In that sense the decisions reveal the inevitable connection between the quality of the contested decision and the status of the primary decision-maker. This is in accord with the more general case law in this area. The most common rationale for affording some deference or respect is that the legislature has made a choice concerning the meaning to be given to a particular right. This may well be contestable, but this may also be true of such decisions reached by the courts, since we often disagree about the detailed implications of rights. The fact that it is the democratically elected legislature that has made the initial considered choice is certainly not determinative of its legality, but nor is it something external to the intrinsic quality of the decision.

Third, Allan's view allows scant room for regard to be given to the considered views of either the executive or the legislature in the determination of whether an infringement of rights has occurred. Thus while he states that courts should defer to the extent to which they find the reasons proffered persuasive, he also makes it clear, as in the preceding quotation, that a judge who allows any aspect of his view to be displaced on the ground of superior expertise, experience or democratic credentials forfeits the neutrality of constitutional adjudication. On this reading the reasons given by the legislature of executive would only be found persuasive if the court would, in any event, have come to the same conclusion itself if it were the primary decision-maker. Allan believes that this is demanded by the separation of powers properly conceived. Space precludes any detailed unpacking of that premise. Suffice it to say for the present that a differing view is possible. It is not in my view contrary to the rule of law or separation of powers for a court to accord respect to the reasoned choice as to the meaning of a particular right expressed in legislation, even if the individual judges might not have made that choice if they had been the primary decision-makers. This does not mean that the relevant legislation will survive scrutiny. The courts might, for example, still conclude that the legislation was discriminatory, or otherwise contrary to Convention rights. To accord respect to the legislative determination does not mean submission,[275] nor does it entail judicial abdication of responsibility. It is reflective of the contested nature of rights' determinations, and a judicial willingness to consider seriously the interpretation given to a right by the democratic branch of government.

6. Rights: The EC Dimension

18–052 An individual may derive rights from Community law and these rights will be capable of being used, inter alia, to challenge primary legislation, discretionary decisions or governmental action inconsistent with them.

---

[275] Dyzenhaus, n.247.

It should be made clear that a breach of EC law will suffice as a ground for challenge for illegality in a judicial review action, irrespective of whether the rule that has been broken concerns fundamental rights. A breach of an agricultural regulation by national authorities will, for example, serve as a ground for judicial review of national measures that are inconsistent with that regulation.

The remainder of this discussion will be concerned with the ways in which EC law might avail an individual in cases concerned with rights of the kind found in the ECHR, or normally included in constitutional documents. There are a number of ways in which such rights can be derived from EC law.

A. Legislative Competence and Human Rights

The EC has a growing legislative competence in the field of human rights. Article 6 of the Treaty of European Union provides that the "Union is founded on the principles of liberty, democracy, respect for human rights and fundamental freedoms and the rule of law, principles which are common to the laws of the Member States".

18–053

Specific legislative competence is found in the addition of art.13 EC, which provides that the Community legislature may, within the limits of the Community's powers, take "appropriate action to combat discrimination based on sex, racial or ethnic origin, religion or belief, disability, age or sexual orientation". This Article does not in and of itself ban such discrimination, but it does empower the Community to adopt measures to combat such discrimination within the scope of the powers otherwise granted in the Treaty. When such measures, on for example race, are enacted they will be capable of being relied upon by individuals within their national courts, assuming that the measures are sufficiently certain and precise.[276]

B. Rights and Direct Effect

Individuals can gain rights from the provisions of the Treaty or norms made thereunder via the concept of direct effect. This concept has been described above,[277] and has been applied to an increasing number of Community norms. Certain directly effective Treaty provisions deal with subject matter that would undoubtedly merit inclusion in any list of constitutional or fundamental rights.

18–054

An obvious example is art.141 EC, which is concerned with equal pay and gender discrimination. This was held to be directly effective in the seminal

---

[276] Council Directive 2000/78/EC of November 27, 2000, Establishing a General Framework for Equal Treatment in Employment and Occupation [2000] O.J. L303/16; Council Directive 2000/43/EC of June 29, 2000, Implementing the Principle of Equal Treatment between Persons Irrespective of Racial or Ethnic Origin [2000] O.J. L180/22.

[277] See, Ch.10.

case of *Defrenne*.[278] Defrenne was employed as an air hostess with Sabena. She argued that her conditions of service were discriminatory, as compared with those of male cabin stewards who performed the same tasks. The ECJ held that art.119 as it then was had direct effect, in some cases at least, that Defrenne therefore derived rights from the Treaty and that these were enforceable against the airline. There have been many other similar cases.

C. Fundamental Rights

18–055   An individual may also make use of the Community concept of fundamental rights, which has been developed by the ECJ.[279] The original Treaty contained no list of traditional fundamental rights as such, in large part because the original rationale for the Treaty was principally economic. The initial catalyst for the creation of such rights was the threat of revolt by the courts of some Member States. Individuals who were dissatisfied with the provisions of, for example, a regulation would challenge it before their national court and contend that it was inconsistent with rights in their own national constitutions. They would moreover argue that these rights could not have been given away by the state when acceding to the Community.

This argument was made before the German courts in *Internationale Handelsgesellschaft*.[280] The threat this posed to the supremacy of Community law was not lost on the ECJ, and it stated that Community norms could not be challenged in this manner. However, in order to stem any possible national rebellion the ECJ declared that fundamental rights were indeed part of the general principles of Community law, and that the compatibility of a Community norm with such rights would be tested by the ECJ itself.[281]

The fundamental rights' doctrine has been used primarily as a way of attacking Community norms, such as regulations or decisions. It is, however, clear that national norms can also be challenged for compliance with fundamental rights in a number of different situations.[282] This will be so where Member States are applying provisions of Community law which based on the protection for human rights[283]; where they are enforcing Community rules on behalf of the Community or interpreting Community rules[284]; or where Member States are seeking to derogate from a requirement of Community law.[285]

It should be made clear that the supremacy doctrine will operate in such instances and national norms, including primary legislation, which are

---

[278] *Defrenne v Sabena* (43/75) [1976] E.C.R. 455.
[279] P. Craig and G. de Búrca, *EU Law, Text, Cases and Materials* (Oxford University Press, 4th edn, 2007), Ch.11.
[280] (11/70) [1970] E.C.R. 1125.
[281] (11/70) [1970] E.C.R. 1125, 1134.
[282] Craig and de Búrca, n.279, 395–402.
[283] *Johnston v Chief Constable of the Royal Ulster Constabulary* (222/84) [1986] E.C.R. 1651.
[284] *Wachauf v Germany* (5/88) [1989] E.C.R. 2609; *R. v Kent Kirk* 63/83) [1984] E.C.R. 2689.
[285] *Elliniki Radiophonia Tileorassi AE v Dimotki Etairia Pliroforissis and Sotirios Kouvelas* (C-260/89) [1991] E.C.R. I-2925; *Society for the Protection of Unborn Children Ireland Ltd v Grogan* (C-159/90) [1991] E.C.R. I-4685.

inconsistent with Community law will have to be altered. This jurisprudence is, therefore, of real importance in giving individuals protected rights, where the ultimate arbiter of the meaning of such rights is the ECJ and not national courts.

D. The EU Charter of Rights

There is also now an EU Charter of Fundamental Rights.[286] The immediate catalyst for the Charter came from the European Council. In June 1999 the Cologne European Council[287] decided that there should be a European Union Charter of Fundamental Rights to consolidate the fundamental rights applicable at Union Level. It was made clear that the document should include economic and social rights, as well as traditional civil and political rights.

18–056

The institutional structure for the discussions about the Charter was laid down in the Tampere European Council in October 1999.[288] It was decided to establish a body called the Convention. It consisted of representatives of the Member States, a member of the Commission, members of the European Parliament, and representatives from national Parliaments. The Convention was instructed to conclude its work in time for the Nice European Council in December 2000. The draft Charter was submitted on October 5, 2000,[289] and was considered at an informal meeting of the European Council at Biarritz on October 14, 2000.[290] The Charter was accepted, and this was reinforced at the Nice European Council.

The Charter includes a broad array of rights, including civil, political, social and economic rights. Chapter VII of the Charter contains important general provisions. Article 51(1) defines the scope of application of the Charter. It is addressed to the institutions and bodies of the Union with due regard to the principle of subsidiarity, and to Member States only when they are implementing Union law.

The Charter was drafted so as to be capable of being legally binding. The precise legal status of the Charter was left undecided in Nice, but was considered in detail at the Convention on the Future of Europe. This Convention drafted a Constitutional Treaty, which stipulated that the Charter should be an integral part of an EU Constitution, and hence legally binding.[291] The Constitutional Treaty was put on hold as a result of the negative results of the referenda in France and the Netherlands. However

---

[286] *Charter of Fundamental Rights of the European Union* [2000] O.J. C364/1.
[287] June 3–4, 1999.
[288] October 15–16, 1999.
[289] Charte 4960/00, Convent 55, October 26, 2000.
[290] Charte 4955/00, Convent 51, October 17, 2000.
[291] A Treaty Establishing a Constitution for Europe [2004] O.J. 310/1, Art I–9.

under the Lisbon Treaty,[292] which was signed by the Member States in December 2007, the Charter,[293] while not incorporated into the Treaty, is made legally binding and given the same legal status as the Treaties.[294] It remains at the time of writing to be seen whether the Lisbon Treaty is ratified by the Member States.

E. The ECHR, HRA and EU

18–057　　It is important by way of conclusion to consider in outline the inter-relationship between protection of Convention rights via the HRA, and protection of rights via the EU.

The ECJ's approach to the ECHR has in the past provided the Convention with a peremptory force in national courts it lacked prior to the passage of the HRA.[295] Community law would take account of the ECHR in fashioning its own fundamental rights doctrine, and this would then bind Member States in the types of case mentioned above. It is still possible, even now, that Convention rights mediated through EC law will provide a more potent weapon than the HRA. This is particularly so where the incompatibility with Convention rights flows from primary legislation. In such instances the courts are limited to making a declaration of incompatibility under s.4 HRA. However, the supremacy law of EC law applies in relation primary legislation itself. It would be perfectly possible for the breach of EC law to consist of failure to comply with the EC fundamental rights' doctrine, or with the Community Charter of Rights. The national courts could then declare that the primary legislation was actually inapplicable to the instant case, rather than simply making a declaration of incompatibility under s.4 HRA.

It is important also to consider the obligation of the national court in circumstances where there is a difference between the ECJ and the ECtHR on the meaning of Convention rights, where the case before the national court has a Community law component. The position from first principle is as follows.

National courts are bound by EC law, and the supremacy doctrine applies to all species of national law. If a national court is applying the HRA and it becomes clear that there is a divergence in the meaning of the relevant Convention right as between the ECJ and the ECtHR then the national court must adopt the interpretation of the ECJ. Under the HRA national courts have an obligation to take account of the Strasbourg case law. They are not bound to follow it. The national courts are bound to apply EC law, irrespective of the way in which the issue arises, or the forum in which it

[292] Conference of the Representatives of the Governments of the Member States, Treaty of Lisbon Amending the Treaty on European Union and the Treaty Establishing the European Community, CIG 14/07, Brussels December 3, 2007; [2007] O.J. C306/1.
[293] The Charter was reissued: Charter of Fundamental Rights of the European Union [2007] O.J. C303/1; Explanations Relating to the Charter of Fundamental Rights [2007] O.J. C303/17.
[294] art.6(1) TEU.
[295] N. Grief, "The Domestic Impact of the European Convention on Human Rights as Mediated through Community law" [1991] P.L. 555.

arises. The binding nature of EC law is applicable just as much to adjudication under the HRA as any other, provided of course that the case has a Community law dimension.

This issue will not necessarily disappear even if the EU accedes to the ECHR.[296] This is because the terms on which the EU accedes may well have provisions analogous to s.2 HRA, to the effect that the Strasbourg jurisprudence must be taken into account, but does not bind. Where there is a case before a national court which does not have any EC component as such, but where there is a ruling by the ECJ which is nonetheless relevant to the interpretation of the Convention right in the instant case, and the interpretation differs from that given by the ECtHR, then the national court would not be under an obligation to follow the ECJ ruling, but could do so if it so wished.

[296] N. Bamforth, "Prohibited Grounds of Discrimination under EU Law and the European Convention on Human Rights: Problems of Contrast and Overlap" (2006–7) 9 C.Y.E.L.S. 1, for discussion of tensions between EU law and ECHR law in relation to discrimination.

CHAPTER 19

RATIONALITY AND PROPORTIONALITY

1. THE LIMITS OF JUDICIAL INTERVENTION

It is important at the outset to be clear about the limits of judicial inter- **19–001**
vention over discretion: it is *not* for the courts to *substitute their choice* as to
how the discretion ought to have been exercised for that of the administrative authority. They should not intervene, reassess the matter afresh and
decide, for example, that funds ought to be allocated in one way rather than
another. Our basic conceptions of political theory and the allocation of
governmental functions are against this approach. Decisions as to political
and social choice are made by the legislature, or by a person assigned the
task by the legislature.[1] To sanction general judicial intervention simply
because the court would prefer a different choice to that of the administrator
runs counter to this fundamental assumption, and would entail a realloca-
tion of power from the legislature and bureaucracy to the courts.

The courts accept that it is not their task to substitute judgment. This is
exemplified by the *Cambridge Health Authority* case[2] The applicant, B, was a
10-year old girl who was extremely ill. She had received a bone marrow
transplant, but the treatment had not proven effective. The hospital, acting
on the advice of specialists, decided that B had only a short time to live and
that further major therapy should not be given. B's father sought the opinion of two further specialists, who thought that a second bone marrow
transplant might have some chance of success. Such treatment could,
however, only be administered privately because there were no beds in the
National Health Service within a hospital which could carry out such
therapy. The proposed treatment would take place in two stages, the first of

[1] *R. v Ministry of Agriculture, Fisheries and Food Ex p. First City Trading* [1997] 1 C.M.L.R.
250, 278.
[2] *R. v Cambridge Health Authority Ex p. B* [1995] 2 All E.R. 129; *R. (on the application of
Walker) v Parole Board, R. (on the application of Wells) v Parole Board* [2007] EWHC 1835,
para.39.

which would cost £15,000 and have a 10–20 per cent chance of success; the second stage would cost £60,000 with a similar 10–20 per cent chance of success. B's father requested the health authority to allocate the funds necessary for this therapy. It refused to do so, given the limited nature of the funds at its disposal and the small likelihood that the treatment would be effective. B's father then sought judicial review of this decision, but failed before the Court of Appeal. Sir Thomas Bingham MR recognised the tragic nature of B's situation, but stressed that the courts were not the arbiters of the merits in such cases. It was not for the courts to express any opinion as to the likely success or not of the relevant medical treatment.[3] The courts should, said the Master of the Rolls, confine themselves to the lawfulness of the decision under scrutiny. The basic rationale for the health authority's refusal to press further with treatment for B was scarcity of resources. The court's role in this respect was perforce limited.[4]

> "I have no doubt that in a perfect world any treatment which a patient . . . sought would be provided if doctors were willing to give it, no matter how much it cost, particularly when a life was potentially at stake. It would however, in my view, be shutting one's eyes to the real world if the court were to proceed on the basis that we do live in such a world. It is common knowledge that health authorities of all kinds are constantly pressed to make ends meet. They cannot pay their nurses as much as they would like; they cannot provide all the treatments they would like; they cannot purchase all the extremely expensive medical equipment they would like; they cannot carry out all the research they would like; they cannot build all the hospitals and specialist units they would like. Difficult and agonising judgments have to be made as to how a limited budget is best allocated to the maximum advantage of the maximum number of patients. That is not a judgment which the court can make. In my judgment, it is not something that a health authority such as this authority can be fairly criticised for not advancing before the court."

While all accept that it is not for the courts to substitute judgment, it is also recognised that there should be some control over the rationality of the decisions made by the administration. This is exemplified by *Rogers*.[5] The defendant had funds available to provide treatment with a breast cancer drug for all patients who fulfilled the clinical requirements for such treatment and whose clinician had prescribed it. However, its policy was to refuse funding for such treatment, save where exceptional personal or clinical circumstances could be shown. The Court of Appeal held that the defendant's policy was irrational, since there were no relevant exceptional

---

[3] *B*, n.2, 135–136.
[4] *B*, n.2, 137.
[5] *R. (on the application of Rogers) v Swindon NHS Primary Care Trust* [2006] 1 W.L.R. 2649. See also, *R. (on the application of Walker) v Secretary of State for the Home Department* [2008] EWCA Civ 30.

circumstances that could justify giving the drug to one patient rather than another.

The theme that runs throughout this area is therefore the desire to fashion a criterion that will allow judicial control, without thereby leading to substitution of judgment or too great an intrusion on the merits. It is nonetheless important at the outset to recognise that the distinction, found in some of the case law and the literature, between merits review and non-merits review, is unhelpful. All tests of substantive judicial review entail the judiciary in taking some view of the merits of the contested action. This is so even in relation to the classic *Wednesbury* test.[6] What distinguishes different tests for review is not whether they consider the merits or not, but in the stringency of the judicial scrutiny of those merits. It is possible in this regard to range different tests for review along a spectrum. Classic, limited *Wednesbury* review is at one end of the spectrum, judicial substitution of judgment, whereby the court imposes what it believes to be the correct meaning of the term or issue in question, lies at the opposite end of the spectrum. Heightened *Wednesbury* review and proportionality occupy intermediate positions,[7] with the latter being more intensive than the former.

2. WEDNESBURY UNREASONABLENESS: PAST, PRESENT AND FUTURE

A. Wednesbury Unreasonableness: "The Touchstone of Legitimate Judicial Intervention"

This section will consider the "past" of *Wednesbury* unreasonableness, and examine the conceptual rationale for the meaning given to unreasonableness in that case.

19–002

We have already seen in an earlier chapter[8] that Lord Greene M.R. used the word unreasonableness in two different senses. It was used to describe the various grounds of challenge which went to the legality of the public body's actions. This "umbrella sense" of unreasonableness was used to describe actions based on illegality, irrelevancy and the like. He also gave unreasonableness a "substantive" meaning in its own right. If an exercise of discretion successfully negotiated the hurdles of propriety of purpose and relevancy it could still be invalidated if it was so unreasonable that no reasonable body could reach such a decision. The two senses of unreasonableness were designed to legitimate judicial intervention over discretionary decisions, and to establish the limits to any such intervention.

The first meaning of the term allowed the courts to intervene where the decision was of a type that could not be made at all, and was therefore illegal. It was outside the four corners of the power that Parliament had

---

[6] *Associated Picture Houses Ltd v Wednesbury Corporation* [1948] 1 K.B. 223, 233–234.
[7] *R. v Ministry of Agriculture, Fisheries and Food Ex p. First City Trading* [1997] 1 C.M.L.R. 250, 278–279.
[8] See, Ch.17.

given to the decision-maker, and it was therefore right and proper for the courts to step in. Where, however, the primary decision-maker was within the four corners of its power then the courts should be reluctant to interfere. The courts should not substitute their view for that of the public body, nor should they overturn a decision merely because they felt that there might have been some other reasonable way for the agency to have done its task. Some control over decisions that were within the four corners of the public body's power was, however, felt to be warranted and legitimate.

This was the rationale for the substantive meaning of unreasonableness. If the challenged decision really was so unreasonable that no reasonable body could have made it, then the court was justified in quashing it. The very fact that something extreme would have to be proven legitimated the judicial oversight, and served to defend the courts from the charge that they were overstepping their remit and intervening too greatly on the merits. It is clear from Lord Greene M.R.'s judgment that he conceived of it being used only in the extreme and hypothetical instance of "dismissal for red hair type of case". Lord Diplock in *GCHQ* was equally clear that this species of irrationality would only apply to a "decision which is so outrageous in its defiance of logic or of accepted moral standards that no sensible person who had applied his mind to the question could have arrived at it".[9] We shall consider in due course whether the test needs to be this limited in order that the court should not be regarded as overstepping its proper bounds.[10]

It should be recognised that the courts have always had an inherent discretion as to whether to classify a case as relating to illegality or unreasonableness in its substantive sense. Let us take the classic example of the unreasonable decision, dismissal of a teacher because of the colour of her hair.[11] If the considerations relevant to dismissal of a teacher are broadly defined as "any physical characteristic" then of course dismissal on the above ground is relevant. However, common sense dictates that this is not the way that we would approach the matter. The question would be posed more specifically, distinguishing between the types of physical characteristics that were felt to be relevant to teaching and those, such as hair colour, which were not. Other decisions could equally be resolved through traditional conceptions of purpose and relevancy[12]

B. Wednesbury Unreasonableness: The Present Law

19–003   The *Wednesbury* test has been the major tool used by our courts to control discretionary decisions, which have passed the legality hurdles of propriety of purpose, etc. The wording of the test, combined with the overlay provided by Lord Greene and Lord Diplock as to when it would apply, might lead one to think that few cases would be condemned. The reality is, however, that the courts have developed the substantive meaning of unreasonableness

[9] *Council of Civil Service Unions v Minister for the Civil Service* [1985] A.C. 374, 410.
[10] See below, para.19–004.
[11] *Short v Poole Corporation* [1926] Ch.66.
[12] See, e.g., *Williams v Giddy* [1911] A.C. 381; *UKAPE v ACAS* [1981] A.C. 424.

in two ways, and they have also articulated a test for review independent of *Wednesbury*, based on abuse of power. These will be considered in turn.

i. The application of Wednesbury *in cases not concerned with rights*

The courts have "loosened" the *Wednesbury* test even in cases that have nothing to do with fundamental rights. They have, for example, applied the test to discretionary decisions that could not, whether right or wrong, be classified as of the "red hair type". The test has been used in the planning sphere to invalidate conditions attached to planning permission. An obligation on the developer to construct an ancillary road over the frontage of the site, to which rights of passage should be given to others,[13] was struck down; so too was an obligation that a property developer should allow those on a council housing list to occupy the houses with security of tenure for 10 years.[14] The test has also been adopted in the context of industrial relations.[15] These cases may have been correctly decided. It is, however, difficult to regard the subject-matter under attack as determinations which were so unreasonable that no reasonable authority could have made them, at least not when viewed as Lord Greene M.R. visualised the notion. The test was applied in a way that made it closer to asking whether the court believed that the exercise of discretion was reasonable.[16]

19–004

This has become more explicit in later cases. In *Saville*,[17] Lord Woolf M.R. held that to label a decision as irrational would often not do justice to the decision-maker, who could be the most rational of persons. In many such cases the true explanation for the decision being flawed was that although such perversity could not be established, the decision-maker had misdirected itself in law. In *Balchin*,[18] Sedley J. held that a decision would be *Wednesbury* unreasonable if it disclosed an error of reasoning, which robbed the decision of its logical integrity. If such an error could be shown then it was not necessary for the applicant to demonstrate that the decision-maker was "temporarily unhinged". In *Coughlan*,[19] the court held that rationality

---

[13] *Hall & Co Ltd v Shoreham-by-Sea Urban District Council* [1964] 1 W.L.R. 240.
[14] *R. v Hillingdon London Borough Council Ex p. Royco Homes Ltd* [1974] Q.B. 720.
[15] *UKAPE*, n.12; See also, *R. v Boundary Commission for England Ex p. Foot* [1983] Q.B. 600; *R. v Crown Court of St. Albans Ex p. Cinnamond* [1981] Q.B. 480.
[16] See also, *Niarchos v Secretary of State (No.2)* [1981] J.P.L. 118; *West Glamorgan County Council v Rafferty* [1987] 1 W.L.R. 457; *R. v Bridgnorth DC Ex p. Prime Time Promotions Ltd* [1999] C.O.D. 265; *R. v Secretary of State for the Home Department Ex p. Tawfick* [2001] A.C.D. 28; *R. v Secretary of State for Health Ex p. Wagstaff* [2001] 1 W.L.R. 292; *R. (on the application of Howard) v Secretary of State for Health* [2002] EWHC 396; *R. (on the application of Von Brandenburg) v East London and the City Mental Health Trust* [2002] Q.B. 235; *R. (on the application of Paul-Coker) v Southwark LBC* [2006] EWHC 497; *Walker*, n.2; *R. (on the application of LH) v Lambeth LBC* [2006] EWHC 1190; *Rogers*, n.5; *R. (on the application of Bradley) v Secretary of State for Work and Pensions* [2008] EWCA Civ 36; A. Le Sueur, "The Rise and Ruin of Unreasonableness?" [2005] J.R. 32.
[17] *R. v Lord Saville of Newdigate Ex p. A* [1999] 4 All E.R. 860, para.33.
[18] *R. v Parliamentary Commissioner for Administration Ex p. Balchin* [1997] C.O.D. 146.
[19] *R. v North and East Devon Health Authority Ex p. Coughlan* [2001] Q.B. 213.

covered not only decisions that defied comprehension, but also those made by "flawed logic".[20] It is nonetheless still the case that the *Wednesbury* test can be a significant hurdle for claimants.[21]

The loosening of Lord Greene's test received explicit support from Lord Cooke in the *ITF* case.[22] He regarded the formulation used by Lord Greene as tautologous and exaggerated. It was not, said Lord Cooke, necessary to have such an extreme formulation in order to ensure that the courts remained within their proper bounds as required by the separation of powers. He advocated a simpler and less extreme test: was the decision one that a reasonable authority could have reached. Lord Cooke returned to the topic in more forthright terms in *Daly*.[23]

> "[I] think that the day will come when it will be more widely recognised that . . . *Wednesbury* . . . was an unfortunately retrogressive decision in English administrative law, insofar as it suggested that there are degrees of unreasonableness and that only a very extreme degree can bring an administrative decision within the legitimate scope of judicial invalidation. The depth of judicial review and the deference due to administrative discretion vary with the subject matter. It may well be, however, that the law can never be satisfied in any administrative field by a finding that the decision under review is not capricious or absurd."

ii. The application of Wednesbury *in cases concerned with rights*

19–005 The courts have varied the intensity with which they apply the *Wednesbury* test in cases concerned with rights. We have already considered the approach of the common law courts prior to the passage of the Human Rights Act 1998.[24] The growing recognition of the importance of rights was accommodated by modification of the substantive meaning of unreasonableness. It is now common to acknowledge that the courts apply the principles of judicial review, including the *Wednesbury* test, with varying degrees of intensity depending upon the nature of the subject-matter.[25]

Lord Bridge in *Brind*[26] said that, in cases concerned with rights, the court must inquire whether a reasonable Secretary of State could reasonably have made the primary decision being challenged. The court should begin its inquiry from the premise that only a compelling public interest would justify

---

[20] *Coughlan*, para.65.
[21] See, e.g., *R. (on the application of J) v Special Educational Needs and Disability Tribunal (SENDIST)* [2005] EWHC 3315; *R. (on the application of AA (Afghanistan)) v Secretary of State for the Home Department* [2006] EWCA Civ 1550.
[22] *R. v Chief Constable of Sussex Ex p. International Trader's Ferry Ltd* [1999] 2 A.C. 418, 452.
[23] *R. v Secretary of State for the Home Department Ex p. Daly* [2001] 2 A.C. 532, 549; *R. (on the application of Louis Farrakhan) v Secretary of State for the Home Department* [2002] 3 W.L.R. 481, para.66.
[24] See, Ch.17.
[25] Sir John Laws, "*Wednesbury*", in C. Forsyth and I. Hare (eds), *The Golden Metwand and the Crooked Cord, Essays in Honour of Sir William Wade* (Oxford University Press, 1998), 185–202.
[26] *R. v Secretary of State for the Home Department Ex p. Brind* [1991] 1 A.C. 696, 748–749.

the invasion of the right. Sir Thomas Bingham M.R.'s formulation was very similar.[27] The court was to consider whether the decision was beyond the range of responses open to a reasonable decision-maker, and the greater the interference with human rights the more the court would require by way of justification.

It is possible to argue that this is merely the *Wednesbury* test, which is being applied with due regard to the nature of the subject matter.[28] Much, however, depends upon what one means by the word "same". The idea that heightened scrutiny in cases concerning rights can be seen *simply* as a variant of the original *Wednesbury* test is problematic in both linguistic and conceptual terms.[29]

In linguistic terms, it is difficult to regard the tests as the same, which is readily apparent when they are juxtaposed. Lord Greene's formulation required the decision to be so unreasonable that no reasonable public body could have made it. The formula applied in cases concerned with rights directs the court to consider whether the decision was beyond the range of responses open to a reasonable decision-maker, and the greater the interference with human rights the more the court would require by way of justification. The court does not rest content with inquiring whether the decision of the minister interfering with rights was so unreasonable that no reasonable minister could have made it. It is true that the degree of linguistic difference between the two fades if one adopts the formulation proposed by Lord Cooke. This is of course because this latter formulation is itself a modification of Lord Greene's test.

In conceptual terms, it is equally difficult to regard judicial review in rights' cases merely as a variant of traditional *Wednesbury,* since the premises that underlie review in the two contexts differ. The premise that underpins the classic *Wednesbury* approach, as overlaid by Lord Diplock, is that the courts should be aware of their limited role. Social and political choices have been assigned by Parliament to a minister or agency and it was not for the courts to overstep their legitimate bounds when engaged in judicial review. It was this premise which shaped the *Wednesbury* test itself. The court would intervene to ensure that the agency remained within the four corners of its powers, through concepts such as propriety of purpose and relevancy, but would only exercise very limited control over the rationality of the decision through *Wednesbury* unreasonableness. The premise differs in cases concerned with rights. The courts continue to accept that they should not substitute judgment. It is also generally accepted that traditional notions of sovereignty mean that the courts cannot invalidate primary legislation on the ground that it infringes rights.[30] The courts do not, however, operate on the assumption that decisions about rights made

---

[27] *R. v Ministry of Defence Ex p. Smith* [1996] Q.B. 517.
[28] Sir John Laws, "*Wednesbury*", n.25.
[29] P. Craig, "Unreasonableness and Proportionality in UK Law", in E. Ellis (ed.), *The Principle of Proportionality in the Laws of Europe* (Hart, 1999), 85–106.
[30] See, however, Sir J. Laws, "Law and Democracy" [1995] P.L. 72 and "The Constitution: Morals and Rights" [1996] P.L. 622; Lord Woolf, "Droit Public-English Style" [1995] P.L. 57.

by the political arm of government, or another public body, must necessarily be accorded the same respect or judicial deference as, for example, allocative decisions of an economic nature. The majoritarian will is quite properly accorded less force in rights-based cases than in others. It is this premise which serves to explain, and which is reflected in, the different meaning given to "reasonableness review". The level of unreasonableness which the applicant must prove is less extreme than in the traditional *Wednesbury* formula,[31] and the court requires more compelling justification before it is willing to accept that an invasion of rights was warranted.

iii. The non-application of Wednesbury in legitimate expectation cases: rationality and abuse of power

19–006
The case law on legitimate expectations will be examined in the following chapter. This case law is however of more general relevance for the standard of review. In *Coughlan*,[32] the court held that judicial intervention could be premised on bare rationality, as reflected in the *Wednesbury* test. This test was rejected as being insufficiently searching in cases where a public body sought to resile from a substantive legitimate expectation.[33] The court held that intervention could, alternatively, be premised on abuse of power, citing *Preston*[34] as the principal authority. The court's task was to ensure that the power to alter policy was not abused by unfairly frustrating an individual's legitimate expectations. This standard of review was more far-reaching than bare rationality.[35] While it was for the public body to decide when to change policy, the applicant's substantive legitimate expectation could not be frustrated unless there was an overriding public interest, and whether this existed or not was a matter for the court.[36] The appropriate standard of review in legitimate expectation cases will be considered in detail below.[37] Two points should be emphasised in the present context.

On the one hand, abuse of power may properly be regarded as the *conceptual rationale* for judicial intervention to protect substantive legitimate expectations. It encapsulates the conclusion that the applicant had some normatively justified expectation, since there would otherwise been no foundation for finding such an abuse. The term abuse of power can also capture the conclusion that the court has found the public body's argument for going back on the expectation to be unconvincing.

On the other hand, it must also be recognised that abuse of power does not, in itself, furnish a *standard of review* for deciding whether a public body can resile from a proven substantive expectation.[38] Abuse of power can

---

[31] This is so even taking account of the discussion in the previous section.
[32] *Coughlan*, n.19.
[33] *Coughlan*, n.19, para.66.
[34] *R. v Inland Revenue* Commissioners *Ex p. Preston* [1985] A.C. 835.
[35] *Coughlan*, n.19, paras 74, 77.
[36] *Coughlan*, n.19, para.76.
[37] See below, paras 20–018—20–022.
[38] See also, *R. (on the application of S) v Secretary of State for the Home Department* [2007] EWCA Civ 546, paras 39–45.

express the conclusion reached under any such standard, but does not constitute a standard of review itself. The standard should, as recognised in *Coughlan*, be more searching than bare rationality. There are two possible standards of review that could be employed: a modified *Wednesbury* test, and proportionality. The choice between these tests, in legitimate expectation cases, will be considered below.[39] The following discussion in this chapter is also of relevance.

C. Wednesbury Unreasonableness: The Future of the Test
The *Wednesbury* test has long occupied centre stage in the control of discretion. Its very malleability has helped it to survive. Whether it continues to do so is dependent upon three factors.

19–007

First, there is the empirical issue as to how many cases which have, up until now, been adjudicated pursuant to this test, will be recast as rights-based claims under the Human Rights Act 1998 (HRA). There can be no doubt that some factual challenges will be recast in this manner, and the indications since the HRA came on line is that many cases do include a rights-based claim as one of the grounds of challenge. This is important because, as we have seen,[40] the test for review under the HRA is different and more demanding than the *Wednesbury* test as originally conceived. It would, for example, be a "nice" question as to how the factual allegations in *Wednesbury* itself would be argued under the HRA.[41] The applicants might well contend that the restriction imposed in that case, to the effect that a cinema could open on a Sunday, but could not admit children under 15, was contrary to the right to family life, or perhaps even free speech. This might be thought to be fanciful, or it might be felt that the courts would decide that there had been no breach of the relevant Convention right. The general point holds true none the less: many of the cases litigated under the *Wednesbury* test could be pleaded under the HRA. This is obviously true in relation to cases such as *Brind*, *Smith* or *McQuillan*, which clearly involve rights-based claims. It is, however, also true of other cases, such as those concerning the imposition of conditions on a planning permission. There is little doubt that some of these cases would now be brought under the HRA.

The second factor that will affect the status of the *Wednesbury* test is more normative in nature. This is the impact of the standard of review under EU law and the HRA. It is clear that Community law uses proportionality as a criterion for review. It is clear also that proportionality is the test applied under the HRA. We shall consider proportionality immediately hereafter. For the present we are concerned with the affect this might have on the *Wednesbury* test itself.

It may be that *Wednesbury* will survive and continue to be used in cases where there is no link with EU law, and where there is no claim under the

---

[39] See, Ch.20.
[40] See above, paras 18–038—18–039.
[41] Sir Robert Carnwath, "The Reasonable Limits of Local Authority Powers" [1996] P.L. 244, 247–248.

HRA. Indeed, some courts might feel that precisely because there are no connections with EU law or the HRA, therefore the traditional *Wednesbury* test remains the most appropriate standard for review.

It may, however, transpire that *Wednesbury* ceases to operate as an independent test in its own right. It might be caught in the "pincers" of the tests used in EU law and the HRA. This is in part because a proportionality test can, as will be seen below, be applied with varying degrees of intensity. The constitutional concerns about the limits of the judicial role that underpinned *Wednesbury* could, therefore, perfectly well be accommodated within a proportionality inquiry. It is in part because it will be increasingly difficult, or impractical, for courts to apply different tests to different allegations made in an application for judicial review. It will be common for cases to feature claims under the HRA, and independent assertions of ultra vires conduct. It would be possible in theory for courts to use different tests for review in relation to each of these claims. The attractions of applying a single test, albeit one which can be applied with varying degrees of intensity may, however, prove to be difficult to resist over time. This is particularly so given that the courts will become more accustomed to a proportionality inquiry via the HRA. We shall see that Lord Slynn in *Alconbury* called for proportionality to be recognised as an independent head of review.[42]

The third factor is related to, but distinct, from the second. This is the precise meaning given to the *Wednesbury* test. If the courts adopt the modified version of the test suggested by Lord Cooke it raises the issue of how different this is from a proportionality test. This will be considered when proportionality has been analysed.

3. Proportionality in UK Law: Status, Meaning and Application

19–008   The discussion will begin with the present status of this concept within our law, to be followed by more general consideration of the meaning of proportionality and the desirability of developing this head of review.[43]

---

[42] *R. (on the application of Alconbury Developments Ltd) v Secretary of State for the Environment, Transport and the Regions* [2003] 2 A.C. 295, para.51.
[43] J. Jowell and A. Lester, "Beyond Wednesbury: Substantive Principles of Administrative Law" [1987] P.L. 368; Craig, n.29; G. de Búrca, "Proportionality and Wednesbury Unreasonableness: The Influence of European Legal Concepts on UK Law", in M. Andenas (ed.), *English Public Law and the Common Law of Europe* (Key Haven, 1998), Ch.4; G. Gerapetritis, *Proportionality in Administrative Law* (Sakkoulas, 1997); M. Elliott, "The Human Rights Act and the Standard of Substantive Review" [2001] C.L.J. 301; T. Hickman, "Proportionality: Comparative Law Lessons" [2007] J.R. 31; R. Clayton and K. Ghaly, "Shifting Standards of Review" [2007] J.R. 210; J. Rivers, "Proportionality and the Variable Intensity of Review" [2006] C.L.J. 174.

A. Legal Status of Proportionality

i. Proportionality in domestic law: Brind
A leading authority on the status of proportionality is the House of Lords'   **19–009**
decision in *Brind*.[44] The Home Secretary issued directives under the
Broadcasting Act 1981 requiring the BBC and the IBA to refrain from
broadcasting certain matters by persons who represented organisations that
were proscribed under legislation concerning the prevention of terrorism.
The ambit of this proscription was limited to direct statements made by the
members of the organisations. It did not, for example, prevent the broadcasting of such persons on film, provided that there was a voice-over
account paraphrasing what had been said. The applicants sought judicial
review on a number of grounds. The arguments relating to a breach of the
European Convention have been considered above.[45] The other main
ground of challenge was that the directives were disproportionate. The
objective was both to deny such organisations any appearance of political
legitimacy, and also to prevent intimidation.

Their Lordships rejected the argument based upon proportionality. Lord
Bridge held that the restrictions on freedom of speech were not unreasonable in scope, and he did not believe that the applicants' case could be
improved by invoking proportionality.[46] Lord Bridge, however, agreed with
Lord Roskill that proportionality might at some time be incorporated
within our law. Lord Roskill acknowledged that Lord Diplock had, in the
GCHQ case,[47] held this open as a possible future development. Lord Roskill
did not however think that this was an appropriate case for such a development, believing that this would lead the courts into substituting their view
for that of the Home Secretary.[48] Similar concerns are apparent in the
judgments of Lord Ackner and Lord Lowry. Thus Lord Ackner reasoned
that if proportionality were to add something to our existing law, then it
must be by imposing a more intensive standard of review than traditional
Wednesbury unreasonableness. This would mean that an "inquiry into and a
decision upon the merits cannot be avoided", in the sense that the court
would have to balance the pros and cons of the decision being challenged.[49]
Lord Lowry felt that the judges were not well equipped by training or
experience to "decide the answer to an administrative problem where the
scales are evenly balanced".[50] He also feared that recognition of proportionality would lead to an increase in the number of applications for
judicial review, with a consequential increase in costs both for litigants and
in terms of court time.[51]

It is not surprising, in the light of *Brind*, to find cases where the courts

[44] *R. v Secretary of State for the Home Department Ex p. Brind* [1991] 1 A.C. 696.
[45] See above, para.18–002.
[46] *Brind*, n.44, 748–749.
[47] n.9, 410.
[48] *Brind*, n.44, 696, 749–750.
[49] *Brind*, n.44, 762.
[50] *Brind*, n.44, 767.
[51] *Brind*, n.44, 767.

have declined to apply proportionality as an independent standard of review. Thus in the *International Stock Exchange* case[52] Popplewell J. stated that it was accepted that proportionality was not a free-standing principle in domestic law, and that it would not be proper for a judge at first instance to take steps to incorporate the concept. A similar reluctance to engage in review over and beyond the *Wednesbury* principle is also apparent in *Absalom*.[53] Popplewell J. rejected proportionality as a ground of review in an application to quash a decision of the Chief Constable that required the applicant police constable to retire from the police force. A reluctance to stray beyond the confines of the traditional *Wednesbury* formula is equally evident in *Hargreaves*,[54] which will be analysed in the discussion of legitimate expectations.[55] More recently in the *ABCIFER* case,[56] Dyson L.J. held proportionality was only applicable in cases concerned with Community law and the HRA, and that it was not for the Court of Appeal to perform the burial rites to the *Wednesbury* test, this being something that would have to be done by the House of Lords. Dyson L.J. nonetheless added that he had difficulty in seeing what purpose was served by retention of the *Wednesbury* test.

ii. Proportionality in domestic law: direct or indirect recognition

19–010 It should however be recognised that there are purely domestic cases where the courts have either explicitly applied proportionality, *or* have reasoned in a manner analogous thereto. This current in the jurisprudence is especially noteworthy in cases dealing with penalties or fundamental rights. There may of course be differences of opinion as to whether a particular case should be regarded as being "about" proportionality.[57]

There are a number of decisions where the courts have applied proportionality expressly or impliedly. This is exemplified by *Hook*,[58] where a stallholder had his licence revoked for urinating in the street and using offensive language. Lord Denning M.R. struck down the decision in part because the penalty was excessive and out of proportion to the offence.[59]

---

[52] *R. v International Stock Exchange Ex p. Else* [1992] BCC 11.
[53] *R. v Chief Constable of Kent Ex p. Absalom*, May 5, 1993.
[54] *R. v Secretary of State for the Home Department Ex p. Hargreaves* [1997] 1 All E.R. 397.
[55] See below, para.20–013.
[56] *R. (Association of British Civilian Internees: Far East Region) v Secretary of State for Defence* [2003] Q.B. 1397, paras 34–35.
[57] Compare J. Jowell and A. Lester, "Proportionality: Neither Novel nor Dangerous", in J. Jowell and D. Oliver (eds), *New Directions in Judicial Review* (Sweet & Maxwell, 1988), 51–73, and S. Boyron, "Proportionality in English Administrative Law: A Faulty Translation" (1992) 12 O.J.L.S. 237.
[58] *R. v Barnsley MBC Ex p. Hook* [1976] 1 W.L.R. 1052, 1057.
[59] See also, *R. v Warwick Crown Court Ex p. Smalley* [1987] 1 W.L.R. 237; *R. v Highbury Magistrates' Court Ex p. Uchendu* (1994) 158 J.P. 409; *R. v Secretary of State for the Environment Ex p. NALGO* [1993] Admin. L.R. 785; *R. v Manchester Metropolitan University Ex p. Nolan*, The Independent, July 14, 1993; *Bolton v Law Society* [1994] C.O.D. 295; *R. v Admiralty Board of the Defence Council Ex p. Coupland* [1996] C.O.D. 147; *B v Secretary of State for the Home Department* [2000] HRLR 439; *South Buckinghamshire DC v Porter* [2003] 2 A.C. 558; *Chaudhury v General Medical Council* [2002] UKPC 41; *R. (on the application of Livermore) v Nursing and Midwifery Council* [2005] EWHC 2339.

More recently in *Nadarajah*[60] Laws L.J. held that a public body could resile from a prima facie legitimate expectation only where it had a legal duty to do so, or where it was otherwise a proportionate response having regard to a legitimate aim pursued by the public body in the public interest.

A similar trend is apparent in cases where the affected interest is a fundamental right. While the House of Lords in *Brind* denied that proportionality was an independent ground of review, a number of their Lordships reasoned in an analogous manner. Lord Templeman[61] held that the court was not restricted in such cases to asking whether the governmental action was perverse or irrational. The judge must rather inquire whether a reasonable minister could reasonably conclude that the interference with the right in question was justifiable. Any such interference must be necessary and proportionate to the damage that the restriction was designed to prevent. Lord Bridge's reasoning was similar. While his Lordship denied that proportionality could advance the applicant's claim, he none the less made it clear that the real inquiry was as to whether the reasonable minister could reasonably reach the conclusion being challenged. In answering this inquiry the court was entitled to start from the premise that any restriction of the right to freedom of expression must be justified, and that nothing less than an important competing public interest would suffice in this respect. The same approach is evident in other cases involving rights.[62] These cases have been considered in an earlier chapter and reference should be made to that discussion.[63] It should nonetheless be recognised that the European Court on Human Rights did not think that this heightened scrutiny was sufficient to meet the necessity and proportionality tests under the European Convention on Human Rights.[64] The House of Lords has, as will be seen below, fashioned a proportionality test under the HRA to meet the strictures laid down by the Strasbourg Court.

The jurisprudence considered thus far has applied proportionality, or a test akin thereto, in specific types of case. The range of such cases is however expanding beyond the strict confines of cases concerned with EU law and the HRA. Thus as we have seen proportionality has been applied in cases concerned with legitimate expectations. In *Walker*, Laws L.J. opined that *Wednesbury* unreasonableness now seemed an "old-fashioned legal construct".[65] The courts were, said Laws L.J., increasingly accustomed to the framing of substantive challenges to public decisions in terms of proportionality, and not only in the context of EU law and human rights. Lord

---

[60] *R. (on the application of Nadarajah) v Secretary of State for the Home Department* [2005] EWCA Civ 1363.
[61] *Brind*, n.44, 751.
[62] *Smith*, n.27; *Bugdaycay v Secretary of State for the Home Department* [1987] A.C. 514, 531; *R. v Secretary of State for the Home Department Ex p. Leech* [1994] Q.B. 198; *R. v Secretary of State for the Home Department Ex p. McQuillan* [1995] 4 All E.R. 400; *Saville*, n.17, paras 34–37.
[63] See above, paras 17–019—17–020.
[64] *Smith and Grady v United Kingdom* (1999) 29 E.H.R.R. 493, para.138.
[65] *Walker*, n.2, para.38.

Slynn in *Alconbury* expressed the view that proportionality should indeed be recognised as a general head of review within domestic law. [66]

"I consider that even without reference to the Human Rights Act the time has come to recognise that this principle [of proportionality] is part of English administrative law, not only when judges are dealing with Community acts but also when they are dealing with acts subject to domestic law. Trying to keep the *Wednesbury* principle and proportionality in separate compartments seems to me to be unnecessary and confusing. Reference to the Human Rights Act however makes it necessary that the court should ask whether what is done is compatible with Convention rights. That will often require that the question should be asked whether the principle of proportionality has been satisfied."

iii. Proportionality in domestic law: The Human Rights Act 1998

19–011 We have already considered in detail the role of proportionality in HRA cases, and reference should be made to that discussion.[67] In *Daly*,[68] Lord Steyn held that there was a material difference between a rationality test cast in terms of heightened scrutiny, and a proportionality test. He accepted that many cases would be decided the same way under either test, but acknowledged that the intensity of review would be greater under proportionality. Proportionality could require the reviewing court to assess the balance struck by the decision-maker, not merely whether it was within the range of reasonable decisions. A proportionality test could also oblige the court to pay attention to the relative weight accorded to relevant interests, in a manner not generally done under the traditional approach to review. It had to be shown that the limitation of the right was necessary in a democratic society, to meet a pressing social need, and was proportionate to the legitimate aim being pursued.

iv. Proportionality: cases with a Community law component

19–012 It is clear that national courts are bound to apply EU law principles, and they have applied proportionality in cases which have a Community law element.[69]

---

[66] *Alconbury*, n.42, para.51.
[67] See above, paras 18–038—18–046.
[68] *Daly*, n.23, 547. See also, *Sudesh Madan v General Medical Council* [2001] A.C.D. 3; *Samaroo v Secretary of State for the Home Department* [2001] EWCA Civ 1139, paras 29–35; *R. (on the application of L) v Manchester City Council* [2002] A.C.D. 45, para.21; *Southampton Port Health Authority v Seahawk Marine Foods Ltd* [2002] EWCA Civ 54, para.34; *Farrakhan*, n.23, para.65; *Chaudhury*, n.59.
[69] See, e.g., *R. v Minister of Agriculture, Fisheries and Food Ex p. Bell Line* [1984] 2 C.M.L.R. 502; *R. v Ministry of Agriculture, Fisheries and Food Ex p. Roberts* [1990] 1 C.M.L.R. 555; *R. v Secretary of State for the Home Department Ex p. Adams* [1995] All E.R. (E.C.) 177; *First City Trading*, n.1; *R. v Ministry of Agriculture, Fisheries and Food Ex p. Astonquest Ltd* [2000] Eu. L.R. 371.

This is exemplified by the *ITF* case.[70] The applicants were exporters of live animals across the Channel. There were serious protests against such exports at the docks. The Chief Constable of Sussex deployed significant manpower to control the protests, but then decided that, because of his limited resources, he could only provide the requisite police cover for the exporters on two days a week. ITF argued that this decision was irrational under domestic law and that it was contrary to Community law. The domestic law argument failed: it was for the Chief Constable to decide how to use his limited resources, and that decision was not *Wednesbury* unreasonable. The Community law claim was that the Chief Constable's decision constituted an export ban, which was prohibited by art.34. The House of Lords accepted that if there had been a breach of what is now art.29, proportionality would be relevant in deciding on the application of what is now art.30. This latter Article allows a defence for limitations placed on the free movement of goods for reasons of, inter alia, public security or public health, provided that the limitation is not disproportionate. The Chief Constable's decision was held to be a proportionate response.

A further example is to be found in the *International Stock Exchange* case.[71] The decision of the Stock Exchange to delist the shares of a company pursuant to powers contained in a Community directive was challenged on the grounds of proportionality. The court accepted that proportionality was the appropriate standard of review, but found against the applicant. The relevant committee of the Stock Exchange had considered less drastic means of controlling the company short of delisting, and the court saw no reason to conclude that its findings were disproportionate.[72]

B. Proportionality: Place and Meaning

It is important at the outset to ascertain the *place* of proportionality within the general scheme of review, and its relationship with other methods of control. It is clear, as a matter of principle, that to talk of proportionality assumes that the public body was entitled to pursue its desired objective. The presumption is, therefore, that the general objective was a legitimate one, and that the public body was not seeking to achieve an improper purpose. If the purpose was improper then the exercise of discretion should be struck down upon this ground, without any investigation as to whether it was disproportionate. Proportionality should then only be considered once the controls considered in the previous chapter have been satisfied. If we bypass this level of control then the danger is that the courts will assume that the public body *was* able to use its discretion for the purpose in question, the only live issue being whether it did so proportionately.

19–013

Let us turn now to the *meaning* of the concept itself. It is obvious that at a

---

[70] *International Trader's Ferry*, n.22.
[71] n.52.
[72] See also, *B*, n.59; *R. (on the application of Hoverspeed Ltd) v Customs and Excise Commissioners* [2002] EWHC 1630; *R. (on the application of Castille Ltd) v Secretary of State for Trade and Industry* [2002] EWHC 16; *Gough v Chief Constable of Derbyshire* [2002] 3 W.L.R. 289.

general level proportionality involves some idea of balance between interests or objectives, and that it embodies some sense of an appropriate relationship between means and ends. We must therefore identify the relevant interests, and ascribe some weight to them. A decision must then be made as to whether the public body's decision was indeed proportionate or not, in the light of the preceding considerations. The most common formulation[73] is a three-part analysis. The court considers,

(i) Whether the measure was suitable to achieve the desired objective.

(ii) Whether the measure was necessary for achieving the desired objective.

(ii) Whether it none the less imposed excessive burdens on the individual. The last part of this inquiry is often termed proportionality *stricto sensu.*

It will be apparent from the subsequent analysis that the court will decide how *intensively* to apply these criteria. It should also be recognised that the criteria may require the court to consider *alternative strategies* for attaining the desired end. This follows from the fact that the court will, in fundamental rights' cases, consider whether there was a less restrictive method for attaining the desired objective. The need to consider alternative strategies may well also arise in other cases. Where the decision is of a technical or professional nature it may require specialist evidence as to the practicability of alternative strategies.[74]

C. Proportionality: Application

19–014   It is readily apparent that the application of the test might well produce differing results depending upon the circumstances of the case. That much is obvious. We can, however, go further in providing some guidance as to how proportionality will be applied in differing *types* of case. Three types of case can be differentiated. It will be seen that proportionality is easier to apply in the first two situations than it is in the third.

i. Proportionality and rights

19–015   The first type of situation is one in which the exercise of discretion impinges upon, or clashes with, a recognised fundamental right. We have already seen that proportionality is part of the test for review under the HRA. Our courts must take the jurisprudence of the European Court of Human Rights on proportionality into account, even though it is not binding on them. It is, however, clear as a matter of principle that some such test should apply in this area, quite apart from the persuasive force of the Strasbourg case law.

---

[73] Hickman, n.43, provides a valuable analysis of different versions of the proportionality test.
[74] *Seahawk Marine Foods*, n.68, paras 34–35.

The reason is as follows. If we recognise certain interests as being of particular importance, and categorise them as fundamental rights, then this renders the application of proportionality necessary or natural, and easier.

Proportionality is *necessary or natural* because the very denomination of an interest as a fundamental right means that any invasion of it should be kept to a minimum. Society may well accept that rights cannot be regarded as absolute, and that some limitations may be warranted in certain circumstances. Nonetheless there is a presumption that any inroad should interfere with the right as little as possible, and no more than is merited by the occasion. It is natural therefore to ask whether the interference with the fundamental right was the least restrictive possible in the circumstances. In this sense, the recognition of proportionality is a natural and necessary adjunct to the recognition of fundamental rights.

Proportionality is also *easier* to apply in such cases. The reason why this is so is that one of the interests, such as freedom of speech, has been identified *and* it has been weighted or valued. We do not have to fathom out this matter afresh on each occasion, precisely because the fundamental nature of the right has been acknowledged. To be sure we still have to decide whether the invasion of the right was proportionate, and this may well be controversial. But this is less problematic than in cases of the third type considered below.

ii. Proportionality and penalties

The second type of case is where the penalty is deemed to be disproportionate to the offence committed. People may disagree as to the precise penalty which is appropriate for a particular offence. Yet here too, as in the first type of case, proportionality is less problematic than it is in the third type of situation. We know the penalty that has been imposed; we know the offence; and we know also the interest affected by the penalty. This interest may be personal liberty in the case of imprisonment, or it may be loss of livelihood as in *Hook*. It *is* a recognised principle of justice that penalties should not be excessive, as acknowledged in the Bill of Rights 1689. A court is unlikely to intervene unless the disproportionality is reasonably evident,[75] and judicial review of this kind is to be welcomed. The application of proportionality in this type of case is also made easier because the applicant will not normally be challenging the administrative rule itself, but simply the penalty imposed for the breach.

19–016

iii. Proportionality and the exercise of administrative discretion

The third type of case is harder. This category includes those situations not covered by the previous two. There are no fundamental rights at stake, and no excessive penalties. The paradigm of this third category is the case where the public body decides to exercise its discretion in a particular manner, this

19–017

---

[75] *Commissioners of Customs and Excise v P & O Steam Navigation Co* [1993] C.O.D. 164.

necessitates the balancing of various interests, and a person affected argues that the balancing was disproportionate. The application of a proportionality test may be more difficult in this type of case.

This is in part because it requires us to weight, for example, the respective values of ratepayers and transport users in a *Fares Fair*[76] type of case. It is in part because many administrative decisions involve balancing, which is the essence of many political determinations and administrative choices. It cannot therefore be right for the judiciary to overturn a decision merely because the court would have balanced the conflicting interests differently. This would amount to substitution of judgment by any other name.

This does not mean that proportionality has no role to play in this type of case. This is especially so given that administrative policy choices should be susceptible to judicial scrutiny.[77] What it does mean is that we must decide on whether the proportionality inquiry is confined to the particular administrative decision under attack, or whether the court is also to consider alternative policy strategies. Consideration of the former will often push the analysis in the direction of the wider ranging inquiry.[78] What it also means is that we must decide on the intensity with which proportionality will be applied. A less intensive form of review can be utilised for cases in this area, as exemplified by the EC jurisprudence on proportionality.

D. Proportionality, the Role of the Court and the Standard of Review

19–018　The discussion thus far has considered the legal status of proportionality within UK law. The precise role of the courts in the proportionality analysis has been the subject of discussion in prominent recent cases in the House of Lords, notably in *Denbigh*,[79] *Huang*,[80] and *Miss Behavin' Ltd*.[81] This issue was addressed in the previous chapter,[82] and reference should be made to that discussion. A further point concerning the nature and standard of judicial review should nonetheless be considered here.

The cases mentioned above contain a number of statements contrasting the judicial role in HRA cases, with its role in ordinary judicial review. Thus Lord Hoffmann in *Denbigh* stated that in domestic judicial review the court was usually concerned with whether the decision-maker reached its decision in the right way, rather than with whether he got what the court might think is the right answer, whereas under the HRA the court was concerned with substance and not procedure,[83] and this view was echoed in later cases.[84]

---

[76] *Bromley London Borough Council v Greater London Council* [1983] 1 A.C. 768.
[77] I. Harden and N. Lewis, *The Noble Lie, The British Constitution and the Rule of Law* (Hutchinson, 1986).
[78] *Seahawk Marine Foods*, n.68.
[79] *R. (on the application of Begum) v Denbigh High School Governors* [2007] 1 A.C. 100.
[80] *Huang v Secretary of State for the Home Department* [2007] 2 W.L.R. 581.
[81] *Belfast City Council v Miss Behavin' Ltd* [2007] 1 W.L.R. 1420.
[82] See above, paras 18–038—18–046.
[83] *Denbigh*, n.79, para.68.
[84] See, e.g., *Miss Behavin'*, n.81, para.31, Baroness Hale; para.45, Lord Mance.

This contrast should not be pressed too far. The reality is that the court is concerned with substance and procedure in HRA cases and ordinary judicial review.

In relation to HRA cases, it is true that the court will be concerned with ensuring that the result reached by the public body is compliant with Convention rights, and that the mere fact that the public body has used immaculate procedure will not prevent the decision from being struck down, if it is felt not to be a correct interpretation of the Convention right. In that respect the focus is indubitably on substance. However, as we have seen,[85] the court is still willing to give a discretionary area of judgment to the public body when deciding whether the Convention right has been broken, and insofar as it does so it is acknowledging that, within the confines of that area, there may be more than one substantive result that is consistent with the Convention right. Moreover the extent to which the public body's decision-making process consciously addressed Convention issues will influence the extent to which the court is willing to accept the decision.

In relation to ordinary judicial review, it is true that some aspects of the standard doctrinal armoury address the decision-making process, rather than stipulating a particular substantive conclusion that must be reached. It would nonetheless be mistaken to conceptualise these doctrines as solely, or even primarily, about the decision-making process. Thus judicial intervention on grounds of relevancy or propriety of purpose will not directly stipulate one substantive result that should be reached, although it may do so indirectly, but the very denomination of what constitutes a relevant consideration or a proper purpose will be a substantive determination, which constrains the range of results that the public body can arrive at. The same is true for proportionality in cases that are not concerned with human rights. Judicial application of the necessity and suitability tests will involve consideration of the administrative decision-making process, but it will also indubitably place substantive limits on outcome or result.

4. PROPORTIONALITY: THE EC DIMENSION

Proportionality is a general principle of EC law, and therefore our courts are obliged to apply it in cases with a Community law dimension.[86] These general principles have been developed by the ECJ and draw their inspiration from the laws of the Member States. They can be relied upon in actions to contest the legality of Community measures, or national measures

19–019

---

[85] See above, Ch.17.
[86] P. Craig, *EU Administrative Law* (Oxford University Press, 2006), Chs 17–18; P Craig and G de Búrca, *EU Law, Text, Cases and Materials* (Oxford University Press, 4th edn, 2007), 554–551; T. Tridimas, *The General Principles of EC Law* (Oxford University Press, 2nd edn, 2006), Chs 3–5; G. de Búrca, "The Principle of Proportionality and its Application in EC Law" (1993) 13 Y.B.E.L. 105.

designed to implement Community law. Proportionality has been applied in all three types of case described above.

A. Proportionality and Rights

19–020 There have been a number of cases concerned with proportionality in the context of rights granted by the Community Treaties. A common scenario is where the Member State seeks to take advantage of a public policy exception to, for example, the free movement of workers. This right is guaranteed by art.39, and the public policy exception finds expression in art.39(3). The ECJ has, however, insisted that derogation from the fundamental principle of art.39 can only be sanctioned in cases which pose a genuine and serious threat to public policy, and then only if the measure is the least restrictive possible in the circumstances.[87] The same principle is evident in cases upon freedom to provide services, which is protected by art.49. In *Van Binsbergen*[88] the Court held that residence requirements limiting this freedom may be justified, but only where they were strictly necessary to prevent the evasion, by those resident outside the territory, of professional rules which were applicable to the activity in question. A similar approach is evident in cases concerning the right to free movement of goods. Thus in the famous *Cassis de Dijon* case[89] the ECJ considered whether a German rule which prescribed a minimum alcohol content for a certain alcoholic beverage constituted an impediment to the free movement of goods under art.28. Having decided that it did do so, the Court assessed the defence that the rule was necessary in order to protect consumers from being misled. The Court rejected the defence, because the interests of the consumers could be safeguarded in other less restrictive ways, by displaying the alcohol content upon the packaging of the drinks.

Application of proportionality can also be seen in cases where individuals claim that Community regulations infringe their fundamental rights. Thus in the *Hauer* case[90] the ECJ held that the validity of a regulation which restricted the areas in which wine could be grown, and thus limited the applicant's property rights, must not constitute a disproportionate and excessive interference with the rights of the owner.[91]

---

[87] *Rutili v Minister of the Interior* (36/75) [1975] E.C.R. 1219; *R. v Bouchereau* (30/77) [1977] E.C.R. 1999.

[88] *Van Binsbergen v Bestuur van de Bedrijfsvereniging Metaalnijverheid* (33/74) [1974] E.C.R. 1299; *Coenen v Sociaal Economische Raad* (39/75) [1975] E.C.R. 1547; *Corsten* (C-58/98) [2000] E.C.R. I-7919; *Canal Satelite Digital SL v. Aministacion General del Estado and Distribuidora de Television Gigital SA (DTS)* (C-390/99) [2002] E.C.R. I-607.

[89] *Rewe-Zentrale AG v Bundesmonopolverwaltung fur Branntwein* (120/178) [1979] E.C.R. 649; *Commission v Germany* (178/84) [1987] E.C.R. 1227; *Commission v United Kingdom* (40/82) [1984] E.C.R. 2793; *Commission v Belgium* (C-217/99) [2000] E.C.R. I-10251; *Kemikalieinspektionen v Toolex Alpha AB* (C-473/98) [2000] E.C.R. I-5681; *Criminal Proceedings against Burmanjer, Van der Linden and de Jong* (C-20/83) [2005] E.C.R. I-4133.

[90] *Hauer v Land Rheinland-Pfalz* (44/79) [1979] E.C.R. 3727.

[91] See also *Council v Hautala* (C-353/99) [2001] E.C.R. I-9565.

B. Proportionality and Penalties

The principle has been often applied where the applicant claims that the penalty is disproportionate to the offence committed.[92] This is exemplified by *Man (Sugar)*.[93] The applicant was required to give a security deposit to the Board when seeking a licence to export sugar outside the Community. The applicant was four hours late in completing the relevant paperwork. The Board, acting pursuant to a Community regulation, declared the entire deposit of £1,670,370 to be forfeit. Not surprisingly the company was aggrieved. The ECJ held that the automatic forfeiture of the entire deposit in the event of any failure to fulfil the time requirement was too drastic.[94]

    In addition to cases dealing with penalties *stricto sensu* the ECJ has applied proportionality in the field of economic regulation, scrutinising the level of charges imposed by the Community institutions. Thus in *Bela-Muhle*[95] the Court held that a scheme whereby producers of animal feed were forced to use skimmed milk in their product, in order to reduce a surplus, rather than soya, was unlawful because skimmed milk was three times more expensive than soya. The obligation to purchase the milk, therefore, imposed a disproportionate burden on the animal feed producers.

19–021

C. Proportionality and Discretion

Proportionality has also been applied in cases of the third type described in the previous section. What is of particular interest is the meaning given to the concept in many of the cases of this kind. *Fedesa*[96] provides a good example. The applicants challenged the legality of a Council directive prohibiting the use of certain substances which had a hormonal action in livestock farming. The challenge was based on a number of grounds including proportionality. The ECJ stressed that the Community institutions must indeed pursue their policy by the least onerous means, and that the disadvantages must not be disproportionate to the aims of the measure. It then continued as follows.[97]

19–022

> "However, with regard to judicial review of compliance with those conditions it must be stated that in matters concerning the common agricultural policy the Community legislature has a discretionary power which corresponds to the political responsibilities given to it by Articles 40 and 43[98] of the Treaty. Consequently, the legality of a measure adopted in that sphere can be affected only if the measure is manifestly

---

[92] Craig, n.86, 681–685.
[93] *R. v Intervention Board Ex p. Man (Sugar) Ltd* (181/84) [1985] E.C.R. 2889.
[94] *Man*, n.93, para.29; *Atlanta Amsterdam BV v Produktschap voor Vee en Vlees* (240/78) [1979] E.C.R. 2137; *Buitoni SA v Fonds d'Orientation et de Regularisation des Marches Agricoles* (122/78) [1979] E.C.R. 677; *Portugal v Commission* (C-365/99) [2001] E.C.R. I-5645.
[95] *Bela-Muhle Josef Bergman v Grows-Farm* (114/76) [1977] E.C.R. 1211.
[96] *R. v The Minister of Agriculture, Fisheries and Food and the Secretary of State for Health Ex p. Fedesa* (C-331/88) [1990] E.C.R. I-4023.
[97] *Fedesa*, n.96, 4063; *Schrader v Hauptzollamt Gronau* (265/87) [1989] ECR 2237.
[98] Now arts 34–37.

inappropriate having regard to the objective which the competent institution is seeking to pursue."

The guiding principle is, as stated in *British American Tobacco* case[99] that
this measure of review will be deemed appropriate whenever the Community
legislature exercises a broad discretion involving political, economic or
social choices requiring it to make complex assessments. It is readily
apparent that if the ECJ adopts a less intensive standard of review in a
particular area then this will carry across to proportionality, as well as to
other grounds of illegality. A decision will only be overturned if it is
"manifestly inappropriate" to the objective being pursued.

It would nonetheless be mistaken to conclude that there is no difference
between proportionality as interpreted in this manner and *Wednesbury*
unreasonableness. The test may be cast in terms of manifest disproportionality, but the reality is that the Community courts will normally
examine the claimant's allegations in considerably more detail than is
commonly to be found within *Wednesbury* review.[100] There are moreover, as
will be seen below, advantages to the use of proportionality, even in this
type of case.

The case law furnishes, moreover, interesting insights into why the ECJ
has adopted this more limited form of review. Space precludes any detailed
discussion of this issue. An important consideration is that the ECJ does not
wish to be continually faced with challenges to EC norms in an area where
the Community institutions possessed of discretionary power have to balance a number of variables, which can often conflict among themselves. If
the ECJ countenanced more intensive review for proportionality in the
agricultural sphere then it would be continually faced with challenges by
groups, arguing that the variables should have been balanced in some other
way. Evidence of reluctance to overturn the Community's choices in relation
to agriculture is evident in other cases,[101] and in the secondary literature.[102]

The relative intensity with which proportionality is applied in the agricultural sphere may not necessarily be indicative of how the concept will be
used in other cases that come within this third category. There may, as noted
above, be other areas where the ECJ is willing to intervene with a more

---

[99] *R. v Secretary of State for Health Ex p. British American Tobacco (Investments) Ltd and
Imperial Tobacco Ltd* (C-491/01) [2002] E.C.R. I-11453, para.123; *Commission v European
Central Bank* (C-11/00) [2003] E.C.R. I-7147; *The Queen, on the application of Swedish Match
AB and Swedish Match UK Ltd v Secretary of State for Health* (C-210/03) [2004] E.C.R. I-
11893, para.48.

[100] Craig, n.86, Ch.17.

[101] See among many, *Balkan Import-Export GmbH v Hauptzollamt Berlin Packhof* (5/73) [1973]
E.C.R. 1091; *Stolting v Hauptzollamt Hamburg-Jonas* (138/78) [1979] E.C.R. 713; *Racke v
Hauptzollamt Mainz* (98/78) [1979] ECR 69; *Ludwigshafener Walzmuhle Erling KG v Council*
(197–200, 243, 245, 247/80) [1981] E.C.R. 3211; *Zardi v Consorzio Agrario Provinciale di Ferrara*
(8/89) [1990] E.C.R. I-2515, 2532–2533; *Bocchi Food Trade International GmbH v Commission*
(T-30/99) [2001] E.C.R. II-943, para.92; *R. (on the application of Omega Air Ltd) v Secretary of
State for the Environment, Transport and the Regions* (C-27/00) [2002] E.C.R. I-2569; *Maatschap
Toeters and M C Verberk v Productschap Vee en Vlees* (C-171/03) [2004] ECR I-10945.

[102] C. Vajda, "Some Aspects of Judicial Review within the Common Agricultural Policy-Part
II" (1979) ELRev. 341, 347–348.

searching form of inquiry, particularly where the area is one in which the administrative authorities possess a narrower discretionary power, or one which is more clearly circumscribed. This third category of cases may, therefore, have to be broken down into more discrete categories to reflect this fact.

5. REASONABLENESS, PROPORTIONALITY AND REVIEW

It is appropriate at this juncture to stand back and consider how the general **19–023** shape of substantive review might develop.[103]

A. The Retention of Traditional *Wednesbury* alongside Proportionality

The courts could persist with *Wednesbury* review outside those areas where **19–024** they have to apply proportionality. Different grounds of challenge would be dealt with under different heads of review, and *Wednesbury* would be interpreted in the traditional sense articulated by Lord Greene as overlaid by Lord Diplock. The applicant would have to show that the public body's action really was so unreasonable that no reasonable body would have made it. It would, however, be accepted that this standard of review could vary in intensity, as exemplified by the application of the test in cases concerned with human rights.

Those who favour this approach would argue that it prevents the courts from intruding too far into the merits and obviates the need for any complex balancing, both of which are said to be undesirable features of pro-portionality. It is argued that the traditional approach will preserve the proper boundaries of judicial intervention. This claim is, however, undermined, in two ways.

First, it is true that if we take Lord Greene's language literally the need for any meaningful balancing is obviated by the extreme nature of the test: you simply do not use the colour of a person's hair as the criterion for dismissal. The reality is, as we have seen, that the courts, while preserving the formal veneer of the *Wednesbury* test, have increasingly applied it to decisions which could not be regarded as having being made in defiance of logic or of accepted moral standards. The realisation that the courts have been applying the test to catch less egregious administrative action casts doubt on the claim that *Wednesbury* review can be conducted without engaging in some balancing. It raises the question as to the difference between this and the balancing that occurs within proportionality.

Second, the juridical device of varying the intensity with which the test is

[103] See also, M. Taggart, "Reinventing Administrative Law", in N. Bamforth and P. Leyland (eds), *Public Law in a Multi-layered Constitution* (Hart, 2003), Ch.12.

applied functions as a mechanism whereby the courts can exercise the degree of control which they believe to be desirable in a particular area, without thereby being accused of improper intrusion into the merits, or inappropriate balancing. The very malleability in the standard of review means, however, that it is within the courts' power to shift the line as to what is regarded as a proper or improper intrusion into the merits.

B. The Retention of Modified *Wednesbury* alongside Proportionality

19–025 The courts could, alternatively, retain the *Wednesbury* test for those areas not covered by the EC or the HRA, but give it the tougher meaning ascribed by Lord Cooke: a decision would be overturned if it was one which a reasonable authority could or should not have made. This standard of review could also vary in intensity, depending upon the subject matter. This option is, somewhat paradoxically, more unstable than that just considered, and the reasons why this is so are revealing.

The essential premise of Lord Cooke's thesis is undoubtedly correct. His Lordship argued that the proper boundaries between courts and administration could be secured by a test which was less exaggerated than the traditional *Wednesbury* formulation. To be sure the courts should not substitute their judgment on the merits for that of the administration, but this could be avoided even where the reasonableness test was formulated in the manner articulated by Lord Cooke.

The instability of this option becomes apparent once we probe a little further. We should recall that the "virtue" of the traditional Lord Greene reading of the test was that there was no need to press further. The really outrageous decision would be all too evident and indefensible. If we shift to Lord Cooke's reading of the test this no longer holds true. It would be incumbent on the judiciary to articulate in some ordered manner the rationale for finding that an administrative choice was one which could not reasonably have been made, where that choice fell short of manifest absurdity. If the courts are not obliged to explain their own findings in this manner then the new test will create unwarranted judicial discretion.

It is, however, difficult to see that the factors which would be taken into account in this regard would be very different from those used in the proportionality calculus. The courts would in some manner, shape or form want to know how necessary the measure was, and how suitable it was, for attaining the desired end. These are the first two parts of the proportionality calculus. It is also possible that under Lord Cooke's formulation a court might well, expressly or impliedly, look to see whether the challenged measure imposed excessive burdens on the applicant, the third part of the proportionality formula.

If these factors are taken into account, and some such factors will have to be, then it will be difficult to persist with the idea that this is really separate from a proportionality test. There will then be an impetus to extend proportionality from the areas where it currently already applies, the EC and the HRA, to general domestic law challenges.

C. Proportionality as the General Criterion of Review

Proportionality should neither be regarded as a panacea that will cure all **19–026** ills, real and imaginary, within our existing regime of review, nor should it be perceived as something dangerous or alien. It seems likely that it will be recognised as an independent ground of review within domestic law. This is because: the courts are already applying the test directly or indirectly in some areas; the *Wednesbury* test itself is moving closer to proportionality; the EC and the HRA will acclimatise our judiciary to the concept; and the concept is accepted in a number of civil[104] and common law jurisdictions.[105] It might therefore be of help to pull together some of the advantages and alleged disadvantages of this criterion.

There are a number of advantages in having proportionality as a general standard of review.

(1) It would, other things being equal, be advantageous for the *same test* to be used to deal with claims arising under EC law, the HRA, and other non-HRA domestic law challenges. This is particularly so because it will be common to find at least two such claims in an application for judicial review, and it will not be uncommon to find cases where all three may be of relevance. It should, moreover, be recognised that there will be difficult borderline cases concerning the application of the HRA. The nature of the test to be applied should not differ radically depending upon which side of the borderline a case is said to fall.

(2) The proportionality test provides a *structured form of inquiry*. The three-part proportionality inquiry focuses the attention of both the agency being reviewed, and the court undertaking the review. The agency has to justify its behaviour in the terms demanded by this inquiry. It has to explain why it thought that the challenged action really was necessary and suitable to reach the desired end, and why it felt that the action did not impose an excessive burden on the applicant. If the reviewing court is minded to overturn the agency choice it too will have to do so in a manner consonant with the proportionality inquiry. It will be for the court to explain why it felt that the action was not necessary, etc. in the circumstances. It is precisely this more structured analysis which has often been lacking when the "monolithic" *Wednesbury* test has been applied.

(3) A corollary is that proportionality facilitates a *reasoned inquiry* of a kind that is often lacking under the traditional *Wednesbury* approach. This is brought out forcefully by Laws J. who stated that under proportionality "it is not enough merely to set out the problem, and assert that within his jurisdiction the Minister chose this

---

[104] An indirect consequence of the EC has been greater inter-penetration of the domestic laws of the differing Member States.
[105] Hickman, n.43.

or that solution, constrained only by the requirement that his decision must have been one which a reasonable Minister might make". It was rather for the court to "test the solution arrived at, and pass it only if substantial factual considerations are put forward in its justification: considerations which are relevant, reasonable and proportionate to the aim in view".[106] It will often only be possible to test the soundness of an argument by requiring reasoned justification of this kind.

(4)   EC law shows that proportionality can be applied with *varying degrees of intensity* so as to accommodate the different types of decision subject to judicial review.[107] There is moreover an emerging sophisticated body of work elaborating the types of factor that should be taken into account in deciding on the appropriate intensity of review in cases concerned with resource allocation and social and economic rights.[108]

(5)   EC law also *reveals the benefits of proportionality review, even in those instances where it is applied with low intensity*. It is often assumed that low intensity proportionality review is much the same as the *Wednesbury* test. The conclusion reached on the respective tests may be the same, but this nonetheless masks equally important differences in the way in which they are applied. Thus the structured form of the proportionality inquiry will normally lead the ECJ to examine the arguments of the parties in a degree of detail that is rarely found in cases employing the *Wednesbury* test.[109]

19–027   A number of arguments have been advanced against proportionality as an independent ground of review. These must be separated and assessed carefully.

(1)   It is argued, as seen above, that proportionality allows too great an intrusion into the merits and demands that the court undertakes a balancing exercise for which it is ill-suited. We have already commented on this argument, but it is important to address the matter directly since fears in this regard have been so prominent in the debate about proportionality. Proportionality does not entail substitution of judgment on the merits by the courts for that of the agency.[110] Proportionality does entail some view about the merits, since otherwise the three-part inquiry could not be undertaken. We

---

[106] *First City Trading*, n.1, 279.
[107] Craig, n.86, Chs 17–18; Rivers, n.43.
[108] K. Syrett, "Opening Eyes to the Reality of Scarce Health Care Resources?" [2006] P.L. 664; J. King, "The Justiciability of Resource Allocation" (2007) 70 M.L.R. 197; A. Pillay, "Courts, Variable Standards of Review and Resource Allocation: Developing a Model for the Enforcement of Social and Economic Rights" [2007] E.H.R.L.R. 616; C. Newdick, "Judicial Review: Low-Priority Treatment and Exceptional Case Review" [2007] Med. L.R. 236.
[109] Craig, n.86, Ch.17.
[110] *First City Trading*, n.1, 278–279.

have, however, already seen that the way in which Lord Greene's test has been applied in practice to strike down agency action falling short of the absurd, also demands some view of the merits. The same can be said a fortiori about the revised meaning of the reasonableness test proposed by Lord Cooke.

(2) There are said to be difficulties if we apply proportionality, particularly in those cases which have nothing to do with fundamental rights or penalties. This has been touched on in the earlier discussion.[111] It is right to acknowledge such difficulties, but they should be kept within perspective. The variability in the intensity with which proportionality is applied will itself be of assistance in this regard. It should, moreover, be recognised that analogous difficulties will be equally present if we adopt Lord Cooke's modified reasonableness test. This test can only be applied if, as seen above, we ask questions which are in substance the same as those posed in the proportionality inquiry.

(3) It has been argued that there may well be certain types of question that are unsuited to a proportionality analysis.[112] Thus in the *Sunday Trading* cases Hoffmann J. concluded that it would have been incorrect for the courts to substitute their view on the legality of Sunday Trading for that of the legislature.[113] It was not, he said, the court's function to carry out a balancing exercise, or form a view as to whether the legislative objective could have been achieved by other means. Such matters involved compromises between competing interests which in a democratic society were to be resolved by the legislature, and the judicial function was limited to deciding whether the compromise adopted by the UK Parliament, insofar as it affected Sunday Trade, could have been reached by a reasonable legislature. This was surely correct in relation to the inquiry before the court in the instant case.[114] Stages one and two of the proportionality inquiry were virtually meaningless in this context, while stage three required the national court to undertake an inquiry which was not in reality suitable for legal resolution. This is, however, not an argument for rejecting proportionality as a general head of review, but for ensuring that its application is subject to the same threshold

---

[111] See above, paras 19–017, 19–022.

[112] Lord Hoffmann, "The Influence of the European Principle of Proportionality upon English Law", in Ellis (ed.), n.29, 107–115.

[113] *Stoke on Trent City Council v B & Q* [1991] 1 A.C. 49.

[114] Whether all compromises between competing interests in a democratic society must be resolved by the legislature, and whether it is inappropriate for a court ever to ask whether an objective could have been achieved by other means, is of course, more controversial. There are strong arguments to the contrary, more especially where the action being challenged is not enshrined in legislation as such, but is rather the result of ministerial or agency choice.

principles which apply generally within administrative law. The
reach of proportionality must be limited by justiciability.[115]

6. SUBSTANTIVE CONTROL, SEPARATION OF POWERS AND THE LIMITS OF JUDICIAL REVIEW

19–028   It may be helpful at this point to stand back and consider, in more general
terms, the principles which should govern substantive review. We have
already seen that it is not for the courts to substitute judgment for that of
the primary decision-maker. This is acknowledged by all. We have seen also
that how far the courts should interfere with the merits is still a matter on
which opinion differs.

A. The Traditional Approach

19–029   The traditional approach has been based on the *Wednesbury* formula. The
controls of purpose and relevancy are used to decide what ends the
authority should be entitled to pursue, and what considerations must be
taken into account. If the authority is within the four corners of its powers
the courts will intervene, but only if the decision is manifestly unreasonable.
It is clear that the decision as to what are legitimate purposes, and what are
relevant considerations, can never be value-free. The underlying reason is
that statutes do not really have "corners" in the neat way postulated by
theory. The language is, as Lord Diplock recognised,[116] often elliptical,
ambiguous and inherently open-textured. It is not therefore surprising that
some decisions in high profile cases such as *Tameside*[117] or *Bromley*[118] should
be controversial.

It is equally clear that the courts possess creative choice as to the general
intensity of review that should operate within a particular area. The concepts of purpose, relevancy and reasonableness can be used in an intensive
or less intensive fashion. Thus the courts have, for example, limited their
intervention in cases concerning homeless persons,[119] using arguments
concerning the subjectivity of administrative discretion which found little
favour in other cases.[120] They have counselled restraint in circumstances
where propositions of law are interwoven with issues of social and ethical

---

[115] W. Van Gerven, "The Effect of Proportionality on the Actions of Member States of the EC:
National Viewpoints from Continental Europe", in Ellis (ed.), n.29, 37–63.
[116] *Bromley*, n.76, 822–823.
[117] *Secretary of State for Education and Science v Tameside Metropolitan Borough Council* [1977]
A.C. 1014.
[118] *Bromley*, n.76.
[119] *Puhlhofer v Hillingdon London Borough Council* [1986] A.C. 484, 510–511, 518.
[120] *Tameside*, n.117.

controversy concerning the scope of parental rights,[121] while being more willing to intervene where legal issues are intertwined with questions of social and economic choice in other cases.[122] These points must, nonetheless, be kept within perspective. The value laden nature of determinations concerning propriety of purpose, and the varying intensity of review, will be present in any system of judicial review, even if its formal structure is different from our own.

There is little doubt that the courts' reluctance to depart from *Wednesbury* has been coloured by their desire not to stray beyond their proper role in relation to the political arm of government. It has been the *Wednesbury* test which has served to define the bounds of judicial propriety. The two senses of unreasonableness employed by Lord Greene M.R. were designed to legitimate judicial intervention over discretionary decisions and to establish the limits to any such intervention. If a decision was outside the four corners of the power Parliament had given to the decision-maker, it was therefore right and proper for the courts to step in. Where, however, the primary decision-maker was within the ambit of its power then the courts should be reluctant to interfere. Some residual control over such decisions was, however, felt to be warranted and legitimate. This was the rationale for the substantive meaning of unreasonableness. If the challenged decision really was so unreasonable that no reasonable body could have made it, then the court was justified in quashing it. The very fact that something extreme would have to be proven to come within this criterion provided both the legitimation for the judicial oversight, and served to defend the courts from the allegation that they were thereby overstepping their remit and intervening too greatly on the merits. The desire to remain within the traditional frame is reinforced by the fact that the courts' role in fundamental rights' cases is expressed in terms of *Wednesbury* unreasonableness. The idea that this can be seen simply as a variant of the original *Wednesbury* test is, however, strained.[123]

The courts have clung to the legitimating frame of the *Wednesbury* test, while at the same time exerting more extensive control than would be allowed by a literal reading of the test. They have used the test to intervene in cases where the challenged action could not plausibly be regarded as so unreasonable that no reasonable body would have taken it. The courts have also interpreted the test more intensively in fundamental rights' cases. It might, with some justification, be felt in the light of these developments not that the Emperor has no clothes, but rather that they no longer fit. Lord Cooke's contributions are therefore to be welcomed. He recognised the separation of powers principle which underlies this area, but believed that this could be properly respected by framing a reasonableness test in less extreme terms than articulated by Lord Greene.

---

[121] *Gillick v West Norfolk and Wisbech Area Health Authority* [1986] A.C. 112, 193–194, 206. See further, *e.g. British Airways Board v Laker Airways Ltd* [1985] A.C. 58.
[122] *Bromley*, n.76.
[123] Craig, n.29.

B. An Alternative Approach

19–030   An alternative approach to substantive review can be presented as follows. The courts should intervene if the authority exceeded the ambit of its power by acting *illegally*, in the sense of using that power for an improper purpose, or taking an irrelevant consideration into account. The courts should also intervene if the authority infringed *substantive principles of fair administration*[124] The nature of such principles is, of course, a matter for debate. Obvious candidates for inclusion would include an expanded concept of reasonableness or preferably proportionality, fundamental rights, legal certainty, legitimate expectations, and equality. Procedural principles, such as transparency and reasons, will often be integrally linked with substantive principles. These principles supplement, not merely implement, legislative intent. The principles will be fashioned by the courts in accord with normative considerations as to the constraints on public power that are felt to be warranted in a democratic society.[125]

It should be accepted that under this approach there will still be contentious cases as to whether, for example, a purpose was lawful or not. Controversy over such matters is a feature of any scheme of review, irrespective of its particular form. It must also be acknowledged that decisions will still have to be made concerning the intensity with which the principles of judicial review are to be applied. This is readily apparent from the previous discussion concerning proportionality.

It should also be recognised that the application of substantive principles will require the proper articulation of some background theory which will serve to explain why a principle is said to demand a particular result in a given case. Intellectual honesty does demand a better explanation as to why an act should be struck than that provided through traditional techniques of *Wednesbury* review. Concepts such as fundamental rights, proportionality or legal certainty will provide a more finely tuned approach. These concepts are not, however, self-executing. Their content will often be dependent upon the identification of the particular theory that is said to warrant the conclusion being drawn[126] Various background theories may well recognise the same general right, such as freedom of speech or equality, but the more particular *conception* of that right may be markedly different. This is equally true in the context of proportionality. Thus, whether a measure which is prima facie discriminatory can be regarded as proportionate to a legitimate aim being pursued may well be viewed differently by a utilitarian, a Rawlsian liberal, or a modern communitarian. Legal labels will not in this instance provide a ready-made answer. They can only serve as the repository for the conclusion reached from a particular system of political thought. The

---

[124] Jowell and Lester, n.43; T. Allan, "Pragmatism and Theory in Public Law" (1988) 104 L.Q.R. 422; J. Bell, "The Expansion of Judicial Review Over Discretionary Power in France" [1986] P.L. 99.
[125] P. Craig, "Ultra Vires and the Foundations of Judicial Review" [1996] C.L.J. 63.
[126] R. Dworkin, *Law's Empire* (Fontana, 1986).

task will not therefore be an easy one, but intellectual honesty will not be served by assuming that there is any easier route[127]

7. The Interrelationship between Procedural and Substantive Principles of Review

The interrelationship between procedural and substantive principles is of **19–031** particular interest and importance in any scheme of review. This is especially so in relation to procedural notions of reasoned justification. The proper application of, for example, a proportionality test requires that reasoned justification be provided by the agency in order that the court can properly assess whether the test has been met or not. This is equally true in relation to, for example, governmental justifications for departing from an established policy with respect to a particular individual.

It may be difficult to decide how much to demand by way of reasoned justification. There must be enough in order that the principles of substantive review can operate meaningfully. Bland statements set at a high level of generality, or justifications rationalised ex post facto, do not ensure proper accountability.[128] This is particularly so given that much decision-making will take place within "bounded rationality"[129] It will normally be incremental. Officials rarely have the full range of choices before them. Since officials will often not be viewing the whole picture comprehensively, it is all the more important that the reasons for a particular course of conduct should be articulated. Moreover, while we should be aware that no official can ever literally take *all* relevant considerations into account, the courts do have a role[130] in redressing a bureaucratic tendency to adopt a very narrow bounded rationality, which thereby forecloses policy choices[131]

The courts should, at the same time, be wary of requiring too much by way of reasoned justification. This is because decisions may have to be made in, for example, areas of scientific uncertainty.[132] Public bodies will make

---

[127] P. Craig, *Public Law and Democracy in the U.K. and the U.S.A.* (Oxford University Press, 1990); M. Loughlin, *Public Law and Political Theory* (Oxford University Press, 1992).

[128] *First City Trading*, n.1, 279; *Manchester City Council*, n.68, paras 15–16.

[129] C. Lindblom, "The Science of Muddling Through" (1959) 19 Pub. Adm. Rev. 79; D. Braybrooke and C. Lindblom, *A Strategy of Decision, Policy Evaluation as a Social Process* (Free Press, 1963).

[130] Harden and Lewis, n.77.

[131] How effective the judiciary can be in fulfilling such a role is another matter. The fact that review may occur relatively rarely for any one agency, the fact that the agency may still be subject to pressures of time and cost which incline it towards a narrow bounded rationality, the relative strength of different interest groups pressing upon the agency, and the competence of the court to assess whether such an authority has improperly excluded a particular policy option, can all combine to limit the effectiveness of this aspect of judicial scrutiny. Compare, e.g., J. Sax, "The (Unhappy) Truth About NEPA" (1973) 26 Okla. L. Rev. 239 and W. Pedersen "Formal Records and Informal Rulemaking" (1975) 85 Yale L.J. 38.

[132] I have benefited from discussions on this issue with Elizabeth Fisher, and see E. Fisher, *Risk Regulation and Administrative Constitutionalism* (Hart, 2007).

decisions about the level of acceptable risk where there is imperfect information about the consequences of a certain substance on the environment or on human physiology. There may well be many instances where "we do not even know what we do not know", but where regulation is nonetheless warranted. To wait until we have more perfect information may mean that the problem cannot be tackled, or that there will already have been consequences that cannot be remedied. To demand "perfect" reasoned justification in such instances would stultify important regulatory initiatives. It could also lead to "paralysis by analysis", whereby those opposed to the regulation seek to use the courts to overturn such initiatives on the grounds that not every piece of data relied on by the agency could be perfectly proven. This can lead to public bodies becoming excessively cautious, or unwilling to suggest a regulation unless they have a veritable mountain of data.

19–032   The interrelationship between procedure and substance can be appreciated by a brief look at the standard of review in the USA, in particular the "hard look" test. The term "hard look" evolved by way of contrast with the previous, narrow standard of review generally employed by United States courts. Agency findings could be set aside if they were found to be "arbitrary, capricious or an abuse of discretion"[133] This criterion was narrowly interpreted in a number of cases, it being sufficient for the agency to show some minimal connection between the statutory goal and the choice actually made[134] The standard of review was akin to having Lord Greene M.R.'s narrow sense of unreasonableness as the only basis for attack.

The label "hard look" developed because the United States courts began to desire more control[135] than allowed by this limited test. In the *State Farm*[136] case the Supreme Court founded its intervention on the arbitrary and capricious test, but then gave a broader reading to that phrase than in earlier cases. The court accepted that it should not substitute its judgment for that of the agency. It could, however, intervene if any of the following defects were present: if the agency relied on factors which Congress had not intended it to consider; failed to consider an important aspect of the problem; offered an explanation which ran counter to the evidence before the agency; was so implausible that it could not be sustained; or failed to provide a record which substantiated its findings.

The hard look doctrine therefore represented a shift from a previously more minimal standard of review, where judicial intervention would occur

---

[133] Administrative Procedure Act 1946 s.706(2)(a).

[134] S. Breyer, R. Stewart, C. Sunstein and M. Spitzer, *Administrative Law and Regulatory Policy* (Aspen Law & Business, 5th edn, 2002), 415.

[135] *Greater Boston Television Corp v Federal Communications Comm.* 444 F. 2d 841, 850–853 (D.C. Cir. 1970), cert denied 403 U.S. 923 (1971); *Environmental Defense Fund Inc v Ruckelshaus* 439 F. 2d 584 (D.C. Cir. 1971); H. Leventhal, "Environmental Decision making and the Role of the Courts" (1974) 122 U. Pa. L. Rev. 509; R. Stewart, "The Development of Administrative and Quasi-Constitutional Law in Judicial Review of Environmental Decision making; Lessons From the Clean Air Act" (1977) 62 Iowa L. Rev. 713.

[136] *Motor Vehicle Manufacturers Assn v State Farm Mutual Automobile Insurance Co* 463 U.S. 29, 42–43 (1983). The case was concerned with the adequacy of an agency's explanation for rescinding a regulation concerned with passive restraints in motor vehicles.

only if there was serious irrationality, to one where the courts would interfere where the broader list of defects set out above are present. That list bears analogy to the totality of Lord Greene M.R.'s list, purpose, relevancy and reasonableness. Viewed in this light hard look appears as a movement away from the earlier approach of the American courts, to the tougher standard which we have had in the United Kingdom for over 100 years[137] Controversial issues touching on the merits occur, not surprisingly, just as often in the US case law as they do here[138]

The hard look test was however a more powerful tool than the *Wednesbury* formula, because of the greater concern for the provision of reasons, and the demand for a more developed record. It also provided a foundation for interested parties to express their views, particularly in the context of rule-making[139] This is not to say that the system of review in the USA has been unproblematic. There have been problems resulting from an excessive demand for information and justification by the courts, which has led to the very phrase "paralysis by analysis".

The point being made here is, however, a more general one. The substantive principles of review cannot be considered in isolation. Two legal systems can have similar substantive grounds for review, but these may have differing degrees of force as a result of the way in which procedural principles, such as reason giving and the like, are applied.

---

[137] The *Wednesbury* decision did not create, but merely synthesised, what the U.K. courts had been doing for considerable time. Many important decisions on purpose and relevancy pre-date Lord Greene M.R.'s decision

[138] S. Breyer, "Vermont Yankee and the Courts' Role in the Nuclear Energy Controversy" 91 Harv. L. Rev. 1833 (1978); J. Skelly Wright, "The Courts and the Rulemaking Process: The Limits of Judicial Review" (1974) 59 Cornell L. Rev. 375. *Cf.* Harden and Lewis, n.77, 205–206, 234, 263.

[139] R. Stewart, "The Reformation of American Administrative Law" (1975) 88 Harv. L. Rev. 1667.

CHAPTER 20

LEGITIMATE EXPECTATIONS

The discussion in the previous chapter focused on reasonableness and proportionality and the way in which these concepts controlled abuse of discretion. The present chapter will focus on the way in which legal certainty and legitimate expectations influence the way in which discretion can be exercised.

    The procedural role of legitimate expectations has been discussed earlier.[1] The present discussion will consider how legitimate expectations substantively constrain the way in which discretion is exercised.[2] The phrase *procedural legitimate expectation* denotes the existence of some process right the applicant claims to possess as the result of behaviour by the public body that generates the expectation. The phrase *substantive legitimate expectation* refers to the situation in which the applicant seeks a particular benefit or commodity, such as a welfare benefit or a licence. The claim to such a benefit will be founded upon governmental action which is said to justify the existence of the relevant expectation.

20–001

---

[1] See, Ch.12.
[2] C. Forsyth, "The Provenance and Protection of Legitimate Expectations" [1988] C.L.J. 238; P. Elias, "Legitimate Expectation and Judicial Review", in J. Jowell and D. Oliver (eds), *New Directions in Judicial Review* (Sweet & Maxwell, 1988), 37–50; P. Craig, "Legitimate Expectations: A Conceptual Analysis" (1992) 108 L.Q.R. 79; R. Singh, "Making Legitimate Use of Legitimate Expectations" (1994) 144 N.L.J. 1215; P. Craig, "Substantive Legitimate Expectations in Domestic and Community Law" [1996] C.L.J. 289; P. Craig, "Substantive Legitimate Expectations and the Principles of Judicial Review", in M. Andenas (ed), *English Public Law and the Common Law of Europe* (Key Haven, 1998), Ch.3; Y. Dotan, "Why Administrators should be Bound by their Policies" (1997) 17 O.J.L.S. 23; P. Craig and S. Schonberg, "Substantive Legitimate Expectations after *Coughlan*" [2000] P.L. 684; S. Schonberg, *Legitimate Expectations in Administrative Law* (Oxford University Press, 2000); R. Clayton, "Legitimate Expectations, Policy, and the Principle of Consistency" [2003] C.L.J. 93; P. Sales and K. Steyn, "Legitimate Expectations in English Public Law: An Analysis" [2004] P.L. 564; I. Steele, "Substantive Legitimate Expectations: Striking the Right Balance?" (2005) 121 L.Q.R. 300.

1. The Nature of the Problem

20–002   The connected concepts of legal certainty and legitimate expectations are to be found in many legal systems, as well as in EU law,[3] although their precise content may vary from one system to another.[4]

A. Actual and Apparent Retroactivity
20–003   The most obvious application of legal certainty is in the context of rules or decisions that have an *actual retroactive effect*. Following Schwarze,[5] actual retroactivity covers the situation where a rule is introduced and applied to events that have already been concluded. Retroactivity of this nature may occur either where the date of entry into force precedes the date of publication; or where the regulation applies to circumstances which have actually been concluded before the entry into force of the measure. The arguments against allowing such measures to have legal effect are simple and compelling. A basic tenet of the rule of law is that people ought to be able to plan their lives, secure in the knowledge of the legal consequences of their actions.[6] This precept is violated by the application of measures which were not in force at the time that the actual events took place. It is not therefore surprising that legal systems have tended to take a very dim view of attempts by legislators or administrators to apply their rules in this manner.

Of more direct concern to the present analysis are the problems presented by cases of *apparent retroactivity*.[7] A person may have planned her actions on the basis of a policy choice made by the administration, and seeks redress when the chosen policy alters, even though this alteration is only prospective and not retrospective. The problem of apparent retroactivity can arise in relation to measures, whether individual or general, which change previous measures or representations with effect for events that have already occurred, but which have not yet been wholly concluded, or with effect for some transaction which is in the process of completion.[8] The moral arguments against allowing laws to have actual retroactive effect are powerful and straightforward. The category of apparent retroactivity is more problematic because the administration must obviously have the power to alter its policy for the future, even though this may have implications for the conduct of private parties planned on the basis of the pre-existing legal regime.

---

[3] P. Craig, *EU Administrative Law* (Oxford University Press, 2006), Ch.16.
[4] J. Schwarze, *European Administrative Law* (Sweet & Maxwell, 1992), Ch.6.
[5] Schwarze, n.4, 1120.
[6] J. Raz, *The Authority of Law* (Clarendon, 1979), Ch.11.
[7] The distinction between actual and apparent retroactivity is sometimes expressed alternatively in terms of a division between primary and secondary retroactivity, *Bowen v Georgetown University Hospital* 488 U.S. 204 (1988).
[8] I have benefited from discussion of this issue with Soren Schonberg.

B. Legal Certainty, Legitimate Expectations and Legality

A public body may have made a representation that it would exercise its **20–004** discretion in a particular manner, which has been reasonably relied on by the individual. This representation may be said to generate a legitimate expectation that the power would indeed be exercised in this way. In this sense the *principle of legal certainty* would indicate that the individual ought to be able to plan his or her action on that basis.[9] There can, however, be a clash between this principle and the *principle of legality*. It is important to understand that the principle of legality has two different meanings in this context.

First, a public body may have made a representation within its power, but then seeks to depart from it. Or it may have published policy criteria for dealing with a particular issue, which criteria were intra vires, but it might now wish to adopt new tests for dealing with the same topic, these new criteria also being lawful. The individual may seek to rely on the initial representation or original statement of policy. A traditional objection to the individual being able to do so is that this would be a fetter on the discretion of the public body, which should be able to develop policy in the manner it believes to be best in the public interest. In this type of case the principle of legality is apparent in the doctrine that such a fetter on discretion would itself be ultra vires.

Second, the representation itself may have been outside the power of the public body or the officer who made it. The principle of legality manifests itself here in the simple form that the representation was ultra vires and therefore should not bind the public body in any way.

The discussion within the first half of this chapter will be concerned with cases where the representation itself was intra vires, the first type of situation. This will be followed in the second half of the chapter by analysis of cases where the representation was ultra vires, the second type of situation.

2. Intra Vires Representations: Types of Case

Problems of legal certainty and legitimate expectations can arise in a variety **20–005** of circumstances, which may be characterised in the following manner. The second type of case also raises issues concerned with consistency of treatment and equality.

(1) A general norm or policy choice, which an individual has relied on, has been replaced by a different policy choice.

---

[9] For a detailed consideration of the problem in other European systems see, Schwarze, n.4, 874–1173.

(2) A general norm or policy choice has been departed from in the circumstances of a particular case.

(3) There has been an individual representation relied on by a person, which the administration seeks to resile from in the light of a shift in general policy.

(4) There has been an individualised representation that has been relied on. The administrative body then changes its mind and makes an individualised decision that is inconsistent with the original representation.

The EU and many continental systems properly recognise that all these cases raise problems concerning legal certainty and legitimate expectations, and they are discussed accordingly,[10] although the legal systems may well draw distinctions between the types of case when devising the appropriate rules. Cases falling into the fourth category are normally treated as the strongest. This is because an unequivocal representation made to a person carries a particular moral force, and because holding the public body to that representation is less likely to have serious consequences for the administration as a whole. Cases falling into the first category are, by way of contrast, generally regarded as more problematic for reasons to be discussed below. Different principles of judicial review may, therefore, be appropriate in this type of case.

3. Intra Vires Representations and Substantive Legitimate Expectations: The Contending Arguments

20–006 It is helpful to read the complex case law in the light of the arguments for and against the existence of substantive legitimate expectations.[11]

A. The Arguments in Favour

i. Fairness in public administration

20–007 In *Hamble Fisheries*, Sedley J. put the case for the recognition of substantive legitimate expectations in terms of fairness in public administration.[12] The argument is a strong one which can well provide the principled foundation for such a doctrine. The essence of the argument is contained in the following extract.[13]

---

[10] Schwarze, n.4, Ch.6.
[11] Schonberg, n.2, Ch.1.
[12] *R. v Ministry of Agriculture, Fisheries and Food Ex p. Hamble (Offshore) Fisheries Ltd* [1995] 2 All E.R. 714, 729. See also *Nadarajah*, n.65.
[13] *Hamble*, n.12, 724.

"[T]he real question is one of fairness in public administration. It is difficult to see why it is any less unfair to frustrate a legitimate expectation that something will or will not be done by the decision-maker than it is to frustrate a legitimate expectation that the applicant will be listened to before the decision-maker decides whether to take a particular step. Such a doctrine does not risk fettering a public body in the discharge of public duties because no individual can legitimately expect the discharge of public duties to stand still or be distorted because of that individual's peculiar position."

It is especially important in this regard to recognise that there are different values that should properly be taken into account in this regard. The way in which we initially conceptualise a particular problem will have a marked impact upon what is perceived to be the correct legal rule. We should acknowledge that it would be wrong to allow changes of policy to be unduly fettered. We should, however, also recognise that there is the value of legal certainty, which encapsulates, in this context, the fundamental idea that those who have relied on a particular policy choice made by an agency may have a valid claim for some protection when that policy alters. This is so notwithstanding that there may be room for debate as to the more detailed conditions that should have to be satisfied before such a claim can proceed.

ii. Reliance and trust in government
The normative argument for according protection to substantive legitimate **20–008** expectations is especially strong where the individual has detrimentally relied on a specific representation made by a public body. The meaning of detrimental reliance will be explored below.

Suffice it to say for the present that where the individual has suffered such detriment as a result of justified reliance on a specific representation made by a public body, this generates a normative argument that some legal protection should be accorded. This is so notwithstanding the fact that the public body may need to resile from the expectation where the public interest so demands, since this can be part of the doctrinal legal rule.

The very fact that a legal system does accord protection to substantive legitimate expectations will moreover serve to enhance trust in government, which is not only a good in itself, but may well also render the discharge of government business more efficient.

iii. Equality
Equality provides a further normative argument in favour of protecting **20–009** substantive legitimate expectations, in some cases at least. It is especially relevant in those instances where a public body seeks to depart from an existing policy in relation to a particular individual, while otherwise preserving the policy in tact. The basic precept that like cases should be treated alike is clearly infringed in such instances.

iv. Rule of law

20–010 The argument thus far can be reinforced by rule of law considerations. The concept of legal certainty, which underlies much of continental and EC thinking in this area,[14] has self-evident connections with mainstream thinking about the formal conception of the rule of law, with its concern for autonomy and the ability to plan one's life.

There is one aspect of the rule of law that is of particular relevance to the present analysis. It is concerned with the importance within adjudication of considering matters across time. This idea is to be found in Raz's work.[15] Space precludes any detailed examination of his thesis. Suffice it to say for the present that Raz stresses the "principled faithful application of the law",[16] in which the courts, while faithful to legislation, act in a principled manner so as to "facilitate the integration of particular pieces of legislation with the underlying doctrines of the legal system".[17] This is justified in part to mix "the fruits of long-established traditions with the urgencies of short-term exigencies".[18]

It is precisely because the legislature or the executive can be susceptible to short-term influences, whether generated by elections or the need to respond quickly to public pressure, that the courts should have a role as the guardians of longer-term tradition. This argument is of importance where the applicant possesses an expectation which is normatively justified. Raz's thesis can best be met in such circumstances by ensuring that the new policy choice should be interpreted by the courts in a manner which takes account of that expectation.

B. The Arguments Against

20–011 The central argument put against a doctrine of substantive legitimate expectations, which is especially prevalent to cases falling within category one, is that the liberty to make changes in policy is inherent in our constitutional form of government,[19] and therefore that existing policy should not be ossified or unduly fettered. Part of the answer to this concern has been given above, viz, the need to balance this value against that of legal certainty. There are however other issues to be addressed. Six points are of particular importance.

First, those who deploy the "ossification or fettering of policy argument" often miss a crucial aspect of substantive legitimate expectation cases, which is the temporal limit of the applicant's claim. A doctrine of substantive legitimate expectations does not lead to ministerial policy becoming ossified or fettered. If a minister wished, for example, to abolish or alter home leave

---

[14] Schwarze, n.4, Ch.6.
[15] J. Raz, *Ethics in the Public Domain* (Oxford University Press, 1994), Ch.17.
[16] Raz, n.15, 373.
[17] Raz, n.15, 375.
[18] Raz, n.15, 376.
[19] *Hughes v Department of Health and Social Security* [1985] 1 A.C. 776, 778.

from prison,[20] that choice remains open. Substantive legitimate expectation claims of the kind under consideration merely speak to the *temporal dimension*, in the sense of questioning when the new policy choice takes effect. This does not entail the courts expressing any preference as to a particular regime on home leave. The applicants in such cases are merely asking that where a new policy has implications for those who have relied upon a prior norm that this should be of significance in determining the class of people affected by the shift in policy.

Second, it should not be forgotten that the government itself often recognises the problems created by change in policy, as shown by the existence of transitional or pipeline provisions when a new policy is adopted. Given that this is so, and given also that such provisions themselves constitute administrative choices, it is difficult to see why it should be thought odd for the courts to review their existence and adequacy.

Third, a doctrine of substantive legitimate expectations still requires an applicant to prove the existence of the requisite expectation on the facts of the case.[21] The mere fact that there has been some change of policy does not mean that those who in some way operated under the old policy would be able to prove the existence of such an expectation. EU law and German law, both of which protect substantive legitimate expectations, contain helpful jurisprudence on this issue.

Fourth, even if the applicant is able to prove the existence of the substantive legitimate expectation on the facts of the case, this does not mean that she wins. The proof of the expectation is but the first step in the analysis. Legal systems that recognise the existence of substantive expectations have a second legal step, in which the courts inquire whether the public body had sufficient reasons to depart from the expectation. The precise nature of the test that should apply at this level will be examined in more detail below.

Fifth, the preceding points help to explain why in more general terms there is no evidence that the recognition of a doctrine of substantive legitimate expectations in other legal systems has had any undue impact on the administration's freedom to develop policy.

Finally, it should be recognised that some limitations on administrative freedom in the policy field are, for the reasons given above, warranted because of the principle of legal certainty.

---

[20] *R. v Secretary of State for the Home Department Ex p. Hargreaves* [1997] 1 All E.R. 397.
[21] Compare, e.g., in the immigration field, *R. v Secretary of State for the Home Department Ex p. Golam Mowla* [1992] 1 W.L.R. 70, with *Oloniluyi v Secretary of State for the Home Department* [1989] Imm. A.R. 135.

4. Intra Vires Representations and Legitimate Expectations: Coughlan

20–012   It may be helpful to provide a guide to the remainder of this section, which concerns the case law on substantive legitimate expectations. The analysis will begin with the case law prior to the important decision in *Coughlan*.[22] It will be seen that there was, at this time, uncertainty as to whether substantive legitimate expectations was part of UK law. The decision in *Coughlan* will then be analysed. This will be followed by a consideration of the factors taken into account in deciding whether an expectation is legitimate or not. The focus will then shift to the standard of review that applies in deciding whether a public body can resile from a substantive expectation that has been found to exist. We shall then discuss the application of the doctrine to the different types of case set out above.

A. The Law Prior to *Coughlan*

20–013   There was, prior to *Coughlan*, uncertainty as to whether substantive legitimate expectations were recognised within UK law.

It was, in particular unclear as to whether any such doctrine existed in *the first type of case*, where a general policy or practice, which has been relied on, was replaced by a different policy choice. In *Hamble Fisheries*,[23] Sedley J. argued strongly in favour of substantive legitimate expectations. Hamble Fisheries had purchased two small fishing vessels with the purpose of transferring fishing licences from those vessels to a larger vessel already operated by the company. At the time of purchase, the policy of the Ministry was to allow such transfers. When that policy was subsequently changed, Hamble Fisheries claimed a breach of legitimate expectations. It accepted that policy could be altered for the future, but argued that the introduction of severe measures such as a moratorium with immediate effect constituted a breach of its legitimate expectations, more especially since it had expended large sums of money in reliance on the previous policy. Sedley J. held, for the reasons given above, that a policy or practice could create legitimate expectations protected by administrative law. Moreover, the test to be used to review the legality of a change of policy was not bare irrationality. The courts would intervene if, in all the circumstances of a case, the expectation "has a legitimacy which in fairness outtops the policy choice".[24] Moreover, in *Unilever*,[25] the Court of Appeal held that the Inland Revenue could not without prior warning discontinue a practice, applied consistently for about 25 years, of accepting annual tax refund claims after the expiry of a statutory time limit. Although the Revenue had neither followed any deliberate general policy, nor made a clear and unambiguous

---

[22] *R. v North and East Devon Health Authority Ex p. Coughlan* [2001] Q.B. 213.
[23] n.12; See also, *R. v Gaming Board of Great Britain Ex p. Kingsley* [1996] C.O.D. 241.
[24] n.12, 731.
[25] *R. v Inland Revenue Commissioners Ex p. Unilever Plc* [1996] S.T.C. 681.

representation, its sudden change of conduct was an unfair breach of the applicant's legitimate expectations and therefore an abuse of power. It is clear that the court reached the finding of abuse of power because it was felt to be unfair for the administration to resile from an administrative practice. This finding only made sense on the basis that the applicant possessed some normatively justified expectation, derived from the administrative practice of not insisting upon the strict time limit.

There was, however, another line of authority, which cast doubt on the existence of substantive legitimate expectations. In *Hargreaves*,[26] the Home Secretary had changed policy on prisoners' home leave with immediate effect in the light of concerns over crimes committed by prisoners on leave. This change had, as the court acknowledged, a severely traumatising effect on some of the prisoners it affected. However, the Court of Appeal held that the Home Office had acted lawfully. Relying primarily on *Findlay*,[27] it rejected the approach taken in *Hamble Fisheries* as "heresy" and "wrong in principle"[28] and stated that the court could interfere only if the administration's decision to apply a new policy was irrational, perverse or *Wednesbury* unreasonable.[29] The impact of *Hargreaves* on the existence of any doctrine of substantive legitimate expectations was not entirely clear. There were aspects of the judgment that could be read as being opposed to any doctrine of substantive legitimate expectations. An alternative reading of the judgment was that no such expectation existed on the facts, and if one were found to have existed the court would review the change of policy which disappointed that expectation only on the *Wednesbury* test, as opposed to any more searching principle of judicial review.

There was however authority for a concept of substantive legitimate **20–014** expectations in the *second type of case*, where a general policy or practice had been departed from in the circumstances of a particular case. In the *Khan*[30] case the applicant alleged that the Home Office had departed from a policy, communicated to him in writing, concerning approval of adoption of family members from abroad. Parker L.J. held, drawing upon Lord Denning's dicta in *HTV*[31] and *Laker Airways*,[32] that a public authority could only go back on a legitimate expectation which it had created by its own policy after granting a hearing and then only if the overriding public interest demanded it.[33] Further authority was provided by the *Ruddock* case.[34] The applicant sought judicial review of a decision to intercept her telephone calls. Taylor J. accepted her argument that fairness might require more than

[26] *R. v Home Secretary Ex p. Hargreaves* [1997] 1 W.L.R. 906; *R. v Secretary of State for Transport Ex p. Richmond upon Thames London BC* [1994] 1 W.L.R. 74; *R. v Secretary of State for Health Ex p. US Tobacco International Inc* [1992] Q.B. 353, 368–369.
[27] *Re Findlay* [1985] A.C. 318.
[28] *Hargreaves*, n.26, 921.
[29] *Hargreaves*, n.26, 924.
[30] *R. v Home Secretary Ex p. Khan* [1984] 1 W.L.R. 1337.
[31] *HTV v Price Commission* [1976] I.C.R. 170, 185.
[32] *Laker Airways v Department of Trade* [1977] Q.B. 643, 707.
[33] n.30, 1344.
[34] *R. v Home Secretary Ex p. Ruddock* [1987] 1 W.L.R. 1482, 1487.

procedural protection, and that she could legitimately expect that the police would comply with published criteria for when telephone interception would take place, unless a departure from those criteria was required for reasons of national security. In *Gangadeen*,[35] the Court of Appeal reaffirmed that "the Home Secretary is in ordinary circumstances obliged to act in accordance with his declared policy"[36] concerning deportation of foreigners with children lawfully residing in Britain.[37]

There was also authority for a concept of substantive legitimate expectations in the *fourth type of case*, where a public body made an individual representation, which was relied on by a person, and the body subsequently sought to resile from the representation. In *Preston*[38] the applicant was assured by the Revenue in 1978 that it would not raise further inquiries on certain tax affairs if he agreed to forgo interest relief which he had claimed and to pay certain capital gains tax. The House of Lords held that the Revenue could not bind itself not to perform its statutory duties. It was therefore in principle entitled to go back on its assurance when it received new information about the applicant's dealings. A court could however hold the Revenue to its assurance where the unfairness to the applicant caused by exercising the statutory duty would amount to an abuse of power. The principles laid down in *Preston* were developed further in *MFK*.[39] Bingham L.J. held that the Revenue could not withdraw from a representation if this would cause substantial unfairness to the applicant, if the conditions for relying upon any such representation were fulfilled, and if holding the Revenue to the representation did not prevent it from exercising its statutory duties. These judgments were couched in terms of abuse of power and substantive fairness, rather than explicitly in terms of legitimate expectations. The reason *why* the administration's actions could be deemed unfair and abusive was that representations had created normatively justified expectations and reliance in the affected individuals.

B. *Coughlan*

20–015   The law on substantive legitimate expectations must now be seen in the light of *Coughlan*.[40] Coughlan had been very seriously injured in a traffic accident in 1971, and was cared for in Newcourt Hospital. The hospital was considered to be unsuited for modern care, and therefore Coughlan and other patients were moved to Mardon House in 1993. The patients were

---

[35] *R. v Home Secretary Ex p. Gangadeen* [1998] 1 F.L.R. 762.
[36] *Gangadeen*, n.35, 766.
[37] See also, *R. v Home Secretary Ex p. Urmaza* [1996] C.O.D. 479.
[38] *R. v Inland Revenue Commissioners Ex p. Preston* [1985] A.C. 835.
[39] *R. v Inland Revenue Commissioners Ex p. MFK Underwriting Agencies Ltd* [1990] 1 W.L.R. 1545. See also *Matrix Securities Ltd v Inland Revenue Commissioners* [1994] 1 W.L.R. 334.
[40] *Coughlan*, n.22. See also, *R. v Merton, Sutton and Wandsworth Health Authority Ex p. P* [2001] A.C.D. 9; *R. (on the application of Theophilus) v London Borough of Lewisham* [2002] 3 All E.R. 851; *R. (on the application of B) v London Borough of Camden* [2001] EWHC Admin 271.

persuaded to move by representations made on behalf of the Health Authority that Mardon House would be more appropriate for their needs. The patients relied on an express assurance or promise that they could live there "for as long as they chose". In October 1998 the Health Authority decided to close Mardon House, and to move the patients to other facilities. A consultation paper issued in August 1998 preceded this decision, and it recognised the force of the promise made to the residents in 1993. The consultation paper was placed before the Health Authority when it made its decision in October 1998. The Health Authority recognised that it had a number of options. It could continue to support Mardon House; it could, in breach of the original promise, assist residents to move elsewhere; or it could move other NHS services into Mardon House. In October 1998 the Health Authority decided to close the facility and to move the residents elsewhere. The applicant challenged this as being in breach of the promise that she would have a home for life. The Court of Appeal distinguished between three situations.

In the first, the court might decide that the public authority was only required to bear in mind its previous policy or other representation, giving it the weight it thought fit, but no more, before deciding to change course. In such cases the court was confined to reviewing the decision on *Wednesbury* grounds. *Findlay*[41] and *Hargreaves*[42] were treated as examples of this type of case.[43]

The second situation was where the court decided that there was a legitimate expectation of being consulted before a decision was taken. In such cases the court would require there to be an opportunity for consultation, unless there was an overriding reason to resile from the undertaking. The court would judge for itself the adequacy of the reason advanced for the change of policy, taking into account what fairness required.[44] This situation was regarded as one where the court would exercise "full review", in the sense that the court would decide for itself whether what happened was fair.[45] The decision in *Ng Yuen Shiu*[46] was cited as an example of this type of case.

The third situation was where the court considered that a lawful promise **20–016** had induced a substantive legitimate expectation. In this type of case it was held that there was authority that the court would decide whether the frustration of the expectation was so unfair that to take a new and different course of action would amount to an abuse of power. When the legitimacy of the expectation had been established, the court would have the task of "weighing the requirements of fairness against any overriding interest relied upon for the change of policy".[47] Most cases within this category were likely

[41] n.27.
[42] n.26.
[43] *Coughlan*, n.22, para.57.
[44] *Coughlan*, n.22, para.57.
[45] *Coughlan*, n.22, para.62.
[46] *Att-Gen For Hong Kong v Ng Yuen Shiu* [1983] 2 A.C. 629.
[47] *Coughlan*, n.22, para.57.

to be those where the expectation was confined to one person, or a few people.[48] *Preston*,[49] *Laker Airways*,[50] *HTV*,[51] *MFK*[52] and *Unilever*[53] were cited as authority for the court's power of review for cases within this third category.[54] *Khan*,[55] *Ruddock*,[56] *CCSU*[57] and *Findlay*[58] were seen[59] as recognising substantive legitimate expectations, even though in a case such as *Findlay* the claim failed on the facts.

The present case was held to come within this third category. This was because of the importance of what was promised to the applicant; because the promise was limited to a few individuals; and because the consequences to the Health Authority of having to honour its promise were only financial.[60]

The recognition that the doctrine of substantive legitimate expectations is part of UK law is to be welcomed. The House of Lords has acknowledged the concept in subsequent cases.[61] The divide between the three types of case in *Coughlan* should, nonetheless, be treated with some caution. It may well be that the first category was created in order to "deal with" cases, primarily *Hargreaves*, that might otherwise have hindered the recognition of substantive legitimate expectations within UK law. This category now appears confined to cases where the original promise was merely to consider taking action.[62] It is clear that the second category, which is concerned primarily with procedural legitimate expectations, is distinct from the other two. The dividing between the first and third categories cannot however be regarded as "hermetically sealed".[63]

We shall consider below the standard of review that applies when a public body seeks to resile from a proven legitimate expectation. Before doing so it is important to address in more detail the factors that will be of relevance in deciding whether a legitimate expectation exists at all.

---

[48] *Coughlan*, n.22, para.59.
[49] n.38.
[50] n.32.
[51] n.31.
[52] n.39.
[53] n.25.
[54] *Coughlan*, n.22, paras 61, 67–69.
[55] n.30.
[56] n.34.
[57] *Council of Civil Service Unions v Minister for the Civil Service* [1985] A.C. 374, 410–411.
[58] n.27.
[59] *Coughlan*, n.22, para.77.
[60] *Coughlan*, n.22, para.60.
[61] *R. v Ministry of Defence Ex p. Walker* [2000] 1 W.L.R. 806; *R. v Secretary of State for the Home Department Ex p. Zeqiri* [2002] UKHL 3, Lord Hoffmann, para.44.
[62] *R. (on the application of Abbasi) v Secretary of State for Foreign and Commonwealth Affairs* [2002] EWCA Civ 1598, para.99.
[63] *R. v Secretary of State for Education and Employment Ex p. Begbie* [2000] 1 W.L.R. 1115, 1130, 1133–1134.

5. INTRA VIRES REPRESENTATIONS: THE DETERMINATION OF WHETHER THE
EXPECTATION IS REASONABLE AND LEGITIMATE

The court will consider a number of factors when determining whether an **20–017**
expectation was reasonable and legitimate.

(1) The most important factor concerns the nature of the representation
itself. A clear and unambiguous promise, undertaking or representation provides the strongest foundation for a claim.[64] Thus
where a public authority had issued a promise or adopted a practice
that represented how it was supposed to act in a given area, the law
would require the promise or practice to be honoured unless there
was a good reason not to do so.[65] The representation may arise from
words or conduct or from a combination of the two.[66] There is,
however, authority that consistent conduct over a long period of
time may give rise to an expectation, even if it was not a clear and
unambiguous representation.[67]

(2) A representation may be based on a variety of sources, including an
individual statement, a circular, a report or an agreement. It will
normally be easier to establish a reasonable expectation the more
specific was the representation in question.[68]

(3) An expectation will not be regarded as reasonable or legitimate if the
applicant could have foreseen that the subject matter of the representation was likely to alter, or that it would not be respected by the
relevant agency. Similarly if the person claiming the benefit knew
that the representor did not intend his statements etc to create an
expectation then this will tell against the expectation being reasonable or legitimate.[69]

---

[64] *MFK*, n.39; *R. v Independent Television Commission Ex p. Flextech plc* [1999] E.M.L.R. 880;
R. (on the application of Montpeliers and Trevors Association) v City of Westminster [2005]
EWHC 16. For cases where the court decided that there was no such representation, or that it
was not deemed to be clear or sufficiently precise, see, e.g., *R. (on the application of Godfrey) v
Conwy County Borough Council* [2001] EWHC Admin 640; *R. v Marie L, The Mayor and
Burgesses of the London Borough of Barking & Dagenham* [2001] 2 F.L.R. 763; *R. (on the
application of Nemeth) v West Berkshire District Council*, December 8, 2000; *R. (on the appli-
cation of C, M, P) v Brent, Kensington and Chelsea and Westminster Mental NHS Trust* [2002]
EWHC 181; *R. (on the application of Association of British Civilian Internees (Far East
Region)) v Secretary of State for Defence* [2002] EWCA Civ 473; *R. (on the application of Vary)
v Secretary of State for the Home Department* [2004] EWHC 2251; *R. (on the application of
Fivepounds.co.ukLtd) v Transport for London* [2005] EWHC 3002; *R. (on the application of
Niazi) v Secretary of State for the Home Department* [2007] EWCA Civ 1495.
[65] *R. (on the application of Nadarajah) v Secretary of State for the Home Department* [2005]
EWCA Civ 1363; *R. (on the application of Greenpeace Ltd) v Secretary of State for Trade and
Industry* [2007] EWHC 311.
[66] *MFK*, n.39; *R. v Gaming Board of Great Britain Ex p. Kingsley* [1996] C.O.D. 241.
[67] *Unilever*, n.25.
[68] *Hamble*, n.12, [1995] 2 All E.R. 714; *United States Tobacco*, n.26.
[69] *Kingsley*, n.66.

(4) If an individual knew or ought to have known that an assurance could only be obtained in a particular way, and a purported assurance was obtained in a different way, it will not be an abuse of power to go back on the assurance.[70]

(5) Detrimental reliance will normally be required in order for the claimant to show that it would be unlawful to go back on a representation.[71] This is in accord with policy, since if the individual has suffered no hardship there is no reason based on legal certainty to hold the agency to its representation. It should not, however, be necessary to show monetary loss, or anything equivalent thereto. There may be moral detriment flowing from disappointment when an expectation is not honoured,[72] although disappointment will not suffice in this respect.[73] While in a strong case there will be both reliance and detriment, there may also be cases where there is reliance, without measurable detriment. It may still be unfair to thwart a legitimate expectation in such circumstances.[74]

(6) Where an agency seeks to depart from an established policy in relation to a particular person detrimental reliance should not be required. Consistency of treatment and equality are at stake in such cases, and these values should be protected irrespective of whether there has been any reliance as such.[75]

(7) An expectation will not be regarded as reasonable or legitimate if the potential beneficiary has not placed "all cards face up on the table".[76] All relevant issues must therefore be disclosed.

(8) The courts will not readily infer a legitimate expectation where it would confer an unmerited or improper benefit, which offended against considerations of fairness and justice.[77]

(9) The court might decide that the nature of the subject matter renders the application of legitimate expectations more problematic. Thus in the context of planning, which is regulated by a comprehensive statutory code, the courts have held that a legitimate expectation arising from the conduct of a local planning authority could only

---

[70] *Matrix Securities*, n.39.
[71] *R. v Secretary of State for the Environment Ex p. NALGO* [1992] C.O.D. 282; *R. v Jockey Club Ex p. RAM Racecourses* [1993] 2 All E.R. 223; *Matrix Securities*, n.39; *Walker*, n.61; *Begbie*, n.63, 1123, 1131, 1133; *R. v London Borough of Newham and Manik Bibi and Ataya Al-Nashed* [2002] 1 W.L.R. 237, para.29; *R. (on the application of Association of British Civilian Internees (Far East Region)) v Secretary of State for Defence* [2002] EWHC 2119, paras 34–35; *R. (on the application of Lindley) v Tameside MBC* [2006] EWHC 2296.
[72] *Bibi*, n.71, paras 54–55.
[73] *The Association of British Civilian Internees*, n.64, para.36.
[74] *Bibi*, n.71, para.31.
[75] *Bibi*, n.71, paras 29–30; *R. (on the application of Rashid) v Secretary of State for the Home Department* [2005] EWCA Civ 744.
[76] *MFK*, n.39, 1569; *Matrix Securities*, n.39.
[77] *Kingsley* [1996] C.O.D. 241, 243; *Matrix Securities*, n.39.

occur in exceptional circumstances, for example where there was no third party or public interest.[78]

(10) Even if the expectation is reasonable and legitimate there may be good reasons why the public body needs to act so as to defeat it. The standard of review which should apply in such circumstances is crucial, and it is to this issue that we should now turn

6. INTRA VIRES REPRESENTATIONS: THE STANDARD OF REVIEW APPLIED WHEN THE ADMINISTRATION SEEKS TO DEFEAT A LEGITIMATE EXPECTATION

A. *Coughlan*

i. The court's reasoning
The distinction between the types of case was regarded as important in **20–018** *Coughlan* for the standard of review. In the first type of case the normal *Wednesbury* test would apply. In the second, the court would engage in "full review", deciding for itself whether the departure from a procedural legitimate expectation was fair. It is the standard of review in the third type of case that is of particular interest. This will be a live issue where, as in *Coughlan*, the public body seeks to resile from the legitimate expectation on the ground that the public interest demands that this should be so.

The Court of Appeal in *Coughlan* accepted that public bodies must be able to change policy, and that undertakings were therefore open to modification or abandonment.[79] It followed that the court's task in such cases was "not to impede executive activity but to reconcile its continuing need to initiate or respond to change with the legitimate interests or expectations of citizens or strangers who have relied, and have been justified in relying, on a current policy or an extant promise".[80] This was all the more so given that there were two lawful exercises of power in this type of case: the promise and the policy change.[81] It was this consideration which led the court to distinguish between two standards of judicial review of discretion.

There was, on the one hand, bare or intrinsic irrationality, which allowed the court to intervene to quash a decision which defied comprehension in the sense articulated by Lord Greene[82] and Lord Diplock.[83] Such cases were

---

[78] *Henry Boot Homes Ltd v Bassetlaw DC* [2002] EWCA Civ 983; *R. (on the application of Wandsworth LBC) v Secretary of State for Transport, Local Government and the Regions* [2003] EWHC 622.
[79] *Coughlan*, n.22, para.64.
[80] *Coughlan*, n.22, para.65.
[81] *Coughlan*, n.22, para.66.
[82] *Associated Picture Houses Ltd v Wednesbury Corporation* [1948] 1 K.B. 223, 228–230.
[83] *Council of Civil Service Unions*, n.57, 410–411.

rare. Rationality also embraced decisions made on the basis of flawed logic. The court in *Coughlan* rejected this criterion.[84] Where there were, as here, two lawful exercises of power, a "bare rationality test would constitute the public authority judge in its own cause, for a decision to prioritise a policy change over legitimate expectations will almost always be rational from where the authority stands, even if objectively it is arbitrary or unfair".[85]

There was, on the other hand, intervention on the grounds of abuse of power. A power which had been abused had not been lawfully exercised.[86] The court's task was to ensure that the power to alter policy was not abused by unfairly frustrating individual legitimate expectations. *Preston*[87] was treated as the principal authority for judicial review for abuse of power, although a number of other cases[88] were cited in support.[89] Abuse of power could take many forms. To renege on a lawful promise made to a limited number of individuals without adequate justification was one such type of case. There was, said the Court of Appeal, no suggestion in *Preston*, or other relevant cases,[90] that the final arbiter of a decision which frustrated a substantive legitimate expectation was, rationality apart, the decision-maker rather than the court.[91] Nor was there any suggestion that judicial review in such instances was confined to the bare rationality of the decision.[92] The court would intervene where there had been an abuse of power, and this was a matter for the court to determine.[93] Policy and the reasons for changing it, were for the public authority. The court's task "is then limited to asking whether the application of the policy to an individual who has been led to expect something different is a just exercise of power".[94] The applicant's substantive legitimate expectation could not be frustrated unless there was an overriding public interest, and whether this existed or not was a matter for the court.[95] The court found in favour of the applicant on the facts of the case.

ii. Assessment

20–019 The reasons given in *Coughlan* for rejecting the *Wednesbury* test,[96] in the original manner conceived of by Lord Greene M.R. are convincing. The test does not strike the right balance between the needs of the administration,

---

[84] *Hargreaves*, n.20, was distinguished in part by placing it in the first of the *Coughlan* categories, to which the *Wednesbury* test was applied, and in part by treating the more general statements about the standard of review as obiter.
[85] *Coughlan*, n.22, para.66.
[86] *Coughlan*, n.22, para.70.
[87] n.38.
[88] *Unilever*, n.25; *HTV*, n.31; *Laker*, n.32; *MFK*, n.39.
[89] *Coughlan*, n.22, paras 67–69.
[90] *R. v Devon County Council Ex p. Baker* [1995] 1 All E.R. 73.
[91] *Coughlan*, n.22, paras 69, 74.
[92] *Coughlan*, n.22, paras 74, 77.
[93] *Coughlan*, n.22, para.81.
[94] *Coughlan*, n.22, para.82.
[95] *Coughlan*, n.22, para.76.
[96] n.82.

and fairness to the individual. It would require the individual to show that the agency's decision to act in a manner inconsistent with the legitimate expectation was so unreasonable that no reasonable agency would have done it. It would, as recognised in *Coughlan*, be almost impossible for the individual to succeed on this criterion.[97]

The court in *Coughlan* preferred, as seen above, to use abuse of power as the criterion for testing whether a public body could resile from a prima facie legitimate expectation. This is however problematic for the following reason. Abuse of power may well properly be regarded as the *conceptual rationale* for judicial intervention to protect substantive legitimate expectations.[98] It encapsulates the conclusion that the applicant had some normatively justified expectation, since there would otherwise have been no foundation for finding such an abuse. The term abuse of power can also capture the conclusion that the court has found the public body's argument for going back on the expectation to be unconvincing. It must however also be recognised that abuse of power does not, in itself, furnish a *standard of review* for deciding whether a public body can resile from a proven substantive expectation. Abuse of power can express the conclusion reached under any such standard, but does not itself constitute a standard of review.[99]

B. *Nadarajah*

i. The court's reasoning

The decision in *Nadarajah* is to be welcomed for clarifying this issue.[100] The facts were as follows. The normal position under the 1999 Asylum Act was that an asylum seeker who sought asylum in another country and then sought asylum in the UK would be returned to the other country, provided it was regarded as safe. This was qualified by the Family Links Policy, FLP, which provided that potential third country cases would nonetheless be considered in the UK where, inter alia, the applicant's spouse was in the UK. This included presence of the spouse in the UK as an asylum seeker. N's spouse came to the UK, was refused asylum, but sought to appeal that decision. N did not know of the FLP. The Secretary of State said that the FLP was not applicable, because N's spouse had been denied entry as an

20–020

---

[97] *Coughlan*, n.22, para.66.
[98] *Coughlan*, n.22, *Unilever*, n.25, *Zeqiri*, n.61; *R. (on the application of Bancoult) v Secretary of State for Foreign and Commonwealth Affairs* [2007] EWCA Civ 498, para.60.
[99] See further, *R. (on the application of S) v Secretary of State for the Home Department* [2007] EWCA Civ 546, paras 39–42.
[100] *Nadarajah*, n.65; P. Sales, "Legitimate Expectations" [2006] J.R. 186; C. Hilson, "Policies, the Non-Fetter Principle and the Principle of Substantive Legitimate Expectations: Between a Rock and a Hard Place?" [2006] J.R. 289; M. Elliott, "Legitimate Expectations and the Search for Principle: Reflections on *Abdi & Nadarajah*" [2006] J.R. 281; C. Knight, "The Test that Dare not Speak its Name: Proportionality Comes out of the Closet?" [2007] J.R. 117; see also, *R. (on the application of Bamber) v Revenue and Customs Commissioners* [2005] EWHC 3221; *R. (on the application of Fingle Glen Junction Business and Community Action Group) v Highways Agency* [2007] EWHC 2446.

asylum seeker, even though she was appealing that decision. The High Court decided that the Secretary of State's construction of the term asylum seeker was wrong, and held that she was still an asylum seeker while her appeal was pending.

N claimed that he had a legitimate expectation that the FLP should be applied to him and that there was in effect a departure from that policy in the instant case. The Secretary of State argued that there had been no abuse of power, since N had not known of the FLP, and hence there was no reliance.

The judgment of the Court of Appeal was given by Laws L.J. He held that the concept of abuse of power might well underlie the law in this area, in the sense that it captured the idea that an act of a public authority that was not legally justified would be an abuse of power, but he recognised that the concept of abuse of power would not in itself tell one whether in a particular case public action really was lawful or not. It could therefore be a conclusory label but little more.

Laws L.J. then addressed more specifically the nature of the legal test that should apply when a public body sought to depart from a legitimate expectation. He held that where a public authority issued a promise or adopted a practice which represented how it proposed to act in a particular area the law required the practice or promise to be honoured unless there was a good reason not to do so.[101] The underlying rationale was good administration.

A public body's promise or practice could, said Laws L.J., only be denied or departed from where to do so was the public body's legal duty, or was otherwise a proportionate response of which the court was the last judge having regard to a legitimate aim pursued by the public body in the public interest. The "principle that good administration requires public authorities to be held to their promises would be undermined if the law did not insist that any failure or refusal to comply is objectively justified as a proportionate measure in the circumstances".[102] The existence of detrimental reliance was no more than a factor to be weighed in deciding whether denial of the expectation was proportionate.[103] This approach was held to apply to both procedural and substantive legitimate expectations.

ii. Assessment

20–021 The judgment in *Nadarajah* is important, and has more general implications for proportionality as a test for review.[104] Two comments can be made about the test in the context of legitimate expectations.

Firstly, the proportionality test articulated by Laws L.J. for deciding whether a public body can go back on or depart from a legitimate

---

[101] *Nadarajah*, n.65, para.68.
[102] *Nadarajah*, n.65, para.68.
[103] *Nadarajah*, n.65, para.70.
[104] See above, para.19–010.

expectation has beneficially clarified this area of the law.[105] Abuse of power does not in reality encapsulate a standard of review, although it might well be a fitting conclusory label to append to the application of any other test. The traditional *Wednesbury* test would be too narrow; the applicant would almost never win on such a test and it was ruled out by *Coughlan*. It is true that the *Wednesbury* test could be applied more intensively in cases of this kind,[106] or the courts could adopt the interpretation of the reasonableness test by Lord Cooke.[107] We have, however, seen that the more particular factors taken into account when reasonableness is interpreted in this manner would be very like those considered in proportionality.[108]

Proportionality review is therefore the best option, and it will of course only ever come into play if the applicant manages to establish that there is a substantive legitimate expectation in the first place. If the applicant does surmount this hurdle then it is fitting in normative terms that a pro-portionality test should be used to determine the legality of action that purports to resile or depart from the substantive legitimate expectation. The proportionality test provides a structured analysis which facilitates review, and forces the agency to give a reasoned justification for its course of action. Indeed the reasoning actually used in *Coughlan* to decide whether the public body could resile from the applicant's substantive expectation was very close to a proportionality inquiry. The way in which the standard of review is applied will depend on the nature of the case. The courts will be more reluctant to interfere with general changes of policy, than with cases where a representation is made to a discrete group.[109] This variability can however be accommodated within a proportionality inquiry.

Second, while the general test adopted by Laws L.J. is to be welcomed, the precise meaning of the condition that a public authority could depart from a prima facie expectation where it had the legal duty to do so, is not entirely clear. It could be intended to capture the situation where the initial repre-sentation was intra vires, but where there was then some supervening legal duty embodied in a subsequent statute that required the public authority to depart from the representation. It could, in addition, be intended to cover the case where the initial representation was ultra vires, although doubt has

---

[105] The application of the test to the facts was more questionable. The court found against the applicant in part because he had not relied on the FLP. It is however generally acknowledged that absence of reliance is less important in departure cases, see *Rashid*, n.75. The other reason for finding against the applicant was that he was said to be seeking a windfall gain from the Secretary of State's misinterpretation of the FLP concerning the meaning of asylum seeker. If however the Secretary of State's interpretation of the term was wrong in the view of the reviewing court, the applicant should be entitled to rely on the correct reading of the term and have the policy applied accordingly. The effect of the judgment on the facts was to allow the Secretary of State to modify the FLP and then apply the modified FLP retrospectively to the original claimant.

[106] C. Forsyth, "*Wednesbury* Protection of Substantive Legitimate Expectations" [1997] P.L. 375.

[107] *R. v Chief Constable of Sussex Ex p. International Trader's Ferry Ltd* [1999] 1 All E.R. 129.

[108] See above, para.19–025.

[109] *Begbie*, n.63, 1130–1131.

been cast as to whether this should always preclude a claim based on legitimate expectations.[110]

C. *Bibi*

i. *The court's reasoning*

20–022 The court might decide to remit the case back to the original decision-maker, where a legitimate expectation has been found to exist.

The *Bibi* case provides a good example.[111] The applicants had been provided with accommodation for the homeless. The local authority promised that it would provide them with security of tenure. It had made this promise because it thought, wrongly, that it was under a duty to provide permanent accommodation. The local authority sought to renege on the promise, having become aware that it did not have a duty to give permanent accommodation. Schiemann L.J. held that the promise had created a substantive legitimate expectation.[112] He held further that when an authority, without even considering that it is in breach of a promise giving rise to a legitimate expectation, acts at variance with the promise, then the authority is abusing its power.[113]

The court did not however order the local authority to provide the secure accommodation. It remitted the case to the local authority and imposed a duty on it to consider the applicants' housing on the basis that they had a legitimate expectation that they would be given secure accommodation. The reason for this strategy was that while the applicants had a legitimate expectation, so too did other people on the council's accommodation list, and the overall stock of housing was limited. It might also be open to the local authority to help the applicants in some other way, if it felt unable to give them secure housing.[114] The court nonetheless made it clear that the assumption was that effect should be given to the legitimate expectation. If the local authority decided not to do so, it had to provide reasons, and it would be open to the applicants to test those reasons in court.[115]

ii. *Assessment*

20–023 The option of remitting the case back to the public body is useful. This is especially so, in cases such as *Bibi*, where there are others who can be directly affected by enforcement of the legitimate expectation. The assumption is that the public body will give effect to the expectation, and if this transpires it side steps difficult issues about the standard of review. If

[110] *Rowland v Environment Agency* [2005] Ch.1.
[111] *Bibi*, n.71. See also, *Theophilus*, n.40, paras 27–29; *B*, n.40, para.32.
[112] *Bibi*, n.71, para.46.
[113] *Bibi*, n.71, paras 39, 49–51.
[114] *Bibi*, n.71, para.58.
[115] *Bibi*, n.71, para.59.

this assumption is not borne out, the applicant can challenge the resultant decision.

7. Intra Vires Representations and Legitimate Expectations: Types of Case

We have examined the criteria used to determine whether a legally **20–024** enforceable expectation exists, and the test for deciding whether a public body can resile from such an expectation. We should now consider in more detail the application of these precepts to the different types of legitimate expectation case.

A. Changes of Policy
There is no doubt that cases that fall within this category are the most **20–025** problematic. They should nonetheless be capable of generating a legitimate expectation. This is so for reasons of principle, as supported by authority.

In terms of principle, public bodies must of course be able to change their policy. A substantive legitimate expectation does not however normally prevent any such policy change, but the time at which it is to take effect. Moreover, if the courts were to say that the doctrine could never apply to this type of case, it would create difficult boundary problems between this category and the others. The line between a general policy and an individual representation may well be difficult in cases where, for example, there is some administrative practice or representation, which affects a group of people across time.

In terms of authority, the fact situations in cases such as *Hamble Fisheries*,[116] *Hargreaves*,[117] and *Godfrey*[118] provide examples of situations in which a change of policy might give rise to a substantive legitimate expectation claim. This is so notwithstanding the fact that the claims failed in these cases. The individual may nonetheless properly argue that she had a legitimate expectation based on representations flowing from things said or done under the old policy, and that this was ignored in the transition from the old policy to the new. This argument would be even stronger in circumstances where there were no transitional or "pipeline" provisions between the two policies. Whether the individual can show the legitimate expectation will of course depend on the facts, and it will be open to the public body to argue that there was an overriding public interest to defeat any such expectation.

---

[116] n.12.
[117] n.20.
[118] n.64.

This is exemplified by *Bancoult*.[119] The inhabitants of the Chagos Islands were compulsorily removed from their land by an Immigration Ordinance in 1971, which was quashed on the ground that the exclusion of an entire population from its land was ultra vires the relevant Order. The government stated that it accepted the court's ruling and would allow the Chagossians to return home. However, the government later decided that resettlement was not feasible and that the territory was still wanted for defence purposes. It therefore enacted Orders in Council, which prevented the Chagossians from returning home.

The court held that the Secretary of State had impermissibly frustrated the claimants' legitimate expectation that they would be allowed to return home.[120] The public promise made by the Secretary of State to right the wrong exposed by the earlier judgment had been implemented by the enactment in 2000 of a right of return for Chagossians, and the Orders in Council of 2004 had gone back on that undertaking. The court did not accept that the reasons cited for doing so, the non-feasibility of resettlement and use of the territory for defence purposes, outweighed the claimants' legitimate expectations. The government had not proffered evidence to show that matters had changed in this regard since 2000, more especially given the importance of the claimants' interest in being able to return to their home.

B. Departure from an Existing Policy

20–026 There are cases where the public authority seeks to depart from an existing policy in relation to a particular applicant. Such cases are somewhat less difficult than those where there is a general change of policy for the future. This is because it will normally be less drastic for a court to compel an agency to apply an existing policy to a particular applicant, and because considerations of equality as well as legitimate expectations will be relevant here. It is indeed the case that even if the applicant is unable to prove a legitimate expectation, considerations of equality should, in and of themselves, suffice as the basis of the claim, unless the agency can show convincing reasons for departure from the policy in this instance.[121] The judicial approach is exemplified by the following two cases.

In *Ruddock*[122] the applicant, who had been a prominent member of the Campaign for Nuclear Disarmament, sought judicial review of a decision to intercept her telephone calls. She argued that she had a legitimate expectation that the published criteria as to when this would be done would be followed. Taylor J. recognised that where *ex hypothesi* there would be no right to be heard before making the interception order, it would be particularly important that the ministerial undertaking should be followed. He accepted that the Minister's power could not be fettered, but correctly

---

[119] *Bancoult*, n.98. See also, *R. (on the application of BAPIO Action Ltd) v Secretary of State for the Home Department* [2008] 2 W.L.R. 1073.
[120] *Bancoult*, n.98, paras 72–76, 100.
[121] *Bibi*, n.71, paras 29–30; *Dotan*, n.2.
[122] *Ruddock*, n.34.

placed this idea in perspective: the publication of a policy did not preclude any future change; nor did it prevent the non-application of that policy in a particular case for reasons of national security. The Minister had not, however, argued that the policy should be dispensed with on these grounds, and therefore the applicant had a legitimate expectation that the published criteria would be applied.[123]

In *Rashid*[124] the applicant was an Iraqi Kurd who was initially denied asylum. However this decision was made without taking account of Home Office policy to the effect that from October 2000 the possibility of internal relocation from government-controlled Iraq to the Kurdish Autonomous Zone would not be treated as a reason for refusing a claim for refugee status.[125] The case workers who initially dealt with the case did not know of this policy and therefore the applicant did not benefit from it. The Home Office nonetheless sought to uphold the decision, arguing that it could be regarded as valid in the light of the situation now prevailing in Iraq and because the applicant had not relied on the Home Office policy, since he had no knowledge of it. The Court of Appeal held that there had been an abuse of power, by reason of the failure to apply the correct policy to the applicant, and there was no countervailing public interest to justify this. It was irrelevant that the applicant had not relied on the policy, since it would said the Court be grossly unfair if the ability of the court to intervene was dependent on whether the applicant had heard of the policy or not, more especially given that some of the Home Office officials were themselves unaware of the policy.

The status of policy, and the legal rules which should apply when an agency seeks to depart from an established policy, were also considered in *Urmaza*[126] and *Gangadeen*.[127] A number of propositions can be distilled from these cases, read together with *Ruddock*, *Rashid* and *Munjaz*.[128]

(1)   The legal principle of consistency in the exercise of public law powers creates a presumption that the agency or minister will follow a declared policy. This presumption flows from the very purpose of such a policy, which is to secure consistency.

(2)   If there is a departure from the policy then reasons must be given to justify this.

---

[123] The applicant failed on the facts because the court held that the minister could have concluded that the criteria were applicable.

[124] *Rashid*, n.75; M. Elliott, "Legitimate Expectation, Consistency and Abuse of Power: The *Rashid* Case" [2005] J.R. 281.

[125] The rationale for this policy was because it had come to light that the Kurdish authorities would not, because of limited resources and infrastructure facilities, admit those who had not previously been resident in the area.

[126] *Urmaza*, n.37. See also, *R. v Secretary of State for the Environment Ex p. West Oxfordshire District Council* [1994] C.O.D. 134; *R. (on the application of Coghlan) v Chief Constable of Greater Manchester* [2005] 2 All E.R. 890; *R. (on the application of Gill) v Lord Chancellor's Department* [2003] EWHC 156.

[127] *Gangadeen*, n.35.

[128] *R. (on the application of Munjaz) v Mersey Care NHS Trust* [2006] 2 A.C. 148.

(3)   The agency should, when considering a departure from an established policy, weigh the interests of those affected by the existing policy with the need to depart from it in the instant case.

(4)   The courts will construe the meaning of such policies. Thus where the policy is framed in ordinary English, the court will ensure that it is not given an interpretation which is inconsistent with its plain and ordinary meaning. Similarly, where the decision is predicated on the existence of certain legal categories the court will hold the agency to these. Thus, "consistency, in the eye of the law, does not extend to being consistently wrong".[129] Where the policy contains specialist terms, or jargon, the court respects evidence as to its meaning, but not so as to subvert the object of the policy.

(5)   There is a difference of opinion as the standard of review that should be applied to determine the legality of a departure from an established policy. In *Urmaza* Sedley J. held that the courts were not restricted to a bare rationality test in this regard.[130] In *Gangadeen* the Court of Appeal took a different view. Hirst L.J. held that review should be limited to traditional grounds,[131] and disapproved of Sedley J.'s suggestions that it should be more intensive. This ruling was however given prior to *Coughlan*.[132] The argument in *Coughlan* for more intensive review than bare rationality is especially apposite here, given that it is a departure from an existing policy which is in issue.

C. Individualised Representations

20–027   We have seen that the problem of apparent retroactivity covers measures, whether individual or general, which change previous measures or representations with effect for events that have already occurred, but which have not yet been wholly concluded, or with effect for some transaction which is in the process of completion. Where the representor makes a decision to depart from a prior representation we are therefore dealing with a problem of apparent retroactivity. It is clear that the courts will protect the individual in some such cases and that in doing so it is protecting substantive legitimate expectations.

In *Preston*[133] P made an agreement with the Revenue in 1978 to forgo interest relief which he had claimed and he also paid some capital gains tax. In return, the inspector said that he would not raise any further inquiries on certain tax affairs. The Revenue however decided to apply provisions of the tax legislation in 1982, following receipt of new information concerning the same transaction. P sought judicial review of this decision. Lord

---

[129] *Urmaza*, n.37, 484.
[130] *Urmaza*, n.37, 483–485.
[131] [1998] C.O.D. 216, 218.
[132] n.22.
[133] *Preston*, n.38.

Templeman, giving the judgment, stated that P would have no remedy for breach of the representation as such, because the Revenue could not bind itself in 1978 not to perform its statutory duty in 1982.[134] Judicial review was, however, available[135]: a court could direct the Revenue to abstain from performing its statutory duties or exercising its powers where the unfairness to the applicant of doing so rendered such insistence an abuse of power.[136] Conduct by the Revenue that was equivalent to a breach of representation could constitute such abuse of power.[137] Although the judgment was framed in terms of abuse of power, the Revenue's action could only have been thus regarded if its prior representation gave rise to some normative expectation which was worthy of protection.

Further authority is provided by the *MFK* case.[138] The applicants **20–028** approached the Inland Revenue as to whether certain investments would be taxed as capital or income. The initial response from the Revenue convinced the applicants that the investments would be taxed as capital, but the Revenue later resolved to tax the assets as income. Bingham L.J. held that the applicants must fail if the representation was in breach of the Revenue's statutory duty. No such breach was present on the facts, since the Revenue was merely acting in pursuance of its proper managerial discretion. In such circumstances the Revenue could not withdraw from its representation *if* this would cause substantial unfairness to the applicant, and *if* the conditions for relying upon any such representation were present. Those conditions were that: the applicant should give full details of the transaction on which the Revenue's ruling was being sought; the applicant should make it apparent that it was seeking a considered ruling which it intended to rely upon; and the ruling itself would have to be clear and unambiguous.[139] The applicants failed on the facts, but the case clearly demonstrates that a representation given by a public body pursuant to the exercise of its statutory discretion can, subject to the above conditions, be relied upon.

It is, moreover, clear from *Matrix Securities*[140] that the courts will insist strictly on full disclosure of the relevant material, more particularly where the purported assurance has been given in relation to, for example, a tax avoidance scheme which should never have been authorised in this manner.

It was not entirely clear what test for review the courts would use in such cases if the public body argued that there was some public interest for departing from its initial representation. It is now clear that there are two aspects to review in such cases. The public body must give the person who has a substantive legitimate expectation the opportunity to present arguments as to why the expectation should not be defeated by the public body's

---

[134] *Preston*, n.38, 862.
[135] *Preston*, n.38, 862–863.
[136] *Preston*, n.38, 864G. Lord Templeman drew on a similar formulation of Lord Denning MR in *HTV* n.31, 185–186.
[137] [1985] A.C. 835, 866–867. The applicant failed on the facts, 867–871.
[138] *MFK*, n.39.
[139] *MFK*, n.39, 1568–1569.
[140] *Matrix Securities*, n.39.

subsequent change of view.[141] *Coughlan* made it clear that a standard of review going beyond bare rationality should be applied in this type of case,[142] and the test from *Nadarajah*[143] will be applicable to this type of case. The argument for more intensive review is especially forceful in the *Preston* type of case. In cases where a public body seeks to go back on an individual representation, there will be no wider repercussions of the kind that can arise where there is a shift from one policy to another.

The assumption in the preceding cases was that the representation was intra vires.[144] However, if a court believes that no balancing should be undertaken if the representation is ultra vires, but it wishes to consider the effects of the representation on the individual, this may cause the court to categorise the representation as intra rather than ultra vires.[145] This is particularly so because, as will be seen below, if a public authority has made an ultra vires representation the courts will be reluctant to allow the representation to have any binding force.

D. Decisions, Final Determinations and Estoppel by Record

i. Final Determinations

20–029 The discussion in the previous section was concerned with cases where there has been a representation, which the individual seeks to rely on. This should be distinguished from the case where there has been a final determination, which cannot be altered because it is a dispositive decision in that case.

This is exemplified by the *Denton Road* case.[146] The plaintiff's house was damaged during the war and later demolished by the local authority. The preliminary determination by the War Damage Commission was that the property was a total loss. This was later altered, the Commission saying that the loss was non-total. A third turn of the wheel caused them to revert to the categorisation of total loss. Greater compensation would be paid where the loss was non-total. It was held that the second determination was final and that where Parliament had imposed a duty of deciding any question the deciding of which affected the rights of subjects, such a decision, when made and communicated in terms which were not preliminary, was final and conclusive. It could not, in the absence of express statutory power or the consent of the person affected, be withdrawn.[147] The intra vires decision was binding as a valid decision, in and of itself.[148]

---

[141] *R. (on the application of Machi) v Legal services Commission* [2002] A.C.D. 8.
[142] n.22.
[143] *Nadarajah*, n.65.
[144] See *MFK*, n.39.
[145] See, e.g., the approach in *MFK*, n.39; *Bibi*, n.71.
[146] *Re 56 Denton Road, Twickenham, Middlesex* [1953] Ch.51. See also, *Livingstone v Westminster Corporation* [1904] 2 K.B. 109, 120; *R. v Ministry of Agriculture, Fisheries and Food Ex p. Cox* [1993] 2 C.M.L.R. 917.
[147] *56 Denton Road*, n.146, 56–57.
[148] *56 Denton Road*, n.146, 57. No reliance on the original decision will be possible where that decision was based upon facts which have been falsified by the applicant, *R. v Dacorum Borough Council Ex p. Walsh* [1992] C.O.D. 125.

The scope of the holding in this case is not, however, clear. In *Rootkin*[149] the plaintiff's daughter was given a place at a school, which the local authority believed to be over three miles from her home. They thereby were obliged to provide transport or to reimburse travelling expenses, and decided upon the latter. They later measured the distance once again and, having decided that it was less than three miles, withdrew the funding. The plaintiff relied, inter alia, on the *Denton Road* case. The argument was rejected, the court saying that it had no application where the citizen was receiving only a discretionary benefit as opposed to a statutory right, since this would fetter the discretion of the public body.[150]

The principle in *Denton Road* is surely correct. When a public body makes what is a lawful final decision this should be binding upon it, even in the absence of detrimental reliance. A citizen should be entitled to assume that it will not be overturned by a second decision, even if the latter is equally lawful. The principle of legal certainty has a particularly strong application in these circumstances, and the ideal that there must be an end to litigation is equally apposite here as elsewhere. Where the initial decision is changed because of a mistake or misinterpretation of the facts then, if there has been detrimental reliance, compensation should be granted. Provided that the applicant has not misled the public body then the onus of ensuring that the facts are correctly applied should be on the public body.

It should make no difference whether the initial decision was the determination of a statutory right or the exercise of discretion. The line between the two may well be a fine one. Moreover, once discretion is definitively concretised in its application to a particular person the argument that the person should be able to rely upon it is equally strong as in the case of a decision about rights. This is supported by the decision in the *MFK* case.[151] The applicant failed on the facts, but the case clearly demonstrates that a discretionary determination will not necessarily be defeated by the argument that to sanction such a result would be a fetter on the general discretion of that body.[152] Any lawful decision will perforce limit the way in which discretion can be used by ruling out other options.

ii. Estoppel by Record

A decision may also be final because of the doctrine of estoppel by record or, as it is often known, estoppel *per rem judicatem*.[153] There are two species of this estoppel. One is known as cause of action estoppel. If the same cause of action has been litigated to a final judgment between the same parties, or their privies, litigating in the same capacity, no further action is possible, the principle being that there must be an end to litigation. The other form of

20–030

---

[149] *Rootkin v Kent County Council* [1981] 1 W.L.R. 1186.
[150] *Rootkin*, n.149, 1195–1197, 1200.
[151] [1990] 1 W.L.R. 1545.
[152] See also, *Preston*, n.38; *Gillingham Borough Council v Medway (Chatham) Dock Co Ltd* [1992] 3 W.L.R. 449.
[153] *Cross and Tapper on Evidence* (Oxford University Press, 11th edn, 2007), 94–105.

estoppel by record is issue estoppel. A single cause of action may contain several distinct issues. Where there is a final judgment between the same parties, or their privies, litigating in the same capacity on the same issue, then that issue cannot be reopened in subsequent proceedings.[154]

The application of the res judicata doctrine in the public law context was reaffirmed in *Thrasyvoulou*.[155] It was held that in relation to adjudication, which was subject to a comprehensive self-contained statutory code, the presumption was that where the statute had created a specific jurisdiction for the determination of any issue which established the existence of a legal right, the principle of res judicata applied to give finality to that determination, unless an intention to exclude that principle could be inferred as a matter of construction from the statutory provisions.[156]

Res judicata expresses the binding nature of a matter litigated to final judgment. In administrative law jurisdictional matters decided by a tribunal or other public body are not final in this sense. They will be determined by the reviewing court.[157] This is exemplified by *Hutchings*.[158] A local Board of Health applied to the justices under the Public Health Act 1875 to recover the expenses of repairing a street from a person whose property was on that street. The claimant contended that it was a public highway repairable by the inhabitants at large. This contention was upheld by the justices. Some years later the Board of Health made an application against the same person, and on this occasion the justices did order payment of expenses. The plea that the matter was res judicata because of the earlier decision was rejected. It was held that, on construction, the justices had no power to decide whether the street was or was not a public highway; that was a matter only incidentally cognisable by them. Their only jurisdiction was to determine whether a sum of money should be paid or not.[159] Even where the subject-matter is clearly within the jurisdiction of the tribunal, there may be a temporal limit to the conclusiveness of that tribunal's findings which limits the application of res judicata. This is illustrated by cases concerning rating and taxes.[160]

Provided that the issue is within the subject-matter and temporal jurisdiction of the public body, res judicata will prevent the same matter being litigated before the original tribunal over again. Whether the public body is performing administrative rather than judicial tasks is not relevant for the application of res judicata, nor is the existence of a *lis inter partes*.[161]

---

[154] See *R. (on the application of Shamsun Nahar) v Social Security Commissioners* [2002] A.C.D. 28, for a recent, unsuccessful, attempt to plead issue estoppel against a public body.
[155] *Thrasyvoulou v Secretary of State for the Environment* [1990] 2 A.C. 273, 289.
[156] See, e.g., *Special Effects Ltd v L'Oreal SA* [2007] EWCA Civ 1; there can be exceptional circumstances justifying non-application of the cause of action estoppel rule, *R. (on the application of East Hertfordshire DC) v First Secretary of State* [2007] EWHC 834.
[157] See, Ch.14.
[158] *R. v Hutchings* [1881] 6 Q.B.D. 300, 304–305; *R. v Secretary of State for the Environment Ex p. Hackney London Borough Council* [1984] 1 W.L.R. 592.
[159] Cf. *Wakefield Corporation v Cooke* [1904] A.C. 31.
[160] *Society of Medical Officers of Health v Hope* [1960] A.C. 551; *Caffoor v Commissioner of Income Tax* [1961] A.C. 584.
[161] *Caffoor* [1961] A.C. 584, 597–599.

The label res judicata is, however, only required where an applicant attempts to litigate the matter over again before the original decision-maker. In circumstances where the individual has received one decision from the public body, and then attempts to have this reversed on appeal or review, the label is not really required. If the original decision is intra vires then it is binding simply because it is a lawful decision given by the appropriate body. The term res judicata is of use to prevent frequent attempts to determine the same point. Thus, if an applicant attempts to obtain a decision from one tribunal, fails, tries later on the same point, still fails, and then seeks appeal or review, res judicata is an appropriate label to apply provided that the original decision was intra vires.

8. ULTRA VIRES REPRESENTATIONS AND LEGITIMATE EXPECTATIONS: THE CURRENT LAW

The discussion thus far has been concerned with intra vires representations. It is now necessary to consider the law and policy relating to ultra vires representations. A representation will be ultra vires if it is outside the power of the public body, or the officer who made it. The topic will be analysed in the following way.   **20–031**

First, the present law concerning ultra vires representations will be examined. The law in this area has been based on the jurisdictional principle, which has traditionally been taken to mean that representations made by an agent who lacks authority, or representations leading to decisions which are ultra vires the public body itself, cannot be binding.[162] It is for this reason that it is said that estoppel can have no role in this area. Second, the jurisdictional principle will be reassessed. It will be argued that there are circumstances in which it is possible to allow even an ultra vires assurance to bind without the dire results predicted by traditional theory. Third, criteria will be suggested for judging whether such representations should be allowed to bind.

A. The Jurisdictional Principle: The Relationship of Ultra Vires, Agency and Delegation

It is necessary to distinguish between two questions that may arise when a public body makes a representation. The first is whether the agent acting for   **20–032**

---

[162] G. Treitel, "Crown Proceedings: Some Recent Developments" [1957] P.L. 321, 335–339; G. Ganz, "Estoppel and Res Judicata in Administrative Law" [1965] P.L. 237; M. Fazal, "Reliability of Official Acts and Advice" [1972] P.L. 43; P. Craig, "Representations By Public Bodies" (1977) 93 L.Q.R. 398; A. Bradley, "Administrative Justice and the Binding Effect of Official Acts" (1981) C.L.P. 1; M. Elliott, "Unlawful Representations, Legitimate Expectations and Estoppel" [2003] J.R. 71; M. Elliott, "Legitimate Expectations and Unlawful Representations" [2004] C.L.J. 261; D. Blundell, "*Ultra Vires* Legitimate Expectations" [2005] J.R. 147.

the public body had authority, actual or apparent, to make the representation in question. This is dependent upon the law of agency. The second is whether the decision resulting from the representation made by the public body or agent is intra vires or ultra vires. This is dependent upon the extent of the powers given to that body.

For the jurisdictional principle to be effective a limit must be imposed upon the apparent authority of the agent, which cannot extend to a matter that is ultra vires in either of two senses. The decision resulting from the representation may be outside the powers of the public body itself, or within its power but incapable of being made by that public officer. Thus, in theory at least, it can be said that whenever a public official has apparent authority the decision itself must be intra vires, since otherwise the agent would not have had authority.

This is not an exceptional position. Company law had to deal with the relationship of ultra vires and agency arising from the limitations on the corporation imposed by its memorandum and articles of association.[163] The similarity between the formulation laid down above and that of Diplock L.J. in *Freeman*[164] is due to the conceptual identity of the problem in public law and company law.

The *Silva* case[165] exemplifies the application of these principles in a public law context. The Collector of Customs in Ceylon advertised certain property for sale by auction in March 1947. He was mistaken in treating this as saleable, for in November 1946 an officer of the Ministry of Supply had taken over the goods and had contracted to sell them to a Ceylon firm in January 1947. The plaintiff was the buyer at the sale organised by the Collector of Customs. The Collector became aware of the earlier sale, and refused to deliver the goods to the plaintiff, who brought an action for breach of contract. The case turned upon whether the Collector had any authority to make the sale.

20–033　　The Privy Council considered first whether the Collector had actual authority to make the sale. Such authority could be derived from the Customs Ordinance, or, arguably, independently of it. The Court rejected the argument on both grounds. As to the former, the argument was dismissed because the Court found that the Customs Ordinance did not, on construction, bind the Crown.[166] As to the latter, it was said that the mere fact that the Collector was a public officer did not give him the right to act on behalf of the Crown in all matters concerning the Crown. The right to do so must be established by reference to statute or otherwise.[167] This is an application of the theory stated above: even if the act of selling was intra

---

[163] *Gower's Principles of Modern Company Law* (P.L. Davies, Sweet & Maxwell, 6th edn, 1997), Ch.10.

[164] *Freeman and Lockyer v Buckhurst Park Properties (Mangal) Ltd* [1964] 2 Q.B. 480, 506. See generally, *Bowstead and Reynolds on Agency* (Sweet & Maxwell, 18th edn, 2006), arts 3–6, 22, 72, 73.

[165] *Att-Gen for Ceylon v AD Silva* [1953] A.C. 461. See also, *R. (on the application of Bloggs 61) v Secretary of State for the Home Department* [2003] 1 W.L.R. 2724.

[166] *AD Silva*, n.165, 473–478.

[167] *AD Silva*, n.165, 479.

vires, the contract could not be upheld if the agent had no authority to make it.

The Privy Council then considered whether the Collector had apparent authority to sell the goods. The answer again was in the negative.[168] Such authority involved a representation by the principal as to the extent of the agent's authority. No representation by the agent could amount to a holding out by the principal.

The Court went on to consider whether the defendant was bound because the Collector had authority, simply from his position qua Collector, to represent that the goods delivered were saleable even though they were not. This argument was also rejected.[169] The Collector might have authority to do acts of a particular class, namely to enter on behalf of the Crown into sales of certain goods. Such authority was, however, limited to those areas actually covered by the Ordinance. Thus, although the Collector had authority derived from his position as Collector this would not extend beyond the limits of the Ordinance: he could not have authority to commit an ultra vires act.

B. The Jurisdictional Principle: Application

While the principles are clear, they have not always been applied. Confusion has been compounded by the vague use of the terms delegation and agency. The strain placed upon legal language stems partly from the hardship that can be produced if the representation cannot bind the public body.[170] A method of avoiding the undesirable conclusions of the traditional logic was to side-step the problem by allowing estoppel to operate on the assumption that the decision was intra vires, even though it was extremely dubious whether the decision could be so regarded.

20–034

Lever Finance[171] is one such case. Developers had obtained planning permission in March 1969. They later made a slight alteration in their plans. The local authority planning officer said no further consent was required. The developers went ahead with their altered plans and the local residents objected. The planning authority then told the developers that they would require planning permission for the variation. It was the practice of planning authorities to allow their planning officers to decide whether any proposed minor changes were material or not and, if not, for the developer to continue without any further planning permission. Lord Denning M.R., with whom Megaw L.J. agreed, referred to the many statements[172] that public authorities cannot be estopped from performing their public duty, but said that

---

[168] *AD Silva*, n.165, 479–480.
[169] *AD Silva*, n.165, 480–481.
[170] B. Schwartz, *Administrative Law* (Little Brown, 1976), 134. This hardship was acknowledged in the *Silva* case, [1953] A.C. 461, 480–481.
[171] *Lever Finance Ltd v Westminster (City) London Borough Council* [1971] 1 Q.B. 222.
[172] See cases in nn.200, 206.

these statements must be taken with reserve. He propounded the following principle,[173]

"There are many matters which public authorities can now delegate to officers. If an officer acting within the scope of his ostensible authority makes a representation on which another acts, then the public authority may be bound by it, just as much as a private concern would be."

We have seen that a decision may be ultra vires in one of two senses: the decision resulting from the representation may be outside the powers of the public body itself, or within its power but incapable of being made by that public officer. The decision in *Lever* was clearly not ultra vires in the former sense, but it appears that it was in the latter sense. When the statutory powers at issue in the *Lever* case are examined it is evident that there was no power to delegate to the officer.[174] It does not therefore matter whether the language of the officer's power is expressed in terms of delegation or ostensible authority as an agent. If delegation is forbidden by a statute expressly or impliedly then a purported delegation will be ultra vires. That is obvious. That cannot be converted into an intra vires act by saying that what the officer does with ostensible authority will bind the principal. There cannot, as we have seen, be ostensible or apparent authority to bind the principal where the act committed is ultra vires in either sense identified above.[175] Even if the delegation had been permissible in the *Lever* case, Lord Denning M.R.'s words were clearly broad enough to allow estoppel to validate ultra vires decisions. This is inconsistent with higher authority.[176]

20–035   The decision in *Western Fish*[177] reaffirmed orthodoxy. The plaintiff company purchased an industrial site which had previously been used for the production of fertiliser from fish and fishmeal. The company intended to make animal fertiliser from fishmeal and also to pack fish for human consumption. It alleged that it had an established user right, which would entitle it to carry on business without the need for planning permission. The planning officer wrote a letter which, the plaintiff claimed, represented that the officer had accepted the established user right.[178] Work on renovating the factories was begun even though no planning permission had yet been obtained. This permission was subsequently refused by the full council and enforcement notices were served on the plaintiff. The latter claimed, *inter*

---

[173] [1971] 1 Q.B. 222, 230. See also, *Robertson v Minister of Pensions* [1949] 1 K.B. 227 in which Denning J. used estoppel against a public authority. The case was criticised in *Howell* [1951] A.C. 837.
[174] See Craig, n.162, 405–406.
[175] *Southend-on-Sea Corporation v Hodgson (Wickford) Ltd* [1962] 1 Q.B. 416; *R. v Leicester City Council Ex p. Powergen UK Ltd* [2000] J.P.L. 629; Craig, n.162, 406.
[176] See below, paras 20–042—20–043.
[177] *Western Fish Products Ltd v Penwith District Council* [1981] 2 All E.R. 204; *Brooks and Burton Ltd v Secretary of State for the Environment* (1976) 75 L.G.R. 285, 296; *Rootkin*, n.149.
[178] The planning officer also said that the application for an established user right was a pure formality.

alia, that the statements of the planning officer estopped the council from refusing planning permission. This was rejected by the Court of Appeal.

Megaw L.J. stated that the planning officer, even acting within his apparent authority, could not do what the Town and Country Planning Act 1971 required the council itself to do. The Act required that the decision concerning planning permission be made by the council, not the officer.[179] No representation by the planning officer could inhibit the discharge of these statutory duties. While specific functions could be delegated to the officer, the determination of planning permission had not been thus delegated.[180]

The requirement that the officer must act within the scope of his actual or ostensible authority before a public body could be bound by a representation was reaffirmed by Keene L.J. in *Flanagan*.[181]

C. The Jurisdictional Principle: The Conceptual Language, Estoppel or Legitimate Expectations

The discussion thus far has used the language of estoppel, since that was the language used in the case law. This will now have to be revised in the light of the *Reprotech* case.[182] Lord Hoffmann, giving judgment for their Lordships, held that private law concepts of estoppel should not be introduced into planning law.[183] He acknowledged that there was an analogy between estoppel and legitimate expectations, but held that it was no more than an analogy because "remedies against public authorities also have to take into account the interests of the general public which the authority exists to promote".[184] Lord Hoffmann recognised that earlier cases had used the language of estoppel, but that was explicable because public law concepts of legitimate expectations and abuse of power were under-developed at that time. Public law had now absorbed whatever was useful from the moral values underlying estoppel, and "the time has come for it to stand upon its own two feet".[185] Three comments are relevant here.

First, it should for the sake of clarity be noted that the shift from the language of estoppel to that of legitimate expectations does not in any way touch the substance of the jurisdictional principle as explicated above. Representations made by an agent who lacks authority, or representations leading to decisions which are ultra vires the public body itself, will not bind that body. The consequence, prior to *Reprotech*, was to say that estoppel

20–036

[179] Town and Country Planning Act 1971, s.29.
[180] [1981] 2 All E.R. 204, 219. Compare the more liberal approach to delegation in *R. v Southwark London Borough Council Ex p. Bannerman* [1990] C.O.D. 115.
[181] *South Bucks DC v Flanagan* [2002] 1 W.L.R. 2601, para.18.
[182] *R. v East Sussex County Council Ex p. Reprotech (Pebsham) Ltd* [2003] 1 W.L.R. 348. See also, *Powergen*, n.175; *Flanagan*, n.181; *Powergen UK Plc v Leicester City Council* [2000] J.P.L. 1037; *Coghurst Wood Leisure Park Ltd v Secretary of State for Transport, Local Government and the Regions, Rother District Council* [2002] EWHC 1091; *R. (on the application of Clear Channel UK Ltd) v Southwark LBC* [2006] EWHC 3325.
[183] *Reprotech*, n.182, para.33.
[184] *Reprotech*, n.182, para.34.
[185] *Reprotech*, n.182, para.35.

cannot apply in such circumstances. This result would now be expressed by saying that there was no legitimate expectation in such circumstances.[186] The result in, for example, *Western Fish* would not have been any different had the language of legitimate expectation been used, rather than estoppel.[187]

Second, we should nonetheless be aware of the close analogy between estoppel and legitimate expectations. The foundation of both concepts is a representation, which provides the rationale for holding the representor to what had been represented, where the reliance was reasonable and legitimate in the circumstances. The fact that any remedy against a public body would have to take account of the broader public interest was moreover recognised by those judges who used the language of estoppel.[188]

Third, cases that would, under the previous terminology, have been pleaded in terms of estoppel, are now considered by the courts under the heading of legitimate expectations.[189]

D. The Jurisdictional Principle: Qualifications

20–037   *Western Fish* reaffirmed, as we have seen, the traditional view. Apparent authority cannot allow an officer to do what is assigned to the council. If the representation is ultra vires either because it is outside the powers of that body, or because, although within its powers, it cannot be delegated to this officer, then it cannot operate as an estoppel. It remains to consider whether there are any exceptions to this principle and to consider their legal status in the light of *Reprotech*.

i. Procedural irregularity

20–038   There is authority that a procedural irregularity *may* be subject to estoppel. Whether it in fact is depends upon the construction of the statutory provision setting out the procedure.[190] This exception may survive *Reprotech*, subject to the caveat that it has to be expressed in the language of legitimate expectation rather than estoppel.

ii. Delegation and finality of decision

20–039   There was also authority that where a power had been delegated to an officer to determine specific questions any decision made could not be revoked, this being regarded as akin to *res judicata*.[191] This suggests that the conceptual rationale for the exception was more akin to the finality of

---

[186] *Flanagan*, n.181, para.18.
[187] As noted by Dyson J. in *Powergen*, n.175.
[188] See, e.g., *Laker Airways*, n.32, 707.
[189] *Flanagan*, n.181, paras 16–17.
[190] *Western Fish*, n.177, 221 referring to *Wells* [1967] 1 W.L.R. 1000. See also, *Re L. (AC) (an infant)* [1971] 3 All E.R. 743, 752.
[191] *Western Fish*, n.177, 221–222.

completed decisions,[192] than estoppel by representation. Sullivan J. doubted whether this exception survived *Reprotech*.[193]

The exception, even if it does survive, is limited. Thus the delegation must be lawful. The statute must allow the relevant power to be delegated to this type of officer, since otherwise the whole force of the basic proposition, that a representation cannot validate an ultra vires act, would be negated. If the delegation is lawful there is a further issue as to how far an individual can assume that it has occurred. The answer from *Western Fish* was that it depends on the circumstances.[194] The individual could not assume that any resolution necessary to delegate authority had been passed, nor was the seniority of the officer conclusive. If, however, there was some further evidence that the officer regularly dealt with cases of a type which the individual might expect that official to be able to determine, this could be sufficient to entitle the individual to presume that delegation had occurred even if it had not.

iii. European Convention on Human Rights

The jurisdictional principle is however qualified to a certain extent by the ECHR, as exemplified by *Stretch*.[195] The claimant complained that the refusal to exercise a renewal option on the ground that it was ultra vires the local authority landlord's powers violated his property rights under art.1 of the First Protocol ECHR. The claimant was granted a 22–year lease on industrial land by the local authority in 1969, with an option to renew for an additional 21 years. When the initial lease expired, S entered into negotiations for a renewal, but was then informed that the option had been granted in excess of the authority's powers.

The Strasbourg Court found that there had been a breach of art.1 of the First Protocol, because the refusal on ultra vires grounds was a disproportionate interference with the claimant's peaceful enjoyment of his possessions. He had entered into the lease on the basis of the option and in reliance on it he had built on the land, paid ground rent to the authority and granted subleases. The ultra vires nature of the grant was only raised late in the renewal negotiations, with the result that S had a legitimate expectation that the lease would be renewed. The court acknowledged that the ultra vires doctrine was important in preventing abuse of power, but concluded that application of the doctrine did not respect proportionality in the instant case. In reaching this conclusion it took into account the fact that there was no third party interest affected, nor would any other statutory function be prejudiced by giving effect to the renewal option.

In *Rowland*[196] the court acknowledged the force of the ECHR jurisprudence. It held that a legitimate expectation relating to property could

20–040

---

[192] See above, para.20–029.
[193] *Wandsworth*, n.78, paras 20–21.
[194] *Western Fish*, n.177, 220–222.
[195] *Stretch v United Kingdom* [2004] 38 E.H.R.R. 12.
[196] *Rowland*, n.110, paras 88, 152.

be a "possession" protected by art.1 of the First Protocol ECHR, even if the representation giving rise to the expectation was ultra vires. It would then be for the public body to show that interference with that possession was justified and proportionate, which was held to be so on the facts of the case.

9. ULTRA VIRES REPRESENTATIONS: REASSESSING THE JURISDICTIONAL PRINCIPLE

20–041 The preceding conclusions have a pristine symmetry. The logic of the jurisdictional principle is followed through to its inexorable end. A moment's reflection will, however, make evident the hardship to the individual. The person who reasonably relies upon a representation made by a public body will be left without any remedy. It may be possible in theory for the individual to ascertain the limits of the public body's and public officer's power, but theory does not always accord with practical reality. This hardship may well incline courts to construe the empowering legislation so as to, for example, confer validity on a mistaken certificate unless and until it has been revoked,[197] or otherwise interpret the legislation so as to render the public body's action intra rather than ultra vires.[198] This will however not always be plausible and the cogency of the traditional theory must now be examined.[199]

A. The Policy behind the Jurisdictional Principle: The First Rationale
20–042 The first rationale was stated by Lord Greene M.R. in *Hulkin*:[200] if estoppel were to be allowed to run against the government the donee of a statutory power could make an ultra vires representation and then be bound by it through the medium of estoppel, or legitimate expectations. This would lead to the collapse of the ultra vires doctrine with public officers being enabled to extend their powers at will.[201] The jurisdictional principle is said to protect the public or that section of it to which the duty relates.[202] The soundness of

---

[197] *Ejaz v Secretary of State for the Home Department* [1995] C.O.D. 72.
[198] *MFK*, n.39; *Bibi*, n.71.
[199] It has been shown that sovereign immunity did not prevent estoppel applying against the Crown, F. Farrer, "A Prerogative Fallacy—'That the King is not Bound by Estoppel'" (1933) 49 L.Q.R. 511; H. Street, *Governmental Liability, A Comparative Study* (Cambridge University Press, 1953), 157.
[200] *Minister of Agriculture and Fisheries v Hulkin*, unreported but cited in *Minister of Agriculture and Fisheries v Mathews* [1950] 1 K.B. 148.
[201] Examples of similar reasoning appear in the US both at Federal and State level. *Utah Power and Light Company v United States* 243 U.S. 389 (1917); *Federal Crop Insurance Corporation v Merrill* 332 U.S. 380 (1947); *Schweiker v Hansen* 450 U.S. 785 (1981); *Office of Personnel Management v Richmond* 496 U.S. 414 (1990); *San Diego County v California Water and Telephone Co* 186 P. 2d 124 (1947); *Boren v State Personnel Board* 234 P. 2d 981 (1951); *Bride v City of Slater* 263 S.W. 2d 22 (1953); *Fulton v City of Lockwood* 269 S.W. 2d 1 (1954).
[202] *Silva*, n.165, 481; *Merrill, Bride, Fulton*, n.201.

this reasoning can be tested against the two ways in which a public body might extend its powers: intentionally or inadvertently.

The cases on representations by public officers do not, on their facts, contain any example of *intentional* extension of power, but let us presume that this has occurred. The jurisdictional principle deals with this by preventing the representee from relying on the representation as against the public body. To prevent intentional extension of power the "burden" is imposed upon the innocent representee. It is not clear that this is the most effective way to deal with the problem. For the rare cases of intentional excess of power the appropriate person to penalise would be the public officer involved.[203]

The typical situation is, however, *inadvertent* extension of power. A public officer will place a particular construction on a statute, which is later overturned by a higher officer in the same department.[204] A practice will have developed that a particular individual should undertake a certain task when the statute places the duty on a different body.[205] Any deterrence that the reasoning of Lord Greene M.R. is intended to have will be of limited effect. It may be possible to deter negligent conduct by making the actor more careful. However, in the present context the officer has often taken all due care. The official will normally be acting in the bona fide belief that the construction of the statute is correct, or that the representation is within that officer's authority. Moreover, even where there has been carelessness there is little in the present system to deter the officer. The sole effect of a careless representation, which turns out to be ultra vires, is that the representee cannot rely.

B. The Policy behind the Jurisdictional Principle: The Second and Third Rationales

The second argument underlying the jurisdictional principle is that estoppel or legitimate expectations cannot be applied to a public body so as to prevent it from exercising its statutory powers or duties,[206] and the third is that to allow an ultra vires representation to bind a public body would be to prejudice third parties who might be affected, and who would have no opportunity of putting forward their views.

20–043

There is force in these arguments. It should nonetheless be recognised that there will be circumstances where the detriment to the public, who are the beneficiaries of the ultra vires doctrine, will not always outweigh the harsh effect upon the individual.

---

[203] See, e.g., Local Government Act 1972 s.161, and *Dickson v Hurle-Hobbs* [1947] K.B. 879.
[204] *Clairborne Sales Co v Collector of Revenue* 99 So. 2d 345 (1957).
[205] *Lever Finance*, n.171.
[206] *Maritime Electric Company Ltd v General Dairies Ltd* [1937] A.C. 610, 620; *Commissioners of Inland Revenue v Brooks* [1915] A.C. 478, 491; *Thrasyvoulou v Secretary of State for the Environment* [1990] 2 A.C. 273, 289; *R. v Inland Revenue Commissioners Ex p. MFK Underwriting Agents Ltd* [1990] 1 W.L.R. 1545, 1568; *R. v Criminal Injuries Compensation Board Ex p. Keane and Marsden* [1998] C.O.D. 128; *Rowland*, n.110, paras 67, 81

This can be exemplified by *Robertson*.[207] The plaintiff had relied upon a representation given by the wrong body that his injury was attributable to military service, as a result of which he had not obtained an independent medical opinion to confirm this. It may be presumed for the sake of argument that the representation was ultra vires.[208] The immediate effect of allowing the ultra vires assurance to bind would be a loss to the department concerned. The loss would be in the form of having to pay a pension that could have been withheld.

In any system there is bound to be a certain percentage of such mistakes. The question is who should bear the loss? The alternatives are either to leave the loss with the representee, or to pass it to the department. The effect of doing the latter would be to spread the loss in minute proportions through those who benefit from performance of the public duty. The inadvertent misrepresentation could have happened to any person. It was fortuitous that it befell this individual. The effect of allowing the representation to bind would be to impose the loss upon those who take the benefit. It does not seem at all self-evident that the detriment to the public interest would outweigh the harm to the individual.[209]

There are of course many situations where the loss to the public will outweigh that of the individual. This will be dependent upon the context, planning, social security or tax, in which the representation occurs. Planning is a prime example of an area where the public interest in the strict enforcement of the statutory norms is especially strong. This is reinforced by the detriment to third party interests that would occur if invalid representations could be relied on.[210]

10. Ultra Vires Representations: Three Possible Strategies

20–044   It is nonetheless important to consider other possible approaches to the problem of ultra vires representations, apart from the jurisdictional principle. Three such approaches will now be considered.

A. Limited Qualifications to the Jurisdictional Principle

i. Government-proprietary distinction
20–045   The distinction between governmental and proprietary functions is not a test

---

[207] *Robertson*, n.173.
[208] The representation in *Robertson* is usually regarded as intra vires. It is far from clear whether this was so, see G. Ganz, "Estoppel and *Res Judicata* in Administrative Law" [1965] P.L. 237, 244–245. It is, however, the factual situation presented by *Robertson* that is of interest.
[209] This would also be so in cases of the *Clairborne* type, n.204.
[210] See cases, nn.78, 182.

separate from the jurisdictional principle.[211] It has been developed in some US jurisdictions as an exception to the general rule that estoppel should not bind a public body.[212] It permits the application of the doctrine when the body is acting in a proprietary rather than governmental capacity, and where the agent making the representation had authority to do so.[213] This approach does, however, have limitations. The distinction between what is a governmental and what is a proprietary function is difficult to draw.[214] More important is that it is based upon the premise that it should not apply to governmental matters which the law "does not sanction or permit". This takes us back to the jurisdictional principle itself.

ii. Internal dealing

A representation could be allowed to bind so far as the internal management of the public body is concerned, but not to those matters which are substantively ultra vires. The idea has obvious analogies with company law. In the public law context it would operate to validate certain types of representation.[215] It would apply to situations where the subject-matter of the representation was within the power of the public body itself, and the officer who gave the assurance was not prohibited, expressly or impliedly, from doing so. For example, if a public body has power to delegate certain functions to an officer, the representee would be entitled to assume that the appropriate procedure had been followed and that the delegation had taken place, provided that there was nothing in the surrounding circumstances to put the individual on inquiry. We have seen that a limited exception of this nature was allowed by *Western Fish*.[216]

20–046

B. Balancing the Public and Individual Interest

i. Balancing legality and legal certainty: the nature of the argument

It is, however, possible to think of a modification to the ultra vires principle which goes further than the options considered above. The ultra vires principle is the embodiment of the *principle of legality*. This principle can, however, clash with the *principle of legal certainty*, and does so when an individual has detrimentally relied upon an ultra vires representation. Where the harm to the public would be minimal compared to that of the individual, there is good reason to consider allowing the representation to bind. This

20–047

---

[211] J.F. Conway, "Equitable Estoppel of the Federal Government and Application of the Proprietary Function Exception to the Traditional rule" (1987) 55 Fordham L.R. 707.
[212] A. Aman and W. Mayton, *Administrative Law* (West Publishing, 2nd edn, 2001), 334–336.
[213] *Branch Banking and Trust Company v United States* 98 F. Supp 757 (1951) (US Court of Claims); *United States v Georgia–Pacific Company* 421 F. 2d 92 (1970) (US Court of Appeals, Ninth Circuit); *FDIC v Harrison* 735 F. 2d 408 (1984) (11th Cir.); *Mobil Oil Exploration & Producing Southeast Inc v US* 530 U.S. 604 (2000).
[214] As admitted in the *Georgia-Pacific* case, 421 F. 2d 92, 100 (1970).
[215] Lord Denning M.R. drew the analogy with company law in *Lever Finance*, n.171, 230–231.
[216] n.177.

would be to recognise that the principle of legality might, on occasion, be trumped or outweighed by that of legal certainty. There will nonetheless be many situations where the public interest must take precedence over that of the individual.

The concept of legitimate expectations should play the same general role in this type of case, as in relation to intra vires representations. It is a necessary, but not sufficient, condition for the representation to bind the public body. Reasonableness of reliance is a *necessary* condition for a legitimate expectation. It might be objected that a representee could never have a "legitimate" expectation if the representation was ultra vires. This is, however, merely a restatement of the general rule that ultra vires representations cannot ever bind, which is the very question in issue. It adds nothing to that statement. It is in any event inconsistent with Convention jurisprudence, which is premised on the assumption that an expectation can be legitimate even if it is based on an ultra vires representation. It is also misleading in that it conveys the impression that the individual somehow harboured an illegitimate or unwarranted expectation that the representation would be fulfilled. The reality is that the representee may have had no reason to expect that the representation was outside the complex powers of the public body.

The existence of a legitimate expectation is not, however, a *sufficient* condition for binding the public body, precisely because the representation is ultra vires. The existence of a legitimate expectation serves, however, as a signal that issues of legal certainty are involved in a case. The existence of such an expectation should, therefore, operate as a trigger to alert a court that a balance between the principles of legality and legal certainty may be required.

ii. Balancing legality and legal certainty: case law and statute

20–048 The application of a balancing approach through the *courts* is apparent in some American jurisdictions. Many Federal decisions and most State jurisdictions have followed the Supreme Court in the *Federal Crop*[217] case, denying estoppel where it would validate an ultra vires decision. Other Federal[218] and State decisions have, however, qualified the Supreme Court's ruling.

California has developed a flexible rule. In *Mansell*,[219] the Supreme Court of California acknowledged the existence of two competing lines of authority, one of which applied estoppel where justice and right required it,

---

[217] 332 U.S. 380 (1947). See also, n.201, and *United States v Certain Parcels of Land* 131 F. Supp. 65, 73–74 (1955) (US District Court); *Montilla v United States* 457 F. 2d 978, 985–987 (1972) (US Court of Claims).

[218] *United States v Lazy FC Ranch* 481 F. 2d 98 (1973) (US Court of Appeals Ninth Circuit). See also, *Moser v United States* 341 U.S. 41 (1951); *Vestal v Commissioner of Internal Revenue* 152 F. 2d 132 (1945) (US Court of Appeals District of Columbia); *California Pacific Bank v Small Business Administration* 557 F. 2d 218 (1977) (US Court of Appeals, Ninth Circuit); *United States v Ruby Company* 588 F. 2d 697 (1978) (US Court of Appeals, Ninth Circuit).

[219] *City of Long Beach v Mansell* 476 P. 2d 423 (1970).

the other which denied estoppel where the representation was beyond the power of the public body and where it would defeat a policy adopted to protect the public. The court propounded the following principle.[220]

"The government may be bound by an equitable estoppel in the same manner as a private party where the elements requisite for such an estoppel against a private party are present, and in the considered view of a court of equity the injustice which would result from a failure to uphold an estoppel is of sufficient dimension to justify any effect upon public interests or policy which would result from the raising of an estoppel."

There is some authority for the balancing approach within our own law. Not surprisingly it came from Lord Denning M.R. His Lordship stated,[221]

"The underlying principle is that the Crown cannot be estopped from exercising its powers, whether given in a statute or by common law, when it is doing so in the proper exercise of its duty to act for the public good, even though this may work some injustice or unfairness to the private individual.[222] . . . It can, however, be estopped when it is not properly exercising its powers, but is misusing them; and it does misuse them if it exercises them in circumstances which work injustice or unfairness to the individual without any countervailing benefit to the public."[223]

Not only does Lord Denning M.R. provide support for the balancing approach, he conceptualises it in a most interesting manner. The formulation makes the binding nature of the representation flow from fulfilment of, not derogation from, the ultra vires principle: where the public body exercises its powers such as to work injustice to the individual without any countervailing benefit to the public this is itself a misuse of powers. If the jurisdictional principle is the trump card, his Lordship trumps this by making this notion of fairness part of the constraints on the use of discretion.

The balancing approach in later cases appears to be confined to cases where the representation was intra vires, and this view has been reinforced by recent case law.[224] However, if a court believes that no balancing should be undertaken if the representation is ultra vires, but it wishes to consider the effects of the representation, this may incline the court to categorise the representation as intra rather than ultra vires.[225] It should also be recognised

---

[220] *Mansell*, n.219, 448. The court did, however, reserve the question of what would happen where the body totally lacked the power to achieve that which estoppel would accomplish against it, 450. See also, *Strong v County of Santa Cruz* 543 P. 2d 264 (1975); *Longshore v County of Ventura* 151 Cal. Rptr 708 (1979); *Lentz v McMahon* 231 Cal. Rptr 622 (1986).
[221] *Laker Airways*, n.32, 707.
[222] Citing *Maritime Electric*, n.200.
[223] Citing *Robertson*, n.173; *R. v Liverpool Corporation Ex p. Liverpool Taxi Fleet Operators' Association* [1972] 2 Q.B. 299 and *HTV*, n.31.
[224] See cases in n.182.
[225] See, e.g., *MFK*, n.39; *Bibi*, n.71 *Ejaz*, n.197.

that there will be often be balancing within the ultra vires principle itself. This can take the form of a value judgment as to whether to categorise an error as one of law, fact, discretion or no error at all.

20–049　　A balancing approach is however, as we have seen,[226] undertaken by the Strasbourg Court and by the ECJ,[227] and in *Rowland* May L.J. considered favourably the general idea of a balancing approach.[228] The court in *Rowland* recognised that some balancing might be required as a result of the Convention jurisprudence. It held, as we have seen, that a legitimate expectation relating to property could be a "possession" protected by art.1 of the First Protocol ECHR, even if the representation giving rise to the expectation was ultra vires. The expectation would not necessarily entitle the party to its realisation, but could entitle him to some other form of relief that was within the powers of the public body. This might take the form of the benevolent exercise of discretion to alleviate the injustice, or the payment of compensation.

The balancing approach has the advantage of allowing the court the very flexibility that the jurisdictional principle treats as a foregone conclusion. It manifests a willingness to inquire whether the disadvantages to the public interest really do outweigh the injustice to the individual. In many of the areas where the representation relates to a purely financial matter, such as a claim by the Government for tax or a citizen seeking social security benefits, the hardship to the individual who has detrimentally relied will outweigh any public disadvantage. There are, of course, many other areas where the balance would be different. It is clear that third party interests and the public interest are of particular importance in the planning context. This explains the reluctance to consider the modification of the general statutory scheme through giving effect to representations, which would have the effect of modifying the scheme in relation to a particular individual.[229]

It is also possible for balancing to be sanctioned or mandated by *legislation*. This could take one of two forms. A clause dealing with the problem might be inserted in particular statutes.[230] Alternatively, there could be a general statute. This could provide a defence for bona fide reliance upon a rule or opinion, where the rule or opinion was made by the body responsible for administering that law, and the rule was promulgated to guide the class of persons to which the representee belonged. The particular statutes to which this defence would apply could be stipulated and additions could be made.[231] These statutes provide a defence to money claims against the

---

[226] See above, para.20–040.

[227] Craig, n.3, 621–626.

[228] *Rowland*, n.110, paras 115–120.

[229] *Powergen*, n.175; *Flanagan*, n.181; *Powergen UK Plc v Leicester City Council* [2000] J.P.L. 1037; *Reprotech*, n.182; *Coghurst Wood Leisure Park Ltd v Secretary of State for Transport, Local Government and the Regions, Rother District Council* [2002] EWHC 1091; *Henry Boot Homes Ltd v Bassetlaw DC* [2002] EWCA Civ 983.

[230] See, e.g., in the US see, Portal-to-Portal Act 1947, 29 USCA ss.258, 259; Trust Indenture Act 1939, 15 USCA s.77(c); Public Utility Holding Act 1939, 15 USCA s.79 I(d); Defence Production Act 1950, 50 USCA s.2157.

[231] F. Newman, "Should Official Advice be Reliable?—Proposals as to Estoppel and Related Doctrines in Administrative Law" (1953) 53 Col. L. Rev. 374.

representee. This is a valuable first stage in the protection of the representee, but it will often not be sufficient in itself. The individual may need not just relief from a penalty, but the ability to pursue the course of conduct which he was induced to follow by the representation.

iii. *Balancing legality and legal certainty: objections*

The central objection to any judicial balancing test is that it would offend **20–050** against constitutional principle. If Parliament has laid down certain limits to the powers of a body it might be felt that the courts should not balance the public versus individual interest in the manner suggested above.[232]

There is obvious force in this objection. The strength of the argument is, however, diminished because we do allow such balancing in other areas. There are at least three areas in which the jurisdictional principle is compromised, and balancing is accepted as legitimate or inevitable. This can be seen in the law relating to invalidity, waiver, and delay.

In the law relating to invalidity there are situations where the courts have qualified the concept of retrospective nullity, because its effect on the administration or on an individual are regarded as unacceptable.[233] We allow waiver to operate with the effect that there will be no remedy for what was an ultra vires decision.[234] This is so also in relation to remedies and delay. The detailed rules on delay will be considered below.[235] Suffice it to say for the present that s.31(6) of the Supreme Court Act 1981 allows the court to refuse a remedy where there has been undue delay in making the application, if it considers that the granting of relief would cause substantial hardship to, or substantially prejudice the rights of, any person or would be detrimental to good administration.

The effect of the law in these three areas is to countenance balancing, usually against the individual, where an ultra vires act has occurred, even though we deny any such balancing in favour of the innocent individual who has been misled by an ultra vires representation made by a public body. A number of objections might be made to this analysis.

First, it might be argued that such a balancing is justified in the context of, **20–051** for example, delay because the balancing has legislative sanction. This will not withstand examination. The argument misconstrues the position at common law prior to the Supreme Court Act 1981.[236] The courts, prior to this Act, took a wide variety of factors into account in determining whether to withhold a remedy or not, including: administrative convenience, effectiveness, hardship to third parties, and broad notions of justice.[237] The courts were, in such instances, balancing the ultra vires nature of the

---

[232] For similar concerns in the United States see, Aman and Mayton, n.232, 328–329.
[233] See Ch.23.
[234] See above, Ch.25.
[235] See below, Ch.26.
[236] Moreover, if legislative sanction was held to be required then Ord.53, r.4 would have been ultra vires prior to the passage of the Supreme Court Act 1981.
[237] See below, Ch.25.

conduct against the consequences of granting a remedy. Viewed in this way s.31(6) was little more than a declaration of the previous common law position.

A second objection to the analogies drawn from invalidity, waiver and delay might be cast as follows. In these instances the ultra vires nature of the act is not touched. It is simply the remedy that is refused or modified. This will not do. There may well be reasons why we would wish the courts to exercise their balancing discretion at the remedial level, rather than by manipulating vires itself.[238] Let us not, however, allow form to blind us to substance: in whichever way the balancing is expressed it is still balancing. The full effects of the ultra vires principle are still being compromised. There is in any event no reason to suggest that the balancing which would take place in the context of representations could not be expressed in the same way. If such balancing were to be allowed we would not be saying that the public body could now lawfully do something outside its powers. We would accept that the public body had made an ultra vires representation, but conclude that because of the minimal effect on the public interest, as compared to the harm to the representee, that the representation should bind in this instance.

A third possible objection is that there might be third party interests affected, who would have no opportunity to put their views when determining whether the representation should bind. This is correct, and will be taken into account in the balancing process.[239] The problem of third party interests is, however, every bit as real when the balancing takes place in relation to invalidity, waiver or delay, yet it has not been regarded as a reason for rejecting balancing in these areas.

A final objection would be to argue that the balancing within invalidity, waiver and delay is justified because it is in favour of the public body, and that such balancing is warranted because the public body represents a wider public interest. A process of weighing is not, it might be argued, legitimate "the other way round", where the only interest affected by the misleading representation is that of the individual. This objection is unconvincing. Granted that the public body represents a wider public interest, this does not explain why an ultra vires representation should never be allowed to bind *if* the detriment to the individual does outweigh the harm to the public interest. In any event the argument is mistaken even in its own terms. When the courts balance within invalidity, waiver, and delay they do not only take account of administrative convenience. They have considered a much broader range of factors, such as effectiveness, third party interests, the detriment to the applicant, and more amorphous considerations of justice.

C. Compensation

20–052   It might be argued that it would be much simpler to give compensation to

---

[238] See below, Ch.25.
[239] e.g. *Raley v California Tahoe Regional Planning Agency* 137 Cal. Rptr 699 (1977).

the aggrieved representee than to allow an ultra vires representation to bind. A monetary remedy would be helpful in this context.[240] There are however two points that should be made in relation to this suggestion.

The first is that in some circumstances it would be tantamount to doing the same thing. Giving compensation in cases like *Robertson*[241] would have the same effect as holding the agency to the representation.

The second point is more important. Two examples will serve as illustrations. Let us assume that X has been given an assurance that certain alterations to property do not require further planning permission. X builds the property with the alterations. The assurance given was ultra vires the representor. The cost of compensating X will be £20,000.[242] The second example has analogies with the *Skytrain*[243] case. Y has received an assurance that he can operate a new transport service. In reliance thereon he invests £5 million. The assurance turns out to be ultra vires the body that made it.

Any system of compensation will derive its funds from a certain section of society, directly or indirectly. It may, for example, be through general taxation or from the local rates. It is a trite, though important, proposition that funds for compensation are scarce. If by balancing the public and private interest it can be shown that the detriment to the former is outweighed by that of the latter, it is not clear why we should give compensation rather than allow the representation to bind. The ultra vires principle operates to keep bodies within the ambit of their powers, and does so to protect society or a certain section of it.

If it can be shown that society is not going to suffer in comparison to the individual, then to insist that, for example, Y's investment should lay idle, and that Y should be compensated, would be a waste of these resources. Society is compensating X and Y for the destruction of things the presence of which did not really harm it. It is doubtful whether this is the most pressing object on which to spend scarce societal resources. Compensation for wrongful administrative action may well be needed.[244] It should not, however, be an alternative to allowing the representation to bind when there has been an ultra vires assurance. It should only be a complement.

[240] *Rowland*, n.110, para.80.
[241] n.173.
[242] *Lever Finance*, n.171.
[243] *Laker Airways*, n.32.
[244] See Ch.29. There may, e.g., be good reason to compensate Z who has suffered loss of amenity due to the ultra vires assurance given to X.

CHAPTER 21

EQUALITY

1. INTRODUCTION

The relevance of equality in cases of judicial review has been touched on in   21–001
previous discussion. It is nonetheless important to treat this topic separately
in its own right.[1] This chapter does not purport to cover all equality law,
since this would require book-length treatment. The focus will rather be on
the role of equality as a precept of judicial review.

2. COMMON LAW

A. The Principle of Treating Like Groups Alike: The Basic Precept
It would be inaccurate to portray the common law, from a historical per-   21–002
spective, as at the forefront in the protection of equality and the proscription
of discrimination. The common law was, as McCrudden states, often a
source of discrimination itself,[2] especially for women, although there were,
as he points out, several islands of non-discrimination norms in the common
law, as exemplified by those dealing with the obligations of common
carriers.[3]

The idea that like groups should be treated in a like manner, and that
different groups should be treated differently, is a central precept of equality.

---

[1] J. Jowell, "Is Equality a Constitutional Principle?" (1994) 7 C.L.P. 1; Lord Lester, "Equality
and United Kingdom Law: Past, Present and Future" [2001] P.L. 77; C. McCrudden, "Equality
and Discrimination", in D. Feldman (ed.), *English Public Law* (Oxford University Press, 2003),
Ch.11, which contains a valuable analysis of the underlying aims served by equality law; R.
Singh Q.C., "Equality: The Neglected Virtue" [2004] E.H.R.L.R. 141.
[2] See, e.g., *Nairn v University of St Andrews* [1909] A.C. 147.
[3] n.1.

The very decision as to whether a certain group should or should not be regarded as the same or different from another inevitably requires the making of value judgments. It should also be recognised that the basic precept of treating like cases alike conceals choices as to whether to think of equality in terms of consistency, results or opportunity.[4] The choice can have a marked impact on the legitimacy of distinctions drawn by government, including the legitimacy of affirmative action.[5]

Thus formal equality or equality as consistency dictates that like cases should be treated alike and that different cases should be treated differently. This important precept is integral to equality law in most legal systems. It does not however dictate any particular substantive result, and can be met whether people are treated equally badly or equally well.[6]

Equality of results, by way of contrast, "goes beyond a demand for consistent treatment of likes, and requires instead that the result be equal", thereby recognising that "apparently identical treatment can in practice reinforce inequality because of past or on-going discrimination".[7] There are, however, as Fredman notes, ambiguities in the meaning accorded to results for these purposes. The focus might be on the particular individual, it might be on the group to which the individual belongs, or it might be on equality of outcome designed to overcome under-representation of a particular group within certain types of employment.[8]

Equality of opportunity constitutes a third conception of equality, and is a *via media* between formal equality and equality of result. Using the metaphor of a race, equality of opportunity is premised on the assumption that real equality cannot be achieved if individuals begin this race from different starting points. There are once again difficulties with the more precise meaning of this conception of equality, with some emphasising its procedural dimension, and others placing greater emphasis on substance so as to ensure that "persons from all sections of society have a genuinely equal chance of satisfying the criteria for access to a particular social good".[9]

B. The Principle of Treating Like Groups Alike: The Case Law

21–003   The dictate that like cases should be treated alike, and that different groups should be treated differently, has been taken into account by our courts. This has sometimes been under existing heads of review, such as improper purpose or relevancy. The more recent tendency is, as will be seen below, to ground intervention openly on the basis of equality.

In *Kruse*[10] the court held that a bylaw could not be partial or unequal in its operation as between different classes. Lord Denning in *Edwards*[11] held

[4] S. Fredman, *Discrimination Law* (Clarendon Press, 2002), Ch.1.
[5] Fredman, n.4, Ch.5.
[6] Fredman, n.4, 7–11.
[7] Fredman, n.4, 11.
[8] Fredman, n.4, 11–14.
[9] Fredman, n.4, 15.
[10] *Kruse v Johnson* [1898] 2 Q.B. 91.
[11] *Edwards v SOGAT* [1971] Ch.354.

that the courts would not allow a power to be exercised arbitrarily or with unfair discrimination. In *Ali*[12] the court held that the devolution of power by a local authority to neighbourhoods to decide on the allocation of property to the homeless was unfair and irrational, since variable criteria were applied. In *Urmaza*[13] and *Gangadeen*[14] it was held that the legal principle of consistency in the exercise of public law powers created a presumption that the agency or minister would follow a declared policy. This presumption flowed from the very purpose of such a policy, which was to secure consistency. A departure from such a policy would require the giving of reasons, and would have to be justified in substantive terms.

The centrality of non-discrimination as a common law concept has been increasingly emphasised by the courts. Thus Lord Woolf C.J. in *A v Secretary of State* stated that the right not to be discriminated against was one of the most significant requirements of the rule of law, and that the common law recognised the importance of not discriminating long before the HRA came into force.[15] In *Hall*[16] Lord Hoffmann adverted to the fundamental principle of justice that people should be treated equally and that like cases treated alike. In *Gurung*,[17] the applicants were Gurkhas. They claimed that the decision of the Ministry of Defence to exclude them from an ex gratia scheme of compensation for prisoners of war held by the Japanese was contrary to common law principles of equality. McCombe J. held that their exclusion was irrational and inconsistent with the principle of equality that formed a cornerstone of UK law.[18] Lord Hoffmann in *Matadeen*[19] reinforced the basic precept concerning equality, while adverting to the difficulties that could attend adjudication thereon. Referring to the precept that persons should be treated uniformly, unless there was some valid reason for differential treatment, Lord Hoffmann stated that:

"Their Lordships do not doubt that such a principle is one of the building blocks of democracy and necessarily permeates any democratic constitution. Indeed, their Lordships would go further and say that treating like cases alike and unlike cases differently is a general axiom of rational behaviour. It is, for example, frequently invoked by the courts in proceedings for judicial review as a ground for holding some administrative act to have been irrational. . . . But the very banality of the principle must suggest a doubt as to whether merely to state it can provide an answer to the kind of problem which arises in this case. Of course persons should be

---

[12] *R. v Tower Hamlets LBC Ex p. Ali* (1992) 25 H.L.R. 158, 314.
[13] *R. v Home Secretary Ex p. Urmaza* [1996] C.O.D. 479. See also, *R. v Secretary of State for the Environment Ex p. West Oxfordshire District Council* [1994] C.O.D. 134.
[14] *R. v Home Secretary Ex p. Gangadeen* [1998] 1 F.L.R. 762.
[15] *A v Secretary of State for the Home Department* [2004] Q.B. 335, para.7. The decision on the facts was reversed by the House of Lords, but this did not affect the substance of the point made in the text, *A v Secretary of State for the Home Department* [2005] 2 A.C. 68.
[16] *Arthur JS Hall v Simons* [2002] 1 A.C. 615, 688.
[17] *R. (on the application of Gurung) v Ministry of Defence* [2002] EWHC Admin 2463.
[18] Compare, *The Association of British Civilian Internees Far East Region v Secretary of State for Defence* [2002] EWHC 2119, paras 53–54.
[19] *Matadeen v Pointu* [1999] 1 A.C. 98, 109.

uniformly treated, unless there is some valid reason to treat them differently. But what counts as a valid reason for treating them differently? And, perhaps more important, who is to decide whether the reason is valid or not? Must it always be the courts? The reasons for not treating people uniformly often involve, as they do in this case, questions of social policy on which views may differ. These are questions which the elected representatives of the people have some claim to decide for themselves. The fact that equality of treatment is a general principle of rational behaviour does not entail that it should necessarily be a justiciable principle—that it should always be the judges who have the last word on whether the principle has been observed. In this, as in other areas of constitutional law, sonorous judicial statements of uncontroversial principle often conceal the real problem, which is to mark out the boundary between the powers of the judiciary, the legislature and the executive in deciding how that principle is to be applied."

3. Statutory Intervention and Statutory Interpretation

21–004 This is not the place for any detailed analysis of the complex body of statute law concerning various aspects of equality.[20] Suffice it to say for the present that Parliament has intervened and dealt with discrimination on a variety of grounds. These include race,[21] gender discrimination and equality,[22] and disability.[23] The very existence of these prohibitions on discrimination means that groups cannot be validly distinguished merely because of, for example, their respective ethnic backgrounds: disadvantageous treatment of one such group cannot be defended by claiming that they are different groups merely because of racial origin. These foundational statutes have been amended, in part because of the need to comply with initiatives from EU law.

The centrality of non-discrimination can also be seen in the way in which the courts use this principle as an interpretative device when considering statutes. Thus in *Fitzpatrick*[24] the House of Lords was willing to construe the word "family" within certain legislation to include a same sex partner. The word could legitimately bear a different meaning in 1999, as compared to the meaning when it was initially enacted in 1920.[25]

---

[20] Fredman, n.4; McCrudden, n.1.
[21] Race Relations Act 1976; Race Relations (Amendment) Act 2000; *R. (on the application of European Roma Rights Centre) v Immigration Officer, Prague Airport* [2005] 2 A.C. 1; *R. (on the application of Elias) v Secretary of State for Defence* [2006] EWCA Civ 1293.
[22] Equal Pay Act 1970; Sex Discrimination Act 1975; Equality Act 2006.
[23] Disability Discrimination Act 1995; Disability Rights Commission Act 1999.
[24] *Fitzpatrick v Sterling Housing Association Ltd* [2001] 1 A.C. 27.
[25] See also, *R. v R.* [1992] 1 A.C. 599; *Ghaidan v Godin-Mendoza* [2002] 2 A.C. 557.

4. THE HRA

A. Article 14 and Protocol 12 ECHR

Most cases raising issues of equality and discrimination will now rely on the   **21–005**
Human Rights Act 1998, which brought Convention rights into domestic
law, including art.14 ECHR. This Article does not enshrine equality as a
free-standing principle. It does, however, provide that the enjoyment of the
rights and freedoms set out in the Convention shall be secured without
discrimination on any ground such as sex, race, colour, language, religion,
political or other opinion, national or social origin, association with a
national minority, property, birth or other status.[26] It is clear that while
there cannot be a violation of art.14 in isolation,[27] there may be a breach of
this article when considered together with other Convention articles, even if
there would have been no breach of those other articles.[28]

This important proposition was established in the *Belgian Linguistic*
case.[29] An example cited by the court will make this clear. Article 6 ECHR
does not compel states to establish appeal courts. If, however, such courts
are set up then access must not be discriminatory since this would violate
art.14. The ECtHR in the same case also gave important guidance on the
meaning of discrimination. It made it clear that art.14 did not prohibit every
difference in treatment, but only those which had no objective and reasonable justification. This was to be assessed in relation to the aims and
effects of the measure in question. The differential treatment must not only
pursue a legitimate aim. It had to be proportionate: there had to be a
reasonable relationship of proportionality between the means employed and
the aim sought to be realised.[30]

Mention should also be made of Protocol 12 ECHR. It is important
because it provides for a general prohibition of discrimination, by way of
contrast to art.14 ECHR, which only prohibits discrimination in the
enjoyment of one of the other rights guaranteed by the Convention. Protocol 12 removes this limitation and guarantees that no-one shall be discriminated against on any ground by any public authority. Thus art.1 of the
Protocol states that,

> "1 The enjoyment of any right set forth by law shall be secured without
> discrimination on any ground such as sex, race, colour, language, religion,
> political or other opinion, national or social origin, association with a
> national minority, property, birth or other status.

[26] The UK courts have acknowledged that the list in art.14 is not exhaustive, while holding that
the phrase "other status" means that the list is not unlimited, *R. (on the application of Clift) v
Secretary of State for the Home Department* [2007] 1 A.C. 484.
[27] *Abdulaziz, Cabales and Balkandali v UK* (1985) 7 E.H.R.R. 471, para.71.
[28] Jacobs and White, *The European Convention on Human Rights* (Oxford University Press, 3rd
edn, 2002), Ch.19.
[29] Judgment of July 23, 1968, Series A, No.6.
[30] See also, *Lithgow v UK* (1986) 8 E.H.R.R. 329.

2 No one shall be discriminated against by any public authority on any ground such as those mentioned in paragraph 1."

The Protocol entered into force in 2005 for those states that had ratified, when the requisite 10 ratifications had been secured. The UK has however not signed or ratified this Protocol.

B. The Determination of Discrimination

i. Michalak

21–006 Article 14 ECHR has been applied by the UK courts pursuant to the HRA. The issues to be considered were initially laid down by Brooke L.J. in *Michalak*.[31] We shall see that the House of Lords has expressed reservations about this approach, but it was influential in the early case law and in any event their Lordships' reservations can only be properly understood once we are aware of Brooke L.J.'s approach.

"i) Do the facts fall within the ambit of one or more of the substantive Convention provisions. . . . ii) If so, was there different treatment as respects that right between the complainant on the one hand and other persons put forward for comparison ("the chosen comparators") on the other? (iii) Were the chosen comparators in an analogous situation to the complainant's situation? (iv) If so, did the difference in treatment have an objective and reasonable justification: in other words, did it pursue a legitimate aim and did the differential treatment bear a reasonable relationship of proportionality to the aim sought to be achieved? The third test addresses the question whether the chosen comparators were in a sufficiently analogous situation to the complainant's situation for the different treatment to be relevant to the question whether the complainant's enjoyment of his Convention right has been free from article 14 discrimination."

The initial question was therefore whether the facts fell within the ambit of one of the Convention rights. If the facts fall within the ambit of a Convention right, the court had to consider whether there was different treatment as respects that right as between the complainant and other persons put forward for comparison, the chosen comparators. It was for the court to decide whether the chosen comparators were in an analogous situation to the complainant. It was also for the court to decide whether the difference of treatment was on a ground that fell within art.14 ECHR. This article lists a number of specific discriminatory grounds, but these are prefaced by the words "on any grounds such as". It has been held that if the ground relied

---

[31] *Michalak v London Borough of Wandsworth* [2003] 1 W.L.R. 617, para.20.

on is not specifically listed in art.14 then it must be broadly of the same kind.[32]

If there is some prima facie discriminatory treatment judged by the above criteria, the court will then determine whether there is an objective and reasonable justification for the difference in treatment. This requires the court to decide whether the difference in treatment was in pursuit of a legitimate aim, and whether there was a reasonable relationship to the aim sought to be achieved. In general terms the test for review will be that laid down by Lord Steyn in *Daly*.[33] This test and the later case law have been considered in detail above and reference should be made to that discussion.[34]

ii. Carson

The approach used in *Michalak* for deciding on art.14 ECHR was however called into question in *Carson*,[35] the facts of which will be considered below. Their Lordships in *Carson* doubted the utility of the *Michalak* approach to discrimination cases. Doubts had been raised in this respect in earlier case law,[36] and these concerns were voiced once again in *Carson* and later cases.[37] The essence of the concern was that the *Michalak* catechism could be over rigid, and that there could be overlap between the different stages of the analysis, more especially questions two, three and four.[38] There is force in this view and it is certainly true that taxonomy of the issues to be decided in discrimination cases should not hinder the resolution of cases by forcing the courts to divide stages of the analysis in an overly rigid manner.

21–007

It should however also be recognised that the substance of the issues set out in the *Michalak* formula will normally have to be addressed by the court. Thus it is axiomatic that an applicant will have to satisfy the court that the facts fall within one or more of the substantive provisions of the ECHR, since if they do not then art.14 cannot be invoked. It is also clear that the applicant will have to show that the alleged discrimination is on one of the grounds covered by art.14. Nor is it possible to avoid discussion of comparators. To be sure this discussion should not obscure resolution of the case before the court, but it is nonetheless central to the very idea of discrimination. It is important moreover to recognise that objective justification is a separate issue that becomes pertinent once a prima facie case of discrimination has been found to exist.

Given that this is so, it is interesting to reflect on the reasons why the

[32] *Waite v London Borough of Hammersmith and Fulham* [2002] EWCA Civ 482.
[33] *R. (on the application of Daly) v Secretary of State for the Home Department* [2001] 2 A.C. 532, para.26.
[34] See above, paras 18–031—18–046.
[35] *R. (on the application of Carson) v Secretary of State for Work and Pensions* [2006] 1 A.C. 173.
[36] *Nasser v United Bank of Kuwait* [2002] 1 W.L.R. 1868, para.56; *Ghaidan v Godin-Mendoza* [2004] 2 A.C. 557, para.134; *Shamoon v Chief Constable of the Royal Ulster Constabulary* [2003] 2 All E.R. 26, para.11.
[37] *Esfandiari v Secretary of State for Work and Pensions* [2006] H.R.L.R. 26; *AL (Serbia) v Secretary of State for the Home Department* [2006] EWCA Civ 1619.
[38] *Carson*, n.35, paras 29–33, 61–70; *Esfandiari*, n.37, para.8.

Michalak test has proven problematic. The difficulty with the *Michalak* formula resides in the division between questions two and three and in that between questions three and four.

The very division between question two and three was premised on the assumption that one could identify in relatively abstract terms a person or group as the appropriate comparator with the applicant, and then make a separate, more concrete determination as to whether the chosen comparators were in an analogous situation to the applicant, this latter inquiry being designed to decide whether the difference in treatment really did constitute discrimination. It is readily apparent that this division can be problematic and artificial, especially where on closer examination the applicant and the chosen comparator are not truly in a sufficiently analogous situation for the difference in treatment to constitute prima facie discrimination. The natural inclination is to run together questions two and three from *Michalak* and simply ask whether the applicant and the chosen comparator really are in an analogous situation.

21–008   This is in effect the approach taken by the Strasbourg Court, as exemplified by a case such as *Van der Mussele*.[39] The applicant argued that provisions of Belgian law requiring advocates to give legal assistance to those who needed it were contrary to arts 4 and 14 ECHR, given that such obligations were not placed on other professionals such as doctors, dentists, veterinary surgeons and the like. The Strasbourg Court rejected the claim, holding that the applicant and the other professionals were not in an analogous situation in this respect, since there were salient differences concerning their legal status, manner of entry to the profession, the nature of their functions and the manner in which they were performed. Each profession was characterised by a corpus of rights and obligations and it would be artificial to isolate one aspect thereof.[40]

The Strasbourg Court did not in this and other cases consider whether the applicant and another individual or group might in abstract terms be regarded as comparators, and then decide whether in more concrete terms they were in an analogous situation. It rather proceeded directly to the latter stage of the inquiry to decide whether in relation to the provision of services to those in need, the applicant and members of other professions were in an analogous situation. It did not thereby ignore the comparator issue. This is, as stated above, central to the very idea of discrimination. The Strasbourg approach indicates that it is only by paying attention to the specific allegations of differential treatment that one can decide whether the two individuals really are in an analogous situation and hence whether there has been discrimination.

The division between stages three and four of the *Michalak* formula can also be problematic. Courts may simply go straight to the issue of objective justification, where they believe that this is the heart of the issue, without bothering unduly with the other stages of the inquiry. It should however be

[39] *Van der Mussele v Belgium* (1984) 6 E.H.R.R. 163.
[40] *Van der Mussele*, n.39, para.46.

recognised that the very idea of objective justification can be brought into play within stage three as well as within stage four.[41] Thus it is open to a court to conclude that a relevant difference between two groups means that they are not in analogous situation and hence that there has been no discrimination; the existence of the relevant difference is the justification for the difference in treatment. The concept of objective justification is also used in those cases where a court has found that the two groups are in an analogous situation, and hence the differential treatment is prima facie discriminatory, but that it can be saved because there is some objective justification for the difference, such as the need to correct past discrimination. It will normally be for the state or public body to discharge the burden of proof if a case is resolved on objective justification in this second sense.[42]

The difficulties of maintaining the distinction between questions two and three, and between questions three and four are exemplified by *Carson* itself. The applicant had immigrated to South Africa from the UK. She received a pension to which she was entitled at the age of 60, since she had paid all necessary national insurance contributions. Pensioners who were resident in the UK received annual cost of living increases, as did those living in countries which had reciprocal Treaty arrangements with the UK, but the applicant did not receive any such increases. She argued that this constituted discrimination contrary to art.14 ECHR, read in conjunction with art.1 of the First Protocol.

The House of Lords rejected the claim. The relevant comparator for the applicant was the way in which pensioners in the UK were treated in relation to annual increments to the pension. The essence of their Lordships' decision was however that while pensioners in the UK and abroad might, in abstract terms, be regarded as the appropriate comparator, closer inquiry revealed that they were not in an analogous situation because the provision of pensions was regarded as but one part of the overall regime of taxation and social security and the former paid tax in the UK while the latter did not. The distinction between the two groups was therefore justified, in the first of the senses identified above: this relevant difference was the justification for the difference in treatment.

C. Strict Scrutiny and Rationality Review

The issue as to how far the court should defer to the executive, or accord it a discretionary area of judgment, has arisen in litigation under art.14, in much the same way as it has in relation to other Convention articles. There was an interesting tension in the courts' jurisprudence. Some courts were willing to accord such a discretionary area of judgment where the justification for the differential treatment raised issues of social and economic policy.[43] Other courts were less willing to do so, even where the subject matter related to

21–009

---

[41] This was recognised by Lord Hoffmann in *Carson*, n.35, paras 30–32.
[42] See however the cautionary observations by Lord Walker, *Carson*, n.35, para.69.
[43] See, e.g., *Michalak*, n.31, para.41; para.115; *Matadeen*, n.19, 109.

social and economic policy. The very fact that the claim concerned discrimination in relation to such policy was seen as raising issues of high constitutional importance, with the consequence that there was searching scrutiny to determine whether there was a proper and rational justification for the difference in treatment.[44] This issue should now be seen in the light of the House of Lords' decision in *Carson*.

i. Strict scrutiny and rationality review

21–010   It is common for legal systems to distinguish between different types of equality claims and to apply different degrees of scrutiny accordingly. This approach has been endorsed by the House of Lords' decision in *Carson*,[45] the facts of which were set out above. It was accepted that pension rights constituted possessions within the meaning of art.1 of the First Protocol and that her foreign residence was a "personal characteristic" for the purposes of art.14 ECHR. The key issue before the House of Lords was whether the differential treatment between the applicant and those who received annual increases constituted discrimination for the purposes of art.14. The House of Lords held that it did not.

It was acknowledged that the applicant was treated differently from a pensioner who lived in the UK. Discrimination meant however the failure to treat like cases alike, or treating cases alike where there were differences between them.[46] Whether cases were sufficiently alike was "partly a matter of values and partly a matter of rationality".[47] A differential standard of review applied depending on the ground of the alleged discrimination.

Thus Lord Hoffmann stated that characteristics such as race, caste, noble birth, membership of a political party, gender and sexual orientation were seldom if ever acceptable grounds for difference in treatment and the courts would carefully examine the reasons for differential treatment in relation to such characteristics. Discrimination on such grounds could not be justified on utilitarian grounds, since that would offend the "notion that everyone is entitled to be treated as an individual and not a statistical unit".[48] Lord Walker also followed US law and treated such grounds of discrimination as suspect, such that they would be subject to especially severe scrutiny.[49]

The standard of review for other forms of discrimination was less demanding. Where differences of treatment were made on grounds such as ability, occupation, wealth or education the courts would demand some rational justification. These differences in treatment were said Lord Hoffmann normally dependent on considerations of the public interest, which

---

[44]   *Ghaidan*, n.24, paras 18, 44.
[45]   *Carson*, n.35. The leading judgments were given by Lord Hoffmann and Lord Walker. Lord Nicholls and Lord Rodger agreed with both of these judgments. Lord Carswell dissented.
[46]   *Carson*, n.35, para.14, Lord Hoffmann.
[47]   *Carson*, n.35, para.15, Lord Hoffmann.
[48]   *Carson*, n.35, para.16.
[49]   *Carson*, n.35, para.55.

were "very much a matter for the democratically elected branches of government".[50] Lord Walker also endorsed less exacting rationality scrutiny for this second general category of differential treatment.[51]

Their Lordships placed the present case firmly in the second category. There was no discrimination on a suspect ground such as sex or race. The case therefore fell to be decided on criteria of rationality, taking due account of the choices made by the democratically elected government. The differential treatment of pensioners at home and abroad was justified in essence because pensions were regarded as part of the overall system of taxation and social security. The fact that the applicant had paid national insurance contributions was not a sufficient condition for entitlement to the same retirement pension as paid to pensioners in the UK. Such contributions were not exclusively linked to pensions, but were rather a source of revenue used to fund social security in general as well as the NHS. The interlocking nature of the taxation and social security system viewed as whole meant that it was impossible to separate a single element, retirement pensions, and treat it in a disaggregated manner.[52] There were therefore valid reasons for differentiating between the applicant resident abroad, and pensioners resident in the UK. Given that this was so, the courts should moreover respect the choice made by Parliament as to how much she should receive.[53]

ii. Strict scrutiny and rationality review: application

The idea that strict scrutiny review should be applied to cases of the kind listed in *Carson* fits with other prominent decisions, such as *A v Secretary of State for the Home Department*.[54] The claimants were foreign nationals who had been certified by the Secretary of State as suspected international terrorists under s.21 of the Anti-Terrorism, Crime and Security Act 2001, on the ground that they posed a threat to national security under s.23 of the Act. They were detained without trial or charge and argued, inter alia, that s.23 was discriminatory since it did not provide for the detention of suspected international terrorists who were UK nationals. The House of Lords agreed. Their Lordships held that the legislation, which had been introduced to combat threats posed by Al-Qaeda post 9/11, was discriminatory and disproportionate, because of the differential treatment of nationals and non-nationals who might constitute a terrorist threat. In reaching this conclusion their Lordships made it clear that deference was not appropriate in cases of discrimination where the effect of the challenged measure entailed a significant deprivation of liberty.

The *Carson* approach has been followed in subsequent cases. Thus in

21–011

---

[50] *Carson*, n.35, para.16.
[51] *Carson*, n.35, para.55.
[52] *Carson*, n.35, paras 21–22, 76–78.
[53] *Carson*, n.35, paras 25–27.
[54] [2005] 2 A.C. 68. See also, *Clift*, n.26.

Baiai[55] Silber J. considered the legality of a statutory regime designed to prevent sham marriages. The new regime required that those who were subject to immigration control and who wished to marry, other than according to the rites of the Church of England, had to apply to the Secretary of State for a certificate of approval at a cost of £135. The marriage could only take place if approval was given by the Secretary of State. The applicants challenged the regime under arts 12 and 14 ECHR. It is the latter claim that is of interest here. The applicants contended that the statutory scheme discriminated on grounds of religion and nationality, since the requirement for a certificate of approval did not apply to those who married in the Church of England. Silber J. held, following the approach in *Carson*, that discrimination on grounds of religion and nationality should be subject to strict scrutiny, and that weighty reasons would have to be proffered to justify such discrimination. He concluded that when judged by this criterion the scheme could not be upheld, since there was no reason to believe that sham marriages were more likely when the ceremony occurred in a place other than the Church of England.

The *Esfandiari* case[56] provides a useful contrast. In that case the applicants argued that the refusal to apply certain regulations under which contributions would be made to funeral expenses, in circumstances where Muslims chose to send the deceased back to their home state for burial, constituted discrimination contrary to art.14 ECHR. The Court of Appeal dismissed the claim, on the ground, inter alia, that the characterization of the applicants as part of a group, that of recent migrants, that was more likely to be affected by the non-contribution policy than others, was artificial. It also held that even if recent migrants had an identifiable status for the purpose of art.14 the case would not attract the highest scrutiny, but would rather fall within the second category laid down in *Carson*, since the allocation of public funds was an issue of social policy. The rationale given by the Secretary of State for not contributing to the cost of such burials, that it would render the system more complex and considerably more expensive, was moreover held to be defensible.

21–012   *AL (Serbia)*[57] provides a further interesting application of the *Carson* decision. The appellant was born in 1984 in Kosovo, left the country in 1999 after being threatened by the authorities, became separated from his parents and arrived in the UK in 2000. His claim for asylum was rejected, but he was granted exceptional leave to remain until his 18th birthday in 2002. His application for an extension was refused. He argued that his removal would however be contrary to arts 8 and 14 ECHR. This was because in 2003 the Home Secretary announced the family amnesty policy, which involved the grant of indefinite leave to remain in the United Kingdom. In order to qualify, a person had to be an adult who, inter alia, had at least one

---

[55] *R. (on the application of Baiai and others) v Secretary of State for the Home Department, Joint Council for the Welfare of Immigrants* [2006] EWHC 853.
[56] *Esfandiari*, n.37, paras 11–13.
[57] *AL (Serbia)*, n.37.

dependant who was under 18, and the appellant did not satisfy this condition because he had arrived in the UK alone.

The Court of Appeal acknowledged that it was not entirely easy to decide whether the instant case fell within the strict scrutiny category of *Carson*, or whether it was to be judged by rationality review. Neuberger L.J., giving judgment for the Court of Appeal, decided ultimately that the case fell within the latter category, notwithstanding that it came within the general field of asylum, because the case concerned challenge to a policy conceding a right to remain to those who would probably have no ECHR basis for resisting removal from this country. The court was therefore willing to accord a significant margin of discretion to the executive. The challenged policy was perforce a blunt instrument, which was inevitably the case unless every asylum-seeker since 2000 was to be given the right to remain. There were rational administrative and economic reasons to limit the policy to families.[58]

A final example of the need for care in the application of the principles in *Carson* can be found in the decision in *Wilson*.[59] The claimant, a Romany gypsy, sited a residential caravan in breach of planning control on land owned by her family. The council issued a "stop notice" under the planning legislation,[60] requiring her to cease using the land for the stationing of caravans. The claimant argued that the legislation was discriminatory, since it exempted dwelling houses, but not residential caravans, from the stop notice regime, and therefore indirectly discriminated against gypsies, in breach of Arts 8 and 14 ECHR. The Secretary of State accepted that the legislation was indirectly discriminatory, but argued that it was justified by the need to protect the public against the serious environmental harm caused by unauthorised caravan sites.

The Court of Appeal found against the claimant. Richards L.J. found that the inclusion of residential caravans within the general stop notice regime was aimed legitimately at protecting the public against serious harm to amenity. The indirect discriminatory impact on gypsies made it appropriate, said Richards L.J., for the court to examine with intense scrutiny the Secretary of State's objective justification for the rule. This did not however preclude according to the legislature some discretionary area of judgment, albeit narrower than that usually given in matters of planning policy. Thus there was, said Richards L.J., no objection in art.14 cases to the adoption of a bright line rule with regard to residential caravans. Provided that the rule fell within the discretionary area of judgment allowed to the legislature, it could not be impugned on the ground that a different balance might have been struck or a less restrictive rule devised, although the existence of a less restrictive alternative might be relevant in examining the cogency of the claimed justification, so that the narrower the discretionary area of judgment, or the more intense the degree of scrutiny required, the more

---

[58] *AL (Serbia)*, n.37, paras 35, 37.
[59] *R. (on the application of Wilson) v Wychavon DC* [2007] Q.B. 801.
[60] Town and Country Planning Act 1990 s.183.

significant it might be that a less restrictive alternative could have been adopted. The court concluded that there were cogent reasons for a simple bright line rule exempting dwelling houses, but not residential caravans, from the stop notice regime.

D. Gender and Positive Discrimination

21–013 While *Carson* is important for judicial endorsement of differential standards of review depending on the nature of the discrimination, *Hooper*[61] is significant for judicial acceptance of justification for discrimination cast in terms of remedying past disadvantages.

The claimants were four widowers, whose wives had died in the period 1995–2000. If they had been widows, they would have received one of a number of widows' benefits depending on their particular circumstances: a widow's payment of £1,000, a widowed mother's allowance for those who had children until they ceased to be dependent, and a widow's pension. Legislation dating from 1999 abolished the widow's benefits for widows whose husbands died on or after April 9, 2001.[62] A new scheme of benefits was introduced that were payable to widows and widowers alike, but the rights of existing widows to the widow's pension were preserved. The claimants argued that once the HRA came into force the denial to them of benefits paid to widows constituted discrimination through a combination of arts 14 and 8 ECHR.

The House of Lords held that there was objective justification for the differential treatment in relation to payment of widow's pensions. Lord Hoffmann surveyed the rationale for and history of such pensions. The payment of this pension was not dependent on the means or resources of the particular widow: it was paid to all widows who satisfied the age criterion, the premise being that "older widows as a class were likely to be needier than older widowers as a class".[63] The rationale for the provision of widow's pension was that "in the social conditions which prevailed for most of the last century, it was unusual for married women to work and that it was unreasonable to expect them to be equipped to earn their own living if they were widowed in middle age".[64] While the proportion of older women active in the labour market had increased by the turn of the century, a significant proportion of these worked part-time and there was a higher concentration of women than men in relatively low paid occupations: "the comparative disadvantage of women in the labour market had by no means disappeared".[65]

21–014 It was against this background that the House of Lords considered whether the continued payment of the widow's pension in the period 1995–

---

[61] *R. (on the application of Hooper) v Secretary of State for Work and Pensions* [2005] 1 W.L.R. 1681.
[62] Welfare Reform and Pensions Act 1999.
[63] *Hooper*, n.61, para.16.
[64] *Hooper*, n.61, para.17.
[65] *Hooper*, n.61, para.31.

2001 and its continuation for women bereaved before April 9, 2001 was objectively justified. The Court of Appeal had concluded that there was no such justification, reversing the decision of Moses J. The House of Lords reversed the Court of Appeal in this respect. The House of Lords' reasoning in *Hooper* indicates that while the courts should, as stated in *Carson*, review gender based discrimination strictly this does not necessarily translate into substitution of judgment.

Lord Hoffmann, with whom the other Law Lords agreed on this issue, stated that the Strasbourg Court allowed Member States to treat groups unequally in order to correct factual inequalities and that in making decisions about social and economic policy, in particular those concerned with the equitable distribution of public resources, the Strasbourg Court allowed Member States a margin of appreciation. In a domestic system these decisions were "ordinarily recognized by the courts to be matters for the judgment of the elected representatives of the people",[66] and the mere fact that the complaint concerned gender discrimination was not "in itself a reason for a court to impose its own judgment".[67]

> "Once it is accepted that older widows were historically an economically disadvantaged class which merited special treatment but were gradually becoming less disadvantaged, the question of the precise moment at which special treatment is no longer justified becomes a social and political question within the competence of Parliament."[68]

The recognition that the remedying of past disadvantage can constitute objective justification for differential treatment under the HRA is to be welcomed.[69] The nature of the judicial review undertaken was finely tuned. The nub of the issue was the timing of the shift from the old regime according special benefits to widows, to the new regime under which benefits were granted to widows and widowers alike. The House of Lords did not impose its own judgment on this matter. Its willingness to afford Parliament some latitude as to the timing of the change should nonetheless be seen against the fact that the House of Lords had satisfied itself that there was valid reason for differential treatment in relation to widow's pensions in the past.

---

[66] *Hooper*, n.61, para.32.
[67] *Hooper*, n.61, para.32.
[68] *Hooper*, n.61, para.32.
[69] S. Fredman, "Affirmative Action and the Court of Justice: A Critical Analysis", in J. Shaw (ed.), *Social Law and Policy in an Evolving European Union* (Hart, 2000), Ch.9.

5. EU Law

21–015 EU law is of relevance for equality in a number of ways.[70] The principle of equality and the prohibition of discrimination are found expressly within a number of Treaty articles,[71] but the ECJ held at an early stage that these were merely specific enunciations of the general principle of equality as one of the fundamental principles of Community law,[72] which must be observed by any court.[73]

A. Discrimination and Nationality

21–016 EU law proscribes any discrimination on the grounds of nationality. This is a central feature of EU law and is enshrined in general terms in art.12 EC. The general prohibition on discrimination on grounds of nationality contained in art.12 EC has been especially significant, in particular when read with the provisions on citizenship contained in arts 17–18 EC.[74] The proscription of nationality discrimination finds more specific recognition in, for example, arts 39, 43 and 49 EC, which prohibit discriminatory treatment in relation to free movement of workers, freedom of establishment and freedom to provide services in another Member State. These provisions have direct effect, both vertical and horizontal, and thus can be relied upon in national courts against either the state or a private individual. The proscription of discrimination on grounds of nationality has an economic and a social rationale.[75]

The basic economic objective is to ensure the optimal allocation of resources within the Community, by enabling factors of production to move to the area where they are most valued. Thus, for example, labour is one of the factors of production. It may be that this factor of production is valued more highly in some areas than in others. This would be so if there were an excess of supply over demand for labour in southern Italy, and an excess of demand over supply in certain parts of Germany. In this situation labour is worth more in Germany than it is in Italy. The value of labour within the Community as a whole is, therefore, maximised if workers are free to move

---

[70] P. Craig, *EU Administrative Law* (Oxford University Press, 2006), Ch.15. For tensions between EU law and the ECHR, N. Bamforth, "Prohibited Grounds of Discrimination under EU Law and the European Convention on Human Rights: Problems of Contrast and Overlap" (2006–7) 9 C.Y.E.L.S. 1.

[71] K. Lenaerts, "L'Egalite de Traitement en Droit Communautaire" (1991) 27 C.D.E. 3.

[72] *Ruckdeschel v Hauptzollamt Hamburg-St. Annen* (117/76 and 16/77) [1977] E.C.R. 1753, para.7.

[73] *Milac GmbH v Hauptzollamt Freiburg* (8/78) [1978] E.C.R. 1721, para.18.

[74] *Maria Martinez Sala v Freistaat Bayern* (C-85/96) [1998] E.C.R. I-2691; *Rudy Grzelczyk v Centre Public D'Aide Sociale d'Ottignes-Louvain-la-Neuve (CPAS)* (C-184/99) [2001] E.C.R. I-6193; *Trojani v Centre Public D'Aide Sociale de Bruxelles (CPAS)* (C-456/02) [2004] E.C.R. I-7573; *The Queen (on the application of Bidar) v London Borough of Ealing and Secretary of State for Education* (C-209/03) [2005] E.C.R. I-2119.

[75] *Phil Collins v Imtrat Handelsgesellschaft mbH* (C-92/92) [1993] E.C.R. I–5145, 5163, AG Jacobs.

within the Community to the area where they are most valued and such movement is not impeded by discrimination on grounds of nationality.

There has however always been a social as well as an economic rationale underlying the proscription of discrimination on grounds of nationality within the four freedoms. This is at its most fundamental the idea that it should be regarded as natural and something to be encouraged that, for example, workers should be employed or firms should carry on business in Member States other than their home state, and that when they did so they could not be treated in a disadvantageous manner as compared with nationals of that state. This was integral to the very idea of a "community". There are of course barriers to the realisation of this ideal, some practical, others cultural in nature, which provisions embodied in a Treaty cannot in themselves dispel. This can be accepted, while at the same time recognising that the four freedoms are designed to facilitate this integration.

B. Discrimination and Gender

The Treaty has, since its inception, prohibited discrimination in relation to **21–017** pay on gender grounds, and this was extended to cover equal treatment, art.141 EC. The principles concerning gender discrimination were further elaborated through Community legislation, in particular Directive 75/117[76] and Directive 76/207.[77] Action by the state or a private party, which infringes art.141, can be challenged via art.234 in the national courts.

This is exemplified by the well-known *Defrenne* case.[78] The applicant, who was an air hostess, brought an action for discrimination against her employer Sabena, because she was paid less than male colleagues who did the same job. The principal issue was whether art.119 EEC, now art.141 EC, should have direct effect. The ECJ said that this question should be considered in the light of the "nature of the principle of equal pay, the aim of this provision and its place in the scheme of the Treaty".[79] The ECJ held that there were two aims underlying this article. The market-integration objective was designed "to avoid a situation in which undertakings established in States which have actually implemented the principle of equal pay suffer a competitive disadvantage in intra-Community competition as compared with undertakings established in States which have not yet eliminated discrimination against women workers as regards pay".[80] The second aim was social in nature: art.119 "forms part of the social objectives of the Community, which is not merely an economic union, but is at the same time intended, by common action, to ensure social progress and seek the constant

---

[76] Council Directive 75/117/EEC of February 10, 1975, On the Approximation of the Laws of the Member States Relating to the Application of the Principle of Equal Pay for Men and Women [1975] O.J. L45/19.
[77] Council Directive 76/207/EEC of February 9, 1976, On the Implementation of the Principle of Equal Treatment for Men and Women as regards Access to Employment, Vocational Training and Promotion, and Working Conditions [1976] O.J. L39/40.
[78] *Defrenne v Société Anonyme Belge de Navigation Aérienne* (43/75) [1976] E.C.R. 455.
[79] *Defrenne*, n.78, para.7.
[80] *Defrenne*, n.78, para.9.

improvement of the living and working conditions of their peoples, as is emphasized by the Preamble to the Treaty".[81]

This double aim, economic and social, was indicative of the foundational role played by the principle of equal pay within the EC.[82] This conclusion reinforced the Court's resolve that what is now art.141 should have direct effect, notwithstanding the fact that it was couched in general terms and required further elaboration through Community legislation.

In *Schröder*[83] the ECJ went further, holding that the social objective underlying art.141 took precedence over the economic. The case was concerned with entitlement to membership of an occupational pension scheme by part-time workers, the great majority of whom were women. If the social aim were accorded priority, then it would be permissible for German law to apply the equal pay principle retroactively so as to permit part-time workers access to such a scheme. However if the economic aim were to take priority the opposite result might be reached, since it was argued that by allowing retroactive membership of the scheme German firms would be placed at a competitive disadvantage as compared with those in other Member States.

The ECJ reiterated the twin objectives of art.141 that had been elaborated in *Defrenne*. It then pointed to subsequent decisions where it had held that the right not to be discriminated against on grounds of sex was a fundamental human right, whose observance the Court had a duty to ensure.[84] The ECJ concluded in the light of this case law that the economic aim pursued by art.141, namely the elimination of distortions of competition between undertakings established in different Member States, "is secondary to the social aim pursued by the same provision, which constitutes the expression of a fundamental human right".[85]

C. Discrimination and Article 13 EC

21–018 The third way in which EC law relating to equality will have an impact on domestic law stems from the addition of a new art.13 by the Treaty of Amsterdam. It gives the Community legislative competence to take appropriate action to combat discrimination based on sex, racial or ethnic origin, religion or belief, disability, age or sexual orientation.[86] Two directives were adopted in 2000.

There is a directive prohibiting discrimination on grounds of race and ethnic origin.[87] There is also the so-called framework employment Directive, covering discrimination in the field of employment on the grounds listed in

---

[81] *Defrenne*, n.78, para.10.
[82] *Defrenne*, n.78, para.12.
[83] *Deutsche Telekom v Schröder* (C-50/96) [2000] E.C.R. I-743.
[84] *Deutsche Telekom*, n.83, para.56, citing *Defrenne III* (149/77) [1978] E.C.R. 1365, paras 26–27, *Razzouk and Beydoun v Commission* (75 and 117/82) [1984] E.C.R. 1509, para.16, and *P v S and Cornwall County Council* (C-13/94) [1996] E.C.R. I-2143, para.19.
[85] *Deutsche Telecom*, n. 83, para.57.
[86] M. Bell, *Anti-Discrimination Law and the EU* (Oxford University Press, 2002).
[87] Council Directive 2000/43/EC of June 29, 2000 implementing the principle of equal treatment between persons irrespective of racial or ethnic origin [2000] O.J. L180/22.

art.13 (other than race, ethnic origin or sex, which are already covered by other legislation): religion, belief, disability, age and sexual orientation.[88] While the jurisdictional limitation in art.13 specifies that the EC can only act within the limits of the Community's powers, art.3 of the anti-racism Directive gives it an apparently wide scope, including a prohibition on discrimination in relation to social protection, healthcare, housing and education.

Individuals will be able to rely on provisions of the directives in national courts where those provisions meet the conditions for direct effect. This means that a person aggrieved by government action may have recourse both to Convention rights concerning discrimination, and EC measures passed pursuant to art.13. It should also be recognised that the latter are more potent in an important respect. National law that is inconsistent with art.13 will be invalid, and even primary legislation can be declared inapplicable where it conflicts with a Community norm.[89]

D. Discrimination and Common Policies

Discrimination is also relevant in relation to the Community's common policies, such as the Common Agricultural Policy, CAP. The principle of non-discrimination performs what More[90] aptly terms a regulatory role in these areas, in that it constrains the regulatory choices that can be made by the administration.

21–019

Article 33 EC is the foundational provision of the CAP. It is of a broad discretionary nature and sets out a range of general objectives to be served by the CAP. They include increase in agricultural productivity, with the object, inter alia, of ensuring a fair standard of living for the agricultural community; the stabilisation of markets; assuring the availability of supplies; and reasonable prices for consumers. It is readily apparent that these objectives can clash with each other.[91] The Commission and Council therefore have to make difficult discretionary choices. Whether the resultant choices discriminate between producers may be contentious. The ECJ has, not surprisingly, accepted that the Community institutions have a considerable degree of choice as to how to balance the objectives which are to be pursued.[92] The principle of non-discrimination must therefore be viewed against this background. Article 34(2) EC provides that,

---

[88] Council Directive 2000/78/EC of November 27, 2000 establishing a general framework for equal treatment in employment and occupation [2000] O.J. L303/16.
[89] See Ch.10.
[90] G. More, "The Principle of Equal Treatment: From Market Unifier to Fundamental Right", in P. Craig and G. de Búrca (eds), *The Evolution of EU Law* (Oxford University Press, 1999), 530–535.
[91] *Germany v Commission* (34/62) [1963] E.C.R. 131; *Beus v Hauptzollamt München* (5/67) [1968] E.C.R. 83.
[92] *Ludwigshafener Walzmühle Erling KG v Council* (197–200, 243, 245, 247/80) [1981] E.C.R. 3211; *KG in der Firma Hans-Otto Wagner GmbH Agrarhandel v Bundesanstalt für Landwirtschaftliche Marktordnung* (8/82) [1983] E.C.R. 371; *Firma A Racke v Hauptzollamt Mainz* (283/83) [1984] E.C.R. 3791.

"The common organisation established in accordance with paragraph 2 may include all measures required to attain the objectives set out in Article 33, in particular regulation of prices, aids for the production and marketing of the various products, storage and carryover arrangements and common machinery for stabilising imports or exports.

The common organisation shall be limited to the pursuit of the objectives set out in Article 33 and shall exclude any discrimination between producers or consumers within the Community.

Any common price policy shall be based on common criteria and uniform methods of calculation."

A necessary condition for an applicant to be able to rely successfully on non-discrimination in art.34(2) is therefore that it is in a comparable situation to that of another producer or consumer and is being treated differently, or that it is in a different situation and is being treated in the same manner. Comparability is a necessary condition for successful invocation of art.34(2). It is not however sufficient. The applicant will also have to rebut arguments advanced by the defendant concerning objective justification. Thus the defendant, normally the Commission and/or the Council, may argue that the differential treatment was objectively justified in order to attain one of the objectives in art.33. The interplay between comparability and objective justification is apparent in the leading cases.[93]

E. Discrimination and the Charter of Rights

21–020   EU law is also of relevance for consideration of equality because of the Charter of Fundamental Rights. The Lisbon Treaty[94] will come into force in 2009 if duly ratified by the Member States. The Charter is, according to the Lisbon Treaty, not incorporated in the Treaties, but it is given the same legal value as the Treaties.[95] The Lisbon Treaty is premised on the version of the Charter as amended by the Intergovernmental Conference in 2004,[96] and this version has been reissued in the Official Journal.[97]

The UK and Poland negotiated a Protocol designed to limit the application of the Charter in certain respects.[98] The Protocol contains a lengthy preamble, which, inter alia, reaffirms that art.6 TEU requires the courts of the UK and Poland to interpret and apply the Charter in accord with the explanations referred to in that article. The preamble moreover "notes" the

[93] *Ruckdeschel*, n.72; *Royal Scholten-Honig v. Intervention Board for Agricultural Produce* (103 and 145/77) [1978] E.C.R. 2037.
[94] Conference of the Representatives of the Governments of the Member States, Treaty of Lisbon Amending the Treaty on European Union and the Treaty Establishing the European Community, CIG 14/07, Brussels December 3, 2007; [2007] O.J. C306/1.
[95] art.6(1) TEU LT.
[96] Brussels European Council, June 21–22, 2007, 25.
[97] Charter of Fundamental Rights of the European Union, [2007] O.J. C303/1; Explanations Relating to the Charter of Fundamental Rights, [2007] O.J. C303/17.
[98] Protocol on the Application of the Charter of Fundamental Rights of the European Union to Poland and to the United Kingdom, LT.

wish of Poland and the United Kingdom to clarify certain aspects of the application of the Charter.

The Protocol has two substantive articles. Article 1(1) states that the Charter does not extend the ability of the Community courts, or any court or tribunal of Poland or of the United Kingdom, to find that the laws, regulations or administrative provisions, practices or action of Poland or of the United Kingdom are inconsistent with the fundamental rights, freedoms and principles that it reaffirms. Article 1(2) further states that nothing in Title IV of the Charter, which concerns solidarity rights, creates justiciable rights applicable to Poland or the United Kingdom except in so far as Poland or the United Kingdom has provided for such rights in its national law. Article 2 provides that insofar as a provision of the Charter refers to national laws and practices, it shall only apply to Poland or the United Kingdom to the extent that the rights or principles that it contains are recognised in the law or practices of Poland or of the United Kingdom.

It will be for the ECJ to interpret the ambit and meaning of this Protocol, assuming that the Lisbon Treaty is duly ratified. Subject to this, the Lisbon Treaty renders the Charter binding. Chapter III of the Charter deals with equality. It contains a basic equality before the law guarantee, as well as a provision similar, though not identical, to that in art.13. There is also a reference to positive action provisions in the field of gender equality, protection for children's rights, and some weaker provisions guaranteeing "respect" for cultural diversity, for the rights of the elderly and for persons with disabilities. The Charter is binding on Member States when they implement EU law,[99] the best reading of which, and that which is in accord with the explanatory memorandum, is that Member States are bound by Charter provisions whenever they act within the scope of EU law. The Charter may also have an indirect horizontal impact as between private parties.[100]

Assuming that the Charter is rendered legally binding as a result of the Lisbon Treaty, applicants wishing to assert equality claims will therefore be able to rely not only on the HRA and Convention rights, but also on EU law, at least insofar as the facts of the case fall within the scope of EU law.

[99] art.51(1) Charter.
[100] Craig, n.70, 498–505.

CHAPTER 22

RULE-MAKING

1. INTRODUCTION

People may be affected not only through individualised adjudication, but 22–001
also through the application of pre-determined rules. These rules will have
to be applied to the case at hand, but they will often be determinative of the
result, or will strongly influence the outcome. This chapter is concerned with
the controls over rule-making.

The term rule-making is used here instead of the more customary
appellation of delegated legislation. The reason is simple. The latter is but
one species of the former. The test of whether a rule is subject to our
legislative checks is one of form. A primary statute that empowers a minister
to make rules will specify whether they are to be regarded as statutory
instruments for the purposes of the Statutory Instruments Act 1946. It is this
Act which contains the provisions for publication and legislative scrutiny.
There are, therefore, three areas not touched by our legislative controls.

First, there are rules that are not expressed to be statutory instruments
and are therefore outside of the 1946 legislation. Second, there are areas in
which administrative institutions will develop rules, even if they are not
expressly empowered to do so. This leads directly to the third area not
covered by our existing controls. This is, ironically, where no rules are made.
Although bureaucracies will often develop rules to guide the exercise of their
discretion, there are still large areas in which they will not. Decisions will be
made by the informal exercise of discretion. Such decisions may be made
against the background of an officially understood policy; or they may
simply be the exercise of judgment by a particular hearing officer. The key
issue is how far we should encourage the crystallisation of this informal
discretion into a series of rules.

There are four broad mechanisms for the control of rule-making: consultation, publication, legislative scrutiny and judicial review. Consultation
is designed to secure consideration of the rule by interested parties prior to

its passage. Publication ensures knowledge of the rule. Legislative supervision takes the form of parliamentary scrutiny. Consultation and legislative scrutiny are general methods of control, and the focus will be upon the merits of the rule as well as its technical legality. Judicial supervision by way of contrast is ex post facto, particular and focuses on the legality of the measure and not its merits. It will take place once the rule has been passed.[1] It is dependent upon an individual invoking the court's assistance and is in this sense particular, and because of the constitutional position of our courts they cannot, overtly at least, attack the merits of the rule. This is not to deny that judicial pronouncements may have an effect upon the making of future rules by prescribing procedural standards, or by decisions upon aspects of legality. The nature of the judicial process is nonetheless unsuited to any generalised control over the content of rules. For this, checks in the form of consultation, legislative supervision and publication must remain the chief weapons. Where the courts could be more adventurous is, as will be seen, in the standards imposed upon the bureaucracy with respect to the making of administrative rules.

It is easy when discussing the plethora of forms of rule-making, to lose sight of why such constraints are required. We are concerned about rule-making, whatever form it takes, because our ideas of representative government tell us that legislative norms achieve validation and legitimacy through the expression of consent by the legislature itself. The existence of rules of a legislative character, other than primary statutes, poses the problem of how this validation and control is to be accomplished. That is the central concern of this chapter.

We will examine first the existing constraints upon delegated legislation and then take a closer look at the whole problem of administrative rule-making. The final section of the chapter will touch on the more general importance of Community law.

2. Delegated Legislation: History, Rationale and Form

A. History

22–002 Delegated legislation is not a new phenomenon.[2] While the Statute of Proclamations 1539 giving Henry VIII extensive powers to legislate by proclamation proved to be a relatively short-lived measure, the Statute of Sewers 1531 was the harbinger of a more general trend. The latter vested the

---

[1] Subject to the judicial role in enforcing compliance with the requirements of, for example, consultation. As to whether the courts would intervene by injunction to prevent the passage of delegated legislation, see below para.25–034.

[2] C. Allen, *Law and Orders: An Inquiry into the Nature and Scope of Delegated Legislation and Executive Powers in English Law* (Stevens, 3rd edn, 1965), Ch.2; C. Carr, *Delegated Legislation: Three Lectures* (Cambridge University Press, 1921); J. Griffith and H. Street, *Principles of Administrative Law* (Pitman, 5th edn, 1973), Chs 2 and 3; R. Baldwin, *Rules and Government* (Oxford University Press, 1995).

Commissioners of Sewers with full powers to make laws and decrees concerning drainage schemes and the levying of rates to pay for them.[3]

It was, however, the social and economic reforms of the 19th century that was the origin of delegated legislation on the scale to which we have now become accustomed. We have already seen how the Poor Law Amendment Act 1834 vested the Poor Law Commissioners with power to make rules for the management of the poor.[4] Many other 19th-century statutes contained power to make rules. After 1890 statutory rules and orders were published annually. Between 1901 and 1914 the average number of orders made was 1,349, which increased in the war years to 1,459.[5]

The advent of war increased not only the amount, but also the complexity and generality of delegated legislation. The Defence of the Realm Act 1914 gave the Government power to make regulations for securing the public safety and the defence of the realm, a power liberally used. Regulations were made on dog shows and the supply of cocaine to actresses, neither of which appears to be of prime concern to the war effort. While the generality of the empowering provisions diminished immediately after the First World War, it did not entirely wane. Thus the Emergency Powers Act 1920 gave the Government extensive powers to deal with peace-time emergencies.[6] The advent of the Second World War found the draftsmen ready with the Emergency Powers (Defence) Acts 1939 and 1940. This legislation empowered the Crown to make regulations, inter alia, for public safety, the defence of the realm, the maintenance of order, the maintenance of supply and the detention of persons whose detention appeared to the Secretary of State to be expedient in the interests of public safety or the defence of the realm.

While wide delegated powers could be accepted during war or civil emergency, there was growing disquiet about their scope in peacetime. Some, like Lord Hewart,[7] felt that delegated legislation was out of control, raising fears that we were to be ruled by the bureaucracy. While controls over delegated legislation were desirable Lord Hewart's general attack upon such delegation was overplayed, as was made apparent by the Committee on Ministers' Powers. The Committee was appointed to consider delegated legislation and the making of judicial or quasi-judicial decisions by ministers.[8] Its conclusions can be summarised briefly: delegated legislation was inevitable but could be improved by a clearer use of terminology; by defining the delegated powers as clearly as possible; and by adequate facilities for publication and legislative scrutiny.[9]

---

[3] The Commissioners of Sewers are also a good example of a body vested with administrative, judicial and executive powers.
[4] See above, Ch.2.
[5] Allen, n.2, 32.
[6] The Act was used in the General Strike of 1926, the 1948 and 1949 dock strikes, the 1955 rail strike, the 1966 seamen's strike, the 1970 dock strike and the coal strike of 1973.
[7] Lord Hewart, *The New Despotism* (Ernest Benn, 1929).
[8] Cmd. 4060 (1932).
[9] For a complete list of the recommendations, Cmd. 4060, n.8, 64–70.

B. Rationale and Constitutional Concerns

22–003 Few have doubted the continuing need for delegated legislation: 3,471 statutory instruments were made in 2006 and 3,601 in 2005.[10] The exigencies of the modern state have increasingly led to statutes containing delegated power. This is so for a number of reasons.

First, the area may be technically complex, making it difficult to set out all the permutations in the original statute. Second, the subject-matter may be novel. Time may be needed to experiment and to determine how the legislation is operating. Only then can all the details be filled in. This process may best be carried out over a period of time, making delegated legislation the most appropriate tool. Third, even where the area is well known, the executive may wish to implement the legislation at a later stage or to alter its detail. Delegated legislation is a useful mechanism for achieving these ends. A fourth reason is the advantage that such legislation gives to the executive. For a government with an onerous legislative timetable, or only a small majority, there is always the temptation to pass skeleton legislation with the details being etched in by the minister. These details may contain important aspects of the legislation, and legislative scrutiny may not always be effective.

While all accept the general need for delegated legislation there are certain types which give rise to particular constitutional concern. The Scott Report[11] was, for example, very critical of the broad delegated powers given to the executive by statutes such as the Import, Export and Customs Powers (Defence) Act 1939, which was used to control exports until 1990, and its successor statute the Import and Export Control Act 1990.[12] More generally the use of skeleton legislation, adverted to above, is a cause for especial concern. The passage of such legislation is now common, with power being given to the executive not merely to fill in technical details, but also to decide broad issues of policy, thereby leading to a consequential shift in the balance of power between Parliament and the Executive.[13]

The type of delegated legislation that is most objectionable is that which contains a "Henry VIII" clause. This is the nickname for clauses that allow a minister to amend the primary statute, or some other statute, through delegated legislation. The use of such clauses has increased as of late,[14] as exemplified by the Deregulation and Contracting Out Act 1994, and the Regulatory Reform Act 2001.[15] It should also be remembered that the Human Rights Act 1998 contains what is in effect a Henry VIII clause to

---

[10] Joint Committee on Statutory Instruments, *Scrutinising Statutory Instruments: Departmental Returns 2006, First Special Report 2006–7* (HL 153, HC 917; 2007), para.2, fn.2.
[11] *Report of the Inquiry into the Export of Defence Equipment and Dual-Use of Goods to Iraq and Related Prosecutions* (HC 115; 1996).
[12] G. Ganz, "Delegated Legislation: A Necessary Evil or a Constitutional Outrage?", in P. Leyland and T. Woods (eds), *Administrative Law Facing the Future: Old Constraints and New Horizons* (Blackwell, 1997), Ch.3.
[13] *Ibid* 63–64.
[14] Lord Rippon, "Henry VIII Clauses" (1989) 10 Stat. L. Rev. 205, and "Constitutional Anarchy" (1990) 11 Stat. L. Rev. 184.
[15] Ganz, n.12, 65–66; M. Freedland, "Privatising *Carltona*: Part II of the Deregulation and Contracting Out Act" [1995] P.L. 21, 21–22.

enable a minister expeditiously to alter legislation which a court has held to be inconsistent with the Convention rights recognised by the Act.[16]

C. Form

There are a bewildering variety of names for delegated legislation. Orders in Council, rules, regulations, byelaws and directions all jostle one another upon the statute book. The key to sanity is the realisation that nothing turns upon the precise nomenclature.[17] A word about the differing devices is nonetheless necessary.

Orders in Council tend to be the more important pieces of subordinate legislation. The executive will draft the legislation, but it will be enacted as an Order of the Privy Council. The authority to make such Orders will be derived from a statute.[18] *Regulations* and *rules* are used widely to denote subordinate law-making power. The power will normally be conferred upon a minister of the Crown. Agencies and local authorities may also pass regulations, rules or orders. *Byelaws* are commonly promulgated by local authorities, but can also be made by agencies.[19]

22–004

3. DELEGATED LEGISLATION: PASSAGE AND PUBLICATION

A. The Statutory Instruments Act 1946

Section 1(1) of the 1946 Act states,[20]

22–005

"1(1) Where by this Act or any Act passed after the commencement[21] of this Act power to make, confirm, or approve orders, rules, regulations or other subordinate legislation is conferred on His Majesty in Council or on any Minister of the Crown then, if the power is expressed—

(a) in the case of a power conferred on His Majesty, to be exercised by Order in Council;

(b) in the case of a power conferred on a Minister of the Crown, to be exercisable by statutory instrument,

---

[16] Human Rights Act 1998 s.10.
[17] The Donoughmore Committee recommended that each of these terms should be used for a specific purpose, but their ideas were not implemented, Cmd. 4060, 64.
[18] The Privy Council can, however, pass legislation which is not subordinate legislation at all on matters within the Royal Prerogative, provided that the power to do so has not been restricted by statute, *Att-Gen. v De Keyser's Royal Hotel* [1920] A.C. 508.
[19] For special problems concerning byelaws see J. Garner, *Administrative Law* (B. Jones and K. Thompson, Butterworths, 8th edn, 1996), 99–106. There are also devices known as Provisional Orders and Special Procedure Orders (for the latter see the Statutory Orders (Special Procedure) Act 1945) which are intended to expedite the passage of private Acts, see Allen, n.2, 76–82.
[20] Statutory Instruments Act 1946 s.1(1A) makes provision for Wales.
[21] January 1, 1948.

any document by which that power is exercised shall be known as a "statutory instrument" and the provisions of this Act shall apply thereto accordingly."

The Act therefore provides for two different types of cases. All Orders in Council made in pursuance of a statutory power must be exercised by statutory instrument.[22] Other rules, regulations or orders must be exercised by statutory instrument only when the particular statute states that the power must be so exercised. The test is one of form. Moreover, s.1(1)(b) only applies when the power is conferred on a minister of the Crown. This is defined flexibly: if there is any question whether any board, commissioner or other body on whom any such power is conferred is a government department, or which minister of the Crown is in charge of them, the question is to be referred to the Minister for the Civil Service.[23] As s.1 makes clear, it is sufficient if the Minister of the Crown has power to make, confirm or approve the subordinate legislation.[24]

B. Publication and Making

22–006   A principal purpose of the 1946 Act is to provide for the publication of statutory instruments. This is dealt with in s.2(1): immediately after the making of any statutory instrument it shall be sent to the King's printer of Acts of Parliament and numbered in accordance with regulations made under the 1946 Act. Copies shall be printed[25] and sold as soon as possible, subject to any exceptions made by Acts passed after the 1946 Act, or contained in any regulations made under the 1946 Act. Statutory instruments must contain a statement of the date on which they will become operative.[26]

The main exceptions from the requirement for publication are as follows: local instruments, which connote local and personal or private Acts[27]; and general instruments[28] certified by the responsible authority to be a class of documents which would otherwise be regularly printed.[29] The Reference Committee[30] may direct that such an instrument should be published.

---

[22] Orders in Council made in pursuance of the Royal Prerogative are not covered.
[23] Statutory Instruments Act 1946 s.11(2).
[24] A third type of case is dealt with in the Statutory Instruments Act 1946 s.1(2), which covers statutes passed before 1946, and provides the criterion as to when rules passed pursuant to such statutes after 1946 should count as statutory instruments. See further Statutory Instruments Regulations 1947 (SI 1948/1).
[25] The Statutory Instruments (Production and Sale) Act 1996 was passed in order to facilitate the contracting-out of the printing of statutory instruments.
[26] Statutory Instruments Act 1946 s.4(2).
[27] Statutory Instruments Regulations 1948 (SI 1948/1), reg.4(2).
[28] General instruments are those in the nature of a public general Act, SI 1948/1 reg.4.
[29] SI 1948/1 reg.5.
[30] Two or more persons nominated by the Lord Chancellor and Speaker of the House of Commons, reg.11(1).

Exemptions from publication also exist for temporary instruments,[31] the publication of bulky schedules,[32] and for confidential instruments.[33]

It might be thought that a failure to publish would affect the validity of the statutory instrument, since the public would not otherwise have the opportunity to know the law being applied to them. This is not however the case. Primary statutes take effect as soon as they have received the Royal Assent.

It was at one time thought that subordinate legislation required publication in order to be valid. There is some authority for this proposition,[34] but the weight of authority is against this view. In *R. v Sheer Metalcraft Ltd*,[35] a company was prosecuted for infringing an Iron and Steel Prices Order. The Order had been printed but certain schedules had not, and no certificate of exemption had been obtained. Streatfeild J. held that the existence of s.3(2) of the 1946 Act indicated that the Order was valid despite failure to publish. That section provides a defence to an action for contravention of a statutory instrument where the instrument has not been issued at the date of the contravention, unless it can be shown that reasonable steps were taken to bring it to the public's knowledge. If an Order was ineffective before publication then s.3(2) would be redundant, as there would be no law contravened. Streatfeild J. stressed that the making of the instrument was one thing and the issue of it another. An instrument was valid once it was made by the Minister and laid before Parliament.[36]

This still leaves open the question as to when the instrument is "made" by the Minister. The enabling legislation may state that an instrument shall not be made until it has been laid before Parliament. There may also be a provision stipulating when the instrument should come into operation. In the absence of such provisions the statutory instrument would appear to be made when either enacted by the Queen in Council, or signed by the competent authority, who will normally be a minister or a civil servant with authority to sign for the Minister.[37]

Whatever the deficiencies of the 1946 Act, it does in general ensure the publication of statutory instruments. There are, however, five categories of case where there is no guarantee of publication.

22–007

(1) Statutory instruments may, as noted above, be exempted from publication under regulations made pursuant to the 1946 Act.

---

[31] SI 1948/1 reg 6.

[32] SI 1948/1 reg 7.

[33] SI 1948/1 reg 8. This exception only applies so as to restrict publication before the instrument comes into operation

[34] *Johnson v Sargent* [1918] 1 K.B. 101.

[35] [1954] 1 Q.B. 586. See also, *Jones v Robson* [1901] 1 Q.B. 673.

[36] There is some doubt whether validity requires the instrument even to be laid before Parliament, *Starey v Graham* [1899] 1 Q.B. 406, 412, and in any event not all instruments are required to be laid. On the other hand, when a statute provides that a statutory instrument is to be laid before Parliament after being made the general rule is that it must be laid before coming into operation, Statutory Instruments Act 1946 s.4.

[37] Allen, n.2, 114.

(2) There is no requirement for publication where Orders in Council are made in exercise of the Prerogative.

(3) No publication is required where delegated legislation is passed in furtherance of a statute that does not deem that legislation to be a statutory instrument.

(4) It is doubtful whether sub-delegated legislation is covered by the 1946 Act: this is legislation made under a power conferred by a regulation or other legislative instrument not being itself an Act of Parliament. The 1946 Act requires that the delegated legislation be made under powers conferred by an Act of Parliament. Whether this really excludes all sub-delegated legislation is questionable. The answer is ultimately dependent upon three issues. First, the meaning of "confer". If this word is interpreted so as to include "derive" then some, at least, sub-delegated legislation will be included. Such legislation can be traced back to the primary statute, which originally conferred the power to make the rules from which the sub-delegated legislation originated. Second, it depends upon the breadth given to the term "Minister of the Crown", which is left open-ended by s.11 of the 1946 Act. The third question is how much of the sub-delegated legislation is actually legislation, as opposed to administrative direction or executive order. While circulars and the like may be published by departments, if they are not the citizen will be faced with a mass of literature which may well be dispositive of the case, but the contents of which cannot be ascertained. As Streatfeild J. has said, such power is four times cursed,[38]

> "First, it has seen neither House of Parliament; secondly, it is unpublished and is inaccessible even to those whose valuable rights of property may be affected; thirdly it is a jumble of provisions, legislative, administrative, or directive in character and sometimes difficult to disentangle one from the other; and, fourthly, it is expressed not in the precise language of an Act of Parliament or an Order in Council but in the more colloquial language of correspondence, which is not always susceptible of the ordinary canons of construction."

(5) Administrators may make rules to guide their discretion. What distinguishes these from sub-delegated legislation is that there may be no express power to make rules, whether derived from an Act of Parliament or other legislative instrument. This does not mean that administrative rule-making is either unlawful or to be regretted. It is neither as we shall see below. Such rules may be unpublished and

---

[38] *Patchett v Leathem* (1949) 65 T.L.R. 69, 70. See also, *Blackpool Corporation v Lockyer* [1948] 1 K.B. 349, 369. Allen, n.2, 194–195, reaches no definite conclusion on the publication of sub-delegated legislation

hence unknown. This problem will be considered in the discussion of administrative rule-making.

4. Delegated Legislation: Control by Parliament

A. Scrutiny by the House

There are instances where there is no requirement that the subordinate legislation be laid before Parliament.[39] Where delegated legislation must come before the House there are numerous ways in which this can occur.[40] Three principal methods can, however, be identified.

22–008

First, the empowering legislation may simply require the subordinate legislation to be laid before the House. In such cases the laying is simply a mechanism to inform Parliament of the content of the legislation before it becomes operative. Questions may be asked, but no direct attack upon such delegated legislation is possible. If a document has been presented to the House it has been laid,[41] and the laying should take place before the instrument comes into force. Where it is vital that it should become operational before being laid this can occur provided that notification is sent to the Lord Chancellor and the Speaker of the House of Commons.[42]

The second mechanism does offer some measure of parliamentary control: this is the affirmative resolution procedure. This requires the subordinate legislation to be subject to an affirmative resolution of each House or the House of Commons alone. This procedure can operate somewhat differently in different areas. A statute may state that instruments made thereunder do not have any effect until parliamentary approval has been secured. If there is no such provision the instrument will have effect as soon as it is made, with a rider that if it is not approved within the requisite period it should not be invalidated retrospectively.[43] The debate on the measure will automatically take place within a delegated legislation standing committee, unless the government agrees to a debate on the floor of the House. The standing committee can, however, only vote on an unamendable motion that it has considered the measure. The substantive vote on whether the measure should be approved takes place on the floor of the House without further debate. Instruments taken on the floor of the House are debated for up to an hour and a half, also on an unamendable motion. Relatively few instruments are subject to the affirmative procedure for the very reason that the

---

[39] J. Kersell, *Parliamentary Scrutiny of Delegated Legislation* (Stevens, 1960), 19.
[40] Allen, n.2, 122–125.
[41] *R. v Immigration Appeal Tribunal Ex p. Joyles* [1972] 1 W.L.R. 1390. The effect of the Laying of Documents before Parliament (Interpretation) Act 1948 is that each House is a master of the meaning of laying. The general rule is that the instruments will be laid at the Votes and Proceedings Office of the House of Commons, and at the Office of the Clerk of Parliaments for the House of Lords.
[42] Statutory Instruments Act 1946 s.4.
[43] Allen, n.2, 123.

government then has to find time to secure their passage. There are now approximately 1,500 statutory instruments subject to parliamentary procedure each year and, on average, only 170 are subject to the affirmative procedure.[44]

22–009   The third principal way in which statutory instruments are processed through Parliament is by the negative resolution procedure. It is the private member who must secure time to attack the delegated legislation. The instrument is open to a prayer for annulment within 40 days of being laid. Such instruments are as a general rule to be laid before becoming operative.[45] The prayer for annulment may be moved in either House, but it is not easily secured. A member must ensure a quorum to retain the House in session. There is no provision for amendment, only outright rejection. Debates on annulment resolutions are subject to time limits. There is insufficient time for such debates, so that in, for example, 1990–1991 78 per cent of prayers for annulment were not debated.[46] Even if a prayer for annulment succeeds this does not of itself administer the death-blow to the subordinate legislation. A successful prayer precludes further action from being taken under the instrument and empowers Her Majesty to pass an Order in Council revoking it. It does not invalidate anything done prior to the prayer, nor does it bar the making of a new statutory instrument.[47] Approximately 1,350 statutory instruments are subject to this procedure each year.[48]

Many instruments are, therefore, subject to the negative resolution procedure,[49] but no real principle seems to guide the choice between the available options. It is clear that the most important types of instrument should be subject to the affirmative resolution procedure and only purely technical matters should be exempt from the need to be laid. While it is true that the affirmative procedure does seem to have been used for important matters such as those affecting statutes and the grant of very broad delegated powers, this practice is by no means uniform. It is common to find the affirmative and negative procedures used indiscriminately to implement the same statute. Moreover, while instruments not subject to the requirement of laying should be reserved for minor matters, subordinate legislation of such "peripheral importance" as the alteration of county council electoral boundaries and the constitution of Regional Hospital Boards have been passed in this manner.[50]

Some oversight is exercised by the House of Lords' Delegated Powers

---

[44] A. Adonis, *Parliament Today* (Manchester University Press, 2nd edn, 1993), 113; Select Committee on Procedure, First Report, *Delegated Legislation* (HC 48; 2000), paras 24–25.
[45] This is the effect of s.5 of the 1946 Act which applies s.4 to the negative resolution procedure.
[46] *Making the Law, The Report of the Hansard Society Commission on the Legislative Process* (1993), 93.
[47] Statutory Instruments Act 1946 s.5.
[48] Select Committee on Procedure, n.44, para.25.
[49] A fifth mechanism is for laying the instrument in draft, see the 1946 Act s.6.
[50] Allen, n.2, 128–133. The Second Report of the Joint Committee on Delegated Legislation (HL 204; 1972–1973), (HC 408; 1972–1973) recommended that the affirmative procedure should be used for rules which substantially affect the provisions of primary legislation, impose or increase taxation, or otherwise involve special considerations.

Scrutiny Committee, which was established in 1992 and is now called the Delegated Powers and Deregulation Committee. It has the power to report whether the provisions of a Bill inappropriately delegate legislative power, or whether they subject the exercise of legislative power to an inappropriate degree of Parliamentary scrutiny.[51]

The effectiveness of control on the floor of the House is constrained by the shortage of time for debate and the difficulty of securing sufficient support to move a prayer for annulment. Some such prayers are moved after the period in which the instruments can be annulled, in which case they can only be discursive, while others are attended by relatively few members. Nor is there any requirement that there be consultation with Members of Parliament prior to the promulgation of the rules.[52] Sir Carleton Kemp Allen concluded that it was a constitutional fiction to say that Parliament exercised any real safeguards over delegated legislation.[53]

B. Scrutiny in Committee: Delegated Legislation Committees
Statutory instruments may be referred to Delegated Legislation Commit-   **22–010**
tees, which are according to the standing orders of the House of Commons regarded as General Committees.[54] There shall be one or more Delegated Legislation Committees at any point in time and the Speaker of the House of Commons distributes such instruments as are referred between them.[55] The remit of these committees is however limited. The Delegated Legislation Committee cannot make any amendments to the measure and merely "considers" the instrument. The meetings are limited to one and half hours, but normally last no longer than 30 minutes.

C. Scrutiny in Committee: The Joint Committee on Statutory Instruments
Control on the floor of Parliament is supplemented by scrutiny in com-   **22–011**
mittee. In 1944 a Scrutiny Committee was appointed and in 1973 a Joint Committee on Statutory Instruments was formed from the committees of the Commons and Lords. Its terms of reference require that it should examine every statutory instrument, rule, order or scheme laid or laid in draft before Parliament in order to determine whether the attention of the House should be drawn to an instrument for any of the following reasons[56]: that it imposes a tax or charge; that it is made under a statute which prevents challenge in the courts; that it appears to make an unusual or unexpected use of powers conferred by the statute; that it purports to have retrospective effect without statutory authorisation; that there seemed to be unwarranted

---

[51] C. Himsworth, "The Delegated Powers Scrutiny Committee" [1995] P.L. 34.
[52] J. Beatson, "Legislative Control of Administrative Rulemaking: Lessons from the British Experience" (1979) 12 Corn. I.L.J. 199, 213–215.
[53] Allen, n.2, 136.
[54] Standing Orders of the House of Commons (HMSO, 2007), Order 84 (h).
[55] Standing Orders, n.54, Order 118.
[56] Standing Orders, n.54, Order 151.

delay in the publication or laying of the instrument; that the statutory instrument has not been laid and that notification to the Speaker has not been prompt; that it is unclear whether the instrument is intra vires; that for any special reason its form or purport requires elucidation; that the drafting appears to be defective.

Scrutiny of technical legality has been of value.[57] In 2006 the Joint Committee scrutinised 1,285 statutory instruments and found cause to draw the special attention of each House to 76 instruments, 6 per cent of the total scrutinised.[58] The attentions of the Joint Committee have improved drafting and increased the number of explanatory notes provided by departments. The very presence of the Committee sounds a warning to departments. The Joint Committee monitors departments in order to determine the action taken on instruments in relation to which the Committee has drawn special attention.[59]

There are nonetheless limitations to the existing controls. Only about one third of statutory instruments are reviewed by the Joint Committee in any one year. It is moreover clear that the departmental response to Joint Committee reports drawing special attention to a particular instrument is mixed Some departments provide "little meaningful information",[60] and there is marked variance in the extent to which different departments address the concerns raised by the Joint Committee.[61] The Committee's power is moreover limited. It can refer an instrument to the House, but it has no means of ensuring that a prayer for annulment or debate will occur following its report. Nor can it even be sure that its report will reach the House before the period for annulment is over, and debate may well ensue on the merits of an instrument before technical scrutiny has occurred.[62] Beatson concluded that,[63]

"The British system of legislative veto has proved less than satisfactory in rendering administrators accountable to their political superiors and protecting those affected by administrative rules. This limited success stems from many factors. These include *de facto* executive control of the legislature, the unavailability of information about the substance of a rule in the time available for control, the limited time available for debate, and the apparent unwillingness of Members of Parliament to take an interest in scrutiny, especially of technical infirmities."

[57] Joint Committee on Statutory Instruments, Thirty-Ninth Report (HL 178, HC 135 xxxix; 2002).
[58] Joint Committee on Statutory Instruments, *Scrutinising Statutory Instruments* (HL 153, HC 917; 2007), n.10.
[59] *Scrutinising Statutory Instruments*, n.58, para.7.
[60] *Scrutinising Statutory Instruments*, n.58, para.10.
[61] *Scrutinising Statutory Instruments*, n.58, paras 14–17.
[62] Beatson, n.52, 215, 218. See also, J. Hayhurst and P. Wallington, "The Parliamentary Scrutiny of Delegated Legislation" [1988] P.L. 547.
[63] n.52, 222.

These sentiments were echoed by Alan Beith M.P.,[64] who emphasised the control wielded by government business managers over the scrutiny of delegated legislation, whether on the floor of the House or in committee. This is all the more important given the fact that delegated legislation will often be concerned not just with issues of detail, but also with major issues of social policy.[65]

D. Scrutiny in Committee: The House of Lords Merits of Statutory Instruments Committee

In 2003 the House of Lords established the Merits of Statutory Instruments **22–012** Committee, the initial catalyst for which came from recommendations of the Royal Commission on the Reform of the House of Lords in 2000, the Wakeham Commission. The Merits Committee considers, subject to certain exceptions,[66] every instrument (whether or not a statutory instrument), or draft of an instrument, which is laid before each House of Parliament and upon which proceedings may be, or might have been, taken in either House of Parliament under an Act of Parliament; and every proposal which is in the form of a draft of such an instrument and is laid before each House of Parliament under an Act of Parliament.

It draws the attention of the House to an instrument, draft or proposal on the grounds that: it is politically or legally important or gives rise to issues of public policy likely to be of interest to the House; it may be inappropriate in view of changed circumstances since the enactment of the parent Act; it may inappropriately implement European Union legislation; or it may imperfectly achieve its policy objectives. The criteria for referring a matter to the House therefore allow the Committee to consider the merits of a statutory instrument in the way that is not normally undertaken by the Joint Committee. The Merits Committee has however no power to block the passage of a statutory instrument.

The Committee has performed a valuable function since its inception. It has made perceptive comments on particular statutory instruments. It has also undertaken more general studies, concluding that defective management processes used by government departments when making statutory instruments were responsible for some of the defects found in particular instruments.[67] The Committee made a number of recommendations for improvement in departmental management of statutory instruments,[68] which will be considered below when discussing possible reforms in relation to delegated legislation.

---

[64] "Prayers Unanswered: A Jaundiced View of the Parliamentary Scrutiny of Statutory Instruments" (1981) 34 Parliamentary Affairs 165, 170.
[65] Hayhurst and Wallington, n.62, 573–574.
[66] The principal exceptions are remedial orders under the Human Rights Act 1998 s.10, and draft orders under the Legislative and Regulatory Reform Act 2006 ss.14 and 18.
[67] House of Lords Merits of Statutory Instruments Committee, Twenty-Ninth Report, *The Management of Secondary Legislation* (HL 149; 2006).
[68] *The Management of Secondary Legislation*, n.67, para.126.

E. Scrutiny of Regulatory Reform: A Special Regime

22–013   A separate procedure operates for statutory instruments dealing with regulatory reform. The Regulatory Reform Act 2001 modified the earlier scheme enshrined in the Deregulation and Contracting Out Act 1994. The Regulatory Reform Act 2001 has now largely been repealed and replaced by the Legislative and Regulatory Reform Act 2006. The 2006 Act enables a Minister of Crown to make an order for the purpose of reforming legislation that has the effect of imposing burdens on persons carrying on any activity. The substantive details of the legislation have been considered in the context of the discussion of regulation.[69] It is the procedure for the making of such orders that is relevant here.

The Legislative and Regulatory Reform Act 2006 stipulates that an order made under the legislation must be made by statutory instrument.[70] The Minister has an obligation to consult about the content of any proposed order.[71] A draft of the order and an explanatory document setting out the reasons for the order and the way in which it fulfils the conditions of the Act is then laid before Parliament.[72] The Minister provides a reasoned recommendation in the explanatory document as to whether the order should be subject to the negative resolution procedure, the affirmative resolution procedure or the super-affirmative resolution procedure. The Minister's recommendation applies unless, within thirty days of the draft being laid before the House, either House of Parliament specifies that a more onerous procedure should apply.[73] It is also open to the Regulatory Reform Committee of the House of Commons or the Delegated Powers and Regulatory Reform Committee of the House of Lords[74] that report on draft orders under the Act to recommend that a particular draft order is subject to a higher level of procedure than recommended by the Minister, and if it does so this will prevail unless it is rejected by resolution of the House.[75]

If the negative procedure is adopted then within 40 days of the draft being laid either House of Parliament must resolve that the draft order should not be adopted.[76] The 2006 Act however also in effect gives the committee of each House charged with reporting on the draft order a veto power, in the sense that it may, after 30 days and before the expiry of the 40-day period, recommend that the draft order should not be made. The Minister may not then make the order, unless the committee recommendation is rejected by resolution of that House.[77]

22–014   If the affirmative procedure is adopted the draft must be approved by resolution of each House of Parliament within 40 days of its being laid. The relevant committees once again have a form of veto power: if either

---

[69] See above, Ch.11.
[70] Legislative and Regulatory Reform Act 2006 s.12.
[71] Legislative and Regulatory Reform Act 2006 s.13.
[72] Legislative and Regulatory Reform Act 2006 s.14.
[73] Legislative and Regulatory Reform Act 2006 s.15.
[74] See Ganz, n.12, 67–68, for operation of the House of Lords' Committee.
[75] Legislative and Regulatory Reform Act 2006 s.15(6).
[76] Legislative and Regulatory Reform Act 2006 s.16.
[77] Legislative and Regulatory Reform Act 2006 ss.16(4)–(5).

committee recommends after 30 days and before the expiry of the 40-day period that the draft order should not be made, then no proceedings can be taken in relation to that draft order unless the recommendation is rejected by resolution of that House in the same Session.[78]

The super-affirmative procedure operates as follows.[79] The Minister must have regard to any representations, any resolution of either House of Parliament, and any recommendations of a committee of either House of Parliament charged with reporting on the draft order, made during the 60-day period with regard to the draft order. If, after the expiry of the 60-day period, the Minister wishes to make an order in the terms of the draft, he must lay before Parliament a statement indicating whether any representations were made and if so he must give details of them. The Minister can then make an order in the terms of the draft if it is approved by a resolution of each House of Parliament. The relevant committees once again have a form of veto power: the committee of either House charged with reporting on the draft order may, at any time after the laying of the ministerial statement and before the draft order is approved by that House, recommend that no further proceedings be taken in relation to the draft order. If it does so then no proceedings may be taken in relation to the draft order in that House unless the recommendation is, in the same Session, rejected by resolution of that House. There is provision for the minister to make a revised version of the order with material changes after the 60-day period. This too must be approved by each House and the relevant committees have the same power in relation to the revised order as they do in relation to the original draft order.

The "super affirmative" procedure that applied under the Regulatory Reform Act 2001 generally worked well and enabled detailed scrutiny of draft deregulation and regulatory reform orders.[80] This was however the only procedure for the making of orders under the 2001 Act. The 2006 Act, as we have seen, provides for the possible use of the negative and affirmative procedures as well as the super-affirmative procedure. It is true that the committees' powers are enhanced, in the sense that they can play a role both in the choice of procedure to govern the making of a particular order, and also have the qualified veto power set out above as to whether a particular order is approved. The degree of scrutiny will therefore depend on how far ministers seek to use the lower level procedures and how far the committees

---

[78] Legislative and Regulatory Reform Act 2006 ss.17(3)–(4).
[79] Legislative and Regulatory Reform Act 2006 s.18.
[80] D. Miers, "The Deregulation Procedure: An Expanding Role" [1999] P.L. 477; Deregulation and Regulatory Reform Committee, Third Special Report, *The Handling of Regulatory Orders (III)* (HC 1272; 2002); Deregulation and Regulatory Reform Committee, First Special Report, *The Handling of Regulatory Reform Orders* (HC 389; 2001); Deregulation and Regulatory Reform Committee, Second Special Report, *The Operation of the Regulatory Reform Act: Government's Response to the Committee's First Special Report of Session 2001–02* (HC 1029; 2002).

exercise their power to press for higher level procedures and how far they recommend against the making of particular orders.[81]

F. Scrutiny of European Legislation

22–015   The United Kingdom's accession to the European Community produced novel problems of supervision and control. European legislation, may, as we have seen,[82] be directly applicable within the Member States. This means that once enacted by the Community it is automatically incorporated into municipal law without the normal requirements of adoption or transformation.

In terms of machinery,[83] Committees of the House of Commons have been established to consider whether delegated legislation is necessary in order to implement,[84] for example, an EC directive, and also to scrutinise proposals that emerge from the EC, in order to provide Parliament with information about impending European legislation. Concern that legislation from Europe was not receiving proper attention led the House of Commons' Procedure Committee to propose the establishment of five standing committees. Only three were in fact established, in part because of the difficulty of finding M.P.s willing to staff more committees.

The system works in the following way. The European Scrutiny Committee examines EU documents, such as draft proposals for legislation, and reports on the "legal and political importance" of each document. It considers approximately 1,000 documents each year, half of which are deemed to be of legal or political importance, such that the Scrutiny Committee reports on them. It recommends approximately 40 such documents per year for further consideration by one of the European Standing Committees, and approximately three per year for debate on the floor of the House. The latter only occurs if the House decides that they should be considered in this way. The relevant European Standing Committee will consider the merits of the issues.

The new regime has undoubtedly had a positive impact.[85] It has been hampered in part by the brevity of time left for discussion before the Community legislation is considered by the Council, and by the way in

[81] The Regulatory Reform Committee, in considering the changes required to its standing orders as the result of the 2006 Act, pressed hard for the power to refer a draft order for debate in a Delegated Legislation Committee, in order to provide M.P.s with the opportunity to consider such draft orders that warranted such scrutiny because of their political or legal significance, Regulatory Reform Committee, Second Special Report 2006–07, *Revised Standing Orders* (HC 385; 2007).

[82] See above, Ch.10.

[83] T. St J N Bates, "European Community Legislation before the House of Commons" (1991) 12 Stat. L.R. 109; E. Denza, "Parliamentary Scrutiny of Community Legislation" (1993) 14 Stat. L.R. 56; The European Union Scrutiny System in the House of Commons (2005) available at   http://www.parliament.uk/parliamentary_committees/european_scrutiny/the_european_ scrutiny_system_in_the_house_of_commons.cfm.

[84] The Legislative and Regulatory Reform Act 2006 s.27 amended the European Communities Act 1972, s.2(2) by providing that Community provisions could be implemented in the UK not only by regulations, but also by orders, rules or schemes.

[85] The European Union Scrutiny System in the House, n.83.

which such legislation is often drafted.[86] These problems are exacerbated by the fact that M.P.s are not overly eager to take on such unglamorous work, and by the fact that those who do participate in the standing committees are often extreme partisans on one side or the other of the domestic European debate.[87] It would nonetheless be wrong to underestimate the value of the work performed by the European Scrutiny Committee itself. Its reports are clearly and succinctly presented.[88] They show an awareness of the legal and political importance of complex issues. The committee's evaluation will sometimes support that of the relevant government minister, and will sometimes take a differing line. The very fact that there is a body within the UK looking at such issues, other than the relevant department of state, is undoubtedly beneficial. The European Scrutiny committee will also liaise where necessary with departmental select committees.

There is also a House of Lords' Select Committee on the European Union. It is chaired by a salaried officer of the House[89] and considers any Community proposal that it believes should be drawn to the attention of the House. The Committee functions through a number of subcommittees which are subject-matter based.[90] The House of Lords' Select Committee is therefore different from that in the House of Commons. The latter will sift through Community legislation and refer matters on to the standing committee where this is warranted. The House of Lords' Committee will produce its own valuable, detailed reports on particular issues.[91]

---

[86] Twenty-Seventh Report of the Select Committee on European Legislation (HC 51-xxvii; 1995–6).

[87] Adonis, n.44, 156.

[88] See Twenty Seventh Report of the Select Committee on European Scrutiny (HC 34-xxvii; 1999), dealing with diverse matters such as the extension to third-country nationals of social security rights, the decommissioning of nuclear research facilities, and the revision of Community competition law; Third Report of the European Union Scrutiny Committee, *The European Union's Annual Policy Strategy 2006* (HC 34-iii; 2005); Fourteenth Report of the European Union Scrutiny Committee, *Aspects of the EU's Constitutional Treaty* (HC 38-xiv-1; 2005).

[89] The chairman will decide which issues are of sufficient importance to warrant scrutiny by one of the subcommittees.

[90] There are seven such subcommittees which deal with: economic and financial affairs, trade and international relations; internal market; foreign affairs, defence and development policy; environment and agriculture; law and institutions; home affairs; social policy and consumer affairs.

[91] See, e.g., Third Report of the Select Committee on the European Communities (HL 23; 1999), dealing with reforms to Comitology procedures; Nineteenth Report of the Select Committee on the European Communities (HL 101; 1999), dealing with the then forthcoming European Council meeting which was the first such meeting to deal with justice and home affairs.

5. Delegated Legislation: Consultation

22–016 Consultation may be required by the terms of a particular statute, or there may, in certain instances, be a duty to consult imposed by the common law.[92]

A. Consultation Rights and Statute

22–017 It should be made clear that there is no *necessary* connection between the existence of a statutory obligation to consult about the making of an order or regulation and the characterisation of this order as a statutory instrument. It all depends upon the enabling legislation. It is therefore perfectly possible for there to be a statutory duty to consult, and for the resulting measure to be a statutory instrument.[93] It is equally possible for there to be such an obligation where the resultant order or regulation is not a statutory instrument.[94]

When consultation is specified by statute this may be a mandatory requirement or it may only be directory. Where the statute states that consultation *shall* take place the former construction is more common.[95] The legislation will determine who must be consulted. In some areas there will be a general discretion to consult such interests as appear to be appropriate; in other areas the statute may be more explicit as to which interests should be consulted.[96]

Where a duty to consult exists it requires the authority to supply sufficient information to those being consulted to enable them to tender advice, and a sufficient opportunity to tender that advice before the mind of the authority becomes unduly fixed.[97] Where the obligation to consult is mandatory, failure to comply with the duty will result in the order subsequently made being held void. The courts' approach is evident in *Gunning*[98]:

---

[92] J. Garner, "Consultation in Subordinate Legislation" [1964] P.L. 105; A Jergesen, "The Legal Requirement of Consultation" [1978] P.L. 290.
[93] See, e.g., Local Government Act 1992 s.8(3)(4).
[94] See, e.g., Competition and Service (Utilities) Act 1992 s.1.
[95] *May v Beattie* [1927] 3 K.B. 353; *Rollo v Minister of Town and Country Planning* [1948] 1 All E.R. 13; *Re Union of Benefices of Whippingham and East Cowes, St. James's* [1954] A.C. 245; *Port Louis Corp v Att-Gen. of Mauritius* [1965] A.C. 1111; *Sinfield v London Transport Executive* [1970] Ch.550, 558; *Agricultural, Horticultural and Forestry Industry Training Board v Aylesbury Mushrooms Ltd* [1972] 1 W.L.R. 190; *Powley v ACAS* [1978] I.C.R. 123.
[96] Compare *Post Office v Gallagher* [1970] 3 All E.R. 712 and *Rollo v Minister of Town and Country Planning* [1948] 1 All E.R. 13.
[97] See *Rollo, Port Louis* and *Sinfield*, n.95.
[98] *R. v Brent London Borough Council Ex p. Gunning* (1985) 84 L.G.R. 168. See also, *R. v Secretary of State for Social Services Ex p. Association of Metropolitan Authorities* [1993] C.O.D. 54; *R. v British Coal Corporation and Secretary of State for Trade and Industry Ex p. Price* [1993] C.O.D. 482; *R. (on the application of Wainwright) v Richmond upon Thames LBC* [2001] EWCA Civ 2062; *R. (on the application of Partingdale Lane Residents Association) v Barnet LBC* [2003] EWHC 947.

"First, that consultation must be at a time when proposals are still at a formative stage. Second, that the proposer must give sufficient reasons for any proposal to permit intelligent consideration and response. Third, that adequate time must be given for consideration and response and finally, fourth, that the product of the consultation must be conscientiously taken into account in finalising statutory proposals."

Consultation may also take place on a more informal, non-statutory basis. Advisory committees abound and will commonly be brought into discussions concerning proposed rules,[99] as will other interest groups.

B. Consultation Rights and the Common Law

There is however no general duty to consult, imposed either by common law or statute. There is no common law duty to consult where the order is of a legislative nature;[100] the right to a reasoned decision does not apply where the order is of a legislative character[101]; and question marks hang over the application of the prerogative orders to legislative instruments. The absence of any common law duty to consult is matched by the lack of any such general statutory duty.[102]

22–018

Consultation rights have, however, been accorded by case law in certain instances. The present discussion is concerned with when such rights exist. How far an individual can insist that a particular policy or representation will be applied, and the scope of substantive legitimate expectations, has been considered above.[103]

(1) If a public body has made a representation to a specific individual or group of individuals that a particular policy will be followed, or that they will be informed before any such change in policy takes place, then the individuals will be entitled to comment before any such change occurs, or before there is a departure from that policy.[104] The change in policy may, moreover, only be countenanced for the instant case if the public interest so demands.

[99] Garner, n.92.
[100] *Bates v Lord Hailsham* [1972] 1 W.L.R. 1373, 1378; *R. (on the application of BAPIO Action Ltd) v Secretary of State for the Home Department* [2007] EWCA Civ 1139, paras 33–47.
[101] Tribunals and Inquiries Act 1992 s.10(5)(b).
[102] The Rules Publication Act 1893 was the nearest which we have ever come to providing any general duty to consult.
[103] See above, Ch.20.
[104] *Att-Gen of Hong Kong v Ng Yuen Shiu* [1983] 2 A.C. 629; *R. v Liverpool Corporation Ex p. Liverpool Taxi Fleet Operators' Association* [1972] 2 Q.B. 299; *R. v Secretary of State for the Home Department Ex p. Khan* [1985] 1 All E.R. 40; *Council of Civil Service Unions v Minister for the Civil Service* [1985] A.C. 374, 408–409; *R. v Secretary of State for the Home Department Ex p. Ruddock* [1987] 1 W.L.R. 1482; *R. v Secretary of State for the Home Department Ex p. Gangadeen* [1998] C.O.D. 216; *R. (on the application of Niazi) v Secretary of State for the Home Department* [2007] EWCA Civ 1495.

(2) If an individual has in the past enjoyed a benefit or advantage which could legitimately be expected to continue, that person may be entitled to a statement of reasons for the change of position, and an opportunity to be consulted thereon.[105]

(3) The principle of consistency creates a presumption that a public body will follow its own policy. If it seeks to depart from that policy then there must be good reasons for the departure and these must be given to the applicant.[106]

(4) The existence of any legitimate expectation, whether arising from a representation or past practice, will be a matter of construction. Thus in *Khan*,[107] Parker L.J. held that a Home Office circular concerning adoption procedure for foreign children generated a legitimate expectation that the procedures would be followed. The Minister could not depart from them without affording the applicants a hearing and then only if the public interest demanded it. In *Robson*,[108] a council decided to allow those who opposed or supported the grant of planning permission to address the relevant committee. It was held that the council was bound to operate this policy properly and fairly within its own terms. In the recent *Greenpeace* case[109] a government White Paper on energy policy indicated that the Government was not minded to support "new nuclear build" and stated that there would be full public consultation before the Government reached any decision to change its policy. A consultation exercise was held and the government decided that it would support some element of "nuclear new build". The court held that there was a legitimate expectation that consultation would occur and that the consultation process that took place was seriously flawed for a number of reasons. However, in *Findlay*[110] a change of policy concerning parole was not held to infringe the legitimate expectations of certain prisoners, notwithstanding the fact that they would, under the previous policy, have expected earlier release. The content of the prisoners' legitimate expectations was held to be that their cases would be individually considered under whatever policy the Minister sought fit to adopt.

---

[105] *CCSU* [1985] A.C. 374, 408–409; *Khan*, n.104; *Ruddock*, n.104; *R. v Birmingham City Council Ex p. Dredger* [1993] C.O.D. 340. Cases may be difficult to classify as type (i) or (ii) particularly where, as in *Khan* or *Ruddock*, there is a circular in question. This could be regarded either as a representation, or as the past practice justifying the legitimate expectation.

[106] *R. v Secretary of State for the Home Department Ex p. Urmaza* [1996] C.O.D. 479; *R. v Secretary of State for the Home Department Ex p. Gangadeen* [1998] C.O.D. 216.

[107] [1985] 1 All E.R. 40.

[108] *R. v Alnwick District Council Ex p. Robson* [1998] C.O.D. 241.

[109] *R. (on the application of Greenpeace Ltd) v Secretary of State for Trade and Industry* [2007] EWHC 311.

[110] [1985] A.C. 318, 338. See also, *R. v Secretary of State for the Home Department Ex p. Hargreaves* [1997] 1 All E.R. 397.

(5) The content of the duty to consult held to flow from the legitimate expectation may also depend upon the circumstances. The applicant may, as in *Khan*, be allowed to argue why the pre-existing policy should continue to be applied to the instant case. The duty may, however, be more extensive, and the applicant may be enabled to contest the soundness of the new policy itself. Thus, in *Dredger*,[111] stall-holders were held to have a legitimate expectation of being consulted about a major change in rental policy for market stalls. This was held to entail consultation rights very similar to those set out in the *Gunning* case. The council had to provide details of its proposals; the applicants were to be given sufficient time to respond; the council had to listen to the applicants' responses with an open mind; and these responses had to be taken into account when reaching a final decision.

(6) It is doubtful whether there is a duty to consult derived from the duty to act fairly, which applies independently of any legitimate expectation based on a prior representation or a prior practice of consultation.[112] Thus in *Kelly*,[113] the applicant, who was blind, complained that there had been a failure to consult before the BBC closed a local radio station that was of particular importance to people such as him. The application failed because there was nothing in the BBC's charter, or other relevant documentation, which suggested that there was any promise, undertaking or representation by the BBC that it would consult about the future of local radio, and hence nothing to establish an arguable case based on legitimate expectations.

C. Consultation Rights and Future Prospects

i. The benefits of consultation rights

There are a number of advantages/benefits of a more general concept of **22–019** prior consultation. The Rippon Commission, as we shall see below, rightly regarded developments with respect to consultation as an important way to improve the quality of secondary legislation. Moreover the Cabinet Office has, as will be seen below, issued a Code of Practice on Consultation. The principal arguments for participation rights are as follows.[114]

---

[111] *R. v Birmingham City Council Ex p. Dredger* [1993] C.O.D. 340.
[112] There are some indications in the Court of Appeal in *R. v Devon County Council Ex p. Baker* [1995] 1 All E.R. 73, that such a duty might exist. However Popplewell J. in the same case [1993] C.O.D. 138 denied the existence of any such obligation. Hutchison J. in *Dredger*, n.111, held that no duty to consult could be based on the duty to act fairly, in the absence of a legitimate expectation. The approach in *BAPIO*, n.100, was similar, albeit less restrictive. The case was decided on other grounds by the House of Lords [2008] 1 W.L.R. 1073.
[113] *R. v BBC Ex p. Kelly* [1998] C.O.D. 58. See also, *R. v Secretary of State for Education Ex p. London Borough of Southwark* [1994] C.O.D. 298.
[114] For a valuable general discussion of participation see, D. Galligan, *Due Process and Fair Procedures* (Oxford University Press, 1996), Ch.4.

(1)   It enables views to be taken into account before an administrative policy has hardened into a draft rule.

(2)   It can assist Parliament with technical scrutiny. This is not a job that is best performed by Members of Parliament, nor one which they are particularly interested in.

(3)   It is hoped that there will be better rules as a result of input from interested parties, particularly where they have some knowledge of the area being regulated.

(4)   The duty to consult has a wider significance. It allows those outside government to play some role in the shaping of policy. In this sense it enhances participation.

(5)   It is not immediately self-evident why a hearing should be thought natural when there is some form of individualised adjudication, but not where rules are being made. The unspoken presumption is that a "hearing" will be given to a rule indirectly in Parliament, via representative democracy. We have already seen how far reality falls short of this ideal. Moreover, many of the rules are not statutory instruments and have, therefore, never seen the Parliamentary light of day at all.

ii. Issues to be addressed

22–020   Commentators who favour increased participation rights look approvingly at the position in the USA where such rights are fostered to a greater extent than here, although that regime is not without difficulties.[115] Three principal issues can be identified if we wish to develop such rights.

First, there is the *type of consultative process* that might be established. There are a range of options. Thus, by way of example, the Administrative Procedure Act 1946 in the USA provides that notice of any proposed rule-making is to be published in the Federal Register, including a statement of the time and place of the rule-making proceedings and the terms or substance of the proposed rule.[116] There are three different modes of participation, with varying degrees of formality. Most administrative rules are subject to what is termed *notice and comment*: the proposed rule is published and interested parties can proffer written comments. A small number of rules are subject to a *full trial type hearing*, which can include the provision

---

[115] See, e.g., the important article by R. Stewart, "The Reformation of American Administrative Law" (1975) 88 Harv LR 1667, is ambivalent about the value of such participatory rights and addresses many of the problems produced by such an approach; Baldwin, n.2, 74–80.
[116] Except where notice or hearing is required by statute, this does not apply to interpretative rules, general statements of policy, rules of agency organisation, procedure or practice, or in any situation in which the agency for good cause finds that notice and public procedures are impracticable, unnecessary, or contrary to the public interest.

of oral testimony and cross-examination.[117] Yet other rules are governed by an *intermediate* or *hybrid process*, which entails more formality than notice and comment, but less than the trial type hearing.[118]

Second, there is the possibility that *dominant groups may exert excessive pressure* on the rulemaking authority. Thus pluralist writers in the UK recognised the existence of groups that influenced the political process.[119] They did not, however, regard groups as equal in power. Corporatist arguments, which postulate the existence of a dominant group, which possesses a "monopoly" of representational status, serve to underline this point. Some theorists go further and argue that agencies can be "captured" by the group they regulate. The agency comes to protect the client group and its interests rather than advancing the public interest.[120]

While the problem of inequality of group power is a real one it must, however, be kept within perspective. Given that such inequality exists, it is difficult to believe that the less advantaged groups will do better where there are no participatory rights. The more powerful groups will exert influence upon a public body even where there are no formal rights, through the very fact of their power. The introduction of a more structured system of participatory rights does at least give the less advantaged groups a chance to air their views.

The problem can in any event be tackled in a number of differing ways. The courts should insist that the agency gives adequate consideration to the range of groups who proffered evidence. This is valuable, but such intervention may come "too late". Certain less powerful groups may simply not be in a good position to advance their views before the agency. We may therefore need to devise strategies to help such disadvantaged groups put their case. This may entail direct financial aid, relief from costs and the provision of assistance in formulating and advancing their views.

Third, it might be argued that greater participatory rights can cause problems of *time, cost, and delay*. There are, however, a number of responses to such concerns. It can be contended that such costs are worth bearing. If an autocrat made all decisions, they would doubtless be made more speedily. A cost of democracy is precisely the cost of involving more people. The argument for increased participatory rights is moreover based upon the idea that the people consulted may have something to offer the administrator.

---

[117] This more formal procedure operates when rules are required by statute to be made on the record after opportunity for an agency hearing, s.553(c). This criterion is narrowly construed, *United States v Florida East Coast Railway* 410 U.S. 224 (1973).

[118] *International Harvester Co v Ruckelshaus* 478 F. 2d 615 (DC Cir 1973); *Portland Cement Assn v Ruckelshaus* 486 F. 2d 375 (DC Cir 1973). The development in this direction was, however, slowed by *Vermont Yankee Nuclear Power Corp v Natural Resources Defence Council, Inc.* 435 U.S. 519 (1978). See generally, S. Breyer, R. Stewart, C. Sunstein and M. Spitzer, *Administrative Law and Regulatory Policy, Problems, Text, and Cases* (Aspen Law & Business, 5th edn, 2002), Ch.6; A. Aman and W. Mayton, *Administrative Law* (West, 2nd edn, 2001), Chs 2–4; A. Aman, *Administrative Law and Process* (Matthew Bender, 1993), Ch.6.

[119] See above, para.1–037.

[120] M. Bernstein, *Regulating Business by Independent Commission* (Princeton University Press, 1955), 270. For scepticism about the capture thesis see, R. Posner, "Theories of Economic Regulation" (1974) 5 Bell Jnl of Econ. & Mgmt. Sci. 335, 342.

The resultant rule will, it is hoped, be better. If a less good rule emerges where there is no consultation then the total costs may be greater because, for example, the rule fails to achieve its objective. It would in any event be recognised that there are certain areas where participatory rights are not suitable, for example, where time is of the essence, such as when it is necessary to combat an outbreak of foot and mouth disease.

D. Consultation and the Code of Practice

22–021   While there is no general statutory right to be consulted in the UK, there have nonetheless been important political developments in this area. The Cabinet Office issued a Code of Practice on Written Consultations, which applies to consultation documents issued after January 1, 2001, and the current version dates from 2004.[121]

The object of the Code is to make written consultations more effective, to improve decision-making and to open up decision-making to a wider group of people. It does not have legal force, but is regarded as binding on UK departments and their agencies, unless ministers conclude that exceptional circumstances require departure from it.[122] Non-departmental public bodies and local authorities are encouraged to follow the Code. There is a list of consultation websites for government departments, with information about current consultation exercises.[123] Compliance with the Code of Practice is measured every year and is reported in the Annual Report on Consultation.[124]

The Code of Practice sets out six criteria for consultation. The relevant departments and agencies should:

(1)   Consult widely throughout the process, allowing a minimum of 12 weeks for written consultation at least once during the development of the policy.

(2)   Be clear about the proposals, who may be affected, what questions are being asked and the timescale for responses.

(3)   Ensure that the consultation is clear, concise and widely accessible.

(4)   Give feedback regarding the responses received and how the consultation process influenced the policy.

---

[121] Cabinet Office, Better Regulation Executive, *Code of Practice on Consultation* (2005), available at http://www.cabinetoffice.gov.uk/regulation/documents/consultation/pdf/code.pdf.
[122] Ministers retain discretion not to conduct a formal written consultation exercise under the terms of the Code, for example where the issue is very specialized and where there is a very limited number of stakeholders who have been directly involved in the policy development process. In such circumstances the general principles of the Code should however still be followed as far as possible, and departments must consider how to ensure that the public is made aware of the policy, for example through a press notice or statement on the department's website. This should state the Minister's reason for the decision.
[123] http://www.cabinetoffice.gov.uk/regulation/consultation/government/index.asp.
[124] Cabinet Office, *Annual Report on Consultation* (2006), available at http://www.cabinetoffice.gov.uk/regulation/documents/consultation/pdf/2006.pdf.

(5) Monitor the department's effectiveness at consultation, including through the use of a designated consultation coordinator.

(6) Ensure that the consultation follows better regulation best practice, including carrying out a Regulatory Impact Assessment if appropriate.

The Government undertook a review of consultation policy in 2007, in order to see whether improvements could be made in the Code.[125] This review was itself subject to consultation, and the Government then came forward with further proposals in late 2007.

E. Conclusion

The Code of Practice on Consultation has been a welcome development. **22–022**
The very fact that there is a centralised initiative that is regarded as binding on government departments and agencies, even if it is not enshrined in law, represents a considerable step forward. The willingness to review the Code to see what improvements can be made is also to be welcomed. It can moreover be argued that this approach to consultation avoids the excessive legalism that can be attendant upon affording legally binding consultation rights. There is some force in this argument.

The limits of the non-legal approach should however also be borne in mind. Thus there is evidence of room for improvement in the way that consultation exercises are conducted in relation to, for example, delegated legislation.[126] Departments and agencies moreover still retain considerable discretion as to whether to undertake consultation in the terms of the Code. There were 571 formal consultation exercises in 2006.[127] This may seem a lot, but the figure must be kept in perspective. The number covers consultation exercises conducted by all government departments and agencies, but it is clear from the Report that some departments and many agencies undertook no such consultations. The figure of 571 should also be viewed against the volume of legislation enacted during 2006: 53 Acts of Parliament, 3,471 statutory instruments and a large number of rules of a legislative nature made by the administration that are not classified as statutory instruments, but the impact of which for those affected may be identical. There is no claim here that consultation is necessary in all such instances. It is rather to place in perspective the impact of the Code.

We should moreover not forget that where the relevant statute does not mandate consultation, claimants who are not consulted will have no legal redress, unless they can show a legitimate expectation in the manner analysed above. This will be so even though they are affected very significantly

---

[125] Cabinet Office, *Effective Consultation: Asking the Right Questions, Asking the Right People, Listening to the Answers* (2007), available at http://www.cabinetoffice.gov.uk/regulation/documents/consultation/pdf/effectiveconsultationpdf.
[126] House of Lords Merits of Statutory Instruments Committee, *The Management of Secondary Legislation*, n.67, paras 91–93.
[127] n.124.

by the change in policy.[128] The *Greenpeace* case[129] demonstrates however the potential implications of the legitimate expectations doctrine. If a government department or agency formally announces that it will engage in consultation on a particular policy matter then it is arguable that this will in itself create a legitimate expectation that such consultation will occur, and allow the courts to adjudicate on the adequacy of the consultation exercise. This could therefore open the door to judicial review of the adequacy of consultation exercises that are undertaken pursuant to the Code of Practice on Consultation.[130]

6. Delegated Legislation: Judicial Review

22–023 Subordinate legislation is susceptible to judicial control. It can be challenged in the following ways.

A. Procedural Ultra Vires and Formal Invalidity

22–024 We have already seen that delegated legislation may be enacted by a variety of procedures. If the requisite rule is not followed, and that procedure is held to be mandatory rather than directory, it will lead to the invalidation of the legislation. We have already come across an example of this in the discussion of the statutory requirement for consultation.

The secondary legislation will also be invalidated if it is formally outside the parent Act. In one case a notice requisitioning certain property was held to be void because the notice did not exclude furniture and the power to requisition did not extend to furniture.[131] In another, a byelaw restricting access to a military site was impugned because the enabling legislation only allowed such byelaws to be made on condition that they did not infringe upon any rights of common.[132] On some occasions it may be necessary to pass legislation to correct an earlier mistake, such as when it was realised that certain regulations concerning fire services had never been laid as required by the parent Act. An Act of Indemnity was passed to correct the error.[133]

---

[128] *BAPIO*, n.100, but the applicants succeeded on other grounds, *R. (on the application of BAPIO Action Ltd) v Secretary of State for the Home Department* [2008] 2 W.L.R. 1073.

[129] *Greenpeace*, n.109.

[130] The court was influenced in *Greenpeace* by the fact that the UK was a signatory to the Aarhus Convention, which required the government to provide opportunities for public participation in relation to the environment. This consideration however affected the issue of whether it was open to the Government to grant or withhold consultation in this area. It does not affect the point being made in the text that if the Government does promise consultation then this can trigger a legitimate expectation allowing the court to adjudicate on the adequacy of the consultation.

[131] *Patchett v Leathem* (1949) 65 T.L.R. 69.

[132] *Director of Public Prosecutions v Hutchinson* [1990] 2 A.C. 783.

[133] National Fire Service Regulations (Indemnity) Act 1944.

B. Substantive Ultra Vires

Delegated legislation may also be struck down because its substance **22–025** infringes the parent Act, another primary statute, or constitutional principle. The courts have on occasion, especially during wartime, liberally construed statutory instruments,[134] but they generally undertake more searching review.

i. Infringement of the Primary Act

A court may decide that the challenged regulation was illegal because it was **22–026** outside the powers of the enabling legislation, or conflicted with rights granted by other legislation. The process of statutory interpretation will be affected by the importance of the rights at stake.

In the *Joint Council for the Welfare of Immigrants*[135] the Secretary of State had made certain regulations acting under powers conferred by the Social Security Contributions and Benefits Act 1992 in order to discourage asylum claims by economic migrants. The effect of the regulations was to remove benefits from many of those seeking asylum. Simon Brown L.J. held the regulations ultra vires, primarily because they rendered nugatory the rights of asylum seekers under the Asylum and Immigration Appeals Act 1993. Parliament could not, he said, have intended a significant number of genuine asylum seekers to be impaled on the horns of an intolerable dilemma[136]: "the need either to abandon their claims to refugee status or alternatively to maintain them as best they can but in a state of utter destitution". This could only be done by primary legislation.

In *Javed*[137] the Court of Appeal held that it was entitled to review subordinate legislation on grounds of illegality, impropriety or irrationality, notwithstanding that it had been approved by affirmative resolution, but that when reviewing for irrationality account would be taken of the nature and purpose of the enabling legislation. In the instant case the applicant challenged the legality of the subordinate legislation on the ground that it wrongly designated Pakistan as a country in respect of which there was no serious risk of persecution. The court accepted that the minister had a margin of appreciation in deciding whether there was such a risk in Pakistan, but decided nonetheless on a review of the evidence that there was such a risk for women, especially those who belonged to the applicant's minority sect.

ii. Breach of Constitutional principle

Although we have no written constitution the courts use certain **22–027**

---

[134] *R. v Halliday* [1917] A.C. 260; *Liversidge v Anderson* [1942] A.C. 206.
[135] *R. v Secretary of State for Social Security Ex p. Joint Council for the Welfare of Immigrants* [1997] 1 W.L.R. 275.
[136] *Joint Council*, n.135, 293.
[137] *R. (on the application of Asif Javed) v Secretary of State for the Home Department* [2002] Q.B. 129.

constitutional principles when construing delegated legislation. An instrument that contravenes such principles will be declared void, unless there is express statutory authority to justify the action.

In *Wilts United Dairies*,[138] the Food Controller was empowered to regulate the sale, purchase, etc. of food and to regulate price. A dairy company was granted a licence to trade in milk, but it had to pay a charge of 2d per gallon. This condition was initially accepted by the company, but it later resisted and refused to pay. Despite its express consent to the condition, the court held that its refusal to pay was justified. The charge infringed the provision in the Bill of Rights 1689 that no money should be levied to the use of the Crown without the consent of Parliament. A power to charge would not be implied from the general power to control that trade.

The use of constitutional presumptions is also apparent in the *Leech* case.[139] The court struck down a rule that authorised a prison governor to read every letter from a prisoner and stop any that were objectionable or of inordinate length. In reaching this conclusion the court reasoned on the basis that the more fundamental the right interfered with, and the more drastic the interference, the more difficult was it to imply a rule-making power of this kind. The fundamental right in question was the right of access to court and it was held that the contested rule could not be upheld because of the extent to which it impeded the exercise of that right.[140]

iii. Purpose, relevancy and reasonableness

22–027 Subordinate legislation will also be subject to the substantive controls that apply to administrative action in general. The courts will apply notions of purpose, relevancy and reasonableness to constrain discretionary power.[141]

Powers are granted for certain purposes. If it can be shown that subordinate legislation is being used for an *improper purpose*, other than that intended by the parent Act, it will be declared void.[142] Thus in *Bancoult*,[143] it was held that a power to make laws for the peace, order and good government of a territory, did not allow the removal of the territory's entire population.

The courts will also intervene if the exercise of the delegated power is held to be *unreasonable*. An instrument will not be held to be unreasonable merely because the particular judge disagrees with its content, or believes that it goes further than is prudent, necessary, or convenient. The

---

[138] *Att-Gen v Wilts United Dairies Ltd* (1921) 39 T.L.R. 781.

[139] *R. v Secretary of State for the Home Department Ex p. Leech (No.2)* [1994] Q.B. 198. See also, *Joint Council for the Welfare of Immigrants*, n.135.

[140] See also, *R. v Lord Chancellor Ex p. Witham* [1998] Q.B. 575; *Chester v Bateson* [1920] 1 K.B. 829.

[141] See above, Chs 17, 19.

[142] *Att-Gen. for Canada v Hallett & Carey Ltd* [1952] A.C. 427; *R. v HM Treasury Ex p. Smedley* [1985] Q.B. 657.

[143] *R. (on the application of Bancoult) v Secretary of State for Foreign and Commonwealth Affairs* [2001] Q.B. 1067. See also *R. (on the application of Bancoult) v Secretary of State for Foreign and Commonwealth Affairs* [2007] EWCA Civ 498.

instrument must be manifestly unjust, involve the oppressive or gratuitous interference with the rights of those subject to it such as could find no justification in the minds of reasonable men, disclose bad faith, or be partial and unequal in its operation as between different classes.[144]

An instrument may also be unreasonable if it is too *vague*, but the courts have in some instances construed statutory instruments generously. In *McEldowney*,[145] a regulation was challenged that created a criminal offence of belonging to an organisation describing itself as a "republican club" or "any like organisation howsoever described". The person convicted belonged to such a club, and a majority upheld the conviction. This was despite the fact that no threat to public order was apparent, and notwithstanding that the wording of the regulation was vague to say the least. By way of contrast in *Bugg*,[146] the court struck down a byelaw restricting access to a military base on the ground that the area covered by the byelaw was not delineated clearly enough. This ruling must, however, now be seen in the light of *Percy*.[147] The court held that a byelaw should be regarded as valid unless it was so uncertain in its language as to have no ascertainable meaning, or so unclear in its effect as to be incapable of certain application in any case.

These substantive controls can be applied with varying degrees of *intensity*. This has been discussed above,[148] and is apparent in the *McEldowney* case. The courts have, moreover, made this explicit. In the *Nottinghamshire County Council* case,[149] the local authority challenged expenditure limits imposed by the Secretary of State. Failure to comply with those limits led to a reduction in the rate support grant available to the local authority. The limits required the approval by resolution of the House of Commons before they could take effect. The local authority argued, inter alia, that these limits were unreasonable. Lord Scarman held that the courts should be reluctant to intervene on this ground. This was in part because the subject matter, public financial administration, inevitably involved political judgment by the minister. It was also because approval of the House of Commons had been given. The court would intervene if there had been a misconstruction of the statute. It would however be constitutionally inappropriate for the court to interfere on the ground of unreasonableness unless the minister had abused his power, in the sense of deceiving the House or producing

---

[144] *Kruse v Johnson* [1898] 2 Q.B. 91. See also, *Monro v Watson* (1887) 57 LT 366; *Repton School Governors v Repton Rural District Council* [1918] 2 K.B. 133; *Sparks v Edward Ash Ltd* [1943] 2 K.B. 223.
[145] *McEldowney v Forde* [1971] A.C. 632.
[146] *Bugg v DPP* [1993] Q.B. 473.
[147] *Percy v Hall* [1997] Q.B. 924. The Court of Appeal preferred the formulation by Lord Denning in *Fawcett Properties Ltd v Buckingham CC* [1961] A.C. 636, 677–678, to that of Mathew J. in *Kruse v Johnson* [1898] 2 Q.B. 91, 108.
[148] See above, para.17–008.
[149] *R. v Secretary of State for the Environment Ex p. Nottinghamshire County Council* [1986] A.C. 240.

expenditure limits so absurd that he must have taken leave of his senses.[150]
The House of Lords has endorsed this approach.[151]

While the subject-matter in such cases, economic regulation, may warrant
less intensive review, the relevance of a resolution by the Commons may be
questioned. We have already seen that the passage of such a resolution does
not indicate any meaningful legislative scrutiny, and hence the effect of this
approval is largely symbolic. This was acknowledged in *Orange Personal
Communications*.[152] The court held that, when making regulations pursuant
to s.2(2) of the European Communities Act 1972, the executive must tell
Parliament in clear terms what primary legislation was being repealed or
amended for the purposes of applying the Community law in question. This
was especially so, given that parliamentary scrutiny under s.2(2) was so
limited.

C. Delegation

22–028 The normal principles concerning delegation apply. These were dealt with in
detail above,[153] and may be briefly summarised here. The general rule is that
a power must be exercised by the person on whom it is conferred. A
necessary qualification exists in the case of ministers, where officials will
exercise powers in the name of the Minister. How far delegation will be
allowed will depend upon the nature of the power in question and the
general circumstances of the case. In principle, legislative power should be
exercised by those in whom it is vested.[154]

D. Remedies

22–029 The presumption is that invalidity may be raised collaterally or directly.[155]
This is particularly so when a criminal sanction may be imposed on an
individual pursuant to, for example, a byelaw which the individual claims to
be invalid. There may then be a collateral challenge by way of defence to the
criminal action. Collateral challenge may also take the form of, for example,
a defence to a contract suit.

There may, however, be instances where the statute is held to indicate that
a direct challenge by way of an application for judicial review is the only
way to raise certain kinds of error.[156]

---

[150] *Nottinghamshire County Council*, n.149, 247, 250–251.
[151] *R. v Secretary of State for the Environment Ex p. Hammersmith and Fulham London Borough
Council* [1990] 1 A.C. 521.
[152] *R. (on the application of Orange Personal Communications Ltd) v Secretary of State for
Trade and Industry* [2001] 3 C.M.L.R. 36.
[153] See above, Ch.16.
[154] See *Hawke's Bay Raw Milk Products Co-operative Ltd v New Zealand Milk Board* [1961]
N.Z.L.R. 218. In the First World War sub-delegation of legislative power was not expressly
authorised, but the Emergency Powers (Defence) Act 1939 allowed further delegation. This
could produce as many as five tiers of authority; a veritable wedding cake of regulations.
[155] *Boddington v British Transport Police* [1999] 2 A.C. 143, overruling in this respect *Bugg*,
n.146.
[156] *R. v Wicks* [1998] A.C. 92.

A statutory instrument may be attacked directly through the declaration. Subject to the doubts voiced below,[157] the direct action should be brought as an application for judicial review for a declaration or injunction.

The scope of locus standi to challenge secondary legislation is not entirely clear. It has traditionally been assumed to be quite wide. However, in *Bugg* it was held that individuals have no right to complain of procedural defects in delegated legislation unless they have been prejudiced by the default.[158] It is unclear whether this aspect of the ruling survives the overruling of the case on other grounds.

The possibilities of an injunction to prevent a minister from proceeding with making an instrument[159] and the possible immunisation of delegated legislation from judicial control[160] are considered later.

The prerogative orders of certiorari and prohibition were traditionally regarded as applying only to judicial functions and hence as being inapplicable to delegated legislation. The inroads that have been made on this principle are considered in the discussion of remedies.[161]

7. Delegated Legislation: Possible Reforms

There is no ready-made solution to solve, at the stroke of a pen, the problems with delegated legislation. Improvements are, however, possible. The Rippon Commission highlighted the problems.[162] Its recommendations for change in the primary legislative process have already been discussed. The Commission recognised that much delegated legislation was of real importance.[163] It stated that "we consider the whole approach of Parliament to delegated legislation to be highly unsatisfactory".[164] The Commission made a number of serious suggestions for improving the existing regime.

22–030

A. Rippon Commission

i. Publication and access to the law
The Commission made its views on the present arrangements for publication and access to the law very clear.[165]

22–031

---

[157] See below, para.25–007.
[158] *Bugg*, n.146.
[159] See below, para.25–034.
[160] See below, Ch.27.
[161] See below, para.25–007. Mandamus seems to be subject to no such limitations and has been used in relation to byelaws, *R. v Manchester Corporation* [1911] 1 K.B. 560.
[162] *Making the Law, The Report of the Hansard Society Commission on the Legislative Process* (1993).
[163] *Making the Law*, n.162, 89.
[164] *Making the Law*, n.162, 89–90.
[165] *Making the Law*, n.162, 108.

"At present the accessibility of statute law to users and the wider public is slow, inconvenient, complicated and subject to several impediments. To put it bluntly, it is often very difficult to find out what the text of the law is—let alone what it means. Something must be done."

It recommended that as far as possible new laws should not come into effect before they are published, and that the government should press ahead as fast as possible with a Statute Law Database, which would facilitate the publication and updating of statute law.[166] There should, moreover, be financial assistance provided to those bodies, such as Citizens Advice Bureaus, in order to help them to explain the law to the public.[167]

The Commission also addressed the problems that exist where a primary statute is to be implemented by delegated legislation. It suggested that the Government should indicate the general nature of the regulations it intended to introduce, and that this could be done by a White Paper or through an explanatory statement published with the Bill.[168]

ii. The subject matter scrutinised by Parliament

22–032 We have already seen that the definition of a statutory instrument is purely formal, with the consequence that many rules of a legislative nature are not open to scrutiny by Parliament. The Commission did not consider this matter in any depth, but it did touch on the issue in passing. The Commission noted that much sub-delegated legislation was not, and could not be, debated in Parliament. This was not, said the Commission, acceptable. It recommended that all Acts and delegated legislation should be drafted so that all important regulations and delegated legislation can be debated in Parliament.[169] The realisation of this particular recommendation is, as will be seen below, problematic.

iii. Debates on Statutory Instruments

22–033 The ineffectiveness of the present regime for debating statutory instruments on the floor of the House has been noted above. The Rippon Commission proposed a number of significant alterations, which centred on greater use of standing committees.

For those statutory instruments subject to *affirmative resolution* the Commission suggested the following new procedure.[170] Unless the House otherwise ordered, all statutory instruments which require affirmative resolution should be automatically referred to standing committee for debate.[171] Longer or more complex instruments could be referred to a special

---

[166] *Making the Law*, n.162, 109.
[167] *Making the Law*, n.162, 113.
[168] *Making the Law*, n.162, 112.
[169] *Making the Law*, n.162, 93.
[170] *Making the Law*, n.162, 91–93, 149.
[171] This does now represent current practice, Ganz, n.12, 70.

standing committee. Such standing committees should have the power to question ministers on the meaning, purpose and effect of the instrument. The Minister responsible for the instrument would move a motion recommending its approval, and members of the committee would then be able to move amendments recommending either that the instrument should not be approved, or that it should be approved subject to changes. There would, in general, be no time limit on debates. If the committee recommended approval of the instrument this should then be put to the House without debate. Where the committee recommended that the instrument should be rejected, or approved subject to amendments, there would then be a debate in the House constrained by time limits.

For those statutory instruments subject to *negative resolution* then, unless the House otherwise ordered, all prayers for the annulment of such instruments should be referred to a standing committee. The procedure within the committee would be the same as for affirmative instruments, except that the M.P. who tabled the prayer would either move a motion for annulment of the instrument concerned, or a motion recommending its amendment. The Minister could then move amendments to such motions. If the M.P.'s motion failed that would be an end of the matter. If this motion succeeded in committee then the M.P. who moved the motion should then have the right to move a formal motion in the House for the annulment of the instrument. Debates would be subject to time limits.

These suggestions are to be welcomed. The centrality accorded to the standing committee as an initial vehicle for scrutiny is designed to alleviate the real difficulty of finding time to conduct the whole procedure on the floor of the House.

iv. Committee scrutiny

The function of the standing committees described above is to render the debate by Parliament more workable and thorough. There is still room for reform of the pre-existing committee regime. The Commission suggested a number of such reforms.   **22–034**

Some relate to the work of the *Joint Committee on Statutory Instruments*. It proposed that, except in cases of emergency, no statutory instrument should be debated until the Joint Committee reported. Furthermore, if that committee reported that an instrument is ultra vires or otherwise defective, there should be no motion approving the instrument without a resolution to set aside the committee's findings.[172]

A further suggestion is for scrutiny of delegated legislation to be assigned to the *departmental select committee* responsible for that area, which would then report on those instruments that raise matters of public importance.[173] There is much to be said for this idea, and it may go some way to alleviating the present malaise.

[172] *Making the Law*, n.162, 91.
[173] *Making the Law*, n.162, 90.

The current committee system is beset by difficulties. These include the workload placed on the Joint Committee; its lack of expertise in many subject matter areas; lack of interest among M.P.s in the committee's work; and the hazy division between technical scrutiny and the merits. If departmental select committees reviewed statutory instruments then this would, at the least, meet some of these problems. The workload would be spread amongst a number of committees. The departmental select committees are staffed by those with knowledge of the area. It is often not easy for those who are unfamiliar with a topic to know whether a new piece of delegated legislation is sound either in technical terms, or in terms of its merits, without having some background expertise in that area. Members of select committees are more likely to possess the understanding that is a prerequisite for reasoned scrutiny. Given the evidence of the workings of the present system this idea must be worth a trial.

The Procedure Committee also recommended the use of a departmental select committee for very important orders, coupled with the two-stage procedure which applies in the case of deregulation orders.[174]

v. Consultation

22–035   The Rippon Commission prefaced its recommendations about consultation and delegated legislation with this observation.[175]

> "The importance of proper consultation on delegated legislation should not be underestimated. For many bodies its importance is equal to-or greater than- the importance of consultation on bills. And from the point of view of those directly affected, it is equally important to get delegated legislation right. Delegated legislation may be of secondary importance to Ministers and those in Parliament . . . but to those to whom the law applies or to the practitioners . . . who have to apply it, the method by which the law is made is of little significance. Primary and delegated legislation are equally the law of the land."

This observation is to be welcomed, as are the suggestions which flow from it. The Commission recommended that there should be consultation where appropriate at the formative stage of delegated legislation, and that wherever possible departments should consult outside experts and affected bodies on the drafts of instruments which they propose to submit to Parliament. Moreover, the guidelines for consultation on primary bills should be applied with suitable modification to delegated legislation.[176]

The problem with this proposal relates not to its substance, but to its application. The force of law may well be required in order to ensure that departments really do consult in the desired manner, rather than by

---

[174] Procedure Committee, n.179, para.9.
[175] *Making the Law*, n.162, 42.
[176] *Loc.cit.*

"marking" certain groups which are regarded as acceptable, with the consequence that others are unable to play any real part in this consultative process. It is for this reason, among others, that developments along the lines described in the USA would be desirable.

B. The Select Committee on Procedure
The Select Committee on Procedure also made valuable suggestions for   **22–036**
reform of delegated legislation. It issued a major report in 1996,[177] and
returned to the topic in a report in 2000,[178] in which it endorsed the conclusions reached in the earlier study. Both reports stressed the failings of the existing system, describing it as palpably unsatisfactory.

First, statutory instruments do not receive scrutiny in proportion to their importance or merits. This was because certain trivial matters were subject to the affirmative procedure, while some important matters were dealt with by the negative resolution procedure. The Committee recommended the establishment of a Sifting Committee, which would examine all statutory instruments subject to annulment.[179] The Committee would recommend those instruments that were of sufficient political importance for debate in standing committee and put down a motion to this effect. The debate would then take place before the time limit for prayers had expired. This committee would also liaise with departmental select committees, a proposal welcomed by the Liaison Committee.[180]

Second, the debates on such instruments in standing committee were criticised as being meaningless, because they did not take place on a substantive amendable motion. The Committee recommended that the motions in delegated legislation standing committees should be substantive and amendable, and that where the government was defeated there should be up to an hour's further debate in the House.

Third, the Committee felt that there was need for a "super-affirmative" procedure, to allow more thorough scrutiny of a small number of complex statutory instruments by departmental select committees. This would be modelled on the procedure used for deregulation and regulatory reform orders. The later report of the Committee also left open the possibility of greater use of departmental select committees more generally in relation to delegated legislation.[181]

C. The House of Lords' Merits of Statutory Instruments Committee
The House of Lords' Merits of Statutory Instruments Committee also made   **22–037**

---

[177] Select Committee on Procedure, *Delegated Legislation* (HC 152; 1996). See also, *First Report of the Select Committee on Modernisation of the House of Commons* (HC 190; 1997), para.83.
[178] Select Committee on Procedure, First Report, *Delegated Legislation* (HC 48; 2000).
[179] Select Committee on Procedure, n.177, (HC 152; 1996), paras 33–36; Select Committee on Procedure, First Report, n.178, (HC 48; 2000), paras 14–15.
[180] Liaison Committee, First Report (HC 323-I; 1997), para.33.
[181] Select Committee on Procedure, First Report, n.178, (HC 48; 2000), para.54.

recommendations for improvement, and focused on departmental management of statutory instruments.[182]

It recommended that in each department there should be one member of top management accountable to the relevant minister for the efficiency and effectiveness of the process of preparing statutory instruments, as well as for ensuring that the finished products met the requirements of good regulation. Departments should prepare annual management plans for their statutory instruments, and they should be given guidance on best practice regarding the planning and management of secondary legislation programmes. Statutory instruments and their explanatory memoranda should be subject to review in the course of preparation by a senior official who was sufficiently detached from the subject matter to be able to assess its intelligibility to the layman reader. Departmental plans for secondary legislation should also include a target date for post-implementation review of each statutory instrument.

The Merits Committee also had reservations about the existing consultation regime. Thus it recommended that: the Government should take action to ensure that the 12-week consultation requirement from the Consultation Code of Practice was met other than in exceptional cases; consultation should be mandatory for all instruments that transpose EU obligations into UK law; there should be an opportunity for ordinary citizens, as well as representative groups, to make their views known; and departments should report the outcome of the consultation in the explanatory memorandum.

The Merits Committee also directed certain recommendations towards government rather than individual departments. The Government should take action to ensure that no instrument is laid before Parliament less than 21 days before it is due to come into force unless there are clear and compelling reasons doing so. The Government should moreover put more impetus behind the process of consolidation and should aim to publish consolidated electronic versions of each instrument following amendment. Once a public database of statute law is available, it should be extended as quickly as possible to cover secondary as well as primary legislation.

8. Rules Made by the Administration

A. Type and Rationale

22–038   There is a duality latent in the term legislative instrument. When we speak of delegated legislation we mean the grant of power by the parent legislature to a minister or other body to make rules or regulations. While the test of what

---

[182] *The Management of Secondary Legislation*, n.67, para.126.

is to count as a statutory instrument in the 1946 Act is primarily one of form,[183] the idea of publication and legislative scrutiny is premised upon the hypothesis that the rules thus made are themselves legislative in nature. Legislative in this sense signifies that the rule has a generality of application that distinguishes it from a mere executive order. Sub-delegated legislation poses problems at both levels. It may be unclear whether Parliament delegated power to a particular person, and it may be questionable whether the rule that that person made really was legislative in character or not.

What is clear is that there exists an important category quite outside that of sub-delegated legislation. There may be no express legislative mandate to make rules, but it is clear nonetheless that the administration makes rules that are legislative in character, using that term in the second sense. They are of a generality of application such that if they were juxtaposed to real statutory instruments they would be indistinguishable in terms of their nature or content. Thus, although such rules may be made by the administration, they are not necessarily administrative rules. Some of them may be, but many are not. Such rule-making can moreover enhance justice in that it allows interference with private interests only on the condition that the individual knows of the rule in advance and can plan his or her actions accordingly.

There is a tremendous variety in the *types* of such rules. Codes of practice, circulars, directions, rules and regulations are all to be found within the administrative landscape. These labels are not, however, terms of art, and the precise label does not therefore "solve" the problem of classification. A suggested classification categorises administrative rules in the following manner[184]: procedural rules; interpretive guides; instructions to officials; prescriptive/evidential rules; commendatory codes; voluntary codes; rules of practice, management and operation; and administrative pronouncements.

There are not surprisingly a number of differing *rationales* for such rules,   **22–039**
and for preferring them to more formal delegated legislation. Four such reasons can be distinguished.[185] First, even where no explicit power to make regulations is granted to an agency, it will often make rules to indicate how it will exercise its discretion. This is a natural tendency for bureaucracies when faced with a recurring problem. The debate about rules versus discretion has been addressed above.[186] Second, non-legal rules facilitate the use of non-technical language, exemplified by the Highway Code, and the Health and Safety Codes. Third, such rules may be preferred because they are more flexible than statutory instruments, and hence can be changed more easily. Finally, these rules may be preferred to delegated legislation precisely because they are not legally binding. They enable policies to be

---

[183] Except for rules made after the 1946 Act came into force under statutes existing prior to that date.
[184] R. Baldwin and J. Houghton, "Circular Arguments: The Status and Legitimacy of Administrative Rules" [1986] P.L. 239, 240–244.
[185] G. Ganz, *Quasi-Legislation: Recent Developments in Secondary Legislation* (Sweet & Maxwell, 1987), Ch.6; Baldwin, n.2, Ch.4.
[186] See above, Ch.16.

developed voluntarily in the sense that "persuasion may be preferable to compulsion".[187]

We should not therefore deprecate the use of such rules. The cogency of particular arguments used in favour of informal rules must nonetheless be carefully analysed. For example, the argument that informal rules are preferred because they reflect a voluntary approach whereby reliance is placed on co-operation and consent rather than the force of law, could mean three very different things.

It could indicate that a policy approved by the legislature is then implemented by a code, rather than formal legislation, because it is felt that this will be more efficacious. It could alternatively exemplify a "corporatist strategy", whereby the executive and a major interest group bargain independently of the legislature to attain a goal, which may be opposed by other less powerful interest groups, and/or the legislature. It could finally mean that a powerful executive implements a code or rule which the relevant interest groups oppose, but which they are powerless to fight. Legislative scrutiny can be avoided, and the minimum of legal formalism troubles the executive in pursuit of its aim. Not all informal rules are therefore necessarily more truly consensual in nature than those norms which emerge as legislation.

B. Legal Status

22–040   The precise legal status of these rules may differ depending upon the type of rule in question. Three points of general importance can, however, be made.

First, the fact that an agency does not have express power to make rules does not, per se, render them invalid. The capacity to make such rules flows from the way in which agencies are allowed to exercise their discretion. The courts have held, as we have seen,[188] that rules or policy guidelines are valid provided that they are not too rigidly applied, and provided that certain other conditions are met.

Second, the precise *legal status* of any particular rule can only be discerned by examining the relevant statutory provisions, and the judicial interpretation thereof. Thus legislation may, for example, stipulate that a code, such as the Highway Code, should have a certain degree of legal force in legal proceedings, by identifying the weight to be given to a breach of the code in any such action.[189] Codes may also possess "indirect" legal effect.[190] Non-compliance with the provisions may provide a reason why, for example, a television programme contractor should not have its franchise renewed.[191] Non-compliance with a code may also furnish the rationale for the passage of a statutory instrument, the object of which is to provide

---

[187] Ganz, n.185, 97–98.
[188] See above, Ch.16.
[189] See, e.g. Transport Act 1982 s.60.
[190] Ganz, n.185, 16–18.
[191] Independent Broadcasting Act 1973 ss.5, 9, 13.

"full" legal force for the attainment of the code's objectives.[192] It is not therefore surprising that the judiciary can be divided as to the status of a rule, even within a particular area.[193]

Third, even if a particular rule is not "related to" primary legislation in any of the ways considered above, it may still have *legal consequences* in a double sense. On the one hand, provided that the rule is not too rigidly applied, it can be dispositive of a person's case.[194] On the other hand, the existence of such a rule may, as we have seen, generate consultation rights if the public body seeks to resile from the application of its rule.[195]

C. Rules made by the Administration: Problems

The first problem presented by the existence of such rules is that their **22–041** promulgation by the executive, together with the relevant interest group, may bypass the legislature and foreclose the possibility of parliamentary scrutiny. As Stewart states,[196]

"The ultimate problem is to control and validate the exercise of essentially legislative powers that do not enjoy the formal legitimation of one-person one-vote election."

A second problem follows from the first, in that particular pressure groups may exercise excessive influence over the rules that emerge. The ability of the public more generally to have input into the proposed rule may be absent, or vary in degree from area to area.

A third cause for concern centres upon the rule of law. Many of the rules under consideration are unpublished, or not readily accessible. The intended and actual legal status of others is unclear. Yet other rules fit poorly with the relevant parent legislation, and appear to countenance action inconsistent with the enabling statute.

Finally, such rules have been used on issues of considerable political contention, thereby rendering the law "most vague at the points where it should be most clear".[197]

D. Rules made by the Administration: Possible Solutions

i. Direct control by Parliament

Direct control would require any rule of a legislative character to be subject **22–042**

---

[192] Local Government, Planning and Land Act 1980 ss.2, 3.
[193] Compare *R. v Heathrow Airport Immigration Officer Ex p. Bibi* [1976] 1 W.L.R. 979, *R. v Home Secretary Ex p. Hosenball* [1977] 1 W.L.R. 766 and *R. v Immigration Appeal Tribunal Ex p. Bakhtaur Singh* [1986] 1 W.L.R. 910, on the status of immigration rules.
[194] See above, Ch.16.
[195] See above, para.22–018.
[196] "The Reformation of American Administrative Law" (1975) 88 Harv. L.R. 1667, 1668. An excellent article which is to be recommended.
[197] Baldwin and Houghton, n.184, 268.

to parliamentary scrutiny. This would reverse the premise of the Statutory Instruments Act 1946, which adopts a formalistic approach: delegated legislation will be subject to parliamentary scrutiny and publication only where the instrument is described as a statutory instrument.[198] If we desire direct validation by Parliament the basic premise of the 1946 Act would, therefore, have to be modified so that any legislative rule formulated by a public body, whether under express delegation or not, would be subject to legislative oversight. Exceptions could of course be made for certain types of rules. It might be felt for example that rules of internal organisation should not be subject to such scrutiny.[199] There are two immediate difficulties with this approach.

The *first problem* is that it may be difficult to decide what constitutes a "legislative rule". This point must, however, be kept within perspective. The criticism voiced of the distinctions between legislative and executive, or legislative and administrative, has force because it is thought not to be relevant as a criterion for the application of natural justice or certiorari. The position is different here. The distinction *is* important and relevant in this context. It is rules of a legislative character that we believe ought to be controlled by the legislature. The 1946 Act with its formalistic approach simply ducks the whole matter. More precisely, it allows the decision to reside with the Government. The Executive will frame the legislation, and will therefore decide whether the delegated powers should be termed statutory instruments.

The *second problem* is the effectiveness of any such control. We have already seen the constraints on effective legislative scrutiny. Adding extra tasks to an already overburdened system of legislative control, both on the floor of the House and in committee, will give cause for hope only to the most sanguine.[200]

These problems should, therefore, be borne in mind when assessing the proposal from the Rippon Commission noted above, that Acts and delegated legislation should be drafted to ensure that all important regulations can be debated in Parliament.[201] This recommendation was framed with the problem of sub-delegated legislation in mind. Even if the 1946 Act were amended to accommodate this suggestion this would still leave many rules outside the realm of legislative scrutiny. Many agencies make rules of a legislative character, even though those rules would not be classified as sub-delegated legislation.

ii. Legislative specification of standards
22–043 Parliament in its initial grant of authority could specify the standards it

---

[198] Although all Orders in Council made under statutory as opposed to prerogative power are automatically so regarded.
[199] Administrative Procedure Act 1946 s.553(b) (USA).
[200] Certain pieces of quasi-legislation are subject to legislative oversight, and scrutiny by select committee, Ganz, n.185, 26–32.
[201] *Making the Law*, n.162, para.382.

wishes the public body to apply. It could, alternatively, empower the relevant minister to supply guidelines or directions to the body in the course of its operations. This is a device that has been used in relation to nationalised industries and other agencies. There is no doubt that it could be used to a greater extent than at present.

Legislative specification of standards may, however, be of limited utility for novel problems, where the precise interests to be weighed are unclear at the outset. This problem can be partially circumvented by granting power to the minister to give directions after consultation with the public body. This is in itself constrained by the type of public institution in question. If it is one that warrants a high degree of autonomy from party political pressures then ministerial directives will be inappropriate.

iii. Consultation
Consultation in the rule-making process is another option. The extent to **22–044**
which statute and the common law presently provide consultation rights has been considered above. Consultation is even more central here than it is in the context of delegated legislation. The latter will at least see the light of day through publication and will be subject to some legislative scrutiny. If we decide that other forms of rule-making are not suited to legislative scrutiny, then validation and control by a different method becomes more important. Consultation through the representation of interested parties can go some way to achieving this. The previous discussion is relevant here, as is the Cabinet Office's Code of Consultation.

iv. Judicial control
There is clearly an overlap between judicial control and consultation rights, **22–045**
since it is the judiciary who will interpret or develop such rights. However the judiciary have a role to play in this area independent of the issue of consultation. The role of the courts can be presented as follows.[202]

First, the court will decide whether the code or circular is susceptible to judicial review. For example, in *Gillick*[203] Lord Bridge stated that the general rule was that the reasonableness of advice contained in non-statutory guidance could not be subject to judicial review, but that there was an exception to this general rule. If a government department promulgated advice in a public document that was erroneous in law the court could correct this.

Second, in so far as codes, circulars, etc. are given certain evidentiary or

---

[202] Ganz, n.185, 41–46; Baldwin, n.2, 85–119.
[203] *Gillick v West Norfolk and Wisbech Area Health Authority* [1986] A.C. 112; *R. v Secretary of State for the Home Department Ex p. Westminster Press Ltd* [1992] C.O.D. 303; *R. (on the application of Axon) v Secretary of State for Health* [2006] Q.B. 539; *R. (on the application of Association of British Travel Agents Ltd (ABTA)) v Civil Aviation Authority* [2006] EWHC 13.

substantive force within legal proceedings, it is the judiciary who will interpret the meaning they should bear.[204] They will also review the interpretation of such a code where it has been applied by an administrative agency.[205] The intensity of any such review may vary from area to area,[206] and courts may disagree upon the appropriate intensity of review within a particular area.[207]

Third, the existence of an agency rule or code will generate an obligation of consistency in relation to its application, such that it should not be departed from without cogent reasons,[208] and it might lead to enforceable legitimate expectations.[209]

Finally, the courts can apply the tests of purpose, relevancy, reasonableness and fettering of discretion to determine whether a particular rule is within the ambit of the relevant empowering legislation, or whether undue weight has been given to one circular and another has been ignored.[210] These tests are normally applied to the individual exercise of discretion. It is, however, clear on principle that agency choices should not be immune from such oversight merely because they assume the form of a rule.[211] The courts' willingness to invalidate a particular rule on the grounds of, for example, unreasonableness may well differ from area to area. It appears that the courts are more willing to consider this where the rule is made in the context of a relatively clear statutory framework, against which its vires and reasonableness can be judged.[212] The court will then pronounce upon the legality of the rule, even if it is non-statutory.

v. Conclusion

22–046 Quasi-legislation has been present for a considerable time. The term was already current in the 19th century,[213] and concern over its existence was expressed over 50 years ago.[214] Renewed interest in the topic is timely,[215] and reflects the importance of the issue addressed. No single, simple solution is likely to be forthcoming. There is a range of options, none of which is free from difficulty. At the very least quasi-legislation should be published, and rendered accessible to those affected by it.

---

[204] *R. v Secretary of State for the Home Department Ex p. Lancashire Police Authority* [1992] C.O.D. 161.
[205] *HTV v Price Commission* [1976] I.C.R. 170.
[206] *R. v Secretary of State for the Home Department Ex p. Gangadeen* [1998] C.O.D. 216.
[207] See, e.g., *R. v Criminal Injuries Compensation Board Ex p. Schofield* [1971] 1 W.L.R. 926; *R. v Criminal Injuries Compensation Board Ex p. Thompstone* [1984] 1 W.L.R. 1234.
[208] *R. (on the application of Munjaz) v Mersey Care NHS Trust* [2006] 2 A.C. 148.
[209] See above, Ch.20.
[210] *JA Pye (Oxford) Estates Ltd v West Oxfordshire District Council and the Secretary of State for the Environment* [1982] J.P.E.L. 557.
[211] See above, Ch.16.
[212] *Gillick*, n.203; *Royal College of Nursing of the U.K. v Department of Health and Social Security* [1981] A.C. 800.
[213] A. Todd, *On Parliamentary Government in England* (1867–1869), Vol. I, 288; H. Parris, *Constitutional Bureaucracy* (1969), 193–194.
[214] R. Megarry, "Administrative Quasi-Legislation" (1944) 60 L.Q.R. 125.
[215] Baldwin and Houghton, n.184; Ganz, n.185; Baldwin, n.2.

9. THE IMPACT OF COMMUNITY LAW

We have already considered the existing mechanisms for the scrutiny of EC **22–047** law by parliamentary committees. The discussion would, however, be incomplete if it did not also advert to the broader significance of Community law for rule-making. This is not the place for any detailed exegesis on the Community's legislative process and the criticisms made of it. Discussion of such matters can be found elsewhere.[216] The object of the present discussion is to make clear at a general level the impact of Community law on the subject at hand.

First, it should be recognised that regulatory competence in many areas has shifted upwards to the EC and away from the nation state. In many areas the main body of rules will emanate from the Community.

Second, it would, however, be mistaken to conclude that all regulatory competence within these areas now resides with the Community. The precise allocation of power as between national and Community authorities varies from area to area. It is not uncommon to find regulatory competence shared between the nation state and the Community. It is this fact, amongst others, which has led commentators to depict the regulatory process as multi-level governance, in which sub-national, national and Community actors take part.

Third, the process by which the Community makes rules which would, in all probability, otherwise have been made by national delegated legislation or rule-making, is problematic. Space precludes any detailed exegesis of the complex procedures that operate within the Community. Suffice it to say for the present that the Comitology process as it is known, whereby the Council delegates power to the Commission, subject to conditions, to make such rules, has been the cause of concern. There is, however, no ready consensus on the best way of tackling the problem, and there is indeed disagreement as to the very way in which we should characterise the Comitology process.[217] What this debate does show is that the problems of ensuring legitimacy, accountability and control are just as difficult when rules are made by the Community as when they are made by a nation state.

---

[216] P. Craig and G. de Búrca, *EU Law, Text, Cases and Materials* (Oxford University Press, 4th edn, 2007), Ch.4; P. Craig, "The Nature of the Community: Integration, Legitimacy and Democracy", in P. Craig and G. de Búrca (eds), *The Evolution of EU Law* (Oxford University Press, 1999), Ch.1.

[217] P. Craig, *EU Administrative Law* (Oxford University Press, 2006), Ch.4.

CHAPTER 23

INVALIDITY

1. DIRECT AND COLLATERAL ATTACK

A. Classification

This chapter is concerned with the result of finding that a decision is ultra **23–001** vires, or that there is an error of law on the face of the record, and with the status of the decision pending such a finding. However, before doing so it is necessary to consider the different methods of attack available to an aggrieved individual.

A person who wishes to challenge a decision may do so directly or collaterally. The dividing line between the two is not entirely clear, and is to some extent dependent upon terminology. There are two ways of looking at the matter, neither of which is entirely satisfactory.

Direct and collateral attack may be taken to refer to the form of remedy sought. Thus, direct attack would cover the prerogative orders, injunction, declaration and possibly habeas corpus. The individual here is seeking a remedy that directly impugns the administrative order. The problem with this classification is that it groups together remedies that go only to the validity of the challenged finding, with those which pertain to the merits. Examples of the latter are certiorari when used to challenge an error within jurisdiction and appeal. On this hypothesis collateral attack would cover the many ways in which a decision can be challenged indirectly, such as by way of defence to enforcement proceedings or in a tort action. The link between the forms of collateral attack is that they challenge the decision incidentally.

Alternatively, the distinction between direct and collateral methods of attack may be determined by the scope of review given by the remedy and not by its form. Collateral proceedings would be those in which the nullity of the decision is at issue, and direct proceedings would cover challenges to the merits.[1] The difficulty with this classification is that a remedy such as

---

[1] A. Rubinstein, *Jurisdiction and Illegality* (Oxford University Press, 1965), 37–39.

declaration, which is traditionally regarded as available only for jurisdictional defects, would be regarded as a collateral challenge while having little connection with an incidental form of attack by way of a tort action.

It is, however, clear that collateral attack covers many forms of incidental challenge and has been recognised for over 300 years. It constituted the early method of attacking decisions and predated the general development of the prerogative writs.[2] For example, in the *Case of the Marshalsea*[3] the plaintiff brought an action for trespass and false imprisonment, claiming that the Marshalsea Court possessed no jurisdiction over him as he was not of the King's House. The Court held that an action would lie where the challenged authority had no jurisdiction over the case, the entire proceedings being *coram non judice*; no such action would lie where the error was one within jurisdiction.

In this type of case the plaintiff brings an action in tort, the defendant relies upon, for example, a warrant from a magistrate and the plaintiff then rebuts that defence by proving a jurisdictional defect in the warrant. There are many other ways in which collateral attack can occur.[4] An accuser's guilt may be dependent upon the validity of an administrative or ministerial order. If the order is ultra vires then the accused will be exonerated.[5] A ratepayer can resist a demand for rates or charges by claiming that the demand is invalid.[6]

B. The Relationship between Direct and Collateral Attack: The General Principle

23–002   Collateral attack will only be an option where the defect alleged is jurisdictional.[7] Errors of law on the face of the record could therefore not be impeached collaterally, but only by way of certiorari. The rationale was that the court in a collateral action could take account of the invalidity of a challenged order; it was acting in a "declaratory" role. If, however, the decision was valid, albeit tainted with some error, it could only be challenged by appeal, or by certiorari where the error was one of law and was on the face of the record. A court not possessed of appellate jurisdiction could not obliquely assume such.[8] This point is, however, less important now given the expansion of jurisdictional error and the consequential demise of error of law within jurisdiction.

The general principle is, therefore, that any defect that would be treated as

---

[2] Rubinstein, n.1, Ch.4.
[3] (1612) 10 Co. Rep. 68b; *Terry v Huntington* (1668) Hard. 480. See also, *Fuller v Fotch* (1695) Carth. 346; *Doswell v Impey* (1823) 1 B. & C. 163.
[4] Rubinstein, n.1, 39–46.
[5] *DPP v Head* [1959] A.C. 83. Whether the validity of the act should always be relevant will be considered below.
[6] *Daymond v Plymouth City Council* [1976] A.C. 609.
[7] See further, *Groenvelt v Burwell* (1700) 3 Salk 354; *Gahan v Maingay* (1793) Ridg. L. & S. 20.
[8] *Gahan v Maingay*, n.7.

jurisdictional in direct proceedings is equally available in a collateral action. Thus in *Foster*[9] it was held that Social Security Commissioners hearing appeals under the Social Security Act 1975 had jurisdiction to determine any challenge to the vires of a provision in regulations made by the Secretary of State, on the ground that it was beyond the scope of the enabling power, whenever this was necessary in order to decide whether a decision under appeal was erroneous in point of law.

This general principle was re-affirmed in *Boddington*.[10] Boddington was convicted by a stipendiary magistrate for smoking in a railway carriage, contrary to a byelaw of the British Railways Board. The House of Lords held that it was open to a defendant in criminal proceedings to challenge subordinate legislation, or an administrative decision made thereunder, where the prosecution was premised on its validity, unless there was a clear legislative intent to the contrary. It was, said their Lordships, unacceptable in a democracy based on the rule of law for a magistrate to be able to convict a person who would be precluded from relying on a defence that he might otherwise have had. A direct action for judicial review was, for a number of reasons, an inadequate safeguard. The defendant might be out of time before becoming aware of the byelaw; he might not have the resources for such a challenge; leave might be refused; or a remedy might be denied pursuant to the court's discretionary power over such matters.

Their Lordships held, moreover, that there was no distinction in this respect to be drawn between cases of substantive and procedural invalidity and overruled *Bugg*.[11] In that case Woolf L.J. had drawn a distinction between procedural and substantive invalidity. So far as procedural invalidity was concerned Woolf L.J. held that subordinate legislation and byelaws were valid until they had been set aside by the appropriate court with jurisdiction to do so. The consequence was that a person accused of breaking a byelaw could not raise such a matter by way of defence to the criminal charge. Where the alleged defect was, however, substantive Woolf L.J. held that the position was different: no citizen was compelled to comply with a law which was bad on its face, and law tainted by this species of invalidity could simply be ignored.

Lord Steyn in *Boddington* rightly pointed to the two weaknesses of the substantive/procedural dichotomy.[12] It did not, on the one hand, make sense in its own terms. There could be issues of substantive invalidity which were very complex, where the error was not apparent from the face of the impugned norm. There could, equally, be instances of procedural invalidity which were relatively simple and required little by way of extrinsic evidence.

[9] *Chief Adjudication Officer v Foster* [1993] A.C. 754; *Howker v Secretary of State for Work and Pensions* [2003] I.C.R. 405.
[10] *Boddington v British Transport Police* [1999] 2 A.C. 143; *Howker*, n.9; *R. v Searby (Alan Edward)* [2003] 3 C.M.L.R. 15; P. Craig, "Collateral Attack, Procedural Exclusivity and Judicial Review" (1998) 114 L.Q.R. 535; C. Forsyth, "Collateral Challenge and the Foundations of Judicial Review: Orthodoxy Vindicated and Procedural Exclusivity Rejected" [1998] P.L. 364.
[11] *Bugg v DPP* [1993] Q.B. 473.
[12] *Boddington*, n.10, 168–171.

There was, therefore, no reason to conclude that magistrates would be better able to deal with substantive as opposed to procedural challenges. It was, on the other hand, often impossible, or at least very difficult, to preserve the distinction between procedural and substantive invalidity. The test laid down by Woolf L.J. would therefore force magistrates to engage in difficult categorisation exercises to decide whether they were able to consider the invalidity. This was particularly undesirable given that the categorisation of the invalidity one way or the other could mean the difference between committing a criminal offence and not committing such an offence.

C. The Relationship between Direct and Collateral Attack: Qualifications to the General Principle

23–003 The general principle that defects that can be raised in direct actions can also be raised collaterally is, however, subject to certain qualifications.

i. Interpretation of the particular statute

23–004 A court may interpret a particular statute to preclude or limit collateral attack.[13] Moreover, merely because one individual might have a direct action should not necessarily mean that a different individual should be able to use this invalidity in a collateral action.[14] It was accepted in _Boddington_ that there could be cases where a collateral challenge to the validity of an order could be defeated by statutory provisions, which indicated that only a direct action was possible.

This is exemplified by _Wicks_.[15] The House of Lords held that whether a defendant charged with failing to comply with an order made under statutory powers was entitled by way of defence in criminal proceedings to challenge the lawfulness of the order depended on the construction of the statute. There could be cases where the statute allowed any public law claim to be raised collaterally by way of defence. There could also be cases where the statute on its true construction merely required that the act which had been done under statutory authority appeared to be formally valid and had not been quashed by judicial review. In this latter type of case, only the formal validity of the act was of relevance before the court in a prosecution.[16]

The premise behind _Boddington_ is, however, that the normal position is that a defendant should be able to raise the invalidity of the byelaw, or an administrative decision based on it, by way of defence in a criminal case. It will be for the prosecution to convince the court that the exception based on the reasoning in _Wicks_ is applicable in the instant case.

---

[13] _R. v Davey_ [1899] 2 Q.B. 301.
[14] See, e.g., Rubinstein's cogent critique of _DPP v Head_ [1959] A.C. 83, n.1, 47.
[15] _R. v Wicks_ [1998] A.C. 92. See also, _DPP v Memery_ [2003] R.T.R. 18; _DPP v T_ [2007] 1 W.L.R. 209.
[16] Compare _Palacegate Properties Ltd v London Borough of Camden_ [2001] A.C.D. 23, with _Dilieto v Ealing London Borough Council_ [2000] Q.B. 381.

ii. The impact of the general law on remedies
The reform of remedies raised important questions as to how far an indi-   **23–005**
vidual should be able to challenge a decision outside the Ord.53 procedure.
This issue will be considered in detail later,[17] but a very brief summary can
be provided here.

The House of Lords held in *O'Reilly v Mackman*[18] that the application for
judicial review was the only way to secure a remedy against a public body
(procedural exclusivity), the rationale being that this procedure contained
certain protections for a public body that would be circumvented by
bringing an action in another way. This was always subject to exceptions,
most notably where the invalidity of the decision arose as a collateral matter
in a claim for the infringement of private rights. Later case law has made it
clear that procedural exclusivity will only be insisted upon where the sole
object of the action is to challenge a public law act or decision. It does not
apply in a civil case when an individual seeks to establish private law rights
that cannot be determined without examining the validity of the public law
decision. Nor does it apply where a defendant in a civil or criminal case
seeks to defend himself by questioning the validity of the public law
decision.[19]

iii. Positive and negative decisions
Collateral attack will by its nature not normally be available to challenge   **23–006**
decisions denying an individual something which the person desires, unless
the individual can show some common law or statutory right to it. If a
public body refuses a licence or a supplementary benefit then if the applicant
does nothing no licence will be granted or no benefit will be paid. Attack by
prerogative order or declaration is the only recourse available to the
aggrieved individual. This may be contrasted with a demand by the public
body for rates or duties. The individual can wait to be sued and then assert
the invalidity of the order.

iv. De facto judges and officers
A long-standing exception to collateral attack applies where the appoint-   **23–007**
ment of judges or public officers is defective. The courts have not allowed
collateral challenge where the judge or officer was acting de facto as such
even though the appointment was de jure invalid.[20] The rationale for this
limitation is essentially practical: annulment of all the officers' subsequent
acts because the appointment was invalid could have serious consequences.[21]

The protection accorded to de facto officers appears to have its origin in
connection with officers or judges whose appointment was valid when made,

---

[17] See Ch.26.
[18] [1983] 2 A.C. 237.
[19] Subject to the point about the interpretation of a particular statute made above.
[20] Rubinstein, n.1, 205–208.
[21] *Crew v Vernon* (1627) Cro. Car. 97.

but where the appointment was subsequently rendered invalid.[22] The doctrine has, however, been extended to encompass appointments invalid at their inception. Thus, a justice who had not taken the requisite oath was still to be regarded as a de facto justice[23]; the acts of assessors and collectors of taxes who did not fulfil residency requirements were treated as valid[24]; a rate levied by vestrymen, one of whom was not duly elected, was not annulled[25]; and the doctrine also covered a judge who was mistaken as to the status of the court in which he was sitting, rather than as to the nature or the extent of his own jurisdiction.[26]

It has moreover been held in *Coppard*[27] that the doctrine not only validated acts done by a de facto judge, but validated the judge's office itself. Thus a person who was believed and believed himself to have the necessary judicial authority was regarded in law as possessing such authority. A de facto judge was a tribunal whose authority was established by the common law. This complied with art.6 ECHR, provided that the doctrine did not lead to the ratification of acts of those who knew themselves to lack authority, did not operate arbitrarily and was limited to the correction of mistakes of form rather than of substance.

There are nonetheless limits to the doctrine. It appears to operate only where there is some "colour of authority".[28] It is in any event now clear from *Coppard*[29] that the de facto doctrine cannot validate the acts, nor ratify the authority, of a person who, though believed by the world to be a judge of the court in which he sits, knows that he is not. A person who knows he lacks authority includes a person who has shut his eyes to that fact when it is obvious, but not a person who has simply neglected to find it out. Such a person is termed a usurper.

2. VOID AND VOIDABLE: CORRECT AND INCORRECT USES

23–008   If a public body makes a decision that is ultra vires this means that it had no power to make such a decision, and the decision should in principle have

---

[22] *Re Aldridge* (1893) 15 N.Z.L.R. 361, 369–370.
[23] *Margate Pier Company v Hannam* (1819) 3 B. & Ald. 266.
[24] *Waterloo Bridge Company v Cull* (1858) 1 El. & El. 213, affirmed (1859) 1 El. & El. 245.
[25] *Scadding v Lorant* (1851) 3 H.L.C. 418.
[26] *Baldock v Webster* [2006] Q.B. 315.
[27] *Coppard v Customs and Excise Commissioners* [2003] Q.B. 1428.
[28] *Baldock*, n.26, para.15. This is in accord with the preponderance of earlier authority. In *Crew*, n.21, the commissioners' acts seemed only to be valid until they received notice of the death of James I. In *R. v Bedford Level Corporation* (1805) 6 East 356 the officer in question was a deputy whose principal had died. It was held that once the principal dies and this becomes known the *de facto* authority of the deputy ceases. In *Adams v Adams* [1971] P. 188 the court rejected the argument that a Rhodesian judge held office *de facto* if not *de jure*, one reason being that the illegality of the Rhodesian regime was widely known. The court in *Aldridge*, n.22, was more divided on this question
[29] *Coppard*, n.27, para.18. See also *Fawdry & Co v Murfitt* [2003] Q.B. 104.

"no effect", although, as we shall see, it might have to be compromised in certain cases because of the draconian consequences which can ensue.

A. Void: A Relative not Absolute Concept

The effect of finding that a decision is ultra vires is best approached from first principles. If the decision-maker had no power then the decision should have no effect. Translated into the lingua franca of our profession, we would say that such a decision was void ab initio, retrospectively null. Void is, however, a relative not an absolute concept, the meaning of which can be explained as follows.[30]

23–009

In administrative law there are rules of locus standi, time limits, and other reasons for refusing a remedy such as acquiescence. It is only if an applicant for relief surmounts these hurdles that a remedy will be given. The sequence is therefore as follows. An administrative decision is taken. An individual feels aggrieved and challenges the decision. *If* the court finds that the individual has standing, is within the time limits, and that there is no reason to deny a remedy *then* the decision will be found to be void ab initio. This is a description of the conclusion that an ultra vires act has occurred, and that it is being challenged by the right person in the correct proceedings.[31] It is, as Lord Diplock said,[32] confusing to speak of the terms void or voidable before the validity of an order has been pronounced on by a court of competent jurisdiction.

If, by way of contrast, void were to be used in an absolute as opposed to a relative sense the word "void" would, in effect, be moved earlier in the sentence. This would now read: if there is an ultra vires act, the finding thus made is void ab initio and therefore any person can take advantage of it.

---

[30] H.W.R. Wade, "Unlawful Administrative Action: Void or Voidable?" (1967) 83 L.Q.R. 499, (1968) 84 L.Q.R. 95; M. Akehust, "Void or Voidable? Natural Justice and Unnatural Meanings" (1968) 31 M.L.R. 2, 138; P. Cane, "A Fresh Look at Punton's Case" (1980) 43 M.L.R. 266; D. Oliver, "Void and Voidable in Administrative Law: A Problem of Legal Recognition" [1981] C.L.P. 43; G. Peiris, "Natural Justice and Degrees of Invalidity of Administrative Action" [1983] P.L. 634; M. Taggart, "Rival Theories of Invalidity in Administrative Law: Some Practical and Theoretical Consequences", in M. Taggart (ed.), *Judicial Review of Administrative Action in the 1980s: Problems and Prospects* (Oxford University Press, 1986), 70–103; C. Forsyth, "'The Metaphysic of Nullity': Invalidity, Conceptual Reasoning and the Rule of Law", in C. Forsyth and I. Hare (eds), *The Golden Metwand and the Crooked Cord* (Oxford University Press, 1998), 141–160 .

[31] In *Calvin v Carr* [1980] A.C. 574 the plaintiff had been found guilty of an offence connected with horse racing, and his conviction upheld on appeal to the Jockey Club. He argued that since the original hearing was a nullity owing to a procedural defect, therefore the internal appeal body could not cure any defect in the original hearing. This was rejected by the court. It should, however, be made clear that nothing within the traditional idea of void justified the plaintiff's argument. Until the original decision was challenged it remained valid. If it was never challenged at all it would always be valid. If and when it was challenged it would be void *if* there was a breach of natural justice: *whether* there had been such a breach depended on whether the internal appellate proceeding could cure any defect in the original hearing, the very question before the court. The traditional concept of void tells us nothing about this one way or the other.

[32] *Hoffmann-La Roche Co AG v Secretary of State for Trade and Industry* [1975] A.C. 295, 366; *Isaacs v Robertson* [1985] A.C. 97; *Bugg*, n.11; *R. v Hendon Justices Ex p. DPP* [1993] C.O.D. 61.

Applied literally there could be no limits of standing and no discretion in granting the remedy.

Two examples of the use of void or nullity in this absolute sense may be given. In *Ridge*, Lord Evershed stated that because the declaration is a discretionary remedy, therefore a breach of natural justice must render the decision voidable and not void. This was because his Lordship felt that if the decision was a complete nullity the court would have to say so in some form or another.[33] A similar usage is apparent in *Durayappah*.[34] A minister dissolved the Jaffna City Council after a commissioner had made a report to him. The commissioner had inquired into the council's activities, but had not given a hearing to any member of it. The mayor sought certiorari, claiming that the dissolution was in breach of natural justice. Lord Upjohn, giving the decision of the Privy Council, found that there had been a breach of natural justice, and then considered whether the mayor could complain of this. His Lordship stated that this depended upon whether the decision was a complete nullity, of which any person having a legitimate interest could complain, or whether it was voidable only at the instance of the party affected.[35] Lord Upjohn found that it was the latter. It could not therefore be attacked by the mayor when the council had chosen not to challenge it.[36]

23–010   Lord Evershed and Lord Upjohn used void or nullity in the absolute sense described above. An ultra vires act was found, and it was said not to be void because that would leave the court no discretion in granting the remedy and no control over standing. This can be juxtaposed to the relative meaning of the term void: it is only if, in addition to finding an ultra vires act, the person has standing and there are no other reasons to refuse the remedy that the decision will be held to be void ab initio.

Lord Diplock endorsed this relative concept of void in *Hoffmann-La Roche*,[37] where he stated that *Durayappah* was best explained as a case relating to standing. There is, therefore, nothing odd in a decision that can be rendered void by one person but not another, or in a decision which would be void if challenged within the correct time, being valid if not so challenged.[38] When a successful challenge is made by the right person in the correct proceedings the decision is retrospectively null.

It should not, however, be thought that an aggrieved individual must always challenge an action directly via the prerogative orders. If the decision requires, for example, a payment by the individual to a public body then the individual could resist the demand, wait to be sued, and then attack the

---

[33] *Ridge v Baldwin* [1964] A.C. 40, 87–88, 91–92.
[34] *Durayappah v Fernando* [1967] 2 A.C. 337.
[35] *Durayappah*, n.34, 353–354. Lord Upjohn stated that in *Ridge* Lord Reid and Lord Hodson had used the word void in the sense that Lord Upjohn is using the word nullity here. There is, with respect, no evidence for this.
[36] *Durayappah*, n.34, 354–355. Lord Upjohn went on to say that if it was challenged by the right person then the decision would be void *ab initio*.
[37] *Hoffmann-La Roche*, n.32, 366. See also, Lord Wilberforce, 358.
[38] *Smith v East Elloe Rural District Council* [1956] A.C. 736, 769, *per* Lord Radcliffe.

decision collaterally. In this limited sense statements by Lord Denning M.R. that there is no need for an order to quash a nullity are correct[39]; the individual can impugn the decision collaterally rather than directly. If the finding is not attacked directly or collaterally it will, however, remain valid irrespective of whether, if it had been challenged, it would have been ultra vires. It will not in some Houdini sense disappear.

B. The Decision as to whether an Error Renders the Administrative Act Void

We have seen thus far that if a decision is challenged by the right person, in the right proceedings, within the relevant time limits, it will be void. The applicant must however show that the error was of kind that led to the challenged action being outside the decision-maker's power. This will normally not be problematic. Where a jurisdictional error, abuse of discretion or failure to comply with natural justice has been proven, the court will regard the decision as being outside the power of the decision-maker.

23–011

The courts have been more cautious in relation to procedural irregularities. The traditional approach was to distinguish between procedural requirements that were mandatory and those that were directory.[40] The assumption was that any breach of the former would render the decision void. The courts now pay less regard to the mandatory/directory distinction.

In *London and Clydeside Estates*,[41] Lord Hailsham held that the terms mandatory and directory could often be expressive of over-rigid classification. In *Ravichandran*,[42] Lord Woolf M.R. accepted that if statutory language states that a certain procedural requirement "shall" be done, then the requirement is not optional. It was nonetheless for the court to determine the consequences of non-compliance with such a requirement. A court should, said Lord Woolf, be slow to find that any departure from the procedural requirement rendered the decision retrospectively null. The decision as to whether a procedural requirement was mandatory or directory was only the first step. The court should also take account of other factors in deciding on the consequences of non-compliance. The court should consider whether there had been substantial compliance with the requirement, and whether this could meet the statutory condition. It should consider whether the non-compliance was capable of being waived, and whether it had been waived in the particular case. If the provision was not capable of being waived, or had not been waived, the court should then address the consequences of the non-compliance.

---

[39] *Head*, n.5, 111–112; *R. v Paddington Valuation Officer Ex p. Peachey Property Corporation Ltd* [1966] 1 Q.B. 380, 402. Reference should, however, be made to the discussion of the presumptive exclusivity of s.31 of the Supreme Court Act 1981, Ch.26.

[40] See, e.g., *Johnson v Secretary of State for Health* [2001] Lloyds Rep. Med. 385.

[41] *London and Clydeside Estates Ltd v Aberdeen District Council* [1980] 1 W.L.R. 182.

[42] *Secretary of State for the Home Department v Ravichandran* [2000] 1 W.L.R. 354; *Westminster City Council v Mendoza* [2001] EWCA Civ 216; *Apex Asphalt & Paving Co Ltd v Office of Fair Trading* [2005] C.A.T. 4; *R. (on the application of McKay) v First Secretary of State* [2005] EWCA Civ 774. Compare *Wallace v Quinn* [2004] N.I. 164; *Seal v Chief Constable of South Wales* [2005] 1 W.L.R. 3183.

C. The Consequences of Holding that an Act is Void

23–012   If the correct person successfully challenges the administrative act in the correct proceedings, within the time limits, and there are no bars to relief then the act will be void in the sense of retrospectively null. The implications that this has for other acts done after the act which was successfully challenged, is a separate conceptual issue, as exemplified by the case law on de facto officers considered above. The initial invalid act will often appear to be factually valid and people may well have acted on that assumption. Forsyth correctly points out that the validity of the later acts depends on the legal powers of the second actor: "the crucial issue to be determined is whether that second actor has legal power to act validly notwithstanding the invalidity of the first act", and this is to be decided against the background that "an unlawful act is void".[43]

This issue will be determined by looking at the relationship between the two sets of acts. It should nonetheless be recognised that the empowering statute will normally provide little if any guidance as to this issue, and that it will be for the reviewing court to decide whether any of the acts done pursuant to the initial unlawful act can be regarded as valid.

In some circumstances, the nullity of the initial act will not render unlawful everything done thereunder.[44] In *Boddington*, Lord Browne-Wilkinson stated that an ultra vires act may be capable of having some legal effect between the doing of the act and the recognition of its invalidity by a court, since people will have regulated their lives on the basis that the act is valid: "the subsequent recognition of its invalidity cannot rewrite history as to all other matters done in the meantime in reliance on its validity".[45] This is exemplified by *Percy*.[46] The plaintiffs had been arrested for breach of certain byelaws later held to be invalid. They brought an action for damages against the police for false imprisonment and wrongful arrest. The court rejected the claim. It reasoned that at the time when the plaintiffs were arrested the byelaws were apparently valid. While a subsequent finding that the byelaws were invalid entitled the plaintiffs to have the conviction set aside, it did not transform what, judged at the time, was a lawful discharge of the police officer's duty into what might later be regarded as tortious conduct.

In other circumstances, the nullity of the initial act will have more far-reaching consequences for acts done prior to the nullity being found to exist. This is evident from *Evans (No.2)*.[47] The applicant had been sentenced to a term of imprisonment, and was entitled to conditional release after a specified period. The prison governor calculated this period in the light of the prevailing case law. This method of calculation was held to be wrong in a subsequent case, the consequence being that she should have been released

---

[43] Forsyth, n.30, 159.
[44] Forsyth, n.30, 146–150.
[45] n.10, 164. See also, Lord Slynn, 165.
[46] *Percy v Hall* [1997] Q.B. 924, 950–952; *R. v Central London County Court Ex p. London* [1999] Q.B. 1260.
[47] *R. v Governor of Brockhill Prison Ex p. Evans (No.2)* [2001] 2 A.C. 19.

earlier. She claimed damages for false imprisonment for this period. The House of Lords held that false imprisonment was a strict liability tort, and that a court decision was declaratory of the law as it had always been, even when overruling prior case law on the point. The assumption was that where previous authorities are overruled, decisions to that effect operate retrospectively.[48] The imprisonment was therefore not lawful and the damages action could lie. Lord Browne-Wilkinson did not however think that the ruling in *Evans (No.2)* was necessarily decisive of the issues that arise where a defendant acted in accord with statutory provisions that are later held to be ultra vires and void.[49]

D. Voidable: Different Uses

The term voidable has not been used uniformly in the case law. At least four distinct meanings have been attributed to the term.   **23–013**

i. Indicative of the need to challenge

Lord Morris of Borth-y-Gest used the term voidable in this sense in *Ridge*.[50]   **23–014**
In this context voidable is simply descriptive of the need for the Chief Constable to challenge his dismissal. Unless he did so the decision of the Watch Committee would prevail. In this sense all decisions are voidable. His Lordship went on to say that if and when the court found for the individual the decision would be null and void.[51]

ii. An alternative to locus standi

This connotation of the term voidable is exemplified by *Durayappah*.[52] The   **23–015**
Privy Council clearly did not wish the mayor to be able to challenge the dissolution of the City Council. The Privy Council therefore drew a dichotomy between defects which any person having a legitimate interest could take advantage of, which were nullities, and those defects which only the person affected could raise. The term voidable was used to describe errors of the latter type, and the Court held that the case fell within this category. The distinction between acts which are null, and those which are merely voidable, manifested itself in the rules of standing. Why the Privy Council did not wish the mayor to succeed will be considered later.

---

[48] *Evans (No.2)*, n.47, 36.
[49] *Evans (No.2)*, n.47, 27.
[50] n.33, 125.
[51] In *Durayappah* [1967] 2 A.C. 337, 354 Lord Upjohn stated that Lord Morris of Borth-y-Gest had agreed with Lord Evershed and Lord Devlin in *Ridge* in holding that a breach of the *audi alteram partem* rule only made the decision voidable. This is, with respect, not so. Lord Morris was not using voidable in the same sense as Lord Evershed and Lord Devlin See, *Hounslow London Borough Council v Twickenham Garden Developments* [1971] Ch.233, 258.
[52] n.34.

iii. The gravity of the error

23–016 In some cases the term voidable has been used to indicate the relative gravity of the defect. This is exemplified by the *Paddington* case.[53] The basis on which a rating list had been compiled was challenged in the courts. The rating authority argued that if the list were struck down there would be widespread administrative upheaval, particularly if the invalidity meant that the list was retrospectively null. To circumvent this problem Lord Denning M.R. said that a grave invalidity would render the list a nullity. There would be no need for an order to quash a list tainted by such a defect. Less serious defects would only render the list voidable, with the result that any invalidity would only be prospective, not retrospective. The rating assessments could remain valid until replaced by a new list.

This reasoning is questionable. The concept of a grave defect leading to a nullity which need not be challenged either directly or collaterally, and yet can still be ignored without ill-effects to the individual, is difficult to comprehend. The offending order will not somehow disappear of its own accord. The formulation of the term voidable is equally questionable. On traditional theory, as it stood at that time, a non-jurisdictional error could only be struck down if it was an error of law on the face of the record. It is hard to discern such a patent error in the *Paddington* case. The reasons why Lord Denning M.R. distorted the meanings of void and voidable in order to avoid the consequences of retrospective nullity will be discussed below.

iv. Errors of law within jurisdiction

23–017 The one context within which it was legitimate to use the term voidable was as descriptive of an error of law within jurisdiction. Such errors are not, by definition, jurisdictional. They indicate that the tribunal made a mistake, not that it lacked the power to act. Such mistakes are valid until quashed, and actions taken in pursuance of an order tainted by a patent non-jurisdictional error remained valid, even when the order had been quashed.

Thus, in *Head*[54] a man was convicted of carnal knowledge with a mental defective. He argued by way of defence that he could not be guilty since the medical certificates did not contain any evidence showing the woman to be a moral defective. The majority of the House of Lords upheld this argument and set the conviction aside. Lord Denning concurred in this result, but his reasoning differed. He stated that the defect in the detention order only rendered it voidable and not void. A voidable order would remain good until set aside. Thus at the time of the offence the detention order was still good, the woman was legally held, and the accused could be guilty of the crime charged.

The expansion in the scope of jurisdictional error, and the corresponding

[53] n.39, 401–402.
[54] n.5. Moral defective was one category of mental defective under the Mental Deficiency Act 1913 s.1.

demise of the category of error of law within jurisdiction means, however, that voidable will no longer have a role to play in this regard.

3. Void and Voidable: Theory, Reality and Judicial Discretion

It might well be thought that we have come to the end of our inquiry. We revealed the reasons why the courts used the term voidable; we found that the only justifiable use related to errors of law within jurisdiction; and we know that this category of error no longer generally exists. This all seems to point to the conclusion that we can discard the language of void and voidable. This is, in one sense, obviously true, since it is no longer needed to describe the differing effects of jurisdictional and non-jurisdictional errors.[55] There are, however, reasons for pressing the inquiry further.

23–018

The expanded scope of error of law still requires us to consider the consequences of such an error. The error will mean that the decision-maker had no power to make that decision and that, prima facie, it should be devoid of any effect from the date on which it was made. The language of nullity, voidness or invalidity describes those consequences.

It is moreover evident that the courts have not always used the term voidable to signify non-jurisdictional errors. They have employed it for other reasons, and it is necessary to understand why they have done so. The general answer is that some courts have sought to escape from the conclusions that will follow if they find that the contested decision was made outside jurisdiction and hence retrospectively null or invalid. They have used the term voidable in order to express the conclusion that the contested order should only be ineffective from the date when it was found to be invalid by the court, and not from the date when it was first made.

The general argument that will be made below is that the concept of retrospective invalidity, in the relative sense considered above, is the correct starting point in principle. We should not lose sight of this. Cases will arise in which the full effects of retrospective invalidity will be unacceptable, and where the principle will, therefore, have to be modified. The most appropriate manner in which to express these modifications is through discretion exercised at the remedial level, not by manipulating the concepts of void or voidable.

A. The Reasons for Judicial Departure from the Traditional Meanings of Void and Voidable: Administrative Convenience, Justice and Rigidity

Traditional theory, derived from first principles, is that an ultra vires decision should be void, using that term in its relative sense. The voidness will be

23–019

---

[55] *Boddington*, n.10, 158–159, Lord Irvine of Lairg L.C.; Sir John Laws, "Illegality: The Problem of Jurisdiction", in M. Supperstone and J. Goudie (eds), *Judicial Review* (Butterworths, 2nd. edn, 1997), Ch.4, 6–4.11.

retrospective, invalidating action taken in the period between the making of the order and the court decision. Voidable decisions involve only prospective and not retrospective invalidity. The tribunal remains within its jurisdiction, but makes a mistake. Action taken in reliance on the order until the time at which it is struck down will be upheld. The invalidity will be only prospective. The only type of defect that should be termed voidable is an error of law on the face of the record. Other non-patent errors of law within jurisdiction would also be voidable, but could only be subject to appeal and not review. It is apparent that not all courts have used the terms void and voidable in this way, the common denominator being a dislike of the results produced by retrospective nullity. Three reasons for this can be discerned.

Administrative convenience was the prime consideration in the *Paddington* case.[56] Lord Denning M.R. wished to characterise the error as voidable in order that the challenged rating list could remain in existence until a new list was prepared. If the error made the list retrospectively void then it, and possibly other such lists, would never have existed and there would have been a gargantuan unravelling task for the rating authorities to perform. Considerations of administrative convenience have not been the only factors at work.

A second reason for departing from traditional ideas of retrospective nullity has been to facilitate the attainment of a *"just result"*. In *Head*[57] Lord Denning was reluctant to allow an accused to escape a criminal charge by relying upon a defect in the certificate. Hence his Lordship's characterisation of the defect as making the certificate only voidable: the woman was therefore lawfully detained at the time of the offence, and the accused could be found guilty.[58] The whole case proceeded on the assumption that the accused should be able to take advantage of the defect within the certificate. There is however, as noted by Rubinstein,[59] no necessary reason why conditions for detention, which could have been legitimately raised by the detainee, should have been available for the benefit of the accused.

More recently in *Ejaz*[60] the court declined to find that a mistaken certificate of naturalisation was a nullity, primarily because this could lead to great hardship, since a person's status could be affected retrospectively many years after the certificate had been granted. The court therefore construed a mistaken certificate to have validity unless and until it was successfully revoked by the Home Secretary.

A third reason why some courts have expressed dissatisfaction with traditional ideas of nullity is that they are felt to be *too rigid*. In *London and Clydeside Estates*,[61] Lord Hailsham held that terms such as mandatory and

---

[56] n.39. Similar fears appear to underlie *Durayappah*, n.34.

[57] n.5, 111–112. Lord Denning did not in the end dissent, 113, 114.

[58] See also, *Ridge*, n.33, 87–92, where Lord Evershed appeared to believe that it was only by terming a breach of natural justice "voidable" that the court could prevent undeserving applicants from seizing upon a technical breach of these rules. This is a *non-sequitur* even in its own terms.

[59] n.1, 47.

[60] *R. v Secretary of State for the Home Department Ex p. Ejaz (Naheed)* [1994] Q.B. 496.

[61] n.41.

directory, void and voidable, and nullity could often be expressive of over-rigid classification. When a public body failed to comply with a statutory requirement there could be different results. At one end of the spectrum, there would be instances of egregious breach of a fundamental obligation: the individual could simply use that defect as a defence without having to take positive action. At the other end of the spectrum there could be trivial defects that would probably be ignored by the courts. In the middle, however, there was a large group of cases in which it would be wise for the individual to challenge the public action, and where the effect of the breach would be dependent upon the circumstances. Terms such as void and voidable should not cramp the exercise of judicial discretion in determining the consequences of the breach.[62] We shall consider below whether concepts such as void and voidable entail unwarranted rigidity.[63]

B. Resolving the Problem

i. First principles

It is not uncommon to see statements that the concepts of void and voidable   **23–020**
are unnatural inhabitants of the administrative law world. They are perceived as alien concepts grafted onto public law from the world of contract and status.[64] This is mistaken. Even if those terms originated within private law, and this is by no means clear, they have been in administrative law ever since we have had such jurisprudence for over 300 years.[65]

The traditional meaning of the term void, in the sense of retrospective nullity, captures the natural conclusion that if a decision-maker had no power to act then the act should be of no consequences. As Lord Diplock stated,[66]

"It would, however, be inconsistent with the doctrine of ultra vires as it has been developed in English law as a means of controlling abuse of power by the executive arm of government if the judgment of a court in proceedings properly constituted that a statutory instrument was ultra vires were to have any lesser consequence in law than to render the instrument incapable of ever having had any legal effect upon the rights or duties of the parties to the proceedings . . ."

The danger of Lord Hailsham's reasoning in *London and Clydeside Estates*[67] is that this important point of principle will be lost sight of. His Lordship

---

[62] *London and Clydeside Estates Ltd*, n.41, 190. See also, Lord Keith, 203. See further, Lord Hailsham's comments in *Chief Constable of the North Wales Police v Evans* [1982] 1 W.L.R. 1155, 1162–1163.
[63] See below, paras 23–020—23–022.
[64] e.g. *Isaacs v Robertson* [1985] A.C. 97, 102–103.
[65] Rubinstein, n.1, Chs 1–4.
[66] *Hoffmann-La Roche*, n.32, 365; *R. (on the application of Wirral HA) v Mental Health Review Tribunal* [2001] EWCA Civ 1901.
[67] n.41, 189.

was correct to point out that there might be some statutory provisions where the consequences of the breach should be taken into account when determining the remedy.[68] This has been affirmed in *Ravichandran*.[69]

The recognition that this is so is, nonetheless, a separate issue from the void/voidable distinction. A condition precedent to the application of retrospective nullity is that the error is regarded as taking the decision-maker outside its power. Whether this should be the case is, as we have seen,[70] problematic in relation to procedural irregularities. The courts have decided that the consequences of the breach should be considered in order to determine the result. This does not affect the conclusion that where the consequences are serious enough, the result should be retrospective nullity.

It is true that the concept of retrospective invalidity can give rise to awkward problems. The problems are the exceptions. Retrospective nullity is and should be the rule. If we need to depart from the principle so be it, but let us be clear that we are departing from the norm, and let us provide cogent explanations for doing so. It is for this reason, amongst others, that the exceptions should operate via the discretion to refuse or limit the remedy, rather than through a sleight of hand over the meanings of void and voidable. There are three related problems with the manipulation of the terms void and voidable.

First, it conceals what is taking place. It provides a convenient mask of legal form to hide reality. Instead of saying that an applicant cannot, because of the administrative consequences, be granted the desired remedy, the applicant is told that the nature of the defect unfortunately only renders the decision voidable. Second, such manipulation produces confusion by ascribing numerous meanings to the same terms, which when analysed make little sense. Third, there is a danger that what may have been intended as only an ad hoc exception to the norm of retrospective nullity, an exception justified by the facts of the particular case, will become unintentionally generalised. The terminology takes on a life of its own, a result easily arrived at when the original rationale for using that language is concealed. Legal form, like Frankenstein's creation, becomes unresponsive to the commands of its creator.

ii. The preferable approach: remedial discretion

23–021   The most appropriate way to resolve problems is through discretion to refuse a remedy, or limit its application, so that it only operates prospectively.[71] This does not mean that we should play fast and loose with this

---

[68] There are obvious analogies here with the condition-warranty distinction in the law of contract and the development of innominate terms.

[69] n.42.

[70] See above, para.23–011.

[71] For examples of cases where the courts have exercised discretion to refuse relief on a variety of grounds, see amongst many, *R. v Herrod Ex p. Leeds City Council* [1976] Q.B. 540; *R. v Mayor of Peterborough* (1875) 44 L.J. Q.B. 85; *R. v Hampstead Borough Council Ex p. Woodward* (1917) 116 L.T. 213; *Re Bristol and North Somerset Railway Co* (1877) 3 Q.B.D. 10, 12; *R. v Bristol Corporation Ex p. Hendy* [1974] 1 W.L.R. 498, 503. For detailed consideration of the factors which the courts will regard as precluding relief, see below paras 25–009—25–010, 25–018, 25–036, 26–055—26–057.

discretion. It means that if a departure from the norm of retrospective nullity is warranted we should say that the decision is void, but that for reasons of, for example, practicality the effects must be confined to the future, or that the remedy must be monetary, rather than a physical undoing of what has transpired. There are indications that our courts see the utility of prospective rulings,[72] although there are also differences of judicial view.[73] The ECJ has employed the technique on a number of occasions.[74]

It is also possible to vest the courts with a more general power to determine the remedial consequences of invalidity.[75] Thus art.231 EC, para.2, provides that in the case of a regulation the ECJ shall, if it considers this necessary, state which of the effects of the regulation it has declared void shall be considered as definitive. This has been used to limit the temporal effect of the Court's ruling when it annuls a regulation. The ECJ has extended this power to directives[76] and decisions.[77] Considerations of legal certainty will often be paramount in this respect. The ECJ will be inclined to apply the second paragraph of art.231 in order to retain in force the contested measure until a new measure can be adopted in order to avoid the drastic consequences that can be attendant on retroactive nullity.[78]

iii. The relevance of compensation

It has been argued that manipulation of the terms void and voidable is often a mask to avoid paying damages. Thus if English law developed a more general compensatory remedy for harm caused by ultra vires acts many of the problems concerned with void and voidable would disappear. Lord Wilberforce expressed a powerful argument along these lines.[79] There is no doubt an argument in favour of developing a remedy for loss caused by ultra vires administrative action which will be considered below.[80]

23–022

The relevance of this to the general debate on void and voidable must, however, be kept within perspective. It is not a panacea that will solve all complexities attendant upon use of these terms. The common type of case is

---

[72] C. Lewis, "Retrospective and Prospective Rulings in Administrative Law" [1988] PL 78; Sir Harry Woolf, *Protection of the Public—A New Challenge* (Sweet & Maxwell, 1990), 53–56; Lady Justice Arden, "Prospective Overruling" (2004) 115 L.Q.R. 7.

[73] *Evans (No.2)*, n.47, 26–27, 35–37.

[74] *Defrenne v Sabena* (43/75) [1976] E.C.R. 471; *Blaizot v University of Liege* (24/86) [1988] E.C.R. 379.

[75] P. Craig, *EU Administrative Law* (Oxford University Press, 2006), Ch.20.

[76] *European Parliament v Council* (C-295/90) [1992] E.C.R. I–4193; *European Parliament v Council (Road Taxes)* (C-21/94) [1995] E.C.R. I-1827.

[77] *European Parliament v Council (Government Procurement)* (C-360/93) [1996] E.C.R. I-1195, paras 32–36; *European Parliament v Council (Telematic Networks)* (C-22/96) [1998] E.C.R. I-3231.

[78] *Commission v Council (Generalized Tariff Preferences)* (51/87) [1988] ECR 5459, paras 21–22; *European Parliament v Council* (C-392/95) [1997] E.C.R. I-3213, paras 25–27; *Portugal v Commission* (C-59/96) [1998] E.C.R. I-7379, paras 52–53; *Austria v Council* (C-443/00) [2003] E.C.R. I-8549, paras 103–106; *European Parliament v Council* (C-93/00) [2001] E.C.R. I-10119, paras 47–48.

[79] *Hoffmann-La Roche*, n.32, 358–359.

[80] See Ch.29; P. Craig, "Compensation in Public Law" (1980) 96 L.Q.R. 413.

where the individual asserts the invalidity of an administrative act, and the public body raises the argument that this could have drastic administrative consequences. A developed system of damages could be useful. Presuming that the public body's fears are well founded, a court could say that the action was void, but that the only remedy was compensation, and not an order to quash the act or declare it to be null. This could well be the most equitable solution.

It is, however, important to understand that the addition of a damages remedy does not dispel the need for judicial discretion. Where there was a real prospect of administrative upheaval the court would use its discretion to restrict the results of the decision being void instead of juggling with void and voidable. The invalidity would show only in the legal liability of the public body to pay compensation. This may be a preferable way forward. At present, faced with pleas of administrative chaos, the court either rejects them, or manipulates void and voidable, or the grant of the remedy, to give effect to such arguments. The ability to give compensation would provide added flexibility. The presence of such a remedy would not, however, show that judicial discretion was unnecessary. It would, rather, provide a more convenient and equitable framework within which to exercise that discretion.

iv. The relevance of parliamentary redress

23–023 The courts could turn a deaf ear to pleas of injustice or administrative chaos, and contend that it would be for Parliament to redress any resulting confusion. This may be warranted in some cases. There are however practical and conceptual difficulties with the idea that Parliament can remedy the problem.

In *practical* terms, the possibility that Parliament could pass a series of one-off pieces of legislation to remedy the effects of retrospective nullity is distinctly unlikely. The *conceptual* or *constitutional* problems are more severe. Let us make the sequence of events clear. The court states that administrative action is retrospectively void and this produces problems because it will, for example, involve large expenditure, or losses in terms of the destruction of half-finished buildings. Parliament is pressed to intervene. The problem with any such intervention is that it would constitute retrospective legislation, which takes away peoples' rights, those having been given by the court's judgment. Such legislation has always been frowned upon, and correctly so.[81]

---

[81] *Burmah Oil Co Ltd v Lord Advocate* [1965] A.C. 75, and the subsequent War Damage Act 1965.

4. VOID AND VOIDABLE: NATURAL JUSTICE

The problem of whether decisions are void or voidable has been particularly **23–024**
prevalent in the context of natural justice.

A. Hearings
The majority view in *Ridge*[82] was that failure to comply with the rules as to **23–025**
hearings rendered the decision void. This is in accord with precedent and
principle. The rationale for regarding such a failure as leading to a void
decision was expressed by Lord Selbourne L.C.: "there would be no decision
within the meaning of the statute if there were anything of that sort done
contrary to the essence of justice".[83]

There have been many other cases where the courts have stated that
a failure to hear renders the decision void or a nullity. Thus, the action of a
committee, which purported to expel a person from a club without a hearing,
was held to be null and void, as was the refusal of a pension to a policeman
who had resigned from the force.[84] Cases of collateral attack are also
instructive.[85] A number of these cases explicitly held that a failure to hear
rendered the decision void.[86] Even where this was not so stated it was implicit
in the ability to attack the decision collaterally: if a failure to hear constituted only an error within jurisdiction the decision could not have been
attacked collaterally.

Despite this long line of authority Lord Evershed in *Ridge*[87] decided that
failure to hear only made the decision voidable. His Lordship did not find
the above cases convincing, and relied on *Osgood*[88] as support for the proposition that the court should only interfere if there had been a real and
substantial miscarriage of justice. This, said Lord Evershed, meant that the
decision must be voidable and not void.[89] Three comments are warranted.

---

[82] n.33, 80, *per* Lord Reid; 125–126, *per* Lord Morris of Borth-y-Gest; 135–136, *per* Lord
Hodson
[83] *Spackman v Plumstead District Board of Works* (1885) 10 App. Cas. 229, 240.
[84] *Fisher v Keane* (1878) 11 Ch. D. 353; *Lapointe v L'Association de Bienfaisance et de Retraite
de la Police de Montreal* [1906] A.C. 535. See also, *R. v North Ex p. Oakey* [1927] 1 K.B. 491; *R.
v Huntingdon Confirming Authority Ex p. George and Stanford Hotels Ltd* [1929] 1 K.B. 698;
Abbott v Sullivan [1952] 1 K.B. 189; *Disher v Disher* [1965] P. 31; *Hounslow London Borough
Council v Twickenham Garden Developments Ltd* [1971] Ch.233; *Firman v Ellis* [1978] Q.B. 886.
[85] *Cooper v Wandsworth Board of Works* (1863) 14 C.B. (N.S.) 182; *Hopkins v Smethwick Local
Board of Health* (1890) 24 Q.B.D. 712; *Capel v Child* (1832) 2 C. & J. 558; *Innes v Wylie* (1844) 1
Car. & K. 257; *Bonaker v Evans* (1850) 16 Q.B. 162; *Wood v Woad* (1874) L.R. 9 Ex. 190.
[86] As in *Capel, Innes, Bonaker* and *Wood*.
[87] n.33, 87–92.
[88] *Osgood v Nelson* (1872) L.R. 5 H.L. 636.
[89] *Ridge*, n.33, 91–92.

First, his Lordship's reasons for distinguishing those cases holding that a failure to hear made the decision void were unconvincing. Second, the *Osgood* case does not in reality support Lord Evershed's argument.[90] Third, even if the *Osgood* case did provide support for the idea that a finding should only be quashed if there had been a substantial miscarriage of justice, the conclusion that therefore the decision must be voidable rather than void does not follow. It is, like his Lordship's reasoning concerning the declaration, based upon an absolute rather than relative meaning of the term void.

Lord Diplock has stated[91] that a breach of the rules of natural justice should render the decision void. This has hopefully laid the argument to rest.

B. Bias

23–026   There are also several authorities for the proposition that bias results in a decision being void: a biased judge ceases to be a judge at all.[92] Further, if bias only made a finding voidable then declaration would not on traditional theory have been available, and the court could not have quashed in the presence of a no certiorari clause. Both have, however, occurred.[93] Despite these arguments some maintain that bias only renders a decision voidable.[94]

This view is based upon *Dimes*.[95] A decision of the Lord Chancellor in the Court of Chancery was challenged on appeal on the basis that the Lord Chancellor possessed a financial interest in the company that was the subject of the litigation. Parke B., in giving advice to the House of Lords, stated that such bias only resulted in the decision being voidable and not void. There are, however, a number of points to notice about the case.[96] First, it was concerned with an appeal from one superior court to another and not with review. Appeal is the classic instance of a voidable act,[97] whereas for review to be applicable the act must be void, or voidable in the area hitherto

[90] There is no reference in the *Osgood* case to void or voidable. The notion of substantial miscarriage of justice appears in the judgment of Martin B. (1872) L.R. 5 H.L. 636, 646. However, there is no indication that Martin B. intended to use the notion in the sense used by Lord Evershed.

[91] *O'Reilly v Mackman* [1983] 2 A.C. 237. The remainder of their Lordships concurred. *cf. R. v Dorking JJ Ex p. Harrington* [1983] Q.B. 1076, 1082.

[92] *Serjeant v Dale* (1877) 2 Q.B.D. 558, 566, 568; *Allinson v General Council of Medical Education and Registration* [1894] 1 Q.B. 750, 757; *R. v Furnished Houses Rent Tribunal for Paddington and St. Marylebone Ex p. Kendal Hotels Ltd* [1947] 1 All E.R. 448, 449; *R. v Paddington North and St Marylebone Rent Tribunal Ex p. Perry* [1956] 1 Q.B. 229, 237; *Anisminic Ltd v Foreign Compensation Commission* [1969] 2 A.C. 147, 171.

[93] *Cooper v Wilson* [1937] 2 K.B. 309 (declaration); *R. v Cheltenham Commissioners* (1841) 1 Q.B. 467 and *R. v Hertfordshire JJ* (1845) 6 Q.B. 753 (no certiorari clauses).

[94] Rubinstein, n.1, 203.

[95] *Dimes v Grand Junction Canal Co Proprietors* (1852) 3 H.L.C. 759, 785–786. See also, *Wildes v Russell* (1866) L.R. 1 C.P. 722, 741–742; *Phillips v Eyre* (1870) L.R. 6 Q.B. 1, 22.

[96] The case is cogently criticised in H.W.R. Wade, "Unlawful Administrative Action: Void or Voidable?" (1968) 84 L.Q.R. 95, 106–108.

[97] Rubinstein, n.1, 5–6.

covered by patent errors of law within jurisdiction. Secondly, the authorities cited by Parke B., do not support his proposition.[98]

C. Waiver

An argument used to support the proposition that a breach of the rules of **23–027** natural justice only makes a decision voidable and not void is that such rules can be waived.[99] The argument is as follows: jurisdictional defects cannot be waived,[100] and therefore if the rules of natural justice can be waived this is indicative that the defect is not jurisdictional. It is true that there are cases indicating that a plaintiff can be barred from obtaining a remedy by waiver.[101] These cases will be discussed in detail later.[102] However, although the premise is to some extent correct, the conclusion that, therefore, a defect of natural justice only renders a determination voidable is open to question.

In terms of principle, the rationale for saying that jurisdictional defects cannot be waived is that the limits to an administrator's jurisdiction are imposed by statute, and by common law principles. It should not, therefore, be open to the individual alone, or in collaboration with the authority, to disregard those boundaries. The boundaries are not established solely for the individual's benefit but, for the general public interest. They cannot therefore be waived at the instance of an individual. This may be correct as a starting point. It is, however, modified in a number of respects.[103] It can be argued that defects of natural justice should be susceptible to waiver, without this involving the conclusion that such defects are only voidable and not void. A primary purpose of natural justice is to protect the individual. If the individual is aware that the rules are not being fully complied with, but is content to proceed, she should not be able to raise the defect thereafter.[104] There is nothing inconsistent in admitting a doctrine of waiver and still regarding a procedural defect if not waived as producing a void decision.

In terms of the case law, a number of cases see no inconsistency between waiver and voidness. It would of course be open to society to say that there is a wider public interest underlying the procedural rules over and beyond that of the particular individual. The result would be that procedural defects could never be waived. However, the current case law does not in general

---

[98] *Brookes v Earl Rivers* (1668) Hardr. 503; *Company of Mercers and Ironmongers of Chester v Bowker* (1726) 1 Stra. 639.
[99] Rubinstein, n.1, 221.
[100] *Essex Incorporated Congregational Church Union v Essex County Council* [1963] A.C. 808, 820–821.
[101] *R. v Salop JJ* [1859] 2 El. & El. 386, 391; *Mayor and Alderman of City of London v Cox* (1867) L.R. 2 H.L. 239, 279–283; *Farquharson v Morgan* [1894] 1 Q.B. 552, 559; *R. v Williams Ex p. Phillips* [1914] 1 K.B. 608, 613–614; *R. v Comptroller-General of Patents and Designs Ex p. Parke Davis* [1953] 2 W.L.R. 760; *R. v British Broadcasting Corporation Ex p. Lavelle* [1983] 1 W.L.R. 23, 39.
[102] See below, paras 25–009—25–010.
[103] The sanctity of the ultra vires principle is compromised by the balancing process inherent within the time limits for remedies, and in the rules concerning delay, acquiescence and the effect of alternative remedies, see Chs 25–26. See also, the discussion of representations, para.20–050.
[104] *Ravichandran*, n.42.

adopt this attitude. While it continues to regard the procedural rules as imposed primarily for the benefit of the individual, there is no conceptual inconsistency in admitting that such rules can be waived and yet denominating a breach of those rules as jurisdictional leading to a void decision.[105] It is to be hoped that the remarks of Lord Diplock mentioned above will be taken to have settled the law in this area.

5. PROBLEMS OF PROOF

A. The Burden of Proof

23–028 The question of who has the burden of proof when the validity of administrative action is challenged is as follows.

The general rule is that the claimant wishing to assert the invalidity of administrative action must produce some evidence which throws doubt upon the apparent validity of that action before the burden shifts to the public body. In this sense the presumption is that the actions of the public body are lawful, and it is for the claimant to lead evidence to the contrary. There is, however, no rule that unlawful acts should be treated as valid. That is an entirely different proposition. The individual will none the less normally have the initial onus of showing some defect in the relevant order. Thus, as Lord Steyn held in *Boddington*, while there is no rule giving validity to invalid acts, the court will assume that subordinate legislation and administrative acts are valid unless persuaded otherwise.[106] This is in accord with the leading authorities.

In *Wrights' Canadian Ropes*,[107] the Minister had power to disallow any expense that he felt to be in excess of what was normal or reasonable for the taxpayer's business. The court held that it was for WRC to show that there was some ground for interfering with the Minister's determination. A number of other cases support the same proposition.[108] In *Rossminster*,[109] tax legislation empowered revenue officers to seize documents where they had reasonable cause to believe that they would be required as evidence of tax fraud. Lord Diplock[110] stated that the court should proceed on the presumption that the officers acted intra vires, until the applicant had displaced that presumption.

---

[105] Akehurst, [1968] 31 M.L.R. 138, 149, and Wade (1968) 84 L.Q.R. 95, 109 express a similar idea.

[106] n.10, 174.

[107] *Minister of National Revenue v Wrights' Canadian Ropes Ltd* [1947] A.C. 109, 122.

[108] *Point of Ayr Collieries Ltd v Lloyd-George* [1943] 2 All E.R. 546, 547; *Potato Marketing Board v Merricks* [1958] 2 Q.B. 316; *Wilover Nominees Ltd v Inland Revenue Commissioners* [1973] 1 W.L.R. 1393, 1396, 1399, affirmed [1974] 1 W.L.R. 1342, 1347; *Fawcett Properties Ltd v Buckingham County Council* [1959] Ch.543, 575, affirmed [1961] A.C. 636.

[109] *R. v Inland Revenue Commissioners Ex p. Rossminster Ltd* [1980] A.C. 952.

[110] *Rossminster*, n.109, 1013. See also, Viscount Dilhorne, 1006–1007. The case was complicated by the fact that the revenue officers claimed public interest immunity for not disclosing the grounds of their belief.

How much evidence will be required in order to shift the burden of proof will depend upon the type of case. If the defect is apparent on the face of the decision, the burden will not be a heavy one. Equally, where the applicant is claiming that the decision-maker has misconstrued a condition of jurisdiction, there is unlikely to be a difficulty. A reasoned assertion that the tribunal misinterpreted, for example, the term employee, would normally suffice in order to force the tribunal to defend its interpretation. The position will, however, be different where the ground of attack is that of unreasonableness or bad faith. The applicant will also have a heavier task where the statute requires the decision-maker to be satisfied of some matter, or where it is required to form some opinion.[111]

This general rule is subject to two qualifications. First, where the applicant alleges what would be a tort in the absence of statutory authority, it seems that the claimant only has to prove the facts which would constitute the wrong. The burden of proof is then on the public body to show justification. This is exemplified by *Rossminster*.[112] Lord Diplock stated that since the handling of a man's property without his permission was prima facie tortious, then in a civil action for trespass to goods based on the seizure of the property, the onus would be on the officer to satisfy the court that there were reasonable grounds for believing that the documents were evidence of a tax fraud.[113] It seems that this qualification will only apply where the allegation is that a statutory condition has not been complied with, and not where the allegation is, for example, one of bad faith.[114]

23–029

The second possible qualification arises from the law on habeas corpus. The law in this area is, however, unclear. In one case the court held that the public body must show that it had complied with the statutory conditions. It was insufficient for a detaining authority to make a return that was valid on its face. A detainee could be put to proof of an allegation of bad faith, but it was otherwise where the allegation related to compliance with the statutory conditions.[115] This case has been distinguished, the court holding that where the return was good on its face it was for the detainee to show that the detention was illegal.[116] The present position none the less seems to be that the burden of proof rests upon the detaining authority. In *Khawaja*,[117] Lord Scarman stated that the initial burden was on the applicant, but that this was transferred to the detaining authority once the applicant had shown

---

[111] See cases, nn.107–108.
[112] *Rossminster*, n.109, 1011. See also, *R. v Secretary of State for the Home Department Ex p. Khawaja* [1984] AC 74.
[113] This was not relevant in the actual case, which was concerned with an application for judicial review, and return of the documents. See also, *St Pancras Borough Council v Frey* [1963] 2 Q.B. 586, 592; *Harpin v St Albans Corporation* (1969) 67 L.G.R. 479. But see, *Bristol District Council v Clark* [1975] 1 W.L.R. 1443, 1448 where doubt was cast upon these cases.
[114] *R. v Governor of Brixton Prison Ex p. Ahsan* [1969] 2 Q.B. 222, explaining *Greene v Secretary of State for Home Affairs* [1942] A.C. 284.
[115] *Ahsan*, n.114. See also, *Eshugbayi Eleko v Government of Nigeria* [1931] A.C. 662.
[116] *R. v Governor of Risley Remand Centre Ex p. Hassan* [1976] 1 W.L.R. 971, 976–979.
[117] *R. v Secretary of State for the Home Department Ex p. Khawaja* [1984] A.C. 74, 111–112; *R. (on the Application of Abbasi) v Secretary of State for Foreign and Commonwealth Affairs* [2002] EWCA Civ 1598, para.60.

that there was a prima facie case that liberty or property were being interfered with. The burden of proof would then be on the detaining authority to
justify the detention. Thus, on the facts of that case, once the applicant had
shown that he had entered the United Kingdom with the leave of the
immigration officer, the burden of proving that he had obtained leave by
deception was on the Executive.

The issue being considered in this section should not be confused with a
separate, albeit connected one. We have been considering the status of an
order or decision once made, and the question of who has the initial onus of
proving a defect. The general answer is that the onus is initially on the
person alleging the invalidity. A related but separate question is what will
the court demand of the public body if it is to justify its action? In other
words if the individual does shift the burden of proof to the public body,
what will that body have to prove and what will be the standard of review?
This will depend upon the statutory context. Normally, as we have already
seen, if the allegation relates to a jurisdictional fact the court will substitute
its judgment for that of the public body. Where the question is whether the
evidence justifies the application of a certain statutory term the standard of
proof will differ depending upon the area in question.[118]

B. Validity Pending Determination

23–030   The basic principle set out above means that it will be for the individual to
persuade the court that there are grounds for invalidating an administrative
decision. This has implications for interim proceedings, as exemplified by
Hoffmann-La Roche.[119] The Secretary of State, acting pursuant to a
Monopolies Commission report on the company's profits on certain drugs,
laid before Parliament statutory orders directing the company to reduce its
price. The company informed the Secretary of State that it would not obey
the relevant Order. It claimed that the procedures of the Monopolies
Commission contravened the rules of natural justice and that the order was
ultra vires. The Secretary of State responded by claiming an interim
injunction to restrain the company from charging prices in excess of those
specified in the Order. The main argument was whether the interim
injunction should be conditional on the Crown giving an undertaking to pay
damages, should the company prove successful in the main action. The
Secretary of State had refused to give any such undertaking. Their Lordships found against the company. Their reasoning may be summarised as
follows.

The statutory instrument is, unless and until successfully challenged, the
law of the land. It has a presumption of validity. If and when it is successfully impugned it will be retrospectively null. The normal judicial
practice is to condition the grant of an interim injunction upon an undertaking in damages given by the person in whose favour the injunction issues.

---

[118] See above, Ch.15.
[119] *Hoffmann-La Roche & Co AG v Secretary of State for Trade and Industry* [1975] A.C. 295.

This is to safeguard the position of the party against whom the injunction issues, should this party prove successful in the main action, and has suffered loss in the period between the interim injunction and the final decision. It was at one time maintained that the Crown would never be required to give such an undertaking, but this rule had been rendered out of date by the Crown Proceedings Act 1947. In principle, therefore, such an undertaking could be extracted from the Crown and would be normally required where the Crown was asserting its purely private law rights of a proprietary or contractual nature.

The position was, however, different where the Crown was enforcing the law of the land. In such cases, although an undertaking in damages could be required as a condition for the grant of an injunction, the private party would have to show a strong case for imposing this condition. The factors which the court would take into account in deciding whether to impose the undertaking in damages included: the strength of the company's prima facie case of invalidity; the financial interest of the Crown, given that the National Health Service was the main buyer of the drugs; the viability of a plan proposed by the company under which it would charge the higher prices, but recompense buyers should the Order be upheld; and the effect upon members of the public who were not parties to the action.[120]

Lord Wilberforce dissented.[121] The Statutory Order could not, said his Lordship, have any presumption of validity since it was now being challenged by the right person in the correct proceedings. The optimum position would be to issue the interim injunction, since the only loss suffered would be pecuniary, but to require the Crown to provide compensation should the final decision be in favour of the company. **23–031**

The difficulty with the decision is that the issues involved therein, the status of the Order and the undertaking in damages, were linked both in the majority and dissenting judgments, in a way which is apt to mislead.

The majority judgment should be accepted in relation to the status of the Order. It should be regarded as presumptively valid. The argument to the contrary put by Lord Wilberforce is, with respect, flawed. The Order must be presumptively something: it must be either presumptively valid or invalid. A neutral stance is not possible, since it would not be possible to assess the demands for injunctive relief, and it would not be possible to decide who had the burden of proof. Lord Wilberforce's argument that no such presumption of validity should exist, because the correct person was challenging the order in the correct proceedings, does not take account of the time scale, and the normal burden of proof. The problems concerning the time scale reflect the fact that the claim was for interim relief. The presumption of validity voiced by the majority is a presumption that applies unless and until the order is challenged in the final action. The burden of proof in this action will rest initially on the person disputing the validity of the order. More

---

[120] *Hoffmann-La Roche*, n.119, 341–342, *per* Lord Reid, 351–354, *per* Lord Morris of Borth-y-Gest, 361–370, *per* Lord Diplock, 370–372, *per* Lord Cross of Chelsea.
[121] *Hoffmann-La Roche*, n.119, 354–360.

recently, Lord Hoffmann in *Wicks* stated that the presumption of validity was an evidential matter at the interlocutory stage of proceedings, and the presumption existed pending a final decision by the court.[122]

There is, however, no logical connection between regarding the order as presumptively valid and the undertaking in damages. It was the latter that Lord Wilberforce was most concerned with, and in this respect his opinion is to be preferred to that of the majority. The fact that the statutory order is presumptively valid does not, in and of itself, tell us anything concerning the basis on which it should be enforced in interim proceedings.

The link between presumptive validity and the undertaking in damages seen by the majority is part conceptual and part practical. The *conceptual* connection is said to be that because the Order is presently the law of the land, and because the Crown has a duty to enforce it, therefore the Crown should not always be fettered by the requirement of a damages undertaking.[123] This is overlaid by the *pragmatic* consideration that such a requirement could be a deterrent to the Crown bringing an action at all.[124] Neither of these reasons is convincing.

23–032   Let us consider the *conceptual* argument first. It is true that the Crown may have a duty to enforce the law, but this premise does not warrant the conclusion drawn from it. The presumption of validity is just that, a presumption. It can be rebutted. The presumption does not tell us who should bear the loss from an order that is found to be invalid. The equation of a duty to enforce the presumptive law, with the absence of responsibility if that presumption proves unfounded is open to serious question. The Crown or a public body is generally given responsibility for law enforcement because it represents the public interest, even if it does not have a financial stake.[125] The people benefit from such law enforcement. If it transpires that the public body was wrong then the public generally should shoulder the burden, through the losses being placed upon it via taxation. Any distributive windfall gain or loss to a section of society[126] is minimal compared to the burden placed on the private party if no undertaking in damages is required.

The *pragmatic* argument concerning deterrence is equally suspect. A public body could of course be deterred from bringing an action if there was the possibility that it could be liable to pay substantial sums in compensation should it prove to be unsuccessful. But this amounts to no more than saying that doing something with no risk of financial liability is less risky than doing something where there is some such risk. It begs the whole question of where losses from invalid governmental action ought to lie.

---

[122] n.15, 116. This view was supported by Lord Steyn in *Boddington*, n.10, 174.
[123] *Hoffmann-La Roche*, n.119, 364, 367, *per* Lord Diplock.
[124] *Hoffmann-La Roche*, n.119, 371, *per* Lord Cross.
[125] *Gouriet v Union of Post Office Workers* [1978] A.C. 435.
[126] *Hoffmann-La Roche*, n.119, 367; *Rochdale Borough Council v Anders* [1988] 3 All E.R. 490. cf. *Director General of Fair Trading v Tobyward Ltd* [1989] 1 W.L.R. 517.

The availability of interim relief against the Crown will be considered more fully below.[127] The House of Lords had occasion to consider the validity of laws pending their final determination in *Factortame (No.2)*.[128] The plaintiffs sought interim relief against the Crown to prevent it from applying a national law, which they argued was in breach of Community law. It was held that there was no *rule* that a party challenging the validity of a law must show a strong prima facie case that the law was invalid. The court had *discretion* in the matter. However, their Lordships also held that the court should not restrain a public authority by interim injunction from enforcing an apparently valid law, unless it was satisfied that the challenge was, prima facie, so firmly based as to justify this exceptional course of action being taken.[129]

C. Partial Invalidity

A court may under certain conditions hold that the invalid part of an order   **23–033**
can be severed, while the remainder is still valid. The court will not, however, "rewrite" the order, and the invalid part must not be inextricably
interwoven with the whole order.[130]

The leading decision is *Hutchinson*.[131] The appellants were convicted of offences under the Greenham Common Byelaws, in that they entered a protected area as defined by the byelaw. They contended by way of defence that the byelaw was invalid, because it was in breach of the enabling legislation. The parent statute had stated that byelaws could be made provided that they did not interfere with rights of common, and the appellants claimed that these byelaws interfered with such rights. The issue for the House of Lords was, therefore, whether the invalid part of the byelaw could be severed. Their Lordships distinguished between two situations.

The first was where textual severance was possible. In this instance a test of substantial severability was to be applied, which would be satisfied when the valid text was unaffected by, and independent of, the invalid. The second situation was where textual severance was not possible. The test was whether the legislative instrument with the parts omitted would be a substantially different law from what it would have been if the omitted parts had been included.

More recently in the *National Association of Health Stores*[132] Sedley L.J. extended the reasoning in *Hutchinson* to cases of curable omissions in

---

[127] See below, para.28–019.
[128] *R. v Secretary of State for Transport Ex p. Factortame Ltd (No.2)* [1991] 1 A.C. 603.
[129] *Factortame Ltd (No.2)*, n.128, 674.
[130] *Potato Marketing Board v Merricks* [1958] 2 Q.B. 316; *Kingsway Investments (Kent) Ltd v Kent County Council* [1971] A.C. 72; *Dunkley v Evans* [1981] 1 W.L.R. 1522; *Thames Water Authority v Elmbridge BC* [1983] Q.B. 570; *R. v Secretary of State for Transport Ex p. GLC* [1986] Q.B. 556; *R. v North Hertfordshire District Council Ex p. Cobbold* [1985] 3 All E.R. 487.
[131] *DPP v Hutchinson* [1990] 2 A.C. 783; A. Bradley, "Judicial Enforcement of *Ultra Vires* Byelaws: The Proper Scope of Severance" [1990] P.L. 293.
[132] *R. (on the application of National Association of Health Stores) v Secretary of State for Health* [2005] EWCA Civ 154.

regulations. He stated that "to strike down an entire regulation because of a curable omission which appears to have affected nobody, however cogent the case in legal theory for doing so, would represent a triumph of logic over reason".[133] If therefore "an omission can be made good without disrupting the existing, presumptively lawful, text, and if so far the omission appears to have done no harm, I see no good reason why, instead of permitting the rule-maker to insert the missing brick, the entire structure should be pulled down".[134]

[133] *National Association of Health Stores*, n.132, para.16.
[134] *National Association of Health Stores*, n.132, para.20.

PART 3

REMEDIES

CHAPTER 24

REMEDIES: STANDING

1. INTRODUCTION

Locus standi is concerned with whether a particular claimant is entitled to **24–001**
invoke the jurisdiction of the court. This issue must be distinguished from
that of justiciability, which asks whether the judicial process is suitable for
the resolution of this type of dispute, whoever brings it to court. It is also
distinct from the issue known in the USA as ripeness,[1] under which premature questions are not adjudicated upon. There is case law on both justiciability and ripeness in the UK,[2] although the concepts are not as
developed as they are in the United States.

The issue of who should be enabled to invoke the judicial process has been
much debated,[3] and the policy arguments will be considered below.[4] We
shall see that assumptions concerning the nature of administrative law, and
the role of the courts, are inherent in any response. The law will be examined
both prior to and consequent upon the reforms of administrative law
remedies.[5] A brief historical perspective is necessary for a proper understanding of the present law. Following this, some of the broader questions
about the scope of standing will be examined.

---

[1] A. Aman and W. Mayton, *Administrative Law* (West Publishing, 2nd edn, 2001), 413–420.
[2] J. Beatson, "Prematurity and Ripeness for Review", in C. Forsyth and I. Hare (eds), *The
Golden Metwand and the Crooked Cord, Essays on Public Law in Honour of Sir William Wade*
(Oxford University Press, 1998), 221–252.
[3] S. Thio, *Locus Standi and Judicial Review* (Singapore University Press, 1971); J. Vining, *Legal
Identity, The Coming of Age of Public Law* (Yale University Press, 1978); P. Van Dijk, *Judicial
Review of Governmental Action and the Requirement of an Interest to Sue* (Sijthoff & Noordhoff,
1980).
[4] See below, paras 24–028—24–041.
[5] SI 1977/1955; SI 1980/2000; Supreme Court Act 1981 s.31.

2. THE LAW BEFORE 1978[6]

24–002   There is considerable diversity in the older case law on standing, both within each remedy and as between them. Even when the same words, such as "private right", "special damage", "person aggrieved" or "sufficient interest" are used, it cannot be assumed that they bear the same meaning. This is evident not only when these phrases appear in different remedies, but also when cases concerning the same remedy are juxtaposed. The main cause for this confusion was the failure to adopt a clear view as to what the remedies were seeking to achieve, which reflected at one stage removed a lack of clarity as to the purpose of administrative law.

A. Certiorari

24–003   There were at least two views as to standing requirements for certiorari. The first was that certiorari had no standing limits as such. Any person could apply for an order, and standing would only be relevant to the granting of the remedy. If the application was made by a person aggrieved, then the court would intervene *ex debito justitiae*, in justice to the applicant; where the applicant was a stranger, the court considered whether the public interest demanded intervention.[7] A second view was that an applicant must show some interest before being accorded standing.[8] The weight of authority appeared to favour the former view.[9] The degree of practical difference between them should not, however, be over-emphasised. If a court did not wish to grant an applicant standing, it could reach that conclusion either by adopting the first view, but refusing in its discretion to admit the applicant, or by adopting the second view and deeming the person not to be an interested party.

B. Prohibition

24–004   The case law on standing to seek prohibition makes that on certiorari seem simple.[10] There was, however, one line of authority that was clear. The cases held that prohibition must be granted whoever the applicant was, the reason

---

[6] SI 1977/1955 came into effect on January 11, 1978.
[7] *R. v Surrey JJ* (1870) L.R. 5 Q.B. 466, 473; *R. v Butt Ex p. Brooke* (1922) 38 T.L.R. 537; *R. v Stafford JJ Ex p. Stafford Corporation* [1940] 2 K.B. 33; *R. v Brighton Borough JJ Ex p. Jarvis* [1954] 1 W.L.R. 203; *R. v Thames Magistrates' Court Ex p. Greenbaum* (1957) 55 L.G.R. 129.
[8] Thio, n.3, Ch.5; D.M. Gordon, "Certiorari and the Problem of Locus Standi" (1955) 71 L.Q.R. 483, 485. Certain cases are said to support this view, *R. v Bradford-on-Avon Urban District Council Ex p. Boulton* [1964] 1 W.L.R. 1136; *R. v Paddington Valuation Officer Ex p. Peachey Property Corporation* [1966] 1 Q.B. 380; *R. v Russell Ex p. Beaverbrook Newspapers Ltd* [1969] 1 Q.B. 342.
[9] Cases cited for the second view appear to be either obiter dictum, *Boulton*, n.8, or ambiguous, *Paddington*, where Lord Denning M.R. purported to apply the *Greenbaum* case, n.7, which is supportive of the first view.
[10] See, the lamentation in J. Shortt, *Informations, Mandamus and Prohibitions* (Blackstone Publishing Company 1888), 441.

being that an excess of jurisdiction by an inferior court was contempt against the Crown, in the sense of being an infringement of the royal prerogative.[11] The applicant therefore approached the court to represent the public interest. This reasoning was indicative of a citizen action[12] approach towards standing. There were, however, also cases that adopted a private rights perspective. Thus some authorities appeared to require a specific interest in the applicant,[13] while others sought to side-step the reasoning in the first line of authority by arguing that it applied only to patent and not to latent jurisdictional defects.[14]

C. Mandamus

The diversity of approach towards standing is clearly evident in the confused **24–005** case law on mandamus. Two approaches can be discerned.

One line of cases required the applicant to show infringement of a legal right in the traditional private law sense, such that a cause of action in contract, tort, etc. could be maintained against the public body.[15] Other cases which employed the terminology of private right, however, gave the term "right" a broader meaning by granting standing even where no contractual or tortious right had been affected.[16]

Another line of authority explicitly regarded a sufficient or special interest as satisfying the requirements for standing. Thus in the *Paddington* case,[17] a company was allowed to challenge a valuation list for rating purposes without showing that it was more aggrieved than any other ratepayer. Lord Denning M.R. held that the court would listen to anyone whose interests were affected, but not to a mere busybody.

D. Injunction and Declaration

Declarations and injunctions were available through Ord.15 r.16, or by way **24–006** of application to the High Court respectively. They may now also be claimed by way of application for judicial review under s.31 of the Supreme Court Act 1981. Two reasons have reduced the importance of the restrictive rules described below. First, the test for standing under s.31 is more liberal

[11] *De Haber v Queen of Portugal* (1851) 17 Q.B. 171; *Worthington v Jeffries* (1875) L.R. 10 C.P. 379; *R. v Speyer* [1916] 1 K.B. 595. See also, the way in which *Forster v Forster and Berridge* (1863) 4 B. & S. 187 was distinguished in *Worthington*.
[12] See below, para.24–031.
[13] *Forster*, n.11; *R. v Twiss* (1869) L.R. 4 Q.B. 407, 413–414.
[14] *Mayor and Aldermen of City of London v Cox* (1867) L.R. 2 H.L. 239; *Farquharson v Morgan* [1894] 1 Q.B. 552.
[15] *R. v Lewisham Union* [1897] 1 Q.B. 498, 500; *R. v Industrial Court Ex p. ASSET* [1965] 1 Q.B. 377.
[16] *R. v Hereford Corporation Ex p. Harrower* [1970] 1 W.L.R. 1424; *R. v Commissioners of Customs and Excise Ex p. Cook* [1970] 1 W.L.R. 450.
[17] *R. v Paddington Valuation Officer Ex p. Peachey Property Corporation Ltd* [1966] 1 Q.B. 380, 401; *R. v Commissioners for Special Purposes of Income Tax* (1888) 21 Q.B.D 313; *R. v Manchester Corporation* [1911] 1 K.B. 560; *R. v Commissioner of Police of the Metropolis Ex p. Blackburn* [1968] 2 Q.B. 118.

than that which existed previously. Second, the courts have emphasised that public law cases should be brought under the new procedure. There will, none the less, still be cases in which a declaration or injunction can be sought outside s.31, and what follows is an analysis of the tests for standing in such cases. The effect of the new procedure will be considered thereafter.

The circumstances in which an individual can seek an injunction or declaration have, in general, been narrowly construed. In *Boyce*,[18] Buckley J. held that an action for an injunction could only be maintained without joining the Attorney-General in two types of case. The plaintiff had to show either that the interference with the public right constituted an infringement of a private right, or there had to be special damage. The House of Lords endorsed this criterion,[19] and later cases on declaration adopted the same reasoning. Thus in *Gregory*,[20] the plaintiff was denied standing to challenge a grant of planning permission. Paull J. reasoned directly by analogy with private law, and concluded that the plaintiff could not succeed unless he could show either that the statute had been passed to benefit a class of people including himself, or that other private law rights had been infringed. There are two reasons, neither of which is convincing, why the courts adopted these narrow rules for standing.

First, the test established in *Boyce* was based upon the criteria for public nuisance, as is clear by the authorities cited therein.[21] This argument is however flawed. In private law there is no separation of standing and the merits. Who can sue is not treated as a distinct issue, but is part of the definition of the cause of action. Thus, for example, a person placed in fear of her bodily safety can claim in assault, or one whose reputation is injured can claim in defamation. The argument from public nuisance therefore tells us who should be able to sue in that action. To infer that the same test should apply generally within public law is a non-sequitur.[22]

A second argument concerning declarations was based on the wording of Ord.15 r.16.[23] Something akin to a private law right was said to be required because the Order was cast in terms of "declarations of rights". This argument is unconvincing. The declaration fulfils both an original and a supervisory role. In the former sense it is used in many circumstances that have nothing to do with public law, for example, to declare the parties' respective rights under a contract. In such cases it will obviously be apposite to know what rights X and Y have so that declarations can be made about

---

[18] *Boyce v Paddington Borough Council* [1903] 1 Ch.109, 114; *Stockport District Waterworks Co v Manchester Corporation* (1863) 9 Jur. (N.S.) 266; *Pudsey Coal Gas Co v Corporation of Bradford* (1872) L.R. 15 Eq. 167.

[19] *London Passenger Transport Board v Moscrop* [1942] A.C. 332, 342.

[20] *Gregory v Camden London Borough Council* [1966] 1 W.L.R. 899; *Anisminic v Foreign Compensation Commission* [1968] 2 Q.B. 862, 910–911; *Wilson, Walton International (Offshore Services) Ltd v Tees and Hartlepool Port Authority* [1969] 1 Lloyd's Rep. 120; *Booth and Co (International) Ltd v National Enterprise Board* [1978] 3 All E.R. 624.

[21] *Winterbottom v Lord Derby* (1867) L.R. 2 Ex. 316; *Benjamin v Storr* (1874) L.R. 9 C.P. 400.

[22] P. Cane, "The Function of Standing Rules in Administrative Law" [1980] P.L. 303, 305.

[23] Declarations can still be sought under this Order, but the courts have held that public law cases must generally be brought within the new procedure save in exceptional cases, see below, Ch.26.

them. Where, however, the declaration is being used in its supervisory role, to control excess of power by public bodies, there is no reason why the remedy can only be granted where a private law right is present.

Not all cases required a private law right, in the sense of a cause of action in contract or tort, before the plaintiff could proceed.[24] The prospect of broadening the standing requirement was however curtailed by *Gouriet*.[25] The Post Office Act 1953 ss.58 and 68, made it an offence to interfere with the mail. The Union of Post Office Workers (UPW) had called on their members not to handle letters being sent to South Africa. Gouriet sought the consent of the Attorney-General to a relator action, but this was not forthcoming. When the case went to the House of Lords the plaintiff no longer asserted that this refusal of consent could be reviewed, rather that the failure to secure the approval was not fatal to the claim. Their Lordships rejected this argument. They were clearly concerned because the case was about a relator action "in support" of the criminal law: the injunction was being sought to prevent the commission of a criminal offence. Although the Attorney-General had been granted injunctive relief in this context before,[26] their Lordships felt that the power should be utilised with caution.[27]

It is however the more general reasoning that is of relevance. The House of Lords' reasoning is permeated by a conception of the role of the citizen in public law. Put shortly the citizen has no such role. In the absence of the Attorney-General a citizen could enforce his or her private rights, but public rights could be enforced only through the Attorney-General as representative of the public interest. It therefore followed that consent to a relator action was not something fictitious or nominal, to be circumvented at will: it was the substantive manifestation of the principle that public rights were to be represented by the Attorney-General.[28] The precise ambit of the term private right was not clear,[29] and there was some uncertainty as to whether

24–007

---

[24] (a) on declaration: *Nicholls v Tavistock Urban District Council* [1923] 2 Ch.18; *Prescott v Birmingham Corporation* [1955] Ch.210; *Brownsea Haven Properties v Poole Corporation* [1958] Ch.574; *Eastham v Newcastle United Football Club* [1964] Ch.413; *Thorne Rural District Council v Bunting* [1972] Ch.470; *Tito v Waddell (No.2)* [1977] Ch.106, 260; *R. v Greater London Council Ex p. Blackburn* [1976] 1 W.L.R. 550. (b) on injunction: *Chamberlaine v Chester and Birkenhead Ry Co* (1848) 1 Ex. 870; *Bradbury v Enfield London Borough Council* [1967] 1 W.L.R. 1311. *cf. RCA Corporation v Pollard* [1982] 3 W.L.R. 1007 and *Lonrho Ltd v Shell Petroleum (No.2)* [1982] A.C. 173, restrictively interpreting *Ex p Island Records Ltd* [1978] Ch.122; and *Barrs v Bethell* [1982] Ch.294 not following *Prescott*, or *R. v Greater London Council Ex p. Blackburn*.
[25] *Gouriet v Union of Post Office Workers* [1978] A.C. 435.
[26] *Att-Gen v Smith* [1958] 2 Q.B. 173; *Att-Gen v Chaudry* [1971] 1 W.L.R. 1614.
[27] Because sanctions and methods of proof could differ between prosecution for a crime, and the grant of injunctive relief; problems of double jeopardy also worried their Lordships; D. Feldman, "Injunctions and the Criminal Law" (1979) 42 M.L.R. 369.
[28] [1978] A.C. 435, 477–480, 483, 495, 498–499, 508. *cf.* the view in the Court of Appeal [1977] 1 Q.B. 729, 768–772, 773–779.
[29] Lord Wilberforce stated that a plaintiff could seek a declaration in his own name whenever a plaintiff asserted a legal right which was being denied, or threatened, or claimed an immunity, [1978] A.C. 435, 483–484; Lord Diplock stated that an existing cause of action was not required, but did seem to require that such an action could eventuate, [1978] A.C. 435, 501–502; Viscount Dilhorne spoke of the need for a personal right or interest without further elucidation, [1978] A.C. 435, 495; Lord Edmund-Davies stated that a private right was necessary, but that a cause of action in contract or tort was not, [1978] A.C. 435, 514–515.

special damage was still an alternative basis for declaratory or injunctive relief.[30]

The decision illustrates a conception of standing based on the vindication of private rights. The difficulties of this approach will be considered below,[31] but a particular difficulty should be mentioned here. An applicant who sought a prerogative order was not tied to the enforcement of private law rights. The person was in effect vindicating the public interest to some degree. The premise underpinning *Gouriet*, to the effect that individuals enforce private rights and the Attorney-General enforces public rights, cannot therefore be unqualifiedly accepted as an accurate description of what the courts had been doing.[32] Gouriet argued that the broader notion of interest for standing within the prerogative orders should apply in injunction/declaration cases. Their Lordships rejected this argument, and the cogency of the reasoning will be examined below.[33]

3. The Attorney-General, Public Authorities and Statutory Appeals

24–008 The rules of standing that operate in certain areas are distinct, and therefore require separate treatment. These will be examined before considering the general rules on standing that operate in ordinary judicial review actions.

A. Attorney-General

24–009 The Attorney-General as the legal representative of the Crown represents the interests of the Crown *qua* Sovereign, and also *qua parens patriae*. This jurisdiction was initially invoked in relation to public nuisance and the administration of charitable and public trusts. The initial impetus seemed to stem from private law proprietary interests, the Crown possessing a *jus publicum* for the use of highways and rivers, coupled with the desire to prevent multiplicity of litigation. The Attorney-General may act on his own initiative, as guardian of the public interest, to restrain public nuisances and prevent excess of power by public bodies.[34]

Particular problems arise where the Attorney-General seeks to buttress the criminal law. In *Att-Gen v Smith*[35] an injunction was granted to prevent S from making repeated applications for planning permission for a caravan

---

[30] Lord Wilberforce was the only one of their Lordships to mention special damage, but this might be because special damage was not pleaded. In *Barrs*, n.24, it was held that an individual could proceed in his own name if he could prove such damage.

[31] See below, para.24–029.

[32] See also Wade, Note (1978) 94 L.Q.R. 4.

[33] See below, para.24–014.

[34] *Att-Gen v PYA Quarries Ltd* [1957] 2 Q.B. 169; *Att-Gen v Manchester Corporation* [1906] 1 Ch.643; *Att-Gen v Fulham Corporation* [1921] 1 Ch.440.

[35] [1978] 2 Q.B. 173, 185.

site, despite the presence of penalties in the relevant legislation. In *Att-Gen v Harris*[36] a flower vendor who contravened police regulations many times was prevented from continuing to do so by an injunction. Their Lordships in *Gouriet*[37] felt that this power should be used sparingly, and should be reserved for cases where there were continued breaches of the law, or serious injury was threatened.[38]

It is not entirely clear whether the Attorney-General seeking an injunction is in an especially privileged position. The law appears to be as follows. The Attorney-General has discretion to decide whether to bring an action or not.[39] If an action is brought and the breach proven the court is not bound to issue an injunction in the Attorney-General's favour, but exceptional circumstances would have to exist before the claim was refused. It will be regarded as a wrong in itself for the law to be flouted.[40]

The Attorney-General may proceed at the relation of an individual complainant where she does not possess the requisite interest to bring a case in her own name. The consent of the Attorney-General is necessary, the procedure being known as a relator action. We have already seen that the failure to secure this consent cannot be circumvented.[41] In a relator action the Attorney-General is the plaintiff, but in practice the private litigant will instruct counsel, and will remain liable for costs.

B. Public Authorities

The courts have in the past restrictively construed the *locus standi* of public **24–010** authorities. The public authority was required to show an interference with proprietary rights, special damage, or that it was the beneficiary of a statutory duty, in order that the action could be maintained without the Attorney-General. Thus, in *Tozer*,[42] the corporation failed to obtain an injunction when complaining that the defendant's building constituted the laying out of a new street in contravention of the byelaws. No proprietary interest of the plaintiff was affected and the courts deprecated the bringing of such actions in the absence of the Attorney-General. Even where standing seemed to be accorded by a specific statute the courts tended to construe such provisions restrictively,[43] as they have done with more general statutory terms.[44]

[36] [1961] 1 Q.B. 74; *Att-Gen v Premier Line Ltd* [1932] 1 Ch.303.
[37] [1978] A.C. 435. See also, the restrictive observations in *Stoke-on-Trent City Council v B & Q (Retail) Ltd* [1984] A.C. 754; *Att-Gen v Able* [1984] Q.B. 975.
[38] *Chaudry*, n.26.
[39] *London County Council v Att-Gen* [1902] A.C. 165, 169; *Gouriet* [1978] A.C. 435.
[40] *Att-Gen v Bastow* [1957] 1 Q.B. 514; *Att-Gen v Harris* [1961] 1 Q.B. 74.
[41] See above, para.24–007.
[42] *Devonport Corporation v Tozer* [1903] 1 Ch.759; *Att-Gen v Pontypridd Waterworks Co* [1909] 1 Ch.388.
[43] *Wallasey Local Board v Gracey* (1887) 36 Ch. D. 593; cf. *London City Council v Metropolitan Gas Company* [1904] 1 Ch.76.
[44] *Prestatyn Urban District Council v Prestatyn Raceway Ltd* [1970] 1 W.L.R. 33, disapproving a more liberal approach by Lord Denning M.R. in *Warwickshire County Council v British Railways Board* [1969] 1 W.L.R. 1117 concerning the construction of the Local Government Act 1933 s.276.

The legislature responded to the restrictive judicial approach through the enactment of s.222 of the Local Government Act 1972. This allows a local authority to maintain an action in its own name where the authority considers it expedient for the promotion and protection of the interests of the inhabitants of its area. It enables the local authority to sue without joining the Attorney-General, and has been liberally interpreted.[45]

C. Statutory Appeals

24–011 The question of standing can also arise where a statute allows a "person aggrieved" to challenge a decision.

The case law on this topic has considerable similarities with that discussed above. Thus one line of cases adopted a narrow, restrictive meaning of the term person aggrieved, requiring the infringement of a private right or something closely akin thereto. The modern case law has, however, embraced a more liberal philosophy.

A leading example of the more restrictive line is *Sidebotham*.[46] S had been declared bankrupt. It was alleged that the trustee in bankruptcy had not been performing his duties properly, an allegation verified by the Comptroller in Bankruptcy who recommended that the trustee make good certain losses. The latter did not do so and was taken to the County Court, which made no order compelling the trustee to make good the deficiency. The Comptroller did not appeal this decision, but S attempted to do so as a person aggrieved. He was unsuccessful, the court interpreting a person aggrieved to require something more than one who was disappointed in a benefit which he might have received. There had to be a legal grievance, a wrongful deprivation of something to which the appellant was entitled.

The decision became the *locus classicus* on the subject and was often applied,[47] even though it could have been distinguished.[48] Thus in *Buxton*[49] B, an owner of land adjacent to a chalk pit, was held not to be a person aggrieved so as to be able to challenge the grant of planning permission for the quarrying, even though his pedigree pigs and landscape garden would be affected by the dust. He had no legal rights affected by the decision to grant planning permission and thus could not complain. The courts recognised that some financial burdens could qualify one as a person aggrieved,[50] thereby indirectly broadening this limited interpretation.

---

[45] *Solihull Metropolitan BC v Maxfern Ltd* [1977] 1 W.L.R. 127; *Stafford Borough Council v Elkenford Ltd* [1977] 1 W.L.R. 324; *Thanet DC v Ninedrive Ltd* [1978] 1 All E.R. 703; *Kent CC v Batchelor (No.2)* [1979] 1 W.L.R. 213; *Stoke-on-Trent*, n.37; *Monks v East Northamptonshire DC* [2002] EWHC 473; *Guildford BC v Hein* [2005] EWCA Civ 979.
[46] *Ex p. Sidebotham* (1880) 14 Ch. D. 458.
[47] *R. v London Quarter Sessions Ex p. Westminster Corporation* [1951] 2 K.B. 508; *Ealing Corporation v Jones* [1959] 1 Q.B. 384.
[48] The court in *Sidebotham* was influenced by the structure of the relevant legislation and the fact that the debtor had an independent cause of action against the trustee: (1880) 14 Ch. D. 458, 466.
[49] *Buxton v Minister of Housing and Local Government* [1961] 1 Q.B. 278.
[50] *R. v Quarter Sessions Ex p. Lilley* [1951] 2 K.B. 749; *Phillips v Berkshire County Council* [1967] 2 Q.B. 991.

This restrictive approach was challenged by Lord Denning.[51] The *Sidebotham–Buxton* interpretation was held to be too narrow. While busybodies should, of course, be excluded, any person with a genuine grievance whose interests were affected should be admitted. The House of Lords applied the more liberal philosophy in *Ende*.[52] Their Lordships held that a ratepayer living in the same borough or even in the same precepting area could qualify as a person aggrieved so as to be able to challenge the assessment of another's rates as too low. The applicant did not have to show financial detriment, and a fortiori the infringement of a legal right was not a necessary prerequisite in order to be able to maintain a claim.[53]

The law in this area has now been clarified by *Cook*.[54] Woolf L.J. reviewed the authorities in this area. He recognised that some of the earlier decisions had taken a restrictive view of the term "person aggrieved", but pointed to the liberal approach adopted in more recent jurisprudence, and held that some of the foundational cases supporting the restrictive view should no longer be treated as good law.[55] Henceforth the following principles should apply whenever the phrase "person aggrieved" appeared in any statute concerning appeal rights, subject to a clear contrary intent in the particular statute.[56]

(1) A body corporate, including a local authority, was just as capable as being a person aggrieved as an individual.

(2) Any person who had a decision made against him, particularly in adversarial proceedings, would be a person aggrieved for the purposes of appealing against that decision, unless the decision amounted to an acquittal of a purely criminal case.

(3) The fact that the decision against which the person wished to appeal reversed a decision which was originally taken by that person, and did not otherwise adversely affect him, did not prevent that person being a person aggrieved. To the contrary, it indicated that he was a person aggrieved who could use his appeal rights to have the original decision restored.

---

[51] *Att-Gen of the Gambia v N'Jie* [1961] A.C. 617, 634; *Maurice v London County Council* [1964] 2 Q.B. 362, 378; *Turner v Secretary of State for the Environment* (1973) 28 P. & C.R. 123, 134, 139.
[52] *Arsenal Football Club Ltd v Ende* [1979] A.C. 1.
[53] Being a taxpayer was not, however, sufficient. *Cf.* the *IRC* case [1982] A.C. 617.
[54] *Cook v Southend Borough Council* [1990] 2 Q.B. 1.
[55] *Westminster Corporation*, n.47, was overruled.
[56] *Cook*, n.54, 7.

4. STANDING IN JUDICIAL REVIEW ACTIONS

A. Introduction

24–012 To describe the common law as unnecessarily confused would be to pay it a compliment. While the general trend was towards liberalisation of standing, particularly in the context of the prerogative orders, the stricter test for injunctions and declarations remained. There were, moreover, differing tests even within the prerogative remedies, particularly between certiorari and mandamus.

The Law Commission disapproved of the restrictive formulations of the legal right test, and of the different requirements that governed each of the remedies. It recommended that any person adversely affected by a decision should have locus standi.[57] In its subsequent report the Law Commission adopted the general flexible approach favoured by the earlier Working Paper and proposed that a person should have standing when there was a sufficient interest in the matter to which the application relates. This was felt to represent the existing position with regard to the prerogative orders. The law relating to declarations and injunctions was to be liberalised by the application of the sufficiency of interest test.[58]

The test proposed by the Law Commission was adopted in Ord.53 r.3(7). This has now been incorporated in the Supreme Court Act 1981[59] s.31(3), which states,

"No application for judicial review shall be made unless the leave of the High Court has been obtained in accordance with rules of court; and the court shall not grant leave to make such an application unless it considers that the applicant has a sufficient interest in the matter to which the application relates."

The procedures for judicial review are now governed by Pt 54 of the Civil Procedure Rules, CPR. This will be discussed below.[60] The test for standing however continues to be governed by the 1981 Act, s.31(3).

B. The IRC Case

24–013 The *IRC* case[61] was the first important decision on the sufficiency of interest test. Casual labour was common on Fleet Street newspapers, the workers

---

[57] Working Paper No.40 (1970), 125–132.
[58] Report on Remedies in Administrative Law, Law Com No.73, Cmnd. 6407, 22, 33.
[59] The Supreme Court Act is to be renamed the Senior Courts Act 1981, the change has been brought about by the Constitutional Reform Act 2005 Sch.11(1) para.1.
[60] See below, Ch.26.
[61] *R. v Inland Revenue Commissioners Ex p. National Federation of Self-Employed and Small Businesses Ltd* [1982] A.C. 617; P. Cane, "Standing, Legality and the Limits of Public Law" [1981] P.L. 322. When the IRC case was decided the test for standing was still to be found in Ord.53. It had not yet been incorporated within a statute. This was important because the Rules of the Supreme Court can only alter matters of procedure and not substance. If standing were to be regarded as substantive then no change could be effectuated through Order 53, although the change could have been made by the court itself.

often adopting fictitious names and paying no taxes. The Inland Revenue, IRC, made a deal with the relevant unions, workers and employers whereby if the casuals would fill in tax returns for the previous two years then the period prior to that would be forgotten. The National Federation argued that this bargain was ultra vires the IRC, and sought a declaration plus mandamus to compel the IRC to collect the back taxes. The IRC argued that the National Federation had no standing. Their Lordships found for the IRC, but it would be misleading to say that they upheld the entirety of the IRC's claim. In order to understand the test adopted by the House of Lords it is necessary to comprehend how it dealt with the *Gouriet* case.

i. Distinguishing the Gouriet case
In the lower courts the IRC relied on *Gouriet*, arguing that the National **24–014** Federation lacked standing to apply for a declaration because no legal right of its own had been affected.

The *Gouriet*[62] decision was treated as referring only to locus standi for declaration and injunction in their private law roles, and as having nothing to say about the standing for those remedies in public law. Order 53 r.1(2)[63] was interpreted to allow an applicant to claim a declaration or injunction instead of a prerogative order, but only in those areas or circumstances where a prerogative order would itself have been available. If an applicant would have had standing to seek a prerogative order then a declaration or injunction could be granted instead, even though the traditional standing requirements for declaration or injunction would not have been met.

To regard *Gouriet* as concerned only with standing in private law is to allow form to blind one to substance. The parties in *Gouriet* might appear "private": a trade union and a private citizen. The real argument in that case was, however, as to whether a private citizen should be able to vindicate the public interest without joining the Attorney-General. This was how the case was argued, and this was how their Lordships responded to the argument.[64]

Gouriet and the *IRC* case in fact reflect different philosophies. The former conceived the private citizen as having no role in enforcing the public interest, and thus preserved the dichotomy in the standing criteria for the prerogative orders and declaration and injunction. This ignored the fact that the private citizen was to some extent vindicating the public interest when seeking prerogative relief. The *IRC* case eschewed the historical distinction between the remedies, and took as its touchstone the more liberal rules for

---

[62] [1978] A.C. 435.
[63] Ord.53, r.1(2) allows a declaration or injunction to be claimed via an application for judicial review in certain circumstances.
[64] Insofar as this was the real question at stake in *Gouriet*, it clearly was "about" public law, and this is nonetheless true even though the issue of whether a citizen should be able to vindicate the public interest can arise in a non-public law case. This view is reinforced by the fact that both older and more recent authority, in what were indubitably public law cases, have expressed the test for standing in terms of private rights and special damage, where a declaration is being sought outside of s.31. See, *Gregory*, n.20; *Barrs*, n.24; *Stoke-on-Trent*, n.37.

prerogative relief, to which standing for declaration and injunction were then assimilated.

ii. Sufficiency of interest: a uniform test

24–015   The *IRC* case is complex because two matters were interwoven in the judgments: whether there should be a uniform test for the prerogative orders and whether there should be a uniform test for all the remedies. Lord Diplock answered both questions affirmatively.[65] The other judgments were less clear. Lord Fraser felt that the differences between the prerogative orders had been eradicated, but that not all the older law had been over-thrown.[66] Lord Scarman held that there should be no difference in standing between the prerogative orders, and that the same test should apply when a declaration or injunction was sought in a public law context.[67] Lord Roskill was clear that many of the old technical distinctions between the remedies, particularly the prerogative orders, should be swept away. The inference was that there should be a uniform test for all the remedies, but this was never made absolutely clear.[68] Lord Wilberforce was, by way of contrast, of the opinion that there should be a distinction even between the prerogative orders, with certiorari being subject to a less strict test than mandamus.[69]

The general thrust of the *IRC* case was, nonetheless, that standing should be developed to meet new problems, and that there should not be an endless discussion of previous authority. This furthered the tendency towards a unified conception of standing based upon sufficiency of interest,[70] not-withstanding the ambiguities in some of the judgments. Arguments that the test for standing should differ depending upon the particular remedy being sought have been generally absent from subsequent case law. It should however be recognised that even when the courts adopt a uniform test this does not mean that individual judges share the same view as to what should count as a sufficient interest. This is evident from the *IRC* case itself.[71]

iii. The determination of sufficiency of interest: fusion of standing and merits

24–016   We noted earlier that in private law the merits and standing were not gen-erally regarded as distinct: who could sue was answered by the definition of the cause of action. In public law, by way of contrast, standing was one matter, the merits another. This has to be revised to some extent at least in the light of the *IRC* case.

Their Lordships agreed that standing and the merits could often not be separated in this way. It might be possible to do so in relatively

---

[65] [1982] A.C. 617, 638, 640.
[66] [1982] A.C. 617, 645–646.
[67] [1982] A.C. 617, 649–653.
[68] [1982] A.C. 617, 656–658.
[69] [1982] A.C. 617, 631.
[70] Lord Denning MR in *O'Reilly v Mackman* [1982] 3 W.L.R. 604 stated that there was a uniform test.
[71] Compare, [1982] A.C. 617, 644 *per* Lord Diplock, 661 *per* Lord Roskill.

straightforward cases, but for more complex cases it would be necessary to consider the whole legal and factual context to determine whether an applicant possessed a sufficient interest. The term merits here meant that the court would look to the substance of the allegation in order to determine whether the applicant had standing. This included *the nature of the relevant power or duty, the alleged breach, and the subject-matter of the claim*. The term *fusion* will be used to refer to the process whereby the court considers these factors in order to determine whether the applicant has standing in a particular case.

To appreciate fully how this operates it is necessary to understand that the Supreme Court Act 1981, s.31(3), requires the court to consider sufficiency of interest at the leave stage. This would, prior to the CPR reforms, often be ex parte, and thus the court might only have evidence from one side. A court might feel at this stage that the applicant demonstrated a sufficient interest. The second stage is the hearing of the application itself, at which point the court will consider evidence from both parties. At this stage the court might well form the view that, on consideration of fuller evidence, the applicant did not possess the interest claimed. This conclusion will be reached from an appraisal of the nature of the duty cast upon the public body, the nature of the breach, and the position of the applicant. Thus, in the *IRC* case the only evidence at the ex parte stage was from the National Federation. By the time of the hearing the IRC had prepared affidavits giving its view of the case. This caused the House of Lords to dismiss the case.

The reasoning of their Lordships was, however, subtly different. Some[72] relied most heavily on the statutory framework and background to reach the conclusion that the applicant possessed no sufficient interest. A qualification was added that such a person or group might possess sufficient interest if the illegality were to be sufficiently grave. Other Law Lords, while referring to the statutory context, placed more emphasis on the absence of illegality. If at the hearing of the application itself the applicant had established the allegations made at the leave stage then the case would have proceeded.[73]

iv. Summary

   (1)   The general message from the *IRC* case was that there would be a unified test of standing based upon sufficiency of interest, shorn of archaic limitations, which would probably operate in the same way irrespective of the particular remedy sought. In this sense the test for standing is uniform.

24–017

---

[72] [1982] A.C. 617, 632–633, *per* Lord Wilberforce, 646, *per* Lord Fraser, 662–663, *per* Lord Roskill.
[73] [1982] A.C. 617, 637, 644, *per* Lord Diplock, 654, *per* Lord Scarman

(2) The relationship between standing at the leave stage and at the substantive hearing was summarised by Lord Donaldson M.R. in *Argyll*[74] as follows. At the leave stage an application should be refused only where the applicant has no interest whatsoever, and is a mere meddlesome busybody. Where, however, the application appears to be arguable and there is no other discretionary bar such as dilatoriness, the applicant should be given leave and standing can then be reconsidered as a matter of discretion at the substantive hearing. At this stage the strength of the applicant's interest will be one of the factors to be weighed in the balance. More recently Sedley J. in *Dixon*[75] emphasised that the criterion at the leave stage is set merely to prevent an applicant from intervening where there was no legitimate interest. This did not, however, mean that the applicant must show some pecuniary or special personal interest.

(3) The fusion technique means that standing may vary from area to area. It will depend upon the strength of the applicant's interest, the nature of statutory power or duty in issue, the subject-matter of the claim and the type of illegality asserted.

(4) The application of these criteria may, however, be unclear or uncertain. Where this is so, the determination of standing will depend upon certain more general assumptions of the judge as to the role which individuals should generally play in public law. This point will be developed later, but it is readily apparent from the *IRC* case itself. Thus, Lord Diplock approached the process of statutory construction with the explicit assumption that it would be a grave lacuna in our law if an interest group, or a private citizen, could not "vindicate the rule of law and get the unlawful action stopped".[76] This is close to a citizen action view of standing. This assumption was not shared by all of their Lordships, and differences of this kind can impact on the interpretative process.

C. Interpretation of the Test

24–018 The cases decided after the *IRC* case may be categorised in the following manner. It will become apparent that not all courts have in fact applied the fusion approach.

i. Individual challenges: a liberal approach, but no real fusion

24–019 There are a number of cases in which the courts have treated the *IRC* decision as a liberalisation of the pre-existing standing rules. The cases

---

[74] *R. v Monopolies and Mergers Commission Ex p. Argyll Group plc* [1986] 1 W.L.R. 763, 773; *Brown v The Executors of the Estate of HM Queen Elizabeth the Queen Mother, The Executors of HRH the Princess Margaret Countess of Snowdon, HM Attorney General* [2007] EWHC Fam 1607, para.62.
[75] *R. v Somerset County Council and ARC Southern Ltd Ex p. Dixon* [1998] Env. L.R. 111.
[76] [1982] A.C. 617, 644.

discussed in this section do *not* however show attachment to the fusion technique. In reaching the decision to accord the applicant standing the courts did not undertake any *detailed* analysis of the nature of the relevant statutory powers, apart from adverting to the seriousness of the alleged illegality.

Thus in *Smedley* a taxpayer who raised a serious question concerning the legality of governmental action in connection with the EC was accorded standing.[77] In *Leigh* a journalist as a "guardian of the public interest" in open justice was held to have a sufficient interest to obtain a declaration that justices could not refuse to reveal their identity.[78] In *Percival* the head of a set of chambers was accorded standing to contest a decision by the Bar Council that another barrister should be charged with a more serious, rather than a less serious, charge.[79]

Attempts to argue that an applicant must possess something akin to a narrow legal right before being accorded standing have not been successful.[80] Thus in *Dixon*[81] the applicant who was a local resident, a local councillor and a member of various bodies concerned to protect the environment, sought to challenge the grant of planning permission to extend quarrying in a particular area. Sedley J. held that standing at the leave stage should only be refused if it was clear that the applicant was a busybody with no legitimate interest in the matter. The applicant in the instant case was not a busybody, and he was perfectly entitled as a citizen to draw the attention of the court to what he considered to be an illegality in the grant of planning permission which was bound to have an impact on the natural environment. This more liberal approach has also been endorsed extra-judicially.[82]

ii. Individual challenges: a more restrictive approach, and the use of the fusion technique

The fusion technique is dependent upon statutory construction and results will therefore differ from area to area. It is also evident that the application of the test can lead to broad or narrow categories of applicant being afforded standing. Some decisions *have* adopted the fusion approach, but the results have been relatively restrictive.

Thus, in *Bateman*[83] it was held, on construction of the relevant statutory provisions, that a legally-aided client did not have standing to contest an

24–020

---

[77] *R. v Her Majesty's Treasury Ex p. Smedley* [1985] Q.B. 657, 667, 669–670.
[78] *R. v Felixstowe JJ Ex p. Leigh* [1987] Q.B. 582, 595–598.
[79] *R. v General Council of the Bar Ex p. Percival* [1990] 3 All E.R. 137.
[80] *R. v Secretary of Companies Ex p. Central Bank of India* [1986] Q.B. 1114, 1161–1163. See also, *R. v Secretary of State for Social Services Ex p. Child Poverty Action Group* [1990] 2 Q.B. 540; *R. v International Stock Exchange of the United Kingdom and the Republic of Ireland Ex p. Else (1982) Ltd* [1993] 1 All E.R. 420, 432; *R. v London Borough of Haringey Ex p. Secretary of State for the Environment* [1991] C.O.D. 135.
[81] *Dixon*, n.75. See also *R. (on the application of Edwards) v Environment Agency (No.1)* [2004] 3 All E.R. 21.
[82] Sir Harry Woolf, "Public Law–Private Law: Why the Divide? A Personal View" [1986] P.L. 220, 231.
[83] *R. v Legal Aid Board Ex p. Bateman* [1992] 3 All E.R. 490.

order made as to the taxation of her solicitor's costs, since she was not affected by the result of the taxation. The action could only be brought by the solicitor, and the fact that the applicant was genuinely concerned to see that her solicitor was properly remunerated did not suffice to afford her a sufficient interest for the purposes of judicial review.[84]

In *Johnson*[85] it was held that the applicant did not have standing to question the validity of a notice served on his wife obliging her to answer inquiries into a fraud investigation currently under way against her husband.

In *Moses*[86] the applicant objected to the grant of planning permission for the extension of an airport runway. She had previously lived close to the end of the runway, but now lived six miles away. She argued that no environmental assessment had been made prior to the grant of planning permission. Scott Baker J. considered the approach in *Dixon*,[87] but adopted a narrower approach. He held that standing should not be accorded where the applicant has no real or justifiable concern about a public law decision. The court's time should not be expended on cases that were bound to fail. The applicant did not, on this criterion, possess a sufficient interest.

Moreover, in *Kides*[88] the claimant was refused standing to challenge the grant of planning permission. This was because she sought to challenge the permission on a ground related to the provision of affordable housing, whereas the court held that she had no interest in this matter, and was rather using it to prevent the building of any housing at all. She was, therefore, said to be a mere busybody in relation to affordable housing.

There may well be good policy reasons for limiting standing in certain types of case. Thus in *Bulger*[89] the father of a murdered child sought to challenge the Lord Chief Justice's decision fixing the tariff term to be served by those who had murdered his son. Rose L.J. held that in criminal cases there was no need for a third party to intervene to uphold the rule of law, since the traditional parties to criminal proceedings, the Crown and the defendant, could do so. The Lord Chief Justice when fixing the sentence had taken account of the views of the victim's family. This did not however amount to an invitation to indicate their views on the appropriate tariff, and the claimant could not therefore raise the matter by judicial review.

---

[84] Nolan L.J. accepted that, in cases where it was appropriate, a member of the public could represent the public interest, but regarded the applicant's behaviour here as "at best quixotic", *Bateman*, n.83, 496. See also, *R. v Lautro Ex p. Tee* [1993] C.O.D. 362; *R. v Secretary of State for Defence Ex p. Sancto* [1993] C.O.D. 144.

[85] *R. v Director of the Serious Fraud Office Ex p. Johnson* [1993] C.O.D. 58.

[86] *R. v North West Leicestershire District Council Ex p. Moses* [2000] J.P.L. 733.

[87] *Dixon*, n.75.

[88] *R. (on the application of Kides) v South Cambridgeshire DC* [2001] EWHC Admin 839, para.109.

[89] *R. (on the application of Ralph Bulger) v Secretary of State for the Home Department, and The Lord Chief Justice of England and Wales* [2001] 3 All E.R. 449.

iii. Group challenges: associational, surrogate and public interest
Cane[90] has argued persuasively that there are three kinds of group challenge: **24–021**
associational, surrogate and public interest. There may be instances where
the line between these categories can become blurred or contestable, but the
taxonomy is helpful nonetheless.

Associational standing is typified by an organisation suing on behalf of its
members. Standing has been accorded in such circumstances where the
group consists of persons who are directly affected by the disputed decision.[91] There can equally be cases where one member of a group brings the
action on behalf of the group as a whole.[92]

Surrogate standing covers the case where a pressure group represents the
interests of others, who may not be well placed to bring the action themselves. The courts have allowed challenges brought by the Child Poverty
Action Group to decisions concerning social security that affected claimants. Woolf J. reasoned that the CPAG was a body designed to represent
the interests of unidentified claimants, who stood to be deprived of benefits
by the Secretary of State and that it had a sufficient interest to argue the
case.[93] The court also construed the Highgate Projects, a charitable body
providing hostel accommodation to young offenders, as being a "person
affected" within the meaning of regulations concerning housing benefit. The
young people could have acted for themselves, and were therefore competent to authorise the Project to act as their agent in review proceedings.[94]

Public interest standing is asserted by those claiming to represent the wider
public interest, rather than merely that of a group with an identifiable
membership. In this type of case the decision may affect the public generally,
or a section thereof, but no one particular individual has any more
immediate interest than any other, and a group seeks to contest the matter
before the courts. We shall see that some claims of this nature have failed,
but a number have succeeded.

iv. Public interest challenges by a group or an individual
An individual or a group may bring a public interest challenge, although it is   **24–022**
now more common for groups to advance such claims.

A well-known claim that failed was the *Rose Theatre* case.[95] Developers,
who had planning permission for an office block, discovered the remains of
an important Elizabethan theatre. A number of people formed a company

---

[90] "Standing up for the Public" [1995] P.L. 276.
[91] *Royal College of Nursing of the UK v DHSS* [1981] 1 All E.R. 545, 551; *R. v Chief Adjudication Officer Ex p. Bland*, February 6, 1985; *R. (on the application of National Association of
Guardians ad Litem and Reporting Officers) v Children Family Court Advisory Service* [2002]
A.C.D. 44.
[92] *R. v Dyfed County Council Ex p. Manson* [1994] C.O.D. 366.
[93] *Child Poverty Action Group*, n.80, detailed argument on the standing issue was not heard by
the court, 556.
[94] *R. v Stoke City Council Ex p. Highgate Projects* [1994] C.O.D. 414.
[95] *R. v Secretary of State for the Environment Ex p. Rose Theatre Trust Co* [1990] 1 Q.B. 504; Sir
Konrad Schiemann, "Locus Standi" [1990] P.L. 342; P. Cane, "Statutes, Standing and
Representation" [1990] P.L. 307.

seeking to preserve the remains. They sought to persuade the Secretary of State to include the site in the list of monuments under the Ancient Monuments and Archaeological Areas Act 1979. The Secretary of State could do so if the site appeared to him to be of national importance. If the site was thus designated no work could be done without his consent. Although the Secretary of State agreed that the site was of national importance he declined to include it within the relevant legislation. Schiemann J. found that there had in fact been no illegality, but he also held that the applicants had no locus standi. He accepted that a direct financial or legal interest was not necessary in order for an applicant to have standing, and that it was necessary to consider the statute to determine whether it afforded standing to these individuals in this instance. However, he also approached the matter with the express view that not every person will always have sufficient interest to bring a case; that the assertion of an interest by many people did not mean that they actually possessed one; *and* that there might be certain types of governmental action which no one could challenge. On the facts of the case he held that no individual could point to anything in the statute which would give him a greater right or interest than any other that the decision would be taken lawfully. Schiemann J. concluded that while in a broad sense we could all expect that decisions be made lawfully that was insufficient to give the applicants standing.[96]

In other cases public interest challenges have been successful. In the *Equal Opportunities Commission* case,[97] the EOC sought locus standi to argue that certain rules concerning entitlement to redundancy pay and protection from unfair dismissal were discriminatory and in breach of EC law. The duties of the EOC included working towards the elimination of discrimination, and promoting equality of opportunity between men and women.[98] The House of Lords held that the EOC had standing. Lord Keith, giving the majority judgment, reasoned that if the contested provisions were discriminatory then steps taken by the EOC to change them could reasonably be regarded as working towards the elimination of discrimination. It would, said his Lordship,[99] be a retrograde step to hold that the EOC did not have standing to "agitate in judicial review proceedings questions related to sex discrimination which are of public importance and affect a large section of the population".

In *Greenpeace*[100] the applicant group challenged the regulation of the Sellafield nuclear site. Otton J. made it clear that interest groups would not automatically be afforded standing merely because the members were concerned about a particular matter, but found that the group had standing, and declined to follow the *Rose Theatre* decision. He reached his conclusion

---

[96] See also, *R. v Secretary of State for the Home Department Ex p. Amnesty International*, January 31, 2000; *Rape Crisis Centre v Secretary of State for the Home Department* [2001] S.L.T. 389; Lord Hope, "Mike Tyson comes to Glasgow—A Question of Standing" [2001] P.L. 294.
[97] *R. v Secretary of State for Employment Ex p. Equal Opportunities Commission* [1995] 1 A.C. 1.
[98] Sex Discrimination Act 1975 s.53(1).
[99] [1995] 1 A.C. 1, 26.
[100] *R. v Her Majesty's Inspector of Pollution Ex p. Greenpeace Ltd (No.2)* [1994] 4 All E.R. 329.

by taking a number of factors into account, including: the fact that Greenpeace was a respected international organisation with a large membership; that a number of its members lived in the Cumbria region; that the issues were serious and complex; that Greenpeace was well-placed to argue them; and that if it did not have standing there might not be any effective way to bring the matter before the court.

A liberal attitude towards public interest challenges is also apparent in the *World Development Movement* case.[101] The WDM sought to challenge the Minister's decision to grant aid to fund the construction of the Pergau dam in Malaysia, on the ground that it was outside the relevant statutory powers. The court accorded the group standing, taking into account the fact that no other challenger was likely to come forward, and the importance of vindicating the rule of law by ensuring that the minister remained within his statutory powers.[102] It is moreover clear from *Blackfordby*[103] that the court will not readily find that the incorporation of an action group is a bar to the bringing of an action for judicial review.

v. Group challenges and unincorporated associations

Special problems have been encountered with actions brought by unincorporated associations, and the courts are presently divided as to whether such a body can bring proceedings in its own name.   **24–023**

Auld J. in the *Darlington* case,[104] relying on the general principle that such bodies could not sue or be sued in their own name, held that they could not seek review in their own name, and that legal capacity was distinct from the issue of standing.

Turner J. in the *"Brake"* case[105] reached the opposite conclusion. He reasoned that in private law a person asserted private rights, and such rights could only be enjoyed by a legal person. In public law it was the legality of the public body's actions that was of prime concern. The applicant who claimed a sufficient interest was invoking the supervisory jurisdiction of the court to control excess of power by a public body. Such actions could therefore be brought by an unincorporated association.

In the *Pig Industry* case, Richards J. took the view that there was nothing to prevent an unincorporated association seeking judicial review, provided that adequate provision could be made as to costs.[106]

---

[101] *R. v Secretary of State for Foreign Affairs Ex p. World Development Movement* [1995] 1 W.L.R. 386.
[102] See also, *R. v Secretary of State for Foreign and Commonwealth Affairs Ex p. Rees-Mogg* [1994] Q.B. 552; *Dixon*, n.75; *R. v Leicester County Council, Hepworth Building Products Ltd and Onyx Ltd Ex p. Blackfordby & Boothcorpe Action Group Ltd* [2000] E.H.L.R. 215.
[103] n.102.
[104] *R. v Darlington BC and Darlington Transport Company Ltd Ex p. the Association of Darlington Taxi Owners and the Darlington Owner Drivers Association* [1994] C.O.D. 424.
[105] *R. v Traffic Commissioner for the North Western Traffic Area Ex p. "Brake"* [1996] C.O.D. 248.
[106] *R. v Ministry of Agriculture, Fisheries and Food Ex p. the British Pig Industry* [2001] A.C.D. 3.

vi. Standing, fusion and the judicial role

24–024　Two more general points are apparent from the courts' jurisprudence, and these should be borne in mind when reading the cases in this area.

First, it is clear that the fusion approach has been used by the courts to varying degrees, and also that the process of statutory construction demanded by the *IRC* methodology can lead to differences of opinion from members of the same court. This is exemplified by the *EOC* case in the Court of Appeal, where three differing views emerged from the process of statutory construction as to whether the applicant body should have standing. The members of the court differed as to whether the nature of the EOC's duties and the subject-matter of the claim should, as a matter of statutory construction, be held to afford the body standing.[107]

Second, there is the less obvious point that the very process of statutory construction demanded by the *IRC* case will often turn upon more general views concerning the purpose of standing. This is unsurprising. The very process of statutory construction, looking to the nature of the duties and the subject-matter of the claim, will often not be self-executing: the answer will not leap out from the relevant materials, as exemplified by the differences in the *EOC* case. In reaching a conclusion the court will, therefore, fall back on certain more general beliefs about the role of standing.

The judgment in the *Rose Theatre* case[108] was, for example, premised on the assumption that a citizen action view of standing was not to be accepted, in this area at least. The idea underpinning the citizen action, that citizens generally should be able to vindicate the public interest without showing any individual harm over and above that of the general community, particularly in cases where such harm would be difficult to substantiate, was rejected.

The *EOC* case provides a good contrast.[109] The differences of view as to the standing of the EOC as between the Court of Appeal and the House of Lords are not explicable solely on the basis of differences as to statutory interpretation. It is clear that Lord Keith disagreed with the majority in the Court of Appeal in part because he took a different view as to the role that the EOC should have in the regime of sex discrimination. His Lordship approached the process of statutory interpretation with the view that it was right and proper that the EOC should be able to raise questions concerning discrimination, which were of public importance and affected large sections of the population.

D. Locus Standi under the Human Rights Act 1998

24–025　We have seen that the Human Rights Act 1998 s.6, created a new statutory head of illegality, which can be used in judicial review actions.[110] The criteria for standing is however not the normal test of sufficiency of interest. It is

---

[107] *R. v Secretary of State for Employment Ex p. Equal Opportunities Commission* [1993] 1 All E.R. 1022, 1030–1032, 1039–1041, 1048–1051.
[108] [1990] 1 Q.B. 504.
[109] [1995] 1 A.C. 1.
[110] See above, Ch.18.

narrower than this, and s.7(1) states that only a victim can plead this head of illegality concerned with breach of Convention rights.[111] This is reinforced by s.7(3), which states that if proceedings are brought for judicial review the applicant is to be taken as having a sufficient interest in relation to the unlawful act only if he is, or would be, a victim of that act. Concerns were expressed about the narrowness of this test during the passage of the Bill, and it remains to be seen how the courts will interpret the term victim. Section 7(6) of the Act stipulates that the criterion as to whether a person is a victim is to be found in the jurisprudence under art.34 ECHR.[112]

This article provides that the European Court of Human Rights (ECtHR) may receive a petition from any person, non-governmental organisation or group of individuals claiming to be the victim of a violation of a Convention right. It is clear from the jurisprudence that there is no *actio popularis* in this area.[113] This is to be expected given the wording of the article in terms of "victim". Article 34 is nonetheless broader than might appear at first sight. It does expressly allow for actions to be brought by organisations such as trade unions, and it seems that such bodies can sue on behalf of their members.[114] It also expressly countenances actions by groups of individuals, provided that each member of the group can show a violation of the relevant right.[115] The term victim has been further expanded by the recognition of potential and indirect victims.[116] The idea of the potential victim has been held to cover the situation where a law has been enacted criminalising homosexuality, and a complaint has been admitted even though the law had not been applied to the complainant.[117] The concept of the indirect victim has been used to admit cases brought by, for example, close relatives of the direct victim, and those who have had a close relationship with the direct victim.[118]

A claimant who has been given some remedy by the ECtHR may still be regarded as a victim for the purposes of a subsequent judicial review action.[119] A claimant under the HRA may nonetheless have difficulty in establishing that he or she is a victim. Thus in the *PAGB* case it was held that a trade association for manufacturers in the pharmaceutical industry

---

[111] J. Miles, "Standing under the Human Rights Act 1998: Theories of Rights Enforcement and the Nature of Public Law Adjudication" [2000] C.L.J. 133.

[112] The jurisprudence was in fact made under art.25 ECHR. This contained the requirement that the applicant be a victim in order to bring a case before the European Commission of Human Rights. The Convention has been modified by Protocol 11, which abolished the Commission and re-modelled the Court. The requirement that the applicant be a victim in order to bring a case before the Court is now to be found in art.34 of the Convention, but the jurisprudence decided under art.25 will doubtless continue to be applied.

[113] D. Gomien, D. Harris and L. Zwaak, *Law and Practice of the European Convention on Human Rights and the European Social Charter* (Council of Europe, 1996), 42–47.

[114] Gomien, Harris and Zwaak, n.113, 44.

[115] Gomien, Harris and Zwaak, n.113, 43.

[116] Gomien, Harris and Zwaak, n.113, 44–46; *Campbell and Cosans v UK* (1982) 4 E.H.R.R. 293; *Open Door Counselling and Dublin Well Woman v Ireland* (1993) 15 E.H.R.R. 244.

[117] *Norris v Ireland* (1991) 13 E.H.R.R. 186.

[118] Gomien, Harris and Zwaak, n.113, 46; *Abdulaziz, Cabales and Balkandali v U.K.* (1985) 7 E.H.R.R. 471.

[119] *Re McKerr* [2004] UKHL 12.

was not a victim for the purposes of an action alleging a breach of art.6 ECHR.[120] In *Adams* the claimant sought to challenge Scottish legislation that criminalised foxhunting, on the ground, inter alia, that it was in breach of the HRA. The court held that membership of a club that supported foxhunting was not equivalent to being actively engaged in it, and therefore the claimant was not a victim for the purposes of the HRA.[121] In *Taylor*[122] the court held that the victim test under s.7 HRA meant that it had not been intended that members of the public should use the Act or the Convention to change legislation which they considered was incompatible with the Convention, but which they were not adversely affected by.

If a claimant is unable to satisfy the victim test all is not lost. It may still be possible to bring an application for judicial review without directly using the HRA, and relying instead on the common law jurisprudence concerning fundamental rights.[123] It should also be remembered that the test for standing under the HRA will not apply where a claimant seeks to vindicate Convention rights via EC law.[124]

E. Locus Standi Outside Section 31

24–026   The passage of the revised Ord.53 did not abrogate the previous methods of seeking a declaration or injunction. A plaintiff could, for example, still seek a declaration outside Ord.53, subject to the case law concerning the presumptive exclusivity of this procedure, which will be considered below.[125] We have already seen that the *IRC*[126] case restricted the *Gouriet*[127] test of private rights and special damage to the private law role of declaration and injunction. The difficulty of regarding *Gouriet* as a purely private law case, and hence the artificiality of the way in which the case was distinguished, have already been discussed.[128] It appears nonetheless that the test for standing outside s.31 is still private rights and special damage.[129]

We have seen that the legal right test has been effectively rejected *within* s.31, and it is therefore important to consider why it should continue to furnish the criterion in actions for a declaration or injunction brought *outside* that section. Two reasons can be identified, neither of which is convincing.

First, there is the argument that removal of the Attorney-General would

---

[120] *Director General of Fair Trading v Proprietary Association of Great Britain* [2002] 1 W.L.R. 269.
[121] *Adams v Lord Advocate* (2003) S.L.T. 366.
[122] *Lancashire County Council v Taylor* [2005] 1 W.L.R. 2668.
[123] See above, Ch.17.
[124] See above, para.18–057.
[125] See below, Ch.26.
[126] [1982] A.C. 617.
[127] [1978] A.C. 435.
[128] See above para.24–014.
[129] *Barrs*, n.24; *Steeples v Derbyshire City Council* [1985] 1 W.L.R. 256, 290–298; *Ashby v Ebdon* [1985] Ch.394; *Stoke-on-Trent*, n.37, 766–767, 769–771; *Mortimer v Labour Party*, January 14, 2000.

mean unrestricted access for individuals wishing to assert a public right.[130] This does not follow. The issue is *who* is to decide the limitations upon standing, the courts as in the case of s.31, or the Attorney-General for cases outside that section. There are a number of reasons for preferring the courts. The Attorney-General is a quasi-political figure, and the day-to-day process of political responsibility may not be the most appropriate backdrop from which to make decisions about whether a case should proceed. The public interest is not, as counsel for Gouriet observed,[131] one and indivisible. It is often an amalgam of intersecting and conflicting interests. A balancing process is entailed and the Attorney-General may not be best placed to make this determination.

The second argument[132] is that the two-stage procedure within s.31 means that frivolous applications will normally be weeded out without troubling the public body since the application will be ex parte. Since there is no such procedure in an ordinary action the public body will have to appear and argue that the plaintiff has no standing. There are a number of difficulties with this argument. It has never been made before even though it would have been equally relevant prior to the reform of remedies since the pre-rogative orders have always had a two-stage procedure. If people who do not have private rights are not regarded as vexatious in proceedings under s.31, it is difficult to see why they should suddenly become so when the form of relief alters.

5. INTERVENTION IN JUDICIAL REVIEW ACTIONS

An issue that is closely related to, but distinct from, standing is that of intervention. The rules on intervention by a third party in judicial review proceedings are as follows. Order 53 r.5(3) provided that the claim form must be served on all persons directly affected, and r.5(7) allowed the court to hear representations from those who ought to have been served. The requirement that a person be directly affected was narrowly construed in *Muldoon*[133] to mean that the person had to be affected without the impact of any intermediate agency. Order 53 r.9(1) allowed the court to admit a person who wished to be heard in opposition to the application for review where the court considered that he was a proper person to be heard.[134]

The Civil Procedure Rules (CPR), which came into force on April 29, 1999, now govern this area.[135] The CPR have been further modified so as to

24–027

---

[130] *Gouriet* [1978] A.C. 435, 483, 501–502.
[131] *Gouriet*, n.130, 461.
[132] *Barrs*, n.24. The point was not developed in *Gouriet* [1978] A.C. 435.
[133] *R. v Rent Service Officer Ex p. Muldoon* [1996] 1 W.L.R. 1103.
[134] *R. v The Monopolies and Mergers Commission, and the Secretary of State for Trade and Industry Ex p. Milk Marque Ltd and the National Farmers' Union* [2000] C.O.D. 329.
[135] Lord Woolf, *Access to Justice: The Final Report to the Lord Chancellor on the Civil Justice System in England and Wales* (1997); SI 1998/3132.

apply to all judicial review applications lodged on or after October 2, 2000.[136] CPR 54.1(2)(f) allows an interested party, other than the claimant and defendant, who is directly affected by the claim, to be served. CPR 54.17 provides that any person may apply for permission to file evidence or make representations at the hearing.[137]

The "amicus brief" is used quite extensively in other countries such as the USA, Canada, and by the European Court of Human Rights. It can perform a valuable informational function by bringing relevant evidence to the court, which it would not otherwise have heard. The recent liberalisation of standing by our courts has made them more receptive to such interventions.[138]

6. THE FUNCTION OF STANDING

24–028   It is time now to stand back from the detail of the case law and to look more generally at the role of locus standi. Any definition of sufficient interest presupposes a particular view of the function to be performed by standing.

A. Vindication of Private Rights

24–029   It is interesting the way in which legal systems, for all their diversity, nevertheless display interesting points in common. Standing is one such instance. There was an early insistence on the presence of a legal right, in the sense of a private cause of action, and a gradual movement away from that criterion.[139] There are two principal reasons why the legal right test assumed such a central role.

On the one hand, there was the unthinking adoption of rules from private law causes of action into the realm of challenges against public bodies, as exemplified by cases such as *Boyce*.[140] On the other hand, there was the more abstract argument found in *Gouriet*.[141] A role for the individual was specifically etched out and that role was the vindication of private rights, with the public interest being protected by the Attorney-General. This function of the individual mirrored that of the courts, which perceived their role as the settling of private dispute. The courts would adjudicate on a matter of

---

[136] SI 2000/2092.
[137] *R. (on the application of the Howard League for Penal Reform) v Secretary of State for the Home Department (No.1)* [2002] EWHC 1750.
[138] *R. v Home Secretary Ex p. Sivakumaran* [1988] A.C. 958; *R. v Coventry City Council Ex p. Phoenix Aviation* [1995] 3 All E.R. 37; *R. v Secretary of State for the Home Department Ex p. Venables* [1998] A.C. 407; *R. v Secretary of State for the Home Department Ex p. Hargreaves* [1997] 1 W.L.R. 906; *R. v Lord Chancellor Ex p. Witham* [1998] Q.B. 575; *R. (on the application of Northern Ireland Human Rights Commission) v Greater Belfast Coroner* [2002] UKHL 25; C. Harlow, "Public Law and Popular Justice" (2002) 65 M.L.R. 1.
[139] The test has been relaxed in the USA, Canada, and Australia.
[140] [1903] 1 Ch.109.
[141] [1978] A.C. 435.

public law at the instance of an individual, provided that it was settling the rights of the latter and because it was doing so. This perspective on the role of the individual and the court proved inadequate for a number of reasons.

First, as argued above, it became clear that this presented a distorted picture of what the courts *had* been doing. The approach within the prerogative orders could not be fitted into a conceptual strait-jacket called private dispute settling. Individuals were to a greater or lesser degree vindicating the public interest. This tension between the prerogative orders, and declaration and injunction, was largely ignored and de facto resolved in favour of the latter in the *Gouriet* case, whereas in *IRC* it was faced more openly, inadequately explained, and resolved in favour of the prerogative orders.

A second reason why the private right model proved inadequate was that new values developed that people felt should be protected, but which could not be accommodated by the traditional restrictive standing criteria. Broader social, economic, religious and non-economic values are justly prized and protection is sought against their infringement. Traditional legal rights in such values will often not exist. No established cause of action arises if they are infringed. If standing were limited to situations in which such a cause of action arose no person could invoke the protection of the court. It could of course be argued that the law should develop new "rights" or new concepts of "property" to provide protection for these emerging values. This has happened to some extent. There are, however, dangers in pressing the concept of property or legal right too far, and thereby diluting their content.[142] The expansion in the concept of right or property does, moreover, undermine the argument that the government is settling a private dispute with an individual.[143]

The final reason why the legal right test was inadequate was that the underlying premise was flawed. The premise was that these cases really were primarily about private rights, and that the court would consider matters of public law only incidentally, in so far as necessary to decide whether the private right was infringed or not. Thus, Sarah claims that a public body has trespassed upon her property. The defence is raised that this is justified by a compulsory purchase order. Sarah will have standing to challenge the legality of the order because her private rights are at stake. However in deciding on the legality of the order, Sarah's status as an injured property owner is not determinative. The principal arguments will focus on public law matters concerning the legality of the order, and Sarah will be voicing the interests of the public at large. The *effect* of a finding that a legal right has been infringed will tell one that the order was invalid and hence that a trespass action lies, but that conclusion only follows from the decision that the order was illegal.[144]

---

[142] Compare, C. Reich, "The New Property" (1964) 73 Yale L.J. 733 and W. Simon, "Rights and Redistribution in the Welfare System" (1986) 38 Stan. L.R. 1431.
[143] *Legal Identity*, n.3, 25; Cane, n.22.
[144] Vining, n.3, 20.

B. Fusion of Standing and Merits

24–030   The argument for the fusion approach is that it is only by looking at matters
such as the type of injury, the aims of the legislation, and the interest
affected, that one can decide who should be able to claim. It has been argued
that attempts to decide such matters in the abstract are productive of misleading and unhelpful generalisation.[145] It is argued, moreover, that this is
not very different from the way in which such factors are used in private law
to determine the existence of a cause of action. These sentiments are clearly
evident in the *IRC*[146] decision, and the House of Lords' insistence that
sufficiency of interest should be seen against the subject-matter of the
application, including the nature of the duty and the nature of the breach.[147]

The closest analogy is to the rules for determining whether an action lies
at the suit of an individual for breach of statutory duty: who is enabled to
sue will be dependent upon construction of the particular statute. This
analogy is also indicative of the problems with the fusion approach. Statutory construction is a notoriously difficult operation quite simply because
the legislature has often given no thought as to who should be able to claim.
Search for actual legislative intent becomes impossible. This leads the courts
to infer intent from such matters as the nature of the duty and subject-
matter of the claim. It is interesting that in cases on breach of statutory duty
the courts' inference is not in fact drawn from detailed consideration of all
points relevant to the statute. Rather, the judicial process abstracts certain
matters and regards these as central or strongly presumptive, such as whether a penalty exists, and the class of persons affected by the statute.
Inferences are then drawn as to civil actionability from the answers to these
questions.[148] The very process of abstracting such criteria recreates standing
as a preliminary issue. Moreover, because who can sue is meant to be a
result of detailed consideration of the individual statute, and because in
many cases it is palpably not,[149] there is a judicial disenchantment with the
process. This manifests itself in a refusal to be led through the competing
lines of cases. The conclusion is both the ultimate generalisation and the
ultimate in the ad hoc: the court will allow a person to be a beneficiary of the
statute if it thinks it right that this should be so.[150]

This is not to suggest that a court should decide standing completely

---

[145] L. Albert, "Standing to Challenge Administrative Action: An Inadequate Surrogate for
Claims to Relief" (1973–1974) 83 Yale L.J. 425 and "Justiciability and Theories of Judicial
Review: A Remote Relationship" (1976–1977) 50 So Calif. L.R. 1139.
[146] [1982] A.C. 617.
[147] Their Lordships framed their judgments as if the fusion technique had been an accepted part
of the legal vocabulary. With respect, this was not so. It is true that one can point to cases in
which the courts have considered the ambit and purposes of a statutory scheme in order to
determine standing. However, these are far outweighed by the cases in which the issue of locus
standi has been decided by abstracted categories, such as ratepayers or competitors, without
any detailed analysis of the scope of the duty or nature of the breach
[148] *Markesinis and Deakin's Tort Law* (S. Deakin, A. Johnston and B. Markesinis, Oxford
University Press, 5th edn, 2003), 358–374.
[149] *Booth & Co (International) Ltd v National Enterprise Board* [1978] 3 All E.R. 624.
[150] *Ex p. Island Records Ltd* [1978] Ch.122, 134. The case has been limited by *RCA Corporation
Ltd v Pollard* [1983] Ch.135, but this does not affect the general point being made in the text.

independent of the merits. The argument is that it is unlikely that standing will disappear as an independent issue, to be swallowed up by the merits and re-emerge as a number of distinct "causes of action", in which those who can sue will depend entirely on the subject-matter area.[151] Even if this aim could be realised it would have serious disadvantages. Access to the courts should, in principle, be as clear as possible and this would not be so under the fusion doctrine.

It is apparent from their Lordships' judgments in the *IRC* case that they did not conceive of having to look to the merits on every occasion. It seems clear that a busybody can be excluded, or an applicant with a strong interest can be admitted, without venturing into any detailed consideration of the merits.

Later case law has shown that many courts have not engaged in detailed analysis of the nature of the statutory power, or subject matter of the claim, when determining who has standing. When the fusion technique has been applied in detail it has, on occasion, generated significant differences of opinion as between the members of the same court as to whether the particular applicant was intended to have standing. Moreover, as we have seen,[152] uncertainty as to what the legislature intended means that the court's judgment will be influenced by more general perceptions as to the role that the individual should have in public law.

C. Citizen Action

i. The arguments for such an action

A citizen action or *actio popularis* is based on the premise that the main aim of public law is to keep public bodies within their powers. The presumption is that citizens generally should be enabled to vindicate the public interest without showing individual harm over and above that of the general community. The arguments in favour of such an approach are as follows.[153] The first was put succinctly by Lord Diplock in the *IRC* case.[154]

24–031

> "It would, in my view, be a grave *lacuna* in our system of public law if a pressure group, like the federation, or even a single public-spirited taxpayer, were prevented by outdated technical rules of locus standi from bringing the matter to the attention of the court to vindicate the rule of law and get the unlawful action stopped."

Second, there are instances of unlawful conduct, which affect the public at large on matters of importance, but which do not in any real sense affect the interests of one individual more than another. Such illegalities should be capable of being challenged in our society.

---

[151] [1982] A.C. 617.
[152] See above, para.24–024.
[153] See also, Sir Konrad Schiemann, n.95, 346.
[154] [1982] A.C. 617, 644.

Third, even if the interests of more specific individuals are affected by the disputed governmental action, there may be reasons why such individuals have not directly raised the point and could not be expected to do so. This was acknowledged by Woolf L.J. in the *CPAG* case, when he recognised that the Child Poverty Action Group, which gives advice to social security claimants, might well contest general matters of importance which individual claimants for social welfare would not be expected to raise.[155]

A number of objections have been voiced against the adoption of such an approach. They can be broadly divided into the practical and the conceptual.

ii. Practical objections

24–032 There are a number of different practical objections raised against the citizen action, the most oft-repeated being that it would open the courthouse doors to vexatious litigants and busybodies. Scott has provided the most succinct response to this criticism,

"The idle and whimsical plaintiff, a dilettante who litigates for a lark, is a spectre which haunts the legal literature, not the courtroom."[156]

A second practical objection is that an applicant who has no personal interest will not be the most effective advocate of the issue. This is a non sequitur. No one has demonstrated any correlation between the degree of interest that an applicant has and the effectiveness of the advocacy, and there is no reason to suspect that any such correlation exists. Indeed the public spirited citizen who challenges governmental action, even though there is no personal stake in the outcome, may well be a more effective litigant simply because the person will normally feel particularly strongly about the matter before bothering to bring a claim.

A final practical objection is that the greater number of suits against government would distract those in government from their primary task by taking up their time in defending legal actions. Moreover, such challenges would take up court time, the costs of which are borne by the public purse, with the consequence that there would be less money available for other matters, such as legal aid.[157]

This argument is open to question. It is, of course, true that the primary task of those who govern or administer is to do just that, but it is equally true that they should administer or govern according to the law. The key issue is, therefore, *who* should be able to bring any potential illegality before the court. It is not clear why an action that affects the public at large, in

---

[155] [1990] 2 Q.B. 540, 546–547.
[156] K. Scott, "Standing in the Supreme Court—A Functional Analysis" (1973) 86 Harv. L.R. 645. If this spectre were ever to be a problem it is one which could be solved through provisions as to costs. See also, J. Jolowicz, "Protection of Diffuse, Fragmented and Collective Interests in Civil Litigation: English Law" [1983] C.L.J. 222.
[157] Sir Konrad Schiemann, n.95, 348.

which no individual is necessarily affected more than any other, is a less deserving distraction from the primary task of governing, or a less deserving use of court time, than an action in which the applicant has some more particularised interest. This is particularly so given that the subject-matter in the former type of case may well be more important than in the latter.

A number of conceptual objections to a citizen action have been advanced in the literature. These must, for the sake of clarity, be distinguished.

iii. Conceptual objections: the need for a person
Vining[158] posits a situation in which the courts have discarded the legal **24–033** rights test and put nothing in its place, and asks whether that would be possible, answering that it would not. He argues that people possess a number of different identities such as father, businessman, sports player, etc. When a person comes to the court he comes not as a "natural person", but in one of the more particularised guises set out above.

The problem with this argument is that the conclusion follows inevitably from the premise, but it is the premise which is in issue. *If* the courts continue to require some harm personalised to the applicant then it will follow that the applicant will fail if he does not fall into the category, such as fathers, which the courts regard as harmed by the activity impugned. However, nothing in the argument demonstrates that the courts have to require such harm. It would be possible for a court, faced with the above example, to say that whether the applicant is or is not a father is not conclusive, and that he possesses a citizen's interest in preventing the challenged regulations from being promulgated. The only identity that the court would be concerned with would be the applicant's position as a citizen. The possibility of citizen actions cannot be rejected on the basis that they would somehow be logically inconsistent with the way in which courts "see" people who come before them.

iv. Conceptual objections: inconsistent with the traditional judicial role
A more complex objection to the citizen action is that it would be incon- **24–034** sistent with the traditional judicial role, or at least place it under severe strain. The argument is as follows.[159]

The common law case method serves, inter alia, to prevent the use of the judicial process for the articulation of abstract principles of law, as opposed to the settlement of concrete disputes. To this end ripeness focuses on the temporal immediacy of the harm, justiciability on the suitability of the subject-matter for judicial resolution, and standing on the nature of the person's interest. Where the connection between the interest asserted and the type of judicial intervention requested becomes more attenuated, so the possibility

---

[158] n.3, Ch.4.
[159] R. Brilmayer, "Judicial Review, Justiciability and the Limits of the Common Law Method" (1977) 57 Boston U.L.R. 807.

of broadly framed challenges increases.[160] The focus of the courts shifts from the remedying of private wrongs to the making of abstract determinations of legal principle. Any interest asserted becomes simply an excuse for engaging a court in a discussion of administrative practice that the applicant does not like.[161] Moreover, the more broadly framed the initial challenge, the more likely it will be that the applicant may fail adequately to represent future applicants who will be affected by the dispute. Narrower standing criteria, by way of contrast, implicitly look to the scope of those affected if the applicant wins or loses, and determine whether the harm alleged by the applicant is proximate enough to that suffered by other possible challengers in order that the former may "represent" the latter.

There is however an ambiguity as to the meaning of the words "abstract" or "broadly framed". Three interpretations are possible, none of which in fact support the argument advanced.

The first sees "abstract" or "broadly framed" as meaning that the principles which the courts will propound will be vague or unripe, in the sense of premature, this being juxtaposed to the settlement of "concrete" disputes. This does not follow from the existence of a citizen action. Allowing a broad range of persons to challenge administrative action does not mean that the principles thereby propounded will be vague or untimely. Limits of ripeness *and* justiciability would still exist. In the *IRC* case the illegality asserted by the National Federation was not abstract in the sense of vague or hypothetical. Nor was it unripe in the sense of being premature. Nor was the issue unsuited for legal resolution. The issue was sharply defined and current, albeit in the end unproven.

A second meaning of "abstract" and "broadly framed" is that a decision will not be concrete, and thus will be abstract, if no person is individually affected. But this proves too much for it is a tautology. It amounts to saying no more than that abstract determinations are bad and are determinations not affecting a specific person more than others; therefore, a citizen action is bad because abstract. A person may take such a view and defend it, but it has nothing to do with the traditional role of the courts. It is simply a value judgment. Moreover, such a meaning of abstract would automatically preclude challenges to important areas of governmental activity, which did not affect any person more than another.

A third interpretation of the phrases "abstract" and "broadly framed" is more complex and can be presented as follows. The premise behind the argument is that the traditional common law model of adjudication can be applied to public law, provided that we observe certain limits in terms of justiciability, ripeness, and standing. The traditional model is one in which the contest is between two individuals, is retrospective in the sense of concerning a completed set of past events, and one in which right and remedy are interdependent, the defendant compensating the plaintiff for some

---

[160] *Gouriet* [1978] A.C. 435, 501–502.
[161] See also, Schiemann, n.95, 348–349; Harlow, n.138; T.R.S. Allan, *Constitutional Justice, A Liberal Theory of the Rule of Law* (Oxford University Press, 2001), Ch.6.

breach of duty committed by him. Further, the judge will be a neutral umpire and the court's involvement will end with the conclusion of the case.[162]

However, whether the traditional model of adjudication can be applied to public law has very little if anything to do with standing, be it broad or narrow, and much to do with the subject-matter of public law. Public law litigation often sits uneasily with the traditional model. There may be a wide range of persons affected by the case, and the judicial focus may be more prospective than retrospective, being concerned with the modification of a public body's conduct in the future. These differences are reflected in the remedy, which will be formed ad hoc, be forward looking, and one that the judge takes an active role in formulating. All of these distinctions rest ultimately upon the fact that the subject-matter in a public law case will often involve broad issues of social and political choice. The more "abstract" or "general" nature of the issues presented for judicial determination is *not* a corollary of who has standing, but of the *subject-matter* itself. Nor is there any necessary connection between broad standing rules and problems of polycentricity. The fact that the action is brought by a public interest group, does not mean that the issue before the court is polycentric.[163] It may well be technical, and hard-edged, albeit one that does not affect any particular person more than another.

24–035

An example may help to make these points clearer. Let us take the facts of the *Prescott* case, in which the challenge was to the provision of free bus rides for old age pensioners.[164] Imagine first that only those with private rights are accorded standing. The court will have to consider a broad range of issues, as to the way local authorities hold their funds and the uses to which they can be put, in determining the legality of the scheme. The result may be the vindication of private rights, but the substance of the case will turn on the broader public interest as reflected in the vires issue. Alter the hypothesis so that a broader range of persons is accorded standing. The nature of the judicial inquiry will not be altered in any way by having broader standing rules.

What *is* undeniably true is that because public law issues have this broad reach there is a problem of interest representation, of ensuring both that those interested in the suit do have a chance to make representations, and that the "person" presenting the case adequately represents future interests. This is, however, because of the subject-matter, not the rules of standing. Narrow rules of locus standi do not solve this problem, they brush it under the carpet. In the example drawn from *Prescott*, if society only allowed those with private rights to argue the public interest about the legality of free bus rides for pensioners this would not somehow magically mean that others were not very concerned with the issue, nor would it ensure that the

---

[162] A. Chayes, "The Role of the Judge in Public Litigation" (1976) 89 Harv. L.R. 1281.
[163] *Cf.* Harlow, n.138, 10.
[164] [1955] Ch.210.

applicant who possessed the private rights would do the job of arguing the public interest adequately.

v. The limits to the citizen action: the relativity of ultra vires

24–036 The most important qualification to the citizen action has been voiced by one of its main proponents. Jaffe advocated broad rules of standing to allow the "private attorney-general" or "non-Hohfeldian plaintiff" to vindicate the public interest.[165] However, Jaffe favoured a two-part test for standing in which those with some interest would have standing as of right, whereas the standing of the citizen applicant would be at the discretion of the court. The rationale for this divide is that there may well be cases in which the interests the law chooses to protect are content with the situation. If this is so a stranger should not be allowed to raise a possible cause of invalidity. For example, if a restaurant is placed in an area where it should not have been allowed, but the residents are content with it, why should a stranger be allowed to complain?[166] Any test of standing should therefore include a concept of the zone of interests which the legislation is intended to protect, since this places control of the situation in the hands of those most immediately concerned. Where however the court feels that those possessing a defined legal interest do not adequately represent all interests intended to be protected by the legislation, and if there are no other devices for public control, or if those devices are unresponsive to unrepresented interests, then the court in its discretion can take jurisdiction at the instance of a private attorney-general.

Leaving aside the difficulties of defining who should be regarded as having a protected legal interest and who should be a stranger, Jaffe performs a valuable service by pointing to an aspect of the standing argument not often addressed. The existence of a citizen action is normally considered against the background of public activity which affects all, or a large number of people, but no one person in particular. Many, including myself, feel that this should not preclude a challenge. The difficulty is to formulate a rule that will allow this to happen, while not encroaching on the type of case that Jaffe has in mind. The essence of his argument is that invalidity is relative and that those who come within the "protected ambit" will differ depending upon the nature of the legislation involved. Thus, there are many cases where, if those affected do not complain, others should not be able to do so. In *Ridge v Baldwin*,[167] if the person affected had decided not to challenge his dismissal, should any one else have been able to do so? This is the key question.

---

[165] "Standing to Secure Judicial Review: Public Actions" (1960–1961) 74 Harv. L.R. 1265; "Standing to Secure Judicial Review: Private Actions" (1961–1962) 75 Harv. L.R. 255; "The Citizen and Litigant in Public Actions: The Non-Hohfeldian or Ideological Plaintiff" (1967–1968) 116 U. of Penn. L.R. 1033; "Standing Again" (1970–1971) 84 Harv. L.R. 633; R. Stewart, "The Reformation of American Administrative Law" (1975) 88 Harv. L.R. 1667, 1735–1737.
[166] See also, R. Cranston, "Reviewing Judicial Review", in H. Genn and G. Richardson (eds), *Administrative Law and Government Action* (Clarendon, 1994), 59–61.
[167] [1964] A.C. 40.

The answer will of course be a value judgment. The most extreme view would be to say that any citizen has an interest in any government wrong-doing and therefore should have standing. Many would, however, believe that this is wrong. If the Chief Constable does not wish to challenge the decision that is his affair and his life should not be upset by someone else doing so. The example from *Ridge* is of course capable of extension. What if, two, three, 20 people are affected; what then?

Jaffe is surely correct in principle. The citizen action is premised upon the sound reasoning that just because a very large number of people are equally affected this does not mean that no one should have standing if the subject-matter of the dispute is otherwise capable of judicial resolution. This does not logically or inexorably mean that any person must always be accorded standing. There will be "*Ridge* type" cases where none but the person or persons concerned will be granted locus standi. If they choose not to complain, so be it.

D. Injury in Fact

Davis favoured a test based purely upon injury in fact.[168] He argued strongly **24–037** against the other part of the test established by the United States' Supreme Court, the zone of interests test, saying that it was unworkable, conceptually unsound, and historically unnecessary. Davis is undoubtedly correct in pointing out the dangers and pitfalls in attempting to define legislative intent, but his insistence that injury in fact can provide the sole requirement for standing is questionable.

For Davis, such injury is both a necessary and a sufficient test of standing. The effect of regarding such injury as a necessary test for locus standi is the outright rejection of the citizen action in so far as that allows a citizen who can demonstrate no such injury, apart from a citizen's concern for legality, to impugn governmental action. The problem is that this leads to fortuitous distinctions being made, which reflect little credit on legal reasoning. Thus cases in which there is ephemeral and indirect injury are approved, even if this reaches the extreme of finding one applicant who has used a park and allowing him to dispute proposed action in relation to it, while disapproving attempts by an environmental group to do the same thing.

Treating injury in fact as a sufficient requirement for standing is also open to the objection that such injury is not, in many instances, self-defining. What constitutes injury is itself a normative value judgment, not simply an empirical observation. This value judgment cannot be made in a vacuum and must in fact be decided against the legislative or constitutional back-ground in question. The essence of the zone of interests test, rejected by the front door, reappears in a veiled form by the side entrance.

---

[168] "Standing: Taxpayers and Others" (1967–1968) 35 U. Chic. L.R. 601; "The Liberalised Law of Standing" (1969–1970) 37 U. Chic. L.R. 450. See also K.C. Davis, "Judicial Control of Administrative Action: A Review" (1966) 66 Col L.R. 635, 659–669.

7. Standing and Intervention: Looking to the Future

A. Standing

24–038 The optimal solution would be an approach akin to that propounded by Jaffe. This involves acceptance of citizen actions, particularly in those areas where a large number of people are equally affected by governmental irregularity, but where no particular person is singled out. To deny any access in such a case seems indefensible. If the subject-matter of the case is otherwise appropriate for judicial resolution, and the application is timely or ripe, to deny standing would be to render important areas of governmental activity immune from censure for no better reason than that they affect a large number of people. Common sense would indicate the opposite conclusion: that the wide range of people affected was a positive reason for allowing a challenge by someone.[169] Judicial support for this approach can be found in Sedley J.'s judgment in the *Dixon* case.[170] Public law was concerned with the abuse of power, even where there were no private rights at stake. A person or organisation with no personal stake in the outcome might wish to call the attention of the court to such an abuse of power, and there were a number of areas where any individual, simply as a citizen, had a sufficient interest to bring the matter before the court.[171]

This does not, as seen above, mean that any person should be allowed to raise any issue of invalidity. There will be "*Ridge* type cases": if the person directly affected does not challenge the act then no one should be able to do so. The precise dividing line between this type of case, and that in which any person should be accorded standing will not be easily drawn. It will necessarily involve a view of the merits to determine the ambit of those primarily entitled to invoke the illegality. Difficult borderlines will, however, always have to be drawn in this area.

24–039 A citizen should therefore be entitled at the discretion of the court to bring an action alleging invalid public activity, except where it can be shown from a consideration of the statutory framework that the range of persons with standing was intended to be narrower than this. In this latter instance standing should be as of right and limited to the protected class. This should be subject to the qualification that there might be cases where those with a protected legal interest do not adequately represent a wider group affected by the legislation. The wider group should be admitted at the discretion of the court. The presumption is therefore that citizens simply *qua* citizens have a sufficient interest in governmental legality. All else should be seen as a qualification of this.

This formulation may be juxtaposed to that proposed by Lord Woolf. He advocated a two-track test for standing, similar to that adopted in Canada, and similar also to the old test for standing and certiorari. The applicant will

---

[169] See the observations of Lord Diplock to this effect in the *IRC* case [1982] A.C. 617, 644.
[170] n.75.
[171] Sedley J. expressly placed reliance on older case law which in effect endorsed a citizen action view of standing: *De Haber*, n.11; *Worthington*, n.11; *Speyer*, n.11.

have a sufficient interest in cases where he or she has been personally adversely affected by the challenged decision. In other cases standing will be at the discretion of the court, which will take into account matters such as the allocation of scarce resources, the relationship between courts and Parliament, and the screening out of busybodies.[172] In a similar vein the Law Commission proposed a two-track system.[173] An applicant who is personally adversely affected will generally be admitted as a matter of course. Public interest challenges will lie at the discretion of the court, the test being whether the court considers that it is in the public interest for the applicant to make the application.

How far these formulations differ from that presented above depends upon the construction of the term "personal adverse effect"; and upon how a court exercises its discretion to admit cases which come within the second category. The broader the construction of the term personal adverse effect, and the more liberally the court interprets the discretion to admit a case which comes within the second category, then the closer will this formulation be to that proposed above.

B. Standing: Individuals and Groups

When we consider the appropriate test for standing, and whether it should **24–040** be different for individuals as opposed to groups, we should also be mindful of the important insights provided by the literature on public choice concerning the logic of collective action.[174] This literature may be controversial in certain respects, but it is nonetheless of value for the insights as to why people pursue their claims collectively rather than individually.

Collective action entails both direct and indirect costs. The direct costs are those of organising the group. The indirect costs arise from the fact that some individual autonomy is foregone. The choice made by the group will be dependent on the views of the members, which will normally be expressed through majority voting. Collective action also has benefits. The group will often be more powerful than any single individual; it will bring together expertise from diverse areas; the workload will be spread among the members; and it will normally have greater resources than any individual. Collective action will be the preferred option when the benefits of organising in this manner outweigh the costs. It is increasingly the case in modern society that this calculus comes down in favour of collective action. The complexity of many issues that involve confrontation between state and citizen, the very power of the state itself, and the demands which everyday life imposes on individuals, will often mean that collective action is preferred. It is therefore to be expected that much of the pressure brought to

---

[172] "Judicial Review: A Possible Programme for Reform" [1992] P.L. 221, 232–233.
[173] Law Commission, *Administrative Law: Judicial Review and Statutory Appeals* (Report No. 226, 1994), 41–44.
[174] J. Buchanan and G. Tullock, *The Calculus of Consent: Logical Foundations of Constitutional Democracy* (University of Michigan Press, 1962); M. Olson, *The Logic of Collective Action: Public Goods and the Theory of Groups* (Harvard University Press, 1965).

bear on governments will come from groups.[175] An understanding of these basic insights is of importance when we think about standing, and the tests for individuals and groups.[176]

Associational standing is an obvious manifestation of the logic of collective action. If the court is faced with a group that directly represents its members then it should not treat this body less favourably than if the action had been brought by an individual member: if the individual would be admitted to court as a matter of right, then so should the group.[177]

The courts should also be sympathetic to surrogate standing by groups, especially where the applicant represents a section of the public affected by the challenged decision and the case is unlikely to be brought by those immediately affected. In this type of case the logic of collective action combines with the relative weakness of those immediately affected.

Public interest challenges by groups will always be more controversial. It may well be that the test for standing in these instances should be discretionary, along the lines of the two-track approach considered above. When considering how this discretion should be exercised we should, however, be mindful of the fact that a group challenge to a matter that affects many individuals equally may be the only realistic option. It is in these areas that the arguments for collective action will be especially strong.

C. Intervention

24–041 Cases raising matters of public concern would be the most obvious category in which to allow intervention.[178] This is more especially so if we accept that public interest challenges are warranted in some circumstances, and if we acknowledge that public law litigation may well have implications for people other than those who actually bring the case.

A study by *Justice* and the Public Law Project[179] proposed a new rule of court which would have the effect of recognising public interest interveners as a class of litigant in its own right. Leave to intervene would be needed, the court would have to be satisfied that the case raised a matter of public interest and that the intervention would assist the court. There would also be limits or guides to the form and length of any intervention.

This suggestion has, however, not gone unchallenged. Sir Konrad Schiemann[180] has expressed concern at the breadth of discretion that would be given to judges as to who should address the court and on what issues. He

---

[175] C. Harlow and R. Rawlings, *Pressure through Law* (Routledge, 1992); R. Rawlings, "Courts and Interests", in I. Loveland (ed.), *A Special Relationship? American Influences on Public Law in the UK* (Oxford University Press, 1995), 104–105.

[176] P. Cane, "Standing up for the Public" [1995] P.L. 276 and "Standing, Representation and the Environment", in Loveland (ed.), n.175, Ch.5; M. Sunkin, "The Problematical State of Access to Judicial Review", in B. Hadfield (ed.), *Judicial Review: A Thematic Approach* (Gill and MacMillan, 1995).

[177] For suggestions that there should be some mechanism to ensure that the group really does represent the views of its members, see, Cane, n.176, 278.

[178] S. Grosz, "A Matter of Public Interest: A Justice/P.L.P. Report" (1996) 1 J.R. 147.

[179] Justice/Public Law Project, *A Matter of Public Interest* (1996).

[180] Sir Konrad Schiemann, "Interventions in Public Interest Cases" [1996] P.L. 240.

is worried that such interventions would force the court to consider social policy to a greater extent than hitherto, and that the traditional judicial role would be undermined. Harlow has voiced similar concerns that intervention could undermine the bipolar, adversarial nature of adjudication, and that intervenors are not necessarily impartial or representative.[181] These concerns should be taken seriously, but intervention can nonetheless be very valuable, and Fordham has recently renewed the call for enhanced intervention rights.[182]

---

[181] Harlow, n.138, 10–11.
[182] M. Fordham, " 'Public Interest' Intervention: A Practitioner's Perspective" [2007] P.L. 410.

CHAPTER 25

JUDICIAL REMEDIES

A citizen who is aggrieved by a decision of a public body has a variety of **25–001** remedies available.[1] The prerogative orders of mandamus, prohibition and certiorari are, after amendment to the Supreme Court Act 1981 in 2004, known as mandatory, prohibiting and quashing orders.[2] The High Court has jurisdiction to make mandatory, prohibiting and quashing orders in those classes of case in which, immediately before May 1, 2004, it had jurisdiction to make orders of mandamus, prohibition and certiorari respectively.[3] Thus the grounds on which mandatory, prohibiting and quashing orders can be made remain largely the same as prior to 2004. In addition both the declaration and the injunction have been applied to public bodies. These are the main remedies, although reference will also be made to others.

The law of remedies was until recently highly complex, with differing procedures applying to the prerogative orders and to declaration and injunction. Some of this disorder was swept away by the reform considered in the following chapter. The reform is, however, principally one of form or procedure. The grounds on which the remedies can be given are not altered.[4] It is for this reason that each of the remedies will be examined in turn, making reference to the reforms where appropriate. In the following chapter there will be a more detailed look at the procedural reforms.

---

[1] C. Lewis, *Judicial Remedies in Public Law* (Sweet & Maxwell, 3rd edn, 2004).
[2] Supreme Court Act 1981 s.29, as amended by SI 2004/1033, art.3. The Supreme Court Act 1981 will henceforth to be known as the Senior Courts Act 1981, see Constitutional Reform Act 2005 Sch.11(1), para.1.
[3] Supreme Court Act 1981 s.29(1)(A).
[4] Supreme Court Act 1981 s.29(1)(A).

1. Certiorari/Quashing Order and Prohibition/Prohibiting Order

A. Introduction

25–002   Certiorari and prohibition have long been remedies for the control of administrative action. The former had its origins as a royal demand for information. The exact history of the development of the writ is complex, but Rubinstein argues convincingly that certiorari was originally developed to fill a gap left by collateral attack and the writ of error.[5] Collateral attack, in the form of an action for assault, trespass, etc., lay only for jurisdictional defects, while the writ of error was restricted to some courts of record.[6] Certiorari developed to fill a gap that might arise. The area left unfilled was an error within jurisdiction by an institution not amenable to the writ of error. The remedy was thus initially aimed at errors within, as opposed to errors going to jurisdiction.[7]

It was in response to the development of finality clauses that certiorari began to be used more generally for jurisdictional defects. The courts restrictively construed such clauses to render them applicable only for non-jurisdictional error; where the error went to jurisdiction certiorari was held to be still available. The reach of certiorari was augmented further by the acceptance of affidavit evidence to prove that a jurisdictional defect existed.[8]

Whereas certiorari operated retrospectively to quash a decision already made, prohibition was prospective in its impact, enjoining the addressee from continuing with something that would be an excess of jurisdiction. It was a particularly useful weapon wielded by the King's Bench Division in the struggles between it and the more specialised or ecclesiastical courts. The law reports are replete with judges of the King's Bench castigating such assumptions of authority.[9] Prohibition was, however, used more generally, like certiorari, to control a wide spectrum of inferior bodies both before and after the reforms in municipal government of 1832, and statements approving of its liberal usage were not uncommon.[10]

---

[5] *Jurisdiction and Illegality* (Oxford University Press, 1965), Ch.4. See also S.A. de Smith, *Judicial Review of Administrative Action* (Sweet & Maxwell, 4th edn, 1980), App.1; *de Smith's Judicial Review* (Lord Woolf, J. Jowell, and A. Le Sueur, Sweet & Maxwell, 6th edn, 2007), Ch.15; E. Henderson, *Foundations of English Administrative Law* (Harvard University Press, 1963); L. Jaffe and E. Henderson, "Judicial Review and The Rule of Law: Historical Origins" (1956) 72 L.Q.R. 345.

[6] Such courts had power to fine and imprison or had jurisdiction to try civil causes according to common law where the sum involved exceeded 40 shillings, Rubinstein, n.5, 57.

[7] *Groenvelt v Burwell* (1700) 1 Ld. Raym. 454. See also, the reports in (1700) 1 Comyns 76; (1700) 12 Mod. 386. Other important early decisions were *Commins v Massam* (1643) March N.C. 196, 197; *R. v Hide* (1647) Style 60; *R. v Plowright* (1686) 3 Mod. 94.

[8] Rubinstein, n.5, 71–80. The original basis of certiorari, for the control of errors within jurisdiction, was forgotten until *R. v Northumberland Compensation Appeal Tribunal Ex p. Shaw* [1952] 1 K.B. 338.

[9] See, e.g., *Mayor and Aldermen of City of London v Cox* (1867) L.R. 2 H.L. 239.

[10] See, e.g., *R. v Local Government Board* (1882) 10 Q.B.D. 309.

It should however be made clear, as emphasised in *Ben-Abdelaziz*,[11] that the Crown's involvement in judicial review proceedings is nominal, and that the action is between the applicant and the public authority.

B. The Scope of Certiorari/Quashing Orders and Prohibition/Prohibiting Orders

In 1924 Atkin L.J. produced the most frequently quoted dictum as to the scope of certiorari,[12]   **25–003**

"Whenever any body of persons having legal authority to determine questions affecting the rights of subjects, and having the duty to act judicially, act in excess of their legal authority, they are subject to the controlling jurisdiction of the King's Bench Division exercised in these writs."

Prohibition is in general subject to the same rules as certiorari; any points of distinction will be mentioned.[13] While not a statutory definition, the dictum of Atkin L.J. provides a useful starting point when considering the scope of the remedies.

i. Which persons and what type of authority?

The general starting point is that certiorari and prohibition will apply to quash any decision of a public law nature.[14] The scope of public law for these purposes will be considered in detail within the following chapter, and the material within this section should be read in the light of that discussion.[15]   **25–004**

Certiorari and prohibition cannot be used to challenge the decision of a superior court.[16] The orders will issue to any body that exercises statutory

---

[11] *R. (on the application of Ben-Abdelaziz) v Haringey LBC* [2001] 1 W.L.R. 1485.
[12] *R. v Electricity Commissioners Ex p. London Electricity Joint Committee Co (1920) Ltd* [1924] 1 K.B. 171, 205.
[13] In the *Electricity Commissioners* case Atkin L.J. explicitly ties the two remedies together, [1924] 1 K.B. 171, 194.
[14] Neither certiorari nor prohibition will lie against decisions of superior courts. Certiorari will not it seems lie against ecclesiastical courts, but as noted above, prohibition will issue to prevent excess of power by such courts.
[15] See below, paras 26–016—26–036.
[16] *Re Racal Communications Ltd* [1981] A.C. 374. The exception to this is Crown courts which are superior courts, but are amenable to the prerogative orders by virtue of the Supreme Court Act 1981 ss.28 and 29.

authority, including departments of state,[17] local authorities,[18] individual ministers,[19] magistrates[20] and public bodies.[21]

It is assumed that they will not be available against the Crown itself, the reason being that the orders are punishable by contempt, being commands from the court. This is unsatisfactory and anachronistic: the existence of a potentially coercive remedy against the Crown as an institution does not necessarily imply that such measures would or could be taken against Her Majesty in person. However, other provisions are based upon similar reasoning.[22] The availability of the prerogative orders against the Crown will be considered in more detail below.[23]

It would, however, be mistaken to assume that the remedies could only issue to those whose authority was based strictly upon statute. The prerogative orders are available to protect common law rights of a public nature,[24] and also to prevent institutions or persons acting under prerogative powers from exceeding their authority.[25]

It is unclear how far these decisions will be taken. The traditional assumption has been that certiorari will not be available where a body is exercising powers that may be of a public nature if the derivation of that power is contractual.[26] There are however statements that the prerogative orders could be available even if the source of the power was contractual.[27] It is, nonetheless, still doubtful whether an institution which derives its powers solely from contract will be amenable to the prerogative orders.[28] The case law will be discussed in more detail in the following chapter.[29]

The argument underlying such cases does not, however, appear to be that there is some "analytical" reason precluding the application of the prerogative orders to bodies that derive their power from contract. It is rather

---

[17] *Board of Education v Rice* [1911] A.C. 179.
[18] *R. v London County Council Ex p. The Entertainments Protection Association Ltd* [1931] 2 K.B. 215.
[19] *R. v Minister of Health Ex p. Yaffe* [1930] 2 K.B. 98.
[20] *R. v Bedwelty Justices Ex p. Williams* [1997] A.C. 225.
[21] *R. v Milk Marketing Board Ex p. North* (1934) 50 T.L.R. 559. See also, *R. v Blundeston Prison Board of Visitors Ex p. Fox-Taylor* [1982] 1 All E.R. 646, where it was held that certiorari could issue to the prison board, even though the breach of natural justice had been caused by the prison authorities. See also, *R. v Leyland Magistrates Ex p. Hawthorn* [1979] 1 All E.R. 209. *cf Cheall v APEX* [1983] A.C. 180.
[22] Crown Proceedings Act 1947 s.21.
[23] See below, para.28–017.
[24] *R. v Barnsley Metropolitan Borough Council Ex p. Hook* [1976] 1 W.L.R. 1052, 1057, 1060.
[25] *R. v Criminal Injuries Compensation Board Ex p. Lain* [1967] 2 Q.B. 864, 880–881, 884; *Council of Civil Service Unions v Minister for the Civil Service* [1985] A.C. 374.
[26] *R. v National Joint Council for the Craft of Dental Technicians (Disputes Committee) Ex p. Neate* [1953] 1 Q.B. 704; *Vidyodaya University Council v Silva* [1965] 1 W.L.R. 77; *Herring v Templeman* [1973] 3 All E.R. 569, 585, and *R. v Post Office Ex p. Byrne* [1975] I.C.R. 221, 226, disapproving of the contrary assumption made in *R. v Aston University Senate Ex p. Roffey* [1969] 2 Q.B. 538.
[27] *O'Reilly v Mackman* [1982] 3 W.L.R. 604 (Lord Denning M.R.), [1983] 2 A.C. 237, 279 (Lord Diplock).
[28] *R. v BBC Ex p. Lavelle* [1983] 1 W.L.R. 23, 31; *Law v National Greyhound Racing Club Ltd* [1983] 3 All E.R. 300; *R. v Panel on Take-overs and Mergers Ex p. Datafin plc* [1987] Q.B. 815, 847, approving *Ex p. Neate* [1953] 1 Q.B. 704.
[29] See below, paras 26–025—26–026.

that the facts of these cases disclosed no "public" law issue, but simply one of a private or domestic character.[30] The courts have, moreover, clearly shown themselves willing to look beyond the source of a body's power, and to inquire into its nature, in order to determine whether that body was susceptible to judicial review.[31]

ii. The determination of rights

Two separate issues are involved here. First, what does determination mean? Second, what does the term right encompass?   **25–005**

On the meaning of determination, it is clear that the decision challenged need not be absolutely final. In the *Electricity Commissioners*[32] case, the commissioners had to report their findings to the Minister who would confirm them or not, and if the former he would then lay them before Parliament. Nevertheless, the court held that this did not preclude certiorari. A number of other authorities explicitly[33] or implicitly[34] affirm the same point. However, there are other cases that regard the necessity for approval or confirmation by another as preventing the orders from issuing.[35] The Supreme Court Act 1981 s.31(2) has made this issue less important: if the decision is felt not to be final enough for certiorari then declaratory or injunctive relief may be claimed instead.

The word "rights" has been broadly interpreted. It clearly includes personal security,[36] traditional property interests[37] and a person's interest in continued membership of a profession.[38] It is not, however, restricted to these categories and includes many interests that would, in Hohfeldian terms, be described as privileges.[39] Two cases illustrate how liberally the courts have interpreted this requirement.

In *Lain*[40] the applicant sought certiorari to quash a decision made by the

---

[30] This appears to be the reasoning in *Lavelle*, n.28, 31, and in *Datafin*, n.28, 834–837, 847–849.
[31] See below, para.26–027.
[32] [1924] 1 K.B. 171, 192, 208; *Church v Inclosure Commissioners* (1862) 11 C.B. (N.S.) 664.
[33] *Estate and Trust Agencies (1927) Ltd v Singapore Investment Trust* [1937] A.C. 898, 917.
[34] *R. v Kent Police Authority Ex p. Godden* [1971] 2 Q.B. 662; *R. v Board of Visitors of Hull Prison Ex p. St Germain* [1979] Q.B. 425.
[35] *R. v St. Lawrence's Hospital Statutory Visitors Ex p. Pritchard* [1953] 1 W.L.R. 1158.
[36] *R. v Boycott Ex p. Keasley* [1939] 2 K.B. 651.
[37] *R. v Agricultural Land Tribunal for the Wales and Monmouth Area Ex p. Davies* [1953] 1 W.L.R. 722.
[38] *General Medical Council v Spackman* [1943] A.C. 627, provided that the body has the necessary statutory authority and that the relationship is not deemed to be one of master-servant, *Vidyodaya University Council v Silva* [1965] 1 W.L.R. 77.
[39] *R. v Woodhouse* [1906] 2 K.B. 501; *R. v Gaming Board for Great Britain Ex p. Benaim and Khaida* [1970] 2 Q.B. 417; *R. v Liverpool Corporation Ex p. Liverpool Taxi Fleet Operators' Association* [1972] 2 Q.B. 299.
[40] *R. v Criminal Injuries Compensation Board Ex p. Lain* [1967] 2 Q.B. 864. Lord Parker CJ was content that the Board was a body of a public as opposed to private character and affected subjects, [1967] 2 Q.B. 864, 882; Diplock L.J. doubted if certiorari could go to a body which did not have any effect on legal rights in any circumstances, but was content that the determination made by the Board rendered lawful a payment which would otherwise be unlawful, 884, 889; Ashworth L.J. thought it sufficient if subjects were affected and believed that the word rights could be omitted, 892.

Criminal Injuries Compensation Board. It was argued that the Board made ex gratia payments and therefore did not determine any rights. The court rejected this contention. It was not necessary that the Board make decisions creating or affecting rights in a narrow sense. Although the precise formulations given by the court differed, they all concurred in holding the Board amenable to certiorari. In *St Germain*,[41] there was a challenge to disciplinary proceedings before a prison visitor consequent upon a prison riot. One defence raised was that the visitor's decision did not interfere with any of the prisoners' rights, but only affected their expectations of having a privilege conferred on them, the privilege in question being remission for good behaviour. Counsel's endeavour to convince the court of the need for accurate Hohfeldian categorisation was to no avail. It was, said the court, irrelevant whether a privilege or right was at stake. This is obviously correct. Administrative law has been plagued for long enough by distinctions based upon rights versus privileges. One shudders to think of the jurisprudential intricacies that lie enmeshed in "expectation of having a privilege conferred", and can only be thankful that the court dismissed the argument so conclusively.

iii. A duty to act judicially

25–006 If the dichotomy between rights and privileges has been one plague visited upon administrative law, a second has been that between administrative and judicial functions. The history of the rise and fall of this confusion can be traced as follows.

In the early years certiorari and prohibition were used partly to control inferior courts, and hence bodies exercising judicial functions. However, even in their early infancy the writs were used to control a wide variety of activities which, if labels must be attached, could only be called administrative: commissioners of sewers or of tithes were regarded as natural defendants in a certiorari action.[42] As both remedies developed they encompassed a whole spectrum of activities, which although they might be termed "judicial", bore little relationship to a formal trial: governmental departments, individual ministers and quasi-governmental undertakings were all brought within their purview. Defences to the application of certiorari or prohibition based upon the non-judicial nature of the proceedings were treated dismissively by the courts.[43]

Unfortunately, some later cases placed emphasis on the fact that Atkin L.J. spoke of certiorari applying where the rights of subjects were affected and where the body had the duty to act judicially.[44] It was clear from the context of his judgment that Atkin L.J. saw the judicial element being inferred from the nature of the power and its consequential effects on

---

[41] *R. v Board of Visitors of Hull Prison Ex p. St Germain* [1979] Q.B. 425; *O'Reilly v Mackman* [1983] 2 A.C. 237, where Lord Diplock talks of common law or statutory rights and obligations.
[42] *Commins v Massam* (1643) March N.C. 196; *R. v Hide* (1647) Style 60.
[43] *R. v Woodhouse* [1906] 2 K.B. 501, 534–535; *Electricity Commissioners*, n.12, 198.
[44] *Electricity Commissioners*, n.12, 205.

individuals. Nonetheless, in certain subsequent decisions courts held that apart from an effect on the rights of individuals there must be a superadded duty to act judicially. Some, but not all such cases, concerned natural justice and are the reverse side of the coin concerning the interaction between rights and remedies discussed above[45]: the requirement that proceedings be judicial before natural justice applied appeared in tandem with the judicial requirement in certiorari. Sometimes the substantive right took the driving seat, infecting the remedy with the same condition. On other occasions the fertilisation process was reversed with the remedy leading the right.[46] This conceptual confusion led to bad decisions: the courts held, for example, that disciplinary proceedings, not being judicial, were not susceptible to certiorari.[47]

All was not however darkness in these years, but the occasional ray of clarity was the more apparent for being exceptional.[48] It was clear that it would require a decision of the House of Lords to restore rationality. This came in 1964 in *Ridge v Baldwin*.[49] The interaction between rights and remedies was again evident. One of the reasons given by Lord Reid for natural justice becoming unduly restricted was the confusion introduced by the requirement of a superadded duty to act judicially as a condition for certiorari, which was adopted in certain natural justice cases. The judicial element was, said Lord Reid, simply to be inferred from the nature of the power.[50] Forty years on the stance adopted by Atkin L.J. in the *Electricity Commissioners* case was restored both for remedies and natural justice.

The extent to which categorisation of a function as judicial still plays a role in natural justice was considered earlier.[51] The law on remedies has been relatively free of such shackles and there are statements that it is no longer relevant how the function is described in determining the applicability of certiorari.[52] Moreover, decisions have been reached which, if the facts had arisen prior to *Ridge*, would almost certainly have been decided the other way. Certiorari has thus been held applicable to discipline by a prison visitor[53] and to decisions by a local planning authority.[54] The court in both

---

[45] See above, para.12–006.
[46] An early clear example of the requirement of a superadded duty to act judicially appears in *R. v Legislative Committee of the Church Assembly Ex p. Haynes-Smith* [1928] 1 K.B. 441. This case had nothing to do with natural justice, but was clearly influential in *Nakkuda Ali v Jayaratne* [1951] A.C. 66, 77–78, a case about natural justice and certiorari: the remedy thus infects the right. In *R. v Metropolitan Police Commissioner Ex p. Parker* [1953] 1 W.L.R. 1150 the same type of process is evident.
[47] *Parker*, n.46.
[48] *R. v Manchester Legal Aid Committee Ex p. R A Brand and Co Ltd* [1952] 2 Q.B. 413, 425–431.
[49] [1964] A.C. 40.
[50] [1964] A.C. 40, 74–78.
[51] See above, para.12–012.
[52] *R. v Barnsley Metropolitan Borough Council Ex p. Hook* [1976] 1 W.L.R. 1052, 1058; *cf. Jayawardane v Silva* [1970] 1 W.L.R. 1365.
[53] *R. v Board of Visitors of Hull Prison Ex p. St. Germain* [1979] Q.B. 425.
[54] *R. v Hillingdon London Borough Council Ex p. Royco Homes Ltd* [1974] Q.B. 720. See, however, the earlier decision in *R. v Hendon Rural District Council Ex p. Chorley* [1933] 2 K.B. 696 decided by Lord Hewart C.J.

instances imposed qualifications, but these related to factors other than the necessity of finding a judicial function. The argument that the judicial or administrative nature of the proceedings should not be relevant for the purposes of certiorari was confirmed by *O'Reilly v Mackman*.[55] Lord Diplock, giving the unanimous decision of the court, stated that there was no longer a requirement of a superadded duty to act judicially before the prerogative orders could apply. It was, said his Lordship, no longer necessary to distinguish between judicial and administrative acts.

iv. Certiorari and subordinate legislation

25–007 It has been assumed in the past that certiorari should not readily apply to legislative functions. In *Ridge*, Lord Reid, while disapproving of the superadded duty requirement, agreed with the result in the *Church Assembly*[56] case, because the process involved was legislative.

It is by no means self-evident that this should be so. The prerogative orders cannot be used to challenge primary legislation, but the reason for this resides in the sovereignty of Parliament. It is not evident why other "legislation" should be immune from the prerogative orders, more particularly given that the declaration will issue against secondary legislation. It is in fact clear that those orders have issued to stages in the legislative process. This was so in the *Electricity Commissioners*[57] decision, and in other cases the courts have expressed their willingness to award certiorari where the function has been defined as legislative.[58] On principle there seems no reason why the prerogative orders should not be available against secondary legislation *stricto sensu* and to impugn rules of a legislative character made by a public body.[59]

Insofar as the scope of the prerogative orders is meant to reflect the ambit of "public law", the orders will be defective in not covering an important area which, judged by any substantive criterion, is public. The line between decisions made individually or ad hoc, and those institutionalised into rules, may be fine and fortuitous.

The more one looks at the early development of the prerogative orders, the greater is the impression that these remedies were interpreted flexibly to meet the new institutions developing at that time. Real conceptual restrictions appeared later. It is to be regretted that flexible tools become, like equity has on occasion, ossified and confined.

The tendency of more recent authority has been to consider applying the prerogative orders to secondary legislation. Thus in one case it was assumed that certiorari was available to quash a statutory instrument which set out

---

[55] [1983] 2 A.C. 237.
[56] [1928] 1 K.B. 411; *Ridge* [1964] A.C. 40, 72.
[57] [1924] 1 K.B. 171; *Church v Inclosure Commissioners* (1862) 11 C.B. (N.S.) 664.
[58] *Minister of Health v R Ex p. Yaffe* [1931] A.C. 494, 532, 533.
[59] *Att-Gen of Hong Kong v Ng Yuen-Shiu* [1983] 2 A.C. 629, and *R. v Secretary of State for the Home Department Ex p. Khan* [1985] 1 All E.R. 40, in both of which certiorari was granted to prevent the public body from altering rules of a legislative character.

regulations on housing benefits, even though the court ultimately decided not to order the remedy as a matter of discretion,[60] and a court has awarded certiorari in relation to a statutory instrument.[61]

C. Grounds for the Award of Certiorari and Prohibition

The grounds for the award of certiorari and prohibition are those set out in Part II: jurisdictional defects including natural justice, and excess, abuse, or failure to exercise a discretionary power. Errors of law on the face of the record were also susceptible to certiorari, but as seen earlier this concept is now largely redundant. This is of course subject to the proviso that the above conditions are met and that none of the limitations detailed below are present.

25–008

D. Limitations on the Grant of the Remedies

i. Waiver

Unless there is a statutory exception the general rule is that jurisdiction cannot be conferred upon a public body by acquiescence.[62] A decision made without jurisdiction is void. However, this general statement does not in fact accurately reflect all the case law, which is somewhat confused. What exceptions exist in the case law and what exceptions should exist in principle must now be examined.

25–009

The most problematic part of the case law concerns prohibition and the problem is exacerbated both by the overlap between standing and waiver, and by the confusing welter of terminology used. Light may be shed by attempting to cut through to the core of the difficulty. We have seen when discussing standing that some 19th-century courts took the view that any person could have standing to seek prohibition on the dual hypotheses that for an inferior court to exceed its jurisdiction was an infringement of the royal prerogative, all courts deriving their authority from the Crown, and because to allow a patent defect to stand could establish a bad precedent.[63] Neither the lateness of the application, nor the triviality of the sum was a bar, since the essence of the action was not the vindication of a personal right, but of the royal prerogative. Logically this reasoning would admit no conception of waiver at all.

However, certain other cases reflected a different attitude, a willingness to accept the basic premise of the above argument and yet a desire to prevent an unworthy applicant from securing prohibition. A line was drawn or, as it

---

[60] *R. v Secretary of State for Social Services Ex p. Association of Metropolitan Authorities* [1986] 1 W.L.R. 1.

[61] *R. v Secretary of State for Health Ex p. United States Tobacco International Inc* [1992] Q.B. 353.

[62] *Essex Incorporated Congregational Church Union v Essex CC* [1963] A.C. 808; *Rydqvist v Secretary of State for Work and Pensions* [2002] 1 W.L.R. 3343.

[63] *De Haber v Queen of Portugal* (1851) 17 Q.B. 171; *Worthington v Jeffries* (1875) L.R. 10 C.P. 379.

might be more accurately put, etched. If the want of jurisdiction was patent on the face of the proceedings, then acquiescence or waiver was irrelevant: the protection of the royal prerogative and preventing the establishment of a bad precedent were supreme. Where however the defect was latent, not patent, and particularly where the defect lay within the knowledge of the applicant who neglected to bring it forward in the lower courts, then the court in its discretion could refuse to issue the writ or order. Here the fault or tardiness of the applicant was allowed to outweigh the public interest represented in the royal prerogative.[64]

25–010   The distinction between patent and latent defects was overlaid by that between total and partial want of jurisdiction. Some cases were explained on the hypothesis that a total want of jurisdiction could not be cured, but that a partial one could.[65] It is by no means clear whether the pairings patent/latent and total/partial were treated as synonymous and it is clear that in principle they need not be. In any event, the leading authorities used the former terminology more consistently. In addition to the above case law, there was authority from the area of natural justice to show that defects could be waived.[66]

We should now consider the issue in terms of principle. The basic proposition should be as stated at the outset: a defect should not be curable by acquiescence or waiver. The rationale is that the limits upon a tribunal are imposed for the public interest. An individual should not be able to extend that tribunal's jurisdiction by waiving limits to its authority. In this sense the ultra vires principle holds supreme and a void act cannot be validated by the individual. The defect itself cannot be cured.

However, unmitigated application of this general rule could lead to undesirable results. The mendacious or crafty could, knowing of a defect, seemingly acquiesce in it in the hope of gaining a profit of some type and then, if this did not occur, seek a prerogative order. One's sense of justice is liable to be touched in such instances if the general rule were to be applied remorselessly. A way to vindicate the ultra vires principle, while avoiding the above scenario, would be to state that the action of the public body was ultra vires, but that the waiver or acquiescence would affect the discretion to grant a remedy. This is, in effect, what happened in the leading 19th-century authorities: the actions of the individual placed a remedy out reach, rather than cured the defect itself.[67]

Waiver, in this sense of precluding a remedy rather than curing the defect,

[64] *Mayor and Alderman of City of London v Cox* (1867) L.R. 2 H.L. 239; *Farquharson v Morgan* [1894] 1 Q.B. 552; *R. v Comptroller-General of Patents and Designs Ex p. Parke Davis* [1953] 2 W.L.R. 760.
[65] *Jones v Owen* (1845) 5 D. & L. 669; *Moore v Gamgee* (1890) 25 Q.B.D. 244.
[66] *R. v Williams Ex p. Phillips* [1914] 1 K.B. 608, 613–614; *R. v Comptroller-General of Patents and Designs Ex p. Parke Davis* [1953] 2 W.L.R. 760.
[67] de Smith, *Judicial Review* (4th edn, 1980), n.5, 422–423 suggests that the nineteenth century authorities talk in terms of curing the defect itself. In the leading authorities the only evidence of this is the way in which Davey L.J. in *Farquharson v Morgan* [1894] 1 Q.B. 552, 563 distinguishes *Jones v James* (1850) 19 L.J. Q.B. 257. See also, *R. v Knightsbridge Crown Court Ex p. International Sporting Club (London) Ltd* [1982] Q.B. 304; *cf. R. v Knightsbridge Crown Court Ex p. Marcrest Properties Ltd* [1983] 1 W.L.R. 300.

should in principle be possible whatever the type of defect. Clearly however the importance of the ultra vires activity, the knowledge of the defect possessed by the applicant, and the extent to which the defect was personal to the applicant or could have wider ramifications, would be relevant factors to be taken into account.

ii. Delay
An applicant may also be denied relief because of undue delay in seeking **25–011** relief. The relevant rules will be considered below.[68]

iii. Alternative remedies
Whether the existence of an alternative remedy precludes the application of **25–012** any of the prerogative orders will be considered within a separate section.[69]

E. The Effect of an Award of Certiorari/Quashing Order
When certiorari is issued it will serve to quash the offending decision and **25–013** render it retrospectively null. The meaning of retrospective nullity has been considered above.[70]

The reviewing courts now possess a further useful power. In circumstances where there are grounds for quashing the decision the court can remit the case to the original decision-maker with a direction to reconsider the matter and reach a decision in accord with the judgment of the court.[71]

Thus instead of merely quashing the original decision and leaving the applicant to make a fresh application, the court can now, for example, quash the refusal to grant a benefit to the applicant, and remit the matter for reconsideration by the decision-maker in the light of the court's judgment.

The court also has the power, subject to any statutory provision giving power to a specific tribunal, person or body, to take the decision itself where there is no purpose to be served by remitting the matter to the initial decision-maker.[72]

2. MANDAMUS/MANDATORY ORDER

A. Introduction
The early history of the writ of mandamus is by no means clear. Commands **25–014** from the King were, as de Smith points out, a common feature amongst the

---

[68] See below, paras 26–045—26–046.
[69] See below, paras 26–056—26–058.
[70] See above, Ch.23.
[71] Supreme Court Act 1981 s.31(5); SI 2000/2092, CPR 54.19(2).
[72] SI 2000/2092, CPR 54.19(3).

early writs, but he shows that it is doubtful whether any real connection existed between these early writs and what we now know as mandamus.[73] The seminal case for the emergence of the writ is *Bagg's Case*[74] and few legal rules can be said to have had so colourful a birth. Bagg was a chief burgess of Plymouth who had been removed from office for unseemly conduct, consisting inter alia of calling the mayor "a cozening knave", threatening to make his "neck crack" as well as other offensive gestures. Despite this behaviour a mandamus was issued against Plymouth, because Bagg had been disenfranchised without a hearing. Similar cases of deprivation of office or position followed.[75] It was however Lord Mansfield who fully exploited the potential in mandamus stating that,[76]

"It was introduced, to prevent disorder from a failure of justice, and defect of police. Therefore it ought to be used upon all occasions where the law established no specific remedy, and where in justice and good government there ought to be one."

From these beginnings a large jurisprudence developed, which compelled Tapping[77] to undertake the Herculean task of categorising the case law by subject-matter. A glance through the treatise reveals the diversity of this subject-matter, including Abbots and Yeoman. The reform of local government in the 19th century diminished the need for mandamus, as did the gradual disappearance of the freehold office, and the emergence of alternative remedies such as appeal.

B. The Ambit of Mandamus/Mandatory Order

i. Type of duty

25–015 For mandamus to lie there must be a public duty owed to the applicant. This involves two distinct requirements.

First, the duty must be of a public as opposed to a private character. The remedy was therefore held to be inappropriate when requested against a private arbitral tribunal, and when sought in relation to reinstatement in a trade union.[78] Whether these duties would still be characterised as private as opposed to public is now more questionable. Provided that the duty is

---

[73] de Smith, n.5, App. I, 591–592; Henderson, n.5, 45–65.
[74] (1615) 11 Co. Rep.93b.
[75] See, e.g., *R. v Chancellor of the University of Cambridge* (1723) 1 Str. 557.
[76] *R. v Barker* (1762) 3 Burr 1265, 1267; *R. v Askew* (1768) 4 Burr 2186.
[77] T. Tapping, *The Law and Practice of the High Prerogative Writ of Mandamus, as it obtains both in England and Ireland* (Lond. 1848).
[78] *R. v Industrial Court Ex p. ASSET* [1965] 1 Q.B. 377. See however, *Imperial Metal Industries (Kynoch) Ltd v AUEW (Technical, Administrative and Supervisory Section)* [1979] I.C.R. 23, 33 where the court approved of the principle but disapproved of its application in the *ASSET* case; *Armstrong v Kane* [1964] N.Z.L.R. 369.

public, it may flow from statute, prerogative, common law, charter, custom, or even contract.[79]

Second, even if the duty is of a public character it must be owed to an individual or type of individual. In *R. v Secretary of State for War*[80] an officer sought mandamus to compel the Secretary of State to upgrade the amount of compensation he had received upon his retirement. He failed. The duty incumbent upon the Secretary of State was held to be owed to the Crown alone. This clearly need not be so, as was admitted in the case. Whether it is or not will be a matter of construction. In the modern day the general rule of construction is that duties imposed upon ministers are owed to the public, or a section thereof, rather than to the Crown alone.

A different type of situation in which the courts might decline mandamus is where, although the duty is of a public character, its terms are so open textured as to indicate that the statute is not enforceable by individuals. The courts might reach this conclusion by saying that the issue is not justiciable. It is, however, more likely that the courts will retain control in principle. They will assert that mandamus might issue, but will find that on the facts of the case there is no cause. This approach will be considered in more detail below.

ii. Type of defect

Mandamus will issue where the tribunal has made a jurisdictional error, and **25–016** has thereby declined to exercise a power that it ought to have exercised. Older cases tended to distinguish between two situations: those in which the tribunal reached an erroneous decision on the merits, and those in which it refused to consider the merits at all, because it felt that they were outside its power. Mandamus would issue in the latter, but not in the former situation.

This traditional approach to mandamus is now of questionable validity. The case law that drew this distinction was based upon the narrow commencement theory of jurisdiction, under which very few defects would be categorised as jurisdictional. The necessary corollary was that no remedy would be available. For example in *Dayman*[81] the applicant claimed that expenses he had incurred for paving a new street had not been met. The magistrate decided after hearing the parties that the street was not a new street, and the applicant sought mandamus. His application failed. The magistrate had, said the court, heard and determined the matter. That was all that was required of him. It was irrelevant that the court might believe that the magistrate's view of "new street" was mistaken. The expansion in the concept of jurisdictional error considered above[82] would be likely to

---

[79] *ex p Napier* (1852) 18 Q.B. 692, 695; *R. v Secretary of State for War* [1891] 2 Q.B. 326, 335; *R. v Criminal Injuries Compensation Board Ex p. Clowes* [1977] 1 W.L.R. 1353. *cf. ex p Mann* (1916) 32 T.L.R. 479.
[80] [1891] 2 Q.B. 326; *Napier*, n.79.
[81] *R. v Dayman* (1857) 7 El. & Bl. 672, 676, 677, 679; *R. v Cheshire JJ Ex p. Heaver* (1913) 108 L.T. 374.
[82] See above, Ch.14.

produce a different result. The reviewing court would reassess for itself the meaning of "new street", the magistrate would be held to have made a jurisdictional error, and mandamus would issue.

Mandamus can also be used to correct a mistaken exercise of discretion. Thus, the remedy is available if a decision is reached on the basis of irrelevant considerations or improper purposes,[83] if a pre-determined policy is applied too rigidly,[84] if the wrong question is answered,[85] if the body has not properly considered whether to exercise its discretion[86] or for other misuses of power.[87] Where, however, the duties are broadly framed and involve competing claims upon limited resources the court is less likely to find any ultra vires behaviour or, even if it does, it may in its discretion refuse the remedy.[88]

iii. Demand and refusal

25–017   The traditional approach was that before seeking mandamus the applicant must have made a specific demand to the respondent that the latter perform the relevant duty. In exceptional circumstances this requirement could be dispensed with,[89] and the duty to make a specific demand was never an absolute one.[90] It is doubtful whether this formalistic requirement will be insisted upon in the modern day. It will normally be unrealistic to expect an individual to make a formal demand that the duty should be performed.[91]

C. Limits on the Availability of Mandamus/Mandatory Order

i. Discretion in the award of the remedy

25–018   It is generally accepted that mandamus is a discretionary remedy.[92] A variety of factors have influenced the court in deciding how the discretion should be exercised. The need for constant supervision has been one factor taken into account in refusing the award of the order,[93] as has been the willingness of the public body to comply voluntarily.[94] Public inconvenience or chaos has

---

[83]   *R. v Birmingham Licensing Planning Committee Ex p. Kennedy* [1972] 2 Q.B. 140.
[84]   *R. v Port of London Authority Ex p. Kynoch Ltd* [1919] 1 K.B. 176.
[85]   *Board of Education v Rice* [1911] A.C. 179.
[86]   *R. v Tower Hamlets London Borough Council Ex p. Chetnik Developments* [1988] A.C. 858.
[87]   *Padfield v Minister of Agriculture, Fisheries and Food* [1968] A.C. 997.
[88]   *R. v Commissioner of Police of the Metropolis Ex p. Blackburn* [1968] 2 Q.B. 118, 136, 148–149; *R. v Commissioner of Police of the Metropolis Ex p. Blackburn (No.3)* [1973] Q.B. 241, 254; *R. v Bristol Corporation Ex p. Hendy* [1974] 1 W.L.R. 498; *R. v Kensington and Chelsea (Royal) London Borough Council Ex p. Birdwood* (1976) 74 L.G.R. 424.
[89]   For more detail on this see de Smith, n.5, 556–557.
[90]   *R. v Hanley Revising Barrister* [1912] 3 K.B. 518.
[91]   See, however, *R. v Horsham DC Ex p. Wenman* [1995] 1 W.L.R. 680.
[92]   See, e.g., *R. v Churchwardens of All Saints Wigan* (1876) 1 App. Cas. 611, 620; *Chief Constable of the North Wales Police v Evans* [1982] 1 W.L.R. 1155.
[93]   *R. v Peak Park Joint Planning Board Ex p. Jackson* (1976) 74 L.G.R. 376, 380; *Chief Constable of the North Wales Police v Evans* [1982] 1 W.L.R. 1155.
[94]   *R. v Northumberland Compensation Appeal Tribunal Ex p. Shaw* [1952] 1 K.B. 338, 357; *Peak*, n.93.

received varying treatment, some courts viewing this as an improper consideration in deciding whether to issue the order,[95] others being willing to take it into account.[96]

The applicant's motives will normally not be relevant in deciding whether an order should be issued. However, in some instances the courts have stated that a particular statutory provision can only be enforced by one who is advancing the general interests of the community, as opposed to his or her own private concerns.[97]

The court will not normally order a respondent to undertake the impossible,[98] nor will it make orders that cannot be fulfilled for other practical or legal reasons.[99] Moreover, as has already been seen, if a public body has a wide discretion and limited resources this will enter into the court's decision as to whether a remedy should be given.[100]

ii. Alternative remedies

The relevance of an alternative remedy for the grant of mandamus will be considered below.[101]

25–019

3. DECLARATION

A. Introduction

The development of declaration in English law is interesting, largely because the main catalyst was not the courts.[102] Indeed, it might well be said that, with some exceptions, declaration flowered despite opposition from the judiciary.

25–020

Declaratory judgments, as opposed to purely declaratory orders, appear to be a relatively novel development. A wealth of dicta can be found in the

---

[95] See, e.g., *R. v Kerrier District Council Ex p. Guppys (Bridport) Ltd* (1976) 32 P. & C.R. 411, 418.
[96] See, e.g., *R. v Paddington Valuation Officer Ex p. Peachey Property Corporation Ltd* [1966] 1 Q.B. 380, 402, 416, but *cf.* 419, *per* Salmon L.J.
[97] *R. v Mayor of Peterborough* (1875) 44 L.J. Q.B. 85; *R. v Hampstead Borough Council Ex p. Woodward* (1917) 116 L.T. 213.
[98] *Re Bristol and North Somerset Railway Co* (1877) 3 Q.B.D. 10, 12; *cf. R. v Birmingham and Gloucester Ry* (1841) 2 Q.B. 47.
[99] *R. v Pembrokeshire JJ* (1831) 2 B. & Ad. 391; *R. v National Dock Labour Board Ex p. National Amalgamated Stevedores and Dockers* [1964] 2 Lloyds L.R. 420, 429; *Evans*, n.92.
[100] *R. v Bristol Corporation Ex p. Hendy* [1974] 1 W.L.R. 498, 503; *R. v Inner London Education Authority Ex p. Ali* [1990] C.O.D. 317; *R. v Lancashire County Council Ex p. Guyer* [1980] 1 W.L.R. 1024.
[101] See below, paras 26–056—26–058.
[102] I. Zamir, Lord Woolf, J. Woolf and Lord Clyde, *The Declaratory Judgment* (Sweet & Maxwell, 3rd edn, 2002).

mid-19th century asserting that the courts should not give a declaration of rights per se.[103] Moreover, as de Smith observes,[104] Lord Brougham's campaign advocating the introduction of the declaration only makes sense against such a background. Certain limited exceptions existed in which the courts could grant some declaratory relief.[105]

There was, however, judicial reluctance to make use of declaratory relief and this was clearly evident in the courts' treatment of the Court of Chancery Procedure Act 1852 s.50. This stated that no suit should be open to objection on the ground that a merely declaratory decree or order was being claimed, and that the courts could make binding declarations of right without granting consequential relief. The possibilities inherent within this legislation were largely nullified by judicial interpretation: declaratory relief was held to be available unaccompanied by any consequential relief, but only in those instances in which the plaintiff would have been entitled to other relief if it had been sought.[106]

In 1883, consequent upon powers conferred by the Judicature Acts, the Rule Committee passed Ord.25 r.5. This repeated the substance of the 1852 legislation with the important alteration that a declaration could be made whether any consequential relief "is or could be claimed, or not". This was intended to circumvent the restrictive interpretation given to the 1852 legislation, but it was to be nearly 30 years before the courts exploited this new potential fully.

The occasion for the breakthrough came in *Dyson*.[107] Dyson was served with a notice by the Inland Revenue Commissioners, which required him to supply certain particulars under pain of a penalty if he did not comply. Dyson refused. He sought declarations that the demand was unauthorised and was ultra vires the Finance Act. For authority he relied both upon Ord.25 r.5, and upon the Exchequer precedents prior to 1842. The Court of Appeal accepted that his method of proceeding was a proper one. The importance of the case lies in the fact that the court not only upheld this method of proceeding, but also regarded it as a convenient and beneficial one through which to test the legality of government action. Moreover, the availability of collateral attack, of declining to furnish the particulars, being sued for the penalty, and raising the invalidity of the demand by way of

---

[103] *Elliotson v Knowles* (1842) 11 L.J. Ch.399, 400; *Clough v Ratcliffe* (1847) 1 De G. and S. 164, 178–179; *Barraclough v Brown* [1897] A.C. 615, 623.

[104] *de Smith's Judicial Review*, n.5, 806.

[105] e.g. the practice of the old Court of Exchequer which awarded relief against the Crown. The latter was represented by the Attorney-General and the power to grant the relief had its origins in the Crown Debts Act 1541. Its relevance here is that the judgments were normally declaratory in form. It is unclear whether this jurisdiction passed to the Court of Chancery, but in any event the jurisdiction does not seem to have been exercised after 1841; it was rediscovered in *Dyson v Att-Gen*. [1911] 1 K.B. 410.

[106] *Jackson v Turnley* (1853) 1 Dr. 617, 628.

[107] *Dyson v Att Gen* [1911] 1 K.B. 410. See also, [1912] 1 Ch.159.

defence, was not regarded as a bar to the more direct approach of the declaration. Whether any form of consequential relief would have been available in such a case is questionable.[108] Despite certain infelicities in the court's reasoning,[109] the *Dyson* case represented a landmark in the development of the declaration.[110]

The current rule omits any reference to rights and provides that the court may make binding declarations whether or not any other remedy is claimed.[111]

B. The Scope of Declaration

i. The broad reach of the declaration

The period following *Dyson* was still characterised by judicial restraint. Statements were made that the declaration should be used sparingly.[112] However, as time progressed the courts became more used to the remedy and more aware of its flexibility, especially when contrasted with the limitations surrounding the prerogative orders. Judicial statements appeared which countenanced the broad reach of the declaration and the freedom from constraint provided by the "new" remedy.[113] **25–021**

No finite list of areas to which declaration applies can be provided. All that can be done is to indicate the broad context within which the remedy operates. It should be made clear that the declaration can operate both as an original and a supervisory remedy. In the former instance a court will declare what rights the parties have, for example, under a contract or over land. In the latter case, the remedy will control acts or decisions made by other bodies, such as declaring the attachment of certain planning conditions to be invalid. This duality of role is one of the strengths of the declaration. It allows a court to declare invalid certain action by a public body, in pursuance of the supervisory role, and then, if appropriate, to pronounce on the parties' rights, in pursuance of the original role.

---

[108] In *Gouriet v Union of Post Office Workers* [1978] A.C. 435, 502, Lord Diplock stated that if Dyson had paid the penalty he could have recovered it in an action for money had and received. It is in fact unclear whether this restitutionary claim would have succeeded, P. Craig, "Compensation in Public Law" (1980) 96 L.Q.R. 413, but see now, paras 29–051—29–053.

[109] The court mistakenly assumed that Exchequer precedents were equally relevant in the Court of Chancery and did not avert to the question of whether Ord.25, r.5 bound the Crown

[110] In *Guaranty Trust Co of New York v Hannay and Co* [1915] 2 K.B. 536, the court rejected the argument that Ord.25, r.5 was itself ultra vires.

[111] CPR 40.20.

[112] *Smeeton v Att-Gen* [1920] 1 Ch.85, 97; *Russian Commercial and Industrial Bank v British Bank of Foreign Trade Ltd* [1921] 2 A.C. 438, 445.

[113] *Pyx Granite Co Ltd v Ministry of Housing and Local Government* [1958] 1 Q.B. 554, 571; *Ibeneweka v Egbuna* [1964] 1 W.L.R. 219, 224.

The types of subject-matter to which the declaration has applied include administrative decisions or orders,[114] subordinate legislation,[115] and, in areas covered by EC law, primary legislation.[116] Rights to pursue a trade[117] and issues of status[118] are also subject to declaration. In addition, the scope of a person's financial obligations is subject to the declaratory procedure,[119] as are questions relating to the scope of obligations imposed upon a public body,[120] or sporting body,[121] and the construction of contracts with public authorities.[122]

ii. Types of defect

25–022 While the subject-matter covered by the declaration is therefore broad, there has been uncertainty as to the type of defects that it will operate against. It is clearly available against jurisdictional defects, but it was doubtful whether it would issue to control an error of law on the face of the record. The rationale for this limitation was that such an error only rendered the decision of the tribunal voidable and not void. The original decision would stand and therefore if the plaintiff were to seek a declaration of her rights she would be faced with the problem that the tribunal had already determined what those rights were, and that the court could not assume an appellate jurisdiction for itself to make a second decision different from the one still extant made by the tribunal. Such a declaration would be of no effect unless the tribunal had power to rescind its original finding, or unless the declaration prevented the tribunal from acting on the decision.[123]

It is doubtful whether this reasoning is correct in its own terms,[124] but in any event the courts have rendered the concept of error of law within jurisdiction largely redundant and the problem outlined above is, therefore, no longer a real one. The defect will in future be regarded as jurisdictional.

---

[114] *Hall and Co Ltd v Shoreham-by-Sea Urban District Council* [1964] 1 W.L.R. 240; *Congreve v Home Office* [1976] Q.B. 629.
[115] *Nicholls v Tavistock Urban District Council* [1923] 2 Ch.18; *Brownsea Haven Properties Ltd v Poole Corporation* [1958] Ch.574. *cf.* the criticism of *London Association of Shipowners and Brokers v London and India Docks Joint Committee* [1892] 3 Ch.242 in *Gouriet v Union of Post Office Workers* [1978] A.C. 435, 480, 493.
[116] *R. v Secretary of State for Employment Ex p. Equal Opportunities Commission* [1995] 1 A.C. 1.
[117] *Eastham v Newcastle United Football Club Ltd* [1964] Ch.413; *Nagle v Feilden* [1966] 2 Q.B. 633; *Bucknell & Son Ltd v Croydon London Borough Council* [1973] 1 W.L.R. 534; *Racal Communications Ltd v Pay Board* [1974] 1 W.L.R. 1149.
[118] *Sadler v Sheffield Corporation* [1924] 1 Ch.483; *Ridge v Baldwin* [1964] A.C. 40.
[119] *Nyali v Att-Gen* [1957] A.C. 253.
[120] *Att-Gen v St. Ives Rural District Council* [1961] 1 Q.B. 366; *Human Fertilisation & Embryology Authority v Amicus Healthcare Ltd* [2005] EWHC 1092.
[121] *Mullins v McFarlane* [2006] EWHC 986.
[122] *Staffordshire Area Health Authority v South Staffordshire Waterworks Co* [1978] 1 W.L.R. 1387.
[123] *Punton v Ministry of Pensions and National Insurance* [1963] 1 W.L.R. 186; *Punton v Ministry of Pensions and National Insurance (No.2)* [1964] 1 W.L.R. 226.
[124] P. Cane, "A Fresh Look at Punton's Case" (1980) 43 M.L.R. 266.

C. Limits on the Availability of Declaration

i. Exclusion of original jurisdiction

The declaration may, as stated above, be used in an original and a super-   **25–023**
visory role. Both of these may, however, be excluded.

The possibility of the original jurisdiction being excluded operates in the
following manner. Parliament may assign a certain topic to a particular
tribunal, minister or other public authority. When it does so the question
arises as to whether an individual can nevertheless have the same matter
adjudicated upon by the High Court in the exercise of its original jurisdiction to grant a declaration. If the determination made by the tribunal is ultra
vires then this will be subject to the court's supervisory jurisdiction, subject
to any possible limits to this role. The issue here is whether the grant of
power will exclude the original jurisdiction of the court.

In answering this question two principles have to be reconciled. One is the
presumption that when the legislature has created new rights and obligations and has empowered a specific tribunal to adjudicate upon them then
recourse must be had to that body. The other principle is the courts' dislike
of anything that takes away their jurisdiction. The outcome of particular
cases has depended upon which principle has been accorded greater weight.

There are a number of cases holding that the jurisdiction of the High
Court has been excluded, one of the best known of which is *Barraclough*.[125]
The plaintiff was empowered to remove boats that had sunk in a river if the
owner did not do so. Expenses of the operation were recoverable from the
owner in a court of summary jurisdiction. The plaintiff sought a declaration
in the High Court that he was entitled to these expenses. His action failed
despite the permissible words of the statute. The plaintiff could not at one
and the same time claim to recover by virtue of the statute and insist on
doing so by means other than those prescribed by that statute.[126] Other
authorities have reached the same conclusion, holding that exclusive jurisdiction resided in a minister or some other public body.[127]

There are, however, cases that deny exclusive jurisdiction to the appointed
public body, one of the best known of which is *Pyx Granite*.[128] The plaintiffs
carried on the business of quarrying and claimed that they should be able to
pursue this without recourse to planning permission.[129] This was denied by
the defendants, who further argued that under the relevant legislation there
was a specified procedure for determining whether planning permission was

---

[125] *Barraclough v Brown* [1897] A.C. 615.
[126] *Barraclough*, n.125, 619–620.
[127] *Baron Reitzes de Marienwert v Administrator of Austrian Property* [1924] 2 Ch.282; *Wilk-inson v Barking Corporation* [1948] 1 K.B. 721; *Gillingham Corporation v Kent County Council* [1953] Ch.37; *Healey v Minister of Health* [1955] 1 Q.B. 221; *Square Meals Frozen Foods Ltd v Dunstable Corporation* [1974] 1 W.L.R. 59; *Waltham Forest LBC v Roberts* [2004] EWCA Civ 940; *Autologic Holdings Plc v Inland Revenue Commissioners* [2006] 1 A.C. 118.
[128] *Pyx Granite Co Ltd v Ministry of Housing and Local Government* [1960] A.C. 260.
[129] The reason being that they claimed entitlement to do so under a private Act of Parliament, and further argued that such statutes were exempt from the requirement of planning permission.

required or not,[130] which procedure was exclusive and prevented an application for a declaration. The House of Lords distinguished the *Barraclough* decision. Whereas in that case the statute had created new rights to be determined by a certain procedure, in the *Pyx* case the plaintiff was simply relying on his common law rights, the only question being how far they had been removed.[131]

The distinction drawn between common law and statutory rights is questionable both in its application to the facts of the case[132] and on principle. Whether an original jurisdiction granted to a public body should be taken to be exclusive or not should be determined by a consideration of the entire subject-matter, and not by whether the rights are derived from common law or statute. The ability to side-step the enacted procedure should be dependent upon the type of procedure and its suitability for resolving the kind of question in issue. If there is little dispute as to the facts, and a point of general legal importance is at stake, then a declaration may well be more appropriate,[133] but unless such special considerations exist the particular regime established to determine the issue should be used, and this has been emphasised in more recent judgments.[134]

ii. Exclusion of supervisory jurisdiction

25–024 Whether the supervisory jurisdiction of the High Court has been excluded will be considered as a separate topic.[135] The difference between exclusion of original and supervisory jurisdiction is brought out clearly in *Fullbrook*.[136] Section 35 of the Local Government Superannuation Act 1937 provided that any question concerning the rights and liabilities of an employee should be determined initially by the local authority and then, if the employee was dissatisfied, by the minister whose decision would be final. The plaintiff was deprived of his superannuation benefits. He challenged this by a declaration claiming that he had been denied a hearing. The defendants relied on s.35 and on cases mentioned in the previous section. This argument failed. While s.35 might exclude the original jurisdiction to grant a declaration, the essence of the plaintiff's claim was the invocation of the supervisory jurisdiction of the courts, a power to declare void action that was ultra vires. This survived and could not be abrogated by the finality clause within s.35.

---

[130] Town and Country Planning Act 1947 s.17(1).
[131] [1960] A.C. 260, 286–287, 290, 302, 304.
[132] G. Borrie, Note [1960] P.L. 14–17.
[133] These factors influenced the court in the *Pyx Granite* case [1960] A.C. 260. See also, *Ealing London Borough Council v Race Relations Board* [1972] A.C. 342.
[134] *Roberts*, n.127; *Autologic Holdings*, n.127.
[135] See below, Ch.27.
[136] *Fullbrook v Berkshire Magistrates' Courts Committee* (1970) 69 L.G.R. 75.

iii. Hypothetical questions: ripeness and mootness

Declaration by its nature offers a greater possibility of raising hypothetical **25–025** questions than do the other remedies.[137] The problems surrounding such declarations are closely linked with those concerning future rights, and to questions of how far utility should play a role in deciding whether the remedy should be granted. Some of the cases within this section involve public authorities, others do not. Even the latter are however instructive. The issues of ripeness and mootness are integral to a rational system of remedies, but are not as fully developed in the UK as they are in the USA.[138] Some examples drawn from private disputes are useful in examining how such concepts could operate.

The courts have long set themselves against deciding hypothetical questions for a number of reasons, one being historical. The dislike of such hypothetical, abstract or academic questions stems from the close association between them and advisory opinions. Such opinions were once commonly asked for and given but, like much else, this practice was abused by the Stuarts. Since the judges could be dismissed by the Crown, the responses to these royal interrogatives were not always accompanied by Olympian detachment by the judiciary. Recognition of judicial independence from the executive had yet to be accepted. Even in the different climate of the 20th century reversion to the practice of giving advisory opinions raised strong passions. Thus, the proposed inclusion of such a power in the Rating and Valuation Bill 1928, hardly the most explosive piece of legislation, was attacked as redolent of the power wielded by the Stuart monarchs.[139]

A number of other reasons have been advanced as to why hypothetical questions should not be answered. There is the endemic fear of a flood of litigation,[140] and the worry that a court, having given its opinion on an abstract matter, might be embarrassed when the case came up again in a more concrete form. There is also the concern that the parties most primarily interested in the dispute might not be before the court to argue the matter,[141] placing the court in the invidious position of having to make a decision when it had not heard full argument from all sides.[142] The dislike of abstract determinations has been reinforced by the fact that if the event never occurs then the judicial time expended will have been wasted.[143] Even if the event does materialise the facts may have altered, thereby casting doubt upon the probative value of the earlier judgment. There is moreover the concern that judicial review could inhibit the giving of pre-transaction

---

[137] J. Jaconelli, "Hypothetical Disputes, Moot Points of Law and Advisory Opinions" (1985) 101 L.Q.R. 587.
[138] J. Beatson, "Prematurity and Ripeness for Review", in C. Forsyth and I. Hare (eds)., *The Golden Metwand and the Crooked Cord, Essays on Public Law in Honour of Sir William Wade* (Oxford University Press, 1998), 221–252.
[139] Lord Hewart, *The New Despotism* (Ernest Benn, 1929), 119.
[140] *Re Clay* [1919] 1 Ch.66, 78–79.
[141] *R. v DPP Ex p. Merton LBC* [1999] C.O.D. 358.
[142] *Maerkle v British Continental Fur Co Ltd* [1954] 1 W.L.R. 1242, 1248.
[143] *R. (on the application of Rusbridger) v Attorney General* [2004] 1 A.C. 357.

advice by a body such as the Inland Revenue.[144] If advice on obscure or difficult points is required then provision already exists within the Judicial Committee Act 1833, s.4 of which empowers the Crown to seek legal advice from the Privy Council.

25–026   There is, however, the important counter-argument that a legal system should enable people to operate their lives with as much certainty as possible. We all make decisions for the future, and they will be influenced by the legal rights and obligations thereby entailed. If the concept of abstract or hypothetical question is drawn too broadly it will prevent this function of a legal system from being performed. It has indeed been held that the courts possess an inherent jurisdiction to make advisory declarations as a matter of discretion.[145] Lord Woolf noted that it may be advantageous for a public body to be able to obtain an anticipatory ruling, particularly in circumstances where there is doubt as to the legality of its proposed course of action.[146] Recommendations that there should be power to make advisory declarations on matters of general public importance were made by Lord Woolf in his report on the civil justice system,[147] and by the Law Commission.[148]

The courts have treated as hypothetical, questions which come too early and are thus unripe, or which come too late and are therefore moot. An example of the former is *Draper*.[149] The defendant optical association informed the plaintiff that it believed him to be in breach of its code of ethics, and that a meeting would be held to determine whether his name should be removed from the list of members. In advance of this the plaintiff sought a declaration that the association could not enforce the code against him or remove him from the list of members. Farwell J. held the application premature: the association had not yet done anything to the plaintiff and the meeting had not yet been held. The court is more likely to take jurisdiction over a case when it feels that a legal decision will prevent possible disruptive action. In *Lee*[150] the plaintiff local authority asked for a declaration that the defendant's caravans were temporary buildings and thereby liable to be removed. The defendant argued, inter alia, that no dispute existed. In rejecting this argument the court was influenced by the possibility of a fight

---

[144] *R. v Inland Revenue Commissioners Ex p. Bishopp* [1999] S.T.C. 531.
[145] *R. v Secretary of State for the Home Department Ex p. Mehari* [1994] Q.B. 474, 491; *R. v Ministry of Agriculture, Fisheries and Food Ex p. Live Sheep Traders Ltd* [1995] C.O.D. 297; Sir John Laws, "Judicial Remedies and the Constitution" (1994) 57 M.L.R. 213.
[146] *Protection of the Public—A New Challenge* (Sweet & Maxwell, 1990), 47.
[147] Lord Woolf, *Access to Justice: The Final Report to the Lord Chancellor on the Civil Justice System in England and Wales* (1997), 251.
[148] Law Commission, *Administrative Law: Judicial Review and Statutory Appeals* (Report No.226, 1994), paras 8.9–8.14.
[149] *Draper v British Optical Association* [1938] 1 All E.R. 115; *Re Carnavon Harbour Acts* [1937] Ch.72; *Re Barnato* [1949] Ch.258; *Lever Brothers & Unilever Ltd v Manchester Ship Canal Co* (1945) 78 Ll. L.R. 507; *R. v Personal Investments Authority Ombudsman Ex p. Burns Anderson Independent Network plc* [1997] C.O.D. 379; *R. (on the application of Robinson) v Torridge DC* [2007] 1 W.L.R. 871.
[150] *Ruislip-Northwood Urban District Council v Lee* (1931) 145 L.T. 208, 214, 215.

or riot if the local authority attempted to remove the caravans without having first clarified the legal position.

Disputes may also be held to be hypothetical when they come too late and are in this sense moot,[151] where the point has become of academic interest,[152] or where the dispute has ceased to be of practical importance.[153] Thus the courts refused to issue a declaration in relation to the legality of a statutory scheme concerning the export of live animals where the scheme had been repealed prior to the application for judicial review.[154] However, where the courts feel that an important point of legal principle is involved they may give judgment even though the matter has ceased to have practical import for the parties.[155] In *Salem*,[156] Lord Slynn held that the courts have discretion to hear a case even where there is no longer a live claim that will affect the rights and obligations of the parties. Lord Slynn held that this discretion should however be exercised with caution. Appeals that were academic between the parties should not be heard unless there was a good reason in the public interest for doing so. There would be a good reason where there was a discrete point of statutory construction, which did not involve detailed consideration of facts, and where there were likely to be a large number of similar cases so that the point would, in any event, have to be decided in the near future. The decision in *Salem* was overruled by the House of Lords in *Anufrijeva*.[157] The reasons for the overruling did not however affect the issue of whether the courts have discretion to hear a case even where there is no longer a live claim.

Closely allied to, but distinct from, the cases discussed in the last paragraph are those in which a declaration is refused because of the practical impossibility of its terms being fulfilled, or because the inconvenience caused by issuing the remedy would be great compared with the benefits to be obtained. *Coney*[158] provides an example of the latter. A school reorganisation scheme was challenged for failure to comply with minor requirements concerning the posting of notices. The court characterised the requirements as directory rather than mandatory, but it made clear that it would in any event have exercised its discretion to refuse relief. Granting the remedy would at most have postponed the whole scheme for a year.

---

[151] *Everett v Ryder* (1926) 135 L.T. 302; *Whyte, Ridsdale & Co Ltd v Att-Gen* [1927] 1 Ch.548; *Harrison v Croydon London Borough Council* [1968] Ch.479; *Howard v Pickford Tool Co* [1951] K.B. 417.
[152] *R. v Her Majesty's Inspectorate of Pollution Ex p. Ch.man* [1996] C.O.D. 154.
[153] *R. v Head Teacher and Governors of Fairfield Primary School and Hampshire County Council Ex p. W* [1998] C.O.D. 106.
[154] *Live Sheep Traders Ltd*, n.145.
[155] *Eastham v Newcastle United Football Club Ltd* [1964] Ch.413; *West Ham Corporation v Sharp* [1907] 1 K.B. 445; *R. v Secretary of State for the Home Department Ex p. Abdi* [1996] 1 W.L.R. 298.
[156] *R. v Secretary of State for the Home Department Ex p. Salem* [1999] 1 A.C. 450, 456–457.
[157] *R. (on the application of Anufrijeva) v Secretary of State for the Home Department* [2004] 1 A.C. 604.
[158] *Coney v Choyce* [1975] 1 W.L.R. 422, 436–437; *Maerkle v British and Continental Fur Co Ltd* [1954] 1 W.L.R. 1242; *Att-Gen v Colchester Corporation* [1955] 2 Q.B. 207.

iv. Justiciability

25–027 To ask whether a dispute is justiciable or not is to ask whether the type of dispute is suitable for resolution by the judicial process, irrespective of who is bringing the action. Justiciability has been most explicitly recognised in tort actions against public authorities.[159] The term itself is used relatively rarely in other areas, but it underlies or has influenced a number of different decisions, some of which concern the declaration.

For example, in reaching the conclusion that broadly framed duties under the Education Act 1944 were to be enforced through the Minister, the courts were clearly influenced by the difficulties of adjudicating upon such subject-matter. While the possibility of judicial intervention was not totally excluded, it was restricted to the more extreme and obvious forms of unlawful behaviour.[160] In some cases the courts have been more willing to tackle such issues, but this must be read against the type of illegality being asserted.[161]

The nature of the subject-matter has influenced the courts in other areas, aside from education. The effect has been either that the courts have declined to intervene, or they have done so on narrower grounds, given the broad discretion granted to the public body. Alleged breaches of duty by university examiners provide an example of the former[162] and the provision of accommodation by a local authority an example of the latter.[163] The categorisation of treaties as giving rise to no legally enforceable obligations until they have been incorporated into municipal law has been partly influenced by the concept of justiciability,[164] as was the related decision that no declaration would be granted to preclude the Crown from undertaking an international obligation.[165]

v. Alternative remedies

25–028 The effect of alternative remedies on the availability of the declaration will be considered in a later section.[166]

D. The Impact of the Declaration

25–029 The normal impact of a declaration is to render the decision challenged retrospectively invalid or void ab initio. There may, however, be instances in which its impact is prospective rather than retrospective. The court may in effect refuse to grant relief in the instant case, but nonetheless proceed to

---

[159] See below, Ch.29; *Anns v Merton London Borough Council* [1978] A.C. 728; *Rowling v Takaro Properties Ltd* [1988] A.C. 473.
[160] *Watt v Kesteven County Council* [1955] 1 Q.B. 408; *Bradbury v Enfield London Borough Council* [1967] 1 W.L.R. 1311; *Cumings v Birkenhead Corporation* [1972] Ch.12.
[161] In *Meade v Haringey London Borough Council* [1979] 1 W.L.R. 637 the Court of Appeal was clearly strongly influenced by what it felt was closure of the schools for non-educational reasons. See also, *Thornton v Kirklees Metropolitan Borough Council* [1979] 3 W.L.R. 1.
[162] *Thorne v University of London* [1966] 2 Q.B. 237.
[163] *R. v Bristol Corporation ex p Hendy* [1974] 1 W.L.R. 498 (mandamus).
[164] *Buck v Att-Gen* [1965] Ch.745.
[165] *Blackburn v Att-Gen* [1971] 1 W.L.R. 1037.
[166] See below, paras 26–056—26–058.

give a declaration on the general point of law.[167] The reasons for employing this technique are similar to those encountered when discussing invalidity.[168] To render the contested decision retrospectively null may have a profound effect on the administration, or may adversely affect the rights of third parties. The court may decide to refuse to give relief in the instant case,[169] or it may, while declining relief in the instant case, take the opportunity to clarify the law in the area.[170] The desirability of modifying the concept of retrospective nullity in this fashion have been considered in the earlier discussion of invalidity.[171]

E. Practice and Procedure

A court can grant a binding declaration irrespective of whether any other remedy is claimed.[172] The judicial review procedure may be used in a claim for judicial review where the claimant is seeking a declaration.[173] This procedure will be analysed in the following chapter. The Supreme Court Act, s.31(2), sets out the circumstances in which a court can grant a declaration in a claim for judicial review, and this will be considered in detail in the chapter that follows. Where the claimant is seeking a declaration or injunction in addition to a mandatory, prohibiting or quashing order, then the judicial review procedure must be used.[174] A "gap" in the courts' jurisdiction was the inability to grant an interim declaration of rights. This was important when claims were brought against the Crown since injunctive relief was not available.[175] The Civil Procedure Rules now provide for an interim declaration.[176]

25–030

---

[167] *R. v Panel on Take-overs and Mergers Ex p. Datafin* [1987] Q.B. 815; *R. v Secretary of State Ex p. Association of Metropolitan Authorities* [1986] 1 W.L.R. 1; C. Lewis, "Retrospective and Prospective Rulings in Administrative Law" [1988] P.L. 78; Sir Harry Woolf, *Protection of the Public-A New Challenge* (Sweet & Maxwell, 1990), 53–54.
[168] See above, Ch.23.
[169] *R. v Monopolies and Mergers Commission Ex p. Argyll Group plc* [1986] 1 W.L.R. 763.
[170] As indicated by Lord Donaldson M.R. in the *Datafin* case [1987] Q.B. 815.
[171] See above, paras 23–020—23–023.
[172] CPR 40.20.
[173] SI 2000/2092, CPR 54.3(1).
[174] CPR 54.3(1).
[175] *Underhill v Ministry of Food* [1950] 1 All E.R. 591; *International General Electric Co of New York Ltd v Customs and Excise Commissioners* [1962] Ch.784; *R. v Inland Revenue Commissioners Ex p. Rossminster Ltd* [1980] A.C. 952; *Clarke v Chadburn* [1985] 1 W.L.R. 78. For more detailed discussion of this issue see below, para.28–021.
[176] CPR 25.1(1)(b); *X NHS Trust v T (Adult Patient: Refusal of Medical Treatment)* [2005] 1 All E.R. 387.

4. INJUNCTION

A. Introduction

25–031 The injunction has had an impact on public law for many years,[177] as exemplified by case law on public nuisance and the administration of charitable or public trusts. The latter was, as de Smith pointed out,[178] of particular importance. The Attorney-General's intervention was founded upon the position of the Crown as *parens patriae*. This role existed not only for charities, infants and those infirm in mind, but also included a visitatorial authority over those charitable and ecclesiastical corporations that lacked visitors of their own. Proceedings by the Attorney-General often arose out of default by such bodies in the performance of their functions and took the form of actions to ensure that they observed their duties. The general right of the Attorney-General to prevent ultra vires action grew out of a broad conception of the prerogative of protection.[179]

Despite the respectability of its historical lineage, the injunction remained largely on the periphery of public law, compared to the position in the USA where it developed into an all-purpose public law remedy. There are a variety of reasons for this. The existence of the prerogative orders as the main control over invalid public action was undoubtedly a factor. More important is the fact that it has remained shackled by its own history. The criteria for individual standing were derived from those of public nuisance.[180] If these were not satisfied the Attorney-General had to bring the action. The reasoning underlying these cases has already been criticised in the discussion of standing.[181] Those rules were, however, reaffirmed in the *Gouriet*[182] case. The fetters binding the injunction have indeed been tightened. Whereas the old rules from public nuisance could have been liberalised, the reasoning in the *Gouriet* case rendered this much less likely. Those rules were upheld because they reflected a view of the role of the individual in public law. The citizen could not protect the public interest unless he or she was settling a private dispute, or one in which he or she had a special interest, with a public body.

The main hope is s.31 of the Supreme Court Act 1981, through which declarations and injunctions can be obtained if the subject-matter concerns public law. The discussion of standing has shown that the courts take a more liberal attitude under s.31 than at common law.[183] The general rules concerning injunctions will be considered here. Problems arising from the interpretation of s.31 will be considered later.

---

[177] Many of the cases brought against local authorities were injunction cases.
[178] *de Smith's Judicial Review*, n.5, 800–804.
[179] de Smith, n.5, 433; *de Smith's Judicial Review*, n.5, 803–804
[180] *Boyce v Paddington Borough Council* [1903] 1 Ch.109.
[181] See above, para.24–014.
[182] [1978] A.C. 435; *Barrs v Bethell* [1982] Ch.294.
[183] See above, Ch.24.

B. The Types of Injunction

Injunctions can be negative or positive, prohibiting certain action from being done or commanding the performance of certain action. In addition, an injunction can be perpetual or interim. The former is granted at the end of the action and conclusively determines the respective rights and liabilities of the parties. How long the injunction is awarded for will be dependent upon the type of dispute.

25–032

Interim injunctions are designed to preserve the status quo pending trial of the main action.[184] The plaintiff must show that there is some arguable point of law and that the balance of convenience indicates that relief should be granted pending trial of the main action.[185] It has, however, been held by Lord Goff that a public authority should not normally be restrained from enforcing an apparently valid law unless the court is satisfied that the challenge to the validity of the law is prima facie so firmly based as to justify "so exceptional a course being taken".[186] It may be particularly difficult to assess the balance of convenience in public law cases, because the public body will be representing a wider public interest when it is making the challenged decision. It is, therefore, unsurprising that the courts are likely to take into account the strength of the applicant's case in challenging the act when deciding where the balance of convenience actually lies.[187] The party in whose favour the interim relief is granted will normally have to give an undertaking in damages lest he or she proves to be unsuccessful and the defendant suffers loss.

The award of an interim injunction will be affected by rules of EU law where there is a challenge involving EU law.[188] It will also be affected by the Human Rights Act 1998 s.12(3), which provides that where a claim might affect the right to freedom of expression, no such relief is to be granted so as to restrain publication before trial unless the court is satisfied that the applicant is likely to establish that publication should not be allowed.[189]

C. The Scope of Injunctive Relief

i. Injunctions: general

Injunctions can be issued in a whole range of situations: to prevent a public

25–033

---

[184] CPR 25.1(1)(a).
[185] This is, in brief, the two stage test established by the House of Lords in *American Cyanamid Co v Ethicon Ltd* [1975] A.C. 396; *R. v Secretary of State for Transport Ex p. Factortame (No.2)* [1991] 1 A.C. 603; *Douglas v Hello! Ltd (No.1)* [2001] Q.B. 967; J. Martin, "Interlocutory Injunctions: *American Cyanamid* Comes of Age" (1993–94) King's Coll. L.J. 52.
[186] *Factortame (No.2)*, n.185.
[187] *Factortame (No.2)*, n.185.
[188] *R. v Ministry of Agriculture, Fisheries and Food Ex p. Monsanto Plc* [1999] Q.B. 1161; *R. v Secretary of State for Health Ex p. Scotia Pharmaceuticals International Ltd (No.2)* [1997] Eu. L.R. 650. See also, *R. v Secretary of State for Health Ex p. Imperial Tobacco Ltd* [2001] 1 W.L.R. 127, for discussion of possible differences between the *American Cyanamid* test, and the test for interim relief developed by the ECJ.
[189] *Cream Holdings Ltd v Banerjee* [2005] 1 A.C. 253; *Greene v Associated Newspapers Ltd* [2005] Q.B. 972.

body from committing what would be a private wrong such as a trespass[190] or a nuisance[191]; to restrain a public body from acting unlawfully[192]; to restrain the implementation of an unlawful decision[193]; and to enforce public duties, provided that they are not too vague.[194]

The remedy can also be used by the Attorney-General, who can seek an injunction to prevent a public body from acting ultra vires.[195] The Attorney-General has also used the injunction to prevent repeated breaches of the criminal law, or in circumstances where injury to the person is threatened.[196] Two more specific uses of the injunction should be mentioned here.

ii. Injunctions and parliament

25–034 Possible challenge to the legality of ordinary public statutes immediately enmeshes one in debates on sovereignty, and the efficacy or otherwise of rules requiring special majorities. This is not the place to consider this debate.[197] Even before a measure has received the Royal Assent it is dubious whether it could be successfully challenged in the courts.[198]

The courts have, however, asserted that, in principle, they would be willing to issue an injunction to prevent a breach of contract where that breach consists of a promise not to oppose a private bill. The key word in the above sentence is "principle", since the courts have in fact declined to intervene even in what appears to be a strong case. Thus in *Bilston Corporation v Wolverhampton Corporation*[199] the latter had contracted with Bilston Corporation that it would not oppose any application to Parliament by Bilston whereby Bilston sought a local Act of Parliament for securing a water supply. Despite this promise and the fact that it had been enshrined in an earlier local Act, the court declined to issue the injunction, the reasoning being that Parliament should have the opportunity to hear the argument of both parties in order to decide whether Wolverhampton Corporation should be released from its obligations by statute.

Challenge to subordinate legislation is subject to different considerations. When such legislation has been passed it is open to attack as being ultra vires, and a declaration or injunction can be granted to a claimant. If a

---

[190] *Broadbent v Rotherham Corporation* [1917] 2 Ch.31.
[191] *Pride of Derby and Derbyshire Angling Association Ltd v British Celanese Ltd* [1953] Ch.149.
[192] *Bradbury*, n.160.
[193] *R. v North Yorkshire County Council Ex p. M* [1989] Q.B. 411.
[194] *R. v Kensington and Chelsea London Borough Council Ex p. Hammell* [1989] Q.B. 518; *South Buckinghamshire DC v Porter (No.1)* [2003] 2 A.C. 558.
[195] *Att-Gen v Manchester Corporation* [1906] 1 Ch.643; *Att-Gen v Fulham Corporation* [1921] 1 Ch.440.
[196] *Att-Gen v Smith* [1958] 2 Q.B. 173; *Att-Gen v Chaudry* [1971] 1 W.L.R. 1614. For more detailed consideration of these authorities and for the qualifications imposed on them in *Gouriet* [1978] A.C. 435, see above, Ch.24.
[197] P. Craig, "Parliamentary Sovereignty after *Factortame*" (1991) 11 Y.B.E.L. 221.
[198] de Smith, n.5, 465–466; de Smith, Woolf and Jowell, *Judicial Review of Administrative Action* (Sweet & Maxwell, 5th edn, 1995), 725–726.
[199] [1942] Ch.391. *cf. Att-Gen v London and Home Counties Joint Electricity Authority* [1929] 1 Ch.513, in which it was accepted that the Attorney-General could have an injunction to prevent unauthorised expenditure of corporate funds to promote a bill.

person wishes to bring an action prior to the final enactment of the order the issue is more problematic. The prerogative orders do not it seems run against legislative proceedings, although as noted above the position in this respect appears to be changing. An injunction will not issue against Her Majesty in Council, nor it seems against a Minister of the Crown who is making a statutory instrument. A declaration might be possible if an appropriate defendant could be found. Where an order has been laid before Parliament, and has been approved by both Houses of Parliament, the courts are likely to feel reluctant to intervene.[200]

Even where the legislative process is not involved, the courts will not award an injunction where to do so would be an interference with the right of the House to regulate its own internal proceedings.[201] There are, however, dicta that it would be possible, albeit unusual, for a court to grant a mandatory injunction ordering a minister to lay a statutory instrument before Parliament.[202]

The position with respect to Community law and the legislative process is different. We have already seen that our courts have accepted that Community law must take supremacy in the event of a clash with domestic law. This was the essence of the holding in *Factortame (No.2)*.[203] The House of Lords held that an interim injunction could be granted under s.37 of the Supreme Court Act 1981 preventing the enforcement of the domestic legislation, pending the final resolution of the disputed matter before the ECJ. It remains to be seen what the courts would do if it were alleged that the domestic legislature was about to enact legislation that was felt to be in breach of Community law. It is clear that, as a matter of Community law, Parliament is under an obligation not to pass legislation contrary to Community obligations. However, it is likely that our courts would require strong evidence before accepting that such domestic legislation that was to be enacted was in breach of Community law. If such evidence were forthcoming then it is not inconceivable that an interim injunction could be issued pending the final resolution of the substantive issue by the ECJ. In the event that the ECJ found that the proposed legislation was contrary to Community law then a final order could be addressed to the relevant minister. This could be in the form of a prohibiting order, or in the form of an injunction.

iii. Injunctions and public offices

An information in the nature of *quo warranto* was, until 1938, the procedure by which challenges to the usurpation of a public office were made. In 1938 the information in the nature of *quo warranto* was abolished and replaced by

25–035

[200] *Harper v Home Secretary* [1955] Ch.238; *Nottinghamshire County Council v Secretary of State for the Environment* [1986] A.C. 240. See, however, *Hoffman-La Roche & Co AG v Secretary of State for Trade and Industry* [1975] A.C. 295.
[201] *Bradlaugh v Gossett* (1884) 12 Q.B.D. 271.
[202] *R. v HM Treasury Ex p. British Telecomunications Plc* [1995] C.O.D. 56.
[203] [1991] 1 A.C. 603.

the injunction.[204] The substance of the action however remained the same, with the old rules still governing; only the form of the remedy was altered.

Thus, the office must be public in character, and the usurper must have actually acted in pursuance of it; a claim per se was insufficient. The office itself had to be not only public but "substantive", as distinct from mere employment at the will of others. Standing to secure the remedy was broadly construed,[205] but acquiescence or undue delay would operate to defeat the plaintiff. Specific statutory provisions govern challenges to particular types of office.[206]

D. Limits to Injunctive Relief

25–036 The injunction is an equitable remedy and equitable principles will influence the way in which it is applied by the courts. Undue delay or acquiescence will bar the claimant. The adequacy of a monetary remedy will also influence the court.

Considerations of practicality have been treated differently by the courts. They will not, on the one hand, order a defendant to do the impossible[207] and they will weigh the inconvenience caused by the public body's defective action with the cost of requiring it to comply with the statutory procedure to the letter.[208] On the other hand, general pleas by a public institution of the disruptive effects or difficulty of complying with a court order will not, in general, bar the remedy.[209]

Particular problems have surrounded the award of injunctive relief against the Crown. This topic is dealt with separately below.[210] The availability of a different remedy, and the effect of this upon the ability to claim injunctive relief, will be considered below.[211]

E. Practice and Procedure

25–037 Injunctions, like declarations, can be claimed under s.31 of the Supreme Court Act 1981, and independently of this procedure. The judicial review procedure may be used in a claim for judicial review where the claimant is seeking an injunction.[212] The Supreme Court Act, s.31(2), sets out the circumstances in which a court can grant an injunction in a claim for judicial review, and this will be considered in the following chapter. Where the

---

[204] Administration of Justice (Miscellaneous Provisions) Act 1938 s.9. See now, Supreme Court Act 1981 s.30.
[205] *R. v Speyer* [1916] 1 K.B. 595, (affirmed [1916] 2 K.B. 858.)
[206] See, e.g., Local Government Act 1972 s.92 applies to challenges to the qualifications of members of a local authority.
[207] *Att-Gen v Colchester Corporation* [1955] 2 Q.B. 207.
[208] *Coney v Choyce* [1975] 1 W.L.R. 422.
[209] *Pride of Derby*, n.191; *Bradbury*, n.160.
[210] See below, para.28–018.
[211] See below, paras 26–056—26–058.
[212] SI 2000/2092, CPR 54.3(1).

claimant is seeking an injunction in addition to one of the prerogative orders, then the judicial review procedure must be used.[213]

An injunction may also be sought independently of a judicial review action. In 1875 the power to grant an injunction, which had previously resided solely with courts of equity, was made available to all divisions of the High Court where the award of the remedy appeared to be just and convenient.[214] The effect of the provision was to allow the High Court to grant an injunction where it would previously have granted a common law remedy. Where no remedy would have been available at common law or equity an injunction could not be given.[215]

5. OTHER REMEDIES

A. Habeas Corpus

If an individual is detained, the writ of habeas corpus may be sought to challenge the legality of the administrative order on which the detention was based.[216] A brief outline of this remedy will be provided here. Fuller treatment may be found elsewhere.[217]

25–038

The immediate progenitor of the present writ was the writ of habeas corpus *cum causa*, which developed in the 14th century as a mechanism for testing the legality of detention. Reforms expediting the procedure were introduced by the Habeas Corpus Act 1679, which also contained financial penalties for those, whether they were judges or jailers, who refused service of the writ or impeded its effective execution. The detainee will normally make the application, unless the circumstances of the imprisonment preclude this and the writ will be served on the person who has the applicant in custody.[218]

The cases on scope of review in a habeas corpus action are a minefield, evidencing a bewildering variety of terminology. Starting from first principles, it seems clear that the writ cannot be used to challenge the correctness of the detention, but only its validity. Correctness can only be challenged on appeal.[219] This is simply an application of the traditional principles of judicial review, but it remains to be seen how far the expansion of jurisdictional error affects this area so as to render the above distinction redundant. Jurisdictional errors provide a clear reason for awarding the writ.[220] It is less clear whether habeas corpus can be awarded for an error on

---

[213] CPR 54.3(1).
[214] Supreme Court of Judicature Act 1873 s.25(8). See now, Supreme Court Act 1981 s.37.
[215] *North London Ry v Great Northern Ry.* (1883) 11 Q.B.D. 30.
[216] For related challenges based on collateral attack, see Ch.23.
[217] R. Sharpe, *The Law of Habeas Corpus* (Clarendon, 2nd edn, 1989); de Smith, n.5, App.2; *de Smith's Judicial Review*, n.5, 865–871.
[218] CPR Sch.1, Pt 54.
[219] *Ex p. Hinds* [1961] 1 W.L.R. 325.
[220] *Eshugbayi Eleko v Government of Nigeria* [1931] A.C. 662.

the face of the record, but the answer appears to be in the affirmative,[221] and the courts will also consider whether the evidence justifies the holding of the detainee.[222] In general, while the courts insist that they are looking at validity rather than correctness, they will not normally be prevented from releasing a detainee who they feel ought to be released by inquiry into the jurisprudential niceties of errors going to and errors within jurisdiction.[223] Such distinctions are, in any event, now of historical interest only given the courts' expansion of the concept of jurisdictional error. A purely technical flaw in the process leading to detention may lead the court to decline to issue the writ.[224]

Habeas corpus will be available to determine whether the detention itself was valid, and the courts will normally apply the general principles of administrative law when determining this issue.[225] Where, however, an applicant seeks to attack the underlying administrative decision, which was the cause of the detention, then judicial review should be used rather than habeas corpus.[226] There is a more general tendency to prefer challenges by way of judicial review, with resort to habeas corpus where no other mode of challenge is available.[227] Where a claimant challenged via judicial review and habeas corpus, the proceedings should be harmonised.

The Lord Chancellor put forward proposals that affect the relationship between judicial review and habeas corpus.[228] The principal recommendation was that habeas corpus should, subject to permission, be available in judicial review proceedings for all civil cases. The Lord Chancellor also sought views on whether habeas corpus should be wholly subsumed into judicial review, and whether the discretionary elements of judicial review in relation to permission, time limits and remedies, should also apply to a claim for habeas corpus within judicial review proceedings.

B. Private Law Remedies

25–039   A person aggrieved with action taken by a public body may be able to bring

---

[221] *R. v Governor of Brixton Prison Ex p. Armah* [1968] A.C. 192.
[222] *Armah*, n.221; *Knowles v Government of the United States of America* [2007] 1 W.L.R. 47, para.14; *Gibson v The Government of the United States of America* [2007] UKPC 52, para.18; *R. v Board of Control Ex p. Rutty* [1956] 2 Q.B. 109.
[223] Rubinstein, n.5, 115.
[224] *R. v Governor of Pentonville Prison Ex p. Osman (No.3)* [1990] 1 W.L.R. 878.
[225] *R. v Governor of Pentonville Prison Ex p. Osman* [1990] 1 W.L.R. 277.
[226] *R. v Secretary of State for the Home Department Ex p. Cheblak* [1991] 1 W.L.R. 890; *R. v Secretary of State for the Home Department Ex p. Muboyayi* [1992] Q.B. 244; *Re S-C (Mental Patient)* [1996] Q.B. 599; *R. v Stoke-on-Trent Justices Ex p. Cawley* [1996] C.O.D. 292; *Re Rahman* [1996] C.O.D. 465.
[227] *MB v The Managers of Warley Hospital*, July 30, 1998; *R. v BHB Community Healthcare NHS Trust Ex p. B* [1999] 1 F.L.R. 106; *R. v Leeds Crown Court Ex p. Hunt* [1999] 1 W.L.R. 841; *Sheikh v Secretary of State for the Home Department* [2001] A.C.D. 33; Sir Simon Brown, "Habeas Corpus—A New Chapter" [2000] P.L. 31.
[228] Lord Chancellor's Department Consultation Paper, *The Administrative Court: Proposed Changes to Primary Legislation following Sir Jeffrey Bowman's Review of the Crown Office List* (2001), paras 3–10.

a civil claim in tort or contract. The scope of these causes of action will be considered in the final chapter.

C. Default Powers

As a final sanction many statutes contain provisions which enable a more **25–040** senior body in the administrative hierarchy or the Minister to exercise powers where it is felt that the original grantee has failed to do so. Normally the defaulting authority will be warned and given time within which to fulfil its duties. Failing this, the duties will be transferred to the minister, to an independent body, or new members may be appointed to replace those in default.

On some occasions the courts have treated the existence of such powers as excluding other remedies. Thus in *Pasmore*[229] the existence of default powers in the Public Health Act 1875 was held to prevent a private person from obtaining mandamus to enforce a duty to provide such sewers as might be necessary for draining a district. In other cases the courts have not adopted this construction. Other remedies have been available despite the presence of default powers in cases involving, for example, education,[230] and television.[231]

It is odd to regard default powers as an alternative remedy that is equally beneficial as a declaration or mandamus. In some ways it is not a legal remedy at all.[232] The cases which regard default powers as excluding other remedies should therefore be narrowly construed. Those cases where such powers have been regarded as exclusive are perhaps better explained as ones in which the nature of the duty rendered it unsuited to enforcement by individuals. There are indications in the case law that the courts have had this factor in mind when construing the relevant statute.[233]

Although default powers will only be used as a last resort they are a potent threat, particularly in times when the relationship between central and local government is under strain.[234] The exercise of such powers will be subject to judicial review. If the minister acts on irrelevant considerations or misdirects himself in fact or law, then the intervention will be ultra vires. The court should not interfere simply because they took a different view from that of the minister.[235]

---

[229] *Pasmore v Oswaldtwistle Urban District Council* [1898] A.C. 387, applying *Doe d. Bishop of Rochester v Bridges* (1831) 1 B. & Ad. 847; *Bradbury*, n.160; *Wood v Ealing LBC* [1967] Ch.364; *Southwark LBC v Williams* [1971] Ch.734.
[230] *Meade v Haringey LBC* [1979] 1 W.L.R. 637.
[231] *Att-Gen, ex rel McWhirter v Independent Broadcasting Authority* [1973] Q.B. 629.
[232] *R. v Leicester Guardians* [1899] 2 Q.B. 632, 639.
[233] *Southwark LBC*, n.229, 743.
[234] *Asher v Secretary of State for the Environment* [1974] Ch.208.
[235] *R. v Secretary of State for the Environment Ex p. Norwich County Council* [1982] Q.B. 808. Lord Denning M.R. also suggests that the Minister has a procedural duty to hear the local authority's view before exercising his powers.

CHAPTER 26

REMEDIES AND REFORM

1. THE REFORMS

A. The Need for Reform

The range of remedies available to a potential claimant has always been a **26–001** mixed blessing. There were, as seen in the previous chapter, uncertainties about the scope of the individual remedies. Moreover, the principal remedies of certiorari and declaration had both advantages and disadvantages.

Certiorari could apply to all types of error, including non-jurisdictional error while that concept still existed, the standing rules were relatively wide, and interim relief was available. Its disadvantages included the impossibility of combining a claim for certiorari with a damages action, a relatively short time limit, and the difficulty of adjudicating upon contested questions of fact.

The declaration was meant, by way of contrast, to be the shining white charger cutting through outmoded limitations encrusted upon the pick and shovel prerogative orders,[1] and so it might have been. It was unencumbered by the limitations mentioned above and its dual capacity as supervisory and original remedy gave it added flexibility. It could, moreover, be combined with other claims for relief, was not subject to a short time limit, and could be attended by full discovery. The promise that declaration might bloom into a general, all purpose remedy, with the prerogative orders being left to atrophy from lack of use, did not however come to pass. It was thought that no interim declaration could be granted, there were question marks surrounding the availability of declaration for non-jurisdictional error of law, and the standing criteria, as laid down in the *Gouriet* case,[2] were restrictive.

---

[1] *Barnard v National Dock Labour Board* [1953] 2 Q.B. 18.
[2] [1978] A.C. 435.

B. The Ordinary Courts: The Legal Foundations of the Existing Procedure

26–002 Given that neither the effluxion of time, nor the application of Darwinian principles, had produced a single, strong remedy, reform was clearly required. The Law Commission's Report No.73 was the culmination of earlier studies,[3] the most wide-ranging of which had been the second. By the time that Report No.73 was published the Law Commission felt that it must confine itself more narrowly to questions of procedure. The earlier Working Paper had undertaken a wider ranging study encompassing, *inter alia*, time limits, ouster clauses, and damages. These were felt to be outside the scope of the Law Commission's brief.

What emerged was a revised Ord.53,[4] as amended by a later statutory instrument.[5] Some of the key provisions were incorporated into the Supreme Court Act 1981[6] s.31. The legal foundations for the public law procedures continued to be the revised Ord.53, and the 1981 Act, for 20 years.

These legal foundations have now changed.[7] The catalyst was the general reform of the civil justice system flowing from the Woolf Report.[8] This led to a radical revision of the rules on civil procedure. The initial impact of these reforms on judicial review was marginal, since Ord.53, subject to minor change, was appended to the new Civil Procedure Rules. The position altered as a result of the Bowman Report into the Crown Office.[9] Judicial review is now governed by CPR 8, as modified by a new Pt 54. These provisions apply to all judicial review applications lodged on or after October 2, 2000.[10] The legal foundations for judicial review will henceforth be based on the CPR, the Supreme Court Act 1981 s.31, and relevant Practice Directions. The detailed procedure under CPR 54 will be considered below.[11] The Crown Office has been renamed the Administrative Court.[12] It is clear that although the claim for judicial review is brought in

---

[3] Law Comm No.20, Cmnd. 4059 (1969); Law Comm Working Paper No.40 (1971); Law Comm. No.73, Cmnd. 6407 (1976).
[4] SI 1977/1955.
[5] SI 1980/2000.
[6] The Supreme Court Act is to be renamed the Senior Courts Act 1981, the change has been brought about by the Constitutional Reform Act 2005 Sch.11(1), para.1.
[7] See generally, C. Lewis, *Judicial Remedies in Public Law* (Sweet & Maxwell, 3rd edn, 2004).
[8] Lord Woolf, *Access to Justice: The Final Report to the Lord Chancellor on the Civil Justice System in England and Wales* (1997); SI 1998/3132.
[9] *Review of the Crown Office List* (LCD, 2000); Lord Chancellor's Department Consultation Paper, *The Administrative Court: Proposed Changes to Primary Legislation following Sir Jeffrey Bowman's Review of the Crown Office List* (2001).
[10] SI 2000/2092; M Fordham, "Judicial Review: The New Rules" [2001] P.L. 4; T. Cornford and M. Sunkin, "The Bowman Report, Access and the Recent reforms of the Judicial Review Procedure" [2001] P.L. 11.
[11] See below, paras 26–053—26–054.
[12] Practice Direction, [2000] 1 W.L.R. 1654.

the name of the Crown, the Crown's involvement is nominal. The real contest is between the claimant and the defendant.[13]

C. The Upper Tribunal: Legal Foundations for New Judicial Review Power

The power of judicial review has traditionally vested in the ordinary courts. The Tribunals, Courts and Enforcement Act 2007 altered this. The Act was considered in detail an earlier chapter.[14] Suffice it to say for the present that it enables, subject to certain conditions, the new Upper Tribunal to exercise judicial review functions,[15] and allows for the transfer of certain judicial review cases to it from the High Court.[16] The procedure for judicial review before the Upper Tribunal is however largely the same as that in ordinary judicial review applications to the High Court, in relation to matters such as the need for permission, time limits and the like.

26–003

D. The Application/Claim for Judicial Review

The 1977 reform was based on the application, or as it is now termed, claim for judicial review. The prerogative orders and declaration and injunction are subject to this mechanism, and the remedies may be sought in the alternative or cumulatively depending upon the type of case.[17] When the revised Ord.53 was first passed it was thought that declaration and injunction would still be obtainable under their pre-existing procedures. It would, however, be inappropriate for those remedies to be claimed under the new procedure unless the case was of a public law nature.

26–004

Section 31(2) of the Supreme Court Act 1981, defines when cases will be of this kind. Declarations and injunctions can be granted pursuant to an application for judicial review if the court considers, having regard to the nature of the matters and the nature of the persons and bodies against whom a remedy may be granted by the prerogative orders, and all the circumstances of the case, that it would be just and convenient for the declaration to be made or for the injunction to be granted. The test is therefore both functional and institutional. It is clear, after some earlier doubts,[18] that a declaration or an injunction can be granted even if a pre-

---

[13] *R. (on the application of Ben-Abdelaziz and Kryva) v London Borough of Hackney and the Secretary of State for the Home Department* [2001] 1 W.L.R. 1485, para.29.
[14] See above, Ch.9.
[15] Tribunals, Courts and Enforcement Act 2007 s.15.
[16] Tribunals, Courts and Enforcement Act 2007 s.19, inserting s.31A into the Supreme Court Act 1981.
[17] Supreme Court Act 1981 s.31(1).
[18] *R. v Inland Revenue Commissioners Ex p. National Federation of Self-Employed and Small Businesses Ltd* [1982] A.C. 617, 647–648.

rogative order would not be available,[19] provided that the subject-matter of the application is of a public law nature and hence suited to judicial review.[20]

This general approach has been retained by CPR 54, Pt 1 of which deals with judicial review. A claim for judicial review is defined in CPR 54.1(2)(a) to be a claim to review the lawfulness of an enactment, or decision, action or failure to act in the exercise of a public function. CPR 54.2 provides that the judicial review procedure must be used where the claimant is seeking a mandatory, prohibiting or quashing order,[21] or an injunction under the Supreme Court Act 1981 s.30. It must also be used where the claimant seeks a declaration or injunction in addition to a mandatory, prohibiting or quashing order. CPR 54.3(1) provides that the judicial review procedure may be used in a claim for judicial review where the claimant is seeking a declaration or an injunction. The Supreme Court Act 1981 s.31(2) continues to provide the circumstances in which a claimant can seek a declaration or injunction in a claim for judicial review. Damages, restitution or the recovery of a sum due can be claimed in conjunction with the other remedies, but a claim for judicial review may not seek such remedies alone, CPR 54.3(2). This does not, however, create a new remedy where none existed before. The court must be satisfied that if the claim had been made in an ordinary action the applicant would have been awarded the remedy.[22]

E. O'Reilly v Mackman

26–005   The application for judicial review must be read in the light of the decision in *O'Reilly v Mackman*.[23] This case limited the circumstances in which a declaration or an injunction in a public law case could be sought outside of the Supreme Court Act 1981 s.31. Lord Diplock gave judgment for the House of Lords, and reasoned as follows.

The prerogative orders had, prior to the reforms, been subject to a number of limitations. There was no right to discovery, damages could not be claimed in conjunction with one of the orders and cross-examination upon affidavits occurred very rarely if at all. These limitations justified the use of the declaration under Ord.15 r.16. However, the reformed Ord.53 had removed these defects by providing for discovery, allowing damages to be claimed, and making provision for cross-examination. The reformed procedure also provided important safeguards for the public body, including the requirement of leave to bring the case and a time limit short enough so that the public body would not be kept unduly in suspense as to whether its actions were valid or not.

---

[19] *R. v Secretary of State for Employment Ex p. Equal Opportunities Commission* [1995] 1 A.C. 1.
[20] *R. v British Broadcasting Corporation Ex p. Lavelle* [1983] 1 W.L.R. 23, 30–31.
[21] These are the new names for mandamus, prohibition and certiorari, Supreme Court Act 1981, s.29, as amended by SI 2004/1033, art.3.
[22] Supreme Court Act 1981 s.31(4).
[23] [1983] 2 A.C. 237.

It would therefore normally be an abuse of process to seek a declaration outside of s.31. Two exceptions were mentioned: certain types of collateral attack and cases where none of the parties objected to a remedy being sought outside s.31. The possibility that other exceptions might exist was left open to be decided upon a case by case basis.

Lord Diplock also felt that within s.31 the prerogative orders should be the main remedies. The declaration was seen as useful, while the prerogative orders were unduly limited. Now that the latter had been liberated from their constraints, they should assume pride of place within s.31. When the sole aim was to quash a decision, certiorari and not declaration should be used.

The decision in *O'Reilly* raised a number of important questions. First, what are the exceptions to *O'Reilly*: how do you "get out" of the judicial procedure? Second, how public must a case be to be brought within the judicial review procedure: how do you "get into" this procedure? Finally, do we need a separate procedure for judicial review cases?

2. THE EXCEPTIONS: "GETTING OUT" OF THE JUDICIAL REVIEW PROCEDURE

A. The Reasons for Seeking to Proceed outside Section 31

Lord Diplock in *O'Reilly* mentioned two types of exception. First, Ord.15 r.16 could be used where none of the parties objected. Second, a person could proceed outside of s.31 where the claim arose as a collateral issue in an action for infringement of a right of the plaintiff arising under private law. Attention has not surprisingly been focused upon the second of these exceptions. It is important to understand why applicants have sought to proceed outside s.31.

26–006

The *principal reason* is that if they were forced to bring their cases within s.31 they would be outside the short time limit and hence their claims would fail. This problem can be particularly acute when the person seeking to raise the public law issue is the defendant in the action, and is, therefore, not in control of the time within which it has been brought.

A *secondary reason* for seeking to bring the claim outside s.31 is that the applicant may wish to investigate factual issues relating to the case, and to undertake cross-examination. While this can occur within s.31 proceedings it is not normal. This point requires a brief explanation.

Prior to 1977 grant of leave to cross-examine under the prerogative orders was very rare. This was one of the main reasons why people preferred to use the declaration or the injunction, since unless one could cross-examine it might be impossible to prove the alleged error. The new procedure made provision for discovery and cross-examination. Notwithstanding these provisions there were early indications that the ability to cross-examine should be used sparingly, and that the ordinary trial procedure was preferable for complex factual questions.[24] Later judicial[25] and extra-judicial[26] statements appeared to confirm the reluctance to allow discovery and cross-examination within s.31, because of the delays and extra costs generated by such concessions to the individual.

This was somewhat paradoxical. A principal reason for making the new procedure exclusive was that the reforms removed defects in the previous law, including the inability to cross-examine and seek discovery. This was the justification for confining the individual to s.31, with its protections for the public body. If however the individual applicant is rarely allowed to use these procedural aids, the applicant may be unable to prove the invalidity alleged. The courts have sometimes allowed a case to proceed outside s.31 because of the complex nature of the factual issues which are involved. It will also be seen that the courts have, more recently, indicated that disclosure should be somewhat more readily available in judicial review cases than hitherto.[27]

It will become apparent from reading the materials within this section that the interpretation accorded to the private rights exception has altered over the years since *O'Reilly*. It is for this reason that the analysis will consider the approach to this exception in the period immediately after *O'Reilly*, and then focus upon the interpretation given to it in the more recent case law.

B. Collateral Attack and Private Rights: The Initial Approach

26–007 The difficulty of applying this exception can be exemplified by contrasting three of the leading cases decided in the years shortly after *O'Reilly*.

In *Cocks*,[28] the plaintiff claimed a declaration and damages alleging a breach by the defendant council of its duties under the Housing (Homeless Persons) Act 1977. The House of Lords insisted that the action should be brought via judicial review under the Supreme Court Act, s.31 for the following reason. The existence of a duty to inquire whether the applicant might be made homeless, and the question whether the applicant might be entitled to temporary or permanent housing, were public law questions. The

---

[24] *R. v Inland Revenue Commissioners Ex p. Rossminster Ltd* [1980] A.C. 952, 1027.
[25] See *O'Reilly* [1983] 2 A.C. 237 itself, where Lord Diplock, having stated that cross-examination will be allowed whenever the justice of the case so requires, then stated that it will normally only be so required when there is a case of natural justice; *R. v Secretary of State for the Home Department Ex p. Khawaja* [1984] A.C. 74, cross-examination should be used sparingly; *Air Canada v Secretary of State for Trade (No. 2)* [1983] 2 A.C. 394, discovery only in exceptional cases; *Lonrho Plc v Tebbit* [1992] 4 All E.R. 280, one reason for allowing the case to proceed outside s.31 was the complex nature of the factual issues involved. Other cases indicating the limited availability of discovery include, *R. v Inland Revenue Commissioners Ex p. Taylor* [1989] 1 All E.R. 906; *R. v Secretary of State for the Environment Ex p. Doncaster Borough Council* [1990] C.O.D. 441; *R. v Secretary of State for the Home Department Ex p. BH* [1990] C.O.D. 445; *R. v Secretary of State for Education Ex p. J* [1993] C.O.D. 146; *R. v Secretary of State for Transport Ex p. APH Road Safety Ltd* [1993] C.O.D. 150; *R. v Secretary of State for Health Ex p. London Borough of Hackney* [1994] C.O.D. 432; *R. v Arts Council of England Ex p. Women's Playhouse Trust* [1998] C.O.D. 175.
[26] Woolf [1986] P.L. 220, 229, 231.
[27] *Tweed v Parades Commission for Northern Ireland* [2007] 1 A.C. 650.
[28] *Cocks v Thanet District Council* [1983] 2 A.C. 286.

determination of these issues in the applicant's favour was a condition precedent to the establishment of a private law right. Such issues must therefore be brought within s.31, because at that stage the applicant did not yet have private law rights allowing him to proceed outside s.31 by way of an ordinary action.[29]

The decision in *Cocks* can be contrasted with *Davy*.[30] The plaintiff was the owner of premises making pre-cast concrete. He made an agreement with the council in 1979 that he would not oppose an enforcement notice terminating his right to use the premises, provided that the council did not enforce this notice for three years. In 1982 the plaintiff brought a damages action claiming that he had been negligently advised of his rights under the planning legislation, and that the 1979 agreement was ultra vires and void. The council argued, inter alia, that the action should be brought under s.31, since any defence that Davy had to the enforcement notice was a right to which he was entitled to protection under public law. The House of Lords rejected this argument. Lord Fraser[31] regarded the negligence claim as "simply" an ordinary tort action, which did not raise any matter of public law as a "live issue".[32] The *Cocks* case was distinguished.[33] In that case the plaintiff had to impugn the defendant's decision that he was intentionally homeless, the "public law" issue, as a condition precedent to the establishment of a private law right. In *Davy* the plaintiff's private right did not depend upon the enforcement notice. The plaintiff was not challenging the enforcement order, but rather claiming damages because he had lost his chance to impugn it. The council would not, therefore, be kept "in suspense" as to the validity of their enforcement notice.[34]

Winder[35] exemplified a further dimension to the private rights exception. The plaintiff local authority had raised the rent of Winder's flat. Winder refused to pay the increase, paying only such an amount as he considered reasonable. The local authority sued for arrears of rent and possession of the flat. Winder argued in defence that the council had acted ultra vires by charging excessive rents. The authority contended that the legality of the rent could only be tested via judicial review under s.31. The House of Lords found for Winder. *O'Reilly* and *Cocks* were distinguished for two reasons. First, the plaintiffs therein did not have private rights, whereas Winder complained of the infringement of a contractual right in private law. Second, the individual had initiated the action in the earlier cases, whereas Winder was the defendant who did not select the procedure to be adopted.

---

[29] It has now been held that there is no private law cause of action for damages arising from the Housing Act 1985 s.63, *O'Rourke v Camden LBC* [1998] A.C. 188.
[30] *Davy v Spelthorne Borough Council* [1984] A.C. 262.
[31] Lord Roskill, Lord Brandon and Lord Brightman agreed with Lord Fraser.
[32] [1984] A.C. 262, 273.
[33] [1984] A.C. 262, 273–274.
[34] [1984] A.C. 262, 274 F.
[35] *Wandsworth London Borough Council v Winder* [1985] A.C. 461.

C. Collateral Attack and Private Rights: Broadening the Exception

26–008   The cases decided in the immediate aftermath of *O'Reilly* revealed the difficulty of deciding whether a particular interest should be characterised as a private right. The precise effect of this characterisation was also unclear. Did the presence of a private right mean that the principle in *O'Reilly* should be deemed no longer applicable at all? Or was the existence of such a right merely an important factor, which could lead the court to make a discretionary exception to the *O'Reilly* principle?

This ambiguity was brought to the fore in the important House of Lords' decision in *Roy*.[36] The applicant was a doctor who was paid certain sums under National Health Service (NHS) regulations for treating patients. The relevant regulations provided, however, that the doctor would only be paid the full basic rate if he devoted a substantial part of his time to treating patients on the NHS, as opposed to private practice. The Kensington Committee decided that the applicant was not complying with this condition and therefore reduced his allowance by 20 per cent. The applicant claimed that this was a breach of contract by the Committee. The Committee argued that the action should have been brought under s.31 by way of judicial review. The application would then have failed since it would have been outside the time limit.[37] The House of Lords found for the applicant, with judgments given by Lord Bridge and Lord Lowry.

Lord Bridge[38] acknowledged that *O'Reilly* had been subject to much academic criticism, but was not persuaded that it should be overruled. He did, however, believe that the principle in that case should be kept within proper bounds. *If* the case turned exclusively on a purely public law right, then the only remedy was by way of judicial review under s.31, with its attendant constraints of leave and strict time limits. *If*, by way of contrast, the case involved the assertion of a private law right, whether by way of defence or by way of claim, the fact that the existence of the private law right might incidentally involve the examination of a public law issue did not prevent the applicant proceeding by way of an ordinary action outside s.31. The present case came within the latter category. It did not matter whether one regarded the applicant as asserting private law rights based on contract, or as asserting private law rights derived from the relevant statute. The result was the same: the applicant could proceed outside s.31 by way of ordinary action.

26–009   Lord Lowry gave the other judgment and proffered two possible interpretations of the exception in *O'Reilly v Mackman*.[39]

"The 'broad approach' was that the 'rule in *O'Reilly v Mackman*' did not apply generally against bringing actions to vindicate private rights in all

---

[36] *Roy v Kensington and Chelsea and Westminster Family Practitioner Committee* [1992] 1 A.C. 624.
[37] The Committee's original decision was in October 1984, and was only challenged in July 1986.
[38] [1992] 1 A.C. 624, 628–630.
[39] [1992] 1 A.C. 624, 653.

circumstances in which those actions involved a challenge to a public law act or decision, but that it merely required the aggrieved person to proceed by judicial review only when private rights were not at stake. The 'narrow approach' assumed that the rule applied generally to *all* proceedings in which public law acts or decisions were challenged, subject to some exceptions when private law rights were involved. There was no need in *O'Reilly v Mackman* to choose between these approaches, but it seems clear that Lord Diplock considered himself to be stating a general rule with exceptions. For my part, I much prefer the broad approach, which is both traditionally orthodox and consistent with the *Pyx Granite* principle. . . . It would also, if adopted, have the practical merit of getting rid of a procedural minefield. I shall, however, be content for the purpose of this appeal to adopt the narrow approach, which avoids the need to discuss the proper scope of the rule, a point which has not been argued before your Lordships and has hitherto been seriously discussed only by the academic writers."

In deciding in favour of the applicant, Lord Lowry took account of the following factors. First, the applicant had a bundle of rights derived from statute, even if they were not actually regarded as contract rights. When individual rights were claimed there should be no need for leave or a special time limit and the relief should not be discretionary. Secondly, although the applicant sought to enforce performance of a public duty under the relevant National Health Service regulations, his private rights dominated the action. Thirdly, this was a case in which the facts were in dispute, and this was better done in an ordinary action. Fourthly, Roy was seeking the payment of a specific sum by way of a remedy, as opposed to damages. An ordinary action was therefore better, since orders for specific sums could not, at that time, be made in judicial review actions. Finally, procedural barriers to claims were not desirable and should be interpreted liberally.

It is clear that Lord Lowry preferred the broad view of the exception, the effect of which is to render the rule in *O'Reilly* inapplicable when cases involve private rights: applicants can proceed unencumbered outside s.31. This view has been generally adopted in later cases.[40]

In *Boddington*,[41] the House of Lords held that it was open to a defendant **26–010** in criminal proceedings to challenge a byelaw, or an administrative decision made thereunder, where the prosecution was premised on its validity, unless there was a clear parliamentary intent to the contrary. The challenge to the measure did not have to be brought by way of judicial review. The inability to plead the invalidity of a byelaw in the course of a criminal prosecution was, said Lord Steyn, contrary to principle and precedent.[42]

His Lordship felt that it was wrong in principle for a magistrate to be able

---

[40] *Lonrho Plc v Tebbit* [1991] 4 All E.R. 973, [1992] 4 All E.R. 280; *Trustees of the Dennis Rye Pension Fund v Sheffield City Council* [1998] 1 W.L.R. 840; *British Steel Plc v Customs and Excise Commissioners* [1997] 2 All E.R. 366; *Bunney v Burns Anderson Plc* [2007] EWHC 1240.
[41] *Boddington v British Transport Police* [1999] 2 A.C. 143.
[42] *Boddington*, n.41, 172.

to convict a person who would be precluded from relying on a defence he might have. That was unacceptable in a democracy based on the rule of law. This general argument of principle was reinforced by the case law on procedural exclusivity. Lord Steyn held that later case law[43] had made it clear that procedural exclusivity would only be insisted upon where the sole object of the action was to challenge a public law act or decision. It did not apply in a civil case when an individual sought to establish private law rights, which could not be determined without an examination of the validity of the public law decision. Nor did it apply where a defendant in a civil case sought to defend himself by questioning the validity of the public law decision. Nor equally did it apply in a criminal case where the liberty of the subject was at stake.[44]

Judicial review was felt by Lord Steyn to be an inadequate safeguard for the individual. The defendant might be out of time before becoming aware of the very existence of the byelaw. He might not have the resources for such a challenge. Leave might be refused, or a remedy denied pursuant to the court's discretionary power over such matters. The possibility of judicial review could not therefore be said to compensate the individual "for the loss of *the right to* defend himself"[45] in the criminal proceedings.

It was accepted in *Boddington*[46] that there could be cases where a challenge to the validity of an order other than by way of judicial review could be defeated by special statutory provisions, as exemplified by *Wicks*.[47] In *Wicks* the House of Lords adopted a functional approach. Whether a defendant who was charged with failing to comply with an order made under statutory powers was entitled by way of defence in criminal proceedings before the court to challenge the lawfulness of the order depended on the construction of the statute under which the prosecution had been brought, and also upon whether the relevant statute indicated which forum was appropriate for a challenge to the validity of the order.[48] The premise behind *Boddington* is nonetheless that a defendant should normally be able to raise the invalidity of the byelaw, or an administrative decision based on it, by way of defence in a criminal case. It will be for the prosecution to convince the court that the exception based on the reasoning in *Wicks* is applicable in the instant case.

---

[43] Lord Steyn referred to *Roy* [1992] 1 A.C. 624, *Winder* [1985] A.C. 461, *Chief Adjudication Officer v Foster* [1993] A.C. 754 and *Mercury Communications Ltd v Director General of Telecommunications* [1996] 1 W.L.R. 48.

[44] n.41, 172.

[45] *Boddington*, n.41, 173. Italics in the original.

[46] *Boddington*, n.41, 173.

[47] *R. v Wicks* [1998] A.C. 92.

[48] There could, on the one hand, be cases where the statute required the prosecution to prove that the contested act was not open to challenge on any ground available in public law, or where it might be a defence to show that it was open to challenge in that way. In such cases it would be for the court before which the prosecution was brought to rule on the validity of the act. There could, on the other hand, be cases where the statute on its true construction merely required that the act which had been done under statutory authority appeared to be formally valid and had not been quashed by judicial review. In this latter type of case, only the formal validity of the act was of relevance to an issue before the court in a prosecution

D. Collateral Attack: Beyond Private Rights

It may well be that the exceptions to *O'Reilly* go beyond those established   **26–011**
by the case law considered in the previous section.[49] This seems to be so from
a reading of the House of Lords decision in *Mercury*.[50] In 1986 two companies, Mercury (M) and British Telecommunications (BT), made an
agreement for the provision of services pursuant to condition 13 of BT's
licence. The agreement provided for a reference to the Director General of
Telecommunications (DGT) where there was a dispute between M and BT.
The parties referred a matter to the DGT concerning pricing for the conveyance of calls. The DGT made his determination and M challenged this,
arguing that the DGT had misinterpreted the costs to be taken into account
when resolving the pricing issue. M's challenge was by way of originating
summons for a declaration. The DGT and BT argued that the case should
have been brought by way of Ord.53. Lord Slynn gave the judgment for a
unanimous House of Lords in favour of M.

His Lordship acknowledged the rationale for the presumptive exclusivity
of this procedure given in *O'Reilly*, but noted also that this exclusivity was
only ever presumptive rather than conclusive in nature. The criterion that
should be used to decide whether a case could be brought outside Ord.53
was whether "the proceedings constitute an abuse of the process of the
court".[51]

The abuse of process test does not on its face require the existence of any
private right as a condition precedent for an applicant to be able to proceed
outside Ord.53. That this is so is further confirmed by the way in which this
test was applied in *Mercury* itself. In allowing M to bring its case by way of
originating summons Lord Slynn did not mention the rights-based criterion
derived from *Roy*. Nor did he frame his judgment that M should be allowed
to bring its case by way of originating summons on the ground that its
private rights were at stake. It would have been difficult to find private rights
that M had as against the DGT. Lord Slynn held that there was no abuse of
process, in part because the essence of the action was a contractual dispute
between M and BT, and in part because the relevant issues could be better
determined by the Commercial Court, rather than via Ord.53.[52]

It would seem that if an applicant has private rights then the case will be
allowed to proceed outside Ord.53, even if it does involve a public law
matter, and this will be deemed *ipso facto* not to be an abuse of process.
However, even where there are no such rights it will be open to an applicant
to convince the court that recourse to an ordinary action does not constitute
an abuse of process.

---

[49] P. Craig, "Proceeding Outside Order 53: A Modified Test?" (1996) 112 L.Q.R. 531.
[50] *Mercury*, n.43.
[51] *Mercury*, n.43, 57.
[52] It might be argued that there was no public law issue at stake in *Mercury* and there are some
passages in Lord Slynn's judgment which could be read in this manner. When the case is read as
a whole it cannot, however, be thus interpreted. If Lord Slynn had intended to decide the case
on this ground there would have been no need to advert to the more general principles concerning the exclusivity of the Ord.53 procedure at all. Those principles only bite if there is a
public law issue involved in the case.

The impact of this reasoning on the holding in *O'Reilly* is significant. In *O'Reilly* the assumption was that it would be an abuse of process for an applicant to proceed outside Ord.53, precisely because this would deprive the public body of the protections enshrined in the Ord.53 procedure. This starting assumption was qualified, but not undermined, by the exceptions concerning consent and private rights. In *Mercury* the same concept, abuse of process, has a very different meaning. Here the assumption is that an applicant should be allowed to bring a case outside Ord.53, unless this constitutes an abuse of process. The fact that the public body will be deprived of the protections contained in Ord.53 does not, however, appear to constitute, in itself, such an abuse. Provided that the applicant can convince the court that there are good reasons for allowing the claim to be brought by way of ordinary action, no such abuse will be found.

E. The Impact of the Human Rights Act 1998

26–012 The Human Rights Act 1998 (HRA) has been considered in detail above.[53] The present discussion is concerned with its impact on the types of case that may be brought outside s.31 by way of ordinary action.

It is clear from s.7 HRA that a person who claims that a public authority has acted unlawfully in breach of s.6(1) may bring proceedings against the authority in the appropriate court or tribunal as determined in accordance with rules to be made on the matter. An application for judicial review is one way in which such proceedings may be brought, as is apparent from s.7(3).

Claimants may, however, have an incentive to proceed other than by way of judicial review where there is a danger that they will otherwise be out of time. Section 7(5) specifies a basic time limit of one year for violations of s.6 in cases where the illegality is used offensively by the individual, but qualifies this by providing that it is subject to any rule imposing a stricter time limit in relation to the procedure actually used. This means that if an application for judicial review is brought for a breach of s.6 HRA, then the time limit for judicial review actions will operate.

This limit will be considered in detail below,[54] but suffice it to say for the present that the basic rule is three months. We have already seen that a major reason why claimants sought to proceed outside s.31 is that they would otherwise be time barred, and this is likely to continue to be a significant consideration in cases brought under the HRA. There may also be other reasons for not proceeding by way of judicial review, such as the limits on discovery and cross-examination.

The fact that s.6 actions may be brought other than by way of judicial review is, in formal legal terms, unproblematic. Section 7 expressly contemplates that actions can be brought other than by way of judicial review. Furthermore, the general jurisprudence considered above, concerning the circumstances in which cases can proceed outside s.31 of the Supreme Court

---

[53] See above, Ch.18.
[54] See below, paras 26–045—26–046.

Act, has made it clear that this is possible where private rights are at stake. If claims that Convention rights have been violated in breach of s.6 are treated in this way then proceedings for breach of the HRA will simply be another exception to procedural exclusivity. The scope of this new qualification to procedural exclusivity may, however, be greater than might initially be thought.

There will be many public law cases where the claim will be cast as a breach of the HRA. Such claims will not however exist in isolation. They may arise as one of a number of allegations of ultra vires conduct. A colourable allegation that there has been a breach of s.6 may serve to take a case outside s.31 of the Supreme Court Act, even if it ultimately proves to be unfounded. The other allegations may well normally have been brought within the judicial review procedure, because they were pure public law claims. Where the HRA claim fails it is, however, unlikely that the court will insist that the case revert to the judicial procedure, more particularly if the applicant would be out of time. It is more likely that the judge will hear argument on the other allegations of ultra vires conduct. We may well therefore see more pure public law claims being litigated by way of ordinary action, where the initial rationale for proceeding in this manner was an allegation of a breach of s.6 that proved unfounded.

F. The Impact of the CPR

It is now clear that the Civil Procedure Rules (CPR), introduced as a result **26–013** of the Woolf reforms, will have a marked impact on the relationship between the public law procedures, and the ordinary procedures for civil action. This is because a central theme of the CPR is to accord the court more control over ordinary civil actions than previously existed.

The implications for procedural exclusivity and the exceptions thereto are apparent from the *Clark* case.[55] The claimant brought a contract action against a University in relation to the classification of her degree. The University argued that the claim should have been brought by judicial review. It contended that the ordinary contract action was an abuse of process, by allowing suit well beyond the three-month time limit for judicial review. Lord Woolf M.R. held that the whole issue of exclusivity should now be seen in the light of the new CPR. This was because the CPR contained safeguards for public bodies *even where* there was an ordinary civil action. The safeguards related to the stopping of the action, and the time in which it could be brought.

If proceedings involving public law issues were begun by ordinary action under CPR Pts 7 or 8, they would be subject to CPR Pt 24. This enabled the court to give summary judgment where it believed that the applicant had no real prospect of success. This restricted the inconvenience to public bodies by the pursuit of hopeless claims.[56]

---

[55] *Clark v University of Lincolnshire and Humberside* [2000] 1 W.L.R. 1988.
[56] *Clark*, n.55, paras 27–28.

The normal time limit for a civil action is six years. Lord Woolf acknowledged that it would in the past not have been appropriate to regard delay within the six-year period as a reason for characterising the action as abusive. The position was, said Lord Woolf, different under the CPR. Delay in commencing proceedings under the CPR could be a factor in deciding whether the proceedings were abusive. This was especially so where the action could have been brought by judicial review.[57]

G. Summary

26–014 It might be helpful to summarise the law and to state when an individual will be allowed to proceed by an ordinary action outside s.31.

(1) The courts will only insist on a case being brought via the judicial review procedure if the sole aim is to challenge a public law act or decision.

(2) A civil case can be brought outside s.31 where the individual seeks to establish private rights, even if this requires an examination of the validity of the public law decision.

(3) A defendant in a civil case can challenge a public law decision in the course of defending the private law action. It is not absolutely certain whether it is enough to be the defendant or whether the defendant must also be able to assert that his rights are being infringed. Some cases have emphasised the first of these factors, without inquiring too closely whether the individual had private rights which were affected, or what the precise nature of these rights were.[58] Other cases suggested that an individual should have some private right in order to be able to raise the invalidity of a public body's action by way of defence in an ordinary action outside s.31.[59] However, the formulation by Lord Steyn in *Boddington* indicated that being a defendant was sufficient in itself.[60]

(4) A defendant in a criminal case will normally be able to raise the invalidity of the subordinate legislation or order on which the prosecution is based by way of defence to the criminal charge, unless there is a clear indication from the relevant statute that such a challenge can only be made via judicial review.

(5) A person may be able to proceed outside s.31 even where no private rights are present, provided that the court decides that to do so is not an abuse of process.

[57] *Clark*, n.55, paras 35–36.
[58] *West Glamorgan County Council v Rafferty* [1987] 1 W.L.R. 457; *R. v Crown Court at Reading Ex p. Hutchinson* [1987] 3 W.L.R. 1062.
[59] *Waverley Borough Council v Hilden* [1988] 1 W.L.R. 246; *Avon County Council v Buscott* [1988] 2 W.L.R. 788.
[60] [1999] 2 A.C. 143, 172–173.

(6) In cases of doubt the advice of Lord Woolf[61] was that the action should be brought by way of judicial review. If the matter was raised in an ordinary action and there was an application to strike out the case on the ground that it should have been brought by way of judicial review, it was open to the court to consider whether leave would have been granted under the s.31 procedure. If the answer was in the affirmative then this was a good indication that the ordinary action should not be struck out.

(7) The degree of difference between bringing an ordinary civil action and a claim for judicial review has however diminished under the CPR, as interpreted in *Clark*.[62] The court read the CPR to provide some protection for public bodies even in ordinary civil actions, thereby diminishing to some extent the incentive to proceed outside the judicial review procedure.

H. Assessment

It is clear that the approach in *Roy, Boddington, Mercury* and other cases has limited the force of *O'Reilly* itself.[63] The principle of presumptive exclusivity in *O'Reilly* was based on the assumption that public bodies warranted the protections of narrow time limits and leave, or permission as it is now known, *and* that these protections should not be circumvented by allowing applicants to proceed through a different action. The reasoning in later cases indirectly undermined this assumption in two ways, one practical, the other conceptual.

    26–015

It undermined that principle in *practical* terms simply because there were fewer cases to which the protections afforded to the public body would apply. Those protections would not apply in cases concerning private rights, or in the other instances set out above. The term "private right" is, moreover, a malleable one. This is exemplified by the *Roy* case, in which the House of Lords gave a broad construction to "private rights", without too nice an inquiry as to the nature of the rights possessed by the applicant. If statutory payments to individuals, which payments are subject to a plethora of evaluative criteria, are to be treated as private law rights, then the number of instances in which litigants can bring actions outside of s.31 will be broad indeed. The very determination of whether a right should be characterised as a private, as opposed to a public right, *and* whether it can be viewed as

---

[61] *Dennis Rye Pension Fund*, n.40.
[62] n.55.
[63] See also, J. Alder, "Hunting the Chimera—The End of *O'Reilly v Mackman*" [1993] 13 L.S. 183.

distinctive from a "public law" issue which the case raises, is not resolvable by some easy mechanical formula.[64]

The *conceptual* foundation of *O'Reilly* was also weakened by these later decisions. The premise behind the post-*O'Reilly* jurisprudence was that protections for the public body, in terms of time limits and leave, were overridden when an individual asserted private rights against a public body, *and* that this was so even if the case involved public law issues. It is clear that even where a case concerns private rights it would be mistaken to believe that it is principally "about" private rights as opposed to public law. This can be easily demonstrated. A public body makes a demolition order on the plaintiff's property, which is said to be ultra vires.[65] The plaintiff brings an action in trespass. The action involves a private right, but it is clear that the action is not solely "about" private rights. *Whether* the plaintiff wins or not in the trespass action will be dependent upon the validity of the demolition order. This will be *the* issue in the case, and this is manifestly a public law matter, the resolution of which will be dependent upon the construction of the relevant legislation. The *consequence* of this finding will determine whether the plaintiff can succeed in the tort claim, and in that sense vindicate her private rights, but this does not mean that the case is principally about private rights.[66]

The reality is that the courts were, and still are, ambivalent about the principle in *O'Reilly*. They wished to preserve the protections afforded by s.31, in terms of short time limits and leave or permission. This explained the approach in *Roy*, where the House of Lords refused to question *O'Reilly* directly, notwithstanding the significant criticism to which it had been subjected. There was, by way of contrast, a recurring theme in the case law, that the hurdles created by *O'Reilly* were merely technical and legalistic, using those terms in a pejorative sense. Judges referred to the complexity of the law in this area and compared it to the forms of action in the 19th century,[67] or to the difficulties in civil law systems based on the public/private divide.[68] The corollary was that it really did *not* matter too much whether individuals were allowed to proceed outside s.31.

The *Clark* decision[69] is however of real importance in this respect. The premise underlying the case was that the differences between an ordinary

---

[64] See, e.g., (a) the criticism of the *Winder* case by the Rt. Hon Sir H Woolf, "Public Law—Private Law: Why the Divide? A Personal View" [1986] P.L. 220, 233–236. *cf.* J. Beatson, " 'Public' and 'Private' in English Administrative Law" (1987) 103 L.Q.R. 34, 59–61; (b) the reasoning in *Gillick v West Norfolk and Wisbech Area Health Authority* [1986] A.C. 112, 163, 177–178.

[65] *Cooper v Wandsworth Board of Works* (1863) 14 C.B. (N.S.) 180.

[66] This point applies equally to *Roy*, n.36. The case involved private rights, arising from Roy's relationship with the Family Practitioner Committee and the fact that he was seeking a contract-type remedy. However, the case also raised general public law matters. The committee had statutory powers to allocate fees derived from public funds. *Whether* Roy won on the substance of the case turned on the construction of the relevant statutory norms, in order to determine what it meant to say that a doctor must devote a substantial amount of his time to NHS work.

[67] *Doyle v Northumbria Probation Committee* [1991] 4 All E.R. 294, 300.

[68] *Mercury* [1996] 1 W.L.R. 48.

[69] n.55.

action and one for judicial review should be minimised. It recognised that an action involving private rights may well involve public law issues. The CPR on ordinary civil actions were interpreted so as to allow protection for public bodies, in terms of the ability to stop hopeless actions, and modify the time in which they must be brought. *Clark* therefore accepted that cases involving private rights could proceed by ordinary action, as opposed to judicial review, but sought to diminish the incentives for doing so. It should nonetheless be recognised that these incentives, although diminished, still exist. In a judicial review action the claimant must still seek permission to proceed, and the time limit is three months. In an ordinary action, even as interpreted by *Clark*, it will be for the defendant to establish that the case should be stopped because it has no prospect of success. It will also be for the defendant to convince the court that bringing the action within, for example, 18 months, constituted an abuse of process, even though it was well within the limitation period.

We shall consider in more detail below whether there are sound reasons for preserving separate procedures for judicial review and ordinary actions in the light of the CPR.

3. PUBLIC LAW CASES: "GETTING INTO" THE JUDICIAL REVIEW PROCEDURE

A. The Reasons for wishing to use the Section 31 Procedure

The preceding discussion has concentrated upon cases where individuals **26–016** wish to proceed outside s.31. The traffic has not, however, been purely "one way". There have been many cases where individuals have sought to argue their way into s.31, what one judge[70] has termed the "obverse" of the situation in *O'Reilly*. There are three principal reasons why litigants have been anxious to avail themselves of the application for judicial review.

The first and most obvious reason for wishing to use s.31 is that the applicant may have *no other cause of action*. In the *Datafin* case, the applicants could not frame a convincing cause of action in contract or tort against the Take-Overs Panel, and this predisposed the court in their favour.[71] Some employment cases are also explicable on this ground. Thus in *Benwell* a prison officer was dismissable at pleasure. He could not use the employment protection legislation, and this inclined the court to admit him into s.31.[72]

A second reason prompting applicants to use the public law procedures is

---

[70] *R. v East Berkshire Health Authority Ex p. Walsh* [1985] Q.B. 152.
[71] *R. v Panel on Take-Overs and Mergers Ex p. Datafin plc* [1987] Q.B. 815.
[72] *R. v Secretary of State for the Home Department Ex p. Benwell* [1985] QB 554, 571, 572; *R. v Bishop of Stafford Ex p. Owen* [2001] A.C.D. 14.

because they believe that the *remedy will be more effective*. This explains some of the other employment cases considered below.[73] The reasons why the public law remedy appears to be more attractive can only be touched upon here. An employee will be entitled to certain procedural hearing rights as part of the general law on unfair dismissal. Breach of these rights will give the employee a damages action, compensation for unfair dismissal and a possible order for reinstatement. The public law remedy may nonetheless be preferred because the applicant perceives that it will afford more chance of getting the job back. Certiorari will quash the dismissal, and leave the applicant in "possession" of the job. This result reflects the historical status of employment in a public office: the office was regarded as akin to a property right which the applicant was entitled to have restored if he or she was improperly deprived of it. The question of whether employees should have job security rights is a complex one, and the rationale for differential treatment between public and private employment may well be historically outdated. It is clear that the courts are wary of expanding indirect job security rights by allowing potentially large categories of employees into s.31. Cases are likely therefore to turn upon the court's perception of whether a type of individual should have such security. The statutory material will then be interpreted so as to be consonant with this conclusion.

The third reason why applicants are keen to use the application for judicial review is because the *scope of the obligations* imposed upon the defendant body exceeds those that would be imposed in a private law cause of action. Thus in the *Aga Khan* case[74] the principal reason why the applicant sought to use the public law procedures was not because there was no remedy in private law. It was because he sought to test the legality of the Club's actions against the range of substantive and procedural norms used to test the validity of a public body's behaviour.

B. Public Law: Possible Tests

26–017		The meaning of public law for the purposes of s.31 is obviously crucial in a double sense. Only public law cases are subject to the presumptive exclusivity of the *O'Reilly* decision, and have therefore to be brought within s.31, and only cases that are about public law are allowed into s.31. Unfortunately no simple test exists to determine the meaning of public law for these purposes. Three possibilities can be briefly considered.[75]

---

[73] See, e.g., *Walsh*, n.70.
[74] *R. v Disciplinary Committee of the Jockey Club Ex p. Aga Khan* [1993] 1 W.L.R. 909.
[75] See generally, Beatson, n.64; P. Cane, "Public Law and Private Law: A Study of the Analysis of and Use of a Legal Concept", in J. Eekelaar and J. Bell (eds), *Oxford Essays in Jurisprudence, 3rd Series* (Oxford University Press, 1987), Ch.3; J. Allison, *A Continental Distinction in the Common Law: A Historical and Comparative Perspective on English Public Law* (Oxford University Press, 1996); N. Bamforth, "The Public Law-Private Law Distinction: A Comparative and Philosophical Approach", in P. Leyland and T. Woods (eds), *Administrative Law Facing the Future: Old Constraints and New Horizons* (Blackstone, 1997), Ch.6.

i. The source of the power

The most obvious test is to consider the source of the authority's power: if **26–018** that power is derived from statute then the body is presumptively public. There are two difficulties with this test. First, applied literally it would bring within public law the activities of any body regulated by statute, even if the body generally operated within the private commercial sphere. The second problem is a converse of the first. A body may owe the source of its authority to statute, but not all of its operations should nonetheless be regarded as raising public law issues. Local authorities and other public bodies frequently operate in an ordinary commercial capacity.[76]

ii. The scope of the prerogative remedies

If we are to have a separate set of remedies for public law, then to regard the **26–019** scope of the prerogative orders as prima facie evidence of the scope of public law might be reasonable, particularly given the centrality accorded to such orders within s.31.

The problem with this criterion is that there has been a tendency to see the ambit of such orders as fixed. There is little justification for this. Historically the orders were used flexibly to provide a remedy against institutions not covered by existing forms of redress.[77] There are indications that they could be used to cover any duty of a public nature, whether it was derived from statute, custom, prerogative or contract, a view echoed by Lord Diplock.[78] The tendency to ossify them, to regard their boundaries as immutable, is a more recent phenomenon. There is no reason why a duty may not be of a public law nature, whatever its derivation.

To focus upon the scope of the prerogative orders as the criterion for the meaning of public law does, however, lead to the following conundrum. If their scope is interpreted flexibly in the above manner they cease to furnish a criterion that is distinguishable from the third test to be considered below. The nature of a "public" as opposed to a "private" duty still has to be determined, and if the ambit of the prerogative orders simply covers any "public law" obligation we are no further forward in deciding whether such an obligation exists in any particular case.[79] If, however, a narrow definition of the prerogative orders is adopted, so that they apply only to bodies created by statute, or pursuant to the prerogative, then we have a formalistic criterion. This renders the applicability of different procedures turn upon the fortuitous incident of whether an authority's powers were derived from a particular source, irrespective of the real power wielded by such a body.[80]

---

[76] Lloyd L.J. in *Datafin* [1987] Q.B. 815, 847 implied that if the source of the power was statutory then the body would be subject to judicial review. For the reasons given in the text I doubt, with respect, whether the source test can be taken so generally.

[77] See above, Ch.25; *Groenvelt v Burwell* (1700) 1 Ld. Raym. 454 is particularly instructive.

[78] *O'Reilly* [1983] 2 A.C. 237, 279.

[79] See the observations of Lord Donaldson M.R. in *Walsh* [1985] Q.B. 152, 162.

[80] See also, H.W.R. Wade, "Procedure and Prerogative in Public Law" (1985) 101 L.Q.R. 180.

iii. The "nature" of the power

26–020 The difficulties of a formalistic test have inclined the courts towards a more open-textured criterion, which requires them to consider the nature of the power wielded by the particular body. The formulation of this test has varied. For example Lloyd L.J. in *Datafin*[81] stated that if the source of the power was statutory then the body would be subject to judicial review, but would not if the source of power were contractual, but that between these "extremes" one had to look at the nature of the power. Thus if the body was exercising public law functions, or such functions had public law consequences, then s.31 would be applicable. This formulation appears to beg the question,[82] as do statements that a public duty will be subject to public law. Lord Donaldson M.R., by way of contrast, seemed only to be concerned with the source of a body's power in order to exclude those institutions whose power was based upon contract or consent.[83] Any other body could be subject to review if there was a sufficiently public element. How far power that is based upon contract or consent is subject to judicial review will be considered more fully below.

The uncertainty of this third test is to be expected. It is the price to be paid for moving away from formalistic tests based upon the source of power, or upon the narrow definition of the prerogative given above. Statements that a body must have a sufficiently "public element", or must be exercising a public duty, cannot function as anything other than conclusory labels. They cannot guide our reasoning in advance. In *Datafin* the court was influenced by a number of such factors including: the undoubted power wielded by the Panel, the statutory cognisance given to its existence, the penalties, direct and indirect, which could follow from non-compliance with its rules, and the absence of any other redress available to the applicants.

It is now time to consider more closely the types of institution that have been deemed to be susceptible to judicial review.

C. The Boundaries of Public Law

26–021 It is clear that traditional public bodies will be able to use the application for judicial review, and that they can be subject to such actions. We are concerned here with other cases in which applicants have sought to bring claims within s.31.

i. Public bodies and Executive Agencies

26–022 The applicability of public law principles to Executive Agencies has been considered above.[84] In principle it is clear that such agencies must be subject to the s.31 procedure, given that they are not formally separate from their

---

[81] [1987] Q.B. 815, 846–869.
[82] As admitted by Lloyd LJ, [1987] Q.B. 815, 847, who nonetheless denied the circularity.
[83] [1987] Q.B. 815, 838–839.
[84] See above, Ch.4.

sponsoring department, and given also that most of these agencies are engaged in public service delivery.

ii. Public authorities and contracting-out

We have seen that contracting-out has been used increasingly by govern-   **26–023**
ment as a method of service delivery.[85] It is clear that a judicial review action may still be maintained against the public body that has contracted-out the power. This may however be of limited utility, since there may be no viable claim against the public body in such instances. Whether the private body to whom power has been contracted-out can be subject to judicial review is therefore important.

This can be exemplified by *Servite Houses*.[86] The applicants were elderly residents at a home run by Servite Houses, a charitable housing association. Wandsworth Council had, pursuant to their statutory duties, assessed them as being in need of residential accommodation.[87] The Council was allowed to contract-out the provision of such accommodation.[88] Servite decided to close the home in which the applicants lived. They objected claiming that they had been promised a home for life.[89] The court therefore had to decide whether the private service provider was amenable to judicial review. This was all the more important, given that there was no obvious private law form of redress.[90] Moses J. recognised the importance of the issue, as to how the courts should respond to the increasing contractualisation of government,[91] but held that Servite was not amenable to judicial review.

Moses J. considered whether Servite could be amenable to review because there was a *statutory underpinning* to its function. There must, said Moses J., be sufficient statutory penetration, which went beyond the statutory regulation of the manner in which the service is provided. This depended on whether the relevant legislation could be said to enmesh Servite's provision of residential accommodation into a statutory system of community care. Moses J. denied that this was so, and held that the effect of the legislation was to create a mixed economy provision for community care services, some being provided in house, others through contracting-out. It followed that the relationship between Servite and the applicants was to be governed solely by private law.[92] Moses J. held moreover that the legislation empowering the contracting-out could not constitute the statutory underpinning to enable Servite's functions to be regarded as public functions. The

---

[85] See above, Ch.5.
[86] *R. v Servite Houses and the London Borough of Wandsworth Council Ex p. Goldsmith and Chatting* (2000) 2 L.G.L.R. 997.
[87] National Health Service and Community Care Act 1990 s.47.
[88] National Assistance Act 1948 s.26.
[89] *R. v North and East Devon Health Authority Ex p. Coughlan* [2001] Q.B. 213.
[90] Servite had lawfully terminated its contract with Wandsworth, the applicants had no contract with Servite, and Wandsworth had discharged its obligation by making the initial arrangements with Servite. Wandsworth could not compel Servite to keep the house open, although the local authority would be under an obligation to find alternative accommodation for the applicants.
[91] *Servite Houses*, n.86, 1010, 1025.
[92] *Servite Houses*, n.86, 1018.

applicants could not successfully contend that "because legislation permits a public authority to enter into arrangements with a private body, the functions of that body are, by dint of that legislation, to be regarded as public functions".[93]

26–024   Moses J. considered also *whether the functions performed by Servite could be regarded as public in the absence of any statutory underpinning.* Moses J. found "enormous attraction" in this approach,[94] but felt unable, in the light of existing precedent to adopt it. He held that *Datafin* and *Aga Khan* stood for the proposition that the courts cannot, in the absence of sufficient statutory penetration, impose public standards upon a body the source of whose power is contractual. *Servite*'s powers were said to derive from a purely commercial relationship.

The conclusion that *Servite* was not amenable to review was regrettable.[95] There is nothing in the logic of contracting-out that dictates whether the service provider should be subject to private law or public law obligations. The conclusion that the case could not be resolved via statutory underpinning was premised on the irrelevance of the enabling legislation. This is unwarranted. The concept of statutory underpinning was developed in cases where there was no contracting-out. It served to identify when bodies that were not public in the strict sense of the term, should nonetheless be regarded as susceptible to judicial review. The fact that such a body was recognised directly or indirectly in legislation was relevant in determining the ambit of judicial review. It is axiomatic to this reasoning that the legislation, where it exists, is central to deciding whether the body is amenable to review.

Consider then the application of this idea to situations where there is contracting-out. There is a public function, the provision of care facilities for certain people. The legislation expressly provides that the function can be undertaken in house or contracted-out. It might well be felt with justification that this is a stronger instance of statutory underpinning than that in a *Datafin* type case. In the case of contracting-out there is legislation that explicitly and directly, not implicitly and indirectly, tells us that a private party can perform the public function cast on the local authority. However, whereas in the *Datafin* type of case it is regarded as axiomatic that the legislation is central to deciding whether the body is amenable to review, in the case of contracting-out we are told that it cannot be taken into account.

---

[93] *Servite Houses*, n.86, 1019.
[94] *Servite Houses*, n.86, 1020; M. Hunt, "Constitutionalism and the Contractualisation of Government", in M. Taggart (ed), *The Province of Administrative Law* (Hart, 1997), Ch.2; Lord Steyn, "The Constitutionalisation of Public Law" (Constitution Unit, 1999).
[95] P. Craig, "Contracting-out, the Human Rights Act and the Scope of Judicial Review" (2002) 118 L.Q.R. 551.

iii. Public authorities and contracting power: the need for a "public law element"

It is clear that if a public body acts pursuant to statutory or prerogative **26–025** powers[96] then its decisions will be subject to judicial review. What then is the position when a *public body* exercises a *contractual form of power*? Is this also subject to judicial review?[97]

The traditional tendency was to see contracts, even those made by public bodies, as essentially private matters. The courts have now moved away from this stance, but their attitude towards such contracts is still somewhat ambivalent. The preponderant approach has been to regard contracts made by public authorities as subject to judicial review if there is a sufficiently "public law element" to the case. This phrase can, however, be subject to different interpretations.

In *Hook*[98] the cancellation of a trader's licence was held to be susceptible to review because the council's powers affected a pre-existing common law right to trade in the market. The courts have also held that a public body's powers as landlord are subject to review.[99] There is, moreover, authority that procurement decisions are capable of being judicially reviewed. Thus in the *Shell* case the court reviewed a local authority decision not to deal with Shell, because other companies in the same corporate group had contacts with South Africa.[100] In *Donn*[101] it was held that a legal aid committee was susceptible to judicial review when deciding to award a contract for the conduct of multi-party litigation. Ognall J. held that such a case might be regarded as being within public law either because there was a statutory underpinning; or because, irrespective of any connection with a statute or policy, the process might in any event have a sufficient public law element.

There are however cases where the court has been unwilling to find the requisite "public law element".[102] Thus in *Hibbit and Saunders*,[103] the Lord Chancellor's department invited tenders for court reporting services. The unsuccessful applicant sought judicial review on the ground that it had a legitimate expectation that discussions would not be held with some tenderers to enable them to submit lower bids. The court, while sympathetic, held that the decision was not amenable to review, because it lacked a

---

[96] See, however, the uncertainty as to whether the BBC is subject to judicial review, *R. v BBC and ITC Ex p. Referendum Party* [1997] C.O.D. 459.
[97] S. Arrowsmith, "Judicial Review and the Contractual Powers of Public Authorities" (1990) 106 L.Q.R. 277; S.H. Bailey, "Judicial Review of Contracting Decisions" [2007] P.L. 444.
[98] *R. v Barnsley Metropolitan Borough Council Ex p. Hook* [1976] 1 W.L.R. 1052; *R. v Birmingham City Council Ex p. Dredger and Paget* [1993] C.O.D. 340.
[99] *Cannock Chase District Council v Kelly* [1978] 1 W.L.R. 1; *Sevenoaks District Council v Emmett* (1979) 79 L.G.R. 346.
[100] *R. v Lewisham Borough Council Ex p. Shell UK Ltd* [1988] 1 All E.R. 938; *R. v Enfield London Borough Council Ex p. Unwin* [1989] C.O.D. 466.
[101] *R. v Legal Aid Board Ex p. Donn & Co* [1996] 3 All E.R. 1.
[102] See, e.g., *R. (on the application of Tucker) v Director General of the National Crime Squad* [2003] I.C.R. 599.
[103] *R. v Lord Chancellor's Department Ex p. Hibbit and Saunders* [1993] C.O.D. 326; *R. v Leeds City Council Ex p. Cobleigh* [1997] C.O.D. 69; *R. (on the application of Menai Collect Ltd) v Department for Constitutional Affairs* [2006] EWHC 724.

sufficiently public law element. It was not sufficient to create a public law obligation that the respondent was a public body carrying out governmental functions. If such a body entered a contract with a third party then the contract would define the nature of the parties' obligations, unless there was some additional element giving rise to a public law obligation. A public law element might be found either where there was some special aim being pursued by the government through the tendering process which set it apart from ordinary commercial tenders. Or where there was some statutory underpinning, such as where there was a statutory obligation to negotiate the contract in a particular way, and with particular terms. In *Pepper* it was held that the mere fact that a public authority was exercising a statutory power when it sold land was not enough by itself to render its decision a public law matter. There had to be an additional public law element to the case.[104]

26–026   It is important to consider whether the idea of a "public law element", which serves to distinguish those contracts that are subject to review, is really needed. It is clear in principle that *some* contracts made by public authorities ought to be susceptible to judicial review. It may be entirely fortuitous whether the government chooses to advance its policy objectives through a regulatory scheme involving statutory discretionary power, or whether it seeks to attain the same regulatory end through the use of a contractual relationship. The choice of method should not affect the application of public law principles.[105] It can however be questioned whether *all* contracts entered into by public bodies should be subject to judicial review, in particular if this is taken to mean that the substantive and procedural principles of public law should be applied. These principles may not be appropriate when a public body makes an ordinary commercial contract for furniture, a lease or the like. It is not self-evident that a private contractor who makes such a contract with a public body should have greater substantive and procedural rights than any other contracting party.

The case law on what constitutes the requisite "public law element" is nonetheless complex and has been justly criticised.[106] The phrase "public law element", while not capable of exact definition, should as a matter of principle be interpreted to focus on two related issues. It should, first, denote whether the task being performed by the public body when it makes the contract really partakes in some manner of "governing" or "public regulation" as opposed to pure private contracting. It should, assuming an affirmative answer to the initial inquiry, then capture the ground of the claimant's challenge. If this relates to abuse of power broadly construed then it should surely be amenable to judicial review.

---

[104] *R. v Bolsover DC Ex p. Pepper* (2001) 3 L.G.L.R. 20.
[105] See above, Ch.18. See also, T. Daintith, "The Techniques of Government", in J. Jowell and D. Oliver (eds), *The Changing Constitution* (Oxford University Press, 3rd edn, 1994), Ch.8; S. Fredman and G. Morris, "The Costs of Exclusivity: Public and Private Re-examined" [1994] P.L. 69, 76–78.
[106] Arrowsmith, n.97, 291; Bailey, n.97, 462–463.

This can be exemplified by the reasoning in *Molinaro*.[107] The council leased certain land to the claimant for use as a delicatessen. The claimant started to use it as a café. The council served an enforcement notice under the planning legislation. The claimant sought a licence for the new use from the council as landlord, but the council refused, notwithstanding the fact that the claimant received considerable support from local residents for use of the premises as a café. Elias J. held that the council's decision was amenable to judicial review.

The judgment can be seen in terms of the analysis in the preceding paragraph. Thus Elias J. acknowledged, first, that contract cases might involve no issue of public law and judicial review would be inappropriate, even where the contract was made pursuant to a statute. Cases where, for example, the public body sued for arrears of rent raised no special public law principles and there would be no justification for treating the public body differently from private bodies.[108] However in this case the Council was not acting simply as a private body when it gave effect to its planning policy through contract, but was rather using the contract to effectuate its planning objectives, and this sufficed to inject a public law element into its decision.[109] Second, if the relevant power was abused it should be amenable to review.[110] Public bodies were given powers to be exercised in the public interest, and "the public has an interest in ensuring that the powers are not abused",[111] more especially because contracting power enabled "a public body very significantly to affect the lives of individuals, commercial organisations and their employees".[112]

iv. Regulatory bodies: the "privatisation of the business of government"
Hoffmann L.J. coined this phrase in the *Aga Khan* case,[113] and it provides an apt description of regulatory bodies which are private, but which have been integrated, directly or indirectly, into a system of statutory regulation.

26–027

Datafin is the seminal decision in this category.[114] The applicants complained that the Panel on Take-Overs and Mergers (The Panel) had incorrectly applied their takeover rules, and had thereby allowed an advantage to be gained by the applicant's rivals who were bidding for the same company. The Panel was a self-regulating body which had no direct statutory, prerogative or common law powers, but it was supported by certain statutory powers that presupposed its existence, and its decisions could result in the imposition of penalties. The Panel opposed judicial review, arguing that it was not amenable to the prerogative orders, which had been restricted to

---

[107] *R. (on the application of Molinaro) v The Royal Borough of Kensington and Chelsea* [2001] EWHC Admin 896; *R. (on the application of A) v B Council* [2007] EWHC Admin 1529.
[108] *Molinaro*, n.107, para.66.
[109] *Molinaro*, n.107, paras 63–64.
[110] *Molinaro*, n.107, para.65.
[111] *Molinaro*, n.107, para.67.
[112] *Molinaro*, n.107, para.67.
[113] *Aga Khan*, n.74.
[114] *Datafin*, n.71.

bodies exercising powers derived from the prerogative or statute. The court rejected this view. The "source" of a body's powers was not the only criterion for judging whether a body was amenable to public law. The absence of a statutory or prerogative base for such powers did not exclude s.31 if the "nature" of the power rendered the body suitable for judicial review. The nature of the Panel's powers was held to satisfy this alternative criterion for a number of reasons.

First, the Panel, although self-regulating, did not operate consensually or voluntarily, but rather imposed a collective code on those within its ambit.[115] Second, the Panel was performing a public duty as manifested by the government's willingness to limit legislation in this area, and to use the Panel as part of its regulatory machinery.[116] There had been an "implied devolution of power"[117] by the government to the Panel, and certain legislation presupposed its existence. Third, its source of power was only partly moral persuasion, this being reinforced by statutory powers exercisable by the government and the Bank of England.[118] Finally, the applicants did not appear to have any cause of action in contract or tort against the Panel.[119]

Similar reasoning can be found in other cases, such as the *Advertising Standards Authority* case.[120] The applicant complained that an adverse report on it made by the ASA was procedurally irregular. The initial question was whether the ASA was susceptible to judicial review. The court held that it was, following the *Datafin* case. The ASA had no powers granted to it by statute, and had no contractual relationship with the advertisers whom it controlled. It was, however, part of a scheme of government regulation of the industry in the following sense. A Community directive required Member States to make provision for the control of misleading advertising. This was implemented by regulations, which gave the Director General of Fair Trading powers to investigate complaints of misleading advertising. The essence of this regulatory scheme was that the Director General would only take legal proceedings if the matter had not been satisfactorily resolved through the ASA. The court held that in these circumstances the ASA was susceptible to control through judicial review.

---

[115] *Datafin*, n.71, 825–826, 845–846.
[116] *Datafin*, n.71, 838–839, 848–849, 850–851.
[117] *Datafin*, n.71, 849.
[118] *Datafin*, n.71, 838–839, 851–852.
[119] *Datafin*, n.71, 838–839. See also, *R. v Panel on Take-Overs and Mergers Ex p. Guiness plc* [1990] 1 Q.B. 146; *R. v Civil Service Appeal Board Ex p. Bruce* [1988] I.C.R. 649, [1989] I.C.R. 171.
[120] *R. v Advertising Standards Authority Ex p. The Insurance Services Plc* [1990] C.O.D. 42. See also, *Bank of Scotland v Investment Management Regulatory Organisation Ltd* (1989) S.L.T. 432; *R. v Financial Intermediaries Managers and Brokers Regulatory Association Ex p. Cochrane* [1990] C.O.D. 33; *R. v Code of Practice Committee of the Association of the British Pharmaceutical Industry Ex p. Professional Counselling Aids Ltd* [1991] C.O.D. 228; *R. v Visitors to the Inns of Court Ex p. Calder* [1994] Q.B. 1; *R. v Governors of Haberdashers' Aske's Hatcham College Trust Ex p. Tyrell* [1995] C.O.D. 399; *R. v BBC and ITC Ex p. Referendum Party* [1997] C.O.D. 459; *R. v London Metal Exchange Ltd Ex p. Albatross Warehousing BV*, March 30, 2000; *R. (on the application of Beer (t/a Hammer Trout Farm)) v Hampshire Farmers Markets Ltd* [2004] 1 W.L.R. 233.

v. Regulatory bodies: contract, power and control
The courts have experienced more difficulty in determining the boundaries **26–028**
of judicial review in a group of cases not far removed from those in the
preceding section. These cases also concern regulatory bodies that exercise
control over a particular industry. However, what serves to distinguish these
cases from those considered above is that there is no governmental involvement in these areas as such. These regulatory institutions are not part of a
schema of statutory regulation. Whether this should make a difference will
be considered in due course. The courts have on the whole been unwilling to
extend judicial review to cover such cases.

The story begins with the decision in the *Law* case.[121] The plaintiff was a
greyhound trainer whose licence was suspended and he sought a declaration
outside s.31 that the decision was ultra vires. The NGRC argued that the
case should have been brought within s.31. This was rejected by the court. It
held that the power exercised by the Greyhound Racing Club was derived
from contract, and was of concern only to those who took part in this sport.
While the exercise of this power could benefit the public by, for example,
stamping out malpractice, this was true for many other domestic tribunals,
which were not subject to judicial review.

The force of the ruling in *Law* was felt in relation to other regulatory
authorities. A number of actions arose concerning the Jockey Club, in which
the court reluctantly declined to use judicial review because of the holding in
the greyhound case.[122]

An opportunity to reconsider the point arose in the *Aga Khan* case.[123] The
applicant was an owner of racehorses and was therefore bound to register
with the Jockey Club, and to enter a contractual relationship whereby he
adhered to its rules of racing. The applicant's horse was disqualified after
winning a major race, and he sought judicial review. The Court of Appeal
found that in general the Club was not susceptible to judicial review. It
rejected the argument that the decision in *Law* had been overtaken by
Datafin. The court acknowledged that the Club regulated a national activity,
and Sir Thomas Bingham M.R. accepted that if it did not regulate the sport
then the government would in all probability be bound to do so. Notwithstanding this the court reached its conclusion because the Club was not
in its origin, constitution, membership or history a public body, and its
powers were not governmental. Moreover, the applicant would have a
remedy outside s.31, because he had a contract with the Jockey Club. The
court did, however, leave open the possibility that some cases concerning
bodies like the Jockey Club might be brought within the public law procedures, particularly where the applicant or plaintiff had no contractual

---

[121] *Law v National Greyhound Racing Club Ltd* [1983] 1 W.L.R. 1302.
[122] *R. v Disciplinary Committee of the Jockey Club Ex p. Massingberd-Mundy* [1993] 2 All E.R.
207; *R. v Jockey Club Ex p. RAM Racecourses Ltd* [1993] 2 All E.R. 225.
[123] [1993] 1 W.L.R. 909. See also *R. (on the application of Mullins) v Jockey Club Appeal Board
(No.1)* [2005] EWHC 2197. Compare however *Bradley v The Jockey Club* [2005] EWCA Civ
1056, where the court treated the case as one of private law, but reasoned in a very similar
manner to a public law case.

relationship with the Club, or where the Club made rules which were discriminatory in nature.[124]

26–029   A similar reluctance to subject the governing authorities' of sporting associations to judicial review is apparent in the *Football Association* case.[125] The FA was the governing authority for football and all clubs had to be affiliated to it. The FA sanctioned various competitions, the most important of which was the Football League (FL). The FL ran the four divisions comprising the league and had a contractual relationship with the FA. The dispute arose from the decision by the FA to establish the Premier League, which would be run by it and not by the FL. In order to facilitate the top clubs breaking away from the FL and forming the Premier League, the FA declared void certain rules of the FL that made it difficult for clubs to terminate their relationship with the FL. The FL sought judicial review of this decision. It argued that the FA had a monopoly over the game, and that although there was a contract between the FA and the FL the rules of the FA were, in reality, a legislative code which regulated an important aspect of national life, in the absence of which a public body would have to perform the same function. Rose J. rejected the application and held that the FA was not susceptible to judicial review, notwithstanding its monopolistic powers. It was not underpinned in any way by any state agency, nor was there any real governmental interest in its functions, nor was there any evidence that if the FA did not exist a public body would have to be created in its place.

The disinclination to intervene via judicial review with such bodies is not restricted to those in the sporting arena. In the *Lloyds* case,[126] it was held that Lloyds of London was not amenable to judicial review in an action brought by "names" who had lost money in insurance syndicates that had covered asbestosis and pollution claims. The court held that Lloyds was not a public body regulating the insurance market, but rather a body that ran one part of the market pursuant to a private Act of Parliament. The case was concerned solely with the contracts between the names and their managing agents.

The cases discussed in this section raise in stark form the boundaries of public law. There are three principal strands in the courts' reasoning.

The first is that *not all power is public power*. The courts undoubtedly recognise that these regulatory authorities exercise power over their area, but they do not necessarily accept that this should be characterised as a species of public power. Thus in the *Aga Khan* case Hoffmann L.J. had this to say about the Jockey Club.[127]

---

[124] In neither *RAM*, n.122, nor *Massingberd-Mundy*, n.122, did the applicant have a contractual relationship with the Club.
[125] *R. v Football Association Ltd Ex p. Football League Ltd* [1993] 2 All E.R. 833; *R. v Football Association of Wales Ex p. Flint Town United Football Club* [1991] C.O.D. 44.
[126] *R. v Lloyds of London Ex p. Briggs* [1993] 1 Lloyd's Rep.176. See also, *R. v Insurance Ombudsman Ex p. Aegon Life Insurance Ltd* [1994] C.O.D. 426; *R. v Panel of the Federation of Communication Services Ltd Ex p. Kubis* [1998] C.O.D. 5; *R. v Association of British Travel Agents Ex p. Sunspell Ltd* [2001] A.C.D 16; *R. v British Standards Institution Ex p. Dorgard Ltd* [2001] A.C.D 15; *R. (on the application of West) v Lloyd's of London* [2004] 3 All E.R. 251.
[127] *Aga Khan*, n.74, 932–933.

"But the mere fact of power, even over a substantial area of economic activity, is not enough. In a mixed economy, power may be private as well as public. Private power may affect the public interest and the livelihoods of many individuals. But that does not subject it to the rules of public law. If control is needed it must be found in the law of contract, the doctrine of restraint of trade, the Restrictive Trade Practices Act 1976, arts 85 and 86 of the EEC Treaty and all the other instruments available for curbing the excesses of private power."

A second strand in the courts' reasoning is related to the first. It concerns **26–030** the *suitability of the public law controls* for the types of body under discussion. The volume of case law on the public/private divide can lead us to forget that there are *consequences*, in terms of the procedural and substantive norms held to be applicable to such bodies, of attributing the label "public" to them. There is concern as to whether such norms are always well-suited to such bodies and this finds expression in the judgment of Rose J. in the *Football Association* case.[128]

"[F]or my part, to apply to the governing body of football, on the basis that it is a public body, principles honed for the control of the abuse of power by government and its creatures would involve what, in today's fashionable parlance, would be called a quantum leap."

A third factor that has influenced the courts is more pragmatic: if these bodies are deemed to fall within public law then *where should we stop*? Rose J. had this in mind when reflecting that if the FA were sufficiently public for the purposes judicial review, then so too would the governing authorities of virtually all other sports, from tennis to motor racing and from golf to cricket.[129] If this was so then why should not the exercise of power by private corporate undertakings with a monopolistic position be subject to the strictures of public law?[130] This then leads to consequential concerns about the capacity of the courts to deal with this breadth of material without becoming "even more swamped with applications than they are already".[131]

Commentators differ as to the cogency of these reasons. Pannick has argued that the exercise of monopolistic power should serve to bring bodies within the ambit of judicial review. To speak of a consensual foundation for a body's power is largely beside the point where those who wish to partake in the activity have no realistic choice but to accept that power.[132] Black has argued that the emphasis given to the contractual foundations for a body's power as the reason for withholding review are misplaced. She contends that the courts are confusing contract as an instrument of economic exchange,

---

[128] *Football Association*, n.125, 849.
[129] *Football Association*, n.125, 849.
[130] G. Borrie, "The Regulation of Public and Private Power" [1989] P.L. 552.
[131] *Football Association*, n.125, 849.
[132] D. Pannick, "Who is Subject to Judicial Review and in Respect of What?" [1992] P.L. 1.

with contract as a regulatory instrument.[133] She argues further that the reliance placed on private law controls, such as restraint of trade and competition law, may be misplaced here. Such controls are designed for the regulation of economic activity in the market place, and they may not be best suited to control potential abuse of regulatory power itself.[134]

vi. Employment relationships: the straining of the public/private divide

26–031 Numerous cases have come before the courts concerning employment relationships, with employees seeking to argue that the case was sufficiently public to warrant judicial review, while employers have resisted this argument. The employees have had mixed success in their attempts to use judicial review.

In *Lavelle*,[135] the applicant claimed that she had been dismissed by the BBC in breach of natural justice, and sought judicial review. Woolf J. decided that this claim could not proceed under s.31, since it was restricted to matters of a public as opposed to a private or domestic nature. The relationship between Lavelle and the BBC was private, and therefore judicial review was inappropriate.[136] The same result was reached in *Walsh*,[137] where a senior nursing officer was dismissed and sought judicial review for breach of natural justice. The defendant contested the suitability of s.31 proceedings, and this challenge was upheld. The court reasoned that judicial review was only available for issues of public law. Ordinary master–servant relationships did not involve any such issue, the only remedy being damages, or relief under the relevant employment legislation. A public law issue could arise if Walsh could be said to hold an office where the employer was operating under a statutory restriction as to the grounds of dismissal.[138] However employment by a public authority did not per se "inject" a public law element; nor did the seniority of the employee; nor did the fact that the employer was required to contract with its employees on special terms. An employee could, however, be a "potential candidate" for administrative law remedies where Parliament "underpinned" the employees' position by directly restricting the freedom of the public authority to dismiss.

The preceding cases can be contrasted with *Benwell*,[139] where a prison officer was allowed to seek judicial review, the court holding that there was a sufficient statutory underpinning to inject the requisite public law element. It is, however, clear that a prison officer is not compelled to use the s.31 procedure. In the *McLaren* case,[140] a prison officer who sought to argue that

---

[133] J. Black, "Constitutionalising Self-Regulation" (1996) 59 M.L.R. 24, 41.
[134] Black, n.133, 42.
[135] *R. v British Broadcasting Corporation Ex p. Lavelle* [1983] 1 W.L.R. 23.
[136] Woolf J. did, however, find that an action for an injunction outside of s.31 could be pursued, and that the BBC did have the duty to comply with natural justice.
[137] *Walsh*, n.70; *R. v Derbyshire County Council Ex p. Noble* [1990] I.C.R. 808.
[138] Following *Ridge v Baldwin* [1964] A.C. 40, 65, and *Malloch v Aberdeen Corporation* [1971] 1 W.L.R. 1578, 1582, 1595.
[139] *Benwell*, n.72.
[140] *McLaren v Home Office* [1990] I.C.R. 824.

new working practices were in breach of a collective agreement known as Fresh Start was allowed to bring his action by way of ordinary writ.

In the *McLaren* case[141] Woolf L.J. distilled some of the more general principles which should apply in employment cases. **26–032**

(1) The starting point, said Woolf L.J., was that employees of public bodies should pursue their cases in the normal way *outside* s.31, by way of ordinary action for a declaration, damages and the like. This was so even if the particular employee held an office from the Crown, which was dismissable at pleasure: "whatever rights the employee has will be enforceable normally by an ordinary action".[142] Judicial review was therefore neither necessary, nor appropriate in normal cases.

(2) Judicial review could, however, be sought if the public employee was affected by a disciplinary body established under statute or the prerogative to which the employer or employee was required or entitled to refer disputes affecting their relationship. Provided that the tribunal had a sufficiently public law element then s.31 could be used.

(3) A public employee could also seek judicial review if attacking a decision of *general* application and doing so on *Wednesbury* grounds. The *GCHQ*[143] case was regarded as an example of this.

(4) Even where review was not available because the disciplinary procedures were purely domestic in nature, it might still be possible for the employee to seek a declaration outside s.31 to ensure that the proceedings were conducted fairly.[144]

The guidelines in *McLaren* will hopefully render matters clearer than in the past. The current position is nonetheless still open to question.

First, the whole issue of how employment cases are to be tried, whether within s.31 or by ordinary action, has generated a complex body of case law, which has been difficult to interpret.[145] The matter has been exacerbated by the fact that public bodies have played the procedural complexities from both sides. When civil servants attempted to use the public procedures the Crown argued that the issue was private and unsuited to review[146]; when an ordinary action was begun the public body contended that it should have been brought within s.31.[147]

---

[141] *McLaren*, n.140, 836–837.
[142] *McLaren*, n.140, 836.
[143] [1985] A.C. 374.
[144] *Lavelle*, n.135.
[145] S. Fredman and G. Morris, "Public or Private: State Employees and Judicial Review" (1991) 107 L.Q.R. 298, and "A Snake or a Ladder?: *O'Reilly v Mackman* Reconsidered" (1992) 108 L.Q.R. 353.
[146] See, e.g., *R. v Civil Service Appeal Board Ex p. Bruce* [1988] I.C.R. 649, [1989] I.C.R. 171.
[147] See, e.g., *McLaren*, n.140.

Second, it is evident that changes in the pattern of governance have rendered it more difficult to distinguish between public and private employment.[148] This does not mean that the distinction between the two spheres has been entirely eroded. It does mean that the "appropriate question is not whether employment is or is not 'public' . . . but rather . . . whether an individual provision should be applicable to particular employment in light of the purpose which it is designed to serve".[149]

Third, whether the approach adopted in *McLaren* achieves the correct balance is open to question. The starting assumption is that all employment actions should be brought by ordinary action, on the hypothesis that the employment relationship is intrinsically private, whether the employer operates in the public or private sector. The assumption is then qualified in the manner described above. What unites these exceptions is the idea that something more general is at stake than in the normal employment dispute. However, as Fredman and Morris point out the exceptions could prove to have a wider application than might have been thought.[150]

"The problem is that this exception could easily engulf the rule. Not only do decisions respecting public employees affect a large number of employees, but they also frequently concern issues which are of public interest and in respect of which the public has the right to expect responsible and accountable behaviour. This is well illustrated by *McLaren*: although McLaren appeared to be an individual litigating an individual point, in fact, he was testing the applicability of a collective agreement to all the prison officers at his establishment; and more fundamentally was pursuing a general public policy issue about the administration of the Prison Service and the Fresh Start agreement. It is difficult to argue that this latter point is not one that affects the public."

vii. Activities within Parliament's proper sphere

26–033 In the *Fayed* case,[151] it was held that the Parliamentary Commissioner for Standards was not amenable to review. His focus was on the activities and workings of those engaged within Parliament. It would therefore be inappropriate for the court to use its supervisory powers in relation to such an investigation, more especially since there was a Committee on Standards and Privileges of the House which performed that role.

---

[148] See above, Ch.5.
[149] G. Morris and S. Fredman, "Is There a Public/Private Labour Law Divide?" (1993) 14 Comparative Labor Law Jnl. 115, 123.
[150] "The Costs of Exclusivity: the Case of Public Employees", paper delivered to Cambridge Conference on the Law Commission's proposals, 1993, n.5–6; "Public or Private" (1991) 107 L.Q.R. 298, 307.
[151] *R. v Parliamentary Commissioner for Standards Ex p. Fayed* [1998] 1 W.L.R. 669.

viii. Activities which are "Inherently Private"

Some activities are regarded as inherently private, and hence unsuited to   **26–034**
judicial review. *Wachmann*[152] provides an example. The applicant sought
judicial review of a disciplinary decision removing him as a Rabbi, because
of conduct rendering him morally unfit to continue in the position.

Simon Brown J. refused the application, holding that the jurisdiction of
the Chief Rabbi was not susceptible to judicial review. He held that the s.31
procedure could only be used when there was not merely a public, but a
governmental interest in the decision-making power in question. The Chief
Rabbi's functions were said to be essentially intimate, spiritual and religious,
and the government could not and would not seek to discharge them if he
were to abdicate his regulatory responsibility, nor would Parliament con-
template legislating to regulate the discharge of these functions. Moreover,
the reviewing court was not in a position to regulate what was essentially a
religious function, whether a person was morally fit to carry out their
spiritual responsibilities.

It should however be recognised that the courts have exercised their
review powers on numerous occasions in relation to Church of England
clergy. This jurisdiction was re-affirmed in *Owen*,[153] where the court judicially reviewed the decision not to extend a clergyman's term of office.

ix. The impact of the Human Rights Act 1998

We have already had occasion to consider the impact of the Human Rights   **26–035**
Act 1998 (HRA) on the types of case which can proceed other than by way
of judicial review. The HRA may also have some impact on the converse
situation, the claims which can be brought via judicial review.

The relevance of the HRA in this regard stems from the definition of
public authority for the purpose of liability under s.6. The HRA contemplates "pure public authorities", all of whose activities are within the
ambit of the HRA. However only the public and not private actions of
"hybrid public authorities" are covered. This may affect the type of claim
that can be brought by way of judicial review. Employment relationships
may serve as an example. We have seen that the basic premise is that disputes over such matters should be brought by way of ordinary action. It
might well now be possible for an employee of a pure public authority,
which is bound by the HRA in respect of all of its actions, to argue that it
can therefore proceed by way of judicial review to vindicate a breach of
Convention rights in the employment context.

x. Future prospects

It remains to be seen how far the courts will be willing to take the scope of   **26–036**
judicial review. The reservations of some judges have been noted above.

---

[152] *R. v Chief Rabbi of the United Congregations of Great Britain and the Commonwealth Ex p.
Wachmann* [1992] 1 W.L.R. 1036; *R. v Iman of Bury Park Jame Masjid Luton Ex p. Sulaiman Ali*
[1994] C.O.D. 142.
[153] n.72.

Others advocate a broader approach. Thus Lord Woolf would, it seems, extend review to cover all bodies that exercise authority over another person or body in such a manner as to cause material prejudice to that person or body. These controls could, in principle, apply to bodies exercising power over sport and religion.[154]

If the scope of review is extended thus far then careful attention will have to be given to whether the procedural and substantive norms applied against traditional public bodies should also be applied against private bodies. Many of the cases considered within this section were concerned with the application of procedural norms. If we were to follow Lord Woolf's suggestion then we would also have to consider whether substantive public law should be applied to such bodies.

Would we insist that sporting bodies with monopoly power, or large companies with similar power, take account of all relevant considerations before deciding upon a course of action? Would we demand that their actions be subject to a principle of proportionality, assuming that it becomes an accepted part of our substantive control? If there is an affirmative answer, then the change would be significant to say the very least. It would have ramifications for other subjects, such as company law, commercial law and contract. It would increase the courts' judicial review case load.[155] It would involve difficult questions as to how such substantive public law principles fit with previously accepted doctrines of private law. This is not to deny that similar broad principles can operate within the public and private spheres.[156] It is to argue that the broader the reach of "public law", the more nuanced we would have to be about the application of public law principles to those bodies brought within the ambit of judicial review.[157]

4. Evaluation of the Present Law

A. The Unavoidable Issue: Which Bodies are Amenable to Review?

26–037   It should be made clear at the outset that the problem of deciding which bodies should be amenable to public law principles would be present even if we had a radically different system of remedies. This can be simply demonstrated. Let us imagine that we had a unified system of remedies, based broadly on the ordinary civil action. It would *still* be necessary to decide which bodies were sufficiently "public" for public law principles to be

---

[154] "Judicial Review: A Possible Programme for Reform" [1992] P.L. 221, 235.
[155] This would surely be so notwithstanding Lord Woolf's caveat that review would only be available if there was no suitable alternative remedy, [1992] P.L. 221, 235.
[156] Sir John Laws, "Public Law and Employment Law: Abuse of Power" [1997] P.L. 467; D. Oliver, "Common Values in Public and Private Law and the Public/Private Divide" [1997] P.L. 630; *Bradley*, n.123.
[157] P. Craig, "Public Law and Control over Private Power", in Taggart, n.94, 196–216.

applied to them. The difference between such a regime and the existing one is that at present the resolution of these questions leads to different procedural routes being deemed appropriate, whereas this would not be so under the new regime being posited. The substantive questions themselves would not, however, disappear, and it would be idle to pretend otherwise. These questions were present long before the 1977 remedial reforms. Put shortly, the substantive issues presented by cases such *Aga Khan* and the like are here to stay.

B. The Central Issue: Do Public Bodies Require Special Protection?

The central issue concerning procedural reform is whether public bodies require special protection through permission and time limits. *If* public bodies require such protection then some species of exclusivity, *or* some other form of protection, should follow in order to prevent the protections from being by-passed.

26–038

It is for this reason that the idea of presumptive exclusivity, for all its difficulties, was not illogical. The Law Commission did not intend the 1977 procedure to be exclusive,[158] but it failed to reason through the implications of its own proposals. It was the Law Commission that proposed the new procedure, complete with leave requirements and time limits, in order to protect public bodies. Given this initial choice the courts were placed in a dilemma. They could treat the procedure as *non-exclusive*, but the consequences would be odd. The same factual situations would be treated in radically different ways, depending on which remedial route the applicant chose. It could not be rational to allow one applicant to proceed without leave and with no formal time limit, while, on the same facts, another applicant would be subject to leave and a very much shorter time period. As Lord Woolf said,[159] it seems "to be illogical to have a procedure which is designed to protect the public from unnecessary interference with administrative action, and then allow the protection which is provided to be by-passed". The courts could alternatively insist, as they have done, that s.31 *is presumptively exclusive* for public law cases, with all the attendant problems this has entailed.

If we believe that public bodies merit some special protection we could alternatively move to a unified system, but modify or apply this procedure to accommodate the particular needs of public bodies. This will be considered below.

---

[158] Law Comm No.73 Cmnd. 6407 (1976), para.34.
[159] "Judicial Review: A Possible Programme for Reform" [1992] P.L. 221, 231.

C. Protecting Public Bodies: Permission

i. The rationale for permission

26–039 It follows that the central issue is whether we should retain the protection for public bodies in the form of permission, which has only been required since 1933.[160] Two senses of "protection" should be distinguished.

It could be argued that public bodies must be protected from vexatious litigants and that permission achieves this. This argument is highly suspect. The vexatious litigant appears to be a hypothetical rather than a real problem. In so far as this spectre assumes a solid form the problem can be solved by adequate provisions as to costs.[161] The case law and literature on the declaration and injunction prior to 1977 contains no evidence that this was a problem even though there was no permission requirement, and evidence about the reformed procedure indicates that the frivolous nature of the application is a very rare ground for refusing permission.[162]

It could alternatively be argued that public bodies must be protected in a broader sense. The argument is that public bodies exist to perform public duties, which are for the benefit of the general public. In deciding whether an action should proceed this wider public interest must be taken into account, as well as that of the applicant, because the public has an interest in seeing that litigation does not unduly hamper the governmental process.[163] A corollary is that the permission requirement exists to protect public bodies from applicants who do not really have a chance of winning their case. It is a screening mechanism to prevent the public body from being troubled by cases that are unlikely to succeed. A crucial issue concerns the *test* to be applied at the permission stage. This was addressed by Lord Donaldson M.R. in *Doorga*.[164] His Lordship gave directions to judges hearing applications for leave, and said that they should distinguish between three categories of case.

"The first is the case where there are, prima facie, reasons for granting judicial review. In such a case leave shall duly be granted. There are other cases in which the application for judicial review is wholly unarguable, in which case, quite clearly leave should be refused. However, there is an intermediate category—not very frequent but it does occur—in which the judge may say, 'Well, there is no prima facie case on the applicant's

---

[160] Administration of Justice (Miscellaneous Provisions) Act 1993 s.5.

[161] The court has, in any event, an inherent jurisdiction to strike out vexatious claims. In addition there are statutory powers to strike out vexatious claims, Supreme Court Act 1981 s.42, and there are Rules of the Supreme Court which enable provision to be made as to costs; *R. (on the application of Ewing) v Office of the Deputy Prime Minister* [2006] 1 W.L.R. 1260.

[162] A. le Sueur and M. Sunkin, "Applications for Judicial Review: the Requirement of Leave" [1992] P.L. 102, 120.

[163] The Rt. Hon Sir H Woolf, "Public Law–Private Law: Why the Divide? A Personal View" [1986] P.L. 220, 230; Sir H. Woolf, *Protecting the Public–A New Challenge* (Sweet & Maxwell, 1990).

[164] *R. v Secretary of State for the Home Department Ex p. Doorga* [1990] C.O.D. 109, 110; *R. v Secretary of State for the Home Department Ex p. Begum* [1990] C.O.D. 107, 108.

evidence but, nevertheless, the applicant's evidence leaves me with an uneasy feeling and I should like to know more about this.' Alternatively he may say, 'The applicant's case looks strong but I nevertheless have an uneasy feeling that there may be some very quick and easy explanation for this.' In either case it would be quite proper, and, indeed, reasonable for him to adjourn the application for leave in order that it may be further heard inter partes. At such a hearing it is not for the respondent to deploy his full case, but he simply has to put forward, if he can, some totally knock-out point which makes it clear that there is no basis for the application at all."

ii. The need for the permission requirement: an evaluation

The preceding argument is an essentially pragmatic one about the need to protect public bodies against cases that do not have the requisite chance of success to warrant proceeding to a full hearing. This practical justification is given added force by the rise in the number of applications for judicial review, which has served to convince many within the judiciary that some filter mechanism is essential. There are however two possible interpretations of Lord Donaldson M.R.'s criterion.

26–040

On a literal interpretation permission should only be refused if the case is indeed "unarguable" or "wholly unarguable".[165] This is strong language and it would seem prima facie unlikely that there will be many such cases. If there are a large number of such cases then there must be something very wrong further back in the system. Public or private money would be wasted by lawyers encouraging the pursuit of such cases. The rational individual is unlikely to wish to press a case if advised by a lawyer that the action was wholly unarguable.

The other possible interpretation would be that a judge should refuse permission where he believed that there was no reasonable chance of success, or that the case was not reasonably arguable. There are, however, problems with this formulation. It does not fit with the actual wording used by Lord Donaldson, and is also inconsistent with the third intermediate category set out by his Lordship. Moreover, to refuse permission because the judge believed that the applicant did not have a reasonable chance of success, or some similar test, is problematic. The judge will be making a difficult evaluation on fact and law, and this evaluation will, after the CPR, be based on written documentation. As Megarry J. has stated, albeit in a different context, the law is full of cases which appeared to be open and shut, but which turned out not to be so straightforward.[166]

There is therefore a choice to be made. The courts could only refuse

---

[165] In *Doorga* [1990] C.O.D. 109, 110, Lord Donaldson M.R. used the language "wholly unarguable", whereas in *R. v Secretary of State for the Home Department Ex p. Begum* [1990] C.O.D. 107, 108, he stated that if there was no arguable case leave should be refused; in *R. v Legal Aid Board Ex p. Hughes* (1992) 24 H.L.R. 698, the formulation was that there must be a clearly arguable case for leave to be granted *ex parte*.

[166] *John v Rees* [1970] Ch.345, 402.

permission where the case really was unarguable. Relatively few such cases
are likely to exist, and one may well wonder whether the whole edifice
erected to protect public bodies is worth the effort. The courts could,
alternatively, exclude cases that do not have some reasonable chance of
success, or that are not reasonably arguable. This hurdle would be more
difficult to surmount, and in this sense would give more protection to public
bodies. It is however open to the objections mentioned above.

   The new Civil Procedure Rules have, unfortunately, not shed light on this
important issue. The Bowman Report, which led to the new CPR on judicial
review, was in favour of retaining the permission stage, with explicit criteria
as to when permission should be granted, and a presumption that it should
be granted.[167] CPR 54.4 retained the leave requirement, subject to the linguistic alteration from leave to permission, but contains no criteria as to
when permission should be granted.

iii. The need for the leave/permission requirement: empirical evidence

26–041 Valuable empirical work has been done on the leave requirement by Le
Sueur and Sunkin.[168] Their findings were as follows.

   (1) Approximately 37 per cent of applications for leave were refused; 40
        per cent of renewed applications were successful. This demonstrates
        the significant rate of error at the initial application stage.

   (2) The reasons for refusing leave varied. Lack of sufficient interest was
        only rarely the reason why the applicant failed. The most important
        grounds for applications failing were: delay, the inappropriateness of
        the public law procedure and the fact that the case was held to be
        unarguable.

   (3) The last of these reasons accounted for the great majority of
        unsuccessful applications, and the study made two important points
        about the criterion of arguability. One is that the authors found it
        difficult to differentiate the three categories of case identified by Lord
        Donaldson M.R. The other is that even where a judge did express
        himself in forthright language, and declared a case to be unarguable,
        such cases were far from clear: "cases characterised as wholly
        unarguable at the leave stage have gone on to win on the merits at
        the full hearing".[169] Many cases were found to be neither wholly
        unarguable, nor patently arguable, with the consequence that the
        judge was forced into playing a dangerous guessing game on fact and
        law.[170] Moreover, the largest category of cases deemed to be unar-
        guable were those in which it was said that the facts or evidence did
        not sustain the applicant's claim. This however demonstrated the

[167] n.9, para.13.
[168] n.162.
[169] n.162, 122.
[170] n.162, 122.

need for applicants to be able to present the factual basis of their claim, with consequential ramifications for discovery and the like.

(4) The authors argued that there should at the very least be more structuring of the judicial discretion at the leave stage, in order to imbue the vague term "arguability" with greater precision, or to replace it with some other related concept such as "serious issue to be tried". There should then be a presumption that leave should be granted unless one of a number of grounds for refusing relief existed.

(5) The authors rightly point out the dangers of using leave as a method for managing overall case load. There is, as they say, "something profoundly ambiguous in giving to the judiciary 'administrative' powers to allocate scarce court resources in a context where the courts are required to supervise the 'administrative' decisions of government", more particularly so where the criteria for decision-making are unclear.[171]

The other important empirical work has been done by Sunkin, Bridges and Meszaros.[172] Some of their main findings over a series of studies can be summarised as follows.

26–042

(1) The authors placed the increase in judicial applications in perspective. They revealed that while the number of review applications increased fourfold since 1981 two main areas accounted for a large number of cases: nearly half of all applications related to immigration and homelessness.[173] There has, more recently, been a decline in the homelessness cases, and a rise in those dealing with other aspects of housing, and asylum.[174] The total number of judicial review applications rose to 4,437 in 1999, from 3,200 in 1994–1995.

(2) The authors found that leave has become a rather more substantial hurdle for applicants in recent years. Whereas leave was granted in 73 per cent of cases in the early 1980s, this figure fell to 56–61 per cent in the period 1987–1989. The study also found that an applicant's likelihood of success could vary dramatically depending upon the judge hearing the application. Some were conservative in this respect, granting leave in only 25 per cent of cases; others were more liberal, allowing 82 per cent to proceed; yet others were in the middle of this range, giving leave in 40–60 per cent of cases. This rendered the application process something of a lottery for individuals. The

---

[171] n.162, 126.
[172] *Judicial Review in Perspective: An Investigation of Trends in the Use and Operation of the Judicial Review Procedure in England and Wales*, Public Law Project, 1993.
[173] There is however a higher withdrawal rate in these areas than in others, L. Bridges, G. Meszaros and M. Sunkin, *Judicial Review in Perspective* (Cavendish, 1995).
[174] L. Bridges, G. Meszaros and M. Sunkin, "Regulating the Judicial Review Case Load" [2001] P.L. 651, 654–657.

later version of this study[175] confirmed the variation in the rates at which individual judges grant leave, thereby providing further evidence that the judicial discretion is not applied consistently.

(3) Many cases are withdrawn (between 31–42 per cent), the majority of these after leave *has* been given.[176] One implication of this is that respondents were sheltering behind the leave requirement, and only considered a negotiated settlement once leave has been obtained.

Two general conclusions can be drawn from these informative studies. The first concerns the test for the permission requirement. Even when the courts are purportedly applying the criterion of arguability they have been refusing roughly 40 per cent of cases. This could mean, contrary to what was suggested above, that the number of wholly unarguable cases really is this high. The figures of failed applications could, alternatively, mean that the courts are in reality applying a more stringent test, and only allowing cases to proceed if there is some reasonable chance of success, or if the case really appears to be arguable on the merits. This certainly appears to be so with respect to some judges who have a very low rate of allowing leave. The dangers of this test have been adverted to above. Even where the courts have been applying the test of arguability, some of the cases deemed initially to be wholly unarguable have gone on to win on the merits at the full hearing, or have been granted leave on a renewed application. Given that this is so, the "error rating" on leave applications is likely to be even higher should the courts generally adopt a more stringent test. This is because there is more room for difference of opinion when a test is framed in terms of "reasonable chance of success", as compared with "wholly unarguable".

The second point relates to the impact of the permission requirement on unmeritorious claims. The Bowman Report recommended the retention of this requirement in part because of a case study that concluded that without the permission requirement more than 1,000 court days would have been spent on unmeritorious claims, defined as those where permission was refused. The calculus of court days saved is however based on questionable assumptions. It "appears to have been assumed that cases currently refused permission would, if this requirement were removed, proceed to substantive hearings at a rate twice as high as that which actually occurs at present".[177]

---

[175] n.173.
[176] M. Sunkin, "Withdrawing: A Problem in Judicial Review?", in P. Leyland & T. Woods (eds), *Administrative Law Facing the Future: Old Constraints & New Horizons* (Blackstone, 1997), Ch.10.
[177] Bridges, Meszaros and Sunkin, n.174, 665.

iv. The need for permission: the impact of the CPR

The permission requirement has been retained by CPR 54.4, following the **26–043** recommendation of the Bowman Report,[178] and the earlier recommendation of the Law Commission.[179] The judiciary and the government believe that it is necessary for the protection of public bodies.

The issue addressed above, concerning the *criterion for the grant of permission*, becomes all the more important. It is to be regretted that CPR 54.4 contains no criterion for the grant of permission, given that there is a plethora of possible tests. These include refusal of permission where the case is "wholly unarguable", "if it is not reasonably arguable", "if there is no serious issue to be tried", or "if there is no real prospect of success". The claimant's chances of securing permission may be very different under these different tests.[180] The courts should not employ a test framed in terms of "serious issue to be tried", since it could be taken to give a court discretion to refuse permission because it felt that the potential illegality was not serious enough to warrant a substantive hearing. The test should be framed in terms of "arguability". A choice then has to be made as to whether to refuse permission only where a case is unarguable, or whether a more rigorous test is to be applied, which requires the claimant to demonstrate a reasonable chance of success or the like.

CPR 54 modified *the permission stage so that it is now more inter partes than hitherto*. The leave stage was traditionally ex parte, and the respondent might only become involved if leave was given. This has been altered by CPR 54.6–9, which has made the permission stage more inter partes than hitherto. The claim form must be served on the defendant, and any person the claimant considers an interested party. Any person served with the claim form who wishes to take part in the judicial review must file an acknowledgement of service. The acknowledgement must state, inter alia, the grounds on which the party is contesting the claim. The rationale for the change was to get defendants to think about the challenge at the outset, and to ensure that the court was well informed at the permission stage.[181] There are however concerns that the inter partes procedure may disadvantage claimants. The court may regard the defendant's brief response as a knock out blow to the claimant, even where it is not fully supported by evidence.[182] There is also a concern that the permission stage as modified by the CPR will be performing two roles, that of mediating access to judicial review, and managing the substantive dispute, and that it may be difficult to reconcile these roles.[183]

---

[178] n.9.
[179] Law Commission Report, *Administrative Law: Judicial Review and Statutory Appeals* (Report No.226, HC 669, 1994), para.5.7. For comment, see, N. Bamforth, "Reform of Public Law: Pragmatism or Principle?" (1995) 58 M.L.R. 722; R. Gordon, "The Law Commission and Judicial Review: Managing the Tension between Case Management and Public Interest Challenges" [1995] P.L. 11.
[180] Gordon, n.179, 14.
[181] Fordham, n.10, 6.
[182] Cornford and Sunkin, n.10, 19.
[183] Cornford and Sunkin, n.10, 15.

It is important to realise that *the gap between the judicial review procedure and that for the ordinary action has also narrowed because of changes in the rules governing the latter*. A central theme of the Woolf reforms was to give the courts greater control over the management of civil litigation than existed hitherto. This is apparent in the general provisions of the CPR.[184] CPR 3.4(2) enables the court to strike out a case if it discloses no cause of action, or if it is an abuse of the court's process. CPR 24 empowers the court to give summary judgment, where it considers that the claimant has no real prospect of success. Increased judicial control over ordinary litigation is also evident in the judicial interpretation of the CPR, as exemplified by *Clark*.[185] The court, as we have seen, made it clear that the CPR relating to ordinary actions would be interpreted to prevent a party gaining unwarranted procedural advantages by proceeding via an ordinary action, as opposed to judicial review.

There are nonetheless still real differences between the judicial review procedure and that for ordinary actions. Public law applicants are not entitled to pursue a case of their own accord. They must secure permission and argue their way into court, subject to a short time limit. In an ordinary action the plaintiff is entitled to proceed without any requirement of permission. The onus is on the defendant to argue that the case should be struck out, and the time limit is considerably longer.

v. The need for permission: conclusion

26–044   It is questionable whether the dichotomy between ordinary actions and those for judicial review is justifiable.[186] It was argued prior to the new CPR that suitable techniques for protecting public bodies in ordinary actions could be devised when such protection was really warranted. These could take the form of expedited procedures, and dismissal of the claim on the ground of undue delay. This choice was favoured by many academics, who were sceptical of the need for leave and short time limits.[187] It has been argued that the changes enshrined in the CPR, especially those relating to striking out and summary judgment, could be used to protect public bodies even if separate public law procedures were abolished.[188]

Many amongst the judiciary and government remained convinced that these protections were nonetheless necessary, particularly in the light of the increase in the number of applications for judicial review. It was felt that the ordinary procedures would be too cumbersome for most judicial review applications.[189]

---

[184] CPR, Pts 1, 3.
[185] n.55.
[186] P. Craig, "Procedures, Rights and Remedies" (1990) 2 E.R.P.L. 425, 437–440.
[187] S. Fredman and G. Morris, "The Costs of Exclusivity [1994] P.L. 69.
[188] Cornford and Sunkin, n.10, 15; D. Oliver, "Public Law Procedures and Remedies — Do We Need Them?" [2002] P.L. 91, 93.
[189] LCCP para.5.8; Law Commission, *Administrative Law: Judicial Review and Statutory Appeals* (Report No 226, HC 669, 1994), para.3.5; Sir John Laws, "Procedural Exclusivity", paper delivered at Robinson College, Cambridge, May 15, 1993.

The Tribunals, Courts and Enforcement Act 2007 is relevant here. It was based on the recommendations of the Leggatt Report[190] on tribunals. It is clear that those who favour the retention of the permission requirement are influenced in part by the case-load on judicial review in the ordinary courts. The Tribunals, Courts and Enforcement Act 2007 should alleviate this problem. First-tier Tribunal decisions are subject to a right of appeal on law to the Upper Tribunal, and then, subject to certain limits, to the Court of Appeal.[191] The Act also makes provision for the Upper Tribunal to exercise judicial review powers, and enables the High Court to transfer a judicial review case to an upper tribunal.[192]

D. Protecting Public Bodies: Time Limits

i. The rules on time limits
The rules on time limits and delay are complicated.[193] Before 1977 only   **26–045** certiorari was subject to a six-month time limit, albeit with a discretion to extend beyond this period which was rarely exercised. Declarations and injunctions were not subject to formal limitation periods, but delay could be a factor in the court deciding whether in its discretion to refuse relief.

The rules concerning delay were altered by the 1977 reforms. Order 53 r.4 contained the provision for delay. This was ambiguous[194] and was replaced in 1980.[195] The basic rule was that an application for permission to apply for judicial review should be made promptly, and in any event within three months from the date when grounds for the application first arose, unless the court considered that there was good reason for extending time.

Order 53 r.4 has now been replaced by CPR 54.5(1). This states that the claim form must be filed promptly and in any event not later than three months after the grounds to make the claim first arose. This rule does not apply when any other enactment specifies a shorter time limit for making the claim for judicial review, CPR 54.5(3). The time limit may not be extended by agreement between the parties, CPR 54.5(2). It can however be extended by the court, pursuant to the general power in CPR 3.1(2)(a).[196]

The Supreme Court Act 1981 s.31(6) also contains provisions on delay, but is framed in somewhat different terms. This states that where the High

---

[190] Report of the Review of Tribunals by Sir Andrew Leggatt: *Tribunals for Users — One System, One Service*, August 16, 2001, www.tribunals-review.org.uk.
[191] Tribunals, Courts and Enforcement Act 2007 ss.11–14.
[192] Tribunals, Courts and Enforcement Act 2007 ss.15–21.
[193] M. Beloff, "Time, Time, Time It's On My Side, Yes It Is", in C. Forsyth and I. Hare (eds), *The Golden Metwand and the Crooked Cord, Essays on Public Law in Honour of Sir William Wade* (Oxford University Press, 1998), 267–295.
[194] J. Beatson and M. Matthews, "Reform of Administrative Law Remedies: The First Step" (1978) 41 M.L.R. 437, 442–444.
[195] SI 1980/2000, r.3, amending Ord.53 r.4.
[196] *R. v Lichfield District Council Ex p. Lichfield Securities Ltd* [2001] 3 L.G.L.R. 35, para.28; *R. on the application of M) v School Organisation Committee, Oxford City Council* [2001] A.C.D 77, para.16.

Court considers that there has been undue delay in making an application for judicial review, the court may refuse to grant leave for making the application, or any relief sought on the application, if it considers that the granting of the relief sought would be likely to cause substantial hardship to, or substantially prejudice the rights of, any person, or would be detrimental to good administration.

There are three key differences between the formulation in CPR 54.5 and that in the Supreme Court Act, s.31(6).

(1) Section 31(6) contains no actual time limit, whereas CPR 54.5 sets a general limit of three months.

(2) Section 31(6) provides that detriment to good administration and prejudice to a party's rights are to be taken into account when there is undue delay. These factors are not found in CPR 54.5.

(3) Section 31(6) applies both at the permission stage, and at the substantive hearing, whereas CPR 54.5 applies at the permission stage.[197]

26–046 The continued existence of two provisions dealing with time limits, cast in different terms, is to be regretted. The complications flowing from this duality have been apparent for over 20 years, and continue to pose problems for the courts.[198] It would be perfectly possible for there to be a single provision dealing with time limits. The fact that this was not done pursuant to the recent CPR reforms of the judicial review procedure is all the more surprising. The rules on time limits flowing from CPR 54.5 and s.31(6) are as follows.

(1) The initial issue concerns the point at which time begins to run.[199] This may be clear in some situations, but may be less certain in others, in particular where a challenge is made to a policy determination or rule.[200] The issue is of real importance, given the need to apply promptly and the brevity of the three month period. It is possible for an applicant to be ruled out of time if the action was

---

[197] *R. v Stratford-on-Avon DC Ex p. Jackson* [1985] 1 W.L.R. 1319.
[198] See, e.g., *Lichfield*, n.196.
[199] Ord.53 r.4 stated that where an order of certiorari is sought in respect of any judgment, order, conviction or other proceeding, the date when grounds for the application first arose shall be taken to be the date of that judgment, order, conviction or proceeding. There is no such provision in CPR 54.5.
[200] In *R. v London Borough of Redbridge Ex p. G* [1991] C.O.D. 398, it was assumed that time ran from when a policy was actually made, but that the fact that the applicant had no knowledge of the policy until it was published later was regarded as a good reason for extending the time limit. However in *R. v Secretary of State for Trade and Industry Ex p. Greenpeace (No.2)* [2000] C.O.D. 141, the court held that time did not begin to run from the date of the contested regulations, since any such claim at that date would have been made in a vacuum.

brought against a later act when it should have been brought against an earlier one.[201] It was however made clear in *Burkett*[202] that it was open to a claimant to challenge an actual grant of planning permission, notwithstanding the fact that there might have been a challenge to an earlier resolution to give the planning permission. Lord Steyn stated more generally that time limits operated to bar review where a public body might have committed an abuse of power. They should be interpreted with this in mind. Courts should not therefore engage in a broad discretionary exercise of determining when the claimant could first reasonably have made the application.[203] The same rules should moreover apply irrespective of the fact that the claimant is a public interest group.[204]

(2) CPR 54.5(1)(a) requires that the decision be made promptly, and in any event within three months after the grounds to make the claim arose. These are separate requirements.[205] It is clear that applications have been held not to be prompt, even if made within three months.[206] In *Burkett*,[207] doubts were raised as to whether the obligation to act promptly was sufficiently certain to comply with the ECHR. The matter was not decided, but a number of their Lordships were concerned that the provision was too uncertain to satisfy Convention jurisprudence. However in *Hardy*[208] the Court of Appeal examined this contention in more detail and concluded that the requirement to act promptly did conform to the ECHR jurisprudence. The concerns expressed in *Burkett* should nonetheless be taken seriously: courts should hesitate before finding that a claim made in less than three months should be struck out because it was not made promptly. It was in any event made clear in *Burkett* that the three-month limit should not be regarded as having been judicially replaced by a period of six weeks.[209]

(3) When an application for leave is not made promptly, and in any event within three months, the court can refuse permission on the grounds of delay, unless it considers that there is a good reason for extending the period.[210] The court, in deciding whether to extend

---

[201] *R. v Avon County Council Ex p. Terry Adams* [1994] Env. L.R. 442; *R. v Commissioners of Customs and Excise Ex p. Eurotunnel Plc* [1995] C.O.D. 291; *R. v Secretary for Trade and Industry Ex p. Greenpeace Ltd* [1998] C.O.D. 59.
[202] *R. v London Borough of Hammersmith and Fulham Ex p. Burkett* [2002] 1 W.L.R. 1593.
[203] *Burkett*, n.202, paras 44–49, disapproving of the first *Greenpeace* case, n.201.
[204] The suggestion, in the first *Greenpeace* case, n.201, that such groups must be especially prompt was not accepted in the second *Greenpeace* case, n.200, or in *Burkett*, n.202.
[205] *Hardy v Pembrokeshire CC (Permission to Appeal)* [2006] EWCA Civ 240.
[206] *Hilditch v Westminster City Council* [1990] C.O.D. 434; *R. v ITC Ex p. T.VNi Ltd and TVS Ltd, The Times*, December 30, 1991; *R. v Minister of Agriculture, Fisheries and Food Ex p. Dairy Trade Federation* [1995] C.O.D. 3; *R. v Bath City Council Ex p. Crombie* [1995] C.O.D. 283.
[207] *Burkett*, n.202, paras 6, 53.
[208] *Burkett*, n.202, paras 11–18.
[209] *Hardy*, n.208, para.53, disapproving *R. v Ceredigion County Council Ex p. McKeown* [1998] 2 P.L.R. 1.
[210] *R. v Dairy Produce Quota Tribunal Ex p. Caswell* [1990] 2 A.C. 738.

time, will consider whether there was a reasonable objective excuse for late application, the possible impact on third-party rights, and the administration, and the general importance of the point raised.[211] The issues must be of genuinely public importance, and must be such that they could be best ventilated in the public law context.[212] The courts have held that attempting to reach a negotiated solution with the respondent will not normally be a reason for extension of time,[213] although there are some instances where this has been taken this into account.[214]

(4)   It is clear from *Caswell*[215] that where the claim is not made promptly, or within three months, there is undue delay for the purposes of the Supreme Court Act 1981 s.31(6), even if the court extends the time for making the claim. The phrase "undue delay" is the condition precedent for invoking s.31(6). The court may then have regard to hardship to third parties, and detriment to good administration, in deciding whether to refuse permission, or refuse relief at the substantive hearing. The court should not however refuse to grant permission at the substantive hearing on the basis of hardship to third parties or detriment to good administration, where permission has already been given, since it is too late to "refuse" permission in such instances. The court should rather refuse relief under s.31(6).[216]

(5)   It is clear from *Lichfield*,[217] that the same factors will generally be relevant to promptness under CPR 54.5, and undue delay under s.31(6). It is nonetheless in principle open to a court to consider undue delay at the substantive hearing, even where promptness has been considered at the permission stage. The judge at the substantive hearing should however only do so where new and relevant material is introduced at the substantive hearing, or if exceptionally the issues as developed at the substantive hearing put a different aspect on promptness, or where the first judge has overlooked a relevant matter.[218]

(6)   Where there is undue delay, it will be for the court to decide whether hardship to third parties or detriment to the administration will lead to the denial of relief. Where the impact on third party interests is insufficient in this respect, it will be rarely in the interests of good administration to leave an abuse of power uncorrected.[219]

---

[211] The second *Greenpeace* case, n.200.

[212] *R. v Secretary of State for the Home Department Ex p. Ruddock* [1987] 1 W.L.R. 1482; *R. v Collins Ex p. MS* [1998] C.O.D. 52; *School Organisation Committee*, n.196, paras 21–31.

[213] *R. v London Borough of Redbridge Ex p. G* [1991] C.O.D. 398, 400.

[214] *Owen*, n.72; A. Lindsay, "Delay in Judicial Review Cases: A Conundrum Solved?" [1995] P.L. 417, 425–426.

[215] *Caswell*, n.210.

[216] *R. v Criminal Injuries Compensation Board Ex p. A* [1999] 2 A.C. 330, 340–342.

[217] *Lichfield*, n.196, para.33.

[218] *Lichfield*, n.196, para.34.

[219] *Lichfield*, n.196, para.39.

ii. Justification for the present rules

Shorter time limits are said to be required in public law cases because of the greater need for certainty than in private law. There is a wider public interest involved in ensuring that the public service knows whether its actions will be valid or not.[220] There is clearly a need for public bodies to have certainty as to the legal validity of their actions. The following points should nonetheless be borne in mind.

First, there is no evidence that the longer limitation periods in the declaration and injunction cases decided prior to 1977 caused problems. The courts use common law concepts of delay, acquiescence and personal bar to control untimely actions.[221] The Law Commission was however against abandoning specific time limits for public law proceedings and against relying on the ordinary limitation periods for civil actions. It believed that the existing three-month period was desirable,[222] subject to a discretion to admit cases beyond this period.

Second, in so far as there is a need for short time limits, this is undermined by allowing applicants with private rights to proceed outside s.31.[223] It is true, as we have seen, that in *Clark*[224] the court held that it would exercise control over the time in which ordinary actions were brought, where such actions entailed a challenge to the legality of a public body's decision. It nonetheless remains to be seen how often a court will exercise this power where the claimant in an ordinary action is bringing the claim well within the six year limit, albeit beyond three months.

Third, there are a number of techniques for dealing with this problem. In areas where there is a high premium on certainty, specific statutory provision could be made to ensure that the challenge was brought within a certain defined period. Such provisions are already common in legislation concerning planning. The exercise of discretion in granting particular types of relief, and the development of prospective as opposed to retrospective invalidity, could also be employed to resolve problems in particular cases. Moreover, the CPR vest the courts with greater control over actions in general. *Clark*[225] shows the court's willingness to interpret the CPR rules to control the timing of ordinary actions that involve a challenge to the legality of a public body's decision.

The final comment on time limits is somewhat different. The increase in the volume of applications for judicial review has been a principal reason for the retention of the permission requirement. The short time limits may, in a

26-047

26-048

---

[220] *O'Reilly v Mackman* [1983] 2 A.C. 237, 249.
[221] Lord Clyde and D. Edwards, *Judicial Review* (Green, 2000), para.13.4.; *Burkett*, n.202, paras 59–66.
[222] Law Commission Report, n.179, para.5.26.
[223] Beatson, n.64, 44–45.
[224] *Clark*, n.55.
[225] *Clark*, n.55.

paradoxical sense, increase the amount of litigation against the administration.[226] An individual who believes that the public body has acted ultra vires now has the strongest incentive to seek a *judicial resolution* of the matter immediately, as opposed to attempting a *negotiated solution*, quite simply because if the individual forbears from suing he or she may be deemed not to have applied promptly or within the three-month time limit.[227] This has been acknowledged by the courts.[228]

> "[A]ny citizen who had a problem with local government, or with any other bureaucracy, was faced with a choice: he could either seek by political means to influence the decision, or could consider whether he had any legal remedy. If he elected to adopt the first course, and achieved nothing, he could not rely on that as a ground for extending time."

It is therefore unsurprising if legal advisers tell their clients that an application for judicial review should be made at once, rather than attempting to negotiate a solution first. Negotiated solutions are of course possible once litigation has begun. However, the existence of a formal suit can polarise existing positions, rendering each party more intransigent. There is in this sense a tension between the rules on time limits and the desire, expressed forcefully by Lord Woolf,[229] that individuals should have resort to any dispute resolution mechanism before seeking judicial review.

Lord Woolf C.J. returned to this theme in the *Cowl* case.[230] He stated that litigation should be avoided wherever possible, and that maximum use should be made of alternative dispute resolution (ADR), and complaints procedures. It was held that the court could, of its own initiative, hold an inter partes hearing, at which the parties would be asked what use they had made of such procedures. There is obvious good sense behind the drive to use ADR. Legal advisers will however only be able to advise their clients to use such mechanisms, if they feel that this will not prejudice a claim for review by it being declared out of time.

E. The Exclusivity Principle

26–049 The "fate" of the exclusivity principle is, as stated above, intimately connected with the decision as to whether special protections for public bodies, in terms of permission and time limits, should be retained. *If* one believes that special protections are needed for public bodies then this requires rules

---

[226] A similar point is made by Bridges, Meszaros and Sunkin, n.173. They argued that a somewhat longer time limit before applications have to be lodged, *combined with* fuller information on the reasons for the disputed decision, might facilitate pre-leave settlement and hence reduce the workload of the courts.

[227] This was recognised in *Burkett*, n.202, para.53.

[228] *R. v London Borough of Redbridge Ex p. G* [1991] C.O.D. 398, 400.

[229] Lord Woolf, *Access to Justice: The Final Report to the Lord Chancellor on the Civil Justice System in England and Wales* (1997), 251.

[230] *Cowl v Plymouth City Council* [2002] 1 W.L.R. 803; *Practice Statement (Administrative Court: Listing and Urgent Cases)* [2002] 1 W.L.R. 810.

to prevent those protections from being side-stepped. It is of course possible to have a unified procedure *if* one assumes that the protections are not required, or that any needs of public bodies could simply be met by the ordinary rules of civil procedure.[231]

This is reflected in the three options canvassed by the Law Commission in its discussion of the exclusivity principle.[232]

The principle could be abolished, with the consequence that there would be no special rules for dealing with public law cases. The Law Commission did not favour this option, and it has not been adopted in the recent changes to civil procedure. CPR 54 has retained a separate procedure for judicial review, with the distinctive features of permission and short time limits.

The principle could be extended, with the consequence that the current exceptions to the principle would cease to operate. The experience of the last decade has shown that cases involving public law can arise in a number of ways. To impose requirements of permission *and* short time limits in all instances could well cause hardship to litigants, and would run counter to the courts' jurisprudence, which had built upon the exceptions to *O'Reilly*. It was therefore not surprising that this option did not find favour with the Law Commission.

The boundaries of the principle could be delineated more clearly. Cases involving private rights could be brought by ordinary action outside CPR 54. The judicial review procedure would be required only in pure public law cases. The Law Commission endorsed this position in its Report.[233] This is broadly the view the courts have adopted. There are, as seen, problems with this "result". However, given that exclusivity was unlikely to be abolished, or extended to all proceedings, this option was inevitable.

F. Disclosure and Inspection

We have already seen the role played by discovery in the 1977 reforms. The reforms made improved provision for discovery, and this was regarded in *O'Reilly* as part of the justification for procedural exclusivity. The reality is that discovery is rarely awarded in judicial review proceedings, because of the cost and time implications.[234] The normal criterion was that discovery would be allowed when it was necessary either for disposing fairly of the cause or for saving costs.[235]

26–050

The problem for the individual can be formidable. It can be extremely difficult to sustain certain types of challenge without discovery, and cross-examination. Allegations that an administrator has taken irrelevant considerations into account, or has acted for improper purposes, are but two

---

[231] S. Fredman and G. Morris, "The Costs of Exclusivity: Public and Private Re-examined" [1994] P.L. 69, 83–84.
[232] Law Commission Consultation Paper No.126, *Administrative Law and Statutory Appeals* (1993), 18–19, hereafter LCCP.
[233] Law Commission Report, n.179, para.3.15, 25.
[234] n.25.
[235] RSC Ord.24 r.13(1).

such instances. The need for discovery will, moreover, be needed if the courts are to develop emerging doctrines such as proportionality. Openness of decision-making is of real importance, but as Gordon notes, "the restrictive rules that have bedevilled discovery in recent years only permit access to documentation where such is necessary to undermine an apparent lack of candour in the affidavits lodged".[236] It is moreover clear from the empirical work done by Le Sueur and Sunkin that the most common reason for refusing permission was that the claimant could not, without discovery, establish the factual foundation for the case so as to convince the judge that the claim was arguable.[237]

It remains to be seen how far the CPR make any difference in this respect. It should be noted that CPR 54 is regarded as a modification of CPR 8, which deals with claims where there is no substantial dispute as to fact. CPR 31 deals with disclosure and inspection of documents. A party discloses a document by stating that the document exists or has existed.[238] A party to whom a document has been disclosed has, subject to certain exceptions, a right to inspect it.[239] An order to give disclosure is, unless the court otherwise directs, an order to give standard disclosure.[240] It is open to the court to dispense with or limit standard disclosure.[241] Where a court does make such an order then it requires a party to disclose the documents on which it relies, and the documents which adversely affect its own, or another party's, case, or support another party's case, and such documents which it is required to disclose by a relevant practice direction.[242] A party is under an obligation to make a reasonable search for such documents.[243] The court is also empowered to make an order for specific disclosure or specific inspection, requiring the party to disclose those documents specified in the order.[244] There is little doubt that these rules give the court ample powers through which to require the public body to provide the information needed for the applicant to sustain its case. It is, however, open to the court to dispense with or limit standard disclosure, and the court also has discretion in relation to requests for more specific disclosure. Much will, therefore, depend upon how the courts use the powers at their disposal.[245]

26–051   The House of Lords' decision in *Tweed* is important in this respect.[246] The claimant sought judicial review of a decision placing restrictions on a parade in Northern Ireland, on the ground that it infringed his rights to assembly and free speech protected by the Human Rights Act 1998. He sought disclosure of documents referred to in an affidavit sworn by the chairman of

---

[236] n.179, 16.
[237] n.162, 102.
[238] CPR 31.2.
[239] CPR 31.3.
[240] CPR 31.5(1).
[241] CPR 31.5(2).
[242] CPR 31.6.
[243] CPR 31.7(1).
[244] CPR 31.12.
[245] See *Three Rivers DC v Bank of England (Disclosure) (No.1)* [2003] 1 W.L.R. 210 for analysis of disclosure from a person who is not a party to the case, pursuant to CPR 31.17.
[246] *Tweed v Parades Commission for Northern Ireland* [2007] 1 A.C. 650.

the Parades Commission, which made the decision. Their Lordships acknowledged that disclosure had been ordered less readily in judicial review cases than in ordinary actions, in part at least because judicial review cases often turned on issues of law rather than fact.

They held that disclosure would however be more necessary in judicial review cases raising issues of proportionality. This was so in the instant case, since the decision of the Parades Commission that imposed restrictions on Convention rights had to be proportionate. The disclosure of documents referred to in affidavits would not however always take place where proportionality was in issue. The proportionality issue formed part of the context in which the court had to consider whether it was necessary for fairly disposing of the case to order the disclosure of such documents. It did not give rise automatically to the need for the disclosure of all the documents. Whether disclosure should be ordered would depend on a balancing of several factors, of which proportionality was only one, albeit one of some significance. In cases involving issues of proportionality, disclosure should be carefully limited to the issues which required it in the interests of justice.

Their Lordships also modified the previous practice concerning disclosure and general judicial review actions. The House of Lords held that disclosure would only be necessary in limited cases, but that it was no longer the rule that disclosure would only be ordered where the decision-maker's affidavit could be shown to be materially inaccurate or misleading and the courts should now adopt a more flexible, less prescriptive approach and judge the need for disclosure on the facts of the individual case to see whether it was required to resolve the matter fairly and justly.[247]

There are also some decisions showing a greater willingness to order cross-examination in judicial review proceedings. Thus in *Wilkinson*[248] the Court of Appeal held that cross-examination should be ordered where there was a challenge to a decision to administer medical treatment to a patient in judicial review proceedings. The court would have to form its own view as to whether the treatment infringed the applicant's human rights, and cross-examination would be required in order to do this where there were disputed questions of fact. This decision must however be seen in the light of the ruling by the Court of Appeal in *N*.[249] It held that it should not often be necessary to adduce oral evidence with cross-examination where there are disputed issues of fact and opinion in cases where the need for forcible medical treatment of a patient is being challenged on human rights grounds, and that *Wilkinson* should not be regarded as a charter for routine applications to the court for oral evidence in human rights cases generally. Much would depend on the nature of the right that had allegedly been breached, and the nature of the alleged breach.

[247] *Tweed*, n.246, paras 3, 32, 56.
[248] *R. (on the application of Wilkinson) v Broadmoor Special Health Authority* [2002] 1 W.L.R. 419; *R. (on the application of B) v Haddock (Responsible Medical Officer)* [2006] EWCA Civ 961.
[249] *R. (on the application of N) v M* [2003] 1 W.L.R. 562, paras 36, 39.

G. Conclusion

26–052 There is no doubt that the CPR have narrowed the differences between the judicial review procedure, and that in ordinary actions. The former has become more inter partes, and to that extent more like an ordinary action. The latter are now subject to greater judicial control pursuant to the general strategy behind the Woolf reforms.

There are nonetheless still real differences between the two forms of procedure. CPR 54 has retained the essential features of Ord.53, the need for permission, plus the short time limits. There continue to be differences of view as to whether these protections are needed, and whether, if they are, they could be provided in the context of ordinary actions, without the need for a separate judicial review procedure.

5. PROCEDURE

A. Permission

26–053 A claimant must seek permission to apply for judicial review, CPR 54.4, and the application must be made promptly and in any event within three months after the grounds for making it first arose, CPR 54. 5. The court has powerful weapons to deter vexatious litigants.[250] The claim for judicial review is made using the CPR 8 claim form, which must in addition to the usual requirements state the following information, CPR 54.6. The claimant must give the name and address of any person considered to be an interested party. The claimant must state that he is requesting permission to seek judicial review, and the remedy being claimed. Where the claimant is raising a point under the HRA, he must specify, inter alia, the Convention right alleged to have been infringed. A Practice Direction issued pursuant to CPR 54 stipulates that the claim form must also state, or be accompanied by, inter alia, a detailed statement of the claimant's grounds for bringing the claim, a statement of the facts relied on, copies of documents relied on by the claimant, relevant statutory material, and a copy of any order that the claimant seeks to have quashed.[251]

The claim form must be served on the defendant and other interested parties within seven days of the date of issue, CPR 54.7. If a person served with the claim form wishes to take part in the judicial review proceedings, he or she must acknowledge service within 21 days of being served, CPR 54.8(2)(a). This acknowledgement must be served on the claimant and any other person named in the claim form, CPR 54.8(2)(b). The acknowledgement must state whether the person intends to contest the claim, the grounds for doing so, and give the names and addresses of any other person

---

[250] *Bhamjee v Forsdick* [2004] 1 W.L.R. 88.
[251] Practice Direction (PD) 54, paras 5.6–5.7.

considered to be an interested party, CPR 54.8(4). A person who fails to file an acknowledgement is not allowed to take part in the permission hearing, unless the court allows him to do so, CPR 54.9(1). There is provision for urgent cases.[252]

The criterion that applies to the grant of permission has been considered above.[253] Permission will not be granted unless the applicant has a sufficient interest in the matter to which the application relates.[254] Where permission is given the court may give directions, which may include a stay of the proceedings to which the claim relates, CPR 54.10. Permission decisions will often be made without a hearing. The court is obliged to provide reasons for its decision, CPR 54.12(2). A claimant that is refused permission without a hearing may not appeal, but may request, within seven days, for the decision to be reconsidered at a hearing, CPR. 54.12(3). It is not however open to the defendant or any other person served with the claim form to apply to have the permission set aside, CPR 54.14. Where permission has been refused after a hearing, the applicant may apply to the Court of Appeal for permission to appeal, which may, instead of giving permission to appeal, give permission for judicial review, CPR 52.15. The case will then be heard in the High Court unless the Court of Appeal indicates to the contrary, CPR 52.15(4).

B. The Substantive Hearing

The defendant and any other person served with the claim form who wishes to contest the claim, or support it on additional grounds, must provide detailed grounds for doing so, together with any written evidence, CPR 54.14. This must be done within 35 days of service of the order giving permission. A claimant must seek the court's permission to rely on grounds other than those for which he has been given permission to proceed, CPR 54.15. Written evidence may not be relied on unless it has been served in accordance with a rule under CPR 54, or direction of the court, or the court gives permission, CPR 54.16. Any person may apply for permission to file evidence, or make representations at the judicial review hearing, CPR 54.17.[255] The court may decide the claim for judicial review without a hearing where all the parties agree, CPR 54.18.

Where a quashing order is sought, the court may remit the matter to the decision-maker, directing it to reconsider the matter in the light of the court's judgment. Where the court considers that this would serve no useful purpose, it may in addition, subject to any statutory provision, substitute its own decision for the decision in question. However it can only substitute its

26–054

---

[252] Practice Statement (Administrative Court: Administration of Justice) [2002] A.C.D 64.
[253] See above, para.26–039.
[254] Supreme Court Act 1981 s.31(3). See above, Ch.24.
[255] *R. (on the application of the Howard League for Penal Reform) v Secretary of State for the Home Department (No.1)* [2002] EWHC 1750; *R. v National Lottery Commission Ex p. Camelot Group Plc* [2001] E.M.L.R. 3, para.3; M. Fordham, " 'Public Interest' Intervention: A Practitioner's Perspective [2007] PL 410.

own decision if the decision in question was made by a court or tribunal, the decision was quashed for error of law and without the error there was only one lawful decision that the court or tribunal could have reached.[256] If the court does substitute its decision in accord with the previous conditions then, unless the High Court otherwise directs, the substituted decision takes effect as if it were a decision of the relevant court or tribunal.[257]

There are provisions allowing cases to be transferred to and from the Administrative Court, CPR 30. It is open to the court to order a claim to continue as if it had been started under CPR 54, and to give directions about the future management of the claim, CPR 54.20. It is also open to the court, where the relief sought is a declaration or injunction, and the court considers that such relief should not be granted in a claim for judicial review, to order that the case continue as a common law claim under CPR 7. There are also provisions concerning the transfer of cases to and from the High Court[258] pursuant to the new power accorded by the Tribunals, Courts and Enforcement Act 2007 to the Upper Tribunal to exercise judicial review functions.[259]

Where the parties have agreed on terms for resolving the case, an order may be obtained from the court to put the agreement into effect, without the need for a hearing. It will be for the judge to decide whether the case can be resolved in this manner.[260] If the judge decides that it would not be appropriate to make such an order, then the case will be heard in the normal manner.

There is power to make a protective costs order, to allow claimants of limited means access to the court without the fear of substantial orders for costs being made against them.[261] Such an order may be made at any stage of the proceedings, on such conditions as the court thinks fit, provided that the court is satisfied that: the issues raised are of general public importance; the public interest requires that those issues be resolved; the applicant has no private interest in the outcome of the case; having regard to the financial resources of the applicant and the respondent and to the amount of costs that are likely to be involved, it is fair and just to make the order; if the order is not made the applicant will probably discontinue the proceedings and will be acting reasonably in so doing. If those acting for the applicant are doing so pro bono, that will be likely to enhance the merits of the application for a protective costs order.

---

[256] Supreme Court Act 1981 s.31(5)–(5A), as amended by the Tribunals, Courts and Enforcement Act 2007 s.141.
[257] Supreme Court Act 1981 s.31(5B), as amended by the Tribunals, Courts and Enforcement Act 2007 s.141.
[258] Supreme Court Act 1981 s.31A, as amended by the Tribunals, Courts and Enforcement Act 2007 s.19.
[259] Tribunals, Courts and Enforcement Act 2007 ss.15–19. See above, Ch.9.
[260] PD 54, para.17.
[261] *R. (on the application of Corner House Research) v Secretary of State for Trade and Industry* [2005] 1 W.L.R. 2600.

C. Discretion to Refuse Relief

We have already seen that the courts exercise discretion in deciding whether **26–055** to grant a remedy, and take into account a variety of factors. These include waiver, bad faith, the premature nature of the application, the absence of any injustice, the impact on third parties and the administration, and whether the decision would have been the same irrespective of the error.[262]

Whether they ought to do so is a matter on which opinions could well differ. Lord Bingham expressed the view that such discretion is acceptable provided that it is strictly limited and the rules for its exercise are clearly understood.[263] There is much to be said for this view. Two further comments are in order.

The first is that, as Lord Bingham clearly accepts, differing considerations should apply to the various grounds for refusing relief. Commentators have, for example, been critical of decisions denying a remedy where there has been a failure to comply with natural justice, because the court believed that the outcome would not have been different.[264] It is doubtful whether this should ever be a ground for refusing relief, and the strong judgment by Lord Bingham pointing out the dangers of denying relief on this ground is to be welcomed.[265] This may be contrasted with the situation where the court decides not to award a coercive order because the respondent authority is doing all that it can to comply with its statutory duty,[266] where the error has been substantially cured,[267] where the problem is now moot,[268] or where there would be serious public inconvenience in upsetting the impugned order.[269]

The second comment is as follows. The discretion to refuse relief operates *against* the individual when the public body has committed an ultra vires act. This is so whether the discretion assumes the form of denying the remedy entirely, or rendering the relief only prospectively rather than retrospectively applicable. Either way the ultra vires principle is being qualified for good reason. If we are willing to do this then we should also be willing to qualify the ultra vires principle *in favour* of the individual in circumstances where, for example, a person has relied upon an ultra vires representation and has suffered loss, provided that there are no dire consequences for the public interest.[270]

---

[262] See above, Ch.25.
[263] "Should Public Law Remedies be Discretionary?" [1991] P.L. 64.
[264] See above, Ch.12.
[265] *R. v Chief Constable of the Thames Valley Police Forces Ex p. Cotton* [1990] I.R.L.R. 344. Courts have, however, held that in cases of failure to comply with the rules on bias because of a pecuniary interest the court may in its discretion refuse relief, *R. v Governors of Bacon's School Ex p. Inner London Education Authority* [1990] C.O.D. 414.
[266] *R. v Bristol Corporation Ex p. Hendy* [1974] 1 W.L.R. 498.
[267] *R. v Secretary of State for Social Services Ex p. AMA* [1986] 1 W.L.R. 1.
[268] See above, Ch.25.
[269] *R. v Secretary of State for Social Services Ex p. AMA* [1993] C.O.D. 54.
[270] See above, Ch.20.

6. The Effect of Alternative Remedies

A. Choice of Remedies under CPR 54

26–056   The traditional view was that the availability of prerogative relief did not operate as a bar to seeking a declaration.[271] The position may now have changed. The removal of many of the restrictions upon the prerogative orders, and the availability of all the remedies under a unified procedure, has inclined some courts to the view that the prerogative orders should be used whenever the validity of a decision is attacked.[272] Notwithstanding this, it is common for claimants to seek a declaration when challenging the legality of a public body's action.

B. Alternative Statutory Remedies

26–057   The effect of statutory appeal procedures upon the availability of judicial review[273] raises two issues which, although linked, should be distinguished.

First, while it is clear that the existence of such a procedure does not operate as a jurisdictional bar to judicial review, it is less clear how far such a procedure creates a presumption that resort should be had to that procedure rather than judicial review. In *Preston*[274] the House of Lords stated that judicial review should only rarely be available if an appellate procedure existed. This may be contrasted with the more liberal approach of Lord Denning M.R. in the *Paddington Valuation* case,[275] where his Lordship stated that review would be available where the alternative appellate procedure was "nowhere near so convenient, beneficial and effectual". The courts have on the whole adopted the approach in *Preston*. Lord Woolf,

---

[271] *Pyx Granite Co. Ltd v Ministry of Housing and Local Government* [1960] A.C. 260, 290.
[272] *Cocks v Thanet District Council* [1983] 2 A.C. 286.
[273] C. Lewis, "The Exhaustion of Alternative Remedies" [1992] C.L.J. 138; J. Beatson, "Prematurity and Ripeness for Review", in Forsyth and Hare, n.193, 229–235.
[274] *R. v Inland Revenue Commissioners Ex p. Preston* [1985] A.C. 835, 852, 862. See also, *R. v Poplar Borough Council (No.1) Ex p. London County Council* [1922] 1 K.B. 72, 84–85, 88, 94; *R. v Epping and Harlow General Commissioners Ex p. Goldstraw* [1983] 3 All E.R. 257, 262; *R. v Chief Constable of the Merseyside Police Ex p. Calveley* [1986] Q.B. 424, 433–434; *Pasmore v Oswaldtwistle Urban District Council* [1898] A.C. 387, 394; *R. v Panel on Take-Overs and Mergers Ex p. Guiness plc* [1990] 1 Q.B. 146; *R. v Police Complaints Authority Ex p. Wells* [1991] C.O.D. 95; *R. v Special Educational Needs Tribunal Ex p. Fairpo* [1996] C.O.D. 180; *R. v Secretary of State for the Home Department Ex p. Capti-Mehmet* [1997] C.O.D. 61; *R. v Secretary of State for the Home Department Ex p. Watts* [1997] C.O.D. 152; *R. v Falmouth and Truro Port Health Authority Ex p. South West Water Ltd* [2001] Q.B. 445, 472–473, 476, 486; *R. (on the application of Sivasubramaniam) v Wandsworth County Court* [2002] EWCA Civ 1738; *R. (on the application of G) v Immigration Appeal Tribunal* [2005] 1 W.L.R. 1445; *R. (on the application of Sinclair Gardens Investments (Kensington) Ltd) v Lands Tribunal* [2005] EWCA Civ 1305.
[275] *R. v Paddington Valuation Officer Ex p. Peachey Property Corporation* [1966] 1 QB 380, 400. See also, *R. v Leicester Guardians* [1899] 2 QB 632, 638–639; *R. v North Ex p. Oakey* [1927] 1 K.B. 491; *Stepney Borough Council v John Walker and Sons Ltd* [1934] A.C. 365; *Ex p. Jarrett* (1946) 52 T.L.R. 230.

writing extra-judicially,[276] has stated that judicial review should normally be a matter of last resort. Lord Woolf C.J. returned to this theme in *Cowl*.[277] He stated that litigation should be avoided wherever possible, and that maximum use should be made of alternative dispute resolution (ADR), and complaints procedures. The court could, of its own initiative, hold an inter partes hearing, at which the parties would be asked what use they had made of such procedures.

Second, the courts have nonetheless been willing to recognise exceptions and allow the judicial review application. A number of factors can be identified which the courts will take into account in deciding whether to allow an application for judicial review, even though an alternative appellate structure exists.

(1) Judicial review is unlikely to be ousted where doubt exists as to whether a right of appeal exists,[278] or whether such an appellate right covers the circumstances of the case.[279]

(2) Judicial review will also be available where the statutory appeal mechanism is deemed inadequate as compared to judicial review. Thus in *Leech*,[280] a prisoner was allowed to seek judicial review of a disciplinary decision reached by a prison governor, notwithstanding the existence of a petition procedure to the Secretary of State. Their Lordships were influenced by the fact that the Secretary of State did not have the formal power to quash the disciplinary decision reached by the governor, but merely the power to remit the punishment inflicted on the prisoner.

(3) In deciding whether to allow an applicant to use judicial review the courts will take into account more general factors concerning the nature of the appellate procedure, and consider how onerous it is for the individual to be restricted to the statutory mechanism. This is clearly sensible, although the results of this analysis may appear unjust. Thus in *Calveley*,[281] the court took account of the fact that the alternative procedure was likely to be slow, and thus allowed police officers to seek judicial review. However, in *Swati*,[282] an immigrant was restricted to the statutory appeals procedure, save in exceptional circumstances, notwithstanding the fact that this entailed leaving the United Kingdom in order to avail himself of that right.

---

[276] Lord Woolf, "Judicial Review: A Possible Programme for Reform" [1992] P.L. 221, 235.
[277] n.230.
[278] *R. v Hounslow London Borough Council Ex p. Pizzey* [1977] 1 W.L.R. 58, 62; *R. v Board of Visitors of Hull Prison Ex p. St. Germain* [1979] Q.B. 425, 456, 465.
[279] *Preston* [1985] A.C. 835, 862.
[280] *Leech v Deputy Governor of Parkhurst Prison* [1988] A.C. 533.
[281] [1986] Q.B. 424, 434, 440.
[282] *R. v Secretary of State for the Home Department Ex p. Swati* [1986] 1 W.L.R. 477; *Doorga*, n.164, 111.

(4) The courts have in the past held that review is more likely to be available where the alleged error is one of law. Thus in the *Paddington Valuation* case,[283] Lord Denning M.R. stated that while the statutory appeal procedures might be suitable for individual challenges to the rating list, review was more appropriate where the legality of the whole rating list was impugned. Similarly in *Royco Homes*,[284] Lord Widgery C.J. felt that review was particularly well suited to errors of law. In *Wells*,[285] it was held that while an applicant should normally be left to pursue the statutory remedy, judicial review would be available if the tribunal had plainly misdirected itself on a matter of law. The general attitude of the courts has, however, changed somewhat. The mere existence of an alleged error of law will not in itself serve to displace the presumption that statutory appeal procedures should be used.[286]

(5) An applicant is likely to be restricted to the statutory appeal procedure where the case turns on mixed questions of law and fact,[287] disputed questions of fact, the appellate tribunal possesses expertise,[288] or where issues of criminal law are involved.[289]

(6) The reforms contained in the Tribunals, Courts and Enforcement Act 2007 may well lead the courts to insist that the possibilities of appeal or judicial review within the tribunal system should be used before any possible recourse to judicial review before the High Court.

(7) The long-standing supervisory jurisdiction exercised over magistrates should generally continue to be exercised notwithstanding rights of appeal to the Crown Court.[290]

C. Conclusion

26–058   The courts have been mindful not to usurp Parliament's choice where it has established a special statutory mechanism to adjudicate on a particular topic. The assumption that litigants must use available statutory machinery has also been influenced by the courts' desire to control the case load on judicial review. Specialised statutory appeal mechanisms may, in addition, be better suited to resolving complex issues of fact, and possess expertise in

---

[283] [1966] 1 Q.B. 380.
[284] *R. v Hillingdon London Borough Council Ex p. Royco Homes Ltd* [1974] Q.B. 720; *Pyx Granite*, n.271.
[285] *Wells*, n.274; *R. v Devon County Council Ex p. Baker* [1993] 1 All E.R. 73.
[286] See cases, n.274.
[287] *R. v Epping Forest District Council Ex p. Green* [1993] C.O.D. 81.
[288] *Clark v Epsom Rural District Council* [1929] 1 Ch.287; *Preston* [1985] A.C. 835; *Smeeton v Att-Gen* [1920] 1 Ch.85; *Coney v Choyce* [1975] 1 W.L.R. 422, 434; *Hilditch v Westminster City Council* [1990] C.O.D. 434.
[289] *R. v DPP Ex p. Camelot Group Ltd* [1998] C.O.D. 54.
[290] *R. v Hereford Magistrates' Court Ex p. Rowlands* [1998] Q.B. 110.

the relevant area. These are sensible considerations for the courts to take into account. However, as the Law Commission stated,[291] there may well be advantages in determining the effect of alternative remedies at the permission stage.

7. Conclusion

There will be no attempt to summarise the entirety of the discussion in this **26–059** and the previous chapter concerning remedies. Cane has rightly pointed out that the way in which we think about remedies in public law should not however be taken for granted. The applicant is presently required to choose from the range of remedies on offer, and these remedies may be subject to technical limitations. The applicant cannot come to court, state the desired object and then ask the court to select a remedy to achieve this end.[292]

> "Just as, under the modern system of pleading, claimants plead facts and ask the court to recognise those facts as giving rise to a cause of action in law, so public law claimants should be free to specify the result they want to achieve by their claim and ask the court to provide an appropriate remedy. A claimant should not be required to specify which remedy is sought; rather it should be for the court to decide if a remedy is available to achieve the claimant's desired end."

---

[291] LCCP, n.232, para.14.14.
[292] "The Constitutional Basis of Judicial Remedies in Public Law", in P. Leyland and T. Woods (eds), *Administrative Law Facing the Future: Old Constraints and New Horizons* (Blackstone, 1997), 245.

CHAPTER 27

REMEDIES: EXCLUSION OF REVIEW

1. COMPLETE EXCLUSION

Ever since Coke, Holt and Mansfield laid the foundations for judicial review   27–001
the legislature has attempted to prevent those principles from being applied.
Various formulae have been inserted into legislation with the intent of
precluding judicial intervention. These efforts have not been successful, as
the courts have time and again restrictively construed such legislation. The
interpretation given to ouster clauses will be considered in this section, to be
followed by discussion of clauses that limit rather than exclude the courts
totally.

A. Finality Clauses

Finality clauses are statutory terms that purport to render the decision of a   27–002
particular agency unassailable. The courts have given them short shrift,
holding that they only protect decisions made on facts and not law.[1] Jurisdictional defects were not immune from judicial scrutiny by such clauses,[2]
nor were errors on the face of the record. Thus, in *Gilmore*[3] it was held that
the decision of the tribunal was open to attack despite the existence of a
finality clause. Denning L.J. reviewed the authorities and concluded that the
only effect of the clause was to prevent an appeal. Judicial review, whether
for jurisdictional error or error on the face of the record, remained
unimpaired.[4]

---

[1] *R. v Plowright* (1686) 3 Mod. 94.
[2] *R. v Moreley* (1760) 2 Burr 1040; *R. v Jukes* (1800) 8 T.R. 542; *cf.* where certiorari is the
creature of statute, *R. v Hunt* (1856) 6 El. & Bl. 409.
[3] *R. v Medical Appeal Tribunal Ex p. Gilmore* [1957] 1 Q.B. 574.
[4] *Gilmore*, n.3, 583–585. See also, *R. v Nat Bell Liquors Ltd* [1922] 2 A.C. 128, 159–160; *R. (on
the application of Sivasubramaniam) v Wandsworth County Court* [2002] EWCA Civ 1738, paras
43–45.

Even this limited effect has been subsequently diminished. Thus the high authority that a finality clause can prevent an appeal[5] has been characterised as out of date. The Court of Appeal has held that, notwithstanding the existence of finality provisions, it was still possible to state a case, at least where declaration or certiorari would themselves have been available.[6]

B. "No Certiorari" Clauses

27–003   Part of the reason for the legislative dislike of judicial review was that the courts could overturn decisions for technical errors with an excess of vigour that bordered upon the pedantic. The legislature responded, inter alia, by the insertion of no certiorari clauses within statutes. The judiciary acknowledged that they had been over-technical.[7]

Jurisdictional defects continued, however, to remain unaffected by no certiorari clauses.[8] In *R. v Wood*[9] a byelaw compelling home owners to remove snow from in front of their houses was attacked as ultra vires the parent legislation. The statute concerned the removal of dirt, manure, dung and soil. Lord Campbell C.J. held that the no certiorari clause was ineffective. The Secretary of State could only give authority to byelaws which were in conformity with the parent legislation, and Lord Campbell rejected any generic identity between these substances and snow.[10]

"It might possibly have been advisable to extend the power to the case of all snow; but that is not done: the words of the section cannot, by any strain of construction, be extended to untrodden and unsunned snow, which is proverbially pure."

Such clauses, while ineffective to insulate jurisdictional error, could exclude review for error of law on the face of the record, while this concept still had currency. If the clause is contained in a statute enacted prior to August 1958 it will be subject to the Tribunals and Inquiries Act which will be discussed below.

Where, however, the preclusive clause is contained in a statute passed after that date, it can be effective, as exemplified by the *South East Asia Fire*[11] case. The Malaysian Industrial Relations Act 1967 s.29(3)(a) contained an "omnibus" exclusion clause. Parliamentary draftsmen had obviously decided that, *ceteris paribus*, the more types of exclusions the better. Thus, s.29(3)(a) contained a finality clause, a shall not be challenged

---

[5] *Kydd v Liverpool Watch Committee* [1908] A.C. 327; *Piper v St. Marylebone Licensing JJ* [1928] 2 K.B. 221.
[6] *Tehrani v Rostron* [1972] 1 Q.B. 182, 187–188, 192. See also, *Pearlman v Keepers and Governors of Harrow School* [1979] Q.B. 56, 68–69, 79, *cf.* 74.
[7] *R. v Ruyton (Inhabitants)* (1861) 1 B. & S. 534, 545; *Gilmore*, n.3, 586.
[8] *R. v Cheltenham Commissioners* (1841) 1 Q.B. 467; *R. v Somersetshire JJ* (1826) 5 B. & C. 816.
[9] (1855) 5 El. & Bl. 49.
[10] (1855) 5 El. & Bl. 49, 55. See also *Ex p. Bradlaugh* [1878] 3 Q.B.D 509, 512–513.
[11] *South East Asia Fire Bricks Sdn Bhd v Non-Metallic Mineral Products Manufacturing Employees Union* [1981] A.C. 363.

or questioned section, and a term providing that awards of the industrial court should not be quashed. A dispute between a company and a union was referred to the industrial court, which found in favour of the union. The company sought to have this quashed for error of law on the face of the record.

The Privy Council declined to interfere. Lord Fraser, giving judgment, agreed with the company's argument that the finality provision did not protect the industrial court.[12] The provision within s.29(3)(a) that an award should not be quashed was however sufficient to achieve this end. If it would not suffice by itself, the addition of the words "shall not be called in question in any court of law" were wide enough to cover certiorari. Only errors of law within jurisdiction were immune from attack.[13] A jurisdictional error could still be impugned. The Privy Council rejected the argument that any error of law was now to be regarded as jurisdictional, but, as we have seen, later developments have effectively spelt the end for the concept of error of law within jurisdiction.[14] The expansion of jurisdictional error means that it will be difficult for the legislature to employ this clause to exclude the courts.

C. "Shall not be Questioned" Clauses

Another formula used to exclude the courts has been the "shall not be questioned clause". Any hope that persevering parliamentary draftsmen might have had that this formula would work where all else had failed was to prove unfounded.

27–004

In *Anisminic*,[15] s.4(4) of the Foreign Compensation Act 1950 stated that a determination of the Commission should not be called in question in any court of law. Their Lordships unanimously held that this only protected intra vires determinations. Ultra vires determinations were not really determinations at all. They were nullities, which could be of no effect. Section 4(4), or any equivalent provision, could, therefore, only immunise from attack errors of law within jurisdiction and this concept has itself now largely ceased to exist.[16]

D. "As if Enacted" and "Conclusive Evidence"

A different technique has been used to insulate subordinate legislation, by providing that a statutory order shall have effect "as if enacted in this Act", or that confirmation by a designated minister "shall be conclusive evidence

27–005

---

[12] [1981] A.C. 363, 369–370 following *Gilmore*, n.3. See also, *Re Waldron* [1986] Q.B. 824.
[13] [1981] A.C. 363, 370.
[14] See above, Ch.14.
[15] *Anisminic Ltd v Foreign Compensation Commission* [1969] 2 A.C. 147, 170–171, 181, 200–201, 210; *R. v Secretary of State for the Home Department Ex p. Mehta* [1992] C.O.D. 484.
[16] *Cf. R. v Acting Returning Officer for the Devon and East Plymouth European Constituency Ex p. Sanders* [1994] C.O.D. 497, distinguishing *Anisminic* in a case concerned with a "shall not be questioned clause" in the context of a returning officer's duties in relation to the acceptance of nomination papers on the ground that the ouster was not absolute.

that the requirements of this Act have been complied with, and that the order has been duly made and is within the powers of this Act".

Such clauses were condemned by the Committee on Ministers' Powers,[17] which doubted whether they would safeguard an order that was flagrantly ultra vires from judicial censure. Other preclusive clauses have not proven effective even where the invalidity was not extreme.[18] Despite this, both formulations have been successful in excluding review. The authorities upholding the efficacy of the "conclusive evidence" formula date mainly from the earlier part of this century.[19] However more recent authority has continued to uphold the effectiveness of such clauses.[20]

The current status of the "as if" formula is that there are two decisions of the House of Lords that indicate opposite conclusions and are difficult to reconcile. In the earlier decision their Lordships interpreted the effect of the clause as being to render secondary legislation as immune from censure as if it were part of the parent legislation, the cloak of sovereignty protecting all.[21] If this ruling had been taken literally then the executive could have governed the country de jure as well as de facto. Its scope has, however, been limited. The House of Lords has subsequently held that the "as if" formula does not provide protection for secondary legislation which conflicts with the parent Act.[22] This latter statement appears not simply to limit the former but to contradict it, and indeed there are judgments in the second decision that are difficult to reconcile with the earlier authority. It may be that the clause will be effective if the statutory order in dispute relates generally to the statutory scheme, even though it may be subject to relatively minor errors which would nevertheless, in the absence of the clause, render the decision ultra vires.[23]

The difficulty of interpreting the case law is compounded by uncertainty and disagreement as to the purpose of such clauses. One argument is that the formula had and was intended to have a substantive impact, giving subordinate legislation the same standing as a primary Act. The other is that the magic words were a survival from medieval times and now possessed only a formal function. According to this latter view, the clause was used to

---

[17] Cmd. 4060 (1932), 41.

[18] *R. v Wood* (1855) 5 El. & Bl. 49.

[19] *Ex p. Ringer* (1909) 73 J.P. 436; *Reddaway v Lancs County Council* (1925) 41 T.L.R. 422; *Minister of Health v R. Ex p. Yaffe* [1931] A.C. 494, 520, 532–533, but see also *Graddage v Haringey London Borough Council* [1975] 1 W.L.R. 241; *County and Nimbus Estates Ltd v Ealing London Borough Council* (1978) 76 L.G.R. 624.

[20] *R. v Registrar of Companies Ex p. Central Bank of India* [1986] Q.B. 1114, distinguishing such clauses from the type used in the *Anisminic* case.

[21] *Institute of Patent Agents v Lockwood* [1894] A.C. 347.

[22] *Minister of Health v R. Ex p. Yaffe* [1931] A.C. 494.

[23] This is the view adopted by de Smith, *Judicial Review of Administrative Action* (Sweet & Maxwell, 4th edn, 1980), 375–376. The formulation in *de Smith's Judicial Review* (Lord Woolf, J. Jowell and A. Le Sueur, Sweet & Maxwell, 6th edn, 2007), 187–188, is somewhat different. See also, *Foster v Aloni* [1951] V.L.R. 481.

indicate that the authority for the creation of secondary legislation was based upon Parliament.[24]

E. Statutory Intervention

In 1958 parliamentary intervention took a different form. Criticism about the use of exclusion clauses had been voiced by many. The Franks Committee advocated the removal of clauses that purported to oust the prerogative orders.[25] The Tribunals and Inquiries Act 1958 implemented a number of the proposals of the Franks Committee. That Act was replaced by the Tribunals and Inquiries Act 1971, which has itself now been replaced by the Tribunals and Inquiries Act 1992, s.12(1) of which provides that,[26]

27–006

> "(a) any provision in an Act passed before 1st August 1958 that any order or determination shall not be called into question in any court, or
>
> (b) any provision in such an Act which by similar words excludes any of the powers of the High Court,
>
> shall not have effect so as to prevent the removal of the proceedings into the High Court by order of certiorari or to prejudice the powers of the High Court to make orders of mandamus."

Three important points about this section should be noted. First, it is subject to two exceptions which are set out in s.12(3), the effect of which is that s.12(1) does not apply to orders or determinations made by courts of law, or to clauses which exclude the courts after a limited period of time. Second, the section only applies to certiorari and mandamus. The declaration is not included. There appears to be no rational reason why this should be so.[27] Third, s.12 has been held not to apply to "conclusive evidence" clauses.[28]

---

[24] W. Graham-Harrison, *Notes on the Delegation by Parliament of Legislative Powers* (Eyre and Spottiswoode, 1931), 26–68; J. Willis, *The Parliamentary Powers of English Government Departments* (Harvard University Press, 1933), 62–101.

[25] Cmnd. 218 (1958), para.117.

[26] s.12(1) applies to England and Wales. Section 12(2) makes similar provision for Scotland.

[27] In *Ridge v Baldwin* [1964] A.C. 40, 120–121, Lord Morris of Borth-y-Gest was of the view that the Act did cover the declaration. But in *O'Reilly v Mackman* [1983] 2 A.C. 237 it was said that this limit showed a preference for the prerogative orders.

[28] *R. v Registrar of Companies Ex p. Central Bank of India* [1986] Q.B. 1114, 1170, 1178, 1182.

2. TIME LIMITS

27–007   In a number of different contexts it may be particularly important to know whether a decision can safely be acted upon. This is particularly so in areas such as planning, compulsory acquisition and the like. Statutes in such areas normally provide a cut-off period of six weeks, after which the decision shall not be called in question in any legal proceedings whatsoever. Within the allowed time there are statutory grounds on which an order can be attacked. Two problems require consideration. First, what is the effect of the expiry of the six weeks? Second, what is the scope of review within that period? The first question will be considered in this section, the second has already been considered in earlier discussion.[29]

The starting point for discussion is the rather confusing *Smith* case.[30] Smith alleged that a local authority had compulsorily acquired her property in bad faith. Despite the possible presence of fraud their Lordships held that the clause protected the local authority after the expiry of the six weeks.[31] It was unclear how far *Anisminic* had affected this decision.[32] The latter also involved a shall not be questioned clause, the difference being that the provision in the Foreign Compensation Act 1950 purported to exclude the courts altogether, whereas in the *Smith* case there was a six weeks time limit within which an order could be challenged. In the *Anisminic* case little favour was shown to the *Smith* decision. It was not expressly overruled, but it was distinguished upon a variety of grounds. The distinction between complete ouster of jurisdiction and time limitations was not, however, foremost in their Lordships' reasoning.[33]

Smith has survived despite this censure. In *Ostler*[34] the applicant sought to quash a road scheme and compulsory purchase order, alleging breach of natural justice and bad faith. The facts of the case were particularly strong. Ostler argued that he was only applying outside the six-week time limit because a covert agreement between a departmental officer and a local merchant had been hidden from him and had changed the whole complexion of the scheme. If the full facts had been revealed at the appropriate time he would have objected and been within the time limits.

27–008   The six-week time limit was, nonetheless, upheld. *Anisminic* was distinguished for a number of reasons. The distinction between a complete ouster clause and a time limit;[35] the administrative nature of the proceedings in *Smith* as compared with the more judicial nature of the Foreign Compensation Commission[36]; and the allegedly differing degrees of nullity

---

[29] See above, para.14–037.
[30] *Smith v East Elloe Rural District Council* [1956] A.C. 736.
[31] See also, *Woollett v Minister of Agriculture and Fisheries* [1955] 1 Q.B. 103. *Cf. Webb v Minister of Housing and Local Government* [1965] 1 W.L.R. 755.
[32] [1969] 2 A.C. 147.
[33] [1969] 2 A.C. 147, 170–171, 200–201, 210.
[34] *R. v Secretary of State for the Environment Ex p. Ostler* [1977] Q.B. 122.
[35] *Ostler*, n.34, 135 (Lord Denning MR); *cf.* 138 (Goff LJ).
[36] *Ostler*, n.34, 135 (Lord Denning M.R.), 138 (Goff LJ).

ensuing from the defects in the two cases,[37] were advanced to uphold the clause. The Court of Appeal was undoubtedly also influenced by the fact that a significant part of the scheme had been begun and that nullification would have resulted in considerable disruption and expense.[38]

The decisions in *Smith* and *Ostler* have been followed on a number of occasions. Thus in *Huntington*[39] it was held that an order subject to a six-week time limit clause could only be challenged within that period, and by the method stipulated in the statute. An applicant could not choose to use the ordinary judicial review procedure instead. It made no difference whether the body whose decision was being challenged was quasi-judicial or administrative; and it was irrelevant whether the invalidity was fundamental or not.

However more recently in *Richards*[40] the Court of Appeal held that time limit clauses should, for constitutional reasons, be narrowly construed. This meant that even if the initial order was immune from review after six weeks because of *Ostler* and *Huntington*, it did not necessarily preclude judicial review of instruments made under that order, since the validity of those instruments depended ultimately on the enabling statute.

The problem considered within this section is now of considerably greater importance given that the time limits for seeking judicial review within s.31 proceedings are short, and given also that the judiciary have insisted that some cases can only be brought by this route. While these provisions on time limits do not contain any explicit shall not be challenged clause the courts have not, on the whole, been willing to allow actions outside this period.[41]

3. The Effect of the Human Rights Act 1998

The HRA is relevant to the viability of ouster clauses. The preclusion of **27–009** review may offend against the requirement contained in art.6 ECHR that a decision must be made by an independent tribunal. This will be of relevance where there is an ouster clause and the initial decision-maker does not qualify as independent for the purposes of the Strasbourg jurisprudence. The relevant case law has been considered above.[42] Thus in *Richards*[43] Neuberger L.J. indicated, without deciding the matter, that a time limit

---

[37] *Ostler*, n.34, 135, 139, 140.
[38] See also, *Jeary v Chailey Rural District Council* (1973) 26 P. & C.R. 280; *Routh v Reading Corporation* (1971) 217 E.G. 1337.
[39] *R. v Cornwall County Council Ex p. Huntington* [1992] 3 All E.R. 566, affirmed [1994] 1 All E.R. 694; *R. v Secretary of State for the Environment Ex p. Kent* [1990] J.P.L. 124; *R. v Secretary of State for the Environment Ex p. Upton Brickworks Ltd* [1992] C.O.D. 301; *R. v London Borough of Camden Ex p. Woolf* [1992] C.O.D. 456.
[40] *R. (on the application of Richards) v Pembrokeshire County Council* [2004] EWCA Civ 1000, paras 46-47.
[41] See above, paras 26–045—26–048.
[42] See above, Ch.13.
[43] *Richards*, n.40, para.37.

clause might not be consistent with art.6 ECHR. A complete ouster would clearly be even more suspect in this regard.

4. CONCLUSION

A. Complete Ouster Clauses

27–010 Whether it would be possible to devise an ouster clause that excluded review is less a matter of semantics than of judicial attitude and legislative response. The courts have always been able to interpret an Act of Parliament and, thus, they can, if they choose, construe it as only precluding errors within jurisdiction, or appeal. Short of provoking a constitutional clash by rejecting this judicial interpretation, there is nothing that Parliament can do.

Until recently the courts could, in formal terms, continue to accept Parliamentary authority, even when restrictively construing an ouster clause, by according such clauses some impact, in the sense of protecting errors of law within jurisdiction from attack. The expansion of jurisdictional control, and the corresponding demise of error within jurisdiction, means that this route is no longer open to the judiciary. The options for the future are that the courts either restrictively interpret the clause and deny it any effect, except perhaps in preventing an appeal; or they give the clause some effect by stating that the presumption that all errors of law are open to review has been displaced in a particular area. Even if the courts choose this latter approach some judicial control can still be maintained, as experience in other jurisdictions demonstrates.[44]

The determination of the courts to preserve judicial review in the face of ouster clauses raises important issues. Whatever the courts' interpretation of these clauses has been, the parliamentary intent was to limit or remove the courts from the particular area in question.[45] It is however clear that the judicial attitude towards ouster clauses has hardened over the years. Thus the government's attempt to include an ouster in legislation relating to asylum provoked a storm of protest from the senior judiciary, which ultimately caused the government to amend the legislation.[46]

It is not clear what would have happened if the constitutional clash between courts and Parliament had not been averted. The courts might have had recourse to arguments based on the Human Rights Act 1998 concerning

---

[44] The Australian courts have retained power in the face of such terms if there is a clear excess of power, while not interfering if the agency has made a bona fide attempt to exercise its authority in a matter relating to the subject with which the legislation deals, M. Aronson and B. Dyer, *Judicial Review of Administrative Action* (LBC Information Services, 4th edn, 2008), Ch.18.

[45] This statement must be qualified in two ways: (a) Parliament has enacted the Tribunals and Inquiries Act 1992 s.12; (b) it has acquiesced, in the sense of continuing to use certain terms even after the legal effect ascribed to them by the courts has become clear.

[46] R. Rawlings, "Review, Revenge and Retreat" (2005) 68 M.L.R. 378; *de Smith's Judicial Review*, n.23, Appendix C.

the need for a decision to be made by an independent tribunal, although it is not clear that this would have availed them in this particular instance. The courts might, alternatively, have made explicit what has been implicit in their existing jurisprudence on ouster clauses. This case law is ultimately premised on the constitutional principle that access to the courts should not be denied, and that such access is a precondition for the protection of other rights guaranteed in our constitutional order.

Given the present judicial attitude to ouster clauses a legislature which is minded to limit judicial intervention might, however, do better by introducing a time limit clause. We have seen that the courts have accepted that such clauses prevent challenges outside the stipulated period, and that any action brought within that time must be by the procedure laid down in the enabling statute, although this case law remains to be tested in the light of the Human Rights Act 1998.

B. Time Limits

Statutes containing time limit clauses raise somewhat different problems. In the modern state there will necessarily be a trade-off between the need for administrative certainty, on the one hand, and justice for the individual and administrative legality on the other. This balancing appears in varying guises throughout administrative law. It arises in the creative decision as to how to categorise an alleged error, as jurisdictional or not, or as law or fact. It rears its head in the way in which we deal with waiver, delay, and representations. It lies behind some of the judicial manipulation of void and voidable.

27–011

The effect to be given to time limits is another manifestation of this problem. If the *Ostler*[47] decision had gone the other way then some other device, judicial or legislative, would have been required. Where an expensive planning and building project is undertaken then the traditional response of retrospective nullity will be difficult to apply. The method of distinguishing *Anisminic* may or may not have been convincing,[48] but some time limit to challenge is required in such areas.

This does not mean that we can be complacent, or that there is no room for improvement. Two matters require especial attention. The first is to consider whether the length of the time limit is adequate. Six weeks is short and thought needs to be given as to what would be the appropriate balance between the needs of the individual and the requirements of the administration. Second, the provision of a compensatory remedy for those unable to

---

[47] [1977] Q.B. 122.
[48] J. Alder, "Time Limit Clauses and Judicial Review" (1975) 38 M.L.R. 274; N. Gravells, "Time Limit Clauses and Judicial Review—The Relevance of Context" (1978) 41 M.L.R. 383; N. Gravells, "Time Limit Clauses and Judicial Review—Some Second Thoughts" (1980) 43 M.L.R. 173; J. Alder, "Time Limit Clauses and Conceptualism—A Reply" (1980) 43 M.L.R. 670.

complain needs to be thought through. This is particularly important where the individual's recourse to the statutory machinery is effectively foreclosed by bad faith or fraud. The possibility of such a remedy will be considered below.[49]

CHAPTER 28

PUBLIC INTEREST IMMUNITY AND CROWN LIABILITY

The Crown's contractual liability has already been considered,[1] and its **28–001** tortious liability will be discussed below.[2] Three matters will be discussed in this chapter all of which are concerned with the process of litigation. First, there is the extent to which the Crown and other public bodies may withhold evidence. Second, we will examine the law relating to the Crown and statutes. The final topic to be considered is the position of the Crown in litigation.

1. PUBLIC INTEREST IMMUNITY

A. "Crown Privilege"
When an action takes place discovery of documents will often be necessary. **28–002** One party will ask the other to produce such documents as are in their possession, which may be material to any question in issue. Where a party resisted disclosure the court would not order the production of the documents unless it believed that the order was necessary either for disposing fairly of the cause or matter, or for saving costs.[3]

Until 1968 the Crown possessed what was known as Crown privilege.[4] It could refuse to reveal certain documents because to do so would be contrary to the public interest. This principle was widely drawn as exemplified by *Duncan*.[5] A submarine built by the defendants for the Admiralty sank while on trial. The plaintiff, the widow of one of those drowned, brought an action

---

[1] See above, para.5–043.
[2] See below, Ch.29. See M. Sunkin, "Crown Immunity from Criminal Liability in English Law" [2003] P.L. 716, for discussion of Crown immunity from criminal liability.
[3] RSC, Ord.24, r.13.
[4] J. Jacob, "From Privileged Crown to Interested Public" [1993] P.L. 121.
[5] *Duncan v Cammell, Laird & Co Ltd* [1942] A.C. 624.

for negligence. She sought discovery of certain documents including plans of the submarine. The Admiralty withheld them and claimed Crown privilege. The House of Lords found for the Crown and propounded a broad rule allowing the Crown to withhold documents of two types. They could be withheld either if the disclosure of the *contents* of a particular document would injure the public interest, or where the document was one of a *class* of documents that must be withheld in order to ensure the proper functioning of the public service. Moreover, a statement by a minister in the proper form that a document fell into one of these two categories would it seems not be challenged by the courts.

There is little doubt that the *Duncan* case sanctioned the withholding of documents to a greater extent than had been allowed previously.[6] The potential breadth of the "class category" enabled the government to protect documents of a type that might not have required blanket protection.[7] Dissatisfaction with this state of affairs led the Lord Chancellor in 1956 to announce that the government would henceforth not claim privilege in certain areas. These areas were: reports of witnesses of accidents on the road, on government premises, or involving government employees; medical reports concerning civilian employees; medical reports where the Crown was sued for negligence, including reports made by prison doctors; materials required for the defence against a criminal charge and witnesses' statements to the police; and certain reports on factual matters relating to liability in contract.[8]

While this self-denying ordinance was welcomed, it proved to be a double-edged sword. The areas where privilege would not be claimed had little if any analytic coherence. Pressure for judicial reconsideration of the *Duncan* case came from both Scotland[9] and the Court of Appeal.[10] The common link between them was the refusal to accept that the court was bound by every class claim put forward by the government. Despite these promising omens, the Court of Appeal[11] then returned once more to the rigidity of the *Duncan* approach. Happily, the case went on appeal to the House of Lords, which took the opportunity for a thorough revision of the law.

B. From Crown Privilege to Public Interest Immunity

28–003 In *Conway v Rimmer*[12] the plaintiff was a former probationary police constable who began an action for malicious prosecution against his former superintendent. The Secretary of State objected to the production of five

[6] See, e.g., *Robinson v South Australia (No.2)* [1931] A.C. 704; *Spiegelman v Hocker* (1933) 50 T.L.R. 87.
[7] *Ellis v Home Office* [1953] 2 Q.B. 135; *Broome v Broome* [1955] P. 190.
[8] HL Deb, Vol. 197, col. 741 (June 6, 1956).
[9] *Glasgow Corporation v Central Land Board* 1956 S.C. 1.
[10] *Re Grosvenor Hotel (London) Ltd (No.2)* [1965] Ch.1210; *Merricks v Nott-Bower* [1965] 1 Q.B. 57; *Wednesbury Corporation v Ministry of Housing and Local Government* [1965] 1 W.L.R. 261.
[11] *Conway v Rimmer* [1967] 1 W.L.R. 1031.
[12] [1968] A.C. 910.

documents, certifying that they fell within classes of document whose disclosure would be injurious to the public interest. The defendant made four of the reports about the plaintiff during his probationary period. The fifth was a report made by him to his chief constable in connection with the prosecution of the plaintiff on a criminal charge on which he was acquitted. It was this criminal charge which was the foundation of the action for malicious prosecution.

The *Duncan* case was overturned.[13] The House of Lords expressly asserted the power of the courts to hold a balance between the public interest as expressed by the minister who wished to withhold certain documents, and the public interest in ensuring the proper administration of justice. While their Lordships were unanimous in this respect, the formulations as to how the balancing was to operate differed somewhat. Two aspects of the balancing operation may be cited by way of example.

First, it was unclear from *Conway* whether there were documents of a kind which would always be privileged. Lord Reid thought that Cabinet minutes and high level policy-making should never be disclosed, irrespective of their content.[14] Lord Pearce recognised an exception in similar terms.[15] It is, however, unclear from his judgment whether this meant that the court could in principle inspect the documents, or whether no inspection whatsoever was warranted in these areas. The same is true of Lord Upjohn's judgment.[16] By way of contrast, Lord Morris[17] began with the principle that the court must always balance the competing interests whatever the type of document, albeit with the recognition that there were certain classes of documents which would by their nature be excluded. This ambiguity has persisted in later cases.

A second aspect of the balancing which was unclear related to the type of reasons put forward by the minister to justify non-disclosure. Lord Reid stated that if these reasons were such that a court was not competent to weigh them, then the minister's view must prevail.[18] A similar but not identical idea was put forward by Lord Morris.[19] Lord Pearce agreed[20] with Lord Reid in general terms, but did not allude to this specific point. The issue was not specifically addressed by Lord Hodson or Lord Upjohn.

These ambiguities should not, however, be allowed to cloud the importance of the main principle that was unequivocally asserted by the House of Lords: the courts would balance the competing public interests to determine whether disclosure should be ordered. If the court was in doubt as to the outcome of this balancing it could inspect the documents before ordering

28–004

---

[13] Some of their Lordships preferred to distinguish the case as covering only situations where discovery would involve a real danger to the public interest, Lord Reid, 938–939, Lord Upjohn, 990–991; others, such as Lord Morris of Borth-y-Gest, preferred a more direct attack, 958–959.
[14] [1968] A.C. 910, 952–953. See also, *Att-Gen v Jonathan Cape Ltd* [1976] Q.B. 752.
[15] [1968] A.C. 910, 986–987. See also, Lord Hodson, 973.
[16] [1968] A.C. 910, 993.
[17] [1968] A.C. 910, 971.
[18] [1968] A.C. 910, 952.
[19] [1968] A.C. 910, 971–972.
[20] [1968] A.C. 910, 980.

production. This was in fact done and the court concluded that the documents should be produced. It is important to understand that class claims and contents claims for public interest immunity persisted after *Conway*. What the House of Lords' judgment made clear was that all such claims would be subject to the balancing test.

Given the nature of the balancing operation the *Conway* case required, the name "Crown privilege" was obviously inappropriate. The Crown could not simply decide whether to withdraw a category of documents from the court. That the title was misleading was recognised in *Rogers*.[21] An application for a gaming certificate had been refused and Rogers wished to know the contents of a letter written by the Chief Constable to the Gaming Board about him. The Home Secretary sought to prevent discovery of the document and pleaded Crown privilege. While the House of Lords agreed that the letter should not be produced, they disapproved of the term Crown privilege. Lord Reid[22] stated that the term privilege was misleading, and that the real issue was whether the public interest in not disclosing the document outweighed the interest of the litigant in having all the evidence before the court.

C. Public Interest Immunity: The Type of Body that can claim Immunity

28–005 This question arose for consideration in *D v National Society for the Prevention of Cruelty to Children*.[23] The Court of Appeal decided that public interest immunity was only available where the public interest related to the effective functioning of departments or other organs of central government. This view was rejected by the House of Lords. The NSPCC was an authorised person for the purpose of bringing care proceedings under the Children and Young Persons Act 1969. Although it was not under a statutory duty to bring such actions, this was not decisive. Ensuring the confidentiality of the information was as important here as it had been in *Rogers*.[24]

It is questionable how far beyond the organs of central government one may go and still have the defence available. Their Lordships rejected the view that it only operated where the effective functioning of departments or other organs of central government were involved. They also rejected the very broad approach posited by the NSPCC that whenever a party to legal proceedings claims that there is a public interest to be served by withholding documents it is the duty of the court to weigh that interest against the countervailing public interest in the administration of justice, and to refuse

---

[21] *Rogers v Secretary of State for Home Department* [1973] A.C. 388.
[22] *Rogers*, n.21, 400. See also, 406, 408, 412.
[23] [1978] A.C. 171.
[24] n.21.

disclosure if the balance tilts that way. Which bodies are entitled to raise the issue must therefore be decided upon a case by case approach.[25]

It should however also be noted that the Civil Procedure Rules allow a person to apply for an order permitting him to withhold documents on the ground that disclosure would damage the public interest.[26] This provision is held not to affect any rule of law that permits or requires a document to be withheld from disclosure on the ground that its disclosure or inspection would damage the public interest.[27]

D. Public Interest Immunity and Confidentiality

A number of cases have been concerned with the protection of information given in confidence.[28] It is, however, clear that confidentiality is not by itself a separate ground for withholding evidence. This was established by *Alfred Crompton*.[29] The company claimed that the assessment of purchase tax based upon the wholesale value of amusement machines was too high. The customs and excise commissioners, as part of their investigation, obtained from Crompton's customers and other sources information concerning the value of the machines. No agreement was reached as to the appropriate tax rate. When the matter went to arbitration the commissioners claimed that the information received from these customers and other sources should be immune from disclosure since it would reveal the commissioners' methods and contained information supplied confidentially. The House of Lords upheld this claim. Disclosure of the information could hinder the commissioners in the discharge of their functions. However, the fact that the information was supplied in confidence was not in itself a reason for non-disclosure. It was not a separate head of privilege, but could be a material consideration when privilege was claimed on the ground of public interest.

Confidentiality also played a part in *D v National Society for the Prevention of Cruelty to Children*.[30] The NSPCC relied heavily upon members of the public to give information about possible child abuse. In the instant case the society acted upon information that subsequently proved to be untrue. The mother claimed damages against the NSPCC, alleging a failure to take reasonable care before investigating an allegation of maltreatment. She demanded discovery of all the documents the society had relating to the case. The House of Lords upheld the public interest defence. They reiterated

28–006

[25] *BL Cars Ltd (Formerly Leyland Cars) v Vyas* [1980] A.C. 1028; *Buckley v Law Society (No.2)* [1984] 1 W.L.R. 1101; *British Steel Corporation v Granada Television Ltd* [1981] A.C. 1096.
[26] CPR 31.19(1); *Frankson v Secretary of State for the Home Department* [2003] 1 W.L.R. 1952, para.9.
[27] CPR 31.19(8).
[28] *Rogers*, n.21. See also, *Lonrho Ltd v Shell Petroleum Co Ltd (No.2)* [1982] A.C. 173; Y. Cripps, "Judicial Proceedings and Refusal to Disclose the Identity of Sources of Information" [1984] C.L.J. 266.
[29] *Alfred Crompton Amusement Machines Ltd v Customs and Excise Commissioners (No.2)* [1974] A.C. 405.
[30] [1978] A.C. 171; *Re D (Infants)* [1970] 1 W.L.R. 599; *Gaskin v Liverpool City Council* [1980] 1 W.L.R. 1549; *Buckley v Law Society (No.2)* [1984] 1 W.L.R. 1101.

the point that confidentiality is not itself a defence but, reasoning by analogy from the case of police informants, it was decided that the documents did not have to be disclosed. Sources of information would dry up if the names of the informants were to be made public, hampering the society in the discharge of its duties. This was held to outweigh the interest of the individual in knowing the name of the informant.[31]

E. Public Interest Immunity: Duty or Discretion

28–007 It was held in *Makanjuola*,[32] that public interest immunity could not be waived. The reasoning was that the litigant who asserted public interest immunity was not claiming a right, but observing a duty. Immunity was accorded in certain circumstances where this was warranted by the public interest. It was for this reason that the immunity could not be waived. The court also gave important indications as to when documents should in fact be withheld. The court stated, on the one hand, that documents should not be kept back in every case where they might be prima facie immune if, on any weighing of the public interest for and against disclosure, there would be a clear balance in favour of disclosure. On the other hand, the court also held that where a litigant possessed documents within a class, which was or might be prima facie immune from disclosure, then public interest immunity should, save for exceptional cases, be claimed and disclosure should be denied, since the ultimate judge of where the balance of public interest lies was not the litigant but the court itself.

The judgment in the *Makanjuola* case led government departments to believe that they should withhold documentation, with the consequence that plaintiffs would have to overcome the hurdles, considered below, which are necessary in order to obtain documents. Thus in the Matrix Churchill saga, concerning the sale of arms to Iraq, government ministers were advised by the Attorney-General that they had no discretion and had to sign certificates claiming public interest immunity.[33]

This matter must now be seen in the light of the decision of the House of Lords in *Wiley*,[34] which overruled *Makanjuola*.[35] Lord Woolf, speaking for the House, accepted that public interest immunity could not be waived *after* the court had determined that the public interest against disclosure outweighed that of disclosure. Matters were, however, different in relation to the situation *before* that final determination had been made. His Lordship held that ministers possessed discretion as to whether to claim public interest immunity. Thus it was open to the Secretary of State acting on behalf of his department, or the Attorney-General, to decide that the public interest in

---

[31] See also, *Norwich Pharmacal Co v Customs and Excise Commissioners* [1974] A.C. 133.
[32] *Makanjuola v Commissioner of Police of the Metropolis* [1992] 3 All E.R. 617; *Halford v Sharples* [1992] 1 W.L.R. 736.
[33] A. Bradley, "Justice, Good Government and Public Interest Immunity" [1992] P.L. 514; A. Tomkins, "Public Interest Immunity after Matrix Churchill" [1993] P.L. 650, 662–665.
[34] *R. v Chief Constable of the West Midlands Police Ex p. Wiley* [1995] 1 A.C. 274.
[35] The court also overruled *Neilson v Laugharne* [1981] Q.B. 736.

documents being withheld from production was outweighed by the public interest in disclosure. While the court was the ultimate arbiter on this balance his Lordship made it clear that it would be extremely rare for the court to reach a different conclusion where the Minister was of the view that the documents could be disclosed. This was equally true of class claims and contents claims.

Where however parties other than government departments were in possession of documents in respect of which immunity could be claimed on a class basis matters were rather different. It would not, said Lord Woolf, be right for the individual to decide that the documents should be disclosed, since this could undermine the claim for immunity of documents within that general category. It might, on the facts, be possible for the individual to consult other relevant parties, and the Attorney-General, and then to decide that disclosure was not problematic. This view as to the balance of the public interest would in all likelihood be accepted by the court. Where this was not possible then public interest immunity should be claimed and the balancing would be undertaken by the court.

F. Public Interest Immunity: Duty, Discretion and the ECHR

The discussion in *Wiley* focused primarily on the extent to which a minister **28–008** had discretion to decide that public interest immunity was, on balance, not required in a particular case. It is clear that the ECHR has an impact in the converse case, concerning the discretion to withhold information on public interest immunity grounds. Applicants have argued that withholding documents on the ground of public interest immunity infringes the right to a fair trial in art.6 ECHR. The European Court of Human Rights (ECtHR) has enunciated the following principles.[36]

It has held that a fundamental aspect of Article 6 is equality of arms, which meant, inter alia, that the prosecution should normally disclose all evidence for or against the accused. The ECtHR accepted that this did not constitute an absolute right, and that there might be circumstances where the public interest justified the withholding of information on public interest immunity grounds. It was for the national court, not the ECtHR, to decide whether the non-disclosure was strictly necessary. It was however not open to the prosecution to withhold evidence without notifying the trial judge, thereby preventing the latter from making the assessment of whether the claim for public interest immunity was really warranted on the facts, unless the defect had been remedied by a full inter partes hearing by the Appeal Court.[37]

Moreover, where evidence was withheld any difficulties caused for the defence must be counterbalanced by the procedures adopted by the judicial

---

[36] *Edwards v United Kingdom* (1993) 15 E.H.R.R. 417; *Rowe and Davis v United Kingdom* (2000) 30 E.H.R.R. 1; *Jasper v United Kingdom* (2000) 30 E.H.R.R. 441; *Atlan v United Kingdom* (2002) 34 E.H.R.R. 33; *Edwards and Lewis v United Kingdom* [2005] 40 E.H.R.R. 24.
[37] The application of these principles was considered in *R. v Jawad Botmeh and Samar Alami* [2002] 1 W.L.R. 531; *R. v H* [2003] 1 W.L.R. 3006.

authorities. Thus, the defence should be kept informed and permitted to make submissions in the decision-making process about public interest immunity, so far as this was possible without revealing the material that the prosecution sought to keep secret.

These principles have been acknowledged by the House of Lords. Thus in *R. v H*[38] the House of Lords held that having regard to the overriding principle that the trial process, viewed as a whole, should be fair and to the rule obliging the prosecution to make full disclosure of unused material tending to undermine its case or assist that of the defence, the trial judge on a public interest immunity application was required to give detailed consideration to the material sought to be withheld in the context of the prosecution and defence cases. The trial judge should identify the public interest in question and assess the prejudice claimed, and ensure that any derogation from the full disclosure rule was the minimum necessary to secure the required protection. An application made ex parte without notice to the defence was permitted only in exceptional circumstances. Appointment of special counsel to represent a defendant as an advocate on such an application might in an exceptional case be necessary in the interests of justice, but such an appointment should not be ordered unless the trial judge was satisfied that no other course would adequately meet the overriding requirement of fairness to the defendant. Material that was damaging to the defendant was not in any event disclosable and should not be brought to the court's attention. Provided the existing procedures were operated in accordance with these principles there would be no violation of art.6.

G. Public Interest Immunity: The Change in Governmental Approach

28–009 The use of public interest immunity certificates was criticised in the Scott Report into the Arms to Iraq affair.[39] The inquiry that led to this report considered the use of such certificates in the abortive attempt to prosecute the directors of Matrix Churchill. It was this report, combined with the decision in *Wiley*, which caused the Government to rethink its approach to this issue. There was a consultation exercise, followed by statements from the Lord Chancellor and the Attorney-General.[40] The new approach only applies when it is the government that is claiming immunity.

i. The new approach

28–010 Ministers will only claim public interest immunity when it is believed that disclosure of a document will cause real damage or harm to the public interest. The harm might be direct or indirect. Ministers will therefore perform the balancing exercise specified in *Wiley*. The damage might relate to the safety of an individual, to the regulatory process, to international

---

[38] *R. v H* [2004] 2 A.C. 134; *R. v May* [2005] 1 W.L.R. 2902; *R. v Lewis* [2005] EWCA Crim 859.
[39] *The Report of the Inquiry into the Export of Defence and Dual Use Goods to Iraq and Related Prosecutions* (1995–96; HC 115).
[40] Hansard, cols 1507–1508 HL, cols 949–950 HC, December 18, 1996.

relations, the nation's economic interests or national security. The nature of the harm will be explained by the minister when immunity is claimed.

The former division into class claims and contents claims will no longer be applied. Ministers will not therefore claim immunity to protect, for example, internal advice or national security merely by pointing to the general nature of the document. The factors which will be taken into account in a properly reasoned certificate relating to, for example, internal advice, will include: the public importance of the topic; the level of the discussion; the degree of controversy; the expectation of the parties that the exchanges would be confidential; and the likelihood that the disclosure will have damaging consequences of a specific and important nature.

ii. Evaluation

The new approach to public interest immunity by the Government is to be **28–011** welcomed. There are however features of the new policy which are still a cause for concern.[41]

First, the criterion of real damage or harm used by the Government should not be read as a lower standard than that of substantial harm set out by Lord Templeman in *Wiley*.[42]

Second, it is encouraging that the Government does not wish to persist with class claims. Public interest immunity claims of this nature have long been criticised.[43] It must, however, be acknowledged that the dividing line between a class claim and a contents claim can be a fine one. Thus while the government has stated that it will not use class claims, it is also clear that it will use "sampling": ministers may assert immunity "for a number of documents after examining a sample of the documents, rather than each one".[44] The Government accepts that it will be for the court to decide whether the sampling that has been done is sufficient, but the very idea of sampling blurs the line between class and contents claims.

Third, the same approach was to be applied to civil and criminal cases.[45] While it was recognised that the balancing might operate differently within the criminal context, it is questionable whether the balancing approach is really suited to criminal cases. Sir Richard Scott has argued cogently that it cannot readily be transferred to such cases. Thus referring to the balancing process that applies in civil cases, he questions whether that has anything to do with the public interest that a defendant should have a fair trial and that an innocent man should not be convicted.[46] It should in any event be borne in mind that the principles applied by the courts in criminal cases discussed

---

[41] M. Supperstone and J. Goudie, "A New Approach to Public Interest Immunity" [1997] P.L. 211.
[42] [1995] 1 A.C. 274, 281.
[43] Sir Richard Scott, "The Acceptable and Unacceptable Use of Public Interest Immunity" [1996] P.L. 427, 436–443.
[44] *Report on Public Interest Immunity*, December 18, 1996, para.6.3.
[45] *Report on Public Interest Immunity*, n.44, para.1.9.
[46] Sir Richard Scott, "The Acceptable and Unacceptable Use of Public Interest Immunity" [1996] P.L. 427, 434.

in the previous section will be controlling, and that criminal procedural rules now deal with this issue.[47]

H. Public Interest Immunity: The Balancing Process

28–012   A number of important points concerning the nature of public interest immunity and the balancing process must be distinguished.

(1)   In the past the person claiming discovery had to show that the documents were necessary for fairly disposing of the cause or matter or for saving costs, within the rules of discovery normally applicable to litigation.[48] If this could not be shown then the documents did not have to be disclosed and there was no need to raise a claim of public interest immunity. It might, however, be unclear whether the documents *were* necessary until they were looked at. The person who was seeking discovery was in danger of being caught in a "Catch 22" dilemma: it might only be possible to show that they were necessary for disposing of the case by seeing the very documents themselves. Yet the courts did not wish to sanction fishing expeditions by people who were seeking to establish a cause of action. The resolution of this conundrum was for the applicant to prove that the documents might well be of use to the case. The precise standard demanded by their Lordships differed. In *Burmah Oil*,[49] Lord Wilberforce stated that the court should not inspect the documents unless the party could show a strong positive case that they might be of help to him. Lord Keith[50] used a test of reasonable probability, while Lord Edmund-Davies[51] adopted a test of likelihood. Only if the person seeking access to the documents surmounted this hurdle would the court undertake the balancing operation.

(2)   It remains to be seen how far these criteria will apply under the new Civil Procedure Rules (CPR).[52] CPR, Part 31, is framed in terms of orders for "standard disclosure" and for "specific disclosure". A party discloses a document by stating that the document exists or has existed.[53] A party to whom a document has been disclosed has, subject to certain exceptions, a right to inspect it.[54] An order to give disclosure is, unless the court otherwise directs, an order to give standard disclosure.[55] It is open to the court to dispense with or limit standard disclosure.[56] Where a court does make such an order then it

---

[47] Criminal Procedure Rules 2005 (SI 2005/384), Pt 25.
[48] RSC, Ord.24, r.13; *Air Canada v Secretary of State for Trade (No.2)* [1983] 2 A.C. 394.
[49] *Burmah Oil Co Ltd v Bank of England* [1980] A.C. 1090, 1117.
[50] *Burmah Oil*, n.49, 1135–1136.
[51] *Burmah Oil*, n.49, 1126.
[52] *In Re R* [2002] 1 F.L.R. 755.
[53] CPR 31.2.
[54] CPR 31.3.
[55] CPR 31.5(1).
[56] CPR 31.5(2).

requires a party to disclose the documents on which it relies, and the documents which adversely affect its own, or another party's, case, or support another party's case, and such documents which it is required to disclose by a relevant practice direction.[57] A party is under an obligation to make a reasonable search for such documents.[58] The court is also empowered to make an order for specific disclosure or specific inspection, requiring the party to disclose those documents specified in the order.[59] There is little doubt that these rules give the court ample powers through which to require the public body to provide the information needed for the applicant to sustain its case. It is, however, open to the court to dispense with or limit standard disclosure, and the court also has discretion in relation to requests for more specific disclosure. The extent to which the courts will order disclosure in judicial review proceedings has been considered in an earlier chapter.[60]

(3)   The person arguing against disclosure raises the public interest in favour of immunity. How strong a case must be made out is not entirely clear,[61] although as we have seen the Government's practice is not to claim immunity unless it believes that disclosure would cause real damage or harm to the public interest. If there is doubt about whether a document should be included within a particular class claim the court may inspect it.[62]

(4)   We have already seen that the government policy is, subject to what was said above, not to make class claims. We saw also that this policy is not binding on claims advanced by non-governmental bodies. If a class claim is advanced by such a body it will be for the court to decide whether the claim is sustainable. This was the ground for the decision in *Wiley*,[63] where it was held that a class claim did not attach generally to all documents coming into existence in consequence of an investigation against the police under Pt IX of the Police and Criminal Evidence Act 1984. There were, however, differences of view as to whether class claims in respect of some reports could be sustained. Lord Woolf expressed reservations as to whether this could be so. Lord Slynn did not share these reservations, since he felt that much turned on the breadth of the relevant class, as did Lord Lloyd.

28–013

---

[57] CPR 31.6.
[58] CPR 31.7(1).
[59] CPR 31.12.
[60] See, Ch.26.
[61] Thus in *Burmah Oil* Lord Wilberforce speaks of a claim for public interest immunity having been made on a strong and well fortified basis, n.49, 1112, while Lord Edmund-Davies speaks of the Chief Secretary establishing a good prima facie case for withholding the documents, 1125; in *Wiley* Lord Templeman speaks of the need for disclosure unless this will cause substantial harm to the public interest, n.34, 281.
[62] *Conway*, n.12, 995; *Burmah Oil*, n.49.
[63] n.34.

(5)   The balancing stage is then reached. An important issue is whether
       there are any categories in relation to which balancing does not
       apply. We have already seen that their Lordships in *Conway*[64] dif-
       fered as to whether certain types of documents should automatically
       be regarded as beyond the reach of the courts and not subject to the
       balancing approach. The question of whether such a category existed
       arose in *Burmah Oil*.[65] Burmah Oil was in financial difficulty and a
       rescue package was put together under which Burmah sold their
       British Petroleum stock to the Bank. The original intent was that
       because BP stock was low at the time of the sale, any profit from the
       resale of the stock would be divided between the Bank and Burmah
       Oil. The Government did not, however, accept this part of the
       scheme. BP stock rose in value, and Burmah Oil alleged that the sale
       of the stock was unconscionable. It sought to discover certain
       documents including those from meetings at which ministers had
       been present, and those relating to meetings of government officials.
       The object of such discovery was to find evidence that the Govern-
       ment's rejection of the profit sharing scheme was unfair. Their
       Lordships held that no classes of document were entirely excluded
       from the balancing process. Even high level governmental policy
       could be subjected to this process. This emerged most clearly from
       the judgments of Lord Keith[66] and Lord Scarman.[67] It was accepted,
       albeit less forcefully, by Lord Wilberforce[68] and was implicit in the
       judgment of Lord Edmund-Davies.[69] It was, however, clear that the
       importance of the documents would be a key factor in the balancing
       process.

(6)   The Human Rights Act 1998 has had an impact on the balancing
       process. Thus in *McNally*[70] the fact that rights protected by the
       ECHR were in play inclined the court to accept that there should be
       a more case-specific balancing to decide whether it should be
       revealed that a person was a police informer. The courts are more
       generally demanding that those who advance a public interest
       immunity claim should set out with greater particularity than
       hitherto the harm that will be caused to the public interest by the
       production of the relevant material.[71]

(7)   Various arguments have been used to justify non-disclosure, parti-
       cularly of high policy documents. The two most oft-repeated are that
       disclosure would place candour within the public service at risk, and
       that it would fan ill-formed or captious public or political criticism

---

[64] See above, para.28–003.
[65] *Burmah Oil*, n.49.
[66] *Burmah Oil*, n.49, 1134–1135.
[67] *Burmah Oil*, n.49, 1143–1144.
[68] *Burmah Oil*, n.49, 1113.
[69] *Burmah Oil*, n.49, 1129.
[70] *Chief Constable of the Greater Manchester Police v McNally* [2002] 2 Cr. App. R. 37.
[71] *In Re R* [2002] 1 F.L.R. 755.

by those without real understanding of how government worked. The candour argument is no longer regarded as such an important factor. There are nonetheless differences of judicial opinion as to its relevance. For example, Lord Reid in *Conway* did not believe that the possibility of disclosure would inhibit candour.[72] This sentiment was echoed even more strongly by Lord Keith in *Burmah Oil*,[73] who regarded the notion that candour would be diminished by the off-chance of disclosure as grotesque. Similarly dismissive statements are to be found in other cases.[74] To be contrasted with these views are those of Lord Wilberforce in *Burmah Oil*.[75] He felt that the candour argument had received an excessive dose of cold water. Lord Scarman[76] in the same case was of the opinion that both the candour argument and the captious public criticism argument were of importance.[77]

I. Public Interest Immunity: Inspection

We have already touched upon inspection in the preceding discussion. It is **28–014** important to realise that inspection may be of relevance at four different stages of the proceedings. Judicial opinion has differed on the desirability of ordering inspection. Comment is rendered more difficult because the judicial statements do not always refer to inspection at the same level, and it is clear that differing policy considerations apply at the four stages. Some attempt must however be made to disentangle the authorities.

(1)   There may be doubts as to whether a particular document should be included within a class for which immunity is claimed. Inspection by the judge can resolve this matter. Arguments of principle and authority are in favour of inspection. If there is doubt as to whether a particular document should or should not be part of a class of documents for which immunity might properly be claimed, not to inspect in order to determine whether the document was properly included would make it possible for the party against disclosure to protect material under the umbrella of a class to which it did not in reality belong. Authority is in favour of inspection in such instances.[78]

---

[72] *Conway*, n.12, 952.
[73] *Burmah Oil*, n.49, 1133.
[74] *Science Research Council v Nasse* [1980] A.C. 1028, 1070 (Lord Salmon), 1081 (Lord Fraser); *Campbell v Tameside Metropolitan Borough Council* [1982] 3 W.L.R. 75 where Ackner L.J. regarded the candour doctrine as having been given its quietus; *Williams v Home Office* [1981] 1 All E.R. 1151.
[75] *Burmah Oil*, n.49, 1112.
[76] *Burmah Oil*, n.49, 1145. Even where the balance is against disclosure there may be a temporal limit upon the secrecy, *R. v Inland Revenue Commissioners Ex p. Rossminster Ltd* [1980] A.C. 952.
[77] See also the opinion of Lord Fraser in *Air Canada* [1983] 2 A.C. 394.
[78] *Conway*, n.12, 995; *Burmah Oil*, n.49, where it appears to have been accepted that inspection should take place on this first level, see, 1111–1112, 1129.

(2) It may be necessary to inspect the documents to determine whether their disclosure is necessary for fairly disposing of the case or for saving costs. This was the issue on which *Burmah Oil*[79] ultimately turned. *Burmah Oil* is authority that inspection can be ordered at this level. This must be correct on principle. Provided that the claimant can show that there is a likelihood, or reasonable probability, or strong positive case, to use the different formulations of their Lordships, that there might be documents that are necessary for fairly disposing of the case then, unless inspection is undertaken, the point cannot be answered. There are nonetheless two problems in this area. The *degree of likelihood* that the claimant must show in order for the court to inspect the documents continues to divide the judiciary. Thus in *Air Canada*[80] their Lordships refused to inspect on this second level, but their formulations differed. Three of their Lordships held that in order to warrant inspection the claimant must show that there was a reasonable probability that the material was necessary for fairly disposing of the case, and that the documents would help his or her case or damage that of the other side.[81] Two of their Lordships held that the claimant must show that the documents were likely to be necessary for fairly disposing of the case, and that the court could inspect the documents when it considered that their disclosure might materially assist either of the parties or the court in the determination of the issues.[82] There is a danger in the stricter formulation. If the standard is set too high then we could find ourselves back in a position not very different from that prior to *Conway*. If the courts refuse to inspect documents in respect of which immunity has been claimed unless, to use one of their Lordships' formulations, the claimants can show that the documents are very likely to contain material which would give substantial support to their contentions, then the claimants are unlikely to reach the balancing stage at all. The other problem is that *some cases object to such inspection at this second level because the court may not be in a good position to assess the relevance of the material for the case.*[83] There may indeed be such difficulties, but there is no real alternative. Either the court refuses to inspect at all, but then it could not tell whether the material *was* necessary for fairly disposing of the case. Or having inspected the documents it would then show the material to the plaintiffs to allow them to indicate its importance. This would, however, automatically answer the case in favour of disclosure, in the sense that the documents would be known. The same issue concerning inspection at the second level could arise in relation to

---

[79] *Burmah Oil*, n.49.
[80] *Air Canada*, n.48.
[81] The precise degree or probability differed, *Air Canada*, n.48, Lord Fraser, 435; Lord Wilberforce, 439; Lord Edmund-Davies, 442–443.
[82] Lord Scarman, 445–446; Lord Templeman, 447–449.
[83] *Gaskin v Liverpool City Council* [1980] 1 W.L.R. 1549, 1555.

applications for specific disclosure under the new Civil Procedure Rules. Whether the courts will continue to employ the same criteria in relation to inspection remains to be seen.

(3) Inspection may be required at the balancing stage in order to determine whether the public interest is for or against disclosure. The judgments in *Conway*[84] endorsed inspection where necessary, in order to decide where the balance lay. In *Burmah Oil*,[85] the House of Lords was also willing, if necessary, to inspect the documents to determine whether the balance was in favour of disclosure. Notwithstanding these statements from high authority, some courts have been more circumspect about the desirability of such inspection.[86] Varying reasons have been given for this more wary approach. A recurring theme is that to inspect infringes the broad rule of justice that documents should be available to both sides. This point was well answered by Lord Upjohn[87]: when the judge demands to see the documents for which privilege is claimed he is not considering the main cause of action between the parties, but a distinct issue, viz whether the public interest in withholding the document outweighs the public interest that all relevant documents not otherwise privileged should be displayed in litigation.

(4) If on balance the court considers that the document should be produced, it may inspect it before ordering production. The House of Lords in *Conway* clearly felt that inspection should take place before ordering production of a document, if the document had not been seen by the court before that stage.

2. STATUTES AND THE CROWN

A. Statutes Binding the Crown

Whether statutes bind the Crown is problematic, because early decisions **28–015** have been interpreted in a way they do not warrant, and those subsequent interpretations have become the law. The commonly stated rule is that the Crown is not bound by statute in the absence of express provision or necessary implication. This was not always the case. Street has traced the history of this rule and has demonstrated the subtle change of meaning in the case law.[88]

In the 16th century the position was that the Crown was bound by a

---

[84] *Conway*, n.12, 953, 972, 980, 989, 995–996.
[85] *Burmah Oil*, n.49, 1121–1122, 1129, 1134–1135, 1145; *Goodridge v Chief Constable of Hampshire Constabulary* [1999] 1 All E.R. 896.
[86] *Gaskin*, n.83.
[87] *Conway*, n.12, 995–996.
[88] "The Effect of Statutes upon the Rights and Liabilities of the Crown" (1948) 7 U.T.L.J. 357.

statute intended to bind it.[89] Where the statute touched upon the rights of subjects generally then the Crown would normally be bound also. There was, however, a presumption that a general statute would not affect the prerogative rights of the King unless he was named therein. The transition from this position to the commonly stated rule set out above occurred largely by accident and misinterpretation.[90] By the 20th century a rule began to be propounded in texts upon statute law that the Crown, if not named, would be bound by a statute only if that was the necessary implication. Such an implication would only be necessary if to do otherwise would be to render the statute "unmeaning".[91] This test will only be met if it can be affirmed at the time when the statute was passed that it was apparent from its terms that its purpose would be wholly frustrated if the Crown were not to be bound. The House of Lords has endorsed this general rule of construction, and has made it clear that it applies irrespective of whether the statute in question has been passed for the public benefit or not.[92]

The immunity should in principle be shared by any person who could show that application of the statute to him or her would prejudice the Crown. On this hypothesis being a Crown servant would be neither a sufficient nor a necessary condition for immunity. It would not be sufficient because it would be possible for a person to be a Crown servant, but for the application of the statute not to be prejudicial to the Crown. It would not be necessary, because it would be possible for independent contractors and others to argue that the application of a statute to them would prejudicially affect the Crown.

A number of problems flow from the existing law. It is unclear when the exception to the present rule will apply. The retention of the present presumption also creates problems with the application to the Crown of statutes concerning tortious liability. The present presumption was left unaltered by the Crown Proceedings Act 1947 s.40(2)(f), except as otherwise expressly provided. Section 2 of the same legislation imposes liability in tort upon the Crown as if it were a private person. A neat question therefore arises as to whether such statutes passed before and after the 1947 Act are rendered automatically applicable to the Crown through the operation of s.2, or whether express provision in the particular statute is required.[93]

The present state of the law is unsatisfactory. The shift from a rule sensibly based upon general legislative purpose to the present position has been the result of accident and misinterpretation of earlier authority. Little thought has been given to the justification, if any, for this position. It might be argued that the present rule gives rise to no great problems because the Crown can easily be expressly included in the statute. This argument is

---

[89] *Willion v Berkley* (1561) 1 Plowden 223.
[90] *Magdalen College Case* (1615) 11 Co. Rep.66b.
[91] *Province of Bombay v Municipal Corporation of the City of Bombay* [1947] A.C. 58; *Madras Electric Supply Co Ltd v Boarland* [1955] A.C. 667; *Gorton Local Board v Prison Commissioners* [1904] 2 K.B. 165; *British Broadcasting Corporation v Johns* [1965] Ch.32. *cf. Att-Gen v De Keyser's Royal Hotel Ltd* [1920] A.C. 508.
[92] *Lord Advocate v Dumbarton District Council* [1990] 2 A.C. 580.
[93] G. Treitel, "Crown Proceedings: Some Recent Developments" [1957] P.L. 321, 322–326.

premised upon an ideal, whereby legislators will carefully decide whether to extend an Act to the Crown. The legislative process will often not operate in this way. Whether the Crown should be bound may receive scant attention or simply be forgotten. A reversal of the present presumption would provide a simple solution: the Crown should be bound unless there is a clear indication to the contrary. This would force the Government to take the initiative in practical terms if it wished to secure immunity, and also place upon it the onus of arguing why immunity was required.

B. Statutes Benefiting the Crown

It appears to be the law that the monarch can take the benefit of statutes 28–016 even though not named therein.[94] The point has been doubted,[95] but appears to be correct. If on true construction of a statute it seems as if the Crown should receive a benefit, then that benefit should indeed be forthcoming even if the Crown is not named expressly therein. This seems to give the Crown a power to claim the benefit but not to take the burden. The problem lies not, however, with the fact that the Crown can take a benefit, even though not named, if the statute was intended to grant the benefit, but with the inflexible rule about the Crown not being bound by statutes unless named therein. A related but separate question is whether the Crown could take the benefit of certain statutory rights without the restrictions attendant upon them. The answer, on authority, appears to be negative.[96]

The common law position is left unchanged by the Crown Proceedings Act 1947, s.31(1) of which states that the Act shall not prejudice the right of the Crown to take advantage of the provisions of a statute although not named therein and that, in any civil proceedings against the Crown, the Crown, subject to express provision to the contrary, may rely upon the provisions of any Act of Parliament which could, if the proceedings were between subjects, be relied on by the defendant as a defence.

3. Procedure, Remedies and the Crown

A. General

In general the rules of civil procedure apply to actions by and against the 28–017 Crown. This general rule is, however, subject to certain modifications. The Crown is not a party to the proceedings. It is represented, whether as

---

[94] H. Street, *Governmental Liability: A Comparative Study* (Archon Books, 1975), 154–156; P. Hogg, *Liability of the Crown in Australia, New Zealand and the United Kingdom* (Law Book Co, 1971), 180–183.
[95] *Cayzer, Irvine & Co Ltd v Board of Trade* [1927] 1 K.B. 269, 274; *Nisbet Shipping Co Ltd v Queen* [1955] 1 W.L.R. 1031, 1035.
[96] *Crooke's Case* (1691) 1 Show K.B. 208; *Nisbet*, n.95. However, as Hogg, n.94, 182 points out, this would not be logically impossible as Parliament might intend the Crown not to be subject to certain restrictions.

plaintiff or defendant, by a government department or by the Attorney-General. A list of such departments is provided. Where none of these is appropriate, or where there are reasonable doubts as to which is appropriate, the Attorney-General should be made the defendant.[97] The most notable distinction between ordinary actions and those brought against the Crown is in relation to the remedies available. There are two particular points to note in this context.

The first is that it has been argued by Wade and Forsyth that the prerogative remedies cannot lie against the Crown itself since they emanate from the Crown.[98] This is said, however, to be no impediment to the availability of certiorari or prohibition since these remedies lie to control all inferior jurisdictions and therefore apply to Ministers of the Crown on whom powers are conferred by Parliament in their own names. It is said to be a problem in relation to mandamus since the Crown itself has public duties. The consequence, in the context of mandamus, is said to be that where the servant of the Crown is merely an instrument selected by the Crown for the discharge of the Crown's duty, any complaint must lie against the Crown itself. Where, however, Parliament has imposed the duty upon a person acting in a particular capacity mandamus will lie even though such a person is acting upon the Crown's behalf.[99]

Whether this particular limit upon the availability of mandamus really exists is questionable. In general terms the prerogative orders will issue to Ministers of the Crown, and the previous chapters of this book are replete with examples of this. It is clear also that mandamus can issue to a minister who is acting in an official capacity.[100] The objection to the applicability of the prerogative remedies against the Crown itself is also questionable. The authority cited for this proposition[101] gives two reasons for holding that mandamus cannot apply to the sovereign: that it would be incongruous for the sovereign to command herself, and that disobedience results in a writ of attachment.

These arguments would have force if one were thinking of mandamus applying to the sovereign in a personal capacity. They lose much of this force when applied to the sovereign as personified in and through the government of the day. Viewed in this light it does not appear to be incongruous for the prerogative orders that emanate from the Crown, in the sense that historically the Crown had a judicial capacity, to be applied to the Crown in its governmental capacity. Moreover, as Lord Woolf noted[102]: when a minister is sued in his or her official capacity then unless the minister is treated as being distinct from the Crown then the incongruity of the Crown suing the Crown would still be present.

---

[97] Crown Proceedings Act 1947 s.17.
[98] *Administrative Law* (Oxford University Press, 9th edn, 2004), 615.
[99] *Administrative Law*, n.98, 628–629.
[100] *Padfield v Minister of Agriculture, Fisheries and Food* [1968] A.C. 997; *R. v Customs and Excise Commissioners Ex p. Cooke and Stevenson* [1970] 1 W.L.R. 450, 455; *M v Home Office* [1994] 1 A.C. 377.
[101] *R. v Powell* (1841) 1 Q.B. 352, 361.
[102] *M v Home Office* [1994] 1 A.C. 377.

The second point to note is that much of the machinery for enforcing a judgment is excluded. Thus, no execution or attachment or process can issue for enforcing payment by the Crown,[103] and the Crown is not susceptible to an order for specific performance, an injunction or for an order compelling the delivery of property. The plaintiff must be content with a declaratory judgment.[104] This will normally create no problem since the Crown will satisfy the judgment. It has, however, given rise to difficulties where the plaintiff was seeking interim relief as will be seen below. Where the redress required is a money payment, the Act states that the appropriate government department shall pay the amount to the person entitled[105] out of moneys provided by Parliament.[106] The normal rules of indemnity and contribution apply.[107]

B. Injunctions and Interim Relief

The root cause of the problem was that injunctions and interim injunctions were thought not to be available against the Crown or its officers.

28–018

i. Extending injunctive relief

The courts have, as will be seen below, taken different views as to whether the Crown or its officers are subject to injunctive relief, and hence whether they are also liable for interim injunctive relief. It is necessary to review some of the important case law in this area in order to understand the present position.

28–019

(1)   Section 21 of the Crown Proceedings Act 1947 allows the court in civil proceedings to award any relief against the Crown as it could in proceedings between subjects, provided that it cannot grant injunctions or specific performance, but can instead make a declaratory order. Section 21(2) further provides that the court should not grant an injunction against an officer of the Crown if the effect of doing so would be to give any relief against the Crown, which could not have been obtained in proceedings against the Crown itself. Civil proceedings do not include proceedings for judicial review,[108] but prior to the reform of Ord.53 injunctions could not be sought in judicial review actions. The accepted wisdom was, therefore, that injunctive relief could not be sought against the Crown or its officers.

---

[103] Crown Proceedings Act 1947 s.25(4).
[104] Crown Proceedings Act 1947 s.21. See G. Williams, *Crown Proceedings, An Account of Civil Proceedings by and against the Crown as affected by the Crown Proceedings Act, 1947* (Stevens, 1948), Ch.7, for further matters such as the Crown's privilege in choice of forum.
[105] Crown Proceedings Act 1947 s.25(3).
[106] Crown Proceedings Act 1947 s.37.
[107] Crown Proceedings Act 1947 s.4.
[108] Crown Proceedings Act 1947 s.38(2).

(2)   The reforms in the law of remedies then allowed injunctions to be claimed when applying for judicial review, and this was given statutory force by s.31 of the Supreme Court Act 1981. Certain decisions suggested that the absence of injunctive relief had been cured by these reforms, and that injunctions could be sought against officers of the Crown pursuant to judicial review.[109]

(3)   These decisions were, however, overruled in the first *Factortame* case,[110] where Lord Bridge stated that the reforms in the law of remedies could not be taken to have changed the law in this respect: interim injunctive relief against the Crown or officers of the Crown acting as such was not possible. The reasoning was, in essence, as follows. The Crown Proceedings Act 1947 s.21(1) precluded injunctive relief in civil proceedings against the Crown. This prohibition did not, on its face, extend to proceedings for judicial review,[111] but no such prohibition was, however, necessary because injunctions were, in any event, not available in judicial review proceedings prior to, or even after, 1947. Injunctions against officers of the Crown were also prohibited.[112] Section 31 of the Supreme Court Act 1981 could not be held to have altered this position, since a more explicit legislative indication of a change was required.

(4)   It was, somewhat paradoxically, the *Factortame* litigation that fuelled the demand for this gap to be filled. In the first *Factortame* case the House of Lords asked the ECJ whether the absence of interim relief against the Crown was *itself* a breach of Community law. The applicants contended that national legal systems must provide protection for Community rights, and that this required some form of interim protection when those rights were in danger of being irremediably impaired in the period pending the final resolution of the dispute. The ECJ responded by stating that the absence of any such protection was indeed a breach of Community law, and that any national rule preventing this relief from being claimed must be set aside.[113]

28–020   (5)   The case then returned to the House of Lords for consideration in the light of the ECJ's opinion. In *Factortame (No.2)*[114] their Lordships accepted the ECJ's ruling and acknowledged that, as a matter of Community law, interim relief had to be applicable against the Crown. The more specific legal manner of reaching this result was not considered in any detail by the court. Lord Goff relied upon the

---

[109]   *R. v Licensing Authority Established under the Medicines Act Ex p. Smith Kline and French Laboratories Ltd (No.2)* [1990] 2 Q.B. 574; *R v Secretary of State for the Home Department Ex p. Herbage* [1987] Q.B. 872.
[110]   *R. v Secretary of State for Transport Ex p. Factortame Ltd* [1990] 2 A.C. 85.
[111]   Because of the definition of civil proceedings within s.38(2) of the 1947 Act.
[112]   By s.21(2) read with s.23(2)(b).
[113]   *R. v Secretary of State for Transport Ex p. Factortame Ltd* (213/89) [1990] 3 C.M.L.R. 867.
[114]   *R. v Secretary of State for Transport Ex p. Factortame Ltd (No.2)* [1991] 1 A.C. 603.

general power to award injunctive relief contained in the Supreme Court Act 1981, and then applied the principle to the facts of the case.[115]

(6) In purely formal terms the decision in *Factortame (No.2)* only applied to cases with a Community law element. This created an uneasy dualism: interim injunctive relief could be obtained in cases with a Community law element, but not in those that were wholly domestic in character. The very existence of the remedy in the one type of case added weight to the suggestion that it should be equally available in the other. This provides a good example of the indirect influence that Community law can have upon our jurisprudence: it might only apply in certain areas, but this then creates pressure for reform in domestic law.[116]

(7) The matter rested there until the decision of the House of Lords in *M v Home Office*.[117] The facts of this case will be set out more fully below. However, the question of injunctive relief came before the court, in essence, because the Home Secretary was being held in contempt of court for action he had taken in relation to M who had been refused political asylum. The availability of injunctions against the Crown was relevant because if the courts had no power to make such coercive orders then the judge who had made the finding of contempt might have done so without jurisdiction. Lord Woolf, giving the judgment of the court, in effect reversed the holding in the first *Factortame* case, and held that injunctions, including interim injunctions, were available against ministers of the Crown. The reasoning is complex and cannot be fully explored here. The essence of the argument was, however, as follows. Lord Woolf's judgment can be conveniently divided into two parts, which dealt respectively with the interpretation of the 1947 Act and the 1981 Act.

(8) His Lordship began his interpretation of the *1947 Act* by considering the legal position prior to its passage. He held that prior to the 1947 Act a plaintiff could sue the actual wrongdoer, even if this was a minister acting in his official capacity, and that an injunction could be issued. This was so even after 1947, since s.21(2) of the Act only prevented actions against a minister acting in a representative capacity. If a statute placed a duty on a specific minister, as opposed to the Crown, then an action could be brought and an injunction could be obtained. A minister could, therefore, be personally liable for wrongs done when acting in an official capacity.[118]

---

[115] P. Craig, "Administrative Law, Remedies and Europe" (1991) 3 E.R.P.L. 521, 527.
[116] See above, Ch.10.
[117] [1994] 1 A.C. 377. See also *Davidson v Scottish Ministers (No.1)* [2005] UKHL 74; *Beggs v Scottish Ministers* [2007] 1 W.L.R. 455.
[118] Lord Woolf doubted the correctness of the judgment in *Merricks v Heathcoat-Amory* [1955] Ch.567.

(9) With this reasoning behind him Lord Woolf then turned to the *1981 Act*. The analysis of the 1947 Act was, however, crucial, when interpreting the later legislation because a cornerstone of Lord Bridge's opinion in *Factortame*[119] was that no injunctive relief against ministers had been available under the 1947 regime, and that therefore any change from this position would have been dramatic. Lord Woolf's contrary interpretation of the 1947 legislation blunted the edge of this critique. He further pointed out that prohibition and mandamus were applicable to ministers, so that the only consequence of reading s.31 as enabling injunctions to be granted against ministers would be to provide an alternative to those remedies and to allow interim relief.[120] Lord Woolf's conclusion was that injunctive relief, both final and interim, should be available against officers of the Crown, given the unqualified language of s.31. These remedies could, moreover, be issued even prior to the granting of leave where this was appropriate.

(10) The general jurisdiction to issue injunctions should, however, only be exercised in limited circumstances, and his Lordship left open the possibility of the courts being able to grant interim declarations. It is to this issue that we should now turn.

ii. Interim declarations

28–021 The courts, in the past, set their face against the grant of interim declarations.[121] In *Rossminster*[122] their Lordships differed as to whether interim relief should be available against the Crown. Lord Wilberforce, Viscount Dilhorne and Lord Scarman all expressed doubts about the availability of interim relief against the Crown, and about the advisability of providing this remedy.[123] Lord Diplock was of a different view: the absence of such relief was seen as a serious procedural defect.[124] There have been three main objections to the granting of such relief.

The first was that the very idea of an interim declaration, even between private parties, was simply illogical. A declaration necessarily declared the final rights of the parties and could not simply preserve the status quo. This reasoning is questionable. Thus, it is said that there cannot be an interim declaration because declarations exist to tell people what their rights are and this cannot be achieved until the final judgment.[125] But the claimant is not seeking a final determination of her rights at this stage. The claimant is

---

[119] [1990] 2 A.C. 85.
[120] [1994] 1 A.C. 377.
[121] *Underhill v Ministry of Food* [1950] 1 All E.R. 591; *International General Electric Co of New York Ltd v Customs and Excise Commissioners* [1962] Ch.784.
[122] *R. v Inland Revenue Commissioners Ex p.Rossminster Ltd* [1980] A.C. 952.
[123] *Rossminster*, n.122, 1001, 1007, 1027.
[124] *Rossminster*, n.122, 1014–1015.
[125] *International General Electric*, n.121, 789; *R. v Collins Ex p. S (No.2)* [1998] C.O.D. 396, 399.

simply asking the court to preserve the status quo. This objection to the grant of interim declaratory relief has been rejected by some other high authorities, which have seen nothing odd or illogical about an interim declaration.[126] It has also been argued that the final declaration might be in different terms from the interim order, and therefore should not be available.[127] Yet it is difficult to see the logic of the argument that because a final order can differ from the interim relief, therefore the interim relief cannot be given. Final injunctions will often differ from an interim injunction granted to preserve the status quo.

The second argument was that to grant an interim declaration would indirectly infringe against the principle that the decisions of the state are presumptively valid unless and until they are shown to be wrong.[128] This argument is flawed. There is nothing inconsistent in regarding, quite correctly, such decisions as presumptively valid and still leaving open the possibility of granting interim relief. The presumption of validity places the burden of proof upon the party challenging the decision. It does not tell us whether that party should be able to claim interim relief. Provided that the claimant is required to show a sufficiently strong prima facie case of invalidity and provided that the balance of convenience is properly assessed, interim relief is not be inconsistent with this principle.[129]

The third argument against the interim declaration was that it would have much the same effect as would the grant of an injunction.[130] This argument is difficult to understand. Section 21 of the Crown Proceedings Act 1947 provides for a declaration to be granted instead of an injunction or specific performance. The argument might be that the Crown would feel duty bound to abide by the court's order. This could, however, be said just as much about final declarations. The Crown does comply with them. It might mean a wariness of granting interim relief on incomplete evidence.[131] This is a valid reason for not giving such relief on the facts of a particular case,[132] because the claimant cannot meet the required standard of proof. It is difficult to see how it provides an objection in principle to the interim declaration.

The procedure for judicial review is now governed by CPR, Pt 54. The judicial review procedure under CPR, Pt 54 is a modification of CPR, Pt 8. CPR, Pt 25, sets out a number of interim orders that a court can grant, including an interim declaration.[133] This is to be welcomed since it provides a valuable additional remedy that can be used against the Crown where it is felt that an injunction is inappropriate.

---

[126] Such as in the Israeli courts.
[127] *Underhill*, n.121, 593; *Rossminster*, n.122, 1027.
[128] *Rossminster*, n.122, 1027, Lord Scarman
[129] Lord Diplock saw no inconsistency between the presumption of validity and the availability of interim relief, *Rossminster*, n.122, 1013, 1014–1015, and it was Lord Diplock who gave the exposition of that presumption in *Hoffmann-La Roche & Co AG v Secretary of State for Trade and Industry* [1975] A.C. 295, 366–367.
[130] *Rossminster*, n.122, 1001, 1007.
[131] Lord Wilberforce, *Rossminster*, n.122, 1001.
[132] As in *Rossminster* itself where the material necessary to challenge the legality of the seizure was protected by public interest immunity at the time of the action
[133] CPR 25.1(1)(b); *R. v R* [2000] 1 F.L.R. 451; *X NHS Trust v T* [2005] 1 All E.R. 387.

iii. Conclusion

28–022   The immunity of the Crown from interim relief was not sustainable on grounds of legal principle.[134] The decision in *M v Home Office* is, therefore, to be welcomed, as is the introduction of the interim declaration.

C. Contempt

28–023   The leading decision on this point is *M v Home Office*.[135] The applicant, M, arrived from Zaire and sought political asylum in the UK. The claim for asylum was rejected by the Secretary of State and he made a direction for the removal of M back to Zaire. M then sought leave to apply for judicial review. The judge thought that there was an arguable point and wished M to remain in the UK until the following day when the point could be fully argued. Counsel for the Secretary of State then gave what the judge believed to be an undertaking that M would not be removed from the UK pending the hearing. There followed a series of mistakes and mishaps, which culminated in M being returned to Zaire. The judge then issued a mandatory order to the Home Secretary demanding that M be returned to the UK. The Home Secretary challenged this order, after taking legal advice, and the judge, at a hearing on the issue, discharged the order on the basis that he, the judge, had no power to make it. An action was then brought on behalf of M for contempt of court by the Home Secretary on the basis that he had broken the undertaking and the judge's order while it was in force.

The House of Lords held that coercive orders, such as injunctions, could lie against Ministers of the Crown, and that if a minister acted in disregard of an injunction made against him in his official capacity the court had jurisdiction to make a finding of contempt against him or his department, albeit not against the Crown itself. The contempt proceedings would, however, differ from normal proceedings of this kind, in that they would not be either personal or punitive: fines and sequestration of assets would not be appropriate in cases involving departments or ministers, although they might be necessary in other instances. There would, said Lord Woolf, still be a point in the finding of contempt since such a finding would vindicate the requirements of justice, and this could be underlined by awarding costs against the government. It would then be for Parliament to decide upon the consequences of the contempt. Any such finding of contempt would be against the authorised department, the Minister or the Attorney-General, rather than the Crown. It would, moreover, be more normal to make the finding of contempt against the department as opposed to the Minister personally. The constitutional precept that the Crown itself can do no wrong was preserved, by presuming that the Minister had acted without the authority of the Crown in such circumstances.

The decision in the case is undoubtedly of significance in emphasising that the government must obey the law not just as a matter of choice, but

---

[134] LCCP No.126, 46.
[135] [1994] 1 A.C. 377.

ultimately by way of compulsion. Instances of contempt are likely to be rare in practice, but this should not diminish the important point of principle in the House of Lords' ruling. It is fitting to conclude this discussion with the following words of Lord Templeman.[136]

"My Lords, the argument that there is no power to enforce the law by injunction or contempt proceedings against a minister in his official capacity would, if upheld, establish the proposition that the executive obey the law as a matter of grace and favour and not as a matter of necessity, a proposition which would reverse the result of the Civil War."

---

[136] [1994] 1 A.C. 377, 395. See also *Beggs v Scottish Ministers* 2005 S.L.T. 305; *Beggs*, n.117.

CHAPTER 29

TORT AND RESTITUTION

INTRODUCTION

It may be helpful at the outset to consider the foundations of the present law[1] and the options at our disposal when thinking about damages liability.

29–001

A. Foundations of the Present Law

All legal systems have to decide on the conceptual foundation for damages liability in actions involving public bodies. The principles that underlie the common law regime can be succinctly stated.

29–002

A public body that acts ultra vires is liable in tort if a cause of action is established, just like any private individual would be. There is no general cloak of immunity.[2] However, the basic premise is that an ultra vires act per se will not give rise to damages liability.[3] The claim must therefore be capable of being fitted into one of the recognised private law causes of action.

Thus in the X case Lord Browne-Wilkinson identified three possible

---

[1] H. Street, *Governmental Liability* (Cambridge University Press, 1953), Ch.2; C. Harlow, *Compensation and Government Torts* (Sweet & Maxwell, 1982); S. Arrowsmith, *Civil Liability and Public Authorities* (Earlsgate Press, 1992); B. Markesinis, J.-B. Auby, D. Coester-Waltjen and S. Deakin, *Tortious Liability of Statutory Bodies, A Comparative Analysis of Five English Cases* (Hart, 1999); J Wright, *Tort Law and Human Rights* (Hart, 2001); D. Fairgrieve, M. Andenas, and J. Bell (eds), *Tort Liability of Public Authorities in Comparative Perspective* (BIICL, 2002); D. Fairgrieve, *State Liability in Tort: A Comparative Law Study* (Oxford University Press, 2003); C. Harlow, *State Liability, Tort Law and Beyond* (Oxford University Press, 2004); T. Cornford, *Towards a Public Law of Tort* (Ashgate, 2008).
[2] *Entick v Carrington* (1765) 19 St. Tr. 1030; *Leach v Money* (1765) 19 St. Tr. 2002; *Cooper v Wandsworth Board of Works* (1863) 14 C.B. (N.S.) 180; *Pride of Derby and Derbyshire Angling Association Ltd v British Celanese Ltd* [1953] Ch.149; P. Craig, "Compensation in Public Law" (1980) 96 L.Q.R. 413. On the availability of exemplary damages see *AB v South West Water Services Ltd* [1993] 1 All E.R. 609.
[3] *X (Minors) v Bedfordshire CC* [1995] 2 A.C. 633, 730G.

causes of action which might avail a plaintiff in a case against a public body.[4] These were an action for breach of statutory duty simpliciter, without the need to prove any carelessness; an action for breach of a common law duty of care arising from the imposition of a statutory duty or from its performance; and misfeasance in a public office. His Lordship made it clear that there could be no cause of action based simply upon the careless performance of a statutory duty in the absence of any other common law right of action.

We do not therefore have what would be recognised by other legal systems as a general principle of damages liability, nor do we have any wholly separate body of law dealing with damages actions against public bodies.

B. The Available Options

29–003　It is important to be aware of the range of options at our disposal when thinking about monetary liability. There are eight basic options available.

(1)　Liability can be imposed on the basis of illegality or ultra vires action per se.

(2)　Liability can be based on negligence.

(3)　Liability can be based on the existence of some serious breach.

(4)　Liability can be based on intentional wrongdoing.

(5)　There can be immunity from suit.

(6)　There can be a requirement to compensate even in respect of some lawfully caused governmental loss.

(7)　Compensation can be given on an ex gratia basis.

(8)　There can be an obligation to grant restitutionary relief.

The term "fault" may prove to be an imperfect guide for distinguishing between these options, since it is used differently in different legal systems. Thus, it may be treated as equivalent to illegality, which is the approach in some civil law systems.[5] Thus in France the starting assumption is that illegality connotes fault and hence responsibility in damages. This is also the case in EU law for acts where there is no real discretion. The only circumstance in which the common law approximates to this position is where there has been a finding that a breach of a statute gives rise, in and of itself, to liability in damages.

Fault may, however, be seen as distinct from illegality, which is the general approach taken in common law jurisdictions. Proof of illegality, in the sense of an ultra vires act, will not be treated as the equivalent of fault

---

[4]　*X*, n.3, 730–740.
[5]　Thus in France the starting point is that "toute illegalite constitue par elle-meme une faute".

for the purposes of damages liability. The plaintiff will still have to prove the existence of a duty of care, a breach thereof, and recoverable damage.

A third sense of the term fault is to be found in EU law. Where there is some significant measure of discretion, and/or where the meaning of the Community norm is imprecise, illegality *per se* will not suffice for liability. The applicant will have to prove that the breach was sufficiently serious. There is however no requirement of fault going beyond proof of the serious breach of EU law.

2. NEGLIGENCE, STATUTORY DUTIES AND STATUTORY POWERS

It is fitting to begin with discussion of negligence, which is the most common **29–004** action against a public body. The law concerning negligence liability and public bodies is complex, and is still evolving.[6] The tort requires the existence of a duty of care, breach of that duty, causation and damage. This apparently simple formulation conceals a plethora of interpretative issues, which have been especially problematic in relation to public bodies. It is clear that there can be no cause of action based simply upon the careless performance of a statutory duty or power in the absence of any other common law right of action.[7] It is for the plaintiff to establish that there is a common law duty of care arising from the imposition of a statutory duty or from its performance.[8] The more precise circumstances in which the courts would be willing to impose a duty of care on public bodies have however altered over time. Three approaches can be identified.

[6] Street, n.1, 40, 56–80; Harlow, n.1; Arrowsmith, n.1, Ch.6; G. Ganz, "Compensation for Negligent Administrative Action" [1973] P.L. 84; C. Harlow, "Fault Liability in French and English Public Law" (1976) 39 M.L.R. 516; P. Craig, "Negligence in the Exercise of a Statutory Power" (1978) 94 L.Q.R. 428; M. Bowman and S. Bailey, "Negligence in the Realms of Public Law—A Positive Obligation to Rescue" [1984] P.L. 277; T. Weir, "Governmental Liability" [1989] P.L. 40; M. Andenas and D. Fairgrieve, "Sufficiently Serious? Judicial Restraint in Tortious Liability of Public Authorities and the European Influence", in M. Andenas (ed.), *English Public Law and the Common Law of Europe* (Key Haven, 1998), Ch.14; S. Bailey and M. Bowman, "Public Authority Negligence Revisited" [2000] C.L.J.; P. Craig and D. Fairgrieve, "*Barrett*, Negligence and Discretionary Powers" [1999] PL 626; D. Fairgrieve, "Pushing Back the Frontiers of Public Authority Liability" [2002] P.L. 288; T. Hickman, "Tort Law, Public Authorities and the Human Rights Act 1998", in Fairgrieve, Andenas and Bell, n.1, Ch.2; T. Hickman, "The Reasonableness Principle: Re-assessing its Place in the Public Sphere" [2004] C.L.J. 166; R. Bagshaw, "Monetary Remedies in Public Law — Misdiagnosis and Misprescription" [2006] L.S. 4; Sir B. Markesinis and J. Fedtke, "Damages for the Negligence of Statutory Bodies: The Empirical and Comparative Dimensions to an Unending Debate" [2007] P.L. 299.

[7] *X*, n.3, 732–733.

[8] *X*, n.3, 735–736.

A. The "Liberal Approach"

29–005 After some initial doubts[9] it was established in *Mersey Docks and Harbour Board Trustees v Gibbs*[10] that a public body could be liable in negligence when exercising a statutory power.[11] The decision was affirmed by the House of Lords,[12] and applied in a number of later cases.[13] The general tendency was to impose liability on public bodies when they failed to take care and caused reasonably foreseeable loss pursuant to a statutory power or duty.

This was in accord with the more general tendency in the law of negligence post *Donoghue v Stevenson*.[14] The years after this landmark decision saw the courts reassessing areas that were not subject to the normal precepts of negligence liability and they often concluded that such areas should be brought within the framework of the principles laid down by Lord Atkin in *Donoghue*, even if, as for example in the case of liability for negligent misstatement, the principles were modified in their operation in a particular area.

This approach was then embodied in Lord Wilberforce's test in the *Anns* case.[15] If there was sufficient proximity between plaintiff and defendant such that reasonably foreseeable loss would be caused to the plaintiff by the defendant's failure to take care then prima facie there was liability, unless the defendant could advance good public policy reasons for this not to be so.

The application of this reasoning to public bodies was tempered by the policy/operational distinction. The distinction had been alluded to in earlier cases.[16] Thus in *Dorset Yacht*,[17] borstal boys, who had been working on an island under the supervision of officers, escaped and damaged the plaintiff's yacht. The Home Office had instituted a system of open rather than closed borstal institutions, because it felt that it would enhance reform of offenders. This necessarily involved a higher risk of escape, and therefore a correlative increase of damage to property. The House of Lords rejected the wide claim for immunity advanced by the Home Office. Their Lordships nonetheless acknowledged that to ask whether the Home Office had been negligent in adopting this policy choice would require the court to balance society's

---

[9] The doubts were raised by a misinterpretation of earlier cases such as *Sutton v Clarke* (1815) 6 Taunt 29, and due to an obiter dictum of Lord Cottenham L.C. in *Duncan v Findlater* (1839) Macl. & R. 911. See, *Mersey Docks and Harbour Board Trustees v Gibbs* (1864–1866) 11 H.L.C. 686, 719–721.

[10] (1864–1866) 11 H.L.C. 686.

[11] (1864–1866) 11 H.L.C. 686, 719–721.

[12] (1864–1866) 11 H.L.C. 686, 725–734.

[13] e.g. *Geddis v Proprietors of Bann Reservoir* (1878) 3 App. Cas. 430, 438, 452, 455–456; *East Fremantle Corporation v Annois* [1902] A.C. 213, 217–219; *Great Central Ry Co v Hewlett* [1916] 2 A.C. 511, 519, 525; *Fisher v Ruislip-Northwood Urban District Council and Middlesex County Council* [1945] K.B. 584.

[14] [1932] A.C. 562.

[15] *Anns v Merton LBC* [1978] A.C. 728.

[16] *East Suffolk Rivers Catchment Board v Kent* [1940] 1 K.B. 319, CA, [1941] A.C. 74, HL.

[17] *Dorset Yacht Co Ltd v Home Office* [1970] A.C. 1004.

interest in the reform of the offender, the interest of the offender, and the danger to private property, which was something that a court should not do.[18] The decision was one of policy and was non-justiciable. Liability could, however, still exist at the operational level. *Given* that the authorities had chosen a more open prison system, the issue was whether there had been negligence within that framework.[19]

The planning/operational dichotomy was made explicit in *Anns*.[20] The plaintiffs alleged that the council had been negligent in their inspection of foundations, causing cracks in their maisonettes. Assuming that there had been a careless inspection, Lord Wilberforce[21] held that it would be easier to impose a duty of care on the operational rather than the planning level. The latter would encompass the scale of the resources that should be made available to carry out the powers, the number of inspectors, and the type of inspections to be made.[22] Therefore, if the defendants had decided that their inspectors could only carry out limited tests, the costs of more extensive checks being prohibitive, an individual could not claim in negligence merely because a further test would have revealed the defect. Where the inspector was simply careless in performing the prescribed tests, liability would ensue, since this would be purely operational negligence.[23]

Later authority focused directly on justiciability, which underlies the policy/operational dichotomy. In *Rowling*,[24] their Lordships held that this distinction did not itself provide a touchstone of liability.[25] It was rather expressive of the need to exclude altogether those cases in which the decision under attack was unsuitable for judicial resolution, as in cases concerning the discretionary allocation of scarce resources or distribution of risks. Classification of a decision as a policy or planning decision could, therefore, exclude liability. A public authority would not, however, simply be able to assert that it, for example, balanced thrift and efficiency in order to evade liability. It would have to show that it reached its decision in this manner, and it would then be for the court to decide whether the issue was non-justiciable.

29–006

There has been considerable discussion of the planning/operational dichotomy. The following points should be borne in mind in this respect.

First, the division was never self-executing. The terms were used in a

---

[18] This is most explicit in the judgment of Lord Diplock, [1970] A.C. 1004, 1066–1068, but it is also evident in the judgments of Lord Reid, 1031–1032, Lord Morris of Borth-y-Gest, 1036–1037, and Lord Pearson, 1055–1056.

[19] For an interesting comparison see, *Evangelical United Brethren Church of Adna v State* 407 P 2d 440 (1965).

[20] *Anns*, n.15.

[21] Lord Diplock, Lord Simon and Lord Russell concurred

[22] [1978] A.C. 728, 754.

[23] On the alternative hypothesis that the defendant had not exercised the power, Lord Wilberforce held that although the defendant was under no duty to inspect it was under a duty to consider whether it should inspect or not. Negligence liability would ensue if the defendant failed to take reasonable care in its acts or omissions to secure compliance with the bylaws, [1978] A.C. 728, 755

[24] *Rowling v Takaro Properties Ltd* [1988] A.C. 473.

[25] See also, *Stovin v Wise* [1996] A.C. 923, 951–952; *Barrett v Enfield LBC* [2001] 2 A.C. 550.

conclusory role. A court faced with an allegation of negligence would consider the negligence claim, and decide whether the allegation was suitable for judicial resolution. When the court felt that it was unsuited for judicial resolution it would apply the label planning decision to express that conclusion.

Second, given that justiciability underlies the planning-operational dichotomy, it is preferable to focus directly on this, thereby avoiding any possible confusion caused by misinterpretation of the terms planning and operational.

Third, the mere presence of some discretion does not entail the conclusion that the matter is thereby non-justiciable. Discretionary judgments made by public bodies, which the courts feel able to assess, should not therefore preclude the existence of negligence liability. This does not mean that discretion will be irrelevant to the determination of liability. It will, as seen below, be relevant in deciding whether there has been a breach of the duty of care.

Fourth, the preceding analysis does not necessitate any "separate" tort for public bodies.[26] Where justiciability is relevant it will be one factor which the court will consider in determining whether a duty of care should be excluded.[27] This analysis will take place within the reformulated concept of duty, under which the court considers a range of factors to determine whether a duty of care exists.[28]

Finally, notwithstanding the academic and judicial ink devoted to this topic, neither the planning/operational distinction, nor justiciability, has been the principal reason why the courts have denied the existence of a duty of care in relation to public authorities. The duty of care has been excluded, as will be seen from the subsequent section, because the courts have felt that it would not be fair, just and reasonable to impose a duty of care in particular cases for a variety of reasons that have had little if anything to do with justiciability.

B. The "Cautious" or "Restrictive Approach"

29–007 A more cautious or restrictive approach to the existence of the duty of care was apparent in cases such as *X v Bedfordshire*[29] and *Stovin*.[30] This label is warranted for three related reasons.

i. Incrementalism and the restriction of the duty of care

29–008 These cases were premised on developments in the general law of negligence that emphasised caution. *Anns* quickly became the subject of judicial criticism, and the House of Lords turned away from Lord Wilberforce's two

---

[26] *Cf.* Bowman and Bailey, n.6; Harlow, n.6.
[27] *Rowling*, n.24.
[28] nn.31–32.
[29] *X*, n.3.
[30] *Stovin v Wise* [1996] A.C. 923.

stage test. It emphasised the cautious and incremental development of the law of negligence. The existence of a duty of care was dependent on the following three factors: there had to be reasonably foreseeable loss as a result of the failure to take care; there had to be sufficient proximity between plaintiff and defendant; and the imposition of a duty of care had to be fair, just and reasonable.[31]

In deciding whether it was fair just and reasonable to impose a duty of care the courts would, inter alia, construe the relevant statutes to determine the scope of any such duty of care. Thus in *Peabody*[32] it was held that a local authority was not liable in negligence to building developers because the purpose of the relevant statutory powers was not to safeguard such developers against economic loss, but rather to safeguard occupiers of houses and the public generally against dangers to health and safety flowing from defective drainage installations. In *Curran*,[33] a statutory authority which provided funds for accommodation and home improvement was held not liable in negligence to a purchaser to whom they had provided a mortgage when the extension to the house which he had purchased proved to be seriously defective. The statutory authority had furnished funds for the extension to the previous owner, but it was held that since the relevant provisions gave the authority no power to control the actual building operation, it could not be sued in negligence for the defects to the property.

In deciding whether it was fair just and reasonable to impose a duty of care, the courts would also take account of a wide range of other policy factors. In practice the most important factor limiting liability was not the policy/operational distinction or justiciability, but rather the judicial determination that it was not fair, just and reasonable to impose such a duty.[34] Justiciability may have been part of this determination, but in many cases there have been other factors leading the courts to conclude that there should be no duty of care. This is apparent from a number of leading decisions.

In *Hill*,[35] it was decided that there was no duty of care on the police in **29–009** relation to the investigation or suppression of crime. Lord Keith was influenced in reaching this conclusion by the fact that the chief police officer had a wide discretion as to the manner in which the duty to prevent crime was discharged. It was for him to decide how the available resources should be deployed, whether particular lines of inquiry should be followed and whether certain crimes should be prosecuted. It was not therefore

---

[31] *Caparo Industries Plc v Dickman* [1990] 2 A.C. 605.
[32] *Governors of the Peabody Donation Fund v Sir Lindsay Parkinson and Co Ltd* [1985] A.C. 210, 241, 245; *Investors in Industry Commercial Properties Ltd v South Bedfordshire District Council* [1986] Q.B. 1034; *Murphy v Brentwood District Council* [1991] 1 A.C. 398.
[33] *Curran v Northern Ireland Co-Ownership Housing Association Ltd* [1987] A.C. 718, 728.
[34] *Peabody*, n.32; *Curran*, n.33; *Yuen Kun-Yeu v Att-Gen. of Hong Kong* [1988] A.C. 175; *Rowling v Takaro Properties Ltd* [1988] A.C. 473; *Hill v Chief Constable of West Yorkshire* [1989] A.C. 53; *Calveley v Chief Constable of the Merseyside Police* [1989] A.C. 1228; *Clough v Bussan* [1990] 1 All E.R. 431; *Richardson v West Lindsey District Council* [1990] 1 W.L.R. 522; *Kirkham v Chief Constable of the Greater Manchester Police* [1990] 2 Q.B. 283; *Davis v Radcliffe* [1990] 1 W.L.R. 821; *Welsh v Chief Constable of the Merseyside Police* [1993] 1 All E.R. 692.
[35] *Hill*, n.34.

appropriate for there to be any general duty of care to members of the public. It was also felt that such a duty of care would lead to defensive policing and the inefficient diversion of resources.[36]

The decision in *Capital and Counties Plc*[37] was concerned with the existence and extent of the liability the fire brigade owed when attending a fire. The Court of Appeal decided that there was no common law duty of care to answer the call for help. It also held that there was no sufficiently proximate relationship between the fire brigade and the owner of premises so as to give rise to a duty of care merely because the fire brigade came to fight the fire. Liability in negligence could only arise if the fire brigade had increased the risk of danger to the plaintiff and caused damage that would not otherwise have occurred. The same result was reached in relation to the coastguard services in the *OLL* case.[38]

In *X*[39] there were a number of joined cases, some of which were concerned with allegations of negligence relating to child abuse, others of which were concerned with allegations of negligence relating to the provision of special educational needs. The House of Lords held that there was no direct duty of care owed by the local authorities in the child abuse cases. Lord Browne-Wilkinson held that it would not be fair, just and reasonable to impose such a duty. Five reasons can be identified from his judgment.

First, he felt that a duty of care would "cut across the whole statutory system set up for the protection of children at risk".[40] Protection of children from abuse was not the exclusive preserve of the local authority's social services. There was an interdisciplinary system involving the participation of the police, educational bodies, doctors and others. To impose liability for negligence on only one such body would, said Lord Browne-Wilkinson, be manifestly unfair. To impose it on all such bodies would lead to impossible problems of disentangling the respective liability of each of the participants.[41] The second reason was because the local authority's task in dealing with children at risk was "extraordinarily delicate".[42] The relevant legislation required the local authority to have regard to the physical well-being of the child, and also to the need not to disrupt the child's family. This duality was reflected in the claims before the court, one of which alleged that the child had been moved precipitately, the other that the child had not been removed soon enough. The third reason that led to the denial of a duty of care was that it could well lead the local authorities to adopt a "more cautious and defensive approach to their duties".[43] Speed of action was

---

[36] See also, *Alexandrou v Oxford* [1993] 4 All E.R. 328; *Vellino v Chief Constable of Greater Manchester* [2002] 1 W.L.R. 218; *Cowan v Chief Constable of Avon and Somerset* [2002] H.L.R. 44. Compare however *Swinney v Chief Constable of the Northumbria Police* [1997] Q.B. 464; *Swinney v Chief Constable of the Northumbria Police (No.2)* [1999] Admin. L.R. 811.
[37] *Capital and Counties plc v Hampshire CC* [1997] Q.B. 1004.
[38] *OLL Ltd v Secretary of State for Transport* [1997] 3 ALL E.R. 897.
[39] *X*, n.3.
[40] *X*, n.3, 749.
[41] *X*, n.3, 750.
[42] *X*, n.3, 750.
[43] *X*, n.3, 750.

often vital in such cases. If the local authority could be made liable for a negligent decision to remove a child then "there would be a substantial temptation to postpone making such a decision until further inquiries have been made in the hope of getting more concrete facts".[44] This would increase the risk of the child being abused, and would reduce the time available for dealing with other such cases. The availability of alternative remedies laid down in the relevant statute was the fourth reason for denying a duty of care. The final rationale for this conclusion was that in deciding whether to develop novel categories of negligence liability the courts should proceed with caution, particularly where Parliament had charged a body with the task of protecting society from the wrongdoing of others.[45]

ii. Discretion and the restriction of the duty of care
The second reason why the label "cautious" or "restrictive" is warranted in relation to these cases is that the House of Lords placed further constraints on a negligence action against a public body, which were related to the existence of statutory discretion. Lord Browne-Wilkinson, who gave judgment in *X*, acknowledged that most statutory duties involved discretion as to the extent to which, and the methods by which, the statutory duty was to be performed.[46]

29–010

It was held that nothing which the body did within the ambit of its discretion could give rise to an action at common law. In determining whether the challenged action was outside its statutory discretion, the court could not assess factors which were felt to be non-justiciable, or within the policy category of the policy/operational dichotomy. In that sense, "a common law duty of care in relation to the taking of decisions involving policy matters cannot exist".[47] Even if a matter were justiciable, the plaintiff, in seeking to show that the authority had acted outside its discretion, would have to prove that it acted manifestly unreasonably so that its action falls entirely outside the ambit of the statutory discretion.[48]

If the challenged decision did fall outside the statutory discretion, it might give rise to a common law duty of care, but whether it did so would depend on the application of the standard tests for the determination of such a common law duty. The court would take into account, inter alia: whether the statute was intended for the protection of those such as the plaintiff;[49] whether the existence of this common law duty would be inconsistent with or discourage the performance of the statutory duties;[50] and whether the public body was acting pursuant to a statutory duty or statutory power, the

---

[44] *X*, n.3, 750.
[45] *X*, n.3, 751.
[46] *X*, n.3, 736.
[47] *X*, n.3, 738.
[48] *X*, n.3, 736H–737A, 749C–D, 761A–B.
[49] *Peabody*, n.32; *Curran*, n.33.
[50] *X*, n.3, 739; *Stovin*, n.30, 952–953.

courts being more reluctant to impose a common law duty of care in the latter instance than in the former.[51]

iii. Omissions and the restriction of the duty of care

29–011 The third reason for the appellation "cautious" or "restrictive" is the approach taken to omissions. It was clear from Lord Hoffmann's majority judgment in *Stovin* that the courts would only rarely impose a duty of care on a public body for failure to exercise a statutory power. He reasoned as follows.

It was for the court to decide in the light of the statute conferring the power whether the authority was not only under a duty in public law to consider exercising the power, but also under a private law duty to act, which might give rise to a claim in damages.[52] The plaintiff had to show that it was irrational for the authority not to have exercised the power, so that there was in effect a public law duty to act; and there had to be exceptional grounds for holding that the policy of the statute conferred the right to compensation on those who suffered loss if the power was not exercised. The very fact that Parliament had conferred discretion on the public body, rather than a duty, was some indication that the policy of the statute was not to create a right to compensation.[53]

Lord Hoffmann accepted the doctrine of general reliance, developed in the Australian High Court,[54] but only in limited circumstances. The doctrine as propounded by Mason J. was based on the idea that the legislature might well have imposed powers on a public body in relation to matters of such complexity or magnitude that individuals could not be expected to take adequate steps for their own protection. Such a situation generated a general expectation on the part of the individual that the power would be exercised, and a realisation on the part of the public authority that there would be general reliance on the exercise of that power.

Lord Hoffmann held[55] that it was essential to this doctrine that the benefit or service provided under statutory powers should be of a uniform or routine nature, so that one could describe exactly what the public authority was supposed to do, as in the case of inspection for defects. If a service were provided as routine it would therefore be irrational for a public authority to provide it in one case and arbitrarily to withhold it in another. It was, however, also necessary for the plaintiff to show that there was some policy to provide compensation where the power had not been exercised.

---

[51] *Stovin*, n.30, 949, 953. It was also made clear that any such claim would be limited to those instances where the action of the public body had made things worse than if it had not acted at all. There would be no such claim where the plaintiff alleged that there had been a failure to confer a benefit on the plaintiff or a failure to protect him from loss, *Stovin*, n.30, 949.

[52] *Stovin*, n.30, 949–950.

[53] *Stovin*, n.30, 953.

[54] *Sutherland Shire Council v Heyman* (1985) 157 C.L.R. 424, 464, Mason J. The doctrine now seems to have passed out of favour, *Pyrenees Shire Council v Day* (1998) 192 C.L.R. 330.

[55] *Stovin*, n.30, 953–955.

C. The "Middle Way"

The law must now be seen in the light of the House of Lords' decisions in **29–012**
Barrett[56] and *Phelps*.[57] The hallmarks of this approach are twofold: a greater
unwillingness to allow the duty of care to be excluded in its entirety, with a
correlative willingness to consider problems concerned with the exercise of
discretionary power at the breach level. These will be considered in turn. It is
nonetheless also important to qualify the extent of the change by recog-
nizing that the courts have in certain instances denied the existence of the
duty of care and that the judicial approach towards omissions continues to
be very restrictive.

i. Greater unwillingness to exclude the duty of care in its entirety
The greater unwillingness to exclude the duty of care in its entirety is evident **29–013**
in two ways in the more recent case law.

First, there is a greater reluctance to decide cases on claims that the action
should be struck out. Many important cases in this area had been decided in
this way. This involved a preliminary determination of whether the facts as
pleaded disclosed a cause of action or not. The dangers of dealing with cases
in this way were acknowledged in *Barrett*, in particular by Lord Browne-
Wilkinson,[58] but also by Lord Slynn and Lord Hutton. Thus Lord Hutton
stated that the court simply could not really know at this stage of the
proceedings whether there were non-justiciable matters involved in the
plaintiff's claim, since it was not known what factors the defendant took into
account when making decisions about the plaintiff. It might, said his
Lordship, transpire that there were not such issues in the case, so that the
trial judge could decide the matter according to normal principles, involving
a determination as to whether the defendant had been negligent as judged by
the standards to be expected from that profession.[59]

Second, we have seen that it was common for claims to fail because the
court decided that it was not fair, just or reasonable to impose a duty of
care. The decisions in *Barrett* and *Phelps* indicate a greater reluctance to
exclude a duty of care on this ground.

In *Barrett*,[60] the defendant local authority contended that it would not be
fair, just and reasonable to impose a duty of care in relation to the
responsibilities which it exercised when undertaking foster care for a child.
This argument found favour in the Court of Appeal.[61] Lord Woolf M.R.
held that the local authority stood in place of the natural parents, and in the
same way that a child should not be able to sue the latter for the decisions
made as to the child's future, neither should he be able to sue the local

---

[56] *Barrett v Enfield LBC* [2001] 2 A.C. 550.
[57] *Phelps v Hillingdon LBC* [2001] 2 A.C. 619.
[58] *Barrett*, n.56, 557–558.
[59] *Barrett*, n.56, 586–587; *Phelps*, n.57, 659–660, 662; *Richards (t/a Colin Richards & Co) v
Hughes* [2004] EWCA Civ 266.
[60] *Barrett*, n.56.
[61] *Barrett v Enfield LBC* [1998] Q.B. 367.

authority. The House of Lords disagreed. Lord Hutton stated that the comparison between the local authority and the parent was not entirely apt, since the former would have to take a number of decisions, such as whether a child should be placed with foster parents or sent to a residential home, which would never have to be taken by natural parents.[62] His Lordship also distinguished the policy considerations taken into account in the *X* case, set out above. Lord Hutton felt that these were less persuasive in relation to fostering, than they were in relation to child abuse.[63]

An unwillingness to reject the existence of a duty of care is apparent once again in *Phelps*.[64] There were four separate cases concerning errors allegedly made in the educational system, such as the failure to diagnose dyslexia, and the provision of inadequate education to a person with muscular dystrophy. The House of Lords adverted to the considerations that had caused Lord Browne-Wilkinson to exclude the duty of care in the *X* case, but concluded that they were not sufficiently compelling to exclude a duty of care in the instant cases.[65]

ii. Greater willingness to consider issues at the level of breach rather than duty

29–014   There are two aspects of the recent case law that are pertinent to the shift in emphasis from duty to breach.

First, the House of Lords in *Barrett* and *Phelps* limited the instances in which the courts would deem the matter to be non-justiciable, and emphasised that matters concerning discretion could often be dealt with when determining whether there was a breach of the duty of care. Thus Lord Hutton in *Barrett* accepted that the effect of prior decisions[66] was that the courts would not permit a claim in negligence to be brought where a decision on the existence of negligence would involve the courts in considering matters of policy raising issues which were not justiciable. This covered issues that the courts were ill-equipped and ill-suited to assess, where Parliament could not have intended that the courts would substitute their views for those of the minister or other primary decision-maker. It was, said Lord Hutton, only where the decision involved the weighing of competing public interests which the courts were not fitted to assess that they would hold that the matter was non-justiciable on the ground that it was made in the exercise of a statutory discretion.[67] It followed said his Lordship that there was nothing to preclude a ruling in the instant case that although the decisions of the defendant were within the ambit of its statutory discretion, nevertheless those decisions did not involve the type of policy considerations which rendered the decisions non-justiciable.[68] It followed also that provided that

[62] *Barrett*, n.56, 587–588.
[63] *Barrett*, n.56, 589–590.
[64] *Phelps*, n.57.
[65] *Phelps*, n.57, 674–675.
[66] *Dorset Yacht*, n.17; *Anns*, n.15; *Rowling*, n.24.
[67] *Barrett*, n.56, 583.
[68] *Barrett*, n.56, 585.

no such non-justiciable matters were raised in a particular case, it was preferable for the courts to decide the matter by applying directly the common law concept of negligence. There was no need to advert to any preliminary public law test of *Wednesbury* unreasonableness to determine whether the decision was outside the ambit of the statutory discretion.[69] Lord Slynn in *Barrett* reasoned somewhat differently, but reached a similar conclusion.[70]

Lord Slynn reaffirmed the *Barrett* approach in *Phelps*.[71] He confirmed that the fact that the acts claimed to be negligent were carried out within the ambit of a statutory discretion did not in itself preclude a negligence action. It was only where what was done involved the weighing of competing public interests, or was dictated by considerations that Parliament could not have intended that the courts would substitute their views for those of the relevant officials, that the courts would hold that the issue was non-justiciable. A public law hurdle would therefore only be relevant where the allegation of negligence raised by the plaintiff was felt to raise matters that were not justiciable in the above sense. In other cases the courts would consider the case within the ordinary framework of the negligence action, as laid down in *Caparo*.[72]

This approach is clearly sensible. It avoids the necessity for the courts to become embroiled in issues of vires, which are not necessary for the resolution of the case. This conclusion is reinforced by the fact that a finding of ultra vires will not, in itself, be determinative in a subsequent negligence action. Thus if a policy decision to inspect all buildings of a certain type by tests one and two, rather than half of them by tests one to four, is found to be ultra vires because it was, for example, based upon irrelevant considerations, this merely tells us that the public body in fact took irrelevant considerations into account. It does not in itself show negligence.[73]   **29–015**

Second, if the courts decide that there is a duty of care, the nature of the statutory discretion and the way in which it was exercised will therefore be relevant in deciding whether there was a breach of that duty.[74] The courts take into account, when assessing breach, the probability that harm will occur, the degree of harm that will occur if that probability comes to pass, and the cost of taking precautions. These factors feature in the determination of whether the defendant has taken reasonable care in all the circumstances.

It will not be easy for the plaintiff to show that a defendant public

---

[69] *Barrett*, n.56, 586.
[70] *Barrett*, n.56, 570–572.
[71] *Phelps*, n.57, 653.
[72] n.31; Compensation Act 2006 s.1.
[73] The plaintiff might argue that the public body failed to take reasonable care in determining the limits of its powers. However to reason from a decision of invalidity, to the conclusion that the policy choice when made prior to that decision was made without reasonable care as to the limits of the public body's statutory powers, will only be possible in rare cases where those statutory limits are laid down in clear unambiguous terms. This is not often the case, see, e.g., *Dunlop v Woollahra Municipal Council* [1982] A.C. 158; *Rowling*, n.24.
[74] *Barrett*, n.56, 591; *Phelps*, n.57, 655, 665, 667–668, 672.

authority is in breach of its duty of care, more especially where, as in *Barrett*, there were difficult discretionary decisions to be made as to the appropriate foster home. The plaintiff raised various claims of negligence as to the way in which he had been frequently moved between foster homes. It is clear that their Lordships did not regard all such matters as non-justiciable. It is equally clear that they accepted that in determining whether any duty of care had been broken the court would have regard to the difficult nature of the tasks involved. It will be necessary for the plaintiff to show that the defendant was in breach of the duty of care, as judged by the *Bolam* test.[75] This test requires a professional to exercise the ordinary skill of an ordinary competent person exercising that particular art. It was made clear in *Phelps* that this test would apply to determine breach in actions brought against professionals such as teachers, and educational psychologists.[76] It was made equally clear that the courts would not look kindly on those who sought to use negligence actions to pursue ill-founded claims that, for example, a child had under-performed at school.

iii. Instances where the courts deny the existence of the duty of care

29–016 The impact of *Barrett* and *Phelps* is apparent in subsequent cases. The general pattern has been for the courts to decide that a duty of care exists and then to determine whether the duty has been breached.[77]

There are however instances in the post *Barrett/Phelps* case law where the courts have felt that the relevant policy concerns are sufficiently strong to deny the existence of the duty of care in its entirety. It can still be accepted on the *Barrett/Phelps* approach that in some cases it may be correct to decide that it is not fair, just and reasonable to impose a duty of care at all. What *Barrett* and *Phelps* properly emphasise is that this conclusion should only be reached when it is clear that the relevant policy factors really do warrant such a conclusion, and there may be disagreement on whether this is so by judges and commentators.

Thus in *JD*[78] the House of Lords decided that no duty of care was owed by the health care officials to parents accused of child abuse. The majority of the House of Lords felt that the imposition of such a duty would lead to a conflict of interest on the part of the officials in the protection of the child and the protection of the parent. Lord Bingham dissented on the ground that that a duty of care could nonetheless be imposed in favour of the

---

[75] *Bolam v Friern Hospital Management Committee* [1957] 1 W.L.R. 582, 586–587.
[76] *Phelps*, n.57, 655, 672. See also, *Bradford-Smart v West Sussex CC* [2002] E.L.R. 139.
[77] *Reeves v Commissioner of Police of the Metropolis* [2000] 1 A.C. 360; *G (A Child) v Bromley LBC* [2000] 2 L.G.L.R. 237; *Larner v Solihull MBC* [2001] R.T.R. 32; *Watson v British Boxing Board of Control Ltd* [2001] Q.B. 1134; *S v Gloucestershire CC* [2001] 2 W.L.R. 909; *Kane v New Forest DC (No.1)* [2002] 1 W.L.R. 312; *A v Essex CC* [2002] EWHC 2707; *Orange v Chief Constable of West Yorkshire* [2002] Q.B. 347; *Bradford-Smart*, n.76; *Devon CC v Clarke* [2005] EWCA Civ 266; *Carty v Croydon LBC* [2005] 1 W.L.R. 2312; *Skipper v Calderdale MBC* [2006] EWCA Civ 238. *Cf Vellino*, n.36; *Cowan*, n.36.
[78] *JD v East Berkshire Community Health NHS Trust* [2005] 2 A.C. 373. See also, *B v Attorney General of New Zealand* [2003] UKPC 61; *Lawrence v Pembrokeshire CC* [2007] 1 W.L.R. 2991.

parents, albeit making clear that it would be difficult for them to succeed at trial in proving a breach. Whatever one's view about the rightness of the decision reached in this case, it clearly does raise singular problems. The decision that a duty of care should not be imposed in this case should not lead to retreat from the *Barrett/Phelps* approach more generally.

In *Brooks*[79] the House of Lords, while not endorsing all the statements made in *Hill*,[80] nonetheless reaffirmed the general principle that the police owed no duty of care to victims or witnesses in their investigation of crime. Their Lordships rejected the plaintiff's attempts to fashion certain more specific duties of care that should be imposed on the police in relation to victims and witnesses of crime. They held that this would have detrimental effects on law enforcement, since police officers would in practice be required to ensure that in every contact with a potential witness or a potential victim time and resources were deployed to avoid the risk of causing harm or offence. Such legal duties would therefore inhibit a robust approach in assessing a person as a possible suspect, witness or victim, and would lead to an unduly defensive approach in combating crime.

iv. Misfeasance and nonfeasance

The preceding discussion has been principally concerned with negligence   **29–017**
caused by some positive act of the defendant. It is however important to consider the applicable legal rules in cases of omissions,[81] more especially because there are indications that the courts have become more restrictive in relation to such cases.

The general rule is that a person is not liable for a negligent omission: a person owes no general duty to assist another. A corollary is that the law will often only award compensation to the person who does intervene, but does so carelessly, if the intervention has actually made the position of the injured party worse than it would otherwise have been.[82]

This general proposition is subject to a number of well-recognised exceptions. Thus, it is clear that a case will be regarded as one of misfeasance rather than nonfeasance if the defendant was already under some pre-existing duty, such as in the instance of the driver who fails to apply the brakes. It is equally well established that there may be duties to act affirmatively for the assistance of others in certain situations because of the relationship between the parties.[83] There are moreover circumstances in which the courts will impose a duty on the defendant to take care that a third party does not act to the detriment of the plaintiff, as exemplified by

---

[79] *Brooks v Commissioner of Police of the Metropolis* [2005] 1 W.L.R. 1495.
[80] *Hill*, n.34.
[81] D. Nolan, "The Liability of Public Authorities for Omissions" (forthcoming).
[82] Markesinis and Deakin's, *Tort Law* (Oxford University Press, 5th edn, 2003), 149–153; *East Suffolk*, n.16.
[83] B. Markesinis, "Negligence, Nuisance and Affirmative Duties of Action" (1989) 105 L.Q.R. 104.

Dorset Yacht,[84] and cases where liability will be imposed because the defendant is taken to have assumed a responsibility to the plaintiff.

Notwithstanding these exceptions, part of the disquiet caused by *Anns* was because of Lord Wilberforce's willingness to impose liability even on the assumption that the council had not inspected the building at all. His Lordship stated that a public body did not have an unfettered discretion as to whether to exercise its powers, since this discretion could be subject to judicial review. This, said Lord Wilberforce, undermined the argument that if there was no duty to inspect, there was no duty to take care in inspection.[85]

Later authorities have not endorsed this reasoning and some commentators were critical of this aspect of *Anns*.[86] Thus, the link between a public law duty concerning the control of discretion, and the imposition of a duty of care, has been contested.[87] Lord Bridge in *Curran*[88] was critical of *Anns* for extending the circumstances in which a public body might be under a duty to control the actions of a third party, and for blurring the distinction between misfeasance and nonfeasance.

29–018   Lord Hoffmann in *Stovin*[89] was equally reluctant to impose liability for nonfeasance. There were, said his Lordship, two minimum conditions for basing a duty of care on the existence of a statutory power in respect of an omission to exercise the power. It must have been irrational for the authority not to have exercised the power, so that there was in effect a public law duty to act; and there must be exceptional grounds for holding that the policy of the statute conferred the right to compensation on those who suffered loss if the power was not exercised. The very fact that Parliament had conferred discretion on the public body, rather than a duty, was some indication that the policy of the statute was not to create a right to compensation.

This restrictive approach was further emphasised in *Gorringe*.[90] The claimant suffered serious injuries when her car collided with a bus. She had braked sharply just before the crest in the road, but her brakes locked, and she skidded into the bus. She argued that the local highway authority was liable, since it had not painted the word "SLOW" on the road surface just below the crest. The House of Lords denied liability. Lord Hoffmann stated that the exceptions he had adverted to in *Stovin* may have been ill-advised and that he now found it "difficult to imagine a case in which a common law duty can be founded simply upon the failure (however irrational) to provide some benefit which a public authority has power (or a public law duty) to provide".[91] This statement applies to both powers and duties and renders it even more difficult for a claimant to succeed than hitherto. Lord Scott was similarly restrictive, stating that "if a statutory duty does not give rise to a

[84] n.17.
[85] n.15, 755.
[86] Bowman and Bailey, n.6.
[87] *Sutherland Shire Council*, n.54, 31.
[88] *Curran*, n.33, 724, 726.
[89] *Stovin*, n.30.
[90] *Gorringe v Calderdale Metropolitan Borough Council* [2004] 1 W.L.R. 1057.
[91] *Gorringe*, n.90, para.32.

private right to sue for breach, then the duty cannot create a duty of care that would not have been owed at common law if the statute were not there".[92] The decision is problematic and not easy to reconcile with other relevant case law.[93]

While liability for omissions raises difficult issues we should nonetheless be wary of being too restrictive for the following reasons. Firstly, the position of a public body vested with a discretionary power is not the same as that of a private individual who simply "happens" upon some accident. The reasons for the reluctance to impose liability in cases of pure omission concerning private individuals are questionable,[94] and are not necessarily transferable to public bodies with discretionary powers. As Arrowsmith notes, [95]

> "[O]ne of the main policy reasons for the reluctance to develop duties in private law is that it would impose an unfair burden, and constitute an excessive interference with private autonomy, to require positive action. This argument has no application where there is a public duty to consider whether and how to exercise a particular power."

Second, it is overly formalistic to draw a radical division between those instances in which a public body is granted a statutory discretionary power, with the implication of no liability for omissions, and those areas where it is vested with a statutory duty, with the contrary implication. The very distinction may be difficult to draw as a matter of statutory interpretation. The legislature will often not have given any great thought as to whether the statute is framed in one form rather than the other. Many statutory duties contain discretionary elements. Perhaps most important is the fact that the general assumption underlying the grant of discretionary powers is that they *will* be exercised in some shape, manner or form. The reason for casting the statute in discretionary rather than mandatory terms is normally reflective of the fact that the problem requires choices to be made by the public body as to how it carries out the statutory remit.

Third, any extension of liability for cases of omission would, in any event, be circumscribed. Thus where a public body makes a legitimate planning decision to exercise its powers in a certain manner, the inevitable consequence will be that it chooses not to act in particular circumstances. However, this species of "omission" is simply the necessary consequence of a policy decision to exercise the powers in one way.

v. The impact of the ECHR
The considerations that have shaped the law discussed thus far have been   **29–019**

---

[92] *Gorringe*, n.90, para.70.
[93] Nolan, n.81, 7–12.
[94] Atiyah's, *Accidents, Compensation and the Law* (Weidenfeld & Nicolson, 5th edn, 1993 by Cane), 63–72.
[95] n.1, 183–184.

domestic in nature. It is, however, also necessary to advert to the impact of the ECHR, and the judgment of the ECtHR in *Osman*.[96] The case arose out of a teacher's obsession with a pupil, which culminated in the teacher killing two people and wounding two others. There was a negligence action against the police for a failure to take care in the investigation of the matter prior to the fatal shootings. This action failed in the domestic court: the House of Lords in *Hill*[97] had held that, for reasons of policy, the police owed no duty of care.

Osman took his case to the ECtHR, which held that the "immunity rule" was contrary to art.6 ECHR. It held that the rule granting "immunity from suit" was in breach of art.6 because it was disproportionate. It did not allow for other public interest considerations to be taken into account, which might favour liability, such as the degree of negligence and the degree of harm in issue in any particular case.[98] The plaintiff had to be able to argue his case on the merits, so that such matters could be investigated, rather than having his case struck out on the basis of *Hill*. The ECtHR held that *Hill* infringed art.6 ECHR.

This use of art. 6 was problematic, since it is a procedural provision that guarantees a hearing by a tribunal in the determination of a person's civil rights and obligations. The UK argued that the applicant had no "right" in this respect. The very existence of a tortious right was dependent upon proof of all the constituent elements of a negligence action: proximity, foresight of harm and whether it was fair, just and reasonable to impose a duty of car on the defendant, in this case the police. The House of Lords, which was clearly an independent tribunal, had already determined this issue after full argument. The ECtHR's decision transformed art.6 into a provision that allowed it to pass judgment on the substantive scope of tort liability within a contracting state.

29–020 The difficulties with *Osman* were addressed by Lord Browne-Wilkinson in *Barrett*[99]: a finding that it was fair, just and reasonable to impose liability was a prerequisite to the existence of a duty of care. Moreover, a decision that it would not be fair, just and reasonable to impose liability was dependent on an aggregate weighing of the detriment to the public interest should negligence liability be held to exist, with the total loss to all would-be plaintiffs if there were held to be no cause of action. When this determination had been made there should not, said his Lordship, be a further weighing of such matters in the context of a particular case. There was also considerable academic criticism of *Osman*.[100]

---

[96] *Osman v United Kingdom* (1998) 5 B.H.R.C. 293.
[97] *Hill*, n.34.
[98] *Osman*, n.96, para.151.
[99] n.56, 558–560.
[100] Lord Hoffmann, "Human Rights and the House of Lords" (1999) 62 M.L.R. 159; T. Weir, "Down Hill — All the Way" [1999] C.L.J. 4; M. Lunney, "A Tort Lawyer's View of *Osman v UK* [1999] K.C.L.J. 238; Craig and Fairgrieve, n.6. Support for *Osman* can be found in J. Wright, "The Retreat from *Osman*: *Z v United Kingdom* in the European Court of Human Rights and Beyond", in Fairgrieve, Andenas and Bell, n.1, Ch.3.

The ECtHR reconsidered the matter in *Z v UK*,[101] which arose out of the decision in the *X* case.[102] It was argued that the absence of a duty of care in the child abuse cases constituted, *inter alia*, a breach of art.6 ECHR, by parity of reasoning with *Osman*. The ECtHR found that there had been a breach of arts 3 and 13 ECHR, but in effect reversed its ruling in *Osman* concerning the effect of art.6. The absence of a duty of care did not, said the ECtHR, constitute a denial of access to court in violation of art.6. There was simply no substantive right, as judged by UK tort law.[103]

It should nonetheless be recognised that, as in the *Z* case, a claimant may well be able to show a violation of a Convention right other than art.6, and then argue that there must be an effective remedy pursuant to art.13. The latter Article was not incorporated into domestic law by the HRA, but Sedley L.J. has held that art.13 reflected the long-standing principle that where there is a right there should be a remedy.[104]

Domestic law should be able to satisfy the requirements of art.13 in most instances. This is in part because there is now the damages remedy under the HRA. It is in part because the decisions in *Barrett* and *Phelps* signal that the courts are less likely to deny the existence of a duty of care. It is in part also because the courts may, in the face of a gap, choose to develop the common law so as to provide an appropriate remedy.

3. BREACH OF STATUTORY DUTY[105]

A. Criteria for Liability
Until the 19th century the courts did not inquire closely whether the breach   **29–021**
of a statute was intended to give a cause of action to individuals, or whether it was only to be enforced by a penalty provided within the statute. A number of 18th- and early 19th-century authorities, some of which dealt with public officers or public bodies, expressed the liability in very general terms: when a public body had a duty imposed upon it an action lay at the suit of anyone injured by the neglect or refusal to perform it.[106]

---

[101] (2002) 34 E.H.R.R. 3.
[102] n.3.
[103] *Z*, n.101, paras 96, 101.
[104] *R. (on the application of K) v Camden and Islington Health Authority* [2002] Q.B. 198, para.54.
[105] Markesinis and Deakin, n.82, 358–374; K. Stanton, *Breach of Statutory Duty in Tort* (Sweet & Maxwell, 1986); R. Buckley, "Liability in Tort for Breach of Statutory Duty" (1984) 100 L.Q.R. 204; K. Stanton et al, *Statutory Torts* (Sweet & Maxwell, 2003); K. Stanton, "New Forms of the Tort of Breach of Statutory Duty" (2004) 120 L.Q.R. 324.
[106] Com. Dig. tit. "Action Upon Statute," F; *Sterling v Turner* (1672) 1 Ventris 206; *Rowning v Goodchild* (1772) 2 W. Black. 906; *Schinotti v Bumsted* (1796) 6 T.R. 646; *Barry v Arnaud* (1839) 10 Ad. & E. 646; *Ferguson v Kinnoull* (1842) 9 Cl. & F. 251; *Pickering v James* (1873) L.R. 8 C.P. 489.

However, by the latter part of the 19th century the courts began to restrict the action.[107] Whether an action would lie at the suit of an individual was dependent upon a number of factors. The prime consideration was to look to the intent of the legislation.[108] When determining whether the statute was intended to give a cause of action the courts considered, inter alia, whether the existing law of torts provided adequate compensation. If it did it would usually mean that no action under the statute would lie.[109] Conversely, where a statute simply enacted a pre-existing common law duty this would give rise to an action under the statute.[110] The mere fact that the statute was for the benefit of the public at large would not in itself preclude an action for breach of statutory duty,[111] although it might be easier to prove such an action where the statute protected a particular class of which the plaintiff was a member.[112] Another factor the court considered was whether the statute provided a penalty for breach. If it did then it might be more difficult to establish a cause of action for an individual, though it was not an impossible hurdle to overcome.[113] In addition, the harm suffered had to be within the risk that the statute was designed to prevent.[114] The courts regarded alternative remedies laid down in the statute, such as default powers, as precluding a civil action.[115] The nature of the duty allegedly broken, and the extent to which the court regarded this as justiciable, influenced its decision as to whether to restrict the plaintiff to the pursuit of a statutory remedy.[116]

It is clear therefore that a plaintiff who seeks to rely on breach of statutory duty will have to prove the existence of this cause of action in accord with the normal criteria applicable in this area. The plaintiff will have to show that the statute was intended to confer private rights of action, and that he

---

[107] *Atkinson v Newcastle Waterworks Co* (1877) 2 Ex. D. 441 restricting the broad approach in *Couch v Steel* (1854) 3 E. & B. 402. Despite occasional reference to the broad view as in *Dawson v Bingley Urban District Council* [1911] 2 K.B. 149, 159, the courts have in the main applied the criteria which govern breach of statutory duty generally, e.g. *Pasmore v Oswaldtwistle Urban District Council* [1898] A.C. 387; *Read v Croydon Corporation* [1938] 4 All E.R. 631; *Reffell v Surrey County Council* [1964] 1 W.L.R. 358; *De Falco v Crawley Borough Council* [1980] Q.B. 460; *Booth v NEB* [1978] 3 All E.R. 624; *Lonrho Ltd v Shell Petroleum (No.2)* [1982] A.C. 173; *R. v Deputy Governor of Parkhurst Prison Ex p. Hague* [1992] 1 A.C. 58; *X v Bedfordshire CC* [1995] 2 A.C. 633, 731–732. See, moreover, the cases on statutory powers which use analogous reasoning: *Peabody*, n.32; *Curran*, n.33.
[108] See, e.g., *Atkinson*, n.107, 448; *Hague*, n.107; *X*, n.3, 731–732.
[109] *Phillips v Britannia Hygienic Laundry Co Ltd* [1923] 2 K.B. 832.
[110] See, e.g., *Ashby v White* (1703) 2 Ld. Raym. 938, 954.
[111] *Phillips*, n.109; *Lonrho*, n.107.
[112] Evidence that the plaintiff is a member of a class covered by the statute will not, however, serve to prove that the plaintiff has a private law right flowing from the statute. It will still have to be shown that the legislature intended to confer such rights, *Hague*, n.107.
[113] *Atkinson*, n.107; *Groves v Lord Wimborne* [1898] 2 Q.B. 402; *Cutler v Wandsworth Stadium Ltd* [1949] A.C. 398.
[114] *Gorris v Scott* (1875) L.R. 9 Ex. 125. See also, *Peabody*, n.32; *Curran*, n.33.
[115] *Watt v Kesteven County Council* [1955] 1 Q.B. 408; *Wood v Ealing London Borough Council* [1967] Ch.364; *Cumings v Birkenhead Corporation* [1972] Ch.12. Cf. *Meade v Haringey London Borough Council* [1979] 1 W.L.R. 637; *Att-Gen. ex rel Mcwhirter v Independent Broadcasting Authority* [1973] Q.B. 626, 649; P. Cane, "Ultra vires Breach of Statutory Duty" [1981] P.L. 11.
[116] Compare *Ching v Surrey County Council* [1910] 1 K.B. 736 and *Reffell v Surrey County Council* [1964] 1 W.L.R. 358, with *Watt* [1955] 1 Q.B. 408 and *Wood* [1967] Ch.364.

or she came within the protected class. The normal rules of construction will be applied when determining these issues, and the courts have been reluctant to impose strict liability for breach of statutory duty per se.

B. Application of the Criteria

Thus in *X* Lord Browne-Wilkinson found that general social legislation of the type in question, although passed for the protection of those affected by it, was enacted for the benefit of society as a whole, and therefore no action for breach of statutory duty would lie.[117] A similar reluctance to subject public bodies to liability for breach of statutory duty is equally apparent in later cases.   **29–022**

Thus in *Barrett*[118] the claim for breach of statutory duty *per se* was not pursued before the Court of Appeal or the House of Lords, in the context of an action against a local authority which had taken a child into care, the only live issue being whether there could be a negligence claim.

In *O'Rourke*[119] the House of Lords found that there could be no cause of action for damages for breach of statutory duty arising from s.63 of the Housing Act 1985. Lord Hoffmann, giving the judgment of the House, reasoned that the duty to provide accommodation was enforceable in public law via judicial review, but that breach of that duty did not sound in damages. The Act was, said his Lordship, intended for the benefit of society in general, and the existence of the duty to house was dependent on the local authority's discretion. These factors indicated that the plaintiff's complaint did not give rise to a cause of action in private law for breach of statutory duty.

In *Phelps*,[120] the House of Lords held that the duties cast on local authorities in relation to special educational needs were for the benefit of all children that fell within the relevant area, and were not intended to sound in an action for breach of statutory duty. A similar reluctance to impose liability for breach of statutory duty per se is apparent in other cases.[121]

C. Comment

Three related comments on this jurisprudence are relevant. The first is that there has been a marked reluctance to find that the conditions for breach of statutory duty have been met in the major cases concerning public bodies. The exercise of statutory construction demanded by the criteria for breach of statutory duty has been explicitly or implicitly underpinned by unwillingness to impose damages liability, more especially where the state is   **29–023**

---

[117] *X*, n.3, 731–732.
[118] *Barrett*, n.56.
[119] *O'Rourke v Camden LBC* [1998] A.C. 188.
[120] *Phelps*, n.57, 652.
[121] *Clunis v Camden & Islington Health Authority* [1998] Q.B. 978; *Olotu v Home Office* [1997] 1 W.L.R. 328; *Cullen v Chief Constable of the Royal Ulster Constabulary* [2003] 1 W.L.R. 1763; *Gorringe*, n.90; *Neil Martin Ltd v Revenue and Customs Commissioners* [2007] EWCA Civ 1041.

undertaking welfare functions to which the plaintiff, in the absence of the relevant legislation, would have no "right". The courts' jurisprudence has therefore been premised on certain background assumptions about the correlation, or lack thereof, between statutory duties and consequent monetary claims that are contestable.

The second comment concerns the standard of liability in cases of breach of statutory duty. The impression given in the *X* case is that breach of statutory duty will or must always mean strict liability.[122] This does not have to be so. The standard of liability will depend upon the construction of the legislation.[123] The duty may be strict, it may simply be one of reasonable care, or it may be an obligation to take action that is reasonably practicable.[124] There is moreover no reason in principle why the courts should not be able to apply other standards of liability such as the serious breach test used by the ECJ in assessing state liability in damages. This criterion gives a court room for manoeuvre, which a strict liability standard does not readily provide. The House of Lords decided not to find for the plaintiffs in *X* and *O'Rourke* in part because this would impose strict liability on the defendants. The prospect of imposing such an onerous strict duty on the defendants when they had to make complex discretionary determinations was not an attractive one for the House of Lords. A test akin to that used by the ECJ would have given their Lordships an extra option. They could have held that the statute was intended to give rights to individuals, but that proof of a serious breach was required for a damages action.

Third, it is readily apparent that certain statutory duties contain discretion as to how they should be carried out,[125] or they may entail difficult points of statutory construction.[126] The courts have been disinclined to impose strict liability in such circumstances. A test like that used by the ECJ does, however, enable the court to consider such factors in the very determination as to whether there has been a serious breach on the facts of a particular case.

4. THE HUMAN RIGHTS ACT

29-024   The previous section was concerned with whether the courts would read a statutory duty so as to provide for damages liability. It is appropriate at this

---

[122] n.3, 731–732.
[123] Markesinis and Deakin, n.82, 358–363; Buckley, n.105, 222–225; Stanton, "New Forms", n.105, 331–333.
[124] *Jayne v National Coal Board* [1963] 2 All E.R. 220; *Edwards v National Coal Board* [1949] 1 K.B. 704.
[125] *Haydon v Kent County Council* [1978] Q.B. 343 provides a good example of a statutory duty which entails many of the discretionary choices in deciding how to fulfil that duty which are regularly present in cases of statutory powers.
[126] See also, Lord Keith's observations on statutory misconstruction in *Rowling v Takaro Properties Ltd* [1988] A.C. 473, albeit made in the context of statutory powers

juncture to deal with the Human Rights Act 1998, since this contains an express provision for the grant of damages in certain circumstances.[127]

A. Criteria for Liability

Section 8(1) HRA provides that the court can grant such relief or remedy **29–025** within its powers as it considers just and appropriate. This is qualified in s.8(2): damages can only be awarded by a court which has power to do so, or to order the payment of compensation, in civil proceedings. Section 8(3) further qualifies this liability by providing that no award of damages is to be made unless taking account of all the circumstances of the case, including any other relief or remedy granted, or order made in relation to the act in question, by that or any other court, and the consequences of any decision, of that or any other court, in respect of that act, the court is satisfied that the award is necessary to afford just satisfaction to the person in whose favour it is made.

In determining whether to award damages or the amount thereof, the court must, in accord with s.8(4), take into account the principles of the ECtHR in relation to the award of compensation under art.41 ECHR. It is questionable how far this case law will assist the national courts. This is in part because the ECtHR has not developed notably clear principles on this issue.[128] It is in part because the focus of art.41 is somewhat different from the domestic paradigm. Article 41 empowers the ECtHR to award just satisfaction for a violation of the ECHR where the internal law of the defendant state allows only partial reparation to be made. This criterion is only of limited relevance for claims that arise within a particular country.

There is, however, nothing to prevent our courts from considering the jurisprudence of other countries concerning damages claims for breach of constitutional rights. Interesting case law on this issue exists in the USA,[129] New Zealand[130] and India[131] to name but three jurisdictions.[132]

---

[127] Law Com. No.266 and Scot Law Com. No.180, *Damages under the Human Rights Act 1998*, Cm. 4853 (2000); D. Fairgrieve, "The Human Rights Act 1998, Damages and Tort Law" [2001] P.L. 695.

[128] *Damages under the Human Rights Act 1998*, n.127, paras 3.4–3.15; Judge Jean-Paul Costa, "The Provision of Compensation under Article 41 of the European Convention on Human Rights", in Fairgrieve, Andenas and Bell, n.1, Ch.1; A. Mowbray, "'The European Court of Human Rights' Approach to Just Satisfaction" [1997] P.L. 647.

[129] Damages liability for those who act pursuant to *state law* which violates the Constitution is governed by 42 USC section 1983. Liability in damages against *federal officers* who violate the Constitution was developed by the Supreme Court, reasoning from first principle, that protection for constitutional rights demanded a monetary remedy in certain limited circumstances, *Bivens v Six Unknown Named Agents of the Federal Bureau of Narcotics* 403 U.S. 388 (1971).

[130] *Simpson v Attorney General* [1994] 3 N.Z.L.R. 667.

[131] *Nilabati Bahera v State of Orissa* (1993) A.I.R. 1960.

[132] L. Tortell, *Monetary Remedies for Breach of Human Rights: A Comparative Study* (Hart, 2006).

Commentators differed as to the nature of the cause of action in s.8,[133] with some analogising it to breach of statutory duty, while others preferred to see it as a free standing tort. It is however clear, in the light of the court's jurisprudence, that there are marked differences between section 8 and traditional torts and hence it may be better to regard s.8 as sui generis.

B. Development and Application of the Criteria

29–026   It is readily apparent that s.8 leaves many issues open as to the more particular criteria that should be used for assessing damages liability under the HRA. It has therefore been for the courts to develop and apply these criteria under the HRA.

i. Damages and the standard of liability

29–027   The standard of liability is of central importance. The general position in domestic law is, as we have seen, that some species of fault or intentional wrongdoing is required to establish a cause of action. The HRA provides little direct guidance on this issue, subject to s.9(3) HRA, which stipulates that in proceedings under the HRA in respect of a judicial act done in good faith, damages may not be awarded.[134] This could be interpreted to mean that no such defence is open to other public authorities that act in breach of s.6(1) HRA.

The courts might more generally decide that prima facie liability should be strict, in the sense that once a right is violated then damages should follow. They might mitigate this through defences open to the public body that it acted in good faith. They might decide that the breach has to be especially serious etc. Lord Woolf argued extra-judicially that the existence of fault should not be a pre-condition for liability, but that it should not be ignored.[135] It should moreover be recognised that breach of certain Convention rights may well entail fault or intentional wrongdoing.[136] The standard of liability must now be seen in the light of the leading cases.

In *Anufrijeva*[137] the claimant argued that the defendant local authority was in breach of art.8 ECHR by failing to discharge its duty to provide accommodation that met the special needs of one member of the family. It is axiomatic that there must be a violation of a Convention right before you can get damages. It is therefore open to courts to limit damages liability by bringing in an element of fault as a requirement for breach of the relevant right. This is what occurred in *Anufrijeva*. The Court of Appeal accepted

---

[133] Compare Fairgrieve, n.127, 696; *Damages under the Human Rights Act 1998*, n.127, para.4.20; A. Lester and D. Pannick, "The Impact of the Human Rights Act on Private Law: The Knight's Move" (2000) 116 L.Q.R. 380, 382; Lord Woolf, n.135, 432.

[134] Except to compensate a person to the extent required by art.5(5) ECHR.

[135] Lord Woolf, "The Human Rights Act 1998 and Remedies", in M. Andenas and D. Fairgrieve (eds), *Judicial Review in International Perspective: Volume II* (Kluwer Law International, 2000), 433.

[136] Fairgrieve, n.127, 700.

[137] *Anufrijeva v Southwark LBC* [2004] Q.B. 1124.

that art.8 could impose positive obligations on the state to provide the support argued for by the claimant. It held however that mere breach of public law obligation to provide the claimant with something to which he was entitled did not automatically constitute breach of art.8. Before inaction could lead to breach of art.8 there had to be some culpability, in the sense of knowledge that the claimant's family life was at risk. The impact on family life by not giving the support had to be sufficiently serious and foreseeable,[138] and the culpable delay had to cause substantial prejudice.[139]

The implications of *Anufrijeva* for the standard of liability must be kept in perspective. The case is indicative of the way in which considerations of culpability can be taken into account when deciding whether there has been a breach of the relevant Convention right. The nature of such considerations was however affected by the type of case, this being a claim for violation of art.8 ECHR by the state's failure to take positive action to secure for the claimant accommodation sufficient to meet his special needs.

These considerations will not necessarily be relevant in relation to breaches of other Convention rights, more especially where there is the more typical claim that the state infringed the claimant's rights to speech, association, and the like, or that it violated his personal freedom. In such circumstances the courts are more likely to find that breach of the relevant Convention right will at least prima facie allow the claimant to seek damages under s.8 HRA. However, as will be evident from the subsequent discussion, the courts have interpreted s.8 as embodying a broad discretion as to whether damages should be awarded or not, and have regarded the seriousness of the violation, and the manner in which it occurred, as factors to be taken into account in deciding whether to award damages and if so how much. In that sense considerations of culpability have been taken into account, albeit as factors in deciding whether to exercise the discretion to award damages.

ii. Damages and discretion
The standard of liability is therefore of central importance under the HRA. **29–028** The courts have also maintained control by emphasising that damages under the HRA are discretionary, by way of contrast to common law causes of action where recovery is of right.[140] Thus in *Anufrijeva* Lord Woolf C.J. placed emphasis on the wording of section 8 HRA, that the court can provide a remedy that it considers just and appropriate, to reinforce the conclusion that the court has a wide discretion as to the award of damages under the HRA. In deciding whether to award damages, and if so how much, the court should balance the interests of the victim and those of the public as a whole.[141] The seriousness of the violation may also be relevant in deciding whether compensation should be awarded, and the manner in

---

[138] *Anufrijeva*, n.137, para.45.
[139] *Anufrijeva*, n.137, paras 46, 48.
[140] *Anufrijeva*, n.137, paras 50, 55.
[141] *Anufrijeva*, n.137, paras 55–56.

which the Convention right was breached may also be a factor in determining whether the violation was serious so as to warrant damages being
awarded.[142]

This approach is also evident in *Greenfield*.[143] The claimant was charged
with a drugs offence while in prison. His case was heard by the deputy
controller, G was found guilty, and ordered to serve more days in prison. G
argued that this decision was in breach of art.6 ECHR, since it was a
determination of a criminal charge and the deputy controller was not an
independent tribunal as required by art.6. He sought damages under s.8
HRA. Lord Bingham, giving judgment, held that the ECHR case law
indicated that a finding of a violation was often per se just satisfaction for
the violation found, thereby reflecting the ECHR focus, which was the
protection of human rights, and not the award of compensation.[144] This was
especially so because violation of art.6 ECHR did not mean that the outcome would necessarily have been different. It was moreover necessary for
the claimant to show that any loss complained of was actually caused by the
breach of art.6.[145] The House of Lords concluded that damages were not
warranted in the instant case.

iii. Damages and quantum

29–029 There has been some disagreement in the courts as to how quantum of
damages should be calculated under the HRA. In *Anufrijeva* Lord Woolf
C.J. stated that awards should not be on the low side as compared with tort
awards, that domestic courts should be free to depart from the ECHR scale
and that English awards by appropriate courts were the fitting comparator.[146]

However in *Greenfield* Lord Bingham disagreed as to the applicable
principles to guide quantum of recovery.[147] He stated that the HRA was not
a tort statute, and had different objectives. Thus even where a finding of a
violation of Convention rights did not give the claimant just satisfaction,
such a finding would still be an important part of the remedy. The purpose
of incorporating the HRA was, said Lord Bingham, not to give victims
better remedies at home than in Strasbourg, but to give them the same
remedies without the delay and expense of going to Strasbourg. Domestic
courts were therefore obliged by s.8(4) HRA to take account of ECHR
principles not only in deciding whether to award damages, but also in
determining the amount of the award. It followed that domestic courts

---

[142] *Anufrijeva*, n.137, paras 64, 66–68; Lord Woolf, n.135; see also, *R. (on the application of Bernard) v Enfield LBC* [2003] L.G.R. 423; *R. (on the application of KB) v Mental Health Review Tribunal* [2004] Q.B. 936; *R. (on the application of TH) v Wood Green Crown Court* [2007] 1 W.L.R. 1670; *Re C (A Child)* [2007] EWCA Civ 2.
[143] *R. (on the application of Greenfield) v Secretary of State for the Home Department* [2005] 1 W.L.R. 673. See also, *R. (on the application of Baiai) v Secretary of State for the Home Department* [2006] EWHC Admin 1035.
[144] *Greenfield*, n.143, para.9.
[145] *Greenfield*, n.143, paras 10–14.
[146] *Anufrijeva*, n.137, paras 73–74.
[147] *Greenfield*, n.143, para.19.

should look to Strasbourg, not to domestic precedent. While they were not bound inflexibly by Strasbourg case law, "they should not aim to be significantly more or less generous than the ECHR might be expected to be in a case where it was willing to make an award".[148]

C. Comment

It is clear that the courts wish to place limits on the recovery of damages **29–030** under s.8. This is evident in the repeated emphasis on the discretionary nature of the remedy, coupled with the related idea that a declaration is the primary means of vindicating violations of Convention rights. The factors identified by the courts as relevant to the exercise of their discretion under s.8, such as the balancing of public and private interest, and the limits placed on quantum, serve to reinforce this.

There is no doubt that the wording of s.8 HRA renders the award of damages discretionary. This can be accepted, but it can nonetheless be questioned as to whether the courts have interpreted the statutory provisions too restrictively. Thus as Clayton has argued in relation to *Anufrijeva*, while the principle of fair balance as between the individual and the public may be inherent in the ECHR as a whole, the ECtHR has not applied "the fair balance principle to questions of just satisfaction", and hence the "idea that the court should expressly balance an individual's rights with the general interest of the community before awarding damages has no basis in ECtHR case law".[149] It is moreover doubtful whether the language of s.8(4) HRA, which is cast in terms of taking account of the principles from the ECtHR's case law in deciding whether to award damages, and the amount of any such award, justifies the conclusion in *Greenfield* that HRA damages should generally be at the same level as that in Strasbourg.

5. MISFEASANCE IN PUBLIC OFFICE

A. Criteria for Liability

The tort of misfeasance in public office[150] applies specifically to public offi- **29–031** cers, which has been held to cover those who exercise governmental

---

[148] *Greenfield*, n.143, para.19; *Van Colle v Chief Constable of Hertfordshire Police* [2007] 3 All E.R. 122.
[149] R. Clayton, "Damage Limitation: The Courts and the Human Rights Act Damages" [2005] P.L. 429, 435.
[150] B. Gould, "Damages as a Remedy in Administrative Law" (1972) 5 N.Z.U.L.R. 105; C Harlow, "Fault Liability in French and English Public Law" (1976) 39 M.L.R. 516.

power.[151] The ambit of this tort has recently been extensively reviewed in *Three Rivers DC v Bank of England (No.3)*.[152] This case will therefore be used as the basis for analysing the constituent elements of the cause of action. The plaintiffs were depositors with a deposit taker (BCCI) licensed by the Bank of England. They lost their money when BCCI went into liquidation. The plaintiffs brought an action in misfeasance in public office claiming that the Bank had wrongly granted a licence to BCCI and that it had wrongly failed to revoke it.

i. Two limbs of the tort

29–032 In *Bourgoin*[153] it was held that there could be an action where the public body exceeded its powers either maliciously or knowingly. It is accepted that there are two limbs to the tort. A public officer can be liable for misfeasance in public office, either:

(1) Where the public officer performed or omitted to perform an act with the object of injuring the plaintiff, what is known as targeted malice.

(2) Where he performed an act which he knew he had no power to perform, and which he knew would probably injure the plaintiff.

It was made clear in *Three Rivers* that these were alternative and not cumulative ingredients of the cause of action. Malice in the sense of intent to injure was central to the first limb of the tort, while knowledge on the part of the public officer that he did not have the power to do the act in question was the central element of the second limb of the tort. The litigation in *Three Rivers* was directed towards the more specific requirements necessary to prove the second limb of the cause of action, since there was no allegation that the Bank had been guilty of targeted malice. It is however necessary to consider some of the older case law in order to understand the way in which the argument proceeded in the *Three Rivers* case.

ii. The relationship between the two limbs

29–033 It is necessary to take a step back to the origins of the cause of action in order to understand the more recent disputes as to the nature of the tort.

---

[151] *Society of Lloyd's v Henderson* [2007] EWCA Civ 930, it did not therefore cover the insurers Lloyd's.
[152] *Three Rivers DC v Bank of England (No.3) (Summary Judgment)* [2003] 2 A.C. 1; D. Fairgrieve and M. Andenas, "Misfeasance in Public Office, Governmental Liability, and European Influences" (2002) 51 I.C.L.Q. 757; D. Fairgrieve, "Damages Claims against Public Bodies: The Role for Misfeasance in Public Office" [2007] J.R. 169.
[153] *Bourgoin SA v Ministry of Agriculture, Fisheries and Food* [1986] Q.B. 716, 775–778, 788; *Dunlop*, n.73; *Calveley v Chief Constable of the Merseyside Police* [1989] A.C. 1228. The courts have disapproved of the potentially broad application of *Beaudesert Shire Council v Smith* (1966) 120 C.L.R. in *Dunlop* [1982] A.C. 158, 170–171, and in *Lonhro Ltd v Shell Petroleum (No.2)* [1982] A.C. 173, 188.

Malicious excess of power had its origin in *Ashby v White*[154] and the dissent by Holt C.J. The plaintiff was wrongfully prevented from voting and he brought an action on the case against the returning officer. He failed in the King's Bench, where the majority gave a variety of reasons for rejecting the claim.[155] But Holt C.J.'s spirited dissent was upheld by the House of Lords. The plaintiff had a right to vote and he must have a remedy to vindicate that right. It was questionable whether Holt C.J. required malice or not.[156] However, later cases held that malice was the essence of the action.[157]

There is however a crucial ambiguity in the meaning ascribed to malice in this context. This could be taken to mean that there has to be some intent to injure the plaintiff. It could alternatively be taken to mean something rather broader, akin to a deliberate and wilful abuse of power, albeit without the need to prove any intent to injure as such. In the *Three Rivers* case the Bank argued vigorously for the former reading of the older case law, and the plaintiffs for the latter.

This ambiguity as to the meaning of malice persisted in later case law. A number of other authorities provide some support for a tort based upon malicious excess of power. In *Smith*[158] the plaintiff could not set aside a compulsory purchase order because she was outside the six-week time limit. The House of Lords believed however that she could seek damages against the clerk for knowingly, and in bad faith, procuring the confirmation of the order. In *Abdul Cader*[159] the plaintiff alleged that he had been wrongfully and maliciously refused a licence. On the basis that the applicant had done all that was necessary to be granted a licence, the defendant owed some duty to him when exercising the statutory power. If the licence had been maliciously refused an action in damages might lie.[160]

There is also a group of cases that either deny the need for malice entirely, requiring only a knowing excess of power, or so define malice as to make it equivalent to knowledge. *Farrington*[161] concerned the withdrawal of the plaintiff's liquor licence as a result of which he had to close his hotel. Smith J. said that the tort of misfeasance in a public office was constituted by a public officer doing an act which to his knowledge is an abuse of his office and thereby causing damage to another. The defendant had withdrawn the licence knowing that he did not have power to do so. Malice was not

---

[154] (1703) 2 Ld. Raym. 938; 3 Ld. Raym. 320.
[155] The matter was judicial; that it was for Parliament; multiplicity of similar actions, see (1703) 2 Ld. Raym. 938, 941–942, 943, 947; *cf.* Holt C.J., 950–954.
[156] His dissent in the King's Bench did not require malice but, *cf Tozer v Child* (1857) 7 E. & B. 377, 381, (*arguendo* Shee Serjt).
[157] *Drewe v Coulton* (1787) 1 East 563n; *Harman v Tappenden* (1802) 1 East 555; *Cullen v Morris* (1821) 2 Stark 577; *Tozer v Child* (1857) 7 E. & B. 377.
[158] *Smith v East Elloe Rural District Council* [1956] A.C. 736, 752, 753.
[159] *David v Abdul Cader* [1963] 1 W.L.R. 835; A. Bradley, "Liability for Malicious Refusal of a Licence" [1964] C.L.J. 4.
[160] [1963] 1 W.L.R. 835, 839–840. See also, *Jones v Swansea City Council* [1990] 1 W.L.R. 1453.
[161] *Farrington v Thomson* [1959] V.R. 286. See also, *Brayser v Maclean* (1875) L.R. 6 P.C. 398, 405–406; *Whitelegg v Richards* (1823) 2 B. & C. 45.

needed. In *Roncarelli*[162] the plaintiff claimed that his liquor licence had been withdrawn arbitrarily to punish him for his support of the Jehovah's Witnesses. Rand J., in delivering one of the judgments against the defendant, the Prime Minister of Quebec, described the cancellation of the licence on this ground as malicious, but then proceeded to define malice as acting for a reason and purpose knowingly foreign to the administration.[163]

The tensions as to the precise constituent elements of the cause of action for misfeasance in public office were also apparent in Commonwealth cases. In *Mengel*[164] the action was brought by the owners of two cattle stations whose plans to sell their cattle were frustrated by the action of two inspectors who placed the cattle under quarantine without statutory authority to do so. The plurality in the High Court held that misfeasance was not constituted simply by an act of a public officer, which he or she knew was beyond power and which resulted in damage. It was said that policy and principle required that liability should be more closely confined. The tort should be limited in the same way as other torts that imposed liability for the intentional infliction of harm. Liability required an act that the public officer knew was beyond his power, including reckless disregard of the means of ascertaining the extent of his power, and a foreseeable risk of harm, or reckless indifference to the harm which was caused.[165] In a separate judgment there were dicta of Brennan J., which could be taken to mean that foreseeability of damage was not relevant, provided that the other requisite elements of the cause of action, including causation were present.

In *Garrett*[166] the plaintiff claimed in misfeasance against a police sergeant in charge of a police station on the ground that he had failed properly to investigate and deal with her claim that she had been raped by a police constable attached to the station. The New Zealand Court of Appeal adopted the same approach as Clarke J. in the *Three Rivers* case. A plaintiff must show actual foresight or reckless indifference in order to recover: foreseeability as to loss was not sufficient in this regard.[167] The matter was considered once again in *Rawlinson*[168] where the court held that knowledge or recklessness was the test in relation to the illegality itself and the consequences thereof.

B. Development and Application of the Criteria for Liability: Three Rivers

29–034 It was accepted in *Three Rivers* that there were two limbs to the cause of action, the targeted malice limb and the illegality limb. It was the precise constituent elements of the latter that were in issue in the instant case.

The *plaintiffs* argued that malice in the older case law was a relatively

---

[162] *Roncarelli v Duplessis* [1959] 16 D.L.R. (2d) 689.
[163] *Roncarell*, n.162, 706. See also the definition of malice in *Ferguson v Kinnoull* (1842) 9 Cl. & F. 251, 303.
[164] *Northern Territory v Mengel* (1995) 69 A.L.J.R. 527.
[165] *Mengel*, n.164, 540.
[166] *Garrett v Attorney General* [1997] 2 N.Z.L.R. 332.
[167] *Garrett*, n.166, 349.
[168] *Rawlinson v Rice* [1997] 2 N.Z.L.R. 651.

loose term akin to a deliberate and wilful abuse of power, without the need to prove any intent to injure as such. They conceived of the targeted malice limb of the tort in just these terms. The corollary was to argue that the illegality limb of the tort should be cast more broadly than found in the ratio of Clarke J. and the Court of Appeal. They contended that knowledge of the illegality should be extended to cover objective recklessness, and that the test for recoverable loss should be cast in terms of foreseeability, or perhaps directness.

The *defendant* argued that misfeasance was always an intentional tort, and that the early cases that spoke of malice meant that there had to be intent to injure the plaintiff. The defendant's view of the targeted malice limb had implications for their view of the illegality limb. The defendant argued that knowledge of illegality should be limited to actual knowledge and possibly subjective recklessness, but that it should go no further than that. The test for recoverable loss should therefore be relatively narrow, since this served to ensure that the requisite intent could be found or presumed to exist.

Clarke J.'s holding in respect of the illegality limb can be summarised as follows.[169] In order to establish that the public officer knew that he had no power to do the act complained of, it was sufficient that the officer had actual knowledge that the act was unlawful, or in circumstances where he believed or suspected that the act was beyond his powers, that he did not ascertain whether or not that was so, or failed to take such steps as an honest and reasonable person would have taken to ascertain the true position. The same test was to be applied for the purposes of establishing the requirement that the officer knew that his act would probably injure the plaintiff or a person in a class of which the plaintiff was a member: actual knowledge would suffice, and so too would belief or suspicion that his action would probably cause loss to the plaintiff, where the public officer did not ascertain whether or not that was so, or where he failed to make the type of inquiries which an honest and reasonable man would have made.

The case went to the House of Lords twice, in part because the constituent **29–035** elements of the cause of action were not entirely clear from the first of these decisions. The summary of the cause of action is therefore taken principally from the second of these cases.[170]

(1) The first limb of the tort applied to cases where a public power was exercised for an improper purpose with the specific intention of injuring a person or persons.[171]

(2) The second limb of the tort required an unlawful act or omission made or done in the exercise of power by a public officer. Since the essence of the tort was an abuse of power, the act or omission must have been done with the required mental element, and must have

---

[169] *Three Rivers DC v Bank of England (No.3)* [1996] 3 All E.R. 558.
[170] *Three Rivers*, n.152.
[171] *Three Rivers DC v Bank of England (No.3)* [2000] 2 W.L.R. 1220.

been done in bad faith. The claimants must demonstrate that they have a sufficient interest to sue the defendant, and establish that the act or omission caused the loss.[172]

(3)   The requisite mental element for the second limb was satisfied where the act or omission was done or made intentionally by the public officer in the knowledge that it was beyond his powers and that it would probably cause injury to the claimant. The fact that the act or omission was done or made without an honest belief that it was lawful was sufficient to satisfy the requirement of bad faith. This could be demonstrated by knowledge of probable loss on the part of the public officer.[173]

(4)   The requisite mental element for the second limb of the tort could also be satisfied if the act or omission was done or made recklessly, where the public officer, although he was aware that there was a serious risk that the claimant would suffer loss due to the act or omission that he knew to be unlawful, wilfully chose to disregard that risk. In this version of the second limb, knowledge of the illegality will include subjective recklessness that the act or omission was illegal. This was part of the holding in the first House of Lords' decision,[174] and was affirmed in the second decision.[175] Moreover, Lord Hope stated that the fact that the act or omission was done or made without an honest belief that it was lawful was sufficient to satisfy the requirement of bad faith.[176] This could be demonstrated by proof of recklessness on the part of the public officer in disregarding the risk.[177]

(5)   A public body can be vicariously liable for the acts of its officers in this tort.[178] Whether the public body would be so liable would depend upon whether the officers were engaged in a misguided and unauthorised method of performing their authorised duties, or whether the unauthorised acts of the officers were so unconnected with their authorised duties as to be quite independent of and outside those duties.

(6)   A claim for exemplary damages can be made in relation to the tort of misfeasance in public office,[179] but the tort is not actionable per se and hence proof of damage is required.[180]

172   *Three Rivers*, n.152, para.42.
173   *Three Rivers*, n.152, para.44.
174   *Three Rivers DC v Bank of England (No.3)* [2000] 2 W.L.R. 1220.
175   *Three Rivers*, n.152, paras 45–46; *Southwark LBC v Dennett* [2007] EWCA Civ 1091.
176   *Three Rivers*, n.152, para.42.
177   *Three Rivers*, n.152, paras 44–46.
178   *Racz v Home Office* [1994] 2 A.C. 45.
179   *Kuddus v Chief Constable of Leicestershire Constabulary* [2002] 2 A.C. 122.
180   *Watkins v Secretary of State for the Home Department* [2006] 2 A.C. 395.

C. Comment

The contending arguments in *Three Rivers* threw into sharp relief the nature **29–036** and reach of the tort of misfeasance in public office. The plaintiffs wished to extend the tort so as to cover damage caused by unlawful governmental action, and hence argued that knowledge of the illegality should embrace objective recklessness. The House of Lords was unwilling to take this step. Subsequent case law has emphasised that the plaintiff must prove knowledge or subjective recklessness as to the lawfulness of the public officer's acts and the consequences of them, and that mere reckless indifference will not suffice for liability.[181] This renders it difficult for any action to succeed, more especially because it is for the plaintiff to prove the requisite recklessness. The case law on misfeasance therefore directly raises the issue of whether there should be some redress for those who suffer loss as a result of unlawful governmental action, and this issue will be considered below.[182]

6. NUISANCE

A. Criteria for Liability

The tort of nuisance is commonly defined as covering any substantial and **29–037** unreasonable interference with the claimant's land, or any right over or in connection with its enjoyment.[183] While the gist of liability is unreasonable interference with the claimant's interest, caution is required as to the meaning of the word "reasonable" in this context, so as to avoid confusion with the law of negligence. As Markesinis and Deakin state, "in nuisance the law does not concentrate so much on the quality of the "doing" (unreasonableness of the defendant's conduct) as on the quality of the "deed" (unreasonableness of the result to the claimant)".[184] While the two sets of considerations are, as the authors accept, not mutually exclusive, the distinction is important: the fact that the creator of the nuisance has taken all reasonable care will not prevent liability if the court decides that the outcome constitutes an unreasonable interference with the plaintiff's land, or use thereof.[185]

B. Application of the Criteria

The principal hurdle for plaintiffs suing public authorities in nuisance **29–038** resides not in the constituent elements of the cause of action, but rather in

---

[181] *Dennett*, n.175; *Henderson*, n.151; *Chagos Islanders v Attorney General* [2004] EWCA Civ 997.
[182] See below, para.29–064.
[183] Markesinis and Deakin, n.82, 455.
[184] Markesinis and Deakin, n.82, 455.
[185] Failure to take care may be relevant where the defendant did not create the initial nuisance, *Sedleigh-Denfield v O'Callaghan* [1940] A.C. 880; *Goldman v Hargrave* [1967] 1 A.C. 645; *Holbeck Hall Hotel Ltd v Scarborough BC* [2000] Q.B. 836.

the defences, more especially that of statutory authorisation. The courts have held that if the loss is caused pursuant to the lawful exercise of statutory authority no action will lay. If the loss is the inevitable result of the exercise of the statutory power or duty there will be no action.[186]

The difficulty is to determine what "inevitable" means. Where the statute prescribes that the public body should act within defined limits and it is obvious that a nuisance must result, no action will lie. Similarly, where the statute confers a power to, for example, build for a particular purpose on a particular site and an individual complains of a nuisance flowing from the normal use of the building for that purpose the action will fail,[187] unless it can be proven that the public body did not use all reasonable diligence to prevent the nuisance from occurring.[188] Thus, actions brought for nuisance from the running of trains have failed where the above criteria have been met,[189] and restrictive covenants have been held to be unenforceable in so far as they clash with the exercise of statutory powers.[190]

Conversely, if the statute is permissive and allows a wide choice of site, area, and method, it has been held that the discretion must be exercised in conformity with private rights. A decision to site a smallpox hospital in Hampstead in pursuance of a general power to provide such hospitals was held to be an actionable nuisance unprotected by the statute.[191]

These principles were reaffirmed by the House of Lords in *Allen*[192]: where Parliament, by express direction or by necessary implication, has authorised the construction and use of an undertaking, that carries with it the authority to do what is authorised with immunity from any nuisance action, provided only that there is no negligence.[193] The concept of negligence has a special meaning in this context. It connotes a requirement that the statutory undertaker, in order to enjoy immunity, must carry out the work with all

---

[186] *R v Pease* (1832) 4 B. & Ad. 30; *Vaughan v Taff Vale Ry Co* (1860) 5 H. & N. 679; *Hammersmith Ry Co v Brand* (1869) L.R. 4 H.L. 171; *London and Brighton Ry Co v Truman* (1886) 11 App. Cas. 45; *Manchester Corporation v Farnworth* [1930] A.C. 171; *Dept. of Transport v North West Water Authority* [1984] A.C. 336, 359; A. Linden, "Strict Liability, Nuisance and Legislative Authorization" (1966) Osgoode Hall L.J. 196.
[187] See n.186, and *Metropolitan Asylum District v Hill* (1881) 6 App. Cas. 193, 212.
[188] *Farnworth*, n.186; *Tate & Lyle Industries Ltd v Greater London Council* [1983] 2 A.C. 509.
[189] *Brand*, n.186 .
[190] *Re Simeon and Isle of Wight Rural District Council* [1937] Ch.525; *Marten v Flight Refuelling* [1962] Ch.115.
[191] *Hill*, n.187; *Vernon v Vestry of St James Westminster* (1880) 16 Ch.D. 449. Where an actionable nuisance has been committed it is no defence that the public authority did what was reasonable in the public interest, *Pride of Derby and Derbyshire Angling Association Ltd v British Celanese Ltd* [1953] Ch.149; *cf. Smeaton v Ilford Corporation* [1954] Ch.450.
[192] *Allen v Gulf Oil Refining Ltd* [1981] A.C. 1001. The principle also applies where the authorisation is given pursuant to planning permission, *Gillingham Borough Council v Medway (Chatham) Dock Co Ltd* [1993] Q.B. 343.
[193] [1981] A.C. 1001, 1014, 1016, 1023–1024. There is an exception to take account of *Hill*, n.187. In *Allen* this exception is expressed by Lord Wilberforce as applying where the statute is permissive in form [1981] A.C. 1001, 1011: in such circumstances a nuisance action will still lie. It would seem that more is required to reconcile *Brand* and *Hill*, or *Hill* and *Allen*: the statute must not only be permissive, but also allow a wide choice of site or area. This view is supported by Lord Diplock, 1014, and by the fact that there was no real choice of site in the *Allen* case itself. This criterion is critically examined below.

reasonable regard and care for the interests of other persons.[194] On the construction of the statute it was held that, despite the absence of detailed specification as to the building of the refinery, its building and operation were contemplated by the Act, and no nuisance action would lie unless there was negligence.

C. Comment

There are a number of difficulties with the case law in this area. These relate respectively to the internal coherence of the courts' jurisprudence, and its normative foundations.

29–039

There are problems concerning the *internal coherence* of the case law. It is, for example, doubtful whether the test in *Allen* can reconcile all the cases.[195] The test of inevitability set out above may also be inappropriate in the context of statutory powers that require a public body to do a variety of work in a given area as and when the body deems it expedient to do so.[196] More important is the fact that whether the test of inevitability is satisfied can be fortuitous, being dependent upon the wording of the enabling statute. Whether the statute is framed in terms of a duty, or a power, or within the latter category a power that specifies a site and method, is often dependent upon factors which should not be determinative of whether an action for nuisance survives or not. Many modern statutes are framed in permissive terms for administrative reasons and contain no indication of site or method because the matter is too complex or best decided upon by the public body. This tells us nothing about whether a private law action should be sustainable or not.

The *normative foundations* of the courts' jurisprudence are also problematic. It is harsh to make the individual bear the loss arising from socially beneficial activities. There is a strong argument for placing the cost on those who take the benefit of the relevant activity. This was recognised by Lord Blanesburgh in *Farnworth*.[197] It was acknowledged more recently by Lord Phillips M.R. in the Court of Appeal in *Marcic*.[198] He stated that where a single house was at the risk of flooding by sewerage once every five years, this might not justify the investment to remove the risk. It did not however follow that the householder should receive no compensation. The flooding was the consequence of a sewerage system that benefited many. Those who used the sewerage system should therefore be charged a sufficient amount to cover the cost of paying compensation to the minority that suffered damage. The House of Lords reiterated orthodoxy and held that a cause of action in

---

[194] [1981] A.C. 1001, 1011.
[195] It is for example difficult to reconcile *London and Brighton Railway Co v Truman* (1886) 11 App. Cas. 45 with *Hill*, n.187.
[196] *Marriage v East Norfolk Catchment Board* [1950] 1 K.B. 284, 308, 309; *Hawley v Steele* (1877) 6 Ch.D. 521, 528, 530.
[197] *Farnworth*, n.186, 203–204.
[198] *Marcic v Thames Water Utilities Ltd* [2002] Q.B. 929, para.114.

nuisance would be contrary to the statutory scheme,[199] but there were, as will be seen below, dicta recognising the point made by Lord Phillips M.R.

It is, in any event, not clear that nuisance is the most appropriate medium whereby compensation should be granted. The criteria for whether private rights of action survive derived from the above authorities are ill-suited to much modern legislative activity.[200] This is an area where it is necessary to break away from the confines of "normal" legal reasoning, which requires an actionable legal wrong as a precondition for the payment of compensation. Justice may require that compensation should be paid even where the public body's action is lawful.[201] This "just result" has to some extent been achieved by particular statutes, and may flow more generally from the HRA. These will be considered in turn.

29–040   The most apposite legislation is the Land Compensation Act 1973, which provides compensation where the value of an interest in land is depreciated by physical factors caused by the use of public works, whether highways, aerodromes, or other works on land provided or used under statutory powers.[202] Physical factors are defined as noise, smell, smoke, fumes, artificial lighting, and the discharge of any substance onto the land.[203] Interest in land is defined to cover a freeholder, or a leaseholder, with three years of the term unexpired; there is a maximum rateable value where the land is not a dwelling.[204] The Act applies to any nuisance which occurred on or after October 17, 1969.[205] The compensation is assessed at prices current on the first day when a claim could be made.[206] Cases where compensation could be obtained through an action in nuisance are in general excluded from the Act.[207]

The HRA is also of relevance for the attainment of the "just result" set out above. Claimants may be able to plead breach of a Convention right in classic nuisance cases. Thus in *Hatton*,[208] the ECtHR found that the noise flowing from the night-time landing regime at Heathrow airport infringed the applicants' right to family life guaranteed by art.8, and awarded them compensation. However in a subsequent action the ECtHR held in *Hatton* that although a person who was significantly affected by noise or pollution

---

[199] *Marcic v Thames Water Utilities Ltd* [2004] 2 A.C. 42. See, however, *Dobson v Thames Water Utilities Ltd (Water Services Regulation Authority (Ofwat) intervening)* [2008] 2 All E.R. 362.
[200] The view of the House of Lords in the *Allen* case should be compared in this respect to that of Lord Denning M.R. in the Court of Appeal, [1980] Q.B. 156, 168–169. While the Master of the Rolls may have somewhat twisted the authorities, the result he reached may accord better with underlying policy considerations: that the general principle should be that Parliament did not intend to damage innocent people without redress.
[201] *Burmah Oil Co Ltd v Lord Advocate* [1965] A.C. 75.
[202] Land Compensation Act 1973 s.1; *R. (on the application of Plymouth City Airport Ltd) v Secretary of State for the Environment, Transport and the Regions* [2001] EWCA Civ 144; *Chrisostomou v Manchester City Council* [2007] R.V.R. 207.
[203] Land Compensation Act 1973 s.1(2).
[204] Land Compensation Act 1973 s.2.
[205] Land Compensation Act 1973 s.1(8).
[206] Land Compensation Act 1973 s.4; see also ss.5–6.
[207] Land Compensation Act 1973 s.1(6). See also, Local Government, Planning and Land Act 1980 ss.112–113.
[208] *Hatton v UK* (2002) 34 E.H.R.R. 1.

could bring a claim under art.8, States had a margin of appreciation that required them to weigh all the competing interests involved. The extent of the margin of appreciation depended on the facts of each case and the question as to whether the appropriate balance had been struck depended upon the weight given to the different rights and interests involved. When assessing the appropriateness of the balance, the measures available to mitigate the effect of interference with those rights had to be considered and the Strasbourg Court held that the UK had not exceeded the margin of appreciation.[209]

The possibility of using the HRA and Convention rights was considered in *Marcic*. The claimant's garden and house were periodically flooded by water and sewerage from a system that was adequate when initially constructed, but had become inadequate because of the increase in the usage of the system. The Court of Appeal[210] affirmed the claim based on a breach of art.8, protection of the home, and breach of art.1 of the First Protocol, peaceful enjoyment of possessions. The water authority could have prevented the flooding of the claimant's land, but argued that under its system of priorities there was no prospect of the work being carried out in the future. The Court of Appeal decided that the company's scheme of priorities did not strike a fair balance between the competing interests of the claimant and other customers.[211] It doubted moreover whether such a scheme could ever be compatible with art.8, if this meant that the claimant would suffer and receive no compensation. There is Strasbourg case law to the effect that while the building of, for example, a power station may be for the public good, the interference with the applicant's right might nonetheless be disproportionate where the individual had to bear an unreasonable burden.[212] Lord Phillips M.R. said that this case law suggested that "where an authority carries on an undertaking in the interest of the community as a whole it may have to pay compensation to individuals whose rights are infringed by that undertaking in order to achieve a fair balance between the interests of the individual and the community".[213]

The House of Lords reversed the Court of Appeal, and relying on the **29–041** approach in the second *Hatton* case,[214] held that there was no breach of Convention rights because the statutory scheme balanced the interests of the defendant's customers whose properties were subject to flooding, with the remainder of its customers whose properties were drained by the sewers, by imposing a general drainage obligation on the defendant and entrusting enforcement to an independent regulator. Lord Nicholls did however echo the sentiments of Lord Phillips M.R. Thus Lord Nicholls stated that in principle, if it was not practicable for reasons of expense to carry out remedial works for the time being, those who enjoyed the benefit of effective

---

[209] *Hatton v UK* (2003) 37 E.H.R.R. 28.
[210] *Marcic*, n.198.
[211] *Marcic*, n.198, paras 108–110.
[212] *S v France* (1990) 65 DR 250.
[213] *Marcic*, n.198, para.118.
[214] n.209.

drainage should bear the cost of paying some compensation to those whose properties endured the sewer flooding, since the flooding was the consequence of the benefit to those making use of the system. Thus, "the minority who suffer damage and disturbance as a consequence of the inadequacy of the sewerage system ought not to be required to bear an unreasonable burden".²¹⁵ This did not however give rise to any enforceable legal claim, but was regarded as a matter to be considered by the relevant administrative authorities.

The HRA can nonetheless be of assistance. In *Andrews* there was a claim under art.8 ECHR to recover the cost of noise insulation to combat excessive traffic noise consequent upon a traffic regulation made by the defendants.²¹⁶ The court held that a relevant factor in assessing whether the right balance had been struck between the interests of the individual and those of the community was the availability of measures to mitigate the effects of noise. Although the rights of residents were not afforded absolute protection under the 1998 Act, the absence of any possibility of grant, or of any consideration whether such a possibility of compensation should exist, could negative justification for the measure advanced by the defendants. A court subsequently granted compensation.²¹⁷ Similarly in *Dennis*²¹⁸ Buckley J. held that noise flowing from military aircraft engaged in training was justified in the public interest, but that it was not proportionate for specific individuals to bear the cost of the public benefit. The noise was held to constitute a breach of art.8 ECHR and art.1 of the First Protocol and compensation was awarded. There is also authority that where nuisance can be proven damages under the HRA might in certain cases complement those available in a nuisance action.²¹⁹

7. RYLANDS V FLETCHER

A. Criteria for Liability

29–042   The principle in *Rylands v Fletcher*²²⁰ imposes liability on a person who for his own purposes brings on to his land something which was not naturally there that is likely to do mischief if it escapes. The central components of the cause of action are therefore accumulation by the defendant, escape, and non-natural user of the land. The potential breadth of the cause of action has however been dramatically reduced by subsequent case law.²²¹ Thus the concept of non-natural user was almost certainly intended by Blackburn J.

²¹⁵ *Marcic*, n.199, para.45. Lords Steyn, Scott and Hope agreed with Lord Nicholls.
²¹⁶ *Andrews v Reading BC* [2005] Env. L.R. 2.
²¹⁷ *Andrews v Reading BC (No.2)* [2005] EWHC 256.
²¹⁸ *Dennis v Ministry of Defence* [2003] EWHC 793.
²¹⁹ *Dobson v Thames Water Utilities Ltd* [2007] EWHC 2021.
²²⁰ (1866) L.R. 1 Ex 265, 279–280; (1868) L.R. 3 H.L. 330.
²²¹ Markesinis and Deakin, n.82, 532–548; D. Nolan, "The Distinctiveness of *Rylands v Fletcher*" [2005] 121 L.Q.R. 421.

in *Rylands* to cover anything that was not naturally on the land. However in *Rickards* the term was interpreted far more narrowly to mean some special use bringing increased danger to others and not merely the ordinary user of land or such use as was proper for the general benefit of the community.[222] The courts also developed a range of defences that further reduced the potential of the cause of action. These restrictive developments reflected the judicial sense that negligence based liability should be the norm, and hence causes of action that appeared to impose some form of strict liability should be narrowly confined.

B. Application of the Criteria

Attempts to apply the principle in *Rylands* against public bodies have not on the whole succeeded. The courts have only applied the doctrine to bodies exercising *statutory powers* where there is a clause imposing liability in nuisance.[223] Where there is a statutory power, but there is no section expressly preserving liability for nuisance, no action will lie.[224] If the public body acts under a *statutory duty* rather than a power, there is no liability whether a nuisance section exists or not, if what was done was expressly required by statute, or was reasonably incidental to that requirement, and was done without negligence.[225] Even where the statutory duty does not lead inevitably to the loss which occurred, there will be no liability if a nuisance clause is present in the statute.[226]

29–043

C. Comment

The justification for this exemption from liability is questionable in terms of principle. Two arguments are interwoven in the judgments, although the courts have not been uniform in their treatment of them.[227]

There is the "*inevitability argument*" analogous to that found in the nuisance cases discussed above: if the body is required to act and by implication, or even expressly, cause loss thereby, it should not be liable.[228] The response to this argument is the same as in the case of nuisance and statutory authority. The public body, even if its acts are regarded as lawful

29–044

---

[222] *Rickards v Lothian* [1913] A.C. 263, 280; *Cambridge Water Co Ltd v Eastern Counties Leather Plc* [1994] 2 A.C. 264; *Transco Plc v Stockport MBC* [2004] 2 A.C. 1.
[223] *Charing Cross Electricity Supply Company v Hydraulic Power Company* [1914] 3 K.B. 772; *Midwood v Manchester Corporation* [1905] 2 K.B. 597. A nuisance clause is simply a specific section in the enabling statute preserving liability in nuisance. Such a clause which *preserves* liability in nuisance has been construed to *exclude* liability unless the public body has been negligent, *Hammond v Vestry of St. Pancras* (1874) L.R. 9 C.P. 316, 322. Not perhaps the most natural construction of such a clause.
[224] *Dunne v North Western Gas Board* [1964] 2 Q.B. 806, 837–838, (the liability of Liverpool Corporation acting under statutory powers: no nuisance section, no liability).
[225] *Smeaton v Ilford Corporation* [1954] Ch.450, 476–477; *Dunne*, n.224, 834–835; *Department of Transport v North West Water Authority* [1984] A.C. 336, 359.
[226] *Smeaton*, n.225, 477–478.
[227] Compare the view of Sellers L.J. in *Dunne*, n.224, 832, with Upjohn J. in *Smeaton*, n.225, 468–470, 477–478.
[228] *Smeaton*, n.225; *Dunne*, n.224.

rather than tortious, should compensate a person who has suffered loss as a result.

The related argument for denying liability has its roots in the requirements of the *Rylands* doctrine itself: a *body which acts not for its own purposes, but for the benefit of the community should not be liable*. This rationale for excluding the principle reflects mistaken assumptions underlying strict liability. These assumptions have stultified the potential development of this tort into a socially useful instrument by which loss can be spread. Strict liability has no hint of moral censure, nor should it be restricted to socially unusual or abnormal activities. Liability without fault has one of its most important roles to play in relation to normal activities that benefit the community, and which involve a relatively high risk of loss or damage. It is *because* they benefit the community that it is unfair to leave the result of a non-negligent accident to lie fortuitously on a particular individual rather than to spread it among the community generally. Those who take the benefit should bear the burden.[229]

Some piecemeal reform has taken place by statute as, for example, in the Nuclear Installations Act 1965,[230] and the Deposit of Poisonous Waste Act 1972.[231] The Land Compensation Act 1973 will cover some cases where recovery is at present denied.[232] It can only be hoped that further such reform will follow. The preceding comments concerning the HRA and nuisance are equally relevant here.

8. THE CROWN

A. The Law Prior to 1947

29–045 Until 1947 a citizen's redress against the Crown for tortious conduct committed by its servants was at best indirect. The Petition of Right had developed as a means of securing redress against the Crown. In effect the Crown voluntarily referred the content of a Petition by a subject to a court of law, thereby overcoming the objection that the Crown could not be made a defendant in its own courts. By the 19th century it was accepted that the Petition of Right lay for breach of contract or recovery of property, but not for an action which sounded in tort. Such actions were doomed to failure by a combination of the maxim the "king can do no wrong" and a particular conception of vicarious liability. The former embraced the idea that the king has no legal power to do wrong. His powers were derived from the law and the law did not allow him to exceed them. The difficulty of rendering the Crown liable for the torts of its servants was exacerbated by the master's

[229] Law Commission Report No.32 (1970), 20–21.
[230] Nuclear Installations Act 1965 s.12.
[231] Poisonous Waste Act 1972 s.2.
[232] e.g. *Smeaton*, n.225, would be covered, but *Dunne*, n.224, would not, since the Act is not concerned with physical injury, but with depreciation in the value of land.

tort theory, which based vicarious liability upon the employer's fault. Neither the illogicality of allowing the Crown to be liable in contract but not in tort, nor the injustice of the immunity in tort impressed the 19th-century judiciary.

The servant could still be sued in person and a practice developed whereby the Crown would stand behind actions brought against their servants. Damages would be paid out of public funds and, if it was unclear who should be sued, a defendant would be nominated by the government department. This "solution" was problematic in two ways: some torts only make the employer, not the employee, liable, and the House of Lords came out against the use of nominated defendants.[233] Various reforms were posited before 1947, but these were frustrated by opposition from powerful government departments.[234]

B. Crown Proceedings Act 1947

The old rules were swept away by s.2(1) of the Crown Proceedings Act 1947, **29–046** which subjects the Crown to the same general principles of tortious liability as if it were a private person of full age and capacity. The Crown is thus rendered liable for torts committed by its servants or agents,[235] and has the duties commonly associated with ownership, occupation, possession and control of property. The Crown also owes the normal duties of an employer to its servants. Liability will attach to the Crown even where statute or common law imposes the duty directly upon a minister or other servant; the Crown is held liable as if the minister or servant was acting on instructions from the Crown.[236] Although the Act leaves unaltered the presumption that the Crown is not bound by statute unless intent to be so bound is expressed or can be implied,[237] the Crown can, subject to the above proviso, be held liable for breach of statutory duty.[238]

The Crown is made responsible for its servants and agents to the same extent as a private person. The term agent includes an independent contractor.[239] For the Crown to be liable for a servant or agent it is not sufficient that the person would have fallen within the common law definitions. The Crown will only be liable if the particular officer[240] was appointed directly or indirectly by the Crown and was at the material time paid wholly out of money provided by Parliament, or out of certain funds certified by the

---

[233] *Adams v Naylor* [1946] A.C. 543.
[234] J. Jacob, "The Debates behind an Act: Crown Proceedings Reform, 1920–1947" [1992] P.L. 452.
[235] Except where the servant himself would not have been liable. There is no liability outside of the Act, *Trawnik v Lennox* [1985] 1 W.L.R. 532.
[236] Crown Proceedings Act 1947 s.2(3).
[237] Crown Proceedings Act 1947 s.40(2)(f).
[238] Crown Proceedings Act 1947 s.2(2), the duty must be one which is binding on persons other than the Crown or Crown officers alone, and the normal prerequisites for an action in tort must be present.
[239] Crown Proceedings Act 1947 s.38(2).
[240] Defined in s.38(2).

Treasury, or would normally have been so paid.[241] This has the effect of excluding from Crown liability action taken by servants of some statutory corporations and, most importantly, the police who are paid out of local funds. Aside from these specialised provisions, the normal principles will operate to determine whether particular bodies are servants of the Crown.[242] Special rules apply to those discharging responsibilities of a judicial nature,[243] and separate rules used to apply to the armed forces.[244]

9. JUDICIAL IMMUNITY

29–047 The law draws a distinction between liability for intra vires and ultra vires acts, and between different types of courts. The precise metes and bounds of liability are not entirely clear, but would appear to be as follows.

(1) No judge, whether of a superior or inferior court, is liable if acting within jurisdiction, even if this is done maliciously.[245] This immunity would appear to apply to justices of the peace.[246]

(2) No judge of a superior court is liable in damages for an act done outside jurisdiction, provided that this was done by the judge in the honest belief that the act was within jurisdiction.[247] Liability will only attach for knowingly acting outside jurisdiction.[248]

(3) An inferior court is one that is subject to the control of the prerogative orders. It is now clear that justices of the peace can be liable for acts done outside their jurisdiction,[249] and it appears that this liability attaches to other inferior courts.[250] It is, however, also clear that the phrase acting without or in excess of jurisdiction will be interpreted more narrowly here than in the context of an ordinary

---

[241] Crown Proceedings Act 1947 s.2(6).
[242] *Tamlin v Hannaford* [1950] 1 K.B. 18.
[243] Crown Proceedings Act 1947 s.2(5).
[244] Crown Proceedings Act 1947 s.10. *Adams v War Office* [1955] 1 W.L.R. 1116; *Pearce v Secretary of State for Defence* [1988] A.C. 755; *Matthews v Ministry of Defence* [2003] 1 A.C. 1163; *Roche v United Kingdom* [2006] 42 E.H.R.R. 30. The Crown Proceedings (Armed Forces) Act 1987 s.1 repealed s.10 of the 1947 Act except in relation to anything done prior to 1987, subject to s.2 of the 1987 Act which allows for the revival of s.10 in certain circumstances.
[245] *Sirros v Moore* [1975] Q.B. 118, 132–133; *Re McC (A Minor)* [1985] A.C. 528, 540–541; *FM (A Child) v Singer* [2004] EWHC 793.
[246] *McC*, n.245, 533, 541, 559.
[247] *Sirros*, n.245, 134–135; *McC*, n.245, 541, 550.
[248] *Sirros*, n.245, 136, 149; *McC*, n.245, 540GH.
[249] *McC*, n.245, 541, 550, disapproving in this respect of the decision in *Sirros*. See also, *R. v Manchester City Magistrates' Court Ex p. Davies* [1989] Q.B. 631; *Lloyd v United Kingdom* [2006] R.A. 329.
[250] *McC*, n.245, 541, 550. cf. *Everett v Griffiths* [1921] 1 A.C. 631.

action for judicial review which seeks to quash the finding of a public body.[251]

10. RESTITUTION

An individual may wish to claim the return of money that has been paid   **29–048**
over to a public body rather than damages.[252] A claim for judicial review can
include a claim for damages, restitution or the recovery of a sum due, but
the claimant may not seek such a remedy alone, provided that these could
have been awarded on a private law claim.[253] Restitutionary claims present a
strong case for relief. The law has been shaped by important decisions of the
House of Lords in the *Woolwich* case[254] and in *Kleinwort Benson*.[255] In order
to appreciate the impact of these decisions it is necessary to understand the
previous law. It was generally accepted that in order to recover money that
had been demanded without authority an individual would have to bring the
case within one of the recognised categories in which such recovery was
allowed under private law.[256] Duress and mistake were the two principal
foundations for a claim to restitution.

A. Duress
The classic situation is that of money paid to obtain fulfilment of a duty,   **29–049**
which the payee is not entitled to charge for at all, or for which a lesser
amount should be charged.[257] This is an established category within duress.[258] The utility of the action for money had and received depends upon the
meaning given to "compulsion". The broader that the idea of compulsion
becomes, the more closely will a restitutionary claim approximate to a
finding of ultra vires. In *Steele*,[259] the plaintiff applied to the defendant, a
parish clerk, for authorisation to search the parish register. The charge was

---

[251] n.245, 542G, 543B, 544E, 546. The precise breadth of this phrase is, however, unclear, n.245, 546–547.
[252] R. Williams, *Unjust Enrichment and Public Law, A Comparative Study of England, France and the EU* (Hart, forthcoming).
[253] Supreme Court Act 1981 s.31(4); CPR 54.3(2).
[254] *Woolwich Equitable Building Society v Inland Revenue Commissioners (No.2)* [1993] A.C. 70.
[255] *Kleinwort Benson Ltd v Lincoln City Council* [1999] 2 A.C. 349.
[256] P. Craig, "Compensation in Public Law" (1980) 96 L.Q.R. 413, 428–435; P. Birks, "Restitution from Public Authorities" (1980) C.L.P. 191; G. Virgo, "Restitution from Public Authorities: Past, Present and Future" [2006] J.R. 370.
[257] J. Beatson, "Duress as a Vitiating Factor in Contract" [1974] C.L.J. 97; A. Burrows, "Restitution, Public Authorities and *Ultra Vires*", in A. Burrows (ed.), *Essays on the Law of Restitution* (Clarendon, 1991), 39; J. Alder, "Restitution in Public Law: Bearing the Cost of Unlawful State Action" (2002) 22 L.S. 165.
[258] *Irving v* Wilson (1791) 4 T.R. 485; *Lovell v Simpson* (1800) 3 Esp.153.
[259] *Steele v Williams* (1853) 8 Ex. 625.

not levied until the search had been completed and there was no right to make the charge at all. Martin B.[260] based his decision on a broad ground. The defendant had a duty to receive only what the Act of Parliament allowed him to take and nothing more. It was irrelevant whether the actual payment took place before or after the search had been made. To call such a payment a voluntary payment would be an abuse of language.

There is support for treating demands by a public body differently from those made by an individual in the Commonwealth,[261] and in cases concerning public utilities.[262] In the latter the courts have allowed recovery because of the wrongful demand per se. The compulsion flows from the excess charge, and the plaintiff does not have to prove any express threat to withhold the service. The statutes in question are often either technically complex, or contain criteria such as "undue discrimination", which may be difficult for either party to interpret. In this context, to require overt threats by the public body or even protest by the individual is unrealistic.[263] The force implicit in a demand from a public body should suffice. There was a problem that flowed from a wide construction of the term compulsion, in that it came close to granting compensation for pure mistake of law, and such mistakes were, until recently, not thought to ground a restitutionary claim.

B. Mistake

29–050 The general principle was that money paid under mistake of fact was recoverable, but that money paid under mistake of law was not.[264] The inability to recover for mistake of law was criticised both judicially[265] and academically.[266] The problem in the past for those seeking recovery was that the wider recovery for duress became, the finer was the dividing line between cases characterised as involving duress and those classified as involving simple mistake of law.[267]

The typical fact situation that has been dealt with until now has been one where the plaintiff has paid over money for a service, which the public body should provide for less, or for no charge at all. Where, however, the public body simply demanded money that it believed it was entitled to, but the

---

[260] *Steele*, n.259, 632–633. *cf.* the somewhat narrower reasoning of Parke B., 630–631. See also, *Morgan v Palmer* (1824) 2 B. & C. 729.
[261] *Mason v State of New South Wales* (1958–1959) 102 C.L.R. 108.
[262] *Great Western Railway v Sutton* (1869) L.R. 4 H.L. 226; *South of Scotland Electricity Board v British Oxygen Co Ltd (No.2)* [1959] 1 W.L.R. 587.
[263] The courts have not always been so willing to imply a threat, *Twyford v Manchester Corporation* [1946] Ch.236.
[264] *Bilbie v Lumley* (1802) 2 East 469. The reasons given were that: there must be an end to litigation, multiplicity of litigation, and the fact that everyone was presumed to know the law.
[265] *Martindale v Falkner* (1846) 2 C.B. 706, 718–720; *R v Mayor of Tewkesbury* (1868) L.R. 3 Q.B. 629, 635–638; *Kiriri Cotton Co Ltd v Dewani* [1960] A.C. 192, 203–205; *Nepean Hydro Electric Commission v Ontario Hydro* (1982) 132 D.L.R. (3d) 193, Dickson J.
[266] P. Winfield, "Mistake of Law" (1943) 59 L.Q.R. 327; Law Com. No.227, *Restitution: Mistakes of Law and Ultra vires Public Authority Receipts and Payments*, Cm. 2731 (1994).
[267] Compare *Morgan*, n.260, and *Steele*, n.259, with *Slater v Mayor of Burnley* (1888) 59 L.T. 636.

claim was misconceived because of a misconstruction of a statute, the position of the private party was even more difficult. The private party might simply pay, discover the error and attempt to reclaim the money. This would normally fail because the payment would be made on a mistake of law. Alternatively, the private party might resist the claim. This would be met by an express threat by the public body. The threat would, however, normally be a threat to litigate and such threats were held not to be actionable. This was a development of the principle that a judgment is binding between the parties to it.[268]

The law has now been transformed by the decision in *Kleinwort Benson*.[269] The case was one of many[270] that arose out of the interest rate swaps agreements made by local authorities. These agreements were held to be ultra vires.[271] The agreements were thought to be valid at the time they were made, and had been fully performed. The claim by the bank was struck out in the lower courts on the ground that there was no recovery for mistake of law. The case then went to the House of Lords which held that mistakes, whether of fact or law, could ground a restitutionary claim, subject to general restitutionary defences such as change of position. A blanket rule prohibiting recovery for mistake of law was, said their Lordships, inconsistent with a law of restitution based on unjust enrichment. A claim for mistake of law could also cover the case where payments had been made under a settled understanding of the law, which was subsequently departed from by judicial decision. Payment made under a view of the law which later proved to be erroneous was still money paid over under mistake of law, since the payer believed when he made the payments that he was bound to do so. If it subsequently appeared that on the law held to be applicable at the date of payment that he was not bound to do so then he was entitled to recover the amount paid over.

The House of Lords subsequently held in *Deutsche Morgan Grenfell*[272] that the principle from *Kleinwort Benson* could apply to recovery of taxes paid under a mistake of law. The plaintiffs had paid certain moneys to the revenue and the relevant statutory regime had been found contrary to EU law by the ECJ. It was held that the plaintiffs could avail themselves of restitutionary relief for mistake of law. This was important on the facts, since the characterisation of the cause of action as mistake of law affected the limitation period that would apply and when it would start from.[273]

---

[268] Beatson, n.257; *W. Whiteley Ltd v King* (1909) 101 L.T. 741.
[269] *Kleinwort Benson*, n.255.
[270] *Westdeutsche Landesbank Girozentrale v Islington LBC* [1996] A.C. 669.
[271] *Hazell v Hammersmith and Fulham LBC* [1992] 2 A.C. 1.
[272] *Deutsche Morgan Grenfell Group Plc v Inland Revenue Commissioners* [2007] 1 A.C. 558; B. Hacker, "Still at the Crossroads" (2007) 123 L.Q.R. 177; Virgo, n.256; *Sempra Metals Ltd (formerly Metallgesellschaft Ltd) v Inland Revenue Commissioners* [2007] 3 W.L.R. 354.
[273] Limitation Act 1980 s.32(1)(c).

C. Recovery for Ultra Vires Demands

29–051 The state of the law until recently left many possible claimants in an unenviable position. If they were unable to prove duress, some form of compulsion or other limited grounds for relief, then it was difficult to sustain an action.[274] This difficulty was compounded by the possibility that the action would be denied because of the then prevailing rule denying recovery for mistake of law. Legislation made provision for recovery in certain circumstances, but the scope of any such rights varied from area to area.[275] The decision in _Woolwich_,[276] which was prior to _Kleinwort Benson_, placed litigants in a stronger position.

The facts were as follows. The plaintiff building society had paid over money to the Inland Revenue on the basis of certain regulations. These were challenged by the Woolwich in judicial review proceedings and held to be ultra vires.[277] The money was repaid to the Woolwich with interest dated from the judgment in the judicial review action. The Woolwich then began a second action, seeking further payment of interest, covering the period from when the money was first paid over to the date of the judicial review proceedings. Such an action would only be sustainable if there was a restitutionary right to recover the capital sum. The defendant argued that none of the traditional grounds for restitutionary recovery existed in this case, since there was nothing that could be termed compulsion and no mistake of fact.

It was held by a majority of their Lordships that such a right did indeed exist. Money paid by a subject pursuant to an ultra vires demand was prima facie recoverable as of right at common law together with interest. This was regardless of the circumstances in which the tax was paid, since common justice required that any tax or duty paid by the citizen pursuant to an unlawful demand should be repaid, unless some special circumstances or some policy consideration required otherwise. This result was strongly influenced by the provision in the Bill of Rights that taxes should not be levied without the authority of Parliament: a restitutionary right to claim the return of taxes unlawfully levied was seen as a necessary adjunct of this constitutional principle. The right to repayment vested from the moment when the sums were handed over pursuant to the unauthorised demand and therefore interest could be claimed from the date of the original payment. Moreover, it was made clear that whatever the fate of the rule that money paid under mistake of law was not recoverable should prove to be, that rule

---

[274] For qualifications to the general rule that recovery was not possible see, Law Com. No.227, n.266, 53–59.
[275] Law Com No.120, _Restitution of Payments made under Mistake of Law_ (1991), 74–84; Law Com. No.227, n.266.
[276] _Woolwich_, n.254; P. Birks, " 'When Money is Paid in Pursuance of a Void Authority. . .' A Duty to Repay?" [1992] P.L. 580.
[277] _R. v Inland Revenue Commissioners Ex p. Woolwich Equitable Building Society_ [1990] 1 W.L.R. 1400.

was no bar to an action of this kind, based as it was, upon the unlawful nature of the public demand.

The result in the *Woolwich* case is to be welcomed, and academic commentators had been pressing for reform along these lines for some time.[278] A number of issues concerning the nature and extent of the *Woolwich* principle remain to be resolved.

First, there is the all important issue concerning the scope of the principle **29–052** enunciated in that case. The strict ratio of the case has been said to be that a citizen who makes a payment in response to an unlawful demand for tax that was unlawful because of the invalidity of the relevant secondary legislation has a prima facie right to restitution of the money, irrespective of whether the payment is mistaken or made under duress.[279] It has however been convincingly argued by the Law Commission that the true scope of the principle is almost certainly broader.[280] The Law Commission's formulation was that the principle could well be held applicable to all taxes, levies, assessments, tolls or charges, whether for the provision of services or not, collected by any person or body under a statutory provision which is the sole source of the authority to charge.[281] On this view the *Woolwich* principle was not confined to payments of tax, or to governmental or quasi-governmental exactions, or to payments made in accordance with a demand. For the Law Commission, "the crucial element is that the payment is collected by any person or body which is operating outside its statutory authority".[282] The Law Commission also believed that acting ultra vires was not confined to excess of statutory power, but also extended to procedural error, abuse of power and error of law by the charging authority.

The decision in *British Steel*[283] confirmed that the *Woolwich* principle could cover a mistaken view of the legal effect of valid regulations, or a mistaken view of the facts of the case, as well as a claim based on regulations that are themselves ultra vires. The courts will have to decide how to deal with the situation where the invalidity was only technical, or the circumstance where the plaintiff has not actually suffered any loss because the tax or levy has been passed on to another.[284] In *Stringer*[285] a landlord had been overpaid housing benefits in respect of a tenant who had left his premises. He paid over part of the sum demanded from him by the local authority, but then claimed that the sum should be returned because the request for repayment did not comply with relevant formalities. The court refused to order restitution. It distinguished the case from *Woolwich*, since in *Stringer*

---

[278] P. Birks, "Restitution from the Executive: A Tercentary Footnote to the Bill of Rights", in P. Finn (ed.), *Essays on Restitution* (Law Book Co, 1990), 164; W. Cornish, " 'Colour of Office': Restitutionary Redress against Public Authority" [1987] J. Malaysian and Comparative Law 41; S. Arrowsmith, "Ineffective Transactions, Unjust Enrichment and Problems of Policy" [1989] L.S. 307; Virgo, n.256.
[279] Law Com. No.227, n.266, para.6.33.
[280] Law Com. No.227, n.266, paras 6.36–6.41.
[281] Law Com. No.227, n.266, para.6.42.
[282] Law Com. No.227, n.266, para.6.42.
[283] *British Steel Plc v Customs and Excise Commissioners* [1997] 2 All E.R. 366, 376.
[284] Arrowsmith, n.1, 273–275.
[285] *Norwich City Council v Stringer* (2001) 33 H.L.R. 15.

the landlord was seeking to resist repayment of money to which he had no entitlement.

Second, there is the relationship between the common law right to restitution and statutory provisions for recovery where they exist. This is a complex issue, which cannot be considered in detail here.[286] Suffice it to say for the present that much turns on the construction of the relevant statutory provisions. Thus in the *Woolwich* case, Lord Goff held that the provisions in the statute did not apply in the instant case, since they presupposed a valid assessment.[287] In *British Steel*,[288] it was held that an unlawful demand for tax was recoverable in a common law restitutionary claim, unless the claim had been removed by the empowering legislation or other legislation. It was clear also that the court would not lightly infer that the common law claim had been excluded by statute.[289]

29–053   Third, there is the matter of defences and other grounds for refusing relief. There may well be circumstances in which a restitutionary right of the kind that has been recognised could be problematic if it could be brought within a six-year period by large numbers of claimants. The effects upon the finances of public authorities could be significant. This was recognised by their Lordships in *Woolwich*, and there were hints that shorter time limits might have to be set for actions of this kind. It has, moreover, been suggested by Lord Goff in *Kleinwort Benson* that in cases concerned with overpaid taxes there is an argument that payments made in accordance with a prevailing practice, or under a settled understanding of the law, should be irrecoverable.[290] In such a situation a large number of taxpayers could be affected and there was an "element of public interest" which militated against repayment of tax in such circumstances.

The Law Commission gave considerable attention to possible defences. It did not feel that there could be completely unrestricted recovery of sums paid in response to ultra vires demands.[291] At the very least the traditional restitutionary defences such as change of position, submission or compromise, estoppel and the limitation period of six years from the date of payment should apply to claims based on the *Woolwich* principle.[292] The Law Commission also recommended that overpayments of tax should not be regarded as recoverable merely because the taxpayer paid in accordance with a settled view of the law that payment was due, and later decisions departed from that view.[293] Further defences recommended by the Law Commission include submission, contractual compromise,[294] and unjust

---

[286] Law Com. No.227, n.266, Pt VII; J. Beatson, "Restitution of Taxes, Levies and Other Imposts" (1993) 109 L.Q.R. 401.
[287] [1993] A.C. 70, 169–170.
[288] *British Steel*, n.283.
[289] See also, *Deutsche Morgan Grenfell*, n.272.
[290] n.255, 382. See also Law Com. No.227, n.266, para.10.20.
[291] Law Com. No.227, n.266, paras 10.4–10.7.
[292] Law Com. No.227, n.266, para.10.6.
[293] Law Com. No.227, n.266, paras 10.20–10.21. The Law Commission would not apply this bar to relief where there was invalidity in the subordinate legislation which created, or was fundamental to, collection of the tax, para.10.30.
[294] Law Com. No.227, n.266, para.10.35.

enrichment by the payer.[295] The Law Commission was, however, against short time limits for bringing actions of this kind.[296] It was also against the introduction of any direct defence of serious disruption to public finance.[297] It did not favour the use of prospective overruling as a technique to prevent financial disruption.[298] It was opposed to the idea that the courts should be empowered to deny recovery to those who had not brought their claims prior to the court's decision, where to allow subsequent claims for recovery would lead to severe disruption to finances.[299]

The decision in *Deutsche Morgan Grenfell*[300] nonetheless shows that the House of Lords is willing to characterise certain actions for recovery of tax as based on mistake of law, even if the consequence is to extend the limitation period, so that it runs from the date when the mistake was, or could with reasonable diligence, have been discovered.

D. Discretionary Payments

Even if a claimant cannot sustain a right to repayment of sums which have been paid over to a public body an action may still be brought challenging the discretionary refusal to reimburse such money. Thus in *Chetnik Developments*[301] the local authority possessed a statutory discretion to refund overpaid rates, but refused to reimburse the applicant on the grounds, inter alia, that the payments had been made under a mistake of law which would not be recoverable at common law. The House of Lords held that the discretion was not unfettered, and struck down the refusal to reimburse the applicant. It held that such sums paid under a mistake of law or erroneous valuation should not in general be retained unless there were special circumstances warranting the retention. The financial position of the applicant, and the general finances of the local authority should not be relevant considerations for the purposes of the exercise of this discretionary decision. However, there are also indications that the principle in the *Chetnik* case will only apply where there is an express statutory discretion to repay, where the courts will ensure that the discretion is exercised in accordance with the statutory intent.[302]

29–054

E. Restitution from the Individual

The discussion until now has focused upon the ability of the individual to recover money paid over to the public body where the demand was unlawful. Restitutionary claims can arise in the converse situation, where

29–055

[295] Law Com. No.227, n.266, para.10.48.
[296] Law Com. No.227, n.266, para.10.41.
[297] Law Com. No.227, n.266, paras 11.6, 11.23.
[298] Law Com. No.227, n.266, paras 11.7, 11.23–11.25.
[299] Law Com. No.227, n.266, para.11.30.
[300] n.272.
[301] *R. v Tower Hamlets London Borough Council Ex p. Chetnik Developments Ltd* [1988] A.C. 858.
[302] *Woolwich*, n.254, 171.

the public body seeks to claim back money paid over to an individual in circumstances where the payment was ultra vires. It is clear on authority that restitutionary relief is available in this situation.[303] There is some doubt as to whether such a claim applies in the context of any ultra vires payment, but the better view on principle is that it should; and also that it should apply irrespective of whether the money is traceable in a technical proprietary sense.[304] The only defence for the individual should be if there has been a change of position in reliance upon the payment. The Law Commission has recommended that the existing rule should not be altered.[305]

11. EU LAW: DAMAGES LIABILITY AND RECOVERY OF MONEY

A. Criteria for Liability

29–056 The preceding discussion has focused upon domestic law. However, an individual may also be able to claim redress by relying upon EU law,[306] more especially by relying on *Francovich*,[307] which introduced the principle of state liability in damages. Italy had failed to pass the laws necessary to implement Directive 80/987, which was concerned with the protection of employees in the event of the insolvency of their employers. The applicants were therefore left with substantial arrears of salary unpaid, and sought damages from the Italian government for the losses they had suffered. The ECJ held that, in principle, such an action was sustainable. It held that the provisions of this directive did not have direct effect, but that the action could be maintained. It reached this result by using arguments of principle, and by drawing upon more general provisions of the Treaty.

The argument of *principle* was that the full effectiveness of Community law would be called into question, and the protection of the EC law rights would be weakened, if the individuals could not obtain compensation where their rights were infringed by a breach of Community law for which a state was responsible. This reasoning was reinforced by *textual foundation* drawn from what is now art.10 EC, which provides that states are under an obligation to take all appropriate measures to ensure the fulfilment of Treaty obligations. From this the ECJ concluded that states had the duty to make good the unlawful consequences of a breach of Community law.

---

[303] *Auckland Harbour Board v R.* [1924] A.C. 318; *R v Secretary of State for the Environment Ex p. London Borough of Camden* [1995] C.O.D. 203.

[304] P. Birks, "A Duty to Repay" [1992] P.L. 580, 588–589.

[305] Law Com. No.227, n.266, para.17.21.

[306] P. Craig and G. de Búrca, *EU Law: Text, Cases and Materials* (Oxford University Press, 4th edn, 2007), Ch.9; J. Lonbay and A. Biondi (eds), *Remedies for Breach of EC Law* (John Wiley & Son Ltd, 1997); R. Craufurd Smith, "Remedies for Breach of EC Law in National Courts: Legal Variation and Selection", in P. Craig and G. de Búrca (eds), *The Evolution of EU Law* (Oxford University Press, 1999), Ch.8; C. Kilpatrick, T. Novitz, and P. Skidmore (eds), *The Future of Remedies in Europe* (Hart, 2000); M. Dougan, *National Remedies before the Court of Justice, Issues of Harmonisation and Differentiation* (Hart, 2004).

[307] *Francovich and Bonifaci v Italian Republic* (C-6 & 9/90) [1991] E.C.R. I-5357.

The precise *conditions* for liability were said to depend upon the nature of the infringement that gave rise to the damage. In cases of non-implementation of a directive three such conditions had to be satisfied. The directive, if applied, must confer rights on individuals; the content of those rights must be apparent from the directive; and there had to be a causal link between the failure to implement the directive and the loss suffered by the individual.

The decision in *Francovich* raised many interesting and important questions as to the scope of the state's liability in damages for a breach of Community law.[308] A number of these issues have now been clarified by the ECJ's later jurisprudence.

B. Development and Application of the Criteria

In *Brasserie du Pecheur*[309] the claim was brought by a French company against the German Government. The company was forced to discontinue selling beer in Germany because the German authorities considered that the beer did not comply with the purity requirements laid down by German law. In a 1987 decision the ECJ held[310] that this prohibition was contrary to the principle of free movement of goods in art.28 EC. The French company sought damages for losses suffered between 1981–1987. In *Factortame* the applicants challenged Part II of the Merchant Shipping Act 1988 as being incompatible with, inter alia, art.43 EC concerning freedom of establishment. The ECJ held that the conditions relating to the nationality, residence and domicile of the vessel owners and operators laid down by the 1988 legislation were contrary to Community law.[311] The damages claims related to the losses suffered by those who could not fish in the period before the UK amended its law so as to comply with the requirements of Community law. The decision in *Brasserie du Pecheur* and *Factortame* may be summarised in the following manner.[312]

29–057

(1)   The principle of state liability in damages was held to be general in nature and existed irrespective of whether the Community norm that was broken was directly effective or not.

---

[308] M. Ross, "Beyond *Francovich*" (1993) 56 M.L.R. 55; C. Lewis and S. Moore, "Duties, Directives and Damages in European Community Law" [1993] P.L. 151; D. Curtin, "State Liability under Private Law: a New Remedy for Private Parties" [1992] I.L.J. 74; J. Steiner, "From Direct Effects to *Francovich*" (1993) 18 E.L.Rev. 3; P. Craig, "*Francovich*, Remedies and the Scope of Damages Liability" (1993) 109 L.Q.R. 595.
[309] *Brasserie du Pecheur SA v Germany, R. v Secretary of State for Transport Ex p. Factortame Ltd* (C-46 & 48/93) [1996] E.C.R. I-1029.
[310] *Commission v Germany* (178/84) [1987] E.C.R. 1227.
[311] *R. v Secretary of State for Transport Ex p. Factortame Ltd* (C-221/89) [1991] E.C.R. I-3905.
[312] P. Craig, "Once More Unto the Breach: The Community, the State and Damages Liability" (1997) 113 L.Q.R. 67; R. Caranta, "Judicial Protection against Member States: A New Jus Commune Takes Shape" (1995) 32 C.M.L.Rev. 703; C. Deards, "Curioser and Curioser? The Development of Member State Liability in the Court of Justice" (1997) 3 E.P.L. 117; C. Harlow, "*Francovich* and the Problem of the Disobedient State" (1996) 2 E.L.J. 199; W. van Gerven, "Bridging the Unbridgeable: Community and National Tort Laws after *Francovich* and *Brasserie* (1996) 45 I.C.L.Q. 507.

(2)   The Court adopted a unitary conception of the state: liability could be imposed irrespective of which organ of the state was responsible for the breach, the legislature, the executive or the judiciary. The rationale for this was that all state authorities were bound, when performing their tasks, to comply with the rules of Community law.[313]

(3)   The ECJ held,[314] following the opinion of the Advocate General,[315] that in determining the conditions for state liability it was pertinent to refer to its case law under what is now art.288(2) EC,[316] which deals with the damages liability of the Community. The ECJ held that the protection which individuals derived from Community law could not, in the absence of some particular justification, vary depending upon whether a national authority or a Community institution was responsible for the breach.[317] The rules developed under art.288(2) took account, said the Court, of the wide discretion possessed by the Community institutions in implementing Community policies, particularly in relation to liability for legislative measures.[318] The relatively strict approach to the Community's liability under art.288(2) in the exercise of its legislative activities was justified because the exercise of legislative functions must not be hindered by the possibility of actions for damages whenever the general interest of the Community required legislative measures which might adversely affect individual interests.[319] The consequence of this was that, in a legislative context characterised by the exercise of wide discretion, the Community could not incur liability unless a Community institution had manifestly and gravely disregarded the limits on the exercise of its powers. Member States did not always possess such a wide discretion when acting in areas covered by Community law, since the relevant Community norm might significantly restrict this discretion, as exemplified by *Francovich* itself.[320] However, where a Member State acted in an area in which it did have a wide discretion, comparable to that of the Community institutions when implementing Community policies, the conditions for liability in damages must, said the ECJ, be the same as those applying to the Community itself.[321]

---

[313] [1996] E.C.R. I-1029, para.34.
[314] [1996] E.C.R. I-1029, para.42.
[315] Advocate General Tesauro, paras 60, 80, 81, 84.
[316] For general discussion of art.215(2) see, T. Heukels and A. McDonnell (eds)., *The Action for Damages in Community Law* (Kluwer Law International, 1997); Craig and de Búrca, n.306, Ch.16.
[317] [1996] E.C.R. I-1029, para.42.
[318] [1996] E.C.R. I-1029, para.43.
[319] [1996] E.C.R. I-1029, para.45.
[320] [1996] E.C.R. I-1029, para.46.
[321] [1996] E.C.R. I-1029, para.47.

(4) The right to damages was dependent upon three conditions.[322] First, **29–058**
the rule of law infringed must have been intended to confer rights on
individuals. Secondly, the breach of this rule of law must have been
sufficiently serious. Finally, there must have been a direct causal link
between the breach of the obligation imposed on the state and the
damage sustained by the injured parties.

(5) The second of these conditions is of particular importance. The
decisive test for deciding whether the breach was sufficiently serious
was whether the Member State had manifestly and gravely disregarded the limits of its discretion.[323] The following factors may,
said the ECJ, be taken into account when deciding upon this issue[324]:
the clarity and precision of the rule which had been breached; the
measure of discretion left by the rule to the national or Community
authorities; whether the breach and consequential damage were
intentional or voluntary; whether any error of law was excusable or
inexcusable; whether the position adopted by a Community institution contributed to the act or omission causing loss committed by
the national authorities; and whether on the facts the national
measures had been adopted or retained contrary to Community
law.[325] A breach of Community law would, the ECJ said, be sufficiently serious if the state persisted in its behaviour notwithstanding
the existence of a judgment by the ECJ which found the infringement
of Community law to have been established. It would be equally so
where there was settled case law of the Court making it clear that the
action by the Member State constituted a breach of Community
law.[326] It will be for national courts to decide whether there has been
a sufficiently serious breach, although the ECJ may give guidance on
this,[327] or even decide the matter for itself if it feels that it has sufficient facts on which to do so.[328]

(6) There was an ambiguity in the conditions for the application of the
test set out above. It was not entirely clear whether this test only
applied where the form of state action was legislative in nature *and*
there was some significant measure of discretion, or whether it could
apply even where the form of state action was administrative or
executive, provided that the significant measure of discretion existed.

[322] [1996] E.C.R. I-1029, para.51.
[323] [1996] E.C.R. I-1029, para.55.
[324] [1996] E.C.R. I-1029, para.56.
[325] See, e.g., *R. v HM Treasury Ex p. British Telecommunications Plc* (C-392/93) [1996] E.C.R. I-
1631; *Denkavit International v Budesamt fur Finantzen* (C-283, 291 & 292/94) [1996] E.C.R. I-
5063; *R. v Ministry of Agriculture, Fisheries and Food Ex p. Hedley Lomas (Ireland) Ltd* [1996]
E.C.R. I-2553; *Dillenkofer v Germany* (C-178, 179, 188—190/94) [1996] E.C.R. I-4845; *Brinkmann Tabakfabriken GmbH v Skatteministeriet* (C-319/96) [1998] E.C.R. I-5255; *Rechberger v
Austria* (C-140/97) [1999] E.C.R. I-3499.
[326] [1996] E.C.R. I-1029, para.57.
[327] As in *Factortame* itself.
[328] See, e.g., Case C-392/93, *British Telecommunications Plc*, n.325.

The ECJ's judgment pointed to the latter formulation.[329] This must be correct in terms of principle. It may be fortuitous whether Community obligations are implemented via legislation *stricto sensu* or in some other manner. Discretionary decisions, which are administrative or executive in nature, may be as difficult as those made through legislation.[330] The ECJ confirmed in *Bergaderm* that the general or individual nature of the contested measure is not a decisive criterion for identifying the degree of discretion.[331] The requirement to prove a sufficiently serious breach will apply to legislative and non-legislative discretionary action.[332]

(7) It is clear from the ECJ's judgment in *Brasserie du Pecheur* and *Factortame* that while the finding of a serious breach could involve "objective and subjective factors connected with the concept of fault",[333] liability could not depend on any concept of fault *going beyond* the finding of a serious breach of Community law.[334] This requires a word of explanation. Where there is some significant measure of discretion, and/or where the meaning of the Community norm is imprecise, illegality per se will not suffice for liability. The applicant will have to prove that the breach was sufficiently serious. However, once it is shown that the state committed a serious breach of the relevant Community norm, there is no room for any further inquiry. It is not open to the state to argue that there should be no monetary liability because there was no subjective fault relating to the conduct which led to the breach.

(8) The general principle is that the reparation for loss or damage caused to individuals flowing from a breach of Community law must be commensurate with the loss or damage sustained.[335] In the absence of Community rules on this issue, it is for the domestic systems of each Member State to establish the criteria for determining the extent of the reparation. This was subject to the qualification that these criteria must not be less favourable than those which were applied in similar claims based on domestic law, and that they must not be such as to make it impossible or excessively difficult to obtain monetary compensation.[336]

---

[329] [1996] E.C.R. I-1029, paras 43–44.
[330] Craig, n.312, 81–83; *R. v Ministry of Agriculture, Fisheries and Food Ex p. Lay and Gage* [1998] C.O.D. 387.
[331] *Laboratoires Pharmaceutiques Bergaderm SA and Goupil v Commission* (C-352/98) [2000] E.C.R. I-5291, paras 40–47.
[332] Craig and de Búrca, n.306, Ch.13.
[333] [1996] ECR I-1029, para.78.
[334] [1996] ECR I-1029, para.78–79.
[335] [1996] ECR I-1029, para.82.
[336] [1996] ECR I-1029, para.83. See, Craig and de Búrca, n.306, Ch.9.

C. The Implications for Domestic Law

Three issues must be addressed when considering the impact of the EC's **29–059** jurisprudence on domestic law.

First, it is clear that national courts are bound by the ECJ's rulings. A remedy in damages will, therefore, have to be provided in cases with a Community law component, which fall within the above rules. Thus in *Factortame Ltd (No.5)*[337] the House of Lords decided that the Merchant Shipping Act 1988 constituted a sufficiently serious breach of EC law, so as to lead to damages liability. This was in part because certain of the conditions in the legislation, relating to nationality and domicile, were felt to be clearly contrary to EC law. It was in part because the Commission had consistently been of the view that the legislation was contrary to Community law. The fact that the government had sought legal advice as to the compatibility of the 1988 Act with EC law was no defence. By way of contrast Latham J. in *Lay and Gage*[338] held that the respondent had made an excusable error in the construction of a complex regulation which was neither clear, nor precise. There was, therefore, no sufficiently serious breach so as to found a claim in damages.

Second, there is the issue as to the nature of the domestic cause of action applicable in cases with a Community law element. Such cases can be treated as giving rise to an autonomous cause of action, without the necessity of fitting them into any pre-existing domestic heads of liability. This is the most straightforward way of proceeding. On this view a new tort has been created and liability will sound if the three conditions set out by the ECJ are met. There is some older authority for treating liability in damages flowing from a breach of EC law in this manner.[339] It is also evident from case law post *Brasserie du Pecheur* and *Factortame* that the national courts do not feel the need to fit cases into one of the pre-existing heads of liability, and in this sense they provide support for the idea of an autonomous cause of action. It would, by way of contrast, be possible to modify the cause of action for breach of statutory duty.[340] There are, however, a number of potential difficulties in conceptualising matters in this way,[341] and for this reason it is preferable to regard breach of EC law as an autonomous cause of action.

Third, there is the interesting issue as to whether, and in what way, the case law of the ECJ will have an impact on cases where there is no Community law element. It is clear that our courts are not bound by EC law in such instances. It is equally clear that they can have regard to such

---

[337] *R. v Secretary of State for Transport Ex p. Factortame Ltd (No.5)* [2000] 1 A.C. 524.
[338] *R. v Ministry of Agriculture, Fisheries and Food Ex p. Lay and Gage* [1998] C.O.D. 387.
[339] *Application des Gaz v Falks Veritas* [1974] Ch.381, 395–396.
[340] *Garden Cottage Foods Ltd v Milk Marketing Board* [1984] A.C. 130; *R. v Secretary of State for Transport Ex p. Factortame (No.7)* [2001] 1 W.L.R. 942.
[341] Craig, n.312, 88–89; M. Hoskins, "Rebirth of the Innominate Tort?", in J. Beatson and T. Tridimas (eds), *New Directions in European Public Law* (Hart, 1998), Ch.7; compare, Stanton, "New Forms", n.105, 328–329.

jurisprudence when developing domestic case law. This matter will be considered below.[342]

D. Recovery of Money

29–060 Community law will also be of assistance to an individual who has paid over money levied by Member States contrary to Community law, and who seeks relief of a restitutionary nature. The extent to which national remedial rules that limit the vindication of an EC right are lawful under EC law is a complex issue which cannot be fully explored here,[343] but some of the basic principles can be set out.

In *San Giorgio*,[344] the ECJ considered a national rule that prevented the recovery of taxes which had been unduly levied where these had been passed on to third parties. Under the relevant national rule it was presumed, in the absence of contrary evidence, that the charge had been passed on whenever the goods to which the charge related had been transferred. The ECJ held that the passing on of a charge was a factor that could be properly considered by the national courts. However, it would be contrary to EC law if the burden of proof rendered recovery excessively difficult or virtually impossible. This was so even if the same rule operated in the context of purely domestic cases.

More recently the ECJ held in *Comateb*[345] that whether a charge had been passed on was a question of fact for the national court to decide, and that repayment could only be resisted where the charge was borne in its entirety by someone other than the trader. Even where the whole or part of an unlawful charge had been passed on repayment to the trader would not necessarily constitute unjust enrichment, since the imposition of the unlawful charge might have affected the volume of sales. The Court also indicated that a trader might bring a damages action in accord with *Brasserie du Pecheur* and *Factortame* for reparation of loss caused by the levying of unlawful charges, irrespective of whether those charges had been passed on.[346]

---

[342] See below, para.29–067.
[343] M. Dougan, "Cutting your Losses in the Enforcement Deficit: A Community Right to the Recovery of Unlawfully Levied Charges" (1998) 1 C.Y.E.L.S. 233; Craig and de Búrca, n.312, Ch.9.
[344] *Amministrazione delle Finanze dello Stato v San Giorgio* (199/82) [1983] E.C.R. 3595; *Amministrazione delle Finanze dello Stato v Denkavit Italiana* (61/79) [1980] E.C.R. 1205.
[345] *Societe Comateb v Directeur General des Douanes et Droits Indirects* (C-192—218/95) [1997] ECR I-165.
[346] *Societe Comateb*, n.345, para.34. The trader would presumably still have to satisfy the causation requirement of a damages action, which would be problematic if the loss had been passed on.

12. REFORM

Suggestions for reform may be forthcoming from the Law Commission. It **29–061**
published a Discussion Paper in 2004,[347] followed by a Scoping Report in
2006,[348] the latter being designed to consider when and how an individual
should be able to obtain redress against a public body that has acted
wrongfully. A consultation paper is due in the first half of 2008. The following considerations are relevant when thinking about reform.

A. Options for Reform

It is apparent from the preceding discussion that public bodies can cause **29–062**
loss to individuals in situations where there is at present no redress.[349] This
may be either because of the difficulties, considered above, of applying
established tortious principles to public bodies, or because public action
may cause loss to an individual in circumstances that do not fit any of the
recognised heads of liability. If a person is refused a licence loss may well
result, but that loss may not have been occasioned by an established tort.
There may simply have been a misconstruction of the legislation, in the
sense that a court on judicial review may have taken a different view of the
law, or its factual application to this individual. If we wish to develop the
law beyond the established heads of civil liability there are three ways in
which this could be done. Compensation could be given on the basis of a
risk theory, for invalidity, or on an ex gratia basis. Whether the courts or
some other agency should administer such a scheme is a separate question.

B. Compensation via a Risk Theory

The risk theory expresses a conclusion, which is that certain interests in **29–063**
society should be protected against *lawful* or *unlawful* interference by government. It does not, however, provide a criterion as to which interests
should be thus protected. This will be a value judgment for society to make.
The conclusion expressed by the risk theory is that the burden of certain
public activities should be borne by the whole community rather than placed
on an individual who has been harmed, but cannot prove an established
tort. Compensation upon the basis of a risk theory, or something closely

---

[347] Law Commission, *Monetary Remedies in Public Law, A Discussion Paper* (2004), available at
http://www.lawcom.gov.uk/docs/monetary_remedies_disc_paper.pdf; Bagshaw, n.6.
[348] Law Commission, *Remedies against Public Bodies, A Scoping Report* (2006).
[349] P. Craig, "Compensation in Public Law" (1980) 96 L.Q.R. 413, 435–455; J. McBride,
"Damages as a Remedy for Unlawful Administrative Action" [1979] C.L.J. 323; C. Harlow,
Compensation and Government Torts (Sweet & Maxwell, 1982); Markesinis, Auby, Coester-
Waltjen and Deakin, n.1; R. Caranta, "Public Law Illegality and Governmental Liability", in
Fairgrieve, Andenas and Bell (eds), n.1, Ch.10; P. Cane, "Damages in Public Law" (1999) 9
Otago L.R. 489; B. Markesinis, "Unity or Division: The Search for Similarities in Con-
temporary European Law", in Fairgrieve, Andenas and Bell (eds), n.1, Ch.14; M. Fordham,
"Reparation for Maladministration: Public Law's Final Frontier" [2003] J.R. 104; Harlow,
State Liablitry, n.6; Bailey, n.6; Markesinis and Fedtke, n.6; Cornford, n.1.

analogous thereto, is far more developed in some other countries, such as France,[350] than it is in the UK.

There *is some statutory recognition of the risk theory in the UK*, in the sense that this theory underlies legislation in certain areas. Which interests are accorded statutory protection on the basis of a risk theory may depend upon the strength of the relevant pressure groups,[351] or the degree of public sympathy aroused for the plight of injured individuals,[352] rather than an objective assessment of the importance of that interest when compared to the plight of others who remain unprotected.[353]

There *has however been no general common law doctrine based on the risk theory*. Indeed, the courts have made it more difficult to establish tortious liability in nuisance, *Rylands v Fletcher* and breach of statutory duty where the defendant is a public body, as opposed to a private party. A risk theory could be usefully employed in such cases, and in the *Dorset Yacht* type of situation.[354] Society will benefit from the greater reformative effect of open borstals on offenders as compared to closed, high security prisons. The increased risk of individual escape may be an inevitable consequence of such borstals. The cost should be borne by society as a whole, and not by the individual who is unable to prove fault.[355] The legitimacy of this type of reasoning was recognised by Lord Phillips M.R. in *Marcic*, who held that Strasbourg jurisprudence suggested that "where an authority carries on an undertaking in the interest of the community as a whole it may have to pay compensation to individuals whose rights are infringed by that undertaking in order to achieve a fair balance between the interests of the individual and the community".[356] However the House of Lords, as we have seen, was more cautious in this respect.[357]

C. Compensation for Invalidity

29–064 Compensation for invalidity, like the risk theory, also expresses a conclusion: certain activities in society that cause loss should only give rise to liability when they are invalidly performed. Invalidity becomes a necessary condition of liability. The type of subject-matter that would commonly come within this area would be losses arising from modern regulatory

---

[350] N. Brown and J. Bell, *French Administrative Law* (Oxford University Press, 5th edn, 1998), 193–201; Caranta, n.349; S. Flogaitis, "State Extra-Contractual Liability in France, England and Greece", in Fairgrieve, Andenas and Bell (eds), n.1, Ch.13; Markesinis and Fedtke, n.6.
[351] See, e.g., Land Compensation Act 1973, which protects property owners on the basis of a risk theory.
[352] See, e.g., Vaccine Damage Payment Act 1979.
[353] J. Fleming, "Drug Injury Compensation Plans" (1982) 30 Am. J. Comp. Law 297.
[354] n.66.
[355] The Home Office has accepted some responsibility in such instances, see C. Harlow and R. Rawlings, *Law and Administration* (Weidenfeld & Nicolson, 1984).
[356] *Marcic*, n.198, para.118.
[357] *Marcic*, n.199.

legislation such as social welfare or licensing. For example, in *Maguire*[358] the applicants had been refused cab licences by the local authority, succeeded in having the refusal quashed, and then sought damages for the losses suffered in the interim. They based their claim upon, inter alia, breach of statutory duty, negligence and breach of contract. These arguments failed on the facts, and Schiemann J. noted that there was no right to damages for breach of administrative law as such. There are two reasons why invalidity is seen as a necessary condition of liability, one practical, the other conceptual.

The *practical reason* is as follows. Legislation is constantly being passed which is explicitly or implicitly aimed at benefiting one section of the population at the expense of another. This may be in the form of tax changes, or a decision to grant selective assistance to industry. If a firm is refused such assistance intra vires there can be no reason even in principle to grant compensation, since this would defeat the object of the legislation.[359]

The *conceptual reason* is more contestable. The natural tendency is to assign cases with some private law analogy to the risk theory, whereas losses arising from more modern regulatory legislation are held to require proof of invalidity.[360] We differentiate in this way because of a feeling that the establishment of a borstal or the building of roads affects "rights" in a way which a statute altering the conditions of manufacturing does not. This achieves plausibility because the loss from the public works has a private law analogy, which "strengthens" the call for sharing the cost among taxpayers when that loss is caused by lawful governmental action. By way of contrast, the passage of a statute that detrimentally affects a section of industry, by altering the conditions of business through restrictions on exports, produces no private law analogy. No private law rights strengthen the call for cost sharing among the public here. The absence of any such common law background does not, however, automatically settle a hierarchy of values or interests. It is, for example, not immediately self-evident that property interests are more precious than livelihood.

There are in any event a number of problems that would have to be resolved if reform were to proceed.[361] In cases where compensation might be given for invalidity the most serious problem is the breadth of the ultra vires doctrine. To render public bodies liable in damages whenever *any* of the various heads of ultra vires behaviour can be found would be to impose a very extensive liability. A public body may be found to have acted ultra vires for a number of reasons including: breach of natural justice, breach of other

[358] *R. v Metropolitan Borough of Knowsley Ex p. Maguire* [1992] C.O.D. 499. See also, *R. (on the application of Quark Fishing Ltd) v Secretary of State for Foreign and Commonwealth Affairs (No.2)* [2003] EWHC 1743, [2006] 1 A.C. 529.

[359] There may, however, be cases where the disadvantage to the individual is not the object of the legislation, but only an incident of it. This is a difficult line to draw. In France there is a limited principle allowing recovery for losses caused by legislation, Brown and Bell, n.350, 199–200.

[360] Thus a case in which public works affects property values is regarded as a prime candidate for a risk theory, while one in which public action affects the livelihood of a particular manufacturer is regarded as a candidate for compensation only if there is invalidity.

[361] Craig, n.349, 438–443.

mandatory procedural conditions, misconstruction of the enabling statute, or violation of one of the principles governing the exercise of discretion, such as irrelevancy, propriety of purpose, unreasonableness and perhaps proportionality. The consequences of rendering public bodies liable for any species of invalidity per se can be appreciated by focusing upon jurisdictional error and excess of discretion.

29–065   Cases involving allegations of jurisdictional error, such as *Dunlop*[362] and *Takaro*,[363] clearly demonstrate that the ambit of statutory provisions will often involve complex and contestable issues of statutory construction, and as Lord Keith has stated, even judges can misconstrue legislation.[364] Indeed the "correct" interpretation of the enabling legislation is not infrequently a matter on which there is disagreement between the judges. In *Anisminic*[365] four out of the nine judges involved in the case from the High Court to the House of Lords believed that the FCC's construction of the term successor in title was in fact correct. These problems are often also present when the challenge is to the manner in which the public body has exercised its discretion. There are, to be sure, examples of ultra vires discretionary behaviour where the public body really has abused its power and behaved in an overbearing manner. There are, however, also many instances in which the discretionary decision of the body may be overturned when there is nothing of this sort present on the facts. Whether a particular consideration is deemed to be "relevant" or "irrelevant" will be a matter on which the judiciary can disagree,[366] as will be the result of the balancing process required in the context of proportionality.

It is for such reasons that the ECJ has declined to impose liability in damages upon the Community where a regulation made pursuant to a discretionary power has caused loss, unless the applicant can show that there has been a manifest and flagrant breach of a superior rule of law to protect the individual. Invalidity per se will not suffice for liability in damages. This shows the need for wariness about imposing any general liability for invalidity per se. Difficult questions of causation, remoteness and the quantum of recovery would also have to be resolved if any such reform were to be seriously considered.[367]

The reform proposed by the Justice study, which imposes damages liability upon proof of a wide category of wrongful behaviour, should, therefore, be treated with caution,[368] and the need for such caution has been

---

[362] n.73.
[363] n.24.
[364] *Takaro*, n.24.
[365] [1969] 2 A.C. 147.
[366] See, *e.g.*, *Takaro*, n.24 and many others.
[367] Craig, n.349, 437–443. The response by the Justice study, *Administrative Justice, Some Necessary Reforms*, Report of the Committee of the Justice—All Souls Review of Administrative Law in the United Kingdom (Oxford University Press, 1988), 362–363, to these problems is unsatisfactory. It is true that the law copes with issues of causation in other areas, but the particular way in which the problem arises here is certainly distinctive and problematic, Craig, n.349, 438–439.
[368] n.367, 362–364. The breadth of the word "wrongful" is conveyed at 333. In so far as the Report considered these problems they were unmoved by them, 364.

stressed by Lord Woolf.[369] If damages for invalidity were to be granted then the term ultra vires should be more narrowly construed, as it has been in the case law on damages liability of the judiciary. There could alternatively be some qualification as to the manner in which the ultra vires act occurred, requiring the error to be manifest or serious, or there should be proven reliance losses, as in *Maguire*,[370] as a result of a legitimate expectation generated by the defendant's representation.

D. Compensation on an Ex Gratia Basis

The third direction for possible reform would be to grant compensation on an ex gratia basis.[371] As with the criteria of risk and invalidity, this third standard expresses a conclusion, but does not tell us when it should be applied. The conclusion is that compensation should be granted even though there may be no formal legal entitlement to it as such. A person who is injured by the action of a public body may not be able to recover because no established tort has been committed, and because no statute gives any legal entitlement.

    The public body may nonetheless decide to grant compensation without formally admitting any legal liability, as has occurred in certain instances.[372] The reasons for preferring ex gratia payments to one of the other grounds for giving compensation vary, but include: the difficulty of devising an adequate principle of liability, flexibility, and an unwillingness to accept that the individual has an entitlement to monetary recovery. The fact that the payment is ex gratia should not lead one to conclude either that decisions are wholly "open textured", or that the courts play no role in the process. Guidelines of some specificity will often exist, as was so in the case of the Criminal Injuries Compensation scheme administered by the CICB,[373] and the courts have applied principles of judicial review to its decisions.[374]

E. The Impact of Community law and Convention Jurisprudence

The direct impact of Community law upon monetary liability has already been considered. EC law may also have an indirect "spillover" effect on cases which do not have any Community component. This occurred in the *Woolwich* case,[375] where one of the reasons given for extending restitution was that EC law demanded the existence of such relief in cases where there was a Community element. It was clearly felt that the existence of differing

29–066

29–067

---

369 *Protection of the Public—A New Challenge* (Sweet & Maxwell, 1990), 56–62.
370 n.358.
371 For a valuable account, see Harlow, n.349, Pt 4.
372 C. Harlow and R. Rawlings, *Law and Administration* (Butterworths, 2nd. edn, 1997), 607–610.
373 C. Harlow and R. Rawlings, n.372, 610–617. The scheme now has a statutory base, Criminal Justice Act 1988, Pt. VII, Criminal Injuries Compensation Act 1995.
374 *R. v Criminal Injuries Compensation Board Ex p. Lain* [1967] 2 Q.B. 864; *R. v Criminal Injuries Compensation Board Ex p. Schofield* [1971] 1 W.L.R. 926.
375 n.254.

rules to govern situations in which there was or was not a Community law issue would be unsatisfactory. The domestic rules on damages liability might be similarly driven by developments post-*Francovich*, and *Brasserie du Pecheur*. The serious breach test laid down in this case law could well be of use in domestic cases, which have no Community law component.[376] It would enable us, for example, to consider liability for breach of statutory duty in domestic law, without necessarily imposing strict liability for any breach of the statute. Manifest or serious breaches of the relevant statute could serve to ground liability.

The ECHR jurisprudence must be taken into account by our courts under the Human Rights Act 1998, but it is not binding thereon. This jurisprudence will clearly have an influence on the development of the damages remedy under the HRA. The ECHR may also be relevant in other ways. It may shape the contours of tortious causes of action as between private individuals. It may cause a shift in the way that these causes of action are applied as between an individual and a public body. Lord Phillips M.R.'s reasoning in *Marcic*,[377] heralding the possible recognition of a risk theory of liability, was premised on the link with Convention rights.

F. Conclusion

29–068 On one level the general conclusions to be drawn about tort liability and public bodies are deceptively simple: we either live with what we have or we create something new. Living with what we have possesses certain disadvantages. The existing torts have inherent restrictions. The choice between piecemeal and general reform is a personal one. The practical and conceptual difficulties of general reform might indicate that piecemeal reform should be preferred, in the sense that particular areas are considered at different times. However, any decisions made about one particular area will have broader ramifications.

First, in relation to any such area, the choice will have to be made as to whether risk, invalidity or ex gratia payment is to be the basis of compensation.[378] Second, the decision to grant a novel form of compensation in one area necessarily causes one to consider whether it is fair or just that it should be absent in a different context. Third, the effect of such compensation upon the operation of a particular area will have to be considered. Would there, for example, be a tendency for the administrator to play safe by granting the benefit sought on the hypothesis that less actions would be brought as there would be fewer disgruntled applicants? Reform may be piecemeal in practice, but the broader issues outlined above cannot be ignored.

---

[376] P. Craig, "Once More Unto the Breach: The Community, the State and Damages Liability" (1997) 113 L.Q.R. 67.

[377] n.198, para.118.

[378] This will often be contentious: should, e.g. victims of crime be treated in the same formal way as other welfare recipients rather than being given compensation on a nominally *ex gratia* basis?

INDEX

Abuse of discretion
bad faith, 17–015
common law constraints
bad faith, 17–015
improper purposes, 17–010—17–012
introduction, 17–009
relevancy, 17–013—17–014
common law discretionary powers, 17–006
delegated legislation, and, 17–004
discretionary powers, and, 17–006
human rights (common law)
heightened rationality review, 17–018—17–019
interpretation of legislation, 17–020
introduction, 17–015
jurisprudence, 17–017
legality principle, 17–020
secondary literature, 17–021
'illegality', 17–001
improper purposes, 17–010—17–012
intensity of review, 17–008
'irrationality', 17–001
powers capable of control
common law discretionary powers, 17–006
introduction, 17–003
non-statutory bodies' powers, 17–007
prerogative powers, 17–005
statutory powers, 17–004
prerogative powers, and, 17–005
primary legislation, and, 17–004
reasonableness, 17–002
relevancy, 17–013—17–014
secondary legislation, and, 17–004
statutory powers, and, 17–004
Wednesbury unreasonableness, 17–002
Access to information
exempt information, 8–005
Information Commissioner, 8–005
legislative history, 8–003
overview, 8–001

Access to information—*cont.*
public authorities, 8–004
rationale, 8–002
statutory provisions, 8–004—8–005
"Acts of public authorities"
And see **Human rights**
contracting out, 18–022—18–025
core public authorities, 18–019
generally, 18–012
Hooper decision, 18–015
horizontal effect of the Act, 18–026—18–028
hybrid public authorities, 18–020—18–025
illegality, and, 18–012
locus standi, 18–029
qualification, 18–013
relationship between provisions, 18–015—18–016
remedies for breach, 18–030
scope of provisions, 18–017—18–025
standing, 18–029
test for authorities, 18–019—18–020
types of authority, 18–017—18–018
Wilkinson decision, 18–014
Administration-made rules
See **Administrative rules**
Administrative decision-making
bias, and, 13–005
Administrative Justice and Tribunals Council
See also **Tribunals**
background, 9–030
generally, 9–031—9–032
inquiries, and, 9–048
introduction, 9–029
Administrative law
administrative bodies
central regulation, and, 2–002—2–005
Donoughmore Committee, 2–020
Franks Report, 2–020
industrialisation, and, 2–002
introduction, 2–001

Administrative law—*cont.*
  administrative bodies—*cont.*
    Justice-All Souls Report, 2–020
    local government, 2–011—2–014
    machinery of administration, 2–006—
        2–008
    19th century development, 2–002—2–015
    rationale for growth, 2–009—2–010
    statutory inquiries, 2–015
    20th century development, 2–016—2–020
    welfare state, 2–016—2–019
  introduction, 1–001
  judicial review
    constitutionalism, and, 1–030—1–034
    origins, 1–003
    rationale, 1–004
  nature and purpose
    introduction, 1–001
    ultra vires, 1–005—1–016
    unitary democracy, 1–002—1–004
  Parliamentary sovereignty, 1–002
  principles and theories
    And see **Jurispridence**
    conclusion, 1–054
    introduction, 1–035
    market-oriented pluralism, 1–046—
        1–050
    pluralism, 1–036—1–045
    rights-based approach 1–017 —1–034
    "the third way", 1–051—1–053
  ultra vires
    And see **Ultra vires**
    critique of principle, 1–016
    deficiencies, 1–010—1–015
    form of intervention, 1–005
    implications, 1–005—1–009
    introduction, 1–003—1–004
    unitary democracy, 1–002—1–004
Administrative rules
  consultation, 22–045
  judicial control, 22–046
  legal status, 22–040
  overview, 22–001
  Parliamentary controls, 22–043
  problem areas
    generally, 22–042
    possible solutions, 22–043—22–047
  rationale, 22–039
  standards, 22–041
  type, 22–039
Age discrimination
  equal treatment, and, 21–018
Agency
  authority of agents
    breach of warranty, 5–041
    extent, 5–040
    introduction, 5–039
  failure to exercise discretion, and
    creation, 16–005
    introduction, 16–004
  legitimate expectation, and, 20–032—
      20–033

"Aggregate external finance"
  local government finance, and, 6–011
Alternative dispute resolution
  generally, 9–027
Appeals
  tribunals, and
    Court of Appeal, to, 9–018
    First-tier Tribunal, from, 9–017
    generally, 9–019—9–021
    Upper Tribunal, to, 9–017
Applications
  judicial review, and, 26–004—26–005
Appropriation
  contracts, and, 5–042
"As if enacted"
  ouster clauses, and, 27–005
Attorney-General
  locus standi, and, 24–009
Audi alteram partem
  application of maxim, 12–001
  balancing
    causation, 12–024
    factors taken into account, 12–021—
        12–022
    introduction, 12–020
    nature of process, 12–025—12–026
    preliminary hearings, 12–023
  causation, 12–024
  civil rights and obligations, 12–018—
      12–019
  conclusion, 12–048
  consultation, 12–028
  content of procedural protection
    balancing, 12–020—12–026
    specific procedural norms, 12–027—
        12–043
  content of procedural rights, 12–043
  ECHR Art. 6(1), and, 12–018—12–019
  evidence, 12–031
  fairness
    generally, 12–044—12–045
    introduction, 12–009—12–010
    social welfare, 12–047
    statutory inquiries, 12–046
  hearings
    introduction, 12–029
    rules of evidence, 12–031
    type, 12–030
  historical development, 12–001
  human rights
    application of maxim, 12–018—12–019
    reasons for decision, 12–035
    specific procedural norms, 12–043
  inquiries, 12–007
  interests, 12–015
  legitimate expectation, 12–016—12–017
  limitation of principle
    administrative/judicial distinction,
        12–004
    introduction, 12–003
    rights/privileges distinction, 12–006
    rights/remedies distinction, 12–005

Audi alteram partem—*cont.*
nonadjudicative procedures, 12–044—12–047
notice, 12–027
preliminary hearings, 12–023
principle revived, 12–008—12–010
procedural protection
applicability, 12–011—12–019
balancing, 12–020—12–026
content, 12–020—12–043
specific procedural norms, 12–027—
12–043
rationale for rights, 12–002
reasons for decision
common law, 12–036—12–037
human rights, 12–035
indirect procedures, 12–036
importance, 12–033
late evidence, 12–039
procedural fairness, 12–037—12–038
statutory provisions, 12–034—12–035
representation, 12–032
rights, 12–014
rules of evidence, 12–031
specific procedural norms
consultation,12–028
content of procedural rights, 12–043
decisions without hearing, 12–042
hearings, 12–029—12–031
human rights, 12–043
notice, 12–027
reasons for decision, 12–033—12–039
representation, 12–032
statutory hearings, 12–007
Authority (agents)
breach of warranty, 5–041
extent, 5–040
introduction, 5–039

Bad faith
abuse of discretion, and, 17–015
"Balancing"
And see **Audi alteram partem**
causation, 12–024
factors taken into account, 12–021—
12–022
introduction, 12–020
legitimate expectation, and, 20–047—
20–051
nature of process, 12–025—12–026
preliminary hearings, 12–023
"Beacon council scheme"
contracts, and, 5–022
Belief discrimination
equal treatment, and, 21–018
Best value
contracts, and, 5–021—5–022
Bias
administrators, 13–005
exceptions
necessity, 13–009
statute, under, 13–010
waiver, 13–011

Bias—*cont.*
institutional prejudice
administrators, 13–005
judges, 13–005
prosecutors, 13–004
invalidity, and, 23–026
judges, 13–005
necessity, 13–009
pecuniary interest, 13–002
personal interests
other interests, 13–003
pecuniary interest, 13–002
prosecutors, 13–004
statutory exceptions, 13–010
test, 13–006—13–008
waiver, 13–011
Breach of contract
failure to exercise discretion, and, 16–030
Breach of statutory duty
torts, and, 29–021—29–023
Burden of proof
invalidity, and, 23–028—23–029

Capacity
contracts, and
Crown, 5–035
Ministers of the Crown, 5–036—5–037
statutory bodies, 5–038
Capping (rates)
local government finance, and, 6–010
Causation
audi alteram partem, and, 12–024
Central government
contracts, and
contracting out, 5–007—5–013
government contracts, 5–006
Private Finance Initiative, 5–014—5–015
public private partnerships, 5–014—
5–015
public procurement, 5–002—5–005
Certiorari
alternative remedies, 25–012
delay, 25–011
determination of rights, 25–005
duty to act judicially, 25–006
effect, 25–013
grounds, 25–008
introduction, 25–002
limitations, 25–009—25–012
locus standi, and, 24–003
relevant persons and authorities, 25–004
scope, 25–003—25–007
subordinate legislation, 25–007
waiver, and, 25–009—25–010
"Charter of Fundamental Rights"
equal treatment, and, 21–020
"Citizen's Charter"
executive agencies, and, 4–022
regulation of utilities, and, 11–035
Civil Aviation Authority
executive agencies, and, 4–025—4–026

Civil Procedure Rules
judicial review, and, 26–013
"Civil rights and obligations"
audi alteram partem, and, 12–018—12–019
Claims
judicial review, and, 26–004—26–005
"Collateral attack"
invalidity, and
classification, 23–001
de facto judges and officers, 23–007
general principle, 23–002
impact of general law on remedies, 23–005
interpretation of statute, 23–004
inter-relationship, 23–002—23–007
positive and negative decisions, 23–006
qualifications to general principle,
23–003—23–007
private rights, and, 26–007—26–011
"Collateral fact doctrine"
demise of doctrine, 14–038
introduction, 14–004
merits, 14–005
preliminary questions, 14–005—14–006
**Commission for Local Administration in
England**
advice to local authorities, 8–041
establishment, 8–038
internal complaints procedures, and, 8–040
procedure, 8–039
scope of authority, 8–038—8–039
Committee on Public Administration
See **Public Administration Select Committee**
Committee on Standards and Privileges
generally, 8–009—8–010
Committee on Standards in Public Life
generally, 8–007—8–008
Common policies
equal treatment, and, 21–019
Community charge
local government finance, and, 6–009
Compensation
legitimate expectation, and, 20–052
Competition policy
accountability, 11–009
choice of legislative criterion, 11–004
Competition Commission, 11–003
conclusion, 11–036
control, 11–009
effectiveness, 11–004
enforcement, 11–008
importance, 11–010
introduction, 11–001
justiciability, 11–007
method of regulation, 11–004
Monopolies and Mergers Commission,
11–003
procedural rights, 11–005
public interest, 11–006—11–007
purpose of regulation, 11–002
rationale for regulation
introduction, 11–011
private interest, 11–013

Competition policy—*cont.*
rationale for regulation—*cont.*
public interest, 11–012
regulation of utilities
agencies, 11–024
Boards, 11–022
broader context, 11–017
Citizen's Charter, 11–035
common law, 11–019—11–020
departmental supervision, 11–021
economic considerations, 11–016
gas supply, 11–027—11–030
government's approach, 11–015
institutional design, 11–031—11–033
introduction, 11–011
legal powers and constraints, 11–027
limits of public law, 11–034
method of regulation, 11–025—11–035
political considerations, 11–016
privatisation, 11–024
public ownership, 11–023
purpose of regulation, 11–011—11–017
regulatory bodies, 11–018—11–024
sale of state assets, 11–025—11–026
social considerations, 11–016
tribunals, 11–022
regulatory bodies, 11–003
rule-making, 11–006
structural adjustment, 11–014
"Comprehensive performance assessment"
contracts, and, 5–022
Compulsory competitive tendering
contracts, and, 5–020
"Conclusive evidence"
ouster clauses, and, 27–005
Consultation
administrative rules, and, 22–045
audi alteram partem, and, 12–028
secondary legislation, and
benefits, 22–019
Code of Practice, and, 22–0021
common law, at, 22–018
conclusion, 22–022
introduction, 22–016
issues to be addresses, 22–020
statute, under, 22–017
Contempt of court
Crown proceedings, and, 28–023
Contracting out
acts of public authorities, and, 18–022—
18–025
Conservative policy, 5–008
failure to exercise discretion, and, 16–010
formation of contracts, 5–012—5–013
Labour policy, 5–009
legal principle, 5–012—5–013
local government, and, 5–020
overview, 5–007
problems and concerns, 5–010—5–011
Contracts
And see **Public procurement**
appropriation, 5–042

Contracts—*cont.*
  authority of agents
    breach of warranty, 5–041
    extent, 5–040
    introduction, 5–039
  beacon council scheme, 5–022
  best value, 5–021—5–022
  capacity
    Crown, 5–035
    Ministers of the Crown, 5–036—5–037
    statutory bodies, 5–038
  central government
    contracting out, 5–007—5–013
    government contracts, 5–006
    Private Finance Initiative, 5–014—5–015
    public private partnerships, 5–014—5–015
    public procurement, 5–002—5–005
  comprehensive performance assessment,
      5–022
  compulsory competitive tendering, 5–020
  contracting out
    Conservative policy, 5–008
    formation of contracts, 5–012—5–013
    Labour policy, 5–009
    legal principle, 5–012—5–013
    local government, and, 5–020
    overview, 5–007
    problems and concerns, 5–010—5–011
  Crown proceedings, 5–043
  Crown servants
    arrears of pay, 5–046
    dismissal, 5–045
    existence of contract, 5–044
    statutory protection, 5–047
  governance, and
    contract as instrument of policy, 5–032
    executive power, 5–033
    introduction, 5–031
    policy formulation, 5–034
  government contracts, 5–006
  illegal contracts, 5–048—5–049
  introduction, 5–001
  local area agreements, 5–022
  local government
    beacon council scheme, 5–022
    best value, 5–021—5–022
    competitive procedures, 5–017
    comprehensive performance assessment,
        5–022
    compulsory competitive tendering, 5–020
    contracting out, 5–020
    introduction, 5–016
    local area agreements, 5–022
    local public service agreements, 5–022
    non-commercial considerations, 5–018—
        5–019
    Private Finance Initiative, 5–023
  local public service agreements, 5–022
  Ministers, and, 5–036—5–037
  Parliamentary appropriation, 5–042
  Private Finance Initiative
    central government, 5–014—5–015

Contracts—*cont.*
  Private Finance Initiative—*cont.*
    local government, 5–023
    public private partnerships, 5–014—5–015
  public procurement
    application of Directives, 5–028
    competitive dialogue procedure, 5–029
    contracting authorities, 5–028
    contract awards, 5–029
    EC rules, 5–024—5–030
    guidelines, 5–004
    institutional responsibility, 5–003
    introduction, 5–002
    Model Conditions of Contract, 5–004
    negotiated procedure, 5–029
    open procedure, 5–029
    overview, 5–001
    procedures, 5–029
    public contract, 5–028
    range of options, 5–005
    remedies, 5–030
    restricted procedure, 5–029
    technical specifications, 5–028
    UK regulations, 5–028—5–029
  public procurement (EC rules)
    Directives, and, 5–027—5–030
    EC Treaty, and, 5–026
    introduction, 5–024
    object, 5–025
  public service agreements, 5–001
  unlawful contracts, 5–048—5–049
COREPER
  See also **European Union**
  generally, 10–002
Council of the European Union
  See also **European Union**
  generally, 10–002
Council on Tribunals
  See also **Tribunals**
  abolition, 9–029
  generally, 9–030
Council tax
  local government finance, and, 6–009
Crown indemnity
  contempt, 28–023
  declarations, 28–021
  injunctions, 28–018—28–022
  procedure, 28–017
  statutes benefitting the Crown, 28–016
  statutes binding the Crown, 28–015
Crown privilege
  generally, 28–002
Crown proceedings
  government contracts, and, 5–043
Crown servants
  arrears of pay, 5–046
  dismissal, 5–045
  existence of contract, 5–044
  statutory protection, 5–047

Damages
  failure to exercise discretion, and, 16–030

Declarations
alternative remedies, 25–028
Crown proceedings, and, 28–021
defect, 25–022
effect, 25–029
introduction, 25–020
limits on availability
alternative remedies, 25–028
exclusion of original jurisdiction, 25–023
exclusion of supervisory jurisdiction, 25–024
hypothetical questions, 25–025—25–026
justiciability, 25–027
"mootness", 25–025
"ripeness", 25–025
locus standi, and, 24–006—24–007
practice, 25–030
procedure, 25–030
scope, 25–021—25–022
Declarations of incompatibility
human rights, and, 18–004—18–011
Default powers
generally, 25–040
"Deference"
And see **Human rights**
critique, 18–051
factors taken into account, 18–036
generally, 18–035
terminology, 18–037
Delay
certiorari, and, 25–011
Delegated legislation
See **Subordinate legislation**
Delegation
failure to exercise discretion, and
agency, and, 16–004—16–0006
creation, 16–005
general principles, 16–003
government departments, 16–007—16–010
retention of authority by delegator, 16–006
statutory power, 16–011
generally, 16–003—16–011
legitimate expectation, and, 20–032—20–033
Democracy
local authorities, and, 6–014—6–017
Devolution
introduction, 7–001
Northern Ireland, 7–001
Parliamentary Commissioner for Administration, and, 8–023
Scotland
background, 7–002
reflections, 7–025—7–026
Scottish Executive, 7–010
Scottish Parliament, 7–003—7–024
Scottish Parliament
composition, 7–003
executive powers, 7–010

Devolution—*cont.*
Scottish Parliament—*cont.*
judicial challenge to competence, 7–018—7–024
legislative powers, 7–005—7–016
operation, 7–004
political challenge to competence, 7–017
powers, 7–005—7–010
revenue-raising, 7–016
subordinate legislation, 7–011—7–015
Wales
background, 7–027—7–028
reflections, 7–045—7–046
National Assembly for Wales, 7–029—7–044
Welsh ministers, 7–031—7–032
Welsh Assembly Government
Assembly Acts, 7–035
Assembly measures, 7–034
composition, 7–029
executive powers, 7–031—7–032
judicial challenge to competence, 7–038—7–044
operation, 7–030
other bodies, and, 7–037
powers, 7–033—7–037
subordinate legislation, 7–036
Welsh ministers
composition, 7–031
functions, 7–032
Direct effect
Directives
generally, 10–023—10–024
horizontal direct effect, 10–025
incidental horizontal direct effect, 10–030
scope of vertical direct effect, 10–027—10–029
vertical direct effect, 10–025—10–026
human rights, and, 18–054
introduction, 10–015
private enforcement, and, 10–018
public enforcement, and, 10–016—10–017
Regulations, 10–022
rights and remedies, 10–031—10–032
Treaty articles, 10–020—10–021
Van Gend en Loos decision, 10–019
Directives
generally, 10–023—10–024
horizontal direct effect, 10–025
incidental horizontal direct effect, 10–030
scope of vertical direct effect, 10–027—10–029
vertical direct effect, 10–025—10–026
Disability discrimination
equal treatment, and, 21–018
Disclosure
judicial review, and, 26–050—26–051
Discretion
failure to exercise discretion, and
fettering, 16–012—16–034
rationale for intervention, 16–002
types of constraint, 16–001

Discretion—*cont.*
fettering of discretion
contracts, 16–021—16–033
Crown, and, 16–034
existing rule or policy, 16–012—16–015
insufficient rules, 16–016—16–020
no existing rule, 16–016—16–020
present law, 16–012
rules and policies, 16–011A—16–020
mandamus, and, 25–018
proportionality, and
domestic application, 19–017
EC approach, 19–022
Discretionary powers
abuse of discretion, and, 17–006
Discrimination
common law
basic precept, 21–002
case law, 21–003
EC law
age, 21–018
Charter of Fundamental Rights, 21–020
common policies, 21–019
disability, 21–018
gender, 21–017
introduction, 21–015
nationality, 21–016
race and ethnic origin, 21–018
religion or belief, 21–018
sex, 21–017
sexual orientation, 21–018
Human Rights Act
Carson decision, 21–007—21–008
generally, 21–005
Michalak decision, 21–006
positive discrimination, 21–013—21–014
scrutiny and rationality review, 21–009—
21–012
introduction, 21–001
positive discrimination, 21–013—21–014
statutory provision, 21–004
Donoughmore Committee 1932
generally, 2–020

EC law
direct effect
Directives, 10–023—10–030
introduction, 10–015
private enforcement, and, 10–018
public enforcement, and, 10–016—
10–017
Regulations, 10–022
rights and remedies, 10–031—10–032
Treaty articles, 10–020—10–021
Van Gend en Loos decision, 10–019
Directives
generally, 10–023—10–024
horizontal direct effect, 10–025
incidental horizontal direct effect, 10–030
scope of vertical direct effect, 10–027—
10–029
vertical direct effect, 10–025—10–026

EC law—*cont.*
government contracts, and
Directives, and, 5–027—5–030
EC Treaty, and, 5–026
introduction, 5–024
object, 5–025
impact, 10–033
introduction, 10–001
legal order
direct effect, 10–015—10–032
introduction, 10–010
supremacy, 10–011—10–014
private enforcement, 10–018
Regulations, 10–022
Treaty articles, 10–020—10–021
supremacy, 10–011—10–014
ECHR
See **European Convention on Human Rights**
Equal treatment
common law
basic precept, 21–002
case law, 21–003
EC law
age, 21–018
Charter of Fundamental Rights, 21–020
common policies, 21–019
disability, 21–018
gender, 21–017
introduction, 21–015
nationality, 21–016
race and ethnic origin, 21–018
religion or belief, 21–018
sex, 21–017
sexual orientation, 21–018
Human Rights Act
Carson decision, 21–007—21–008
generally, 21–005
Michalak decision, 21–006
positive discrimination, 21–013—21–014
scrutiny and rationality review, 21–009—
21–012
introduction, 21–001
positive discrimination, 21–013—21–014
statutory provision, 21–004
Error of fact
See also **Judicial review**
conclusion, 15–029
de novo review, 15–024
determination of factual error, 15–022—
15–028
*E v Secretary of State for the Home
Department*, 15–005—15–008
fresh evidence 15–021
introduction, 15–001
mistake of fact
meaning, 15–002—15–004
test, 15–009—15–021
role of reviewing court, 15–022—15–028
standard of proof, 15–023
test for mistake of fact
criteria in the *E* decision, 15–014—15–020
generally, 15–009—15–013

Error of law
  See also **Judicial review**
  case law, 14–025—14–037
  collateral fact doctrine
    demise of doctrine, 14–038
    introduction, 14–004
    merits, 14–005
    preliminary questions, 14–005—14–006
  'extensive review' (academic argument)
    critique of theory, 14–016—14–018
    impossibility argument, 14–017
    introduction, 14–012
    Parliamentary intent, 14–016
    preliminary questions, 14–013—14–015
    uniformity argument, 14–018
  'extensive review' (judicial argument)
    assessment, 14–021
    introduction, 14–019
    law/fact distinction, 14–022—14–023
    review for error of law, 14–020
  introduction, 14–001—14–002
  'limited review'
    critique of theory, 14–010—14–011
    demise of theory, 14–038
    introduction, 14–007
    limits, 14–009
    relative /absolute facts distinction,
      14–008
  merits, 14–005
  preliminary questions
    ambit, 14–006
    generally, 14–005
  test for review, 14–038—14–046
  theories of jurisdiction, 14–003—14–024
Estoppel
  legitimate expectation, and, 20–031
"Ethnic origin"
  equal treatment, and, 21–018
EU Charter of Rights
  human rights, and, 18–056
European Commission
  See also **European Union**
  generally, 10–004—10–005
European Convention on Human Rights
  And see **Human rights**
  audi alteram partem, and
    application of maxim, 12–018—12–019
    reasons for decision, 12–035
    specific procedural norms, 12–043
  generally, 18–002
  right to independent and impartial tribunal,
    and
    domestic courts, in, 13–013—13–019
    fairness, 13–013
    housing law, 13–017—13–019
    introduction, 13–001
    legal requirements, 13–012
    planning inquiries, 13–014—13–016
    waiver, 13–013
European Council
  See also **European Union**
  generally, 10–07

European Court of Justice
  See also **European Union**
  generally, 10–008
European Parliament
  See also **European Union**
  generally, 10–006
European Union
  COREPER, 10–002
  Council of the European Union, 10–002
  direct effect
    Directives, 10–023—10–030
    introduction, 10–015
    private enforcement, and, 10–018
    public enforcement, and, 10–016—
      10–017
    Regulations, 10–022
    rights and remedies, 10–031—10–032
    Treaty articles, 10–020—10–021
    Van Gend en Loos decision, 10–019
  Directives
    generally, 10–023—10–024
    horizontal direct effect, 10–025
    incidental horizontal direct effect, 10–030
    scope of vertical direct effect, 10–027—
      10–029
    vertical direct effect, 10–025—10–026
  European Commission, 10–004—10–005
  European Council, 10–07
  European Court of Justice, 10–008
  European Parliament, 10–006
  impact of Community law, 10–033
  institutions
    COREPER, 10–002
    Council of the European Union, 10–002
    European Commission, 10–004—10–005
    European Council, 10–07
    European Court of Justice, 10–008
    European Parliament, 10–006
    introduction, 10–002
  introduction, 10–001
  legal order
    direct effect, 10–015—10–032
    introduction, 10–010
    supremacy, 10–011—10–014
  legislative process, 10–009
  private enforcement, 10–018
  Regulations, 10–022
  supremacy of EC law, 10–011—10–014
  Treaty articles, 10–020—10–021
Evidence
  audi alteram partem, and, 12–031
Executive agencies
  accountability, 4–020—4–021
  Citizen's Charter, 4–022
  Civil Aviation Authority, 4–025—4–026
  constitutional framework, 4–032—4–033
  control, 4–019
  effectiveness, 4–022—4–023
  failure to exercise discretion, and, 16–009
  historical development
    conclusion, 4–007
    Efficiency Unit, 4–003

Executive agencies—*cont.*
  historical development—*cont.*
    Fulton Committee, 4–002
    Next Steps Report, 4–003—4–004
    non-departmental public bodies, 4–005
    Rayner Unit, 4–003
    terminology, 4–006
  institutional design
    Civil Aviation Authority, 4–025—4–026
    introduction, 4–024
    nationalisation, and, 4–027—4–028
    privatisation, and, 4–029—4–031
    public corporations, 4–027—4–028
  introduction, 4–017
  legal framework, 4–032—4–033
  legal status, 4–010
  local authorities, and, 6–013
  nationalisation, and, 4–027—4–028
  organisational framework, 4–010
  overview, 4–001
  privatisation, and, 4–029—4–031
  public corporations, 4–027—4–028
  regulatory control, 4–029—4–031
  staffing, 4–018
  terminology, 4–006
Executive power
  centralisation of legislative initiative,
    3–005—3–006
  governmental responsibility, 3–003—3–004
  introduction, 3–002
  party system, 3–007
  Scottish Parliament, and, 7–010
  Welsh Assembly Government, and,
    7–031—7–032
Extrinsic evidence
  inquiries, and, 9–040

"Failure to exercise discretion"
  agency, and
    creation, 16–005
    introduction, 16–004
  contracting-out, and, 16–010
  damages for breach of contract, 16–030
  delegation
    agency, and, 16–004—16–0006
    creation, 16–005
    general principles, 16–003
    government departments, 16–007—
      16–010
    retention of authority by delegator,
      16–006
    statutory power, 16–011
  discretion
    fettering, 16–012—16–034
    rationale for intervention, 16–002
    types of constraint, 16–001
  executive agencies, 16–009
  fettering of discretion
    contracts, 16–021—16–033
    Crown, and, 16–034
    existing rule or policy, 16–012—16–015
    insufficient rules, 16–016—16–020

"Failure to exercise discretion"—*cont.*
  fettering of discretion—*cont.*
    no existing rule, 16–016—16–020
    present law, 16–012
    rules and policies, 16–011A—16–020
  frustration, 16–031—16–032
  government departments
    application of *Carltona* principle, 16–008
    contracting-out, and, 16–010
    executive agencies, and, 16–009
    general principles, 16–007
  introduction, 16–001—16–002
  rationale for intervention, 16–002
  retention of authority by delegator, 16–006
Fairness
  And see **Audi alteram partem**
  generally, 12–044—12–045
  introduction, 12–009—12–010
  right to independent and impartial tribunal,
    and, 13–013
  social welfare, 12–047
  statutory inquiries, 12–046
Fettering of discretion
  contracts, 16–021—16–033
  Crown, and, 16–034
  existing rule or policy, 16–012—16–015
  insufficient rules, 16–016—16–020
  no existing rule, 16–016—16–020
  present law, 16–012
  rules and policies, 16–011A—16–020
"Finality clauses"
  ouster clauses, and, 27–002
Finance
  local government, and
    aggregate external finance, 6–011
    capital expenditure, 6–012
    community charge, 6–009
    council tax, 6–009
    grants, 6–010—6–012
    introduction, 6–008
    'poll tax', 6–009
    rate support grant, 6–010
    rates, 6–009
    relative needs formula, 6–011
    resources, 6–009
    spending curbs, 6–010—6–012
First-tier Tribunal
  See also **Tribunals**
  appeals to Upper Tribunal, 9–017
  generally, 9–013
  judicial review by High Court, 9–023
  self-review, 9–015—9–016
  transfer of functions, 9–014
Franks Report 1957
  implementation, 9–006
  inquiries, and
    implementation, 9–036
    recommendations, 9–034—9–035
  recommendations, 9–005
  remit, 9–004
  terms of reference, 2–020

Freedom of information
exempt information, 8–005
Information Commissioner, 8–005
legislative history, 8–003
overview, 8–001
public authorities, 8–004
rationale, 8–002
statutory provisions, 8–004—8–005
Fulton Committee 1968
generally, 4–002
Frustration
failure to exercise discretion, and, 16–031—
16–032

Gender
equal treatment, and, 21–017
"Governance"
central government
contract as instrument of policy, 5–032
executive power, 5–033
introduction, 5–031
policy formulation, 5–034
local government, 6–013
Government contracts
And see **Contracts**
generally, 5–006
Government departments
failure to exercise discretion, and
application of *Carltona* principle, 16–008
contracting-out, and, 16–010
executive agencies, and, 16–009
general principles, 16–007
Grants
local government finance, and, 6–010—
6–012

Habeas corpus
generally, 25–038
Health Service Commissioners
establishment, 8–036
functions, 8–036
jurisdiction, 8–037
Hearings
audi alteram partem, and
And see **Audi alteram partem**
generally, 12–007
introduction, 12–029
rules of evidence, 12–031
type, 12–030
invalidity, and, 23–025
judicial review, and, 26–054
House of Lords
Merits of Statutory Instruments Committee
generally, 22–012
reform proposals, 22–038
reform proposals, 3–020—3–021
Housing
right to independent and impartial tribunal,
and, 13–017—13–019
Human rights
acts of public authorities
contracting out, 18–022—18–025

Human rights—*cont.*
acts of public authorities—*cont.*
core public authorities, 18–019
generally, 18–012
Hooper decision, 18–015
horizontal effect of the Act, 18–026—
18–028
hybrid public authorities, 18–020—
18–025
illegality, and, 18–012
locus standi, 18–029
qualification, 18–013
relationship between provisions,
18–015—18–016
remedies for breach, 18–030
scope of provisions, 18–017—18–025
standing, 18–029
test for authorities, 18–019—18–020
types of authority, 18–017—18–018
Wilkinson decision, 18–014
application in domestic courts, 18–003
audi alteram partem, and
application of maxim, 12–018—12–019
reasons for decision, 12–035
specific procedural norms, 12–043
Charter of Rights, 18–056
common law, at
heightened rationality review, 17–018—
17–019
interpretation of legislation, 17–020
introduction, 17–015
jurisprudence, 17–017
legality principle, 17–020
secondary literature, 17–021
constitutional competence, 18–048—18–049
declarations of incompatibility, 18–004—
18–011
deference
critique, 18–051
factors taken into account, 18–036
generally, 18–035
terminology, 18–037
democratic dialogue, 18–050
direct effect, 18–054
discretionary area of judgment
factors taken into account, 18–036
generally, 18–035
terminology, 18–037
discrimination
common law, 21–002—21–003
EC law, 21–015—21–020
Human Rights Act, 21–005—21–014
introduction, 21–001
statutory provision, 21–004
equal treatment
common law, 21–002—21–003
EC law, 21–015—21–020
Human Rights Act, 21–005—21–014
introduction, 21–001
statutory provision, 21–004
domestic approach
deference, 18–035—18–037

Human rights—*cont.*
domestic approach—*cont.*
introduction, 18–033
margin of appreciation, 18–034
proportionality, 18–038—18–046
EC principles
direct effect, 18–054
EU Charter of Rights, 18–056
fundamental rights, 18–055
introduction, 18–052
legislative competence, 18–053
relationship between ECHR and HRA,
18–057
EU Charter of Rights, 18–056
European Convention on Human Rights,
18–002
fundamental rights, 18–055
in accordance with the law, 18–032
institutional competence, 18–048—18–049
interpretation of legislation
case law, 18–007—18–011
common law, at, 17–020
Ghaidan decision, 18–008—18–009
judicial approach, 18–007—18–011
legislative history, 18–006
statutory provisions, 18–004—18–005
introduction, 18–001
judicial review procedure, 26–012
legislative competence, 18–053
legislative history, 18–002—18–003
legitimate aim, 18–032
locus standi, and
acts of public authorities, 18–029
generally, 24–025
margin of appreciation
domestic law approach, 18–034
generally, 18–032
necessary in democratic society, 18–032
ouster clauses, and, 27–009
prescribed by law, 18–032
proportionality
conclusion, 18–046
Daly decision, 18–038
final determination by court, 18–041
generally, 18–038—18–039
introduction, 18–032
role of domestic court, 18–040—18–045
weight accorded to view of initial
decision-maker, 18–042—18–045
respect
factors taken into account, 18–036
generally, 18–035
terminology, 18–037
right to fair trial
domestic courts, and, 13–013—13–019
fairness, 13–013
housing law, and, 13–017—13–018
independent and impartial tribunal,
13–020
legal basis, 13–012
planning law, and, 13–014—13–016
recent developments, 13–019

Human rights—*cont.*
right to independent and impartial tribunal
common law, at, 13–020
domestic courts, in, 13–013—13–019
fairness, 13–013
housing law, 13–017—13–019
introduction, 13–001
legal requirements, 13–012
planning inquiries, 13–014—13–016
waiver, 13–013
standard of review
academic debate, 18–047—18–051
domestic law approach, 18–033—18–046
ECHR precepts, 18–032
introduction, 18–031
status of ECHR, 18–002
torts, and, 29–024—29–030
Illegal contracts
And see **Contracts**
generally, 5–048—5–049
Illegality
acts of public authorities, and, 18–012
bad faith, 17–015
common law constraints
bad faith, 17–015
improper purposes, 17–010—17–012
introduction, 17–009
relevancy, 17–013—17–014
common law discretionary powers, 17–006
delegated legislation, and, 17–004
discretionary powers, and, 17–006
human rights (common law)
heightened rationality review, 17–018—
17–019
interpretation of legislation, 17–020
introduction, 17–015
jurisprudence, 17–017
legality principle, 17–020
secondary literature, 17–021
'illegality', 17–001
improper purposes, 17–010—17–012
intensity of review, 17–008
'irrationality', 17–001
powers capable of control
common law discretionary powers,
17–006
introduction, 17–003
non-statutory bodies' powers, 17–007
prerogative powers, 17–005
statutory powers, 17–004
prerogative powers, and, 17–005
primary legislation, and, 17–004
reasonableness, 17–002
relevancy, 17–013—17–014
secondary legislation, and, 17–004
statutory powers, and, 17–004
Wednesbury unreasonableness, 17–002
Improper motive
abuse of discretion, and, 17–010—17–012
In accordance with the law
See **Prescribed by law**

Independent and impartial tribunal
See **Right to independent and impartial tribunal**
Information Commissioner
And see **Freedom of information**
generally, 8–005
Injunctions
Crown proceedings, and, 28–018—28–022
introduction, 25–031
limits to relief, 25–036
locus standi, and, 24–006
practice, 25–037
procedure, 25–037
public offices, and, 25–035
scope, 25–033—25–035
types, 25–032
Inquiries
Administrative Justice and Tribunals Council, 9–048
audi alteram partem, and, 12–007
background, 9–033
conduct of inquiry, 9–038
decision by appointed persons, and, 9–044
example procedure, 9–042
extrinsic evidence, 9–040
framework
pre-IA 2005, 9–046
Inquiries Act 2005, 9–047
Franks Report, and
implementation, 9–036
recommendations, 9–034—9–035
inspector's reports, 9–039
judicial review, 9–050
limitations, 9–043
Parliamentary Commissioner for Administration, 9–049
planning inquiries, 9–051—9–053
planning inquiry commissions, 9–045
post-inquiry procedure
extrinsic evidence, 9–040
inspector's reports, 9–039
reasons, 9–041
pre-inquiry procedure, 9–037
reasons, 9–041
reforms, 9–034—9–036
statutory framework, 9–047
supervision
Administrative Justice and Tribunals Council, 9–048
judicial review, 9–050
Parliamentary Commissioner for Administration, 9–049
written representations
decision by appointed persons, 9–044
planning inquiries, 9–045
Interpretation of legislation
See **Statutory interpretation**
"Intra vires representations"
application of precepts, 20–024—20–030
contending arguments, 20–006—20–011
Coughlan decision, 20–012—20–016
legitimacy of expectation, 20–017

"Intra vires representations"—*cont.*
reasonableness of expectation, 20–017
standard of review, 20–018—20–023
types of case, 20–005
Invalidity
bias, 23–026
burden of proof, 23–028—23–029
direct and collateral attack
classification, 23–001
de facto judges and officers, 23–007
general principle, 23–002
impact of general law on remedies, 23–005
interpretation of statute, 23–004
inter-relationship, 23–002—23–007
positive and negative decisions, 23–006
qualifications to general principle, 23–003—23–007
hearings, 23–025
natural justice
bias, 23–026
hearings, 23–025
introduction, 23–024
waiver, 23–027
partial validity, 23–033
validity pending determination, 23–030—23–032
void
determining if error renders act void, 23–011
effect of holding act void, 23–012
judicial discretion, 23–018—23–023
natural justice, 23–024—23–027
nature of concept, 23–009—23–010
overview, 23–008
voidable
alternative to locus standi, 23–015
error of law within jurisdiction, 23–017
gravity of error, 23–016
indicative of need to challenger, 23–014
introduction, 23–013
judicial discretion, 23–018—23–023
natural justice, 23–024—23–027
overview, 23–008
waiver, 23–027
Irrationality
See also **Rationality**
And see **Wednesbury unreasonableness**
abuse of discretion, and, 17–001
generally, 19–001
proportionality, and
introduction 19–001
Wednesbury unreasonableness, 19–002—19–007

Joint Committee on Statutory Instruments
secondary legislation, and, 22–011
Judges
bias, and, 13–005
Judicial review
And see under individual headings

Judicial review—*cont.*
  abuse of discretion
    common law constraints, 17–009—
      17–015
    human rights, 17–015—17–021
    illegality, 17–001
    intensity of review, 17–008
    irrationality, 17–001
    powers capable of control, 17–003—
      17–007
    reasonableness, 17–002
  administration-made rules
    legal status, 22–040
    overview, 22–001
    possible solutions, 22–043—22–047
    problem areas, 22–042
    rationale, 22–039
    type, 22–039
  audi alteram partem
    balancing, 12–020—12–026
    conclusion, 12–048
    fairness, 12–044—12–047
    historical development, 12–001
    limitation of principle, 12–003—12–007
    non-judicatative procedures, 12–044—
      12–047
    principle revived, 12–008—12–010
    procedural protection, 12–011—12–043
    rationale for rights, 12–002
    specific procedural norms, 12–027—
      12–043
  bias
    exceptions, 13–009—13–011
    institutional prejudice, 13–004—13–005
    pecuniary interest, 13–002
    personal interest, 13–002—13–003
    test, 13–006—13–008
  constitutionalism, and
    fundamental values, 1–033
    legitimacy, 1–034
    nature of argument, 1–032
    participation, 1–030
    polycentricity, 1–031
  equal treatment
    common law, 21–002—21–003
    EC law, 21–015—21–020
    Human Rights Act, 21–005—21–014
    introduction, 21–001
    statutory provision, 21–004
  errors of law
    case law, 14–025—14–037
    introduction, 14–001—14–002
    test for review, 14–038—14–046
    theories, 14–003—14–024
  failure to exercise discretion
    delegation, 16–003—16–011
    fettering of discretion, 16–012—16–034
    introduction, 16–001—16–002
    rationale for intervention, 16–002
  hearings
    balancing, 12–020—12–026
    conclusion, 12–048

Judicial review—*cont.*
  hearings—*cont.*
    fairness, 12–044—12–047
    historical development, 12–001
    limitation of principle, 12–003—12–007
    non-judicatative procedures, 12–044—
      12–047
    principle revived, 12–008—12–010
    procedural protection, 12–011—12–043
    rationale for rights, 12–002
    specific procedural norms, 12–027—
      12–043
  human rights, and
    acts of public authorities, 18–012—
      18–030
    declarations of incompatibility, 18–004—
      18–011
    EC principles, 18–052—18–057
    interpretation of legislation, 18–004—
      18–011
    introduction, 18–001
    legislative history, 18–002—18–003
    proportionality, 18–038—18–046
    standard of review, 18–031—18–051
  illegality
    common law constraints, 17–009—
      17–015
    human rights, 17–015—17–021
    generally, 17–001
    intensity of review, 17–008
    powers capable of control, 17–003—
      17–007
    reasonableness, 17–002
  independent and impartial tribunal, 13–020
  inquiries, and, 9–050
  intra vires representations
    application of precepts, 20–024—20–030
    contending arguments, 20–006—20–011
    Coughlan decision, 20–012—20–016
    legitimacy of expectation, 20–017
    reasonableness of expectation, 20–017
    standard of review, 20–018—20–023
    types of case, 20–005
  invalidity
    burden of proof, 13–028—23–033
    direct and collateral attack, 23–001—
      23–007
    void and voidable, 23–008—23–027
  irrationality
    common law constraints, 17–009—
      17–015
    human rights, 17–015—17–021
    generally, 17–001
    intensity of review, 17–008
    powers capable of control, 17–003—
      17–007
    reasonableness, 17–002
  jurisdiction
    case law, 14–025—14–037
    introduction, 14–001—14–002
    test for review, 14–038—14–046
    theories, 14–003—14–024

Judicial review—*cont.*
  legitimate expectation
    intra vires representations, 20–005—
      20–030
    introduction, 20–001
    nature of problem, 20–002—20–004
    ultra vires representations, 20–031—
      20–052
  locus standi, and
    fusion approach, 24–024
    human rights, and, 24–025
    group challenges, 24–021—24–023
    individual challenges, 24–019—24–020
    interpretation of the test, 24–018—24–024
    introduction, 24–012
    IRC case, 24–013—24–017
    outside section 31, 24–026
    public interest challenges, 24–022
    sufficiency of interest, 24–015—24–016
    unincorporated associations, 24–023
  natural justice
    audi alteram partem, 12–001—12–047
    bias, 13–002—13–011
    independent and impartial tribunal,
      13–020
    right to fair trial, 13–012—13–019
  nemo judex in sua causa
    exceptions, 13–009—13–011
    institutional prejudice, 13–004—13–005
    overview, 12–001
    pecuniary interest, 13–002
    personal interest, 13–002—13–003
    test, 13–006—13–008
  origins, 1–003
  Parliamentary Commissioner for
    Administration, and, 8–031
  procedural rights
    And see **Audi alteram partem**
    introduction, 12–002
    rationale, 12–002
  proportionality
    application, 19–014—19–017
    discretion, and, 19–022
    EC Dimension, 19–019—19–022
    future developments, 19–024—19–027
    human rights, and, 18–038—18–046
    inter-relationship between principles of
      review, 19–031—19–032
    introduction, 19–008
    legal status, 19–009—19–012
    penalties, and, 19–021
    place and meaning, 19–013
    rights, and, 19–020
    role of court, 19–018
    standard of review, 19–018
    substantive control, 19–029—19–030
  questions of fact
    conclusion, 15–029
    determination of factual error, 15–022—
      15–028
    *E v Secretary of State for the Home
      Department*, 15–005—15–008

Judicial review—*cont.*
  questions of fact—*cont.*
    introduction, 15–001
    mistake and fact, 15–002—15–004
    role of reviewing court, 15–022—15–028
    test for mistake of fact, 15–009—15–021
  rationale, 1–004
  rationality
    introduction 19–001
    Wednesbury unreasonableness, 19–002—
      19–007
  remedies
    And see **Remedies**
    available orders, 25–001—25–040
    exclusion of review, 27–001—27–023
    procedure, 26–001—26–058
    standing, 24–001—24–041
    torts, 29–001—29–066
  right to fair trial
    domestic courts, and, 13–013—13–019
    fairness, 13–013
    housing law, and, 13–017—13–018
    independent and impartial tribunal,
      13–020
    legal basis, 13–012
    planning law, and, 13–014—13–016
    recent developments, 13–019
  rule-making
    administration-made rules, 22–039—
      2–047
    EC law, and, 22–048
    delegated legislation, 22–002—22–038
    introduction, 22–001
  secondary legislation
    breach of constitutional principle,
      22–027
    delegation, 22–029
    formal invalidity, 22–024
    infringement of primary legislation,
      22–026
    introduction, 22–023
    procedural ultra vires, 22–024
    purpose, 22–028
    reasonableness, 22–028
    relevance, 22–028
    remedies, 22–030
    substantive ultra vires, 22–025—22–028
  tribunals, and
    High Court, by, 9–023
    Upper Tribunal, by, 9–022
  ultra vires representations
    agency, 20–032—20–033
    application of principle, 20–034—20–035
    assessment of principle, 20–041—20–043
    balancing, and, 20–047—20–051
    compensation, 20–052
    conceptual language, 20–036
    delegation, 20–032—20–033
    estoppel, and, 20–031
    introduction, 20–031
    jurisdictional principle, 20–032—20–043
    policy behind principle, 20–042—20–043

Judicial review—*cont.*
 ultra vires representations—*cont.*
  qualifications to principle, 20–037—
   20–040
  rationale for principle, 20–042—20–043
  strategies available, 20–044—20–052
 Wednesbury unreasonableness
  future of the test, 19–007
  introduction, 19–002
  present law, 19–003—19–006
Jurisdiction
 case law, 14–025—14–037
 introduction, 14–001—14–002
 test for review, 14–038—14–046
 theories, 14–003—14–024
Jurisprudence (administrative law)
 conclusion, 1–054
 constitutionalism
  fundamental values, 1–033
  generally, 1–028—1–029
  judicial review, and, 1–030—1–034
  legitimacy, 1–034
  nature of argument, 1–032
  participation, 1–030
  polycentricity, 1–031
 human rights, 1–025
 introduction, 1–001
 market-oriented pluralism, and
  implications, 1–047—1–050
  intellectual basis, 1–046
  introduction, 1–035
  process rights, 1–049
  rights, citizenship and society, 1–048
 nature and purpose of administrative law
  introduction, 1–001
  ultra vires, 1–005—1–016
  unitary democracy, 1–002—1–004
 participation, 1–030
 pluralism, and
  accountability of administrative law,
   1–040
  corporatist challenge, 1–039
  critique of unitary thesis, 1–037
  effectiveness of Parliamentary controls,
   1–038
  gateways to administrative law, 1–041—
   1–042
  implications, 1–040—1–045
  intellectual basis, 1–036—1–039
  introduction, 1–035
  locus standi, 1–042
  natural justice, 1–042
  process rights, 1–043
  remedies of administrative law, 1–045
  scope of administrative law, 1–040
  scope of judicial review, 1–044
  standing, 1–042
 polycentricity, 1–031
 rights-based approach
  articulation of principles of good
   administration, 1–019
  critical appraisal, 1–026—1–034

Jurisprudence (administrative law)—*cont.*
 rights-based approach—*cont.*
  human rights, 1–025
  justifications, 1–021—1–025
  meaning, 1–018—1–020
  nature, 1–017
  protection of fundamental rights,
   1–018—1–019
 rule of law, 1–023—1–024
 "the third way", and
  implications, 1–053
  intellectual basis, 1–051—1–052
  introduction, 1–035
 ultra vires
  And see **Ultra vires**
  critique of principle, 1–016
  deficiencies, 1–010—1–015
  form of intervention, 1–005
  implications, 1–005—1–009
  introduction, 1–003—1–004
  unitary democracy, 1–002—1–004
Justice-All Souls Report 1998
 generally, 2–020
Justiciability
 declarations, and, 25–027
 remedies, and, 24–001

Legal certainty
 legitimate expectation, and, 20–004
Legal representation
 audi alteram partem, and, 12–032
Leggatt Report
 See also **Tribunals**
 introduction, 9–007
 recommendations, 9–008—9–010
Legislation
 abuse of discretion, and, 17–004
Legislative proceedings
 centralisation of initiative, 3–005—3–006
 changes, 3–019
 introduction, 3–015
 Rippon Commission, 3–016
 Select Committee on Modernisation,
  3–017—3–018
Legitimate aim
 human rights, and, 18–032
Legitimate expectation
 actual retroactive effect, 20–003
 agency, 20–032—20–033
 apparent retroactive effect, 20–003
 audi alteram partem, and, 12–016—12–017
 balancing, and, 20–047—20–051
 compensation, 20–052
 delegation, 20–032—20–033
 estoppel, and, 20–031
 intra vires representations
  application of precepts, 20–024—20–030
  contending arguments, 20–006—20–011
  Coughlan decision, 20–012—20–016
  legitimacy of expectation, 20–017
  reasonableness of expectation, 20–017
  standard of review, 20–018—20–023

Legitimate expectation—*cont.*
  intra vires representations—*cont.*
    types of case, 20–005
  introduction, 20–001
  legal certainty, and, 20–004
  nature of problem
    introduction, 20–002
    legal certainty, 20–004
    retroactivity, 20–003
  procedural role, 12–016—12–017
  retroactivity, 20–003
  ultra vires representations
    agency, 20–032—20–033
    application of principle, 20–034—20–035
    assessment of principle, 20–041—20–043
    balancing, and, 20–047—20–051
    compensation, 20–052
    conceptual language, 20–036
    delegation, 20–032—20–033
    estoppel, and, 20–031
    introduction, 20–031
    jurisdictional principle, 20–032—20–043
    policy behind principle, 20–042—20–043
    qualifications to principle, 20–037—
      20–040
    rationale for principle, 20–042—20–043
    strategies available, 20–044—20–052
  Wednesbury unreasonableness, and, 19–006
"Local area agreements"
  local government contracts, and, 5–022
Local authorities
  aggregate external finance, 6–011
  beacon council scheme, 5–022
  best value, 5–021—5–022
  capital expenditure, 6–012
  Commission for Local Administration in
      England
    advice to local authorities, 8–041
    establishment, 8–038
    internal complaints procedures, and,
      8–040
    procedure, 8–039
    scope of authority, 8–038—8–039
  community charge, 6–009
  comprehensive performance assessment,
    5–022
  compulsory competitive tendering, 5–020
  conduct in public life, and, 8–011
  contracts, and
    beacon council scheme, 5–022
    best value, 5–021—5–022
    competitive procedures, 5–017
    comprehensive performance assessment,
      5–022
    compulsory competitive tendering, 5–020
    contracting out, 5–020
    introduction, 5–016
    local area agreements, 5–022
    local public service agreements, 5–022
    non-commercial considerations, 5–018—
      5–019
    Private Finance Initiative, 5–023

Local authorities—*cont.*
  council tax, 6–009
  democracy, 6–014—6–017
  executive agencies, 6–013
  finances
    aggregate external finance, 6–011
    capital expenditure, 6–012
    community charge, 6–009
    council tax, 6–009
    grants, 6–010—6–012
    introduction, 6–008
    'poll tax', 6–009
    rate support grant, 6–010
    rates, 6–009
    relative needs formula, 6–011
    resources, 6–009
    spending curbs, 6–010—6–012
  functions, 6–006—6–007
  governance, 6–013
  grants, 6–010—6–012
  internal organisation, 6–004—6–005
  introduction, 6–001
  local area agreements, 5–022
  local public service agreements, 5–022
  'poll tax', 6–009
  powers, 6–006—6–007
  Private Finance Initiative, 5–023
  rate capping, 6–010
  rate support grant, 6–010
  rates, 6–009
  relations with central government, 6–014—
      6–017
  relative needs formula, 6–011
  resources, 6–009
  spending curbs, 6–010—6–012
  standards of conduct in public life, and,
      8–011
  structure, 6–002—6–003
Local government finance
  aggregate external finance, 6–011
  capital expenditure, 6–012
  community charge, 6–009
  council tax, 6–009
  grants, 6–010—6–012
  introduction, 6–008
  'poll tax', 6–009
  rate support grant, 6–010
  rates, 6–009
  relative needs formula, 6–011
  resources, 6–009
  spending curbs, 6–010—6–012
"Local public service agreements"
  local government contracts, and, 5–022
Locus standi
  acts of public authorities, and, 18–029
  'Citizen action'
    arguments in favour, 24–031
    conceptual objections, 24–033—24–035
    limits, 24–036
    practical objections, 24–032
    ultra vires, and, 24–036
  Attorney-General, 24–009

Locus standi—*cont.*
function
citizen action, 24–031—24–036
fusion of standing and merits, 24–030
injury in fact, 24–037
introduction, 24–028
vindication of private rights, 24–029
fusion of standing and merits, 24–030
future issues
generally, 24–038—24–039
groups, 24–040
individuals, 24–040
Human Rights Act 1998, under
acts of public authorities, 18–029
generally, 24–025
injury in fact, 24–037
introduction, 24–001
judicial review actions, in
fusion approach, 24–024
human rights, and, 24–025
group challenges, 24–021—24–023
individual challenges, 24–019—24–020
interpretation of the test, 24–018—
24–024
introduction, 24–012
IRC case, 24–013—24–017
outside section 31, 24–026
public interest challenges, 24–022
sufficiency of interest, 24–015—24–016
unincorporated associations, 24–023
pluralism, and, 1–042
pre-1978 law
certiorari, 24–003
declarations, 24–006—24–007
injunctions, 24–006
introduction, 24–002
mandamus, 24–005
prohibition, 24–004
public authorities, 24–010
section 31, outside, 24–026
statutory appeals, 24–011
third party intervention, 24–027
ultra vires, and, 1–007
vindication of private rights, 24–029

Maladministration
And see **Parliamentary Commissioner for Administration**
generally, 8–015
merits of decision, 8–018
overview, 8–012
political response, 8–019
principles of good administration, 8–016—
8–017
Mandamus
alternative remedies, 25–019
ambit, 25–015—25–017
defect, 25–016
demand and refusal, 25–017
discretion, 25–018
duty, 25–015
introduction, 25–014

Mandamus—*cont.*
limits on availability, 25–018—25–019
locus standi, and, 24–005
refusal, 25–017
Mandatory orders
alternative remedies, 25–019
ambit, 25–015—25–017
defect, 25–016
demand and refusal, 25–017
discretion, 25–018
duty, 25–015
introduction, 25–014
limits on availability, 25–018—25–019
locus standi, and, 24–005
refusal, 25–017
Margin of appreciation
domestic law approach, 18–034
generally, 18–032
Mediation
tribunals, and, 9–027
Ministers
government contracts, and, 5–036—5–037
Misfeasance
torts, and, 29–017—29–018
Misfeasance in public office
torts, and, 29–031—29–036
Mistake of fact
See also **Judicial review**
conclusion, 15–029
de novo review, 15–024
determination of factual error, 15–022—
15–028
E v Secretary of State for the Home Department, 15–005—15–008
fresh evidence 15–021
introduction, 15–001
meaning, 15–002—15–004
role of reviewing court, 15–022—15–028
standard of proof, 15–023
test
basis, 15–009—15–013
criteria in the *E* decision, 15–014—
15–020

National Assembly for Wales
Assembly Acts, 7–035
Assembly measures, 7–034
background, 7–027—7–028
composition, 7–029
executive powers
composition, 7–031
functions, 7–032
judicial challenge to competence
court immediately seised of matter, 7–042
effect of fidning, 7–044
general law on collateral challenge, 7–043
introduction, 7–038
law officer proceedings, 7–040
reference to Supreme Court, 7–039
reference through other courts, 7–041
operation, 7–030
other bodies, and, 7–037

National Assembly for Wales—*cont.*
powers
Assembly Acts, 7–035
Assembly measures, 7–034
introduction, 7–033
subordinate legislation, 7–036
reflections, 7–045—7–046
subordinate legislation, 7–036
Nationalisation
executive agencies, and, 4–027—4–028
Nationality
equal treatment, and, 21–016
Natural justice
audi alteram partem
balancing, 12–020—12–026
conclusion, 12–048
fairness, 12–044—12–047
historical development, 12–001
limitation of principle, 12–003—12–007
non-adjudicative procedures, 12–044—
12–047
principle revived, 12–008—12–010
procedural protection, 12–011—12–043
rationale for rights, 12–002
specific procedural norms, 12–027—
12–043
bias
exceptions, 13–009—13–011
institutional prejudice, 13–004—13–005
overview, 12–001
pecuniary interest, 13–002
personal interest, 13–002—13–003
test, 13–006—13–008
independent and impartial tribunal, 13–020
invalidity, and
bias, 23–026
hearings, 23–025
introduction, 23–024
waiver, 23–027
right to fair trial, 13–012—13–019
ultra vires, 1–007
Necessary in democratic society
human rights, and, 18–032
Necessity
bias, and, 13–009
Negligence
torts, and, 29–004—29–020
Nemo judex in sua causa
exceptions, 13–009—13–011
institutional prejudice, 13–004—13–005
overview, 12–001
pecuniary interest, 13–002
personal interest, 13–002—13–003
test, 13–006—13–008
"No certiorari clauses"
ouster clauses, and, 27–003
Nolan Committee
standards of conduct in public life, and,
8–006
Non-departmental public bodies
accountability
generally, 4–015

Non-departmental public bodies—*cont.*
accountability—*cont.*
introduction, 4–013
appointments, 4–012
control
generally, 4–014
introduction, 4–013
efficiency, 4–016
historical development
conclusion, 4–007
Efficiency Unit, 4–003
Fulton Committee, 4–002
Next Steps Report, 4–003—4–004
non-departmental public bodies, 4–005
Rayner Unit, 4–003
terminology, 4–006
introduction, 4–011
legal status, 4–009
organisational framework, 4–009
overview, 4–001
terminology, 4–006
Non-discrimination
See **Discrimination**
Nonfeaseance
torts, and, 29–017—29–018
Northern Ireland
devolution, and, 7–001
Notice
audi alteram partem, and, 12–027
Nuisance
torts, and, 29–037—29–0412

Ombudsmen
Commission for Local Administration in
England
advice to local authorities, 8–041
establishment, 8–038
internal complaints procedures, and,
8–040
procedure, 8–039
scope of authority, 8–038—8–039
Health Service Commissioners
establishment, 8–036
functions, 8–036
jurisdiction, 8–037
inquiries, and, 9–049
Parliamentary Commissioner for
Administration
generally, 8–012
judicial review, and, 8–031
matters excluded, 8–020—8–023
matters to be investigated, 8–014—8–019
persons to be investigated, 8–013
procedure, 8–024—8–026
remedies, 8–027—8–028
role, 8–032—8–035
Select Committee on Public
Administration, 8–030
workload, 8–029
reform proposals, 8–042
Order 53 procedure
generally, 26–002

Ouster clauses
"as if enacted", 27–005
conclusion, 27–010
"conclusive evidence", 27–005
finality clauses, 27–002
human rights, and, 27–009
introduction, 27–001
"no certiorari" clauses, 27–003
"shall not be questioned" clauses, 27–004
statutory restriction, 27–006

Parliament
conclusion, 3–022
executive power
centralisation of legislative initiative,
3–005—3–006
governmental responsibility, 3–003—
3–004
introduction, 3–002
party system, 3–007
House of Lords reform, 3–020—3–021
introduction, 3–001
legislative process
changes, 3–019
introduction, 3–015
Rippon Commission, 3–016
Select Committee on Modernisation,
3–017—3–018
role, 3–008
select committees
development, 3–010
early assessments, 3–011—3–012
origins, 3–010
recent developments, 3–014
reform initiatives, 3–013
scrutiny, 3–009—3–014
"Parliamentary appropriation"
government contracts, and, 5–042
**Parliamentary Commissioner for
Administration**
background, 8–012
complainants, 8–024
court proceedings, and, 8–021
devolution, and, 8–023
filter procedure, 8–025
generally, 8–012
inquiries, and, 9–049
investigation, 8–026
judicial review, and, 8–031
maladministration
generally, 8–015
merits of decision, 8–018
overview, 8–012
political response, 8–019
principles of good administration,
8–016—8–017
matters excluded, 8–020—8–023
matters to be investigated
administrative functions, 8–014—8–019
judicial functions, 8–014
legislative functions, 8–014
maladministration, 8–015—8–019

**Parliamentary Commissioner for
Administration**—*cont.*
MP filter, 8–025
persons to be investigated, 8–013
principles of good administration, 8–016—
8–017
procedure
complainants, 8–024
investigation, 8–026
MP filter, 8–025
remedies
awards, 8–027
principles, 8–028
role
enhanced remedial power, 8–034
improving administration, 8–035
introduction, 8–032
remedying individual grievances, 8–033
small claims administrative court, 8–034
Select Committee on Public
Administration, 8–030
workload, 8–029
Parliamentary Commissioner for Standards
generally, 8–009—8–010
Pecuniary interests
bias, and, 13–002
Penalties
proportionality, and
domestic approach, 19–016
EC approach, 19–021
Permission
judicial review, and
generally, 26–053
impact of CPR, 26–043
rationale, 26–039—26–044
Personal interests
bias, and
other interests, 13–003
pecuniary interest, 13–002
Planning inquiries
See also **Inquiries**
generally, 9–051—9–053
right to independent and impartial tribunal,
and, 13–014—13–016
Planning inquiry commissions
See also **Inquiries**
generally, 9–045
"Pluralism"
accountability of administrative law, 1–040
ambit of administrative law
general, 1–045
market-oriented pluralism, 1–050
corporatist challenge, 1–039
critique of unitary thesis, 1–037
effectiveness of Parliamentary controls,
1–038
gateways to administrative law, 1–041—
1–042
implications, 1–040—1–045
intellectual basis, 1–036—1–039
introduction, 1–035
locus standi, 1–042

"Pluralism"—*cont.*
  introduction, 1–035
  market-oriented pluralism
    implications, 1–047—1–050
    intellectual basis, 1–046
    introduction, 1–035
    process rights, 1–049
    rights, citizenship and society, 1–048
  natural justice, 1–042
  process rights
    general, 1–043
    market-oriented pluralism, 1–049
  remedies of administrative law, 1–045
  scope of administrative law, 1–040
  scope of judicial review, 1–044
  standing, 1–042
Poll tax
  See **Community charge**
Positive discrimination
  equal treatment, and, 21–013—21–014
Preliminary hearings
  audi alteram partem, and, 12–023
Prerogative powers
  abuse of discretion, and, 17–005
Prescribed by law
  human rights, and, 18–032
"Principles of good administration"
  Parliamentary Commissioner for
    Administration, and, 8–016—8–017
Private Finance Initiative
  And see **Contracts**
  central government, 5–014—5–015
  local government, 5–023
Privatisation
  executive agencies, and, 4–029—4–031
  regulation of utilities, and, 11–024
Procedural rights
  See **Audi alteram partem**
Procedure (judicial review)
  alternative remedies, and, 26–056—26–058
  claims for review, 26–004—26–005
  conclusion, 26–059
  disclosure, 26–050—26–051
  discretion to refuse relief, 26–055
  evaluation of present law, 26–037—26–052
  exclusivity principle, 26–049
  "getting in" the procedure
    activities in Parliament's proper sphere,
      26–033
    boundaries of public law, 26–021—
      26–036
    contracting out, 26–023—26–024
    employment relationships, 26–031—
      26–032
    executive agencies, 26–022
    future prospects 26–036
    human rights, and, 26–035
    'inherently private' activities, 26–034
    public law, 26–017—26–020
    'public law element', 26–025—26–026
    reasons, 26–016
    regulatory bodies, 26–027—26–030

Procedure (judicial review)—*cont.*
  "getting out" of procedure
    assessment, 26–015
    collateral attack, 26–007—26–011
    human rights, 26–012
    impact of CPR, 26–013
    reasons, 26–006
    summary, 26–014
  hearings, 26–054
  introduction, 26–001
  legal foundations, 26–002—26–003
  permission
    generally, 26–053
    impact of CPR, 26–043
    rationale, 26–039—26–044
  time limits, 26–045—26–48
  Upper Tribunal, 26–003
Prohibiting orders
  alternative remedies, 25–012
  delay, 25–011
  determination of rights, 25–005
  duty to act judicially, 25–006
  effect, 25–013
  grounds, 25–008
  introduction, 25–002
  limitations, 25–009—25–012
  locus standi, and, 24–003
  relevant persons and authorities, 25–004
  scope, 25–003—25–007
  subordinate legislation, 25–007
  waiver, and, 25–009—25–010
Prohibition
  alternative remedies, 25–012
  delay, 25–011
  determination of rights, 25–005
  duty to act judicially, 25–006
  effect, 25–013
  grounds, 25–008
  introduction, 25–002
  limitations, 25–009—25–012
  locus standi, and, 24–003
  relevant persons and authorities, 25–004
  scope, 25–003—25–007
  subordinate legislation, 25–007
  waiver, and, 25–009—25–010
Prohibition of discrimination
  See **Discrimination**
Proportionality
  discretion, and
    domestic application, 19–017
    EC approach, 19–022
  domestic application
    discretion, to, 19–017
    introduction, 19–014
    penalties, to, 19–016
    rights, to, 19–015
  domestic law, in
    direct or indirect recognition, 19–010
    Human Rights Act, 19–011
  EC approach
    discretion, to, 19–022
    introduction, 19–019

Proportionality—*cont.*
  EC approach—*cont.*
    penalties, to, 19–021
    rights, to, 19–020
  exercise of administrative discretion, and, 19–017
  future developments, 19–024—19–027
  human rights, and
    conclusion, 18–046
    Daly decision, 18–038
    final determination by court, 18–041
    generally, 18–038—18–039
    introduction, 18–032
    role of domestic court, 18–040—18–045
    weight accorded to view of initial decision-maker, 18–042—18–045
  inter-relationship between principles of review, 19–031—19–032
  introduction, 19–008
  legal status
    Community law component, with, 19–012
    domestic law, in, 19–009—19–011
  penalties, and
    domestic approach, 19–016
    EC approach, 19–021
  place and meaning, 19–013
  rights, and
    domestic approach, 19–015
    EC approach, 19–020
  role of court, 19–018
  standard of review, 19–018
  substantive control, 19–029—19–030
  Wednesbury unreasonableness, and, 19–024—19–025
Prosecutors
  bias, and, 13–004
Public authorities
  And see **Acts of public authorities**
  locus standi, and, 24–010
"Public corporations"
  executive agencies, and, 4–027—4–028
Public interest immunity
  background, 28–002—28–004
  balancing process, 28–012—28–013
  claimants, 28–005
  confidentiality, and, 28–006
  Crown privilege, and, 28–002—28–003
  duty/discretion, 28–007—28–008
  government approach, 28–009—28–011
  human rights, and, 28–008
  inspection of documents, 28–014
  introduction, 28–001
Public private partnerships
  And see **Contracts**
  generally, 5–014—5–015
Public procurement
  And see **Contracts**
  application of Directives, 5–028
  competitive dialogue procedure, 5–029
  contracting authorities, 5–028
  contract awards, 5–029

Public procurement—*cont.*
  EC rules
    Directives, and, 5–027—5–030
    EC Treaty, and, 5–026
    introduction, 5–024
    object, 5–025
  guidelines, 5–004
  institutional responsibility, 5–003
  introduction, 5–002
  Model Conditions of Contract, 5–004
  negotiated procedure, 5–029
  open procedure, 5–029
  overview, 5–001
  procedures, 5–029
  public contract, 5–028
  range of options, 5–005
  remedies, 5–030
  restricted procedure, 5–029
  technical specifications, 5–028
  UK regulations, 5–028—5–029
Public service agreements
  And see **Contracts**
  generally, 5–001

Quangos
  See **Non-departmental public bodies**
Quashing orders
  alternative remedies, 25–012
  delay, 25–011
  determination of rights, 25–005
  duty to act judicially, 25–006
  effect, 25–013
  grounds, 25–008
  introduction, 25–002
  limitations, 25–009—25–012
  locus standi, and, 24–003
  relevant persons and authorities, 25–004
  scope, 25–003—25–007
  subordinate legislation, 25–007
  waiver, and, 25–009—25–010
"Questions of fact"
  conclusion, 15–029
  determination of factual error, 15–022—15–028
  E v Secretary of State for the Home Department, 15–005—15–008
  introduction, 15–001
  mistake and fact, 15–002—15–004
  role of reviewing court, 15–022—15–028
  test for mistake of fact, 15–009—15–021

Race discrimination
  equal treatment, and, 21–018
Rate capping
  See **Capping**
Rate support grant
  local government finance, and, 6–010
Rates
  local government finance, and, 6–009
"Rationality"
  See also **Irrationality**
  And see **Wednesbury unreasonableness**

"Rationality"—*cont.*
  generally, 19–001
Reasonableness
  See also **Wednesbury unreasonableness**
  abuse of discretion, and, 17–002
Reasons
  And see **Audi alteram partem**
  common law, 12–036—12–037
  human rights, 12–035
  indirect procedures, 12–036
  importance, 12–033
  late evidence, 12–039
  procedural fairness, 12–037—12–038
  statutory provisions, 12–034—12–035
Regulations
  direct effect, and, 10–022
"Relative needs formula"
  local government finance, and, 6–011
Relevance
  abuse of discretion, and, 17–013—17–014
Religious discrimination
  equal treatment, and, 21–018
Remedies
  certiorari
    effect, 25–013
    grounds, 25–008
    introduction, 25–002
    limitations, 25–009—25–012
    scope, 25–003—25–007
  Crown liability
    contempt, 28–023
    declarations, 28–021
    injunctions, 28–018—28–022
    procedure, 28–017
    statutes benefitting the Crown, 28–016
    statutes binding the Crown, 28–015
  Crown privilege, 28–002
  declarations
    effect, 25–029
    introduction, 25–020
    limits on availability, 25–023—25–028
    practice, 25–030
    procedure, 25–030
    scope, 25–021—25–022
  default powers, 25–040
  exclusion
    conclusion, 27–010—27–011
    human rights, and, 27–009
    introduction, 27–001
    limiting clauses, 27–007—27–008
    ouster clauses, 27–001—27–006
  habeas corpus, 25–038
  injunctions
    introduction, 25–031
    limits to relief, 25–036
    practice, 25–037
    procedure, 25–037
    scope, 25–033—25–035
    types, 25–032
  justiciability, and, 24–001
  locus standi
    Attorney-General, 24–009

Remedies—*cont.*
  locus standi—*cont.*
    function, 24–028—24–037
    future issues, 24–038—24–041
    Human Rights Act 1998, under, 24–025
    introduction, 24–001
    judicial review actions, in, 24–012—24–028
    pre-1978 law, 24–002—24–007
    public authorities, 24–010
    section 31, outside, 24–026
    statutory appeals, 24–011
  mandamus
    ambit, 25–015—25–017
    introduction, 25–014
    limits on availability, 25–018—25–019
  mandatory orders
    ambit, 25–015—25–017
    introduction, 25–014
    limits on availability, 25–018—25–019
  ouster clauses
    "as if enacted", 27–005
    conclusion, 27–010
    "conclusive evidence", 27–005
    finality clauses, 27–002
    human rights, and, 27–009
    introduction, 27–001
    "no certiorari" clauses, 27–003
    "shall not be questioned" clauses, 27–004
    statutory restriction, 27–006
  Parliamentary Commissioner for
    Administration, and
    awards, 8–027
    principles, 8–028
  private law, 25–039
  procedure
    alternative remedies, and, 26–056—26–058
    claims for review, 26–004—26–005
    conclusion, 26–059
    discretion to refuse relief, 26–055
    evaluation of present law, 26–037—26–052
    "getting in" the review procedure, 26–016—26–036
    "getting out" of review procedure, 26–006—26–015
    hearings, 26–054
    introduction, 26–001
    legal foundations, 26–002—26–003
    permission, 26–053
    Upper Tribunal, 26–003
  prohibition
    effect, 25–013
    grounds, 25–008
    introduction, 25–002
    limitations, 25–009—25–012
    scope, 25–003—25–007
  prohibiting orders
    effect, 25–013
    grounds, 25–008
    introduction, 25–002

Remedies—*cont.*
  prohibiting orders—*cont.*
    limitations, 25–009—25–012
    scope, 25–003—25–007
  public interest immunity
    background, 28–002—28–004
    balancing process, 28–012—28–013
    claimants, 28–005
    confidentiality, and, 28–006
    duty/discretion, 28–007—28–008
    government approach, 28–009—28–011
    human rights, and, 28–008
    inspection of documents, 28–014
    introduction, 28–001
  quashing orders
    effect, 25–013
    grounds, 25–008
    introduction, 25–002
    limitations, 25–009—25–012
    scope, 25–003—25–007
  "ripeness", and, 24–001
  time limits
    conclusion, 27–010
    generally, 27–007—27–008
  torts
    breach of statutory duty, 29–021—29–023
    Crown liability, 29–045—29–046
    EU law, 29–056—29–060
    human rights, and, 29–024—29–0030
    introduction, 29–001
    judicial immunity, 29–047
    legal foundations, 29–002
    misfeasance in public office, 29–031—29–036
    negligence, 29–004—29–020
    nuisance, 29–037—29–041
    options available, 29–003
    reforms, 29–061—29–066
    restitution, 29–048—29–055
    Rylands v Fletcher liability, 29–042—29–044

Representation
  See **Legal representation**
"Respect"
  And see **Human rights**
  factors taken into account, 18–036
  generally, 18–035
  terminology, 18–037
Restitution
  torts, and, 29–048—29–055
Retrospective effect
  legitimate expectation, and, 20–003
Right to fair trial
  domestic courts, and, 13–013—13–019
  fairness, 13–013
  housing law, and, 13–017—13–018
  independent and impartial tribunal, 13–020
  legal basis, 13–012
  planning law, and, 13–014—13–016
  recent developments, 13–019

Right to independent and impartial tribunal
  common law, at, 13–020
  domestic courts, in
    fairness, 13–013
    housing law, 13–017—13–019
    planning inquiries, 13–014—13–016
    waiver, 13–013
  fairness, 13–013
  housing law, 13–017—13–019
  introduction, 13–001
  legal requirements, 13–012
  planning inquiries, 13–014—13–016
  waiver, 13–013
"Ripeness"
  declarations, and, 25–025
  remedies, and, 24–001
Rippon Commission 1992
  legislative proceedings, and, 3–016
  secondary legislation, and, 22–032—22–036
Rules
  administration-made rules
    legal status, 22–040
    overview, 22–001
    possible solutions, 22–043—22–047
    problem areas, 22–042
    rationale, 22–039
    type, 22–039
  consultation, and, 22–001
  EC law, and, 22–048
  introduction, 22–001
  judicial scrutiny, and, 22–001
  legislative scrutiny, and, 22–001
  publication, and, 22–001
  secondary legislation
    constitutional issues, 22–003
    consultation, 22–016—22–022
    form, 22–004
    historical background, 22–002
    judicial review, 22–023—22–030
    legislative passage, 22–005—22–007
    overview, 22–001
    Parliamentary control, 22–008—22–015
    rationale, 22–003
    reform proposals, 22–031—22–038
    scrutiny, 22–008—22–015
  supervision, and, 22–001
***Rylands v Fletcher* liability**
  torts, and, 29–042—29–044

Scotland
  background, 7–002
  reflections, 7–025—7–026
  Scottish Executive, 7–010
  Scottish Parliament, 7–003—7–024
Scottish Parliament
  competence
    judicial challenge, 7–018—7–024
    political challenge, 7–017
  composition, 7–003
  executive powers, 7–010

Scottish Parliament—*cont.*
  judicial challenge to competence
    court immediately seised of matter,
      7–022
    general law on collateral challenge 7–023
    introduction, 7–018
    law officer proceedings, 7–020
    Privy Council reference, 7–019
    result of finding, 7–024
  legislative powers, 7–005—7–016
  operation, 7–004
  political challenge to competence, 7–017
  powers
    executive, of, 7–010
    generally, 7–006
    introduction, 7–005
    limits, 7–007—7–009
    reserved matters, 7–009
    revenue-raising, 7–016
    subordinate legislation, 7–011—7–015
  resolution of devolution issues
    court immediately seised of matter,
      7–022
    law officer proceedings, 7–020
    Privy Council reference, 7–019
  revenue-raising powers, 7–016
  subordinate legislation, 7–011—7–015
Secondary legislation
  See **Subordinate legislation**
Select committees
  development, 3–010
  early assessments, 3–011—3–012
  legislative proceedings, and, 3–017—3–018
  origins, 3–010
  recent developments, 3–014
  reform initiatives, 3–013
  secondary legislation, and, 22–037
Senior President of Tribunals
  See also **Tribunals**
  generally, 9–012
Sex discrimination
  equal treatment, and, 21–017
Sexual orientation discrimination
  equal treatment, and, 21–018
"Shall not be questioned clauses"
  ouster clauses, and, 27–004
Standards of conduct
  Committee on Standards and Privileges,
    8–009—8–010
  Committee on Standards in Public Life,
    8–007—8–008
  development of administrative machinery,
    8–006
  local authorities, and, 8–011
  Nolan Committee, 8–006
  overview, 8–001
  Parliamentary Commissioner for
    Standards, 8–009—8–010
Standing
  See **Locus standi**
Statutory appeals
  locus standi, and, 24–011

Statutory inquiries
  See **Inquiries**
Statutory interpretation
  And see **Human rights**
  case law, 18–007—18–011
  common law, at, 17–020
  Ghaidan decision, 18–008—18–009
  judicial approach, 18–007—18–011
  legislative history, 18–006
  statutory provisions, 18–004—18–005
Statutory powers
  abuse of discretion, and, 17–004
Subordinate legislation
  abuse of discretion, and, 17–004
  certiorari, and, 25–007
  committee scrutiny
    delegated legislation committees, 22–010
    House of Lords Merits of Statutory
      Instruments Committee, 22–012
    Joint Committee on Statutory
      Instruments, 22–011
  constitutional issues, 22–003
  consultation
    benefits, 22–019
    Code of Practice, and, 22–0021
    common law, at, 22–018
    conclusion, 22–022
    introduction, 22–016
    issues to be addressed, 22–020
    statute, under, 22–017
  delegated legislation committees, and,
    22–010
  form, 22–004
  historical background, 22–002
  House of Lords Merits of Statutory
    Instruments Committee
    generally, 22–012
    reform proposals, 22–038
  Joint Committee on Statutory Instruments,
    22–011
  judicial review
    breach of constitutional principle,
      22–027
    delegation, 22–029
    formal invalidity, 22–024
    infringement of primary legislation,
      22–026
    introduction, 22–023
    procedural ultra vires, 22–024
    purpose, 22–028
    reasonableness, 22–028
    relevance, 22–028
    remedies, 22–030
    substantive ultra vires, 22–025—22–028
  legislative passage, 22–005—22–007
  overview, 22–001
  Parliamentary control, 22–008—22–015
  publication, 22–006—22–007
  rationale, 22–003
  reform proposals
    House of Lords' Merits of Statutory
      Instruments Committee, 22–038

Subordinate legislation—*cont.*
  reform proposals—*cont.*
    introduction, 22–031
    Rippon Commission, 22–032—22–036
    Select Committee on Procedure, 22–037
  regulatory reform, 22–013—22–014
  Rippon Commission, 22–032—22–036
  Scotland, 7–011—7–015
  scrutiny
    committee, by, 22–010—22–012
    EU legislation, 22–015
    Houses of Parliament, by, 22–008—
      22–009
    regulatory reform instruments, 22–013—
      22–014
  Select Committee on Procedure, 22–037
  statutory basis, 22–005
  supervision, and, 22–001
  Wales, 7–036
Supremacy of EC law
  generally, 10–011—10–014

Third parties
  locus standi, and, 24–027
Time limits
  conclusion, 27–010
  generally, 27–007—27–008
  judicial review, and, 26–045—26–48
Torts
  bases of liability, 29–003
  breach of statutory duty, 29–021—29–023
  Crown liability, 29–045—29–046
  EU law, 29–056—29–060
  human rights, and, 29–024—29–030
  introduction, 29–001
  judicial immunity, 29–047
  legal foundations, 29–002
  misfeasance, 29–017—29–018
  misfeasance in public office, 29–031—
    29–036
  negligence, 29–004—29–020
  nonfeaseance, 29–017—29–018
  nuisance, 29–037—29–041
  options available, 29–003
  reforms, 29–061—29–066
  restitution, 29–048—29–055
  Rylands v Fletcher liability, 29–042—29–044
  ultra vires, and, 29–002
Transfer of functions
  tribunals, and, 9–014
Tribunals
  See also **Inquiries**
  administration, 9–028
  Administrative Justice and Tribunals
    Council
    background, 9–030
    generally, 9–031—9–032
    introduction, 9–029
  advantages, 9–002
  alternative dispute resolution, 9–027
  appeals
    Court of Appeal, to, 9–018

Tribunals—*cont.*
  appeals—*cont.*
    First-tier Tribunal, from, 9–017
    generally, 9–019—9–021
    Upper Tribunal, to, 9–017
  Council on Tribunals
    abolition, 9–029
    generally, 9–030
  definition, 9–003
  First-tier Tribunal
    appeals to Upper Tribunal, 9–017
    generally, 9–013
    judicial review by High Court, 9–023
    self-review, 9–015—9–016
    transfer of functions, 9–014
  Franks Report, and
    implementation, 9–006
    recommendations, 9–005
    remit, 9–004
  introduction, 9–001
  judicial review
    High Court, by, 9–023
    Upper Tribunal, by, 9–022
  Leggatt Report
    introduction, 9–007
    recommendations, 9–008—9–010
  mediation, 9–027
  nature, 9–003
  procedure
    generally, 9–025—9–026
    pre-TCEA 2007 position, 9–024
  reasons for creation, 9–002
  reforms
    Franks Report, 9–004—9–006
    Leggatt Report, 9–007—9–010
  regulation of utilities, and, 11–022
  review, 9–015—9–016
  Senior President of Tribunals, 9–012
  staffing, 9–028
  statutory provisions, 9–011
  transfer of functions, 9–014
  Tribunals Service, 9–008
  tribunals system, 9–009—9–010
  Upper Tribunal
    appeals to Court of Appeal, 9–018—
      9–021
    generally, 9–013
    judicial review, 9–022
    judicial review by High Court, 9–023
    self-review, 9–015—9–016
    transfer of functions, 9–014
Tribunals Service
  See also **Tribunals**
  generally, 9–008

Ultra vires
  ambit of public law, 1–014
  critique of principle, 1–016
  deficiencies
    ambit of public law, 1–014
    distrust of the state, 1–011
    form of intervention, 1–012—1–013

Ultra vires—*cont.*
  deficiencies—*cont.*
    mistake avoidance, 1–011
    introduction, 1–010
    private rights theme, and, 1–015
    scope of intervention, 1–012—1–013
    straining of principle, 1–014
  distrust of the state, 1–011
  form of intervention
    deficiencies, 1–012—1–013
    generally, 1–005
  implications
    form of intervention, 1–005
    locus standi, 1–007
    natural justice, 1–007
    protected interests, 1–007
    public bodies, on, 1–009
    scope of intervention, 1–006
    shape of intervention, 1–006
    standing, 1–007
    type of protection, 1–008
  indeterminacy of principle, 1–012—1–013
  introduction, 1–003—1–004
  judicial review, and
    agency, 20–032—20–033
    application of principle, 20–034—20–035
    assessment of principle, 20–041—20–043
    balancing, and, 20–047—20–051
    compensation, 20–052
    conceptual language, 20–036
    delegation, 20–032—20–033
    estoppel, and, 20–031
    introduction, 20–031
    jurisdictional principle, 20–032—20–043
    policy behind principle, 20–042—20–043
    qualifications to principle, 20–037—20–040
    rationale for principle, 20–042—20–043
    strategies available, 20–044—20–052
  locus standi, 1–007
  mistake avoidance, 1–011
  natural justice, 1–007
  protected interests, 1–007
  public bodies, and, 1–009
  scope of intervention
    deficiencies, 1–012—1–013
    generally, 1–006
  shape of intervention, 1–006
  standing, 1–007
  torts, and, 29–00
  type of protection, 1–008
"Unitary democracy"
  generally, 1–002—1–004
Unlawful contracts
  See **Illegal contracts**
Upper Tribunal
  appeals to Court of Appeal, 9–018—9–021
  generally, 9–013
  judicial review, 9–022—9–023, 26–003
  self-review, 9–015—9–016
  transfer of functions, 9–014

Utilities (regulation)
  agencies, 11–024
  Boards, 11–022
  broader context, 11–017
  Citizen's Charter, 11–035
  common law, 11–019—11–020
  departmental supervision, 11–021
  economic considerations, 11–016
  gas supply, 11–027—11–030
  government's approach, 11–015
  institutional design, 11–031—11–033
  introduction, 11–011
  legal powers and constraints, 11–027
  limits of public law, 11–034
  method of regulation
    Citizen's Charter, 11–035
    gas supply, 11–027—11–030
    institutional design, 11–031—11–033
    legal powers and constraints, 11–027
    limits of public law, 11–034
    sale of state assets, 11–025—11–026
  political considerations, 11–016
  privatisation, 11–024
  public ownership, 11–023
  purpose of regulation
    broader context, 11–017
    economic considerations, 11–016
    government's approach, 11–015
    introduction, 11–011—11–013
    natural monopoly, 11–014
    political considerations, 11–016
    social considerations, 11–016
  regulatory bodies
    agencies, 11–024
    Boards, 11–022
    common law, 11–019—11–020
    departmental supervision, 11–021
    introduction, 11–018
    privatisation, 11–024
    public ownership, 11–023
    tribunals, 11–022
  sale of state assets, 11–025—11–026
  social considerations, 11–016
  tribunals, 11–022

"Void"
  determining if error renders act void, 23–011
  effect of holding act void, 23–012
  judicial discretion, 23–018—23–023
  natural justice, 23–024—23–027
  nature of concept, 23–009—23–010
  overview, 23–008
"Voidable"
  alternative to locus standi, 23–015
  error of law within jurisdiction, 23–017
  gravity of error, 23–016
  indicative of need to challenger, 23–014
  introduction, 23–013
  judicial discretion, 23–018—23–023
  natural justice, 23–024—23–027
  overview, 23–008
  waiver, 23–027

Waiver
  bias, and, 13–011
  certiorari, and, 25–009—25–010
  invalidity, and, 23–027
  right to independent and impartial tribunal,
      and, 13–013
Wales
  background, 7–027—7–028
  Commission for Local Administration in
      Wales
    advice to local authorities, 8–041
    establishment, 8–038
    internal complaints procedures, and,
        8–040
    procedure, 8–039
    scope of authority, 8–038—8–039
  executive
    composition, 7–031
    functions, 7–032
  National Assembly for Wales
    Assembly Acts, 7–035
    Assembly measures, 7–034
    composition, 7–029
    executive powers, 7–031—7–032
    judicial challenge to competence,
        7–038—7–044
    operation, 7–030
    other bodies, and, 7–037
    powers, 7–033—7–037
    subordinate legislation, 7–036
  reflections, 7–045—7–046
Wednesbury unreasonableness
  abuse of discretion, and, 17–002
  abuse of power, and, 19–006
  future of the test, 19–007

Wednesbury unreasonableness—*cont.*
  introduction, 19–002
  legitimate expectation, and, 19–006
  present law, 19–003—19–006
  proportionality, and, 19–024—19–025
  rationality, and, 19–006
Welsh Assembly Government
  Assembly Acts, 7–035
  Assembly measures, 7–034
  background, 7–027—7–028
  composition, 7–029
  executive powers
    composition, 7–031
    functions, 7–032
  judicial challenge to competence
    court immediately seised of matter,
        7–042
    effect of fidning, 7–044
    general law on collateral challenge, 7–043
    introduction, 7–038
    law officer proceedings, 7–040
    reference to Supreme Court, 7–039
    reference through other courts, 7–041
  operation, 7–030
  other bodies, and, 7–037
  powers
    Assembly Acts, 7–035
    Assembly measures, 7–034
    introduction, 7–033
    subordinate legislation, 7–036
  reflections, 7–045—7–046
  subordinate legislation, 7–036
Written representations procedure
  decision by appointed persons, 9–044
  planning inquiries, 9–045